ביאור תניא

THE STEINSALTZ TANYA

VOLUME II

THE MAGERMAN EDITION
THE STEINSALTZ
TANYA

LIKKUTEI AMARIM
33–53

COMMENTARY & TRANSLATION BY
RABBI ADIN EVEN-ISRAEL STEINSALTZ

Steinsaltz Center
Maggid Books

The Steinsaltz Tanya:
Likkutei Amarim, Volume 2
First edition, 2023

Maggid Books
An imprint of Koren Publishers Jerusalem Ltd.

POB 8531, New Milford, CT 06776-8531, USA
& POB 4044, Jerusalem 9104001, Israel
www.maggidbooks.com

Original Hebrew Edition © The Steinsaltz Center Ltd., 2020
English translation © The Steinsaltz Center Ltd. 2023
Koren Tanakh font © 1962, 2022 Koren Publishers Ltd.

This book was published in cooperation with
the Israeli Institute for Talmudic Publications.
All rights reserved to the Steinsaltz Center Ltd.

We acknowledge with gratitude the generous support of
Terri and Stephen Geifman, *who made possible an earlier edition of this commentary.*

The right of Adin Steinsaltz to be identified as the author
of this work has been asserted by him in accordance
with the Copyright, Designs & Patents Act 1988.
Steinsaltz Center is the parent organization of institutions
established by Rabbi Adin Even-Israel Steinsaltz
POB 45187, Jerusalem 91450 ISRAEL
Telephone: +972 2 646 0900, Fax +972 2 624 9454
www.steinsaltz-center.org

All rights reserved. No part of this publication may be reproduced,
stored in a retrieval system, or transmitted in any form or by
any means, electronic, mechanical, photocopying, or otherwise,
without the prior permission of the publisher, except in the case
of brief quotations embedded in critical articles or reviews.

Cover design by Tani Bayer

ISBN 978-1-59264-586-2, hardcover

Printed and bound in the United States

Executive Director, Steinsaltz Center
Rabbi Meni Even-Israel

Editor-in-Chief
Rabbi Jason Rappoport

Translators
Zev Bannet
Noam Harris
Yaacov David Shulman
Oritt Sinclair

Editors
Noam Harris
Debbie Ismailoff
Rabbi Zalman Margolin
Yaacov Dovid Shulman
Rabbi Michael Siev

Proofreader
Dvora Rhein

Hebrew Proofreader
Avichai Gamdani

Hebrew Edition Editors
Rabbi Meir Hanegbi, Senior Editor
Rabbi Hillel Mondshein
Rabbi David Brokner

Hebrew Vocalization
Rabbi Hillel Mondshein

Technical Staff
Adena Frazer
Adina Mann
Avi Steinhart

Dedicated to

my wife, **Debra**,

and my children,
Elijah, **Zachary**, **Sydney**, and **Lexie**.

May this new translation of the Tanya,
along with the commentary from Rabbi Steinsaltz (*z"l*),
bring us closer to hasidic teaching and
help us connect with the mystical meaning
behind the Torah.

*May all the children of Israel use
the Tanya's knowledge and wisdom
to work together to hasten the coming of Mashiaḥ.*

DAVID M. MAGERMAN

*Dedicated with gratitude
to the high souls of every tradition
who have come to this earth to help show humanity
the path towards a righteous life
and the way back to our Creator.*

Burton G. and Anne C. Greenblatt Foundation

ספר התניא מלמד אותנו שהנפש האלוקית מסורה כל כולה לקב"ה והיא מבחינה זו חסרת אנוכיות או תחושת ישות. הנפש הבהמית לעומת זאת מרוכזת בעצמה ומסורה לקיומה הנפרד.

לפיכך לימד אותנו האדמו"ר האמצעי שכאשר שני יהודים לומדים או משוחחים בעניני עבודת ה' הרי אלו שתי נשמות אלוקיות כנגד נפש בהמית אחת. הנפש הבהמית לא מצטרפת עם חבירתה משום שכאמור היא מסורה לעצמה אבל הנפשות האלוקיות מצטרפות יחד בלי כל חציצה או הבדל.

(מתוך: "היום יום" כ' לטבת)

לזכות
משה ליב בן זיסל שיחי' לאיוש"ט
שולמית בת זהרה שתחי' לאיוש"ט

The *Tanya* teaches us that the divine soul is fully devoted to G-d, and therefore it is selfless. By contrast, the animal soul is selfish, devoted only to maintaining its own existence.

The Mitteler Rebbe, Rabbi Dovber of Lubavitch, taught that when two Jews learn or discuss matters pertaining to service of God, there are two divine souls against one animal soul. The animal soul thinks only of itself and will not attach itself to the animal soul of the other. But the two divine souls are joined together with no division or barrier.

(Cited from *HaYom Yom*, 20 Tevet)

In the merit of
MOSHE LEIB BEN ZISEL
SHULAMIT BAT ZOHARA

A blessing from the Lubavitcher Rebbe, Rabbi Menaḥem Mendel Schneerson, dated 21 Av 5721 (August 3, 1961), viewing with favor Rabbi Steinsaltz's project of writing a short commentary, with longer explanations, on the *Tanya* in a style accessible to the contemporary reader:

(ושאלות ותשובות – כהמצורף למכתבו) בעניינֵי־ המובאים בתניא, כן ביאור קצר או גם ארוך, ובסגנונו, ערוכים בלשון בני דורנו...

בברכה לבשו"ט

In December 2012, the final volume of the Hebrew edition of *The Steinsaltz Tanya* was published. That year, at a hasidic gathering, Rabbi Adin Steinsaltz shared why he wrote the book. He explained that Rabbi Shneur Zalman of Liadi, the author of the *Tanya*, had poured his entire soul, his love and awe, his soul-wrenching oneness with God into that concise book, into pages that obscured his immense spirit so well. Through his commentary, Rabbi Steinsaltz strove to reveal to us this spirit, that powerful fire just barely contained by the words of the *Tanya*.

And he certainly succeeded. Yet he failed to mask his own burning spirit, his own love, awe, and closeness to God, as he had attempted to do his entire life.

The publication of this English edition of *The Steinsaltz Tanya* is the fulfillment of Rabbi Steinsaltz's vision to make the teachings of the *Tanya* accessible to every single individual. At the height of the preparations for this edition, our teacher Rabbi Adin Even-Israel passed away.

In this book, one learns how the life of the tzaddik lives on in this world, in those who learn his works. It is through those students who are open to receiving his teachings and are inspired to build upon his words that his light remains with us. We pray that this commentary of Rabbi Steinsaltz will introduce many generations of Jews to the world of the *Tanya* and to the path of authentic devotion to God.

May it serve to elevate his soul.

Contents

LIKKUTEI AMARIM/A COMPILATION OF TEACHINGS

Chapter 33	1
Chapter 34	25
Chapter 35	47
Chapter 36	79
Chapter 37	107
Chapter 38	167
Chapter 39	207
Chapter 40	261
Chapter 41	307
Chapter 42	375
Chapter 43	423
Chapter 44	453
Chapter 45	491
Chapter 46	507
Chapter 47	545
Chapter 48	557
Chapter 49	585
Chapter 50	623
Chapter 51	647
Chapter 52	673
Chapter 53	705
Afterword	731

Summary of Chapters 733
Glossary 739
Works Cited in This Volume 743

For the Hebrew Tanya Vilna edition, open from the Hebrew side of the book.

Chapter 33

AT THE END OF CHAPTER 31, THE AUTHOR OF THE *TANYA* began to discuss the topic of joy – in particular, joy that emerges from bitterness – and the connection between joy and lowliness and bitterness. He stated that this feeling of joy, which flows from bitterness, occurs when a person emerges from a state of divine concealment and distress. After a brief digression in chapter 32, which focuses on loving one's fellow Jew, the author now returns to the topic of joy, this time not in the context of escape from pain and bitterness but as an independent subject. He explains the benefits of joy and details what a person should contemplate in order to continuously arouse within himself boundless feelings of joy regardless of his life circumstances.

עוֹד זֹאת, תִּהְיֶה שִׂמְחַת הַנֶּפֶשׁ הָאֲמִיתִּית, **In addition, there will be true joy of the soul,**

11 Adar

29 Adar I (leap year)

The joy that will be discussed in this chapter is "true" in the sense that it does not stem from a sense of temporary relief from a state of spiritual inadequacy and distress but rather is continuous, an expression of the existence of the infinite divine oneness. A person only has to think about this in order to attain this unparalleled joy.

This type of joy differs from the joy described in chapter 31 in another way as well. The joy depicted earlier was experienced by the divine soul alone and had to be shielded from and evade the flaws of the body and the animal soul, while the joy described in this chapter may express itself even through the body and the animal soul.

וּבִפְרָט כְּשֶׁרוֹאֶה בְּנַפְשׁוֹ בְּעִתִּים מְזוּמָּנִים שֶׁצָּרִיךְ לְזַכְּכָהּ וּלְהָאִירָהּ, בְּשִׂמְחַת לֵבָב.

especially when a person sees on certain occasions that he must purify and illuminate his soul with joy of the heart.

Sometimes a person goes through a phase of self-induced bitterness which he must leave behind to attain a state of joy. At other times a person must experience joy, not because he was embittered but because he feels the need "to purify and illuminate his soul."[1]

A person can accomplish many things as part of his routine or out of a sense of duty. But sometimes he undergoes such a severe state of spiritual or physical exhaustion that he cannot act. He must experience what the author of the *Tanya* refers to as "joy of the heart" in order to purify and illuminate his soul. This kind of joy – genuine, heartfelt joy, not frivolity – is the optimal state of the soul. When a person experiences this joyful, positive state of mind, all of his actions are animated and effortless. He solves problems and meets challenges, and new paths open up for him.

The Talmud says that a person should pray only out of the joy associated with performing a mitzva.[2] Prayer, which is fundamentally an emotional service, clearly requires an appropriate emotional state. Our Sages broaden the scope of this requirement to include other mitzvot, such as Torah study, in another talmudic dictum[3] which states that the Divine Presence rests only on a person who is imbued with the joy associated with a mitzva. When a person is feeling dejected or melancholy, it is as though he is trying to function in the dark. He cannot fully utilize his abilities. In order to illuminate the darkness and "purify and illuminate his soul," he must experience joy. Then he can look at himself and at the world around him with joy, energy, and ease.

But how can a person reach this state of joy solely from within himself without relying on external stimuli?

---

1. The word "purify" refers to the vessel, whereas "illuminate" indicates drawing light into it. The vessel, that is, the soul, must first be purified and then illuminated (Rabbi Shmuel Gronem Esterman).
2. *Berakhot* 31a.
3. *Shabbat* 30b.

אֲזַי יַעֲמִיק מַחֲשַׁבְתּוֹ וִיצַיֵּיר בְּשִׂכְלוֹ וּבִינָתוֹ עִנְיַן יִחוּדוֹ יִתְבָּרֵךְ הָאֲמִיתִּי, **Then he should contemplate and visualize with his mind and his understanding the concept of God's true unity,**

One way for him to achieve true joy is to "contemplate and visualize with his mind and his understanding the concept of God's true unity." Just as a person must dwell on certain ideas in order to elicit painful feelings, so must he contemplate the concept of God's divine oneness and unity in order to elicit joy.

In order for a person's thoughts to lead to knowledge that is not only theoretical but will change his life, he must direct his thoughts. Directing one's thoughts involves a process of careful analysis whereby a person approaches a concept from multiple angles. In this way, he visualizes the concept in his imagination as tangibly as possible so that his soul can connect itself to that concept fully, both intellectually and emotionally.

This applies to all objects of thought, whether material or spiritual, holy or impure. If a person cannot build frameworks in his soul in which his most personal understanding will become meaningful, he will be unable to emotionally relate to the objects of his thought.

"The concept of God's true unity" as a topic for contemplation is discussed extensively in *Sha'ar HaYiḥud VeHa'emuna*.[4] Here, the author of the *Tanya* touches only briefly on this concept, and only regarding the aspect that leads to joy.

אֵיךְ הוּא מְמַלֵּא כָּל עָלְמִין, עֶלְיוֹנִים וְתַחְתּוֹנִים, **namely, how He fills all worlds, higher and lower,**

"Fills all worlds" is a concept in hasidic thought that refers to one of the two categories of the revelation of the divine light: "fills all worlds" and "encompasses all worlds."[5] That the divine light fills all worlds refers to the revelation of divine light within created beings, animating each one according to its measure and purpose. Analogous to this is the revelation and function of the soul in the body: the power of sight is

---

4. See also chaps. 20–21 above.
5. See the *Kitzur Tanya*.

expressed via the eye, the ability to walk is expressed via the legs, and so forth. The author of the *Tanya* specifies "higher and lower" because with regard to the divine light that fills all worlds, the higher and lower worlds are not equally capable of containing it.

וַאֲפִילוּ מָלֵא כָּל הָאָרֶץ הַלֵּזוּ הוּא כְּבוֹדוֹ יִתְבָּרֵךְ **and how even this earth is filled with God's glory**

The second category of light, the other aspect of God's unity, is that which "encompasses all worlds," including this physical world."[6] On this level, the divine light is transcendent, beyond all existence and encompassing all particulars equally. Regarding this category of divine light, differences between large and small, and upper and lower are meaningless. It brings into existence our lower world just as it does the upper worlds. It creates existence from nothing by virtue of its concealed nature.[7]

When a person contemplates these two aspects of the divine light, the transcendent and the immanent, which generates and animates everything, it can lead him to experience God's true unity. His awareness that even as God is transcendent He is here upon this earth, with all that this implies, is the essence of faith in the true divine unity. This type of faith negates the dichotomous perspective that "God is in the heavens and you are on earth" (Eccles. 5:1), in other words, that God is somewhere above whereas a person resides down below. Faith in God's unity is faith that God is present even where the person is. Therefore, He is truly one and unified, and there is no existence outside Him.

וְכוֹלָּא קַמֵּיהּ כְּלָא חֲשִׁיב מַמָּשׁ, וְהוּא לְבַדּוֹ הוּא בָּעֶלְיוֹנִים וְתַחְתּוֹנִים מַמָּשׁ, כְּמוֹ שֶׁהָיָה לְבַדּוֹ קוֹדֶם שֵׁשֶׁת יְמֵי בְּרֵאשִׁית. **and how everything before Him is literally considered nothingness, and that He is literally alone in the higher and lower worlds just as He was alone before the six days of Creation,**

---

6. See Ezek. 36:35.
7. See chap. 48 below.

God is present whether or not the world exists, whether before or after the six days of Creation. The existence of the world does not in any way conceal God's presence. ☞

AN ALTERNATIVE CONCEPTION OF GOD'S UNITY

☞ A person's initial, simple, and undeveloped understanding of how God fills all worlds is that He is everywhere and fills everything, like the vacuum of space or, in a more concrete analogy, like the air that fills a room. A deeper understanding of this concept is that "there is nothing besides Him," that the multifaceted world that we perceive constitutes nothing other than God.

A material illustration of this idea is a black-and-white image. It is not always clear which is the foreground and which is the background. There are some images (such as those of the Dutch artist M. C. Escher) that are entirely focused on this liminal state. The more a person looks, the more uncertain he grows as to which is the foreground and which is the background.

A similar question, bearing multiple layers of implication, is whether a written letter consists of the black ink or the white paper. Generally speaking, we perceive the black as the letter and the white as the background, but it is possible to reverse this and to view the white as the letter and the black as the background. (Regarding the letters of a Torah scroll, this question has a halakhic basis, because the holiness of the Torah scroll pertains as much to the white parchment as it does to the black letters.)

In the same way, we generally see the world in the foreground and the Divine in the background. However, there is a dimension in which we can contemplate that "everything before Him is literally considered nothingness," and attempt to view the world differently, not with the Divine standing in the background and filling in the gaps between entities that compose the world, but with these entities seen as the gaps within the divine existence. Instead of viewing a tangible world within whose shadowy reaches God does not dwell, we understand that the entire world comprises the divine existence.

Let us use an analogy that our Sages did not employ: that of black and white cinematography. Light is projected through a film onto a screen. Areas of darkness on the film create the images on the screen. This means that the world of a movie, in which characters move and converse, live and die, is created by light and shadows. The light is the backdrop, and the world of the movie appears where the light is hidden, to one degree or another. Similarly, the world is composed of dancing shadows that have no substance compared to the source of light. This is an expression of the concept that "everything before Him is literally considered nothingness." It is the perspective that "He is alone in the upper and lower worlds, just as He was alone before the six days of Creation." The world that appears so tangible to us is not a new, independent existence but only a darkness concealing God's existence. It is an illusion.

וְגַם בַּמָּקוֹם הַזֶּה שֶׁנִּבְרָא בּוֹ עוֹלָם הַזֶּה - הַשָּׁמַיִם וְהָאָרֶץ וְכָל צְבָאָם - הָיָה הוּא לְבַדּוֹ מְמַלֵּא הַמָּקוֹם הַזֶּה. וְגַם עַתָּה כֵּן הוּא לְבַדּוֹ בְּלִי שׁוּם שִׁינּוּי כְּלָל,

and also in this very space in which this world, the heavens and earth and all their hosts, was created – He alone filled this space. He is now also alone, without any change at all,

Prior to the creation of the world, God was fully revealed and manifest everywhere; there was no existence without Him. Now as well, the world's seeming existence does not negate the infinite divine existence. The world does not, so to speak, press upon the divine existence to keep it from being present in the same space. The created world is nothing more than a secondary or tertiary image overlaid onto the true existence. In essence the created world itself is the divine existence.

מִפְּנֵי שֶׁכָּל הַנִּבְרָאִים בְּטֵלִים אֶצְלוֹ בִּמְצִיאוּת מַמָּשׁ,

because the existence of all created beings is literally nullified in relation to Him,

The world is not at all comparable to the Divine. The world is transparent compared to God's existence. From God's perspective, whether or not the world exists makes no difference. In this sense, created beings are nullified within God's existence, since essentially they are part and parcel of that existence, and have no independence beyond Him whatsoever.

כְּבִיטּוּל אוֹתִיּוֹת הַדִּבּוּר וְהַמַּחֲשָׁבָה בִּמְקוֹרָן וְשָׁרְשָׁן, הוּא מַהוּת הַנֶּפֶשׁ וְעַצְמוּתָהּ,

just as the letters of speech and thought are nullified within their source and root, namely, the essence and being of the soul,

The letters of speech and thought make up the concepts and words with which a person thinks and speaks. In a sense, these letters reveal a person's character and essence. When we compare the revealed letters to the original, unrevealed source, that which is revealed is nullified. It has no intrinsic meaning without the source that it reveals.[8]

---

8. See chap. 20 and commentary there.

שֶׁהֵן עֶשֶׂר בְּחִינוֹתֶיהָ: חָכְמָה בִּינָה וָדַעַת כו', שֶׁאֵין בָּהֶם בְּחִינַת אוֹתִיּוֹת עֲדַיִין, קוֹדֶם שֶׁמִּתְלַבְּשׁוֹת בִּלְבוּשׁ הַמַּחְשָׁבָה [כְּמוֹ שֶׁנִּתְבָּאֵר בִּפְרָקִים כ' וְכ"א בַּאֲרִיכוּת עַיֵּין שָׁם].

which are the soul's **ten faculties** – wisdom, understanding, and knowledge, **and so forth. They do not yet possess the aspect of letters before they are clothed in the garment of thought** (as explained at length in chapters 20 and 21; see there).

The ten faculties of the soul constitute its essence and being, which serves as the source of the letters, which are ultimately clothed in the garment of thought. When we consider the soul itself, prior to the expression of its traits, abilities, and potential, we see that what these express in the "garment" of the letters of thought and speech is as nothing compared to the infinite possibilities the soul contains.

This relationship between a person's thoughts and personality is not merely quantitative. An entire world may exist within those thoughts: people, places, events, and actions. But that world has no independent, objective existence outside of his thoughts. It is no more than a shadow of the person's personality. Similarly, the letters of divine speech – whose power creates and maintains the universe and the reality of all of the worlds within it – do not possess substantiality any more than do the letters of human thought. Just as the creations of human thought are nullified relative to the person thinking them, so too, all worlds are nullified relative to the divine essence that creates them.

וּכְמוֹ שֶׁנִּתְבָּאֵר גַּם כֵּן בְּמָקוֹם אַחֵר, מָשָׁל גַּשְׁמִי לָזֶה מֵעִנְיַן בִּיטּוּל זִיו וְאוֹר הַשֶּׁמֶשׁ בִּמְקוֹרוֹ, הוּא גּוּף כַּדּוּר הַשֶּׁמֶשׁ שֶׁבָּרָקִיעַ. שֶׁגַּם שָׁם מֵאִיר וּמִתְפַּשֵּׁט וַדַּאי זִיווֹ וְאוֹרוֹ, וּבְיֶתֶר שְׂאֵת מֵהִתְפַּשְּׁטוּתוֹ וְהֶאָרָתוֹ בַּחֲלַל הָעוֹלָם, אֶלָּא שֶׁשָּׁם הוּא בָּטֵל

This idea was likewise explained elsewhere (see *Sha'ar HaYiḥud VeHa'emuna*, chap. 3) **by employing an analogy to this** from the physical **world, namely, the concept of the nullification of the sun's radiance and light within its source, that is, the body of the sun in the firmament. In there too, the sun's radiance and light certainly shine and radiate, even more than its radiance**

בִּמְצִיאוּת בִּמְקוֹרוֹ וּכְאִילוּ אֵינוֹ בִּמְצִיאוּת כְּלָל. and illumination in the expanse of the universe; **but there,** inside the sun, **its existence is nullified within its source, as though it does not exist at all.**

The light of the sun shines everywhere except within the sun itself. When the light shines outside the sun, it appears as an independent entity that gives vitality to complete worlds. But within the sun none of that has any significance. When the light is in the source from which it is generated, it is nullified. It returns, as it were, to the state prior to its having been created, when it did not exist at all.

וְכָכָה מַמָּשׁ, דֶּרֶךְ מָשָׁל, **In precisely the same way, figuratively speaking,**

One should bear in mind that the light and the source of light are only analogies. An analogy, whether taken from the material or spiritual world, serves to explain something beyond the analogy itself. We must examine the analogy again and again in order to seek its deeper meaning. In this particular analogy, the idea to contemplate is how a derivative is nullified in relation to its source, in the fundamental existence from which it stems.

הוּא בִּיטוּל הָעוֹלָם וּמְלוֹאוֹ בַּמְצִיאוּת לְגַבֵּי מְקוֹרוֹ, שֶׁהוּא אוֹר אֵין סוֹף בָּרוּךְ הוּא, וּכְמוֹ שֶׁנִּתְבָּאֵר שָׁם בַּאֲרִיכוּת. **is the existence of the world and everything in it nullified in relation to its source, which is the light of** *Ein Sof*, **blessed be He, as explained there at length.**

As was explained earlier, the nullification of the world's existence relative to the divine is not due to the lowliness and insignificance of the world but due to the fact that its entire existence is a dim ray of light deriving from the essence of divine light. It is an illumination that appears as an independent entity only when it is disconnected and distanced from the divine source. The world, including everything contained therein, is insubstantial in the context of the divine light source.

וְהִנֵּה כְּשֶׁיַּעֲמִיק בָּזֶה הַרְבֵּה, **When a person contemplates this a great deal,**

Deep contemplation in general consists of thinking about a particular topic until it becomes clear to one and conceptually integrated into one's soul. Contemplation of God's unity is a component of the daily prayer service. It is what one must bear in mind when proclaiming, "Hear, Israel: The Lord is our God, the Lord is one" (Deut. 6:4). The idea expressed in this verse is more than the fact that God is one and not two. A person must be unwavering in his concentration, steadily focused for a period of time, envisioning and clarifying for himself the nature of this oneness, of the fact that "there is nothing besides Him" (Deut. 4:35), that not only is there no other like Him in terms of greatness or strength, but that nothing exists apart from Him. This is not the kind of thought that a person can have fleetingly – "God exists; He is one" – and then go on with his day. A person must meditate on this thought at length, reviewing it again and again.

A significant proportion of hasidic teachings is meant to supply the content for such contemplation and provide a springboard that enables a person to look at this verse anew twice daily, in a fresh light and with new vitality. This is similar to how a person contemplates a physical object placed directly before him, as something he is seeing for the first time. ☞

THE POWER OF THE BEDTIME *SHEMA*

☞ A story is told of a Chabad hasid who reached an inn late at night. The innkeeper asked him if he wanted to eat, but the hasid refused, saying that he was too tired and wanted to go straight to bed. In his room, the hasid washed his hands and began to recite the bedtime *Shema*. Since he was a hasid, he began to deeply meditate on the concept that God is one while standing with one foot on the floor and the other on the bed. The innkeeper found him in that same position the following morning, still pondering this phrase. That hasid's meditation was not the same that he had had on previous occasions, but a new insight into God's oneness. Although he had genuinely intended to go to sleep, his meditation revealed a new reality that gave him enough material to think about until the morning. Not everyone is capable of such a deep meditation, but this story teaches how deep and broad the topic of God's unity is, and how far one can go in meditating upon it.

The deep contemplation that this chapter is discussing is not a purely intellectual and abstract analysis, but something that has an emotional aspect as well. The nullification of the world before the Divine means that no barrier exists, that God is here with us as fully as He is in the highest heavens, and perhaps even more so. The more a person meditates on this, the more he perceives an intensely tangible nearness to God. This nearness is not dependent on a person's righteousness, fulfillment of mitzvot, Torah study, or anything else. Rather, it is a closeness that has no conditions, no limits, where essence meets essence and one may come to feel an intense joy that is without conditions and without limits.

> יִשְׂמַח לִבּוֹ וְתָגֵל נַפְשׁוֹ אַף גִּילַת וְרַנֵּן בְּכָל לֵב וָנֶפֶשׁ וּמְאֹד

his heart will rejoice and his soul will be glad even with joy and song (see Isa. 35:2), **with all his heart and soul and might**

The phrase "With all his heart and soul and might" recalls the commandment to love God mentioned in the first paragraph of the *Shema*: "With all your heart, and with all your soul, and with all your might." That love of God likewise comes from a person's contemplation of God's oneness as he recites the words "Hear, Israel: The Lord is our God, the Lord is one."

> בֶּאֱמוּנָה זוֹ כִּי רַבָּה הִיא, כִּי הִיא קִרְבַת אֱלֹקִים מַמָּשׁ.

in this faith in God's unity. One's joy abounds **because it is a great faith, since it is literally** an experience of **closeness to God.**

Although the chapter began with the notion of intellectually contemplating God's unity, the author of the *Tanya* refers to this concept here as "faith" because it is first and foremost founded upon the faith that, as the psalmist says, "By the word of God the heavens were made" (Ps. 33:6).[9]

As stated earlier, the purpose of contemplating God's unity is not to deny material existence but to attain an experiential awareness of the Divine Presence. By contemplating the nothingness of existence

---

9. As explained by the Lubavitcher Rebbe, Rabbi Menaḥem Mendel Schneerson.

relative to the Divine, we dismantle all the barriers and reveal that God is present. When we contemplate that "there is nothing besides Him," that there is no existence besides the Divine, no existence that has any tangibility that can interpose between us and Godliness, we attain a feeling of closeness to God, of being as close to Him as we can bear to be.

In order to attain closeness with God, a person need not storm the supernal realms or penetrate more and more deeply into the layers of his soul. He need only remove the veil of created reality and reveal that God is present. The question is not whether God is present, but to what degree a person is aware of His presence. For example, there are many things whose existence a person is unaware of and that do not depend on his awareness. Every person has a heart, but only a minority (usually those with a heart condition) are sensitive to the fact. The heart constantly operates; a person's life depends on its continuing activity at every moment, yet he may not be aware of that.

As a rule, the extent to which a person is aware of something bears no correlation whatsoever to how real or close it is to him. If anything, the correlation may be inverse, in that the closer and more familiar something is, the more effort and practice a person requires to be truly aware of its existence. As noted in other contexts, a person's greatest pleasure is that of being alive. Yet one typically takes this for granted, except at a time of crisis, such as after recovering from a serious illness or being granted a reprieve from a death sentence. The meaning of one's "closeness to God" is that the Divine is closer to him than anything else, closer than life itself, closer than the beating of his heart – and that is precisely why he does not sense it. But the moment the veil is lifted, as soon as this notion of God's unity enters into his awareness, then he needs nothing else in his life. He has everything.

וְ"זֶה כָּל הָאָדָם" וְתַכְלִית בְּרִיאָתוֹ, וּבְרִיאַת כָּל הָעוֹלָמוֹת עֶלְיוֹנִים וְתַחְתּוֹנִים, לִהְיוֹת לוֹ דִּירָה זוֹ בַּתַּחְתּוֹנִים, כְּמוֹ שֶׁיִּתְבָּאֵר לְקַמָּן בַּאֲרִיכוּת.

In fact **this is the whole** purpose of man and the purpose of his creation, and of the creation of all the worlds, higher and lower: namely, **in order for this** to be **a dwelling place for Him below**, as will be explained at length below.

God created the world and man in order to have "a dwelling place below,"[10] which, to quote Ecclesiastes (12:13), "is the whole [purpose of] man." God is found in everything and everywhere, including the lower worlds, and this reality is not dependent on man at all. Moreover, from God's perspective, there is no distinction between the higher and lower realms. Therefore, the concept of "a dwelling place below" refers not to God's existence in the lower realms but rather to the fact that His existence is revealed to man both consciously and emotionally. The notion of lower realms as applied to the psyche of the human being relates to a level of his intellect or emotion that does not perceive the divine. When a person becomes aware that God is present in his ordinary state of reality, when he feels close to God, he creates "a dwelling place below" for God, and as such he attains the great goal of the existence of all worlds, from their beginning to their end. ☞

וְהִנֵּה כַּמָּה גְדוֹלָה שִׂמְחַת הֶדְיוֹט וְשָׁפָל אֲנָשִׁים בְּהִתְקָרְבוּתוֹ לְמֶלֶךְ בָּשָׂר וָדָם, הַמִּתְאַכְסֵן וְדָר אִתּוֹ עִמּוֹ בְּבֵיתוֹ,

How great is the joy of a commoner and lowly man when he draws close to a human king who lodges and lives with him in his home!

SEEING THE WORLD OR SEEING THE DIVINE?

☞ Our world was created in such a well-balanced and complete way that it appears to possess an independent existence. As a result, God's existence is not readily apparent. In the analogy given earlier of a black-and-white drawing, one may perceive black shapes resting against a white background or vice versa. That which helps the eye pass from the black shapes to the white shapes are the flaws: a lack of completeness in some point, lines that are unfinished, improper proportions. These allow the eye to switch perspectives. In this vein, our world is so well balanced that a person is equally likely either to perceive or not perceive the divine. Someone who sees only the natural aspect of the world may live all his life without ever discovering that there is another, divine aspect, and it is theoretically possible (although this requires much practice) to perceive this other aspect continuously. A person's perspective may also switch from one point to the other. Suddenly he may discover a new viewpoint so that the proportions drastically change. That which he had considered central he now considers merely decorative. That which he had considered reality he now sees as nothing but a backdrop to reality.

---

10. Further discussed in chaps. 35–36 below. See also *Tanḥuma, Naso* 16 and *Beḥukotai* 3; *Bemidbar Rabba* 13:6.

Until now, the author of the *Tanya* has focused on a person's intellectual contemplation of God's omnipresence. Now he returns to the initial subject of the chapter: the concept of joy and how it emerges from that contemplation.

Were a great, well-known man to stay at the home of a commoner, were he to shake his hand and speak to him even briefly, that meeting would become the focal point of the commoner's life, its apex of light and happiness. It would be an experience he would always remember and that would serve as his source of vitality.

וְקַל וָחוֹמֶר לְאֵין קֵץ לְקִרְבַת וִדִידַת מֶלֶךְ מַלְכֵי הַמְּלָכִים הַקָּדוֹשׁ בָּרוּךְ הוּא. וְכִדְכְתִיב: "כִּי מִי הוּא זֶה אֲשֶׁר עָרַב לִבּוֹ לָגֶשֶׁת אֵלַי נְאֻם ה'" (ירמיה ל, כא).

How **infinitely more so** is a person's joy with regard **to the closeness and dwelling** here below **of the King of kings, the Holy One, blessed be He, as it is written: "For who is it whose heart has dared to approach Me? – the utterance of the Lord"** (Jer. 30:21).

In order to truly sense God's closeness and the resulting joy one experiences, a person must have, on the one hand, a sense of trepidation in the face of awesome, infinite distance, such that "who is it whose heart dared to approach Me?" and he must perceive, on the other hand, the unrivaled closeness of the Divine. When a person experiences these two feelings, a sense of gratitude and tremendous joy bursts into being, as he considers that God, who is immeasurably great and awesome, chooses to be the guest in his home, meaning, in his awareness and his feelings. In and of himself, a person is a small, lowly creature. No matter how much he grows, he can never come close to God, the infinite *Ein Sof*. All human beings, from the simplest and lowest, to Moses, the preeminent human being, stand before *Ein Sof* at the same point: the point of nothingness. But although a person cannot reach the infinite *Ein Sof*, the infinite *Ein Sof* can reach him. Accordingly, it is only when God so desires that a person can be close to him. That is the reason for one's sense of gratitude, which results in a feeling of joy: that as infinitely great as God is, He reaches down infinitely below. "It is true that God is the King of kings, and before whom no one dares to approach, yet here He is! The King of kings visits me. He is always with me." This is the essence of a person's most simple and all-encompassing gratitude for being able to experience God's closeness to him.

12 Adar וְעַל זֶה תִּיקְנוּ לִיתֵּן שֶׁבַח וְהוֹדָיָה לִשְׁמוֹ יִתְבָּרֵךְ בְּכָל בֹּקֶר, וְלוֹמַר: "אַשְׁרֵינוּ מַה טּוֹב חֶלְקֵנוּ וכו' וּמַה יָּפָה יְרוּשָׁתֵנוּ". כְּלוֹמַר, כְּמוֹ שֶׁהָאָדָם שָׂשׂ וְשָׂמֵחַ בִּירוּשָּׁה שֶׁנָּפְלָה לוֹ הוֹן עָתֵק שֶׁלֹּא עָמַל בּוֹ,

It is on account of this that the Sages **instituted that a person should give praise and thanks to God's name every morning, and say, "Happy are we, for how good is our portion** and how pleasant is our lot, **and how beautiful is our heritage!"** That is to say, **just as a person is happy and joyful** in receiving **an inheritance when a great fortune that he had not labored to acquire falls into his possession,**

The most germane clause of this quote is "How beautiful is our heritage."[11] When a person acquires wealth through laborious and extensive efforts, he may feel as if he has received compensation for an investment that he made. But when a person receives an inheritance, something that he did not strive to achieve, something that was given freely, he can experience only pure joy and gratitude.

כֵּן וְיוֹתֵר מִכֵּן לְאֵין קֵץ, יֵשׁ לָנוּ לִשְׂמוֹחַ עַל יְרוּשָׁתֵנוּ שֶׁהִנְחִילוּנוּ אֲבוֹתֵינוּ, הוּא יִחוּד ה' הָאֲמִיתִּי, אֲשֶׁר אֲפִילּוּ בָּאָרֶץ מִתַּחַת אֵין עוֹד מִלְּבַדּוֹ - וְזוֹ הִיא דִּירָתוֹ בַּתַּחְתּוֹנִים.

likewise, and infinitely more so, ought we to rejoice over our heritage that our forefathers bequeathed to us. This inheritance **is the** ability to feel **God's true unity,** the knowledge **that even on earth below there is nothing besides Him.** This awareness **is His dwelling place in the lower worlds.**

Our ancestors bequeathed to us an awareness, a realization that they themselves attained, by devoting their entire lifetimes to study, meditation, and contemplation. It is an inheritance for which we should be more grateful and joyful than for anything material. Our ancestors passed on to us the secret that in essence God is present right here.

---

11. Regarding the phrase "How good is our portion, how pleasant is our lot," see *Iggeret HaKodesh*, epistle 7 and *Sefer HaMa'amarim Admor Yosef Yitzḥak*, 5688.

From generation to generation, fathers, as it were, whispered into the ears of their children: "In your house, in the house that all of us live in, lies a hidden treasure." This deeply personal awareness is the secret of God's true unity. The sense that despite everything, God is here with us and permeates all of existence is more precious than the treasures of all the kings of the earth. This is an inheritance that, although containing everything, is a person's individual awareness that he cannot pass on to anyone else. So in thanks to God, we exclaim: "How good is our portion … and how beautiful our heritage." Compared to this gift, everything else in the world pales into insignificance.

וְזֶהוּ שֶׁאָמְרוּ רַבּוֹתֵינוּ ז"ל: תרי"ג מִצְוֹת נִתְּנוּ לְיִשְׂרָאֵל... בָּא חֲבַקּוּק וְהֶעֱמִידָן עַל אַחַת שֶׁנֶּאֱמַר: "וְצַדִּיק בֶּאֱמוּנָתוֹ יִחְיֶה" (חבקוק ב, ד).

This is the meaning of the statement of our Rabbis, "There were 613 commandments given to Israel… Habakkuk came and established them upon one, the mitzva of *emuna*, as the verse states: "But the righteous will live by his faith" (Hab. 2:4).

Our Rabbis teach that "613 commandments were given to Israel[12]… King David came and established them upon eleven…. Isaiah came and established them upon six…. Micah came and established them upon three…. Habakkuk came and established them upon one, referring to the commandment of faith, as it is stated: 'But the righteous person shall live by his faith.'" This refers to faith in God's unity, which fills a righteous person with life and constitutes his reality. It is the meaning, power, and joy of his life. This joy is intrinsic regardless of his circumstances, whether a person is righteous or evil, rich or poor, fortunate or wretched. He knows what is important: that God is here with him.

כְּלוֹמַר, כְּאִלּוּ אֵינָהּ רַק מִצְוָה אַחַת - הִיא הָאֱמוּנָה לְבַדָּהּ. כִּי עַל יְדֵי הָאֱמוּנָה לְבַדָּהּ - יָבֹא לְקִיּוּם כָּל הַתרי"ג מִצְוֹת.

In other words, it is as though there is only one commandment, which is faith alone, for by means of faith alone a person will come to fulfill all 613 commandments.

This is not to say that faith substitutes for all the other commandments,

---

12. See *Makkot* 23b–24a.

and one who possesses faith is not obligated to fulfill them. On the contrary, faith provides the means by which a person fulfills all of the commandments. This unique quality underscores the importance of faith.[13]

| דְּהַיְינוּ כְּשֶׁיִּהְיֶה לִבּוֹ שָׂשׂ וְשָׂמֵחַ בֶּאֱמוּנָתוֹ בְּיִחוּד ה' בְּתַכְלִית הַשִּׂמְחָה - כְּאִלּוּ לֹא הָיְתָה עָלָיו רַק מִצְוָה זוֹ לְבַדָּהּ, וְהִיא לְבַדָּהּ תַּכְלִית בְּרִיאָתוֹ וּבְרִיאַת כָּל הָעוֹלָמוֹת - | That is to say, **when** a person's **heart will be happy and joyous, with the ultimate joy in his faith in God's unity, as though he is obligated only in this commandment alone, and** that **it alone is the purpose of his being created and the creation of all the worlds,** |

The phrase "the righteous person lives by his faith" means that the greater a person's faith, the more alive, inspired, and vibrant he is. When a person believes that God exists not only somewhere in the heavens above but is here with us and that there is truly nothing besides Him, that is the sole source of his joy and vitality. The purpose of the creation of man and all the worlds is for God to have a dwelling place below, which, as was noted above, is our personal, subjective awareness that God is with us. When a person attains this awareness that God is with him, that God is his life and that there is nothing besides Him, he fulfills his part in the purpose of his being created and of the creation of all the worlds.

| הֲרֵי בְּכֹחַ וְחַיּוּת נַפְשׁוֹ בְּשִׂמְחָה רַבָּה זוֹ תִּתְעַלֶּה נַפְשׁוֹ לְמַעְלָה מַעְלָה עַל כָּל הַמּוֹנְעִים קִיּוּם כָּל הַתְּרִי"ג מִצְוֹת, | then **with the strength and vitality of his soul** experienced **through this great joy, his soul will be elevated far beyond all obstacles that prevent** him **from fulfilling all of the 613 commandments,** |

---

13. The 613 commandments are established on faith. Faith and fulfilling the other commandments are not two separate matters. Rather, when a person fulfills a commandment, he feels faith in the source of that commandment (remark of the Lubavitcher Rebbe, Rabbi Menaḥem Mendel Schneerson).

This feeling of joy is a person's sensation of divine life flowing through him and all existence.

This chapter continues the theme begun in chapter 31, which describes a person who feels dejected on account of his spiritual failings and who therefore cannot serve God by properly fulfilling His commandments. In order to break free of his immobility and overcome the obstacles that are preventing him from serving God, he must attain a state of joy. The path to doing so is the way of "a righteous person, [who] lives by his faith," that is, faith in the unity of God. A person possessing faith can constantly be rejuvenated.

This path is accessible not only to the righteous. Any person can say, "Although I, as lowly and disgraceful as I may be, have committed such and such sins, God is always with me, and when God is with me, what can be bad?" The power of this joy enables anyone to overcome his feelings of dejection and rise above anything that prevents him from serving God by keeping His commandments.

מִבַּיִת וּמִחוּץ. whether those obstacles are **internal or external.**

A person can overcome every obstacle, whether it is the result of entanglements within his own soul and his own life choices, or whether it stems from external circumstances.

Until this point, the author of the *Tanya* has explained the verse "A righteous person lives by his faith" as referring to the sense of renewal and joy experienced by a person who possesses faith in the oneness of God and His closeness to him. From this point onward, the author analyzes the subject on a deeper level.

וְזֶהוּ שֶׁאָמַר "בֶּאֱמוּנָתוֹ יִחְיֶה" - יִחְיֶה דַּיְיקָא - כִּתְחִיַּית הַמֵּתִים דֶּרֶךְ מָשָׁל, כָּךְ תִּחְיֶה נַפְשׁוֹ בְּשִׂמְחָה רַבָּה זוֹ. **Thus** the verse **states, "He shall live by his faith"** – specifying "he shall *live*"; that is, **just as the dead, for example, will be revived, so will his soul be revived by means of this great joy.**

Not only does this faith provide inspiration for the rest of a person's life, but it constitutes a renewal of his current life. When the soul of one whose former life was cause for bitterness, for a fading will to live, is rejuvenated by the joy generated by living by one's faith, a completely new life replaces the old. This phenomenon is analogous to the future resurrection of the dead, when the deceased will be infused with an utterly new and qualitatively different life than we experience at present.

וְהִיא שִׂמְחָה כְּפוּלָה וּמְכוּפֶּלֶת, כִּי מִלְּבַד שִׂמְחַת הַנֶּפֶשׁ הַמַּשְׂכֶּלֶת בְּקִרְבַת ה׳ וְדִירָתוֹ אִתּוֹ עִמּוֹ, **This is a manifold joy, because apart from the joy of the** person's **soul when apprehending God's closeness** to him and His **dwelling together with him,**

This refers to the joy of a person who attains the awareness that God dwells with him.

13 Adar
עוֹד זֹאת יִשְׂמַח בִּכְפְלַיִים בְּשִׂמְחַת ה׳ וְגוֹדֶל נַחַת רוּחַ לְפָנָיו יִתְבָּרַךְ בֶּאֱמוּנָה זוֹ, **he will moreover be doubly joyful** in his awareness of **God's joy and** the **great** degree of **gratification this faith brings God,**

The joy a person's closeness to God generates is twofold: not only does he himself experience joy, but God too may be said to experience joy when a person believes in Him. When one who is trapped inside a body and unable to perceive the Divine is ensconced within a society that denies God, within a world that is turning to other directions, and he becomes aware that "behold, the Lord is standing over him," then God rejoices, and the person partakes of that joy. He consequently experiences a double joy: his own joy at being close to God, and God's joy at being close to him.

דְּאִתְכַּפְיָא סִטְרָא אָחֳרָא מַמָּשׁ, וְאִתְהַפֵּךְ חֲשׁוֹכָא לִנְהוֹרָא, **in that the** *sitra aḥara* **is literally subdued, and darkness is transformed into light.**

The *sitra aḥara*, the "other side," refers to the aspect of existence that is not holy and hides holiness. As has been explained in a number of places (see commentary to chap. 27), there are two aspects to serving God, "subduing" and "transforming." Regarding the first aspect, the concealing veil is torn and a ray of the divine light appears from the other side. But with regard to the second, the concealment (the darkness) itself is transformed into light: the *kelippa* that had concealed the Divine is revealed as itself being divine light.

שֶׁהוּא חֹשֶׁךְ הַקְּלִיפּוֹת שֶׁבָּעוֹלָם הַזֶּה הַחוּמְרִי, הַמַּחֲשִׁיכִים וּמְכַסִּים עַל אוֹרוֹ יִתְבָּרֵךְ עַד עֵת קֵץ, כְּמוֹ שֶׁכָּתוּב: "קֵץ שָׂם לַחֹשֶׁךְ" (איוב כח, ג).	**This** darkness is referring to **the darkness of the *kelippot* in this material world, which obstruct and conceal God's light until the end time,** when, as the verse states: "He sets an end to darkness" (Job 28:3).

In addition to the particular type of darkness associated with each specific sin, there is general darkness associated with the existence of *kelippa* in the most primal sense: *Kelippa* is by definition a covering that prevents us from seeing the essence within, an entity through which we cannot see the Divine. This concealment is due to the fact that the world (*olam*) is by design an occlusion (*he'elem*) of the Divine. At present this concealment is an integral part of the nature of the world, unaffected by people or the passage of time, that will be eradicated only at the end of days, when the world as we know it will be totally shattered.

[דְּהַיְינוּ קֵץ הַיָּמִין, שֶׁיַּעֲבִיר רוּחַ הַטֻּמְאָה מִן הָאָרֶץ "וְנִגְלָה כְּבוֹד ה' וְרָאוּ כָל בָּשָׂר יַחְדָּיו" (ישעיה מ, ה), וּכְמוֹ שֶׁיִּתְבָּאֵר לְקַמָּן].	(**This is** a reference to **the end of days, when** God **will remove the spirit of impurity from the earth, "and the glory of the Lord will be revealed and all flesh will see together"** [Isa. 40:5], **as will be explained below** [chap. 36].)

At the end of days (see Dan. 12:13), when the spirit of impurity will be removed completely and the concealment intrinsic to the existence of the world will be eradicated, then "all flesh will see together." The concealment is a combination of a number of factors: the external world, a person's senses, and the internal structure of his psyche. In order to go beyond concealment, it does not suffice to rectify just one of these factors. Being able to see the Divine via the external world as a result of a miracle or a revelation will in itself not change much. A change in a person's sensory, material awareness will in itself not be enough without a corresponding shift in the internal makeup of his psyche. Lacking that, he will always readjust himself so that the messages from the outside align with his internal preconceptions. It is virtually impossible for a person to see things that, according to his fundamental assumptions, cannot exist. Moreover, in order to attain a perception of the Divine, he must push not only beyond the boundaries of material existence and the perception associated with the material world, but also beyond the confining existence of his own self. In order for God to be revealed in this world, one must make a place for Him, and wherever a person's sense of self is present, God cannot be revealed. Therefore the Talmud states, "Any person who has arrogance within him, the Holy One, blessed be He, said: He and I cannot dwell together in the world" (*Sota* 5a). But at the end of days, at the end of the existence of this world with its present meaning, form, and structure, at a time when the "world" (*olam*) will no longer constitute a "concealment" (*he'elem*), the existence of physicality will itself be a revelation of the Divine. Then "all flesh will see together that the mouth of God has spoken."

וּבִפְרָט בְּחוּץ לָאָרֶץ, שֶׁאֲוִיר אֶרֶץ הָעַמִּים טָמֵא וּמָלֵא קְלִיפּוֹת וְסִטְרָא אָחֳרָא. — This darkness exists **particularly outside the Land** of Israel, **since the air of the land of the nations is impure and full of** *kelippot* **and the** *sitra aḥara*.

The spiritual darkness[14] and concealment outside the Land of Israel is more powerful than in the Land of Israel.[15] As a result of this potent darkness, the divine light is significantly less apparent outside the Land of Israel. ☞

וְאֵין שִׂמְחָה לְפָנָיו יִתְבָּרֵךְ כְּאוֹרָה וְשִׂמְחָה בְּיִתְרוֹן אוֹר הַבָּא מִן הַחֹשֶׁךְ דַּוְקָא. — **There is no** greater **joy before God** as the **light and joy** caused by the **superior** nature of **light that emerges specifically from the darkness.**

---

14. See *Shabbat* 15b, and Rambam, *Sefer Tahara, Hilkhot Tumat Met*, chap. 11.
15. See *Torah Or* 13a.

This darkness refers to the darkness of this world, in particular, the darkness in the lands of the other nations outside the Land of Israel. If a person clearly recognizes God's existence in the midst of this darkness, he creates light from within the darkness. The light that is generated from within the darkness, in which God takes such joy, is not a light that is the opposite of darkness but one that emerges from the darkness. Jeremiah alludes to this concept in the verse "If you extract that which is precious from the worthless" (Jer. 15:19), referring to a unique factor that is not shared by light that does not emerge from darkness. ☞

TO TRULY ENTER THE LAND OF ISRAEL

☞ Not everyone who enters the Land of Israel is immediately aware of a greater divine revelation. One possibility accounting for this phenomenon is that a person brings with him the *kelippot* from outside the land. Therefore, even in the Land of Israel he is in a bubble of sorts that contains the atmosphere from outside the land. As was explained above, a person's ability to perceive the Divine depends not only on his external environment's illumination but also on his internal being's purification. One must train himself to sense the difference between the degree of light radiating from one place and another. One who has yet to do so cannot have truly transitioned from one location to another.

GOD'S JOY

☞ As was mentioned above, when a person is close to God, it generates two elements of joy. The first is the person's joy at recognizing his nearness to God. The second is God's joy at his success in recognizing Him despite the labyrinth of life in which God placed him. God created a universal concealment and distance from Him so that people would discover Him from the midst of the concealment.

This sense of discovery that comes out of concealment has been compared to the entertainment presented before aristocrats, which consists of entirely new and unexpected sights (see *Torah Or* 18a). It has also been stated (*Torah Or* 61b and *Likkutei Torah*, Num. 77c) that laughter and lightheartedness result when something different and new is introduced (*Likkutei Hagahot* on the *Tanya*).

The feeling of joy upon discovering God may be compared to that of a father who asks his child difficult questions and rejoices when he answers them correctly. The most crucial question that God asks us is "Where am I?" To answer this question, a person must overcome stumbling blocks, work his way through errors, and emerge from a labyrinth, after which he can respond, "You are here!" The person rejoices because he feels close to God and because he feels God's joy on his behalf (see *Torah Or* 18a, 61b; *Likkutei Torah*, Num. 77c).

וְזֶהוּ שֶׁכָּתוּב: "יִשְׂמַח יִשְׂרָאֵל בְּעוֹשָׂיו" (תהלים קמט, ב), פֵּירוּשׁ שֶׁכָּל מִי שֶׁהוּא מִזֶּרַע יִשְׂרָאֵל יֵשׁ לוֹ לִשְׂמוֹחַ בְּשִׂמְחַת ה' אֲשֶׁר שָׂשׂ וְשָׂמֵחַ בְּדִירָתוֹ בַּתַּחְתּוֹנִים, שֶׁהֵם בְּחִינַת עֲשִׂיָּה גַּשְׁמִיִּית מַמָּשׁ.

This is the meaning of **the verse "Let Israel rejoice in its Maker"** (Ps. 149:2). **This means that everyone who is of the seed of Israel should rejoice in God's joy, who is happy and joyous that His dwelling place is in the lower worlds, which are on the level of** actual physical *Asiya*.

A Jew must rejoice that God has made him dwell in the lowly and dark world of *Asiya* so that despite the darkness he will be able to perceive the divine light hidden within. The verse "Let Israel rejoice" indicates that this is the characteristic quality of Israel: Every Jew accepts simple belief in God's unity not as a philosophical conclusion nor as the apex of the mystical ladder, but in the same way that a small child does. He acknowledges that God is one not only in the higher worlds but in the lower worlds as well. A Jew accepts this not as the conclusion of his life, but as the starting point for his life. "Let Israel rejoice" because the end point and purpose of a Jew's life, to make a dwelling place for God below, is also imprinted upon every starting point of his life, in his soul and in his body.

וְזֶהוּ שֶׁכָּתוּב 'בְּעוֹשָׂיו', לְשׁוֹן רַבִּים, שֶׁהוּא עוֹלָם הַזֶּה הַגַּשְׁמִי הַמָּלֵא קְלִיפּוֹת וְסִטְרָא אָחֳרָא, שֶׁנִּקְרְאוּ 'רְשׁוּת הָרַבִּים', וְ'טוּרֵי דִפְרוּדָא',

This is the meaning the verse, which **states "its Makers," in the plural form.** This is a reference to the fact **that this material world is filled with** multitudinous *kelippot* **and the** *sitra aḥara*, **which are called a "public domain" and**, in the *Zohar*'s parlance, **"mountains of separation,"**

In terms of the straightforward reading of the verse, either the Hebrew term actually does mean "its Maker" (and the *yod* in the word usually indicating a plural is a linguistic anomaly here), or the reference to a powerful figure in the plural is a standard technique.[16]

---

16. See *Da'at Mikra*.

Whereas a private domain (literally, "the domain of the individual") alludes to a space in which God, the "Individual One of existence," is revealed, and there is nothing besides Him, a public domain (literally, "the domain of the multitude") alludes to our physical world, a realm in which the Individual One is concealed. Instead, we perceive a multiplicity of forces and factors that make up and propel the world.

וְאִתְהַפְּכָן לִנְהוֹרָא וְנַעֲשִׂים רְשׁוּת הַיָּחִיד לְיִחוּדוֹ יִתְבָּרֵךְ בֶּאֱמוּנָה זוֹ. **and which are then transformed into light by means of this faith and become a private domain for the sake of God's unity.**

This world, referred to here as a public domain, i.e., a place where multiple forces seem to be at play and the oneness of God is concealed, must be transformed into a "private domain," i.e., a realm where God's unity and oneness are clearly apparent. It is a transformation in which darkness morphs into light. This occurs when there is a transition from a perspective of multiplicity to a perspective of oneness, from a perspective of a multitude of forces that appear to be acting arbitrarily and aimlessly, of evil and good jumbled together, to a perspective in which all forces act as guided by one clear guideline and in which they are all one.

Transforming darkness into light is the work of the human being. A person is born into a world of disparity, the "mountains of separation." But he slowly learns that all of its barriers, the ominous "mountains of separation," are a deception, that what appear to be disparate entities are elements of one existence. He attains the faith that the divine light exists everywhere and that nothing can obscure it. As a result, the "public domain" is nullified and transformed into a "private domain."

"Let Israel rejoice in its Maker." Israel rejoices in the transition from the so-called public to private domains. A person rejoices not in his personal accomplishments, but in the existence of God, in the fact that as a result of his awareness God illuminates all the worlds, and in the fulfillment of the purpose of his creation and the creation of all the worlds.

The existence of the world is, as it were, God's endeavor to receive a signal, a message from another. The entire framework of creation is built to this end, to transmit that message. Ultimately, the fact that someone below answers Him, that God receives a signal from man saying, "You, God, exist," means that the message has been successfully transmitted from one end of existence to the other. This expresses the divine victory, which floods all of existence with light.

This chapter has discussed God's unity from the human perspective, as something meaningful in a person's awareness and experience. But that faith in His unity does not suffice if one also believes that He exists only on some other plane. That kind of faith will change nothing in a person's life, because if God exists only on another plane, it would make no practical difference whether He were one or three. Rather, a meaningful faith in the unity of God is the awareness that "there is nothing besides Him," in other words, that there is no other power, existence, or meaning apart from Him.

When that faith is authentic and clear, it results in double joy: The person is joyful because God is close to him, and God is joyful, as it were, because this person is close to Him, having overcome all of the obstacles that had been placed in his way.

There is a well-known Chabad melody sung to the words "Indeed, You are God who conceals Himself" (Isa. 45:15). Contrary to what one might suppose, this is a melody of joy, because a person knows that, although seemingly absent, God is "a God who conceals Himself," and this awareness causes him to be joyful. The Ba'al Shem Tov used to say[17] that the verse from the Torah portion of the rebuke, "I will conceal (*haster astir*) My face" (Deut. 31:18), literally means "I will conceal the concealment." The curse in God's doubly concealing His face is that a person does not even know that there is a concealment; he does not sense the darkness and the gaping chasm beneath him. But as soon as a person knows that there is concealment, the concealment ceases. Belief in God's unity does not necessarily disclose the depth of divine existence, but it reveals that a concealment of God exists, that He is hidden right here. The joy in this revelation is not like any other type of joy. It is the crux of every kind of joy in the world, the bedrock of all true joy, which can never be undermined.

---

17. See *Ba'al Shem Tov al HaTorah*, 71–72.

Chapter 34

THE PREVIOUS CHAPTER DISCUSSED THE JOY THAT A person experiences as a result of his awareness of God's unity, an awareness that is every Jew's inheritance from the patriarchs. The deep emotional expression of this awareness of God's unity is a sensation of being close to God, together with an immeasurable feeling of joy arising from this closeness.

The present chapter will continue discussing this feeling of joy as it is manifest on a deeper level: Now, not only is one aware of God's oneness, but he himself becomes a receptacle, a dwelling place, for it. The chapter begins by describing the limitations of a human being, the highest extent to which anyone – even a patriarch or prophet – can reach. The chapter then delineates what each Jew can and must do to attain and maintain his connection with God's unity.

וְהִנֵּה מוּדַעַת זֹאת שֶׁהָאָבוֹת הֵן הַמֶּרְכָּבָה (בראשית רבה פרשה מז, ח), **It is known that the patriarchs are the very chariot** of God (*Bereshit Rabba* 47:8), — 14 Adar / 30 Adar I (leap year)

The statement that the patriarchs – Abraham, Isaac, and Jacob – "are the very chariot" means that there was no distinction between them and the heavenly chariot that Ezekiel described in his prophecy. They were not just *like* the chariot, but they *were* the chariot.

A chariot is a vehicle upon which a rider sits, and upon which he may be seen. The essence of a chariot, or vehicle, is solely utilitarian; it does not choose where to go but is a vehicle that the rider directs as he wishes. Ezekiel's chariot was a vehicle for holiness. When a person is described as a chariot of holiness, it means that his entire being serves as a vehicle for expressing holiness. From the perspective of the rider, he is not a happenstance vehicle, but the authentic vehicle – always and wherever he goes.

שֶׁכָּל יְמֵיהֶם לְעוֹלָם לֹא הִפְסִיקוּ אֲפִילוּ שָׁעָה אַחַת מִלְּקַשֵּׁר דַּעְתָּם וְנִשְׁמָתָם לְרִבּוֹן הָעוֹלָמִים, בְּבִיטוּל הַנִּזְכָּר לְעֵיל לְיִחוּדוֹ יִתְבָּרֵךְ.

who, throughout their lives, never ceased even momentarily from binding their minds and souls to the Master of the Universe with the aforementioned self-nullification to His unity.

As was explained earlier,[1] when a person performs a holy act (a mitzva), he functions as a vehicle for holiness. But he is called a chariot only if he achieves the level of the patriarchs, who never ceased from binding their minds and souls to God by nullifying themselves to His unity. When a person nullifies himself in some small way to perform a holy act, he becomes a vehicle for holiness. But only if he is able to live in such a way that his entire being, whether he is awake or asleep, aware or unaware, is an instrument for the Divine Presence, is he regarded as its "chariot."

VARIOUS LEVELS OF THE CHARIOT

☞ Some people can become a vehicle for the Divine Presence only when they make a conscious effort to do so. When that conscious effort ceases, so does their connection to the Divine. But for unique individuals who have reached perfection in this area, this connection does not depend on a conscious, ongoing decision. Whether they will it or not, they operate from the impetus of the core of their being, which cannot act independently of the Divine. The patriarchs' connection to the Divine not only existed in certain times and situations, but was present uninterrupted throughout their entire lives. In that sense, they attained a total identification with the supernal chariot. They were the chariot and the chariot was they, and so "they are the chariot of God."

---

1. See chap. 23 above.

וְאַחֲרֵיהֶם כָּל הַנְּבִיאִים, כָּל אֶחָד לְפִי מַדְרֵגַת נִשְׁמָתוֹ וְהַשָּׂגָתוֹ.

They were succeeded by all the prophets, each commensurate with the level of his soul and comprehension.

Following the patriarchs (and suffused with their influence), whenever a prophet would, on his level, prophesy, he would become a chariot for the Divine Presence. At that moment, the prophet's unique personality would be nullified before God. The prophet would therefore serve as an instrument through which God expressed Himself within the spiritual realm that the prophet had attained. ☞

וּמַדְרֵגַת מֹשֶׁה רַבֵּינוּ עָלָיו הַשָּׁלוֹם הִיא הָעוֹלָה עַל כּוּלָּנָה,

The level of Moses, our teacher, may he rest in peace, surpasses that of them all,

THE PROPHET AS CHARIOT

☞ When a person becomes a chariot, as did the patriarchs and the prophets, all his words, whether he has thought them out, whether he even intended to say them, are vehicles for holiness. His individual ideas, his thoughts, and his words are no longer his personal decisions. Just as his awareness is a vehicle for holiness, so are his slips of the tongue and even his errors. There are many stories about people who were on such lofty levels that their sharp words were fulfilled "like an error that emerges before the ruler" (see Eccles. 10:5), even when they themselves did not intend these undesired consequences (see, for example, the stories of Rabbi Yoḥanan and Rabbi Kahana in *Bava Kamma* 117a, and Rabbi Yoḥanan and Reish Lakish in *Bava Metzia* 84b). Such a person's words change the world because they are a component of its inner workings.

In that sense, such a person serves as a chariot for the inner forces of existence. He becomes fused with existence to the extent that whatever he says – irrespective of his underlying rationale – will come to fruition, like a stone or a tree that is always part of the natural order. Regardless of our thoughts about why a tree grows in a specific way, regardless of whether we are correct, the tree grows as it will. Whether it grows straight or crooked or fails to grow at all is all part of nature. Similarly, the more a prophet or one imbued with divine inspiration is influenced by that inspiration, the more his individual personality is nullified, so that when he speaks and in so doing creates realities, he does so without his knowledge. In retrospect, he may provide rationales for why he said one thing and not another. But that is only his impression after the fact, as if it were any other person analyzing the facts from an external perspective. That which he said is one thing, and that which he thinks about it afterward, as an individual, is on an altogether different plane.

Moses's self-nullification to the divine light surpassed even that of the patriarchs and the prophets.

שֶׁאָמְרוּ עָלָיו: שְׁכִינָה מְדַבֶּרֶת מִתּוֹךְ גְּרוֹנוֹ שֶׁל מֹשֶׁה. as our Sages said of him: "The Divine Presence speaks from Moses's throat."

Moses's words were not his at all. Since there was no separation between Moses's individual self and the divine being, he possessed no personal speech. ☞

וּמֵעֵין זֶה זָכוּ יִשְׂרָאֵל בְּמַעֲמַד הַר סִינַי, רַק שֶׁלֹּא יָכְלוּ לִסְבּוֹל, כְּמַאֲמַר רַבּוֹתֵינוּ ז״ל, שֶׁעַל כָּל דִּיבּוּר פָּרְחָה נִשְׁמָתָן כו' (שבת פח, ב), שֶׁהוּא עִנְיַן בִּיטוּל בִּמְצִיאוּת הַנִּזְכָּר לְעֵיל. The people of Israel attained something of this level at the revelation at Mount Sinai, yet they were unable to bear it, as our Rabbis state that at each utterance God spoke, their souls flew out of their bodies, and so forth (Shabbat 88b). This refers to the nullification of their existence that was mentioned above.

THE DIVINE PRESENCE SPEAKS FROM THE THROAT OF MOSES

☞ An example of this can be readily found in the second paragraph of the *Shema* (Deut. 11:13–21). The passage apparently begins with the words of Moses: "It shall be, if you will heed my commandments that I command you today, to love the Lord your God...." However, the next verse transitions to convey the words of God: "I will provide the rain of your land...." Then the text reverts to indicate Moses speaking about God: "The wrath of the Lord will be enflamed against you"; "You shall place these words of Mine upon your heart...so that your days will be increased...on the land with regard to which the Lord took an oath to your forefathers." Seamlessly, Moses switches back and forth between his own words and the words of God. He speaks God's words in the third person and in the first person, without any differentiation. Moses never prefaces his words with "So said the Lord," as do the other prophets. This is because whatever Moses says is itself the word of God.

In truth, the divine essence fills all of existence, but our own being creates an interposing barrier by generating an apparently separate, independent reality. Moses, the most humble of human beings, did not have his own individual existence (as he states of himself and Aaron in the verse "what are we?" [Ex. 16:7]), and so there was no cause for any interference. At times, Moses narrates as an outsider, in third person, and at times he speaks from his perspective, in first person. Even when Moses speaks to God, the Divine Presence speaks from his throat. In essence, God wrote the

At Mount Sinai, as the Israelites received the divine words of the Torah, the inner essence of existence, they experienced a level approaching that of the chariot of the patriarchs and the prophets.

Every person has drives, desires, and dreams unique to him and by means of which he lives in his personal reality. But at each of God's utterances, the consciousness and emotions of the people of Israel – their realities – were nullified, the meaning behind their souls flying out of their bodies. As no vestige of their personality remained, they were thus able to become a vessel upon which the Divine Presence rested.

When a person experiences God's presence he cannot relate to anything else and cannot function in this world. Existence as he knows it is suffused with the brilliance of the divine light, which pumps life into him as well. Consequently, as a prophet enters a prophetic state, he encounters a severe crisis,[2] jarred as he is by the traumatic transition in and out of the prophetic state. With great difficulty, the prophet (being a person of great wisdom and strong character)[3] can bear this crisis. But the people of Israel, who merited a semblance of this state at the revelation at Mount Sinai, were unable to sustain the burden of this total and ongoing state of self-nullification.

לָכֵן, מִיָּד אָמַר לָהֶם לַעֲשׂוֹת לוֹ מִשְׁכָּן, וּבוֹ קָדְשֵׁי הַקֳּדָשִׁים, **Therefore**, God **immediately instructed them to make Him a Sanctuary, containing the Holy of Holies**,

Since the people of Israel could not bear having the Divine Presence rest upon them, God immediately instructed them to make Him a Sanctuary containing the Holy of Holies. The Sanctuary was a replacement of sorts for God's presence resting on the people.

Torah and signed it with Moses's name. It is actually the Torah of God, with Moses serving as the scribe. The Torah's description of the death of Moses (see *Bava Batra* 15a) is the most extreme expression of this. As a result of the total identification between Moses and God, Moses wrote, as dictated to him by God, the description of his own death (something that the human mind cannot comprehend).

---

2. See Rambam, *Sefer HaMadda, Hilkhot Yesodei HaTorah* 7:2.
3. See Rambam ad loc., 7:1.

Initially, it was intended that the Divine Presence dwell within the person himself and not be confined to a particular building or geographic placement. This is alluded to in the verse "And I [God] will dwell among them" (Ex. 25:8), literally rendered as "*within* them," in other words, within each and every Jew, no matter their physical location.[4] However, because the souls of Israel were incapable of tolerating that intense state of awareness and being veritable receptacles for the Divine Presence, the physical Sanctuary became necessary. The Sanctuary constituted a site for holiness, in addition to containing a space of even loftier holiness – the Holy of Holies. This space of supreme holiness, the Holy of Holies, was the locus in this world where all barriers were dissolved, where contact was made with the world beyond, where the dimensions of this world were nullified to divine existence.[5] In the Holy of Holies, the divine being is not a light that a person gropes after in the dark, but a tangible existence directly before him. It is the place where ordinarily no one can enter, because his individual existence would be immolated there.[6] Only the High Priest, after purifying and sanctifying himself as mandated by the Torah, entered that place once a year, and in so doing bound together place, holiness, and man.

לְהַשְׁרָאַת שְׁכִינָתוֹ, שֶׁהוּא גִּילּוּי יִחוּדוֹ יִתְבָּרֵךְ, כְּמוֹ שֶׁיִּתְבָּאֵר לְקַמָּן. **for the dwelling of His Divine Presence, that is, the revelation of God's unity, as will be explained below** (chaps. 52–53).

What is the implication of there being a particular location where the Divine Presence dwells? After all, the verse states that "His glory fills the entire world" (Isa. 6:3), meaning that there is no place devoid of the Divine Presence. Moreover, the Divine Presence is the soul

---

4. See Alsheikh, Ex. 31; Ps. 78.
5. This idea is alluded to in the talmudic statement "The place of the Ark of the Covenant is not included in the measurement of the Holy of Holies in which it rested" (*Megilla* 10b).
6. This notion is alluded to in the verse "A man shall not see Me and live" (Ex. 33:20).

that animates all existence, and so it is impossible for there to be any existence in the absence of the Divine Presence.

The explanation is that there is a difference between the "enclothing of the Divine Presence" and the "dwelling of the Divine Presence."[7] The "enclothing of the Divine Presence" refers to the Divine Presence within everything, "filling all worlds" in order to enliven and sustain everything (including evil, as well as an evil gentile, as explained in *Iggeret HaKodesh*, epistle 25, p. 141). But the "dwelling of the Divine Presence" expresses the "revelation of His unity," the revelation of the existence of the Divine Presence not as something mysterious and hidden, but overt and tangible. In this sense, the Holy of Holies is the locus where the Divine Presence, the divine oneness encompassing all being and found everywhere, is revealed.

וּמִשֶּׁחָרַב בֵּית הַמִּקְדָּשׁ, אֵין לְהַקָּדוֹשׁ בָּרוּךְ הוּא בְּעוֹלָמוֹ מִשְׁכָּן וּמָכוֹן לְשִׁבְתּוֹ, הוּא יִחוּדוֹ יִתְבָּרַךְ, אֶלָּא אַרְבַּע אַמּוֹת שֶׁל הֲלָכָה,

But since the destruction of the Temple, the Holy One, blessed be He, has no Sanctuary and place for His dwelling, i.e., His unity, in His world, apart from the four cubits of *halakha* (*Berakhot* 8a),

1 Adar II (leap year)

This statement does not mean that God has no place to be, since it is axiomatic that He fills and encompasses everything. Rather, it means that His unity is not revealed, and so not all elements of existence are aware of it. There are unique individuals who are characterized as "chariots," and there was a unique place characterized as a "place of His dwelling," where God's unity was revealed.

With the destruction of this place, that is, the Temple, God no longer has a means through which to reveal His unity, except for the "four cubits of *halakha*." The place wherein one is able to connect to God's unity, the abode of the Divine Presence, no longer exists in a geographical location. Instead, it exists in an altogether different realm of existence. The concept of the four cubits of *halakha* refers to the space in which one dedicates time and energy to the study of *halakha*. That connects him to God's unity, and God's presence dwells upon him.

---

7. See, for example, *Iggeret HaKodesh*, epistle 25, p. 141.

In this arena alone there is a revelation of the true divine unity. Thus, when a person learns *halakha* and keeps the *halakhot*, he can build a connection with God and enter into partnership with Him.

שֶׁהוּא רְצוֹנוֹ יִתְבָּרֵךְ וְחָכְמָתוֹ הַמְלוּבָּשִׁים בַּהֲלָכוֹת הָעֲרוּכוֹת לְפָנֵינוּ. — that is to say, **God's will and wisdom, which are clothed in the *halakhot* that are set out before us.**

The divine essence that was revealed in the Holy of Holies is now disclosed in a different manner: via the embodiment of God's will and wisdom in *halakha*, which essentially is the unadulterated expression of God's true desire. Only within the four cubits of *halakha* is the Divine Presence revealed and the divine will clear: what we should do, say, and think in order to be with Him. If we leave the four cubits of *halakha*, we lose our connection with the divine will and wisdom that reaches down to us.

The revelation of the divine will within the four cubits of *halakha* does not depend on the practical application of *halakha* – whether a particular *halakha* can be fulfilled, whether it is constantly applicable, or even whether it involves a situation that never existed and never will exist.[8] The *halakhot* express what it is God desires in this world. When a person thinks about these matters and he too desires their fulfillment, he unites with God's will and wisdom, in the sense that he and God share the same desire. The four cubits of *halakha* are therefore the place of the divine unity's revelation, where a person can become as close to God as is humanly possible.

וְלָכֵן, אַחַר שֶׁיַּעֲמִיק הָאָדָם מַחֲשַׁבְתּוֹ בְּעִנְיַן בִּיטּוּל הַנִּזְכָּר לְעֵיל כְּפִי יְכָלְתּוֹ, זֹאת יָשִׁיב אֶל לִבּוֹ, כִּי מִהְיוֹת קָטָן שִׂכְלִי וְשֹׁרֶשׁ נִשְׁמָתִי מֵהָכִיל לִהְיוֹת מֶרְכָּבָה וּמִשְׁכָּן לְיִחוּדוֹ יִתְבָּרֵךְ — **Therefore, after a person deeply contemplates, according to his ability, the idea of self-nullification mentioned above, let him consider the following: "Seeing that my intellect and the root of my soul are too limited in their capacity to constitute a chariot and a sanctuary for God's unity**

---

8. Such as the details of the *halakhot* of *pigul* and similar laws (see *Kuntres Aḥaron* 5, 159b).

When a person deeply contemplates the divine unity, he senses the need to nullify himself to the divine essence and banish the darkness and concealment of his physicality in the face of the unity of the divine existence. When this occurs, he should be aware that as his intellect and the root of his soul are too limited to constitute a chariot and tabernacle for God's unity, he must take another course of action, described below.

Theoretically, if a person's intellect and the root of his soul are sufficiently lofty, similar to those of Abraham or Moses, he should not require a physical Temple, since he himself functions as one. Thus, Moses's private tent, where he would seclude himself, was called "the Tent of Meeting," the same term that is used to refer to (the precursor to the Temple) the Tabernacle (Ex. 33:7), because Moses was in his essence the Holy of Holies, and the Divine Presence would speak from his throat wherever he was, just as it did from "between the two cherubs" (Ex. 25:22). ☞

When a person contemplates the exalted status of a human being

---

THE INTELLECT AND THE ROOT OF THE SOUL

☞ Two elements are required in order for a person to be a chariot and temple: his intellect must be sufficiently developed and the root of his soul must be lofty.

"Intellect" in this sense refers not only to one's ability to intellectually grasp a physical concept, but it also connotes the ability to attain a complete and crystal-clear awareness even of concepts beyond the nature of the material world. Not everyone shares the same capacity for grasping abstract concepts. There are certain limits beyond which some people can push while others cannot, depending on their intellectual capabilities.

In other areas of life we see the power of the intellect and how it is unfettered by reality. For instance, some people can read a musical score and enjoy the music without ever having heard it. Others can read an engineering blueprint for a bridge and appreciate the interrelationships of forces and the beauty of the construction without ever seeing the bridge and without the bridge even existing. Many women can read a recipe and, without even partaking of it, can conjure up an image of the dish and "taste" it in their minds.

This phenomenon occurs by means of the intellectual ability to internalize an abstract concept by circumventing the physical senses. To a certain extent, every act of reading is such a process: the absorption of a reality not via the senses. It is the ability to relate to and envision an abstract topic directly, without resorting to any system of interpretation. The more abstract an issue is and the more distant it is from the senses, the more intellectual ability a person requires to grasp it. This is certainly the case regarding the Divine, which is immeasurably more complex and abstract

who is a chariot and sanctuary for the one God, on the one hand, and contrasts that with his own lowly level on the other, he eventually arrives at the following conclusion: "True, Abraham and Moses were a chariot and tabernacle for the Divine Presence because they possessed the requisite combination of intellectual ability and soul root. But with my inadequate intellect and my particular soul, I cannot expect my body and soul to become a sanctuary for the divine unity."

בֶּאֱמֶת לַאֲמִיתּוֹ, **in absolute truth,**

Even if a person can achieve some semblance of the feeling associated with being a chariot, he cannot achieve it in absolute truth, because his intellectual strength and the root of his soul are inadequate to the task. In this context, "absolute truth" connotes an unwavering and unmalleable connection with God.

Nevertheless, every Jew has some level of a connection to this matter, as each soul is a part of the Divine.[9] If he exerts the requisite effort, he will, on occasion, likely experience this degree of holiness. But in order for this to occur in absolute truth, that state of being must be unaffected by the moment and circumstances, such that this person is capable of feeling the same intensity of holiness while reciting the *Shema* on Tisha B'Av as he does during the climactic closing *Ne'ila* prayer of Yom Kippur.

---

than music or mathematics, and which does not have any expression via the physical senses.

However, intellectual ability does not suffice. In order to be a vessel for holiness, the root of a person's soul must also be lofty. Even a person who is wise, scholarly, and highly educated (including in Jewish matters) will never attain a direct feeling of the essence of holiness if he does not possess a lofty soul. A person with a lofty soul is sensitive to the Divine. This is not a function of his intellect or of any other aspect of his being, but of the root of his soul. Just as there are people who are gifted artistically or musically, there are people who are gifted in regard to the Divine, to holiness. This is not an ability acquired in the course of one's lifetime, but a gift that a person receives (if he receives it at all) from the outset. This is not a quality of the soul, but rather something far beyond: it is the soul's root and essence.

---

9. See chap. 2 above.

CHAPTER 34

Hasidism considers this point of absolute truth, of an unchanging feeling and essence, to be extraordinarily praiseworthy. The Hasidim of Kotzk would speak of "the upright man," a person who is internally integrated from head to toe. The writings of Chabad refer to this as the point of the self, a point of personal being that does not change, that does not undergo stages of training and learning, of fluctuating ascent and descent, because it is a part of a person's inner self.[10]

מֵאַחַר דְּלֵית מַחֲשָׁבָה דִּילִי תְּפִיסָא וּמַשֶּׂגֶת בּוֹ יִתְבָּרֵךְ כְּלָל וּכְלָל, שׁוּם הַשָּׂגָה בָּעוֹלָם וְלֹא שֶׁמֶץ מִנְהוּ מֵהַשָּׂגַת הָאָבוֹת וְהַנְּבִיאִים,

since my thought cannot grasp and apprehend God with any degree of apprehension in the world whatsoever, nor can I achieve even the slightest trace of the level of apprehension attained by the patriarchs and the prophets.

Not only is this individual unable to grasp the divine existence as did the patriarchs (who were chariots), but he is unable to experience even a mere trace of this.

In theory, a direct path to the Divine is open before every human being. The path of the patriarchs and prophets, of becoming a chariot for God's presence, is considered all but inaccessible, not because it is forbidden but because very few people can attain it, and so it is an objective limitation. No one can demand that he or others attain something for which they are unfit. A person must assess himself and his abilities, know that he is not capable of attaining this level, and then learn what he must nevertheless do in order to achieve a connection of absolute truth with God.

אִי לָזֹאת, אֶעֱשֶׂה לוֹ מִשְׁכָּן וּמָכוֹן לְשִׁבְתּוֹ, הוּא הָעֵסֶק בְּתַלְמוּד תּוֹרָה

This being so, I will make Him a sanctuary and a place for His dwelling, by being engaged in Torah study,

This individual tells himself that since he personally cannot be a sanctuary, he must enter God's own sanctuary. At present this sanctuary

---

10. See *Sefer HaMa'amarim* of the Rebbe Rashab, 5678, p. 12.

is not in a geographical location but is found within the Torah, in the four cubits of *halakha*. It follows that when a person engages in Torah study, he thereby enters God's sanctuary. ☞

כְּפִי הַפְּנַאי שֶׁלִּי, **as my free time** permits,"

Everyone, even a person whose full-time occupation is Torah study, has certain limits, because he cannot constantly be in the "sanctuary" of the four cubits of *halakha*. But every person has at least some free time during which he is not obligated to engage in other activities. It is during these moments that he is able – and required – to dwell in the four cubits of *halakha*, God's sanctuary.

בִּקְבִיעוּת עִתִּים בַּיּוֹם וּבַלַּיְלָה, **by designating** fixed **times by day and**
כְּדַת הַנִּיתְּנָה לְכָל אֶחָד וְאֶחָד **by night, as per the prescribed amount**
בְּהִלְכוֹת תַּלְמוּד תּוֹרָה, **for each individual, as set forth in the Laws of Torah Study,**

It is not enough to study Torah sporadically. A person must designate specific times by day and by night, in accordance with the prescribed

ENGAGEMENT IN TORAH STUDY

☞ Studying Torah is not optional; it is an absolute necessity. Torah study possesses an inherent advantage over being a chariot in and of oneself, as were the patriarchs. (That is besides the fact that after the revelation at Mount Sinai the path of being a chariot ceased to exist as it did in the days of the forefathers, since all service of God from then has been mediated through the Torah.) When we study Torah, we need not access God's will and wisdom as they exist in the heavenly realms (something that, as stated above, we are incapable of doing), but rather they are accessible to us as they descend via the Torah precisely to where we are. Every person, according to the level of his comprehension and implementation of the words of the Written and Oral Torah, can connect and unite himself through them to the highest divine will and wisdom.

Torah study also possesses an advantage over performing mitzvot. With respect to the Temple and sacrificial rites, for example, although at present a person cannot construct the Temple or offer sacrifices, every person can study the topics in Torah detailing the Temple service. By engaging in this act of Torah study, he is regarded as though he is actually fulfilling the Temple service. As he studies those topics, he brings into the world the level of the revelation of the divine unity associated with whatever specific topic he is learning.

amount stated in the Laws of Torah Study.[11] The true mitzva of Torah study applies at all times, as alluded to in the verse in reference to Torah observance, "And you shall ponder it day and night" (Josh. 1:8), implying all day and all night. However, since every person has various obligations and constraints, one fulfills the mitzva by dedicating all of his free time to Torah study. This means that after he has discharged all of his practical obligations, he should dedicate his remaining time to engaging in Torah study.

וּכְמַאֲמַר רַבּוֹתֵינוּ ז״ל: אֲפִילוּ פֶּרֶק אֶחָד שַׁחֲרִית כו׳. **and as our Rabbis state: Even one chapter in the morning, and so forth.**

The Talmud states: "Even if a person learned only one chapter [of a Torah subject] in the morning and one chapter in the evening, he has thereby fulfilled the commandment 'This book of the Torah shall not depart from your mouth, and you shall ponder it day and night'" (*Menaḥot* 99b). We often find ourselves exceptionally busy, preoccupied with countless obligations, leaving no time for much else, let alone Torah study. This talmudic passage teaches that even if we can manage but a few meager moments to devote to Torah study, any accomplishment in this regard fulfills our obligation. Moreover, one is viewed as though he has engaged in Torah study the entire day and night. That is because he decides to dedicate his meaningful time, the moments he truly has for himself, solely to God by studying His Torah. These daily and nightly dedications connect his entire life, both his material and spiritual pursuits, to the divine unity, to the four cubits of *halakha*.

וּבָזֶה יִשְׂמַח לִבּוֹ וְיָגִיל, וְיִתֵּן הוֹדָאָה עַל חֶלְקוֹ בְּשִׂמְחָה וּבְטוּב לֵבָב עַל שֶׁזָּכָה לִהְיוֹת אוּשְׁפִּיזָכָן לְגָבוּרָה פַּעֲמַיִם בְּכָל יוֹם, כְּפִי הָעֵת וְהַפְּנַאי שֶׁלּוֹ, כְּמִסַּת יָדוֹ אֲשֶׁר הִרְחִיב ה׳ לוֹ. **His heart shall thereby be gladdened and rejoice, and so he will give thanks to God for his portion, with joy and a glad heart, that he has merited to be a host to the Almighty twice daily, according to the extent of his available time, in keeping with the capacity that God has generously granted him.**

---

11. See *Hilkhot Talmud Torah* 3:4 by the author of the *Tanya*.

Just as the Tabernacle was the locus of the Divine Presence's revelation, where the divine word was spoken from between the two cherubs, so too, a person who engages in Torah study becomes a locus for the revelation of the Divine Presence, which speaks through him (see *Torah Or* 67b). When a person designates specific times to study Torah, at least twice a day, once during the day and once at night, God lodges at his residence, so to speak, so that he becomes a host for God.[12] As stated in the previous chapter, one within whose humble abode God, the King of kings, chooses to lodge, is overcome with immense joy, gladness, and gratitude.

15 Adar	
2 Adar II (leap year)	

וְאִם יַרְחִיב ה' לוֹ עוֹד, **If God graciously grants him more free time,**

The author of the *Tanya* is not referring to an era such as ours, in which labor laws make it possible for every person, even someone who works two jobs, to enjoy ample free time. Instead, he is referring to those who engaged in unregulated, intensive physical labor at home and in the field. If such people were able to squeeze out a few meager minutes to enter the four cubits of *halakha*, they too could become chariots for the Divine Presence.

אֲזַי טְהוֹר יָדַיִם יוֹסִיף אוֹמֶץ **then the clean-handed will add strength,**

Earlier, the author of the *Tanya* defined the very basic requirements of Torah study with which one must grapple in order to create a dwelling place for the Divine Presence. Citing part of a verse from Job (17:9),

---

12. See *Yoma* 12a and *Sota* 37a, which employ this expression regarding the tribe of Benjamin, which "merited...and became a host for the [Divine Presence of the] Almighty," since the Ark was located in Benjamin's territory (see Rashi's comment to *Sota* there). Like God, the Ark is referred to as Almighty (*Gevura*) because the Torah and commandments were given through *tzimtzum*, at times also referred to as the attribute of *Gevura*. Rabbi Shmuel Gronem Esterman points out that this idea is alluded to in another talmudic dictum which states that the children of Israel at Mount Sinai heard the first two of the Ten Commandments, "I am the Lord your God" and "You shall have no other gods," directly from the mouth of the Almighty (*Gevura*) (*Makkot* 24a).

the author now adds that should God grant him additional free time, the beneficiary must take extra care not to squander it by filling it with worthless pursuits. Instead, he must make the effort to fill it with holiness. Productive use of one's free time by engaging in Torah study indicates that holiness is truly important to him.

וּמַחֲשָׁבָה טוֹבָה כו'. and "God links **a good thought** to an action" (*Kiddushin* 40a).

Above, the author of the *Tanya* wrote, "If God graciously grants him *more*." The simple understanding is that it is referring to more time. Here, the author adds that this is not necessarily an increase in free time that he can utilize to perform additional good deeds. It can also be an increase in the sense of an improved intention and focus on matters that he already performs in those few free moments. For instance, he may have a "good thought," i.e., intention, that if he has more free time he will use it to study Torah. Because God links this good thought to an action, it is reckoned as though he has actually engaged in Torah study the entire day and night.

וְגַם שְׁאָר הַיּוֹם כּוּלּוֹ, שֶׁעוֹסֵק בְּמַשָּׂא וּמַתָּן, יִהְיֶה מָכוֹן לְשִׁבְתּוֹ יִתְבָּרֵךְ בִּנְתִינַת הַצְּדָקָה שֶׁיִּתֵּן מִיְּגִיעוֹ, שֶׁהִיא מִמִּדּוֹתָיו שֶׁל הַקָּדוֹשׁ בָּרוּךְ הוּא, מַה הוּא רַחוּם וכו', **The rest of the entire day as well**, when he is engaged in his **business affairs, he will be a dwelling place for God through the charity that he will give from** the profits of **his toil, since** being charitable **is one of the attributes of the Holy One, blessed be He: "Just as He is merciful…,"**

In addition to the time that a person spends studying Torah, and in addition to the time that God considers it as though he had done so (meaning that he wished to learn Torah but circumstances prevented him from doing so), it is possible that even during the rest of his day when he is at work, he will be a dwelling place for God. This is achieved when one gives charity from the money he has earned with the intent to fulfill God's will. Our Sages state, "Just as He is compassionate and merciful, so should you be compassionate and merciful" (*Shabbat* 133b), and "Is it truly possible for a person to go in the way of the

Divine Presence? After all, the Torah says, 'The Lord your God is a consuming fire' (Deut. 4:24). Rather, a person must emulate God's attributes. Just as He clothes the naked…so should you clothe the naked…" (*Sota* 14a). Just as God shows compassion and mercy by "giving charity," meaning, bestowing His bounty upon all creatures, a person who gives charity emulates God. He thus attaches himself to God and becomes a dwelling place for Him.

וּכְמוֹ שֶׁכָּתוּב בַּתִּיקוּנִים (תיקוני זהר, תיקון א): "חֶסֶד דְּרוֹעָא יְמִינָא". **and as it is written in** *Tikkunei* Zohar **(*17a*), "Kindness is the right arm** of God."

The attribute of kindness is, as it were, God's right arm. God's hand gives everything, but sometimes it does so via human hands. When a person gives charity with the intent to fulfill God's will, he serves as an instrument via which the quality of divine kindness gives charity. At that moment, he is God's "right arm." He is a chariot for divine kindness, a resting place for God to dwell.

וְאַף שֶׁאֵינוֹ נוֹתֵן אֶלָּא חוֹמֶשׁ, הֲרֵי הַחוֹמֶשׁ מַעֲלֶה עִמּוֹ כָּל הָאַרְבַּע יָדוֹת לַה', לִהְיוֹת מָכוֹן לְשִׁבְתּוֹ יִתְבָּרֵךְ, **Even though he gives only one-fifth** of his income, yet **that fifth elevates with it all four** remaining **parts to God, so that** the totality **will be a dwelling place for Him,**

According to *halakha*, one is normally not required to give more than one-fifth of his income to charity.[13] Nevertheless, *halakha* views the one-fifth he *does* give as representative of his total income. Thus, as it ascends to God, it raises the remaining four-fifths with it.[14] Moreover, since this money is the expression of all the sweat and blood that a person invested in his work, it represents his entire life, which now ascends to holiness to be a dwelling place for God.

---

13. See *Shulḥan Arukh, Yoreh De'a* 249.
14. This expression is borrowed from the verse in Genesis (47:24), "You shall give one-fifth to Pharaoh, and four parts shall be yours." See also *Likkutei Torah*, Song 6d.

כַּנּוֹדָע מַאֲמַר רַבּוֹתֵינוּ ז״ל, שֶׁמִּצְוַת צְדָקָה שְׁקוּלָה כְּנֶגֶד כָּל הַקָּרְבָּנוֹת,	as is taught in **the well-known statement of our Rabbis, that the mitzva of charity is equivalent to all the** Temple **offerings,**

Giving charity is equivalent to bringing sacrificial offerings, which elevates the world and draws it closer to God.[15]

וּבַקָּרְבָּנוֹת הָיָה כָּל הַחַי עוֹלֶה לַה׳ עַל יְדֵי בְּהֵמָה אַחַת, וְכָל הַצּוֹמֵחַ עַל יְדֵי עִשָּׂרוֹן סֹלֶת אֶחָד בָּלוּל בַּשֶּׁמֶן כו׳.	**and with** regard to **the offerings** sacrificed in the Temple service, **all living creatures ascend to God by means of** sacrificing **one animal, and all vegetation by means of one-tenth** of an ephah **of fine flour mixed with oil, and so forth.**

One animal offered as a sacrifice in the Temple (such as the daily continual offering) represented all living creatures. The measure of fine flour mixed with oil that accompanied each animal offering represented all vegetation, and the salt that accompanied every offering represented all inanimate matter. Similarly, the fifth of a person's income that he gives to charity (which is equivalent to the offerings) represents the entirety of his assets, and by extension the totality of his life and effort he invested into acquiring them.

The essence of an offering is not the physical object designated for and given to God, because in truth nothing can be given to Him, as it states, "For every beast of the forest is Mine" (Ps. 50:10), and "The world and all it contains is Mine" (Ps. 50:12). Rather, the essence of an offering is the self-sacrifice for the sake of God demonstrated by the person bringing it. When one sets aside something that he had earned with his toil, desire, and energy, with his mental and physical exertion, and dedicates it to a purpose that God desires, he thereby becomes a chariot for God's "right arm," His attribute of kindness.

וּמִלְּבַד זֶה, הֲרֵי בִּשְׁעַת הַתּוֹרָה וְהַתְּפִלָּה עוֹלֶה לַה׳ כָּל מַה שֶּׁאָכַל וְשָׁתָה וְנֶהֱנָה מֵאַרְבַּע	**Apart from this, during the moments of Torah** study **and prayer, all that one has eaten, drunk, and enjoyed of the**

---

15. See *Bava Batra* 9a; *Sukka* 49b.

הַיָּדוֹת לִבְרִיאוּת גּוּפוֹ, כְּמוֹ שֶׁיִּתְבָּאֵר לְקַמָּן. remaining **four parts** of his income for the health of his body ascends to God, as will be explained below.

A person's material possessions, along with the efforts he makes with his body and soul to acquire them, are elevated to holiness not only when he gives a portion of them to charity but in another way as well. When one studies Torah, prays, or fulfills the commandments, he utilizes his physical body, energized by the strength that he gained by his eating, resting, and so forth. The remaining four-fifths of his possessions, despite not having been dedicated to God by giving charity, for example, are nevertheless elevated to holiness when used for a holy purpose.

As explained elsewhere (see *Iggeret HaKodesh*, epistle 26), there are three types of eating: eating that is itself the fulfillment of a commandment (such as on the Sabbath), eating in order to have the strength to fulfill a commandment, and eating simply in order to live. Even this last kind of eating, which has no intrinsic holiness, ascends to holiness if afterward a person uses the energy gained thereby to study Torah or to pray (unless it was connected to something forbidden, as explained in *Iggeret HaKodesh* there). Ultimately, all elements of a person's life, even if not used directly for holiness, attain at least a measure of holiness. By analogy, although the ark that contains a Torah scroll is not intrinsically holy, it attains holiness because it serves the Torah scroll.

All elements of a person's life can be channeled to holiness. This holds true not only when he engages in the four cubits of *halakha*, but even when he is not consciously thinking of holiness and even while involved in other matters. A person can reach the divine light from every area of his existence in one way or another, breaking through the thickest darkness that spans the entire universe, and making himself a dwelling place for God. When a person builds a sanctuary for God in his life, he must construct it together with its adjoining courtyards, so that at the very least he may bring all existence into those courtyards, if not into the Holy of Holies itself.

This concludes the discussion of the joy experienced by one who has made himself into a sanctuary for God by having God dwell within him, as it were. Although not every Jew can become this sanctuary through his own efforts, as did the patriarchs and prophets (the veritable "chariot for God"), he can do so by means of divine assistance. When a Jew engages in Torah study, he carves out the space for the four cubits of *halakha*, and in so doing he creates a sanctuary and dwelling place for God. Only when all the elements of one's life are concentrated into this four-cubit space as receptacles for holiness can one emulate the patriarchs and prophets and become a veritable sanctuary for God.

וְהִנֵּה בְּכָל פְּרָטֵי מִינֵי שְׂמָחוֹת הַנֶּפֶשׁ הַנִּזְכָּרִים לְעֵיל, **As for all of the particular types of joy of the soul mentioned above** (chaps. 31, 33–34), 3 Adar II (leap year)

With these forms of joy, a person emerges from any depression and brokenheartedness he is liable to fall into, whether as a result of crushing his ego and shattering his sense of self (as explained in chapters 29–31), or for no particular reason. ☞

JOY OF THE SOUL

☞ Broadly speaking, chapters 31, 33, and 34, respectively, discuss three types of joy the soul experiences. The first is a person's joy in the simple fact that a divine soul exists within him. It is a joy that emanates solely from his unimpeded connection to the divine soul, without regard to the other physical or psychological aspects of his life, without concern for them, and without even attempting to repair them. This type of joy is described as "the exodus from Egypt," regarding which the verse states that "the people had fled" (while Egypt remained as it was) (Ex. 14:5). It is joy in the divine soul in and of itself, a joy experienced as one flees from the sense of self connected to his body and animal soul, which remain in their lowly and imperfect state.

An additional phase in this type of joy is a person's complete detachment from his egocentric outlook and shift in his focus to an objective, God-centered perspective of the world. At that moment, the totality of his sense of self, with its needs and pains, with its sadness and problems, are no longer important. That is not to say that they do not exist, but there is something more important. The question is not what I can do for myself, but what I (my ego) can do for God. The answer is that it can be used to subjugate the evil inclination and perform acts that are pleasing to God. Taking such an approach, there is no room for sadness or lethargy, but only the joy of taking action.

The second type of joy (described in chap. 33) is one that emanates from his faith in the divine unity. This kind of faith (which other people must struggle mightily, sometimes their entire lives, to achieve even in part) is one that every Jew attains without toil, because it is an inheritance from our forefathers. The emotional

אֵין מֵהֶן מְנִיעָה לִהְיוֹת נִבְזֶה בְּעֵינָיו נִמְאָס וְלֵב נִשְׁבָּר וְרוּחַ נְמוּכָה, בִּשְׁעַת הַשִּׂמְחָה מַמָּשׁ, **none prevents** one **from being despised and repugnant in his own eyes and** from having **a broken heart and lowly spirit at the very time of joy,**

The common theme underlying these three types of joy is that they do not result from personal accomplishment, and so they are not accompanied by a sense of self-importance. Accordingly, a person can experience them while simultaneously feeling lowly and far from God, crestfallen that he is not striving and focusing sufficiently. He rejoices in the fact that he is a "sanctuary for God" as a result of his Torah study and a "dwelling place for Him" as a result of his giving charity, but that does not interfere with his being simultaneously "despised and repugnant in his own eyes."

A similar idea is found in Hillel's statement "If I am not for me, who will be? But when I am only for myself, what am I?" (*Avot* 1:14). On the one hand, we have the total nullification of the person and his

---

implication of faith in the divine unity – that "there is nothing besides Him" (Deut. 4:35) – is "the closeness to God," the sense that God dwells with us and is closer to us than anything else. We must rejoice and thank God for this faith, as we say each day in the morning prayers, "Happy are we, how good is our portion...and how beautiful is our heritage."

In addition, beyond the joy a person feels in God's closeness to him, there is God's joy, as it were, in the fact that the person has attained this awareness. The purpose of the world, which hides, obscures, and conceals Godliness, and the purpose of man's being within a coarse body and an animal soul, is to enable him to illuminate the darkness, to reveal the Divine that the world conceals. The purpose of man is to transform the public domain into the private domain by means of faith in God's unity, namely, that "there is nothing besides Him," and that "I the Lord do not change" (Mal. 3:6). With this awareness, a person fulfills the purpose of his existence and the existence of all the worlds. One's recognition of God's unity, despite the apparent disunity of the world, constitutes a response, so to speak, to the call of God from beyond the veil of creation, which itself was brought forth by His word. Man's response to God completes the act of creation. This partnership results in God's great joy, a feeling reciprocated by man himself.

The third type of joy is that discussed in the present chapter. It is experienced by a person when he becomes a "host to the Almighty," hosting God within the four cubits of *halakha* as he engages in Torah study and performs a commandment, or even just intending to do so.

petty value in the face of the Divine, implied in the latter half of Hillel's statement. This creation is exceedingly lowly and perhaps would have been better off having never been created. On the other hand, the individual has inherent value in that he serves as a sanctuary for God. A person can possess this dichotomous makeup when he understands that his being a vessel for God is not a personal accomplishment, that his being a sanctuary for God is a given, just as his being "despised and vile" is a given. Just as a palace may stand atop a mound of trash, so too do these not contradict each other; both are equally true.

מֵאַחַר כִּי הֱיוֹתוֹ נִבְזֶה בְּעֵינָיו וכו' הוּא מִצַּד הַגּוּף וְנֶפֶשׁ הַבַּהֲמִית, וֶהֱיוֹתוֹ בְּשִׂמְחָה הוּא מִצַּד נֶפֶשׁ הָאֱלוֹקִית וְנִיצוֹץ אֱלֹקוּת הַמְלוּבָּשׁ בָּהּ לְהַחֲיוֹתָהּ כַּנִּזְכָּר לְעֵיל [בְּפֶרֶק ל"א].

since his being despised in his own eyes, and so forth, is on account of the body and animal soul, whereas his being joyous is on account of the divine soul and spark of Godliness enclothed within it in order to animate it, as mentioned above (in chapter 31).

When a person contemplates his personal, material self, he truly feels despicable and repugnant (as explained in chaps. 29–30), feelings not obviated by these hitherto discussed types of joy. He feels joy only on account of the divine soul within him giving him life, as mentioned above (in chap. 31). The divine soul is capable of reaching the greatest heights and fulfilling God's will. It can thus be joyful, although a person continues to see his body and animal soul as despised and repugnant and still requiring rectification.

וּכְהַאי גַּוְונָא אִיתָא בַּזֹהַר (חלק ג עה, א): "בְּכִיָּה תְּקִיעָא בְּלִבַּאי מִסִּטְרָא דָא וְחֶדְוָה תְּקִיעָא בְּלִבַּאי מִסִּטְרָא דָא".

A similar idea appears in the *Zohar* (3:75a): "Weeping is lodged in one side of my heart, and joy is lodged in the other."

Weeping out of sadness and feelings of joy can coexist within one heart, because human experience includes both.[16]

---

16. The context of the *Zohar*'s expression is a story in which Rabbi Shimon bar Yoḥai revealed Torah secrets pertaining to the Temple's destruction to his son,

This chapter concludes the discussion spanning the last few chapters regarding various types of sadness and joy. The author of the Tanya concludes that the *beinoni* can, and moreover must, live with both weeping and joy. His joy makes it possible for him to serve God and steadfastly overcome obstacles, while his humble spirit keeps his heart from growing dull. The cause of his joy is the knowledge that he has a holy soul, God is close to him, and that he is a sanctuary for God. The cause of his despondency and brokenheartedness is that he remains imperfect nonetheless. In fact, the knowledge of his positive qualities intensifies his self-criticism. Why does he not feel the holiness of his soul, God's unity, and His ever-present closeness? Why do these feelings of holiness and divine closeness not influence his body and animal soul to a greater extent? But rather than letting his self-criticism plunge him into sadness and inactivity, he willingly surrenders his feelings of pleasure, his natural desire for calm and tranquility, in order to dedicate himself with greater vigor and joy to serving God by nullifying his ego.

Although weeping and joy coincide within the *beinoni*, they do not always do so harmoniously. One may say that they do not stand together but rather proceed side by side in a spiral of ascent and holiness, as each side drives its counterpart toward greater achievements, toward greater heights. This is the path of the *beinoni* throughout his life, a path of simultaneous weeping and joy.

Rabbi Elazar. Rabbi Elazar rejoiced over the revelation of those secrets while simultaneously crying over the pain of the destruction (Rabbi Shmuel Gronem Esterman).

Chapter 35

THE PREVIOUS CHAPTER CONCLUDED AN EXTENSIVE discussion of the inner work of the *beinoni*. In order to emerge victorious in the battle for control of the "small city," i.e., his body, the *beinoni* must be joyful on account of his divine soul and embittered on account of his animal soul. But this inner work is only a prerequisite for the *beinoni* to fulfill the divine service required of him. In the present chapter and in the chapters to follow, the author of the *Tanya* will direct his focus to the nature of this divine service.

The unique quality of the *beinoni* (when compared to the tzaddik and the angels) is the service he must engage in, with his body and evil inclination operating at their full strength. This indicates that the essence of his service takes place in the realm of action, involving both the body and the physical world. Our chapter begins by addressing this point.

| וְהִנֵּה לְתוֹסֶפֶת בֵּיאוּר תֵּיבַת "לַעֲשׂוֹתוֹ". | Let us further clarify the term "to perform it." | 16 Adar
4 Adar II
(leap year) |

Here the author of the *Tanya* revisits the theme of the book, namely, the verse "Rather, the matter is very near to you, in your mouth and in your heart, to perform it" (Deut. 30:14). Why is it so important to emphasize that the service of God involves action? ☞

TO PERFORM IT

☞ In chapter 17, the author of the *Tanya* explained how "the matter" – the love that brings a person to fulfill the mitzvot – "is near to you," since a person's mind is under

47

וְגַם לְהָבִין מְעַט מִזְּעֵיר תַּכְלִית בְּרִיאַת הַבֵּינוֹנִים וִירִידַת נִשְׁמוֹתֵיהֶם לָעוֹלָם הַזֶּה לְהִתְלַבֵּשׁ בְּנֶפֶשׁ הַבַּהֲמִית שֶׁמֵּהַקְּלִיפָּה וְסִטְרָא אָחֳרָא,

Let us also understand a small fraction of the purpose of the creation of *beinonim* and their souls' descent into this world to be clothed in the animal soul, which derives from the *kelippa* and *sitra aḥara*,

The idea of "in your mouth and in your heart to perform it" is part of the broader understanding of the essential nature of a *beinoni* and his role in this world. As was explained, unlike the tzaddik, the *beinoni* will never be able to fully resolve the issues in his life. He can neither completely repair himself nor the world. The first question requiring clarification is: What does a *beinoni* accomplish in the world? Why did God take a pure soul and place it into an impossible setting, a life filled with unending struggle, unsolvable problems, and unanswerable questions? Even the advice presented in this book does not intend to solve his problems, but only to temper them, not curing the illness but ameliorating the pain so it is not intolerable. This is not a rare situation confined to a limited number of *beinonim*. It is equally applicable to all, since the *beinoni* is, in a sense, each and every one of us. Perhaps we are not at present on the actual level of a *beinoni*, but we certainly have the potential to be one. The *beinoni* is an idealization of the human construct, but not an impossible one. The question concerning the purpose of the *beinoni* is a question about man and the world in general, which have been created with inherent imperfection: For what purpose did the soul descend into this world, to be clothed in a body and an animal soul?

מֵאַחַר שֶׁלֹּא יוּכְלוּ לְשַׁלְּחָהּ כָּל יְמֵיהֶם וְלִדְחוֹתָהּ מִמְּקוֹמָהּ מֶחָלָל הַשְּׂמָאלִי שֶׁבַּלֵּב,

since they will not, during their lifetime, be able to banish or expel it, i.e., the animal soul, **from its place in the left chamber of the heart,**

his control and he can focus on whatever he wishes. In chapter 18, the author explained how the matter is *"very* near," referring to the hidden love within every Jew.

Here, the author explains the final part of the verse, "to perform it" (Rabbi Shmuel Gronem Esterman).

The divine and the animal souls struggle over control of the totality of a person's being, which in the case of a *beinoni* is an unremitting battle. Through great effort, a *beinoni* can gain control of the garments of his soul, utterly repelling the animal soul and preventing it from intruding on the *beinoni*'s thoughts, words, and actions. Having said this, he will never be able to banish the animal soul itself, along with its impulses and desires for mundane matters, from its abode in the "left chamber of his heart" (as explained previously in chap. 9).

שֶׁלֹּא יַעֲלוּ מִמֶּנָּה הִרְהוּרִים אֶל הַמּוֹחַ,	so that no distracting **thoughts will arise from it to the brain,**

The animal soul itself, which can never be repaired, remains at full strength in its place in the left chamber of the heart. From there it constantly transmits thoughts and ideas into the brain. The *beinoni* can control his thinking, but only regarding conscious thought. He can avoid consciously thinking about certain topics and can force himself to think about others. But he cannot control the thoughts that constantly intrude into his consciousness from the depths of his soul, since it is not subject to conscious control. In that sense, the *beinoni* will forever be engaged in an unending struggle to control his thoughts and overcome temptation.

כִּי מַהוּתָהּ וְעַצְמוּתָהּ שֶׁל נֶפֶשׁ הַבַּהֲמִית שֶׁמֵּהַקְּלִיפָּה הִיא בְּתָקְפָּהּ וּבִגְבוּרָתָהּ אֶצְלָם כְּתוֹלַדְתָּהּ,	**for in the case** of the *beinonim*, **the essence and being of the animal soul, deriving from the *kelippa*, retains its full power and might as at birth,**

The *beinoni* is born with an animal soul and an evil inclination which remain fixed and unchanging within him throughout his life. As a person's life unfolds, he develops and grows, and the animal soul and the evil inclination grow with him. A toddler has an immature perspective of the world, mirrored by the limited capacity of his evil inclination. A three-year-old wants colored paper and marbles. As he grows older and develops a more mature understanding of life, he desires a different kind of colored paper (money). Despite the change in the object of one's desire, the basic way a person's animal soul pulls him toward what he wants remains the same. An adult does not have the desires of a young child, not because he has conquered them, but because his desires have changed shape. It could very well be that even now, as an adult, he desires these things, and perhaps with a greater intensity. ☞

רַק שֶׁלְּבוּשֶׁיהָ אֵינָם מִתְלַבְּשִׁים בְּגוּפָם, כַּנִּזְכָּר לְעֵיל. **except that its garments do not clothe themselves within their body, as mentioned above** (chap. 12).

The "garments" of the animal soul refers to its expression and realization. The point here is that although the animal soul is ever-present in the *beinoni*, nevertheless, it does not succeed in materializing itself in his body. The animal soul in a *beinoni* is like that of a wicked person, but the *beinoni* is able to prevent the evil within him from being clothed and manifest, and so in every outward respect he is exactly like the righteous.

The *beinoni* perforce contains two opposing forces within himself. These unalterable forces never weaken, nor are they capable of defeating one another. As a result, he lives in constant tension, with no opportunity for respite. In a single moment of complacency, if for but one instant he lowers his guard, he is liable to lose everything.

JEALOUSY, LUST, AND HONOR

☞ A statement in the Mishna (*Avot* 4:21) says: "Jealousy, lust, and honor remove a person from the world." There are three phases in a person's life. In young children, the feeling that is most prominent, motivating them to action, is that of jealousy. A child is not so much desirous of things as he is jealous of others who possess them. When a person becomes an adult, jealousy subsides, and lust burns. Afterward, when a person grows old, lust quiets down, and the desire for honor comes. Jealousy, lust, and honor, with all their differences, are the same in that they are expressions of the animal soul dominating a person. Tradition has it that the last thing the Ba'al Shem Tov said before his death was "Let the foot of pride not come to me" (Ps. 36:12). Similarly, it is told that the holy Arizal's last words were "Protect me from arrogance" (see *Notzar Ḥesed*, *Avot* 4:4). These accounts express, perhaps in the most extreme way, that the struggle with the evil inclination continues until the very last moments of one's life. Even a person who has conquered his evil inclination completely still has the challenge not to succumb to pride due to its defeat. This very fact could lead to his potential downfall. The core essence of the animal soul within the *beinoni* can never be fully eradicated (and perhaps this is true to some extent even in the tzaddik).

The *beinoni* is like a hand grenade that lacks a safety pin, such that if one loosens his grip for only a moment, it explodes. There have been people who spent many years proceeding along the path of the righteous and the just, but in one moment of weakness they discovered that festering deep within were the same desires shared by the wicked.

וְאִם כֵּן, לָמָּה זֶּה יָרְדוּ נִשְׁמוֹתֵיהֶם לָעוֹלָם הַזֶּה, לִיגַע לָרִיק חַס וְשָׁלוֹם, לְהִלָּחֵם כָּל יְמֵיהֶם עִם הַיֵּצֶר וְלֹא יָכְלוּ לוֹ?

If so, why then did their souls descend into this world, to toil in vain, God forbid, to fight the evil inclination all their lives and be unable to vanquish it?

This constant tension a *beinoni* faces and is unable to resolve forces him to repeatedly confront an unanswerable question: What is the purpose of this unending and indecisive battle? A soul descends into this world, resides here for seventy years or so, experiences suffering and struggles, and in that entire time reaches no resolution. What is the justification for such an extensive, inconclusive process?[1]

וּתְהִי זֹאת נֶחָמָתָם לְנַחֲמָם בְּכִפְלַיִם לְתוּשִׁיָּה וּלְשַׂמֵּחַ לִבָּם בַּה׳ הַשּׁוֹכֵן אִתָּם בְּתוֹךְ תּוֹרָתָם וַעֲבוֹדָתָם.

But let this answer to follow **be their consolation, to comfort them with a double measure of wisdom, and to gladden their hearts in God who dwells among them, in their Torah and** divine **service.**

As was explained in previous chapters, there are aspects of the struggle,

---

1. In chap. 27, the author of the *Tanya* explains that when a person subjugates his evil inclination, he brings satisfaction to God. Given this, the efforts of the *beinoni* are not in vain. If so, the question posed here is moot. The explanation, however, is that in order to achieve that subjugation, the divine soul did not need to be clothed *within* the animal soul. On the contrary, the souls should have been distinct from one another and in opposition, so that when the divine soul triumphs, it will do so without the animal soul. Thus, the question posed here still stands: For what purpose is the divine soul enclothed within the animal soul? (Noted by the Lubavitcher Rebbe, Rabbi Menaḥem Mendel Schneerson.)

toil, and suffering of life within which the *beinoni* can find solace and even joy. Though he may not always see reason for rejoicing in his individual situation, he can still delight in the closeness to God generated through his Torah study and divine service. ☞

There is no guarantee that when a person fulfills a mitzva he will feel closeness to God. Similarly, if one studies a particularly technical section of the Talmud, he is not assured a powerful religious experience. But there is a guarantee that someone who immerses himself in Torah and mitzvot will merit becoming objectively close to God, even though he may not feel it. ☞

THE *BEINONI* AND INNER TRANQUILITY

☞ One of the challenges of finding joy in the service of God is that it is not found where one thinks it to be. Throughout history there have been individuals who explored a life of faith in order to reach inner peace, tranquility, and stability. But as mentioned above, apart from a limited number of exceptional people, the average person cannot expect to achieve this. Possessing faith in God and fulfillment of His mitzvot is not necessarily the path to achieving inner peace. On the contrary, a *beinoni* who does not experience the tension of inner conflict, who does not sense any problems, who thinks that everything is going smoothly suffers from the serious disease of "dullness of the heart" (see chap. 29). A person who begins to feel tranquil must attempt to create a crisis in order to extricate himself from that tranquil state. A person can enter Gehenna in one leap or slip slowly into it.

Rabbi Simḥa Bunim of Peshisha once said that every person must see himself as if his head is laid on the executioner's block with Satan standing over him holding an axe to his neck. It is told that one of Rabbi Simḥa Bunim's students asked him, "What happens when a person is unable to see himself in this way?" Rabbi Bunim answered, "It is a sign that Satan has already beheaded him." When a person feels that his world is straight and smooth, that there is no challenge to rising in the morning for prayers or to making blessings before and after eating, or to designating specific times for Torah study, when a person feels that he has no more obstacles on the path to holiness, this is a decisive sign that he is lost. It is indicative that there are no longer any obstacles on his path to Gehenna. If he wants to prevent that outcome, he must take drastic steps. He must undertake to do more.

EXPERIENCING CLOSENESS TO GOD

☞ Experiencing closeness to God and actually being close to Him are not necessarily dependent on one another. This point is especially important to empha-

CHAPTER 35

וְהוּא בְּהַקְדִּים לְשׁוֹן הַיָּנוּקָא [בַּזֹּהַר פָּרָשַׁת בָּלָק (קפ"ז, א)] עַל פָּסוּק: "הֶחָכָם עֵינָיו בְּרֹאשׁוֹ" (קהלת ב, יד): וְכִי בְּאָן אֲתָר עֵינוֹי דְּבַר נָשׁ כוּ'? אֶלָּא קְרָא הָכֵי הוּא וַדַּאי:

For this purpose, we must preface our explanation to the above question with the words of the Yanuka [Zohar, Parashat Balak, 187a] on the verse "The wise man's eyes are in his head" (Eccles. 2:14). The Zohar asks, "But where else could a person's eyes be? Rather, the meaning of the verse is certainly as follows:

5 Adar II (leap year)

One of the figures appearing in the Zohar is the Yanuka, the young child. In our context, he is quoted as questioning the verse in Ecclesiastes "The wise man's eyes are in his head." The verse demands explanation, as the eyes of every person are in his head. What then is the intent of the verse that specifically states that the eyes of a wise person are in his head?

---

size nowadays, as we live in a world where we often measure things through a psychological lens. This may lead to the perspective that the truth of something is less significant than the psychological impact it has on a person. For example, every individual is programmed to eat, and typically does so daily. Yet it is not always true that a person enjoys the food he consumes. Eating and the enjoyment of eating are two separate phenomena. It is possible to eat food that nourishes the body, giving it everything it needs for sustenance, while the food itself is not at all enjoyable. On the other hand, one could eat foods that are incredibly enjoyable and then die from malnutrition. This is a choice that always lies before a person. Does he want the thing itself, or the appearance of the thing? Does a person prefer to *be* close to God, or to *feel* as though he is close to God? There are a wide variety of methods a person can employ in order to feel uplifted and close to God, ranging from drug-induced states to an industry of artificial experiences. But it is possible to be close to God without sensations of ecstasy, divine enlightenment, or spiritual pleasure. This is not to say that it is impossible to feel a closeness to God, but that these two aspects – closeness to God and experiencing that closeness – are not connected. There are times that a person will feel this closeness, and other times he will not. The point here is that even in times when a person does not *feel* any closeness to God, he can console himself in the knowledge of God's closeness to him. He can rejoice in God who dwells with him in his Torah study and divine service, even though he may not have succeeded in resolving his personal issues and even though he may not be on the level of being able to feel that closeness.

דִּתְנַן: לָא יְהָךְ בַּר נַשׁ בְּגִילּוּיָא דְּרֵישָׁא אַרְבַּע אַמּוֹת. מַאי טַעְמָא? דִּשְׁכִינְתָּא שַׁרְיָא עַל רֵישֵׁיהּ.

As we learned: A person should not walk four cubits with an uncovered head. What is the reason? For the Divine Presence dwells upon his head.

We cover our heads not only when we are in a holy place or involved in a holy endeavor, but at all times and in all places. This is because the Divine Presence, which is everywhere, constantly rests on a person's head. Covering our heads symbolizes our awareness of God's presence surrounding and resting upon us everywhere and at all times. ☞

וְכָל חָכָם עֵינוֹהִי וּמִילּוֹי בְּרֵישֵׁיהּ אִינּוּן, בְּהַהוּא דְּשַׁרְיָא וְקַיְּימָא עַל רֵישֵׁיהּ. וְכַד עֵינוֹי תַּמָּן, לִנְדַּע דְּהַהוּא נְהוֹרָא דְּאַדְלִיק עַל רֵישֵׁיהּ - אִצְטְרִיךְ לְמִשְׁחָא.

Now, the eyes and words of every wise person are in his head, that is, **with the One who rests and reveals Himself upon his head. When his eyes are focused there, he must know that the light that shines above his head requires oil.** The expression "the eyes and words of every wise person are in his head" refers to the wise person focusing his attention and awareness on the light of the Divine Presence, which dwells and reveals itself upon his head. This awareness leads to the knowledge that this light that shines above his head requires oil.

COVERING ONE'S HEAD

☞ A head covering, in whatever form a person chooses, expresses feelings of awe and fear. For this reason, the Sages would customarily wrap their heads in coverings at times of legal judgment or the speaking of words of Torah. This is also the reason that most Jewish communities have the custom that during the silent *Amida* prayer the men cover their heads with a *tallit* (prayer shawl). Doing so is a sign of submission to an authority, standing before that authority with awe and fear. Conversely, when a man's head is uncovered, it is a sign of irreverence and moral irresponsibility. There is an Aramaic term, *resh galei* (uncovered head), which refers to this point. This is why the phrase "with a high hand" is translated into Aramaic as "with an uncovered head," with both positive (Ex. 14:8) and negative (Num. 15:30) connotations. A person removes layers of clothes when he feels free in his own home and covers himself when he feels he is being scrutinized from on high.

CHAPTER 35

בְּגִין דְּגוּפָא דְּבַר נַשׁ אִיהוּ פְּתִילָה, וּנְהוֹרָא אַדְלֵיק לְעֵילָא. וּשְׁלֹמֹה מַלְכָּא צָוַח וְאָמַר: "וְשֶׁמֶן עַל רֹאשְׁךָ אַל יֶחְסָר" (קהלת ט, ח). דְּהָא נְהוֹרָא דִּבְרֵאשׁוֹ אִצְטְרִיךְ לְמִשְׁחָא וְאִינּוּן עוֹבְדָאן טָבָאן. וְעַל דָּא "הֶחָכָם עֵינָיו בְּרֹאשׁוֹ". עַד כָּאן לְשׁוֹנוֹ.

The *Zohar* explains the analogy: **For a person's body is the wick, and the light that shines above** him is the light of the Divine Presence. Concerning this, **King Solomon cried out, saying: 'May the oil on your head not be lacking'** (Eccles. 9:8), **for the light above his head requires oil, namely, good deeds. It is in this regard that 'the wise man's eyes are in his head.'"** Here end the Yanuka's **words** in the *Zohar*.

In this analogy, a person's soul is symbolized by a lamp, as in the verse "The spirit of man is the lamp of the Lord" (Prov. 20:27). The wick of the lamp is the person's body, and the flame burning on the wick is the light of the Divine Presence, which dwells upon one's head (that is, atop the wick). The fire takes hold of the wick, but the wick itself does not burn. Instead, it serves as a means for the oil to burn. The wick serves as a focal point by which the fire is localized. It is the channel for the oil (meaning, good deeds) to burn. This then is the meaning of the verse "The wise man's eyes are in his head," namely, the wise man is attentive and careful in order to ensure that the "oil" on his head should never be lacking. He must see to it that he never lacks good deeds, for it is through them that the Divine Presence dwells and shines upon his head.

וְהִנֵּה בֵּיאוּר מָשָׁל זֶה, שֶׁהִמְשִׁיל אוֹר הַשְּׁכִינָה לְאוֹר הַנֵּר שֶׁאֵינוֹ מֵאִיר וְנֶאֱחָז בַּפְּתִילָה בְּלִי שֶׁמֶן, וְכָךְ אֵין הַשְּׁכִינָה שׁוֹרָה עַל גּוּף הָאָדָם שֶׁנִּמְשַׁל לִפְתִילָה, אֶלָּא עַל יְדֵי מַעֲשִׂים טוֹבִים דַּוְוקָא.

The meaning of this analogy is as follows: **The light of the Divine Presence is compared to the light of a lamp,** in that it **neither shines nor takes hold of the wick without oil. Similarly, the Divine Presence will not rest upon a person's body, which is compared to a wick, except by virtue of good deeds alone.**

17 Adar

6 Adar II (leap year)

The meaning of this analogy that "the spirit of man is the lamp of the Lord" is that although the light of the candle is dependent on the wick, the wick is not consumed by the fire, but rather the oil is absorbed by the wick. A wise man's eyes are in his *head* in the sense that he must always make certain that the oil in his head is never lacking. In other words, he must make it a priority of his to constantly supply fuel for the fire so that it can burn continuously without consuming the wick. How does one sustain this divine fire, the light of the Divine Presence that illuminates a person? The answer is through good deeds (the "oil"). When a person fulfills the mitzvot in this world, he thereby creates a bridge linking the Divine and the physical world.

On the other hand, oil cannot burn by itself. A wick is required to serve as an interface between the oil and the fire. This is comparable to the role of man, a soul within a body, who fulfills the mitzvot with his physical actions. The mitzvot are meaningless and insubstantial without man (the wick) who actualizes them. So it is the human being who causes the good deeds, the mitzvot, to come to fruition and have meaning. Only when a human being, with his body, and with a soul inhabiting his body, performs the mitzvot, does the Divine Presence take hold of him, burning and shining through him into the world.

וְלֹא דַי לוֹ בְּנִשְׁמָתוֹ שֶׁהִיא חֵלֶק אֱלוֹהַּ מִמַּעַל, לִהְיוֹת הִיא כְּשֶׁמֶן לַפְּתִילָה. **It is not sufficient that his soul,** which is a veritable **portion of God above**, serve as oil for the wick.

This statement touches upon the core of one of the most fundamental questions regarding the essence of man's service of God: Why does the light of the Divine Presence require our good deeds? Why is the soul incapable of shining on its own? Why is it unable to serve alone as both the oil and the wick? Why is the pure and holy soul inadequate vis-à-vis bearing the light of the Divine Presence, thereby maintaining the connection between man and God? Why does a person need to perform specific, external actions, that is, good deeds, in order to connect to God? Would it not be logical that a more internal, deep love and awe of God serve as an efficacious means of doing so?

מְבוֹאָר וּמוּבָן לְכָל מַשְׂכִּיל, כִּי הִנֵּה נִשְׁמַת הָאָדָם, אֲפִילוּ הוּא צַדִּיק גָּמוּר עוֹבֵד ה' בְּיִרְאָה וְאַהֲבָה בְּתַעֲנוּגִים, **It is obvious and understandable to every intelligent person that** with regard to **man's soul, even if he is a completely righteous individual, serving God with fear and** a love on the level of **love of delights,**

The level of fear referred to here is the most sublime level, namely, fear of His exaltedness. The level of "love of delights" refers to that of one who is enraptured in his love of God and needs nothing else.

אַף עַל פִּי כֵן, אֵינָהּ בְּטֵילָה בִּמְצִיאוּת לְגַמְרֵי, לִיבָּטֵל וְלִיכָּלֵל בְּאוֹר ה' מַמָּשׁ לִהְיוֹת לַאֲחָדִים וּמְיוּחָדִים בְּיִחוּד גָּמוּר. רַק הוּא דָּבָר בִּפְנֵי עַצְמוֹ - יְרֵא ה' וְאוֹהֲבוֹ.

nevertheless, his soul **is not utterly nullified from existence, literally nullified to and absorbed within the light of God so that they are united and unified in total unity. Rather,** the person, along with his soul, **is a separate entity,** defined as **one that fears God and loves Him.**

Even a soul with an unsurpassable rank, such as that found within a complete tzaddik, is still not perfectly and totally unified with the divine being. Even at its peak of love and fear of God, the soul remains an independent entity, one that experiences love toward another. In this case, the object of this person's love is God. Hence, there remain two distinct entities: the lover and the beloved. Even when the soul reaches its ultimate purified state, it merits only to be close to God, yearning and aspiring toward the Divine, but never fully nullified to or unified with God. ☞

LOVE OF GOD

☞ There is a love of "flames of fire" (see Song 8:6 and chap. 3 above), one of "on my bed during the nights I sought the one whom my soul loves" (Song 3:1). These verses speak of a burning love for God, a tormenting desire and yearning for the Divine. Then there is "love of delights" (see Song 7:7 and chap. 9 above), the most sublime love, in which a person is together with God, as it were, delighting in that closeness and needing nothing else. Regarding this it is written, "Whom else do I have in heaven? With You, I desire nothing on earth" (Ps. 73:25).

With regard to both these types of love there remains a distinction, which in a sense creates the enjoyment between the one who loves, namely, the person, and the beloved, namely, God. As long as a person is aware of the fact that "*he* loves God, on any level, the implication is that there is a separate entity, the person, who loves, and so by definition that person is not utterly one with the Divine.

Elsewhere, the author of the *Tanya* states that the challenge for a tzaddik who ascends to a higher world is that he is faced with the following choice: To remain in the Garden of Eden, climbing to and basking in ever-higher levels of love for God, or to

מַה שֶּׁאֵין כֵּן הַמִּצְוֹת וּמַעֲשִׂים טוֹבִים, שֶׁהֵן רְצוֹנוֹ יִתְבָּרֵךְ,

This is not the case with regard to **the mitzvot and good deeds,** both of **which are God's will.**

A mitzva is not the expression of the person but the will of God. In this sense, the mitzva a person fulfills is not part of himself the way his love and fear of God is, as mentioned above. This being the case, a mitzva one performs has the capacity to unite with God in total unity.

וּרְצוֹנוֹ יִתְבָּרֵךְ הוּא מְקוֹר הַחַיִּים לְכָל הָעוֹלָמוֹת וְהַבְּרוּאִים, שֶׁיּוֹרֵד אֲלֵיהֶם עַל יְדֵי צִמְצוּמִים רַבִּים וְהֶסְתֵּר פָּנִים שֶׁל רָצוֹן הָעֶלְיוֹן בָּרוּךְ הוּא וִירִידַת הַמַּדְרֵגוֹת, עַד שֶׁיּוּכְלוּ לְהִתְהַוּוֹת וּלְהִבָּרְאוֹת יֵשׁ מֵאַיִן וְדָבָר נִפְרָד בִּפְנֵי עַצְמוֹ, וְלֹא יִבָּטְלוּ בִּמְצִיאוּת כַּנִּזְכָּר לְעֵיל.

Now God's will is the source of life for all the worlds and created entities, descending to them by means of many constrictions and the concealed countenance (*panim*) **of God's supernal will and by descending** many **levels until they can come into being and be created** as an **existence out of nothingness and as separate entities, so that they will not be nullified from existence, as mentioned above** (chaps. 21–22).

forgo it all and simply nullify himself within God. We can deduce from this that even when a person is no longer encased in a body, he still retains some sense of self, and this self is intrinsically an impediment.

It is told in the name of Rabbi Yeḥiel Mikhel of Zlochov that when the Torah says, "I was standing between the Lord and you" (Deut. 5:5), it is describing the state of man: The "I" of a person, his sense of self, "stands" and separates between himself and God. This barrier of the self is a part of what it means to be human. When the Torah states, "Man shall not see Me and live" (Ex. 33:20), this includes all mankind, even Moses himself.

This is the same fundamental issue underlying the gap between a person's sense of self and the "other." It is impossible to straddle both sides: If I am myself, I am not the other. The greatest person can reach as far as forty-nine gates of understanding but cannot reach the fiftieth, because once opened, he is no longer a person. One who penetrates this barrier has "broken the vessels" and is no longer a part of the existence of man or the world.

This sense of self is not the ego. It is a primal identity necessary for man to exist, which does so even in the person who truly loves God and thinks not of himself nor of his own benefit. Nevertheless, when he loves, it is still "I love." As long as there is "I" and there is God, regardless of the nature of the connection between them, whether it is loving or lined with holy fear,

The divine will is the sole source and vivifying "soul" of all existence, but it is hidden. The life force that flows from it descends level by level through layers of concealment until created beings are brought into existence out of nothingness. That is, they perceive themselves as new creations (creations out of nothingness) that may perhaps be causally related to their Creator, but they still see themselves as independent from Him. They are capable of loving and fearing God, yearning for and connecting to Him, but it is all within the fundamental perspective that they exist as independent entities, distinguishable from the divine existence. This perspective is the defining element that characterizes creation as creation. That which is God is not the world, and that which is the world feels, by the nature of its parameters, that it is not God.

מַה שֶּׁאֵין כֵּן הַמִּצְוֹת שֶׁהֵן פְּנִימִית רְצוֹנוֹ יִתְבָּרֵךְ וְאֵין שָׁם הֶסְתֵּר פָּנִים כְּלָל, **Whereas** with regard to **the mitzvot, which are God's innermost (***penimi***) will, and with regard to which there is no concealed countenance (***panim***) whatsoever,**

The various elements comprising the world all exist and receive their life force from the back (or "hind") aspect of the divine will. By contrast, the mitzvot are the innermost aspect of the divine will. This innermost aspect constitutes God's foremost objective and ultimate goal, while the "hind" aspect of His will relates to the external means used to achieve that goal. In every part of existence there is a front and back. For example, when describing a knife blade, we speak of its sharp edge and blunt spine, i.e., the back of the blade. The blade may be regarded as the "innermost" side, that is, the part that serves the intended function and purpose of the knife. The back of the knife is merely a technical component enabling the "innermost" side to achieve the intended goal: to cut. A more abstract example is that of a person who is giving

---

it is by definition impossible for there to be a complete merging of identity within God. Therefore, the feelings of love for God, though great and holy, cannot serve as something that is utterly burned and consumed, the way that oil burns and is consumed by way of the wick. Love of God, like fear of God and the full array of human emotions, is only a part of the wick, part of human existence, and human existence can never stop being itself.

a public address. His words have both an internal and external aspect. Two different people in the audience hearing the same speech will notice different things. One may focus on the speaker's content and intent, the "innermost" side. The other may remember the "hind," i.e., outer, components: his speaking style, jokes, and analogies that "clothe" and conceal his innermost content. In the same way, all the components constituting the world, from the highest forms of life to the lowest elements, exist in a concealed state and are an expression of "concealed countenance" (*panim*), which means that the innermost (*penimi*) aspect of God's will is concealed. The very fact that the creation seems distinct from God conceals Him and forms the divide between God and the world. By contrast, the mitzvot alone are direct expressions of God's innermost will.

אֵין הַחַיּוּת שֶׁבָּהֶם דָּבָר נִפְרָד בִּפְנֵי עַצְמוֹ כְּלָל, אֶלָּא הוּא מְיֻחָד וְנִכְלָל בִּרְצוֹנוֹ יִתְבָּרַךְ, וְהָיוּ לַאֲחָדִים מַמָּשׁ בְּיִחוּד גָּמוּר. the life force within them is not a distinct entity in and of itself at all, but rather it is unified and merged with God's will, literally becoming one, with complete unity.

A mitzva, as it is manifest here in this world, is the will of God. Although the mitzva appears in our world clothed in a material garb, that garb does not have its own identity. Rather, the mitzva is the pure expression of the unmediated inner divinity, without any distortion of an added sense of self-identity of the item with which the mitzva is performed.

In a dark, distorted world, the mitzva is the unadulterated expression of the Divine. In a world wherein all created entities conceal, a mitzva, by contrast, is unique in that it reveals. The intent here is not of a revelation of the transcendent that bursts forth and shatters the natural order of things. Instead, it refers to a quiet, powerfully deep revelation occurring within and alongside the systems of nature, essentially indicating that the combination of particular things within the world arranged in a specific manner expresses the will of God. There is a mitzva to affix a *mezuza*. This mitzva is comprised of a number of mundane details with which specific actions are performed in the most natural of ways. All of these mundane details and the physical actions associated with them combine to become a single, wondrous unity with the Divine; this is the very definition of a mitzva.

A genuine connection between the physical world and God cannot be generated by the world itself, as the signs and symbols that pass from one side of existence to the other can be created only by God. Therefore, as long as a person speaks to God in his own personal language, through his personal experiences, although this may resonate with the person, it does not truly speak to God. It is not actually transmitted to the supernal realm, from the finite to the infinite. In order to create a true connection with the other side, one must communicate in its language. Therefore, "speech" between a person and God is possible only by means of the language of Torah and mitzvot, which in this sense is God's language, the language He gave us with which to communicate with Him.

וְהִנֵּה עִנְיַן הַשְׁרָאַת הַשְּׁכִינָה הוּא גִּילּוּי אֱלֹקוּתוֹ יִתְבָּרֵךְ וְאוֹר אֵין סוֹף בָּרוּךְ הוּא בְּאֵיזֶה דָבָר, **Now the concept of the dwelling of the Divine Presence refers to the revelation of His Godliness and the light of *Ein Sof*, blessed be He, within a particular object,** 18 Adar

Elsewhere (*Iggeret HaKodesh*, epistle 25), the author of the *Tanya* distinguishes between the terms "the dwelling of the Divine Presence" and "the enclothing of the Divine Presence." The "enclothing of the Divine Presence" refers to the Divine Presence in its capacity to manifest itself within and vivify all of existence, including neutral entities such as trees and rocks, as well as the existence of holiness and the existence of *kelippa*, the latter operating, as it were, counter to the Divine Presence itself. The Divine Presence enclothed within

---

EXPERIENCING A MITZVA

☞ On the one hand, it is possible for a person to comprehend the concept of a mitzva. The idea of it may even be exciting and exhilarating. On the other hand, the notion of a mitzva can be unintelligible, unstimulating, and alien, because the nature of a mitzva is far beyond a person's individual feelings. Its essence constitutes the very nexus between God and man, no matter if the individual personally apprehends its mechanics or not. A mitzva contains a specific code, so to speak, that must be transmitted. The moment the transmission occurs, with or without the comprehension of the person transmitting it, contact with the Divine has been made, and the purpose of the mitzva is achieved.

every being is the divine force which brings about and animates that being. But this force functions within that object in a powerful state of concealment, to the extent that the entity can be so dense that its existence hides the divine energy within. By contrast, the "dwelling of the Divine Presence" within a particular object refers to the revelation of the Divine Presence both within and through the particular entity it creates and vivifies. Examples of this include the manifestation and revelation of the Divine Presence in the Temple, in a prophet experiencing a state of prophecy, and in the words of Torah spoken by a Jew at any time (the four cubits of *halakha*).

וְהַיְינוּ לוֹמַר שֶׁאוֹתוֹ דָּבָר נִכְלָל בְּאוֹר ה' וּבָטֵל לוֹ בִּמְצִיאוּת לְגַמְרֵי, שֶׁאָז הוּא שֶׁשּׁוֹרֶה וּמִתְגַּלֶּה בּוֹ ה' אֶחָד. אֲבָל כָּל מַה שֶׁלֹּא בָּטֵל אֵלָיו בִּמְצִיאוּת לְגַמְרֵי - אֵין אוֹר ה' שׁוֹרֶה וּמִתְגַּלֶּה בּוֹ.

that is to say, that particular **object becomes merged with the light of God and is utterly nullified from existence to it, for** only then is it something **within which the One God dwells and reveals Himself. However, the light of God neither dwells nor is revealed within anything that is not utterly nullified from existence to Him.**

When the Divine Presence dwells within a person, place, or situation, the implication is that it no longer has an independent existence. It is impossible for something to exist independently while simultaneously serving as a vessel for the revelation of the Divine Presence. The object must therefore be nonexistent for the divine being to be revealed within it. The vessel for divine revelation must be transparent. If it is perceived as or views itself as an independent entity, it then is blocked, either partially or completely, from the divine radiance, and the Divine Presence cannot rest within it.

וְאַף צַדִּיק גָּמוּר שֶׁמִּתְדַּבֵּק בּוֹ בְּאַהֲבָה רַבָּה, הֲרֵי לֵית מַחֲשָׁבָה תְּפִיסָא בֵּיהּ כְּלָל בֶּאֱמֶת,

Even in the case of **a completely righteous person who cleaves to Him with a great love,** nevertheless, **no thought** of his **can truly grasp Him at all,**

As defined in chapter 10 above, a completely righteous person is not only someone who does no evil in deed, word, or thought, for this is the rank of a *beinoni*. Rather, he is someone whose quintessential nature, deepest yearnings, and most hidden desires are completely identified with God. He cleaves to Him with every fiber of his soul, experiencing "a great love," referring to the highest levels of closeness with God that a person can attain. Even so, the thoughts of the completely righteous person, and certainly the thoughts of anyone on a lower level, cannot truly grasp God.[2] That is to say, although every thought comprehends something, a truly complete grasp of God does not exist.

כִּי אֲמִיתַּת "ה׳ אֱלֹקִים אֱמֶת" (ירמיה י, י) הוּא יִחוּדוֹ וְאַחְדוּתוֹ שֶׁהוּא לְבַדּוֹ הוּא וְאֶפֶס בִּלְעָדוֹ מַמָּשׁ.

for the truth of the verse "The Lord God is true" (Jer. 10:10) is His unity and oneness, as He is absolutely alone and there is literally nothing besides Him.

Similarly, Rambam (*Sefer HaMadda, Hilkhot Yesodei HaTorah* 1:4) states: "'For the Lord God is true' – He alone is the truth, and nothing else possesses truth like His truth. This is what is meant when the Torah states, 'There is no other besides Him' (Deut. 4:35). It means that there is no other entity besides Him that is true as He is." The phrase "The Lord God is true" implies that God is the only truth, relative to which all else is not true. The phrase "For the Lord God is true" also indicates that God is the true and exclusive existence, as there is absolutely no other existence outside of Him.

וְאִם כֵּן זֶה הָאוֹהֵב, שֶׁהוּא יֵשׁ וְלֹא אֶפֶס - לֵית מַחֲשָׁבָה דִּילֵיהּ תְּפִיסָא בֵּיהּ כְּלָל,

It follows, that with regard to this person who loves God and who is by definition a separate being and not nonexistent, no thought of his can grasp Him at all,

Even the greatest tzaddik, master of spiritual gifts and abilities, is unable to attain a level of thought that grasps Him. This is because if the

---

2. Based on the introduction to *Tikkunei Zohar* 17a.

thought could truly grasp "the Lord God is true," it would understand that in actuality there is no other existence besides God.

There is an expression attributed to the philosophers of the Middle Ages that states, "If I knew Him, I would be Him."[3] This means that for a person to know God, not merely to know *about* Him, but to truly know Him, is to *be* Him. Therefore, if someone claims to know God, then they by definition do not truly know Him. Love of God is similar to knowledge of Him, in the sense that one who loves, even the most sublime level of love, still exists as the lover, a being distinct from the beloved – God. However hidden it may be, there still exists a "someone" who loves or knows God, and whenever there is that someone, there is an unbridgeable gulf between them and the Divine.

Human experiences are ultimately just that – human experiences – and so they form the gaping chasm of the vacated space that separates our existence as finite beings from the true, infinite, divine existence. Even the pinnacle of human truth remains limited as such. This is in contrast to the notion of "God is true," a perspective that not only is not human, but that looms threateningly over all existence, since such a notion bears the implication that there truly is "nothing besides Him." Thus, when a person exists as an independent being and is "not nonexistent," the result is that "no thought of his can grasp Him at all," meaning he is incapable of truly comprehending the notion of "the Lord God is true."

וְאֵין אוֹר ה' שׁוֹרֶה וּמִתְגַּלֶּה בּוֹ, אֶלָּא עַל יְדֵי קִיּוּם הַמִּצְוֹת שֶׁהֵן רְצוֹנוֹ וְחָכְמָתוֹ יִתְבָּרֵךְ מַמָּשׁ, בְּלִי שׁוּם הֶסְתֵּר פָּנִים.	and the light of God does not dwell or reveal itself within him, except through the fulfillment of the mitzvot, which are literally God's will and wisdom, without any concealed countenance.

The advantage of a mitzva is not in the fact that through performing it a person can purify his body or soul, or that it is a method of enhancing and maintaining the social order. Rather, its true value lies in the fact that it is a medium by which God Himself traverses the unfathomable gap of infinity in a process of revelation, not unlike the process of

---

3. See, for example, *Derashot HaRan*, derush 4 (s.v. "*veaḥar shehoda lo*"); see also *Sefer HaIkkarim*, essay 2, end of chap. 30.

Creation, and says to man: "Such and such is My will; such and such is My thought. While engaged in these things, you are engaging in something objective: Me." Based on this perspective, no matter to what degree a person intellectualizes the mitzvot and imbues them with layers of meaning and feeling, he is ultimately creating mere scaffolding to assist him to relate to them. There is nothing wrong with employing these methods; people need them, either temporarily or even for a lifetime, because as human beings we find it difficult without them. But fundamentally, the connection between man and God exists within the action itself, not because the action is good, nice, and useful, but because it is the will of God.

A similar point exists with regard to Torah study (see chap. 4 above). Torah is God's wisdom, yet the bulk of the Torah a person studies deals with very basic topics, mundane concepts which are readily understood. Examples of such subjects include oxen and donkeys, wool and *tzitzit*, and so forth. On the surface, engaging in these commonplace matters bears no relation to God's divine wisdom, which no thought can grasp; on the contrary, these concepts are easily comprehensible.

In order to better understand this we ought to recall the analogy the author of the *Tanya* employs in chapter 4, of a person who embraces the king while the latter is wearing multiple layers of garments. Despite there being several layers of clothing separating the person and the king, ultimately, he is embracing the king. Similarly, God's wisdom is embedded in the Torah we possess, wrapped in layer upon layer of "garments." The idea presented here is that the value of this exterior garment within which the Torah is wrapped, e.g., its ethical values or therapeutic powers, is not as important as the core truth of its inner essence: that the King Himself lies within it. Notwithstanding the ancillary benefits these garments provide, the Torah at its core is God's pure and unalloyed will and wisdom. ☞

THE NOVELTY IN THE TEN COMMANDMENTS

☞ There is a well-known question posed in multiple hasidic writings (see, for example, *Likkutei Torah*, Num. 12c, 15c): When God descended upon Mount Sinai amid overwhelming sounds and thunder and lightning, the world stood still. Birds stopped flying, oxen did not low, and even the angels ceased to sing God's praise. Yet after the thunderous revelation, what did God say? "Do not murder," "Do not

הַגָּהָה: ((וְכַאֲשֶׁר שָׁמַעְתִּי מִמּוֹרִי עָלָיו הַשָּׁלוֹם, פֵּירוּשׁ וְטַעַם לָמָּה שֶׁנֶּאֱמַר בְּעֵץ חַיִּים, שֶׁאוֹר אֵין סוֹף בָּרוּךְ הוּא אֵינוֹ מִתְיַחֵד אֲפִילוּ בְּעוֹלָם הָאֲצִילוּת, אֶלָּא עַל יְדֵי הִתְלַבְּשׁוּתוֹ תְּחִלָּה בִּסְפִירַת חָכְמָה. וְהַיְינוּ מִשּׁוּם שֶׁאֵין סוֹף בָּרוּךְ הוּא, הוּא אֶחָד הָאֱמֶת, שֶׁהוּא לְבַדּוֹ הוּא וְאֵין זוּלָתוֹ, וְזוֹ הִיא מַדְרֵגַת הַחָכְמָה וְכוּ׳)).

Gloss: This follows what I heard from my teacher, the Maggid of Mezeritch, of blessed memory, in explanation and rationale for that which is stated in *Etz Ḥayyim*, that the light of *Ein Sof*, blessed be He, is not united even in the world of *Atzilut*, unless it is first clothed in the *sefira* of *Ḥokhma*. This is because *Ein Sof*, blessed be He, is the true One, that is, He is absolutely alone and there is nothing besides Him, and this is the level of *Ḥokhma*, and so forth.

The author of the *Tanya* corroborates his above assertion, namely, that the light of *Ein Sof* dwells and is fully manifest in something that is completely nullified within Him. The author's teacher, the Maggid of Mezeritch, concurs with this, as deduced from his explanation of a passage in *Etz Ḥayyim*[4] according to which the light of *Ein Sof* is united, even in the world of *Atzilut*, only by first being clothed in the *sefira* of *Ḥokhma*.

The underlying principle here is that in all the worlds, both higher and lower, the innermost aspect of the divine light is revealed only through the *sefira* of *Ḥokhma*.[5] This is because *Ein Sof* is the true One, completely alone and with nothing besides Him. This is the level of

---

commit adultery," "Do not steal" – concepts that were already accepted in most world cultures. Did God descend from the heavens only to tell us what every civilization already knew? The answer given is that the importance did not lie in the words God said, but in the fact that it was God saying them. There is a "Do not murder" that is structurally integral to society, and there is an "Honor your parents" that is an essential component of human moral values. On the other hand, there exist the concepts of "Do not murder" and "Honor your parents" as part of the Ten Commandments. This is a qualitative difference between accepted social norms and a system by means of which a person can connect with God.

---

4. *Etz Ḥayyim* 47:3. See *Sha'ar HaShemot*, chap. 6 (*Likkutei Hagahot LaTanya*).
5. It appears that this refers to Ḥokhma of Adam Kadmon, which could ac-

Ḥokhma, through which this innermost aspect is revealed. As was explained above (see chaps. 3, 19, and commentary there), the word Ḥokhma is comprised of the letters that spell *koaḥ ma*, which can be understood to mean "the power of nothingness." This alludes to the idea that the power to fully absorb something lies at a point which itself is nothing. This is also true regarding a person's soul. Ḥokhma is the power of listening; it is the initial absorption of something into one's consciousness. This capacity is essentially the ability to nullify oneself. It is the capability to be nothing, to not have any independent existence, as that would otherwise constitute an interposition and an interference. Therefore, only the power of Ḥokhma, which is nothing, is able to serve as the vessel to transmit and reveal *Ein Sof*, which is everything.[6]

This gloss is intended to shed light on the central question this chapter addresses: Why is a person unable to attain true attachment to God by means of his soul alone? Why are qualities such as love and contemplation of the Divine incapable of effectuating "the dwelling of the Divine Presence"?

Thus far, it has been explained that the qualities of the soul, whatever they may be, are unable to achieve an absolute fusion with the Divine resulting from the nullification of their own individual existence, as does oil that is consumed by fire. Consequently, the soul on its own cannot achieve that level of contact with *Ein Sof*; it is incapable of attaining that degree of amalgamation with the One Truth besides which there is nothing else.

---

count for why it is the author of the *Tanya* who added the phrase "Even in the world of *Atzilut*" (noted by the fifth Lubavitcher Rebbe, Rabbi Sholom Dovber Schneerson).

6. This refers to the nullification of the vessel of Ḥokhma, which is precisely the reason why it acts as a vessel for the light of *Ein Sof*. We can now understand how these two points are not at all contradictory: The vessel of Ḥokhma was brought into being through the aspect of "something from nothingness," and so it is, in a sense, a "something." Nevertheless, it simultaneously bears the aspect of nullification or "nothing," because it is specifically through it that the truth of absolutely nothing existing besides God is revealed and manifest (based on an insight from the Rebbe Rashab in *Hagahot LeDibbur Hamatḥil Pataḥ Eliyahu* [2008], p. 54).

The gloss now adds that when we speak of the "dwelling of the Divine Presence" in the sense that it reveals the most profound essence of the light of *Ein Sof*, not via the *sefira* of Ḥokhma, we must understand that this phenomenon does not exist even in the world of *Atzilut*, nor in the purest soul whose root is in *Atzilut*. The only exception to this, as noted earlier in this chapter, is when a person fulfills a mitzva. When this occurs, he merges with the essence of that mitzva, and thus becomes integrated within God's innermost will.

19 Adar

וְהִנֵּה כְּשֶׁהָאָדָם עוֹסֵק בַּתּוֹרָה אֲזַי נִשְׁמָתוֹ, שֶׁהִיא נַפְשׁוֹ הָאֱלֹהִית עִם שְׁנֵי לְבוּשֶׁיהָ הַפְּנִימִיִּים לְבַדָּם, שֶׁהֵם כֹּחַ הַדִּבּוּר וּמַחֲשָׁבָה, נִכְלָלוֹת בְּאוֹר ה' אֵין סוֹף בָּרוּךְ הוּא וּמְיֻחָדוֹת בּוֹ בְּיִחוּד גָּמוּר. וְהִיא הַשְׁרָאַת הַשְּׁכִינָה עַל נַפְשׁוֹ הָאֱלֹקִית, כְּמַאֲמַר רַבּוֹתֵינוּ ז"ל: שֶׁאֲפִילוּ אֶחָד שֶׁיּוֹשֵׁב וְעוֹסֵק בַּתּוֹרָה שְׁכִינָה עִמּוֹ (ברכות ו, א).

When a person engages in Torah study, his *neshama*, i.e., his divine soul, along with its two innermost garments alone, namely, the faculties of speech and thought, are then absorbed in the light of God, *Ein Sof*, blessed be He, and are unified with it in complete unity. This constitutes the dwelling of the Divine Presence upon his divine soul. This is **in accordance with our Rabbis' statement that "even regarding one who sits and engages in Torah study, the Divine Presence is with him"** (*Berakhot* 6a).

Torah study employs the innermost garments of one's soul, i.e., thought and speech. When a person thinks and speaks about Torah, his thoughts and words *become* Torah. It follows that the person is transformed into a vehicle by which to express the Torah, the supreme manifestation of Godliness in the world. This constitutes the dwelling of the Divine Presence upon one's divine soul, as evidenced by the talmudic passage.[7] The phrase "The Divine Presence is with him" refers to the idea that it rests upon his divine soul; that is, there occurs the revelation of God as the source of divine light, unimpeded by the exterior casing of the world. All this takes place within one who engages in Torah study.

---

7. See also Mishna *Avot* 3:6.

The very act of engaging in Torah study constitutes one's intimate attachment to the divine wisdom contained therein. In that sense, the particular topic of study and the level of depth one delves into it matters less than the basic fact of his involvement in Torah study. When a person studies Torah, he generates a circuit of divine flow in the world, one of holiness that radiates from the greatest heights to the deepest depths. Granted, Torah exists in the world even without him, but on its own it leaves no imprint. Only when a person engages in its study does he create the revelation, as he becomes a medium through which the connection with the Divine Presence is reignited. ☞

As was previously stated, when a person studies Torah, he closes one circuit. The Torah, which appears in this world as spoken words and as thoughts, is connected to the divine essence that is beyond

THE PARADOX OF MAN

☞ This deeply powerful connection with God through Torah study occurs specifically without human awareness. While it is true that a person functions as the instrument closing the circuit of divine flow, he is not necessarily aware of his role. On the contrary, his very lack of awareness and personal involvement in this incredible process of divine revelation that he himself activates is precisely what allows for its existence. This process, which presumably should be impossible, can in fact become a reality only within the paradoxical structure of man's existence – the irreconcilable combination of body and soul.

The body by its very nature impedes one's capacity to grasp what transpires when he serves God, studies Torah, or fulfills mitzvot. This innate impediment is the very thing allowing a person to study Torah and fulfill mitzvot. The inherent obstruction created by the body is the justification for the hybrid existence of body and soul. Were a person aware of the powerful impact of his actions, he would explode. That a person is able to sit and study Talmud, for example, lies in the fact that he is unaware of the force of his actions. His ability to do so is only on account of the barrier that separates his sense of self from the connection to the Divine, to "the true One," besides whom there is nothing else.

Rabbi Levi Yitzḥak of Berditchev was quoted as saying that if one string of *tzitzit* were brought into the Garden of Eden, the entire garden would be utterly incinerated. The Garden of Eden is the place where the divine light is revealed. Yet the revelation of the Divine that rests in the *tzitzit* would burn the garden itself! If this is true, it begs the question: Why is a person able to wear *tzitzit* on his four-cornered garment and not be burned? The answer is that the person is not in the Garden of Eden. He is within a framework of divine concealment, of body and soul. The combination of body and soul grants him an advantage that allows him to involve himself in things that would destroy the pure soul upon contact with them.

The problem that exists with this combination, which a person must be wary of,

this world. Through this unification of the Divine that is revealed in the world, with the divine essence that is beyond the world, between *Kudsha Berikh Hu* (God in His transcendence) and *Shekhintei* (the Divine Presence within the world), the Divine Presence is able to rest upon the divine soul within a person.

אַךְ כְּדֵי לְהַמְשִׁיךְ אוֹר וְהֶאָרַת הַשְּׁכִינָה גַּם עַל גּוּפוֹ וְנַפְשׁוֹ הַבַּהֲמִית, שֶׁהִיא הַחִיּוּנִית הַמְלוּבֶּשֶׁת בְּגוּפוֹ מַמָּשׁ, צָרִיךְ לְקַיֵּים מִצְוֹת מַעֲשִׂיּוֹת הַנַּעֲשׂוֹת עַל יְדֵי הַגּוּף מַמָּשׁ, שֶׁאָז כֹּחַ הַגּוּף מַמָּשׁ שֶׁבַּעֲשִׂיָּה זוֹ נִכְלָל בְּאוֹר ה' וּרְצוֹנוֹ, וּמְיוּחָד בּוֹ בְּיִחוּד גָּמוּר.

But in order to draw down the light and illumination of the Divine Presence also upon his body and animal soul, the vital soul, which is literally clothed in his body, one must fulfill practical mitzvot, which are performed by means of the physical body itself, as then the literal energy of the body that is utilized in performing this action is absorbed in the light and will of God, and is unified with Him in complete unity.

The animal soul is comprised of elements on varying levels. There are extremely subtle and abstract elements that relate to a person's animal state of being as it pertains to the more refined human level. There are

---

is that of balance. As was explained, in order for a person to tolerate the connection with the Divine, he must be immunized and "anesthetized" to a certain degree. But if he is not careful, that numbness, so to speak, to the Divine can exceed the appropriate amount.

In expounding the deeper meaning of the verse "The Rock that gave birth to you, you forsook, and you forgot God, your Originator" (Deut. 32:18), the Maggid of Dubna said (see *Mishlei Yaakov*, 5717, p. 223): "The Rock (*tzur*) that gave birth to you" refers to when God created (*yatzar*) man. "You forsook" refers to the power to forget, a power that can be used to forget worldly matters, the pain and lusts, in order to serve God with peace of mind. Instead, what does a person do with this power to forget? "You forgot God, your Originator." The force allowing one to involve himself in holiness, in Torah study, and in performance of mitzvot is the same power one can potentially use to numb himself from experiencing holiness. An angel, who sees holiness, is unable to fulfill even one small mitzva, whereas a human being is able to fulfill the mitzvot but cannot see the holiness.

This point captures the essence of man. The power to choose, the possibility of attaching oneself to the true One and the simultaneous potentiality of totally denying His existence, together form the structure that constitutes man's being formed "in the image of God."

also superficial and less refined elements that animate a person's animal state of being pertaining to the baser, more animal level, meaning that of a physical creature who lives in a physical world. This baser aspect of the animal soul is called the "vital soul." In order to extend the Divine onto the vital soul, in which the entire scope of one's physical being lies, one must fulfill *practical* mitzvot, that is, those performed with a physical action. Therefore, it is insufficient to study Torah, using mere words and thoughts; it is also necessary to fulfill the divine mitzvot with physical actions. When one fulfills a practical mitzva with his body, the energy of the vital, animating soul in his body, expressed, for example, through the ability to move his hands or to walk, becomes part of the mitzva and is absorbed in the light of God, becoming "unified with Him in complete unity."

וְהוּא לְבוּשׁ הַשְּׁלִישִׁי שֶׁל נֶפֶשׁ הָאֱלוֹקִית. **This is the third garment of the divine soul.**

The garment of action is the third of the divine soul's three garments, which are thought, speech, and action. When the divine soul clothes itself in all three of these garments and operates through them, a person becomes attached to God with his entire being.

וַאֲזַי גַּם כֹּחַ נֶפֶשׁ הַחִיּוּנִית שֶׁבְּגוּפוֹ מַמָּשׁ שֶׁמִּקְּלִיפַּת נוֹגַהּ, נִתְהַפֵּךְ מֵרַע לְטוֹב, וְנִכְלָל מַמָּשׁ בִּקְדוּשָּׁה, כְּנֶפֶשׁ הָאֱלוֹקִית מַמָּשׁ, **Then the energy of the vital soul, deriving from *kelippat noga*, and which is literally in his body, is also transformed from evil to good, and is actually absorbed in holiness, literally like the divine soul,**

Kelippat noga is the entity that interfaces between holiness and the completely impure *kelippot*, between good and evil. The energy of the vital, animating soul, which derives from *kelippat noga*, is not intrinsically connected to holiness, but its trajectory can be changed and its direction shifted. Thus, in an action of holiness, in the performance of a mitzva, even the vital soul is transformed from evil to good, and, like the divine soul, it becomes absorbed in holiness. When a person performs a mitzva, every component of his body and physical being that relates to the action of that mitzva, such as the hand that straps on *tefillin* and the energy utilized in that act, is integrated in the mitzva.

At that moment, the vital soul, along with the divine soul, is intimately connected with the one God.

מֵאַחַר שֶׁהוּא הוּא הַפּוֹעֵל וְעוֹשֶׂה מַעֲשֵׂה הַמִּצְוָה, שֶׁבִּלְעָדוֹ לֹא הָיְתָה נֶפֶשׁ הָאֱלֹקִית פּוֹעֶלֶת בַּגּוּף כְּלָל,

since it is the vital, animal soul **itself that performs and does the** physical **act of the mitzva. Without** this soul, **the divine soul could not act through the body at all,**

The divine soul cannot act through the body without the mediating presence of the vital, animal soul.

כִּי הִיא רוּחָנִית, וְהַגּוּף גַּשְׁמִי וְחוֹמְרִי, וְהַמְמוּצָּע בֵּינֵיהֶם הִיא נֶפֶשׁ הַחִיּוּנִית הַבַּהֲמִית הַמְלוּבֶּשֶׁת בְּדַם הָאָדָם שֶׁבְּלִבּוֹ וְכָל הַגּוּף.

since it is spiritual, while the body is physical and material. The intermediary between them is the vital, animal soul, which is clothed in a person's blood, which is in his heart and entire body.

There is no direct contact between the spiritual and physical. The only way they can be bridged is by means of the vital, animal soul, which serves as an intermediary between the pure soul and the physical body. Consequently, when a person fulfills a mitzva using his body, it forms a connection between all the elements of his being and the light of *Ein Sof*. The animal soul, which provides the physical infrastructure for the mitzva's execution, links the divine soul – which has attained a deeply intimate connection to God – with the corporeal body, the element that executed the physical act of the mitzva.

20 Adar וְאַף שֶׁמַּהוּתָהּ וְעַצְמוּתָהּ שֶׁל נֶפֶשׁ הַבַּהֲמִית שֶׁבְּלִבּוֹ, שֶׁהֵן מִדּוֹתֶיהָ הָרָעוֹת, עֲדַיִין לֹא נִכְלְלוּ בִּקְדוּשָּׁה.

Although the essence and being of the animal soul that is in his heart, i.e., the animal soul's **evil attributes, have not yet been absorbed into holiness,**

When a person performs a mitzva (and, as was explained previously, a *beinoni* can be in a perpetual state of "performing mitzvot" in his thoughts, words, and actions), his animal soul becomes absorbed into the holiness of that mitzva. It is absorbed as part of the bond forged at that time between the physical world and God. Despite this connection between the physical and the Divine, the animal soul itself is not changed at its core. It remains an animal soul that is drawn to the physical and attracted to the other side that is not divine. As the author of the *Tanya* taught earlier, a *beinoni* must remain constantly aware of this fact, and consequently regard himself as wicked (see chap. 1). In other words, the *beinoni* must understand the potential danger he is in. For if he merely slackens his grip on the reins of self-restraint, he will be relegated to the status of a wicked person.

The dwelling of the Divine Presence within the children of Israel follows the directive mentioned in the verse "They shall make for Me a sanctuary, and I will dwell within them" (Ex. 25:8). The Torah does not say "within it [i.e., the sanctuary]" but rather "within *them*," that is, within each individual person.[8] Located within the sanctuary was the Holy of Holies, the locus of the Divine Presence. All types of people were integral elements of the sanctuary, including those like Koraḥ, Datan, and Aviram.

This is also true within the makeup of an individual. When one fulfills a mitzva, he acts as a sanctuary for God, despite there being evil aspects that still exist within him. Only certain rare individuals succeed in transforming the nature of their souls and purifying them through and through. Most people must content themselves with the knowledge that their darker aspects are buried under many layers, and at best they need to make certain that they are not brought to the fore, as alluded to in the verse "A shameful matter shall not appear among you" (Deut. 23:15).

מִכָּל מָקוֹם מֵאַחַר דְּאִתְכַּפְיָן לִקְדוּשָׁה, וּבְעַל כָּרְחָן עוֹנִין אָמֵן וּמַסְכִּימִין וּמִתְרַצִּין לַעֲשִׂיַּית הַמִּצְוָה, עַל יְדֵי הִתְגַּבְּרוּת נַפְשׁוֹ הָאֱלֹקִית שֶׁבַּמּוֹחַ שֶׁשַּׁלִּיט עַל הַלֵּב,	**nevertheless, since** these evil attributes **are subjugated to holiness, and begrudgingly answer amen, agreeing to and accepting the performance of the mitzva through the strengthening of his divine soul, which is in the brain that rules over the heart,**

A person who is able to overcome the attributes of the animal soul and perform a mitzva has in essence succeeded in quieting the power of

---

8. See, for example, Alsheikh, Ex. 31.

the animal soul within him and forced it to participate in a holy matter. Even if he experiences inner conflict ("two peoples are in your womb" [Gen. 25:23]), it is never manifest in practice. He either fulfills the mitzva or he does not. In order to perform an action, all the disparate parts of the soul must cooperate. At the very least, the discordant elements cannot interfere when the action is being executed.

וְהֵן בְּשָׁעָה זוֹ בִּבְחִינַת גָּלוּת וְשֵׁינָה כַּנִּזְכָּר לְעֵיל, וּלְכָךְ אֵין זוֹ מְנִיעָה מֵהַשְׁרָאַת הַשְּׁכִינָה עַל גּוּף הָאָדָם בְּשָׁעָה זוֹ. **and at this moment they are in a state of exile and sleep, as mentioned above** (chaps. 13, 19); **therefore, this is not an obstacle** preventing **the Divine Presence from dwelling upon the person's body at this moment,**

The Divine Presence is able to dwell, unimpeded, upon the person when he is involved in a mitzva because the evil attributes of the animal soul are neither aroused nor enclothed in the body, but are dormant.

דְּהַיְינוּ, שֶׁכֹּחַ נֶפֶשׁ הַחִיּוּנִית הַמְלוּבָּשׁ בַּעֲשִׂיַּית הַמִּצְוָה **meaning, the energy of the vital soul that is clothed in the performance of the mitzva**

For example, when a person extends his hand and gives charity, that movement serves as a garment for the vital soul. The same applies to all mitzvot. Yet the mitzva of charity is a particularly striking example of this, because in it are clothed the full force and focus of the vital soul, which had been completely invested in the money that this person is now giving to charity.

הוּא נִכְלָל מַמָּשׁ בְּאוֹר ה׳ וּמְיוּחָד בּוֹ בְּיִחוּד גָּמוּר. **is literally absorbed in God's light and is unified with it in complete unity.**

The particular element of the animal soul and body that participates in fulfilling the mitzva becomes absorbed into the supernal holiness, since it becomes a part of the mitzva. This is because a mitzva cannot be performed without the participation of the body and animal soul. The essence of a mitzva is that it creates a bond between the divine essence that issues the command and the person who is the object and executor of the command – doing so with his body and soul – forming one cohesive entity of holiness.

| וְעַל יְדֵי זֶה מַמְשִׁיךְ הֶאָרָה לִכְלָלוּת נֶפֶשׁ הַחִיּוּנִית שֶׁבְּכָל הַגּוּף וְגַם עַל הַגּוּף הַגַּשְׁמִי, | One thereby draws down a ray of light upon the totality of the vital soul that permeates the entire body, as well as upon the physical body, |

The energy directly involved in executing a mitzva is not the sole aspect of one's being connected to it. Not only does the vital soul not interfere with the performance of the mitzva, but in a way it grants it its tacit approval. Consequently, the entirety of the vital soul plays a role in the physical fulfillment of the mitzva.

| בִּבְחִינַת מַקִּיף מִלְמַעְלָה מֵרֹאשׁוֹ וְעַד רַגְלָיו. | this light being expressed **as an encompassing** light **from above,** surrounding them **from head to toe.** |

The concepts of inner light and encompassing light are borrowed to some degree from the world in which we live. If one were to describe them in a more abstract sense, inner and encompassing lights are two types of influence. The inner influence derives from an internal sensation in which a person comprehends and senses something and acts based on that comprehension and those feelings. This type of influence is common, for instance, when one is studying Torah.[9] There is an additional type of influence, also quite common, which is described as being encompassing. An encompassing influence does not become absorbed within one's intellect or feelings. Rather, one is merely situated in a particular atmosphere, in a place and environment that influence him without his knowing and feeling it. In this sense, the dwelling of the Divine Presence upon a person who performs a mitzva is characterized as an encompassing influence (an "encompassing light"). The person is unaware of this influence, as it is inherently unable to be grasped. Yet since his soul and body are vital partners in the

---

9. See, for example, *Likkutei Torah*, Num. 37c, which gives the rather well-known analogy of a teacher and his student.

performance of the mitzva, it is impossible for them not to experience some degree of resonance with or acknowledgement of the influence (or "light") engendered by the mitzva.

וְזֶהוּ שֶׁנֶּאֱמַר (בזהר שם): דִּשְׁכִינְתָּא שָׁרְיָא עַל רֵישֵׁיהּ, "עַל" דַּיְיקָא. וְכֵן: אַכָּל בֵּי עֲשָׂרָה שְׁכִינְתָּא שָׁרְיָא (סנהדרין לט, א).

This is the meaning of that which is stated (Zohar, Parashat Balak, 187a), "For the Divine Presence dwells upon his head"; the term "upon" is used specifically. Likewise the Talmud states, "The Divine Presence dwells upon every gathering of ten Jews" (Sanhedrin 39a).

Both the Zohar and Talmud use the term "upon," alluding to the fact that the Divine Presence is atop and above one's head,[10] meaning in an encompassing manner, and not "in his head," meaning in an internal manner. One who experiences the Divine Presence in his head has attained the status of a prophet who merits seeing the revelation of God's presence."[11]

וְהִנֵּה כָּל בְּחִינַת הַמְשָׁכַת אוֹר הַשְּׁכִינָה, שֶׁהִיא בְּחִינַת גִּילּוּי אוֹר אֵין סוֹף בָּרוּךְ הוּא, אֵינוֹ נִקְרָא שִׁינּוּי חַס וְשָׁלוֹם בּוֹ יִתְבָּרֵךְ וְלֹא רִיבּוּי. כְּדְאִיתָא בְּסַנְהֶדְרִין (שם), דְּאָמַר לֵיהּ הַהוּא מִינָא לְרַבָּן גַּמְלִיאֵל: אָמְרִיתוּ 'כָּל בֵּי עֲשָׂרָה שְׁכִינְתָּא שָׁרְיָא', כַּמָּה שְׁכִינְתָּא אִית לְכוּ? וְהֵשִׁיב לוֹ מָשָׁל מֵאוֹר הַשֶּׁמֶשׁ הַנִּכְנָס בְּחַלּוֹנוֹת רַבִּים כו'.

No amount of drawing down the light of the Divine Presence, meaning the revelation of the light of Ein Sof, blessed be He, is considered a change in Him, God forbid, nor does it indicate a plurality. As it is stated in Sanhedrin (39a) that a certain heretic said to Rabban Gamliel: "You say that the Divine Presence dwells upon any gathering of ten Jews. How many Divine Presences do you have?" Rabban Gamliel replied to him with an analogy of the sun's light, which enters through many windows, and so forth.

---

10. See commentary on chap. 11 above.
11. Sanhedrin 39a.

As was mentioned earlier, the Divine Presence is manifest wherever a person performs a mitzva. This might lead one to think that God has undergone a change, God forbid, as He reveals Himself differently in different contexts. Alternatively, one might erroneously presume that there are multiple elements within God, since the Divine Presence apparently manifests itself in multiple places simultaneously. The incident recorded in the Talmud provides a resolution to this misconception. Rabban Gamliel's analogy teaches that although the windows differ from one another in shape and location, and the light passing through them is ostensibly unique to each one, the fact of the matter is that it is the same sunlight that shines through them all.

וְהַמַּשְׂכִּיל יָבִין. **The intelligent person will understand.**

This analogy alludes to the concept of the dwelling of the Divine Presence. Any time a person merits attaining a certain degree of utter self-nullification to God, namely, through altruistic Torah study and performance of mitzvot, it is as though he has opened a window to the Divine. The exact characteristics of the window itself are less important than the dwelling of the Divine Presence that shines and is revealed through it.

This chapter began with an explanation of the phrase "To perform it," the final words of the verse "Rather, the matter is very near to you, in your mouth and in your heart, to perform it," quoted in the book's title page, which says: "The actions that are performed take place in our physical, practical world, and the one performing these actions is man, a soul within a body. The *beinoni* in particular, within whom the conflict between the divine and animal souls is unceasing, is he who is able 'to perform it,' to act and irradiate holiness into this lower world."

The author of the Tanya then proceeded to explain mortal man's role in this process. He described how specifically the practical performance of mitzvot causes the Divine Presence to dwell in this world. This concept refers to the revelation of God's unity in a particular object whereby that object is utterly absorbed and nullified within the Divine. As was explained, a person cannot achieve total nullification of this sort except by performing the practical mitzvot. The analogy presented in this chapter and mentioned frequently throughout the rest of the book was that of the oil lamp. The "lamp of God" refers to the divine soul within man. The body is the wick. The oil that fuels the wick is analogous to good deeds, the performance of God's mitzvot in this world.

The dwelling of the Divine Presence that results from the performance of mitzvot is not an internal illumination (or influence) that is clothed within the powers of the soul, which the person can understand and feel. Rather, it is an encompassing illumination, on occasion sensed somewhat, and at times not felt at all. Yet as the author of the Tanya stresses here and elsewhere, a person's feelings remain his own personal experience. Though that sensation is important to the person who effectuated the dwelling of the Divine Presence, it is less so for the mitzva itself, for the resultant divine unity, and for the ultimate achievement of creating space for God to dwell in the lower worlds. From the perspective of man, this seems almost tragic. The light is shining above his head, yet he cannot benefit from it. He has turned on the lights, yet his house remains dark. But as was explained in the preceding chapters, the process can be seen on a deeper level. This system engenders even greater joy of the soul, that which is beyond the person's own personal reckoning. It is the joy of someone who performs a mitzva and thereby changes the world, the joy borne of the awareness that not only is he fulfilling the purpose of the creation of all worlds, but he has also gone far beyond this: He has fulfilled God's innermost will to have a dwelling place in the lower worlds.

Chapter 36

IN THE PREVIOUS CHAPTER, THE AUTHOR OF THE *TANYA* began exploring the purpose underlying the creation of *beinonim* and their souls' descent into this physical world. He established that this purpose is for the *beinoni* to fulfill "good deeds," that is, the mitzvot, alluded to in the verse, which states, "To perform it" – the overarching theme of the book.

The previous chapter focused on the implications this has vis-à-vis man: the total nullification of the self when engaged in the performance of a mitzva, and the subsequent dwelling of the Divine Presence upon that person. This chapter will elaborate upon the overall purpose of God's creation, of both the upper and lower worlds, and that through performing mitzvot in this corporeal world (thereby fulfilling the injunction "to perform it"), man effects a transformation that renders this earthly realm into both an instrument of and a dwelling place for Godliness.

וְהִנֵּה מוּדַעַת זֹאת מַאֲמַר רַבּוֹתֵינוּ זִ״ל, שֶׁתַּכְלִית בְּרִיאַת עוֹלָם הַזֶּה הוּא שֶׁנִּתְאַוָּה הַקָּדוֹשׁ בָּרוּךְ הוּא לִהְיוֹת לוֹ דִירָה בַּתַּחְתּוֹנִים.	There is a well-known statement of our Rabbis that the purpose of the creation of this world is because the Holy One, blessed be He, desired to have an abode in the lower worlds.	21 Adar 7 Adar II (leap year)

It is told that the author of the *Tanya* was once asked about the purpose of the creation of this world. He answered with this statement regarding God desiring a dwelling in the lower realms,[1] and then added,

---

1. *Tanḥuma, Beḥukotai* 3, *Naso* 15; *Bemidbar Rabba* 13:6.

"But one does not question the existence of a desire!"[2] Though given humorously, this answer is quite true. It penetrates the essence of the answers given by the greatest philosophers, who didn't elaborate about the purpose of the creation of the world.[3]

וְהִנֵּה לֹא שַׁיָּךְ לְפָנָיו יִתְבָּרֵךְ בְּחִינַת מַעְלָה וּמַטָּה, Now, the concepts of "higher" and "lower" are not applicable to God,

In order to understand the concept of a "dwelling place in the lower worlds," it is necessary to first explain the concepts of higher and lower relative to God, so as to avoid the impression that God exists in some upper level versus a lower one. In relation to God, it is clearly impossible that concepts of up and down are meant to be understood spatially or geographically. To do so is absurd, as His existence is utterly beyond the constraints of time and space.

כִּי הוּא יִתְבָּרֵךְ מְמַלֵּא כָּל עָלְמִין בְּשָׁוֶה. because He permeates all worlds equally.

Relative to God, it is impossible to use concepts of higher and lower, not only in a spatial sense, but even on a more abstract level. The higher, spiritual worlds are distinct from the lower, physical worlds not in the physical sense, as they are not physical, but rather in terms of spiritual levels. The higher worlds are suffused with a greater divine illumination, since, in contrast to the lower worlds, there are fewer interposing "garments" and veils, as explained in chapter 46 below. Therefore, the author of the *Tanya* states that God permeates all the worlds equally, unfettered by distinctions of spiritual levels. Accordingly, the statement of our Sages regarding "a dwelling place in the *lower* worlds" perforce must bear a different meaning, as will be explained.

---

2. See the beginning of *Hemshekh Samekh Vav*, 5666, by the Rebbe Rashab, who mentions this quip in the name of the author of the *Tanya*. This also appears in *Or HaTorah* by the Tzemah Tzedek, *Parashat Balak*, p. 997.

3. The Lubavitcher Rebbe, Rabbi Menahem Mendel Schneerson, notes the *Zohar* (2:42b) and the beginning of *Etz Hayyim*. For more on the subject, see *Hemshekh Samekh Vav*, 5666, p. 3 and onward, s.v. "*shokav amudei shesh*," 5702, and elsewhere (*Likkutei Biurim La Sefer HaTanya*).

CHAPTER 36

אֶלָּא בֵּיאוּר הָעִנְיָן, כִּי קוֹדֶם שֶׁנִּבְרָא הָעוֹלָם הָיָה הוּא לְבַדּוֹ יִתְבָּרֵךְ יָחִיד וּמְיוּחָד, וּמְמַלֵּא כָּל הַמָּקוֹם הַזֶּה, שֶׁבָּרָא בּוֹ הָעוֹלָם,

Rather, the explanation of the matter is that before the world was created God was alone, completely one, permeating this entire space in which He created the world.

Prior to the creation of the world there was no other existence besides God. He was completely one in the sense that there was nothing added to His own essential being.

The expression "permeating this entire space" is to be understood in its broadest sense, as "the space of the world" that God carved out within the constriction[4] in which He created the world.

The creation of the world took place within a space that is ostensibly void of God's presence. From this perspective, before the world was created, God alone existed, with no limits or constraints. No other entity was present outside of God; not even the most infinitesimal speck of otherness existed beyond His being. It is thus impossible to speak of space existing as a geographic location or even an abstract dimension before the creation of the world. It is only possible to speak of the Source from which space and the world were subsequently created. In this sense, before there was a world, God was the "place of the world."[5]

וְגַם עַתָּה כֵּן הוּא לְפָנָיו יִתְבָּרֵךְ,

Now too, after the creation of the world, it is the same from God's perspective,

The truth of the matter is that the existence or non-existence of the world effects no change in God, as we say in the morning prayers, "You are as You were before the world was created, and You are as You were after it was created." From God's perspective, He alone is present throughout all existence, both before and after the creation of the world. Relating to the world and God as distinct entities, or the very notion of the existence of the world, its being created, and the way it operates, is a perspective not shared by God, as will be explained.

---

4. See the Arizal's *Likkutei Torah, Parashat Ki Tisa*, s.v. "*hineh Makom iti.*"
5. *Bereshit Rabba* 68:8.

רַק שֶׁהֲשִׁינּוּי הוּא אֶל הַמְקַבְּלִים the change is only in relation to those
חַיּוּתוֹ וְאוֹרוֹ יִתְבָּרֵךְ, who receive God's life force and light,

While the creation of the world effects no change in God, as mentioned, with respect to created beings the creation of the world is the most significant change, as it is the absolute inception of their existence.

The relationship between the Creator and created beings is not at all mutual. That which is true for one side is not true for the other, and that which appears to be the bedrock of existence for created beings is not at all existence from God's vantage point. The veil interposing between the Creator and creations, between God and those receiving His life force and light, is regarded as an obstruction and concealment for only one side, while for the other side it does not exist at all.

Consider, for example, a one-way mirror. One side is reflective while the other is transparent. One peering into the reflective side sees himself and the entire world around him reflected in the glass, whereas one who looks through the other side sees nothing. From the latter's standpoint there is no obstruction, only transparent glass that conceals nothing and that constitutes no existence vis-à-vis the person looking. ☞

TRANSPARENT LENS

☞ The Talmud states that Moses would prophesy by peering through a transparent lens, while the other prophets would observe their prophecies through a non-transparent lens (a mirror) (*Yevamot* 49b; see *Zohar* 2:82b; *Pardes Rimmonim* 23:1, s.v. "*aspaklaria*"). It would thus be expected that Moses would experience God more clearly than would the other prophets. But as our Sages noted, the verses imply the opposite. Isaiah, who prophesied through a non-transparent lens, said, "I saw the Lord" (Isa. 6:1); Ezekiel said, "I saw, and behold, there was a likeness" (Ezek. 8:2). Yet Moses, who observed his prophecy through a transparent lens, records God as saying, "A man shall not see Me and live" (Ex. 33:20).

When understood correctly, these verses pose no contradiction. A transparent lens is completely clear, and so a person looking through it, unhindered by anything whatsoever, is able to see the truth, which is that he does not see. By contrast, a person looking through an obscure lens, to whatever degree, will perceive some kind of image in it. Therefore, the prophets looking through a non-transparent lens saw something, and the less clear the lens, the more they saw (see *Torah Or* 33a; *Or HaTorah*, Num. 492a, Song 349).

שֶׁמְּקַבְּלִים עַל יְדֵי לְבוּשִׁים רַבִּים הַמְכַסִּים וּמַסְתִּירִים אוֹרוֹ יִתְבָּרֵךְ,

which they receive by means of many garments that cover and conceal God's light,

Created beings do not receive God's light and life force directly, but only when the latter are enclothed in many spiritual garments, layer upon layer. Like physical clothing, these garments conceal the utterly profound divine influence while simultaneously allowing it to be transmitted beyond the divine existence, as it were, into our lower worlds. Were the divine illumination to shine directly upon the created beings without any garment or concealment, these beings would cease to exist as created beings.

כְּדִכְתִיב: "כִּי לֹא יִרְאַנִי הָאָדָם וָחָי"
(שמות לג, כ), וּכְדְפֵירְשׁוּ רַבּוֹתֵינוּ ז"ל:
שֶׁאֲפִילוּ מַלְאָכִים הַנִּקְרָאִים חַיּוֹת
אֵין רוֹאִין כוּ׳.

as it is written: "For no man shall see Me and live [*vahay*]" (Ex. 33:20), and as our Rabbis explained, that even angels that are called *hayot* do not see, and so forth.

This verse is commonly understood as expressing that a person cannot see the Divine and remain alive. But our Sages explain it differently: No man and no living being (*hai*) shall see Me. Included within "living being" are the seraphim, ophanim, and *hayot hakodesh* angels.[6] This verse teaches that God's true essence cannot be perceived, not only by man, who is a soul in a corporeal body, covered by and concealed within a physical makeup, but even the angels, who possess no physical body that obstructs the spiritual, and who stand in the higher worlds where the existence of God's presence is clear, are unable to perceive His essence.

וְזֶהוּ עִנְיַן הִשְׁתַּלְשְׁלוּת הָעוֹלָמוֹת
וִירִידָתָם מִמַּדְרֵגָה לְמַדְרֵגָה עַל יְדֵי
רִבּוּי הַלְּבוּשִׁים הַמַּסְתִּירִים הָאוֹר
וְהַחַיּוּת שֶׁמִּמֶּנּוּ יִתְבָּרֵךְ,

This is the concept of the unfolding succession of the worlds and their descent, level by level, by means of the many garments that conceal the light and life force that emanate from God,

---

6. See *Bemidbar Rabba*, end of *Parashat Naso*.

The "unfolding succession of the worlds" refers to the descent of God's light through the worlds and the manner in which one influences the next, level after level.

What is this process of descending levels, of a lower world emanating from an upper world? A lower world, existing on a lower level, means greater concealment of the Creator from the created beings. In this sense, the distinction between the worlds, like the distinction between levels or people, lies in the number of veils that separate them from God. What defines a particular world's level is the extent to which God's existence is apprehended therein. The more obscure God is, the lower the world. Consequently, the progressive descent of the worlds does not come about through the penetration of divine light into each respective level of existence. To the contrary, it is a concealment of divine light, concealment upon concealment, level after level, world after world.

עַד שֶׁנִּבְרָא עוֹלָם הַזֶּה הַגַּשְׁמִי וְהַחוֹמְרִי מַמָּשׁ. **until the actual physical, material world was created.**

A careful reading yields three distinct terms the author of the *Tanya* uses in describing this world: "physical," "material," and "actual." These depict three specific levels, each below the one preceding it. "Physical" refers to a quantifiable world, with all elements therein being subject to some degree of measurement. Yet it is possible for something quantifiable to not be material, such as in mathematics, for example, and so the author adds that our world is also "material." However, materiality can also be perceived in a manner not directly physical, e.g., visually, auditorily, and cognitively. The author therefore emphasizes that this world is "actual" (in Hebrew, *mamash*). The most basic denotation of the term *mamash* is something which can be touched. Our world is so low, so physical and material, that the determining factor as to its existence is ultimately confirmed through the sense of touch.[7]

The nuanced definitions regarding this world and the emphasis

---

7. See *Iggerot Kodesh* by the sixth Lubavitcher Rebbe, Rabbi Yosef Yitzhak Schneerson, vol. 3, p. 304 (also published in the *HaTamim* journal, p. 32 [vol. 1, p. 30]).

placed on them have important ramifications for us, since we are part of this "actual physical, material world." We are complex creatures, possessing lofty and spiritual elements that exceed the bounds of this world. Yet the awareness we attain on each rung on the spiritual ladder we scale necessarily receives its input and makeup through the lens of the material aspects within us. Man's core struggle to elevate his being is therefore also the struggle to extricate himself from these constraints. He struggles to rid himself of the material perceptions of existence, of physical images, and dependence on his sense of touch. For man, the above-mentioned definitions are more than a mere description of the world; they are meant to illuminate his path by which to push beyond this-worldly limitations and attach himself to the Divine.

וְהוּא הַתַּחְתּוֹן בְּמַדְרֵגָה שֶׁאֵין תַּחְתּוֹן לְמַטָּה מִמֶּנּוּ בְּעִנְיַן הֶסְתֵּר אוֹרוֹ יִתְבָּרֵךְ וְחֹשֶׁךְ כָּפוּל וּמְכֻפָּל, **This world is the bottommost level, beneath which there is none lower vis-à-vis the concealment of God's light and a doubly reinforced darkness,**

Our world is considered the lowest world, because it is the realm in which the Divine is concealed to the greatest degree. It is the place in which the darkness is doubly powerful and the divine light is not at all revealed. (More accurately, our world broadly speaking is the lowest world vis-à-vis the concealment of the divine light, though it can still be revealed. It is the lowest world that can yet be elevated.)

עַד שֶׁהוּא מָלֵא קְלִיפּוֹת וְסִטְרָא אָחֳרָא, שֶׁהֵן נֶגֶד ה' מַמָּשׁ לוֹמַר: "אֲנִי וְאַפְסִי עוֹד" (צפניה ב, טו). **to the extent that it is rife with *kelippot* and the *sitra aḥara*, which are literally antithetical to God, declaring: "I and nothing but me" (Zeph. 2:15).**

The *sitra aḥara*, the other side, can exist and operate only when God is concealed. In our world, that concealment is so dense that the *kelippot* not only exist as an additional reality, ancillary to God's existence, but they are utterly antithetical to Him,[8] proclaiming their exclusive existence.

---

8. The concealment and darkness generated by this world intrinsically clouds

The darkness enshrouding our world, the lowest of all realms, is so powerful that it professes to be light. It is a world in which the created beings, mere shadows and shadows of shadows, claim to exist as independent beings, even going so far as to repudiate the existence of all else, including God. ☞ ☞

Thus far, the author of the *Tanya* has explained, to a certain degree, the concepts of "higher" and "lower" relative to God. When it is said of God that He is not present in the lower realms, it means He is not

I AND NOTHING BUT ME

☞ The definitions of "higher" and "lower" parallel varying degrees of consciousness: The higher the level, the clearer and more direct is one's consciousness of the Divine. At a lofty level, the Divine is the sole existence, while at a lower level, it is a reality that can be perceived. In our world, the lowest of all worlds, the Divine is obfuscated to the extent that it is possible for a created entity to proclaim, "I and nothing but me." Not only does that entity not see the Creator, it even denies His fundamental existence.

The existence of the worlds lies, as it were, between two extremes: between the most sublime state of existence, where "there is nothing besides Him" on the one hand, and the inferior state of "I and nothing but me" on the other. At one extreme, God's presence, permeating all existence, is clearly manifest to the extent that "there is no place void of Him." At the other extreme, existence (*kelippa*), not only fails to perceive the omnipresence of the Creator, but it perceives its own existence as the foundation of everything, as the source and purpose of existence.

THE ROOT OF IDOL WORSHIP

☞ As the gap between the divine revelation and the existence of the world grows, the experience of the divine becomes increasingly blurred. It is incrementally replaced by intervening entities, until at some point it is no longer possible to perceive the apex of the supernal chain. When this occurs, the intermediary becomes the new focal point of all created beings.

Rambam articulates this in his *Mishneh Torah* (*Hilkhot Avodat Kokhavim* 1) from a slightly different angle. He describes a three-step process leading to the inception of idol worship, which he asserts was the result of a protracted degeneration of faith in God's unity. Initially, people saw how the divine energy flowed into the world through various intermediaries. This

---

one's awareness of its divine origin, yet it could be construed that the concealment is not necessarily contrary to God's will. To this, the author of the *Tanya* adds that they are, in fact, diametrically opposed to His will (noted by the Lubavitcher Rebbe, Rabbi Menaḥem Mendel Schneerson).

readily exposed within them. The author will now proceed to explain the purpose of the progressive descent of creation, from the most sublime realms to the lower worlds.

וְהִנֵּה תַּכְלִית הִשְׁתַּלְשְׁלוּת הָעוֹלָמוֹת וִירִידָתָם מִמַּדְרֵגָה לְמַדְרֵגָה אֵינוֹ בִּשְׁבִיל עוֹלָמוֹת הָעֶלְיוֹנִים, הוֹאִיל וְלָהֶם יְרִידָה מֵאוֹר פָּנָיו יִתְבָּרַךְ.

The purpose of the progressive descent of the worlds, and their descent from level to level, is not for the sake of the higher worlds, since for them it is in actuality **a descent from the light of God's countenance.**

8 Adar II (leap year)

The progressive descent of worlds, which constitutes the mammoth process of Creation, is not for the sake of the higher realms, as for them such a descent is a distancing from God's light.

The higher worlds, as lofty as they are, are still worlds. The concept of "world" (*olam*) stems from the Hebrew root and concept of "hiddenness" (*ha'alama*).[9] In this sense, a world means a place wherein the divine existence is hidden, imperceptible in its totality. Even the higher worlds are referred to as *worlds*, connoting hiddenness, in the sense that the light of God's countenance is not completely manifest. As such, even the higher worlds bear no intrinsic justification for their existence, as they cannot be characterized as a perfect reality.

Every world represents a degree of remoteness from the absolute perfection of the divine reality. Each point along the vast configuration

eventually led to their taking note of those intermediaries, as they felt it necessary to forge relationships with them. (This is similar to earthly kingdoms, where people make it their business to establish a good rapport not only with the highest-ranking official, but also with his subordinates.) As time passed, the intermediary gained increasing prominence, while the primary source progressively lost His. The distance between people and the source increased, and their understanding of God weakened, until eventually the primary source became a relic of the past. People not only ceased relating to God, but their original belief in a transcendent cause of existence was utterly lost.

It is thus a reality that purportedly monotheistic religions may become idolatrous, albeit in the guise of venerating local saints. Should this occur, man loses all vestiges of any previous connection with God.

---

9. See, for example, *Likkutei Torah*, Num. 37d.

of the progressive descent of the worlds is necessarily inferior relative to its point of inception – the light of God's countenance – and so it cannot possibly constitute the ultimate intent and purpose of Creation. It is impossible to say that God created such an immensely complex system in order to gain less than He invested. Therefore, as will be explained, the purpose of this descent must be to ultimately generate some type of amplification of the initial state of things. The intention is to effectuate a rectification reaching the Essence that transcends even the very point propelling the progressive descent of creation.

אֶלָּא הַתַּכְלִית הוּא עוֹלָם הַזֶּה הַתַּחְתּוֹן, **Rather, the purpose is for this lower world,**

When we consider the progressive descent of worlds as a totality, as a purposeful system spanning from the "light of God's countenance" to this lowest of all worlds, we note how each point between these two extremes acts only as an intermediary, a means of channeling from above to below and vice versa. It follows that the ultimate purpose of the highest point is to be sought specifically in the lowest point, "in this lower world," the lowest of all worlds. The author of the *Tanya* will soon demonstrate that it is precisely within this lowest, most remote point that the point of greatness is hidden.

שֶׁכָּךְ עָלָה בִּרְצוֹנוֹ יִתְבָּרֵךְ, לִהְיוֹת נַחַת רוּחַ לְפָנָיו יִתְבָּרֵךְ כַּד אִתְכַּפְיָא סִטְרָא אָחֳרָא וְאִתְהַפֵּךְ חֲשׁוֹכָא לִנְהוֹרָא, **as this is what arose in God's will, namely, that He would have gratification when the *sitra aḥara* is subdued and darkness is transformed into light,**

The phrase "This is what arose in God's will" is an alternate form of the expression "The Holy One, blessed be He, desired to have an abode in the lower worlds." Both convey the same idea, that we are incapable of grasping why God derives satisfaction specifically when we subdue the *sitra aḥara* and why the emergence of light from darkness affords Him particular satisfaction.

The notion that "God desired" – the primal divine desire – is fundamentally inexplicable. Because the world was created by virtue of this desire, it by definition is not a part of this world's reality. Anything not lying within the bounds of our reality is utterly beyond our comprehension. Yet, although we are unable to broach the subject of this divine desire in its pristine state, we can attempt to understand it vis-à-vis its manifestation within the worlds. We can appreciate God's desire in the sense that it serves as the foundation and purpose of the worlds in which we dwell and to which we can relate.

שֶׁיָּאִיר אוֹר ה' אֵין סוֹף בָּרוּךְ הוּא בִּמְקוֹם הַחֹשֶׁךְ וְהַסִּטְרָא אָחֲרָא שֶׁל כָּל עוֹלָם הַזֶּה כּוּלוֹ, בְּיֶתֶר שְׂאֵת וְיֶתֶר עֹז וְיִתְרוֹן אוֹר מִן הַחֹשֶׁךְ מֵהָאָרָתוֹ בְּעוֹלָמוֹת עֶלְיוֹנִים, שֶׁמֵּאִיר שָׁם עַל יְדֵי לְבוּשִׁים וְהֶסְתֵּר פָּנִים הַמַּסְתִּירִים וּמַעֲלִימִים אוֹר אֵין סוֹף בָּרוּךְ הוּא שֶׁלֹּא יִבָּטְלוּ בִּמְצִיאוּת.	so that the light of God, *Ein Sof*, blessed be He, will shine in the place of darkness and *sitra aḥara* of this entire world with a greater magnitude and intensity – being that **light is brighter when emerging from darkness** – more **than its illumination in the higher worlds,** where it shines through garments and through **a concealed countenance** both **concealing and hiding the light of** *Ein Sof*, **blessed be He, so that they not be nullified from existence.**

God's light is perceived and revealed to a much greater extent when contrasted with the darkness of this world. In fact, it shines brighter in this earthly realm than it does in the higher worlds. The brilliant rays of God's light are obfuscated by "garments" and a "concealed countenance" in the higher worlds so as not to nullify them from existence.

As was noted above, even in the higher worlds, the divine light is not completely revealed. Each world, by virtue of its being so, is unable to tolerate light beyond a particular degree of exposure. The inner light and its corresponding vessel must be in perpetual consonance with one another. Should there be a lack of harmony, if the illumination exceeds the capacity of the vessel to receive, the vessel will shatter, akin to electrical wiring catching fire if the current running through it exceeds its capacity.

The world and God are in a state of perpetual paradox. There is a qualitative contradiction between them making it impossible for them to coexist. The world can exist only inasmuch as it is unaware of and numb to the divine essence, only when the Divine is hidden, as it were. To express this differently, the existence of each world is fictitious, and so any given world can continue to exist only as long as it is under the illusion that it is real. Yet the very moment it becomes aware of its fictitious nature, it ceases to exist.

The necessity to conceal the divine light in order to perpetuate existence so that the worlds not be nullified from existence is in fact an existential requirement pertaining to all the worlds, higher and lower, yet is more apparent in the higher worlds. The Talmud recounts an incident where a child was studying in his rabbi's house from the book of Ezekiel. The child was able to comprehend the esoteric mystery of the *ḥashmal*, whereupon a fire emerged from the *ḥashmal* and consumed him. When the Sages saw this, they wished to hide away the book of Ezekiel. Ḥananya ben Ḥizkiya replied in wonderment: "If this one is wise, does that mean they all are wise?" (*Ḥagiga* 13a).

In other words, the fear that a person studying the book of Ezekiel would be incinerated due to his ecstatic experience with the holy *ḥayot* angels is not something to be considered in our normal lives. In fact, for this reason the book of Ezekiel was ultimately not hidden away. True, there were people throughout history, and even recently, who were known to have literally died while experiencing euphoric closeness to the Divine. Yet the likelihood of this occurring in our world is far less than it is in the higher worlds, and so it poses no concern. In the higher worlds, the relationship between the light and the vessels is more subtle, the barrier more delicate and sensitive. The slightest variation in that relationship, any increase in light, will cause that world to completely dissolve, disappearing forever in the divine illumination.

Consequently, since the higher worlds are incapable of tolerating even the most negligible of changes and increases in the divine revelation, the purpose of our world, the lowest of all the worlds, is, paradoxically, to contain that revelation. Moreover, the purpose of this world is not merely to reach a state of equilibrium with the higher worlds, but to serve as a means for the exponential increase of the divine illumination, exceeding that in the higher worlds.[10] This is possible precisely in our

---

10. The Lubavitcher Rebbe, Rabbi Menaḥem Mendel Schneerson, noted that

world, as a result of the paradox of the transformation of darkness into light. When the concealment itself will become light, it may have a divine illumination that is without any barriers or parameters at all.

וְלָזֶה נָתַן הַקָּדוֹשׁ בָּרוּךְ הוּא לְיִשְׂרָאֵל אֶת הַתּוֹרָה שֶׁנִּקְרֵאת 'עוֹז' וְ'כֹחַ'. וּכְמַאֲמַר רַבּוֹתֵינוּ ז״ל (סנהדרין ק, ב), שֶׁהַקָּדוֹשׁ בָּרוּךְ הוּא נוֹתֵן כֹּחַ בַּצַּדִּיקִים לְקַבֵּל שְׂכָרָם לֶעָתִיד לָבֹא, שֶׁלֹּא יִתְבַּטְּלוּ בִּמְצִיאוּת מַמָּשׁ בָּאוֹר ה', הַנִּגְלָה לֶעָתִיד בְּלִי שׁוּם לְבוּשׁ,

For this reason the Holy One, blessed be He, gave Israel the Torah, which is called "might" and "strength." This accords with our Rabbis' statement (*Sanhedrin* 100b) that the Holy One, blessed be He, grants the righteous the strength to receive their reward in the World to Come, so that they should not be literally nullified from existence in the light of God, which will be revealed in the future without any garment,

9 Adar II (leap year)

God's people are designated to effectuate a powerful divine illumination in this lowest of all worlds. To this end, God gave them His Torah, which is referred to as "might"[11] and "strength."

What is the purpose behind this God-given strength granted the righteous cited here? The author of the *Tanya* explains that it is to shield them from becoming obliterated in God's light, which will be revealed in the World to Come (that is, when God will dwell in this world) without any obstructing garment. The light that will shine in this world in the future will in a sense be a revelation of the divine essence itself, in its pristine and unalloyed intensity.

As was explained, the perpetuated existence of all created beings hinges on the concealment of the divine essence, a space seemingly

---

this resolves the well-known question of why something great and lofty should be created solely for the sake of something inferior to it. The author of the *Tanya*, therefore, teaches here that this physical world has the potential to be far greater than the higher worlds, as through our spiritual work God's light can shine to a much greater extent than it does in the higher worlds.

11. This is based on Ps. 29:11, which states, "The Lord gives strength to His people," understood as an allusion to the giving of the Torah. See also *Zevaḥim* 116a and *Zohar* 2:58a.

void of God, within which existence can thrive. The point being presented here is that the Torah, referred to as "might," is a unique strength God bestows upon the righteous, enabling them to maintain their presence in this world and avoid becoming nullified from existence. In this context, all Jews are regarded as righteous, as the verse states, "Your nation, they are all righteous."[12] God desires that they remain cognizant and sentient beings, even when the divine light will manifest itself in the world in all its intensity, incinerating all other existence. ☞

כְּדִכְתִיב: "וְלֹא יִכָּנֵף עוֹד מוֹרֶיךָ" (ישעיה ל, כ) [פֵּירוּשׁ, שֶׁלֹּא יִתְכַּסֶּה מִמְּךָ בִּכְנַף וּלְבוּשׁ] "וְהָיוּ עֵינֶיךָ רוֹאוֹת אֶת מוֹרֶיךָ" (שם),

as it is written: "But your Teacher will no longer be concealed (yikkanef)" (Isa. 30:20) (meaning, He will not be concealed from you with the corner of a robe [kanaf] and a garment), "but your eyes shall see your Teacher" (Isa. 30:20),

DIVINE REVELATION IN THE MATERIAL WORLD

☞ As was explained in the previous chapter, the materiality of this world, its density and opacity, renders our world unique among countless spiritual worlds. The advantage this world possesses is its ability to forge within it a bond with the divine essence without being incinerated and nullified. When the divine revelation inundates all existence, we are able, as it were, to take refuge in the material world's opacity and desensitization to the spiritual. Yet this is not possible when it comes to the spiritual worlds. Since those worlds are unidimensional, lacking the additional aspect of the material, they are incapable of providing any protection (see Shlomo Ibn Gabirol, *Keter Malkhut*; Rabbi Yisrael Najara, *Ana Elekh*).

This point is of paramount importance in grappling with recurring issues plaguing mankind. We are often troubled by the existential question: For what purpose did the pure soul descend into this world? To what end did the soul, basking in God's glory, descend into a chiefly evil world rife with *kelippot*? The various answers given all revolve around this point: As low and dense as this world is, its very materiality is what accounts for its durability and capacity to ultimately receive that which all the supernal worlds are unable to receive. Indeed, this world demands hard work and a fierce struggle to acquire even a basic awareness of divine existence. Ours is a world in which only a select few, after extraordinary toil, are privy to live with true awareness of the Divine. Despite, and perhaps because of, these challenges, this world is equipped to absorb the most sublime

---

12. Isa. 60:21. See also *Sanhedrin*, chap. 10, mishna 1.

"Teacher" in this verse refers to God. The verse therefore means that in the World to Come, God will no longer be hidden by "the corner of a garment," alluding to the fact that He will not hide His face from His children. The continuation of the verse reads, "But your eyes shall see your Teacher"; that is, at that time there will be a revelation of the divine essence itself, unobstructed by any form of concealment or garment.

and transcendent divine revelation, that of *Ein Sof* Himself.

This bond between the physical world and the Divine, as absurd as it may seem, is in fact self-evident. The process of progressive descent, eventuating in Creation, explains the descent of spiritual levels and the constriction of the divine light yet does not account for the existence of materiality. Although we ourselves experience within us the nexus between the spiritual and the material, nevertheless, even at the core of its deepest descent, the spiritual is not transformed into corporeality. Indeed, the spiritual may have been relegated to an exceptionally low level, perhaps even ranking lower on the spiritual barometer than a speck of materiality. Even so, it retains its spiritual nature, never morphing into something physical.

The descent of a lofty, abstract idea into raw, simplistic thought is a process of progressive descent. But for that idea to then be expressed in a physical action, there must occur a qualitative shift of an entirely different nature. Within the framework of causal progressive descent, there is no direct cause resulting in material existence. For it to come about, it requires its own, unique creation, expressed as "something created from nothing" (in contrast to "something created from something else").

The coming into being of materiality, a concept diametrically opposed to any spiritual (that is, non-material) entity, is an astounding, novel phenomenon, not deriving from the causal nature of the spiritual worlds. In this sense, materiality is created exclusively from the power of *Ein Sof* Himself, far beyond the process of progressive descent. The existence of corporeality, of total concealment, of the furthermost limit, is possible only with the power of He who transcends all limits. This constitutes the paradox of *Ein Sof*: He cannot be concealed except by He Himself.

This explanation alters our intellectual and emotional perspective of materiality, and in a certain sense even upends it. Instead of saying that materiality is inferior, we are now asserting that it is more hidden. Moreover, since materiality is not spiritual, it can be what the spiritual worlds are not: a vessel for *Ein Sof*. As the author of the *Tanya* explained in the previous chapter, it is for this reason that the physical Torah (the mitzvot and good deeds) is the exclusive path by which one can experience a profound connection with *Ein Sof*. This is in stark contrast to the ostensibly more spiritual faculties of love and fear of God, which do not reach *Ein Sof*. God is able to dwell specifically in materiality, due to the overwhelming concealment of the Divine therein. Thus, the concealment generated by the physical world maintains the comprehensive framework of God's universal concealment. While the material world is not destroyed by God's existence within it, the spiritual worlds cannot maintain their existence in the face of such a powerful presence.

וּכְתִיב: "כִּי עַיִן בְּעַיִן יִרְאוּ" וְגוֹ' (ישעיה נב, ח), **and it is written: "For they shall see eye to eye..."** (Isa. 52:8),

This verse refers to the crystal-clear perception of the divine reality. Unlike our present perception of God, which is indirect and muddled, in the World to Come we will see God's light "eye to eye," in a tangible, unhampered, and unveiled manner.

וּכְתִיב: "לֹא יִהְיֶה לָּךְ עוֹד הַשֶּׁמֶשׁ לְאוֹר יוֹמָם וְגוֹ' כִּי ה' יִהְיֶה לָּךְ לְאוֹר עוֹלָם" וְגוֹ' (ישעיה ס, יט-כ). **and it is written: "The sun will no longer be for light for you by day... as the Lord will be for you an eternal light"** (Isa. 60:19–20).

These verses describe the end of days, when all barriers interposing between the world and God will be broken, allowing for the full revelation of the Divine. Typically, the mechanics of creation are such that when the barriers between God and a particular world are removed, that world ceases to exist. The exception is our physical world, which is capable of maintaining its independent existence together with, and without being obliterated by, the divine revelation.

This concept recalls the opening concept of our chapter: "The Holy One, blessed be He, desired to have an abode in the lower worlds." This is precisely the same concept articulated here, albeit in different words. God desired a world wherein His light would be able to shine unimpeded. To this end, God "needed" to create the lowest and most material of all worlds – our world.

וְנוֹדַע שֶׁיְּמוֹת הַמָּשִׁיחַ, וּבִפְרָט כְּשֶׁיִּחְיוּ הַמֵּתִים - הֵם תַּכְלִית וּשְׁלֵימוּת בְּרִיאַת עוֹלָם הַזֶּה, שֶׁלְּכָךְ נִבְרָא מִתְּחִילָּתוֹ. **It is well known that the messianic era, and especially the time when the dead will be resurrected, is the ultimate purpose and culmination of the creation of this world, for which reason it was originally created.**

This world was originally created for the ultimate purpose of what it will become after the days of the Messiah, when the dead will live again. As will be explained below, this purpose is in a sense the endpoint of this world. Despite this, the new state of the world at the time of the resurrection of the dead will still remain within the framework of this world, as it ultimately emanates from the existence of the world as we know it. As was mentioned at the beginning of the chapter, the purpose of this world was to create an abode in the lower worlds. God Himself, unimpeded by any sort of casing or concealment, can be found and manifest in the space of this lower world. ☞

הַגָּהָה: (וְקַבָּלַת שָׂכָר עִיקָּרוֹ בָּאֶלֶף הַשְּׁבִיעִי כְּמוֹ שֶׁכָּתוּב בְּלִיקּוּטֵי תּוֹרָה מֵהָאֲרִ"י ז"ל).

Gloss: The receiving of reward is primarily in the seventh millennium, as it is written in *Likkutei Torah, Parashat Bereshit*, p. 8, of the Arizal.

In line with his general approach throughout the book, the author of the *Tanya* inserts a gloss to address an issue that diverges from the overall flow of this chapter. The author noted earlier that the

RESURRECTION OF THE DEAD

☞ This is a fundamental theme vis-à-vis understanding the nature and purpose of the world, which is subject to dispute. According to Rambam, the World to Come refers to the time when one's soul will be united with God, a feat that can come about only when the soul is unfettered by the body. The author of the *Tanya*, by contrast, maintains here that a unification of one's disembodied soul with God is essentially impossible. It follows that the ultimate, complete revelation of God, the culmination of creation, takes place not in the Garden of Eden, which is the world of souls, but rather only within and through the medium of the material world. According to this approach, the resurrection of the dead is a logical step in the process of the hereafter, as it is a renewal of life specifically in a physical body.

The soul's confinement to a physical body and a corporeal world is not a mere technicality temporarily required to grant reward and mete out punishment. Rather, it is the core element in creation that ultimately enables the true revelation of the Divine.

It is specifically the paradox of an existence that conceals and repudiates its source of being that will ultimately transform the notion of "Man shall not see Me and live" into a state where "they shall see [God] eye to eye." The statement "Man shall not see Me and live" refers to the present, when a person must remove his "garments" in order to see God, at which point he will automatically cease to live. The phrase "They shall see [God] eye to eye," refers to the World to Come, "when God returns to Zion," meaning, when, at the resurrection of the dead, the pure soul will inhabit a physical body once more (see *Iggeret HaKodesh*, epistle 17).

messianic era and the resurrection of the dead are the culmination of man's service in creating an abode for God in the lower worlds. The emphasis is therefore not on the revelation of the light of *Ein Sof*, but on man's divine service of creating that abode. The revelation of God's light that will result in the future, when "your Teacher will no longer be concealed," and when "they shall see eye to eye," is not the key reward for this service, but is instead a natural consequence of it.[13] Regarding this point, the author of the *Tanya* adds that the primary, true reward God will grant man for his service of creating for Him an abode in the lower worlds will be in the seventh millennium, which is destined to be, in a sense, even loftier than the life of the World to Come.[14]

---

22 Adar
10 Adar II (leap year)

וְגַם כְּבָר הָיָה לְעוֹלָמִים מֵעֵין זֶה בִּשְׁעַת מַתַּן תּוֹרָה,

A semblance of this degree of revelation **has already occurred in this world at the time of the giving of the Torah,**

A taste of what will transpire in the future at the resurrection of the dead, when the abode for God in this world will have been completed, was already experienced at the giving of the Torah at Mount Sinai. The divine revelation at Mount Sinai was on the level of "I am the Lord your God" (Ex. 20:2). It was a degree of revelation where the divine essence transcended all the interposing garments and barriers, all the while sustaining and permeating this corporeal world.

כְּדִכְתִיב: "אַתָּה הָרְאֵתָ לָדַעַת כִּי ה' הוּא הָאֱלֹהִים, אֵין עוֹד מִלְּבַדּוֹ" (דברים ד, לה). "הָרְאֵתָ" - מַמָּשׁ, בִּרְאִיָּה חוּשִׁיִּית,

as it is written in reference to the giving of the Torah, **"You have been shown in order to know that the Lord, He is God; there is nothing besides Him"** (Deut. 4:35). The expression **"have been shown"** is to be taken **literally,** that is, **with physical sight,**

---

13. Reminiscent of the concept stated in the Mishna (*Avot* 4:2): "The reward for fulfilling a mitzva is the mitzva itself."
14. See *Pelaḥ HaRimon, Shemot*, p. 177. Refer also to the lecture delivered by the Lubavitcher Rebbe, Rabbi Menaḥem Mendel Schneerson, on Shabbat *Parashat Ki Tetze* 5751.

This verse describes God as having been "shown" to His people. One could argue that this is meant to be understood figuratively, in the sense that God's existence was demonstrated to them. But the author of the *Tanya* interprets the verse quite literally: The divine revelation in this world was so palpable, it could be physically sensed. The verse does not mean that God's existence was demonstrated through methods of philosophical proofs, nor was it proven by supernatural phenomena. Rather, it was literally seen with everyone's own eyes, as will be the case in the future, when "they shall see eye to eye."

כְּדִכְתִיב: "וְכָל הָעָם רוֹאִים אֶת הַקּוֹלוֹת" (שמות כ, טו), רוֹאִים אֶת הַנִּשְׁמָע, as it is written: "All the people were seeing the thunder" (Ex. 20:15), a description of the fact that **they saw that which is heard,**

Noting the unusual phenomenon described in this verse, the commentaries[15] explain that at the giving of the Torah, the people saw that which is typically heard.

The divine revelation at Mount Sinai was in some way more direct than a regular sensory experience, whereby one merely sees the visible and hears the audible. It was a revelatory experience untainted by even the slightest shade of concealment, a sensation of such a pristine caliber that the people saw the audible and heard the visible. It was an unfiltered, tangible experience of the divine essence that breached the normal boundaries of the senses.

וּפֵירְשׁוּ רַבּוֹתֵינוּ ז"ל (שמות רבה פרשה ה, ט): מִסְתַּכְּלִים לַמִּזְרָח וְשׁוֹמְעִין אֶת הַדִּבּוּר יוֹצֵא "אָנֹכִי" כו', וְכֵן לְאַרְבַּע רוּחוֹת וּלְמַעְלָה וּלְמַטָּה. וְכִדְפֵירֵשׁ בַּתִּיקוּנִים (תיקוני זהר תיקון כב [סד, ב]): דְּלֵית אֲתַר דְּלָא מַלֵּיל מִינֵּיהּ עִמְּהוֹן כו'. **and our Rabbis explained** (see *Shemot Rabba* 5:9): "They looked eastward and heard the divine speech emerging, saying: 'I am,'" and so forth. So did they look **toward the four directions, as well as above and below, as is explained in the** *Tikkunei Zohar* (64b), **that there was no place from which He was not speaking to them, and so forth.**

---

15. See Rashi, based on the *Mekhilta*, there.

The divine speech heard at Mount Sinai was not experienced as emanating from a single direction. No matter the direction a person faced, he could hear God's voice originating from that point. It did not come specifically from Mount Sinai, nor from any hidden locus; it issued forth with equal intensity from the four directions, from above and below, from within and from without. It was a direct revelation shattering the boundaries of space, transcending both the normal parameters of human perception and sensation, rendering meaningless even time and space.

The revelation at Mount Sinai was a semblance of the revelation that will transpire in the World to Come, when "your Teacher will no longer be concealed" and the garments of this lower, material world will have become things of the past. It was a revelation essentially undefined by any material form. All physical sensations (e.g., auditory and visual) associated with it were products of man's finite perception of that divine phenomenon. As a result, the divine speech emanated from every direction a person faced and assumed the finite delineations of whatever physical form that person was prepared to receive.

A revelation of this kind, as it occurred at the giving of the Torah and as it will be in the World to Come, is the revelation of God's abode in the lower worlds. When this occurs, God is revealed in the lower worlds, a physical space apprehended by physical senses. Yet since it is the revelation of *Ein Sof*, it simultaneously obliterates these finite sensory and spatial limitations.

וְהַיְינוּ מִפְּנֵי גִּילּוּי רְצוֹנוֹ יִתְבָּרֵךְ בַּעֲשֶׂרֶת הַדִּבְּרוֹת, שֶׁהֵן כְּלָלוּת הַתּוֹרָה, **This was because of the manifestation of God's will within the Ten Commandments, which constitute the totality of the Torah,**

The concept that the Ten Commandments comprise the totality of the Torah appears in particular in the liturgical poems of Rav Se'adya Gaon, where he traces the source of each mitzva in the Torah to the Ten Commandments. Rashi also comments (Ex. 24:12) that "all 613 mitzvot are included within the Ten Commandments."[16]

---

16. See the mystical work *Otzar HaḤayyim* of the Kamarna Rebbe, Rav Yitzḥak

שֶׁהִיא פְּנִימִית רְצוֹנוֹ יִתְבָּרֵךְ וְחָכְמָתוֹ, וְאֵין שָׁם הֶסְתֵּר פָּנִים כְּלָל,	which is God's innermost will and wisdom, and where there is no concealment of countenance whatsoever,

The concealment of God's countenance exists within creation, in the physical world. Yet, within the Torah – God's innermost will – there is no such concealment, as the Torah itself is a *revelation* of the countenance of God; it is the revelation of the innermost divine will. Granted, the Torah as we have it is clothed in comprehensible words and concepts and can be apprehended by finite beings confined to the human body and corporeal world. Nevertheless, this does not constitute a concealment of countenance; it is merely a translation from one language to another. Although we do not detect the inner divine essence within the Torah revealed to us, nevertheless, the Torah neither distorts nor conceals; it functions solely as a direct translation of God's innermost will and wisdom themselves.

כְּמוֹ שֶׁנֶּאֱמַר: "כִּי בְאוֹר פָּנֶיךָ נָתַתָּ לָּנוּ תּוֹרַת חַיִּים".	as it is stated in the *Amida* prayer, "For by the light of Your countenance You gave us a Torah of life."

The Torah was given with the light of God's countenance, that is, in a state of complete revelation, with no concealment or "darkness" of His countenance. It was given in a manner in which one could experience a direct encounter with God, face-to-face, as it were.

וְלָכֵן הָיוּ בְּטֵלִים בִּמְצִיאוּת מַמָּשׁ. כְּמַאֲמַר רַבּוֹתֵינוּ ז"ל (שבת פח, ב), שֶׁעַל כָּל דִּבּוּר פָּרְחָה נִשְׁמָתָן כוּ',	Therefore, they were literally nullified from existence. This accords with our Rabbis' statement (*Shabbat* 88b) that at each and every utterance of the Ten Commandments **their souls flew** out of their bodies, **and so forth,**

At the giving of the Torah, the divine revelation was so complete, permeating all of existence, that no place was concealed from it. It was

---

Yehuda Yeḥiel Safrin, which correlates each of the 613 mitzvot to one of the 613 letters comprising the Ten Commandments.

so intense that the Israelites' souls could no longer be contained within their bodily encasements.

When He about whom the verse states, "Man shall not see Me and live," reveals Himself, it is impossible for a human being to continue living. When the divine existence is manifest, not only does man cease to exist, but existence as a whole is utterly effaced. The removal of the concealments and barriers effectuates the immediate nullification of all existences that endured prior within the shadows of creation, leaving only the divine reality to remain.

אֶלָּא שֶׁהֶחֱזִירָהּ הַקָּדוֹשׁ בָּרוּךְ הוּא לָהֶן בַּטַּל שֶׁעָתִיד לְהַחֲיוֹת בּוֹ אֶת הַמֵּתִים (שבת שם), וְהוּא טַל תּוֹרָה שֶׁנִּקְרָא עוֹז. כְּמַאֲמַר רַבּוֹתֵינוּ ז״ל: כָּל הָעוֹסֵק בַּתּוֹרָה טַל תּוֹרָה מְחַיֵּיהוּ כו'. but the Holy One, blessed be He, restored their souls to them with the dew with which He will ultimately revive the dead (*Shabbat* 88b). This is the dew of the Torah, which is called "might," as our Rabbis said, "Anyone who engages in Torah study, the dew of Torah will revive him," and so forth.

The concept of dew serving as a vivifying agent in the future is based on the verse in Isaiah (26:19), "Your dead will live...for the dew of light is Your dew."[17]

The giving of the Torah at Mount Sinai was like a momentary penetration of the World to Come into this world. A glimmer of the phenomenon that will take place in the end of days – at the time of the resurrection – was felt at the giving of the Torah: the paradoxical nature of an abode for God in the lower worlds. On the one hand, all concealments and darkness were removed, so that God's light alone shone unimpeded throughout all of existence. Yet in order for existence to continue to endure, in order for human beings to maintain their identities to whatever extent possible, there needed to be a perpetuation of existent reality, of a soul within a body, of the Divine within the physical.

At the giving of the Torah, there occurred a process not unlike that which will transpire at the resurrection of the dead, as our Sages

---

17. See *Ketubot* 111b.

expounded the verse describing the Tablets of the Covenant: "Do not read '*ḥarut* (engraved) on the tablets' (Ex. 32:16), but rather *ḥerut* (free), that is, free from the angel of death (*Shemot Rabba* 41:7). This is how it will be at the end of days. It will be a time when "death will be swallowed up forever" (Isa. 25:8).

The giving of the Torah was a divine revelation whereby "at each and every utterance their souls flew [out of their bodies]." Yet at the same time, the Torah fortified existence with the might necessary to perpetually endure this revelation. The Torah we received and which we are engaged in at all times is itself the revelation and has the power to tolerate that revelation. It itself constitutes the substance that makes it possible to perceive God without dying. It imbues the body with a resilience in the face of the divine revelation without disintegrating or being obliterated from existence. ☞

THE VIVIFYING DEW OF TORAH

☞ A commonly asked question with regard to Torah study is, what purpose is there in studying topics we cannot possibly comprehend, such as certain aggadic sections of the Talmud? What is the point of learning about higher worlds and the various kinds of angels, when the fact is that we have no true understanding of these concepts?

The primary answer given, albeit formulated differently by various sages, is that upon studying a particular concept, even if one does not understand it properly, he nevertheless comprehends a basic structure upon which he may later build. There may initially be no discernable difference between a person who studied Torah uncomprehendingly and someone who did not engage in Torah study at all, but it will become quite clear at a time when "your Teacher will no longer be concealed" and "they shall see eye to eye." At that point, the one who did engage in Torah study will say: "Ah, *this* is what I studied then, though I did not understand it!" He will have a foundational starting point, a framework with which to receive and maintain a grip on the great light.

This is comparable to someone who learns a profound teaching for the second time. The first time he was exposed to it he had absolutely no understanding whatsoever; he merely absorbed a jumble of words and amorphous ideas which to him were unintelligible. The second time, however, the words begin to coalesce into a coherent message, and the ideas start to take shape. The initial exposure to the concepts created the vessel, while the second encounter provided the light that fills that vessel. In a similar though far greater vein, engaging in Torah study provides not only the knowledge but also the key framework that allows for an exponentially greater revelation to follow.

11 Adar II
(leap year)

רַק שֶׁאַחַר כָּךְ גָּרַם הַחֵטְא, וְנִתְגַּשְׁמוּ הֵם וְהָעוֹלָם,

Yet subsequently, the sin of the golden calf caused a change in their spiritual state, whereupon they and the world became physical again,

At the giving of the Torah, the entire world was exposed to the divine illumination to the extent that the physical constraints of the world – space, time, and experience – were nullified. All of existence recognized the divine essence face-to-face. But after the sin of the golden calf, when the bedrock of the world, the people of Israel, disintegrated, the world reverted back to its physical state, in the sense that the parameters of the physical world were reinstated, thus impeding and concealing the divine illumination.

עַד עֵת קֵץ הַיָּמִין, שֶׁאָז יִזְדַּכֵּךְ גַּשְׁמִיּוּת הַגּוּף וְהָעוֹלָם וְיוּכְלוּ לְקַבֵּל גִּלּוּי אוֹר ה׳

until the end of days, at which point the physicality of the body and the world will be refined, and they will be able to receive the revelation of God's light,

The vision of the World to Come is not that materiality will be nullified, but rather that it will be purified. Purification of materiality refers to the transformation of the physical into something transparent. At present, the material reality constitutes the most intense opacity in the face of the divine illumination. The vision of the future is not one wherein physical reality is negated but rather where materiality will be converted from a vessel that obstructs to one that enables the transmission of the divine light, and through which the divine essence, as it were, is manifest.

שֶׁיָּאִיר לְיִשְׂרָאֵל עַל יְדֵי הַתּוֹרָה שֶׁנִּקְרֵאת עֹז.

which will shine forth upon the people of Israel by means of the Torah, which is called "might."

The power ("might") of the Torah will imbue the Jewish people with the ability to absorb the divine illumination while concurrently containing it without losing their own existence.

וּמִיִּתְרוֹן הֶאָרָה לְיִשְׂרָאֵל יַגִּיהַּ חֹשֶׁךְ הָאוּמוֹת גַּם כֵּן. כְּדִכְתִיב: "וְהָלְכוּ גוֹיִים לְאוֹרֵךְ" וְגוֹ' (ישעיה ס, ג).

From the overflow of illumination upon the people of Israel by means of the Torah, called "might," the darkness of the gentile nations will be illuminated as well, as it is written, "Nations shall walk by your light and kings by the glow of your shining" (Isa. 60:3),

וּכְתִיב: "בֵּית יַעֲקֹב לְכוּ וְנֵלְכָה בְּאוֹר ה'" (שם ב, ה),

and it is written, "House of Jacob, go and let us walk by the light of the Lord" (Isa. 2:5),

When God's light shines upon the nations of the world, they will say to the people of Israel, "Go and let us walk...." They will tell the Jews, "You walk ahead, and we will follow after you by the light of God."[18]

וּכְתִיב: "וְנִגְלָה כְּבוֹד ה' וְרָאוּ כָל בָּשָׂר יַחְדָּיו" וְגוֹ' (שם מ, ה),

and it is written: "The glory of the Lord will be revealed and all flesh will see together that the mouth of the Lord has spoken" (Isa. 40:5),

"All flesh," that is, even the gentile nations of the world, will see "that the mouth of the Lord has spoken." Hasidism teaches that the nations will perceive the divine speech of the ten utterances God used to create the world. These utterances constitute the divine energies that operate within the world, animating it and maintaining its existence.

וּכְתִיב: "לָבוֹא בְּנִקְרוֹת הַצּוּרִים וּבִסְעִפֵי הַסְּלָעִים מִפְּנֵי פַּחַד ה' וּמֵהֲדַר גְּאוֹנוֹ" וְגוֹ' (שם ב, כא),

and it is written, "To come into the crevices of the rocks and into the cracks of the crags, out of fear of the Lord and the glory of His majesty..." (Isa. 2:21),

This verse refers to the nations, who will be unable to bear the intensity of the divine revelation, and so will need to shield themselves by hiding

---

18. *Likkutei Biurim La Sefer HaTanya.*

in "the crevices of the rocks," in contradistinction to the people of Israel, who are wrapped in the might of the Torah.¹⁹

וּכְמוֹ שֶׁנֶּאֱמַר: "וְהוֹפַע בַּהֲדַר גְּאוֹן עֻזֶּךָ עַל כָּל יוֹשְׁבֵי תֵבֵל אַרְצֶךָ" וְגוֹ'. **and as we say** in the Rosh HaShana liturgy, "Appear, in the splendor of Your great might, before all those who live in this world, Your land," and so forth.

This divine appearance is the ultimate and complete purpose of the existence of the world. Within the intensely dense darkness of this world, alluded to in the verse "Those who dwell in this world, Your land," God's kingship will be revealed "in the splendor of Your great might," referring to Torah, which is called "might." This phenomenon will transpire in a manner such that all will recognize that "the mouth of the Lord has spoken."

This chapter discussed the purpose of the creation of this world, which essentially is to serve as an abode for God in the lower worlds. As was explained, God is equally present in the higher and lower worlds, unfettered by the bonds of time and space. Thus, the implication of "an abode in the lower worlds" is purely vis-à-vis the lower worlds, not God Himself. The concept that this world functions as an abode for God refers to His self-revelation within the lower realms to the extent that they perceive and sense His presence.

Having said that, the lower worlds must retain their state as such, as it is God's desire to dwell specifically within the lower worlds. A person who breaks through and transcends all the earthly barriers fails in his mission to create an earthly abode.

Some suggest that this was the sin of Aaron's sons (see Lev. 10). Some sins are "ugly," while others are "beautiful." The sin of Aaron's sons, of departing and transcending the lower world, is perhaps the most beautiful sin, a "sin" that can be committed only by a saintly individual. Although in certain cultures such transcendence is regarded as the pinnacle of holiness, it is deemed a sin for a Jew. A person who shirks his responsibility and mission in this physical world acts

---

19. Based on a comment of Rabbi Shmuel Gronem Esterman.

contrary to God, since He expressly desires His abode to be in the lower realms.

The status of the lower worlds as an abode for God is not a current reality. It is a challenge we are faced with, a quest we must embark upon. It is incumbent on us to prepare this world for the ultimate purpose of creation, which will transpire in the World to Come. Our work toward this goal began with the giving of the Torah at Mount Sinai, a glimpse of the culmination of existence as an abode for God, and continues through our keeping the Torah and its mitzvot in this world for all generations until the end of time. Through the study of Torah over the course of history and throughout the generations, we create spiritual infrastructures within our souls and the world that function as a sort of code, allowing us to connect with supernal holiness. By means of continual Torah study and wholehearted devotion to the Torah's timeless message, we gradually attain a certain level in which this at times enigmatic code will be decrypted and rendered intelligible. At that time, there will be a sudden revelation of all that was previously hidden. At that point the Torah and its mitzvot will illuminate the entire world, which will join them in extolling God's glory. (This point is a central theme found in a number of stories recounted by Rabbi Naḥman of Breslov. See, for example, "The Tale of the Exchanged Children.")

He who engages in Torah study and fulfilling its mitzvot is in a sense playing an integral role in creating order in this chaotic world. To illustrate this further, let us consider the magnetization of iron (ferromagnetism). Unmagnetized iron contains electrons that spin at random. To magnetize a piece of iron, a magnet is rubbed against it in the same direction. This action causes an alignment of the electrons, thereby generating a magnetic quality in the iron. The idea here is that the iron already contains the potential for becoming a magnet. All that is required is to align and order the disordered electrons. Our world is full of "noises" that drown out all other sounds. Yet when one succeeds in creating order in this world, he transforms that senseless chatter into intelligible words. The world can be either an enigma or comprehensible speech. The Torah is the tool by which we make the continual change in the world from garbled noise to meaningful speech, from the hidden to the revealed, step by step, until the entire world is transformed from darkness into light.

Chapter 37

IN THE PREVIOUS CHAPTER, THE AUTHOR OF THE *TANYA* explained that God created this world because "the Holy One, blessed be He, desired to have an abode in the lower worlds." This purpose has two implications for us. From one perspective, this world is the lowest world, with the greatest amount of concealment of the divine light. From another perspective, this world has the capability of serving as God's "abode in the lower worlds," with the potential for a wondrously complete, unparalleled revelation of the divine essence. As the previous chapter described, this process will not reach its completion until the messianic era and in particular the time of resurrection of the dead. This chapter explains that this process is not beyond us, neither in this period nor at any other time. On the contrary, it is specifically in our world and our time, within the most opaque materiality, in darkness and exile, that we are to engage in attaining this goal, in order to manifest it at every moment and to reveal it at the end of days.

וְהִנֵּה תַּכְלִית הַשְּׁלֵימוּת הַזֶּה שֶׁל יְמוֹת הַמָּשִׁיחַ וּתְחִיַּית הַמֵּתִים, שֶׁהוּא גִּילּוּי אוֹר אֵין סוֹף בָּרוּךְ הוּא בָּעוֹלָם הַזֶּה הַגַּשְׁמִי - תָּלוּי בְּמַעֲשֵׂינוּ וַעֲבוֹדָתֵנוּ

This ultimate perfection of the messianic era and the resurrection of the dead, which is the revelation of the light of *Ein Sof*, blessed be He, in this material world, depends on our actions and service

23 Adar
12 Adar II
(leap year)

The ultimate perfection of the messianic era and the resurrection of the dead, which is the incredible, paradoxical phenomenon of God's dwelling in the lower worlds, of the manifestation of the light of *Ein Sof* in this material world, depends on our deeds and our service.[1]

כָּל זְמַן מֶשֶׁךְ הַגָּלוּת, **throughout the duration of the exile,**

Redemption is not an arbitrary, unilateral or unidirectional act. It is the outgrowth of a process, the accumulation of deeds and groundwork over generations of exile, which generate the possibility of this revelation. As in all fields, there is a correlation between the investment, the quantity and quality of effort and work, and the eventual outcome.

כִּי הַגּוֹרֵם שְׂכַר הַמִּצְוָה הִיא הַמִּצְוָה בְּעַצְמָהּ (אבות פרק ד משנה ב). **for the cause of the reward of a mitzva is the mitzva itself** (*Avot* 4:2).

The reward for performing a mitzva is not something independent that hinges tangentially upon its fulfillment. Rather, the mitzva itself generates the reward.[2]

The concept of reward and punishment is commonly perceived as a carrot-and-stick approach. But the idea presented here is that reward and punishment are the mitzvot and sins themselves. Mitzvot and sins are not callous, indifferent actions that by divine decree result in a distinct reward or punishment. The action itself intrinsically forms the structure that is its reward or punishment. The reward and punishment are part and parcel of the action and should be treated as an extension of the deed itself, not as an external component.

---

1. As to the distinction between the terms "deeds" and "service," see *Iggeret HaKodesh*, epistle 12, beginning with the words "the act of charity." Another possibility is that "actions" refers to the messianic era, while "service" alludes to the period of the resurrection (*Likkutei Levi Yitzḥak He'arot LeSefer HaTanya*, p. 15).

2. The Lubavitcher Rebbe, Rabbi Menaḥem Mendel Schneerson, notes that this is unlike a case where, for example, a landowner compensates a laborer for plowing and sowing his field. Whereas in this instance, the laborer does not actually create the money he receives in payment, a mitzva one fulfills generates its own reward.

כִּי בַּעֲשִׂיָּתָהּ מַמְשִׁיךְ הָאָדָם גִּילּוּי אוֹר אֵין סוֹף בָּרוּךְ הוּא מִלְמַעְלָה לְמַטָּה, לְהִתְלַבֵּשׁ בְּגַשְׁמִיּוּת עוֹלָם הַזֶּה, בְּדָבָר שֶׁהָיָה תְּחִלָּה תַּחַת מֶמְשֶׁלֶת קְלִיפַּת נוֹגַהּ וּמְקַבֵּל חִיּוּתָהּ מִמֶּנָּה.

That is **because when a person performs** a mitzva in this world, **he draws down the revelation of the light of** *Ein Sof*, **blessed be He, from above to below, so that it becomes enclothed in the materiality of this world,** namely, **in an object that was initially under the dominion of** *kelippat noga*, **from which** the object **had received its life force.**

The essence of each mitzva, particularly those that are action related, is that we take an object from its place in the realm of *kelippat noga*, the realm ranging from neutrality to consummate evil, and bind it to the realm of holiness. By performing a mitzva with such an object, it attains a holy rank, character, and trajectory.

שֶׁהֵם כָּל דְּבָרִים הַטְּהוֹרִים וּמוּתָּרִים שֶׁנַּעֲשֵׂית בָּהֶם הַמִּצְוָה מַעֲשִׂיִּית,

These refer to **all the pure and permissible objects with which the act of the mitzva is performed,**

These items mentioned above – under the dominion of *kelippat noga*, and used in fulfillment of mitzvot – possess no intrinsic holiness, yet at the same time they are not held captive and trapped within the *kelippa*. As a result, they have the capacity to become receptacles for holiness when used in the performance of an action-related mitzva.

כְּגוֹן: קְלַף הַתְּפִילִּין, וּמְזוּזָה, וְסֵפֶר תּוֹרָה. וּכְמַאֲמַר רַבּוֹתֵינוּ ז"ל: לֹא הוּכְשַׁר לִמְלֶאכֶת שָׁמַיִם אֶלָּא טְהוֹרִים וּמוּתָּרִים בְּפִיךָ (שבת קח, א),

such as the parchment used **for** *tefillin*, **a** *mezuza*, **and a Torah scroll, as our Rabbis state, "The only** objects **fit for the service of Heaven are those which are pure and permissible for consumption"** (see *Shabbat* 108a),

It is prohibited to use a horse's hide or pigskin in the manufacture of a Torah scroll.[3] In order to utilize an object in the service of Heaven, that is, for a spiritual matter, and elevate it to the realm of holiness, it must be associated with that which is regarded as permissible and not with something forbidden. The item must be included in the realm of *kelippat noga* and not the domain of the impure *kelippot* (see chap. 8 above). The Hebrew word for "forbidden" is *assur*, which literally means "fettered," while the Hebrew for "permissible" is *mutar*, meaning "unfettered." Something forbidden is "bound" or "fettered" to the *kelippot*, from which they have no possibility of being released and elevated to holiness. But that which is fundamentally permissible, such as the hide of a kosher animal, is associated with *kelippat noga* and as such retains the possibility of being unbound and released from the clutches of *kelippa*. Even though the hide is not intrinsically holy, it has the potential to become so.

וְכֵן אֶתְרוֹג שֶׁאֵינוֹ עָרְלָה **as well as an *etrog* that is not** prohibited on account of its being ***orla*,**

One may fulfill the mitzva of taking the four species on Sukkot using an *etrog* (citron), provided that it is not an *etrog* that is *orla* (fruit growing on a tree during the first three years after it has been planted, which is forbidden to consume). If it were in fact *orla*, the mitzva may not be performed with it, since it is associated with the impure *kelippot*.

הַגָּהָה: (שֶׁהָעָרְלָה הִיא מִשָּׁלֹשׁ קְלִיפּוֹת הַטְּמֵאוֹת לְגַמְרֵי, שֶׁאֵין לָהֶם עֲלִיָּה לְעוֹלָם, כְּמוֹ שֶׁכָּתוּב בְּעֵץ חַיִּים, וְכֵן כָּל מִצְוָה הַבָּאָה בַּעֲבֵירָה חַס וְשָׁלוֹם).

Gloss: For *orla* is of the three utterly impure *kelippot* that can never ascend to the realm of holiness, as is written in *Etz Ḥayyim*. The same goes for any other **mitzva performed through** commission of **a transgression, Heaven forbid.**

---

3. This, and the examples to follow, symbolize respectively three fundamental elements comprising material existence: parchment symbolizes animal life, an *etrog* signifies plant life, and coins represent inanimate objects (*Likkutei Levi Yitzḥak He'arot LeSefer HaTanya*, p. 15).

Halakha dictates that it is prohibited for one to derive any benefit from *orla* fruits, with no possibility of their ever being rendered permissible for consumption.[4] It is explained in *Etz Ḥayyim*[5] that *orla* produce, for example, is included among the three completely impure *kelippot*, the implication being that it can never be released from their clutches.

The author of the *Tanya* adds that the inability of prohibited items to be released and elevated to the realm of holiness applies to any mitzva, not exclusively *orla*, performed through commission of a sin; the resultant mitzva is immaterial.

וּמָעוֹת הַצְּדָקָה שֶׁאֵינָן גֶּזֶל, וְכַיּוֹצֵא בָּהֶם. **or monies** distributed **as charity that were not** obtained through **theft, and** other **similar items.** — 13 Adar II (leap year)

Just as in the case of food, there is also kosher money and non-kosher money. Regarding kosher money, that is, money acquired honestly, though not yet holy, one is nevertheless permitted to derive benefit from it, and so it may be used in the performance of mitzvot. By contrast, it is absolutely forbidden for one to derive benefit from stolen money. Thus, it cannot be used to perform a mitzva and cannot be elevated to the realm of holiness.

In this sense, when the *halakha* rules something to be forbidden or permissible, it is in fact determining that item's essential character. *Halakha* assesses whether it can be rectified and elevated to a state of sanctity. This is not a legal determination, where the court decides whether someone has committed a particular act or not, or whether one is guilty or not. It is not a moral determination founded on an external construct of presumptions. Rather, it is an evaluation of an

---

4. Rabbi Shmuel Gronem Esterman refers the reader to chap. 7 of *Likkutei Amarim*, which states that even prohibited ("fettered") objects can be elevated to holiness. He explains that this poses no contradiction to what is stated here, since they can be elevated only by means of a powerful act of repentance (see chap. 7).
5. *Sha'ar Kelippat Noga* (*Sha'ar* 49), chap. 6. See *Pardes Rimmonim*, end of *sha'ar* 24, which states that the three years of *orla* parallel the three impure *kelippot*. See *Likkutei Torah*, Lev. 29a, s.v. "*vekhi tavo'u el ha'aretz.*" See also *HaMa'amarim Melukat*, vol. 3, p. 135.

entity's intrinsic nature, the final determination of whether or not it can ascend to the realm of holiness.

וְעַכְשָׁיו שֶׁמְּקַיֵּים בָּהֶם מִצְוֹת ה' וּרְצוֹנוֹ, הֲרֵי הַחַיּוּת שֶׁבָּהֶם עוֹלָה וּמִתְבַּטֵּל וְנִכְלָל בְּאוֹר אֵין סוֹף בָּרוּךְ הוּא, שֶׁהוּא רְצוֹנוֹ יִתְבָּרֵךְ הַמְלוּבָּשׁ בָּהֶם,

Now that one fulfills through them God's mitzva and will, the life force within them ascends and is nullified to and absorbed within the light of *Ein Sof*, blessed be He, which is God's will that is clothed in them, i.e., the mitzvot,

When performing a mitzva using an object that is included in the realm of *kelippat noga*, (i.e., an object deemed permissible [*mutar*]), one thereby releases the animating life force – the hidden holiness – within that object from the domain of *kelippa*, and elevates it to its root. Upon its reunion with its source, it becomes absorbed in the quintessence of holiness: the light of the blessed *Ein Sof*.

Note the linguistic nuance employed here. The author of the *Tanya* writes that the *life force* within such objects ascends to its source. He does not, however, say that the object *itself* is elevated and is transformed into holiness. The physical money given as charity undergoes no change to become a holy item. What *does* undergo a transformation is the life force that inheres within the money, the "energy of holiness" that accumulates within it. Through this act of charity, the energy and life force contained within the money is now released and elevated to the realm of holiness.

An *etrog* that we hold as part of the mitzva of taking the four species on Sukkot is an *etrog* like any other. It remains chemically and botanically unchanged after the mitzva is performed. But the life force within it becomes connected with and nullified to holiness, to the divine will that it generated, and which is now clothed within it.

מֵאַחַר שֶׁאֵין שָׁם בְּחִינַת הֶסְתֵּר פָּנִים כְּלָל לְהַסְתִּיר אוֹרוֹ יִתְבָּרֵךְ.

since in them there is no element of concealed countenance whatsoever to hide God's light.

There is no concealment of countenance in the divine will clothed in the mitzvot, since the latter constitute God's very will in this physical realm as it is on high. Although a person is incapable of grasping and relating to the essence and innermost depths of the divine will within the physical world, he is nevertheless able to relate to the mitzva, which is the expression of the divine will within his reality, as is explained elsewhere. This manifestation of divine will, although encased in entirely physical objects and processes, is neither distorted nor concealed. ☞ ☞

THE ACT OF A MITZVA

☞ The author of the *Tanya* often addresses the following question: What is the particular significance of the act of a mitzva? Why is the deep, spiritual bond with God forged by the soul incapable of attaining the supreme level of connection created by the physical act of a mitzva? The author explains that in an emotional or intellectual relationship, even between two people, there inevitably exists a gap resulting from a disparity in understanding and experiences between the two parties. This gap is far greater and more intense with regard to man's relationship with God. In any place, time, or situation in which a true connection cannot be formed, there exist only superficial experiences and illusions of a relationship. By contrast, with respect to a connection founded upon fulfilling another's will, there exist no mediums or intermediaries that interpose between the potentially incomprehensible will and the physical act of fulfilling it. When a person needs only to carry out another's will, but has no need to fully comprehend it, a true and tangible connection is formed.

Consider, for example, a scenario where someone throws a stick to his dog, and shouts, "Catch!" The intellectual gap between the owner and his dog remains unchanged, but there is one point at which they experience complete congruity. The moment the dog catches the stick, he fulfills his master's will. Were the dog to begin meditating, in efforts to connect with his owner's will, it is doubtful whether the dog would succeed. Yet the instant the dog hears "catch!" and he does so, in that moment there is total unity among the one possessing the will, the will itself, and the one fulfilling that will, between the commander, the command, and the commanded.

Some suggest that the word "mitzva" (commandment) is related to the word *tzavta*, meaning "together" (see, for example, *Likkutei Torah*, Lev. 45c). The idea here is that the only way to bridge two otherwise infinitely divergent and uncommunicative poles is through a mitzva. The fact that a commandment is, at its essence, beyond our comprehension is the very thing that allows for the creation of a true bond with God when the mitzva is performed.

INTENT WHEN PERFORMING A MITZVA

☞ It is important to clarify that these ideas are not meant to negate the relevance of intent when performing a mitzva. It is not as though one's focus on the act of the mitzva is rendered meaningless or somehow ruins its performance. In fact,

וְכֵן כֹּחַ נֶפֶשׁ הַחִיּוּנִית הַבַּהֲמִית שֶׁבְּאֶבְרֵי גּוּף הָאָדָם הַמְקַיֵּים הַמִּצְוָה, הוּא מִתְלַבֵּשׁ גַּם כֵּן בַּעֲשִׂיָּה זוֹ וְעוֹלָה מֵהַקְּלִיפָּה וְנִכְלָל בִּקְדוּשַׁת הַמִּצְוָה, שֶׁהִיא רְצוֹנוֹ יִתְבָּרֵךְ, וּבָטֵל בְּאוֹר אֵין סוֹף בָּרוּךְ הוּא.

Likewise, **the energy of the vital-animal soul within the bodily limbs of the person fulfilling the mitzva is also enclothed within this act** of the mitzva. **It then ascends from the *kelippa* and becomes absorbed in the holiness of the mitzva, which is God's will, and is nullified within the light of *Ein Sof*, blessed be He.**

There are two elements in every act of a mitzva: the object with which the mitzva is performed, and the person performing the mitzva. There are even some mitzvot in which one plays both roles (see below). It was mentioned above that a physical object deriving from *kelippat noga* used in the performance of a mitzva (*tefillin*, *etrog*, etc.) is bound thereby to supreme holiness – the light of *Ein Sof*. Here the author of the *Tanya* adds that the body and vital soul of a Jew, both deriving from *kelippat noga* (see chap. 2), are connected to and absorbed within the light of *Ein Sof*.

When a person performs a mitzva, his body, which executes the physical action of the mitzva, as well as the energy of his vital soul, which animates his body to execute this action, are bound to and clothed within that very action, which itself is the manifestation of God's will. At that moment, when the action of the mitzva is being performed, both the body and the vital soul transcend the *kelippa*, becoming deeply ensconced within the divine will, with the very source of divine light, to which they become utterly nullified.

---

the fundamental intention to fulfill God's will through the performance of a mitzva is crucial to its execution (see *Berakhot* 13a: "mitzvot require intention"). Moreover, every inner intention, whether or not based on the secrets of Torah (such as the meditative intentions of the Arizal), has a deeply powerful impact on the mitzva. Even if strictly speaking one's intention is not required in the performance of the mitzvah, should one choose to incorporate an inner meaning into the mitzva he performs, he effects an immeasurably qualitative difference in its execution. This topic will be treated at length in the chapter to follow.

וְגַם בְּמִצְוֹת תַּלְמוּד תּוֹרָה וּקְרִיאַת שְׁמַע וּתְפִלָּה וְכַיּוֹצֵא בָּהֶן, אַף שֶׁאֵינָן בַּעֲשִׂיָּה גַשְׁמִית מַמָּשׁ שֶׁתַּחַת מֶמְשֶׁלֶת קְלִיפַּת נוֹגַהּ,

The same applies with regard to the mitzvot of Torah study, the recitation of *Shema*, prayer, and the like. Although they are not literally performed with a physical action which is under the dominion of *kelippat noga*,

Torah study, the recitation of *Shema*, and prayer are mitzvot in thought and speech alone. The words of Torah that one speaks and studies are not "objects" of the mitzva that derive from the world of action, under the governance of *kelippat noga*. Rather, they possess an intrinsic holiness. ☞

מִכָּל מָקוֹם, הָא קַיְימָא לָן דְּהִרְהוּר לָאו כְּדִבּוּר דָּמֵי וְאֵינוֹ יוֹצֵא יְדֵי חוֹבָתוֹ עַד שֶׁיּוֹצִיא בִּשְׂפָתָיו, וְקַיְימָא לָן דַּעֲקִימַת שְׂפָתָיו הָוֵי מַעֲשֶׂה.

nevertheless, we maintain in *halakha* that contemplation is not tantamount to actual speech, and one does not fulfill his duty with regard to these mitzvot until he utters the words with his lips. We also maintain that moving one's lips while speaking is considered an action,

---

TORAH STUDY ON OUR LEVEL

☞ God does not expect us to comprehend and grasp the Torah we study on its supremely sublime level, to apprehend its wisdom as it is manifest in the world of Atzilut. Rather, God expects us to understand the Torah we study according to our limited capabilities. This expectation parallels the act of a mitzva. Just as God requires us to perform a mitzva only according to *our* abilities (meaning, an action we can physically perform), so it is with regard to Torah study. We are not expected to fully plumb the depths of the divine meaning and intent contained in the subject matter. We are required to understand the Torah only to the extent that our finite capacities allow. Yet we must not allow ourselves to be lulled into a state of laxity in our attempts to comprehend God's Torah. Instead, we must strive diligently to understand what is within our reach as precisely and perfectly as possible. On this level of understanding we are able to form a complete, direct connection with God's wisdom, and with God Himself.

In this sense, there is unique significance to the study of the revealed portion of Torah, particularly the seemingly mundane topics, regarding which it may be expected of us to attain a true, concrete understanding. This is in contrast to the more abstract, spiritual subjects, which cannot be tangibly grasped, and thus are liable to lead us to untrue connections with God, illusions, false experiences, and self-deception.

The two primary modes of fulfilling the mitzvot of Torah study and prayer are speech and thought. The *halakha* states that mere thought is not tantamount to speech, such that if, for example, one is capable of speaking words of Torah yet merely thinks of them in his mind, he has not fulfilled the mitzva of Torah study.[6] *Halakha* also maintains that even the movement of one's lips is regarded as an action. Thus, even these thought-and speech-related mitzvot require a physical action – either being actually uttered, or at the very least, mouthed. ☞

It is thus clear that a person cannot fulfill a mitzva, even one which does not entail a concrete action –such as Torah study or prayer –

HOW TO PRAY

☞ According to *halakha*, one does not fulfill his obligation to recite the *Shema* or the *Amida* should he neglect to verbally express the words he is reading. However, if he does articulate the words of the *Shema* or the *Amida* but has no idea as to their meaning, he can nevertheless fulfill the mitzva – at times in what is even considered a high level of performance of the mitzva.

The required intent in prayer is not what many believe it to be, that a person must understand its grammar and syntactic constructs, or be able to provide some clever explanation of the language used in the prayer. In fact, this is not the case, as evidenced by the following anecdote. There was once a simple Jew who was praying on Rosh HaShana from the prayer book. At some point, he began screaming on the top of his lungs a rather complex Hebrew expression of praise of God from the hymn entitled "God Is the King." The surprised congregants asked him: "Do you know the meaning of the words you were shouting?" He responded: "Of course I know! The words mean 'Master of the world, give me a good livelihood!'" This simple Jew succeeded in penetrating the essence of prayer. A prayer accompanied by that kind of intent is certainly more meaningful than that of a person who, while praying, considers how the name of the author appears in the hymn, when he lived, or if the hymn is composed in a single or double acrostic. Granted, knowing the meaning of the words in a prayer is important, but that knowledge is meaningful provided that it engenders a loving and awe-inspired connection with the Divine. Yet should this knowledge not cause a connection with God, it is completely unrelated to the prayer and serves only as a distraction.

Unlike prayer, the question of whether a person fulfills the mitzva of Torah study even if he does not understand what he is saying is more complex. Similar to the recitation of *Shema* and the *Amida*, Torah study also has a component of "you shall inculcate them in your children, and you shall *speak of them*" (Deut. 6:7), describing the mitzva as orally expressing words of

---

6. See *Berakhot* 20b; *Shulḥan Arukh, Oraḥ Ḥayyim* 62; *Hilkhot Talmud Torah* of the author of the *Tanya*, 2:12.

without some degree of bodily movement. The author of the *Tanya* explains why this is so:

כִּי אִי אֶפְשָׁר לַנֶּפֶשׁ הָאֱלוֹקִית לְבַטֵּא בִּשְׂפָתַיִם וּפֶה וְלָשׁוֹן וְשִׁנַּיִם הַגַּשְׁמִיִּים כִּי אִם עַל יְדֵי נֶפֶשׁ הַחִיּוּנִית הַבַּהֲמִית הַמְלוּבֶּשֶׁת בְּאֵבְרֵי הַגּוּף מַמָּשׁ.

because it is impossible for the divine soul to express itself with the physical lips, mouth, tongue, and teeth except by means of the vital-animal soul that is literally enclothed in the limbs of the body.

As was stated previously, the divine soul bears no direct relationship with the physical body. They are connected only through the medium of the vital soul that is clothed in the body's physical limbs (and organs). Consequently, the divine soul itself cannot directly study Torah or pray, just as it is unable to directly fulfill action-related mitzvot, without the cooperation of the vital soul.

וְכָל מַה שֶּׁמְּדַבֵּר בְּכֹחַ גָּדוֹל יוֹתֵר, הוּא מַכְנִיס וּמַלְבִּישׁ יוֹתֵר כֹּחוֹת מִנֶּפֶשׁ הַחִיּוּנִית בְּדִיבּוּרִים אֵלּוּ.

The more force one puts into his speech, the more energy from the vital soul is introduced and enclothed within those words.

The clearer and more forceful one makes one's words of Torah or prayer, the more he invests in efforts to do so, the more of his vital energy – spiritual and physical – is enclothed within that mitzva.

וְזֶה שֶׁאָמַר הַכָּתוּב: "כָּל עַצְמוֹתַי תֹּאמַרְנָה" וְגוֹ' (תהלים לה, י).

This is the meaning of the verse "All my bones shall declare: Lord, who is like You?" (Ps. 35:10).

---

holiness. This mode of Torah study is typically employed when studying the written Torah. By contrast, when studying the oral Torah, there exists an additional element, namely, the knowledge of Torah, the understanding and resultant intellectual connection with God's wisdom. Thus, one fulfills the mitzva of studying the oral Torah specifically by understanding it. In the event that he does not comprehend the subject matter, even if it is being verbally expressed, it is not regarded as Torah study whatsoever (see *Likkutei Torah*, Lev. 5a).

This verse speaks of one utilizing his entire being, the totality of his body and soul's energy, in this declaration of God's praise.

וְזֶה שֶׁאָמְרוּ רַבּוֹתֵינוּ ז"ל: אִם עֲרוּכָה בְּכָל רְמַ"ח אֵיבָרִים - מִשְׁתַּמֶּרֶת, וְאִם לָאו - אֵינָהּ מִשְׁתַּמֶּרֶת (עירובין נד, א).

This is related to **what our Rabbis stated** regarding the verse "Ordered in every sense, and protected" (II Sam. 23:5): "If the Torah **is ordered in all** your **248 limbs, it will be secure** in your memory; **and if not, it will not be secure.**"

The author of the *Tanya* cites this passage (*Eruvin* 54a)[7] in support of the theme he is developing. Within every person there exist body and soul energies. The more encompassing and profound one's connection to the holy words he utters, by exerting both types of energies, the more these words become a part of him, seared forever in his memory and secure within him. This teaching, stated specifically in the context of Torah study, is also pertinent to a bond one develops with any holy matter, be it Torah, prayer, or otherwise. ☞

The author of the *Tanya* addresses what it is about studying Torah specifically using one's corporeal body that renders it the sole factor in one's eternal retention of those subjects studied. What is the paramount

---

EXERTING BODY AND SOUL IN THE SERVICE OF PRAYER

☞ This idea of body and soul exertion is mentioned elsewhere (see chaps. 30, 42) with regard to the service of prayer. Those contexts speak of one's obligation to pray "with exertion of the soul and exertion of the flesh," meaning that one must galvanize both his body and soul in intense concentration while praying.

Physical exertion is not necessarily expressed through physical movement. It is told that the prayers of the Rebbe of Ruzhin were not particularly lengthy, and that there was no noticeable change in his demeanor while praying. Yet upon concluding his prayers, he would need to change all his clothes, as they had become soaked in sweat. The onlooker observed no extra effort or unusual movements on the part of the Rebbe of Ruzhin as he prayed. Despite this, it was clear that his body expended tremendous energy. It is quite possible that specifically the externally undetectable "movement" is far more difficult and grueling than any external action.

---

7. The Lubavitcher Rebbe, Rabbi Menaḥem Mendel Schneerson, refers the reader to the author of the *Tanya's Hilkhot Talmud Torah* 4:9.

significance of the Torah's being ordered in his 248 limbs, of one using his lips in its study, that secures it in his memory? The author of the *Tanya* proceeds to explain:

כִּי הַשִּׁכְחָה הִיא מִקְּלִיפַּת הַגּוּף וְנֶפֶשׁ הַחִיּוּנִית הַבַּהֲמִית, שֶׁהֵן מִקְּלִיפַּת נוֹגַהּ, הַנִּכְלֶלֶת לִפְעָמִים בִּקְדוּשָׁה. וְהַיְנוּ כְּשֶׁמֵּתִישׁ כֹּחָן וּמַכְנִיס כָּל כֹּחָן בִּקְדוּשַׁת הַתּוֹרָה אוֹ הַתְּפִלָּה.

This is **because forgetfulness derives from the *kelippa* of the body and the vital-animal soul, which stem from *kelippat noga*, which is sometimes absorbed within holiness.** This occurs **when one weakens their power and directs all their energy into the holiness of Torah or prayer.**

The divine soul itself is not subject to forgetfulness. It is inextricably linked to the Torah in a very real and deeply powerful bond, and so it cannot forget. The ability to forget something is a flaw that is rooted in materiality and *kelippa*. When a person is attached to his materiality and the *kelippa* elements within him while studying a particular subject, it is possible that the material aspect will pay no heed to what he is studying, in which case he is liable to forget. But when a person directs the energy of his animal soul into the letters of Torah and prayer, he thereby repairs and nullifies the *kelippa* of the animal soul, automatically resulting in his ability to retain those words in his memory.[8] ☞

FORGETTING THE TORAH

☞ The fact that a person forgets the Torah he studied indicates that he possesses a flaw that he must fix (see *Menaḥot* 99b on the verse "Only beware, and protect yourself greatly lest you forget... [Deut. 4:9]. See also Mishna *Avot* [3:8]). Forgetfulness can be compared to an unintentional sin, the latter indicating a flaw within the person's soul. This is implied by the *halakha* stating that even one who committed an unintentional sin is required to bring a sin offering, whereas one who sinned out of coercion is not required to do so. Whether a person forgets that today is the Sabbath or cannot recall something he studied in a talmudic tractate, the underlying issue is the same; it is a clear indication of a faulty and imperfect relationship with the subject – the Sabbath or the talmudic tractate.

Therefore, in a case where someone is the embodiment of holiness, the Torah he studies will not be forgotten. A similar concept is found in the Talmud (*Berakhot*

---

8. A person's entire soul ascends to the realm of holiness when he devotes all his energy to Torah study. A natural consequence of this devotion is his ability

In the section that follows, the author of the *Tanya* will describe how an action-related mitzva not only impacts the physical object used in the performance of that mitzva as well as the person performing it, but its positive reverberations are felt throughout all of existence.

32b). The passage there states that the early generations of pious men would wait one hour before praying, pray one hour, then wait one hour again. Given that they prayed three times a day, this meant they spent a total of nine hours daily in prayer, leaving little time to review their studies. The Talmud asks: "Since they would spend nine hours per day engaged either in prayer or the requisite waiting periods before and after prayer, how is their Torah preserved?" The Talmud answers: "Because they were pious, their Torah was preserved." It is possible for a person to forget the Torah he studied only because those studies are impeded by the physical body and animal soul. That which fails to penetrate these barriers will remain outside and is doomed to sooner or later become forgotten and lost.

The story is told of a hasidic Rebbe who was discussing a section of the *Tosafot* (a talmudic commentary) with one of his erudite hasidim, debating whether *Tosafot* had stated a particular point or not. The learned hasid said: "I studied this only a few days ago, so I am confident that I am correct." The Rebbe replied: "I have not seen this topic in fifteen years, yet I am certain I am correct." After investigating the issue, it turned out that the Rebbe was in fact correct. The surprised and disheartened hasid asked his master how he was able to recall the passage correctly. The Rebbe answered: "Do you remember your wedding?" "Certainly!" replied the hasid. The Rebbe continued, "Do you remember who escorted you down the aisle, who stood to your right, and what the bride wore?" "Of course!" said the hasid. The Rebbe then said, "For me, each time I study Torah, it is a wedding!"

One's ability to remember the Torah he studies reflects the degree of esteem in which he holds it, how deeply the subject matter penetrates his being, and how much it suffuses his 248 limbs. A famous rabbi, renowned for his great genius and recollective ability, was once asked how it was that he never forgot anything he studied. He replied: "How is it that people never forget that food must be inserted into one's mouth?"

We do not forget something upon which our lives depend. The degree to which a person is involved in his studies, how intense and encompassing they are, determines how deeply they are instilled and preserved within him. Therefore, when a person studies Torah in a manner that it is "ordered" within all of his 248 limbs, that Torah will never be forgotten.

---

to remember those studies with no concern of their ever being forgotten (Rabbi Shmuel Gronem Esterman).

24 Adar
14 Adar II (leap year)

In addition to **this, there is yet another** ramification of performing a mitzva: **The energy of the vital soul, enclothed within the letters of speech** spoken in Torah study or prayer, **and the like, or** while performing **action-related mitzvot, grows and derives its life force from the blood** in one's body, **which literally stems from** *kelippat noga* **itself, that is, all the food one consumed and the drinks one drank that have become blood,**

זֹאת וְעוֹד אַחֶרֶת, שֶׁכֹּחַ נֶפֶשׁ הַחִיּוּנִית הַמִּתְלַבֶּשֶׁת בְּאוֹתִיּוֹת הַדִּבּוּר בְּתַלְמוּד תּוֹרָה אוֹ תְּפִלָּה וְכַיּוֹצֵא בָּהֶן אוֹ מִצְוֹת מַעֲשִׂיּוֹת, הֲרֵי כָּל גִּידוּלוֹ וְחִיּוּתוֹ מֵהַדָּם, שֶׁהוּא מִקְּלִיפַּת נוֹגַהּ מַמָּשׁ, שֶׁהֵן כָּל אוֹכָלִין וּמַשְׁקִין שֶׁאָכַל וְשָׁתָה וְנַעֲשׂוּ דָם,

The blood coursing through our veins, vitalizing and animating our bodies, is a product of *kelippat noga* – the latter comprised of the permissible foodstuffs and beverages belonging to the inanimate, plant, and animal worlds – that one ingests.

that were previously **under its,** that is, the *kelippat noga*'s, **dominion and drew their life force from it.** *Kelippat noga* **is now transformed from evil to good and is absorbed within holiness.** This is achieved **by means of the energy of the vital soul that grows from it,**

שֶׁהָיוּ תַּחַת מֶמְשַׁלְתָּהּ וְיָנְקוּ חִיּוּתָם מִמֶּנָּה, וְעַתָּה הִיא מִתְהַפֶּכֶת מֵרַע לְטוֹב וְנִכְלֶלֶת בִּקְדֻשָּׁה, עַל יְדֵי כֹּחַ נֶפֶשׁ הַחִיּוּנִית הַגָּדֵל מִמֶּנָּה,

The permissible food and drink that one ingests were initially under the "dominion of *kelippat noga*" (another way of expressing that which is *kelippat noga* itself). The energy derived from this food invigorates and strengthens the person's body (itself *kelippat noga*). When this person utilizes the raw energy to perform a mitzva, study Torah, or pray, he transforms it into something holy. As such, it is no longer under the dominion of *kelippat noga*.

שֶׁנִּתְלַבֵּשׁ בְּאוֹתִיּוֹת אֵלּוּ אוֹ בַּעֲשִׂיָּה זוֹ, אֲשֶׁר הֵן הֵן פְּנִימִיּוּת רְצוֹנוֹ יִתְבָּרֵךְ, בְּלִי שׁוּם הֶסְתֵּר פָּנִים, וְחַיּוּתָן נִכְלָל גַּם כֵּן בְּאוֹר אֵין סוֹף בָּרוּךְ הוּא שֶׁהוּא רְצוֹנוֹ יִתְבָּרֵךְ,

and which is now **enclothed in these letters** of Torah or prayer, **or in this action** used for a mitzva, **which constitute the very innermost aspect of God's will, without any concealed countenance. Their life force is also absorbed within the light of** *Ein Sof*, **blessed be He, which is God's will,**

One's vital soul, the source of his physical energy, derives its strength from *kelippat noga* (that is, the permissible food one eats), which becomes one's blood circulating throughout his body. When a person uses his physical energy to study Torah, pray, or perform mitzvot, his energy becomes garbed in these words or mitzvot. Thus, even the food and drink that a person consumed and that fuel his physical energy become absorbed within the light of *Ein Sof* as well.

As was mentioned above, unlike the veiled manifestation of the Divine in this world (referred to here as the "concealment of [God's] countenance"), the Torah, by contrast, constitutes the pristine, unfiltered expression of Godliness. Granted, the divine will at its core is vastly distant from the physical mitzva. Yet it must be emphasized that although this distance is a constriction, God's will is in no way distorted or veiled. The Torah as we have it does not reveal the totality of the divine wisdom and will, but that which *is* revealed is indeed God's very will, exactly so, without any concealment of countenance.

וּבְחַיּוּתָן נִכְלָל וְעוֹלֶה גַּם כֵּן כֹּחַ נֶפֶשׁ הַחִיּוּנִית.

and with their life force, the energy of the vital soul is also absorbed and ascends into the light of *Ein Sof*.

The author of the *Tanya* clarifies the second of the twofold benefit of the physical performance of a mitzva. That is, in addition to the elevation of the physical object used to perform the mitzva, even the person himself – his body and vital soul – is elevated and absorbed into the light of *Ein Sof*.

Moreover, when a person performs a mitzva, he thereby elevates the essential nature of each physical element and act – such as his eating, drinking, and other mundane activities – utilized in the execution of this mitzva. Take, for example, the act of giving some coins to charity.

The effects of this seemingly simple action are far-reaching and powerful. Through this act, the giver effectuates not merely an elevation of the divine life force contained both within those coins and that particular act of giving. But also elevated is the *aggregate* life force of all people and objects involved in the process leading to these particular coins being given as charity.

וְעַל יְדֵי זֶה תַּעֲלֶה גַּם כֵּן כְּלָלוּת קְלִיפַּת נוֹגַהּ, שֶׁהִיא כְּלָלוּת הַחַיּוּת שֶׁל עוֹלָם הַזֶּה הַגַּשְׁמִי וְהַחוּמְרִי. As a result, the totality of *kelippat noga*, which constitutes the totality of the life force of this physical and material world, will ascend as well.

A person's single, limited action effects only a minor change in the whole of reality. On his own, he is incapable of transforming every *etrog* in the world into one with which a mitzva is performed, nor does he have the ability to convert every strip of hide in existence into a parchment on which a Torah scroll is written. But the truth is that there is no need for him to do so. Everything in the world is interconnected, every element drawing others along with it. The ripple effects of each isolated action in this world are felt far beyond its epicenter, and so when a person alters even one particular detail in the world, he thereby affects everything of a similar nature. The totality of existence is elevated along with its particularity. Thus, by elevating the energy of his personal vital soul, being a veritable part of *kelippat noga* in its overarching totality, a person elevates the entirety of *kelippat noga* along with the reality of this physical, material world. ☞

ELEVATING THE ENTIRE WORLD

☞ As will be explained, the purpose of physically performing mitzvot is to ultimately elevate the entire world, to utterly redefine our previously limited understanding of existence in its totality. The point the author of the *Tanya* stresses here is that a mitzva alters not only the physical object with which it is performed but also every element (tangible or not) involved in the process allowing for its performance. Every element of existence without which the mitzva could not have been performed is elevated along with it. Thus, by means of the vastly complex inner workings of existence, and the supreme interconnectedness of elements involved in our every action in this world, which we are often unaware of, with each mitzva we perform there arises to holiness the broadest swath of the world's reality.

15 Adar II (leap year) כַּאֲשֶׁר כָּל הַנְּשָׁמָה וְנֶפֶשׁ הָאֱלֹקִית שֶׁבְּכָל יִשְׂרָאֵל, הַמִּתְחַלֶּקֶת בִּפְרָטוּת לְשִׁשִּׁים רִבּוֹא,

This will occur **when the composite** *neshama* **and divine soul within the Jewish people, which is divided into 600,000 particular** souls,

At the root of all the Jewish people's souls, there is a level at which they are all in fact a single, unified soul, known as *kenesset Yisrael*, the congregation of Israel. This comprehensive soul, incorporating all the souls of the Jewish people, is divided into 600,000 individual souls. Although the census of Jews throughout history often yielded more than 600,000, this number is the root and foundational number comprising the Jewish people, defining and characterizing them. Any number less than this no longer constitutes the Jewish nation.

תְּקַיֵּים כָּל נֶפֶשׁ פְּרָטִית כָּל תרי"ג מִצְוֹת הַתּוֹרָה, שס"ה לֹא תַעֲשֶׂה, לְהַפְרִיד שס"ה גִּידִים שֶׁל דַּם נֶפֶשׁ הַחִיּוּנִית שֶׁבַּגּוּף, שֶׁלֹּא יִינְקוּ וִיקַבְּלוּ חַיּוּת בַּעֲבֵירָה זוֹ מֵאַחַת מִשָּׁלֹשׁ קְלִיפּוֹת הַטְּמֵאוֹת לְגַמְרֵי,

will fulfill, each particular soul, all of the 613 mitzvot of the Torah, namely, **the 365 prohibitions,** which serve **to separate** and thereby obstruct **the 365 sinews of the blood of the vital soul that are in the body, so that they not obtain sustenance and receive** their **life force, by means of a transgression, from one of the three utterly impure** *kelippot*,

Applying the same logic, the converse is also true. When Adam sinned with the tree of knowledge, although he was an individual person and his sin was ostensibly his own personal affair, his singular act led all of existence to sink to such a low level that mankind was fated throughout history, up to and including our present times, to struggle mightily to restore the world to its pre-sin state of purity. Adam's sin, though minor in deed, was cosmic in effect. The initial damage caused to one part of the system, however minimal it may have been, was sufficient to provide evil an entryway by which to penetrate and wreak havoc on the rest.

Man's actions are the determining factor in all creation, in the world's overall condition. Even the isolated action of just one individual can alter the essence of the entire world, for good or evil. Just as Adam's one sin had cosmic reverberations, so can the fulfillment of a single mitzva. The enormous spiritual power of one mitzva is such that, following its fulfillment, were no one to commit a single sin in the world,

In general, there are four *kelippot* (literally, "shells" or "husks") that are spoken of in kabbalistic and hasidic writings: *kelippat noga* and the three wholly impure *kelippot*. The *kelippot* and their appellations are derived from a verse in Ezekiel (1:4) describing the prophet's vision of the divine glory: "I saw, and behold, a storm wind was coming from the north, a great cloud and fire igniting and an aura (*noga*) surrounding it."[9] God's glory is surrounded by four barriers (*kelippot*). The more distant barriers are the three impure *kelippot*, alluded to respectively in the verse: "a storm wind," "a great cloud," and "fire igniting." The barrier closest to His glory is defined as "an aura (*noga*) surrounding it," and is known to be the most translucent of the *kelippot*.

Even the most impure and opaque of the *kelippot* must, by definition, bear some degree of meaning and purpose, namely, the spark of holiness and life force on account of which they can exist at all. The purpose of their existence is analogous, for example, to that of a fruit's outer peel (hence the name *kelippa*), which does not exist solely for itself. With regard to *kelippat noga*, this spark is conspicuous and radiant, thus allowing for the elevation of this *kelippa* to the realm of holiness. By contrast, this spark is concealed and trapped within the impure *kelippot*, unable to radiate. Inaccessible to man, and thus unextractable, the three impure *kelippot* have no way of being elevated to holiness. They are therefore referred to as "impure," alluding to their inability to be rectified.

We can describe these two realms of *kelippot* by employing two

---

all of existence would be restored to its original pristine state. But the reason this has not yet occurred is because our world is comprised of myriad people, each one constituting a dynamic and complex world unto themselves. The nature of such a system is that for each person fulfilling a mitzva, there is someone committing a sin. We are unable to see the big picture: where the world stands, and where we each stand vis-à-vis the world. Despite this (or perhaps even on account of this), we must constantly be aware of the nature of things: each holy act pulls the entire world upward, and vice versa. Even a single action – and we will never know which one – has the capacity to change everything in a split second, for good or otherwise.

---

9. See chap. 6 above.

basic terms used in halakhic parlance: *mutar* and *assur*. In *halakha*, the term *mutar*, literally meaning "that which can be released," is employed to signify that which is permissible. This is in contrast to that which is forbidden, or *assur*, literally meaning "that which is bound or fettered." The realm of *kelippat noga* is the realm of that which is *mutar*. This refers to those elements of the world that can be "released," or elevated to holiness, by using them in the performance of a mitzva. The three impure *kelippot*, by contrast, are included in the realm of that which is *assur*, and comprise the elements of this world that are prohibited and "bound" to the *kelippa*. This latter realm of *kelippa* must be avoided, as it cannot at present be elevated to the realm of holiness.

שֶׁמֵּהֶן נִשְׁפָּעִים שס״ה לֹא תַעֲשֶׂה דְּאוֹרַיְיתָא, וְעַנְפֵיהֶן שֶׁהֵן מִדְּרַבָּנָן. **from which the 365 biblical prohibitions and their rabbinic offshoots receive** their **energy.**

The role of the Torah's 365 prohibitions is chiefly to prevent the soul from clinging to the three impure *kelippot* by creating a separation between the two. Essentially, the prohibitions tell us which objects or actions constitute the impure *kelippot*, which things cannot be elevated to holiness, and where a death trap with no means of escape is hidden. Avoiding transgressing biblical prohibitions, as well as adhering to rabbinically imposed protective guidelines, serves to maintain the borders separating man from the impure *kelippot*. Resisting violation of the prohibitions preserves those elements in the world that have already been rectified and elevated to the realm of holiness – or at the

SEVERING EVIL FROM ITS LIFE SOURCE

☞ Apart from acting as a collective barrier between holiness and *kelippa*, the biblical and rabbinic prohibitions have an additional, more inclusive function, namely, to actively disconnect the *kelippa* from its source of life. As noted previously, nothing exists without being sustained and fueled by holiness. Even the impure *kelippot* exist and are maintained only by virtue of a certain degree of holiness (albeit received indirectly).

It was likewise taught previously that man possesses the power to serve as the conduit channeling holiness to *kelippa*. Endowed with free choice, man is capable of acting in defiance of God's will, unabashedly repudiating the very source of his own life force. This occurs when he violates one

very least have the potential of being so – by preventing their becoming mingled with a reality that does not possess this redeeming quality. These prohibitions are intended to create a separatory infrastructure, the purpose of which is to clearly demarcate between that which is and that which is not capable of being rectified and elevated, allowing for the actual implementation of that holy process when God deems it the appropriate time. ☞ ☞

---

of the 365 prohibitions, whereby he channels the life force from holiness to *kelippa*. Theoretically, were there a way to isolate *kelippa* from people entirely, it would no longer bear any meaning, and in effect cease to exist as *kelippa*. A pig is an impure animal in a certain context, that is, when a Jew eats it. As long as he refrains from doing so, and as long as the pig is "isolated," unconnected to the Jew, it has no power to generate evil.

THE PARASITIC NATURE OF EVIL

☞ The existence of *kelippa*, its growth and sustenance, are analogous to that of a parasite. *Kelippa* latches onto man, sucking its life force from him, and consequently existing on his host's account. Concurrent with the gradual death of its host, *kelippa* is essentially destroying its own source of life. Some sources (see, for example, *Zohar* 2:95b; *Iggeret HaKodesh*, epistle 25) find an allusion to this in the verse "Whenever man controlled man, it was to his detriment" (Eccles. 8:9). They explain the verse to mean that when a *kelippa* dominates a human being, the *kelippa* is doomed, as, at that moment, it is effectively sucking dry its own source of life.

A careful analysis of this analogy yields a more extreme understanding of evil, specifically, that it is in fact *not* similar to a parasite. Whereas the latter is a foreign entity existing on its own and festering within the body, evil in itself has no independent existence and without a host is absolutely nothing. Not only does evil's life force stem from holiness, of which it is a mere distortion, but its very existence hinges solely upon it. Thus, it would be more accurate to say that evil is analogous to a cancer. The body of someone with cancer is not invaded by foreign bodies. Rather the body's own cells mutate by themselves, dividing out of control. Instead of dying when they should, the cancer cells destroy the body and often lead to the patient's death.

Evil is perpetually drawn to places with the highest concentration of holiness, as that is its source of energy and vitality. This explains the talmudic adage "Anyone who is greater than another, his evil inclination is greater than his"(*Sukka* 52a). In other words, the intensity of evil's grip upon a person is commensurate with his level of holiness. The loftier a person's spiritual level, the deeper his devotion to holiness, the more invigorated and impactful is the evil drawing its sustenance from him. Now if the evil inclination is ultimately successful in its mission to destroy the Torah scholar onto whom it is leeched, it no longer has what to gain from his host. Only too late does the evil inclination realize that he has effectively destroyed his very own source of life.

In the not-too-distant past, there were

וְשׁוּב לֹא תּוּכַל נֶפֶשׁ הַחִיּוּנִית לַעֲלוֹת אֶל ה', אִם נִטְמְאָה בְּטוּמְאַת הַשָּׁלֹשׁ קְלִיפּוֹת הַטְּמֵאוֹת, שֶׁאֵין לָהֶן עֲלִיָּה לְעוֹלָם כִּי אִם בִּיטּוּל וְהַעֲבָרָה לְגַמְרֵי, כְּמוֹ שֶׁכָּתוּב: "וְאֶת רוּחַ הַטּוּמְאָה אַעֲבִיר מִן הָאָרֶץ" (זכריה יג, ב).

The vital soul would no longer be able to ascend to God were it defiled with the impurity of the three impure *kelippot*, for they can never be elevated, but must be **utterly nullified and banished** from the world, **as it is written: "I also will remove…the spirit of impurity from the land"** (Zech. 13:2).

Indeed, the Torah's prohibitions and rabbinical decrees maintain the barrier between man and the impure *kelippot*, both isolating the *kelippot* and protecting man. Yet should one breach this barrier by violating one of the 365 prohibitions, thereby contaminating his vital soul with the impurity of the three impure *kelippot*, his soul will be forever tainted and unable to ascend to God, that is, to holiness.

Unlike *kelippat noga*, the impure *kelippot* are not subject to internal rectification and can never be converted to good. They are regarded as rectified only when destroyed. One must completely avoid them, making certain to sever them from their life source by

---

many good, talented Jews who were swept up in the Enlightenment and various revolutionary movements. Interestingly, however, one who was raised to become a great rabbi and community leader but subsequently abandoned that path in pursuit of secular trends did not become a socialist leader or famed poet, for example. Instead, such individuals were generally reduced to a confused shell of their original selves, lacking any sense of purpose, and unremarkable by all accounts.

This degenerative process, while indeed destructive for the Jewish nation, was even more so for those who had experienced it.

Any process in which good turns to evil is a doomed affair. When the doses of life the "good" person funnels to evil exceed a certain limit, an inevitable breaking point is reached. That person, the source of life for evil, eventually implodes, shattering into insignificant shards. Following this logic, every victory of evil simultaneously triggers the beginning of its own downfall. The more powerful and sweeping its victory, the more imminent its demise. Essentially, embedded within the very nature of evil there exists a barrier preventing it from ever surpassing a certain level, beyond which would commence its own self-destruction.

not violating any of the Torah's prohibitions and not even giving them any thought.

It is thus clear that the true weapon against the impure *kelippot* is specifically to refrain from transgressing the Torah's prohibitions. Whereas *kelippat noga* can be rectified by being utilized in the fulfillment of a positive mitzva (as is noted at the beginning of the chapter regarding *etrog* and *orla*), no such possibility exists with the impure *kelippot*. Their rectification occurs only through one's lack of engagement with them, by *not* violating one of the 365 prohibitions. As we have said, this avoidance breaks the connection between the impure *kelippot* and the vital soul, consequently severing the former's ties to the divine holiness which previously sustained it. Once the *kelippa* is cut off from its life source, it gradually atrophies until it is utterly destroyed and vanishes from existence. ☞

PATHS OF REPENTANCE

☞ In the context of a person's journey to self-improvement, there are, broadly speaking, two approaches to repentance. These are reflected in how one regards the evils he committed in his past. The first approach, that which forms the most basic and core element in the repentance process, is a person's dissociation from the past and the evil acts he perpetrated. The second approach involves making an active change in the sinful deeds he performed, in an effort to impart new meaning to them.

The first approach is relatively simple, attainable by any person and for any evil action he may have committed. In this approach, one disentangles himself from the ramifications of the particular deed, escaping from the vicious cycle of sin and evil by taking ownership of those actions and resolving to abandon them completely. To be sure, the damage wrought by his actions woefully remains within existence, in desperate need of repair; he merely breaks his connection with it. This is, in a sense, how a person relates to the impure *kelippot*: He neither repairs them nor transforms them into good, but only disconnects himself from them. The 365 prohibitions provide the framework within which this approach can operate. They represent those actions one must avoid, how to contain them, and how to sever their lifeline, banishing them from existence.

The second approach to repentance, exceedingly rare and far more difficult than the first, is one in which a person succeeds in changing the meaning of his past actions. To undertake this task one must relate to the evil not merely in a passive manner, i.e., by ceasing that action, but by actively elevating and rectifying the evil with a holy action. As we shall see below, this is, in a way, the same manner in which a person relates to the realm of *kelippat noga*.

וְרַמָ"ח מִצְוֹת עֲשֵׂה, לְהַמְשִׁיךְ אוֹר אֵין סוֹף בָּרוּךְ הוּא לְמַטָּה, לְהַעֲלוֹת לוֹ וּלְקַשֵּׁר וּלְיַיחֵד בּוֹ כְּלָלוּת הַנֶּפֶשׁ הַחִיּוּנִית שֶׁבְּרַמָ"ח אֶבְרֵי הַגּוּף, בְּיִחוּד גָּמוּר לִהְיוֹת לַאֲחָדִים מַמָּשׁ. כְּמוֹ שֶׁעָלָה בִּרְצוֹנוֹ יִתְבָּרֵךְ לִהְיוֹת לוֹ דִּירָה בַּתַּחְתּוֹנִים, וְהֵם לוֹ לְמֶרְכָּבָה כְּמוֹ הָאָבוֹת.

Kelippat noga will be elevated when each Jewish soul also fulfills **the 248 positive commandments,** which serve **to draw down the light of** *Ein Sof,* **blessed be He, below, to ascend to Him and bind and unite within Him the totality of the vital soul that is in the 248 organs of the body, in absolute unity, so that they literally become one** with God, **as it arose in His will to have an abode in the lower worlds, and so that they will be a chariot for Him, as were the patriarchs.**

The patriarchs – Abraham, Isaac, and Jacob – constituted the "chariot" for the Divine (see *Bereshit Rabba* 47:6, 82:6, and chap. 34 above). As was previously stated (chap. 36), the purpose of creation was in order that God have an abode in the lower worlds. This is accomplished when human beings emulate the patriarchs and mold themselves into a "chariot," a complete vessel whose sole function is to provide a place for the "resting" of the Divine Presence. These people have converted their entire beings and souls into vessels through which Godliness can be manifest in this lowly world.

Indeed, not every Jew can attain the level of the patriarchs and through his own efforts (i.e., by an awakening from below) become a chariot. But God did grant His people the Torah and mitzvot, equipping us with the necessary tools to help us elevate, bit by bit, the *kelippat noga* within ourselves and within the world. When one seriously engages in this transformative soul work on a consistent and regular basis, not merely as a sporadic pastime, he gradually transforms into a chariot for the Divine Presence. At least one phase in the fulfillment of the overall purpose of creation is achieved when each of us, to the best of our abilities, draws closer to this level of a chariot for the Divine Presence.

CHAPTER 37

וּמֵאַחַר שֶׁכְּלָלוּת נֶפֶשׁ הַחִיּוּנִית שֶׁבִּכְלָלוּת יִשְׂרָאֵל תִּהְיֶה מֶרְכָּבָה קְדוֹשָׁה לַה׳ – אֲזַי גַּם כְּלָלוּת הַחַיּוּת שֶׁל עוֹלָם הַזֶּה, שֶׁהִיא קְלִיפַּת נוֹגַהּ עַכְשָׁיו, תֵּצֵא אָז מִטּוּמְאָתָהּ וְחֶלְאָתָהּ וְתַעֲלֶה לִקְדוּשָׁה, לִהְיוֹת מֶרְכָּבָה לַה׳ בְּהִתְגַּלּוּת כְּבוֹדוֹ. "וְרָאוּ כָל בָּשָׂר יַחְדָּו" (ישעיה מ, ה), וְיוֹפִיעַ עֲלֵיהֶם בַּהֲדַר גְּאוֹן עֻזּוֹ, "וְיִמָּלֵא כְבוֹד ה׳ אֶת כָּל הָאָרֶץ" (במדבר יד, כא).

Once the totality of the vital soul of the community of Israel becomes a holy chariot for God, then the totality of the life force of this world, which at present constitutes *kelippat noga*, will also emerge from its state of **impurity and filth and ascend to holiness to become a chariot for God upon the revelation of His glory,** as it states, **"All flesh will see together"** (Isa. 40:5), and He will appear before them in the splendor of His great might, and **"the entire earth shall be filled with the glory of the Lord"** (Num. 14:21).

When the nation of Israel attains the level of being a chariot for the Divine Presence, the entire world will undergo a transformation. The patriarchs on their own were unable to effectuate this cosmic transformation because, despite their greatness, they were only individual people. The Jewish nation, by contrast, constitutes a totality representative of the entire world, and so the effects of a qualitative transformation within the Jewish people are felt by the rest of creation, generating a global change as well.

25 Adar

16 Adar II (leap year)

In a certain sense, the Jewish people are the nucleus and heart of the world. Their transformation into a state of holiness reestablishes the cosmic coordinates. From that point forward, the entire world operates within a new framework, one in which all elements interrelate the way they were meant to, thus serving as a grand vessel for divine revelation.

וְיִשְׂרָאֵל יִרְאוּ עַיִן בְּעַיִן כִּבְמַתַּן תּוֹרָה, דִּכְתִיב: "אַתָּה הָרְאֵתָ לָדַעַת כִּי ה׳ הוּא הָאֱלֹהִים אֵין עוֹד מִלְּבַדּוֹ" (דברים ד, לה).

At that time, **the Jewish people will have an absolutely clear perception of divine revelation, seeing it "eye to eye,"** as they had at the giving of the Torah, as it is written, **"You have been shown in order to know that the Lord, He is God; there is no other besides Him"** (Deut. 4:35).

The phrase in the verse "You have been shown in order to know" does not refer to an intellectual understanding of the Divine, but rather to physical vision whereby one sees something "eye to eye" (see Isa. 52:8). In other words, the Jewish people will perceive that "the Lord, He is God," in the sense that they will literally see divine existence, apart from which there is nothing else.

At Mount Sinai God forced this awareness on the Israelites by "overturning the mountain above them like a tub" – to borrow the talmudic expression (see *Shabbat* 88a). Through this act, antithetical to human nature and that of the world, God granted them a peek at the perfected state of existence as it will be in the World to Come. Yet this was but an ephemeral glimpse, as both they and the world were unprepared to withstand such a state of existence. The revelatory experience at Sinai did not leave the Israelites changed at their core, and so immediately following their "eye to eye" encounter with the Divine, they committed the sin of the golden calf. Thus, concerning the giving of the Torah, Moses told the Israelites, "You have been shown in order to know," that is, you, Israel, have been privy to this glimpse, but in the future, "all flesh will see."

וְעַל יְדֵי זֶה יִתְבַּלְּעוּ וְיִתְבַּטְּלוּ לְגַמְרֵי כָּל הַשָּׁלֹשׁ קְלִיפּוֹת הַטְּמֵאוֹת, כִּי יְנִיקָתָן וְחַיּוּתָן מֵהַקְּדוּשָּׁה עַכְשָׁיו הִיא עַל יְדֵי קְלִיפַּת נֹגַהּ הַמְמוּצַעַת בֵּינֵיהֶן.

As a result of this, all three impure *kelippot* will be completely swallowed up, i.e., destroyed, and nullified from existence, **for their present nourishment and life force from holiness is through *kelippat noga*, the intermediary between them.**

As was explained earlier, even the *kelippot* receive their sustenance from and are maintained by holiness. Like pure evil, the three impure *kelippot* are incapable of coming into direct contact with holiness, but instead require *kelippat noga* to act as an intermediary. It follows that when *kelippat noga* is converted to holiness, when it ceases to interface between holiness and impurity, the impure *kelippot* are left bereft of any connection to holiness. Lacking nourishment from holiness, the *kelippot* are automatically nullified and "swallowed up"[10] into oblivion, completely disappearing from existence.

---

10. The Lubavitcher Rebbe, Rabbi Menaḥem Mendel Schneerson, notes that this expression is based on the verse "Death will be swallowed up forever" (Isa. 25:8).

Consummate evil cannot exist in a vacuum, and so it seeks to bind itself with a less potent evil, effectively creating an infrastructure allowing for its continued existence. The two evils, and however many more elements this growing structure may comprise, become interlinked to the extent that should just one link in the middle snap, the entire system crumbles. To illustrate this further, take the example of a thief. Without a clientele for his stolen goods, he has no reason to continue his criminal activities. The survival of the black market hinges upon the existence of gray areas, situations where money laundering can thrive. The moment those gray areas disappear, as soon as the passage from the underworld to the rest of society is sealed off, the world of organized crime ceases to exist.

וְנִמְצָא, כִּי כָּל תַּכְלִית שֶׁל יְמוֹת הַמָּשִׁיחַ וּתְחִיַּית הַמֵּתִים, שֶׁהוּא גִּילּוּי כְּבוֹדוֹ וֶאֱלֹקוּתוֹ יִתְבָּרֵךְ וּלְהַעֲבִיר רוּחַ הַטּוּמְאָה מִן הָאָרֶץ, תָּלוּי בְּהַמְשָׁכַת אֱלֹקוּתוֹ וְאוֹר אֵין סוֹף בָּרוּךְ הוּא לְנֶפֶשׁ הַחִיּוּנִית שֶׁבִּכְלָלוּת יִשְׂרָאֵל בְּכָל רְמַ״ח אֵבָרֶיהָ עַל יְדֵי קִיּוּמָהּ כָּל רְמַ״ח מִצְוֹת עֲשֵׂה,

It follows that the entire purpose of the messianic era and resurrection of the dead, that is, the manifestation of His glory and the Divine, and the banishment of the spirit of impurity from the earth, is dependent upon the act of **drawing down the Divine and the light of *Ein Sof*, blessed be He, into the vital soul, which is within the Jewish collective, into all its 248 limbs, by fulfilling all 248 positive mitzvot in the Torah,**

17 Adar II (leap year)

The purpose and fulfillment of the messianic era and the resurrection of the dead is twofold: It is for the true revelation of God's glory and the Divine in the world, and for the utter banishment of evil, both contingent upon our actions. This is accomplished when the Jewish people as a whole draws down the Godly light into its collective vital soul. That is, when each one of us fulfills the 248 positive mitzvot, our individual vital souls (regarded as one collective soul) become infused with this divine light. As explained below, this collective soul is powerful enough to elevate the entire world along with it.

וּלְהַעֲבִיר רוּחַ הַטּוּמְאָה מִמֶּנָּה בִּשְׁמִירָתָהּ כָּל שס"ה מִצְוֹת לֹא תַעֲשֶׂה, שֶׁלֹּא יִינְקוּ מִמֶּנָּה שס"ה גִּידֶיהָ.

as well as by banishing the spirit of impurity from it, that is, the vital soul, **through** the latter's **observance of all 365 prohibitions**, thereby **preventing its 365 sinews from deriving** any sustenance from *kelippa*.

In addition to the vital soul's actively fulfilling the 248 positive mitzvot, thereby becoming suffused with God's light, the ultimate purpose of creation also depends upon the vital soul's refraining from violating any of 365 prohibitions, which would otherwise contaminate it with the spirit of impurity. The observance of the prohibitions likewise prevents the 365 sinews of *kelippa* from deriving sustenance from the vital soul. ☞

REDEMPTION AND THE BIRTH PANGS OF MESSIAH

☞ The final redemption, heralded by the messianic era and the resurrection of the dead, a new epoch in which the revelation of God will permeate all of existence, will arrive after a gradual process of (often imperceptible) events. This process comprises three core phases. The first phase transpires with the divine revelation for the individual as distinct from others. The second is the divine revelation for every Jew as regarded as a part of an organic whole (specifically through the Jewish people's joint fulfillment of the 248 positive mitzvot with their 248 collective limbs). The final phase of the ultimate redemption occurs with the complete revelation of the Divine in all the worlds.

Observing other areas of life, we discover two basic types of processes: those which can be readily understood and tracked, and those which remain a complete mystery to the observer. The first type of process refers to one whose gradual unfolding is immediately detectable. A skilled artist, for example, can clearly visualize in his mind's eye each layer in his painting's evolution. The second type is one which remains an enigma to those involved and affected. In such a case, the true implications of each phase become clear only upon the process's culmination. Throughout the duration of such a process, one often suffers much pain and discomfort, in addition to being plagued by fears of the unknown. Only the end of this painful process can offer him some degree of solace.

For most people, the redemptive process is of the second type; there is no apparent progress and no sense of accomplishment. Until the process is complete, people often feel a sense of despair, lost in the darkness of the unknown, and perhaps even seeing the transpiring events as setbacks. This accounts for the widely accepted view comparing redemption to the typically painful birthing process (see, for example, *Torah Or* 55a). This analogy is the source for the now common expression "the pangs of Messiah" (*Sanhedrin* 98b). This concept is also referenced in *Tanakh*, such as in the verse "The throes

CHAPTER 37

כִּי כְּלָלוּת יִשְׂרָאֵל, שֶׁהֵם שִׁשִּׁים רִבּוֹא נְשָׁמוֹת פְּרָטִיּוֹת, הֵם כְּלָלוּת הַחַיּוּת שֶׁל כְּלָלוּת הָעוֹלָם, כִּי בִּשְׁבִילָם נִבְרָא.

For the totality of the Jewish people, comprising 600,000 individual souls, constitutes the collective vitality that serves as the source of life for the entire world, which was created for them.

18 Adar II (leap year)

In this passage, the author of the *Tanya* asserts that the Jewish people as a whole are the *raison d'être* and life force of the entire world, which was ultimately created for them, and by virtue of whom it remains in existence.

וְכָל פְּרָט מֵהֶם הוּא כּוֹלֵל וְשַׁיָּךְ לוֹ הַחַיּוּת שֶׁל חֵלֶק אֶחָד מִשִּׁשִּׁים רִבּוֹא מִכְּלָלוּת הָעוֹלָם,

Each specific one of them contains and is connected to one part in 600,000 of the life force of the entire world,

Being the ultimate cause for the creation of the world, the Jewish people bear a great responsibility toward existence as a whole. The point here is that this is not a vague, overarching degree of responsibility. Rather, each member of the Jewish nation has direct accountability for the specific part of the world related and connected to his specific soul.

הַתָּלוּי בְּנַפְשׁוֹ הַחִיּוּנִית לְהַעֲלוֹתוֹ לַה' בַּעֲלִיָּיתָהּ,

each part of which depends on his vital soul to elevate it to God through the vital soul's own ascent,

As mentioned above, the vital soul derives from *kelippat noga* and interfaces with the physical world. When a person elevates his vital

---

of a woman in childbirth will come to him," (Hos. 13:13) and "Before a pang comes" (Isa. 66:7).

There are always the rare few who are privy to catch a clear glimpse of the redemptive process as it unfolds. These individuals are endowed with the ability to track the stages in the cosmic recalibration and rectification. They clearly perceive the impact a particular action or mitzva has upon the world, how it effects a change in any given part of existence. But for the overwhelming majority of people, the process of redemption, the ramifications of one's actions vis-à-vis the world's improvement and growth, remains an impenetrable mystery. At present, we can see only the pain and suffering associated with this process, growing ever more acute and bitter the closer we approach the end of days.

soul by using it to engage in holy pursuits, he simultaneously elevates with it that part of the world to which it is connected.

The vital soul within each Jew is responsible for a corresponding part of the world. The relationship between a person and the part of the world he is accountable for can be described as organic in nature, akin to the disparate yet interconnected parts of the body. Though each limb and organ serves a different purpose, they are all necessary components in the overall anatomical structure, impacting and influencing each other. In our context, the person in which the vital soul lies functions as the critical component in this soul-world dynamic, unique in its sentience and thus in its responsibility. Understood in this manner, the person is just one part of a much larger entity, playing the role of the "heart" of a giant body. When he "stands up," the rest of his "body" follows suit. When one engages his vital soul in holy endeavors, he by default engages the part of the world associated with and connected to it.

דְּהַיְינוּ בַּמֶּה שֶׁמִּשְׁתַּמֵּשׁ מֵעוֹלָם הַזֶּה לְצוֹרֶךְ גּוּפוֹ וְנַפְשׁוֹ הַחִיּוּנִית לַעֲבוֹדַת ה׳, כְּגוֹן: אֲכִילָה וּשְׁתִיָּה וְדוֹמֵיהֶם וְדִירָה וְכָל כְּלֵי תַשְׁמִישָׁיו. namely, by utilizing this physical world for the needs of his body and vital soul in the service of God, such as eating, drinking, and the like, his house and all his belongings.

When a person makes use of the world, such as when he eats something, he assumes a great degree of responsibility. He is responsible not only for the food he ingests, but for the entire network involved in its preparation and his ultimate ability to enjoy it: the people, the equipment, the location, and even the heavens and earth.

The whole of existence – inanimate entities, plant life, and the animal world – is perpetually busy preparing and arranging raw ("neutral") reality in a manner such that a critical decision must be made as to its ultimate purpose and trajectory, in any given context and juncture in time. At those crucial points stands the Jew, invested with the power to decide this object's fate: Will it be utilized for a holy purpose or not? One's choice not only affects that isolated object, but impacts the *entire* system that contributed to its current state of being. One can decide to use an object in a holy endeavor, thereby justifying and imparting significance to the existence of this complex network from its very inception, from the beginning of time. Alternatively, he can choose to use an object for an unholy purpose, polluting it with improper deeds or inappropriate thoughts. Either choice one makes, he not only decrees his own destiny and that of the piece of bread he consumes, but he also dictates the fate of an entire part of existence. His decision is a veritable decree, determining an object's "acquittal" or "guilt," success or failure. He determines whether the object will at long last be elevated to holiness, or whether it must remain in limbo as it has been since the beginning of its creation, until it crosses paths with the person who chooses to rectify and redeem it.

אֶלָּא שִׁשִּׁים רִבּוֹא נְשָׁמוֹת פְּרָטִיּוֹת אֵלּוּ הֵן שָׁרָשִׁים, וְכָל שֹׁרֶשׁ מִתְחַלֵּק לְשִׁשִּׁים רִבּוֹא נִיצוֹצוֹת, שֶׁכָּל נִיצוֹץ הוּא נְשָׁמָה אַחַת. These 600,000 individual souls, however, are roots, each one dividing into 600,000 sparks, each spark constituting one soul.

The Jewish people as a unit comprises 600,000 souls (each one correlating to one of the 600,000 parts composing the totality of the world). One may question this assertion based on the plain facts pointing to a greater number of Jews throughout the ages. Addressing this question, the author of the *Tanya* explains that this number represents not the total number of Jewish souls, but rather the number of *root* souls, each of which is splintered into an additional 600,000 derivative souls.

The overwhelming majority of Jews in any given time or place do not possess a root soul, but rather a fragment, a spark of it. ☞

SOUL CONNECTIONS

☞ The subdivision of fundamental root souls accounts for why people who to all appearances share nothing in common – being worlds apart in their opinions, lacking any familial connections or shared educational backgrounds – nevertheless feel a sense of kinship to one another. As mentioned, there is an undetectable, quintessential soul force engendering often inexplicable feelings of closeness among people. Their mutual sense of companionship and compatibility is on account of their kindred souls, each of which is a fragment of the same root soul. Such people

וְכֵן בְּנֶפֶשׁ וְרוּחַ, בְּכָל עוֹלָם מֵאַרְבַּע עוֹלָמוֹת: אֲצִילוּת בְּרִיאָה יְצִירָה עֲשִׂיָּה.

The same goes for the *nefesh* and *ruaḥ* in each of the four worlds: *Atzilut* (Emanation), *Beria* (Creation), *Yetzira* (Formation), and *Asiya* (Action).

A person's soul is composed of levels (*nefesh, ruaḥ, neshama*), paralleling the four worlds: *Atzilut, Beria, Yetzira,* and *Asiya*. The level of *neshama* in one's soul is rooted in the world of *Beria* (and *Atzilut*), *ruaḥ* in *Yetzira*, and *nefesh* in *Asiya*. Thus, the division of 600,000 root souls, along with their 600,000 offshoots, that exist on the level of *neshama*, exist on the levels of *nefesh* and *ruaḥ* as well.

26 Adar
19 Adar II
(leap year)

וְכָל נִיצוֹץ לֹא יָרַד לָעוֹלָם הַזֶּה –

Each spark descended into this world only for the purpose stated below.

Before continuing, the author of the *Tanya* makes a parenthetical remark:

אַף שֶׁהִיא יְרִידָה גְדוֹלָה וּבְחִינַת גָּלוּת מַמָּשׁ, כִּי גַּם שֶׁיִּהְיֶה צַדִּיק גָּמוּר עוֹבֵד ה' בְּיִרְאָה וְאַהֲבָה רַבָּה בְּתַעֲנוּגִים, לֹא יַגִּיעַ לְמַעֲלוֹת דְּבֵיקוּתוֹ בָּהּ' בְּדְחִילוּ וּרְחִימוּ בְּטֶרֶם יְרִידָתוֹ לָעוֹלָם הַזֶּה הַחוֹמְרִי, לֹא מִינָהּ וְלֹא מִקְצָתָהּ, וְאֵין עֵרֶךְ וְדִמְיוֹן בֵּינֵיהֶם כְּלָל,

The soul descends to this world **even though it entails a profound decline** and banishment into **a literal state of exile, for even were one to be a completely righteous individual, serving God with fear and a great love of delights, he would not** be able to experience the quality of his attachment to God through fear and love that his soul had experienced **prior to its descent into this material world, not even a miniscule amount of it. There is no comparison or similarity between them whatsoever,**

Despite such differences, these individuals will feel an inexplicable kinship with each other, like two shards of the same root soul. The collective, root soul is analogous to the defining character of an overarching entity, are not exactly the same because the soul fragments themselves are not necessarily of equal status. For example, a particular soul offshoot may possess a unique intellectual bent, while its counterpart does not.

The descent of the soul – any soul – into this world is very profound indeed. It can be described as suffering a steep fall, a severe decline, from its former position in the supernal heights. The soul experiences this decline not only when placed specifically in the body of a sinner or a person lacking moral scruples, since every person in this world is endowed with free will and can potentially choose to lead a sinful lifestyle, tainting the divine soul within.

The author of the *Tanya* adds here that the soul regards its descent into this world as a painful decline, even were the person housing it to be a complete tzaddik who had forged the most profound and intimate bond with God humanly possible. The soul regards its very descent into a physical body – irrespective of how spiritually refined it may be – as a spiritual "fall," for an embodied soul cannot experience even a modicum of its previous connection to the Divine prior to being forcibly placed within a body.

כַּנּוֹדָע לְכָל מַשְׂכִּיל, שֶׁהַגּוּף אֵינוֹ יָכוֹל לִסְבּוֹל כו'. **as is known to every intelligent person that the body cannot bear, and so forth ….**

The reason the embodied soul is incapable of experiencing even a hint of its pre-descent attachment to God is that the body, by its very definition, cannot tolerate the levels of love and fear of God its newly endowed soul had attained prior to descending into it. Such spiritual levels are far too intense and abstract for the body to bear, and so prevent the soul from accessing any taste of that divine attachment.

Having concluded his parenthetical remark, the author of the *Tanya* continues his explanation of the purpose of the soul's descent.

while its "sparks" are components of that same character. Just as the collective essence of the Jewish people is divided into 600,000 root elements, so each root soul is subdivided into 600,000 sparks. These sparks, reflecting various facets and pre-senting unique perspectives of the root soul from which it originated, are gifted and bound to every one of us, providing the contexts for our unique paths of divine service in this world.

אֶלָּא יְרִידָתוֹ לָעוֹלָם הַזֶּה, לְהִתְלַבֵּשׁ בְּגוּף וְנֶפֶשׁ הַחִיּוּנִית, הוּא כְּדֵי לְתַקְּנָם בִּלְבַד

Rather, its descent into this world, **fated to be clothed in the body and the vital soul, is solely in order to rectify them**

The holy soul descends into a body not for its own sake, but for the benefit of "others." It is on a mission, placed here to rectify the body and its vitalizing animal soul.

וּלְהַפְרִידָם מֵהָרַע שֶׁל שָׁלֹשׁ קְלִיפּוֹת הַטְּמֵאוֹת עַל יְדֵי שְׁמִירַת שס"ה לֹא תַעֲשֶׂה וְעַנְפֵיהֶן,

and to separate the body and vital soul **from the evil of the three impure** *kelippot***, by observing the 365 prohibitions and their offshoots,**

The body and vital soul of a Jew derive from *kelippat noga*, which is comprised of good and evil elements. The initial phase of rectifying and improving the body and vital soul is their separation from the evil elements in *kelippat noga*. This is achieved by observing the 365 prohibitions, the purpose of which is to protect the body and the vital soul from becoming spiritually impure and attached to evil.

וּלְהַעֲלוֹת נַפְשׁוֹ הַחִיּוּנִית עִם חֶלְקָהּ הַשַּׁיָּיךְ לָהּ מִכְּלָלוּת עוֹלָם הַזֶּה וּלְקַשְּׁרָם וּלְיַיחֲדָם בְּאוֹר אֵין סוֹף בָּרוּךְ הוּא, אֲשֶׁר יַמְשִׁיךְ בָּהֶם עַל יְדֵי קִיּוּמוֹ כָּל רמ"ח מִצְוֹת עֲשֵׂה בְּנַפְשׁוֹ הַחִיּוּנִית, שֶׁהִיא הִיא הַמְקַיֶּימֶת כָּל מִצְוֹת מַעֲשִׂיּוֹת כַּנִּזְכָּר לְעֵיל.

and to elevate his vital soul, along **with its corresponding part of the totality of this world, and to bind and unify them with the light of** *Ein Sof***, blessed be He, which** he, the person, **draws down into them by fulfilling all 248 positive mitzvot using his vital soul, the very thing that fulfills all the action-based mitzvot, as mentioned above.**

The second phase in the rectification of the body and vital soul is the binding of the vital soul, together with its corresponding part of the physical world, with the light of *Ein Sof*. In this phase, the good elements in the animating soul are connected to the source of good and divine holiness. The person achieves this by fulfilling the 248 positive mitzvot through the medium of his 248 limbs and vital soul.

These are the only tools through which the action-based mitzvot can be performed, as the holy soul itself cannot fulfill such mitzvot. Its only task is to assist in forming this bond with the light of *Ein Sof*, to spur, motivate, and goad the body and vital soul to fulfill the mitzvot and become elevated through them.

וּכְמוֹ שֶׁכָּתוּב [בְּעֵץ חַיִּים שַׁעַר כ"ו] כִּי הַנְּשָׁמָה עַצְמָהּ אֵינָהּ צְרִיכָה תִּיקוּן כְּלָל כוּ', וְלֹא הוּצְרְכָה לְהִתְלַבֵּשׁ בָּעוֹלָם הַזֶּה וְכוּ' רַק לְהַמְשִׁיךְ אוֹר לְתַקְּנָם כוּ', וְהוּא מַמָּשׁ דּוּגְמַת סוֹד גָּלוּת הַשְּׁכִינָה, לְבָרֵר נִיצוֹצִין וְכוּ'.	It is also written (in *Etz Ḥayyim* 26:1) that the soul itself does not require any rectification whatsoever, and so on, and was required to become clothed in this world, and so on, only to draw down light to rectify the body and vital soul. This is actually similar to the mystery of the exile of the Divine Presence, the purpose of which is to elevate the sparks, and so forth.

The mystery of the exile of the Divine Presence mentioned in this passage in *Etz Ḥayyim* refers to the idea that the "exile" it experiences is not for itself, but for the sake of the world throughout which it wanders. The Divine Presence is represented by the collective souls of Israel, also known as the congregation of Israel. On a deeper level, "the congregation of Israel" alludes to the assembling and gathering of divine light (known as "Yisrael") scattered throughout the worlds. The Divine Presence is exiled in the world in the sense that it roams this physical realm, sifting through its coarseness, gathering and elevating the sparks of holiness that were trapped there since they "fell" when the primordial vessels were shattered.[11]

Like the exile of the Divine Presence within this world, the divine soul "descends" into exile within the body for the express purpose of elevating the elements of holiness contained therein. Its mission is also to elevate the sparks of holiness contained within the vital soul and within the parts

---

11. See *Pesaḥim* 87b, which states, "The Holy One, blessed be He, exiled Israel among the nations only so that converts would join them." This statement not only obviously refers to literal converts, but also alludes to the task of elevating the sparks of holiness that fell with the shattering of the vessels. See, for example, *Siddur Im Dach*, 59c; *Torah Or* 11a; *Ma'amarei Admor HaZaken 5565*, p. 21.

of the world that correspond and are connected to it. The divine soul (or *neshama*) itself is pure, literally a portion of God above, and so it does not require purification and elevation. Yet it descends into a physical body, tasked with refining and rectifying both that body and the parts of this world related to and affected by it. It follows that the more the mitzva is interconnected with physical objects in this world and the broader its reach, so is its cosmic effect. To the extent that the mitzva relates to and impacts this world, so is the *neshama*'s success in its mission.

It is not for naught that the author of the *Tanya* adds the seemingly superfluous expression "actually" ("this is *actually* similar to..."). This term is meant to emphasize the fact that the analogy between the exile of the *neshama* and the Divine Presence is not merely superficial in nature, but is very real and actual indeed. The author uses this expression to underscore the truly quintessential connection between the *neshama* and the Divine Presence, where the former is in a certain sense a mere detail of the latter. The descent of the *neshama* into the body cannot be understood on its own, but only as a particularized instance of the more encompassing exile of the Divine Presence.

---

27 Adar

20 Adar II (leap year)

וּבָזֶה יוּבַן מַה שֶּׁהִפְלִיגוּ רַבּוֹתֵינוּ ז״ל בִּמְאֹד מְאֹד בְּמַעֲלַת הַצְּדָקָה, וְאָמְרוּ שֶׁשְּׁקוּלָה כְּנֶגֶד כָּל הַמִּצְוֹת (בבא בתרא ט, א), וּבְכָל תַּלְמוּד יְרוּשַׁלְמִי הִיא נִקְרֵאת בְּשֵׁם מִצְוָה סְתָם, כִּי כָּךְ הָיָה הֶרְגֵּל הַלָּשׁוֹן לִקְרוֹא צְדָקָה בְּשֵׁם מִצְוָה סְתָם.

In light of the above, one can now **understand why our Rabbis extolled the supreme virtue of** the mitzva of charity, **asserting that it is equivalent to all the mitzvot** combined (*Bava Batra* 9a). Moreover, **throughout the entire Jerusalem Talmud,** the mitzva of charity **is referred to simply as "the mitzva," for the** unmodified **expression "the mitzva" was commonly used in reference to** the mitzva of **charity,**

Whenever the Jerusalem Talmud refers to an unspecified mitzva, such as when discussing an individual who is actually performing a mitzva or merely thinking about one, the intent is inevitably the mitzva of charity and its various offshoots.[12] ☞

---

12. See, e.g., Mishna *Pe'a* 8:8.

מִפְּנֵי שֶׁהִיא עִיקַּר הַמִּצְוֹת מַעֲשִׂיּוֹת וְעוֹלָה עַל כּוּלָּנָה. שֶׁכּוּלָן הֵן רַק לְהַעֲלוֹת נֶפֶשׁ הַחִיּוּנִית לַה', שֶׁהִיא הִיא הַמְקַיֶּימֶת אוֹתָן וּמִתְלַבֶּשֶׁת בָּהֶן, לִיכָּלֵל בְּאוֹר אֵין סוֹף בָּרוּךְ הוּא הַמְלוּבָּשׁ בָּהֶן.

because it is the core of the action-based mitzvot, surpassing them all. For the sole purpose of all of them, i.e., these action-based mitzvot, is to elevate the vital soul to God, as this is the very thing that fulfills them and enclothes itself in them, becoming absorbed in the light of *Ein Sof*, blessed be He, which is enclothed in the mitzvot.

Every action-based mitzva plays two roles, each operating on distinct planes. The first role is to elevate the world – that is, the materiality previously located in the neutral realm intermediating between holiness and impurity (i.e., *kelippat noga*) – to the realm of holiness. The second is to elevate to holiness the vital soul of the person performing the mitzva. Although the action element of the mitzva is a garment of the divine soul (see chap. 4), nevertheless, the divine soul itself cannot be directly involved in the performance of the mitzva (on account of its sublime nature), and so it requires the services of the vital soul, which acts as the force energizing and motivating the body to execute the action element of the mitzva. When the vital soul fulfills its task of driving the body to perform a mitzva, it too is elevated along with this mitzva, becoming absorbed within the divine essence clothed in the mitzva performed. These two roles inhere in the mitzva of charity on a higher and more intensive level than in the other mitzvot.

EQUIVALENT TO ALL THE OTHER MITZVOT

☞ The mitzva of charity is not the only one described as being equal to all the other mitzvot. This declaration is also made with regard to each of the following mitzvot (among others): *tzitzit* (*Nedarim* 25a); circumcision (*Nedarim* 32a); Shabbat (Jerusalem Talmud, *Berakhot* 1:3); and Torah study. In a certain sense, all the mitzvot form a single, unified structure in which each mitzva is viewed independently of the others. Each one possesses a unique function not shared by the other mitzvot. Having said this, there are certain mitzvot that are more universal in nature, relating to, and interconnected with, the other mitzvot comprising this grand structure. As we shall see below, one such mitzva is that of charity.

וְאֵין לְךָ מִצְוָה שֶׁנֶּפֶשׁ הַחִיּוּנִית מִתְלַבֶּשֶׁת בָּהּ כָּל כָּךְ כְּבְמִצְוַת הַצְּדָקָה, — You will find no other mitzva in which the vital soul is enclothed to the same extent as it is in the mitzva of charity,

The vital soul is indeed enclothed in every action-based mitzva, but it is enclothed to a far greater degree in the mitzva of charity.

שֶׁבְּכָל הַמִּצְוֹת אֵין מִתְלַבֵּשׁ בָּהֶן רַק כֹּחַ אֶחָד מִנֶּפֶשׁ הַחִיּוּנִית בִּשְׁעַת מַעֲשֵׂה הַמִּצְוָה לְבַד, — for with regard to all other mitzvot, only one faculty of the vital soul is enclothed in them, and does so only while performing the mitzva.

For example, lighting the Shabbat candles is a single action stimulated by the momentary influence of the person's vital soul. Likewise, when one dons *tefillin*, he is performing a specific action, elevating only one faculty of his vital soul that participated in and motivated this action.

אֲבָל בִּצְדָקָה שֶׁאָדָם נוֹתֵן מִיְּגִיעַ כַּפָּיו, הֲרֵי כָּל כֹּחַ נַפְשׁוֹ הַחִיּוּנִית מְלוּבָּשׁ בַּעֲשִׂיַּת מְלַאכְתּוֹ אוֹ עֵסֶק אַחֵר שֶׁנִּשְׂתַּכֵּר בּוֹ מָעוֹת אֵלּוּ, וּכְשֶׁנּוֹתְנָן לִצְדָקָה הֲרֵי כָּל נַפְשׁוֹ הַחִיּוּנִית עוֹלָה לַה'. — Yet in the case of charity, whereby a person gives money earned from the toil of his hands, all the energy of his vital soul becomes enclothed in the effort exerted in his labor or in another occupation through which he earned this money. Thus, when he gives it to charity his entire vital soul ascends to God.

The mitzva of charity is to give of oneself to another. The giving of money in an act of charity does not fully encapsulate the depths of this mitzva, which in truth extends far beyond what can be discerned by this isolated act. The act of giving can be viewed as a summation of the broad scope of efforts and actions the vital soul expended and executed over the course of time, leading up to and culminating in this single act. The charity money not only expresses the intense labor expended by the vital soul, but also epitomizes its desires and passionate pursuit of wealth – all of which are now condensed within the money being given. In this sense, the money is invested with the energy, labor, time, and essence of the soul. When a person then gives this money to charity, he essentially is giving the value of all the energy spent in its acquisition. The more a person labored and invested in obtaining this money, the more he gives of his soul. The more of himself he devoted to attaining his wealth, the greater and more encompassing is the release and subsequent transformation of his soul's energy into holiness. ☞

וְגַם מִי שֶׁאֵינוּ נֶהֱנֶה מִיגִיעוֹ, מִכָּל מָקוֹם הוֹאִיל וּבְמָעוֹת אֵלּוּ הָיָה יָכוֹל לִקְנוֹת חַיֵּי נַפְשׁוֹ הַחִיּוּנִית, הֲרֵי נוֹתֵן חַיֵּי נַפְשׁוֹ לַה'.

Even someone who is not financially **dependent on his** personal **toil, nevertheless, since he could have used this money to purchase** necessities to sustain **the life of his vital soul,** when he gives this money to charity **he is** thereby **giving his soul's life to God.**

In this brief remark, the author of the *Tanya* adds that even one who gives charity from funds he received without having to expend any personal effort, such as inheritance or allowance money, is still regarded as though he has given his vital soul to God. For the truth is that the source of the funds is immaterial. Since this money can be used to buy something, its possessor can potentially purchase anything necessary for his livelihood, so if he gives this money to charity, he is giving his soul's life to God. Thus, the mitzva of charity entails more than a simple, isolated act of giving some money. It is in fact an act whereby one gives

CHARITY: TO GIVE AWAY ONE'S VITAL SOUL

☞ We find another source alluding to the money-soul connection. The verses state, "Do not rob the impoverished, as he is impoverished, and do not oppress the poor at the gate, for the Lord will fight their battle and will deprive those who deprive them of life" (Prov. 22:22–23). These verses clearly imply that one who robs a poor person of his money robs him of his soul. Additionally, regarding late payment of a worker's wages, the Torah states, "As he is poor, and for he sets his soul upon it..." (Deut. 24:15). Commenting on this verse, our Sages state, "For what reason did this person ascend a tall ramp, risking giving his soul into your hands? This teaches that the Torah regards anyone who withholds the payment of a worker as if he has taken his soul" (*Sifrei*, Deut. 24:15; see *Bava Metzia* 112a). The idea here is that a poor person gives his soul in order to obtain the money he needs. Therefore, if someone steals from him, or even delays his payment, it is as though he has taken his soul! Having established that one's money can at times serve in place of his soul, the converse is also true. When one gives his hard-earned money to charity, it is tantamount to giving away his entire soul. This then is the intent here when the author of the *Tanya* writes that "his entire vital soul ascends to God."

God a complex and highly advanced network of personal soul desires and profound efforts. Through this act, he relinquishes to God a broad swath of life – his very soul.

וְלָכֵן אָמְרוּ רַבּוֹתֵינוּ ז"ל שֶׁמְּקָרֶבֶת אֶת הַגְּאוּלָה (בבא בתרא י, א). **Therefore, our Rabbis state that** charity **hastens the redemption** (*Bava Batra* 10a).

As was mentioned earlier, the redemption is not an isolated event, bearing no relation to events preceding it. Rather, it is an ongoing process, a culmination of the aggregate efforts and divine service of all Jews throughout the generations.

לְפִי שֶׁבִּצְדָקָה אַחַת מַעֲלֶה הַרְבֵּה מִנֶּפֶשׁ הַחִיּוּנִית, מַה שֶּׁלֹּא הָיָה יָכוֹל לְהַעֲלוֹת מִמֶּנָּה כָּל כָּךְ כֹּחוֹת וּבְחִינוֹת בְּכַמָּה מִצְוֹת מַעֲשִׂיּוֹת אֲחֵרוֹת. **For through a single** act of **charity one elevates a significant portion of the vital soul, of which the same number of soul faculties and facets could not be elevated by the** performance of **many other action-based mitzvot** combined.

Every mitzva one performs effectuates a change both in the world and in the soul. Each mitzva constitutes another phase in the unfolding process of redemption, thus ultimately hastening its arrival. The mitzva of charity plays a particularly significant role in the redemptive process by virtue of its far-reaching and profoundly powerful impact on both the soul and the world, more so than other mitzvot.

The author of the *Tanya* now proceeds to address an apparent difficulty posed by a talmudic statement made in reference to the mitzva of Torah study:

28 Adar וּמַה שֶּׁאָמְרוּ רַבּוֹתֵינוּ ז"ל, שֶׁתַּלְמוּד תּוֹרָה כְּנֶגֶד כּוּלָּם (פאה פרק א משנה א), **With regard to our Rabbis' statement that Torah study is equivalent to all** the mitzvot (*Pe'a* 1:1),

This statement in tractate *Pe'a* apparently contradicts the aforementioned assertion (based on another talmudic statement mentioned above) that the mitzva of charity is equal to all the other mitzvot combined. Furthermore, it was taught previously that God's abode in the lower realms is created specifically by the performance of action-based mitzvot. This poses a unique difficulty with regard to the mitzva of Torah study, which, in contrast to other action-based mitzvot, does *not* involve a physical action. Thus, how can the mitzva of Torah study be equivalent to all the other mitzvot, more so than the mitzva of charity, an action-based mitzva?

The author of the *Tanya* resolves this apparent contradiction by enumerating two unique qualities that the mitzva of Torah study does not share with the mitzva of charity.

הַיְינוּ מִפְּנֵי שֶׁתַּלְמוּד תּוֹרָה הִיא בְּדִבּוּר וּמַחֲשָׁבָה, שֶׁהֵם לְבוּשִׁים הַפְּנִימִיִּים שֶׁל נֶפֶשׁ הַחִיּוּנִית.	**this is because** the mitzva of **Torah study** is accomplished **with the faculties of speech and thought, which are the innermost garments of the vital soul.**

The first quality unique to the mitzva of Torah study not shared by any other mitzva is that whereas action-based mitzvot are chiefly performed using the vital soul's external garment of action, the mitzva of Torah study is primarily accomplished by using the vital soul's innermost garments of speech and thought. In this sense, although the connection with the Divine achieved through Torah study is not as expansive and intense as that attained through the mitzva of charity, it is nevertheless of a loftier and more profound nature. Giving charity is primarily a physical act, and so the connection to God generated thereby is (relatively) limited by the physical body. The connection to the Divine formed through the study of Torah, by contrast, is far more profound, for it directly involves human consciousness and not the corporeal body. There is no other mitzva by which a person becomes so deeply and intimately connected with God (see chap. 5 above).

וְגַם מַהוּתָן וְעַצְמוּתָן שֶׁל בְּחִינוֹת חָכְמָה בִּינָה דַּעַת מִקְּלִיפַּת נוֹגַהּ שֶׁבַּנֶּפֶשׁ הַחִיּוּנִית נִכְלָלוֹת בִּקְדוּשָׁה מַמָּשׁ כְּשֶׁעוֹסֵק בַּתּוֹרָה בְּעִיּוּן וְשֵׂכֶל.	**Furthermore, the essence and being** of the **intellectual faculties of** Ḥokhma**, Bina, and** Da'at **of** kelippat noga **in the vital soul are literally absorbed within holiness when one engages in Torah** study **by plumbing its depths and exerting mental effort.**

When one engages in Torah study according to his unique intellectual capability, the faculties of understanding and apprehension utilized in this process become unified with the Torah itself. This is in contrast to other mitzvot, in which the part of a person's body used to perform a particular mitzva serves only as a tool in its execution, but does not become one with it.

Every mitzva one performs creates a bond with the Divine that transcends the individual's intellectual capabilities. The very fact that one fulfills God's will forges a bond and connection with Him, regardless of whether or not the person is aware of it. Torah study, on the other hand, is at a higher level. When engaged in the study of Torah, one employs not only the physical, but also the spiritual elements of his being. It follows that the impact the mitzva of Torah study has upon the person engaged in it is not lost in an ethereal realm, hovering just out of the person's reach. Rather, it penetrates the innermost chambers of his soul, effecting a profound change in the deepest recesses of his consciousness.

When a person uses his hand to give charity, it becomes an extension of God's hand, as it were.[13] Despite this lofty status, there is no noticeable impact or change in the giver's physical hand. Torah study, by contrast, effects a veritable change in one's intellect. His faculty of Ḥokhma (wisdom) literally becomes a vessel of holiness, its essence transforming from a state of indifference to one of holiness. When one employs his intellect by thinking about a particular topic of Torah, he is at that very moment thinking God's thoughts. This person's faculties of Ḥokhma, Bina, and Da'at are instantly converted into Godly intellect.

וְאַף שֶׁמַּהוּתָן וְעַצְמוּתָן שֶׁל הַמִּדּוֹת חֶסֶד גְּבוּרָה תִּפְאֶרֶת כו' לֹא יָכְלוּ לָהֶם הַבֵּינוֹנִים לְהַפְּכָם לִקְדוּשָּׁה, **Although** *beinonim* **are incapable of overpowering the essence and being of the emotive attributes of** *Ḥesed* **(Kindness),** *Gevura* **(Restraint),** *Tiferet* **(Beauty) and so on, to the extent that they can transform them into holiness,**

---

13. This concept is discussed at length in various sources, particularly regarding the verse "You open Your hand and satisfy the desire of every living thing" (Ps. 145:16), which implies that a human has the capacity to fulfill this Godly task.

The ability for the essence of the intellectual faculties (even those of the vital soul) to become absorbed within holiness is a characteristic unique to them (namely, Ḥokhma, Bina, and Da'at). This absorption, occurring while the person studies Torah, renders holy these faculties themselves. By contrast, the emotive attributes of the vital soul of the *beinoni*, the intermediate-level person, such as love and fear, cannot undergo a fundamental change. Granted, there are certain instances, such as during a particularly devotional prayer experience, where these emotive attributes are inactive, posing no distractions. Perhaps they even provide support and serve as intermediaries for the attributes of the divine soul. Yet ultimately their essence cannot transform into holiness. The *beinoni*'s raw attributes of love and fear cannot be converted at their core into love and fear of God.

This distinction is largely a function of the nature of the animal soul. Since a person's inception, the emotions of his animal soul are drawn in very specific directions, tending from the outset to particular objects. When someone experiences feelings of attraction, he is by definition drawn to a particular object, something that already exists. Practically speaking, we are not endowed with the capability of experiencing generic emotions. Each emotion we experience is necessarily directed toward a particular thing or object: a desire for something or an aversion to it. Because the animal soul is, in a certain sense, the spiritual expression of the body, it is thus capable of expressing the body's objects of interest, its passions and desires. This is in stark contrast to the intellectual faculties. Ḥokhma, Bina, and Da'at are inherently undirected. Even in a situation where one consciously applies his intellectual faculty to a particular matter, the faculty of thought present here is not intrinsically linked with the object at which it is directed. Instead, it is an undirected power that can change its object almost effortlessly. Just as it is very difficult, almost impossible, to change the objects of one's desires (an aspect of one's emotions), so is it easy, nearly effortless, to change the direction and object of the intellect from one thing to another, from one direction of contemplation to a completely opposite one. ☞

THE MIND DOMINATES THE HEART

☞ As noted, our emotions and desires are directed toward clearly defined objects, while our intellectual faculties (e.g., thought and awareness) are essentially un-

הַיְינוּ מִשּׁוּם שֶׁהָרַע חָזָק יוֹתֵר בַּמִּדּוֹת מִבְּחָכְמָה בִּינָה דַּעַת, מִפְּנֵי יְנִיקָתָן שָׁם מֵהַקְּדוּשָּׁה יוֹתֵר, כַּיָּדוּעַ לְיוֹדְעֵי חֵן.

this is because evil is stronger in the emotive **attributes than** it is in *Ḥokhma, Bina,* and *Da'at,* as the *kelippot* there derive more nourishment from holiness, as is known to those initiated in the esoteric wisdom of Kabbala.

In his explanation of the deeper reason underlying the fundamental difference between the emotive attributes and intellectual faculties, the author of the *Tanya* hints at one of the core tenets of kabbalistic thought, namely, the shattering of the vessels in the world of *Tohu*. As he explains elsewhere, the shattering of the vessels is the cause of the admixture of good and evil within existence.

This cosmic event is described as having varying degrees of impact upon the *sefirot*. On a very basic level, the shattering of the vessels transpired within the lower seven *sefirot*, the emotive attributes, and not within the intellectual *sefirot* of Ḥokhma, Bina, and Da'at (or at least not to the same extent).[14] Thus, there is a greater presence of evil embedded in the emotive attributes than there is in the intellectual faculties. While it is true that the intellect can in fact choose to do things that are not good, it is not inherently bound to evil.

As explained above, the intellect is characterized by its objectivity; it is by nature not automatically defined or impacted by good and evil. The emotive attributes, by contrast, are characterized by their intrinsic directed. This distinction accounts for the *beinoni*'s ability, despite his inherent limitations, to function in a manner almost identical to the tzaddik. Although he cannot directly change his desires and the focus of his emotions, by mastering the focus of his *thoughts* he can control his desires, preventing them from being an operative force. It is impossible for a person to intentionally make even the slightest move without the involvement of his thoughts, which, as we have said, are capable of being dominated by man. Harnessing the power of thought, one can choose a path of action or non-action, of desire or non-desire. Through sheer willpower, a person can choose to think only holy thoughts, automatically preventing inappropriate desires from materializing.

---

14. See, for example, *Torah Or* 110d and 118c.

directionality and so are necessarily drawn toward either good or evil. Love, for example, does not exist in a vacuum. We cannot describe someone who is experiencing a feeling of love as loving nothing. He must love some *thing*, yet he can choose to direct his love toward good or toward evil.

It is therefore easier to effect a rectification in the intellect than in the emotive attributes. When a person studies Torah, he engages his intellect, which then becomes merged at its core with the Torah studied. Through this process, one's consciousness and the object of his consciousness become one entity. The intellect and subject matter meld into a unified whole, an essence formed of the person's innermost being and the Torah in which he engages.

The entire Torah is suffused with divine holiness. When one studies, for example, the verse "In the beginning, God created..." the holiness contained in those words penetrates the essence of his soul, resulting in a harmonious blend of Torah and soul. The knowledge of that verse, now merged with his soul's essence, is not a mere transient experience, but is seared forever in his memory. This person could in theory subsequently commit every sin in the world, but without focused, concentrated effort, his actions are powerless to excise from his being this newly formed entity. He can no longer erase the knowledge contained within those timeless words, "In the beginning, God created," as they have already penetrated to his core. ☞

INTELLECT AND ATTRIBUTES, GOOD AND EVIL

☞ It is important to note that this is no simple distinction, neither for the higher *sefirot* (as explained in kabbalistic literature) nor for the soul of man. For the truth is that even consciousness cannot be absolutely objective. Human consciousness is always accompanied by a certain degree of emotion, of the desire to resonate and bond with the object of one's awareness.

One of the explanations of the sin of the tree of knowledge is that Adam did not account for the fact that it is impossible to know something without having a relationship with that knowledge. Adam just wanted to observe the world of evil from the outside, and if he could have only seen it objectively, he would never have sinned. But the fact is that it is impossible to be a mere observer, to have the knowledge and awareness of something without becoming emotionally involved to some degree. The deeper one's awareness and knowledge, the more entangled one becomes (see *Torah Or* 5c).

זֹאת וְעוֹד אַחֶרֶת, וְהִיא הָעוֹלָה עַל כּוּלָנָה, בְּמַעֲלַת עֵסֶק תַּלְמוּד תּוֹרָה עַל כָּל הַמִּצְוֹת, עַל פִּי מַה שֶּׁכָּתוּב לְעֵיל בְּשֵׁם הַתִּיקוּנִים (תיקוני זהר, תיקון ל [עד, א]) דִּרְמַ"ח פִּיקוּדִין הֵן רְמַ"ח אֵבָרִים דְּמַלְכָּא.

There is an additional, far more important point pertaining to the advantage engaging in Torah study possesses over all other mitzvot, and it is **based on the above-mentioned statement** (chap. 23) from the *Tikkunei Zohar* (74a), **that the 248 positive mitzvot are the 248 limbs of the King** (God).

Thus far, two reasons have been provided in describing the superiority of Torah study over the other mitzvot. The first reason is that while engaged in Torah study, one activates one's soul's two innermost garments – thought and speech. The second reason given is that Torah study effectuates a core change in the soul's intellectual faculties (*Ḥokhma, Bina,* and *Da'at*). The author of the *Tanya* now presents a third, far more significant reason, surpassing the other two in importance.

This statement from the *Tikkunei Zohar* teaches that when a person fulfills one of the 248 positive mitzvot, he simultaneously functions as one of God's "limbs" within the world. When, for example, one gives charity, he in fact becomes the embodiment of God's hand, as it were, which provides the sustenance for all of existence. Every mitzva thus serves as the vehicle for the manifestation of God in the world. The person fulfilling the mitzva converts, so to speak, another portion of the world into a part, or "limb," of God.

וּכְמוֹ בָּאָדָם הַתַּחְתּוֹן דֶּרֶךְ מָשָׁל, אֵין עָרוֹךְ וְדִמְיוֹן כְּלָל בֵּין הַחַיּוּת שֶׁבִּרְמַ"ח אֵיבָרָיו לְגַבֵּי הַחַיּוּת שֶׁבַּמּוֹחִין, שֶׁהוּא הַשֵּׂכֶל הַמִּתְחַלֵּק לְג' בְּחִינוֹת: חָכְמָה בִּינָה דַּעַת,

Just as, for example, in the case of a mortal man, there is no comparison or similarity whatsoever between the life force animating his **248 limbs and the life force** vivifying **the brain, namely, the intellect, which is divided into the three faculties of** *Ḥokhma, Bina,* **and** *Da'at,*

The expression "mortal man" (literally, "the lower man") used in this analogy is contrasted here with "supernal man" (literally, "the higher man"), the latter being a supernal structure comprised of the "248 limbs of the King."

Even a "lowly" human being is sustained and animated by a life force that courses through his entire body, extending its reach to include the seemingly insignificant toenails as well. Despite this, there is without a doubt a vast distinction between the life force animating the brain and that which energizes the hands and feet, for example. This distinction is not merely quantitative, but is of an immeasurably qualitative nature.

Elsewhere[15] the author of the *Tanya* differentiates between "outer" and "inner" limbs. The outer limbs are calculated as totaling 248, while the inner limbs refer to the organs, such as the brain, heart, liver, etc. From the standpoint of *halakha*, the organs are not considered limbs and so are not included among the 248 limbs enumerated with regard to the laws of ritual impurity, for example.[16] Despite this distinction, the life force flowing through the inner limbs is regarded as a deeper, more impactful force in contrast to that vivifying the outer limbs.[17] In this sense, when comparing the mitzvot to the 248 limbs, Torah study parallels the brain. It follows that Torah study bears an aspect that both transcends and has the same force as all the other mitzvot combined.

Let us take this a step further by considering a view expressed by the author of the *Tanya* pertinent to the subject at hand. In several contexts,[18] the author suggests that there are two unrelated mitzvot pertaining to Torah. One is the mitzva to *study* Torah, which is fulfilled primarily through speech (that is, by articulating the words of the Torah subjects he studies). The other mitzva is to *know* and *understand* the Torah he studies. Knowing and understanding the Torah one studies is not necessarily synonymous with the act of studying Torah.

---

15. See, for example, *Likkutei Torah, Parashat Pekudei* 3c.
16. For the purposes of imparting ritual impurity, the *halakha* defines a limb as a part of the body that is comprised of flesh, sinew, and bone (see Mishna *Oholot* 1:8 and Rambam, *Sefer Tahara, Hilkhot Tumat Met* 2:7).
17. This accounts for the *halakha* which states that even a tiny perforation in one of these limbs renders an animal a *tereifa* (a halakhic status rendering an animal prohibited for consumption). See also Mishna *Arakhin* 5:2.
18. See, for example, *Likkutei Torah*, Lev. 5b.

A person can fulfill the mitzva of Torah study without knowing the Torah, that is, without understanding and knowing the meaning of what he has studied. Conversely, one can know Torah concepts he has studied previously without actively being engaged in Torah study at that moment.

Like any mitzva, the mitzva to study Torah must in some way bear a connection, however minimal it may be, to the physical world. This can come about only by its being enclothed within the 248 limbs. By contrast, the mitzva to *know* Torah is not enclothed in a physical garment, and so parallels the "inner limbs." Though distinct from the 248 outer limbs, the inner limbs are in fact those which the life force of the entire body is dependent upon. The mitzva to know Torah correlates not to the 248 limbs, but instead parallels the vitality of the soul that powers the body.

כָּכָה מַמָּשׁ דֶּרֶךְ מָשָׁל in literally the same manner, figuratively speaking –

This expression, repeated several times throughout the book,[19] seems to be self-contradictory. If it is "literally the same manner," it cannot simultaneously be "figuratively speaking," and vice versa. Yet, this apparent paradox can be resolved as follows: The basic function of an analogy is to compare two things for the purpose of clarification. In this context, the analogy used plays a more significant role. It functions as the medium by which the reader can literally grasp the true meaning and essence of the concept being presented. The essential bond between the limbs of the body and those of the soul is as true in this world as it is on every plane of existence, including those in the higher worlds. Having said that, it is crucial to remember that when dealing with the higher worlds, we are not dealing with physical limbs, but with entirely different entities. It is in this regard that the analogy presented is to be taken in only a figurative sense.

---

19. See, for example, chap. 21 and the commentary there.

לְהַבְדִּיל בְּרִבְבוֹת הַבְדָּלוֹת לְאֵין קֵץ, בְּהֶאָרַת אוֹר אֵין סוֹף בָּרוּךְ הוּא הַמִּתְלַבֵּשׁוּת בְּמִצְוֹת מַעֲשִׂיּוֹת לְגַבֵּי הֶאָרַת אוֹר אֵין סוֹף שֶׁבִּבְחִינוֹת חָכְמָה בִּינָה דַּעַת שֶׁבְּחָכְמַת הַתּוֹרָה, אִישׁ אִישׁ כְּפִי שִׂכְלוֹ וְהַשָּׂגָתוֹ.	though **removed by untold degrees of separation** – is it **with regard to the radiance of the light of** *Ein Sof*, **blessed be He, clothed in action-based mitzvot, compared to the radiance of the light of** *Ein Sof* **clothed in the faculties of** *Ḥokhma, Bina,* **and** *Da'at* of a person immersed **in the wisdom of the Torah, each person** receiving an illumination **commensurate with** what he understood using **his intellect and** according to **his mental grasp.**

The radiance of the light of *Ein Sof* shining upon one who fulfills an action-based mitzva pales in comparison to that which shines upon one who grasps any facet of Torah, no matter how meager his level of comprehension, provided he devoted his every fiber of being and intellect toward that cause. These two levels of illumination are simply beyond comparison.

If the mitzvot are the limbs of God, the Torah is His wisdom. The brain of the greatest fool contains a greater degree of life force than that in the hand of the wisest person. By the same token, a person who is capable of a mere rudimentary grasp of Torah still merits an illumination immeasurably greater than that attained through the fulfillment of mitzvot.

וְאַף שֶׁאֵינוֹ מַשִּׂיג אֶלָּא בְּגַשְׁמִיּוּת,	**Although one grasps** the Torah **only in physical terms,**

It was mentioned above that when a person grasps an aspect of Torah he is essentially grasping the wisdom of God. The Torah as we have it, however, is couched in physical terms, such as the *halakhot* pertaining to an ox that gores a cow and fringes on four-cornered garments. It would seem then that the Torah we grasp – described as the veritable wisdom of God – is ostensibly meager in nature, limited to the physical realm.

הֲרֵי הַתּוֹרָה נִמְשְׁלָה לְמַיִם שֶׁיּוֹרְדִים מִמָּקוֹם גָּבוֹהַּ כו', כְּמוֹ שֶׁנִּתְבָּאֵר לְעֵיל, **yet** it is known that **Torah is compared to water, which descends from a high place** to a low place, **as explained above** (chap. 4),

This analogy is meant to convey that although the Torah we study and understand as it is manifest in our lowly world deals primarily with the physical, it is nevertheless the very same Torah emanating from the highest supernal levels. Like the downward flowing nature of water, so does Torah "flow" downward into this lowly world. Though we may not understand the Torah the way God does, or even the way the angels do, the Torah we *do* grasp is nevertheless also regarded as Torah and divine wisdom, truly and fully.

The lengthy discussion of Torah study presented thus far was a tangential excursus deviating from the main thrust of this chapter, a theme to which the author of the *Tanya* now returns.

29 Adar וְאַף עַל פִּי כֵן אָמְרוּ רַבּוֹתֵינוּ ז"ל: "לֹא הַמִּדְרָשׁ עִיקָּר אֶלָּא הַמַּעֲשֶׂה" (אבות פרק א משנה יז), **yet even so, our Rabbis stated, "The main thing is not the study** of Torah, **but rather the action"** (Mishna *Avot* 1:17),

After describing the Torah's virtues, the author of the *Tanya* revisits the point he made earlier in the chapter, emphasizing that the study of Torah is not of paramount importance, but rather the physical actions involved in the performance of the mitzvot.

TORAH AND WATER

Let us illustrate the concept that the Torah we study is also considered divine wisdom by considering a mathematical equation. Equations can be understood at varying levels of depth, ranging from the most basic to the most complex and abstract. For example, one can determine that $3^2 + 4^2 = 5^2$. Yet because one arrived at this conclusion experimentally, one's understanding of this equation is quite rudimentary. There may perhaps be those with a more advanced level of understanding, such as the ancient Egyptians, who were aware that a 3-4-5 ratio yields a right triangle, yet they did not have an understanding of the Pythagorean theorem. Even one who is aware of the Pythagorean theorem may not grasp its mathematical proofs and implications. Despite their rather basic level of understanding, the knowledge to which they were privy was indeed true in every sense of the word.

When we understand a particular facet of the *halakhot* pertaining to an ox

וְ"הַיּוֹם לַעֲשׂוֹתָם" כְּתִיב (דברים ז, יא). and it is written, "You shall observe the commandment, and the statutes, and the ordinances tha I command you **today, to perform them**" (Deut. 7:11).

The author of the *Tanya* stresses the phrases "today" and "to perform them." "Today" implies the realm of time, or the temporality inherent in a day; it connotes this physical world, which is defined by time and space. The phrase "to *perform* them," implies an action performed with one's physical body and not merely divine service limited to the intellectual and emotional faculties of the soul.

וּמְבַטְּלִין תַּלְמוּד תּוֹרָה לְקִיּוּם מִצְוָה מַעֲשִׂיִּית כְּשֶׁאִי אֶפְשָׁר לַעֲשׂוֹתָהּ עַל יְדֵי אֲחֵרִים, **Furthermore**, the *halakha* dictates that we are required to **interrupt Torah study to fulfill an action-based mitzva when it cannot be done by others**,

There are two instances where an action-based mitzva cannot be fulfilled by one person in another's stead. The first instance is one involving a mitzva done with one's body, such as prayer or *tefillin*, in which case person A cannot practically discharge the obligation incumbent upon person B. The second instance involves a situation where a mitzva must be performed, such as giving charity or tending to a dead body, yet there is no one else in the vicinity at that particular time who can do so. The *halakha* states that when a person is confronted with

goring a cow, we gain a certain degree of true knowledge. Although this knowledge exists on a profoundly low plane in the grander cosmic scheme, it is nevertheless just as much a true knowledge of Torah as is attained in the most supernal spheres of existence. The fact that we are not able to uncover the loftiest levels of truth is certainly unfortunate, but that does not negate the fact that our knowledge of Torah is indeed true and complete. It is possible, in fact, that our grasp of Torah is in a certain sense superior to that of the higher beings, for we possess a true and profound understanding of the physical world.

In any event, the point the author of the *Tanya* is stressing here is that Torah study at any level is still regarded as the study of God's Torah. Even if the subject matter reveals the most infinitesimal facet of the Torah's vastness, and even if the Torah we study is almost laughable relative to the Torah studied in the study halls of Heaven, that does not change the fact that the Torah in which we engage in the physical world and that studied on high are both one true Torah.

one of these two scenarios, he cannot excuse himself from fulfilling that particular mitzva on account of his current involvement in Torah study.[20] Granted, Torah study is equivalent to all the mitzvot combined, and so he is liable to think that he should not fulfill the mitzva in question. Nevertheless, *halakha* teaches that he is in fact required to interrupt his studies to do so.

The unique advantage of Torah study over the performance of another mitzva is relevant only in a situation where the mitzva in question will be performed by someone other than the one engaged in study. Yet the moment there is no one else to fulfill the other mitzva (and it cannot be delayed until some later time), the obligation to physically fulfill this mitzva overrides the otherwise superior mitzva of Torah study.

As will be explained, the purpose of the Torah is, in a certain sense, the practical fulfillment of the mitzvot, as the Sages taught, "The objective of Torah wisdom is to achieve repentance and good deeds" (*Berakhot* 17a). One who shirks this duty has effectively studied Torah not with the intention to fulfill that which he has studied; regarding him the Talmud states that "it would have been better for him had his placenta overturned [in the womb], thus preventing him from emerging into the world" (Jerusalem Talmud, *Berakhot* 1:2).[21]

מִשּׁוּם "כִּי זֶה כָּל הָאָדָם" (קהלת יב, יג), וְתַכְלִית בְּרִיאָתוֹ וִירִידָתוֹ לָעוֹלָם הַזֶּה, לִהְיוֹת לוֹ יִתְבָּרֵךְ דִּירָה בַּתַּחְתּוֹנִים דַּוְקָא, for "this is the entire purpose of man" (Eccles. 12:13) **and the purpose for which he was created and for which his soul descended into this world, namely, so that God has an abode specifically in the lower worlds,**

As mentioned previously,[22] the purpose of creation and of man's divine service is to fashion an abode for God specifically in the lower worlds. It follows that the more profound the descent, the lower and more material the world, the greater is that world's ascent to its original intended purpose.

---

20. *Mo'ed Katan* 9b; Rambam, *Sefer HaMadda, Hilkhot Talmud Torah* 3:4. See also *Hilkhot Talmud Torah* 4:3 of the author of the *Tanya*.
21. See the author of the *Tanya*'s *Hilkhot Talmud Torah*, chap. 4.
22. *Midrash Tanḥuma, Naso* 15 and elsewhere. See also the beginning of chap. 36 above.

לְאַהֲפָּכָא חֲשׁוֹכָא לִנְהוֹרָא, "וְיִמָּלֵא כְבוֹד ה' אֶת כָּל הָאָרֶץ" (במדבר יד, כא), הַגַּשְׁמִית דַּיְיקָא,

and **to transform darkness into light,** thus fulfilling the verse "The entire earth shall be filled with the glory of the Lord" (Num. 14:21), that is, **specifically the physical** earth.

Man's purpose in this physical realm is to transform the darkness of the world into light, thereby creating an abode for God. The term "earth" implies physicality. The verse therefore emphasizes that man's divine service is meant to create an abode for God in this *physical* world, and not merely on some abstract spiritual plane.

"וְרָאוּ כָל בָּשָׂר יַחְדָּו" (ישעיה מ, ה), כַּנִּזְכָּר לְעֵיל.

Then "the glory of the Lord will be revealed **and all flesh will see together...**" (Isa. 40:5), **as mentioned above** (chap. 36).

The prophet does not employ the seemingly more logical phrase "all people," but rather "all flesh," in order to stress the material aspect that characterizes man – a being of "*flesh* and blood." The purpose of creation is to reveal God's glory not only to the soul, but even to the flesh, the physical body. Thus, because action-based mitzvot are, by definition, performed with the physical body (the "flesh") and within the material world, they in particular bring to fruition the purpose of creation – an abode for God. This demonstrates their superiority to Torah study, provided the mitzvot cannot be performed by others, as mentioned above.

מַה שֶּׁאֵין כֵּן כְּשֶׁאֶפְשָׁר לַעֲשׂוֹתָהּ עַל יְדֵי אֲחֵרִים – אֵין מְבַטְּלִין תַּלְמוּד תּוֹרָה (רמב"ם הלכות תלמוד תורה פ"ד ה"ב) אַף שֶׁכָּל הַתּוֹרָה אֵינָהּ אֶלָּא פֵּירוּשׁ הַמִּצְוֹת מַעֲשִׂיּוֹת.

This is not so, however, **when the** mitzva **can be performed by others.** In that case, **we do not interrupt the study of Torah** (Rambam, *Sefer HaMadda, Hilkhot Talmud Torah* 4:2), **even though the entire Torah is only an explanation of the action-based mitzvot.**

Seemingly, the entire Torah is a guidebook instructing us how to fulfill the mitzvot. This certainly appears to be true with regard to the aspects of Torah discussing the practical application of action-based mitzvot. Yet even the more abstract areas of Torah can be perceived as serving as a guide to, and elaboration upon, the mitzvot of faith in God and love of Him.

This being the case, why is it that when a mitzva can be performed by someone else, the *halakha* dictates that one who is engaged in Torah study should continue his study session uninterrupted? It seems counterintuitive that one studying tractate *Sukka* – a mere guide on how to build a *sukka* – should not interrupt his studies and build one himself! Why is it that where there are others available to build one in his stead, he is absolved of this responsibility?

The author of the *Tanya* proceeds to resolve this question:

וְהַיְינוּ מִשּׁוּם שֶׁהִיא בְּחִינַת חָכְמָה בִּינָה דַּעַת שֶׁל אֵין סוֹף בָּרוּךְ הוּא, וּבְעָסְקוֹ בָּהּ מַמְשִׁיךְ עָלָיו אוֹר אֵין סוֹף בָּרוּךְ הוּא בְּיֶתֶר שְׂאֵת וְהֶאָרָה גְּדוֹלָה לְאֵין קֵץ מֵהֶאָרָה וְהַמְשָׁכָה עַל יְדֵי פִּקּוּדִין, שֶׁהֵן אֵבָרִים דְּמַלְכָּא.

This is because the Torah **is the level of** *Ḥokhma*, *Bina*, **and** *Da'at* **of** *Ein Sof*, **blessed be He. Therefore, when one occupies himself with it, he draws down upon himself a far greater intensity of the light of Ein Sof, blessed be He, an illumination infinitely greater than the illumination and influx effectuated by the mitzvot, which are** merely **the limbs of the King.**

One who engages in Torah study taps into the level of *Ḥokhma*, *Bina*, and *Da'at* of *Ein Sof*. This draws down a radiance infinitely more powerful than the influx generated by one who performs a mitzva. Relative to the inner level of *Ḥokhma*, *Bina*, and *Da'at*, the mitzvot are regarded as being on a more external level (symbolized by the limbs of the King).

וְזֶה שֶׁאָמַר רַב שֵׁשֶׁת: "חֲדַאי נַפְשַׁאי, לָךְ קְרָאִי, לָךְ תְּנָאִי" (פסחים סח, ב), כְּמוֹ שֶׁנִּתְבָּאֵר בְּמָקוֹם אַחֵר בַּאֲרִיכוּת.

This is the meaning of Rav Sheshet's statement, "Rejoice my soul, for you I have read *Tanakh*, **for you I have studied** Mishna," **as explained elsewhere at length.**

The soul rejoices in the fulfillment of every mitzva, for through it one attains a oneness with God that transcends any degree of unity resulting from a mystical experience. This talmudic passage[23] demonstrates that the study of Torah generates an even greater sense of joy for the soul. For through this act and the holiness engendered thereby, the soul attains a far more profound oneness with God, felt by the person on both a conscious and tangible level.[24]

| וְהִנֵּה הַמְשָׁכָה וְהָאָרָה זוֹ שֶׁהָאָדָם מַמְשִׁיךְ וּמֵאִיר מֵהֶאָרַת אוֹר אֵין סוֹף בָּרוּךְ הוּא עַל נַפְשׁוֹ, וְעַל נַפְשׁוֹת כָּל יִשְׂרָאֵל, | **This influx and illumination from the radiance of the light of _Ein Sof_, blessed be He, that a person draws down and causes to illuminate upon his soul and upon all the souls of Israel,** | 1 Nisan |

The phrase "upon all the souls of Israel" is similar to that used in the textual formula many say before performing a mitzva: "For the sake of the unification of the Holy One, blessed is He, and His presence, *in the name of all of Israel*." It is proper to have this intent prior to performing every mitzva, to fulfill it "in the name of all of Israel" (see chap. 41 below). Yet whether a person has this intent or not, anything a member of Israel does is essentially "in the name of all Israel."

At its core, "all of Israel" is one body. All the limbs and organs of a living, physical body are interconnected and inextricably linked to one another, such that whatever one part of the body does, whether positive or negative, impacts the other parts. This is true of the people of Israel. The righteous deeds of a righteous person elevate all the other souls of Israel, and, by contrast, the evil acts perpetrated by an evil person drag them down.

| הִיא הַשְּׁכִינָה, כְּנֶסֶת יִשְׂרָאֵל, מְקוֹר כָּל נִשְׁמוֹת יִשְׂרָאֵל, כְּמוֹ שֶׁיִּתְבָּאֵר לְקַמָּן, | **which is** also known as **the Divine Presence, the congregation of Israel, and the source of all the souls of Israel,** as will be explained below (chap. 41), |

The Divine Presence is the reservoir of the souls of Israel. It encompasses all souls, regardless of their particular placement, appearance in

---

23. *Pesaḥim* 68b.
24. The Lubavitcher Rebbe, Rabbi Menaḥem Mendel Schneerson, suggests that the allusion mentioned here may refer to the author of the *Tanya*'s essay in *Torah Or*, the beginning of *Parashat Mishpatim*.

history, and unique characteristics. The Divine Presence is the source from which all souls emanate and to which they return. It is the ocean into which all rivers flow and from which they issue forth. It follows that when an individual person performs an act of divine service, he thereby draws down divine illumination not only upon his personal being but also upon the essence of the entire congregation of Israel, upon the Jewish nation as a whole.

עַל יְדֵי עֵסֶק הַתּוֹרָה, נִקְרֵאת בִּלְשׁוֹן קְרִיאָה, 'קוֹרֵא בַּתּוֹרָה', פֵּירוּשׁ: שֶׁעַל יְדֵי עֵסֶק הַתּוֹרָה קוֹרֵא לְהַקָּדוֹשׁ בָּרוּךְ הוּא לָבוֹא אֵלָיו כִּבְיָכוֹל, כְּאָדָם הַקּוֹרֵא לַחֲבֵירוֹ שֶׁיָּבֹא אֵלָיו,

and which is accomplished **through Torah study, is referred to as *keria*, as** in the expression *korei baTorah*. **The meaning** here **is that by engaging in Torah** study **one calls out to the Holy One, blessed be He, to come to him, as it were, like a person who calls to his friend to come to him,**

The Hebrew term *koreh* can mean either "to read" or "to call out." The word *koreh* in the phrase *koreh baTorah*[25] is typically understood in its first sense, in which case the phrase means "one who is reading [sections of] the Torah." In the present context, the author of the *Tanya* suggests a novel interpretation of the same phrase. He understands it in the *second* sense, namely, "to call out." According to this, the phrase now means "one who calls out by means of the Torah." The idea here is that Torah study is the means by which one calls out to God, as it were, in a manner similar to one who calls his friend's name to get his attention.

וּכְבֵן קָטָן הַקּוֹרֵא לְאָבִיו לָבֹא אֵלָיו לִהְיוֹת עִמּוֹ בְּצַוְותָּא חֲדָא וְלֹא לִיפָּרֵד מִמֶּנּוּ וְלִישָׁאֵר יְחִידִי חַס וְשָׁלוֹם.

or like a young child calls to his father to come to him and join him, and not to part from him, leaving him alone, God forbid.

The meaning of one who "reads the Torah" now takes on an emotional and poetic hue. In a world in which God is not revealed, a person is an isolated existence, and he feels like a child who finds himself alone in a vast and threatening world. What does such a child do? He calls

---

25. See, for example, *Berakhot* 13a.

his father to come and be with him. A person does not want to and cannot remain alone in the world, and therefore, he calls to his Father. How does he call Him? He "reads the Torah," that is, he calls out to God by means of his Torah study. Through the Torah, he creates the togetherness with his Father in Heaven.

וְזֶה שֶׁכָּתוּב: "קָרוֹב ה' לְכָל קוֹרְאָיו לְכֹל אֲשֶׁר יִקְרָאוּהוּ בֶאֱמֶת" (תהלים קמה, יח). וְאֵין אֱמֶת אֶלָּא תּוֹרָה. דְּהַיְנוּ, שֶׁקּוֹרֵא לְהַקָּדוֹשׁ בָּרוּךְ הוּא עַל יְדֵי הַתּוֹרָה דַּוְקָא, לְאַפּוּקֵי מִי שֶׁקּוֹרֵא אוֹתוֹ שֶׁלֹּא עַל יְדֵי עֵסֶק הַתּוֹרָה, אֶלָּא צוֹעֵק כָּךְ: 'אַבָּא! אַבָּא!'

This is the meaning of the verse "The Lord is close to all who call Him, to all who call Him with truth" (Ps. 145:18), **and there is no truth other than Torah. That is, he calls** out to God **specifically by means of the Torah. This is in contrast to one who calls out to Him not through engaging in Torah** study, **but merely shouts, "Father! Father!"**

Based on the context here, the verse from Psalms is understood to mean that God is near, i.e., draws close, to anyone who calls out to Him by means of "truth," which our Sages explain refers to Torah – the only real truth.[26] This is in contrast to one who calls out to God by merely crying: "Father! Father!" One who calls out in this manner is only expressing feelings and deep yearning, and although this too is a form of calling, it does not penetrate the outer edges of existence; its impact is, in a sense, limited. One who calls out through Torah, however, is heard on a cosmic level. The Torah is the name of God, and so through Torah study one taps into that divine essence, thus forming a connection to that which is beyond man's existence, to God Himself.

וּכְמוֹ שֶׁקּוֹבֵל עָלָיו הַנָּבִיא: "וְאֵין קוֹרֵא בְשִׁמְךָ" כו' (ישעיה סד, ו), וּכְמוֹ שֶׁמְּבוֹאָר בְּמָקוֹם אַחֵר.

About him the prophet bemoans, "There is no one calling Your name" (Isa. 64:6), **as explained elsewhere.**

The Torah is the name of God.[27] When a person studies Torah, he is calling out to God by His name. Yet when a person calls out to God

---

26. Jerusalem Talmud, *Rosh HaShana* 3:8; *Eikha Rabba* (Buber), introduction, 2.
27. See Ramban in his introduction to his commentary on the Torah.

not by name, but rather in a less intimate way, it cannot be said that he is "truly" calling out to God. It may be an expression of a person who *wants* to call out to God, which itself has value. Nevertheless, true calling is achieved by using the proper tool, the Torah, in order for the call to reach God, to be heard, and effectively draw down the divine influx.

Elsewhere,[28] the author of the *Tanya* addresses this idea from another angle. On the surface, the prophet's words "Ho, everyone thirsty, go to water!" (Is. 55:1) are strange. What benefit is there in telling a thirsty person to go to water? This is stating the obvious! Moreover, we encounter another difficulty in the following talmudic teaching. The Talmud states that the term "water" referenced in the above verse refers only to [the study of] Torah (*Bava Kamma* 17a). Why must the prophet tell one who wishes to study Torah to go and do so? That is obviously his course of action! Rather, the prophet's words must be understood thus: The phrase "Ho, everyone thirsty" refers not to one who thirsts for Torah, but to one who thirsts for God, while the following phrase, "go to water," refers to Torah. The lesson here is that a person who wishes to quench his soul's thirst for a true and enduring closeness to God – not merely a superficial, transient relationship – can do so only through the study of Torah.

וּמִזֶּה יִתְבּוֹנֵן הַמַּשְׂכִּיל לְהַמְשִׁיךְ עָלָיו יִרְאָה גְדוֹלָה בִּשְׁעַת עֵסֶק הַתּוֹרָה, כְּמוֹ שֶׁנִּתְבָּאֵר לְעֵיל [פֶּרֶק כ"ג].

The intelligent person should reflect upon this in order to draw down upon himself a great awe while engaged in Torah study, **as explained above (chap. 23).**

In his concluding remarks in the chapter, the author of the *Tanya* emphasizes the importance of contemplating these matters and the awe of God such reflection will generate.

One can treat the study of Torah as he does any other subject. He can study it as he does professional studies or as an intellectual pursuit, absent of any inner, emotional connection. In order to prevent this, a person must be aware of the import of his actions when studying Torah. He needs to consider the fact that his involvement in Torah study is

---

28. See chap. 40 below. See also the commentary to chap. 23 above.

essentially a call to God by His name, asking Him to come. In that moment, he is no longer alone, but rather standing before the King of kings, speaking and thinking together with God. In these moments, both his words and thoughts are united and fused with those of God, forming a unified whole. When a person is aware of all this, he will certainly feel a sense of "tremendous awe," the appropriate feeling when studying Torah.

The previous chapter discussed the purpose of the creation of this world, which is to provide God with an abode in this lower world. Put differently, God wishes to manifest His light specifically within this physical world. It was explained that this purpose will be fully realized in the redemptive period of the Messiah and during the resurrection of the dead.

This chapter dealt with the divine service incumbent upon man throughout the duration of the current exile that is needed to bring this cosmic goal to fruition. As was explained, the complete redemption in the future and the divine revelations that will occur at that time hinge on the service of each and every Jew through the study of Torah and fulfillment of its mitzvot. This service is meant specifically for this physical world, since the reward for a mitzva (and the positive spiritual impact it has upon all of existence) is solely through the performance of a mitzva itself, which can be accomplished only in this world.

It was likewise taught that the overall purpose of this service is to elevate the totality of *kelippat noga*, which is the totality of the life force of this world, to a state of holiness. We are able to accomplish a feat of such immense proportions because the Jewish people as an organic whole parallels the totality of the world's sustaining life force, each of us connected to, and impacting, a different part of the physical world. Each individual is charged with elevating the food he eats, the clothes he wears, and anything else used for his general needs, to the realm of holiness.

Based on this, we were able to understand the unique status given to the mitzva of charity, described as bringing the redemption closer, and as equal to all the mitzvot combined. It was explained that because this mitzva involves a plethora of elements, a greater portion of both this world and a person's animal soul is elevated to holiness.

In the final section of this chapter, the author of the Tanya elaborated upon the distinction between the mitzvot of charity and Torah study, both of which are respectively described as being equivalent to all the other mitzvot combined. The chapter concluded by describing the profound power inherent in the study of Torah, which, as the author explains, is a means through which one calls out to God by name, as it were, asking that He literally remain close by – specifically in this physical world.

Chapter 38

THE PREVIOUS CHAPTERS (35–37) DEALT WITH THE importance of the action-related aspect of the mitzvot, the actions of the physical body specifically within the material world. This chapter initially summarizes this issue in the context of *halakha*. The author of the *Tanya* then transitions to discuss the other aspect involved in performing mitzvot: the spiritual intent one should have when fulfilling a mitzva, engaging in Torah study, or while praying.

וְהִנֵּה עִם כָּל הַנִּזְכָּר לְעֵיל יוּבַן הֵיטֵב פְּסַק הַהֲלָכָה הָעֲרוּכָה בַּתַּלְמוּד וּפוֹסְקִים, דְּהִרְהוּר לָאו כְּדִבּוּר דָּמֵי,

In light of all that has been said above, one can now **thoroughly understand the** *halakha* **set forth in the Talmud** and codified **by the halakhic authorities,** namely, **that mere thought is not considered speech,**

2 Nisan
21 Adar II
(leap year)

We learned in chapter 35 (and onward) that the primary spiritual work of man through Torah and mitzvot, in efforts to repair human existence and the world at large, is specifically through physical action. This explains the *halakha*[1] which states that thought alone is not tantamount to actual speech. Thus, with regard to any mitzva requiring speech, be it Torah study or prayer, one is not regarded as fulfilling his obligation by merely thinking the words. Rather, he must actually utter the words, as the lip movement involved is deemed an action.

---

1. See *Berakhot* 20b and Tur and *Shulḥan Arukh, Oraḥ Ḥayyim* 62, 185. See also the author of the *Tanya*'s *Hilkhot Talmud Torah* 2:10.

וְאִם קָרָא קְרִיאַת שְׁמַע בְּמַחֲשַׁבְתּוֹ וּבְלִבּוֹ לְבַד, בְּכָל כֹּחַ כַּוָּנָתוֹ – לֹא יָצָא יְדֵי חוֹבָתוֹ, וְצָרִיךְ לַחֲזוֹר וְלִקְרוֹת.

and, therefore, **if one recited the** *Shema* **solely in his thoughts and heart,** even if he does so **with the full power of his concentration, he has not fulfilled his duty, and he must go back and recite** it verbally.

One who wishes to fulfill the mitzva of "You shall *speak* of them" (Deut. 6:7) by reciting the *Shema* does so only if he physically articulates the words. Merely thinking the words – even with his full focus and concentration – does not accomplish this goal.

וְכֵן בְּבִרְכַּת הַמָּזוֹן דְּאוֹרַיְיתָא, וּבִשְׁאָר בְּרָכוֹת דְּרַבָּנָן, וּבִתְפִלָּה.

Similarly, thought alone is not sufficient **with regard to the biblical mitzva of Grace after Meals, as well as other rabbinically ordained blessings, and prayer.**

Even mitzvot that are chiefly fulfilled with a person's intention are nevertheless not fulfilled through his intent and thought alone, but only through speech (regarded as an action, as mentioned above).[2]

וְאִם הוֹצִיא בִּשְׂפָתָיו וְלֹא כִּוֵּן לִבּוֹ – יָצָא יְדֵי חוֹבָתוֹ בְּדִיעֲבַד וְאֵין צָרִיךְ לַחֲזוֹר,

By contrast, **if one articulated the words with his lips, yet did not concentrate with his heart, he has** nevertheless **fulfilled his duty,** albeit **in a less than optimal manner, and is not required to go back** and repeat them with concentration,

Even if one spoke the words he is obligated to say by rote and without any intent, although this is not the optimal way to recite the *Shema*

---

2. The Lubavitcher Rebbe, Rabbi Menaḥem Mendel Schneerson, points out that the requirement to articulate the words of Grace after Meals applies even though the injunction to "speak of them" is not written in its regard. He also notes that prayer requires actual speech despite its being described as the "service of the heart."

and prayers, and intent should accompany speaking, he has at any rate fulfilled his obligation.

לְבַד מִפָּסוּק רִאשׁוֹן שֶׁל קְרִיאַת שְׁמַע וּבְרָכָה רִאשׁוֹנָה שֶׁל תְּפִלַּת שְׁמוֹנֶה עֶשְׂרֵה, וְכִדְאִיתָא [בְּרֵישׁ פֶּרֶק ב' דִּבְרָכוֹת (יג, ב)]: "עַד כָּאן מִצְוַת כַּוָּנָה מִכָּאן וָאֵילָךְ מִצְוַת קְרִיאָה" וְכוּ'.

except for the first verse of the *Shema* and the first blessing of the *Amida*, **the prayer of eighteen** blessings, **as is stated** (at the beginning of the second chapter of *Berakhot* [13b]), **"To this point, there is the mitzva of intent; from here on,** there is only **the mitzva of recitation,"** and so forth.

These are two instances where the intent to understand the words being recited is a critical requirement, without which the mitzva is not fulfilled. The quote from the Talmud, with regard to the *Shema*, teaches that up to the end of the first verse of *Shema*, intention is a critical factor (in addition to reciting the words). From that point on, although ideally one should have intent, only the recitation is the critical factor, and after the fact, one who has lacked intent has still fulfilled his obligation.

It follows that even with regard to mitzvot that primarily relate to the mind and heart, such as the recitation of the *Shema* and prayer in general, a person does not fulfill his obligation with mind and heart alone, with thoughts and feelings, without action. Conversely, even if he completely lacked inner intent, he still fulfills the mitzva with his spoken words, and is not required to go back and perform it again with words and intent together.

וְהַיְינוּ מִשּׁוּם שֶׁהַנְּשָׁמָה אֵינָהּ צְרִיכָה תִּיקּוּן לְעַצְמָהּ בְּמִצְוֹת,

This is because the divine **soul does not need to repair itself through mitzvot,**

The theoretical basis for this in *halakha* is that the spirit does not need repair for itself through mitzvot.[3] The underlying intent of a

---

3. See chap. 37; *Etz Ḥayyim* 26:1. See the essay of the Tzemaḥ Tzedek printed at the end of *Torah Or*.

commandment is the service of the soul in loving and fearing God, and this service takes place within the soul. However, intrinsically the soul does not need this service, and does not need to perform exercises to practice and progress in these areas.

רַק לְהַמְשִׁיךְ אוֹר לְתַקֵּן נֶפֶשׁ הַחִיּוּנִית וְהַגּוּף, עַל יְדֵי אוֹתִיּוֹת הַדִּבּוּר שֶׁהַנֶּפֶשׁ מְדַבֶּרֶת בָּהּ׳ מוֹצָאוֹת הַפֶּה, וְכֵן בְּמִצְוֹת מַעֲשִׂיּוֹת שֶׁהַנֶּפֶשׁ עוֹשָׂה בִּשְׁאָר אֶבְרֵי הַגּוּף.

but is **solely** meant **to draw down light to repair the vital soul and the body.** This is accomplished **by means of the letters of speech uttered by the soul, using the five organs of articulation, and through action-related mitzvot that the soul performs using the other limbs of the body.**

The divine light that the soul draws down through its service is intended for the body. This light is successfully drawn down into the body when the soul utilizes the latter for holy pursuits, such as holy speech and mitzvot. The soul utilizes the five organs of articulation – the throat, palate, tongue, teeth, and lips – to create physical speech, and animates them.

The purpose of a mitzva in repairing the world is fulfilled specifically when the person executing the mitzva performs an action with his body. Therefore, when a mitzva is not performed through action, it is not truly a mitzva. As was stated, the purpose of mitzvot and of man is to bring divine light into the lower world. The more the mitzva descends into the physical realm, the more it fulfills its purpose and perfects itself. In the upper, spiritual worlds, there is only a very limited expression of a mitzva, an illumination or a spark of its being. Only in the lower, material world can a mitzva be fully manifest. ☞ ☞

ACTION VERSUS INTENT

☞ The spiritual aspects of a mitzva are not important in this context, not because they are worthless, but because the purpose of man in this world is different. Imagine, for example, a person who is responsible for tending a garden. If he only contemplates the plant life, thinking positive thoughts about them, this may be nice for his soul, but the plants need him to fulfill his gardening duties of hoeing, weeding, watering, and so forth. A person's purpose in existence is bound to the material world,

אַךְ אַף עַל פִּי כֵן, אָמְרוּ: תְּפִלָּה אוֹ שְׁאָר בְּרָכָה בְּלֹא כַּוָּונָה הֵן כְּגוּף בְּלֹא נְשָׁמָה.	Nevertheless, it has been said that prayer or any other blessing without intent is like a body without a soul,	22 Adar II (leap year)

That is, despite the crucial role the act of a mitzva plays, as has been explained, nevertheless, it is known that any prayer or blessing uttered without intent is like a disembodied soul.[4]

פֵּירוּשׁ, כִּי כְּמוֹ שֶׁכָּל הַבְּרוּאִים שֶׁבָּעוֹלָם הַזֶּה שֶׁיֵּשׁ לָהֶם גּוּף וּנְשָׁמָה,	meaning, just as all created beings in this world possess a body and soul, i.e., life force,

an environment with which the pure soul, ethereal and sublime, has no direct connection. Spiritual achievements – intent, holy thoughts, and deep feelings – despite being significant and consequential, serve only as scaffolding, not as the building itself. They are tools used to assist one in his divine service, but they are not the service itself. At the end of the day, man's spiritual work takes places specifically in the physical realm.

THE ROLE OF "ACTION" IN HASIDISM

☞ It is somewhat surprising to find a formal approach like this in a hasidic work. It is surprising because a number of scholars researching Hasidism present the opposite perspective, claiming that the essence of Hasidism is actually a protest against formalism. They portray Hasidism as emphasizing the need to put the "soul," that is, spirituality, back into the performance of mitzvot and Torah study. Yet, as will be further explained in this chapter, the approach presented here, stressing the importance of action, is in no way meant to diminish the value of the spiritual ("soul") element. On the contrary, the main thrust of this book revolves specifically around the idea of "in your heart to perform it." Rather, it is essential to clearly define the relationship between these two elements – between the intent one has when fulfilling a mitzva and the physical act of performing it. This relationship, as will be explained, accounts for the emphasis placed at the beginning of this chapter on the performance of a mitzva using one's body and the material world, while simultaneously explaining the continuation of this chapter and the chapters to follow that deal with the significance of the soul's part in divine service, expressed by one's heartfelt intentions when performing a mitzva.

---

4. See *Ḥovot HaLevavot, Sha'ar* 8 (*Ḥeshbon HaNefesh*), chapter 3, s.v. "*vehateshi'i.*" See also Abarbanel in his *Yeshuot Meshiḥo* (Ashkelon edition, 5779) p. 40, and his commentary on *Avot* 2:13; *Midrash Shmuel* on *Avot* 2:15; *Shenei Luḥot HaBerit* on tractate *Tamid, Ner Mitzva*, 10.

In order to explain this statement, it is first necessary to elucidate the analogy and its meaning, and how the body and soul, concepts borrowed from man's existence, align with the ideas of prayer and intent.

As will be explained in the continuation of this chapter,[5] all creations in the world, of all types and levels, are formed of two components, material and form, vessel and light. Regarding man, these two components are the body and the soul.

שֶׁהֵם "נֶפֶשׁ כָּל חַי וְרוּחַ כָּל בְּשַׂר אִישׁ" (איוב יב, י) וְ"נִשְׁמַת כֹּל אֲשֶׁר רוּחַ חַיִּים בְּאַפָּיו" מִכָּל בַּעֲלֵי חַיִּים,   namely, "the soul [*nefesh*] of every living thing, and the breath [*ruaḥ*] of all mankind" (Job 12:10), and "the spirit [*neshama*] of all in whose nostrils there is the breath of life" (see Gen. 7:22) **among all living creatures,**

The terms *nefesh*, *ruaḥ*, and *neshama* represent different levels of man's soul. Like in man (who is a veritable microcosm), these levels constitute the different degrees of the divine life force that continuously vivifies and animates all respective elements within existence.[6]

וַה' מְחַיֶּה אֶת כֻּלָּם,   **all of which God animates** (see Neh. 9:6),

The various levels of life all derive solely from God. He animates them and pumps them with life force by connecting the body and soul – the very definition of life. The verse "The spirit of all in whose nostrils there is the breath of life" speaks of the life resulting from the body-soul blend, a combination inherent in all elements of creation. The verse "God animates them all" refers to His maintaining this body-soul bond. All beings require God's constant influence, an unceasing flow of divine energy, constantly animating them and preserving the life force contained within.

---

5. And at length in *Shaʿar HaYiḥud VeHaʾemuna*, chaps. 1, 7.
6. The Lubavitcher Rebbe, Rabbi Menaḥem Mendel Schneerson, points out that the verse "And the breath of all mankind (*ish*)" is not in fact referring to man (as the plain meaning indicates), for it concludes "among all living creatures." Rather, the term *ish* here is to be understood as it is used in the context of the cherubs: "Their faces of an *ish* to its brother" (Ex. 25:20), where the word is obviously not referring to a human being. Thus, the term *ish* indicates any sort of living creature.

CHAPTER 38

וּמְהַוֶּה אוֹתָם מֵאַיִן לְיֵשׁ תָּמִיד בָּאוֹר וְחַיּוּת שֶׁמַּשְׁפִּיעַ בָּהֶם, שֶׁגַּם הַגּוּף הַחוֹמְרִי וַאֲפִילּוּ אֲבָנִים וְעָפָר הַדּוֹמֵם מַמָּשׁ - יֵשׁ בּוֹ אוֹר וְחַיּוּת מִמֶּנּוּ יִתְבָּרֵךְ, שֶׁלֹּא יַחֲזוֹר לִהְיוֹת אַיִן וָאֶפֶס כְּשֶׁהָיָה,

perpetually bringing them into being from nothingness to existence, by the light and life force with which He infuses them, for even the physical body, and even completely inanimate stones and earth, contain a light and a life force emanating from God in order that they not revert to absolute nothingness as they initially were,

The life force that all creatures receive from God enables them to fulfill their unique purposes in the world. This life force also constitutes the essence of their existence, both spiritual and material, coming into being from absolute nothingness. This is in contrast to the analogy of the soul vivifying the body, for the latter exists independent of the soul.

The physical body of a person or animal, as well as plant life and even completely inanimate stones and earth, all contain a Godly light and life force that establishes their independent, physical existence, preventing their reverting back to a state of absolute nothingness.

This is the meaning of a "soul" of all things in the most general sense. This "soul" does not merely express itself in the life force that acts upon and courses through an entity (whether it be through growth or movement, as is the case with animals and plants). Rather, it is the very essence of the entity, which can come only from the power of constant divine influence flowing through it. As is explained in chapter 2 of *Sha'ar HaYiḥud VeHa'emuna*, the existence of something in the world is not a given, not nature. It is an ongoing marvel, the result of a process of continuous creation that vivifies and sustains everything anew each moment. This leads to the conclusion that the infinite source of life pulses constantly even within an inanimate object that seems to have no life at all.

וְאַף עַל פִּי כֵן, אֵין עֵרֶךְ וְדִמְיוֹן כְּלָל בֵּין בְּחִינַת אוֹר וְחַיּוּת הַמֵּאִיר בַּגּוּף לְגַבֵּי בְּחִינַת אוֹר וְחַיּוּת הַמֵּאִיר בַּנְּשָׁמָה, שֶׁהִיא נֶפֶשׁ כָּל חַי.

nevertheless, there is no comparison or similarity whatsoever between the quality of the light and life force that illuminates the body and the quality of the light and life force that illuminates the *neshama*, which is the soul of every living thing.

Although all things in existence, inanimate and animate, soul and body, contain divine light and life force, nevertheless, the light illuminating the body and that illuminating the *neshama* cannot be compared. The author of the *Tanya* points out that the term *neshama* he uses here refers to "the soul of every living thing." He distinguishes between the soul (*nefesh*), which allows for the "body" of an inanimate object to exist, and the "soul (*nefesh*) of every living thing," referring to the soul that animates the bodies of animals and human beings. The difference between the "soul" (*nefesh*) that shines in the body and soul which is the *neshama* within the body parallels the difference between the physical action of a mitzva and its spiritual intent. ☞

---

3 Nisan
23 Adar II
(leap year)

וְאַף שֶׁבִּשְׁנֵיהֶם אוֹר אֶחָד שָׁוֶה

True, within both of them the light is one and the same

The divine light that animates the body and the divine light that vivifies the soul are not two separate forces, but one force, the force of God, that vivifies the existence of man, body and soul together. On the most basic level, this is the divine force that allows for the existence of everything in our world: inanimate matter, plant life, animals and human beings, the physical and spiritual, as well as the ways that they relate to each other.

בִּבְחִינַת הֶסְתֵּר פָּנִים וּלְבוּשִׁים שָׁוִים, שֶׁהָאוֹר מִסְתַּתֵּר וּמִתְעַלֵּם וּמִתְלַבֵּשׁ בּוֹ,

vis-à-vis the concealed countenance and the garments in which the light conceals, hides, and enclothes itself in equal measure,

---

THE BODY AND *NESHAMA*

☞ The difference between these things is so vast that, as the author of the *Tanya* states, "There is no comparison or similarity between them whatsoever" – neither in terms of their respective value nor in terms of conceptual comparison. As is explained elsewhere (see, e.g., *Torah Or* 90b), the transition from the spiritual to the physical is not achieved through the process of devolution, of cause and effect, but rather in a manner that defies logic. In this sense, the spiritual reality does not explain and apprehend material reality, nor can the material explain or apprehend the spiritual, and so "there is no comparison or similarity whatsoever" between the two. Rabbi Shmuel Gronem Esterman adds that the philosophers also admit that the unfathomable jump from the spiritual realm to physical creation constitutes the greatest demonstration of "creation from nothingness," as the two are truly incomparable.

In the body, as in the soul, as in everything in our world, the divine light is revealed in its essential being not in a manner that enables us to see how God vivifies everything, but rather is hidden, referred to here as a "concealed countenance." Despite the disparity in the levels of existence, the divine essence is equally hidden in them all. We may see a difference in the light and in God's influence upon things, but the Divine itself is completely concealed in equal measure on all levels. ☞

CONCEALED, HIDDEN, ENCLOTHED

☞ These three terms are not arbitrary. The author of the *Tanya* uses them to convey the three-step process of the concealment of the divine light: It is first "concealed," then "hidden," and finally "enclothed." In the first stage, the light is concealed, that is, one knows it exists, but it cannot be seen. In the second stage, the light is hidden in the sense that its existence is no longer recognized or known. The final, most perplexing stage is when the divine energy is enclothed within materiality itself, when it becomes part of its own apparent concealment and hiddenness.

The Ba'al Shem Tov is said to have made the following observation regarding the verse "The enemy said: I will pursue, I will overtake, I will divide" (Ex. 15:9), where the letter *alef* appears at the beginning of each word. The letter *alef* is a reference to God, sometimes referred to as the *Aluf* (leader or master) of the world. The implication here is that the *alef*, the Master of the world, is present not only in the important events throughout history, such as the beginning of creation, or in the word *anokhi*, "I," with which the Ten Commandments open. But it is found even in the above-mentioned words of Pharaoh (see *Ba'al Shem Tov al HaTorah, Beshalah* 9–11).

The enclothing of the divine energy within concealment itself is the very thing that, in a certain sense, renders this concealment impenetrable. It inherently creates an impossibility of penetrating into its core to see the divine soul, the spark, the power of life in it. This is because once the divine light is hidden, it is no longer just invisible but is actually enclothed and assumes the outward appearance of something else.

In the first stage, when the divine light is only concealed, a person is still aware of its existence and that it is merely concealing its ability to be detected. In the second phase, when it is "hidden," it seems to have completely disappeared. There is a dread of darkness, a sense of meaninglessness to life, a fear that the very underpinnings of existence have unraveled. Yet though it appears that existence is deficient at its core, the very fact that a person can still sense this deficiency is indicative of a relationship that can ultimately be cultivated. In the third stage, however, when the divine light is enclothed, even this sense of deficiency, that there is a cosmic lack, is absent. On the contrary, in this stage the world appears so neatly structured, natural, logical, and independent that one cannot relate to anything beyond it.

The first stage is thus the stage of seeking out the Divine. The second stage is that of despair, and the third stage is that in which people see an entirely new edifice. This stage is the darkest and most

כִּי שְׁנֵיהֶם הֵם מֵעוֹלָם הַזֶּה, שֶׁבִּכְלָלוּתוֹ מִסְתַּתֵּר בְּשָׁוֶה הָאוֹר וְהַחַיּוּת שֶׁמֵּרוּחַ פִּיו יִתְבָּרֵךְ,

for they, the body and soul, **are both of this world, in whose totality the light and life force that are from the breath of His mouth are concealed in equal measure,**

God's countenance, or the innermost aspect of divine light, is concealed equally in both the soul and the body (which, without a soul, is incapable of thought or feeling). It is likewise concealed in equal measure in the soul of animal and man, just as it is in the soul of inanimate objects.

The concealment of the divine light (or "countenance") is an essential quality of the world in which both soul and body exist. It is the backdrop, the space that allows for their existence. The concept of a "world" (the world of *Atzilut* or *Beria*, etc.) is similar to that of a "field" (in the scientific sense) in which a certain law, a certain level of concealment of the countenance, exists. Accordingly, the concept of "world" describes a group of entities that share a common level of divine concealment and are therefore regarded as sharing the same plane of existence. In this sense, the degree of divine concealment in this world equally affects all the creations within it, and the distinctions between them are themselves a part of the nature of the world and the divine concealment.

בִּבְחִינַת הֶסְתֵּר פָּנִים וִירִידַת הַמַּדְרֵגוֹת בְּהִשְׁתַּלְשְׁלוּת הָעוֹלָמוֹת, מִמַּדְרֵגָה לְמַדְרֵגָה בְּצִמְצוּמִים רַבִּים וַעֲצוּמִים, עַד שֶׁנִּתְלַבֵּשׁ בִּקְלִיפַּת נֹגַהּ,

through the concealment of countenance and the gradational process of descent of the worlds, from one level to the next, by undergoing numerous and immense constrictions, until it is enclothed in *kelippat noga*, in

concealing, because the edifice people perceive is a mere illusion, dulling one's sense of despair and distracting him from feeling the need to seek out God. The point the author of the *Tanya* is emphasizing in detailing the stages of concealment is that God's light is equally concealed on all levels. This holds true for both the material elements of existence as well as the spiritual, for both the body and soul. The nature of concealment is the same for both; in the same way one's foot cannot see God, so is the soul incapable of doing so.

לְהַחֲיוֹת כְּלָלוּת עוֹלָם הַזֶּה הַחוּמְרִי, דְּהַיְינוּ, כָּל דְּבָרִים הַמּוּתָּרִים וְהַטְּהוֹרִים שֶׁבָּעוֹלָם הַזֶּה.	order to vivify **the totality of this material world,** that is, **all the permissible and pure things that are in this world.**

This material world, with its seemingly independent existence, hides the divine essence that creates and animates it. It receives its life force from, and is primarily comprised of, *kelippat noga*. This *kelippa* is a neutral realm comprising all elements that are intrinsically neither holy nor impure, neither a mitzva nor a prohibition. This neutral realm constitutes the essence of this material world, which contains all pure and permissible objects that can be used for human consumption or other needs. It is a world in which the Divine is hidden, which allows man to exercise his free will and choose whether to elevate those objects to the realm of holiness or pull them down to the realm of impurity, God forbid.

וּמִמֶּנָּה, וְעַל יָדָהּ, מוּשְׁפָּעִים דְּבָרִים הַטְּמֵאִים, כִּי הִיא בְּחִינָה מְמוּצַּעַת, כַּנִּזְכָּר לְעֵיל.	Furthermore, all **impure things** in this world **derive** their **sustenance** both **from and through it, for it,** *kelippat noga,* **acts as an intermediary, as mentioned above** (chaps. 7 and 37).

All elements in the world that are from the three completely impure *kelippot* and are thus forbidden and impure derive their life-giving sustenance from *kelippat noga*. As stated previously, *kelippat noga* is a neutral realm that interfaces between holiness (the source of all life and existence) and impurity, i.e., the three impure *kelippot*, which are inherently lifeless. *Kelippat noga* is the realm where man's choice decides the fate of any given object – either for good or for evil. Thus, *kelippat noga* carries with it the power of life and death, depending on the realm for which it has been used. It is through this process that holiness sustains the impure *kelippot* and everything influenced by them.

אַף עַל פִּי כֵן, הָהֶאָרָה, שֶׁהִיא הַמְשָׁכַת הַחַיּוּת אֲשֶׁר ה' מֵאִיר	**Nevertheless, the** divine **illumination,** namely, **the drawing down**

וּמִחַיֶּה דֶּרֶךְ לְבוּשׁ זֶה, אֵינָהּ שָׁוָה בְּכוּלָן, **of** the life force that God radiates and with which He **grants life by means of this garment,** i.e., *kelippat noga*, **is not the same for all of them,**

The divine concealment within the natural world generated by *kelippat noga* equally incorporates all elements of creation – the living and the inanimate, the body and the soul – in the sense that they all see a world yet do not see the divine essence.[7] Despite this, the divine radiance that is revealed through this concealment, suffusing all creations with life, is not at all of equal measure. Within this world, there are different levels that, although not inherently distinct in terms of their essential awareness of the divine existence, are distinct in terms of their awareness of themselves.

בִּבְחִינַת צִמְצוּם וְהִתְפַּשְּׁטוּת. **in terms of** both **constriction and expansion.**

The difference in the levels of this world lies in the intensity of the divine illumination: whether it is constricted and limited or amplified. ☞

TWO KINDS OF RELATIONSHIPS

☞ There is a distinction here between two categories regarding the types of created beings in the world. From the perspective of an absolute value, such as good and evil, there is essentially no difference between levels, between the inanimate and man. However, there is another side, in which a human being (of whatever sort he may be) is superior to stones, grass, and insects. With regard to the constriction or spreading forth of the vivifying illumination, with regard to the strength of the power of life that is revealed in the illumination's content and scope, there is a recognizable difference between man, animal, plant life, and inanimate matter. These two categories are not at all on the same plane. Therefore, it is possible that an entire realm will be on one level in terms of value, but on completely different levels in terms of the constriction and spreading forth of the illumination of life force within it.

---

7. Hasidim point out that the Hebrew word *teva*, or "nature," is a cognate of the Hebrew word *tove'a*, meaning "drown," suggesting that God is submerged or drowned within the natural order of the world.

כִּי בַּגּוּף הַגַּשְׁמִי וְהַדּוֹמֵם מַמָּשׁ, כָּאֲבָנִים וְעָפָר, הָהָאָרָה הִיא בִּבְחִינַת צִמְצוּם גָּדוֹל אֲשֶׁר אֵין כָּמוֹהוּ, וְהַחַיּוּת שֶׁבּוֹ מוּעֶטֶת כָּל כָּךְ עַד שֶׁאֵין בּוֹ אֲפִילוּ כֹּחַ הַצּוֹמֵחַ,

For in the physical body and utterly inanimate objects, like stones and earth, the divine illumination is in a state of supreme constriction, entirely unparalleled in nature. The life force within it is so minimal that it lacks even the power of growth, _{4 Nisan / 24 Adar II (leap year)}

The life force suffusing inanimate objects is limited to the minimal amount necessary to maintain their existence, preventing them from simply disintegrating. This life force is of the most constricted nature possible – just enough to maintain their basic existence – yet not enough to provide for their growth or reproduction, for which a far greater amount is necessary, such as that which is found only in vegetation.

וּבַצּוֹמֵחַ הָהָאָרָה אֵינָהּ בְּצִמְצוּם גָּדוֹל כָּל כָּךְ.

whereas in vegetation, the light is not as greatly constricted.

The life force within vegetation is conveyed not only in the maintenance of the latter's existence, but in a vitality that goes beyond the limits of its intrinsic survival and is expressed in the elevation of its existence, and in its growth and reproduction.

וְדֶרֶךְ כְּלָל נֶחֱלָקוֹת לְאַרְבַּע מַדְרֵגוֹת: דּוֹמֵם, צוֹמֵחַ, חַי, מְדַבֵּר, כְּנֶגֶד ד' אוֹתִיּוֹת שֵׁם הֲוָיָ"ה בָּרוּךְ הוּא, שֶׁמִּמֶּנּוּ מוּשְׁפָּעִים.

In general, everything is divided into four categories: inanimate, vegetation, animal, and speaking, corresponding to the four letters of the name of *Havaya*, blessed be He, from which they receive their vitality.

The name of *Havaya* is the name of God that brings everything into being. In particular, each of the four categories of existence receives its life force from one of the four letters of the name of God. Inanimate creation is parallel to the last letter *heh* in the name *Havaya* (a letter which in the *sefirot* is the *sefira* of *Malkhut*; in the world it is the earth and inanimate matter; and in the soul it is speech; speech refers to letters, and as *Sefer Yetzira* explains, the letters are like stones and inanimate matter). Vegetation is parallel to the letter *vav* (in the *sefirot* this is the six attributes, which, like vegetation, grow and blossom). The category of animal is parallel to the first letter *heh* (in the *sefirot* it is *Bina*, or "Mother," the mother and source of the attributes, called Ḥaya, "life"). Finally, man is analogous to the letter *yod* (in the *sefirot*, the level of *Ḥokhma*, or "Father"; man is called *medaber*, literally, the speaking, as in the phrase "the Father establishes the daughter," meaning that it is specifically *Ḥokhma*, the Father, that is connected to the daughter, which is *Malkhut* and speech).[8]

וּכְמוֹ שֶׁאֵין עֶרֶךְ וְדִמְיוֹן הָהֶאָרָה וְהַמְשָׁכַת הַחַיּוּת שֶׁבַּדּוֹמֵם וְצוֹמֵחַ לְהֶאָרָה וְהַמְשָׁכַת הַחַיּוּת הַמְלוּבֶּשֶׁת בְּחַי וּמְדַבֵּר –

Just as there is no comparison or similarity between the illumination and the drawing down of the life force that is in inanimate objects and vegetation, and the illumination and the drawing down of the life force that is clothed in animals and man –

In vegetation, we see the life force causing growth beyond that of inanimate objects. In animals and man, we see a life force of an immeasurably greater and different nature. In animals and man, we see life at work: how they move and change, feel and think, etc.

אַף שֶׁבְּכוּלָן אוֹר אֶחָד שָׁוֶה בִּבְחִינַת הֶסְתֵּר פָּנִים, וּמְלוּבָּשׁ בִּלְבוּשׁ אֶחָד בְּכוּלָן, שֶׁהוּא לְבוּשׁ נֹגַהּ –

although all of them contain a light of equal measure in terms of the concealment of countenance, and all are clothed in one garb, namely, the garb of *kelippat noga* –

The light permeating all four categories is of equal measure in that its inner essence is hidden. The reality of our world – whether that of a person or of the chair upon which he sits – belongs to *kelippat*

---

8. See, for example, *Torah Or* 4a, and in the commentary of Rabbi Shmuel Gronem Esterman.

noga. Kelippat noga constitutes the totality of our world, the common denominator of its multitude of components. These components are therefore able to recognize each other, and thus utilize and live off of each other. Thus, despite the differences between these categories, between a person and the food he eats and the chair upon which he sits, a human being has the ability to sit on the inanimate chair and eat the food derived from vegetation.

Until this point, the author of the *Tanya* has spoken of the body and soul, using them as a metaphor. He will now proceed to discuss their underlying meaning, namely, the mitzva and intent.

כָּךְ אֵין עֵרֶךְ וְדִמְיוֹן כְּלָל בֵּין הֶאָרַת וְהַמְשָׁכַת אוֹר אֵין סוֹף בָּרוּךְ הוּא, שֶׁהוּא פְּנִימִיּוּת רְצוֹנוֹ יִתְבָּרֵךְ, בְּלִי הֶסְתֵּר פָּנִים וּלְבוּשׁ כְּלָל, הַמְּאִירָה וּמְלוּבֶּשֶׁת בְּמִצְוֹת מַעֲשִׂיּוֹת מַמָּשׁ. וְכֵן בְּמִצְוֹת הַתְּלוּיוֹת בְּדִבּוּר וּבִיטוּי שְׂפָתַיִם בְּלִי כַּוָּנָה, שֶׁהוּא נֶחְשָׁב כְּמַעֲשֶׂה מַמָּשׁ, כַּנִּזְכָּר לְעֵיל לְגַבֵּי הַהֶאָרָה וְהַמְשָׁכַת אוֹר אֵין סוֹף בָּרוּךְ הוּא הַמְּאִירָה וּמְלוּבֶּשֶׁת בְּכַוָּנַת הַמִּצְוֹת מַעֲשִׂיּוֹת,

so too, there is no comparison or similarity whatsoever between the illumination and drawing down of the light of *Ein Sof*, blessed be He, that is, the innermost aspect of God's will, without any concealed countenance or garment, which illuminates and is clothed in both physical, action-related mitzvot, as well as mitzvot that depend on speech and the expression of the lips that lack intent, which are considered actual actions, as stated above (chap. 37 and elsewhere). There is no comparison between this illumination and the illumination and drawing down of the light of *Ein Sof*, blessed be He, that illuminates and is clothed in the intent of action-related mitzvot,

As was explained in the analogy, the body and soul from *kelippat noga* are not differentiated from each other in terms of their value (that is, it cannot be said that one is more valuable than the other), but rather in terms of the intensity of the revelation of life within them. Just as in the realm of *kelippat noga*, so too in the realm of holiness; there is no difference in value between a mitzva act and its intent in terms of holiness. The divine holiness is equally present in both without any concealment of countenance. The difference between them is with regard to the quality and intensity of the illumination of holiness. In the act of a mitzva itself, although the illumination is holy, it is nevertheless revealed on a lower level, whereas the holy illumination in a mitzva performed with intent is far more intense. ☞

שֶׁהָאָדָם מִתְכַּוֵּין בַּעֲשִׂיָּיתָן, כְּדֵי לְדָבְקָה בּוֹ יִתְבָּרֵךְ עַל יְדֵי קִיּוּם רְצוֹנוֹ, שֶׁהוּא וּרְצוֹנוֹ אֶחָד. namely, the intent a person has when performing them. This intent is to cleave to God by fulfilling His will, since He and His will are one.

PLACE VALUE AND ORDER OF MAGNITUDE

☞ The distinction between these two types of evaluation is similar to the difference between the face value of numbers and their place value. For example, the numerals 1, 2, and 3 have face values that can be objectively compared, where one numeral is greater or less than the others. Having said that, a numeral's value can change depending on its position. A change in position affects the numeral's place value by order of magnitude.

In the decimal system, for example, the numeral 1 appears as 1, 10, 100, 1000, and so forth. Between 1 and 3 there is a qualitative difference (a difference in value). By contrast, the numbers 1, 10, and 100 are, in this sense, equal (as are 1 and -1), as they share the same fixed value. The difference between them is the direction and intensity of the value, which can be 1,000 or 1,000,000 times greater.

In this sense, the relationship between a sin, a mitzva, and a neutral action is like the relationship among absolute values. Each is its own unique entity, a world unto itself. There is a deed that is a mitzva and there is a deed that is a sin. A mitzva possesses the innate quality of a mitzva and is essentially connected to the realm of mitzva. A person who gives charity to a poor person performs a mitzva action, and no matter how he performs that action, it will have the value of a mitzva; it will exist upon the positive scale of mitzvot. At the same time, the intensity of the mitzva is not always uniform but is measured according to the underlying intent with which it was performed. The effort, the soul, that the person invested in attaining the money that he is giving to charity, how much he gives and how he gives, are taken into consideration. One can give charity with a sour expression or with a caring smile. In either case, the mitzva is a mitzva, and the coin is a coin. Yet there is a great difference in the level, and consequently in the intensity, with which the mitzva impacts all the worlds. In this way, through the power of intent, the mitzva of one's giving even a small coin to charity can accomplish more than the giving of a mountain of gold by someone else (see Rambam, *Sefer Zera'im, Hilkhot Matenot Aniyyim* 10:7–14).

CHAPTER 38

The essence of the intent required when performing an action-related mitzva is that through this particular act the person who has been commanded (*metzuveh*) to perform it will become attached to the Commander (*metzaveh*) of that mitzva, in a bond (*tzavta*) that is more real than any experiential bond (as explained previously in chap. 37).

וְכֵן בְּכַוָּונַת הַתְּפִלָּה וּקְרִיאַת שְׁמַע וּבִרְכוֹתֶיהָ וּשְׁאָר בְּרָכוֹת, שֶׁבְּכַוָּונָתוֹ בָּהֶן מְדַבֵּק מַחֲשַׁבְתּוֹ וְשִׂכְלוֹ בּוֹ יִתְבָּרֵךְ.

The same applies to intent in prayer, and the recitation of the *Shema* and its blessings, as well as in other blessings, that through one's intent regarding them, he attaches his thoughts and intellect to God.

The same applies to intent in prayer, and the recitation of the *Shema* and its blessings, and other blessings, which are the commandments that are dependent on speech and enunciation, that when [a person] has intent regarding them, he causes his thoughts and intellect to cleave to God.

The mitzvot mentioned here all involve speech and verbal articulation. When performing these mitzvot, a person's intent should be to focus on the meaning of the words he is saying. He is speaking to God, and so he must also think about God.

Intent in action and speech is accomplished by means of thought. Speech and action are the external garments of the soul, and not necessarily connected to the faculties of the soul. A person can speak and act in a way that is detached from his soul. This is not true regarding thought, which is the inner garment of the soul and which is always attached to and inseparable from the faculties of the soul. When a person not only performs a mitzva but thinks at that moment about the Commander, he attaches his soul to God. That is not to say that the thought itself is the intent. As will be explained further on, the soul of a mitzva is the love and fear of God. Rather, the thought, as the inner garment of the person's soul, arouses and brings along with itself love and fear.

וְלֹא שֶׁדְּבֵיקוּת הַמַּחֲשָׁבָה וְשֵׂכֶל הָאָדָם בּוֹ יִתְבָּרֵךְ הִיא מִצַּד עַצְמָהּ לְמַעֲלָה מִדְּבֵיקוּת קִיּוּם

This does not mean that the cleaving of a person's thoughts and intellect to God is intrinsically loftier than the

5 Nisan
25 Adar II
(leap year)

הַמִּצְוֹת מַעֲשִׂיּוֹת בְּפוֹעַל מַמָּשׁ, כְּמוֹ שֶׁיִּתְבָּאֵר לְקַמָּן. — cleaving achieved through **the actual fulfillment of action-related mitzvot, as will be explained below** (see *Iggeret HaKodesh*, epistle 29).

The cleaving of the faculties of a person's soul to God is certainly no greater than the cleaving that is achieved through the act of performing a mitzva. The attachment of a person's thought and intellect to God will reach as high as a person's strength will allow. Yet this necessarily means that it is limited, just as man is fundamentally limited. By contrast, the attachment to God achieved by performing mitzvot is not sourced in the person but rather in *Ein Sof*, in God Himself. God turns to man and says, "Do such and such." When a person does so, his attachment to God reaches far beyond his own abilities and his very self; it is an attachment that transcends all limitations.

אֶלָּא מִפְּנֵי שֶׁזֶּהוּ גַּם כֵּן רְצוֹנוֹ יִתְבָּרֵךְ, לְדָבְקָה בְּשֵׂכֶל וּמַחֲשָׁבָה וְכַוָּנַת הַמִּצְוֹת מַעֲשִׂיּוֹת, וּבְכַוָּנַת קְרִיאַת שְׁמַע וּתְפִלָּה וּשְׁאָר בְּרָכוֹת. — **Rather, it is because it is also God's will that one should cleave** to Him **with his intellect, thought, and the intent** he has **for action-related mitzvot, and with the intent** he has **for the reading of the *Shema*, prayer, and other blessings.**

The intent a person has while performing a mitzva is, in this sense, equal to the act of performing the mitzva. The superiority of a mitzva, which comes from God and not from man, is actualized through the intent a person has while performing the mitzva, as much as it does in the act of the mitzva. The intent is not an addition to the act of the mitzva that a person contributes to God of his own volition. Rather, it is part and parcel of the performance of the mitzva as God commanded, emanating from God's will, no different from His will for the physical performance of the mitzva.

וְהֶאָרַת רָצוֹן הָעֶלְיוֹן הַזֶּה הַמֵּאִירָה וּמְלוּבֶּשֶׁת בְּכַוָּנָה זוֹ הִיא גְּדוֹלָה לְאֵין קֵץ לְמַעְלָה מַּעְלָה מֵהֶאָרַת רָצוֹן הָעֶלְיוֹן — **The illumination of this supernal will that shines and is enclothed in this** person's **intent is infinitely greater than, and above and beyond, the illumination of the supernal will that**

הַמְּאִירָה וּמְלוּבֶּשֶׁת בְּקִיּוּם הַמִּצְוֹת עַצְמָן, בְּמַעֲשֶׂה וּבְדִבּוּר בְּלִי כַּוָּנָה, — shines and is enclothed in the fulfillment of the mitzvot themselves performed only **with action and speech yet without intent,**

As was stated, the supernal divine will that commanded the act of the mitzva applies equally to the intent a person should have when performing one. However, the illumination of that will that is enclothed within the intent is immeasurably greater than its radiance enclothed solely in the action.

כְּגוֹדֶל מַעֲלַת אוֹר הַנְּשָׁמָה עַל הַגּוּף, שֶׁהוּא כְּלִי וּמַלְבּוּשׁ הַנְּשָׁמָה, כְּמוֹ גּוּף הַמִּצְוָה שֶׁהוּא כְּלִי וּמַלְבּוּשׁ לְכַוָּנָתָהּ. — similar to the vast superiority of the light of the soul over the body – which is a vessel and garment for the soul – just as the body of the mitzva is a vessel and garment for its intent.

Although the body and soul exist on the same plane of life, they are extremely different from each other in terms of the illumination of life force that is revealed in them. More life force is revealed even in the smallest soul than is revealed in the most developed body. The same sort of difference exists when comparing a mitzva performed without intent (even though it too is holy and turns the world toward holiness), with a mitzva performed with intent, that is, with the involvement of the faculties of the soul. The difference is not only with regard to the attachment of a person's body to the mitzva, but also with regard to the attachment of his spirit to the One who commanded the mitzva. Through this attachment and with this intent, the mitzva changes his personal existence and that of the world to one possessing an infinitely greater and expansive degree of holiness. ☞ ☞

THE FUNCTION OF INTENT IN REPAIRING THE WORLD

☞ As is explained elsewhere (chap. 40 below; *Tikkunei Zohar* 21a), the function of intent is to enhance the mitzva, serving as wings that lift it upward. The more intent of the heart (namely, love and fear of God) involved in fulfilling a mitzva, the higher, more encompassing, and powerful it is. This is true for a mitzva that exists in the practical, material world, which transforms one small point from evil to good, as well as for a mitzva that impacts and changes all the worlds, reaching ever higher.

This difference, which is dependent on a person's intent while fulfilling a mitzva, has major significance with regard to man's function in the world. As was explained previously (chaps. 36–37), the purpose of human existence is to prepare the world for redemption so that it will serve as a dwelling place for God, "and all flesh will see together that the mouth of the Lord has spoken" (Isa. 40:5). Every good deed brings the redemption closer, and the performance of every mitzva repairs the world on some level. However, when a person is faced with the overarching purpose of existence, namely, to rectify completely the entire world, there is significance not only in that someone made a repair, but also in the size of the repair, determined by the scope and power of the deed. A mitzva performed only with one's body has a limited scope. But when a person harnesses his power of thought, attaching his soul to the mitzva and to the One commanding it, the mitzva receives immeasurably greater intensity and scope.

As an analogy, the act of a person hoeing a field and the act of a person plowing with a tractor are essentially the same. The tractor does nothing essentially different from the person digging by hand. Yet when a person has the intent, beyond his basic involvement in the task at hand, to plow the entire field and finish the job, then there is without a doubt a great difference between someone digging by hand and a person plowing with a tractor. The tractor in this sense harnesses tremendous power in order to intensify and broaden the scope of the person's act. Similarly, when a person fulfills a mitzva, prays, or says a blessing, he is of course performing an act of holiness. But when one fulfills that act only with the life force of his body (which parallels the power of the life force in inanimate objects), the act will remain on the same level. In order for the holy act to be even more powerful and with a broader impact, a person must incorporate the intent of the heart – fear and love – into the act.

Alternatively, one can say that a mitzva may be understood as a sort of code, a specific, defined mathematical expression. The intent of the mitzva, on the other hand, is like the exponent; it is the power to which that expression can be raised. Similarly, the essence of a mitzva is a constant, always dependent upon the basic expression, namely, the act of the mitzva. By contrast, the intent of the mitzva (or the exponent) can raise the number or expression to the second, third, fourth, or tenth powers. One's intent does not provide a number's face value, but it does add the number of zeros to it.

THE TRUE VALUE OF INTENT

☞ A person's intent forges a bond between his soul and the action he performs. In this sense, the value of the intent is not in its intellectual level but rather in the level of intensity of the relationship between a person's self and the mitzva he fulfills. Therefore, when a person deeply and truly devotes his being when performing a mitzva, he can reach the highest level of connection. This is the case even if he does not know exactly what he is doing and even if his action is not inherently defined as a mitzva.

This last point is borne out in numerous stories. One such account is told of Rabbi Levi Yitzḥak of Berditchev, who one year was engaged in the Passover Seder and utilizing very lofty spiritual inten-

וְאַף שֶׁבִּשְׁתֵּיהֶן, בַּמִּצְוָה וּבְכַוָּנָתָהּ, מְלוּבָּשׁ רָצוֹן אֶחָד, פָּשׁוּט בְּתַכְלִית הַפְּשִׁיטוּת בְּלִי שׁוּם שִׁינּוּי וְרִיבּוּי חַס וְשָׁלוֹם, וּמְיוּחָד בְּמַהוּתוֹ וְעַצְמוּתוֹ יִתְבָּרֵךְ בְּתַכְלִית הַיִּחוּד,

Although it is true that **both of them – the mitzva and its intent – enclothe a single, utterly simple will, without any change or multiplicity, God forbid, and are unified with God's essence and being in absolute unity,**

tions and unifications. At its conclusion, he felt very good that he had prepared such a sublime Seder. The following day, he inquired of Heaven if there was anyone who had conducted a Seder superior to his. The heavenly response was that there was a Jew named Ḥayyim Traiger ("the porter") who had in fact conducted a superior Seder. Immediately, Rabbi Levi Yitzḥak set out to find him. When he found him, he saw that Ḥayyim was a simple Jew who earned his living as a porter. Rabbi Levi Yitzḥak asked him, "Reb Ḥayyim, did you make a Passover Seder?" He answered, "Rebbe, I will tell you the truth. I heard it was forbidden to drink liquor for all eight days of Passover. So, on the morning before Passover, I drank eight days' worth of liquor. This made me very tired, so I went to sleep. That evening, my wife woke me and said, 'Are you a non-Jew that you are not making a Passover Seder?' I got out of bed and dragged myself to my place at the table. Upon seeing how it was beautifully set, with a white tablecloth, and laden with carefully prepared holiday food, I regained my energy. I poured myself first one cup, then another. I said to my wife, 'You know that I am a simple Jew, unable to properly tell you the entire story of our exodus from Egypt. But look, we were enslaved by the Gypsies and they made our lives intolerable and tormented us. Then God saved us from them. Now as well, we are in dire straits, and God will save us from them too!' I ate, drank more wine, and then fell asleep again." Rabbi Levi Yitzḥak heard this and admitted: "This Seder was truly higher than mine." The intentions of Rabbi Levi Yitzḥak were certainly loftier and more sophisticated than those of the simple Jew, but it seems that Ḥayyim's intent was more complete, because it was all he knew.

It is also told of Rabbi Levi Yitzḥak of Berditchev that he was once searching for a person to blow *shofar* for Rosh HaShana in his *beit midrash* (Torah study hall). All the *shofar* blowers were gathered together, and each one displayed his knowledge of the inner intentions and secrets underlying the mitzva of blowing the *shofar*. Despite their expertise, none of them seemed right to Rabbi Levi Yitzḥak. One day, a simple Jew came to him and asked to be the *shofar* blower. The Rabbi asked him what kind of inner intent he has during the blowing. The Jew answered: "Rebbe, I am a simple man, and I have four daughters who have reached marriageable age. When I blow the *shofar* I think: Master of the universe, I am fulfilling Your will and blowing the *shofar*! May You also fulfill my will and help me marry off my daughters!" Upon hearing this, Rabbi Levi Yitzḥak said: "You will blow *shofar* in my *beit midrash*!" What counts is not the level of intent, be it the extent of one's knowledge or the degree of focus. What is important is the intensity of the relationship between the person and the act. This is what truly matters when fulfilling a mitzva.

A mitzva and its intent are, in essence, different aspects of one entity, namely, God's supernal will. The innermost aspect of the divine will, expressed as a mitzva and its intent, is unified within the divine essence. Just as that essence is one and indivisible, so is the divine will. Given this, how can we make a distinction and say that the illumination of the supernal will in the intent of a mitzva is greater than the illumination of the divine will in actually performing the mitzva?

אַף עַל פִּי כֵן, הַהֶאָרָה אֵינָהּ שָׁוָה בִּבְחִינַת צִמְצוּם וְהִתְפַּשְּׁטוּת, **nevertheless, the illumination is not equal with respect to constriction and expansion,**

The world is not one uniform reality, but rather is comprised of different levels (inanimate, vegetation, animal, man), the differences between which emanate from variations in the illumination of the divine life force that flows through them, be it constricted or more expansive. The same goes for God's will within the mitzvot. Although at its root, the divine light is the same light, its illumination in the soul is not of equal measure, both in terms of its constriction and expansion, as mentioned above. The difference between the illumination in a person's intent as he performs a mitzva and the illumination in the act of the mitzva is discernible by one's attachment and connection to God.

הַגָּהָה: (וּכְמוֹ שֶׁכָּתוּב בְּעֵץ חַיִּים, שֶׁכַּוָּונַת הַמִּצְווֹת וְתַלְמוּד תּוֹרָה הִיא בְּמַדְרֵגַת אוֹר, וְגוּף הַמִּצְווֹת הֵן מַדְרֵגוֹת וּבְחִינוֹת כֵּלִים, שֶׁהֵם בְּחִינַת צִמְצוּם. שֶׁעַל יְדֵי צִמְצוּם הָאוֹר נִתְהַוּוּ הַכֵּלִים, **Gloss: as is written in *Etz Ḥayyim*, that the intent in the mitzvot and Torah study is the level of light, whereas the body of the mitzvot is the level and quality of vessels. The vessels represent constriction, because by means of the light's constriction the vessels come into being,**

In this gloss, the author of the *Tanya* clarifies additional facets of what was stated above, by referencing an idea expressed in *Etz Ḥayyim*.[9]

---

9. *Sha'ar Kelippat Noga* (*Sha'ar* 49), chap. 5; *Sha'ar Penimiyut VeḤitzoniyut* (*Sha'ar* 40), derush 2 (*Likkutei Hagahot LaTanya*).

Like the other glosses throughout this book, this gloss addresses a dimension of the higher realm relating to the *sefirot* in the world of *Atzilut*. As was mentioned regarding the soul and the body, and a mitzva and its intent, the author now draws the same distinction regarding the lights and vessels of the *sefirot* in the world of *Atzilut*.

Both the lights and the vessels are truly divine (as stated in the introduction to *Tikkunei Zohar* [3a]: "He and His attributes are one in them, He and His life are one in them"). Despite this, they are separate from each other, as one is called "lights" and the other, "vessels." The light refers to expansion without limits, bringing about *sefirot* and levels without end. The vessel is the constriction of the light, bringing about ten specific *sefirot*: Ḥokhma, Ḥesed, and so forth, which are the characteristics of a particular vessel (i.e., the vessel of Ḥokhma, the vessel of Ḥesed, etc.). Thus, in terms of constriction and expansion there is a major difference between the light, which is the revelation of a simple, unlimited, divine light, and the vessel, namely, the constriction of the light contained in ten vessels.

Applying this to our context, the light is the root of the intent of the mitzvot down below (which is the "simple" and general intent applicable to all mitzvot, namely, "to cleave to Him"). The vessel, on the other hand, refers to the acts of the 613 mitzvot, and in the proper manner that each of them must be performed, as explained by the *halakha*. In that sense, the performance of a mitzva with intent is the drawing down of the light into the vessels on high.

(The additional explanation of the gloss is to explain that the divine revelation shines more in the intent of the mitzva than it does in the act of the mitzva. The reason is that since the "body," i.e., the act of the mitzva, is extremely lofty, as explained in the previous chapters, the illumination would presumably be of an equal quality. The author of the *Tanya* addresses this in the gloss and explains that since the root of the intent of the mitzvot is in the lights, the revelation of that illumination is greater in the intent of the mitzvot than in the act of the mitzvot, whose root is in the vessels, which represent the constriction of the light.)[10]

---

10. See the explanation of Rabbi Shmuel Gronem Esterman.

כַּיָּדוּעַ לְיוֹדְעֵי חֵן).   as known to those initiated in the esoteric wisdom of Kabbala.

The observations in the gloss are not for the masses, but rather specifically for those who know the hidden wisdom of the Kabbala. That is why these ideas were written in this way, so as not to interfere with the flow of ideas for a reader who is not familiar with the hidden wisdom.

וְנֶחְלֶקֶת גַּם כֵּן לְאַרְבַּע מַדְרֵגוֹת.   and is also divided into four levels.

Just as the divine life force in the world is divided into four categories – inanimate, vegetable, animal, and man – so too the divine illumination within a mitzva reveals itself in four general levels, similar to the four categories of created beings. Further on, we will see that this division into four levels is of a double nature. The initial division is between the act (body) and the intent (soul) of a mitzva. There is another division within the act of a mitzva (similar to that between inanimate matter and vegetation), as well as within the intent of a mitzva (similar to that between animals and humans).

כִּי גּוּף הַמִּצְוֹת עַצְמָן מַמָּשׁ הֵן ב' מַדְרֵגוֹת, שֶׁהֵן מִצְוֹת מַעֲשִׂיּוֹת מַמָּשׁ, וּמִצְוֹת הַתְּלוּיוֹת בְּדִבּוּר וּמַחֲשָׁבָה, כְּמוֹ תַּלְמוּד תּוֹרָה וּקְרִיאַת שְׁמַע וּתְפִלָּה וּבִרְכַּת הַמָּזוֹן וּשְׁאָר בְּרָכוֹת.   That is because the body of the actual mitzvot themselves are composed of two levels, namely, actual action-related mitzvot, and mitzvot that are dependent upon speech and thought, such as Torah study, the reading of the *Shema*, prayer, Grace after Meals, and other blessings.

The act of a mitzva can be divided into two types: The first category includes action-related mitzvot, which are mitzvot performed with an action of the body, and which, accordingly, affect and alter material reality. The second category includes mitzvot that are performed using the body, but they do not effect a change in the physical state of the world. Thus, speech is only *considered* an action, since in certain ways it is like an action (an action of the body), but it is not an action in every aspect and in every sense. It follows that there are two levels in the act of the mitzvot. One includes the mitzvot that truly involve action and which affect the physical world. These are analogous to the category of "inanimate matter." The second category includes mitzvot involving speech and thought, and which impact spiritual entities. These mitzvot are analogous to the category of "vegetation."[11]

וְכַוָּנַת הַמִּצְוֹת לְדָבְקָה בּוֹ יִתְבָּרֵךְ, שֶׁהִיא כְּנִשְׁמָה לַגּוּף, נֶחְלֶקֶת גַּם כֵּן לִשְׁתֵּי מַדְרֵגוֹת, כְּמוֹ שְׁתֵּי מַדְרֵגוֹת הַנְּשָׁמָה שֶׁהֵן בַּגּוּף הַחוֹמְרִי, שֶׁהֵן: חַי וּמְדַבֵּר.

The intent of the mitzvot, i.e., one's intent to cleave to God, which is like a soul to the body, is also divided into two levels, corresponding to the two levels of the soul that exists in the material body: animal and man.

In the intent of the mitzvot, as in the soul within the body, there are two levels: the animalistic soul and the human soul. In every person's soul, there is the embodiment of the soul of a human and the embodiment of the soul of an animal, as the verse states, "I will sow the house of Israel with human seed and animal seed" (Jer. 31:26).[12] These two aspects exist among different people, as well as within each person's soul in his divine service as manifest in his intent in performing the mitzvot. Each type of intent injects a "soul" into the "body" (i.e., the act) of the mitzva, and the quality and scope of the intent determine if that will be a human soul or an animal soul.

The author of the *Tanya* begins by explaining the intent of a mitzva belonging to the category of a human soul, namely, the love and fear on the level of "human."

| כִּי מִי שֶׁדַּעְתּוֹ יָפָה לָדַעַת אֶת ה', | A person who has intellectual capacity to know God, | 6 Nisan

26 Adar II (leap year) |

---

11. The idea that there are mitzvot that are dependent on speech and thought indicates that there is an aspect of thought included in the body of the mitzvot, namely, studying Torah in depth on the simple, revealed level, and reciting the *Shema*, prayer, and blessings with an understanding of the meaning of the words. The soul of the mitzvot, however, is only when accompanied by one's manifest love and fear, as is explained elsewhere that "without fear and love, it cannot fly upward" (see *Likkutei Biurim*).

12. See Ḥullin 5b; Torah Or, s.v. "ve'eleh hamishpatim," 74c.

The discussion here is specifically about knowledge (*da'at*), because knowledge is the power of the intellect that leads a person to connection and, as a by-product, generates an emotional experience. The ability of one's consciousness to generate an experience, or, put differently, the ability of the mind to dominate the heart, is so characteristic of man that it is used here to define man's essential nature as it pertains to his path of serving God.

וּלְהִתְבּוֹנֵן בִּגְדוּלָּתוֹ יִתְבָּרַךְ, **and to contemplate His greatness,**

In order to attain this knowledge of God and the emotional experience that comes with it, one must contemplate His greatness. Contemplation is not a random passing thought, but rather, it is focused thinking about a defined topic for a period of time. It involves a person envisioning the issue in his mind and repeatedly contemplating its various angles and components. Such contemplation of the greatness of God is on multiple levels, as is explained in numerous places.[13] There is the level on which a person contemplates the cosmos and is amazed in the face of its grandeur, and asks, "Who created these?" There is a higher level, when a person contemplates the upper spiritual essences. Then there is the highest level, on which one's consciousness actually touches the divine essence itself.

וּלְהוֹלִיד מִבִּינָתוֹ יִרְאָה עִילָּאָה בְּמוֹחוֹ, **and to engender from his understanding (*bina*) a higher-level fear in his mind,**

This type of contemplation generates an emotional response within a person regarding the object of contemplation. It can be a relationship of attraction or repulsion, love or fear. When the objects of one's contemplation are God's infinite greatness and exaltedness, the person experiences an emotional response reflective of the emotive aspect of those objects, namely, a higher-level fear.

There is lower fear and higher fear. Lower fear is a lowly fear causing fright and terror. Higher fear, on the other hand, is a sense of awe engendered by God's exaltedness, fear that stems from a sense of shame

---

13. See, for example, *Torah Or* 47a and *Likkutei Torah*, Lev. 3b.

in the face of such exaltedness. Fear stemming from shame is not fear of punishment, nor is it terror of God's might and awesomeness, but is simply shame.

A story is told of Rabbi Naḥman of Breslov when he was a child. Whenever it seemed to him that he had sinned, he would blush in shame before God. Generally, fear is an emotion of distance, in contrast to love, which is one of attraction. In this sense, the most elevated fear is not a recoiling from that which is undesirable, from that which is painful or frightening, but rather retracting due to the awareness of "Who is it whose heart dared to approach Me? – the utterance of the Lord" (Jer. 30:21), from the feeling of shame one experiences when he is aware of his nothingness in the presence of God. ☞

CONTEMPLATION

☞ Sometimes people think that contemplation is an exercise outside their reach and intended only for unique individuals. But the truth of the matter is that the ability to engage in contemplation exists in everyone, though not necessarily with regard to contemplating the greatness of God. Focusing and concentrating one's thoughts on an abstract topic for a sustained period of time is a difficult feat for anyone. But as a general rule, anyone can direct his thoughts at will. Everyone, before falling asleep, engages in this kind of contemplation, during which he is not thinking about his affairs and problems. If this were not so, he would not fall asleep. Each person also engages in contemplation that engenders and intensifies his character. For example, everyone who gets angry is engaging in this form of contemplation, since, if he were to cease ruminating on whatever is making him angry, his anger would be fleeting and dissipate. But when he repeatedly contemplates that situation and reconstructs it in his mind, thinking about how he was wronged, how unfair it was, and what he and others thought about the incident, he forms a seed of anger that grows the more he continues focusing on what happened.

Contemplation of God's greatness is not qualitatively different from any other contemplation. However, because the divine existence in our world is hidden, contemplation upon it must be more strenuous and prolonged. This contemplation is, in a sense, a kind of solution to an equation or riddle. The difficult equation: God is one, and a person must delve into this and understand it. The riddle: Where is God? A person must solve this as well.

Some suggest the following analogy describing this type of contemplation: There are magicians who seem to produce rabbits from hats and the like. In order to detect the deception and see the truth behind the tricks, a person must contemplate carefully, with full concentration, until he clearly and obviously sees the sleight of hand, the lie of the *kelippa* and the truth hidden behind it. The method of contemplation adopted by Chabad hasidim follows, in a sense, that same approach: A person chooses a topic to ponder, thinking

וְאַהֲבַת ה' בְּחָלָל הַיְמָנִי שֶׁבְּלִבּוֹ, לִהְיוֹת נַפְשׁוֹ צְמֵאָה לַה' לְדָבְקָה בּוֹ עַל יְדֵי קִיּוּם הַתּוֹרָה וְהַמִּצְוֹת, שֶׁהֵן הַמְשָׁכַת וְהֶאָרַת אוֹר אֵין סוֹף בָּרוּךְ הוּא עַל נַפְשׁוֹ – לְדָבְקָה בּוֹ,

and the love of God in the right chamber of his heart, so that his soul thirsts for God, desiring **to cleave to Him by means of the fulfillment of the Torah and the mitzvot, which constitute the drawing down and the illumination of the light of** *Ein Sof,* **blessed be He, upon his soul** – so that he **cleaves to Him** –

Contemplating and relating to God always yield feelings of fear and love. This is the love of the divine soul, which dwells in the right chamber of the heart (see chap. 9). The expression of this love is the fact that the person's soul thirsts for God and desires to come closer

about it and examining it repeatedly, each time from a different angle. He does this until the innermost essence of that topic, despite its foreignness and abstraction, begins to become reified. The more tangible and sensory it becomes, the more it leads to an emotional connection, in the form of love and fear of God that are manifest in one's heart.

As was stated earlier, the purpose of this contemplation is to make the transition from awareness to experience. It is quite likely for one to encounter obstacles in this transition. One of the metaphors for this transition is the "narrow part of the throat." The throat is positioned between the intellectual faculties found in the head and the experiential emotion found in the heart. In the narrow part of the throat there are several obstacles that interfere with passage; these obstacles are described as Pharaoh and his three officers, Amalek, and Amalek's progeny. These prevent passage from the brain to the heart. They create an obstructive barrier that does not allow the mind's faculty of grasping abstract concepts to reach the experiential tangibility of love and fear and similar feelings (see, for example, *Torah Or* 57d and 85c). When this passage is blocked, a person can live in an absurd state, as is described by our Sages: "A thief at the opening of the burglary tunnel calls out to God" (*Berakhot* 63a, as recorded in *Ein Yaakov*). When a thief is poised to steal, he calls out to God in prayer so that God should assist him in his thievery. This means to say that when there is a disconnect between the mind and the heart, a person can contain two opposites within himself, in that he "knows of his Creator and intentionally rebels against Him" (see Rashi, Lev. 26:14). He recognizes God's existence intellectually, but this awareness does not permeate any further. It does not generate within him any emotional experience, neither love nor hate, nor does it impel him to do something or to sacrifice himself for it. As a result, simultaneous with his being aware of his Creator, he is also able to rebel against Him.

to Him. How does one quench this thirst? By cleaving to God, which is achieved by fulfilling the Torah and mitzvot. These constitute the drawing down of the internal aspect of the light of *Ein Sof* into the world and the soul. This is the inner, essential will of God as it is manifest in our world. When a person fulfills the Torah and mitzvot, he draws the internal aspect and essence of the light of *Ein Sof* into his soul, and in that way he achieves the true attachment to God that cannot exist in any other way.

וּבְכַוָּנָה זוֹ הוּא לוֹמֵד וּמְקַיֵּים הַמִּצְוֹת, וְכֵן בְּכַוָּנָה זוֹ מִתְפַּלֵּל וּמְבָרֵךְ, **and with this intent he studies** Torah **and fulfills the mitzvot, and he likewise prays and recites blessings with this intent,**

When the Torah one studies, the words of prayer he utters, or the mitzvot he performs are accompanied by this intent – the embodiment of the human soul – which stems from contemplation and knowledge of God's greatness, as was explained, then his Torah study, words of prayer, and mitzvot he fulfilled constitute the culmination of a process. This is not a spontaneous phenomenon of actions and thoughts, but rather the tip of a hidden process, a process of constructing a world, with each stage emerging from that which preceded it. It is an answer that resolves a question.

From a person's contemplation and knowledge of God's greatness, and through the emotional response that stems from it (arising from the need to build relationships that bring one closer to God and that keep one at a distance from the things He does not want), he can fulfill a mitzva. The fulfillment of a mitzva is a direct result of the spiritual perspective that preceded it. This is the conclusion, the answer, for a person who loves God, who thirsts and yearns for Him. It is the action by which this person can truly draw close to God.

WITH THIS INTENT, ONE FULFILLS THE MITZVOT

☞ In the first paragraph of the *Shema* we say, "Hear Israel, the Lord is our God, the Lord is one." Following this, we say, "Blessed be the name of His honored kingdom forever." As is explained in *Sha'ar HaYihud VeHa'emuna*, this is the contemplation that brings us to an awareness of the "upper unity" and after that the "lower unity." This

הֲרֵי כַּוָּונָה זוֹ, עַל דֶּרֶךְ מָשָׁל, **then this intent is analogous to the soul**
כְּמוֹ נִשְׁמַת הַמְדַבֵּר, **of a human being,**

This is the analogy mentioned earlier, equating prayer (and every mitzva for that matter) lacking intent with a body lacking a soul. As was explained, there is a soul within inanimate objects, vegetation, animals, and man. The intent spoken of here, namely, the love and fear one generates from his understanding (*bina*), is analogous to the soul of a human being.

שֶׁהוּא בַּעַל שֵׂכֶל וּבְחִירָה **who possesses intelligence, freedom**
וּבְדַעַת יְדַבֵּר. **of choice, and is one who speaks with wisdom.**

The Hebrew word designating the level of man is *medaber*, literally, "a speaking being." Man is a being whose thoughts, words, and actions are not detached from the inner faculties of the soul, but rather are part of a single process generated from within those inner faculties and that are ultimately manifest as actions. This is the nature of man: wisdom is recognized in his thought, and his thought also creates the practical tools that bring the wisdom to expression. ☞

---

awareness is meant to transform the soul, like a person who stands before and within the divine oneness, and to arouse the love of "the Lord your God, with all your heart, and with all your soul, and with all your might." The powerful charge that accumulates and is compressed in the soul from the word "hear" until the words "your might" is released in the next stage: "These matters that I command you today...you shall speak of them...you shall bind them...." It is released through the actions spoken of in these verses, namely, Torah study and the fulfillment of mitzvot.

THE SPEAKING BEING

☞ In contrast to the definition of man as "homo sapiens" (wise man), here the definition of man is "a speaking being." The question is: What is man's superiority? What is the thing that a human being can do that animals cannot? It seems that intelligence is not unique to man. But speech, the power to communicate and transfer knowledge and understanding, is a quality of man that is not shared by any other creature. Certainly, other living creatures do communicate, but that is nothing more than an emotional expression. An animal can say "I want," "I am hungry," but it is unable to articulate a concept like "bread." This is not due to a lack of intelligence, as it

CHAPTER 38

After the discussion of the level of intent that is analogous to the human soul, the author of the *Tanya* proceeds to discuss the intent that is analogous to the soul of a living creature.

וּמִי שֶׁדַּעְתּוֹ קְצָרָה לֵידַע וּלְהִתְבּוֹנֵן בִּגְדוּלַת אֵין סוֹף בָּרוּךְ הוּא לְהוֹלִיד הָאַהֲבָה מִבִּינָתוֹ בְּהִתְגַּלּוּת לִבּוֹ, וְכֵן הַיִּרְאָה בְּמוֹחוֹ וּפַחַד ה' בְּלִבּוֹ,

But a person whose mind is too limited to know and contemplate the greatness of *Ein Sof*, blessed be He, and thus **to generate from his understanding a revealed love for God in his heart, as well as fear in his mind and the trepidation of God in his heart,**

Not everyone has the requisite intellectual capacity to "know and contemplate the greatness of *Ein Sof*." Moreover, even if a person does possess this ability, it does not necessarily follow that he can generate a revealed sense of love, fear, and trepidation. A clear intellectual grasp and comprehension can result in different degrees of emotional involvement, none of which will necessarily be expressed as an emotional response. There are people who find it difficult or impossible to grasp abstract concepts, and when they try to contemplate God, they contemplate some reified image, each person on his level. But even if a person were to have a clear, physical image, to whatever degree of physicality, this still will not necessarily lead him to an experiential and emotional connection. This can be observed in children engaged in prayer. There are children who in their minds can imagine God and can achieve a sense of deep emotional involvement. By contrast, there

---

knows the difference between bread and a mouse, for example. What an animal lacks that keeps it from being able to say "bread" is an entire system (which apparently exists only in man) that makes it possible for a person to convert things – sensory stimuli, images, events – into concepts. In contrast to animals, man has the singular ability to transform his intelligence into a framework of symbols that one can think about, to build them through letter combinations, and to transfer them from world to world – from intellect to feeling, and from one person to another. This transformation from idea to symbol is rooted in a very lofty realm, higher than understanding and comprehension, somewhere in the mysteries of the divine speech, of the divine kingship. These mysteries are the qualitative leap that defines this new being, existing nowhere else in creation, that of man, the speaking being.

are children who, while also capable of imagining God (according to their perception), are nevertheless unable to use that image to create a relationship, neither emotional nor intellectual.

רַק שֶׁזּוֹכֵר וּמְעוֹרֵר אֶת הָאַהֲבָה הַטִּבְעִית הַמְסוּתֶּרֶת בְּלִבּוֹ, וּמוֹצִיאָהּ מֵהֶעְלֵם וְהֶסְתֵּר הַלֵּב אֶל הַגִּלּוּי בַּמּוֹחַ עַל כָּל פָּנִים, — but rather, he remembers and awakens the natural love that is hidden in his heart, and brings it forth from the hidden and concealed recesses of his heart, at the very least to a state of awareness in his mind,

There are people who are incapable of attaining constructs within their souls of love and fear for God through intellectual contemplation. So how does such a person attain love and fear through fulfilling the mitzvot? The author of the *Tanya* addresses this question by returning to the fundamental point of the book, which speaks to the elemental nature of the Jewish people. Within every Jew, in the prototypical essence that is passed down hereditarily, there is a hidden love of God. This love is beyond the grasp of the intellect and is indisputable. Because it is a love that is a part of the soul's essence, it is not dependent on the person's intellectual traits and talents. It does not derive from a person's contemplation of the greatness of God, but rather from the person's essential Jewishness that connects him to God. However, because this love is hidden, it is necessary to recall it and mention it, to awaken it, at the very least to raise it within oneself to the level of consciousness, to think about and be aware of this essence that exists within oneself.

שֶׁיִּהְיֶה רְצוֹנוֹ שֶׁבְּמוֹחוֹ וְתַעֲלוּמוֹת לִבּוֹ מַסְכִּים וּמִתְרַצֶּה בְּרִיצּוּי גָּמוּר בֶּאֱמֶת לַאֲמִתּוֹ, לִמְסוֹר נַפְשׁוֹ בְּפוֹעַל מַמָּשׁ עַל יִחוּד ה' — so that his will in his mind and in the inner recesses of his heart should agree and fully consent, with true sincerity, to give up his life in martyrdom in actual practice for the sake of God's unity

As was explained, the nature of this love is one of connection, which eventually matures into a total identification with the divine source and totality. This bond, deeper and stronger than any intellectual understanding and contemplation, transcends the roots of one's individual existence, and is expressed as a tangible readiness on the part of every Jew to give up his life in martyrdom to sanctify God.

כְּדֵי לְדָבְקָה בּוֹ - נַפְשׁוֹ הָאֱלֹהִית וּלְבוּשֶׁיהָ וּלְכָלְלָן בְּיִחוּדוֹ וְאַחְדּוּתוֹ, שֶׁהוּא רָצוֹן הָעֶלְיוֹן הַמְלוּבָּשׁ בְּתַלְמוּד תּוֹרָה וּבְקִיּוּם הַמִּצְוֹת כַּנִּזְכָּר לְעֵיל,

in order to attach to Him his divine soul and its garments of thought, speech, and action, **and to unite them with His unity and oneness,** namely, **the supernal will that is enclothed in Torah study and in the fulfillment of the mitzvot, as stated above** (chap. 19),

As was explained earlier (chap. 19), giving up one's life in martyrdom to sanctify God's name expresses the overwhelming surge of this love that is embedded within every Jew the moment he feels that his essential connection with God threatens to be severed. As this book teaches us, this point of choice – whether to be attached to God or separated from Him – is not limited to the extreme case of choosing to die for the sanctification of God's name. Rather, this choice exists in every expression of the faculties of the divine soul and its garments – in thought, in speech, and in action – when these matters pertain to Torah study and the fulfillment of each mitzva. The moment it is clear to a person that with this mitzva and with this action he clings to God, or the opposite, God forbid, the sheer force of this love is revealed. The intense force of this love is revealed throughout one's entire life, even to the extent that one actually gives up his life in order to fulfill any mitzva.

וְגַם הַיִּרְאָה כְּלוּלָה בָּהּ לְקַבֵּל מַלְכוּתוֹ שֶׁלֹּא לִמְרוֹד בּוֹ חַס וְשָׁלוֹם,

and also fear is included in this hidden love, namely, **accepting His kingship** so as **not to rebel against Him, God forbid** (see chap. 19 above),

This fear is like that of a lover who is afraid of being separated from his beloved. It descends to the level of action (or *Malkhut*) in the soul, so that a person accepts, like a servant, the yoke of God's kingship. Even if he neither understands nor feels love for God, at least he will not rebel against Him, God forbid.

וּבְכַוָּנָה זוֹ הוּא סוּר מֵרָע וְעוֹשֶׂה **and with this intent he turns away**
טוֹב, **from evil and does good,**

This intent is on the level of "the soul of a living creature," and stems from hidden love and the fear that is contained within that love. With such intent one turns away from evil by refraining from violating Torah prohibitions, and does good by fulfilling the positive mitzvot. ☞ ☞

LOVE OF GOD ON THE LEVEL OF A LIVING CREATURE

☞ As was mentioned, the intent one experiences in his soul on this level (like the soul of a living creature) is not a product of a complete human process, of the complete human stature, which extends from the intellect to the emotive attributes and finally to action. Here there is no process of one stage emerging from a preceding stage, of something that is comprehended, necessary, and simple that emerges from that which preceded it, of an awareness that leads to a feeling that leads to an action. The love that already exists within a person is not dependent on his awareness to engender it, and an action is not dependent on the revelation of that love, but only on that love's very existence within him. Accordingly, the intent, and the action that a person performs as a result of this intent, will not necessarily be a primary, experiential feeling and expression, but may be of a secondary level. This person is not like someone who knows, feels, and then acts, but like someone who knows that he must feel and that he must act. He is like someone who acts not out of a live, energizing feeling within him, but on the basis of logical conclusions of an insipid feeling that he has.

INTENT ON THE HUMAN LEVEL

☞ When a person's intent is like that of the human soul, when one who contemplates the greatness of *Ein Sof* experiences an emotional involvement on account of this contemplation and he has sought a way to express his emotion, then at that moment his relationship with Torah and mitzvot (to the point of giving up his life to sanctify God's name) is not something he must learn from an external source, but rather it wells up from within him, from the essence of his being. Because he feels this, he does not need others to teach it to him.

We are all familiar with parallel processes in our daily lives, where the relationship between contemplation, emotion, and action leaves no room for any other conclusion. It is clear to the person that in such a situation he is to continue to do specific things, and he does not need anyone to tell him, "Do this," and "Don't do that."

When a person is deeply in love, no matter the context, there is no need to tell him to think about the object of his love, because he already does so on his own. There is no need to schedule a time for him to do so, because his soul is constantly engaged in those thoughts. So it happens – sometimes as loving-kindness from above and sometimes as the result of contemplation – that a person is privy to experience within himself a similar love of God. On such occasions, not only does that individual not need to arouse love, but the love prevents him from sleeping. He experiences the love not as a codified positive mitzva, one of many things that he is obligated to do, but it is embedded within all his limbs, not specifically during the recitation of the *Shema*, but rather in such a manner that he cannot live otherwise, alluded to in the verses "I meditate on You during the night watches" (Ps. 63:7) and "When I awake, I am still with You" (Ps. 139:18).

Such a person's challenge is not how to arouse love within himself. On the contrary, it is to somewhat clear his mind of the object of his love, so as not to let it interfere with all other aspects of his life.

A story is told of a hasid who had worked as a merchant in the marketplace and eventually became a hasidic master. He was once seen wandering through the marketplace mumbling to himself, "A meter of cloth costs a ruble and a half, a meter of cloth costs a ruble and a half." Someone explained that he was repeating this to himself because if he did not do so, he would forget it. When a person is entirely engaged, mentally and emotionally, in a completely different world, if he does not make space, if he will not remind himself and awaken, repeatedly bringing the matter into his consciousness, the matter will become forgotten and erased from his soul. So when a person is "in love" with God, and "in her love you will always be intoxicated" (Prov. 5:19), it is not his love for God for which he must make room in himself, of which he must remind himself. Love for God burns of itself, grows and spreads and rises of its own accord. Rather, this person must take care to keep strong, to stay alive and not be entirely consumed.

In his *Amud Ha'Avoda* (section on *Mesirut Nefesh*, nos. 5–6), Rabbi Barukh of Kosov describes this type of love for God not as a momentary surge that leads one to sanctify God's name by dying a martyr's death, but as a lifelong love, a love one lives with and which burns within him day after day. The individual experiencing it cannot attain inner peace until he gives up his life to sanctify God's name.

Rabbi Barukh illustrates this with an analogy: There was once a man who did not have children. All his life he prayed and hoped for a child, until finally, toward the end of his life, his wife gave birth to a son who was perfect physically and spiritually. As he grew up and he became more beautiful, wise, and charming, his parents loved him more and more. In order to express their love, they bought him beautiful clothes, and when he wore them and he appeared even more appealing, their love grew. They taught him wisdom, and when he became wiser, their love grew more. Eventually, the love became oppressive, because it was impossible to satisfy. The more they gave, the greater their love became and demanded more. The parents began to suffer from a love that was insatiable, a thirst that increased. This lasted until one day the boy became dangerously ill. The parents were told that they would have to undergo surgery and donate parts of their bodies to him. When they underwent the surgery, they experienced satisfaction, perhaps for the first time, because they could finally give him something.

The story of Rabbi Akiva's martyrdom in sanctification of God's name can also be explained with this analogy. The Talmud (*Berakhot* 61a) relates that when they (the Romans) took Rabbi Akiva out to be executed, it was time for the recitation of *Shema*. They were raking his flesh with iron combs, and he was reciting *Shema*, thereby accepting upon himself the yoke of Heaven. His students said to him: "Our teacher, even now, as you suffer, you recite *Shema*?" He said to them: "All my days I have been pained by the verse 'With all your

וְלוֹמֵד וּמִתְפַּלֵּל וּמְבָרֵךְ בְּפֵירוּשׁ הַמִּלּוֹת לְבַדּוֹ, בְּלֹא דְחִילוּ וּרְחִימוּ בְּהִתְגַּלּוּת לִבּוֹ וּמוֹחוֹ – and studies, prays, and recites blessings, with a focus on **the meaning of the words alone, without fear and love revealed in his heart and mind** –

He prays because there is a mitzva to pray. He recites what is written in the prayer book with the intent that he is now speaking words that are said by a person who loves God. He does this without the feeling of love and fear that are felt by a person who senses the presence of God before him. He knows the meaning of the words that express love and fear. He knows these are the things he is supposed to say, and he says them accordingly, but he feels no revealed love or fear – not in his heart, nor even in his mind.

---

soul,' meaning, even if God takes your soul. I said to myself: When will the opportunity be afforded to me to fulfill this verse? Now that it has been afforded me, shall I not fulfill it?"

Throughout his whole life, Rabbi Akiva felt love for God, just like in the analogy. What does a person who loves God do? He studies more Torah and he dedicates himself more and more. But none of this satisfies his love. On the contrary, the Torah study only gives him a greater picture, loftier and more attractive, of the object of his love, and so his love simultaneously increases, flaming and tormenting him more. This is the meaning of what Rabbi Akiva said to his students: My whole life, I have been pained by the verse "You shall love the Lord your God with all your heart, and with all your soul, etc." All his life, this verse caused Rabbi Akiva tremendous suffering, the pain of an insatiable, relentless passion. Now, when Rabbi Akiva's flesh was being raked with metal combs because he upheld God's honor, his true pain finally subsided. At long last, finding expression for his tormenting pangs of love, Rabbi Akiva was able to feel a sense of satisfaction and tranquility.

Someone who lives with this awareness and this love has no need to remind himself of and arouse the love. But there are those who do not live with such a feeling and are unable to attain such an awareness. In order for someone like this to achieve the proper intent, in order to attain love and fear of God that at the very least motivate him to study Torah and fulfill the mitzvot, he must recall the hidden love that exists within him. He must tell himself: "I am a Jew, and although I do not truly feel or fully live like one, I nevertheless feel that I need to do so. With this conviction, I want to attach myself to God, and I am not willing to be separated from Him." As was mentioned, this is not the optimal type of intent, in which a person thirsts for the love for God and does something (Torah and mitzvot) in order to quench this thirst. This type of intent is not informed by an experience, but rather comes from an awareness and decisiveness that does not undergo passage through an emotional stimulus.

הֲרֵי כַּוָּנָה זוֹ, עַל דֶּרֶךְ מָשָׁל, כְּמוֹ נִשְׁמַת הַחַי שֶׁאֵינוֹ בַּעַל שֵׂכֶל וּבְחִירָה, וְכָל מִדּוֹתָיו, שֶׁהֵן יִרְאָתוֹ מִדְּבָרִים הַמַּזִּיקִים אוֹתוֹ וְאַהֲבָתוֹ לִדְבָרִים הַנֶּאֱהָבִים אֶצְלוֹ, הֵן רַק טִבְעִיִּים אֶצְלוֹ וְלֹא מִבִּינָתוֹ וְדַעְתּוֹ. וְכָךְ הֵן עַל דֶּרֶךְ מָשָׁל הַיִּרְאָה וְהָאַהֲבָה הַטִּבְעִיּוֹת הַמְסוּתָּרוֹת בְּלֵב כָּל יִשְׂרָאֵל. כִּי הֵן יְרוּשָׁה לָנוּ מֵאֲבוֹתֵינוּ, וּכְמוֹ טֶבַע בְּנַפְשׁוֹתֵינוּ, כַּנִּזְכָּר לְעֵיל.

this intent of the hidden love and fear is, metaphorically speaking, like the soul of a living creature that neither possesses intelligence nor is capable of free choice, and all of whose attributes, namely, its fear of harmful things and its love for things it considers pleasant, are merely natural to it, and do not stem from its understanding and knowledge. So too, metaphorically speaking, are the natural fear and love for God that are hidden in the heart of every Jew, for this latent love and fear **are our inheritance from our forefathers, and are like a natural** component **of our souls, as stated above** (chap. 18).

MITZVOT AND PRAYER WITHOUT LOVE AND FEAR

☞ It is impossible for an action to exist without some degree of intent. If a person has no connection whatsoever to something, he will neither act nor refrain from doing so. But there is a difference between an action that a person commits after deciding that it must be done, and an action that a person connects to experientially such that he cannot act otherwise.

For example, people engage in different activities for their livelihoods. Each person chooses a particular job because he has some kind of connection to it. Quite often, that connection is the result of a decision one makes, such as deciding to work in a particular place for one reason or another. This individual can fulfill his duties in this office or another, he can know that his work is important and sustains many people, and he can do his job with complete dedication and to the best of his ability. He can write beautiful letters, behave responsibly, and act with social propriety. Yet despite doing all this, he feels no thrill in it. As the author of the *Tanya* writes here, he does this without revealed love or fear in his heart and mind. It also can happen, and this is true in any field, that a person does his work with the vibrant feeling that he is performing holy work, with a conscious sense of mission and a feeling that he is doing so by devoting his very essence.

There is a Yiddish song that essentially says: "Eating happens by itself, drinking happens by itself, but prayer does not happen by itself." There is no need to teach a person that he must eat, nor does one need to stimulate within himself the intention to eat, since he feels that on his own. It is also possible for a person to feel this way regarding prayer. On the other hand, there are situations where one suffers an illness

The feelings living creatures (i.e., animals) experience, namely, attraction and aversion, are natural instincts which are part of the fundamental structure of their very existence. They have no choice regarding these, just as they cannot choose whether to exist or not.

Similar to an animal's instincts of attraction and aversion, within every Jew there exists love and fear of God. In other words, these feelings of love and fear are not dependent on any intellectual or conscious awareness and are not subject to choice, because they are a part of a Jew's very being on the most basic level of his existence as a Jew – as a descendent of Abraham, Isaac, and Jacob.

As was mentioned, this love is hidden, and a person must remember to awaken it. Awakening this love does not require the use of one's intellect, awareness, or contemplation. Rather, it merely requires one to remember that it is there, to notice its existence within himself. When he does this, the love awakens automatically. Moreover, this natural, hidden love does not just awaken and reveal itself, but can also grow and take on a profound and experiential character and meaning, no less than love that is the result of intellectual contemplation. The only difference between the two is how the process is initiated. There are those who are unable to begin this cycle merely by using their intellect. Therefore, they create a connection with God by resorting to the "animalistic" aspect of their soul, as it were, which entails arousing within themselves experiences that are not dependent upon intellectual understanding.

This chapter dealt with the relationship between the act of performing a mitzva and the intent one has as he performs it. The first part of the chapter discussed the halakhic aspect of this relationship and the pivotal role this aspect plays in the act of the mitzva (including the act

or psychological condition in which the natural mechanism malfunctions. In such instances, those individuals eat – similar to the way people pray – because they know they must eat, and because it is time to eat. Indeed, this state is considered an illness, but at any rate it demonstrates that it is also possible to live like this, that living thus is also considered to have authentic intent and to be an experience that can motivate people to engage in everyday, life-sustaining activities, such as keeping the mitzvot and praying.

of speech). The second part of the chapter dealt with this relationship from a different angle, encapsulated in the phrase "Prayer or any other blessing without intent is like a body without a soul." Just as there is a difference between the illumination of the divine life force in the body and its illumination in the soul, so too is there a difference between the illumination of the light of *Ein Sof* in the act of a mitzva and the illumination in the mitzva's intent. Specifically, just as the illumination of the divine life force is divided into four levels – inanimate, vegetable, animal, and man – similarly, the illumination of the light of *Ein Sof* that is revealed in the act of a mitzva and its intention is divided into four levels. The "body" of the mitzva is divided into two: action and speech, paralleling the levels of inanimate objects and vegetation. The intent of the mitzva is likewise divided into two: inborn love and fear, and intellectual love and fear, paralleling the levels of animals and man. The intent on the level of "man" is complete intent, where intellectual awareness engenders the appropriate emotional sense of relationship that culminates in the act of fulfilling a mitzva. The intent of the mitzvot that is on the level of "animal" is the intent of love and fear that is hidden within the nature of every Jew. This love does not need to be created, for it already exists within the nature of the soul. All a person must do is remember that it exists, and that it is the natural aspiration of the soul to attach itself to its source and root. The ability of this love to be awakened even in the absence of a conscious infrastructure means that at its core this love will be revealed only when it reaches its final level of being expressed through a person's performance of a mitzva, so that his soul will be connected to God. The following chapter will discuss the other aspects of this love, both within man and the holy *ḥayot* angels.

Chapter 39

THE PREVIOUS CHAPTER DEALT WITH TWO LEVELS OF intention that can underlie a person's performance of the mitzvot. These intentions are compared to the soul, in contrast to the performance of a mitzva, which is compared to the body. The first level, which is higher than the second, is analogous to the human soul. It is the of love and fear of God that arise from a person's service of intellectual contemplation. The second, lower, level is analogous to the animal soul. It involves the revealing of the natural love and fear of God hidden within the nature of the soul of every Jew.

This chapter will discuss in further detail these levels of intent. In order to hone its presentation of these ideas, the current chapter begins with a description of the intentions engaged in by the holy *ḥayot* (a class of angels) and their service of God in actuality. The chapter then contrasts these to the service of human souls. Even on their "animal" level, human souls are higher than the *ḥayot*.

וּמִפְּנֵי זֶה גַּם כֵּן נִקְרָאִים הַמַּלְאָכִים בְּשֵׁם חַיּוֹת וּבְהֵמוֹת, כִּדְכְתִיב: "וּפְנֵי אַרְיֵה אֶל הַיָּמִין וְגוֹ' וּפְנֵי שׁוֹר מֵהַשְּׂמֹאל" וְגוֹ' (יחזקאל א, י),	For this reason as well, angels are called by the name of beasts and animals, as it is written: "The face of a lion on the right side… and the face of an ox on the left side…" (Ezek. 1:10),	7 Nisan 27 Adar II (leap year)

The spiritual character of the supernal angels is described, among other ways, in terms of animals and beasts, as it says in the description of the divine chariot: "The face of a lion on the right side… and the face of an ox on the left side…" (Ezek. 1:10). Of course, this description does not refer to an actual lion and ox, nor to faces such as those of actual people or animals. Rather, it refers to spiritual entities that have certain parallels with physical animals and beasts (as was explained at the conclusion of the last chapter). ☞

לְפִי שֶׁאֵינָם בַּעֲלֵי בְחִירָה, וְיִרְאָתָם וְאַהֲבָתָם הִיא טִבְעִית לָהֶם, כְּמוֹ שֶׁכָּתוּב בְּ׳רַעְיָא מְהֵימְנָא׳, פָּרָשַׁת פִּנְחָס.

for they do not have free will, and their fear and love come naturally to them, as it is written in *Raya Meheimna, Parashat Pinḥas.*

The characteristic that angels share with animals and beasts is that they do not have free will. Unlike human beings, angels are like animals in that they lack the strength and ability to choose between good and evil. They cannot choose between loving (taking action) and fearing (refraining from action) God or anything else. Their fear and love of God come naturally to them, as the author of the *Tanya* points out, quoting the *Zohar*.[1] Angels love God or fear God not because they have weighed the matter and made the choice to do so. Rather, it is the essence of their nature. This is how these beings were made: to love or fear God in a particular way, just as it is the nature of all animals in our material world to feel and behave in certain ways and not in others.

וְלָכֵן מַעֲלַת הַצַּדִּיקִים גְּדוֹלָה מֵהֶם,

Therefore, the righteous are on a greater level than they are,

THE NAMES OF ANGELS

☞ Since this passage refers to angels, it seemingly does not belong in the "Book of *Beinonim.*" However, the Lubavitcher Rebbe, Rabbi Menaḥem Mendel Schneerson, explains that this passage is placed here for two reasons: First, to emphasize the greatness of those who serve God with intellectual love and fear; they are even greater than the angels. Second, to show that serving God with natural fear and love has a lesser effect than serving Him with intellectual fear and love. Because of this, the author emphasizes that natural fear and love are on the level of the angels and the chariot.

---

1. Presumably, the author of the *Tanya*'s citation of *Raya Meheimna* is a reference to *Zohar* 3:225a. This requires more research (the Lubavitcher Rebbe, Rabbi Menaḥem Mendel Schneerson).

The angels serve God not out of awareness and choice, but rather because doing so is their nature. By contrast, the righteous serve God out of free choice and the intellectual awareness that it is the correct thing to do. Therefore, the service of man (a righteous person whose service is on the level of "man," and, as will be explained further, the service of the *beinoni* as well, whose spiritual intentions are on the level of "animal"), achieved through intellect and choice, is higher than the service of angels, just as a person's intellect is on a higher level than his attributes.

כִּי מְדוֹר נִשְׁמוֹת הַצַּדִּיקִים הוּא בְּעוֹלָם הַבְּרִיאָה, וּמְדוֹר הַמַּלְאָכִים בְּעוֹלָם הַיְּצִירָה.

since the abode of the souls of the righteous is in the world of *Beria* (Creation), whereas the abode of the angels is in the world of *Yetzira* (Formation).

The abode of the spirit of the righteous is in the world of *Beria* (Creation), whereas the abode of the angels is in the world of *Yetzira* (Formation). The world of *Beria* is above the world of *Yetzira*, as will be explained.

הַגָּהָה: (וְהַיְינוּ בִּסְתָמָם מַלְאָכִים. אֲבָל יֵשׁ מַלְאָכִים עֶלְיוֹנִים, בְּעוֹלַם הַבְּרִיאָה, שֶׁעֲבוֹדָתָם בִּדְחִילוּ וּרְחִימוּ שִׂכְלִיִּים, כְּמוֹ שֶׁכָּתוּב בְּרַעְיָא מְהֵימְנָא' שָׁם, שֶׁיֵּשׁ שְׁנֵי מִינֵי חַיּוֹת הַקֹּדֶשׁ, טִבְעִיִּים וְשִׂכְלִיִּים, וּכְמוֹ שֶׁכָּתוּב בְּעֵץ חַיִּים).

Gloss: This applies to regular angels. However, there are supernal angels in the world of *Beria* who serve with cognitive fear and love of God, as it states in *Raya Meheimna* there that there are two types of holy *ḥayot* angels, natural and cognitive ones, and as it is written in *Etz Ḥayyim*.

This observation, that angels dwell in the world of *Yetzira*, applies to regular angels. However, there are higher-level angels in the world of *Beria* (called seraphim), whose service is with cognitive fear and love of God; as it is written in *Raya Meheimna* there, that there are two types of holy *ḥayot* angels, natural and cognitive ones, and as it states in *Etz Ḥayyim*.[2] In this gloss, the author of the *Tanya* observes that the

---

2. Presumably *Etz Ḥayyim* 50:7 (the Lubavitcher Rebbe, Rabbi Menaḥem

distinction mentioned here between divine souls and angels is not exactly parallel to the distinction between the world of *Beria* and the world of *Yetzira*. Although there is a parallel between them, which is discussed in this chapter, there are elements in which the correlation is more complex.

וְהַהֶבְדֵּל שֶׁבֵּינֵיהֶם הוּא כִּי בְּעוֹלַם הַיְצִירָה מְאִירוֹת שָׁם מִדּוֹתָיו שֶׁל אֵין סוֹף בָּרוּךְ הוּא לְבַדָּן, — The difference between them is that in the world of *Yetzira* the attributes of *Ein Sof*, blessed be He, shine there by themselves alone,

The difference between the worlds of *Beria* and *Yetzira* is not just one of location, but rather (as is true regarding all the spiritual worlds), it is a qualitative difference that completely sets apart the two worlds. The main difference is that in the world of *Yetzira*, the attributes of *Ein Sof*, which are the six *sefirot* of *Ḥesed*, *Gevura*, *Tiferet*, *Netzaḥ*, *Hod*, and *Yesod*, shine there by themselves, unlike the three intellectual *sefirot* of *Ḥokhma*, *Bina*, and *Da'at*, which do not shine there by themselves.

שֶׁהֵן אַהֲבָתוֹ וּפַחְדּוֹ וְיִרְאָתוֹ כו', וּכְמוֹ שֶׁכָּתוּב [בַּתִּיקּוּנִים וְעֵץ חַיִּים] דְּשִׁית סְפִירִין מְקַנְּנִין בִּיצִירָה. — these being the love, dread, and fear of Him, and so forth, and as it is written in *Tikkunei Zohar* and *Etz Ḥayyim*, that the six *sefirot* reside in *Yetzira*.

These six attributes that shine within the world of *Yetzira* are the love, dread, and fear of God, and so forth, for their love and fear of Him is

---

Mendel Schneerson). However, according to this, it is unclear in what way the souls of the righteous are above those of angels. The explanation is given elsewhere: Although some angels have intellectual ability, there is still a difference between angels and human souls. The angels are themselves intellect, and this means that their love and fear is not only natural but in keeping with intellect. Even so, it is not something they can actively use, and they have no free will at all. By contrast, besides the fact that the love and fear of souls are in keeping with intellect and understanding, souls possess free will, and their love and fear can be actualized (*Sefer HaMa'amarim* of the sixth Lubavitcher Rebbe, Rabbi Yosef Yitzḥak Schneerson, 5700, p. 33).

manifest in the world of *Yetzira*. The six *sefirot* reside in *Yetzira*, meaning that the place in which these attributes are revealed and active is the world of *Yetzira*.³

וְלָכֵן זֹאת הִיא עֲבוֹדַת הַמַּלְאָכִים תָּמִיד, יוֹמָם וָלַיְלָה לֹא יִשְׁקוֹטוּ, לַעֲמוֹד בְּיִרְאָה וָפַחַד וכו' וְהַיְינוּ כָּל מַחֲנֵה גַּבְרִיאֵל שֶׁמֵּהַשְּׂמֹאל,

Therefore, this is the constant service of the angels, from which **they do not rest day or night, to stand in fear and dread, and so on, and this is the whole camp of Gabriel that is on the left,**

Therefore, this is the constant service of the angels, from which they do not rest day or night, to stand in fear and dread of God. This is the whole camp of Gabriel, and all the angels connected to this side, which is on the left. The ten *sefirot* are organized in three lines: The left line (*Bina-Gevura-Hod*), the right line (*Hokhma-Hesed-Netzah*) and the middle line (*Da'at-Tiferet-Yesod*). The left line is generally the line of *Gevura*, and therefore the service of the angels and the quality of their service, which relates to this line, involve the fear and dread of God.

וַעֲבוֹדַת מַחֲנֵה מִיכָאֵל, הִיא הָאַהֲבָה כו'.

and the service of the camp of Michael, which is the love, and so forth.

RESIDE IN *YETZIRA*

☞ The general principle is that the *sefirot* of the world of *Atzilut* illuminate the four worlds of *Atzilut*, *Beria*, *Yetzira*, and *Asiya*. The *sefira* of *Hokhma* is in *Atzilut*. *Bina* is in the world of *Beria*. The six attributes are in the world of *Yetzira*. The *sefira* of *Malkhut* is in the world of *Asiya*. The world of *Yetzira* is therefore mainly the world of feelings, and the entities of the world (*Tikkunei Zo-har* 23a; see *Etz Hayyim, Sha'ar Seder Abiya,* chap. 5) of *Yetzira* operate in this area of feelings. Just as the entities in our world, the world of *Asiya*, experience as a natural and primary given the material world and physical action, so too the entities in the world of *Yetzira* experience the higher attributes, the love, dread, and fear of God.

---

3. *Tikkunei Zohar* 23a; see *Etz Hayyim, Sha'ar Seder Abiya,* chap. 5.

The service of the camp of Michael consists of all the angels that belong to the right side, which is the line of *Ḥesed*. The angels of the camp of Michael are those whose service and existence consist of love for God in all its forms and types.

The attributes of *Ḥesed* and *Gevura* are, in a sense, the patriarchs of the six attributes. Therefore, the angels mentioned here, the camps of Michael and Gabriel, include, in this sense, all the camps of the angels and entities of the entire world of *Yetzira*.

The service of the angels in love and fear reaches very high emotional levels. Yet this takes place without any amount of awareness or free choice generating the emotion. An angel loves God the same way that a spider weaves its web and a lion devours its prey. It does so not as an intelligent action, involving examination and choice through awareness, but rather as an instinct inherent in its nature. The angel that loves God is simply expressing its being. It loves God because it does not know anything different and is incapable of doing anything different. Its existence is one of love for God, just as an angel from a different camp is one of fearing God, or glorifying God, each camp having its particular trait and *sefira*. ☞

אֲבָל בְּעוֹלָם הַבְּרִיאָה מְאִירוֹת שָׁם חָכְמָתוֹ וּבִינָתוֹ וְדַעְתּוֹ שֶׁל אֵין סוֹף בָּרוּךְ הוּא, שֶׁהֵן מְקוֹר הַמִּדּוֹת וְאֵם וְשֹׁרֶשׁ לָהֶן. וְכִדְאִיתָא בַּתִּיקּוּנִים, דְּאִימָּא

However, in the world of *Beria*, the wisdom, understanding, and knowledge of *Ein Sof*, blessed be He, shine there. These are the source of the attributes, and their mother and root. As it states in *Tikkunei Zohar* (23a),

THE WORLD OF *YETZIRA*

☞ The world of *Yetzira* is the world of powerful emotions, the world of angels whose love and fear are immeasurably higher than that of man. At the same time, this is a natural world whose creatures all operate only according to instinct. Their instincts are the instincts of the holy *ḥayot*, which are on a much higher level, and involve greater intelligence, than that of a lion or ox of the lower world. Yet despite this, at their root, these creatures are of the same type as these animals. Just like animals, angels lack the power of awareness and choice that lead to love and fear. Their awareness, like their love, is one-dimensional. It has one valence, one meaning, and one end point in the expression of their root quality of love, fear, or glorification, and so forth, of God.

עִילָאָה מְקַנְּנָא בִּתְלָת סְפִירָן the supernal mother resides in the
בְּכָרְסַיָּא, שֶׁהוּא עוֹלָם הַבְּרִיאָה. three *sefirot*, on a throne which is the
world of *Beria*.

The "supernal mother" is the *sefira* of *Bina* of the world of *Atzilut*. It resides in, and is revealed through, the three *sefirot* of the intellect that are incorporated within it (because *Bina* is the main intellectual *sefira*, and in it is revealed the intellectuality that is composed of the three *sefirot*): Ḥokhma, Bina, and Daʾat. That occurs in the "world of the throne," which is the world of *Beria*. As described in Ezekiel's prophecy (1:26), the "throne" is positioned above the holy *ḥayot* (Ḥagiga 13a). This means that above the world of the angels, which is the world of *Yetzira*, there is a complete world, the world of *Beria*, that parallels all the worlds below it. The prophets refer to this world as "the world of the throne."

וְלָכֵן הוּא מְדוֹר נִשְׁמוֹת הַצַּדִּיקִים Therefore, it is the abode of the
עוֹבְדֵי ה' בִּדְחִילוּ וּרְחִימוּ, הַנִּמְשָׁכוֹת souls of the righteous, who serve
מִן הַבִּינָה וָדַעַת דִּגְדוּלַת אֵין סוֹף God with fear and love, these
בָּרוּךְ הוּא. emotions **being drawn from the
understanding and knowledge of
the greatness of *Ein Sof*, blessed
be He.**

Since the world of *Beria* is the world of lofty *Bina*, it is the abode of the souls of the righteous, who serve God with fear and love, emotions that come from the understanding and knowledge of the greatness of *Ein Sof*, blessed be He. These feelings blossom and draw their strength from the awareness associated with Ḥokhma, Bina, and Daʾat.

As stated previously, all service of God is service with one's attributes (such as love and fear, as they are directed toward enhanced holiness). When a person's service of God in the world is on the level of intellectual comprehension, which is the source and root of the attributes of love and fear, his service is connected to the level of the world of *Beria*. In other words, this is serving God with the attributes as they exist in their root, i.e., in *Bina* and *Daʾat*, which constitute the greatness and infinity of God which give rise to sensations of fear and love.

שֶׁאַהֲבָה זוֹ נִקְרָא 'רְעוּתָא For this love, rooted within the intellect, is called "the desire of the heart,"
דְלִבָּא', כַּנִּזְכָּר לְעֵיל, as stated above (chap. 17),

The power of a person's intellectual understanding that this is what his soul desires activates and reveals the love and fear within him, even if he does not feel it. ☞

וּמֵ'רְעוּתָא דְלִבָּא' נַעֲשֶׂה לְבוּשׁ and from "the desire of the heart" it
לְנִשְׁמָה בְּעוֹלָם הַבְּרִיאָה, becomes a garment for the person's soul in the world of *Beria*,

This inner love that emanates from *Bina* and *Da'at* becomes a garment for the soul, that is to say, a mediating layer that allows the soul to be present and to connect, to "live" in that world. Unlike an external feeling, the will of a person's heart and his internal feeling hidden within this level of consciousness is able to connect to the world of *Beria* and to make it possible for the soul to be present in that world, which is the loftier and more abstract world of the intellect.

שֶׁהוּא גַּן עֵדֶן הָעֶלְיוֹן כְּדִלְקַמָּן, which is the higher Garden of Eden,
וּכְמוֹ שֶׁכָּתוּב בַּזֹּהַר וַיַּקְהֵל (רִי, as will be explained **below, and as it is**
ב). **written in the *Zohar*, *Vayak'hel* (210b).**

DESIRE OF THE HEART

☞ There is a distinction between an external feeling, one that does not emanate from within a person's inner being, and a desire of the heart that wells up from within, deriving from a person's contemplation and recognition of something, which leads to his having an emotional connection to it. When a person's love or fear of God is external, like an awareness independent of him that does not emanate from the totality of the forces of his soul, he must examine this feeling and learn how to express it. However, as the feeling is revealed, drawn forth, and develops with the growth of his awareness, it as it were stands on its own. This is the inner "desire of the heart," which requires no external stimulus such as memories and exercises. It is the dread that emanates spontaneously from a person's awareness of the frightening nature of existence, or the love that a person feels when he examines something and automatically begins to love it, since the more he contemplates and scrutinizes it, the more he creates inside himself a love for it.

As will be explained, speaking very generally, there are two levels of the Garden of Eden. There is the supernal Garden of Eden and the lower Garden of Eden. Obviously, this refers not to above and below in any geographical sense (since this is discussing spiritual worlds), but rather to levels. The lower Garden of Eden is in the world of *Yetzira*, and the higher Garden of Eden is in the world of *Beria*. Accordingly, when saying that the soul exists in the Garden of Eden, we do not mean any kind of physical location. Instead, it refers to the connection the soul has to that existence via its "garments of the soul" formed from the love and fear that it possessed (or that it possesses) in this world. When that love and fear are on the level of the person's "desire of the heart," the soul is connected to and located in the world of *Beria*.

אַךְ הַיְינוּ דַּוְוקָא נְשָׁמוֹת מַמָּשׁ, **However, this applies specifically to actual *neshamot*, the highest soul level,** 8 Nisan

The statement that the dwelling place of the souls of the righteous is in the world of *Beria* applies specifically to the *neshama* in the kabbalistic sense of that word. As was explained, the human soul is made up of not one level, but a series of five levels, one above the other (*nefesh, ruaḥ, neshama, ḥaya, yeḥida*).[4] The highest level, the pinnacle of the revelation of a person's spiritual existence, is the level of *neshama* (since the levels of *ḥaya* and *yeḥida* are not revealed within a person).

שֶׁהֵן בְּחִינַת מוֹחִין דְּגַדְלוּת אֵין סוֹף בָּרוּךְ הוּא. **which is the level of the expanded awareness of Ein Sof, blessed be He.**

Only at the highest level of the revealed soul, the level of *neshama*, does awareness of the Divine exist on an expanded level. This is a direct awareness, comparable to sight (not only understanding achieved via examples and analogies), in which a person sees and recognizes God before his eyes. On that level, the divine soul within a person lives and

---

4. It has been explained that the levels of the soul (*nefesh, ruaḥ, neshama, ḥaya, yeḥida*) parallel the four worlds: *Asiya, Yetzira, Beria, Atzilut*. This indicates that the level of *neshama* parallels the world of *Beria*.

is revealed, and in it his love of God pours forth of itself, without any need for external arousal or action.

אֲבָל בְּחִינַת הָרוּחַ שֶׁל הַצַּדִּיקִים, But the level of *ruaḥ* of the righteous,

The level of *ruaḥ*, among the three levels of *nefesh*, *ruaḥ*, and *neshama*, is the level below *neshama*.

וְכֵן שְׁאָר כָּל נִשְׁמוֹת יִשְׂרָאֵל שֶׁעָבְדוּ אֶת ה' בְּדָחִילוּ וּרְחִימוּ הַמְסוּתָרוֹת בְּלֵב כְּלָלוּת יִשְׂרָאֵל, and similarly the rest of all the souls of Israel who have served God with the fear and love that are hidden in the heart of the totality of Israel,

THE *NEFESH*, *RUAḤ*, AND *NESHAMA* OF THE RIGHTEOUS

As has been explained (*Zohar* 2:94b), every Jew possesses all five levels of the soul (*nefesh*, *ruaḥ*, *neshama*, *ḥaya*, *yeḥida*). However, not every person is aware of and lives on all levels of the soul. Every person lives and is present on the level of his *nefesh*, which is the life of the body and the basic feelings related to it. Some, through their service in purifying the *nefesh*, also live in and experience the level of *ruaḥ*, which is the spiritual life of feeling love and fear of God, and so forth. Then there are those – generally speaking, the righteous – who ascend to and come to live as well the level of the *neshama* within them, meaning, intellectual being as it is comprehended by the intellect, which is the level of the most complete awareness and consciousness of the Divine that a person can reach. (The levels of *ḥaya* and *yeḥida* are surrounding layers that are never intellectually grasped or felt.)

EXPANDED AWARENESS AND DIMINISHED AWARENESS

A person's expanded awareness is the level of the intellect itself. In the spiritual worlds, as in the soul, each level is composed of all the levels. There are attributes within the intellect, and there is intellect within the attributes. Intellect is germane to even the level of *Asiya*.

The intellect within the attributes serves the attributes, as it were, in terms of how to present an attribute, how to acquire it, and so forth. This intellect is called diminished awareness, meaning intellectual power that is controlled by the attributes, which lack the clarity and breadth of intellect, and certainly lack the capabilities of the brain that rules over the heart.

Expanded awareness, by contrast, is the intellect itself, the ability to think and understand with the entire range and freedom of the nature of the intellect. There, the intellect rules over the heart and the divine soul rules over the animal soul.

This is true of the rest of all the souls of Israel, whose experience and location are not on the level of *neshama* (but on lower levels of the soul), who have served God not with intellectual love and fear but rather with the natural fear and love that are hidden in the heart of the totality of Israel. As explained previously, this is the "animal" level of the human being in terms of a person's intention and in his divine service overall.

אֵין עוֹלוֹת לְשָׁם, רַק בְּשַׁבָּת וְראֹשׁ חֹדֶשׁ לְבַד, **do not ascend there, except on the Sabbath and Rosh Ḥodesh,**

These souls do not ascend to the supernal Garden of Eden in the world of *Beria* except on the Sabbath and Rosh Ḥodesh. As the verse states, "It shall be that on each and every New Moon and on each and every Sabbath all flesh will come to prostrate themselves before Me, said the Lord" (Isa. 66:23).[5] ☞

EVERY PERSON LIVES ON MORE THAN ONE LEVEL OF EXISTENCE

☞ Just as the body does not exist in the spiritual world, so too, the soul does not exist in the physical world. Therefore, even the lowest person exists in at least two worlds: the physical, material world in which his body exists, and the spiritual world in which the soul of every person exists, even if that is at the lowest point of spirituality. Additionally, in the realm of *ruaḥ* as well, every person exists in more than one world, because parts of his soul are constantly on different levels and in different worlds. Even a person who belongs to an elevated spiritual world has aspects of his soul that reside at that moment in a lower world, in which he remembers a telephone number or deals with other matters that aren't particularly lofty. As a person grows physically, he becomes taller, his head rising higher and higher, but his feet remain on the ground. Accordingly, as a person grows, the breadth of his existence grows as well. As the space between the levels of his being widens, the differences between the levels of his soul and body became sharper and more significant, between the physical and spiritual, and even between spirit and spirit on the levels of spiritual worlds.

This means that the *nefesh*, *ruaḥ*, and *neshama* of the righteous person are spread out over the great expanse from

---

5. The Sabbath and Rosh Ḥodesh are the ascent of the worlds from the beginning of all levels to the end of all levels. Therefore, these souls too then ascend to a higher level. See *Likkutei Torah*, Lev. 41a (commentary of Rabbi Shmuel Gronem Esterman).

In contrast to the level of *neshama* of the righteous, the level of *ruaḥ* of the righteous and the totality of the life of the *ruaḥ* of other people ascend to the upper Garden of Eden only during special times, at supernal times of heavenly favor. There is then a general ascent of the worlds themselves to this high level. Therefore, during these occasions – the Sabbath, or Rosh Ḥodesh – when all the worlds are raised by one or more levels, the souls ascend with them.

דֶּרֶךְ הָעַמּוּד שֶׁמִּגַּן עֵדֶן הַתַּחְתּוֹן לְגַן עֵדֶן הָעֶלְיוֹן, **by means of the pillar that rises from the lower Garden of Eden to the higher Garden of Eden,**

As explained in many works of Hasidism,[6] in order for there to be an ascent from one level to another, an intermediate level of nullification must be traversed. Similarly, when a person is learning, in order to ascend to a higher level of understanding, he must first nullify his previous level.[7] Likewise, in order for a seed to sprout into a tree, it must first rot away in the earth, losing its prior character and becoming nothing. This nullification that exists between the level of the *neshama* in the lower Garden of Eden and the *neshama*'s level in the higher Garden of Eden is referred to by the description of "the pillar of the lower Eden that [rises] from the lower Garden of Eden to the higher Garden of

the physical world of *Asiya* up to the world of *Beria*. The level of the righteous person's *neshama* belongs to the world of the "throne," the world of *Beria*. On the lower levels of the righteous person's being, the level of emotional forces and downward, he is also on lower levels: in the world of *Yetzira* and below it. As explained in other places (see, e.g., *Likkutei Torah*, Lev. 18a), only a few exceptional individuals, who in the essence of their being belong to a different world, exist with all their being and all their lives in a higher state. These people exist in the lower worlds only as a secondary occupation, as it were, like visitors to the activity of our world, while in essence they have no relationship with the structure and components of this world.

---

6. See, e.g., the commentary to the introduction of *Sha'ar HaYiḥud VeHa'emuna*.

7. In many places in Hasidism this concept is mentioned in the context of the story of Rabbi Zeira, who, when he moved from Babylonia to the Land of Israel, fasted a hundred times in order to forget the Babylonian Talmud (see *Bava Metzia* 85a).

Eden."[8] The pillar that connects the floor to the ceiling draws down to the lower level from the very highest level, from an illumination that the lower level is unable to grasp. But it affects the lower level so that the present comprehension and entire existence of the lower level will cease to exist. Following this, via this pillar, the lower level can ascend and reach the comprehension of the higher level, which will become its existence.

שֶׁהוּא עוֹלָם הַבְּרִיאָה הַנִּקְרָא 'גַּן עֵדֶן הָעֶלְיוֹן' לְהִתְעַנֵּג עַל ה' וְלֵיהָנוֹת מִזִּיו הַשְּׁכִינָה. כִּי אֵין הֲנָאָה וְתַעֲנוּג לְשֵׂכֶל נִבְרָא אֶלָּא בַּמֶּה שֶׁמַּשְׂכִּיל וּמֵבִין וְיוֹדֵעַ וּמַשִּׂיג בְּשִׂכְלוֹ וּבִינָתוֹ מַה שֶּׁאֶפְשָׁר לוֹ לְהָבִין וּלְהַשִּׂיג מֵאוֹר אֵין סוֹף בָּרוּךְ הוּא, עַל יְדֵי חָכְמָתוֹ וּבִינָתוֹ יִתְבָּרֵךְ הַמְּאִירוֹת שָׁם בְּעוֹלַם הַבְּרִיאָה.

which is the world of *Beria*, called **the higher Garden of Eden**, which exists for the soul **to take delight in God and to enjoy the radiance of the Divine Presence. For there is no enjoyment and delight for the intellect of a created being other than in what it apprehends, understands, knows, and attains with its intellect and understanding of that which it is capable of understanding and attaining from the light of** *Ein Sof*, **blessed be He, by means of His wisdom and understanding, which shine there in the world of** *Beria*.

In the Garden of Eden, "the righteous sit ... and enjoy the radiance of the Divine Presence" (*Berakhot* 17a). The enjoyment and pleasure of the *neshama* is primarily a pleasure of comprehension. That pleasure comes from the comprehension, and especially when that comprehension is realized and fulfilled (just as the pleasure in every sense and ability is found in its actualization). Therefore, the higher Garden of Eden, which is the Garden of Eden at its highest level, exists in the world of *Beria*, which is the world of higher comprehension (*Bina*), as

---

8. See *Torah Or* 22d, 7c. See also the commentary of Rabbi Shmuel Gronem Esterman: As is known, the concept of the pillar refers to the drawing down to souls of that which is above, until a soul is divested of its initial level, and in this way it can ascend upward.

was explained. This is the world of intellectual attainment in which the *neshama* grasps all that it can of the light of *Ein Sof*. It is in this world that the soul attains a full and complete power of understanding.

All that a person comprehends in this world, even when his comprehension is lofty, is still only a faint glimmer of comprehension when compared to the understanding attained in the higher world. There, comprehension is stripped of the physical, because understanding and wisdom are the essence of that world's existence. They are that reality itself. When a person's soul is ready to enter that world, it attains the distillation of all pleasures, the intellectual pleasure of reaching the most complete comprehension possible (the ultimate purpose of comprehension) of the divine existence. ☞☞☞

THE WORLD OF BERIA

☞ *Hokhma* is in the world of *Atzilut*. However, as was explained, comprehension mainly takes place in *Bina* and not in *Hokhma*. Although *Hokhma* is the source of the intellect, it cannot be contemplated. Meaningful, tangible, intellectual comprehension to which a person can relate, which he can ponder and enjoy, belongs specifically to the world of *Beria*.

FOUR LEVELS OF COMPREHENSION

☞ The *Tanya*'s language, "apprehends, understands, knows, and attains," indicates four levels (related to the four worlds: *Atzilut*, *Beria*, *Yetzira*, and *Asiya*). "Apprehends" indicates the level of *Hokhma* (see *Likkutei Torah*, Song 33a), analogous to the planting of a seed. "Understands" refers to the level of *Bina*, in which the seed grows and develops into a multidimensional entity. "Knows" expresses the level of *Da'at*, when a person connects to that which he comprehends. "Attains" reflects the level of acquisition, which is the ultimate comprehension in the full meaning of the term "intellectual grasp."

It is possible for a person to apprehend, understand, and know something, even to explain it to other people, without truly grasping it in a way that it becomes his, a part of him. It can remain foreign, despite his understanding of it. Attaining comprehension is the level where that which is comprehended has tangibility. It relates to the person not only in an abstract way, but as a part of him that is so tangible that he intuits it as strongly as he intuits his own existence.

THE AUTHOR OF THE TANYA AND THE RAMBAM

☞ The description of the Garden of Eden here, not coincidentally, is similar to the Rambam's description of the World to Come (see *Sefer HaMadda, Hilkhot Teshuva* 8:2). It is noteworthy that the author of the *Tanya* bases himself on the Rambam, and even quotes him in many places, despite having a different perspective

וּמַה שֶּׁזּוֹכוֹת נְשָׁמוֹת אֵלּוּ לַעֲלוֹת לְמַעְלָה מֵהַמַּלְאָכִים, אַף שֶׁעָבְדוּ בִּדְחִילוּ וּרְחִימוּ טִבְעִיִּים לְבַד,	As for the fact that these souls merit to ascend higher than the angels, even though they served with only natural fear and love,

The statement that souls ascend to the upper Garden of Eden, to a level even higher than that of the angels, is understandable regarding the souls of the righteous who serve with intellectual love and fear. Because of this, they are connected to the pleasure of total comprehension found in the world of *Beria*. But why is this so of those souls that served God not with intellectual love and fear, but only with natural love and fear? The divine service of these souls was not on a higher level than the service of angels, and they served God with love and fear that was merely an expression of their natural character, like the animals below and the angels above. In fact, an angel certainly has more revealed love and fear than that found in man. So why, despite this, does the soul of man ascend on the Sabbath and Rosh Ḥodesh above the angels, who dwell in the world of *Yetzira*, as was explained? A person who had a connection only to natural love and fear, not intellectual love and

---

from him (primarily on the topic of reward). Similarly, the author of the *Tanya* bases himself on kabbalistic viewpoints and ideas of scholars besides the Arizal (such as Rabbi Moshe Kordovero).

These are important points in understanding the broad and inclusive approach of the author of the *Tanya*. The kabbalistic thought of the Arizal did not necessarily negate the works of previous scholars. The philosophical perspective of the Rambam and the kabbalistic approach of Rabbi Kordovero are not now viewed as mistaken and wrong, nor as deviant. The idea here is that all these approaches are considered to be true, but they serve as partial perspectives within the all-inclusive framework of the Kabbala of the Arizal. The previous perspective was not wrong, but rather an isolated occurrence, correct within a particular framework, within particular coordinates and limited parameters. It is correct as an individual occurrence and within one world, within a massive, infinite framework of possible worlds.

Accordingly, the perspective of the Rambam is still established and firm, even though it describes only one piece of the picture. The way the Rambam, and somewhat similarly, the author of the *Tanya*, describe the concept of reward is dependent upon a particular approach, and even, to a certain degree, upon a certain personality's intellectual understanding. However, it is understood that other conceptualizations and other perspectives are not to be rejected, but are, in fact, correct in individual occurrences, and they appear when appropriate.

fear, should not be able to ascend to the upper Garden of Eden in the world of *Beria*. ☞

הַיְינוּ מִפְּנֵי שֶׁעַל יְדֵי דְחִילוּ וּרְחִימוּ שֶׁלָּהֶם אִתְכַּפְיָא סִטְרָא אָחֳרָא הַמְלוּבֶּשֶׁת בְּגוּפָם בֵּין בִּבְחִינַת 'סוּר מֵרָע', לִכְבּוֹשׁ הַתַּאֲווֹת וּלְשַׁבְּרָן, וּבֵין בִּבְחִינַת 'וַעֲשֵׂה טוֹב', כַּנִּזְכָּר לְעֵיל.

the reason is that due to their fear and love, the *sitra aḥara*, the *kelippa* that is enclothed in their bodies is subdued, whether in terms of "turning away from evil," conquering one's lusts and breaking them, or whether in terms of "doing good," as stated above (chap. 25).

The service of man, including that performed with his natural love and fear, is higher than the service of the angels. An angel has no body and no dark "other side." An angel is entirely one side, entirely one will and one proclamation. Therefore, an angel does not struggle in its service of God. By contrast, a person must struggle to serve God, whether in the realm of avoiding evil or the aspect of doing good. The breaking of one's lusts, which stem from the *sitra aḥara*, the side of evil, occurs when one refrains from committing evil acts, whether in thought, word, or deed.

THE STATE OF THE SOUL IN THE GARDEN OF EDEN

☞ As was explained, there is a parallel between the soul and the world in which it finds itself. Within the framework of "world-year-soul" (the three dimensions of the world, as formulated in *Sefer Yetzira*), there is necessarily a match between each world and the souls in it. Souls, whether those of human beings or angels, possess the quality and character of that world, and a soul that lacks the quality of a specific world is not found in that world. Although it is possible to give a person any kind of reward, even the Garden of Eden, it is impossible to give him a new "I."

There is a story told of a simple Jew who owned a wagon. He once encountered an opportunity to fulfill the major commandment of saving a life. Stampeding horses were about to pull a wagon filled with passengers off a cliff, and he stood in the path of the horses and stopped the wagon.

Years went by and the man passed away, arriving before the heavenly court. The court ruled that because he had risked his life to save a number of souls of Israel, and when one saves one such person, it is as if he has saved an entire world, then although he had lived most of his life without following the Torah and its commandments, he deserved a share in the World to Come. However, since he was not capable of receiving the pleasure of either the high-

וְהֵם הָיוּ בַּעֲלֵי בְחִירָה לִבְחוֹר בָּרָע חַס וְשָׁלוֹם, וּבָחֲרוּ בַּטּוֹב לְאַכְפְּיָא לְסִטְרָא אָחֳרָא, לְאִסְתַּלְקָא יְקָרָא דְקוּדְשָׁא בְּרִיךְ הוּא כו' כִּיתְרוֹן הָאוֹר כו', כַּנִּזְכָּר לְעֵיל.

They had the free will to choose evil, God forbid, but they chose good, to subdue the *sitra aḥara*, to raise up the glory of the Holy One, blessed be He, in all the worlds, **like the advantage of the light** over the darkness, **as stated above.**

These souls had the free will to choose evil, God forbid, and they chose good, to subdue the *sitra aḥara*, to raise up the glory of the Holy One, blessed be He, in all worlds, like the advantage of the light over the darkness, as stated above.[9] From this perspective, a human being has an advantage over not only a physical animal, but also over the holy *ḥayot*, angels, and seraphim. The difference between a machine, a living creature, and an angel in this sense is only a difference of degree, but they all can be characterized as "stationary."[10] A human being, by contrast, is uniquely characterized as "moving." This means that due to his power of free will, he has the ability to move up and down and

er Garden of Eden or the lower one, it was impossible to give him a place there, where the righteous bask in the radiance of the Divine Presence. The court judges asked him what he wanted, and he said that he would like a new wagon and horse. So they granted him a chariot with six horses, and a straight path without any obstacles. Since then, he has been riding that chariot, the horses constantly galloping.

This man could not comprehend anything more than this, and the vessel of his soul was unable to receive any greater pleasure, so this became his Garden of Eden. In the same vein, the transition from the upper Garden of Eden to the lower one does not involve simply a change of location, of moving a soul from one place to another. Rather, it is a matter of the qualitative essence of a particular soul. A soul that does not belong to a place cannot be brought there, as that place means nothing to it, and therefore, it cannot enter there. However, as will be explained, the soul of man, in contrast to an angel, is also more than that. Like the angel, the soul of man exists in a place, yet it is also always beyond that place. At its root, in the hidden, innermost point, man's soul is embedded in God, who is beyond all worlds. As a result, under certain conditions, such a soul can choose a new place, rising and making that new place its own.

---

9. Chap. 27, and the end of chap. 33. See also *Likkutei Torah*, Num. 65c. Based on the *Zohar* 2:128b, 284a.

10. Zech. 30:7. See the commentary on *Sha'ar HaYiḥud VeHa'emuna*, "Ḥinukh Katan," p. 76a.

within all the worlds. This is the reason why everything depends on man, for only he can raise up the glory of God in all the worlds. ☞

Elsewhere[11] it is written that "raising up the glory of God in all the worlds" means that one draws that which "surrounds all worlds," into that which "fills all worlds." When something is revealed in its proper place, according to its measure and meaning, it "fills all worlds." But when God is revealed in a place that has no holiness at all, this is a revelation of "surrounds all worlds," a piercing of all boundaries of existence. This is accomplished when a person subdues the *sitra aḥara*.

For what connection can a person have with *Ein Sof*? Limited man can never truly reach the absolute *Ein Sof*. Nevertheless, he can at least uncouple himself from the finite. This is not reaching the infinite, but it is still transcending the finite. At the moment that a person breaks that barrier, even in the smallest way, the barrier essentially ceases to exist. When there is a tiny hole in a giant dam, it is only a matter of time before the dam will burst.

Using gravity as an analogy, it is difficult for an object to escape the pull of gravity. At the moment that an object passes the barrier of escape velocity, however, it can reach any place. The instant a

---

SUBDUING THE *SITRA AḤARA* ELEVATES THE DIVINE

☞ The word *olamot* (worlds) is related to *he'elem* (hiddenness). In every revelation, there is necessarily a hidden aspect, something that remains unrevealed. Each world is a revelation of what it contains together with a concealment of that which is beyond it. The entire system of progressive transmutations – descent after descent, devolution after devolution – is a chain of concealments, world beneath world, reaching until the lowest world, which we dwell in with our bodies. This world is the lowest because it contains a *sitra aḥara*, so that it possesses not only a concealment of holiness, but also its denial: a denial of God, the Creator of the world. It is the lowest world because it includes within it the possibility of denying all that exists above it. God is the *Kadosh* (Holy One), who is essentially separated, the Supreme Being who cannot be comprehended by any parameter and in any world. When a person subdues the *sitra aḥara* in the lowest world, he draws the holy divine light to the lowest concealment. When he finds himself in the *kelippa* that says "There is no God!" and he responds, "There is a God!" it is as if he reveals our purpose regarding all worlds: to disclose that even "in the valley of the shadow of death...You are with me" (Ps. 23:4).

---

11. See *Likkutei Torah*, Num. 65c.

person pierces the axiom that a world is a world, at the moment that he discovers, even in the smallest way, that a world (*olam*) is not a world in the sense that it conceals (*he'elem*) God's existence, he is no longer in that world. When a law of nature is disproved even in only one small way, even if in thousands of other incidences it is correct, that law is no longer a law. Similarly, when a person breaks the *kelippa*, even in only one small way, he rises beyond the boundaries of the world, transcending his own limitations. At such times, he is able to reach the upper Garden of Eden, the world of *Beria*, even if he does not truly belong there.

The problem is that when a person subdues the *sitra aḥara*, it does not inform him that it is giving in but rather reappears in a new form and continues to fight. This makes it difficult for a person to see and feel what is happening. But as was said, each subduing of the *sitra aḥara* is essentially a fundamental breaking of its character, of the character of the concealment of the Divine, and the drawing of the Divine that is beyond all worlds into the worlds. This is specifically accomplished by man and specifically in the lowest world.

A human being has an advantage not only over animals but even over the holy *ḥayot*, angels, and seraphim. This advantage stems from the fact that his soul is truly a portion of God on high. Despite this, in this world, with his apparent level of comprehension, he can exist at a very low level, certainly lower than that of the angels. Yet even in this state, he still has within him a spark of the Divine, expressed on every level in his freedom to choose holiness and overcome the *sitra aḥara*. When he succeeds in actualizing this higher power of choice and overpowers the *sitra aḥara*, he connects himself with that supernal part, a portion of God on high, which is higher even than the level of angels.

When a person does not reach high levels of intellectual love and fear of God in this world, it is not because of something missing in his character. Rather, it stems from circumstances or lack of opportunities for success, due to his lack of time or ability. But his essence possesses a spark of the Divine, and therefore, even if he cannot currently achieve that comprehension, since he contains the basis and foundation for this connection, he has the capacity to connect in some way to these things, despite the fact that they are far beyond his ability to understand.

The concept of "an incomplete righteous person" includes one who is lacking because he has not yet finished that which he can and must do. In this sense, each person of Israel, even the simplest one, carries the power to serve God at all levels, though not every individual manages to complete the work. This issue is linked to environment and education; it is related to a long list of possible obstacles. But ultimately, the capacity for growth exists within each person. Consequently, at special times, the soul can develop further, even enabling it to rise to the upper Garden of Eden, accomplishing what even the angels cannot.

וְהִנֵּה כָּל זֶה הוּא בִּמְדוֹר הַנְּשָׁמוֹת וּמְקוֹם עֲמִידָתָן, **All of this** applies **in the abode of the souls and in the place where they stand,**

That which was said about the abode of souls, the world and environment in which the souls live, as well as the place they are able to rise to and stand in at specific times (in the higher Garden of Eden or lower Garden of Eden[12]) was stated in reference to the location of the souls themselves.

אַךְ תּוֹרָתָן וַעֲבוֹדָתָן נִכְלָלוֹת מַמָּשׁ בְּעֶשֶׂר סְפִירוֹת שֶׁהֵן בְּחִינַת אֱלֹהוּת, **but their Torah and service are literally incorporated within the ten** *sefirot*, **which are the level of divinity,**

There is a difference between the place of the souls and the place of the Torah these souls learn and the service of God they perform. Their Torah learning and service of God are not related to the placement and rules of the higher Garden of Eden and lower Garden of Eden, of the worlds of *Yetzira* or *Beria*. Rather, they are actually incorporated into the ten *sefirot* within that particular world, those *sefirot* being on the level of divinity. Just as there are ten broadly inclusive *sefirot* in the world of *Atzilut*, each of the lower worlds also has its own ten *sefirot*. The ten *sefirot* of each world are the manifestation of the Divine in that world. That divinity is the root of *Ḥokhma* in that world, the root

---

12. For the place where they stand is sometimes not in their abode, as on the Sabbath or Rosh Ḥodesh, because they ascend to *Beria* even though their place is in *Yetzira* (the Lubavitcher Rebbe, Rabbi Menaḥem Mendel Schneerson).

of the *Ḥesed* and *Gevura* that construct that world, and so forth. Thus, the soul itself, a created entity, exists in the world relevant to it, either *Asiya* or *Yetzira* or *Beria*. But the Torah that the soul learns and the commandments it fulfills are inherently divine, and they ascend and unite with the level of divinity of that world, that is, its ten *sefirot*.

וְאוֹר אֵין סוֹף מִתְיַיחֵד בָּהֶן בְּתַכְלִית הַיִּחוּד – **and the light of *Ein Sof* is unified with them in the ultimate union –**

The ten *sefirot* in each world – *Beria*, *Yetzira*, and *Asiya* – are not like the creations within each world. They are not like people, animals, and birds that exist in the world of *Asiya*, or like beings on other levels relevant to the worlds of *Yetzira* and *Beria*. The ten *sefirot* are the divine structure, the divine driving force within each world. They are not the revelation of that world's existence, but the divinity that operates within it, the being that is on every level unified with *Ein Sof* Himself.

A person is a being that exists within the world he inhabits, whether on a higher or lower level. His Torah and divine service, on the other hand, are included within the ten *sefirot* of that world, meaning that they are included within *Ein Sof* Himself, Who exists in all levels.

Accordingly, whereas there are differences between people regarding the levels of their soul as well as their levels of comprehension, there is no difference between people regarding the commandments they fulfill. A commandment that was executed with a higher level of comprehension, with loftier love and fear, is not necessarily a holier commandment. There is a difference in the path and in other factors, but each commandment, by virtue of it being a commandment, unites with the infinite divine light which is beyond all factors.

וְהַיְינוּ, בְּעֶשֶׂר סְפִירוֹת דִּבְרִיאָה עַל יְדֵי דְּחִילוּ וּרְחִימוּ שִׂכְלִיִּים, **that is, in the ten *sefirot* of *Beria*, by means of intellectual fear and love,**

When a person engages in Torah and service with intellectual love and fear, they unite with the ten *sefirot* of the world of *Beria*.

וּבְעֶשֶׂר סְפִירוֹת דִּיצִירָה עַל יְדֵי דְּחִילוּ וּרְחִימוּ טִבְעִיִּים, **and in the ten *sefirot* of *Yetzira*, by means of natural fear and love,**

When a person engages in Torah and divine service with natural love and fear, they unite with the ten *sefirot* of the world of *Yetzira*.

וּבְתוֹכָן מְלוּבָּשׁוֹת עֶשֶׂר סְפִירוֹת דַּאֲצִילוּת, וּמְיֻחָדוֹת בָּהֶן בְּתַכְלִית, — in which the ten *sefirot* of *Atzilut* are enclothed, and which are completely unified in them,

As was explained, the ten *sefirot* in each world are, in their inner being, unified with *Ein Sof*. How so? The ten *sefirot* of *Atzilut* are enclothed and are completely unified within the ten *sefirot* of the world of *Beria* and of the world of *Yetzira*. The divine force that operates within the ten *sefirot* within each world, even within our lowest of worlds, is fundamentally the infinite divine power itself that operates within all the worlds. The ten *sefirot* of the world of *Atzilut* are enclothed within the ten *sefirot* of the world of *Beria*, which are themselves clothed within the ten *sefirot* of the world of *Yetzira*, which are enclothed within the ten *sefirot* of the world of *Asiya*.

וְעֶשֶׂר סְפִירוֹת דַּאֲצִילוּת מְיֻחָדוֹת בְּתַכְלִית בְּמַאֲצִילָן אֵין סוֹף בָּרוּךְ הוּא. — and the ten *sefirot* of *Atzilut* are completely unified with their Emanator, *Ein Sof*, blessed be He.

This means that unification with the ten *sefirot* (in any of the worlds) is a unification with the Emanator, with *Ein Sof* Himself. The lower the world, the more concealed the divine force within it. Yet even so, it is the divine light, the light of *Ein Sof* Himself. The difference, as was explained, is only within the experiential sense of the perceiver, but not the level of the essence of the perceived. As an analogy, brought previously (chap. 4), whether a person holds the actual hand of the king or the king's hand wrapped in his sleeve, he is holding the hand of the king himself. Similarly, with regard to divine service, to studying the Torah and performing the commandments, a person is connected to the Divine in each world. Even though God appears in each world according to its level, in His essence He is always the same.

מַה שֶּׁאֵין כֵּן הַנְּשָׁמוֹת, אֵינָן נִכְלָלוֹת בֶּאֱלֹהוּת דְּעֶשֶׂר הַסְּפִירוֹת, אֶלָּא — Which is not the case with regard to the souls. They are not

עוֹמְדוֹת בְּהֵיכָלוֹת וּמְדוֹרִין incorporated in the divinity of the
דִּבְרִיאָה אוֹ יְצִירָה, ten *sefirot*; rather, they stand in the
palaces and abodes of *Beria* or *Yetzira*,

Even when the soul fulfills a commandment, it remains as it was: a created soul. As a result of its Torah study, its performance of the commandments, and its personal divine service, it reaches a higher level of existence in a higher world, and thus experiences the radiance of the Divine Presence. But the soul does not itself transform into a part of the essence of the Divine Presence. The commandment a person performs unites with the Divine, but his soul remains an independent being, part of the world, existing as one of the creatures within the palaces and dwellings of that world. The soul only grasps something, an illumination, a radiance, of the commandment it performs, according to the level of the world within which the commandment exists.

The difference between a commandment and the person performing it lies in the fact that the person has an "I," a soul with its own identity and existence. Because of this, the soul belongs to a specific created world and to a particular level, and it does not completely cleave and become nullified to the Divine (except in rare instances, as will be explained). A commandment, by contrast, has no "I" of its own. A commandment is an angel. God sends an angel via His commanding of the mitzva, and with our fulfillment of the mitzva it is as if we are sending an angel back to God. The commandment from its beginning is divine, a revelation of the divine to the world. The person is not creating that revelation with his intentions or the power of his goodwill. Rather, he just reveals the commandment. When he performs it, he reveals the holiness that is present within existence. ☞

THE STATUS OF A PERSON RELATIVE TO HIS TORAH AND COMMANDMENTS

☞ The entire world is filled with Godliness, with divine sparks, but they have no ability to ascend and connect with the Source, the Creator. Man's purpose in the world is to free them, to position them in a manner and place that will allow them to recreate their connection with the Divine. This action by man is the performance of a commandment. As described by the phrase customarily said before performing a commandment, commandments are "the unification of the Holy One, may He be blessed, and

What becomes of the man himself, the one performing the commandment? He remains a human being. The commandment elevates a person, but it does not transfer its infinite essence, the unity of the performance of the commandment and the divine essence, to him. A person remains a person, and the commandment he performed always remains a commandment. This is true whether he performed the commandment because his father taught it to him when he was a child, because of an inner natural love, because he wishes to act on behalf of God, or out of intellectual love and fear of God.

The action of the commandment the person performs, which connects the Holy One with His Divine Presence, linking the divine light in each world with the divine light transcending all worlds, is truly lofty, far above the person himself. This relationship between the person and his Torah study and service, in which basically he is incapable of comprehending the true greatness of the action, is in a way essential to his capacity to fulfill the commandment, and therefore essential to its fulfillment. ☞ ☞

His Divine Presence." The Divine Presence refers to the divine that is found within the world in exile, within the material and physical, within other entities. The "Holy One, may He be blessed," is the divine existence that transcends the world. The purpose of man is to build the connection, to close the circuit of the divine reality, to connect the divine light that is beyond the world with the divine light within the world. A commandment creates that connection at every level, opening the flow of divine energy between God and the divine truth within the world. This means that a person does not in himself generate the effect brought about by the commandment. Rather, he forms the contact point, as when a person completes an electrical circuit. He did not create the circuit, yet without his action, nothing would have happened. Man has a unique role, since he possesses free will and can freely move within the world and perform commandments. This allows him to move the "switches" that are scattered throughout the world, changing the meaning of things, creating groupings and connections, completing the circuit that allows the Divine to flow into all of existence.

THE POWER OF A SIMPLE PERSON

☞ There is an ancient story about a crown being made for a king. A precious, one-of-a-kind stone must be placed in this crown in a very specific way, or otherwise the stone will break. When the craftsman reaches the stage of placing the stone, he is unsuccessful. His hands shake with fear, because he realizes how each of his movements has the potential to ruin the project. In that situation, the only way to finish the work is to give the stone to a simple worker, who lacks understanding or knowledge of the value of the crown and the danger of fixing the stone in it, and to tell him: "Put this stone here!" The worker does so without becoming self-conscious or distracted, because he does not understand the gravity of the situation. His hands do not shake because he does not feel the danger, and this allows him to complete the task exactly as he was instructed.

In this example, it is specifically the simple person who is able to act. A great person cannot, because he is too great. Along these lines, it is said that the most difficult work for a truly lofty person is not to see the supernal lights. The definition of a truly lofty person in this sense is someone who can continue his divine service while ignoring the supernal lights that he sees. His struggle is not regarding how to ascend but rather how to stop himself from losing touch with the lower aspects of reality as he rises. While for most people, the great challenge is the stripping away of the physical, for the righteous, elevated person, the challenge is how not to be stripped of physicality, how to remain connected to the material world and not be disconnected from it.

Stories are told of a number of righteous people who, while praying, would hold an object in their hands and look at it from time to time. They did this to maintain their connection with reality, with the dimensions of time and space, especially during prayer, so that they would not completely leave the world.

It is said that during the last years of Rabbi Yeḥiel Mikhel of Zlotchov, his family would watch over him. There was a fear that he would ascend to such spiritual heights that he would be unable to return to this world and would be consumed in his clinging to God. Therefore, someone would always make sure to distract him whenever it seemed that he was rising too high. The story is told that one day, his daughter was responsible for watching him, and she went out for a moment. When she returned, she found him pacing in his room, repeating again and again the phrase from the *Zohar* (2:88b), "With this will, Moses left the world; with this will, Moses left the world." She quickly called her brother to help her, and they grabbed their father and shook him, but it was too late. They could no longer reach him. He no longer recognized anyone, and shortly afterward he passed away.

"I THE LORD DID NOT CHANGE"

☞ Elsewhere (*Likkutei Torah*, Deut. 61d), the author of the *Tanya* explains as a question the words of the prophet: "I the Lord did not change, and you, sons of Jacob, did not perish" (Mal. 3:6): The Lord did not change: He was Himself prior to creating the world, and He is Himself after creating the world. The divine existence is infinite, filling all, including our own human reality. The question of the prophet is: How is it possible that "the sons of Jacob did not perish"? How is it possible that human beings are not totally consumed by their yearning for God? That is the starting point of the author of this book. Therefore, one may understand why the book is written the way that it is: organized, almost dry, with traditional frameworks, and no unusual, emotional phraseology. Since the author must constantly expend all his might to contain the intensity of his own passion, since the inner meaning of the book is a storming fire, the author must guard himself like one who guards a volcano to prevent it from exploding. He builds around this passion using technical, rational, and cold terms, in order to preserve the light within the vessel, in order to keep the vessel whole.

וְנֶהֱנִין מִזִּיו הַשְּׁכִינָה, הוּא אוֹר אֵין סוֹף בָּרוּךְ הוּא הַמְיֻחָד בְּעֶשֶׂר סְפִירוֹת דִּבְרִיאָה אוֹ דִּיצִירָה, **and they derive pleasure from the radiance of the Divine Presence, which is the light of** *Ein Sof,* **blessed be He, that is unified in the ten** *sefirot* **of** *Beria* **or** *Yetzira,*

As was stated, the position of a person in the spiritual worlds is lower than the Torah he has studied and the commandments he has performed, so much so that he is essentially unable to comprehend the character of what he is doing. Nevertheless, his Torah study and divine service affect his soul. The *neshama* at best exists in the palaces and abodes of the worlds of *Beria* and *Yetzira*, whereas the person's Torah and service are included within the *sefirot* themselves. The individual *neshama* cannot itself be a part of the essence of the Divine Presence, of the essence of the ten holy *sefirot*, but it can derive pleasure from the glory of the Divine Presence.

וְהוּא זִיו תּוֹרָתָן וַעֲבוֹדָתָן מַמָּשׁ [עַיֵּין זֹהַר וַיַּקְהֵל דַּף ר"י], **and this is the actual radiance of their Torah and service (see** *Zohar, Vayak'hel* **210),**

The radiance of the Divine Presence that the *neshamot* enjoy is the radiance of their Torah and service. When a person studies Torah and performs commandments, even when these activities rise to a level beyond the ability of his soul to comprehend, a connection remains that enables him to perceive the Divine through the Torah he has studied and the commandments he has performed.

כִּי שְׂכַר מִצְוָה - הִיא מִצְוָה עַצְמָהּ. **for the reward of a mitzva is the mitzva itself (see** *Avot* **4:2).**

The highest reward a person can receive for performing a commandment is the commandment itself: to feel – at least to whatever extent a person is capable of – the essence of the commandment, and to derive pleasure from the radiance of the Divine Presence that passes to him through the commandment he has performed.

וְעוֹלַם הָאֲצִילוּת שֶׁהוּא לְמַעְלָה **But the world of** *Atzilut* **lies beyond the intelligence, perception, and**

מֵהַשֵּׂכֶל וְהַהַשָּׂגָה וְהַהֲבָנָה לְשֵׂכֶל נִבְרָא, **understanding of the intellect of a created being,**

As was explained previously, the place where souls receive the reward for performing commandments, where they derive the intellectual pleasure or emotional excitement from the commandments (respectively, the higher Garden of Eden and the lower Garden of Eden), are the worlds of *Yetzira* and *Beria*. As discussed, the world of *Beria* is the world of *Bina*, the world in which the intellectual entities in *Hokhma*, *Bina*, and *Da'at* are revealed. It is understood that there are lofty levels of intellect that not everyone can attain. But when we speak of the world of *Beria* as the world of intellect, it means that it can be intellectually understood, that its character is that of intellect that a created being can grasp. By contrast, the world of *Atzilut* is intrinsically above the intellect, beyond the grasp and understanding of the intellect of a created being. This is true for both small and large intellects: for the intellect of a human being, an angel, or a seraph. Anything that is in the realm of created beings is incapable of grasping the world of *Atzilut*.

כִּי חָכְמָתוֹ וּבִינָתוֹ וְדַעְתּוֹ שֶׁל אֵין סוֹף בָּרוּךְ הוּא מְיוּחָדוֹת שָׁם בּוֹ בְּתַכְלִית הַיִּחוּד, בְּיִחוּד עָצוּם וְנִפְלָא, בְּיֶתֶר שְׂאֵת וְיֶתֶר עֹז לְאֵין קֵץ מִבְּעוֹלַם הַבְּרִיאָה. **because the wisdom, understanding, and knowledge of *Ein Sof*, blessed be He, are unified in Him there with the ultimate union, with an immense and wonderful union, with infinitely greater magnitude and greater power than in the world of *Beria*.**

By its nature, the world of *Beria*, which is a created world, belongs to the parameters and character called "world." The definition of "world" is a reality bounded by rules of some sort, a reality in which *Ein Sof* is concealed and hidden, leading to its sense of having its own separate "I." The *Hokhma* and *Bina* of God are revealed and intelligible to created beings only within the defined and finite frameworks of a world, within a reality that is not completely identified with, unified with, the divine *Ein Sof*. But in the world of *Atzilut* there is essentially no distinction between God and the world. In *Atzilut*, the *Hokhma* and *Bina* of God are no longer *Hokhma* and *Bina* of a world, but *Hokhma* and *Bina* completely unified with God alone. No created being can grasp them.

From the perspective of a created being, just as there is no way to comprehend the essence of God, there is no way to comprehend God's *Ḥokhma, Bina,* or *Da'at* that is intrinsically unified with Him. They can be comprehended only when they are revealed in a created world.

The gap between divine *Ḥokhma* in itself and *Ḥokhma* that relates to creation is unbridgeable. It is said that "it is not the way of a king to deal with mundane issues."[13] Both the higher and lower worlds are "mundane issues" relative to God. Despite this, God does, as it were, engage in the worlds because He is "our Father, our King." Even if a king does not involve himself in mundane issues, a father frequently involves himself with his children, each according to their level, even with trivialities. Those are God's *Ḥokhma* and *Bina* as they are revealed in the worlds of creation. But in regard to God's *Ḥokhma* and *Bina* in the world of *Atzilut*, there, as it were, God is speaking with Himself. No created being can comprehend that world, and it is clear that there is an endless, yawning divide between God and the world.

כִּי שָׁם יָרְדוּ לְהָאִיר בִּבְחִינַת צִמְצוּם כְּדֵי שֶׁיּוּכְלוּ שְׂכָלִים נִבְרָאִים לְקַבֵּל מֵהֶן חָכְמָה בִּינָה דַּעַת לֵידַע אֶת ה' וּלְהָבִין וּלְהַשִּׂיג אֵיזוֹ הַשָּׂגָה בְּאוֹר אֵין סוֹף בָּרוּךְ הוּא, כְּפִי כֹּחַ שְׂכָלִים הַנִּבְרָאִים, שֶׁהֵם בַּעֲלֵי גְבוּל וְתַכְלִית,	For there they descended to shine in a constricted manner, in order that the intellects of created beings would be able to receive wisdom, understanding, and knowledge from them, to know God and to understand and attain some apprehension of the light of *Ein Sof*, blessed be He, in accordance with the strength of the intellects of created beings, which are bordered and bounded.

However, in the world of *Beria*, the intellect of created beings is capable of comprehension. In that world, God's *Ḥokhma* is not revealed in its full essence, but rather in a constricted manner. This is so that the intellects of created beings can receive wisdom, understanding, and

---

13. *Zohar* 3:149b; see also *Likkutei Torah*, Lev. 25d.

knowledge for the purpose of knowing God and attaining something of the light of *Ein Sof*, in accordance with the strength and structures of their intellects, which have defined limits.

All parts of existence have boundaries and limitations. The boundaries can be huge or miniscule. But even a ratio of one to a billion is a specific number, albeit a very small one. It seems so miniscule as to be insignificant, but it is still a defined value that can be measured and used in calculations. By contrast, any number in relationship to *Ein Sof* equals nothing. In this way, the intellects of created beings exist in environments that can be defined, environments that have discernible borders. This is not the case when speaking of the nature of an intellect that is completely different from ours, lacking any of the structures of our intellects. Such an intellect is totally foreign to us, and when encountering it we will find ourselves standing before an unbridgeable abyss separating the limited world from *Ein Sof*.

שֶׁלֹּא יִתְבַּטְּלוּ בִּמְצִיאוּתָם, וְלֹא יִהְיוּ בְּגֶדֶר נִבְרָאִים כְּלָל רַק יַחְזְרוּ לִמְקוֹרָם וְשָׁרְשָׁם שֶׁהוּא בְּחִינַת אֱלֹהוּת מַמָּשׁ.

This constriction ensures **that they will not be nullified** out of **their existence, no** longer **being classified as created beings at all but returning to their source and root, which is the level of actual divinity.**

The nature of the world of *Beria* is that of the revealed intellect – as much as the recipients are capable of receiving. In order for a created being to retain its individual existence, experiencing its existence and its world, it must maintain a constricted perception. If it uninhibitedly perceived the totality of existence, then its environment and, moreover, its individual existence, would dissolve, and it would return to its source, the level of actual divinity, at the moment that a person's gaze would show him with absolutely clarity that "there is no other besides Him."

For this reason, the world of *Beria* is necessarily the place in which the revelation of the divine *Ḥokhma* is constricted. The border of *Beria* is "Man shall not see Me and live," or, as the early sages said, "Were I to know Him, I would be Him." The border of a created being's comprehension of the Creator is also the border of its existence. One cannot be on both sides at once, existing as a created being while also comprehending the Creator. One who crosses this boundary ceases to be a created being.

29 Adar II (leap year)

וְהִנֵּה צִמְצוּם זֶה הִיא סִבַּת הֶהָאָרָה שֶׁמְּאִירוֹת שָׁם חָכְמָה בִּינָה דַּעַת שֶׁל אֵין סוֹף בָּרוּךְ הוּא לִנְשָׁמוֹת אֵלּוּ בְּעוֹלַם הַבְּרִיאָה,

This constriction is the cause of the illumination, where the wisdom, understanding, and knowledge of *Ein Sof*, blessed be He, shine onto these souls in the world of *Beria*,

Constriction is the basis for all comprehension. When there is constriction, there is comprehension, and when there is no constriction, there is no comprehension. Above constriction, on the level where there is no constriction, comprehension is impossible. There, either a created being does not comprehend, or he does but is no longer a created being. All illumination is dependent upon the level and nature of the recipient. These parameters determine the amount of constriction and boundary required to allow for that divine illumination.

מַה שֶּׁאֵין כֵּן בַּאֲצִילוּת, שֶׁאֵינָם בִּבְחִינַת צִמְצוּם כָּל כָּךְ, אִי אֶפְשָׁר לִשְׂכָלִים נִבְרָאִים לְקַבֵּל מֵהֶן, וְלָכֵן לֵית מַחֲשַׁבְתָּא דִּילְהוֹן תְּפִיסָא שָׁם כְּלָל.

which is not the case in *Atzilut*, where they are not as much in a state of constriction. The intellects of created beings cannot receive from them, and therefore their thoughts cannot grasp anything there at all.

In the world of *Atzilut*, Ḥokhma, Bina, and Da'at of *Ein Sof* are not in the same state of constriction. Each world, by virtue of being a world, is constriction. *Atzilut* is different from other worlds in that there the Divine is not concealed and the truth of "there is no other besides Him" is fully recognized. Therefore, the intellects of created beings cannot receive from the *sefirot* of the world of *Atzilut*, which means that their thoughts cannot grasp anything of the world of *Atzilut*. To use an analogy from the physical world, there is weak light that a person can see, and there is strong light that can blind him. There is also light that cannot even be seen by the human eye, such as ultraviolet and infrared light. Similarly, a strong light that blinds is light from a world above the level of the one looking, and light that cannot even be seen corresponds to the light of Ḥokhma in the world of *Atzilut*. This light is not only lofty and subtle, but it cannot be accessed by created beings. Even the righteous, those who serve God with love and fear,cannot comprehend the world of *Atzilut*.

לָכֵן הוּא מָדוֹר לַצַּדִּיקִים הַגְּדוֹלִים, שֶׁעֲבוֹדָתָם הִיא לְמַעְלָה מַעְלָה אֲפִילוּ מִבְּחִינַת דְּחִילוּ וּרְחִימוּ הַנִּמְשָׁכוֹת מִן הַבִּינָה וְדַעַת בִּגְדוּלָתוֹ יִתְבָּרֵךְ, כְּמוֹ שֶׁעוֹלָם הָאֲצִילוּת הוּא לְמַעְלָה מַעְלָה מִבְּחִינַת בִּינָה וְדַעַת לְשֵׂכֶל נִבְרָא.

Consequently, it is an abode for the greatly righteous, whose service is above and beyond even the level of the fear and love that is drawn from the understanding and knowledge of God's greatness, just as the world of *Atzilut* is above and beyond the level of understanding and knowledge of the intellect of a created being.

The souls that reach the world of *Atzilut*, those that can tell us about that world, as it were, are those whose service of God has ascended beyond all previously discussed levels of both natural and intellectual fear and love. This divine service transcends all that a person can reach with his own might, with his intellectual strength, and with the power of his spiritual efforts on all levels. ☞

There are levels that a person with the appropriate talents can reach through intellectual understanding and deep knowledge. But there are also levels (the levels of the righteous that are beyond those of every man) that talent, effort, and spiritual achievement cannot access. Man's fundamental nature cannot connect to these levels. The *Zohar* states

THE DWELLING PLACE OF THE RIGHTEOUS IN THE WORLD OF *ATZILUT*

☞ What is the necessity of discussing the service of the souls in the world of *Atzilut*? The *Tanya* is defined as a book for the *beinoni*, who has "the attributes of every person" (chap. 14). The book refers to the *beinoni*, is geared toward the *beinoni*, and is directed to him. Even the level of the *beinoni* often feels unattainable to us. So what is the point of describing the service of the great, righteous people of the world of *Atzilut*? One answer is that this description is needed to complete the general picture, at least on a theoretical level. A deeper answer is that even if a person cannot reach these levels with his own will and strength, sometimes an aspect of them will appear as he goes on his path.

that the soul has levels, namely, the *nefesh, ruaḥ*, and *neshama*.[14] *Nefesh* is the basic level that every person begins his understanding with, in the world of *Asiya*. If a person merits it, he receives the level of *ruaḥ*, which is higher; it is understanding in the world of *Yetzira*. If he merits further, he receives the highest level, *neshama*, which connects to the world of *Beria*. At this stage, a person no longer strives to comprehend God. He no longer struggles with faith. Rather, his intellectual comprehension of God's existence is on the level of "with actual eyes they will see"; it is a simple and clear truth.

But there is a level that is even higher than this, in which the *ḥaya* aspect of the soul, which is connected to the world of *Atzilut*, is revealed. This level is not attained through merit, as a person cannot reach this level through his own ability. Nothing a person does can raise him to this level. Nevertheless, it is said that sometimes this level can "happen" to a person, not as a result of his actions or because he deserves it, but simply because some aspect of *ḥaya* will be revealed within his soul. At that moment, he will experience an upheaval of his whole essence and will exist in an entirely different reality.

A person feels this kind of spiritual revelation when he gives up his life to sanctify God's name. There is a tradition mentioned in various books[15] that has tragically been experienced by many throughout Jewish history,[16] that a person who intentionally gives up his life to sanctify God's name does not suffer pain. There is a shocking account of a conversation with a person who was being slowly burned alive, sanctifying God's name. He claimed throughout the conversation until he died that he felt nothing. There is a similar account of the last public burning in Spain. A Jew in hiding who had circumcised himself was arrested and sentenced to be burned. At the time of his burning until his soul left him, he sang the words of *Shema Yisrael* (it is said that his singing left such an impression on the spectators that the government canceled future public burnings).

Something of this dynamic exists even in less extreme situations. I heard a story from a person who was imprisoned in Russia because

---

14. See *Zohar* 2:94b.
15. See *Tashbetz Katan*, 415, and also *Kolbo*, end of 67.
16. See Shlomo Ashkenazi, "Sanctifying God's Name in the Middle Ages," *Maḥanayim* 60, 5721.

he observed mitzvot and who was sentenced to death by shooting but was unexpectedly saved and escaped from there. He told me that for some time after that, his whole life was qualitatively different. Prayer, Torah study, divine service, were all on a completely different level. A person cannot reach this state through intellect and contemplation, nor through decision making and choice. It can be achieved only when something happens to a person and he reacts as he does. Since such a phenomenon is not impossible, there is room for this to be discussed even in the "book of the *beinoni*."

אֶלָּא עֲבוֹדָתָם הָיְתָה בִּבְחִינַת מֶרְכָּבָה מַמָּשׁ לְאֵין סוֹף בָּרוּךְ הוּא וְלִיבָּטֵל אֵלָיו בִּמְצִיאוּת וּלְהִכָּלֵל בְּאוֹרוֹ יִתְבָּרֵךְ, הֵם וְכָל אֲשֶׁר לָהֶם, עַל יְדֵי קִיּוּם הַתּוֹרָה וְהַמִּצְוֹת. עַל דֶּרֶךְ שֶׁאָמְרוּ: "הָאָבוֹת הֵן הֵן הַמֶּרְכָּבָה" (בראשית רבה פרשה מז, ו ופרשה פב, ו). וְהַיְינוּ לְפִי שֶׁכָּל יְמֵיהֶם הָיְתָה זֹאת עֲבוֹדָתָם.

However, their service was on the level of an actual chariot for *Ein Sof*, blessed be He, so that their existence is nullified before Him and incorporated into His light, they and all that is theirs, by means of the fulfillment of Torah and mitzvot, in the manner that the Rabbis stated: "The patriarchs, they, they are the chariot" (*Bereshit Rabba* 47:6; 82:6), and the reason is that this was their service all their days.

This level is in the world of *Atzilut* and consists of serving as a chariot for God. It is where a person functions as a vessel for God and nothing else, where his individual entity has ceased to exist. ☞☞☞☞

THEY, THEY ARE THE CHARIOT

☞ This refers not only to the patriarchs but to all the righteous who serve on this level (Rabbi Shmuel Gronem Esterman). In the phrase "They, they are the chariot," the first "they" refers to the patriarchs and the second "they" refers to those like them. Similarly, some souls are nullified constantly, and some are nullified only occasionally (*Likkutei Hagahot LeTanya*, p. 108).

THIS WAS THEIR SERVICE ALL THEIR DAYS

☞ This kind of person does nothing; he does not even lift a finger until he feels that the act is necessary for the honor of God. The question regarding a person like this is not how he prays or studies Torah, for one certainly does not ask such a question. Instead, it is how such a person behaves in the areas of life that have no connection to Torah, to mitzvot, and to prayer. One of the students of the Maggid of Mezeritch, Rabbi Aryeh Leib Sarah's, said that he would visit his teacher not to hear his Torah teachings and not even to observe how he taught Torah. Rather, he would visit to observe how he tied his shoelaces. Even the *beinoni* must constantly engage in divine service, but the level of a lofty righteous person is such that everything he does, every comment and every movement he makes, has meaning. Regarding such a person, the answer to questions like "What is he doing?" "How is he doing this?" "Why is he doing that?" is always the same. As one of the righteous masters expressed it, a righteous person does not always knowingly do what God wants, but what he does is what God wants. That is to say, this person has such a strong connection of identification with God that what motivates him, what directs him, comes solely from the level of supernal holiness. He does not need to engage in mystical intentions and unifications, because everything he does, even when he is not thinking or acting with intent, is a unification.

THE FISH OF THE SEA

☞ Elsewhere (e.g., *Likkutei Torah*, Num. 8c, 18a) there are discussions of souls that are on the level of "fish of the sea." These are people who essentially are not connected to our world. For them, this world exists in a sense for other people. This may be compared to looking through a glass pane which acts partially as a mirror. The viewer sees an external existence through the glass, but it is overlaid with a faint secondary image. Similarly, a person who is referred to as "fish of the sea proceeding on dry land" sees our world as a type of secondary impression, a shadow that overlays tangible reality but is not a part of it. Still, since he sees something, he can live in our world somehow. He can travel on "dry land." He learns that in this world, there are streets, paths, food, meat. But essentially he lives in a different world. He is only visiting this world in order to fulfill a particular mission.

These ideas clarify a story in the Torah about Moses (Num. 11), in which the mob had a craving for meat, and the rest of the people of Israel also wept, and said, "Who will feed us meat?" Moses's reaction was very harsh, as if he could not comprehend what they wanted. He asked, "From where do I have meat?" (Num. 11:13). God listened to Moses's words, and then seemed to respond disjointedly, "Gather for Me seventy people from the elders of Israel" (Num. 11:16). The reason is that since Moses was on the level of "fish of the sea," he did not understand what the mob desired. He was not able to comprehend personally that a person desires meat, that he cares whether he lives or dies. Moses understood these things as we understand the motivations of animals. We realize that a chicken must swallow pebbles to enable its digestive processes, not because we personally relate to this, but due to our knowledge that creatures with such odd needs exist. Therefore, God's answer to Moses's question, "From where do I have meat?" is now intelligible: "Take seventy people who will understand that they need bread, and sometimes they also desire meat."

THE LEVEL OF THE CHARIOT

☞ This is a level of connection that is beyond the intellect. Divine service on the level of the intellect is based on what a person understands. On his level, he understands what God wants, and he knows what he is able and ready to do. On the lev-

When a person merits to serve as a chariot for the Divine Presence, his dwelling place is in the world of *Atzilut*, above the world of intellect, as he is completely nullified to God. There is a level of the divine that "no thought can grasp,"[17] but (as is explained in multiple places[18]) "it can be grasped with the desire of the heart," which occurs when a person is totally and completely nullified to God's will. There, through the will of the heart, a person can comprehend Him, not with the comprehension of thought or intellect, but as the result of contact that is created only through total and complete nullification on the level of will that transcends the intellect.

אַךְ מִי שֶׁשֹּׁרֶשׁ נִשְׁמָתוֹ קָטָן מֵהָכִיל עֲבוֹדָה תַּמָּה זוֹ, לִיבָּטֵל וְלִיכָּלֵל בְּאוֹרוֹ יִתְבָּרֵךְ בַּעֲבוֹדָתוֹ בִּקְבִיעוּת,

By contrast, one whose soul's root is too small to contain this perfect service, to be subsumed and incorporated into His light through serving Him constantly,

1 Nisan (leap year)

As was explained, this refers to the level of the chariot.[19]

el of the chariot, however, a person has no need to understand. Instead, he does what he does because he cannot act otherwise. This is how the story of the binding of Isaac has been explained: "Abraham sent forth his hand and took the knife to slaughter his son" (Gen. 22:10). Abraham heard and understood with his intellect that God told him to slaughter his son. However, since Abraham was a "chariot," he could not do anything against the will of God, who in truth did not want Isaac to be slaughtered. Abraham's hand could not of itself take the knife, so Abraham had to "send forth" his hand, to force his hand to act. Abraham's test was the test of a person who already knows what is right, who does not need to learn these and those *halakhot* in order to know what to do, since he understands the will of God on his own. Such a person, who serves as a chariot for the Divine Presence, comprehends the will of God from the place that is the root of comprehension, from the root where we receive the certain knowledge whether something is right or wrong, true or false.

---

17. Introduction to *Tikkunei Zohar* 17a.
18. *Likkutei Torah*, Deut. 35d, and many other places in Hasidism, in the name of the *Zohar*. See also *Sefer HaMa'amarim*, 5689 (of the sixth Lubavitcher Rebbe, Rabbi Yosef Yitzḥak Schneerson), p. 105, who cites *Zohar* 3:289b along these lines.
19. Previously, beginning of chap. 34.

רַק לִפְרָקִים וְעִתִּים, שֶׁהֵם עֵת רָצוֹן לְמַעְלָה, **but only on occasion and at intervals that are a time of favor on high,**

There are special times, times of divine favor above, when there is an awakening and revealing of the divine will from above. At those times, if a person prepares himself from below, he can reach moments of nullification and subsummation in the divine existence, as it is in the world of *Atzilut*.

וּכְמוֹ בִּתְפִלַּת שְׁמוֹנֶה עֶשְׂרֵה, שֶׁהִיא בַּאֲצִילוּת, **such as during the *Shemoneh Esrei* prayer, which is in *Atzilut*,**

There is a mystical teaching that the morning prayers are structured to go through four phases, parallel to the four spiritual worlds. The section of sacrifices until *Barukh She'amar* parallels the world of *Asiya*. The section of *Pesukei DeZimra* (verses of song) from *Barukh She'amar* until *Barekhu* parallels the world of *Yetzira*. *Keriat Shema* and its blessings parallel the world of *Beria*. The standing prayer of *Shemoneh Esrei* parallels the world of *Atzilut*.[20]

וּבִפְרָט בַּהִשְׁתַּחֲוָואוֹת שֶׁבָּהּ, שֶׁכָּל הִשְׁתַּחֲוָואָה הִיא בִּבְחִינַת אֲצִילוּת [כְּמוֹ שֶׁכָּתוּב בִּ'פְרִי עֵץ חַיִּים' בְּקַבָּלַת שַׁבָּת (שער יח פרק ה)], כִּי הִיא עִנְיַן בִּיטוּל בְּאוֹרוֹ יִתְבָּרֵךְ, לִהְיוֹת חָשִׁיב קַמֵּיהּ כְּלָא מַמָּשׁ. **and especially when one bows during this prayer at the four designated times, for every bow is on the level of *Atzilut* [as written in *Pri Etz Ḥayyim* on the prayer for welcoming the Sabbath (18:5)], since it represents nullification in His light, to be considered as literally nothing before Him.**

The meaning of prostration, that "every being shall bow before You," is the absolute and complete nullification before that which is above us.[21]

Similarly, there are special intentions that a person has when

---

20. *Pri Etz Ḥayyim* 9:1; see also *Likkutei Dibburim* of the sixth Lubavitcher Rebbe, Rabbi Yosef Yitzḥak Schneerson, 12 Tammuz 5707, section 16 and onward.

21. In prayer, the act of prostration has two aspects: nullification and drawing down: "female waters" and "male waters" (see *Torah Or* 28c).

he immerses in a *mikveh* (ritual purification bath): intentions of the heart and kabbalistic intentions. It is taught that the essence of these intentions is as follows: A person descends, and then descends further, and when he reaches the bottom, he crouches. This is the concept of the *mikveh* and it is also the concept of prostration, of the total nullification of one's entire stature and being. Immersion and prostration, purification, repentance and atonement all depend on self-nullification and a return to the source. Only complete nullification of all previous barriers allows the opening of an entry into a new world.

אֲזַי גַּם כֵּן עִיקַּר קְבִיעוּת נִשְׁמָתוֹ הוּא בְּעוֹלָם הַבְּרִיאָה (וְרַק לִפְרָקִים, בְּעֵת רָצוֹן, תַּעֲלֶה נִשְׁמָתוֹ לָאֲצִילוּת, בִּבְחִינַת מַיִּין נוּקְבִין, כַּיָּדוּעַ לְיוֹדְעֵי חֵן).

Then as well, the main fixed place of his soul is in the world of *Beria* (only sometimes, at a time of favor, will his soul rise to *Atzilut*, referring to the feminine waters, as is known to those initiated in the esoteric wisdom of Kabbala).

As was explained earlier, the primary abode of souls that serve God only with hidden love and fear is in the world of *Yetzira*, and they ascend to the world of *Beria* only during special times (the Sabbath and Rosh Ḥodesh). Similarly, the souls that serve God with intellectual love and fear, who primarily reside in the world of *Beria*, merit on occasion, during special times, to ascend to the higher world of *Atzilut* and to attain nullification that transcends the intellect.

וְהִנֵּה שְׂכַר מִצְוָה מִצְוָה (אבות פרק ד משנה ב), פֵּירוּשׁ, שֶׁמִּשְּׂכָרָהּ נֵדַע מַהוּתָהּ וּמַדְרֵגָתָהּ,

"The reward of a mitzva is a mitzva" (*Avot* 4:2) means that from its reward we can know its essence and level,

10 Nisan

2 Nisan (leap year)

The question regarding reward for a commandment, meaning, the place of those who serve God in the higher worlds (whether in the worlds of *Yetzira*, *Beria*, or *Atzilut*) is a question of qualitative essence. This is unlike a person's position in our world, which constantly changes and which says nothing about his essence. In contrast to that, a soul's permanent position in the higher worlds indicates where he truly belongs, his status and true level.²²

וְאֵין לָנוּ עֵסֶק בַּנִּסְתָּרוֹת, שֶׁהֵם צַדִּיקִים הַגְּדוֹלִים, שֶׁהֵם בִּבְחִינַת מֶרְכָּבָה, **and we do not involve ourselves in hidden matters, which refers to the greatly righteous, who have the status of a chariot,**

The expression "we do not involve ourselves in hidden matters"²³ is used here not in its usual sense (as is found in Ḥagiga regarding those topics that are not taught publicly), but rather with regard to the service of those rare people in each generation, the highly righteous, who have the status of a chariot and who serve in the world of *Atzilut*. This level is so rare that we cannot discuss it within the normal human context. Therefore, we do not need to take this path into account.

רַק הַנִּגְלוֹת לָנוּ, שֶׁאַחֲרֵיהֶם כָּל אָדָם יִמְשׁוֹךְ: **but we are engaged only with those things that are revealed to us, which every person should be drawn after:**

In contrast to the hidden levels that are beyond the comprehension and considerations of a normal person, there are also revealed levels. These revealed areas are not what every person already sees and grasps, but levels that "all people should be drawn after." These are levels that every person can acquire, every person can desire to walk upon, and every person must follow. This does not mean that a person has already achieved these levels, nor does it mean that it is easy to reach them. But it does mean that every person is capable of doing so. This is the entire theme of this book, the book of the *beinoni*, which articulates those paths and levels in service of God that "every person should be drawn after." Walking on these paths can be required of all people,

---

22. From the fact that the reward of the mitzva is in the upper Garden of Eden, which is the world of *Beria*, it is clear that the place of the service (the mitzva) is in the ten *sefirot* of *Beria*. And from the fact that the reward for service performed with the natural love and fear in the brain is in the palaces and chambers of *Yetzira*, it is clear that the place of that service is within the ten *sefirot* of *Yetzira* (*Likkutei Biurim*).

23. Based on *Ben Sira* 3:22; see also *Bereshit Rabba* 8:2; *Ḥagiga* 13a.

since every person is capable of doing so, even if he must dedicate his whole life to this pursuit.

לֵידַע נֶאֱמָנָה מַהוּת וּמַדְרֵגַת עֲבוֹדַת ה' בְּדְחִילוּ וּרְחִימוּ בְּהִתְגַּלּוּת לִבּוֹ, **To know for certain the essence and degree of the service of God with fear and love in the awareness of his heart,**

Now the author of the *Tanya* will explain the levels of divine service through revealed love and fear. The first is "the essence and degree of the service of God with fear and love in the awareness of his heart." Fear and love in the awareness of a person's heart (in contrast to love and fear in the hidden parts of the heart, as will be explained further) means an active, living feeling of love or fear of God.

הַנִּמְשָׁכוֹת מִן הַבִּינָה וְדַעַת בִּגְדֻלַּת אֵין סוֹף בָּרוּךְ הוּא, **which are drawn from the understanding and knowledge of the greatness of *Ein Sof*, blessed be He;**

In order for there to be a feeling in a person's heart that he is clearly aware of, there must be a tangible, clear, and active perception in his mind. Only when a person has a good, clear, and conscious idea of the greatness of God, that He is infinite and bestows life on all, can he attain love and fear of God in the revealed awareness of his heart. Only when he has a constructed and structured consciousness (*Bina*), and it is connected (*Da'at*) to the tangible reality that he sees with his eyes, will it draw forth and reveal the feelings of love and fear in his heart. ☞

AWARENESS IN THE HEART FROM REVELATION IN THE MIND

☞ In the Talmud (*Berakhot* 28b), there is a story about Rabban Yoḥanan ben Zakkai, who blessed his students prior to his death with these words: "May it be His will that you shall have fear of Heaven upon you like the fear of flesh and blood." His students were perplexed by the blessing and asked: "Is that all?" He replied: "If only you could do this much! Fear of Heaven is a lofty ideal, but when a person is about to sin, what is more important to him is whether another person is watching him. Even if he is not afraid of that other person, even if he doesn't care what he thinks, what matters to him is that there is an actual person standing there. Because of this, his consciousness of that person's presence is more clear and tangible, giving rise to feelings of revealed love or fear, such that he is unable to sin. Regarding Joseph, our Sages say (*Sota* 36b) that he avoided sinning with Potiphar's wife because he saw an image of

מְקוֹמָהּ בְּעֶשֶׂר סְפִירוֹת דִּבְרִיאָה, **its place is in the ten *sefirot* of *Beria*,**

As was explained, "The reward for a commandment is the commandment itself." Since the reward for this service is in the higher Garden of Eden, in the world of *Beria*, we can assess that the essence of the service (the commandment) performed on this level is positioned in the ten *sefirot* of the world of *Beria*.

וַעֲבוֹדָה בִּדְחִילוּ וּרְחִימוּ הַטִּבְעִיִּים שֶׁבְּמוֹחוֹ, בְּעֶשֶׂר סְפִירוֹת דִּיצִירָה. **and it is service through the natural fear and love that is in his mind, in the ten *sefirot* of *Yetzira*.**

Additionally, there is service of God that is also "revealed to us," in the sense that every person can achieve it, as was explained, but that is in the hidden part of one's heart, not in the revealed part. The service of God that does not emanate from personal, independent consciousness but only from the arousal of a person's root identity as a Jew, an identity that loves and fears God, is positioned in the ten *sefirot* of *Yetzira*. Just as the reward for this service is in the world of *Yetzira*, the person's service of God that leads to this reward belongs to the forces and *sefirot* of the world of *Yetzira* alone, and not to the intellectual world of *Beria*.

---

his father. Joseph already knew that he had a father, but only when his father's image appeared to him before his eyes, as if alive, did he feel that he could not commit that sin. It is known that many people avoid sinning because they are nervous about being caught by "the Rebbe." This fear is not so strong regarding God, but the idea that the Rebbe would find out is unbearable for them. As was explained, this is not an issue of a lack of faith, but rather an issue of clarity, of conscious awareness. This clarity is what determines a person's feelings of love and fear. From this perspective, if only a person could have fear of Heaven like fear of flesh and blood!

FEAR AND LOVE IN THE MIND

☞ Since love and fear are feelings, how is it that they would appear in a person's mind and not in his heart? To illustrate the difference between fear in the mind and fear in the heart, let us look at the fear of a world war that would eradicate the human race. This is a fear that exists in the mind. It is not a living feeling of fear, but rather an awareness that will naturally cause a person to be afraid. By contrast, when a person is walking through a minefield, he experiences fear in his heart. The significant difference between these two fears is not in conscious awareness, but rather in the intensity of the feelings of fear. When a person must walk through a minefield and he is uncertain whether his next step will kill him, he not only knows that he should

אֲבָל עֲבוֹדָה בְּלִי הִתְעוֹרְרוּת דְּחִילוּ וּרְחִימוּ אֲפִילוּ בְּמוֹחוֹ בִּבְחִינַת גִּילּוּי, דְּהַיְינוּ לְעוֹרֵר הָאַהֲבָה הַטִּבְעִית הַמְסוּתֶּרֶת בַּלֵּב, לְהוֹצִיאָהּ מֵהֶעְלֵם וְהֶסְתֵּר הַלֵּב אֶל הַגִּילוּי, אֲפִילוּ בְּמוֹחוֹ וְתַעֲלוּמוֹת לִבּוֹ עַל כָּל פָּנִים, רַק הִיא נִשְׁאֶרֶת מְסוּתֶּרֶת בַּלֵּב כְּתוֹלַדְתָּהּ, כְּמוֹ שֶׁהָיְתָה קוֹדֶם הָעֲבוֹדָה –

However, a service of God **without an awakening of fear and love even in his mind on a revealed level**, that is, so as to awaken the natural love hidden in his **heart, to bring it out from being concealed and hidden** within his **heart into the open** – even, at least, in his mind and the hidden recesses of his heart, **only it remains hidden in** his **heart as when it was formed, as it was before** his **service of God** –

When a person serves God, through Torah study or the performance of commandments, without revealed love and fear, not even within his intellect, not only is he unable to arouse the love as a warm, living feeling in his heart, but he is also unable to reach an understanding in keeping with which he is able to love. Instead, the love remains hidden in his heart as when it was formed, as it was before his service of God.

The definition of this level of service of God, and the basic idea that such a level is a legitimate form of divine service, is one of the fundamental ideas in this book. The goal is not to remain at this level but to establish this as the foundation from which to progress – something that every person can do.

The underlying assumption here is that certain things are embedded in the soul of every Jew. A person need not create these things from

be afraid, but he actually fears! In order for fear to be a living feeling in the heart, a person must have a clear and tangible conscious awareness of his danger. When a person lacks this tangible awareness, even if he possesses a good theoretical understanding of the danger, he cannot experience a fear that will be revealed in his heart as a living feeling.

Many people who smoke cigarettes know the dangers of smoking, yet this awareness does not cause them to stop. This is not because they fail to understand the danger, but rather because the "picture" of the danger is not powerful enough to create a feeling of threat in their hearts that will motivate them to take action. Similarly, when a person is able to imagine and preserve in his mind a sufficiently tangible image of God's greatness, this will create a living and revealed feeling of fear or love. If he cannot do so but can only reach a theoretical understanding of the divine existence, he will reveal natural love and fear in his mind only, but not in his heart.

scratch, but rather need only arouse them in order to cause them to be revealed. This is in contrast to elements that do not lie within the scope of human experience, which a person therefore cannot arouse, and regarding which he at most builds mental constructs that have no true foundation. For example, a human being has the ability to walk on two legs, an ability that a dog does not possess. However, just as one can teach infants to walk upright, so it is possible to train a dog to walk on two legs for short periods. The difference between them (a difference that will become magnified over time) derives from the fact that the biological infrastructure to walk on two legs exists in man and does not exist in dogs.

Similarly, loving and fearing God are an intrinsic part of being human, although people are different in how revealed these traits are within their souls. It is even possible with certain people, under particular personal and social conditions, for these feelings not to be revealed at all. This is the level of divine service discussed here by the author of the *Tanya*. It is the most basic level of intent, "without an awakening of love or fear even in his mind." Even in this state, a person can live a Jewish life. He can perform commandments, refrain from sinning. Yet it is possible that he will not reach love and fear even in his mind, because he finds no experiential connection to his actions. The actions he is taking are right, but they have no parallel in any internal connection. A person can live as a religious Jew within a community of people who follow the commandments, and raise his children accordingly. Perhaps he does this because this is how he was raised and he never had enough interest or motivation to leave this way of life. Or perhaps he decided that this framework is a pleasant and easy lifestyle, without intense shocks, albeit without anything uplifting, and his other options were less optimal.

Commandments performed by such a person are still commandments, and his sins are still sins, even if he does not intend them to be so. As was already explained, commandments and sins have intrinsic meaning and value. Commandments and sins are always two sides of existence, with commandments on the side of holiness and sins on the side of impurity. This may be compared to the difference in value between positive and negative numbers. The difference is quintessential. One set is on the positive side of the zero, the other set on the negative. The smallest of the positive numbers is larger than the largest of the negative numbers. If a person performs a commandment, even by accident, it is still a commandment. When he refrains from committing a sin, even by accident, he is still refraining from sin. The difference between this person and a person who acts with intention is only a question of magnitude. These orders of magnitude are, in the most fundamental sense, the levels under discussion here, and determine whether a soul is connected to the world of *Beria*, *Yetzira*, or *Asiya*.

הֲרֵי עֲבוֹדָה זוֹ נִשְׁאֶרֶת לְמַטָּה בְּעוֹלָם הַפֵּירוּד, הַנִּקְרָא חִיצוֹנִיּוּת הָעוֹלָמוֹת,	this service remains down below in the world of separation, which is called the externality of the worlds,

When a person serves God without any love or fear at all, his service stays down below in the world of separation, which is called the externality of the worlds.[24] The world of separation and the externality of the worlds is a region that identifies itself as being separate from the divine.[25] This is not a sin. It is the service of God. But it lacks any inner relationship between the soul and holiness, and so it remains in the realm of *Asiya* only. A person has performed an act in the world of action, and nothing more. A commandment that is observed as an external action and does not touch a person's internal space remains in the externality of the worlds and does not reach their interior.

וְאֵין בָּהּ כֹּחַ לַעֲלוֹת וְלִיכָּלֵל בְּיִחוּדוֹ יִתְבָּרַךְ, שֶׁהֵן עֶשֶׂר סְפִירוֹת הַקְּדוֹשׁוֹת, וּכְמוֹ שֶׁכָּתוּב בַּתִּיקּוּנִים (תִּיקּוּנֵי זֹהַר תִּיקּוּן י׳ [כה, ב]): דִּבְלָא דְחִילוּ וּרְחִימוּ לָא פָּרְחָא לְעֵילָּא וְלָא יָכְלָא לְסַלְּקָא וּלְמֵיקָם קֳדָם ה׳.	and it does not have the strength to ascend and to be incorporated in His unity, which are the ten holy *sefirot*. As it states in *Tikkunei Zohar* (25b), without fear and love an act of serving God does not fly upward, and it cannot ascend and stand before God.

---

24. See further, chap. 40, where it states that this may also be said of the world of *Yetzira*. This requires some further study, as the word "below" is used here. And see *Kuntres Aḥaron*. Still, from the concluding phrase, "which is called the externality of the worlds," it is clear that this refers to *Asiya* and *Yetzira* (*Likkutei Biurim*).
25. The intent here is not to the region of the *kelippa*, God forbid, for this level is nevertheless considered divine service and related to the region of holiness. See the commentary of Rabbi Shmuel Gronem Esterman on the *Tanya*.

A commandment that is performed without any love or fear lacks "wings" and without these wings, it cannot rise above this world, and so it remains within it. A creature can have large or small wings, and there are wings that are so small as to be unable to lift a coarse body, but nevertheless, that creature still has wings. It knows that it does not belong down here below and must ascend. It tries a little until it succeeds, like a hen, to rise a little off the ground on occasion. But a commandment that has no wings at all remains bound to the earth, moving only within the lower reality, unable to detach itself and approach God's countenance.

---

11 Nisan
3 Nisan
(leap year)

וְהַיְנוּ אֲפִלּוּ אִם אֵינוֹ עוֹסֵק שֶׁלֹּא לִשְׁמָהּ מַמָּשׁ, לְשׁוּם אֵיזוֹ פְּנִיָּה חַס וְשָׁלוֹם,

This is the case **even if he is not literally engaged** in Torah and mitzvot **not for its own sake but for the sake of some** other **motive, God forbid,**

The author of the *Tanya* emphasizes that this is the case even if a person is engaged in Torah and mitzvot for the sake of some other motive. There is a concept of divine service "not for its own sake" (which will be discussed later), in which a person not only lacks intention for the sake of Heaven (love and fear, whether intellectual or natural), but actually has a different intention. An example would be a person studying Torah, performing commandments, or even praying for his own honor, or for some other self-serving purpose. That is not being discussed here.

אֶלָּא כְּמוֹ שֶׁכָּתוּב: "וַתְּהִי יִרְאָתָם אוֹתִי מִצְוַת אֲנָשִׁים מְלֻמָּדָה" (ישעיה כט, יג). פֵּרוּשׁ, מֵחֲמַת הֶרְגֵּל שֶׁהוּרְגַּל מִקַּטְנוּתוֹ שֶׁהִרְגִּילוּ וְלִמְּדוּ אָבִיו וְרַבּוֹ לִירָא אֶת ה' וּלְעָבְדוֹ, וְאֵינוֹ עוֹסֵק לִשְׁמָהּ מַמָּשׁ.

but rather as it states, "Their reverence of Me has become a commandment of men learned by rote" (Isa. 29:13), **meaning that it is a result of habit, which has been ingrained in him from his childhood, when he was made accustomed and taught by his father and teacher to fear God and serve Him, and he is not engaged** in serving God literally **"for its own sake."**

Here, the author of the *Tanya* deals with "not for its own sake" in the sense that a person serves God without having any active intention to do so for the sake of Heaven. When a person is raised in a certain way and remains in that framework, he does things by rote, as a function of routine. He ritually washes his hands in the morning and then prays, not because he is praying to God or wants to, but rather because this is an inseparable component of his daily routine. There are people who wake up in the morning and brush their teeth, and there are people who wake up and recite *Keriat Shema* and pray. If such a person would not pray in the morning, he would have the same feeling that a person who didn't brush his teeth has. If he would think, even for a moment, that he was performing these actions for God's sake, even without an emotional component, it would already be a different situation. Whether for good or ill, it is possible to perform many actions that do not fall within the realm of intent at all, actions performed with no significance whatsoever. ☞

כִּי לִשְׁמָהּ מַמָּשׁ אִי אֶפְשָׁר בְּלֹא הִתְעוֹרְרוּת דְּחִילוּ וּרְחִימוּ הַטִּבְעִיִּים עַל כָּל פָּנִים, לְהוֹצִיאָן מֵהֶסְתֵּר הַלֵּב אֶל הַגִּלּוּי בַּמּוֹחַ וְתַעֲלוּמוֹת לִבּוֹ עַל כָּל פָּנִים. כִּי כְּמוֹ שֶׁאֵין אָדָם עוֹשֶׂה דָּבָר בִּשְׁבִיל חֲבֵירוֹ לְמַלֹּאת רְצוֹנוֹ אֶלָּא אִם כֵּן אוֹהֲבוֹ אוֹ יָרֵא מִמֶּנּוּ,

As it is impossible to act **literally "for its own sake" without at least the awakening of natural fear and love, bringing** these feelings **out from the hidden heart into the open in the mind and the hidden recesses of his heart, at any rate. For just as a person does not do anything on behalf of another to fulfill his will unless he loves him or is afraid of him,**

TRAINED FROM HIS CHILDHOOD

☞ This would be different in a case where a person trained himself when he was an adult (as mentioned in chap. 15 above). In that case, it can be said that the element of "for the sake of Heaven" that existed at the beginning of his service elevates his "not for its own sake" as well. This is similar to the idea that if a person's intent in his prayers has occurred only in bits and pieces over the course of the year, those fragments can be placed together to form one complete prayer with intent (an idea that is touched upon at the end of this chapter). This requires further study, for it is possible that the author used the term "from his childhood" because that is the experience of every person, and this is how things are meant to be, which is why the Torah commands, "You shall inculcate them in your children" (the Lubavitcher Rebbe, Rabbi Menaḥem Mendel Schneerson).

In order for a person to do something "for its own sake," for the purpose of that something, he must first have some basic awakening of awareness and feeling, if no more than in his mind and the hidden areas of his heart. That way, even if there is no revealed emotional feeling, there is at least an experience that constitutes a foundation of a connection to that something that leads to that something being done. Anything one person does for another has an emotional motivation. It can be respect or fear on one level or another, from the fear of death at being threatened with a dangerous weapon to the discomfort of what others will think. It can be love, ranging from love revealed in one's heart, when the soul is filled with awareness and feeling that this action is taken for the sake of the beloved, to love on lower and less revealed levels, to a level of basic courtesy, such as polite people sitting together, in which one asks for the salt and the other fulfills his request. Every action has a minimum basis in a feeling. (However, in the case of people who have been strongly indoctrinated to act politely, it is possible for them to engage in such actions without any emotional connection. This is similar to a person who has been habituated from his childhood to serve God, and who, as was explained, can study Torah and perform commandments purely out of habit, without any arousal of love or fear.)

כָּךְ אִי אֶפְשָׁר לַעֲשׂוֹת לִשְׁמוֹ יִתְבָּרֵךְ בֶּאֱמֶת לְמַלֹּאת רְצוֹנוֹ לְבַד בְּלִי זִכָּרוֹן וְהִתְעוֹרְרוּת אַהֲבָתוֹ וְיִרְאָתוֹ כְּלָל, בְּמוֹחוֹ וּמַחֲשַׁבְתּוֹ וְתַעֲלוּמוֹת לִבּוֹ עַל כָּל פָּנִים.

so too it is impossible to act truly for His name, solely to fulfill His will, without any remembrance or awakening of love for Him or fear of Him at all, in one's mind, thought, and the hidden recesses of one's heart, in any event.

Like a person's relationship with other people, so is his relationship with God. It is impossible to perform divine service that is "for its own sake" without some spark of feeling. The person may have a living and warm feeling, or, alternatively, he may have a feeling that remains in the "hidden recesses of the heart," found only within his mind, in thoughts that it is appropriate to love and fear God, and therefore it is fitting to perform some actions or refrain from performing other actions.

וְגַם אַהֲבָה לְבַדָּהּ אֵינָהּ נִקְרֵאת בְּשֵׁם עֲבוֹדָה בְּלִי יִרְאָה תַּתָּאָה לְפָחוֹת, שֶׁהִיא מְסוּתֶּרֶת בְּלֵב כָּל יִשְׂרָאֵל, כְּמוֹ שֶׁיִּתְבָּאֵר לְקַמָּן.

Also, love by itself is not called by the name of serving God, without at least the lower level of fear, which is hidden in the heart of every Jew, as will be explained below (chap. 41).

The author observes here that a person's service of God does not ascend to Him without both love and fear. As explained in the *Zohar*, love and fear are the wings with which the commandment "flies," rising above this world. Just as a bird cannot fly without wings, it also cannot fly with only one wing. Similarly, in order for a person's service to ascend to God, it must possess both love and fear together. ☞

THERE IS NO TRUE LOVE WITHOUT FEAR

☞ It is impossible for real love to exist unless it is accompanied by fear. When love is serious, it is necessarily accompanied by an aspect of fear, which is the fear of losing the beloved. This is true in a relationship between people and in a relationship between a person and anything else, even an inanimate object that cannot see or feel. When a person has a relationship of affinity toward something, there is perforce also a relationship of respect toward that thing. People have this kind of relationship with work, with beauty, with animals, and even with food and drink. A person who has an affinity for good wine will treat it with a certain amount of respect. One who has an appreciation for special foods will shudder if two different kinds of foods that do not belong together are mixed. Additionally, any situation in which there is love without fear, or the opposite, indicates a flaw, a falsehood or corruption in the relationship.

This can also be seen in the prayer liturgy. In prayer in general, and in each part of the prayer service, there are words, sentences, and sections with themes of love and fear interspersed with each other (see *Likkutei Torah*, Lev. 45b). Between fear and love lie pathways that lead from fear to love and back. The nearly dialectical relationship between the two is built on the fact that love and fear are not separate structures but rather emanate from one another and lead to each other. If there is true fear, it is only a question of time and of depth of feeling until it will lead to love, and vice versa. The full emotional relationship is arranged in a structure in which the first level and the last level are a certain manner of fear, of the creation of distance and maintaining of that distance. Between these levels is love, which removes that distance. (This is reflected in some forms of the liturgy of the formulation "for the sake of divine unification": "for the sake of divine unification...with fear and love, and love and fear.")

12 Nisan
4 Nisan (leap year)

וּכְשֶׁעוֹסֵק שֶׁלֹּא לִשְׁמָהּ מַמָּשׁ, לְשׁוּם אֵיזוֹ פְּנִיָּה, לִכְבוֹד עַצְמוֹ, כְּגוֹן לִהְיוֹת תַּלְמִיד חָכָם וּכְהַאי גַּוְונָא,

When a person **engages** in Torah and mitzvot in a way that is **literally "not for its own sake,"** for the sake of some ulterior **motive, for his own honor – for example, to be a Torah scholar and the like,**

Until this point, the discussion centered on a person who serves God neither for its own sake, nor not for its own sake. However, a person may be occupied with Torah and mitzvot in a way that is literally not for its own sake, meaning for an ulterior motive, when he directs his intentions toward a goal that is completely not for the sake of Heaven. Studying Torah is a commandment, but being a Torah scholar is not. So when a person studies Torah in order to be called a Torah scholar, he is studying with an ulterior motive. When a person wants to acquire the status of a Torah scholar, when he desires any kind of social recognition, whether as a rabbi or a university professor, his motive is not for the sake of Heaven but for his own honor. Not only with Torah study and with divine service overall, but even with prayer it is possible to serve God with such a motive, and with motives that are even lower than that. ☞

A PERSON WHO PRAYS FOR THE SAKE OF HIS OWN HONOR

☞ The story is told of an ascetic who isolated himself in his room for many years, studying Torah and praying. His most basic necessities were passed to him through a slot in the door. Over time, he began to hear sounds near his door, which he assumed were made by Jews who were pushing forward to hear and be moved by his Torah study and divine service. As a result of this assumption, he was energized like a lion during his prayers, and he would pray with a loud voice that could be heard from afar. After twenty years passed, he opened the door and discovered a family of cats that resided outside his door. He realized that he had studied and prayed for twenty years for the benefit of a family of cats (see Rabbi Avraham Ḥazan, *Avaneha Barzel*, 5695, pp. 227–28).

It is possible for a person to study and pray for his entire life and not serve God at all, but rather he serves himself. Serving God "not for its own sake" in this way raises the question: Does this sort of intent poison the commandments one performs, until the actions do not even qualify as performance of the commandments?

CHAPTER 39

אֲזַי אוֹתָהּ פְּנִיָּה שֶׁמִּצַּד הַקְּלִיפָּה דְּנוֹגַהּ, Then that motive, which stems from the *kelippa* of *noga*,

This motive – to be a Torah scholar, a righteous person, and the like – is not a sin that belongs in the realm of impurity. Even if it is not a commandment, neither is it a sin. It belongs to the realm of the mundane, the area defined as *kelippat noga*.

מִתְלַבֶּשֶׁת בְּתוֹרָתוֹ, וְהַתּוֹרָה הִיא בִּבְחִינַת גָּלוּת בְּתוֹךְ הַקְּלִיפָּה, becomes enclothed in his Torah, and the Torah is in a state of being exiled within the *kelippa*,

The Torah that a person studies for the sake of that *kelippa* (the ulterior motive) now serves the directives of the *kelippa*. It becomes enclothed in the *kelippa* and nourishes it. The explanation of this (as discussed elsewhere) is that this Torah is in a state of exile within the *kelippa*.

לְפִי שָׁעָה, temporarily,

The definition of *kelippat noga* is a *kelippa* that is capable of being rectified. The good that is exiled within it can, must, and ultimately will be freed from the evil and elevated to holiness. Therefore, the exile of the Torah enclothed in *kelippat noga* is only temporary.

עַד אֲשֶׁר יַעֲשֶׂה תְּשׁוּבָה שֶׁמְּבִיאָה רְפוּאָה לָעוֹלָם (יומא פו, א). until he repents, which brings healing to the world (*Yoma* 86a).

This healing is the repair of a flawed situation. A person who was ill and is healed is a person with a flaw that was repaired. When it is said that repentance brings healing to the world, the meaning is that repentance repairs and heals that which was flawed. The Torah that a person studies for the sake of some personal motivation is Torah that is ill. When the person repents, it is not only he who is healed, but his Torah and service are also healed and ascend to God.

שֶׁבְּשׁוּבוֹ אֶל ה' גַּם תּוֹרָתוֹ שָׁבָה עִמּוֹ, For in his return to God, his Torah also returns with him,

When a person repents, not only does he return to God, but also the commandments he performed and the Torah that was enclothed and exiled in the *kelippa* returns and rises with him.

וְלָכֵן אָמְרוּ רַבּוֹתֵינוּ ז"ל: "לְעוֹלָם יַעֲסוֹק אָדָם וְכוּ' שֶׁמִּתּוֹךְ שֶׁלֹּא לִשְׁמָהּ בָּא לִשְׁמָהּ" (פסחים ס, ב).

and therefore our Rabbis said: "**A person should always engage** in Torah study and performance of mitzvot… **as** through studying Torah **not for its own sake, one comes** to study it **for its own sake**" (*Pesaḥim* 60b).

Since this Torah that he learned is not enclothed in an impure *kelippa* but is only in the intermediate realm of *kelippat noga*, then ultimately, when it becomes possible, it will be connected to the realm of holiness. All the Torah a person studies, even for ulterior motives, remains in existence. It does not automatically ascend from the world of the *kelippa*, but it is not erased either. It remains stored there and builds up and increases, layer upon layer. When at a certain stage this person repents and studies Torah for its own sake, his present study is built upon and draws from the Torah he had studied previously not for its own sake. The Torah he now studies for its own sake justifies and raises all his deeds and Torah study of the past. A parallel illustration is that of eating and drinking (see chap. 7 and elsewhere). If, after a person eats mindlessly, without intending it to be for the sake of Heaven, he serves God with the energy of that food, he retroactively elevates his act of eating.

בְּוַדַּאי שֶׁבְּוַדַּאי סוֹפוֹ לַעֲשׂוֹת תְּשׁוּבָה בְּגִלְגּוּל זֶה אוֹ בְּגִלְגּוּל אַחֵר,

This is a certainty, since it is certain that he will ultimately repent, whether in this incarnation or in another incarnation,

The author of the *Tanya* adds: The idea that by performing commandments not for their own sake, a person comes to perform them for their own sake is not only a possibility, but rather it is a certainty, since it is guaranteed that he will ultimately repent. Although the Torah studied not for its own sake will not connect on its own to God, it will return to Him when the person repents and studies it again for its own sake. The underlying assumption is that in the end, every person will repent, whether in this lifetime or in another. That is because the Sages said, "A person should always engage," and so forth, and if always (all his days) a person studies Torah not for its own sake, when will his rectification occur? Therefore, the author of the *Tanya* adds that even if he does not attain proper repentance in this lifetime, then in a different lifetime, in a different incarnation, he will certainly repent properly. Then all the Torah he had studied, including his study in previous lifetimes, will be rectified.

כִּי לֹא יִדַּח מִמֶּנּוּ נִדָּח. **for none shall be banished from Him.**

The Torah promises that "none shall be banished from Him."[26] This includes any banished person of Israel who ultimately repents. This includes as well any banished Torah, meaning Torah that was studied not for its own sake. How long this return will take is only a matter of time of time. But ultimately, everything returns to God.

אַךְ כְּשֶׁעוֹשֶׂה סְתָם, לֹא לִשְׁמָהּ וְלֹא שֶׁלֹּא לִשְׁמָהּ, אֵין הַדָּבָר תָּלוּי בִּתְשׁוּבָה, אֶלָּא מִיָּד שֶׁחוֹזֵר וְלוֹמֵד דָּבָר זֶה לִשְׁמָהּ, הֲרֵי גַּם מַה שֶּׁלָּמַד בִּסְתָם מִתְחַבֵּר וּמִצְטָרֵף לְלִימּוּד זֶה, וּפָרְחָא לְעֵילָא, **However, when** a person **acts for no particular reason, neither "for its own sake" nor "not for its own sake," the matter does not depend on repentance. Instead, as soon as he goes back and studies this matter for its own sake, then even that which he had learned for no particular reason combines and joins with this study, and flies upward,**

However, when a person performs an action without any inner intention, neither for the sake of Heaven nor for any other reason, but purely based on habit and the like, a special act of repentance is not required. Instead, when he reviews that topic or section of Torah,

---

26. Based on II Sam. 14:14. See *Hilkhot Talmud Torah* by the author of the *Tanya*, 4:3.

this time studying it for its own sake, then even what he had studied previously for no particular reason combines and joins with this study, and ascends.

מֵאַחַר שֶׁלֹּא נִתְלַבֵּשׁ בּוֹ עֲדַיִין שׁוּם קְלִיפָּה דְּנוֹגַהּ. **since it was not yet enclothed by any** *kelippa* **of** *noga*.

Why is it that when a person studies "not for its own sake" he must repent, but when he studies only by rote, neither "for its own sake" nor "not for its own sake," without any specific intentions, there is no need for repentance, and it is sufficient for the studying itself to be done properly? That is because it lacks a *kelippa* of *noga*. This kind of study lacks any inner meaning, and therefore it is not enclothed by anything, neither holiness nor a *kelippat noga*. It remains an action without intent. This sort of action receives its direction and meaning from the person's subsequent actions.

וְלָכֵן "לְעוֹלָם יַעֲסוֹק אָדָם" כו'. **Therefore "a person should always engage," and so forth,**

The Sages therefore said that a person should always engage in studying Torah, even not for its own sake, because even if currently he is not in a state in which he can study Torah for its own sake, it is still worthwhile to study anyway.

וְכֵן הָעִנְיָן בִּתְפִלָּה שֶׁלֹּא בְּכַוָּונָה, כְּמוֹ שֶׁכָּתוּב בַּזֹּהַר (חלק ב, רמה, ב). **and the same applies to prayer without intention, as it is written in the** *Zohar* (*Zohar* 2:245b).

Since this prayer lacks intention and it lacks love and fear, it does not ascend. Still, as long as it does not contain any foreign intention, it remains in its place. When the person subsequently prays with intent, that lifts all the previous prayers that had lacked intent. ☞

There is a teaching quoted in the name of the Ḥozeh from Lublin[27] regarding the verse "The Lord makes an account of the peoples" (Ps. 87:6): What is the meaning of "an account of the peoples"? The only

---

27. See *Niflaot HaRebbe*, section 73.

digit that exists in the accounts – the mathematics – of other nations but is not in Jewish notation is the zero. When a person prays (and similarly, when he studies Torah or performs other commandments), without any intention or meaning, it is recorded with "the accounts of the peoples," meaning it is recorded as a zero. The next day, he prays again without intention, and a second zero is recorded. But when he finally prays once with intention, the digit of one is recorded before all those zeros.

Continuing with the theme of the previous chapter, this chapter dealt with the issue of intention, and the relationship between intention and Torah study or performing the commandments. The chapter began by continuing the discussion of the two levels of intent: serving God with natural love and fear, on the "animal" level, and serving God with

ACTION AND INTENT IN PRAYER

☞ Every Jew is supposed to pray three times a day, and it is difficult to maintain intentional focus each time. There have been people, however, rare individuals in each generation, who were able to pray each prayer to the exhaustion of the soul. They prayed each morning as if it were the first time they had ever prayed, and as if there would never be another prayer. Regarding the holy Rabbi Uri (the "Angel") from Strelisk, the story is told that before each prayer, he would instruct his household as if he were not returning, since each of his prayers was a deep experience from which he was uncertain he would return (see *Eser Tzaḥtzaḥot*, p. 39). However, in general, out of a person's hundreds and thousands of prayers, there is perhaps one prayer, or one blessing, even just one word, that he said with intention.

Many have wondered: If this is so, why must a person pray so often? One answer given is that the very act of standing in prayer, where a person sets aside time and orients himself to a state of preparation toward divine revelation, develops the vessel, the possibility, that this will open a doorway to God. Another answer is the one brought here, that when a person prays, even if he does so without intent, it is still a prayer. Therefore, when he finally does pray once with intention, he elevates the prayers of that entire past year. A person can recite the blessing "Heal us" a thousand times without thinking, but one time that prayer becomes personally relevant to him (may God protect us), and he recites that blessing with complete intention and a broken heart. At that moment, all his previous recitations of "Heal us" ascend together with it. At that time, all those prayers are rectified. Every prayer leaves an imprint, and sometimes what remains is illegible script, yet it remains writing which one can return to and rewrite. When a person recites one prayer for its own sake, even if that happens once a year or once in a lifetime, that prayer rewrites all the previous prayers and blends them into a single entity that ascends.

intellectual love and fear, on the "human" level. The reward for serving on these two levels is either on the level of the higher Garden of Eden in the world of *Beria* or on that of the lower Garden of Eden in the world of *Yetzira*. All souls, even those that serve God with natural love and fear, ascend during a time of favor (the Sabbath and Rosh Ḥodesh) to the higher Garden of Eden in the world of *Beria* (unlike the angels, who always belong in the world of *Yetzira*).

To complete the discussion, the author described the service of the great and righteous souls, which is related to the world of *Atzilut* ("the Patriarchs: they, they are the chariot"), and the relevance of these matters to the level of the *beinoni*, everyman. Finally, the chapter dealt with service of God without any love or fear of God at all. As was brought from the *Zohar*, this service does not ascend at all from the physical existence in which it was performed. Here too the author differentiates between two types of service that are "not for its own sake." The first is "not for its own sake" in the sense that it only has no active intent toward Heaven. The second is "not for its own sake," in the sense that it has an active intent toward something else (in other words, an ulterior motive). Serving God with an ulterior motive, with an intent that comes from the *kelippa*, cannot be uplifted from the *kelippa* until a person repents (which he will certainly do, as was explained). But service of God that was not for its own sake, in the sense that it lacked only intent for the sake of Heaven, does not require repentance for it to be able to ascend to God. Rather, as soon as a person performs a similar act with intent, it too will ascend.

Chapter 40

IN THE PREVIOUS CHAPTERS, THE AUTHOR DISCUSSED the intentions underlying the fulfillment of the commandments and the study of Torah, as well as the two levels of the soul that are expressed through a person's intent in performing commandments: intellectual love and fear, and natural love and fear. At the end of the previous chapter, the author also discussed Torah study and commandments performed without any intent at all, which are unable to ascend to God. However, he explained that all a person must do to repair this is to perform the commandment or study the Torah again for the sake of Heaven, with love and fear. This will enable the previous actions and study to rise along with them. This is because as long as the original action was not performed with an invalid intent, the latter intent can extend meaning and ascension to it. Therefore, the previous chapter concluded that "a person should always immerse himself in Torah and commandments, even not for their own sake," and so forth (*Pesaḥim* 50b). This chapter will continue to discuss in greater detail the topic of Torah and commandments performed without intent. It will first deal with the question of their status before a person returns to study or perform them with correct intent.

אַךְ כָּל זְמַן שֶׁלֹּא חָזַר וְלָמַד דָּבָר זֶה לִשְׁמָהּ, אֵין לִימּוּדוֹ עוֹלֶה אֲפִילוּ בְּעֶשֶׂר סְפִירוֹת הַמְּאִירוֹת בְּעוֹלָם הַיְצִירָה וְהָעֲשִׂיָּה.

However, as long as a person has not gone back and learned this subject "for its own sake," his study does not rise even to the ten *sefirot* that shine in the world of *Yetzira* (Formation) and *Asiya* (Action).

13 Nisan

5 Nisan (leap year)

As long as a person continues to fulfill commandments, to study Torah, and to pray out of habit and routine, without any associated impetus of experience and vibrancy, without any internal intent regarding the meaning and purpose of his actions, his study does not rise even into the ten *sefirot* of the world of *Yetzira* (Formation) and *Asiya* (Action), and it certainly does not reach the loftier worlds.

כִּי הַסְּפִירוֹת הֵן בְּחִינַת אֱלֹהוּת וּבָהֶן מִתְלַבֵּשׁ וּמִתְיַיחֵד אוֹר אֵין סוֹף בָּרוּךְ הוּא מַמָּשׁ, That is **because the *sefirot* are an aspect of divinity; the light of *Ein Sof*, blessed be He, is literally enclothed and unified in them,**

The *sefirot* in each world, even in the world of *Asiya*, are an aspect of divinity, in the sense that the light of *Ein Sof*, blessed be He, is literally enclothed and unified in them. The ten *sefirot* in each world are the vessels and ways in which the divine exists, acts, and is revealed, in each world according to its level. As was said in the previous chapter, the Torah and commandments that a person fulfills in this world for the sake of Heaven, with love and fear of God, ascend via this love and fear and connect to the Divine. They reach a state of relationship with the ten *sefirot* of the world of *Beria*, or at least with the ten *sefirot* of the world of *Yetzira*. But when there is no love or fear at all, a person's Torah study and service of God do not ascend to the ten *sefirot* at all, not even to those of the world of *Asiya*.

Since the ten *sefirot* are the revelation of the inner being of the divine within a world, a person cannot connect to them without some level of inner intent on his part. When the Torah studied or commandment performed in this world lacks any intent to connect above, they have no way to ascend. When they are performed in the absence of any relationship with the divine within existence, they lack a point of attachment to connect to the divine within existence, not even of the world of *Asiya*.

"וּבְלָא דְּחִילוּ וּרְחִימוּ לָא יָכְלָא לְסָלְקָא וּלְמֵיקָם קֳדָם ה׳", כְּמוֹ שֶׁכָּתוּב בַּתִּיקוּנִים (תיקוני זהר תיקון י [כה, ב]). **"Without fear and love,** the Torah **cannot ascend and stand before God,"** as it is written in the *Tikkunei Zohar* 25b.

A commandment performed without any intent for the sake of Heaven, neither out of or for the sake of love and fear of God, cannot ascend "before God," meaning to the ten *sefirot* that are the inner being of every world and the divine aspect within it.

רַק לִימּוּדוֹ עוֹלֶה לְהֵיכָלוֹת וּמְדוֹרִין שֶׁהֵן חִיצוֹנִיּוֹת הָעוֹלָמוֹת, שֶׁבָּהֶן עוֹמְדִים הַמַּלְאָכִים.

Rather, a person's **study ascends to the palaces and abodes that are the externality of the worlds, where the angels stand.**

The "ten *sefirot*," as was stated, are the inner being and living soul of the world, the divine "active force that activates within the acted upon" that manifests the world, whereas the palaces and abodes are the externality of the worlds, the scaffolds and support structures, within which the angels stand. The Torah that is not for its own sake does not ascend to stand before God, but nevertheless, it does ascend from the existence of this world, the mundane world, to an existence of holiness. The Torah is Torah, and a commandment is a commandment even without intent. Therefore, as was explained in the previous chapter, and as will be further elaborated upon, even if it does not ascend now, it can ascend at a later time, if a person simply attaches the proper intent to it to stand "before God."

THE COMMANDMENT IS A COMMANDMENT

A commandment has value intrinsically, even without intent. As was explained, the qualitative difference between good and evil, between commandment and sin, is not determined based on one's intent. The levels of intent, with their many differences, determine the "size" of the commandment, its quality and level of connection with the supernal worlds, but not the basic essence of the act as a commandment or as a sin, as holy or as a *kelippa*. Every mitzva act, even when executed without any inner substance, creates a reality of holiness. Its holiness is objective and is derived not only from the intent of the thought. An act of holiness is like a holy book in a cabinet. The book does not fulfill any of the commandments written within it, it does not study Torah or ascend to the heavens on its own, but nevertheless, it remains a holy book in an honored place, in a holy place, since it is meant and fit to assist in fulfilling commandments. A commandment performed without intent lacks the energy of holiness, it lacks the point of connection with supernal existence. Therefore, it cannot ascend to stand before God, the King. But the commandment remains a commandment, and even without the intent of holiness, it is an entity of holiness that cannot be erased.

וּכְמוֹ שֶׁכָּתַב הָרַב חַיִּים וִיטַל ז"ל בְּ'שַׁעַר הַנְּבוּאָה' פֶּרֶק ב': שֶׁמֵּהַתּוֹרָה שֶׁלֹּא בְּכַוָּנָה נִבְרָאִים מַלְאָכִים בְּעוֹלַם הַיְצִירָה, וּמֵהַמִּצְוֹת בְּלִי כַּוָּנָה נִבְרָאִים מַלְאָכִים בְּעוֹלַם הָעֲשִׂיָּיה,

As Rabbi Ḥayyim Vital wrote in chapter 2 of *Sha'ar HaNevu'a*, that from Torah studied without intent, angels are created in the world of *Yetzira*, and from mitzvot performed without intent angels are created in the world of *Asiya*,

As Rabbi Ḥayyim Vital wrote in chapter 2 of *Sha'ar HaNevu'a*,[1] from Torah studied not for its own sake angels are created in the world of *Yetzira*, and from mitzvot performed not for their own sake angels are created in the world of *Asiya*. Something similar to this is written in *Pirkei Avot* (*Avot* 4:11), that one who performs a commandment acquires a defender, and one who commits a sin acquires an accuser.[2] This means that when a person performs a good or bad action, a new

---

THE LAW OF CONSERVATION OF MASS AND ENERGY IN SPIRITUALITY

☞ Matter is not destroyed, and it is not created anew. It simply undergoes transitions from one aggregated form to another. Every action in the physical world creates a result. It is not possible for an action to take place and vanish absolutely. Even for the most apparently random, meaningless action, like a person scratching his nose, there are consequences: changes in the material and temperature that result from that action. It is possible that the action has transitioned to a different construct or realm, but in some way, in this place or another, the action continues to exist. This law operates in the spiritual world even more powerfully. The spiritual essence of a commandment that was performed, its meaning and form, generate a particular reality and generate an angel, as was explained. This angel, formed from the particular action of a particular person, is now an existing and active force in the life, framework, and level of that particular person.

---

1. The reference here seems to be to the book called *Sha'ar HaYiḥudim* (its full name, *Sha'ar HaYiḥudim U'Nevu'a VeRu'aḥ HaKodesh*, "Gateway of Unifications, Prophecy, and Holy Spirit"), which is the fourth section of the book *Pri Etz Ḥayyim*, edited by Rabbi Meir Popperos from the writings of Rabbi Ḥayyim Vital (see the work *Kabbalat HaAri* by Rabbi Yosef Avivi, p. 651).
2. The word *koneh*, "acquires," can also mean "creates," as in the verse (Gen. 14:19) "He creates [*koneh*] the heavens and earth"(*HaLekaḥ VeHalibbuv*).

objective reality is created. The actions of a person not only leave behind a balance of merits and sins, they go out beyond a person's subjective existence and become independent, objective realities, a good angel or an evil angel. ☞

When a person learns Torah, just as the physical energy of uttering the words does not vanish, the spiritual content of those words also does not vanish. When a person reads a verse or studies a page of Talmud, it becomes a form of spiritual reality. This spiritual reality is linked to the person, to what and how he studied, in a relationship of cause and effect. It now remains, and it operates according to its place and magnitude. If the person studied Torah without intention for the sake of Heaven, it belongs, as was said, to the externality of the worlds. This generates angels of a lower level, roughly formed angels that are only undirected, blind forces. This is a spiritual reality of holiness that has no essential inner spirit within it, and all it contains is the intellect that was invested into the study, the natural heat of committing the action, and nothing more.

וְכָל הַמַּלְאָכִים הֵם בַּעֲלֵי חוֹמֶר וְצוּרָה. and all angels have matter and form.

Matter and form are, in the language of the Kabbala, "vessels and lights." In this sense, all things in existence are comprised of matter and form, and all existence, spiritual or physical, is built from vessels and lights, from frameworks and content. The framework is the "matter," and the content that animates the matter is its "form." The most relatable example is our own existence as human beings. As human beings, we have a body and a soul. The body is made from matter, and the soul is spiritual. Even so, they are linked to each other, operate together, and influence one another. The body lives the life of the soul – its wants, fears, and dreams. The soul cannot operate, even nonmaterial actions, except within the guidelines and parameters of the body. A soul and body share a personal relationship with each other. A particular soul in a particular body operates in one way, and if that same soul would have been placed in a different body, it would behave differently. This is true not only for entities composed of matter and spirit, but regarding all things, even creations that are purely spiritual. Thought (not only as an activity of the physical brain, but as a concept) is also made from matter and form, of formal structures and parameters that circumscribe and define it (language, concepts), and from the inner content within these structures. This dualism is strikingly visible in literary creations, in which the "form," the inner content, appears in different types of "matter," in different types of expression. Furthermore, when particular content is translated from one language to another, the content (the form) remains, but the language (the matter) changes. Form and matter, like lights and vessels, do not specifically apply only to the physical world, and even spiritual entities like angels are comprised of form and matter, from a formal structure and content.

The matter and form of an angel constitute the particular borders of its existence. Regarding the angels created out of the Torah study and performance of commandments of human beings, their boundaries are essentially the boundaries of the human being, the borders of his actions and thoughts that powered the creation of these angels. The essence of the act or speech created the matter of the angel, and the underlying intent of the act or study generated the form of the angel. In this sense, angels created through Torah and commandments that lacked intention for the sake of Heaven are also holy creations. But their existence is primarily external (the externality of worlds), like holy objects that are left sitting in the corner, like a scroll in its closet. They are not part of the current of divine holiness itself. ☞

LIKE THE ANGELS, SO IT IS WITH THE HARMFUL FORCES

☞ "Burning anger, fury, indignation, and trouble, a band of destroying angels" (Ps. 78:49) that a person receives are his own delegation. He does not receive evil angels of someone else, but his own, the ones he himself sent. They relate to him and are built according to his own format, tied to him such that he cannot cast them behind his back. There are descriptions of how evil forces created by a person escort him in his life, and how they do not leave him even after his death, because, as they tell him, "You are our father." Every person ultimately receives his own, and not those of someone else. Similar to this, there are parasites that live only on human beings, and they cannot survive on other creatures. In the same way, the angels created by a man are tied to him, and cannot operate within someone else. There appears to be an ongoing mechanism (as in the physical world) that kills these parasites. This is a type of "daily kindness of God," which screens and protects us from some of these harmful

In this sense, repentance is characterized by the constant struggle to build barriers, to disconnect the link between a person and the destructive deeds of his past. Yet as was explained, this disconnection is only partial. It is possible to create changes, to prevent a direct connection, and to sterilize the poison, but it is almost entirely impossible to completely detach oneself from those deeds. There is the more rare option of "his willful evil deeds are transformed into merits,"[3] in which a person does not try to disconnect himself from his past deeds, but instead changes their meaning as he moves forward into the future. At the moment that these evil deeds become a force driving toward holiness and form a basis for holiness, they cease to be evil. It has happened to more than one person that, if not for the fact that he was a sinner, he would have remained a nonentity, and it was precisely the fact that he had committed sins that presses with intensified strength toward holiness. It is as if such a person says to himself, "So-and-so the righteous person can sit in peace, but I, the sinner, cannot sit in peace!" Repentance of this high caliber, in which one's sins are transformed into merits, and which is even above the level of the totally righteous, is the only way to change the material and the form of the components of existence, the meaning and direction of the actions of man and what they create.

The Torah that a person studies and the commandments he performs, even those without intent for the sake of Heaven, are therefore forces, without which we would be overrun by them and destroyed. This is similar to what is written in the Talmud, that "if the eye had been given permission to see [them], no creature could stand before the harmful forces" (*Berakhot* 6a). Everything a person does, his actions and thoughts, those that are just "not for God" down to the lowliest ones, are all realities that are attached to him. If a person could see all these, the accumulation of days and years of "normal" life, not necessarily of evil, he could not carry on in the face of his terror. Even though these forces are not depicted in photographs, each person has his own mental image of their appearance. A person has a visual representation of sexual immorality or jealousy or fraud. He himself created them, and they are all attached to him. "Sin crouches at the entrance, and its desire is for you." This evil loves him and wants to be close to him, strangling him with the poison that the person himself secretes into his reality.

---

3. *Yoma* 86b.

not lost. Even if they are performed without internal love or fear, they create angels that escort the person and fill his life with holiness (and they are even influenced by him, if he commits those same actions again but with intentions that are for the sake of Heaven).

אֲבָל תּוֹרָה שֶׁלֹּא לִשְׁמָהּ מַמָּשׁ, כְּגוֹן לִהְיוֹת תַּלְמִיד חָכָם וּכְהַאי גַוְונָא, אֵינָהּ עוֹלָה כְּלָל לְמַעְלָה, אֲפִילוּ לְהֵיכָלוֹת וּמְדוֹר הַמַּלְאָכִים דִּקְדוּשָׁה, אֶלָּא נִשְׁאֶרֶת לְמַטָּה בָּעוֹלָם הַזֶּה הַגַּשְׁמִי שֶׁהוּא מְדוֹר הַקְּלִיפּוֹת,

However, Torah studied truly "not for its own sake," for example, to be a Torah scholar and the like, does not ascend upward at all, not even to the palaces and abode of the angels of holiness. Instead, it remains below in this material world, which is the abode of the *kelippot*,

Torah studied truly "not for its own sake," refers to Torah that was not only not studied actively for the sake of Heaven, having been studied from a place of habit and routine, but was actually studied for a different reason. For example, a person decides that he wants to make a career out of being a Torah scholar, and therefore, he studies Torah. The Torah he studied with this intention does not ascend upward at all. Instead, it remains below in this material world, the abode of the *kelippot*. The "career" of a person (including the career of a Torah scholar) is not something connected to the higher spiritual worlds but rather to this world, and that which belongs to this physical world essentially belongs to the abode of the *kelippot*. The Torah is Torah, and it cannot lose its existence just because the person studied it without intent. But it is Torah that exists together with the other entities of the world, submerged unrecognizably among the existences of this world, and it cannot separate itself from them to ascend and attach itself to the side of holiness.

הַגָּהָה: (כְּמוֹ שֶׁכָּתוּב בַּזֹּהַר חֵלֶק ג' דַּף ל"א עַמּוּד ב' וְדַף קכ"א עַמּוּד ב' עַיֵּין שָׁם: "הַהִיא מִלָּה סָלְקָא וּבָקְעָה רְקִיעִין כו' וְאִתְּעַר מַה דְּאִתְּעַר, אִי טָב - טָב" כו'

Gloss: As written in the *Zohar* I:31b and 121b; see there: "That word ascends and breaks through the heavens, and so forth, and awakens that which it awakens; if it is good – good," and so forth; see there. Then 105a: "A

עַיֵּין שָׁם. וְדַף ק״ה עַמּוּד א׳: "מִלָּה דְּאוֹרַיְיתָא אִתְעֲבִיד מִינֵּיהּ קָלָא וְסָלֵיק" כו׳ וְדַף קס״ח עַמּוּד ב׳: "קָלִין דְּאוֹרַיְיתָא וּצְלוֹתָא בָּקְעִין רְקִיעִין" כו׳).

word of Torah is formed into a sound, which ascends," and so forth, and 168b: "Sounds of Torah and prayer break through heavens," and so forth.

In this gloss, sources are brought from various places in the *Zohar* that words of Torah that a person speaks with intent ascend above our world, breaking through the heavens and reaching supernal worlds (and see *Kuntres Aharon* and *HaLekah VeHalibbuv*).

וּכְמוֹ שֶׁכָּתוּב בַּזֹּהַר (חלק א רכג, ב) עַל פָּסוּק: "מַה יִּתְרוֹן לָאָדָם בְּכָל עֲמָלוֹ שֶׁיַּעֲמוֹל תַּחַת הַשָּׁמֶשׁ" (קהלת א, ג),

as written in the *Zohar* (I:223b) on the verse "What advantage is there to man from all his labor in which he labors under the sun?" (Eccles. 1:3),

The question of Ecclesiastes, "What advantage is there to man from all his labor" is a broadly inclusive question regarding all the things a person does "under the sun," that is, all of the things a person does in our world, the world of nature, physical and spiritual, in the world of dynamism and changes: What value is there to all the accomplishments and achievements? What is their utility? For what purpose are they performed, and what remains of them? In the *Zohar*,[4] the Sages infer from the language of Ecclesiastes that "under the sun" there is no advantage, but in the labor of Torah, which is above the sun, there is an advantage.

דַּאֲפִילּוּ עֲמָלָא דְּאוֹרַיְיתָא, אִי עָבֵיד בְּגִין יְקָרֵיהּ כו׳.

which includes **even the labor of Torah if one acts for his own honor, and so forth.**

The *Zohar* there adds that even regarding Torah study, if one studies for his own honor, and not for Torah's own sake, the Torah study does not ascend.[5] When a person's Torah study and performance of

---

4. See the *Targum*'s translation of this verse, and *Shabbat* 30b.
5. This is also found in *Pesahim* 50b: "It is written, 'For Your kindness is great,

commandments are a part of the structure of his life in this world that is "under the sun," they do not ascend above the sun. Just as a person does not expect to reach the World to Come with his salary pay stub, he also cannot reach the World to Come with the Torah he studied in order to achieve a certain status or position.

וְזֶה שֶׁאָמְרוּ: "אַשְׁרֵי מִי שֶׁבָּא לְכָאן וְתַלְמוּדוֹ בְּיָדוֹ" (פסחים נ, א). This relates to **what our Rabbis stated: "Praiseworthy is the one who arrives here with his studies in hand,"**

This is related to what our Rabbis stated (*Pesaḥim* 50a, and elsewhere) regarding the story of one of the Sages, who became sick and was near death, and when he returned to health, his father asked him, "What did you see when you were there?" Among other things, he said he heard people talking there, saying: "Praiseworthy is the one who arrives here with his studies in hand." We can derive from this that it is possible for a person to arrive in the higher worlds without his studies in hand.

פֵּירוּשׁ, שֶׁלֹּא נִשְׁאַר לְמַטָּה בָּעוֹלָם הַזֶּה. **meaning that it did not remain below, in this world.**

Just as a person leaves his money in this world, he is also liable to leave his Torah. The labor of a person who exerted his effort "under the sun" includes not only his physical assets – his house, clothing, money, and so forth – but also spiritual items, even holy things, and holy acquisitions, since it is possible for all of these to belong only to this world. When a person ascends to the world of truth and stands in judgment, he is asked, as described: "Did you conduct business in good faith? Did you set aside times to study Torah?" (see *Shabbat* 31a), for these are the things that are relevant there and that have value even in the world of truth. If he claims in response: "But I was exceedingly wealthy," "I had an enormous home," "I was a member of parliament," or other similar examples, none of these things are relevant there. Sometimes, as has been explained, even the Torah a person studied in this world is not

---

reaching unto the heavens' (Ps. 57:11), and it is also written, 'For Your kindness is greater than the heavens' (Ps. 108:5). How are these verses resolved? One refers to service for its own sake, and the other refers to service not for its own sake."

relevant there. A person can say: "I studied this many chapters, I wrote this many books," and they check up above and do not find these, since they were presumably sent to a different address. ☞

| וְאַף דְּאוֹרַיְיתָא וְקוּדְשָׁא בְּרִיךְ הוּא כּוֹלָּא חַד, שֶׁהוּא וּרְצוֹנוֹ אֶחָד, | Although the Torah and the Holy One, blessed be He, are all one, because He and His will are one, | 14 Nisan |

Regarding what was said previously, that Torah can remain in this world, one can ask: Since the Torah and God are all one, because He and His will are one, so that the Torah is itself the will of God, the *keter* (that is, the will) that is above the ten *sefirot*, how is it possible that it does not ascend to the ten *sefirot*? The question is, How is it possible to say that Torah will not ascend and will have no meaning in the higher world? One can say regarding an individual's thought that it is mistaken, or that it is meaningless in general, or as applied to a specific topic, but Torah itself is "truth" and holy, because it is unified with God, and it is therefore relevant and meaningful regarding all of existence.

| הֲרֵי קוּדְשָׁא בְּרִיךְ הוּא אִיהוּ מְמַלֵּא כָּל עָלְמִין בְּשָׁוֶה, וְאַף עַל פִּי כֵן אֵין הָעוֹלָמוֹת שָׁוִים בְּמַעֲלָתָם. | the Holy One, blessed be He, fills all worlds equally, and yet the worlds are not equal in their status. |

WHAT ASCENDS TO THE HIGHER WORLD

☞ Whether a person's action will ascend to the higher world or will remain below in this world is determined by the person's intent in committing the action. This is true not only of physical deeds. Even spiritual creations can remain in this world and be irrelevant to the world of holiness. The opposite can also happen, that thoughts of issues of this world are pulled into a structure of holiness. A story is told of a great hasid who was a successful merchant, and he was seen once sitting and summarizing the transactions of that year. Suddenly, they saw that he was deep in thought, and when he completed the summaries of his activity with each batch of inventory, he would write, "There is no other besides Him." He would begin with calculations of his trading, how much he purchased and how much he profited, but when he would reach the line marked "total," something within his soul would awaken and say that he could not just write a number of rubles. Therefore, he would finish the calculation and summarize it in a way that would rise above this world to a completely different one.

The answer is that God fills all worlds equally, and yet the worlds are not equal in status. All the worlds, higher and lower, receive their life force from God, and they are all sustained from His power alone, yet we see that the worlds are not equal to each other at all.

וְהַשִּׁינּוּי הוּא מֵהַמְקַבְּלִים, **The difference is due to the recipients,**

The story is told about Rabbi Yitzḥak Meir Rotenberg-Alter from Gur, known as the author of *Ḥiddushei HaRim*, who asked his hasidim: "Where is God?" His hasidim expressed surprise. "What's the question? God is everywhere!" they said. The Ḥiddushei HaRim replied, "That is not correct. God is found wherever a person allows Him to enter." God is found in all places equally, but the question that relates to us of whether God is found with us depends on the recipient; the amount of God's eternal, unchanging existence is present for him in the way that he thinks of Him, recognizes and understands His greatness, and senses and feels love and fear of Him. All this depends first of all on the individual, on the degree to which he opens his mind and heart, making space for his awareness of and feelings toward the Divine Presence.

בְּב' בְּחִינוֹת: הָאַחַת, שֶׁהָעֶלְיוֹנִים מְקַבְּלִים הֶאָרָה יוֹתֵר גְּדוֹלָה לְאֵין קֵץ מֵהַתַּחְתּוֹנִים, **in two respects: one, that the higher beings receive an infinitely greater illumination than the lower ones;**

This difference between each world, which is dependent on the recipients, is seen in two respects: First, although God is found in all the worlds equally, His illumination and revelation in each world is not the same. The higher a particular world, the more encompassing it is, and the illumination it receives is greater, broader, and more inclusive. This is similar to how a person can be connected to two people equally, and even speak the same words to each of them, yet from their perspective, the revelation is completely different. He is more fully revealed to the person who understands and is knowledgeable of the scope of the words, and is less revealed to the person with a worldview that is more constricted within particular details. This is similar to what is written in Daniel (2:21): "He grants wisdom to the wise."

וְהַשֵּׁנִית, שֶׁמְּקַבְּלִים בְּלִי לְבוּשִׁים וּמָסַכִּים רַבִּים כָּל כָּךְ כִּבְתַחְתּוֹנִים.

and two, that they receive it without as many garments and screens as is the case for the lower ones.

The second difference between the two worlds is as follows. The higher realms receive this illumination without as many garments and screens as do the lower realms. The difference between the higher and lower worlds is in the layers and coverings that increase the more one descends in the structure of devolutions. This difference relates of course only to the divine illumination and revelation, in that in the higher realms there are fewer coverings, so the divine light is clearer. In the lower worlds, the layers and garments are more numerous, so the light is concealed and blurred; the picture is less clear than in the higher worlds.[6]

וְעוֹלָם הַזֶּה הוּא עוֹלָם הַשָּׁפֵל בְּב' בְּחִינוֹת, כִּי הַהֶאָרָה שֶׁבּוֹ מְצוּמְצֶמֶת מְאֹד עַד קָצֶה הָאַחֲרוֹן, וְלָכֵן הוּא חוֹמְרִי וְגַשְׁמִי,

This world is the lowly world in two regards, because the illumination it contains is extremely contracted, to the greatest degree, and therefore it is material and physical,

THE DIFFERENCE BETWEEN THE HIGHER AND LOWER WORLDS

☞ The difference between above and below is thus recognizable in two respects: scope and clarity. The scope of the higher worlds is broader, and therefore, they receive more. But also the vessels of the higher worlds are clearer, more transparent, and therefore, all that they receive is also received with greater clarity. One can draw an analogy from human experience: There is a difference between the intellectual capacity to understand complex matters and the capacity to achieve clarity of understanding. One person can have great talent in both areas, at the same time or at different times, or one person might have great talent in one area and a different person in a different area. Some people are capable of understanding very complex matters but their comprehension lacks full clarity. Others might be limited in what level of information they can understand, but that which they do understand they comprehend with great clarity.

---

6. In other words, the first difference is due to the concept of constriction, and the second is due to the concept of concealment (Rabbi Shmuel Gronem Esterman).

This world is the lowly world in these two regards. First, because the illumination it contains is extremely contracted, to the greatest degree, and therefore it is material and physical. Our world is the lowest because, as a physical, material world, its method of comprehension is primarily physical and material. Any amount of comprehension in this world is fundamentally dependent on physical comprehension, which is, by definition, limited and constricted. Since our existence in this world is dependent on our connection with the body, since the soul lives in this world through a symbiosis with the body and the material reality, we are unable to absorb anything except through the body and in the context of the body. Everything that is comprehended in this world is therefore very constricted and limited to things that can relate to bodily concepts. This limitation of comprehensible concepts that derives from the physical is the primary obstacle we face regarding the revelation of holiness.

וְגַם זֹאת הִיא בִּלְבוּשִׁים וּמָסַכִּים רַבִּים, **and even that is through many garments and screens,**

The second limitation relates to the clarity with which we can absorb these subtle things. The picture we receive is small and constricted, because we are small creatures, but it is a picture that could have been clear. Not only does God, as it were, speak to us in a constricted manner, where we receive less than do the higher worlds, but that which we do receive is with concealment of the countenance, via many layers and garments.

עַד שֶׁנִּתְלַבְּשָׁה בִּקְלִיפַּת נוֹגַהּ לְהַחֲיוֹת כָּל דְּבָרִים הַטְּהוֹרִים שֶׁבָּעוֹלָם הַזֶּה, **until it is enclothed in *kelippat noga*, in order to sustain all the pure things that are in this world,**

Beyond the fact that our world is a physical one and constricted in its comprehension, it is also a world that lacks absolute clarity regarding the differences between good and evil, truth and falsehood. These are two separate areas, and it is possible to distinguish between them even in our world. There are people with tremendous comprehension, able to grasp huge ideas, but they lack clarity about good and evil. There are also people without significant powers of comprehension, but who possess constant clarity on the distinction between good and evil. A person like this knows clearly and sharply what is good and what is evil, what is a commandment and what is a sin within existence. ☞

Our world is "lowly" in these two ways. It is both ignorant and blurred. Its comprehension of matters is rudimentary, because it is limited by its tools for receiving. It also grasps matters in a blurred and distorted form. The Divine is understood in limited, external form, and the relationships between good and evil, truth and falsehood, holiness and impurity are not perceived clearly. This mixing together of good and evil is referred to, as was explained in the initial chapters, as *kelippat noga*.

וּבִכְלָלָם הוּא נֶפֶשׁ הַחִיּוּנִית הַמְדַבֶּרֶת שֶׁבָּאָדָם. **including the vital, speaking soul in man.**

Included within all the things of this world that belong to the realm of *kelippat noga* is the vital, speaking soul in man. The animating soul of a Jew is his starting point, before he damaged and before he repaired. It is his initial existence in this world, which intrinsically is not connected or identified with holiness, but rather is part of the mundane (*kelippat noga*) aspects of this world.

וְלָכֵן כְּשֶׁמְּדַבֶּרֶת דִּבְרֵי תוֹרָה וּתְפִלָּה בְּלֹא כַּוָּנָה, אַף שֶׁהֵן אוֹתִיּוֹת קְדוֹשׁוֹת, וְאֵין קְלִיפַּת נוֹגַהּ שֶׁבְּנֶפֶשׁ הַחִיּוּנִית מָסָךְ מַבְדִּיל כְּלָל לְהַסְתִּיר וּלְכַסּוֹת עַל קְדֻשָּׁתוֹ יִתְבָּרֵךְ הַמְלֻבָּשֶׁת בָּהֶן,

Therefore, when the vital soul speaks words of Torah and prayer without intent, even though they are holy letters, the *kelippat noga* that is in the vital soul is not a separating screen at all, concealing and covering His holiness that is enclothed in them,

---

THE WISE MAN AND THE SIMPLE MAN

☞ There was a well-known family in which the four older brothers were renowned rabbis, while the fifth brother was thought to be a simpleton. Despite this, it was specifically that fifth brother who was known as an astonishingly honest person, who would not take even a penny that did not belong to him. His older brothers certainly attained greater comprehension than he did, but his clarity within the small understanding he attained regarding the division between truth and falsehood, honesty and duplicity, was unblemished. There was no lack of clarity for him in these areas.

As was explained, words of Torah, even without intention, are holy and are not part of this neutral world of *kelippat noga*. *Kelippat noga* only conceals and covers the neutral reality, which is neither intrinsically holy nor impure, but words of Torah, which are intrinsically holy, cannot be concealed or covered.

כְּמוֹ שֶׁהִיא מַסְתֶּרֶת וּמְכַסָּה עַל קְדוּשָּׁתוֹ יִתְבָּרֵךְ שֶׁבַּנֶּפֶשׁ הַחִיּוּנִית כְּשֶׁמְּדַבֶּרֶת דְּבָרִים בְּטֵלִים, וְשֶׁבַּנֶּפֶשׁ הַחִיּוּנִית שֶׁבִּשְׁאָר בַּעֲלֵי חַיִּים הַטְּהוֹרִים, — as *kelippat noga* conceals and covers His holiness in the vital soul when it speaks worthless things and that holiness in the vital soul of other pure creatures.

Kelippat Noga covers over the holiness within the soul of man when that soul speaks worthless things. Worthless things do not necessarily have no value or meaning but rather are part of the mundane needs of the soul within this world, neutral things that are neither prohibited nor required for performance of commandments. When a soul involves itself in these matters, the *kelippat noga* covers over the holiness within it, just as it conceals the holiness in the vital soul of the other pure creatures. Pure animals also have a spark of holiness within them, but it is concealed by the *kelippat noga* as long as these animals remain a part of this world, as long as they do not leave (through the action of fulfilling a commandment, as is explained elsewhere) the realm of the *kelippat noga* and enter the realm of holiness.

דְּאַף דְּלֵית אֲתַר פָּנוּי מִינֵיהּ, — For although there is no place void of Him (*Tikkunei Zohar* 91b),

The question regarding the character of the divine concealment is, How can it be that the Divine, of which no place is void, and which sustains and maintains every part of existence, can be concealed? How is it possible to conceal God?

מִכָּל מָקוֹם אִיהוּ סָתִימוּ דְּכָל סְתִימִין וְנִקְרָא "אֵל מִסְתַּתֵּר", — nevertheless, He is the most hidden of all hidden, and is called "the God who conceals Himself,"

God is the most hidden of all hidden,[7] more concealed than anything concealed. God is present, but not revealed. He is known as "the God who conceals Himself."[8] There are two types of concealment. The first is when a concealed entity becomes concealed. This is built on the fact that there is a certain mechanism for the concealment, of a darkening that prevents revelation. The second category, which in many ways is the more common, is the concealment that does not require any mechanism of concealment, as it is a concealed character that cannot be comprehended. The first type is the result of a smallness of light, since the light is covered and cannot emerge and be revealed outward. The second type derives from the fact that the light is so bright that it cannot be comprehended by existing tools of comprehension. In this sense, among human beings as well, the greatest concealment is not when a person hides something, but rather, when he says everything, and specifically then the receiver does not understand anything. This is concealment that does not derive from too little revelation, but rather from too much, from a lack of connection between the hidden and the one who reveals. When we speak of "the God who conceals Himself," of the concealment of God, we speak primarily of the second type of concealment. For although "there is no place void of Him," it is actually for this precise reason that we cannot see anything. ☞

GOD WHO CONCEALS HIMSELF

☞ Here we also find an answer to the problem with which small and great grapple, namely, why doesn't God reveal Himself? Since ultimately, the concealment of God is of the second type, what will God do in order to be revealed? The difficulty is not because He conceals Himself, but because we are not capable of seeing Him. The problem lies in the vessels, and our tools of comprehension, which are physical tools, are not at all on the level that enable us to comprehend Him. "Man shall not see Me and live" (Ex. 33:20), not because there is concealment blocking man, but because there is man. We cannot see because our reality consists of a world in which the basic perception of its physical nature conceals the existence of God.

---

7. Based on the *Zohar Ḥadash*, vol. 2 (*Megillot*), *Megillat Shir HaShirim* 8a.
8. Isa. 45:2. Also based on the well-known poem of Rabbi Avraham Maimin (Safed, 16th century CE), *El Mistater*.

וְגַם הֶאָרָה וְהִתְפַּשְׁטוּת הַחַיּוּת **and likewise the illumination and**
מִמֶּנּוּ יִתְבָּרֵךְ **expansion of the life force from Him**

The problem of concealment exists not only regarding the divine essence (which is certainly beyond any comprehension), but even includes the reality within which we live. The problem is that we do not sense the causal chain of life, the causality that acts between the holiness of God and mankind, that penetrates into our reality level after level.

There is a difference between the concealment of the Divine itself, "God who conceals Himself," and the concealment of the illumination and spreading forth of life force from Him. God "conceals" Himself because we are unable to comprehend Him. But we should be able to sense God's illumination in the world, the life force that flows from Him and sustains us. Electricity is an analogy for this. No person has ever seen electricity; we have no direct way to perceive it. In fact, we don't have any understanding of what electricity is. Yet even though we don't know what electricity is, we can feel an electrical shock. Beyond this, we can construct devices that harness its power, activate its force, and experience its strength. In this sense, we do not comprehend the entity itself, but we comprehend its illumination; we feel its manifestations.

Every divine revelation, therefore, always involves a manner of change, of breakage in the character of the world. This is seen in the description of the revelation at Mount Sinai, and so it is in all descriptions of individual revelation (see Rambam, *Sefer HaMadda, Hilkhot Yesodei HaTorah* 7:2). The revelation is dependent on a person's ceasing to see as he saw previously, and beginning to see things differently. We do not feel the Divine Presence, just as we do not feel any presence which cannot be directly, tangibly encountered. The Rambam describes something similar to this (in his introduction to *Perek Ḥelek*) when he compares this phenomenon to a person who is blind from birth and cannot comprehend what color is. It can be described and explained to him, but none of these things will ever suffice. Every attempt to explain the difference between green and blue (other than the numerical differences in lightwave frequencies) will immediately expose the inability of language to capture even something that involves our direct human experience. All the more so, when speaking of the Divine, in order for the listener to hear, in order for the comprehending person to relate, he must move to a totally different framework. A person who is tied to the concepts of the body cannot begin to comprehend what the Divine is and what the divine power is. He lacks words and points of relationship needed to construct a relationship.

Therefore, the question regarding the Divine is: Why do we not at least sense the divine force that operates in the world?

מִסְתַּתֶּרֶת בִּלְבוּשִׁים וּמָסַכִּים רַבִּים וַעֲצוּמִים עַד שֶׁנִּתְלַבְּשָׁה וְנִסְתַּתְּרָה בִּלְבוּשׁ נֹגַהּ. **is concealed in many dense garments and screens, until it is enclothed and concealed in the garment of *noga*.**

The answer is that the illumination and the spreading of the life force from Him is concealed by numerous garments and screens, until it is enclothed and concealed in the garment of *kelippat noga*. These concealments, coverings, and screens do not conceal God Himself. His essence and being is here, in our world, as it is in the higher worlds and everywhere. The concealment is of the illumination and spreading forth of His life force with which He animates the worlds, level after level.

מַה שֶּׁאֵין כֵּן בָּאוֹתִיּוֹת הַקְּדוֹשׁוֹת שֶׁל דִּבְרֵי תּוֹרָה וּתְפִלָּה, **This is not the case with regard to the holy letters in words of Torah and prayer,**

The holy letters in words of Torah and prayer are the revelation of the inner aspect of His will, His inner essence, because there is no concealment here, as was mentioned. This is different from our world, the world that is "lowly" in two ways, in terms of the constriction of illumination and in terms of the level of the concealment and its blurring. Torah has only the constriction of light, but it has no concealment or distortion.

דְּאַדְּרַבָּה, קְלִיפַּת נֹגַהּ מִתְהַפֶּכֶת לְטוֹב וְנִכְלֶלֶת בִּקְדֻשָּׁה זוֹ, כַּנִּזְכָּר לְעֵיל. **for on the contrary, *kelippat noga* is transformed to good and it is encompassed into this holiness, as stated above.**

This is the nature of *kelippat noga*, that when it encounters holiness, it is transformed to become a part of that holiness. When we involve ourselves with Torah and holiness in our world, the world of *kelippat noga*, assuming there is no forbidden element, if we have no abased intention, we change the nature of this world. The meaning of this is that when there is contact between Torah and the *kelippat noga*, not only does the *kelippa* not cover the Torah, it is itself transformed into holiness.

מִכָּל מָקוֹם הַהֶאָרָה שֶׁבָּהֶן, מִקְּדוּשָׁתוֹ יִתְבָּרֵךְ, הִיא בִּבְחִינַת צִמְצוּם עַד קָצֶה הָאַחֲרוֹן, מֵאַחַר שֶׁהַקּוֹל וְהַדִּבּוּר הוּא גַּשְׁמִי.

Even so, the illumination these words contain from His holiness is constricted to the utmost degree, since the voice and speech are physical.

The letters of Torah and prayer always contain a direct, clear illumination of holiness, even when they are spoken in the lower, physical world of *kelippat noga*. This illumination of holiness is extremely constricted, however, since both the voice and speech are physical. The Torah resides in this world in physical voice and speech, which are a component of the nature of this physical world in which the illumination is constricted to the utmost degree. One cannot expect there to be a profound and great revelation within something that is a part of the physicality of this world. A person does not have a special mouth for holiness; the mouth that says holy words is the same mouth that says other words. The letters expressing holiness that are printed in books are physical letters. Because of this, the holiness that they intrinsically possess, before a person speaks them, or after he speaks them but without any spiritual intent, is a holiness that is revealed in its lowest level, the level of action and materiality alone. ☞

In this way, the way a person relates to a book, Rabbi Meir related to the Torah of Elisha ben Abuya (*Aḥer*). The Torah that Rabbi Meir learned from the mouth of *Aḥer* did not generate any connection

TORAH IN THIS WORLD

☞ The Torah appears within the vessels of this world, within the screens and concealments in which the world exists, and it cannot transcend this on its own. A holy book is just a holy book, part of the parameters of this world, physical ink on physical pages, it does not in itself rise higher to the upper worlds. Prayer that is spoken by a person when his heart is not in it is still holy, but it possesses only the holiness of the physical. When a person takes a holy book and studies it, whether with holy intent, with intent that is not holy, or with intent not for its own sake at all, the book itself remains unchanged. It remains a book, and it remains a holy book. A person cannot cause the Torah to stop being Torah. All his power lies only in his ability to extract it or not to, from the primary physical level in which it exists without him.

between Rabbi Meir and the man who spoke it. The person was what he was, but the Torah that resided in him remained as it was and did not stop being Torah. There was no flaw in the Torah, but just in its place. It could not ascend, and remained in the parameters of words without rectification, without ascent, without the creation of the appropriate relationship to repair them. This reality of "a holy book lying on the trash heap" is possible precisely in our world. If this world were higher, if it were a world in which holiness was visible and illuminating, a Torah scroll would necessarily fly in the air. However, since our world is not a world of revealed holiness, but rather a world of "nature," the laws of nature affect a book of Torah. In this sense, the thoughts and words of Torah, so long as they are subordinate to the laws of the natural world and not extracted from its parameters through holy intention, are bound by those natural laws.

| אֲבָל בִּתְפִלָּה בְּכַוָּונָה וְתוֹרָה בְּכַוָּונָה לִשְׁמָהּ, הֲרֵי הַכַּוָּונָה מִתְלַבֶּשֶׁת בְּאוֹתִיּוֹת הַדִּבּוּר, הוֹאִיל וְהִיא מָקוֹר וְשֹׁרֶשׁ לָהֶן, שֶׁמֵּחֲמָתָהּ וּבִסִבָּתָהּ הוּא מְדַבֵּר אוֹתִיּוֹת אֵלּוּ. | However, in the case of prayer with intention and Torah with intention "for its own sake," the intention is enclothed in the letters of speech, as it is their source and root, since the person articulates these letters due to and on account of this intent. | 15 Nisan |

What can free the holiness and raise it up from this world is the intention of a person who engages in that holiness. That occurs when a person studies Torah "for its own sake," not for any lower purpose, but only to elevate the Torah to its holy source. This intention allows the Torah to ascend to the revealed holiness of the higher worlds, and to disconnect from the material frameworks of this world.

In order to bring out a commandment from the material realm, there needs to be some point of relationship between the person and God. God is the Commander, and there is a commandment in the Torah. We fulfill His commands, and there is a commandment in the world. But the point that completes the circuit, enabling this commandment to truly have an effect and actively be a bridge between above and below, is the element of a person's intent, of his determination to forge a relationship between below and above. Even if this point is tiny, it still creates the contact, opening the current from below to above. This explains the requirement repeatedly expressed in the book of Deuteronomy: "Now, Israel, what does the Lord your God ask of you? Only to fear the Lord your God...and to love Him" (Deut. 10:12), "so that you will learn to fear the Lord your God always" (Deut. 14:23), and elsewhere. If one should ask: How much must one love and fear Him? From one perspective, a person is required to do as much as he possibly can, but from another perspective, "what does the Lord your God ask of you? Only to fear...and to love," even a tiny amount, "and to observe the commandments of the Lord, and His statutes" (Deut. 10:13). In other words, God wants a person's actions and at least a minimum level of relationship.

לָכֵן הִיא מַעֲלָה אוֹתָן עַד מְקוֹמָהּ בְּעֶשֶׂר סְפִירוֹת דִּיצִירָה אוֹ דִּבְרִיאָה, לְפִי מַה שֶׁהִיא בִּדְחִילוּ וּרְחִימוּ שִׂכְלִיִּים אוֹ טִבְעִיִּים כוּ', כַּנִּזְכָּר לְעֵיל.

Consequently, the intent **raises up** these words **to its own place in the ten** *sefirot* **of either** *Yetzira* **or** *Beria***, depending on whether it is natural or intellectual fear and love, and so forth, as explained above** (chap. 39).

The intention elevates the letters of the spoken words of Torah that a person uttered in this world "to its own place," to the place of the intention. As was explained, when a person speaks words of Torah or prayer

EVEN A TINY AMOUNT OF INTENTION

Something similar is also said regarding *teshuva*. Until what point is a person required to repent? From one perspective, the answer is: always, and at every level. But there is a minimum amount of *teshuva*, and that is when a person decides, "No more!" From this point, a person is able to rise higher endlessly. This is also true regarding commandments. There is a beginning point, a minimum amount of relationship, which is always "the matter is very near to you," and this is "what the Lord your God asks of you." This point, which in itself is a "small thing" (*Berakhot* 33b), generates the contact, changing the nature of the action and giving it "wings," whether small or large. From that moment, it is a different essence, possessing wings that give it the ability to fly. It can fly high or low, but in either case, it can ascend from the ground to float at least somewhat above its starting point.

without any intent, simply uttering words out of habit, he nevertheless is expressing physically audible sounds. These sounds have holiness, for they are the sounds of words of Torah, but this holiness is in the plane of this physical world alone. When these letters are attached to an intention of a higher level, then according to that intention, the words are also elevated above the initially limited physical level at which they were spoken. In that moment, these words can ascend to the higher level of the intention with which they were said, which is in the ten *sefirot* of *Yetzira* or *Beria*, depending on whether it is with natural or intellectual fear and love, as explained in chapter 39 above.

וְשָׁם מֵאִיר וּמִתְגַּלֶּה אוֹר אֵין סוֹף בָּרוּךְ הוּא, שֶׁהוּא רָצוֹן הָעֶלְיוֹן בָּרוּךְ הוּא, הַמְלוּבָּשׁ בָּאוֹתִיּוֹת הַתּוֹרָה שֶׁלּוֹמֵד וּבְכַוָּונָתָן, אוֹ בִּתְפִלָּה וּבְכַוָּונָתָהּ, אוֹ בְּמִצְוָה וּבְכַוָּונָתָהּ, בְּהֶאָרָה גְדוֹלָה לְאֵין קֵץ, מַה שֶּׁלֹּא יָכוֹל לְהָאִיר וּלְהִתְגַּלּוֹת כְּלָל בְּעוֹד הָאוֹתִיּוֹת וְהַמִּצְוָה בָּעוֹלָם הַזֶּה הַגַּשְׁמִי, לֹא מִינָהּ וְלֹא מִקְצָתָהּ,

There the light of *Ein Sof*, blessed be He, shines and is revealed, which is God's supernal favor that is above all the worlds, **that is enclothed in the letters of Torah one studies and in their intention, or in prayer and its intention, or in a mitzva and its intention, with an infinitely great illumination, one that cannot shine and be revealed at all while the letters and the mitzva are** found (if they were committed without intent) **only in this physical world, not even the smallest part of it,**

The revelation of a commandment or words of Torah or prayer that shines in the ten *sefirot* of the world of *Yetzira* or the world of *Beria* is immeasurably higher than the revelation in itself within this world [of *Asiya*].

An explanation is necessary here to respond to some of the fundamental questions raised in these chapters: What is the importance of intention in performing commandments? What is the difference between commandments performed without intention, commandments performed with a specific intention, and commandments performed with a higher intention?

As was said, a commandment is always a commandment, and it is always holy, irrespective of the level of intent. When a commandment (or words of Torah or prayer) lacks any intent, there is still a change effected in the world, for the breath of this mouth is different from the breath of a different mouth, since it serves a holy purpose. Yet on its own, this does not shine and does not reveal the holiness in itself. In the low and material world, the light of holiness that is within Torah and commandments does not shine in any unique or distinct way. This is the nature of this world, a world of concealment in which God hides, and in it an entity of holiness looks no different from something without holiness.

This world can be described as a reality that has a very small number of dimensions, such that when any other reality, even one that is infinitely vast and complex, is revealed within these dimensions, it has no way to appear distinct in its character. As an analogy, a drawing on paper will always be two-dimensional. Even if the design that is drawn on it is one of a three- (or even more) dimensional entity, it is impossible to draw more than two dimensions on the paper. It is possible to create the illusion of more dimensions, but one can never avoid the fact of the limitation inherent in the medium. However, when going out to a three-dimensional expanse, one can create three-dimensional designs, and then one can differentiate tangibly between flat objects and three-dimensional ones. For us, the three-dimensional expanse

THE ASCENT OF THE COMMANDMENT

☞ An additional analogy for the concept of different dimensions: If a colored picture is projected in black and white (with the strongest contrast possible), the image perceived is a sort of silhouette. The dark shapes are reminiscent of the shapes in the original picture, but they all resemble each other; a person looks similar to a tree, and a tree looks similar to a rock. But as hues are added to the picture, whether gray or other colors, the image becomes increasingly enriched and whole. Each hue and color that is added reveals more distinctions between each shape and layer. In the previous analogy of the two-dimensional image, people can learn to differentiate at least the markers of the additional dimensions, even when apparently they are not visible. People who are experts at decoding aerial photographs (in which only two-dimensional shapes and shadows are visible) can tell, for example, that what appears to be a circle is actually a tall building, and what appears to be another circle is actually a well, and so forth. Similarly, regarding holiness, one who understands can identify the markers and differentiate somewhat between holy and mundane, between light and dark, even in this world.

is the limit of our direct comprehension, and we cannot reach above this. Although we know that there are more dimensions, and although we can speak theoretically of four-dimensional expanses and beyond, as human beings existing in a physical, three-dimensional space, we cannot conceive that. Thus, within this analogy, this world is "flat" relative to the revelation of holiness; all of the entities in it have one aspect, conditional to the limits of the world, to the movements that it makes possible, and to its limitations. Anything found within it, whatever it may be, is limited in its ability of expression. Therefore, to the naked eye, there is no difference in our world between a holy book and a book that contains repulsive content. The two books look identical, similar in size, weight, and smell. This is not because there is no difference between them, but rather because this is the dimension of our reality, which everything in it receives. In order for a difference between holy and mundane, light and dark, to be apparent, one must raise the matters to a world that has more dimensions, to the world of *Yetzira* and to the world of *Beria*. There, in a higher, more complex world, the difference between holy and mundane is revealed. ☞

When a commandment ascends from this world to the world of *Yetzira* and the world of *Beria*, it does not change. Instead, it is simply positioned in a different reality, one that is multidimensional and with significantly more meaning, such that the action, letter, or word appears entirely different. ☞

THE ASCENT OF A COMMANDMENT TO HIGHER DIMENSIONS

☞ The higher one ascends into increasingly subtle and spiritual worlds, even within the world of *Asiya*, the more forms receive additional dimensions, the more new, previously unseen aspects are revealed, uncovering dramatic differences between entities that initially seemed absolutely identical. Even in the material world, it is possible to see how things that were identical within a two-dimensional reality are completely different from each other when they pass to three- or four-dimensional reality. In this sense, when a person says words of holiness without intent, those words remain in this world. They belong to this world, as it were, folded and flattened within its dimensions. The words that could be charged with sublime holiness instead remain empty words that sound no different from any other words. However, when they reach (through the power of intention) a higher level, they receive a different form, distinct from any other words, and the more they ascend, the more the dimensions unfold, until the words are revealed in their full stature.

The topic of intent, according to this, is to move the commandment, or words of Torah or prayer, from this world to the level of a world in which it can appear as a revelation of and connection to the Divine; to reach a world in which the words of Torah and prayer should appear as words shining with holiness. As long as the commandment remains in this dark world, its light cannot be perceived at all. Only when it is removed to a place of light, a place in which the difference between light and darkness can be distinguished, can the difference between the act of a commandment and a mundane act be discerned.

עַד עֵת קֵץ הַיָּמִין שֶׁיִּתְעַלֶּה הָעוֹלָם מִגַּשְׁמִיּוּתוֹ, "וְנִגְלָה כְּבוֹד ה'" וְגוֹ', כַּנִּזְכָּר לְעֵיל בַּאֲרִיכוּת.

until the time of the end of days, when the world will ascend from its physical state, "and the glory of the Lord shall be revealed," and so forth, as explained above at length (in chap. 36).

As was explained, in this world and time period, the holiness of a commandment cannot be revealed until the end of days, because then the world itself will ascend from its physical state, "and the glory of the Lord shall be revealed and all flesh will see together that the mouth of the Lord has spoken" (Isa. 40:5). The faintly detectable underlying essence that currently only certain select individuals can guess at will become visible to "all flesh." In the future, when there will be a qualitative change in the nature of this world, when the physical foundation of this world will be completely transformed, when the divine essence will be revealed within the reality of this world, then, instead of a world in itself, everyone will see that "the mouth of the Lord has spoken" the word of God that animates and manifests all of existence.

6 Nisan (leap year)

הַגָּהָה: (וְשָׁם מֵאִיר וּמִתְגַּלֶּה גַּם כֵּן הַיִּחוּד הָעֶלְיוֹן הַנַּעֲשֶׂה בְּכָל מִצְוָה וְתַלְמוּד תּוֹרָה, שֶׁהוּא יִחוּד מִדּוֹתָיו יִתְבָּרֵךְ, שֶׁנִּכְלָלוֹת זוֹ בָּזוֹ, וְנִמְתָּקוֹת הַגְּבוּרוֹת בַּחֲסָדִים,

Gloss: There, supernal unification, which is formed through every mitzva and Torah study, also shines and is revealed. This is the unity of His attributes, which are encompassed in one another, and the *gevurot* are sweetened by the kindness

Until this point, the discussion has focused on one aspect of a commandment, as a revelation of the higher will within the reality of this world, in the sense of "I spoke, and My will was done." In this gloss, the author references another aspect of the commandments, which complements the first aspect: the impact of the performance of commandments upon the higher worlds.

The supernal unification is revealed in the higher worlds, in the ten *sefirot* of the world of *Yetzira* or *Beria*, which is where Torah and commandments ascend when they are performed with intent. This is the unity of His attributes, the unity and oneness of the different *sefirot* when the supernal will, which includes them all, illuminates them. Even the attributes that are apparently opposites of each other, like Ḥesed and Gevura, unite and operate as one. This unity is described as the sweetening of the *gevurot* by kindness, meaning that the sharpness of *Gevura* acts out the sweetness of the kindness (see chap. 27). The *Gevura* remains *Gevura*, but its purpose is that Ḥesed will result. At that point the result and conclusion of all the attributes is wholly Ḥesed.

עַל יְדֵי עֵת רָצוֹן הָעֶלְיוֹן אֵין סוֹף בָּרוּךְ הוּא, הַמֵּאִיר וּמִתְגַּלֶּה בִּבְחִינַת גִּילּוּי רַב וְעָצוּם בְּאִתְעָרוּתָא דִּלְתַתָּא, הִיא עֲשִׂיַּת הַמִּצְוָה אוֹ עֵסֶק הַתּוֹרָה, שֶׁבָּהֶן מְלוּבָּשׁ רָצוֹן הָעֶלְיוֹן אֵין סוֹף בָּרוּךְ הוּא.	**by means of a supernal time of favor of *Ein Sof*, blessed be He, which shines and is revealed in a great and mighty revelation through an awakening from below, which is the performance of a commandment or engagement in the Torah, in which the supernal will of *Ein Sof*, blessed be He, is enclothed.**

The performance of a commandment or the study of Torah down below, in this world, is the execution of the supernal will as it is above, above even the highest *sefirot*. The fulfillment of the divine will above illuminates all of existence until the lowest realms. When this divine revelation passes through the higher attributes, it links and unites them with each other. As is explained in other places, the unification of opposites, of Ḥesed and Gevura, is possible only when they are illuminated by an essence that is above both of them.[9] Here also, the supernal traits are encompassed within each other and the *gevurot* are sweetened by the kindness, in the illumination of the supernal will, which is even higher than *Atzilut*.

אַךְ עִיקַּר הַיִּחוּד הוּא לְמַעְלָה מַעְלָה בְּעוֹלָם הָאֲצִילוּת שֶׁשָּׁם הוּא מַהוּת וְעַצְמוּת מִדּוֹתָיו יִתְבָּרֵךְ, מְיוּחָדוֹת בְּמַאֲצִילָן אֵין סוֹף בָּרוּךְ הוּא, וְשָׁם הוּא מַהוּת וְעַצְמוּת רָצוֹן הָעֶלְיוֹן אֵין סוֹף בָּרוּךְ הוּא. וְהֶאָרָתָן לְבַד הִיא מְאִירָה בִּבְרִיאָה יְצִירָה עֲשִׂיָּה, בְּכָל עוֹלָם מֵהֶן לְפִי מַעֲלָתוֹ.

However, the main unification is above and beyond, in the world of *Atzilut*, where the essence and being of His attributes are united with their Emanator, *Ein Sof*, blessed be He, and there is the essence and being of the supernal will of *Ein Sof*, blessed be He. Only their illumination shines in *Beria*, *Yetzira*, and *Asiya*, in each of those worlds according to its level.

The main unification is above and beyond the worlds of *Yetzira* and *Beria*, in the world of *Atzilut*. The illumination of the unification and its impact are recognizable in all the worlds that are below the world of *Atzilut*, but [that unification] takes place mainly in the world of *Atzilut*. Only the illumination of the higher attributes shines in *Beria*, *Yetzira*, and *Asiya*, in each of those worlds according to its level. Just as the essence of the *sefirot* is in *Atzilut*, so is the unification of the *sefirot* (through the performance of a commandment below) also in *Atzilut*.

וְאַף שֶׁנֶּפֶשׁ הָאָדָם הָעוֹסֵק בְּתוֹרָה וּמִצְוָה זוֹ אֵינָהּ מֵאֲצִילוּת, מִכָּל מָקוֹם הֲרֵי רָצוֹן הָעֶלְיוֹן הַמְלוּבָּשׁ בְּמִצְוָה זוֹ, וְהוּא הוּא עַצְמוֹ הַדָּבָר הֲלָכָה וְהַתּוֹרָה שֶׁעוֹסֵק בָּהּ, הוּא אֱלֹהוּת וְאוֹר אֵין סוֹף הַמַּאֲצִיל בָּרוּךְ הוּא, שֶׁהוּא וּרְצוֹנוֹ אֶחָד,

Although the soul of a person who engages in this Torah and mitzva is not from *Atzilut*, nevertheless, the supernal will is enclothed in this mitzva, and it itself is the matter of *halakha* and the Torah in which he is engaged in study. It is the divinity and the light of *Ein Sof*, the Emanator, blessed be He, for He and His will are one,

---

9. See *Iggeret HaKodesh*, epistle 12.

If so, the following question must be asked: Since the soul of one who engages in Torah and this mitzva is not from the world of *Atzilut*, how can he arouse and draw forth the upper will that is unified with the Emanator, who is above *Atzilut*? The answer is that even though the person who involves himself in Torah and mitzvot is significantly below *Atzilut*, nevertheless, the Torah within which he immerses himself possesses the holiness of the Emanator Himself, who is above *Atzilut*. Torah is the materialized form of divine desire itself, which despite its descent into the lowly material forms of this world remains the divine will itself.

וּבִרְצוֹנוֹ יִתְבָּרֵךְ הֶאֱצִיל מִדּוֹתָיו הַמְיֻחָדוֹת בּוֹ יִתְבָּרֵךְ. וְעַל יְדֵי גִּילּוּי רְצוֹנוֹ הַמִּתְגַּלֶּה עַל יְדֵי עֵסֶק תּוֹרָה וּמִצְוָה זוֹ הֵן נִכְלָלוֹת זוֹ בָּזוֹ, וְנִמְתָּקוֹת הַגְּבוּרוֹת בַּחֲסָדִים בְּעֵת רָצוֹן זוֹ).

and through His will He emanated His attributes, which are united with Him. By means of the revelation of His will, by virtue of a person's engaging in this Torah and mitzva, they are encompassed in one another, and the *gevurot* are sweetened by the kindness at this time of favor.

This supernal divine will is lofty, even above the world of *Atzilut*, and it is therefore the emanator and source for the attributes that are within *Atzilut*. Through the revelation of His will, brought about by a person's engaging in this Torah and mitzva, the attributes of *Atzilut* are encompassed in one another, and the *gevurot* are sweetened by the kindness at this time of favor, at the time of the performance of the commandment down below, which arouses the illumination of the will in *Atzilut*.

A person who performs a commandment and studies Torah in this world is not within the world of *Atzilut*. However, man is the single creature in creation who is able to involve himself in the divine desire that exists above *Atzilut* and to materialize it within reality. Through using his will and his power of choice in fulfilling the Torah and its commandments, he arouses a "time of favor" above. Although man is a tiny being, the supernal will is vast, and a person's capacity to fulfill the supernal will activates infinitely great divine powers to modify and cause even the supernal essences in the world of *Atzilut* to relate to each other, one together with the other.

7 Nisan
(leap year)

וּבָזֶה יוּבַן הֵיטֵב הָא דִּדְחִילוּ וּרְחִימוּ נִקְרָאִים 'גַּדְפִין' דֶּרֶךְ מָשָׁל,

Based on the previous discussion, one can thoroughly understand the fact **that fear and love are figuratively called "wings,"**

The previous discussion dealt with the intentions of the soul when it performs a mitzva with love and fear of God. The analogy here is that the love and fear that a person uses to perform a commandment are like the wings of a bird. Just like wings lift a bird's body upward, so is the role of love and fear to lift the "body" of the commandment or the words of Torah to a higher level. Love and fear are not the essence of the commandment, nor do they create the commandment. But they lift the commandment and position it on a level in which it has the significance of a mitzva, where there is a differentiation between the holy and the mundane.

כְּדִכְתִיב: "וּבִשְׁתַּיִם יְעוֹפֵף" (ישעיה ו, ב)

as it is written: "With two wings **it would fly"** (Isa. 6:2)

The verse in Isaiah describes the seraphim and the wings they use to fly. Seraphim and their wings are spiritual characteristics, not physical ones, and the essence of their "two wings" is the revelation of love and fear, as will be explained.

[וּכְמוֹ שֶׁכָּתַב הָרַב חַיִּים וִיטָאל ז"ל בְּ'שַׁעַר הַיִּחוּדִים' פֶּרֶק י"א], שֶׁהַכְּנָפַיִם בָּעוֹף הֵן זְרוֹעוֹת הָאָדָם כוּ'.

(as Rabbi Ḥayyim Vital wrote in chapter 11 of *Sha'ar HaYiḥudim***), that wings are for a bird what arms are for a person, and so forth.**

Just as the arms of a person symbolize the attributes of *Ḥesed* and *Gevura* (as it is written in the introduction to *Tikkunei Zohar* 17a: "*Ḥesed* is the right arm, *Gevura* is the left arm," so do the wings of a bird (or angel) represent *Ḥesed* and *Gevura*, fear and love.

וּבַתִּיקּוּנִים (תיקוני זהר תיקון ו [כא, א-ב]) פֵּירְשׁוּ שֶׁהָעוֹסְקִים בַּתּוֹרָה וּמִצְוֹת בִּדְחִילוּ וּרְחִימוּ נִקְרָאִים

Then in *Tikkunei Zohar* **(21a–b), it is explained that those who are engaged in Torah and mitzvot with**

'בָּנִים', וְאִם לָאו, נִקְרָאִים 'אֶפְרוֹחִים' דְּלָא יָכְלִין לְפָרְחָא.

fear and love are called "children," and if not, they are called "fledglings" that are unable to fly (based on Deut. 22:6–7).

The reason such people are called "fledglings" is because they are unable to fly, since their wings are undeveloped, like the wings of fledglings. Just as birds and angels have wings, so does man, and the Torah he studies and commandments he performs also possess wings. But sometimes these wings are developed and can fly like one of the seraphim, while at other times they cannot lift man or his actions above the ground level of this world.

הַגָּהָה: (וּבְתִיקוּן מ"ה, דְּעוֹפָא הוּא מטַ"ט, רֵישָׁא דִּילֵיהּ י' וְגוּפָא וָא"ו וּתְרֵין גַּדְפִּין ה' ה' כו'.

Gloss: In *tikkun* 45 it is written that Metatron is depicted by a bird: Its head is a *yod*, its body is a *vav*, and the two wings are each a *heh*, and so forth.

This means that regarding this angel, about whom it is said that "his name is like the name of his Master" (the divine four-letter name of God), its head is the *yod* in the name of God, which is the embodiment of *Ḥokhma*, the main component of the "head," the intellect; its body is the *vav* in the name of God, which represents the six attributes; and the two wings are each one of the two *heh* letters found in the divine name, and so forth. The first, higher letter *heh* is the embodiment of *Bina*, and the second, lower *heh* is the embodiment of *Malkhut*.

וְהַיְינוּ, עוֹלָם הַיְצִירָה שֶׁנִּקְרָא מַטַּ"ט, וּבוֹ הֵן גּוּפֵי הֲלָכוֹת שֶׁבַּמִּשְׁנָה,

This is referring to the world of *Yetzira*, which is called Metatron, which contains the body of *halakhot* of the Mishna;

Yetzira, or Metatron, is the world whose body and primary being are the attributes, that being the world of *Yetzira*. The world of *Yetzira* is primarily the world of the attributes, love and fear and their branches, which indicate relationship: for or against. As is explained in other places,[10] love is the root of all positive commandments, and fear is the root of all negative commandments. In this sense, the expression of the world of *Yetzira* is in halakhic decisions: for and against, permitted and forbidden.

וְרֵישָׁא דִּילֵיהּ הֵן הַמּוֹחִין וּבְחִינַת חָכְמָה בִּינָה דַּעַת, שֶׁהֵן פְּנִימִיּוּת הַהֲלָכוֹת וְסוֹדָן וְטַעֲמֵיהֶן, — and its head is the intellect, *Ḥokhma, Bina*, and *Da'at*, which are the internal embodiment of the *halakhot*, and their secret and reason;

Its head, the head of the world of *Yetzira*, of *halakha*, is the intellect, *Ḥokhma, Bina*, and *Da'at*, which are the internal embodiment of the *halakhot*, and their secret and reason. If the body of *halakha* is the body of the world of *Yetzira*, then the inner meaning of *halakha*, the mystical secrets and reasons of *halakha*, are the aspects of the head – the *Ḥokhma, Bina*, and *Da'at* – of the world of *Yetzira*.[11]

וּתְרֵין גַּדְפִין דְּחִילוּ וּרְחִימוּ הֵן ה' עִילָּאָה שֶׁהִיא רְחִימוּ, וְה' תַּתָּאָה הִיא יִרְאָה תַּתָּאָה, — and the two wings, fear and love, are the higher *heh*, which is love, and the lower *heh*, which is lower fear,

The two wings with which commandments "fly," ascending upward, are fear and love. When compared to the letters of God's name, they are the higher *heh*, *Bina*, which is the embodiment of love, because

FEAR AND LOVE – THE HIGHER *HEH* AND LOWER *HEH*

☞ It is taught that there are four levels of love and fear in the divine service performed by man, from below to above: fear and love and love and fear. Meaning, the beginning of divine service is rooted in fear, which is the lower fear. Above this is "small love" (*ahavat olam*, love based in this world). Above this is "tremendous love," and above this is higher fear. The four letters of God's name reflect this: lower fear is the lower *heh*, small love is the *vav* (*Ze'ir Anpin*), tremendous love is the higher *heh* (*Bina*) and higher fear is the *yod* (*Ḥokhma*) (see *Likkutei Torah*, Deut. 31d).

---

10. See the introduction to *Sha'ar HaYiḥud VeHa'emuna*, "Ḥinukh Katan."
11. The concept of "inner meaning" refers to *Da'at*, which is the inner embodiment and life force of the attributes. The "secrets" refer to *Bina*, which is called "secret." The "reasons" refers to *Ḥokhma*, which is called "reason" (*Likkutei Levi Yitzḥak*).

Ze'ir Anpin, the six attributes, are rooted in *Bina*, and included among them is love, and the lower *heh*, *Malkhut*, which is the embodiment of lower fear. ☞

עוֹל מַלְכוּת שָׁמַיִם וּפַחַד ה׳, כְּפַחַד הַמֶּלֶךְ דֶּרֶךְ מָשָׁל, שֶׁהִיא יִרְאָה חִיצוֹנִית וְנִגְלֵית, מַה שֶּׁאֵין כֵּן יִרְאָה עִילָּאָה יְרֵא בּוֹשֶׁת, הִיא מֵהַנִּסְתָּרוֹת לַה׳ אֱלֹהֵינוּ, וְהִיא בְּחָכְמָה עִילָּאָה יוּ״ד שֶׁל שֵׁם הוי״ה בָּרוּךְ הוּא, כְּמוֹ שֶׁכָּתוּב בְּרַעְיָא מְהֵימְנָא).	of the yoke of the kingdom of Heaven and the dread of God, like the dread of a king, metaphorically speaking. This is an external, revealed fear, whereas higher fear, the fear consisting of shame, is one of "the secrets of the Lord our God" [Deut. 29:28], and is of the higher wisdom, the *yod* of the name of *Havaya*, blessed be He, as it is written in *Raya Meheimna*.

This lower fear is fear of the yoke of the kingdom of Heaven and the dread of God, which is like the dread of a king, metaphorically speaking. This is an external, revealed fear, in the sense that it is fear derived from His external, revealed aspect, fear of [His] actions, not of the Actor. Whereas higher fear, which is referred to elsewhere as the fear consisting of shame, is not fear and dread of what He who is mighty and awesome can do to us, but rather is shame before the very fact of His being "great, powerful, and awe inspiring." This is one of "the secrets of the Lord our God" [Deut. 29:28]. The fear and dread are not of the kind that are garbed in matters of our world; rather, this is fear before that which exists above the parameters of our world (the "secrets"). This fear is of the higher wisdom, and it is known that *Hokhma* and *Bina* are referred to as "the secrets of the Lord" (Deut. 29:28) relative to *Ze'ir Anpin* and *Malkhut*, which are called "the revealed matters" (Deut 29:28). The higher wisdom is the *yod* of the name of *Havaya*, blessed be He, as it is written in the *Zohar* in *Raya Meheimna*. For the *yod* in the name of *Havaya* is in the *sefira* of *Hokhma*, while the first *heh* is in the *sefira* of *Bina*.

Based on this analogy, that love and fear relative to Torah and commandments are like wings relative to a bird, we can explain an additional point regarding the relationship of love and fear to commandments or to the Torah itself that a person performs or studies.

8 Nisan (leap year)

כִּי כְּמוֹ שֶׁכַּנְפֵי הָעוֹף אֵינָם עִיקַּר הָעוֹף, וְאֵין חַיּוּתוֹ תָּלוּי בָּהֶם כְּלָל, כְּדִתְנַן: "נִטְּלוּ אֲגַפֶּיהָ כְּשֵׁרָה" (חולין פרק ג משנה ד),

For just as the wings of a bird are not the main part of the bird, and its life does not depend on them at all, as it is taught: "If its wings have been removed, it is kosher,"

While a bird has wings, and it needs them, they are not the center of its being. They are not a vital limb such that a bird cannot live without them. The author of the *Tanya* brings proof from the *halakhot* of *treifot* (mortally injured or damaged animals): "If its wings have been removed, it is kosher" (*Ḥullin* 3:4).[12] The *halakha* is that a bird with wings that were removed for one reason or another is kosher and is not called a *treifa* (unkosher due to having sustained mortal damage). Meaning, this loss is not a mortal injury for the bird, and it can continue living even without its wings.

וְהָעִיקָּר הוּא רֹאשׁוֹ וְכָל גּוּפוֹ, וְהַכְּנָפַיִים אֵינָם רַק מְשַׁמְּשִׁים לְרֹאשׁוֹ וְגוּפוֹ לִפְרְחָא בְּהוֹן.

and the main parts are its head and its whole body, while its wings merely serve its head and body, so that they may fly with them,

Wings serve an important function enabling a bird to fly, but they do not form the essence and vitality of the bird: If a bird's head is removed, it cannot live. Similarly, if a bird sustains damage to one of its internal organs, it cannot live. If a bird's wings are damaged, however, while it may not be able to fly, it will continue to live.

וְכָךְ דֶּרֶךְ מָשָׁל, הַתּוֹרָה וּמִצְוֹת הֵן עִיקַּר הַיִּחוּד הָעֶלְיוֹן, עַל יְדֵי גִּילּוּי רָצוֹן הָעֶלְיוֹן הַמִּתְגַּלֶּה עַל יְדֵיהֶן,

so too, analogously, the Torah and mitzvot are the main part of the supernal unification, via the revelation of the supernal will, which is revealed by means of them,

Commandments are the will of God, demonstrating that things should be done in a specific way. Torah is the description and explanation of

---

12. There the language employed is "its wings were broken." The author of the *Tanya* infers from this that the same is true if the wings are removed (Lubavitcher Rebbe, Rabbi Menahem Mendel Schneerson).

His will for how something will be done, what is the decree of God's wisdom and the underlying plan of the existence of the worlds. When a person down below fulfills the will of God, he reveals the supernal will down below, which is the essence of unification.

Torah and commandments possess objective holiness that is independent of a person's intentions and feelings when he fulfills them. If one wore *tefillin* without intention, without love or fear, but just out of habit, he has still fulfilled the commandment of *tefillin*. By contrast, if a person dons *tefillin* with "fear and love" but the *tefillin* he is wearing are invalid, then although he has love and fear, he has no *tefillin*. This would be like having a pair of wings but no bird. An invalidation of the main aspect of a commandment negates its existence as a commandment. A flaw in the intention of the mitzva negates only its ability to fly, but not its existence.

וְהַדְּחִילוּ וּרְחִימוּ הֵם מַעֲלִים אוֹתָן לְמָקוֹם שֶׁיִּתְגַּלֶּה בּוֹ הָרָצוֹן, אוֹר אֵין סוֹף בָּרוּךְ הוּא, וְהַיִּחוּד, שֶׁהֵן יְצִירָה וּבְרִיאָה.	and the fear and love elevate them to a place where the will, the light of *Ein Sof*, blessed be He, and the unification will be revealed, which is *Yetzira* and *Beria*.

The fear and love elevate the Torah and commandments to where the will, the light of *Ein Sof*, and the unification, that is, the higher unification that is formed through the fulfillment of commandments down below, which is the unification of His attributes (as was explained in the gloss that began with "There is the illumination"), will be revealed in the place where all these things are revealed, which are the worlds of *Yetzira* and *Beria*. ☞

THE ROLE OF THE "WINGS" OF COMMANDMENTS

☞ A commandment is intrinsically holy even without the wings of love and fear. However, a commandment that lacks intention remains in the physical world in which it was performed, in which the spiritual meaning of the act of the mitzva is not revealed. In order for the commandment to be revealed and serve as a source for divine revelation, in order for it not to remain superficial with no significance among the things of this world, it must be raised to a higher level, to a world that is able to relate

הַגָּהָה: (אוֹ אֲפִילוּ בַּעֲשִׂיָּה, בְּעֶשֶׂר סְפִירוֹת דִּקְדֻשָּׁה, מְקוֹם מִצְוֹת מַעֲשִׂיּוֹת, Gloss: Or even in *Asiya*, in the ten holy *sefirot*, the place of the practical mitzvot,

The gloss expands upon the point that the supernal will and supernal unification are revealed in the world of *Beria* and in the world of *Yetzira*: This is the case even in the world of *Asiya*, in the ten holy *sefirot* of the world of *Asiya*, which is the place of the practical mitzvot. Practical commandments that are committed in the world of *Asiya* with intention for the sake of Heaven, even without an active feeling of natural or intellectual love and fear, but with the acceptance of the yoke of Heaven with a simple action, also ascend from the physical world to the ten *sefirot* of the world of *Asiya*, i.e., to divine existence and to significance that exists even within the existence of a physical action in itself.

וְכֵן מִקְרָא. and likewise Scripture.

This is true not only for practical commandments. In Torah study, too, there is a realm in which a revelation of the divine unification arrives in the world of *Asiya*. When studying Scripture, the Written Torah, the main thing is the verbal expression of the words and letters (and speech is an action). Therefore, just like with practical commandments, there is an expression and revelation within the letters in the world of *Asiya*.

אֲבָל בַּמִּשְׁנָה מִתְגַּלֶּה הַיִּחוּד וְאוֹר אֵין סוֹף בָּרוּךְ הוּא בִּיצִירָה, But with regard to Mishna, the unity and light of *Ein Sof*, blessed be He, are revealed in *Yetzira*,

When studying Mishna, which refers to the study of decisions of *halakha* within the Oral Torah, the unity and light of *Ein Sof*, blessed be He, are revealed in the world of *Yetzira*. The world of *Yetzira* is the world of attributes, love, and fear and their offshoots. It is the world in which is determined the stance regarding matters: for or against, I want to holiness, to a place in which a differentiation between a commandment and not a commandment exists. In order to uplift a commandment above this world, it needs wings. It requires some level of intention, some kind of connection with love and fear to the divine essence that is above this world.

to come close or I want to move away. Accordingly, the study of Mishna, which is the determination of positions – permitted or forbidden, for or against – belongs to the world of *Yetzira*, and the unification and light of *Ein Sof* that is revealed through this study appears in the world of *Yetzira*.

וּבַתַּלְמוּד בַּבְּרִיאָה, **while in the case of Talmud, it is in *Beria*.**

When one studies Talmud, the system of reasons for *halakhot* and their roots, the divine unification is revealed in the world of *Beria*. The world of *Beria* is the world of intellect, the world of consciousness within which exists recognition of concepts: what, who, and why. As a result, the study of Talmud belongs to the world of *Beria*, and the divine unification that is revealed through this study appears in the world of *Beria*.

דְּהַיְינוּ, שֶׁבְּלִימוּד מִקְרָא מִתְפַּשֵּׁט הַיִּחוּד וְאוֹר אֵין סוֹף בָּרוּךְ הוּא מֵאֲצִילוּת עַד הָעֲשִׂיָּה, וּבְמִשְׁנָה עַד הַיְצִירָה לְבַדָּהּ, וּבַתַּלְמוּד עַד הַבְּרִיאָה לְבַדָּהּ. **In other words, through the study of Scripture, the unity and light of *Ein Sof*, blessed be He, emanates from *Atzilut* to *Asiya*, while in the case of Mishna, only to *Yetzira*, and with regard to Talmud, only to *Beria*,**

On the surface, this is difficult to understand, for Scripture is holier than Mishna, and Mishna is holier than Talmud. Yet, as was explained, their revelation is the opposite: Scripture in the lowest world of *Asiya*, Mishna in the world of *Yetzira*, and so forth.[13] Consequently, the author of the *Tanya* adds, "In other words, through the study of Scripture, the unity and light of *Ein Sof*, blessed be He, emanates from *Atzilut*," where, as was stated previously (in the gloss beginning with "there illuminates") the primary unification exists, for there the character and essence of the attributes unite in their Emanator. It is there that the character and essence of the will within the Torah is revealed. It is only the Torah's illumination that shines on the worlds of *Beria*, *Yetzira*,

---

13. See *Torah Or* 17a.

and *Asiya*. Through the study of Scripture, the illumination spreads to and is revealed within the world of *Asiya*, because there, in speech and writing (which are actions) is the essence of studying Scripture. Regarding the study of Mishna, it reaches only to *Yetzira* and does not reach *Asiya*. Regarding the study of Talmud, it reaches only to *Beria*, not to the worlds of *Yetzira* and *Asiya*.

כִּי כּוּלָן בַּאֲצִילוּת.   for they are all in *Atzilut*.

As was stated, the unification itself generated through Torah study, whether Scripture, Mishna, or Talmud, takes place in *Atzilut*, and only its illumination and revelation spread in each lower world, each according to its level.

אֲבָל קַבָּלָה אֵינָהּ מִתְפַּשֶּׁטֶת כְּלָל מֵאֲצִילוּת לִבְרִיאָה יְצִירָה עֲשִׂיָּה,   However, Kabbala does not emanate at all from *Atzilut* to *Beria*, *Yetzira*, and *Asiya*,

Kabbala, the mystical teaching of Torah, does not spread and is not enclothed in any world, but rather it remains hidden by its very nature. It is not revealed through practical concepts nor through feeling or the creation of relationships to its topics, nor even through comprehending intellectual concepts stripped of all materiality. We can comprehend only patterns, without any tangible grasp of what truly lies within that.

In summary, it can be said: Scripture is so lofty that its revelation reaches all the way to *Asiya*. Mishna is lower than Scripture and reaches until *Yetzira*. Talmud reaches only until *Beria*. Kabbala does not have the power to spread and to be revealed at all, in any world, except for the place in which it primarily dwells.

כְּמוֹ שֶׁכָּתוּב בִּ'פְּרִי עֵץ חַיִּים').   as it is written in *Pri Etz Ḥayyim*.

All the points raised in this gloss are as it is written in *Pri Etz Ḥayyim* of the writings of the Arizal.[14]

---

14. *Sha'ar Hanhagat HaLimud*. See also *Sha'ar HaMitzvot, Parashat Va'ethanan*.

וְהִנֵּה אַף דְּדְחִילוּ וּרְחִימוּ הֵם גַּם כֵּן מִתַּרְיַ"ג מִצְוֹת,	Now although fear and love are also included in the 613 commandments,	16 Nisan 9 Nisan (leap year)

Love and fear, which are also included within the 613 commandments,[15] are not merely "wings"; they are not simply psychological elements that accompany a person's act of performing a commandment, but rather they are commandments themselves. There is a positive commandment to love God, and a positive commandment to fear God. This means that every instance of love or fear of God is the fulfillment of a commandment, whether it accompanies a person's actions or simply exists in isolation.

אַף עַל פִּי כֵן, נִקְרָאִין 'גַּדְפִין', לִהְיוֹת כִּי תַּכְלִית הָאַהֲבָה הִיא הָעֲבוֹדָה מֵאַהֲבָה,	they are still called "wings," because the purpose of love is service performed out of love,

The highest level of love is when a person both actualizes his love and studies Torah and [performs] commandments out of love, out of an inner, personal desire. Because of this, although the love itself is a commandment, since love's main purpose is wings for the totality of divine service, love itself is referred to as wings. ☞

There is a similar question that most thinkers have posed in recent generations: What is the commandment to have faith? Seemingly, this is a commandment that either lacks meaning or is extraneous (and indeed there were those who did not count it among the 613

THE MEANING OF THE COMMANDMENT TO LOVE GOD

☞ At the root of this issue is a question that many have discussed: What is the nature of the commandment to love God? We understand that it is possible to command an action, the details of the commandment. But how does one command someone to love? Given that there is such a commandment, what is the nature of this love that is the result of a command?

---

15. See Rambam, *Sefer HaMitzvot*, positive commandments 3–4, and *Sefer HaMadda, Hilkhot Yesodei HaTorah* 2:1.

commandments).¹⁶ For if a person does not believe, how is it possible to command him to believe? If he does believe, what is the purpose of commanding him? But regarding faith, it can be said that the commandment is one of self-preparation, contemplation that leads to the creation of an appropriate spiritual relationship. There were sages, such as the Rambam, who similarly explained the commandment of love of God, that although it is not possible to command someone to love, it is possible to command someone to prepare himself for it. It is feasible to command a person to behave in those ways that will lead to love, and to avoid those that negate it. This will then automatically yield a feeling of love as a result.

The author of the *Tanya* also espouses this perspective, although, as stated here, he does not accept this as a definition and understanding of the nature of the commandment to love God. His understanding of this mitzva is that when the Torah commands us to love or fear, the basic fulfillment of this commandment is conditional not on an emotional relationship, but rather on an intellectual relationship that motivates a person, bringing him to action that is analogous to that of love. There is a similar command which is more recognizable. The command to "love your neighbor as yourself" is not meant to arouse feelings of love of one's friend. If your friend has broken his leg and is sitting in his home, the commandment is not to sit in the house and love him. This is not a fulfillment of the commandment to love one's friend. Can a person tell his friend who needs money in order to save his life, "I love you, and that which has to do with money is something else"? What significance does such love have, and what value is there to such a commandment? Necessarily, this commandment can be understood not on the level of emotion, but rather on the level of behavior. The determinant of this commandment is not the intensity of one's feeling of love but how it is expressed in action, the way one behaves toward a friend. Similarly, the commandment to "love the Lord your God" must also be understood not as a commandment to generate a relationship of feeling, but rather as a commandment that instructs us how to behave toward the object that we are commanded

---

16. *Ba'al Halakhot Gedolot*.

to love, that is, to relate to Him with loving behavior, the way we relate to someone we love.

Love and fear of God, according to this, are not spiritual, emotional commandments that are essentially distinct and different from other commandments. Like all commandments, these commandments too have a specific form of expression. The difference is that the command regarding practical commandments is a command regarding a specific, defined expression. The commandment of love is an inclusive directive, including everything that love can create. When a person loves, he constantly searches for and creates new ways to reveal his love. According to this, the love that the Torah commands is mainly a tangible love. To borrow a term, it is not a "platonic love," but rather, it is a love that moves one to some practical expression. As explained here, the main purpose of love is service out of love.

> וְאַהֲבָה בְּלִי עֲבוֹדָה - הִיא 'אַהֲבָה בְּתַעֲנוּגִים', and love without service is "love of delights,"

The love discussed previously (whose purpose is service out of love) is the love with which we are generally familiar, like the love of yearning for one's beloved. This kind of love is founded in a lack and in the desire to fill that lack. It relates to distance and the need to constrict and traverse that distance to the beloved. However, there is another type of love, which is called "love of delights" in hasidic writings. This love has no lack. It fills itself. It itself constitutes its own satisfaction. It is a love in which the object and subject of love exist on the same level and do not lack one another. In this kind of love, the lover lacks nothing and does not need to do anything that inherently requires expression. This is "love without service."

Love of God in this manner does not require a person to do anything, and he is not required to reach anything. Instead, it is like the words of the poet in one of the greatest expressions of love of God: "Whom else do I have in heaven? With You, I desire nothing on earth. My flesh and my heart may fail, but God is the strength of my heart and my portion forever" (Ps. 73:25–26). When a person feels that God is his portion, he does not want or need anything. A story is told about the author of the *Tanya*,[17] that in moments of spiritual excitement, he would say: "I don't want Your Garden of Eden. I don't want Your World to Come. I only want You!" A person who loves God on this level desires nothing else. One who says, "Hear Israel, the Lord our God, the Lord is one," and then reaches the level of "You shall love the Lord your God" needs nothing else. He does not need "the rain of your land" nor "your grain and your wine," neither in this world nor in the World to Come.

לְהִתְעַנֵּג עַל ה׳ מֵעֵין עוֹלָם הַבָּא וְקַבָּלַת שָׂכָר. **in which one delights in God, a semblance of the World to Come, the receiving of a reward;**

The essence of the Garden of Eden is delight in love of God. Such is also true of a person who reaches this level while living in this world. The level of "love of delights" is, therefore, a semblance of the World to Come, in that it is connected not to the realm of the life of this world, but to the realm of the Garden of Eden, which does not relate anymore to the realm of performance of commandments, but rather it relates to the realm of receiving reward for commandments. When a person loves God and needs nothing else, when he feels pleasure from the very essence of the divine existence, when "nearness to God for me is good" (Ps. 73:28), this is no longer a commandment, but the receiving of a reward.

וְ״הַיּוֹם לַעֲשׂוֹתָם״ (דברים ז, יא) כְּתִיב, וּלְמָחָר לְקַבֵּל שְׂכָרָם. **but it is written: "Today to perform them"** (Deut. 7:11), **and tomorrow to receive their reward.**

But, although this love is of a very high level, nevertheless, it says: "Today to perform them," and tomorrow to receive their reward.[18] The implication is that "today," in this world, it is the time to fulfill the commandments, to serve God, and it is not the time to receive reward.

---

17. This story is brought in *Derekh Mitzvotekha* of the third Lubavitcher Rebbe, Rabbi Menaḥem Mendel Schneerson, the *Tzemaḥ Tzedek*, in *Shoresh Mitzvat HaTefilla* chap. 40 (138b), and copied in *HaYom Yom*, 18 Kislev.

18. See *Eiruvin* 22a.

Only "tomorrow," in the World to Come, is it the time for receiving reward, for then a person can no longer fulfill the commandments and is not obligated to do so. Accordingly, the "world of action" is called by that name not only because it is the physical world, but because it is a world of action, in which love motivates one to action, in which love requires expression, and in which the meaning of love is "service motivated by love."

וּמִי שֶׁלֹּא הִגִּיעַ לְמִדָּה זוֹ, לִטְעוֹם מֵעֵין עוֹלָם הַבָּא, אֶלָּא עֲדַיִין נַפְשׁוֹ שׁוֹקֵקָה וּצְמֵאָה לַה' וְכָלְתָה אֵלָיו כָּל הַיּוֹם, **One who has not attained this level, to taste a semblance of the World to Come, but his soul still yearns and thirsts for God, and pines for Him all day,**

The reference is to one who has not attained the level of the "love of delights," whose reward is not limited to the World to Come, but is even acquired in this world. The soul of a person who has not reached this level still yearns for God constantly since his love of God remains love based on lack, on a thirst for that which is missing, a recognition of distance, and on a yearning to come closer and cleave to the Divine.

וְאֵינוֹ מְרַוֶּה צִמְאוֹנוֹ בְּמֵי הַתּוֹרָה שֶׁלְּפָנָיו, הֲרֵי זֶה כְּמִי שֶׁעוֹמֵד בַּנָּהָר וְצוֹעֵק: 'מַיִם מַיִם לִשְׁתּוֹת!' **and yet he does not quench his thirst in the waters of Torah that are before him; this is like one who stands by a river and shouts: "Water! Water! I need to drink!"**

There is a way for any person to quench his thirst, by partaking of "the waters of Torah that are before him." Apparently, the thirst for God cannot be quenched; this distance is infinite. However, as is explained elsewhere, even if we are unable from our side to bridge the qualitative gap between man and God, God can bridge it. God did so when He gave us the Torah, as a pathway for us to come closer to Him. From then on, a person who feels that he wants to express his love, to consolidate the meaning to his love, a person who wants to reach true connection with Him, and a person who thirsts for God should quench his thirst in the waters of Torah that are currently before him. If he does not do so, he is like a thirsty person who stands by a river, and instead of drinking, he shouts for water to drink. Similarly, a person who has a thirst for cleaving to God should not only scream out that he is thirsty and yearning, but he should also quench his thirst in the Torah that is before him.

כְּמוֹ שֶׁקּוֹבֵל עָלָיו הַנָּבִיא: "הוֹי כָּל צָמֵא - לְכוּ לַמַּיִם" (ישעיה נה, א). כִּי לְפִי פְּשׁוּטוֹ, אֵינוֹ מוּבָן, דְּמִי שֶׁהוּא צָמֵא וּמִתְאַוֶּה לִלְמוֹד - פְּשִׁיטָא שֶׁיִּלְמוֹד מֵעַצְמוֹ, וְלָמָּה לּוֹ לַנָּבִיא לִצְעוֹק עָלָיו: "הוֹי"?

This is like the prophet's complaint about such a person: "Ho, everyone who is **thirsty, go to water**" (Isa. 55:1). For according to a plain reading, its meaning is unclear – it is obvious that one who is thirsty and craves to study should go and study of his own accord. Why does the prophet shout at him, "Ho,"

As our Sages teach that water refers to Torah (*Bava Kamma* 17a), the plain meaning of this verse is unclear – it is obvious that one who is thirsty and craves to study should go and study of his own accord, just as one who is thirsty for water goes and drinks. Why does the prophet shout at him, "Ho"? Rather, it must be that the prophet is not talking about thirst for learning Torah, but instead about thirst for the Divine. This person who wants to cleave to the Divine does not know that the way to do so is by attaching oneself to Torah. This person imagines that there is some direct way to cleave to God, and he yearns and is pained by his longing for this connection. Therefore, the prophet yells at him: "Ho, everyone [who is] thirsty," this is not the way; rather, "go to water." One's thirst for the Divine is not quenched through abstract thought and longing of the soul, but through one's involvement in Torah and the performance of commandments. These are the expression and manner in which a person can connect to the divine essence.

וּכְמוֹ שֶׁנִּתְבָּאֵר בְּמָקוֹם אַחֵר בַּאֲרִיכוּת. as explained elsewhere at length.

(It is not explained elsewhere in this book, and in the original manuscript these words do not appear. It is observed there that this may have been a later addition, after this issue was explained in a different essay.)

In this chapter, the author summarized the topic that was discussed in the previous chapters, of the relationship between intention and action. The concluding principle is, in the language of the Zohar: "Fear and love are called wings." Meaning, the intention of fear and love of God within a person's heart with which he performs commandments or studies Torah are referred to as wings. Just as wings allow a bird to fly skyward, and without them the bird cannot ascend, so do love and fear raise up the Torah studied and commandments fulfilled by a person. Without love and fear, a person's Torah study and performance of commandments cannot ascend from this lower world. This analogy articulates the relationship between intention and action. The act of performing the commandments, like the body of a bird, makes up the main existence of the commandment, and that existence is not conditional on the person's intent. Despite this, like a bird without wings, a commandment in this state cannot fly, cannot ascend from this world.

In summary, and in preparation for the deeper discussions regarding love and fear found in the following chapters, the author touched upon the question of the nature of love of God. He wrote that the commandment to love God is both a commandment and an intention, both a body and wings, because it is a commandment whose goal is "service [of God coming out of] love," not an emotional expression of love, but rather an expression of action in Torah and in all the commandments, and thus, it is a commandment performed with an arousal of love for the Torah and its commandments. The realization of feelings of love in one's soul, when "my soul thirsts for you, my flesh yearns for you," is through involvement in Torah study and performing commandments, because "water refers to Torah."

Chapter 41

IN THE PREVIOUS CHAPTER, THE AUTHOR OF THE *TANYA* concluded his discussion of the complex relationship between mitzvot and the intentions behind them – the love and fear of God. The essential idea is that the love and fear of God are not part of the essence of the mitzva; a mitzva remains a mitzva even without them. However, a mitzva that is performed without the love and fear of God cannot ascend from the realm of action to the upper realms and to the Divine unity. The coming chapters will discuss love and fear not only in terms of their being the reward for serving God or their being "wings" that raise a person in his service of God, but as an integral part of serving God, which, according to the hasidic outlook, which drives, sustains, and elevates its entirety. According to this outlook, love and fear are not the outcome of serving God but its source. This chapter begins with the idea that serving God starts with fear, and not with love.

בְּרַם, צָרִיךְ לִהְיוֹת לְזִכָּרוֹן תָּמִיד רֵאשִׁית הָעֲבוֹדָה וְעִיקָרָהּ וְשָׁרְשָׁהּ. **However, a person must constantly bear in mind the beginning of** divine **service and its essence and root.**

17 Nisan
10 Nisan (leap year)

Although the ways of serving God rise progressively higher, a person must always remember the starting point, the essence and root of divine service, regardless of which particular level he happens to be on.

וְהוּא, כִּי אַף שֶׁהַיִּרְאָה הִיא שֹׁרֶשׁ לְ'סוּר מֵרָע', **This is as follows: that even though the fear of God is the root of turning away from evil,**

Distancing oneself from evil, at any level, is basically an expression of the attribute of fear. Fear in general is a form of distancing, of shrinking into oneself, and of withdrawal. Accordingly, fear is a quality of a person's spirit that is at the foundation of his ability to turn aside from evil, to refrain and distance himself from wrong.

וְהָאַהֲבָה לְ'עֲשֵׂה טוֹב', and the love of God is the basis **for doing good,**

Essentially, a person fulfills the commandments and does God's will because he possesses a love of God. Love is the desire to come close, to be together, and the way to come close and bond with God is through fulfilling the commandments. The word for "commandment," mitzva, is etymologically related to the Hebrew word *tzavta*, which means "connection." Thus, the love of God is the root of the ability of the soul to perform the positive commandments, while the fear of God is the root of the ability of the soul to observe the negative commandments.

אַף עַל פִּי כֵן, לֹא דַי לְעוֹרֵר הָאַהֲבָה לְבַדָּהּ לְ'עֲשֵׂה טוֹב'. nevertheless, **solely awakening** one's **love** of God **in order to** induce **doing good does not suffice.**

Even though it would seem that the root of performing a mitzva is love and not fear, love is not enough for sustainable fulfillment of positive mitzvot. If a person only has love as his intention as he performs a mitzva, without fear, his intention will be faulty. Love alone, especially the love of God, is essentially lacking. Love is the movement of coming close to God. But if it is not preceded by a sense of being distant, then what kind of "coming close" is it? Is this true love, or just some intellectual and emotional diversion? People play around with love, although they do not play around with fear. When a person is merely playing with concepts and with feelings, he lacks a basic foundation of a full life: commitment. Such a love is merely a short-lived "game"; it is not serious. When one "plays" in this way with God, not only is it not serious, but it holds no meaning whatsoever. Such a person is performing the mitzvot because he wants to come closer to God. But if at the basis of his actions he has no concept of obligation and acceptance of the yoke of God's kingship, of God as a great and awesome

King who commands the mitzvot, then in essence what he is doing is not a mitzva. All that he does is more like an amusing game.

There is another, more serious flaw involved in this kind of service. Love creates closeness, and therefore a person whose connection to God is only that of love is unlikely to experience a sense of the acceptance of the yoke and obligation of this relationship, because he has such a strong sense of familiarity with God. Such a person will almost certainly neglect some essential elements of the mitzvot, and will carry out others not as exactly as he should. He behaves this way not because he does not care but because out of his love and his approach to the purpose of these matters, he does not take all of the small details into consideration. In contrast, when a person serves God out of fear, he always pays attention to the smallest details. He will do exactly as he is told, without making any changes. The foregoing is somewhat parallel to the dynamic of human relationships. Some people will go above and beyond what they are told to do, but do not do exactly what they were asked, whereas others will not go above and beyond what they are told to do, because they do not know what else to do, and they do not want to do anything else. Nevertheless, they succeed in doing exactly as they are told. ☞ ☞

LOVE WITHOUT FEAR IS MERELY SELF-LOVE

☞ Love is an expression of a person's feelings, which emerge from his own vantage point. As important as this is, it is lacking, because this approach does not suggest looking beyond oneself to see the relationship from the other person's perspective. The level of love called *ahavat olam*, "world-centered love" (unlike the higher level of love known as *ahava rabba*, "a great love") contains a fundamental limitation, which is the limitation of the self, because such love is, fundamentally, love of the self. The person basically loves himself, but this love is channeled through some other medium. A person often says that he loves someone else with the same meaning as when he says he loves herring. He loves herring because he loves to eat it, and similarly he loves someone else in the sense that the relationship makes him happy. For example, a person might know that a relationship is not good for the other person, and that the best thing would be to end the relationship. Yet it is extremely rare that anyone actually does this. In general, people are not even able to think this way. Thus, from time to time people even kill and are killed because of love: not that this is an expression of love, but because one person cannot let go of the other, due to his own need. Such a person does not love the other person for the sake of that other person, out of consideration for that person and that person's perspective. Rather, such a person loves himself. He requires the other person's cooperation in order to realize his love for himself. The same is true with regard to a person's relationship to holiness: The love is essentially the expression of a person's feelings, one of which is his desire to be closer to God. Yet, regarding the intent of a mitzva, the primary, essential meaning of a mitzva is not what a person wants for himself but what God wants from him. Therefore, the author of the *Tanya* emphasizes that a person must begin with some degree of fear of God, and the relationship must be founded on doing what God wants; the person must act for the sake of God. Only after a person has accepted the yoke and authority of Heaven can he go on to cultivate the bond that has formed between himself and God.

THERE MUST ALSO BE FEAR OF GOD IN THE RECEIVING OF THE TORAH

☞ The Talmud (*Shabbat* 88a) says that at the giving of the Torah, God overturned the mountain above the children of Israel like a tub and forced them to accept the Torah. Numerous verses, however, seem to imply otherwise: In response to God's offer of the Torah, the people said to Moses, "Everything that the Lord has spoken we will perform" (Ex. 19:8), and elsewhere they said, "We will perform and we will heed" (Ex. 24:7). Likewise, we say in our daily prayers, "His kingdom they willingly accepted upon themselves." Why then do the Sages say that the children of Israel were forced to receive the Torah? It is because if the bond formed by the children of Israel with God at the receiving of the Torah was sparked from the outset solely by our desire, then although it would certainly be beautiful, it would have been generated by the Jews, dependent on them, and limited to the confines of the human dimension. On the other hand, when the bond comes from God, it is dependent on Him. This is a relationship whose beginning is a person's self-nullification. Perhaps there is no place for this in relationships between human beings, but any true connection to God must begin with a person's self-nullification, with the nullification of his desires and perceptions. The essence of the bond is expressed in our ancestors' reply to God: "We will perform and we will heed."

There is a difference between that which we receive from the outside and then internalize, and that which comes from within us, which we project outward. What we receive from the outside is objective reality, truth, and it is imposed upon us. On the other hand, that which the thoughts of our heart create is not bound to anything, neither to reality nor to truth; it is free. A person is free to think about anything, whether it is true or not and whether it is realistic or not. This is why it is so important, in every perception, to have the ability to accept things without involving the self, its thoughts, and feelings, that one have the ability to become bound to the objective reality as far as possible, and to be total nothingness before it, so that one will be able to accept it as it is. It is well known that an intrinsic factor in every scientific observation that must be taken into account is the involvement of the observer. The first principle taught to every person who is making a study in any field is to write down exactly what he sees, not what he thinks he has seen or what he would have liked to have seen. At the next stage, he will be able to look for correlations and formulate conclusions, but first he must accept the reality just as it is. The same is true with regard to accepting God's kingship. In order for it to be objective and real, one's self must initially be passive and receptive. A person does something because he was told to do it. It is especially import-

וּלְפָחוֹת צָרִיךְ לְעוֹרֵר תְּחִלָּה הַיִּרְאָה הַטִּבְעִית הַמְסוּתֶּרֶת בְּלֵב כָּל יִשְׂרָאֵל, **Rather, at the least,** in order to do good, a person **must first awaken the natural fear that is hidden in the heart of every Jew,**

The proper order is that fear comes first, without any other faculty of the soul preceding it. This fear is the natural and hidden fear that exists in the heart of every Jew. The revelation of that fear in a person's heart is in accordance with the nature of his heart and the character of his soul. Therefore, the demand for the arousal of fear in a person's heart is necessarily the demand for a minimal measure of emotional capacity. It is not realistic to require everyone to reach the level of fear possessed by the angels. Not everyone is capable of reaching a level of clear perception and emotion in which all his bones shake from fear of God. However, every Jew can awaken and discover within himself the innate sense of fear that is concealed in his heart, which stems from the very fact of his being a Jew.

שֶׁלֹּא לִמְרוֹד בְּמֶלֶךְ מַלְכֵי הַמְּלָכִים הַקָּדוֹשׁ בָּרוּךְ הוּא, כַּנִּזְכָּר לְעֵיל. which guards him so that he does **not rebel against the King of kings, the Holy One, blessed be He, as stated above** (chaps. 19, 38).

This basic fear literally acts upon every single Jew. There are many real-life examples in which a person, even if he is a simple or despicable

ant to say these things in our time, when the very concept of accepting a yoke is perceived as negative, "coercion" is an offensive word, and we feel that we must view this episode as being one in which the children of Israel simply accepted the Torah. In these times in particular, it should be emphasized that the acceptance of the Torah and of God's kingship was not voluntary, but rather, that God overturned the mountain above the children of Israel, not because they did not desire from the outset to understand and accept, but rather because it was necessitated from the nature of the connection between us and God, moving from Him to us. Afterward, the children of Israel could try to understand what they were told about their relationship with the Torah and its meaning. After "we will perform" comes "we will heed." When fear is present, there is a place for love as well, and so with regard to all evolving frameworks, where fear emerges from love and love emerges from fear. However, the author of the *Tanya* emphasizes that the first step, "the beginning of divine service and its essence and root," is to receive, which correlates with the simple fear that inspires the acceptance of the yoke of God's kingship.

individual, reached a crisis point and believed himself to be standing on the brink of rebellion and severance from God, and he then discovered within himself a fear of separation from God, and as a result he took action to the extent of actual self-sacrifice.

שֶׁתְּהֵא בְּהִתְגַּלּוּת לִבּוֹ אוֹ מוֹחוֹ עַל כָּל פָּנִים, **This fear must become manifest in his heart, or at least in his mind.**

It is not enough that this fear exists concealed within the heart and that it emerges only in exceptional cases of self-sacrifice. Rather, a person must constantly bring it forth to be exposed, so that it will be an experience that influences his day-to-day life. Even if a person cannot cause fear to impact his soul in the ideal way, as a palpable emotion within him, he can at any rate meditate on the notion that it is proper and necessary to fear God and to behave accordingly.

דְּהַיְינוּ לְהִתְבּוֹנֵן בְּמַחֲשַׁבְתּוֹ עַל כָּל פָּנִים **That entails** a person's **contemplating, at least in his thoughts,**

In order to awaken this fear within himself, a person must at least engage in mental contemplation, which involves thinking about a particular idea repeatedly and from every angle until it becomes tangible. This is a spiritual process at the end of which a person no longer needs to consciously think about the matter, because it has already become so clear and real to him, as though he literally sees it before his eyes, since it has become embedded in his consciousness.

גְּדוּלַת אֵין סוֹף בָּרוּךְ הוּא וּמַלְכוּתוֹ, אֲשֶׁר הִיא מַלְכוּת כָּל עוֹלָמִים, עֶלְיוֹנִים וְתַחְתּוֹנִים. וְאִיהוּ מְמַלֵּא כָּל עָלְמִין וְסוֹבֵב כָּל עָלְמִין, וּכְמוֹ שֶׁכָּתוּב: "הֲלֹא אֶת הַשָּׁמַיִם וְאֶת הָאָרֶץ אֲנִי מָלֵא" (ירמיה כג, כד), **the greatness of the Infinite One, blessed be He, and His kingship, which is the kingship of all worlds, higher and lower.** A person should also contemplate **that He fills all worlds and encompasses all worlds. As the verse states, "Do I not fill the heavens and the earth?"** (Jer. 23:24),

This process, whereby a person goes from thinking about something to possessing a tangible consciousness of it, operates in all areas of life, and this is equally true in the realm of God. When one contemplates the greatness of the Infinite One, who is the Ruler of all worlds, contemplating that He is the power of life within all worlds and their particulars, and He surrounds all worlds, transcending all worlds and all of the particulars within them.

וּמַנִּיחַ הָעֶלְיוֹנִים וְתַחְתּוֹנִים וּמְיַחֵד מַלְכוּתוֹ עַל עַמּוֹ יִשְׂרָאֵל בִּכְלָל, וְעָלָיו בִּפְרָט. **and he should contemplate that nevertheless God disregards the higher and lower worlds in order to confer His kingship upon His nation, Israel, as a whole, and upon him in particular.**

After a person contemplates this aspect of the Divine exaltedness, of God's greatness, might, and beauty, after he has an awareness of the scope of that greatness, he should contemplate the other aspect, which is that nevertheless "He sets aside the upper and lower universes" and "confers His kingship upon His nation, Israel, as a whole, and upon him in particular," upon this person who is engaged in this contemplation.

This contemplation consists of two parts. One is the contemplation of the infinite greatness of the Divine. The second part involves contemplating the special, unequaled connection between the Divine and the individual. God so to speak disregards all the greatness of the higher and lower worlds and deals only with the Jewish people, and in particular with the individual currently contemplating this fact.

I FILL THE HEAVENS AND THE EARTH

☞ This verse is quoted in many hasidic sources as portraying the light that encompasses all worlds – the heavens and the earth equally – without any differentiation between them. With regard to the One who surrounds and encompasses all worlds, the heavens and the earth are the same. Therefore, "I fill" refers to God Himself. He encompasses all worlds, and is distinct from and more exalted than the worlds, and cannot be grasped or contained by any part of them. By contrast, the verses, "Behold, the Lord stood over him" (Gen. 28:13) and "He fills the entire world with His glory" (Isa. 6:3), refer to the light that fills all worlds (see *Kitzurim U'Biurim LeSefer HaTanya*).

כִּי חַיָּב אָדָם לוֹמַר: "בִּשְׁבִילִי נִבְרָא הָעוֹלָם" (סנהדרין פרק ד משנה ה). **We see that this last assertion is true, because our Rabbis teach that a person is obligated to say, "The world was created for me"** (*Mishna Sanhedrin* 4:5).

From one perspective, a person should see himself as the center and essence of the universe. "I and He" – that is the reality. The human self and the divine self unite with each other, and God is currently involved only with me.

This is not an expression of human egoism, but is a part of divine service. The service is not to regard oneself as the center of the world. Rather, one's task is to bear the responsibility that is implied by this. As the center of the world, the individual is the axis around which all reality revolves. All creatures and all actions come toward him from all directions, and he determines their significance and the direction in which they are to flow onward. This is what "the world was created for me" means: not that everything was made for me, but that I am responsible for all of reality and everything that happens in it. If I am the center of the world, this means that I and my actions, for better or worse, determine the nature of all reality. ☞

THE WORLD WAS CREATED FOR ME

☞ The nation of Israel that we mention in our prayers and blessings is not an abstract, barren concept, nor is it the sum total of a list of names; rather, it is first and foremost "myself," and then everyone connected to me, by varying degrees of closeness. When a Jew mentions in his prayers "the One who chooses His people Israel with love," he should not mean that God chooses a particular rabbi, nor any other individual; he should be referring primarily to himself. When he recites, "to observe, to do, and to fulfill all the words of Your Torah," he should not mean the entire Jewish people, nor a particular institution; once again, he should be referring to himself. One of the tzaddikim expressed it thus: When a person prays, he should see himself as though he is standing in a forest. In the forest, he does not ask himself whether the trees around him are praying too; he is not bothered by this, and he does not rely on their praying. In the forest, he stands alone before God, and alone he must conduct an accounting of himself. This is how every person should view matters when praying with a congregation as well: There is a tree standing in front of him, another beside him, and several behind him, and he is the only one who is praying.

CHAPTER 41

וְהוּא גַּם הוּא מְקַבֵּל עָלָיו מַלְכוּתוֹ, לִהְיוֹת מֶלֶךְ עָלָיו, וּלְעָבְדוֹ וְלַעֲשׂוֹת רְצוֹנוֹ בְּכָל מִינֵי עֲבוֹדַת עֶבֶד.

Subsequently, he accepts upon himself God's **sovereignty, that He will be King over him,** which entails his **serving God and fulfilling His will** by performing **all aspects of a servant's duties.**

After a person contemplates the notion that "the world was created for me," he reaches the conclusion that he must do something. It does not matter what others will do, nor whether they are good or evil, nor whether they are present or absent, because in this regard the entire world is merely the backdrop, merely the environment in which he exists. The same applies to his relationship with God, regarding which he must think: Everyone else in the world is a helper, an attendant, but only I am God's servant in the world. God created the world for me. I am its center and its reason for being, and therefore its existence depends on me. The existence of the entire kingdom hinges on me accepting the yoke of the kingdom, serving Him and doing His will.

Until now, the author of the *Tanya* has discussed contemplation that leads to accepting the yoke of God's kingship, namely a simple acceptance of His yoke; to serve God and do whatever is His will, even without understanding and without the emotion of love or fear. The

---

This is not because the other people are not praying, but because it makes no difference in this context.

The reason the author of the *Tanya* appended the statement of the Mishna, "A person must say, 'The world was created for me,'" to the phrase "upon him in particular," was so that the reader would not mistakenly think that it refers to him simply because he is a member of the Jewish people. Rather, it is referring to him in particular, as an individual. This is clear from the Mishna, because it states that a person is obliged to say, "The world was created for me," as a conclusion to what was said earlier in the Mishna, where it is explained why Adam was created alone. Just as Adam had no one to rely on and needed to act alone in all the worlds, so too every Jew should see himself as being alone. Likewise, just as all the worlds depended on Adam's divine service, which elevated them when he performed that service properly, so too each and every Jew has the same responsibility to serve God in a way that elevates all worlds (based on a talk of the Lubavitcher Rebbe, Rabbi Menaḥem Mendel Schneerson, on this chapter; see *Torat Menaḥem*, vol. 41, pp. 203ff).

author of the *Tanya* will now discuss contemplation that draws a sense of fear into the heart.[1]

11 Nisan (leap year)

"וְהִנֵּה ה' נִצָּב עָלָיו" (בראשית כח, יג) וּ"מְלֹא כָל הָאָרֶץ כְּבוֹדוֹ" (ישעיה ו, ג),

He reflects that "**behold, the Lord stands over him**" (Gen. 28:13), and "**He fills the entire world with His glory**" (Isa. 6:3),

This contemplation not only concerns the infinitely great and distant God, who is above and beyond all reality, but also the divine essence that permeates all worlds. This refers to the divine sovereignty, which does not operate from a distance through written directives, as it were. Rather, God Himself stands directly over the universe.[2]

וּמַבִּיט עָלָיו וּבוֹחֵן כְּלָיוֹת וָלֵב אִם עוֹבְדוֹ כָּרָאוּי.

scrutinizing him, examining the thoughts of his innards and the emotions of his heart to determine whether he is serving Him properly.

God examines not only a person's actions, but his innermost feelings as well. When a person genuinely feels that God is standing over him, he can no longer make excuses such as "I'm nobody," "I'm unimportant," or, "God doesn't care whether or not I put on *tefillin* today." That is because God is truly standing over him, just as He stood over Jacob, and God's glory fills the entire world. ☞

---

1. Accepting the yoke of God's sovereignty without the fear of God is not good. If a person accepts the yoke of God's sovereignty without fearing God, that means that he is undertaking to do God's will only on a superficial level. Therefore, he must have the fear of God as well. Accepting the yoke of God's sovereignty and fearing God correspond, respectively, to the garment of a *tallit* and to the *tzitziyot* (ritual fringes) on its corners. The *tallit* is called the "garment of the King" because it draws down onto a person his acceptance of God's sovereignty. The *tzitziyot*, meanwhile, draw fear down onto the person. Just as a *tallit* must possess *tzitziyot*, even though the *tzitziyot* are seemingly just tiny and insignificant threads, so too we require fear in addition to accepting the yoke of God's sovereignty. Although fear may be only a subtle and faint perception in the mind and heart, it is nevertheless required (Rabbi Shmuel Gronem Esterman).

2. The Lubavitcher Rebbe, Rabbi Menaḥem Mendel Schneerson, treats this subject at length in a talk on *Parashat Noaḥ*, 5725.

וְעַל כֵּן צָרִיךְ לַעֲבוֹד לְפָנָיו **Therefore,** a person **must serve** God
בְּאֵימָה וּבְיִרְאָה כְּעוֹמֵד לִפְנֵי **with trepidation and fear, as though**
הַמֶּלֶךְ. **he were standing before a king.**

This point of contemplation is the starting point at which a Jew must begin his thoughts, meaning that this is how a person views his situation. He is not like someone sitting in an inner room and doing something which will have an effect elsewhere. He is performing his divine service now. He is standing before the King. The King is present here and now, and is watching him. The emotional result of this contemplation of serving God with trepidation and fear is that he actually feels trepidation and fear, triggered by the thought that he is standing before the King.[3]

וְיַעֲמִיק בְּמַחֲשָׁבָה זוֹ **He should delve into this thought**

It has already been said that contemplation in general is not just a passing thought or momentary reflection on a particular subject.

THE FOUNDATION OF THE TRAIT OF FEAR

☞ There are numerous levels of fear, but here the author of the *Tanya* is not discussing that elevated, highly-refined level known as "exalted fear." Rather, he is discussing the very first level of relationship, the initial level required of every person: to awaken within himself a minimal degree of the fear of God. Like everything that is basic, fundamental, and minimal, this is something extremely simple, the tangible feeling that God is standing over him. God has, so to speak, left the upper worlds. He is not concerned about distant galaxies; He is concerned about only one thing: the specific individual. God stands over this person and looks at him. He does not see only the person's actions and speech, but also examines what is inside his innards and heart, how he has acted and spoken, and what he was thinking and feeling at that time. This is the most basic and simple foundation of fear: of having the sense of standing before God, that God is literally standing here. He is not elsewhere, and He is not involved in anything else; rather, there is only God and the individual. This is the reality, and everything else is only shadows in the background. A person cannot evade or deceive God, or conceal anything. In this perspective on reality, it does not matter what others say or think about a person, nor does it matter whether he is happy or not. All that exists is God and the individual. "I am standing before Him, and He is standing over me." There is nothing more fundamental than this.

---

3. See Rema, *Shulḥan Arukh, Oraḥ Ḥayyim* 1.

Rather, it is a concentrated deepening of one's thoughts. The purpose of engaging in contemplation is to consciously create a clear, palpable image that will impact the most intimate, personal aspects of the soul; its experience of love and fear. In and of itself, this topic that a person focuses on is universal, it is a notion that anyone can reflect upon. However, arriving at a particular image specific to himself, which is neither uniform nor fixed, yet truly touches and connects with his soul, is possible only when he concentrates and deepens his thinking. There is no uniform technique with regard to how and where to delve deeper in contemplation. Each individual has his own approach in accordance with his nature, inclinations, and education.

וְיַאֲרִיךְ בָּהּ   and do so at length,

The deepening of a thought in order to give it permanence and tangibility must be done over a period of time; a fleeting reflection is not enough. The necessary contemplation, therefore, consists of two things: deepening the thought and extending its duration.

כְּפִי יְכוֹלֶת הַשָּׂגַת מוֹחוֹ וּמַחֲשַׁבְתּוֹ   in accordance with the capacity of his mind and thought to comprehend,

Contemplation, especially of these issues, requires serious effort. It is not enough to have a particular idea about a matter, or a general thought or understanding of the topic. Rather, a person must delve into it, in order to continuously try to expand his capacity to comprehend, to enter into its inner being in order to understand it to the best of his ability – the whole, as well as its component parts – in order to instill the abstract image in his mind as clearly and concretely as possible. This requires a great deal of work.

וּכְפִי הַפְּנַאי שֶׁלּוֹ,   and in accordance with his available time,

Just as there is a limit to a person's capacity for intellectual attainment, so too there is a limit to the time each person is able to do so. There is no set expectation for each one. Rather, what he can accomplish depends on the amount of time that he is able to devote to the task. After all, these are not topics that one can exhaust within a set amount of time. Rather, they are topics that a person can delve into more and more, spending more and more time on them. They never end. As time goes by, new aspects emerge for him to consider. The deeper he goes, the more depth he discovers.

Once again, these words are addressed not only to exceptional individuals but to those who fit the definition of a *beinoni*. A *beinoni* is a person who is, spiritually speaking, an ordinary person. Therefore, just as he needs to be told that he must engage in contemplation, so too – because of this fact – he needs to be reminded that there are limitations, that he must not allow himself to become immersed in this undertaking and prolong it indefinitely.

לִפְנֵי עֵסֶק הַתּוֹרָה **prior to engaging in Torah** study

The proper time to engage in contemplation is before learning Torah. Before a person studies Torah, he should devote some time to contemplating the essence of the Torah and the One who gives the Torah.

אוֹ הַמִּצְוָה, כְּמוֹ לִפְנֵי לְבִישַׁת טַלִּית וּתְפִילִּין. **or a mitzva, such as before donning** *tallit* **and** *tefillin*.

THE CAPACITY OF HIS MIND AND THOUGHTS

☞ The author of the *Tanya* is addressing every Jew and discussing the most fundamental point, the "beginning of divine service," which is the natural fear that is hidden in the heart of every Jew. Therefore, just as he does not define objectives, he likewise does not stipulate the amount of effort required. Rather, everyone is to act "in accordance with the capacity of his mind and thoughts to comprehend." Not everyone has the mental capability necessary to absorb and analyze abstract matters, and certainly some people cannot do this as well as others. For some, abstract forms are crude, unclear, and almost meaningless, whereas for others they are more clear and real. Therefore, at the outset, the author of the *Tanya* does not discuss contemplating the Torah's mysteries, nor does he use complex, kabbalistic terms. Rather, he employs the simplest of images, which everyone, even a child, can contemplate, each person in accordance with his capabilities.

Before a person performs a mitzva, he should take time to contemplate the fact that God is standing over him, that God has commanded him to fulfill this commandment, and that He scrutinizes the thoughts and emotions of his heart to determine whether a person is serving Him properly. In the past, there were hasidim who would stand with a *tallit* wrapped around their shoulders for hours on end contemplating these matters. Some stayed that way for the majority of the day, because they needed to reach an understanding of certain concepts before they could put on the *tallit* and *tefillin* and begin to pray. There was once a hasid who was asked why he always arrived late for the prayer services. He answered, referring to the first words that a Jew recites upon awakening each morning, "It is because of the *Modeh Ani* prayer. When I wake up in the morning and recite '*Modeh ani lefanekha*,' 'I am thankful before You,' I begin to think: Who am 'I'? What does 'thankful' mean? What does 'before You' mean? And before I know it, half the day has passed by." ☞

Until now, the author of the *Tanya* has discussed one particular topic that a person contemplates. Contemplating this topic arouses a person's most fundamental level of fear of God, in which he recognizes that God is the King, that He is standing above him, and that He examines what is in his innards and heart. This contemplation constitutes the initial, immediate, and generalized perception of a person in God's presence. Next, the author of the *Tanya* will discuss the contemplation of more specific topics: the relations between God and man in the realm of mitzvot and the revelation of Godliness within them, and he will then discuss in much greater detail specific mitzvot, and the aspects of the soul that relate to their observance.

BEFORE DONNING *TALLIT* AND *TEFILLIN*

☞ Not only on Rosh HaShana, when a person recites Psalms 47 seven times, nor on Yom Kippur, when a person cries out *Shema Yisrael* during the *Ne'ila* service, but rather, a person must serve God as His servant also on a regular weekday when he dons the *tallit* and *tefillin*. The existence of all the worlds depends on this (from a talk of Rabbi Menaḥem Mendel Schneerson, the Lubavitcher Rebbe).

CHAPTER 41

18 Nisan
12 Nisan (leap year)

וְגַם יִתְבּוֹנֵן אֵיךְ שֶׁאוֹר אֵין סוֹף בָּרוּךְ הוּא, הַסּוֹבֵב כָּל עָלְמִין וּמְמַלֵּא כָּל עָלְמִין, הוּא רָצוֹן הָעֶלְיוֹן, הוּא מְלוּבָּשׁ בָּאוֹתִיּוֹת וְחָכְמַת הַתּוֹרָה אוֹ בְּצִיצִית וּתְפִילִּין אֵלּוּ, וּבִקְרִיאָתוֹ אוֹ בִּלְבִישָׁתוֹ הוּא מַמְשִׁיךְ אוֹרוֹ יִתְבָּרֵךְ עָלָיו,

He should also contemplate how the light of the Infinite One, blessed be He, which encompasses all worlds and fills all worlds, that light being the supernal will, is clothed in the letters and wisdom of the Torah that he is studying or in these *tzitzit* and *tefillin* that he is donning. Thus, **by reciting** the words of Torah or **donning** the *tallit* or *tefillin*, **he draws** God's **light onto himself,**

The supernal will actualizes and sustains all worlds. A person should contemplate the following questions: What exactly are the Torah and mitzvot? What is the significance of engaging in them? The answer to this is that when a person performs a practical commandment such as donning *tzitzit* or *tefillin*, or when he learns a chapter of Mishna or a verse of the Torah, doing so leads to the revelation of an infinite essence within him.

דְּהַיְינוּ עַל חֵלֶק אֱלוֹהַּ מִמַּעַל שֶׁבְּתוֹךְ גּוּפוֹ, לִיכָּלֵל וְלִיבָּטֵל בְּאוֹרוֹ יִתְבָּרֵךְ.

that is, onto his soul, **the portion of God above that is within his body,** so that his soul **may become incorporated and subsumed in God's light.**

When a person performs a mitzva, he attains, on the highest level that he can, unity with the divine light. Each mitzva is a kind of window, a particular point of view regarding the Divine. The person who performs the mitzva binds himself in this way to the divine essence. In this sense, the *tefillin* and Torah embody this connection only while the person is performing the mitzva. In order for the union between the human "I" and the supernal will to be formed, a person needs to complete the circuit.

This is analogous to the spinal cord. The spinal cord passes through the vertebrae to make a living connection between the upper part of the human organism and its other parts. The spinal cord cannot exist without the vertebrae, and if one of the vertebrae breaks or even moves slightly, the whole structure may be damaged. In the same way, the object comprising a mitzva, such as *tzitzit*, Sabbath candles, or the letters that make up the Torah and prayers, corresponds to the vertebrae. All that the person does is connect the vertebrae-like conduits, or electrical wires, to connect the current between the upper part, which is the infinite light, and the lower part, which is the divine soul in the human body. This idea is found in a verse: "Before the silver cord is severed" (Eccles. 12:6). The cord of silver, *kesef*, is the cord of yearning, *kisufim*, between the upper and the lower, the source of life above, and the place where the soul has been embedded below. Through this silver cord, the yearning soul is connected to the Creator with the infinite light. The soul on one end and the divine light on the other join together in the mitzva, or in the words of Torah or prayer, and thus they establish the "silver" (yearning) connection.

וְדֶרֶךְ פְּרָט בִּתְפִילִּין – לִיבָּטֵל וְלִיכָּלֵל בְּחִינוֹת חָכְמָתוֹ וּבִינָתוֹ שֶׁבְּנַפְשׁוֹ הָאֱלֹקִית, בִּבְחִינוֹת חָכְמָתוֹ וּבִינָתוֹ שֶׁל אֵין סוֹף בָּרוּךְ הוּא,

To give a **specific** example, a person should perform the mitzva of donning *tefillin* with the intent that **the attributes of wisdom and understanding within his divine soul will become subsumed and incorporated into the attributes of the wisdom and understanding of the light of *Ein Sof*, blessed be He,**

The intention behind the mitzva of *tefillin* is that the wisdom and understanding of the person should be subsumed within God's attributes of wisdom and understanding.

הַמְלוּבָּשׁוֹת דֶּרֶךְ פְּרָט בְּפָרְשִׁיּוֹת "קַדֶּשׁ" (שמות יג, ב-י), "וְהָיָה כִּי יְבִאֲךָ" (שם יא-טז),

which are enclothed specifically in the passages, "Sanctify to Me..." (Ex. 13:2–10) and "It shall be when the Lord will take you..." (Ex. 13:11–16), that are written in the *tefillin*.

The upper attributes of wisdom and understanding are enclothed in two of the four passages found in the *tefillin*. The passage that begins "Sanctify to Me every firstborn" (Ex. 13:2) alludes to wisdom, because sanctity and the firstborn are matters that pertain to wisdom (*Likkutei Torah*, Deut. 6c). The passage that begins, "It shall be when the Lord will take you" alludes to understanding, for the verse has the phrase,

"When your son asks you tomorrow, saying: What is this?" (Ex. 13:14), and this pertains to contemplation (*Torah Or* 86c). Moreover, the passage mentions the exodus from Egypt (*Mitzrayim*), which corresponds to the limits (*meitzarim*) of understanding.[4]

דְּהַיְינוּ שֶׁלֹּא לְהִשְׁתַּמֵּשׁ בְּחָכְמָתוֹ וּבִינָתוֹ שֶׁבְּנַפְשׁוֹ בִּלְתִּי לַה׳ לְבַדּוֹ.

That is to say that he will subsume and incorporate the wisdom and understanding in his soul into the higher wisdom and understanding by **not utilizing** the former for any other purpose **than solely serving God.**

In this sense, the *tefillin* are the conduit, the instrument for the connection between the divine powers of wisdom and understanding, and human wisdom and understanding. The meaning of this connection is that human wisdom and understanding are subsumed and incorporated into divine wisdom and understanding.[5] "Incorporation" means that a person's wisdom and understanding, as well as the higher forces of wisdom and understanding, are engaged in the same matter, so to speak. At that moment, a person's wisdom and understanding are solely an expression of God's wisdom and understanding.

וְכֵן לִיבָּטֵל לִיכָּלֵל בְּחִינַת הַדַּעַת שֶׁבְּנַפְשׁוֹ הַכּוֹלֵל חֶסֶד וּגְבוּרָה, שֶׁהֵן יִרְאָה וְאַהֲבָה שֶׁבְּלִבּוֹ בִּבְחִינַת דַּעַת הָעֶלְיוֹן הַכּוֹלֵל חֶסֶד וּגְבוּרָה, הַמְלוּבָּשׁ בְּפָרָשִׁיּוֹת "שְׁמַע" (דברים ו, ד-ט) "וְהָיָה אִם שָׁמוֹעַ" (שם יא, יג-כא).

Likewise, a person should have in mind that **the attribute of knowledge within his soul, which encompasses** the attributes of **kindness and restraint, which** correspond to **the fear and love in his heart, is subsumed** and **incorporated within the** divine **attribute of supernal knowledge, which encompasses** the attributes of **kindness and restraint. This attribute is enclothed in the passages of "Hear, Israel..."** (Deut. 6:4–9) **and "It shall be, if you shall heed..."** (Deut. 11:13–21), which are also in the *tefillin*.

---

4. This is explained at length in *Peri Etz Ḥayyim, Derushei Tefillin; Siddur im Divrei Elokim Ḥayyim, Sha'ar HaTefillin; Imrei Bina.*

5. Incorporation is from above, whereas subsuming is from the human perspective (see *Likkutei Levi Yitzḥak He'arot LeSefer HaTanya*).

Knowledge is an intellectual attribute, but it is a part of the intellect that encompasses kindness and restraint, which are at root the emotions of love and fear. These are incorporated within supernal knowledge, which is enclothed in the two additional passages found in the *tefillin*.

וְהַיְינוּ כְּמוֹ שֶׁכָּתוּב בַּשֻּׁלְחָן עָרוּךְ (אורח חיים סימן כה סעיף ה) לְשַׁעְבֵּד הַלֵּב וְהַמּוֹחַ כו'. — All of **this corresponds to the statement of the *Shulḥan Arukh*** (*Oraḥ Ḥayyim* 25:5), that when a person dons *tefillin* he should have the intent **to subjugate his heart and mind** to God, **etc.**

When a person puts on *tefillin*, he should subjugate his heart and mind to serve God, or, as stated above in more kabbalistic terms, "become subsumed and incorporated."[6]

The essence of the mitzva of *tefillin* is attachment,[7] and the meaning of this attachment, from the individual's perspective, is that he subjugates his heart and mind to God. Regarding the mind, this means that he thinks with God and does not lower his thoughts to other matters. And regarding the heart, it means that he does not employ his emotions for other matters, but only for God.[8]

13 Nisan (leap year)

וּבַעֲטִיפַת צִיצִית יְכַוֵּין כְּמוֹ שֶׁכָּתוּב בַּזֹּהַר לְהַמְשִׁיךְ עָלָיו מַלְכוּתוֹ יִתְבָּרֵךְ, אֲשֶׁר הִיא מַלְכוּת כָּל עוֹלָמִים וכו', לְיַחֲדָהּ עָלֵינוּ עַל יְדֵי מִצְוָה זוֹ. וְהוּא — Also **when** a person **wraps himself in tzitzit**, he should have the intent, **as written in the *Zohar*, to draw upon himself** God's **sovereignty, which is** His **sovereignty over all worlds, etc.** We do so in order **to unify** God's

---

6. The *Shulḥan Arukh* explains that "to subjugate his heart" refers to the arm *tefillin*, and "and [to subjugate his] mind" refers to the head *tefillin*. The *Zohar* explains that "heart" and "mind" refer to the four passages in the head *tefillin* (Rabbi Shmuel Gronem Esterman).

7. The word *tefillin* derives from the same root as the word for "struggle," as in the verse, "I engaged in a great struggle [*naftulei elohim niftalti*]" (Gen. 30:8), and in the rabbinic statement, "One may not smear [*tofelin*] them with clay" (*Tosefta, Pesaḥim* 5:10).

8. The words *tefillin* and *tefilla*, prayer, have the same root, and the meaning of both is the evocation of expanded consciousness (the Lubavitcher Rebbe, Rabbi Menaḥem Mendel Schneerson).

בְּעִנְיַן "שׂוֹם תָּשִׂים עָלֶיךָ מֶלֶךְ" (דברים יז, טו). sovereignty **with ourselves through this mitzva. This corresponds to** the commandment, **"You shall place a king over you"** (Deut. 17:15).

The mitzva of *tzitzit* is the vessel through which a person draws the divine kingdom upon himself. As the *Zohar* states,[9] when a person wraps himself in the *tallit*, he should have the intent to accept God's authority and place himself under God's sovereignty.[10]

Therefore, contemplation of the intent behind the mitzvot has two aspects. General contemplation before performing a mitzva does not relate to the essence of that particular mitzva, but to the act of performing a mitzva in general. A person should contemplate the One who commands us to perform mitzvot: God Himself. Likewise, he should contemplate the nature of a mitzva, which is a conduit through which the human soul unites with God's infinite light. There is also a specific contemplation, which relates to the intention of the particular mitzva. The person performing the mitzva must be aware of what he is doing. All mitzvot possess the same general content: They reveal the connection between the divine soul and God. This connection is revealed in a particular and unique way within each individual mitzva. ☞ ☞

CONTEMPLATION THAT EVOKES TREPIDATION AND FRIGHT

☞ If a person performs this double contemplation properly, and if he has a sensitive soul, it will lead him to experience fear of the divine kingdom. There are various levels, starting from a level where a person feels something small when he acts, and culminating in a level where, out of sheer terror at the realization of what he is doing, the person is unable to act. When a person contemplates that he is standing before God and he is about to achieve a connection with Him, then if this notion is clear enough, he will be overcome with trepidation and fright. This may be compared to someone who has been sentenced to die by the electric chair, who has time to contemplate what an electric chair is, what happens to those who are put it

---

9. See *Zohar* 3:120b, as pointed out by the Lubavitcher Rebbe, Rabbi Menaḥem Mendel Schneerson.

10. Before this, the person has no king, and now he places a king over himself (the Lubavitcher Rebbe, Rabbi Menaḥem Mendel Schneerson). According to Rambam, "You shall place a king over you" is a positive commandment (number 173).

וַאֲזַי, אַף אִם בְּכָל זֹאת לֹא תִּפּוֹל עָלָיו אֵימָה וָפַחַד בְּהִתְגַּלּוּת לִבּוֹ, מִכָּל מָקוֹם, מֵאַחַר שֶׁמְּקַבֵּל עָלָיו מַלְכוּת שָׁמַיִם וּמַמְשִׁיךְ עָלָיו יִרְאָתוֹ יִתְבָּרֵךְ בְּהִתְגַּלּוּת מַחֲשַׁבְתּוֹ וּרְצוֹנוֹ שֶׁבְּמוֹחוֹ,

Then, even if a person **is still not overcome with conscious trepidation and fright in his heart, nevertheless, since he accepts upon himself the kingship of Heaven and draws the fear of God onto himself in his revealed thought and his will in his mind,**

Once a person has contemplated everything described above, if he still does not reach the level of a living, palpable sense of trepidation and fear in his heart, whether because he did not exert enough effort or whether because even with the requisite amount of effort he was unable to reach that level, his intention in itself and whatever change in his thought and emotions it brings about are acceptable; although he does not feel a sense of trepidation and fright, he nevertheless understands the concept that it is proper to feel such trepidation and fright. He thinks about it, identifies with it, and willingly accepts the effect that such trepidation would have on him. He is not afraid of emotion – that is not what is keeping him from experiencing trepi-

in it, and how he soon will experience this fate. Doubtless, that person will be overcome with a terrible fear. Here, the author of the *Tanya* is describing something infinitely more terrifying. A person contemplates God's greatness to the extent that he is able to comprehend it, and then he contemplates the fact that this greatness is not in a distant realm, in a separate space. Rather, it is here, in the present, in the person's very space. Subsequently, when he contemplates the fact that he is about to perform a mitzva and form a connection that will penetrate into the very depths of his being, then if he has the appropriate spiritual sensitivity, he will begin to tremble and he will be exceedingly fearful that he is about to perform the mitzva.

CONTEMPLATION ON EACH PERSON'S LEVEL

The *Tanya* is called the Book of *Beinonim*, i.e., ordinary people. Thus, the words of the *Tanya* here are not meant in relation to people with exceptional souls, but in a sense they apply to everyone. Possessing a lofty soul with a sensitivity to holiness is indeed desirable, but it is not an absolute necessity. As the Sages say (and as will be explained at length in the next chapter), "If a person says to you...I have labored and I have found [success], believe him" (*Megilla* 6b). Anyone can achieve this level; the question is only how hard he is willing to work. Therefore, these matters certainly also pertain to a person who does not have a sensitive soul. If such a person truly wants to succeed in this area, and he is deeply motivated to do so, and he works extremely hard, he will ultimately succeed.

dation. He understands that one should be afraid, and he accepts the yoke of God's kingship upon himself, as if he were experiencing the emotion of trepidation. This too is complete divine service, as will be discussed below.

וְקַבָּלָה זוֹ הִיא אֲמִתִּית בְּלִי שׁוּם סָפֵק, שֶׁהֲרֵי הִיא טֶבַע נַפְשׁוֹת כָּל יִשְׂרָאֵל, שֶׁלֹּא לִמְרֹד בַּמֶּלֶךְ הַקָּדוֹשׁ יִתְבָּרֵךְ, **this acceptance is undoubtedly genuine.** That is **because the nature of every Jew's soul is to not rebel against the blessed, holy King.**

The acceptance of the yoke of God's kingship and the attendant behaviors as described directly above do not stem from a feeling of fear, but rather from a person's thoughts and decision that this is what should be felt. This thought has not reached the emotion of fear, not even on the simplest level of fearing God as the King and accepting his sovereignty. Therefore, one might think that this person's acceptance of the divine yoke is not genuine. So the author of the *Tanya* remarks that this intention to experience fear, where one accepts God's kingship upon himself, is in fact sincere and genuine. Since this attribute is found in the essence of the Jewish soul, even if a person forces it, it is not false. This is similar to the various abilities that human beings possess just by virtue of their being human beings. The ability to speak, for example, is one that every person is born with. Some children learn to speak quickly, while others need to work harder. Some learn on their own, and others need urging and training in order to reach the point where they speak. But since this capacity is a fundamental part of the human psyche, the learning and practicing merely transform potential into actual. This is not like some forms of training of animals, such as when a bird is taught to "talk." The bird is not truly speaking; it is imitating speech. But with regard to a person, even if he requires much urging to learn to speak, it is real speech; it is the realization of his potential. In the same way, the fear of rebelling against God is part of the Jewish potential. Like any potential, it too requires cultivation, practice, and sometimes a little pushing. When a person cultivates it a great deal, he can achieve a great deal. Some people used to work at this extensively, and they found their own fear of God impossible to endure. Reb Zusha once prayed to feel true fear of God, and when he received it, he crawled under his bed weeping for it to be taken away, because he could not stand the terror. While not everyone can be like Reb Zusha, anyone can reach true, sincere fear of God, the fear of being parted from Him, as is explained in several places in the *Tanya*.

When a person accepts God's kingship in thought, this is not merely superficial. Rather, in the depths of his heart, in the root of his soul, he is truly connected to the heavenly kingdom. The act of thinking about accepting the yoke of Heaven leads to the revelation of the force within him. Even if that proper thought does not translate itself into this person's emotions, the thought reflects the sincere desire within the person to accept God's yoke. This desire motivates his acting as though he truly fears God.

הֲרֵי הַתּוֹרָה שֶׁלּוֹמֵד אוֹ הַמִּצְוָה שֶׁעוֹשֶׂה מֵחֲמַת קַבָּלָה זוֹ, וּמֵחֲמַת הַמְשָׁכַת הַיִּרְאָה שֶׁבְּמוֹחוֹ, נִקְרָאוֹת בְּשֵׁם 'עֲבוֹדָה שְׁלֵימָה', כְּכָל עֲבוֹדַת הָעֶבֶד לַאֲדוֹנוֹ וּמַלְכּוֹ.

Accordingly, the Torah that this person **studies or the mitzva that he performs as an outcome of this acceptance** of God's kingship **and of drawing forth the fear of God in his mind are considered a perfect service, no different from any duty** performed **by a servant for his master and king.**

Even if there is no feeling of fear in a person's heart but only the thought of that fear in his mind, his is still a perfect service of God. That is because the essence of a Jew's divine service is like that which a servant performs for his master, as will be mentioned below.

14 Nisan (leap year)

מַה שֶּׁאֵין כֵּן אִם לוֹמֵד וּמְקַיֵּים הַמִּצְוָה בְּאַהֲבָה לְבַדָּהּ, כְּדֵי לְדָבְקָה בּוֹ, עַל יְדֵי תּוֹרָתוֹ וּמִצְווֹתָיו,

By contrast, if a person **studies Torah or performs a mitzva out of love** of God **alone, in order to cleave to Him through His Torah and mitzvot,**

This is the case when a person desires to come closer to and cling to the object of his love. Learning Torah and performing mitzvot are the means of binding oneself to God.

CHAPTER 41

אֵינָהּ נִקְרֵאת בְּשֵׁם ׳עֲבוֹדַת הָעֶבֶד׳.	that is not deemed the service of a servant.

Although it is clear that this person is not simply amusing himself, but is engaging seriously in learning Torah and performing mitzvot in order to come closer to God and cling to Him, nevertheless, since there is no fear involved in his divine service, it is not deemed the service of a servant, which is the service resulting from accepting the divine yoke – a service that comes from fear.

וְהַתּוֹרָה אָמְרָה: "וַעֲבַדְתֶּם אֵת ה׳ אֱלֹהֵיכֶם" וגו׳ (שמות כג, כה) "וְאוֹתוֹ תַעֲבוֹדוּ" וגו׳ (דברים יג, ה).	He does not fulfill his duty, because the Torah stipulates, "You shall serve the Lord your God…" (Ex. 23:25) and "Him you shall serve" (Deut. 13:5).

A person must serve God. He must accept divine service upon himself by accepting the yoke and by means of commitment and servitude, and not just as a voluntary expression of love.

וּכְמוֹ שֶׁכָּתוּב בַּזֹּהַר [פָּרָשַׁת בְּהַר (קח, א)]: "כְּהַאי תּוֹרָא דְיָהֲבִין עֲלֵיהּ עוֹל בְּקַדְמֵיתָא בְּגִין לְאַפָּקָא מִנֵּיהּ טַב לְעָלְמָא כו׳ הָכִי נָמֵי אִיצְטְרִיךְ לְבַר נָשׁ לְקַבָּלָא עֲלֵיהּ עוֹל מַלְכוּת שָׁמַיִם בְּקַדְמֵיתָא כו׳ וְאִי הַאי לָא אִשְׁתְּכַח גַּבֵּיהּ – לָא שַׁרְיָא בֵּיהּ קְדוּשָּׁה" כו׳	As the *Zohar* states (*Parashat Behar* 3:108a), "Just as a yoke must be placed upon the ox from the outset in order for the world to derive benefit from the ox…, so too a person must accept upon himself the yoke of Heaven's kingship from the outset…. If this acceptance is not found in him, holiness will not rest upon him.…"

In order for an ox to plow, a yoke must first be placed upon it. The ox does not voluntarily do anything good and useful out of love for its master. Primarily, it works because it bears a yoke, because it fears its master and has no choice. So too a person must engage in divine service as a result of accepting God's kingship. If he engages in Torah and mitzvot but not from a mindset of accepting the yoke, the holiness of the Torah and the mitzvot will not be upon him.

> וּבְרַעְיָא מְהֵימְנָא שָׁם דַּף קי"א
> עַמּוּד ב] שֶׁכָּל אָדָם צָרִיךְ לִהְיוֹת
> בִּשְׁתֵּי בְּחִינוֹת וּמַדְרֵגוֹת, וְהֵן:
> בְּחִינַת 'עֶבֶד' וּבְחִינַת 'בֵּן'.

Also it is written (in **Raya Meheimna** there, *Zohar* 111b) **that every person must serve God in two distinct modes and levels: namely, the mode of servant and the mode of son.**

As stated in several places, there are two general modes, or levels, of serving God, two realms of connection between a human being and God. The first is that of a servant, as in, "For to Me the children of Israel are slaves" (Lev. 25:55). This means that a person serves God even without a reason and without understanding, like a servant, who does not need to know the reason for his master's commands but obeys them without a reason, even when he has no intrinsic desire to do so. The second mode is that of a son, as in "My firstborn son is Israel" (Ex. 4:22). This means that a person fulfills the commandments out of love. The intention behind his act is to do the will of his father, whom he loves. This does not mean that the two modes must exist separately, that some people are "servants" while others are "children." Rather, as stated in the liturgical hymn sung on Rosh HaShana, "whether as children or as servants," meaning that at certain times and in certain manifestations of our being, we are like children, and at other times, and in certain manifestations of our being, we are like slaves. As the *Tanya* states here, everyone should serve God with both of these modes and levels; a person should not be satisfied with only one of them. When a person worships God as a "servant" only, there is something lacking in his intent and spiritual attachment. However, when a person worships God as a "son" only, solely out of love and desire, something there is lacking as well. The "son" who acts out of love is really doing so for his own gratification, whereas the "servant," who acts out of simple acceptance of a yoke imposed upon him, does so for the sake of his Master. A person who lacks this aspect of servitude is missing something from his divine service. There is a flaw in the meaning and objective value of this service. Divine service must go beyond an individual's personal, selfish desires.

> וְאַף דְּיֵשׁ 'בֵּן' שֶׁהוּא גַם כֵּן 'עֶבֶד',

Although there is such a thing as **a son who is also a servant,**

On a higher level, these two modes can be combined – not each as a different manifestation of who we are, but a complete merging of the two: a "son" who is, at the exact same time and in his present state, also a "servant," in other words, a "son" who is willing to do anything due to his love for his father, yet who acts in a manner of accepting the yoke and the obligation involved, like a "servant."

הֲרֵי אִי אֶפְשָׁר לָבֹא לְמַדְרֵגָה זוֹ בְּלִי קְדִימַת הַיִּרְאָה עִילָּאָה, כַּיָּדוּעַ לַיּוֹדְעִים.

it is impossible to attain that level without first attaining the level of higher fear, as is known to those who are initiated in the esoteric wisdom of Kabbala.

It is not easy to reach this combination of "son" and "servant," where love and fear are blended together. It is not the level of a novice, because in order to reach it, the initial, lower fear is not sufficient. Higher fear, which follows lower fear, is required (as will be explained below). In higher fear, in a sense, closeness and love are combined within that fear itself.

A SON WHO IS A SERVANT

There is a fundamental contradiction between these two states. As stated in *Sha'ar HaYiḥud VeHa'emuna* (chap. 7), "There is no such thing as a king without a nation." The concept of kingship relates to a nation, which is like to a "servant" who accepts the yoke of royalty, but it does not apply to a "son." A king does not rule over his children as a king. Even if he is a great king, and even if he has many children, he is still not a king over them. Therein lies the contradiction: servitude means accepting a yoke and surrendering. When a servant acts, it is not because he desires to do so, but because he is under someone's authority, he is obligated. A "son," on the other hand, acts because he wants to, not out of duty. The son acts out of love rather than fear, whereas the servant acts out of fear rather than love. Love and fear, or attachment and acceptance of the yoke, therefore work in opposite directions. Attachment means closeness, whereas accepting the yoke is based on a perception of distance. Love is an emotion of attraction and involves moving closer, while fear is an emotion of withdrawal and involves moving further away. Thus, simultaneously being close and far, loving and fearing, is not straightforward. For a "son" to be a "servant" at exactly the same time, he must be on a very high level, where there is no element of self-love and there is a great capacity for self-discipline. This is so that he will be able to, so to speak, forget that he is a "son" and act as a "servant," to forget that he loves and act instead out of obligation. The main difficulty is that because

Until now, the author of the *Tanya* has discussed fear as it manifests in feelings and as it manifests in thought. Next, he will address an additional level of fear.

> 19 Nisan
> 15 Nisan
> (leap year)

וְהִנֵּה אַף מִי שֶׁגַּם בְּמוֹחוֹ וּבְמַחֲשַׁבְתּוֹ אֵינוֹ מַרְגִּישׁ שׁוּם יִרְאָה וּבוּשָׁה, — **Now, even someone who does not feel any fear or shame, even in his mind and thought,**

The highest, most perfect level of contemplation leads to emotion. For instance, contemplation on the subject of fear is realized as a feeling of fear in one's heart. This lofty level is not one experienced by exceptional individuals only; anyone can achieve it when he contemplates a topic to which he is sensitive, and when the time and circumstances are right so that he is open to absorbing and deepening the feeling. Some people have such a response to something that they see or hear: a painting or a piece of music moves them. On a lower level, a person fails to achieve an emotional response, such as fear – because he is not sensitive or because he is not in the right frame of mind at that time – but he does achieve intellectual excitement through his intellectual contemplation. He realizes what should be: how he should feel and react. As mentioned above, this too is called "feeling." But here the *Tanya* discusses a level on which a person does not attain that "feeling" – not even in his mind or thoughts. He thinks about God's greatness and about fear of God, but nothing happens within him.

מִפְּנֵי פְּחִיתוּת עֵרֶךְ נַפְשׁוֹ מִמְּקוֹר חוּצְבָהּ מִמַּדְרֵגוֹת תַּחְתּוֹנוֹת דְּעֶשֶׂר סְפִירוֹת דַּעֲשִׂיָּה, — **because of the lowly nature of his soul, due to the origin from which it was hewn, from the lowest levels of the ten** *sefirot* **of the world of** ***Asiya*** **(Action),**

Here, the author of the *Tanya* touches upon the question of why some people achieve some level of arousal and others do not. The souls of

---

of the fact that he loves, he cannot forget that he is a child acting out of love for his father. This inherent contradiction can be solved only on an extremely high level of fear, which is also known as "fear out of shame," or "exalted fear." On this level, love and fear in a sense merge into a single, integrated emotion.

people in this world have a source in the higher worlds from which they are "hewn." Of course, all souls are a "portion of God"; their point of origin is in the highest realm, in the divine essence. Nevertheless, the shape and character of the soul here below is hewn from a particular realm and level within the sequence of spiritual worlds. This quarry from which the soul is hewn is also an aspect of the divine, but it is divinity that relates to those particular levels and realms, i.e., to the ten *sefirot* of the world to which a particular soul's form belongs. Accordingly, the author of the *Tanya* clearly explains that the quarry from which those souls are hewn, souls whose form and level are relatively crude and "lowly," is the quarry of the "lowest levels of the ten *sefirot* of the world of *Asiya*." *Asiya* is the lowest of the four worlds. If a person's soul derives from these levels, even if he works hard and engages in contemplation properly, he will not uncover more than what is found at that level. He will uncover the treasure of the fear of God concealed within his soul, which remained undiscovered until this point. He will polish and reveal the pure soul within himself, no matter what level it has descended to, until it shines of its own accord. But still, it will not shine any more than it did in its source. Therefore, even after first doing all that is necessary – contemplating, working hard, and seeking as much as he can – if he still does not feel, the reason is that his soul originated from a lowly place, from the lower levels of the world of *Asiya*, and it is unable to achieve the subtle feeling of God's presence. ☞

It is entirely possible that a person could have a high soul and an average intellect, whereas someone else could be wise and understand everything written on a subject but lack any sensitivity to and innate

---

HIGH SOULS AND LOW SOULS

☞ The level of a soul is not related to a person's intellectual proficiency, nor to any other physical or spiritual ability (see the end of chap. 23). It is based on one factor only: the soul's sensitivity to holiness. The more sensitive to holiness the soul is, the higher its source. The higher the source of the soul, the deeper and more natural its sensitivity to holiness and to God's presence, and the less illumination and awakening it requires from the outside, because it is drawn to attain this of its own accord. Conversely, when a person possesses a lowly soul, his basic sensitivity to holiness is limited, and it is more difficult for him, perhaps even impossible, to achieve a spiritual awakening, even one that is only in his thought and mind.

understanding of holiness. This dynamic can be seen in other areas as well. Some people are sensitive to certain matters or images, while others are not. There are people who are great experts in a particular field like art or music, yet they lack any emotional sensitivity to the subject. A person might be able to understand the subject matter and explain it to others, but he himself does not become moved, because he lacks the internal mechanism for feeling with regard to this subject.

אַף עַל פִּי כֵן, מֵאַחַר שֶׁמִּתְכַּוֵּין בַּעֲבוֹדָתוֹ כְּדֵי לַעֲבוֹד אֶת הַמֶּלֶךְ, הֲרֵי זוֹ עֲבוֹדָה גְּמוּרָה. **nevertheless, since he serves with the intent to serve the King,** his service **is still considered a complete service.**

Fundamentally, the individual is engaged in doing mitzvot, learning Torah, and praying with the intent to serve God.

כִּי הַיִּרְאָה וְהָעֲבוֹדָה נֶחֱשָׁבוֹת לִשְׁתֵּי מִצְוֹת בְּמִנְיַן תרי״ג, וְאֵינָן מְעַכְּבוֹת זוֹ אֶת זוֹ. That is **because the fear and service** of God **are counted as two** distinct **mitzvot in the list of the 613 commandments, and they are not contingent on each other.**

Because the fear and service of God are two separate mitzvot,[11] they are not contingent on each other. There is a mitzva to fear God and there is also a mitzva to serve Him. Although these two commandments are connected to each other, failure to fulfill one does not prevent the fulfillment of the other. Consequently, a person can serve God and fulfill the mitzvot with acceptance of the yoke, and he thereby fulfills the mitzva of "Him you shall serve," even though he has not yet attained the fear of God.

וְעוֹד שֶׁבֶּאֱמֶת מְקַיֵּים גַּם מִצְוַת יִרְאָה, בַּמֶּה שֶׁמַּמְשִׁיךְ הַיִּרְאָה בְּמַחֲשַׁבְתּוֹ. **Moreover,** this person **actually fulfills the mitzva of the fear** of God **as well by virtue of drawing fear into his thought.**

---

11. According to the count of the *Ba'al Halakhot Gedolot*, as well as *Hasagot HaRamban* on Rambam, *Sefer HaMitzvot*, positive commandment 5.

CHAPTER 41

Although the fear and service of God are two separate mitzvot and can theoretically exist separately, in reality they do not, because when a person fulfills the mitzva of serving God, he likewise fulfills the mitzva of fearing God. The essence of serving God is that a person does what is required of him, which is equivalent to fearing God. This fear is not always apparent, and it is not necessarily an emotional or even an intellectual experience, yet it is there, in the background.

כִּי בְּשָׁעָה וְרֶגַע זוֹ עַל כָּל פָּנִים, מוֹרָא שָׁמַיִם עָלָיו, — This is **because, in any case, at that very moment he is invested with a fear of Heaven,**

When a person serves God, the fear of Heaven is upon him. When he performs a mitzva and is spiritually connected to his act, this means that he has accepted God's kingship upon himself. He might not sense the full significance of his acceptance, nevertheless, the yoke is upon him in a very real way, because he is doing what is required of him, and likewise, he is refraining from that which he should not be doing.

עַל כָּל פָּנִים כְּמוֹרָא מִפְּנֵי בָּשָׂר וָדָם הֶדְיוֹט לְפָחוֹת, שֶׁאֵינוֹ מֶלֶךְ, הַמַּבִּיט עָלָיו, שֶׁנִּמְנָע בַּעֲבוּרוֹ מִלַּעֲשׂוֹת דָּבָר שֶׁאֵינוֹ הָגוּן בְּעֵינָיו, שֶׁזּוֹ נִקְרֵאת יִרְאָה, — which is **at any rate no less than** his **fear of at least a common mortal,** someone **who is not** even **a king, who scrutinizes him, because of** whom he would inhibit himself **from doing anything** that the observer **would deem inappropriate. This is** also **considered fear,**

A person's fear of a king is linked to his recognition of the king's exalted state and the emotion that accompanies this. There is also a simpler sense of fear, when a person refrains from doing certain activities due to his social values, because doing them would make him uncomfortable, since he is wary of the opinions of others. Although this type of fear, a fear of "what will people say," is not like the sense of trepidation and exalted fear, it is still considered fear. The same applies to the fear of Heaven. Take, for example, a person who is afraid and does not steal because there are people around him. It is not because they are policemen, but just because he does not want to be seen stealing. If such a person fears Heaven, he will refrain from stealing for the very same reason even when there are no other people around. His fear of Heaven is on a low level because it does not involve recognition of the divine essence. But it is nonetheless fear, because the person refrains from acting against God's will as a result of it. And for its sake he acts for the sake of God, just as though he possessed the higher level of fear. Such a person seems to be lacking a spiritual connection with God; he does not understand or feel the fear of God. Yet he acts in a particular way that correlates to the fear of God, and his way of life is itself an expression of connection.

כְּמוֹ שֶׁאָמַר רַבָּן יוֹחָנָן בֶּן זַכַּאי לְתַלְמִידָיו (ברכות כח, ב): "יְהִי רָצוֹן שֶׁיְּהֵא מוֹרָא שָׁמַיִם עֲלֵיכֶם כְּמוֹרָא בָּשָׂר וָדָם כו'. תֵּדְעוּ, כְּשֶׁאָדָם עוֹבֵר עֲבֵירָה אוֹמֵר: שֶׁלֹּא יִרְאַנִי אָדָם" כו'. — as Rabbi Yoḥanan ben Zakkai told his students: "May it be His will that the fear of Heaven shall be upon you like the fear of a mortal.... Know that when a person commits a transgression, he says to himself, 'I hope that no man will see me...'" (Berakhot 28b).

When the students of Rabbi Yoḥanan ben Zakkai asked him, "Only as far as that?" he answered, "If a person would only reach that level of fear, that would be enough." After all, by virtue of having this fear, a person refrains from transgressing.

The "fear of a mortal" that Rabbi Yoḥanan ben Zakkai wished upon his disciples is not the fear of being killed or treated badly, but rather it refers to the shame a person feels when he does something that is considered indecent by society. It is the fear of disgrace and discomfort, whether in the eyes of a person or of God. Since this fear makes a person avoid evil just like a fear of tangible harm does, it too is considered fear.

רַק שֶׁיִּרְאָה זוֹ נִקְרֵאת 'יִרְאָה תַּתָּאָה' וְ'יִרְאַת חֵטְא' — However, this type of fear is referred to as lower fear and the fear of sin

The definition of lower fear is, stated simply, any concern a person has that prevents him from sinning. Just as a person does not defy social norms of the place that he lives in, a Jew does not sin because sinning goes against his basic spiritual makeup. As stated above, he is not willing to become separated from the Divine in any way. Therefore, the word *ḥet* in "fear of sin (*ḥet*)," signifies a deficiency or defect.[12]

שֶׁקּוֹדֶמֶת לְחָכְמָתוֹ, **that precedes** a person's **wisdom,**

This is not referring to a fear of something the person recognizes and really understands. Rather, it is an elementary fear that "precedes his wisdom." The language used here connects to a mishna that states, "Rabbi Ḥanina ben Dosa said: Anyone whose fear of sin precedes his wisdom, his wisdom is enduring, but anyone whose wisdom precedes his fear of sin, his wisdom is not enduring" (*Avot* 3:9). This shows that there is a fear – the "fear of sin" – that precedes wisdom.

וְיִרְאָה עִילָאָה׳ הוּא ׳יְרֵא בּוֹשֶׁת׳ כו׳. **whereas higher fear is** called **"fear out of shame,"** and so on.

Higher fear is fear that causes a person to turn aside from evil not because he fears punishment or because he fears sin, but because he is ashamed of sinning.[13] ☞

דְּאִית יִרְאָה וְאִית יִרְאָה כו׳. This is **because "there are two levels of fear,"** etc.

FEAR OUT OF SHAME

☞ This fear stems from feeling the presence of the divine, infinite, omnipotent greatness. As explained above, it is a combination of love and fear. Like love, this type of fear is based on an awareness of God's exaltedness, not just the superficial constraint imposed by embarrassment or fear of harm. Therefore, it is not merely a fear whereby one accepts authority, but it involves a recognition of greatness, exaltedness, and holiness, and as a result, an inability to carry out certain acts due to the shame that that recognition engenders. The Rabbis state with regard to higher fear, "Where there is no wisdom, there is no fear of God" (Mishna *Avot* 3:17), because only after a person has studied and contemplated this matter is he able to recognize God's exaltedness and feel shame before Him.

---

12. See *Likkutei Torah*, Num. 82a.
13. This does not mean that the person is ashamed of the sin; this is "fear of shame," which belongs to the lower fear mentioned above. See *HaLekaḥ VeHalibbuv*; *Hemshekh Mayim Rabbim* 136.

There is lower fear and higher fear.[14] Elsewhere[15] the author of the *Tanya* comments on the statement in *Avot*: "Where there is no wisdom, there is no fear of God; where there is no fear of God, there is no wisdom" (3:17). If this is the case, then where is the starting point? The answer is that there are two levels of fear. Lower fear precedes wisdom, "Where there is no fear of God, there is no wisdom." This is "fear of sin," the initial feeling of accepting the divine yoke, which must precede all the insights of wisdom. Higher fear, on the other hand, comes after wisdom. "Where there is no wisdom, there is no fear of God." After a person has learned and become wise, his wisdom influences his fear, and he possesses fear on a higher level.

It is thus clear that fear is not a single specific sensation, but rather a broad range of phenomena within the soul, from the highest level, where a person trembles in terror at God and His glory, to the level that is considered fear only in a practical sense, because the person is willing to accept authority by performing certain acts and refraining from other acts.

אֲבָל בְּלִי יִרְאָה כְּלָל - לָא פָּרְחָא לְעֵילָּא **However,** if a person has **no fear at all**, a mitzva that he performs **cannot soar upward**

When there is neither lower fear nor higher fear, a mitzva cannot ascend.

בְּאַהֲבָה לְבַדָּהּ, **with love alone,**

Even if a person had focused intent when performing a mitzva, but it only had the quality of love and no fear, the mitzva cannot ascend.

כְּמוֹ שֶׁהָעוֹף אֵינוֹ יָכוֹל לִפְרוֹחַ בִּכְנָף אֶחָד. דִּדְחִילוּ וּרְחִימוּ הֵן תְּרֵין גַּדְפִין **just as a bird cannot fly with** just **one wing.** That is **because the fear and love** of God **are compared to the two wings** of a bird

Here, the author of the *Tanya* returns to the example he used in the

---

14. See *Zohar, Hakdama* 11b; *Tikkunei Zohar* 5 and 74.
15. See chaps. 23, 43; *Likkutei Torah*, Lev. 6d, Num. 15b, 21a, 88a.

previous chapter. Love and fear are like the two wings of a mitzva. A mitzva cannot ascend with only one of these emotions.

(as written in *Tikkunei Zohar* 25b). [כְּמוֹ שֶׁכָּתוּב בַּתִּיקוּנִים].

Likewise, having **fear alone** is analogous to having only **one wing,** and a person's mitzva **cannot soar upward with it alone.** וְכֵן הַיִּרְאָה לְבַדָּהּ הִיא כְּנָף אֶחָד וְלָא פָּרְחָא בָּהּ לְעֵילָא.

There are, however, "love" people and there are "fear" people. There are those for whom the desire and longing for closeness and attachment is their basic perception. That is how they view reality and act within it. Consequently, it is possible that they have only love. Then there are others whose primary approach to reality is one of fear, and it is possible that they possess only fear.

Even though worship that only involves fear **is deemed the service of a servant,** nevertheless **a person must also** engage in service **in the manner of a son.** אַף שֶׁנִּקְרֵאת עֲבוֹדַת עֶבֶד וְצָרִיךְ לִהְיוֹת גַּם כֵּן בְּחִינַת בֵּן,

Although the *Tanya* stated above that the essence of the mitzva of divine service is the service performed by a servant, this is not enough. Just as it is impossible, and forbidden, to be a son without also being a servant, it is likewise forbidden to be a servant without also being a son. The service of a servant is in essence the acceptance of a yoke, but with regard to divine service, a person must not be satisfied with worship that stems only from accepting God's kingship.

This entails a person awakening, at least, the natural love hidden in his heart, לְעוֹרֵר הָאַהֲבָה הַטִּבְעִית עַל כָּל פָּנִים הַמְסוּתֶּרֶת בְּלִבּוֹ

Like the fear of God, the love of God too has various levels. A certain minimum is required. Just as in the case of fear, this love, which is contingent on the essential, internal connection between the Jewish people and God, lies within a person's essence, in the very fact that he is a Jew. It is innate within the Jewish people; it is embedded in the root of the Jewish essence, both on an individual and a universal level. This is why, when this connection is revealed, combining love, fear, and self-sacrifice, its power is greater than that of any other spiritual force.

שֶׁתְּהֵא בְּהִתְגַּלּוּת מוֹחוֹ עַל כָּל פָּנִים לִזְכּוֹר אַהֲבָתוֹ לַה' אֶחָד בְּמַחֲשַׁבְתּוֹ וּבִרְצוֹנוֹ לְדָבְקָה בּוֹ יִתְבָּרֵךְ.

so that at least he has the consciousness in his mind to recall in his thoughts his love for the one God and his will to cleave to God.

All Jews are capable of awakening this love within themselves. Even if a person does not reach the point of revelation in his heart, he can at least gain a general comprehension of the concept in his mind. The complete awakening of God's love in a person is an awakening of his heart, whereby he experiences a real, overt love. But even when a person only thinks about the love of God until his intellect accepts the idea that he should love God and cling to him, this too is considered the love of God.

וְזֹאת תִּהְיֶה כַּוָּנָתוֹ בְּעֵסֶק הַתּוֹרָה אוֹ הַמִּצְוָה הַזּוֹ, לְדָבְקָה בּוֹ נַפְשׁוֹ הָאֱלוֹקִית וְהַחִיּוּנִית וּלְבוּשֵׁיהֶן, כַּנִּזְכָּר לְעֵיל.

This should be a person's intention when he engages in Torah study or a specific mitzva: to bind his divine soul and vital soul, together with their garments, to God (as stated above (chaps. 23, 35, 37; see also chaps. 4, 14).

The intentions outlined here, that a person should have with regard to his love and fear of God, are merely the most basic ones. In the case of fear, this is the fear involved in the acceptance of a yoke and in the service of a servant. A person performs his service because God commanded it, because there are directives stating that "it is forbidden to do this," and "one must do that." Regarding love, the intention discussed here involves a Jewish person's innate need to be attached to God. This contains both an active and a passive aspect. The active aspect involves that which a person does in order to become connected and favored, to come close. The passive aspect involves that which a person refrains from doing so that he does not become distanced. If God does not approve of a particular act, the person will not do it, because if God does not want it, then neither does he. This person just wants to be with his Father. Thus, he recites *Shema* because his Father likes this, and he refrains from eating certain foods because his Father would not like it. This is not the love of a great tzaddik like Abraham; rather, it is the feeling of a simple individual who is filled entirely with love and who does what God loves because he wants to be with God.

אַךְ אָמְנָם אָמְרוּ רַבּוֹתֵינוּ ז"ל: "לְעוֹלָם אַל יוֹצִיא אָדָם עַצְמוֹ מִן הַכְּלָל" (ברכות מט, ב).

However, indeed this is insufficient, because **our Rabbis stated, "A person should never exclude himself from the community"** (*Berakhot* 49b).

20 Nisan

16 Nisan (leap year)

Up to this point, the intentions behind the mitzvot – namely, the love and fear of God – have been discussed in terms of the personal relationship between the individual and God. This relationship has been portrayed as having two polarities: God is on one end and the individual is on the other. Now the author of the *Tanya* will add another factor, which adds a new dimension. This new factor is a fundamental principle, which appears in various forms and which will be explained at length: A person must not exclude himself from the Jewish community.

לָכֵן יִתְכַּוֵּין לְיַחֵד וּלְדָבְקָה בּוֹ יִתְבָּרֵךְ מְקוֹר נַפְשׁוֹ הָאֱלוֹקִית וּמְקוֹר נַפְשׁוֹת כָּל יִשְׂרָאֵל שֶׁהוּא רוּחַ פִּיו יִתְבָּרֵךְ, הַנִּקְרָא בְּשֵׁם 'שְׁכִינָה'.

Therefore, a person **should have the intention to unite and attach** both **the source of his own divine soul, as well as the source of** all **the souls of all of Israel, with God. That source is the breath of God's utterance,** which is **known as the "Divine Presence"** [*Shekhina*],

When a person engages in learning Torah and performing mitzvot, he should have an additional level of intent: that he is acting not only for the sake of his own personal bond with God, but for the sake of the bond of all of Israel with God. This is because the origin of his own soul is the origin of all Jewish souls. This point at which all

Jewish souls are united has various names, all of which are different aspects of the same thing: "the congregation of Israel," "the word of God" and, in the words of the Talmud, "the Divine Presence."[16] From this perspective, the more "internal" and "self-centered" one's actions are, the more universal they are. This is not only the individual's experience, but that of the entire Jewish people. This world does not consist of separate individuals, but of "the word of God," the Divine Presence itself.

עַל שֵׁם שֶׁשּׁוֹכֶנֶת וּמִתְלַבֶּשֶׁת תּוֹךְ כָּל עָלְמִין לְהַחֲיוֹתָן וּלְקַיְּימָן. **because it is immanent** [*shokhenet*] **and clothed within all worlds,** in order **to grant them life and to sustain them.**

As explained in *Sha'ar HaYiḥud VeHa'emuna*, the *Shekhina* is the soul of the world, which dwells [*shokhenet*] within everything. It sustains all worlds and brings them into existence. It is the word of God within the ten utterances with which He created the world. This is the divinity which speaks within reality and constitutes reality.

וְהִיא הִיא הַמַּשְׁפַּעַת בּוֹ כֹּחַ הַדִּבּוּר הַזֶּה שֶׁמְּדַבֵּר בְּדִבְרֵי תּוֹרָה, אוֹ כֹּחַ הַמַּעֲשֶׂה הַזֶּה לַעֲשׂוֹת מִצְוָה זוֹ. **It is this very** Divine Presence **that invests a person with this faculty of speech to speak words of Torah or this capacity for action to perform this mitzva.**

A person's ability to speak, or to do anything else comes from the life force within him, the Divine Presence, which gives him life and sustains him. Therefore, when, by virtue of this force, he performs a mitzva or does anything else related to holiness, his intention should be that this act is not only an expression of his own personal being but of the Jewish collective of which he is a part. He is bringing about union and connection to God not merely with his own superficial existence but with the source of his soul and the souls of the entire Jewish nation, the Divine Presence.

---

16. See *Iggeret HaKodesh*, epistle 25.

וְיִחוּד זֶה הוּא עַל יְדֵי הַמְשָׁכַת אוֹר אֵין סוֹף בָּרוּךְ הוּא לְמַטָּה עַל יְדֵי עֵסֶק הַתּוֹרָה וְהַמִּצְוֹת שֶׁהוּא מְלוּבָּשׁ בָּהֶן,

This union of souls with God is **achieved by drawing down the light of the Infinite One, blessed be He, by means of engaging in Torah** study **and** performing **the mitzvot, since** this light **is enclothed in them,**

Each individual Jew is an expression of the Jewish people. Every Jew expresses in his life the entirety of the Divine Presence, because he is a part of the Divine Presence, since the entirety of his life is an expression of the divine life force in the world, which is the Divine Presence. In contrast, the divine existence that is not part of earthly reality but transcends it is revealed in Torah and mitzvot. When these two polarities, the individual and the mitzva, are united, a union is formed not only between the individual and the mitzva, but between God and all the worlds, which is to say between God and His Divine Presence. ☞

A PERSON'S PERFORMANCE OF A MITZVA CREATES A UNION OF GOD AND HIS DIVINE PRESENCE

☞ When a person performs a mitzva, he brings about this fusion of high and low, of the infinite with the world. The character of a mitzva is that it transforms something that is part of the world into an instrument for the divine light. For instance, wine effects the mitzva of *Kiddush*. However, this mitzva is not performed by itself. It is actualized only when a human being performs it. That is because the human being himself is this combination of high and low, the infinite and the world, in that he is a combination of soul and body. Thus, only in him and through him can the two connect with each other and enter into each other. It is therefore the human being who unites God and His Divine Presence, the light of the Infinite One, which is above and beyond all worlds, with those worlds.

All of existence is like an open electrical circuit. The circuit exists above and below, but there is a gap between the two halves. Once it is closed, nothing more is needed; it will operate on its own. In order for it to be closed, a human being must willingly take action by performing a mitzva. In this sense, all that performing a mitzva does is form a connection, just as pressing the on switch of an electric device activates it. All that the switch does is to connect the positive and negative electrical currents, which are active only when they are linked. A mitzva is this point of connection that joins God with the Divine Presence. It connects the essence beyond all things, the Creator Himself, with the essence within all things, the Divine Presence.

It is therefore understandable why almost all of the mitzvot involve something physical. A mitzva combines the abstract,

וְיִתְכַּוֵּין לְהַמְשִׁיךְ אוֹרוֹ יִתְבָּרֵךְ עַל מְקוֹר נַפְשׁוֹ וְנַפְשׁוֹת כָּל יִשְׂרָאֵל לְיַחֲדָן, וּכְמוֹ שֶׁיִּתְבָּאֵר לְקַמָּן פֵּירוּשׁ יִחוּד זֶה בַּאֲרִיכוּת, עַיֵּין שָׁם.

and by having the intent to draw God's light upon the source of one's own soul, as well as the souls of all of Israel, to unify them with God. (This union will be explained at length later in this chapter. See there.)

When a person performs a mitzva, he draws the light and will of God not only toward the specific aspect of his being on which the action is performed, but deep into his root and essence, where he is completely united with all Jewish souls and his being is an expression of the Divine Presence itself.[17]

intangible essence of the Creator with the core of His power as it is found in the material world. Hence, a mitzva must involve the material.

This is also why the pure soul must be in a physical body. A person is at the epicenter of powerful events, since he connects and activates immense forces. Therefore, he must be protected and isolated from high voltage so that he will not be burned as a result of his performing a mitzva. This explains the talmudic statement, "There is no reward [for performance of] a mitzva in this world" (*Kiddushin* 39b). The entire world is not large enough to contain the reward of one mitzva. Because the world is a place of concealment, a person can perform mitzvot in it, but for the same reason he cannot receive the reward for the mitzva, which is the revelation of the mitzva, in this world. A tzaddik taught that if one pair of *tzitzit* were to be brought into the Garden of Eden, the entire Garden of Eden would be immolated. Since the Garden of Eden is the place of revelation and reward, if a mitzva were to get there, it would cause such a revelation of holiness that the Garden could not bear it and it would be destroyed. The Talmud (*Shabbat* 88b) states that at Mount Sinai, which was a moment of revelation, "[With] each and every utterance that emerged from the mouth of the Holy One, blessed be He, the souls of the Jewish people left [their bodies]. As the verse states: 'My soul departed when he spoke' (Song 5:6)." However, it was not only upon Mount Sinai that God descended; He descends and unites with this world whenever a person performs a mitzva. A person's soul must be concealed and protected so that it will not "see," because if it did see, it would leave his body every time he studied Torah or performed a mitzva. Thus, at Mount Sinai our ancestors requested of Moses: "You speak with us and we will hear, and God should not speak with us, lest we die" (Ex. 20:16). Our ancestors gave up that spiritual experience and sight so that they would be able to continue to fulfill God's word.

---

17. See later in this chapter; and see *Likkutei Biurim*.

וְזֶהוּ פֵּירוּשׁ "לְשֵׁם יִחוּד קוּדְשָׁא בְּרִיךְ הוּא וּשְׁכִינְתֵּיהּ בְּשֵׁם כָּל יִשְׂרָאֵל".

This is the meaning of the formula recited before performing a mitzva, **"For the sake of uniting the Holy One, blessed be He, with His Divine Presence on behalf of all Israel."**

The kabbalists recite this formula before performing a mitzva. The Chabad custom is to say it before the *Barukh She'amar* prayer and to have the intent that it will apply to all the mitzvot that one will perform throughout the day. A mitzva is the revelation of "the Holy One, blessed be He," and a Jew is the revelation of "His Divine Presence." When the two combine, they "unite the Holy One, blessed be He, with His Divine Presence." When a person performs a mitzva, he must have intent that he is doing so not only as an individual, but as a part of the Jewish whole. Each individual's particular personality is part of the entirety of the Divine Presence, of the Jewish people, of *Kenesset Yisrael*, the congregation of Israel.

הַגָּהָה: (וְגַם עַל יְדֵי זֶה יִתְמַתְּקוּ גַּם כֵּן הַגְּבוּרוֹת בַּחֲסָדִים מִמֵּילָא, בְּהִתְכַּלְלוּת הַמִּדּוֹת וְיִחוּדָם עַל יְדֵי גִּילּוּי רְצוֹן הָעֶלְיוֹן בָּרוּךְ הוּא הַמִּתְגַּלֶּה לְמַעְלָה,

Gloss: Moreover, through this unification, the harsh **aspects of *Gevura* will also automatically be sweetened** by the gentle **aspects of Ḥesed, with the incorporation and unification of** these two **attributes. This results from the revelation of God's supernal will, which is revealed on high**

In this note, the author of the *Tanya* adds a comment addressed principally to those who are learned in Kabbala. In it he explains that the union achieved through a person's Torah learning and performance of a mitzva with the intention of uniting God and His Divine Presence do not pertain only to the blending of the light of the Infinite One with this world and the Divine Presence. Beyond this, certain entities in the higher realms are also combined and unified. Now the supernal will, which is higher than all the attributes, is revealed, and that brings about the unification and integration of these attributes. Even the attributes that are opposed to one another now operate in the same direction and for the same purpose. This may be compared to a king and his ministers; when the king reveals his will, all disputes among the ministers are eliminated.

בְּאִתְעָרוּתָא דִלְתַתָּא הוּא גִילוּיוֹ לְמַטָּה בְּעֵסֶק הַתּוֹרָה וְהַמִּצְוָה, שֶׁהֵן רְצוֹנוֹ יִתְבָּרֵךְ.

as the result of an awakening from below. This awakening **constitutes the manifestation** of the supernal will **below**, which occurs **due to** a person's **engaging in Torah** study **and mitzvot, which are God's will.**

Learning Torah and performing the mitzvot constitute the supernal will as it is expressed in our lower world. When a person fulfills the Torah and performs mitzvot, he fulfills the supernal will both on high and below, thereby awakening the revelation of the supernal will that comes from the highest heights.

וּכְמוֹ שֶׁכָּתוּב בְּאִדְּרָא רַבָּא (זהר חלק ג קלו, א) וּבְ׳מִשְׁנַת חֲסִידִים׳ מַסֶּכֶת ׳אֲרִיךְ אַנְפִּין׳ פֶּרֶק ד: שֶׁתַּרְיַ״ג מִצְוֹת הַתּוֹרָה נִמְשָׁכוֹת מֵחִיוָּורְתָא דַּאֲרִיךְ אַנְפִּין, שֶׁהוּא רָצוֹן הָעֶלְיוֹן, מְקוֹר הַחֲסָדִים).

This is **in accordance with what is written in the** *Idra Rabba* (*Zohar* 3:136a) **and in** *Mishnat Hasidim* **(tractate** *Arikh Anpin***, chap. 4) that the 613 commandments of the Torah are drawn from the whiteness** *of Arikh Anpin,* **which is the supernal will, the source of the aspects of Ḥesed.**

Mishnat Hasidim, a foundational work of Kabbala cited in the above gloss, explains that through a person's fulfillment of Torah and mitzvot here below, the source of the aspects of Ḥesed is revealed above. This causes an increasing abundance of Ḥesed to flow, which sweetens the aspects of *Gevura*.

This means that the union created through a person's fulfillment of a mitzva encompasses all of reality, upper and lower. Since the source of Torah and mitzvot transcends reality, fulfilling a mitzva brings about the complete unification of all the different and opposing aspects within reality (*Ḥesed* and *Gevura*) into one complete whole.

וְאַף שֶׁלִּהְיוֹת כַּוָּנָה זוֹ אֲמִתִּית בְּלִבּוֹ, שֶׁיִּהְיֶה לִבּוֹ חָפֵץ בֶּאֱמֶת יִחוּד הָעֶלְיוֹן הַזֶּה,

However, for a person to **sincerely have this intent in his heart,** the intent that his **heart will truly desire this supernal union,** — 21 Nisan

This should not merely be a formula that a person utters, but he should really mean it. However, it is true that even when a person really means it, not every intention is on the level of "sincerely having this intent in one's heart." Every decent person, if asked if he wants the union of God and His Divine Presence, will answer that he does. Why wouldn't he? However, when such a person must decide what he is willing to give up for that, the answer becomes more difficult.

צָרִיךְ לִהְיוֹת בְּלִבּוֹ אַהֲבָה רַבָּה לַה׳ לְבַדּוֹ, לַעֲשׂוֹת נַחַת רוּחַ לְפָנָיו לְבַד וְלֹא לְרַוּוֹת נַפְשׁוֹ הַצְּמֵאָה לַה׳.

he **must have a great love in his heart for God alone,** the desire **only to give** God **gratification and not** the desire **to quench his own soul's thirst for** closeness to **God.**

In order for a person's intent in performing a mitzva to genuinely be to connect the Divine Presence with the Holy One, blessed be He, he must have a great love in his heart for God alone, the desire only to give God gratification and not the desire to quench his own soul's thirst for closeness to God. It is true that wanting to worship God out of longing and desire, in order to quench one's thirst for Him, is a very high level. But the intention discussed here – that the Divine Presence and God's will be united – is even higher. Now the individual self is not in the center of his thoughts. He must forget his own desire, will, and self, and think of God alone. Not only must he forget his earthly desires, but even the fact that he yearns to become attached to God.

אֶלָּא כִּבְרָא דְּאִשְׁתַּדַּל בָּתַר אֲבוּי וְאִמֵּיהּ דְּרָחִים לוֹן יַתִּיר מִגַּרְמֵיהּ וְנַפְשֵׁיהּ כו׳ [כְּמוֹ שֶׁנִּזְכַּר לְעֵיל בְּשֵׁם רַעְיָא מְהֵימְנָא (זהר חלק ג רפא, א).]

Rather, he must be **"like a son who tends to his father and mother, loving them more than** he loves **his own body and soul..."** (as cited previously, in chap. 10, **from** *Raya Meheimna* [*Zohar* 3:281a]).

The love of a son who cares for his parents more devotedly than he cares for himself parallels the intent expressed in the formula, "For the sake of uniting the Holy One, blessed be He, with His Divine Presence."[18] The person's own self is no longer the subject of his intentions. His goal is not that he will cling to God; rather, his goal is that God and the Divine Presence will achieve completion, becoming one. To this end, a person must forget his own existence in his desire and thirst for connection with God. That is because although not contradictory, these two desires, to quench one's thirst for God and to unite God and the Divine Presence, cannot coexist in the same intention. In the place where God and the Divine Presence are united, nothing else exists, especially not the self.

Almost all of the love that a person experiences is to a great extent love of himself. A person loves himself by means of a different entity, meaning another person or even God; he desires to "quench his own soul's thirst for closeness to God." However, when a person acts for the sake of uniting God and His Divine Presence, he forgets himself. At that moment, he does not exist. He has no desires of his own. He wants only God's great desire to be fulfilled. This intention is on such a high level because it contains the deepest act of self-abnegation, of *bitul hayesh* and *bitul bimetziut* (the nullification of existence).

MORE THAN HIS OWN BODY AND SOUL

Self-sacrifice in the context of loving God means that a person renounces his own self. There are different levels of this. On the most basic level, it means the relinquishment of one's own will. The individual gives up the things he wants to have, one by one: his property, his enjoyments, and his way of life, culminating in his giving up his life itself: he sacrifices himself in order to sanctify God's name. However, even this is only a sacrifice of the body, because a person who dies sanctifying God's name does not feel that his spiritual essence has been damaged. On the contrary, he feels that it has become stronger. While he is indeed making a sac-

---

18. The Holy One, blessed be He, is a person's Father, and His Divine Presence is a person's Mother. And the *Zohar* states, "At that time, the Holy One, blessed be He, came and kissed him and said…You are the child of myself and the Divine Presence" (*Raya Meheimna* 3:281b).

מִכָּל מָקוֹם יֵשׁ לְכָל אָדָם לְהַרְגִּיל **Nevertheless,** although this goal is so elevated, **every person should accustom himself to** having **this intention,**
עַצְמוֹ בְּכַוָּנָה זוֹ,

This intention constitutes a very high level, and not everyone can reach it. However, even a person who does not think he can reach it should try to do so in any case. He should prepare himself, stating before performing a mitzva, "For the sake of uniting the Holy One, blessed be He, with His Divine Presence," in order to accustom himself to reaching that high level.

כִּי אַף שֶׁאֵינָהּ בֶּאֱמֶת לַאֲמִיתּוֹ **for even if he is not completely and absolutely sincere**
לְגַמְרֵי

The phrase *emet la'amito*, "absolute truth," which is found in several places in the *Tanya*, refers to the purest truth. Every intention of the heart has levels of refinement and purification: meaning, the extent to which a person truly holds the intention, and the extent to which his feelings are sincere, realistic, and alive within him.

---

rifice, this is in order to receive something even greater, deeper, and more meaningful. There is a higher level of self-sacrifice than this, whereby a person gives up his soul. He relinquishes his soul's desire, dreams, and yearning to reach God. This was the devotion of Abraham in his final test, the binding of Isaac. He had to give up his whole world, his entire experience of reality, his beliefs and visions, the justice and goodness that he had preached, and even his entire future. This is even greater than simple self-abnegation; it is the sacrifice of a person's innermost will, reaching to his very deepest "I." There was once a tzaddik who came to a town where there was no ritual bath. A wealthy man in the town had the means to pay for the construction of a ritual bath, but he refused to do so. The tzaddik promised him that if he would donate the money, then he, the tzaddik, would give this wealthy man his share in the World to Come. The tzaddik was willing to give up his share even in the World to Come, just so that another Jew would reach a point that he believed he needed to reach. There are numerous levels with regard to this type of self-sacrifice. Some are deep and painful. On some levels, a person must break himself, his will, and perhaps even his love for God. But his intent on all of these levels, as he has the intention of "For the sake of uniting the Holy One, blessed be He, with His Divine Presence," must be that of love and fear. That is because the essence of this intention is to shift the person's focus away from himself. It breaks down all personal elements and reveals his bond with God.

בְּלִבּוֹ, שֶׁיַּחְפּוֹץ בָּזֶה בְּכָל לִבּוֹ, מִכָּל מָקוֹם מְעַט מִזְעֵר חָפֵץ לִבּוֹ בָּזֶה בֶּאֱמֶת, — in his heart to the extent of wholeheartedly desiring this, nevertheless his heart does have some genuine, if minuscule, desire for this,

Although a person may not reach this level fully, his words and thoughts regarding his intention are nevertheless not false. They contain a kernel of truth, which grows at a point in the soul that is always prepared for it and truly wants it.

מִפְּנֵי אַהֲבָה הַטִּבְעִית שֶׁבְּלֵב כָּל יִשְׂרָאֵל לַעֲשׂוֹת כָּל מַה שֶּׁהוּא רְצוֹן הָעֶלְיוֹן בָּרוּךְ הוּא. — due to the natural love in every Jew's heart to do anything that constitutes God's supernal will.

This natural love constitutes the essential connection between God and the souls of Israel. By virtue of this love, a Jew naturally desires to do God's will. By virtue of this connection, his soul yearns and thirsts, at its root, for God. His soul longs to strengthen and sustain the connection, and all that this comprises, with God.

At its root, a Jew's natural love for God is not just his desire to love or fear God, but the character of his soul, its indescribable, unexplainable connection with God. Deep down, this is a love that is on the level of self-sacrifice and the binding of Isaac. Every Jew possesses at least a small degree of willingness, and some ability to achieve complete self-sacrifice. Even though he may not consciously feel it, the tiny seed that is the beginning of this feeling exists within him. Therefore, when a person expresses this, he is not saying anything false or mechanical. Rather, he is expressing something sincere that is latent and unconscious within him.

וְיִחוּד זֶה הוּא רְצוֹנוֹ הָאֲמִתִּי, — This union constitutes His true will,

By its nature, every Jewish soul in its truest and innermost will desires to fulfill God's will, which is the achievement of union between God and the Divine Presence.

וְהַיְינוּ יִחוּד הָעֶלְיוֹן שֶׁבָּאֲצִילוּת, — and it constitutes the higher unification in the world of *Atzilut* (Emanation),

CHAPTER 41

Here, the author of the *Tanya* describes the higher, all-encompassing aspect of this union. The union of God and the Divine Presence occurs primarily in the world of *Atzilut*. It is the unification of the levels of *Zeir Anpin* and *Malkhut* in the world of *Atzilut*. This union is in higher worlds that are above and beyond our own reality, and it relates to our world only indirectly. How then can a person in the lower world effect the union of God and the Divine Presence?

הַנַּעֲשֶׂה בְּאִתְעֲרוּתָא דִּלְתַתָּא עַל יְדֵי יִחוּד נֶפֶשׁ הָאֱלֹקִית וְהִתְכַּלְלוּתָהּ בְּאוֹר ה׳, הַמְלוּבָּשׁ בַּתּוֹרָה וּמִצְוֹת שֶׁעוֹסֶקֶת בָּהֶן, וְהָיוּ לַאֲחָדִים מַמָּשׁ, כְּמוֹ שֶׁנִּתְבָּאֵר לְעֵיל.

brought about by an awakening from below when a person **unifies and incorporates** his **divine soul into God's light,** that light **being enclothed in the Torah and mitzvot in which** the soul **is engaged** in learning or performing, **so that** the divine soul and God **literally become one (as explained above** (chaps. 5, 23).

This higher unification is immeasurably higher than a human being in this world. However, as will be explained, it is related to the lower unification that a person can effect in this world. A human being's "divine soul" represents the Divine Presence in its totality, and "God's light" refers to the Holy One, blessed be He. When a person engages in Torah or mitzvot, and especially when he does so wholeheartedly, he becomes one with the Torah or the mitzva. With regard to prayer, a verse states, "I am prayer" (Ps. 109:4).[19] When a person prays, he is not merely himself. Rather, he is the prayer itself; he has become prayer. The Maggid of Mezeritch[20] is quoted as having remarked on the verse "It was as the musician played [*kenagen hamenagen*]" (II Kings 3:15) that the word *nagen* refers not to the musician but to the musical instrument. There is a stage at which a musician becomes the instrument on which he plays. Likewise, when, as a person performs a mitzva, he connects and unites his soul with it, that bond rises beyond the individual and his experience.

---

19. See *Torah Or* 93a.
20. See *Or Torah* 387a in the notes.

כִּי עַל יְדֵי זֶה מִתְיַחֲדִים גַּם כֵּן מְקוֹר הַתּוֹרָה וְהַמִּצְוֹת, שֶׁהוּא הַקָּדוֹשׁ בָּרוּךְ הוּא, עִם מְקוֹר נַפְשׁוֹ הָאֱלוֹקִית הַנִּקְרָא בְּשֵׁם שְׁכִינָה,

That is **because through this, the Source of the Torah and mitzvot – i.e., the Holy One, blessed be He – also unites with the source of** the person's **divine soul,** that source being **called the Divine Presence,**

When a person performs a mitzva that he has been commanded to perform, that creates a connection between him and the One who commands it. More fundamentally, this is the connection between the Divine Presence, of which a person's divine soul is a spark, and the Holy One, blessed be He, who has given the Torah and ordered the performance of the mitzvot.

שֶׁהֵן בְּחִינַת 'מְמַלֵּא כָּל עָלְמִין' וּבְחִינַת 'סוֹבֵב כָּל עָלְמִין' כְּמוֹ שֶׁנִּתְבָּאֵר בְּמָקוֹם אַחֵר בַּאֲרִיכוּת.

and **these** two **correspond to the aspect of "fills all worlds" and the aspect of "encompasses all worlds,"** as explained elsewhere at length (chaps. 48, 49).

The Holy One, blessed be He, and the Divine Presence constitute God's immanence, which fills all of reality, and God's transcendence, which is beyond all reality.[21] ☞

THE UNIFICATION OF THAT WHICH FILLS ALL WORLDS AND THAT WHICH ENCOMPASSES ALL WORLDS

☞ The union of God and His Divine Presence is a union of all reality, from one end to the other. There is a flow, and even an identification, between the immanent and the transcendent, between the divine power that flows in the world and gives it life and the divine essence beyond it, which is concealed from all thought and understanding. When this connection is formed, a light turns on and shines upon all the worlds, from one end to the other.

With this union, the "contradictory" relationship between the Creator and the created disappears or is in any case blurred for a time. The essence of creation is the gap between "encompasses all worlds," and "fills all worlds." When the union between these two will occur totally, in all possible ways and on all levels, that will be the completion and end of creation, the end of days, when "the Lord will be one and His name one" (Zech. 14:9). Nevertheless, in

---

21. This subject is discussed at length in chaps. 48 and 49.

אֲבָל יִחוּד נַפְשׁוֹ וְהִתְכַּלְלוּתָהּ בְּאוֹר ה׳ לִהְיוֹת לַאֲחָדִים, בָּזֶה חָפֵץ כָּל אָדָם מִיִּשְׂרָאֵל בֶּאֱמֶת לַאֲמִיתּוֹ לְגַמְרֵי, בְּכָל לֵב וּבְכָל נֶפֶשׁ,

However, unlike the matter of this cosmic unification, **every Jew fully desires with absolute sincerity, with all** his **heart and soul, the union and incorporation of his own soul into God's light to become one,**

22 Nisan

"Great love," which is like that of a son who loves his father and mother more than he loves himself, a state in which a person thinks of "uniting the Holy One, blessed be He, with His Divine Presence," and not about himself, is apparently the level of a select few. However, every Jew truly possesses the absolutely sincere level of loving God to the degree that he desires to cling to God and have his soul unite with Him.

As mentioned, only a select few can reach a point at which these matters are a living experience for them. Only a person on such a level can sincerely feel that he does not care about himself at all but cares only for the honor of the Divine. Nevertheless, there is always an aspect of truth when any Jew says, "For the sake of uniting the Holy One, blessed be He, with His Divine Presence." That is because effecting such union, even if one does so incompletely, is overall the fulfillment of the purpose of reality. Therefore, even if a person does not know that, and even if he is busy with endless other matters, in some concealed place deep within him, his soul desires this union. And when a person becomes accustomed to thinking in this way and reciting the formula, "For the sake of uniting the Holy One, blessed be He, with His Divine Presence," he awakens something in himself. He is saying something that has a deep impact inside him.

our days, there are intermediate degrees of closeness and distance, of "touching and not touching." There are always connections passing between "encompasses all worlds" and "fills all worlds," and these connections illuminate the world. Some connections involve all the worlds. Some connections relate to time: whether a general or a personal time of favor, whether recurring or a one-time event. Sabbath, which constitutes an elevation of the worlds, is a level of the union of God and the Divine Presence, and this is true of all the other special days of the year. There are also personal connections that come about whenever a person performs a mitzva. When a person performs a mitzva, even if he does so on the lowest possible level, the connection reaches all the way up to the highest level. What the person is doing with his mitzva performance, which is a type of awakening from below, is to close the circuit that connects the high to the low, this world to that which is beyond it.

מֵאַהֲבָה הַטִּבְעִית הַמְסוּתֶּרֶת בְּלֵב כָּל יִשְׂרָאֵל לְדָבְקָה בּה' וְלֹא לִיפָּרֵד וְלִהְיוֹת נִכְרָת וְנִבְדָּל חַס וְשָׁלוֹם מִיִּחוּדוֹ וְאַחְדוּתוֹ יִתְבָּרֵךְ בְּשׁוּם אֹפֶן, אֲפִילוּ בִּמְסִירַת נֶפֶשׁ מַמָּשׁ.

coming **from the natural love hidden in the heart of every Jew to cleave to God and not to be parted, excised, or separated, God forbid, from** God's **unity and oneness in any way, even** if that means **actually sacrificing his life.**

This natural, concealed love, which has been discussed in previous chapters, has two aspects. One aspect is a person's desire to draw nearer to and cling to God, and the other aspect is a person's drive to prevent himself from growing detached from God in any way, even if this involves self-sacrifice to the point of dying. ☞ ☞

NATURAL, HIDDEN LOVE

☞ It is possible that a person will not feel this love. He might need to be shaken up in order to understand that he has within himself this love of God. In other areas as well, a person may ordinarily be unaware of a central factor in his life. For example, a person is not usually cognizant of the presence of his heart, but if something happens to his heart, particularly something bad, he becomes aware of it. There may be a person who is on the lowest possible level, a great sinner who, if told that he possesses the love of God, would laugh out loud, because he has never even considered this or felt that it was relevant to him. And yet, if this person is forced to decide whether he belongs with God or not, that love will undoubtedly arise in him, so much so that he will be willing to give up his life for it. The explanation for this is that the love exists within him; it is his very essence. Whether or not it will be revealed, and whether that revelation will occur through an act of life or an act of death, is only a question of his character, circumstances, and environment.

The desire to cling to God and not be separated from Him exists within a person's soul, and the revelation and propagation of this throughout the soul's powers and "garments" depends only on the person himself: on his ability to remove restraints, screens, and *kelippot* (husks of impurity). Some screens are comprised of coarse *kelippot*, such as when a person follows his desires. This blocks and prevents him from pursuing his love of God. And there are also more subtle *kelippot*, such as ideological *kelippot*, which are in a way even worse because, due to their subtle and intangible nature, they are especially difficult to remove. Furthermore, those *kelippot* are more a mix of good and evil than the coarse *kelippot* and are thus more entwined within the person's soul. If a person desecrates the Sabbath due to his desires, he at least knows where he stands; he knows that he is not on the side of holiness. But if he violates the Sabbath as an act of rebellion, in order to "anger" God, he may believe from his perspective that his act is one of holiness. A person acting on the basis of ideology could continue in this way, building entire false edifices

The author of the *Tanya* now shifts discussion of this love, by virtue of which every Jew is able to sacrifice his life to sanctify God's name, in a different direction, one that is much more important and significant: that a person can reveal this love not only with his death, as in being immolated to sanctify God's name, but he can also reveal it through his daily divine service, in the acts that he can perform in the here and now.

וְעֵסֶק הַתּוֹרָה וּמִצְוֹת וְהַתְּפִלָּה הוּא גַּם כֵּן עִנְיַן מְסִירַת נֶפֶשׁ מַמָּשׁ. **Engaging in learning Torah, performing mitzvot, and praying is also tantamount to actually sacrificing one's life.**

of fear and love of God. The verse states, "God made this corresponding to that" (Eccles. 7:14), meaning that there is a balance in this world between good and evil. Thus, in opposition to the love for God that exists within every Jew, every Jew also has a strong, inexplicable tendency toward idol worship. The distinguishing *kelippa* of the Jewish people does not relate to forbidden relationships or bloodshed, but to idol worship, in all its various shades and levels. The Jewish people become fixated on anything that involves a relationship to the Divine, whether it is holy or not.

WHO IS A JEW?

☞ This love is so characteristic of every Jew that its existence is, practically speaking, the only real definition and test of Jewish identity. This definition is loftier and more profound than any other, including a conversion certificate, or even a record of one's Jewish ancestry. The famous convert, Count Potocki, is reported to have said the following: The Talmud states that before God gave the Torah to Israel, He approached all the nations, asking if they wanted to receive the Torah, but they did not. Then He asked Israel, and they wanted it. How is it possible that all Jews, in all generations, including "him who is here with us standing today... and with him who is not here with us today" (Deut. 29:14), wanted to receive the Torah, without a single exception? And likewise, how is it possible that among all the gentiles of all the generations, there was not one individual who wanted to receive the Torah? He answers that there were Jews who did not want it, and there were gentiles who did. And the matter has been straightened out over the course of the generations: Those gentiles who said that they wanted it eventually found their way in, and those Jews who did not want it left. Similarly, the statement is made in the name of the Ba'al Shem Tov: There was never a gentile who converted, nor a Jew who renounced Judaism. What takes place only demonstrates the person's original essence. Thus, there really is no external sign that can definitively identify a Jew. The only sign is this point of concealed love. If it exists within a person, if he has the power to give up his life to sanctify God's name, then he is a Jew.

Usually, when a person thinks about the idea of self-sacrifice, he imagines a person giving up his life. However, that is not necessarily what is involved. Daily Torah learning, performance of mitzvot, and praying are also considered self-sacrifice. As has been explained, self-sacrifice is simply the relinquishment of the self for the sake of God. Stated more fundamentally, it is the relinquishment of all the possessions and boundaries of the self. This process of self-sacrifice occurs whenever a person engages in Torah or a mitzva. He could have chosen to engage in many other activities that would have served his ego in this world, yet he chose to engage at that moment in serving God. At that time, he is sacrificing himself for God. This is the point that was discussed at the beginning of the chapter with regard to lower fear and the service of a servant. When a person performs a mitzva because it brings him enjoyment, as lofty as that may be, he is not engaged in an act of self-sacrifice. However, when a person does not understand what he is doing and does not feel anything pleasing, when he relinquishes his personal desires, which are in direct opposition to the actions that he now undertakes in serving God, he is engaged in an act of real self-sacrifice. To illustrate, if a person is told to mail a letter, at the moment that he does so, he is not himself. He is not expressing his own personality or desire, but only that of somebody else. He becomes an emissary, and becomes subsumed with respect to the one who sent him. The less he understands the meaning of his act, the more he is nullified, even though this is only a basic level of nullification and relinquishment of the self. Likewise, within a person's performance of any mitzva, learning of any portion of the Torah or any prayer, there is something of this movement of self-sacrifice, of his relinquishing his personal desires out of submission to God's will.

כְּמוֹ בְּצֵאתָהּ מִן הַגּוּף בִּמְלֹאת שִׁבְעִים שָׁנָה, שֶׁאֵינָהּ מְהַרְהֶרֶת בְּצָרְכֵי הַגּוּף, אֶלָּא מַחֲשַׁבְתָּהּ מְיֻחֶדֶת וּמְלֻבֶּשֶׁת בְּאוֹתִיּוֹת הַתּוֹרָה וְהַתְּפִלָּה, שֶׁהֵן דְּבַר ה' וּמַחֲשַׁבְתּוֹ יִתְבָּרֵךְ, וְהָיוּ לַאֲחָדִים מַמָּשׁ, שֶׁזֶּהוּ כָּל עֵסֶק הַנְּשָׁמוֹת

This is **comparable** to the soul **leaving the body after** the proverbial **seventy years,** at which point **it no longer considers the body's needs. Rather, its thought is focused on and invested in the letters of the Torah and prayer, which are the word and thought of God, and they,** the soul and the letters,

בְּגַן עֵדֶן, כְּדְאִיתָא בַּגְּמָרָא (ברכות יז, א) וּבַזֹּהַר (חלק ב פג, א). **actually become one – because** indeed, this is all that souls are occupied with in the Garden of Eden (as stated in the Talmud (*Berakhot* 17a) **and in the Zohar** (2:83a).

Proverbially, a human life in this world lasts seventy years. As the verse states, "The days of our lives in it are seventy years" (Ps. 90:10). When a person dies and his soul is separated from his body, it no longer worries about the affairs that bothered it so much in this life, such as his bank account and mortgage payments. It is, however, very much concerned about its connection to God. In this sense, when a person performs a mitzva, prays, or learns Torah, he is in the world of souls, in his own Garden of Eden. At that time, he leaves his ordinary reality of the life of the body and the physical world, which usually seem so important and urgent, and moves instead into a realm where the soul is paramount and where he is close to and united with God.

אֶלָּא שֶׁשָּׁם מִתְעַנְּגִים בְּהַשָּׂגָתָם וְהִתְכַּלְלוּתָם בְּאוֹר ה'. The **only** difference is **that there,** in the Garden of Eden, people **delight in their comprehension of God's light and their incorporation within it.**

Nevertheless, there is a difference between a person in this world who keeps mitzvot and his soul in the Garden of Eden. The difference lies not in the extent of the person's clinging to God, but in the extent of his awareness of this clinging. A person who performs a mitzva or learns Torah in this world cannot see its effect and thus he is not properly aware of the significance of what he is doing. Therefore, he does not always enjoy it. His thought, which is engaged with the Torah at that moment, is in another world, soaked in attachment to God as much as it would be if he were in the Garden of Eden. However, since the person himself is in this world, which is very far from that realm, he cannot take pleasure in the attachment.

When a person's soul is in this world, in his physical body, it is "deafened" by the noises created by our senses and physical experiences, until it becomes unable to perceive spiritual sensations except in their lowest form. Only after his life in this world has ended, when his soul has separated from his body and all of these noises are silenced, does it begin to hear and see. Then, little by little, another world is revealed to it.

In this world, the act of a mitzva gives an appearance comparable to a rudimentary sketch that does not yet display an image. A person gives charity to the poor, and apart from a very limited perception of cause and effect, he does not see what he has accomplished or the significance of his act, including how it plays out in other worlds. In contrast, in the Garden of Eden the soul is allowed to see. It sees these same things, but in a completely different way. The lines of the sketch connect to one another and take on meaning. This sketch becomes a silent, black-and-white movie, and then the frames take on color and sound. Suddenly, everything is different. Everything becomes clear. What was important before is no longer important, and what was unimportant before is now the center of everything.

וְזֶהוּ שֶׁתִּקְּנוּ בִּתְחִלַּת בִּרְכוֹת הַשַּׁחַר קוֹדֶם הַתְּפִלָּה: "אֱלֹהַי נְשָׁמָה וכו' וְאַתָּה נְפַחְתָּהּ כו' וְאַתָּה עָתִיד לִיטְּלָהּ מִמֶּנִּי" כו',

This is why the Sages **instituted** reciting **at the beginning of the morning blessings, before the prayers, "My God, the soul** that You have placed within me is pure. You have created it; You have formed it. **You have breathed it into me... and You will ultimately take it from me...."**

THE JOY OF A MITZVA IN THIS WORLD

In this world a person can also feel enjoyment from Torah and mitzvot, but this is not usually the pleasure of the mitzva itself, of incorporation within God's light. Rather, it is a this-worldly pleasure. A person who learns Torah may derive intellectual pleasure from it, just as a person who participates in a meal for the sake of a mitzva may enjoy the taste of the food. This is in keeping with the parable that hasidim use to explain why they partake of alcohol: There was once a man who had no legs and who was carried on the back of a deaf man. Once, they arrived in a place where an orchestra was playing. The legless man wanted to dance but he had no legs, and the deaf man could not hear the music. So the legless man gave the deaf man some liquor. As a result, the deaf man began to leap around and dance, and thus the cripple was able to dance to the music by proxy. Like the deaf man, the body

Why do we recite this prayer? What is the purpose of declaring that the soul is actually God's and that He placed it within the person? And why recite it at this time and place, before the morning prayers?

כְּלוֹמַר, מֵאַחַר שֶׁאַתָּה נְפַחְתָּהּ בִּי וְאַתָּה עָתִיד לִיטְּלָהּ מִמֶּנִּי - לָכֵן מֵעַתָּה אֲנִי מוֹסְרָהּ וּמַחֲזִירָהּ לְךָ לְיַחֲדָהּ בְּאַחְדוּתֶךָ.

That is to say, "Since You have breathed my soul into me, and ultimately You will take it from me, I therefore from now already relinquish it and return it to You, to unite it with Your oneness."

Prayer is an act of self-sacrifice comprised of attachment and union with God. Before praying, a person declares that he is ready for that

does not "hear." And like the legless man, the soul has no hands with which to perform mitzvot. So what do we do in order to worship God with the joy of a mitzva? We cause the body to feel joy and pleasure for its own reasons. And when the body dances, the soul dances as well.

THE JOY OF A MITZVA IN THE GARDEN OF EDEN

☞ In this world, a person does not feel the attachment to God and the delight of being incorporated into God's light that derive from performing a mitzva. A person experiences this only in the World to Come. By way of illustration, the world around us is full of electromagnetic waves that carry important information as well as meaningless nonsense, and tuneful melodies as well as mere noises. Had a person been given an additional sense through which he could absorb this information directly, his sense of this world would be incomparably changed. As long as we do not have that sense, we only perceive a part of that spectrum (as light). A person can operate a worldwide communication system without having even the smallest understanding of how the electrical signals he is transmitting work. Likewise, a person in this world does not possess the "sense" that would enable him to directly experience a higher world. Therefore, he cannot truly appreciate the nature of the Torah he is learning or the mitzva he is performing. When a person engages in Torah in this world, he is able to hear only certain "tones" of that activity, which comprise a negligible component of what is really taking place at that moment. In contrast, in the innumerable levels of the Garden of Eden, the soul is capable of perceiving an additional "wavelength." The person then perceives how the act of a mitzva ascends into the highest realms, even beyond the world of *Atzilut*, and he perceives the sublime tones that it emits, which rise into other, infinitely exalted realms. At every stage the soul, so to speak, goes through its life again, including all that it did and experienced in this world, but in a different way, with a different level of revelation.

attachment and union. He announces, in the words of King David, "It is from Your hand, and everything is Yours" (I Chron. 29:16). The person is essentially saying, "Since the soul is Yours and You are going to take it from me in the future, all I can do in the meantime – while it is, so to speak, in my possession – is to do the same: to give You my soul for Your sake."

וּכְמוֹ שֶׁכָּתוּב: "אֵלֶיךָ ה' נַפְשִׁי אֶשָּׂא" (תהלים כה, א). **This is also** the intent of **the verse "To You, Lord, I lift up my soul"** (Ps. 25:1),

The simple meaning of these words is, "I lift my soul up to God. I hand it over, returning it to You." The implication of this is shocking; it describes an actual transfer of one's soul to God.

וְהַיְינוּ עַל יְדֵי הִתְקַשְּׁרוּת מַחֲשַׁבְתִּי בְּמַחֲשַׁבְתְּךָ וְדִיבּוּרִי בְּדִיבּוּרְךָ, בְּאוֹתִיּוֹת הַתּוֹרָה וְהַתְּפִלָּה. **meaning,** I lift up and relinquish my soul to You **by binding my thought with Your thought and my speech with Your speech** through **the letters of the Torah and prayer,**

This certainly does not mean that a person should harm himself and certainly not take his own life. Rather, when a person learns Torah, he is thinking God's thought. When he says the words of the Torah aloud, he is saying God's words. God is saying the words of Torah, and the individual says it along with Him. It is as though God Himself is speaking from within the person, as in the verse, "My words that I have placed in your mouth" (Isa. 59:21).[22] The person's enunciation might not be exactly right, but the speech is God's and the thought is God's. And this is truly an act of devotion and self-nullification, true self-sacrifice, as in the verse, "To You, Lord, I lift up my soul."

וּבִפְרָט בַּאֲמִירָה לַה' לְנֹכַח, כְּמוֹ "בָּרוּךְ אַתָּה", וּכְהַאי גַּוְונָא. **especially** when addressing God directly **in the prayers, as in "Blessed are You, God," and the like.**

---

22. See *Torah Or* 67a.

There are prayers that are predicated on our sense of distance from God. They praise God "in His heavenly stronghold," and describe Him as "He who spoke and the world came into being." Other prayers and blessings are based on our sense of closeness to Him, in which we address God directly. In these latter prayers, a person should contemplate that he is conversing with God, speaking to him in the second person as "You." This is the closest that a person can come to God, whether in this world or the World to Come. ☞

PRAYER AND REVELATION IN THIS WORLD

☞ It is precisely in this world, in a state of unawareness, that we are so close to God. Other states may be more spiritual, and we may be more aware in them, but we are not as close. Right now, we are carrying out the greatest acts and are in the strongest light, and consequently now is the time when we do not see. This is because if we sensed even a small part of what we were doing, we would be immolated.

The Ḥozeh of Lublin, who became famous for his spiritual insight, studied in his youth under the Maggid of Mezeritch. As was common among hasidic rebbes at the time, the Maggid would usually pray alone. Only when he reached *Ein Kelokeinu*, at the end of the morning prayer service, would he summon ten of his disciples in order to finish the prayer with a *minyan*, a prayer quorum. One day, one person was missing from the *minyan*, and since the Ḥozeh was always nearby, he was pulled into the room. When the Maggid saw the Ḥozeh, the Maggid said to his disciples, "Why have you brought him? He is a layabout." They began to recite *Ein Kelokeinu*, and because of what he saw on the spiritual plane, the Ḥozeh immediately fainted. The Maggid said to his disciples, "See? I told you he was a layabout. Remove him and bring someone else who does not see, who is able to say *Ein Kelokeinu*" (Rabbi Shlomo Yosef Zevin, *Sippurei Ḥasidim, Torah* 452; *Reshimot Devarim* 4:116–117). Our ability to recite the entire morning prayer from *Ma Tovu* until *Aleinu* in the short time that we assign to it is due to the fact that we are not aware of what we are saying. Based on the verse, "Come you and your entire household into the ark [*teiva*]" (Gen. 7:1), the Ba'al Shem Tov instructed that a person enter into each word (*teiva*) of prayer with all his vigor, all his concerns, and all that he holds dear (see *Ba'al Shem Tov al HaTorah, Parashat Noaḥ* 15). If a person were to approach prayer in this way, he would pray for increasingly lengthy periods of time. However, in general, in order to be able to function in this world and carry out a certain amount of obligatory Torah study, mitzva observance, and prayer, a person cannot allow himself to feel all this. If a person's eyes are uncovered, he cannot fulfill his duties. Those people who had extraordinary ability of spiritual sight had to accustom themselves not to see, to take care to always be protected. They are like welders who work with extremely strong light. They must wear dark goggles so that they will not see the light that they are producing. If a welder were to directly see the light he is producing, he would

23 Nisan
17 Nisan (leap year)

וְהִנֵּה בַּהֲכָנָה זוֹ, שֶׁל מְסִירַת נַפְשׁוֹ לַה׳, יַתְחִיל בְּבִרְכוֹת הַשַּׁחַר: "בָּרוּךְ אַתָּה" כו׳.

With this preparation of relinquishing one's soul to God, one can begin to recite **the morning blessings: "Blessed are You...."**

When a person knows that his soul is essentially bound to God, and when he is prepared to relinquish it to Him, then he is open to the Divine and is ready to begin praying and learning Torah. In order for the words of prayer and Torah to have value, the person speaking them must be connected to God, which means that he must relinquish his soul to God. Otherwise, what he is doing is only a game that he is playing by himself, whether to gain emotional or intellectual pleasure, in which he may or may not be including the attempt to create a connection with the Creator. The only expression of a true, fundamental relationship between a human being and his Creator is the human being's total and unconditional surrender of his soul to God. The willingness to relinquish one's soul exists within every Jew, but since often this is spontaneously revealed only in moments of crisis, in normal times it must be actively evoked. A person prepares his soul for such an awakening by saying "My God, the soul that You have placed within me..." before he begins an act of divine service such as a mitzva, Torah study, or prayer. ☞

be blinded. Prayer is the highest level of self-sacrifice, even in the case of a person who does not see. Therefore, before praying, a person must recite the formula, "My God, the soul that You have placed within me...," in preparation for relinquishing his soul and raising it in prayer.

PREPARATION FOR PRAYER

☞ The work involved in preparing for prayer is a serious matter, particularly in Hasidism. There were places where this preparation used to take more time and effort than the act of prayer itself. The prayer itself can take a moment, but in order for it to constitute a union of the Holy One, blessed be He, with His Divine Presence, for it to truly join together the upper and lower worlds, a person must engage in thorough, sometimes prolonged, preparation. The hasidim of Kotzk were especially known for this. Some would spend most of the day preparing for prayer, and toward evening they would begin the morning prayer. Among the followers of the Kotzker Rebbe was Rabbi Leibele Eiger, who himself later became a rebbe. Once, when he was about to return home, Rabbi Leibele asked the Rebbe what he should say to his

וְכֵן בַּהֲכָנָה זוֹ יַתְחִיל לִלְמוֹד שִׁעוּר קָבוּעַ מִיָּד אַחַר הַתְּפִלָּה.

Likewise, with this preparation one should commence with a regular course of Torah study **immediately after** morning **prayers.**

As it is written in *Shulḥan Arukh*,[23] immediately after prayer one must set aside time to engage in the words of Torah, in order to connect the Torah to the prayer.[24] One should proceed with the same preparation for the Torah study: "To You, Lord, I lift up my soul," relinquishing his soul to God just as he did before praying.

וְכֵן בְּאֶמְצַע הַיּוֹם, קוֹדֶם שֶׁיַּתְחִיל לִלְמוֹד, צְרִיכָה הֲכָנָה זוֹ לְפָחוֹת.

Also, during the day, before one begins to study Torah, **this preparation is the minimum requirement.**

A person must return to have this intention in preparation for Torah study. There are many levels of preparation of the soul. As mentioned illustrious grandfather, Rabbi Akiva Eiger, when he asked about the prayer customs of the hasidim. The Kotzker Rebbe replied, "Tell him that there is an explicit *halakha*: A laborer who was hired to cut down trees and spent most of the day sharpening his ax must receive his wages in full as one who worked all day cutting down trees." For a person's prayer to be worthy, he must clean, sharpen, and prepare the tools, and this may take time, but it too is considered part of the prayer. A cannon is fired in an instant, but for the shot to be precise, it must be aimed accurately, and this requires time. In a sense, the core of divine service is preparation, for if done properly, it positions the person and the prayer or mitzva in such a way that everything else falls into place. This is in keeping with Rabbi Ḥanina ben Dosa's statement: "If my prayer is fluent in my mouth, I know that it is accepted" (Mishna *Berakhot* 5:5). When prayer is not a painful process, when Torah study no longer involves a painful struggle, this is a sign that the preparation was good and that everything else is developing naturally.

---

23. *Shulḥan Arukh, Oraḥ Ḥayyim* 155:1; see also *Shulḥan Arukh HaRav* there.
24. It is explained in several hasidic sources, with regard to the talmudic idea that one's prayer should be adjacent to one's bed (*Berakhot* 5b), that Torah study should directly follow prayer (see *Likkutei Torah*, Deut. 96b). The Tzemaḥ Tzedek explains: This is because via prayer the revelation of the actual light of *Ein Sof*, which encompasses all worlds, is drawn down, and when one learns Torah immediately after this, it flows to the Torah as well.

previously, there are extremely high levels, where a person achieves perfect preparation and implementation of a holy act. However, only exceptional individuals can reach such levels. That is something that cannot be required of everyone. However, there is a minimal level of preparation, which each individual must require of himself. This involves declaring before prayer and Torah study that he relinquishes his soul to God.

כַּנּוֹדָע שֶׁעִיקַּר הַהֲכָנָה לִשְׁמָהּ לְעַכֵּב הוּא בִּתְחִלַּת הַלִּימוּד בַּבֵּינוֹנִים. **As it is known, for *beinonim* (intermediate-level people) the principal preparation for achieving the indispensable intent to perform a mitzva for its own sake is upon commencing Torah study.**

That which is required of a *beinoni* is, as stated previously, another way of speaking about that which is required of every individual (chap. 14). For every individual, the indispensable, required intention before he learns Torah, without which his learning is not considered to be within the scope of Torah study, must take place before he begins his learning. A tzaddik always has intent. Since his divine service is not only the language of truth but truth itself, his experience of attachment to God is continuous. But that is not the case regarding a *beinoni*. His intention is only the language of truth and not truth itself (see chap. 13). Thus, his intention is superficial and requires particular attention and concentration. Were he to focus on constantly maintaining that concentration, his ability to learn Torah might be compromised. Therefore, he is permitted to not maintain his intent to be attached to God. If a person cannot attain both perfect intention and proper Torah study, he should at least be sure to have proper intent at the beginning of his learning. ☞

SEPARATING FROM GOD DURING TORAH STUDY

☞ The Ba'al Shem Tov is quoted as having commented on the talmudic statement, "A person should only take leave of his friend from [involvement in a] matter of *halakha*" (*Berakhot* 31a), that "his friend" refers to God. There are numerous verses

CHAPTER 41

וּכְמוֹ בְּגֵט וְסֵפֶר תּוֹרָה שֶׁצְּרִיכִים לִשְׁמָהּ לְעַכֵּב, **It is similar to** the *halakha* of writing a bill of divorce and a Torah scroll, in which intent for performing the mitzva **for its own sake is indispensable,**

The *halakha* states[25] that when a scribe writes a bill of divorce he must have the intention that this bill of divorce is for the specific woman and man named in it. Otherwise, the bill of divorce is invalid. Likewise, with regard to a Torah scroll, if the scribe did not write it for the purpose of creating a Torah scroll, it does not possess the sanctity of a Torah scroll.

וְדַיּוֹ שֶׁיֹּאמַר בִּתְחִלַּת הַכְּתִיבָה: הֲרֵינִי כּוֹתֵב לְשֵׁם קְדוּשַּׁת סֵפֶר תּוֹרָה, אוֹ לִשְׁמוֹ וְלִשְׁמָהּ כוּ'. **yet it is sufficient to state** intent at **the outset of writing** a Torah scroll, **"I am hereby writing for the sake of the holiness of the Torah scroll," or,** when writing a bill of divorce, **"In his name and her name…"**

However, this intention is not required at every moment of the act of writing. Once the scribe has stated his intent at the outset as to what he is writing, the bill of divorce or Torah scroll is kosher, even if he does not have this intent as he writes each letter. It is the same for a person's intent that he relinquishes his soul to be attached to God as he will learn Torah, as fully as if he were in the Garden of Eden. It is sufficient for a *beinoni* to state this intention at the beginning of his learning.

in which God and the Jewish people are referred to as friends, such as "your friend or your father's friend" (Prov. 27:10), and "for the sake of my brothers and friends" (Ps. 122:8). One might ask: When is it permitted to "take leave" of God? It is permitted when there is "involvement in a matter of *halakha*." Only when a person is engaged in Torah learning and *halakha* may he cease adhering to God. But with regard to the times when a person is not learning, the verses state, "In all your ways be cognizant of Him" (Prov. 3:6), and (Ps. 16:8), "I have set the Lord before me always" (*Likkutei Biurim* on chap. 41).

---

25. See Mishna *Gittin* 3:1; *Shulḥan Arukh, Even HaEzer* 131:1. Regarding a Torah scroll, see *Shulḥan Arukh, Yoreh De'a* 274:1.

וּכְשֶׁלּוֹמֵד שָׁעוֹת הַרְבֵּה רְצוּפוֹת, יֵשׁ לוֹ לְהִתְבּוֹנֵן בַּהֲכָנָה זוֹ הַנִּזְכֶּרֶת לְעֵיל, בְּכָל שָׁעָה וְשָׁעָה עַל כָּל פָּנִים,

and when a person studies Torah for many consecutive hours, he should stop and contemplate this aforementioned preparation at least once every hour,

However, when a person learns for an extended period of time, declaring his intention once at the beginning is not sufficient. At least once an hour, he must stop his learning and reestablish his intention; he is not learning for the sake of his profession or anything else, but for the sake of God's holiness. ☞

כִּי בְּכָל שָׁעָה וְשָׁעָה הִיא הַמְשָׁכָה אַחֶרֶת מֵעוֹלָמוֹת עֶלְיוֹנִים לְהַחַיּוֹת הַתַּחְתּוֹנִים, וְהַמְשָׁכַת הַחַיּוּת שֶׁבַּשָּׁעָה שֶׁלְּפָנֶיהָ חוֹזֶרֶת לִמְקוֹרָהּ [בְּסוֹד רָצוֹא וָשׁוֹב שֶׁבְּסֵפֶר יְצִירָה],

because in each and every hour, there is a new flow of vitality from the higher worlds to grant life to the lower worlds, while the flow of life force from the previous hour returns to its source (in accordance with the mystical concept of "running and returning" mentioned in *Sefer Yetzira* 1:6),

---

TIME

☞ This passage of the *Tanya* presents part of an overall conception of the nature of time as one of the dimensions, one of the components of reality. Time is not a meaningless, random flow of identical events, one following another, but something with a living character, part of the organic structure of reality. In scientific calculations, we refer to all moments in time as units, and other units, as having equal value. In spiritual calculations, however, we see points in space not as mere mathematical units, but as having a context and a particular significance. So too should we view units of time. Although the length of two units of time may be the same, their characters are not. Just as each individual point in space is unique, so is each individual moment in time. A moment is not merely something that, once passed, we cannot return to. It also has a unique character that cannot be relived. Despite its cyclical and repetitive nature, time also progresses. This results in a spiral that creates points in time that are fundamentally different from one another. Everyone feels that a day is a significant unit in his life, and that no day is like any other. This applies not just to days, but to all units of time, from historical ages and eras, to years, months, and weeks, to days and hours. All are unique units of meaning.

"Running and returning" is the living rhythm of reality, both of the individual and the entire world. The motion of life is that of "running and returning." It is a bidirectional movement of gathering and dispersing, giving and taking. It is like breath, which involves inhaling and exhaling, and like the heartbeat, which involves contraction and dilation. It is the way of the world: "He daily, continuously, renews the work of creation." This motion of running and returning is the nature of time, which is called *shana* ("year") in *Sefer Yetzira*, because time is change (*shinui*). At its root, change is the giving and taking of life force. It is bringing something into being and erasing it. That is the rhythm of "running and returning," which constitutes the expanse of time. In every world and in every soul, the rate of "running and returning" determines the duration and speed of its time.

עִם כָּל הַתּוֹרָה וּמַעֲשִׂים טוֹבִים שֶׁל הַתַּחְתּוֹנִים. along with all the Torah and good deeds of the lower worlds.

Therefore, at every unit of time, there is a renewal of life, of the soul of the world. Renewal is a two-way motion of "running" and "returning." New life is given, and the life that had existed returns to its source. The life that returns to its source does not return as it was given, but as it has been affected by the reality in which it had been, whether by Torah and good deeds, or their opposite, God forbid.

Accordingly, Judaism's strong disapproval of wasting time is understandable. Every mitzva that is performed or not performed, every sin that is committed or not committed at a certain moment takes on a different meaning when one thinks of the moment as a unique, one-time event. A moment that passes by without a remarkable achievement will not return. A person could fully repent and correct his past, but the irreplaceable uniqueness, the particular nature of that particular hour on that particular day will never occur again.

Here, the author of the *Tanya* is discussing something even greater: the unique value of time, not only because of a person's particular action or non-action but because time itself is the essence of change and renewal. As stated in the prayer book, God "daily, continuously, renews the work of creation." Therefore, in order to fill time with meaningful actions, it is not sufficient for a person to continue to do what he has been doing until now, with the same intentions that he had had previously, even if he had acted impeccably. Rather, he must change and renew himself constantly.

כִּי בְּכָל שָׁעָה שׁוֹלֵט צֵירוּף אֶחָד מִי"ב צֵירוּפֵי שֵׁם הוי"ה בָּרוּךְ הוּא בִּי"ב שְׁעוֹת הַיּוֹם, וְצֵירוּפֵי שֵׁם אדנ"י בַּלַּיְלָה כַּנּוֹדָע.

For during **each hour, throughout the twelve hours of the day,** a different **one of the twelve** letter **combinations of the name of** *Havaya* **presides, and throughout the** twelve hours of the **night, the** twelve **combinations of the name of** *Adnut* **preside, as is known.**

The four letters of the name of *Havaya* can be arranged together to form twelve different combinations, as can the four letters of the name of *Adnut*.[26] Just as these names constitute reality as a whole (as explained in *Sha'ar HaYihud VeHa'emuna*, chap. 4), each combination of their letters constitutes one part of reality. For example, each combination gives life to one hour of the day. The twelve combinations of the name of *Havaya* give life to the twelve hours of the day, and the twelve combinations of the name of *Adnut* give life to the twelve hours of the night.[27] ☞

Therefore, every hour constitutes a new reality, and accordingly, at every hour a person must renew himself and his connection to the Divine. When a person is engaged in Torah study for several consecutive hours, at every hour it is fitting that he renew his intention to relinquish his soul to God through this learning. He should not consider his intention from the previous hour sufficient.

---

26. Ostensibly, it is possible to say that the reason that there are twelve combinations of the name of *Havaya*, and not twenty-four is because two of the letters are the same. But this is not the reason, because the name of *Adnut* does not have any double letters, and so it can be arranged into twenty-four combinations, but it is only arranged into twelve combinations. Furthermore, one can say that the two identical letters in the name of *Havaya* are not truly identical, because they are not spiritually equal to each other. Therefore, it appears that the reason each of these names is rearranged in twelve combinations and not in twenty-four combinations is that of each set of twenty-four combinations, only twelve illuminate the hours. The other combinations, not being relevant to the matter of hours, are not discussed here (Lubavitcher Rebbe, Rabbi Menaḥem Mendel Schneerson).

27. The twelve combinations of the name of *Havaya* likewise pertain to the twelve months of the year. In some prayer books, these combinations are presented in the *Musaf* of Rosh Ḥodesh, so that the person praying can have the proper intention each month.

וְהִנֵּה כָּל כַּוָּנָתוֹ בִּמְסִירַת נַפְשׁוֹ לַה', עַל יְדֵי הַתּוֹרָה וְהַתְּפִלָּה, לְהַעֲלוֹת נִיצוֹץ אֱלֹקוּת שֶׁבְּתוֹכָהּ לִמְקוֹרוֹ, תְּהֵא רַק כְּדֵי לַעֲשׂוֹת נַחַת רוּחַ לְפָנָיו יִתְבָּרֵךְ,

Now a person's **sole intention in relinquishing his soul to God through Torah** study **and prayer,** by which **he elevates the divine spark within** the soul **to its source, must be exclusively to give gratification** and joy **to God,**

18 Nisan
(leap year)

As discussed above, there is an absolutely sincere intention in every Jew to have his soul unite with and be incorporated into the Divine. This should be a person's explicit intent when he engages in Torah and prayer: that he intends to take the divine spark concealed within him and elevate it and bind it to God, who is the source of the Torah and the object of his prayers. Although this intention is not "for the sake of uniting the Holy One, blessed be He, with His Divine Presence," it is nevertheless a part of it. In order for a person to connect that partial intent to the whole, as expressed in "for the sake of…," his intention must not be for the sake of his own soul's gratification at being returned to its source. His simple intention is indeed to elevate his soul, but in order to connect this to the greater intention, he should add another

---

DAY AND NIGHT

☞ Daytime is a time of kindness: "The Lord commands His kindness by day" (Ps. 42:9). Accordingly, the twelve hours of the day are combinations of the name of *Havaya*, which expresses the attribute of compassion. The hours of the night, which is a time of judgment, stem from combinations of the name of *Adnut*, which is the name of *Malkhut* and judgment (*din*). Within daytime and nighttime, there are also differences between the various hours. Each hour has its own nature, which expresses a particular combination of the letters of God's name. According to Kabbala, these variations are also expressed in the daily life of a Jew. The morning hours are hours of revealed kindness, the afternoon hours are hours of judgment, and the night hours start with strict judgment and progress toward the awakening of compassion at midnight, which is why people arise at that time and recite *Tikkun Ḥatzot*. This is a time to meditate on the exile of the Divine Presence in relation to God, and in relation to the entire world. The nature of the different hours also varies according to the day of the week. For example, although on weekdays the hour of the afternoon prayer is a time of judgment, on the Sabbath it is a time of ultimate favor. Regarding Torah study, there is daytime Torah and nighttime Torah. This is why, according to the mystical wisdom, one should learn the Written Torah during the day and not at night.

layer, an intention upon an intention, that this act of elevating his soul will give gratification to God.

כְּמָשָׁל שִׂמְחַת הַמֶּלֶךְ בְּבוֹא אֵלָיו בְּנוֹ יְחִידוֹ בְּצֵאתוֹ מִן הַשִּׁבְיָה וּבֵית הָאֲסוּרִים, כַּנִּזְכָּר לְעֵיל. — as in the analogy of the king's joy when his only son returns to him upon leaving captivity or imprisonment, as stated above (chap. 31).

In our world, holiness is concealed within matter. It is in captivity. When a person performs a mitzva with a physical item, he releases the spark of holiness within it, which then reunites with its source. Each spark of divine holiness is like a son of God, whom God cherishes, and misses when he is far away. When a person performs a mitzva, he should have the intent that through this act he is returning the son home to its Father, and in that way he is giving gratification and joy to God.

The essence of higher pleasure and joy is the concept of "extract[ing] that which is precious from the worthless" (Jer. 15:19).[28] This joy is inherent in every mitzva. The entire world is in exile because, even though it receives its life force from God, it does not recognize Him. But as soon as any entity in the world makes a conscious connection to God, recognizing Him as its Father, that entity is redeemed. In this sense, every mitzva we do is redemption from exile. It is the extraction of the precious from the worthless and is part of the process of restoration, whereby we return the world to God. A person's every intention of doing something "for the sake of Heaven" is in essence for the sake of giving gratification to God, because the person is returning the world to God. When a person has the intent to give gratification to God, he ties his individual, personal intent to the overarching intent of "uniting the Holy One, blessed be He, with His Divine Presence."

---

28. See *Bava Metzia* 85b. With regard to the idea that God rejoices, see above, at the end of chap. 33. Regarding the idea that the act of offering a sacrifice gives gratification to God, see *Likkutei Torah*, Num. 73c.

וְהִנֵּה כַּוָּנָה זוֹ הִיא אֲמִתִּית בֶּאֱמֶת לַאֲמִתּוֹ לְגַמְרֵי, בְּכָל נֶפֶשׁ מִיִּשְׂרָאֵל, בְּכָל עֵת וּבְכָל שָׁעָה, מֵאַהֲבָה הַטִּבְעִית שֶׁהִיא יְרוּשָׁה לָנוּ מֵאֲבוֹתֵינוּ.

This intention is completely genuine and absolutely sincere in the soul of every Jew, at any given time or hour, stemming from the natural love that is our legacy from our forebears.

As mentioned earlier, the higher intention of "uniting the Holy One, blessed be He, with His Divine Presence," is not absolutely sincere in all hearts. However, the intention of relinquishing one's desires in order to cling to God to the point of true self-sacrifice is. This love of God, the natural connection between a Jew and God (being the definition and essence of the nature of the Jewish people), is truly present in every Jew. This is true not only of tzaddikim, but of every Jewish soul. In fact, sometimes it is even stronger in the simplest people than in the wisest, most distinguished sages.

רַק **Yet**

Although this is a natural connection, a tremendous force inherent in a Jew at his very foundation, it is concealed. And no one is exempt from attempting to uncover that connection through his own efforts. It is his duty to reveal them. In order to do so, a person must develop and refine his comprehension and emotions, so that they will be tools capable of giving expression to this innermost force: the love of God that is concealed in the heart of every Jew.

שֶׁצָּרִיךְ לִקְבּוֹעַ עִתִּים לְהִתְבּוֹנֵן בִּגְדוּלַּת ה', לְהַשִּׂיג דְּחִילוּ וּרְחִימוּ שִׂכְלִיִּים,

one must establish set times to contemplate God's greatness in order to achieve cognitive fear and love,

In order for a person to comprehend these matters, and for his comprehension to lead him to feeling his closeness to God and to performing mitzvot, he requires effort and persistence. That means that he must establish set times to contemplate God's greatness. This is a matter of practice and habituation. If a person puts in persistent effort, he will reach a point where his soul is able to perceive matters that it previously could not. ☞ ☞

The supernal union attained by engaging in the intention of "uniting the Holy One, blessed be He, with His Divine Presence" is not essentially an ability of a *beinoni* but rather of a *tzaddik*. And as the author of the *Tanya* has explained, the attribute of a *tzaddik* is unattainable for a *beinoni*. Nevertheless, if a *beinoni* engages in persistent hard work to achieve this union, then possibly "from an awakening from below will come an awakening from above." This awakening, a gift from God, will elevate the *beinoni* to a level and spiritual experience that he could not have achieved on his own.

וְכוּלֵי הַאי וְאוּלַי וכו' כַּנִּזְכָּר לְעֵיל. and even with **all this,** only **perhaps will a person succeed.... (as stated above** (chap. 34).

SET TIMES

☞ The need to establish set times to contemplate God's greatness is emphasized, because when a person thinks consistently about something, he is within it. A statement quoted in numerous places in the name of the Ba'al Shem Tov (see, e.g., Toledot Yaakov Yosef, Bereshit, s.v. "omnam"; Degel Mahaneh Efrayim, Shemot, s.v. "vata'al") is that a person is to be found wherever his thoughts are. When a person stays in a certain place over a period of time, even if initially he does not belong there, over the course of time – perhaps even thirty or forty years – he will certainly be affected, so that he will acquire some degree of openness to it. This can be seen, for example, on the faces of veteran museum security guards. Over the years, the atmosphere of the museum refines and affects them, and that may be seen in their appearance and sometimes even their personality. After a number of years, one can see the difference between a museum guard and a guard who works elsewhere. Analogously, there is a noticeable difference between a person who works in a *beit midrash*, a house of study, and a person who does the same work elsewhere, and between a person who establishes set times to think about God and a person who does not.

ACHIEVING COGNITIVE FEAR AND LOVE

☞ Achieving cognitive love and fear involves a wide array of abilities, such as intellectual prowess and sensitivity of the soul. These are present in everyone, but to different degrees. As mentioned above, the *Shulhan Arukh*, which is certainly written for everyone, begins with the laws of waking up in the morning, stating that a person should strengthen himself like a lion to get up in the morning to serve his

The effort that a *beinoni* expends in focusing on "for the sake of the union..." does not guarantee that he will reach such a union, because that attainment is, after all, something that is only achieved by a tzaddik. Reaching that merely becomes a possibility; perhaps God will grant him something from above, but perhaps not.

This chapter has discussed the intention a person should have when performing the mitzvot. He should intend to awaken his love and fear of God. The first part of the chapter dealt with the connection between love and fear. A person's divine service cannot involve love alone or fear alone, but requires both together, just as a bird requires two wings to fly. A person who worships out of love, who is like a son to God, must also awaken within himself the natural fear of God that is concealed in the heart of every Jew, so that he will not rebel against God but will be like a servant who fearfully follows the orders of his king. On the other hand, if a person is like a servant, he must strive to be like a son as well, to awaken within himself the natural love that is concealed in the heart of every Jew. The second part of the chapter spoke of the higher, encompassing level of the intention of the mitzvot: "for the sake of uniting the Holy One, blessed be He, with His Divine Presence." This reflects the supernal union in the world of Atzilut. Every person must say this phrase and accustom himself to mean it, although this intent is not absolutely sincere for every person. However, on a lower level, every Jew sincerely desires his own union, his own personal attachment to God. A person should begin his day with this intention; he should pray with it and then engage in Torah and mitzvot with it. And he should return to it

Creator. The gloss there adds, "When a person contemplates how the great King, the King of kings, the Holy One, blessed be He, whose glory fills the entire world, stands over him and sees his deeds...immediately he will be filled with fear." Some have commented that this description was apparently true of the author of the *Tanya*. When he opened his eyes and recalled the great King, the Holy One, blessed be He, he would immediately jump out of bed in terror. However, some people, after thinking of God, then turn over and go back to sleep. Clearly, this thought does not work on everyone equally at all times. Some people are in a constant state of spiritual alertness, and a thought can spur them to cling to God. But others are in a deep sleep, and they must establish set times to contemplate God's greatness with persistent effort.

afresh at every hour throughout the day. If a person intends in that way to give gratification to God – so that God feels joy, just as a king feels joy when his son returns to him – this will mirror the joy of the supernal union of God and His Divine Presence.

Chapter 42

THE PREVIOUS CHAPTER INITIATED A SERIES OF CHAPters on serving God: in particular, on how to worship God with love and fear, and thereby to sincerely study Torah and observe mitzvot for the sake of Heaven. The previous chapter discussed the fear of God as the beginning of divine service, dividing that fear into two subcategories: higher fear and lower fear. The present chapter will focus on the lower fear of God.

וְהִנֵּה בְּמַה שֶּׁנֶּאֱמַר לְעֵיל בְּעִנְיַן יִרְאָה תַּתָּאָה, יוּבַן הֵיטֵב מַה שֶּׁכָּתוּב בַּגְּמָרָא (ברכות לג, ב) עַל פָּסוּק: "וְעַתָּה יִשְׂרָאֵל מָה ה' אֱלֹהֶיךָ שׁוֹאֵל מֵעִמָּךְ כִּי אִם לְיִרְאָה אֶת ה' אֱלֹהֶיךָ" (דברים י, יב), "אַטּוּ יִרְאָה מִילְּתָא זוּטַרְתִּי הִיא?"

On the basis of what was stated earlier (chap. 41) **about the lower fear** of God, the reader **may clearly understand the** Talmud's comment (*Berakhot* 33b) on the verse "Now, Israel, what does the Lord your God ask of you? Only to fear the Lord your God" (Deut. 10:12). The Talmud asks, "But is the fear of God a minor matter?"

24 Nisan
19 Nisan (leap year)

The verse in Deuteronomy implies that the fear of God is a trivial matter. Yet anyone who has tried to attain it knows that it is no small matter at all, and that a person can strive to attain it his entire life without success. Moreover, the Talmud demonstrates from another verse (elided here in the *Tanya*) that God Himself does not consider such fear inconsequential. That verse states: "The fear of the Lord is His treasure" (Isa. 33:6), meaning that it is so precious to God that He stores it away in His treasury.

However, this question may be answered in light of the statement in the previous chapter that there are two types of fear of God. A person can attain the lower fear – which means that he does not do the opposite of God's will – simply by engaging in contemplation.

אִין, לְגַבֵּי מֹשֶׁה מִילְתָא זוּטַרְתִּי הִיא" וְכוּ'. The Talmud answers, "**Indeed, for Moses, [fear of God] is a minor matter...**" (*Berakhot* 33b).

The Talmud answers this question: Yes, the fear of God is a minor matter for Moses. The Talmud offers a parable: When a person is asked for something that he possesses, that request seems to him to be a small matter, whereas if he is asked for something that he does not possess, it seems to him to be substantial. Thus, since the verse in Deuteronomy is referring to the lower fear, which Moses possessed, it was a small matter for him. (In fact, as explained elsewhere, Moses was on the level of "higher fear," complete self-nullification, as expressed in the verse "And what are we" (Ex. 16:7). Therefore, lower fear was certainly a minor matter for him.

דִּלְכְאוֹרָה אֵינוֹ מוּבָן הַתֵּירוּץ, דְּהָא "שׁוֹאֵל מֵעִמָּךְ" כְּתִיב. This answer apparently does not make sense, since the verse specifically states, "**ask of you.**"

Moses explicitly asks, "What does the Lord your God ask of *you*? Only...." God is asking this not only of Moses but of every Jew for whom even this lower fear of God is not a minor matter.

אֶלָּא הָעִנְיָן הוּא, כִּי כָּל נֶפֶשׁ וָנֶפֶשׁ מִבֵּית יִשְׂרָאֵל, יֵשׁ בָּהּ מִבְּחִינַת מֹשֶׁה רַבֵּנוּ עָלָיו הַשָּׁלוֹם. Rather, the idea is that each soul of the house of Israel contains an aspect of Moses, our teacher, may he rest in peace.

Moses is not just a historical figure. He is part of each Jew's current spiritual existence. Every Jew, by virtue of the fact that he is a Jew, possesses some level of illumination and influence from Moses.[1]

---

1. See *Tikkunei Zohar* 112a, 114a, which speaks of "the extension of Moses in each generation...until sixty myriad" (the Lubavitcher Rebbe, Rabbi Menaḥem Mendel Schneerson).

כִּי הוּא מִשִּׁבְעָה רוֹעִים הַמַּמְשִׁיכִים חַיּוּת וֶאֱלֹהוּת לִכְלָלוּת נִשְׁמוֹת יִשְׂרָאֵל, שֶׁלָּכֵן נִקְרָאִים בְּשֵׁם רוֹעִים.

This is **because** Moses **is one of the seven shepherds who channel life force and divinity to the totality of the souls of Israel – for which reason** these leaders **are called shepherds.**

Just as a shepherd provides for his flock's physical needs, these shepherds provide sustenance for the spiritual needs of all Jewish souls in all generations by bestowing the divine life force upon them. ☞

וּמֹשֶׁה רַבֵּינוּ עָלָיו הַשָּׁלוֹם הוּא כְּלָלוּת כּוּלָּם,

Moses, our teacher, may he rest in peace, is the totality of them all,

THE SEVEN SHEPHERDS

☞ The concept of seven shepherds is mentioned in the Prophets: "We shall appoint over them seven shepherds..." (Mic. 5:4). It appears in greater detail in the kabbalistic works (where they are identified as Abraham, Isaac, Jacob, Moses, Aaron, Joseph, and David), via which it has entered the realm of Jewish custom: for example, the seven *ushpizin*, guests, who visit the *sukka*. The significance of these seven people as "shepherds" lies in their existence that transcends time, in their being embedded in the spirit of every Jew in every generation. Thus, we learn that "David, king of Israel, lives and endures" (as we say in *Kiddush Levana*), "Our patriarch Jacob did not die" (*Ta'anit* 5b), and "Joseph still lives" (Gen. 45:26). It may be said that with their personal deaths these individuals began to live forever within the Jewish collective. Their personalities are impressed in the soul of every Jew and in the character of the Jewish people, so that each "shepherd" guides the nation in his own way.

It is said that the seven branches of the candelabrum – the most recognizable symbol of *Kenesset Yisrael*, the congregation of Israel – represent the seven shepherds (see *Torah Or* 33d; *Likkutei Torah*, Num. 39c). Every Jew receives something from each of the seven shepherds, but within each Jew certain aspects are especially prevalent. Some people are "children of Abraham"; others "children of Isaac." There are "children of Jacob," as well as "children of Joseph," "children of Aaron," and so forth. Some souls are more drawn toward love and others toward fear. All seven shepherds, all seven branches of the candelabrum, illuminate us. Although they do not illuminate each person equally, the Jewish people as a whole contains the complete candelabrum. Therefore (as explained elsewhere), the complete redemption hinges on the ingathering and unification of the Jewish people. As long as they remain divided, the spiritual forces scattered among them are dormant. Only when all of Israel comes together do these forces reawaken, and the seven shepherds are reborn into reality as a single whole.

As has been stated, each of the seven shepherds nourishes Israel with one of the seven attributes: *Gedula, Gevura, Tiferet,* and so forth. But Moses is unique in that he encompasses all seven attributes, which includes the understanding of the reality in which emotions such as love and fear develop. (In a non-mystical sense, as well, Moses had a special status: during his lifetime, he was a prophet, king, and priest.)

וְנִקְרָא רַעְיָא מְהֵימְנָא. **and he is called the faithful shepherd.**

God Himself refers to Moses's faithfulness: "Not so My servant Moses; in all My house he is trusted" (Num. 12:7).[2]

There is another, related interpretation of the term "faithful shepherd": he shepherds faith.[3] The inner being and character of Israel is faith.[4] The person who leads them on that level is the faithful shepherd. He sustains the faith of the nation as a whole and of each individual, providing it with the conditions and nourishment it needs to grow and develop.

דְּהַיְינוּ שֶׁמַּמְשִׁיךְ בְּחִינַת הַדַּעַת **That is to say, he channels the faculty of knowledge**

THE FAITHFUL SHEPHERD

God gave Moses all the keys to the world to do with them as he pleased: to plant or uproot, to build or destroy, to give or take. But because he was faithful to God, Moses did not make use of these keys.

The greatest tzaddikim act the same way. When a person views reality from below, he sees torment, illness, and injustice, so he prays for change. But when he looks from above, from God's point of view (so to speak), he sees things differently. There, cause and effect are interconnected, and relationships between elements appear different. God gives all the keys to the tzaddik who is able to see this way. However, because such a tzaddik is faithful to what God wants, he does not change anything.

---

2. For this reason, no other prophet can change anything in the Torah, which is called the "Torah of Moses." See Rambam, *Sefer HaMadda, Hilkhot Yesodei HaTorah* 8:3, 9:1–3.
3. See *Torah Or* 75a; *Ma'amarim Melukatim*, vol. 6, p. 130, s.v. "*ve'ata tetzaveh 5741*."
4. For they are "believers, the children of believers." See *Torah Or* 111a.

Moses transmits the faculty of knowledge to the souls of the people of Israel. This knowledge is the intellect and consciousness within the seven attributes. It influences the attributes, modifying and cultivating them. Each of the other seven shepherds guides and nurtures one of the attributes. But Moses shepherds all of them with knowledge, which is their inner essence. ☞

לִכְלָלוּת יִשְׂרָאֵל, לֵידַע אֶת ה', כָּל אֶחָד כְּפִי הַשָּׂגַת נִשְׁמָתוֹ וְשָׁרְשָׁהּ לְמַעְלָה וִינִיקָתָהּ מִשֹּׁרֶשׁ נִשְׁמַת מֹשֶׁה רַבֵּינוּ עָלָיו הַשָּׁלוֹם, הַמּוּשְׁרֶשֶׁת בְּדַעַת הָעֶלְיוֹן שֶׁבְּעֶשֶׂר סְפִירוֹת דַּאֲצִילוּת, הַמְיֻחָדוֹת בְּמַאֲצִילָן בָּרוּךְ הוּא, שֶׁהוּא וְדַעְתּוֹ אֶחָד, וְהוּא הַמַּדָּע כוּ'.

to the totality of the people of Israel, leading them to know God, each individual according to his soul's capacity, its root on high, and the degree to which it is nurtured from the root of the soul of Moses, our teacher, may he rest in peace, whose soul is rooted in the sefira **of supernal** Da'at **(Knowledge) within the ten** sefirot **of the world of** Atzilut, **which are unified with the One who emanated them, blessed be He, since "He and His knowledge are one, and He is the knowledge...."**

The extent to which a person can know God in accordance with the soul's root is dependent on the level from which the root is quarried. The higher the root, the greater is the soul's perception and its nurturance from the root of the soul of Moses, and the greater the amount of holiness it can bear. As explained previously, Jewish souls derive nourishment from the seven shepherds. Thus, the da'at of every Jew

---

THE FAITHFUL SHEPHERD WHO CHANNELS THE FACULTY OF KNOWLEDGE

☞ The point here is that Moses sustains the connective faculty of knowledge rather than that he sustains faith. This is because the context is the connection to the attributes – in particular, to lower fear, to how it is a "minor matter" – and not to faith. So here the emphasis is on Moses's role as a faithful shepherd rather than his role as the shepherd of faith (the Lubavitcher Rebbe, Rabbi Menaḥem Mendel Schneerson).

derives its nourishment from the soul of Moses, which is rooted in the supernal *da'at* in the ten *sefirot* of *Atzilut*, which in turn are united in their Emanator. In the language of Rambam, "He and His knowledge and His life are one, and He is the knowledge" (an alternative reading: "He is the Knower and He is the known and He is the knowledge itself") (*Sefer HaMadda, Hilkhot Yesodei HaTorah* 2:10; this is explained in the gloss in chap. 2, and in *Sha'ar HaYiḥud VeHa'emuna*, chap. 7). Thus, when an individual draws knowledge from Moses's soul, he is drawing it from supernal *Da'at*, which in essence is not only knowledge, but also the Knower and the known. It is knowledge about God, which is also God's knowledge.

When the people of Israel stood at Mount Sinai – which included all Jewish souls, past and future[5] – they said to Moses, "If we shall continue to hear the voice of the Lord our God, we shall die" (Deut. 5:22). They therefore suggested, "You approach, and hear everything that the Lord our God will say, and you speak to us everything that the Lord our God will speak" (5:24). From that moment on, Moses, the faithful shepherd, conveys divine knowledge to the souls of Israel.

וְעוֹד זֹאת יָתֵר עַל כֵּן, Furthermore,

HE CHANNELS KNOWLEDGE TO THE TOTALITY OF ISRAEL, EACH ONE ACCORDING TO HIS CAPACITY

The Sages explain the verse "Do not touch My anointed ones" (Ps. 105:15) as referring to schoolchildren. It has been said that every Jewish child possesses something of the Messiah. Every Jewish child at some point wants to redeem the world. This shows that he contains a spark of the Messiah. This is a spark of David, or a spark of Abraham, or Moses, and it can become a flame. And as a child grows more whole, many sparks grow, and they can eventually come together to become a candelabrum.

Tanna deVei Eliyahu Rabba (chap. 23) states that every person should say, "When will my deeds reach those of Abraham, Isaac, and Jacob?" It is audacious to demand that everyone be as great as Abraham, Isaac, Jacob, as all-encompassing as Moses. But it is reasonable to demand that everyone be at least somewhat similar to the seven shepherds. That is because the shepherds are a part of each Jew's being, since a spark of who they are is the seed of his existence.

A key question comes up again and

---

5. *Shemot Rabba* 28:6.

In addition to the knowledge that every Jew receives from the root of his soul – which is the root of Moses's soul – he also receives knowledge from books, scholars, and the sages of the generation.

בְּכָל דּוֹר וָדוֹר יוֹרְדִין נִיצוֹצִין מִנִּשְׁמַת מֹשֶׁה רַבֵּינוּ עָלָיו הַשָּׁלוֹם וּמִתְלַבְּשִׁין בְּגוּף וְנֶפֶשׁ **in every generation, sparks descend from the soul of Moses, our teacher, may he rest in peace, and clothe themselves in the body and soul**

In every generation, sparks descend from the soul of Moses. They are clothed in a person's body and soul. The sparks are clothed in his body directly and not merely by first being clothed in his soul, because this process mirrors how sparks were clothed in Moses's body.[6] Furthermore, as explained elsewhere, the higher something is, the lower the entity in which it clothes itself.

שֶׁל חַכְמֵי הַדּוֹר "עֵינֵי הָעֵדָה" (במדבר טו, כד) לְלַמֵּד דַּעַת אֶת הָעָם וְלֵידַע גְּדוּלַת ה' וּלְעָבְדוֹ בְּלֵב וָנֶפֶשׁ. **of the sages of the generation, the "eyes of the congregation" (Num. 15:24), so that they may teach the people knowledge and teach them to know the greatness of God and to serve Him with heart and soul.**

In this sense, every Jewish spiritual leader is, to a greater or lesser extent, an aspect of "Moses." And the role of these leaders is to "teach again in the teachings of the Ba'al Shem Tov and in Hasidism in general (see chap. 17): How to reconcile the Torah's descriptions of long-past events with the idea that the Torah is eternal and relates to our lives right now? The answers to this question indicate that the Torah's narratives are describing what is happening in our lives at present. The Torah is the true reality of our lives, which we incarnate and live again and again, every individual in every generation. The Torah is like a play, and we are the actors, and each one of us plays all of the parts, every time another role in a different way. We are the figures in the Torah, and the events that take place in the Torah are, on an inner level, the events of our own lives. In this sense, "Moses" is found in each of us. And just as the role of Moses is central in the Torah, so is it central within our being.

---

6. The Lubavitcher Rebbe, Rabbi Menaḥem Mendel Schneerson.

the people knowledge and to [teach them] to know the greatness of God and serve Him with heart and soul."⁷

כִּי הָעֲבוֹדָה שֶׁבַּלֵּב הִיא לְפִי הַדַּעַת, כְּמוֹ שֶׁכָּתוּב: "דַּע אֶת אֱלֹהֵי אָבִיךָ וְעָבְדֵהוּ בְּלֵב שָׁלֵם וְנֶפֶשׁ חֲפֵצָה" (דברי הימים א כח, ט).

That is **because** a person's **service of the heart** functions **in accordance with** his **knowledge. As it is written, "Know the God of your father and serve Him with a whole heart and with a willing mind"** (I Chron. 28:9).

Service of the heart depends upon one's knowledge. As stated elsewhere, "The mind rules over the heart."⁸ One's intellect and consciousness generate the contours and substance of his attributes, but here the author is speaking more specifically about knowledge. As will be explained below, a person loves and fears God in accordance with how much he "knows" God, not how much he understands intellectually.

וְלֶעָתִיד הוּא אוֹמֵר: "וְלֹא יְלַמְּדוּ אִישׁ אֶת רֵעֵהוּ לֵאמֹר דְּעוּ אֶת ה' כִּי כוּלָּם יֵדְעוּ אוֹתִי" וְגוֹ' (ירמיה לא, לג).

And with regard to the messianic **future, the verse states, "No longer will they teach, each man his neighbor... saying: 'Know the Lord,' because all of them will know Me..."** (Jer. 31:33).

At present, our knowledge of God is in accordance with what we learn from the "the sages of the generation, the 'eyes of the congregation.'" But at the time of the full redemption, every individual will possess an inherent knowledge of God. Thus, it is possible to learn from that future state about the nature of knowledge in general, including the inner character of the knowledge that we seek at present, which is the root of all divine service (as will be explained below).

אַךְ עִיקַּר הַדַּעַת אֵינָהּ הַיְדִיעָה לְבַדָּהּ, שֶׁיֵּדְעוּ גְּדוּלַּת ה' מִפִּי סוֹפְרִים וּמִפִּי סְפָרִים,

However, the essence of knowledge is not the knowledge itself, the knowledge of God's greatness from the teachings of scholars and books.

---

7. See *Iggeret HaKodesh*, epistle 14.
8. See chaps. 3, 12, and 16.

The essence of knowledge is not primarily the information that a person acquires from the sages of the generation or from the books written by sages of previous generations. Of course, this does not mean that a person should not learn from them. On the contrary, it is essential that he do so. However, it is not enough for a person to know what others say. Just because a person is an expert in theology, well versed in all the works of the sages, or conversant with the kabbalistic texts does not mean that he knows God.

אֶלָּא הָעִיקָּר הוּא לְהַעֲמִיק דַּעְתּוֹ בִּגְדוּלַּת ה' וְלִתְקוֹעַ מַחֲשַׁבְתּוֹ בָּהּ בְּחוֹזֶק וְאוֹמֶץ הַלֵּב וְהַמּוֹחַ, עַד שֶׁתְּהֵא מַחֲשַׁבְתּוֹ מְקוּשֶּׁרֶת בָּה' בְּקֶשֶׁר אַמִּיץ וְחָזָק, כְּמוֹ שֶׁהִיא מְקוּשֶּׁרֶת בְּדָבָר גַּשְׁמִי שֶׁרוֹאֶה בְּעֵינֵי בָשָׂר וּמַעֲמִיק בּוֹ מַחֲשַׁבְתּוֹ. Rather, the main thing is that a person meditate on God's greatness and affix his thought on God with the strength and might of his heart and mind until his thought is bound with God with a mighty and strong bond, just as it is bound to a physical object that he sees with his corporeal eyes and that he thinks deeply about.

A person's knowledge of God does not mean that he knows only what other people know. Therefore, a person must work on his own knowledge and understanding. He must invest time and effort until his knowledge of God will be at least of the same quality and level of conviction as his knowledge of himself and of the most basic aspects of his physical reality.

Knowledge is connection: connection to what one knows and thinks about, leading to a clear sense of its tangible presence. Therefore, the first test of knowledge is always: Does a connection exist? Does a relationship – for instance, an attraction or rejection – exist? When a connection exists, one can add to it and fill it with feelings, ideas, and so forth. But if no connection exists, then all of these additions have no meaning and value. ☞

KNOWLEDGE OF GOD SHOULD BE AS TANGIBLE TO HIM AS A PHYSICAL OBJECT BEFORE HIS EYES

☞ Many questions are asked about God and the Torah. Individuals may have questions based on their own life experiences, and there are general philosophical ques-

כַּנּוֹדָע שֶׁדַּעַת הוּא לְשׁוֹן הִתְקַשְּׁרוּת, כְּמוֹ "וְהָאָדָם יָדַע" וְגוֹ' (בראשית ד, א).

As known, *da'at*, "knowledge," connotes connection, as in "And the man had been intimate [*yada*] with Eve, his wife…" (Gen. 4:1).

Knowledge means connection, union, pairing. Just hearing about the existence of something does not mean that we know it. "Knowing" means being connected with something.

25 Nisan
20 Nisan (leap year)

וְכֹחַ זֶה וּמִדָּה זוֹ לְקַשֵּׁר דַּעְתּוֹ בַּה', יֵשׁ בְּכָל נֶפֶשׁ מִבֵּית יִשְׂרָאֵל, בִּינִיקָתָהּ מִנִּשְׁמַת מֹשֶׁה רַבֵּינוּ עָלָיו הַשָּׁלוֹם.

This capacity and attribute of connecting one's mind to God is intrinsic to every soul of the house of Israel via the spiritual sustenance it derives from the soul of Moses, our teacher, may he rest in peace.

The ability to know God exists in all Jews, including those who have little knowledge of other matters and those who do not generally grasp abstract concepts. Moses possessed this capacity completely and – as one of the shepherds of Israel – he conveyed it to every Jew, in accordance with each person's spiritual level and his deeds. ☞

---

tions. All of these doubts and misgivings may be summed up in the question "Is this really true?" If something is true, then any questions about it are irrelevant. And if it is not true, then the whole matter is irrelevant. By analogy, people may ask why historical events occurred, why people acted in a particular manner, and the like. But fundamentally, the main point is, did the event take place or not. If it did, the questions surrounding it are purely academic. If it did not, the entire discussion is meaningless. In the same way, all of the questions on the Torah, the prophets, and Moses are irrelevant either way. If something is true, then that is how it is. And if not, then why ask about it? In a sense, this is the message of the book of Job. Two verses near its end state: "I had heard You with the hearing of the ear, and now my eye has seen You; therefore, I despise [my life] and I will be consoled on dust and ashes" (Job 42:5–6). In other words, Job concludes: "Until now, I had learned from scholars and books that there is a God. I believed, but like everyone else, I had questions. But now 'my eye has seen You.' Since You are before me, all of my questions are no longer relevant. Now I view them as nothing but foolishness." There is a story about a man who went to the zoo and, after standing before the giraffe for a while, he exclaimed, "Such an animal cannot exist!" The absurdity of this remark is self-evident. When something exists, one cannot deny it. Knowing God means knowing Him in the same way that one knows the tangible reality of this world. Once the knowledge exists, the love of God, fear of God, and service of God follow automatically.

רַק מֵאַחַר שֶׁנִּתְלַבְּשָׁה הַנֶּפֶשׁ בַּגּוּף, צְרִיכָה לִיגִיעָה רַבָּה וַעֲצוּמָה Yet since the soul is clothed within the body, it requires huge and immense exertion,

A person must exert himself tremendously in order to bring forth his soul's innate capacity for knowledge. That is because his soul is clothed in the body. Even thoughts are not purely spiritual, because they go through the brain, which is just as much a part of the body as is the hand or foot. The body's envelopment of the soul imposes many significant limitations – in particular, on the soul's capacity to know God. A person must exert effort to remove this envelope and reveal the potential that lies beneath it. Breaking free of the limiting, concealing constructs of the body and its concepts requires "huge and immense exertion." ☞

THE CAPACITY TO KNOW GOD

☞ The ability to connect one's mind to God is intrinsic to every Jewish soul. A person may possess a certain ability that bears no relation to his overall level of intelligence. One can have natural ability and expertise in a certain area even if he is not well endowed in others. A similar phenomenon exists in the animal kingdom. It is presently believed that migratory birds navigate by using the stars. This level of ability does not mean that a swallow is more intelligent than a human being, who is incapable of such navigation. But in this area it has knowledge that is lacking in a human being. Similarly, every Jew possesses the capacity to know God, no matter what his general nature or intellectual capacity.

THE BODY AS GARMENT AND THE KNOWLEDGE OF GOD

☞ The confines of the body affect a person from the moment he is born. These confines are due not only to the body itself but to everything that it absorbs from the environment, which from an early age obscures his ability to know God and separates him from all genuine spiritual connection, from any capacity for real knowledge, and uproots his soul from any way of life that touches on what lies beyond. The soul's ability to see, know, and connect with God is its lifeline, but the body and the world of physical gratification constantly work to blur this ability, to block the conduits, to obscure the sight. They are not necessarily acting against the soul, but they prevent it from connecting to anything spiritual. When a person moves through the day in a habitual cycle of eat-work-family, that leaves no opening for anything else. In order to withstand this pressure and remain open to our soul's divine powers, we must constantly struggle against our environment, our experiences, and our constraints.

כְּפוּלָה וּמְכוּפֶּלֶת. הָאַחַת הִיא 'יְגִיעַת בָּשָׂר' לְבַטֵּשׁ אֶת הַגּוּף וּלְהַכְנִיעוֹ שֶׁלֹּא יַחְשִׁיךְ עַל אוֹר הַנֶּפֶשׁ כְּמוֹ שֶׁנִּתְבָּאֵר לְעֵיל בְּשֵׁם הַזֹּהַר (חלק ג קסח, א): "דְּגוּפָא דְּלָא סָלִיק בֵּיהּ נְהוֹרָא דְּנִשְׁמָתָא - מְבַטְּשִׁין לֵיהּ"

which is twofold. First is exertion of the flesh. A person must crush and subdue his body so that it will not dim the soul's light, as explained above (chap. 29) in the name of the Zohar (3:168a): "A body in which the soul's light does not penetrate must be crushed."

This exertion functions on two planes. The first is the "exertion of the flesh." That is exertion whose function is to remove the confines imposed by the body and the material reality in which we live. A body that is not imbued with the soul's light must be "broken," just as a thick log that does not catch fire must be split. One way to do this is by fasting and engaging in physical self-deprivation. Although there are situations in which this is effective, the author of the *Tanya* does not speak of this approach here. One reason is that this does not reach the root of the matter. The problem is not how much a person eats, but how he eats, not what the body does or does not do, but how the soul relates to that. Another problem with this approach discussed by the hasidic masters is that a person cannot impose on the body without imposing on the soul. Whereas a person can take off a garment in order to beat it and shake off the dust, he cannot remove his body from his soul. When he shakes and beats his body, his soul is also being shaken and beaten. When the body's strength and desires are weakened, the powers of the soul are likewise weakened. Because of the problematic nature of this approach, the author of the *Tanya* prefers to discuss other methods.

וְהַיְינוּ עַל יְדֵי הִרְהוּרֵי תְּשׁוּבָה מֵעוֹמֶק הַלֵּב, כְּמוֹ שֶׁנִּתְבָּאֵר שָׁם.

This is achieved **through thoughts of repentance from the depths of the heart, as explained there.**

Since it is impossible to weaken the body and its concealing forces by beating them without weakening the soul, one may attempt to do so by breaking the heart. Breaking the heart means breaking the sense of oneself as the center of the world. As a person deeply considers his sins, flaws, and imperfection, he breaks his heart.

The body is a barrier to knowledge because a person constructs a world that is centered entirely around his body, a sense of "I" that is separate from the rest of reality. A person's growth and the development of his knowledge depend on his ability to forget himself, to reduce and nullify his self. In order to receive, he must be an empty receptacle. A full vessel has no room to receive. It can only pour out what it contains. A person who is filled with himself may travel all across the globe and remain provincial. He may pass through worlds without his own world changing at all. On the other hand, a person who is empty embraces the entire world even while sitting in a corner. Therefore, in order to attain knowledge – in particular, in order to know God – a person must break his feeling of "I and no other," the sense of self that stems primarily from his physical being.

Sometimes such a breakthrough comes to a person from the outside, when events cause him such distress that he begins to see and feel things differently and on a different scale than he had before. This does not mean that one finds God as an attempt to escape adversity, but rather the adversity breaks the veil around his self. He now sees what he did not see before and connects with what he had not connected with before. However, a person may not deliberately attempt to cause himself this kind of anguish. Instead, the approach proposed here by the author of the *Tanya* is that a person engage in "thoughts of repentance from the depths of the heart," which cause him to feel that it would be better not to speak about himself or even think about himself. At that moment, the door is opened for the spark within him to connect to the transcendent Divine.

וְהַשֵּׁנִית הִיא יְגִיעַת הַנֶּפֶשׁ And second is exertion of the soul

21 Nisan (leap year)

The work of "exertion of the flesh," of breaking the barriers that pertain to the body, is mainly preparatory. After a person has removed the obstacles and neutralized external disruptions, he reaches a stage that involves more internal work: the "exertion of the soul."

A person must know what this "exertion of the soul" requires. He must understand that he will be required to devote time and effort toward this goal. If he is not prepared to invest more effort in this than he puts into buying a theater ticket, he should not expect to receive more in return.

It does happen on occasion that even without exertion a door suddenly opens. Everything grows clear, and a person feels that he can see from one end of the world to the other. Yet these illuminations, as brilliant as they are, do not really change anything. The person does not become another person, nor does he learn anything he did not know before. This is a gift, an illumination from above, but it does not become his. The significance of such an experience is similar to Rambam's metaphor for prophecy: A person is walking in the dark and does not know his way. A brief flash of lightning illuminates the entire landscape and then it is again swallowed up in darkness. What he sees during that split-second shows him the direction in which to walk, even in the dark. The lightning flash did not change his character or his path, it did not become his, but it opened up a new possibility for him. It helped him change direction.

Another limitation of such a moment is that it does not depend on the person. It is gifted to him, perhaps only once in a lifetime, and does not return. Therefore, the author of the *Tanya* does not mention those fleeting moments of illumination. Rather, he discusses what a person can generate by himself at any time.

שֶׁלֹּא תִכְבַּד עָלֶיהָ הָעֲבוֹדָה לִיגַּע מַחֲשַׁבְתָּהּ, לְהַעֲמִיק וּלְהִתְבּוֹנֵן בִּגְדוּלַּת ה' שָׁעָה גְדוֹלָה רְצוּפָה.	so that it will not be overburdened by the work of exerting its thoughts in order to delve into and contemplate God's greatness for a lengthy, uninterrupted period of time.

In order to connect to the knowledge of God, a person must engage in contemplation for "a lengthy, uninterrupted period." This is hard work, which requires a great deal of ability and practice so that the soul "will not be overburdened."

Focusing one's thoughts for even one minute is hard, and extending that concentration is extremely difficult. Two great spiritual masters were once talking. One said, "I can bring fire down from heaven." The other retorted, "I can think about one matter for three days in a row." In other words, thinking about one topic for three days is inestimably harder than bringing down fire from heaven. But although engaging in such contemplation for a lengthy period of time is difficult, it is not impossible. For a person to genuinely do this so that he will be able to contemplate God, and even more so, so that the knowledge of God will constantly flood his consciousness, he must practice and work very hard, so that his soul "will not be overburdened." Then this knowledge will be drawn into his life and personality. This is the only way that anyone can, even when in this body, uncover the "knowledge of God" within himself, which the faithful shepherd, Moses, instills and reveals within him. ☞

CONTEMPLATING FOR A LENGTHY, UNINTERRUPTED PERIOD

☞ Several methods of non-Jewish meditation involve intense concentration on one topic, resulting in almost physical phenomena, similar to self-hypnosis. These methods culminate in an experience of strong excitement or of peace of mind, clarity, and lucidity, but nothing more. Here, however, the purpose is not to attain an experience, but to acquire tools for serving God that a person will be able to use repeatedly. A moment of enlightenment can provide a person with a moment of serenity. However, the *Tanya* is not concerned with serenity or enlightenment, but with knowledge of God, a true connection with Him. Knowledge means that after a person's contemplation and exertion, God is tangibly present in his reality. The person is required not just to ascend spiritually but, and primarily, to bring this capacity down and realize it in his own personality and in his own realm.

To understand why such intense, ongoing exertion is required, it is necessary to understand the broader, implicit context. This may be illustrated by a similar phenomenon reported by people who are in isolation for extended periods of time. After a while, certain things in their previous lives cease to be real for them. When a concept has no external reinforcement, when it has nothing to grasp in the reality in which a person lives, it ceases to be real. Some methods of brainwashing are based on this principle. A person is put into a reality in which certain matters do not exist, and after some time passes, his entire worldview changes. Although he knows that those matters exist, they lose their reality because he does not have any present experiences that relate to them. It may appear to a person in isolation that certain animals are mythical, even though he himself has seen them. This phenomenon is so powerful that there were men who, after many years in a remote prison camp, were unsure about the existence of women. This sheds light on the *Tanya*'s description of the need for extensive exertion. The soul belongs to other worlds and other realms. When it is clothed in a body, it is in a small, dark dungeon that allows it only a narrow view. The soul is locked in this "prison" for around seventy years, and during that entire time it sees only the cage around it. It is no wonder, then, that after a while it ceases to believe that anything exists beyond this cage. Even if the soul has

כִּי שִׁיעוּר שָׁעָה זוֹ אֵינוֹ שָׁוֶה בְּכָל נֶפֶשׁ. יֵשׁ נֶפֶשׁ זַכָּה בְטִבְעָהּ, שֶׁמִּיָּד שֶׁמִּתְבּוֹנֶנֶת בִּגְדוּלַּת ה' - יַגִּיעַ אֵלֶיהָ הַיִּרְאָה וָפַחַד ה'. כְּמוֹ שֶׁכָּתוּב בְּשֻׁלְחָן עָרוּךְ אוֹרַח חַיִּים סִימָן א': "כְּשֶׁיִּתְבּוֹנֵן הָאָדָם שֶׁהַמֶּלֶךְ הַגָּדוֹל, מֶלֶךְ מַלְכֵי הַמְּלָכִים הַקָּדוֹשׁ בָּרוּךְ הוּא, אֲשֶׁר מְלֹא כָל הָאָרֶץ כְּבוֹדוֹ, עוֹמֵד עָלָיו וְרוֹאֶה בְמַעֲשָׂיו - מִיָּד יַגִּיעַ אֵלָיו הַיִּרְאָה" וְכוּ'.

The length of this period is not the same for every soul. There is a type of soul that is naturally refined. Immediately upon contemplating God's greatness, it is invested with fear and dread of God. As it is written in the *Shulḥan Arukh, Oraḥ Ḥayyim, siman* 1: "When a person contemplates how the great King, the King of kings, the Holy One, blessed be He, whose glory fills the entire world, stands over him and sees his deeds, immediately he will be invested with the fear of God...."

Every soul requires a measure of exertion in order to attain knowledge. However, the more sensitive and pure a soul is, the less exertion it requires. There are people with lofty souls who have a high level

---

ing and contemplating that which was beyond their present reality, so as not to be broken and swept away. And we too: If we do not wish to sink into forgetfulness, if we want to know God, if we want to feel the divine reality, we must constantly remember, strive, and not surrender to obscuring images. We exist in a reality in which the divine seems not to exist, in a world of perceptions that overwhelm us and sweep us along. Our challenge is not just to peek at a greater reality and then immediately disconnect from it but to remain connected to that reality. To do so, we must engage in contemplation for lengthy, uninterrupted periods, making sure that the work does not overburden us and that we not only achieve a momentary experience but build ourselves up and position ourselves "below," just as we are "above."

memories, that does not make much of a difference, since even the most real memories seem mere dreams after a time, and the soul no longer believes in them.

Accordingly, a person must act similar to someone in isolation. He must exert himself so that he will not be broken by his earthly circumstances. He must repeatedly revive himself and remind himself that another world exists. All the stories of people who maintained their sanity in isolation describe one thing: They engaged in a constant effort to remember and think, so as not to forget what the outside world looks like. They clung to every memory, sensation, and scrap of information in order to preserve their concepts of the outside world. They did not suffer a breakdown but emerged whole as a result of constant practice, exertion of the soul and exertion of the flesh, remember-

of sensitivity to holiness, as described by the Rema in his gloss to *Shulḥan Arukh*. When such people open their eyes in the morning, they immediately recall the King of kings and a great dread falls upon them, and they leap out of bed to serve the Creator.

וְיֵשׁ נֶפֶשׁ שֶׁפָּלָה בְּטִבְעָהּ וְתוֹלַדְתָּהּ, מִמְּקוֹר חוּצְבָהּ, מִמַּדְרֵגוֹת תַּחְתּוֹנוֹת דְּעֶשֶׂר סְפִירוֹת דַּעֲשִׂיָּה, וְלֹא תּוּכַל לִמְצוֹא בְּמַחֲשַׁבְתָּהּ הָאֱלֹקוּת כִּי אִם בְּקוֹשִׁי וּבְחָזְקָה,	By contrast, **there is a** type of **soul that is lowly in its nature and origin from the source from which it is hewn,** that being **from the lowest levels of the ten** *sefirot* of the world of *Asiya*. **It is not able to discover divinity in its thought without difficulty and forceful effort,**

This type of soul comes from a relatively low spiritual level. It has no deep perception, and "it is not able to discover divinity in its thought without difficulty and forceful effort." When such a person opens his eyes in the morning, he recalls other matters, and even if he does think of the greatness of the Creator, he is not moved, and he can go back to sleep.

A person with such a low soul requires especial exertion to connect to holiness, to an image of holiness to which his soul can relate.

וּבִפְרָט אִם הוּטְמְאָה בְּחַטֹּאת נְעוּרִים, שֶׁהָעֲוֹנוֹת מַבְדִּילִים כוּ' [כְּמוֹ שֶׁכָּתוּב בְּסֵפֶר חֲסִידִים סִימָן ל"ה].	**especially if it has been defiled by the transgression of youth, since iniquities separate** a person from God, and so on **(as written in** *Sefer Ḥasidim*, **chap. 35).**

"The transgression of youth" refers to those sins that almost no one can avoid at a certain stage in his life. A sin has consequences on two planes. First, a person is judged and punished, whether in the heavenly court, in an earthly court, or in his everyday life. All factors are taken into account: the act, the intention, the awareness, his society and its influence on him. The outcome – called "punishment" – does not relate directly to the sin, but to these factors. Second, sin has an intrinsic effect on a person. It prevents his soul from functioning properly. It causes a stain, a fracture, interference, which prevents the soul from attaining certain achievements. Regarding forbidden food, the Sages explain (*Yoma* 39a) that the term *venitmetem* in the verse "And you shall not be rendered impure by them, and become impure [*venitmetem*] through them" (Lev. 11:43) connotes a secondary meaning, foolishness (*timtum*), because sin stupefies the soul and blocks (*otem*) its access to holiness. Even if a person ate forbidden food unknowingly and is not subject to punishment, the sin affects his soul. Thus, a person's difficulties related to the low level of his soul plus the burden of his transgressions mean that he must invest much effort and time in order to "know" God.[9]

וּמִכָּל מָקוֹם, בְּקוֹשִׁי וּבְחָזְקָה, שֶׁיִּתְחַזֵּק מְאֹד מַחֲשַׁבְתּוֹ בְּאוֹמֶץ וִיגִיעָה רַבָּה וְעוֹמֶק גָּדוֹל לְהַעֲמִיק בִּגְדוּלַּת ה' שָׁעָה גְדוֹלָה, — Nevertheless, with difficulty and forceful effort, by greatly exerting his thoughts with immense effort and exertion, along with deep concentration in order to meditate on God's greatness for a lengthy period,

Even a person with an inherently low soul or one who has sinned can, despite all obstacles, constraints, and concealments, achieve knowledge of God if he works hard. To do so, he must first resolve to set out on this difficult path from which, in a sense, there is no going back. Secondly, he must work with unremitting effort. He must implement his resolution day after day and hour after hour. He must practice constantly, and that practice requires not only a courageous decision but also the great effort needed to consistently pursue its aims.

בְּוַדַּאי תַּגִּיעַ אֵלָיו עַל כָּל פָּנִים הַיִּרְאָה תַּתָּאָה הַנִּזְכֶּרֶת לְעֵיל. — he will certainly be invested with at least the lower level of fear discussed above (chap. 41).

After all this, there is no guarantee that the person will reach the level of attaining an inner emotional connection to God. However, he will at least attain the lower fear of God. Even if he himself does not feel anything, he can still attain the fear of God.

---

9. "Rather, your iniquities have separated between you and your God" (Isa. 59:2); see chap. 29; *Iggeret HaTeshuva*, chap. 5.

וּכְמוֹ שֶׁאָמְרוּ רַבּוֹתֵינוּ ז״ל: "יָגַעְתִּי וּמָצָאתִי - תַּאֲמִין" (מגילה ו, ב). As our Rabbis stated, "If someone tells you, 'I have exerted myself and I have found success,' believe him" (*Megilla* 6b).

The complete talmudic passage is: "If someone tells you, 'I have exerted myself and I have not found success,' do not believe him. [Similarly, if he says to you:] 'I have not exerted myself but I have found success,' do not believe him. [If, however, he tells you:] 'I have exerted myself and I have found success,' believe him."

How should we understand the phrase "If someone tells you, 'I have exerted myself and I have not found success,' do not believe him"? Why shouldn't he be believed? The answer is that we believe that he did not find success, but we do not believe that he exerted himself sufficiently. Of course, as in other matters of the soul, this does not apply to everyone in exactly the same way, and it is difficult to quantify what different individuals require. Some people exert themselves a little and find much success, whereas others exert themselves a great deal but find only limited success. The outcome depends on the individual's nature, ability, and background. The principle, however, is the same for everyone: As long as a person exerts himself sufficiently, he will attain success.

EXERTING ONESELF AND FINDING SUCCESS

The Tzemaḥ Tzedek spoke of a particular individual who was a perfect model of a person who exerted himself and found success. This was a hasid by the name of Yekutiel Liepler who lived in the days of the second Lubavitcher Rebbe, Rabbi Dovber Schneuri, also known as the Mitteler Rebbe. Although he was an ardent hasid, he was a simple Jew who barely knew how to learn. The Mitteler Rebbe's hasidic discourses were extremely deep and complex, and whenever the hasidim would pass through Yekutiel's town and repeat the Rebbe's discourses, his lack of understanding would dishearten him, and he grew despondent. Finally, he went to the Rebbe and asked him what he should do. The Rebbe essentially recounted the words of the Sages that if a person says that he exerted himself and found success he should be believed, and added that nothing stands in the way of a person's will, and that a person can achieve anything with the right amount of exertion. When Yekutiel heard the Rebbe tell him that this was only a matter of hard work, he sent a message home saying that an important matter required him to stay in Lubavitch, and his family should attend to his business until he returned. He re-

וּכְדִכְתִיב: "אִם תְּבַקְשֶׁנָּה כַכָּסֶף וְכַמַּטְמוֹנִים תַּחְפְּשֶׂנָּה אָז תָּבִין יִרְאַת ה'" (משלי ב, ד-ה). פֵּרוּשׁ: כְּדֶרֶךְ שֶׁמְּחַפֵּשׂ אָדָם מַטְמוֹן וְאוֹצָר הַטָּמוּן בְּתַחְתִּיּוֹת הָאָרֶץ, שֶׁחוֹפֵר אַחֲרָיו בִּיגִיעָה עֲצוּמָה - כָּךְ צָרִיךְ לַחְפּוֹר בִּיגִיעָה עֲצוּמָה לְגַלּוֹת אוֹצָר שֶׁל יִרְאַת שָׁמַיִם הַצָּפוּן וּמוּסְתָּר בְּבִינַת הַלֵּב שֶׁל כָּל אָדָם מִיִשְׂרָאֵל.

This is also the meaning of the verse "If you will seek it like silver and search for it like hidden treasures, then you will understand the fear of the Lord" (Prov. 2:4–5). Just as a person searches for hidden treasure buried deep underground, digging for it with immense exertion, so must a person dig with immense exertion to uncover the treasure of fear of Heaven, which is hidden and concealed in the inner **understanding of every Jew's heart.**

The understanding of the heart is home to a person's deepest emotions, even if he is not consciously aware of them, and they are hidden, as they are in its silent root in *bina* ("understanding"), the *sefira* that is the mother of all feelings. Every Jew possesses, hidden in the understanding of his heart, the fear of Heaven.

---

mained in Lubavitch for a few months and worked hard at developing his ability to contemplate: to take a subject, isolate it in his thoughts, and consider and analyze it until it became totally clear to him from every angle. He exerted himself tremendously, reviewing each concept dozens of times, accustoming himself to think about one subject without interruption until finally, after a few months, he felt something beginning to change within himself. Many years later, the Mitteler Rebbe's grandson, the fourth Lubavitcher Rebbe, Rabbi Shmuel Schneerson, also known as the Rebbe Maharash, who had met Yekutiel, said of him, "He was not an outstanding scholar, but with regard to understanding hasidic concepts, there was no one like him." A leading hasid, Rabbi Shmuel Dov of Borisov, said that he had never met anyone as intelligent, deep, sharp, and organized as Rabbi Yekutiel. His ability to delve into a subject for seven or eight hours without interruption and then explain it clearly was extraordinary even among the greatest Chabad hasidim. It is said that the Mitteler Rebbe wrote each of his books with a particular individual in mind, and that he wrote *Imrei Bina*, which is one of the deepest works of hasidic thought, for Rabbi Yekutiel Liepler.

When a simple person undergoes such a transformation, it is not because he has an innate aptitude or a refined and sensitive soul. Yekutiel Liepler was in truth simple, but since the ability to contemplate deeply was more important to him than all his personal affairs and because he invested all his energy in this endeavor, that effort brought about a change in his soul.

Although this treasure is concealed, whoever seeks it can find it. But a person must exert himself to do so. If a person says, "I have exerted myself and I have found success," believe him. If a person applies himself in a lackluster fashion, he will not succeed. If a person is not prepared to invest more in the fear of God than he does in paying for his groceries, he cannot complain if he achieves nothing. But if he invests effort, fervor, and persistence, then he will "understand the fear of the Lord."

The fear of God exists within everyone, whether concealed or easily accessible. Therefore, a person may be certain that if he will search thoroughly for it he will find it. If he digs with exertion and persistence, utilizing the understanding of his heart, then he will find and understand the fear of God, just as a miner will find gold or silver when he knows where it is. ☞ ☞

"IF YOU WILL SEEK IT LIKE SILVER"

☞ In addition to denoting the intensity of the search, this image has other relevant aspects. A person must dig in the right place in order to extract silver or gold. Otherwise, he might dig and not find anything of value. If a person does not direct his hard work properly, his efforts will be wasted. He may invest much effort and time in seeking God, only to discover years later that the knowledge he seeks is elsewhere: on a different path, with another teacher. Thus, regarding the assurance that a person will achieve results after a certain amount of exertion, one must add the caveat that he requires guidance so that his efforts will be directed properly.

A group of young people once asked the Lubavitcher Rebbe, Rabbi Menaḥem Mendel Schneerson, the meaning of the term "Rebbe." He quoted a verse that describes the Jewish people as "a desired land" (Mal. 3:12). "Desired land" refers to land that contains precious materials such as gold, silver, and gemstones. But even in such a land, one can dig and find only rocks and mud. Therefore, a person must go to an expert who knows where the gold, silver, and diamonds are to be found. Similarly, in the "desired land" of the Jewish soul, one needs to know where and how to dig. A person may dig extremely deep and conclude that the human being is made up entirely of sludge or stones. The proper guide finds the silver (the love of God), gold (the fear of God), and gemstones (faith) that are hidden in a person. That is the role of the Rebbe, a person who knows where to dig in the Jewish soul in order to bring forth its treasures.

This is not a general search, an attempt to extract and develop all the abilities concealed in a person. It is a search for a specific outcome: a person's ability to create a real connection between himself and God. Knowing God is the root and essence of the character of Israel. Other treasures and strengths also exist, concealed within the soul and able to affect the soul. However, they are not the essence of a Jew's character. They are not God's treasure, the treasure that we are seeking.

שֶׁהִיא בְּחִינָה וּמַדְרֵגָה שֶׁלְּמַעְלָה מֵהַזְּמַן, וְהִיא הַיִּרְאָה הַטִּבְעִית הַמְסֻתֶּרֶת, הַנִּזְכֶּרֶת לְעֵיל.

This quality and level of understanding of the heart **transcends time. And this is the natural, hidden fear discussed above** (chap. 41).

Every Jew is prepared to fear God in the "understanding of his heart." This ability is not active on the plane of the regular life of the soul. It is above time in the sense that it does not proceed in consonance with the pace of our ordinary lives. Therefore, it cannot be integrated into the soul's normal, day-to-day operations unless a crisis should occur, which brings a person to a state of being without time and limits. However, as long as life goes on as usual, a person does not make contact with this layer of his soul. Someone can live for sixty or seventy years without discovering that he possesses understanding of the heart and fear of God, or that he even possesses a soul.

רַק שֶׁכְּדֵי שֶׁתָּבֹא לִידֵי מַעֲשֶׂה, בִּבְחִינַת 'יִרְאַת חֵטְא', לִהְיוֹת 'סוּר מֵרָע' בְּמַעֲשֶׂה דִּבּוּר וּמַחֲשָׁבָה, צָרִיךְ לְגַלּוֹתָהּ מִמַּצְפּוּנֵי 'בִּינַת הַלֵּב' שֶׁלְּמַעְלָה מֵהַזְּמַן, לַהֲבִיאָהּ לִבְחִינַת מַחֲשָׁבָה מַמָּשׁ שֶׁבַּמֹּחַ,

Yet in order for that **fear to be actualized as fear of sin, so that one may avoid evil in action, speech, and thought, it must be revealed from the hidden recesses of the understanding of the heart that transcends time, so as to bring it to the dimension of actual thought in the brain,** as a

---

EXERTION IS EXHAUSTING

☞ This search is not easy; it is taxing, and the reality is that people get tired. Few can continue the search year after year. There is usually a period in a person's life when he searches. Most people do so when they are young, or following a significant event in their lives, but after a while, having invested a certain degree of exertion and achieved a certain level of success, they remain there – not because they are unable to do more, but because they are tired.

There was once a prominent hasidic elder who did not afford honor to others except for one hasid, before whom he would always stand. He explained, "We all came to the Rebbe and we all began to plow our souls. One person plowed for half a year, another for a year, and yet another for two years. But since the day this man placed his hand on the plow, he has not removed it."

לְהַעֲמִיק בָּהּ מַחֲשַׁבְתּוֹ מֶשֶׁךְ זְמַן person **actually meditates on it for a**
מַה מַּמָּשׁ, **substantial duration of time,**

In order for this hidden fear, which is disengaged from a person's this-worldly life, to be actualized as the fear of sin – a fear that comes to expression in a person's deeds when he turns away from evil in action, speech, and thought (the three garments of the soul in which the soul's powers are clothed and are revealed in the world (see chap. 4) – a person must transfer the concealed fear of Heaven from the inner, subconscious "understanding of the heart" to conscious thought in his mind. The "understanding of the heart" is the innermost point of the soul's existence, which does not depend on thoughts but lies concealed beyond them. It is the point where the heart understands but the mind does not, the point that is sometimes called "the heart's desire," the inner point that precedes even the attributes that lead to thought. In a sense, it is identical to the essence and character of the soul. Its essence is a person's ongoing and unexplainable connection with God. Every Jew is born with this ability, the ability to find his way, the "silver cord" that binds the soul to God. Since this ability is hidden in the "understanding of the heart," a person might fail to discover it. The author of the *Tanya* explains here and throughout the book how a person can draw this concealed connection, which transcends time, into his day-to-day existence.

There is an almost impenetrable barrier between the "understanding of the heart" – the connection of a person's essential character with God – and the life that a person leads. One way in which this barrier may be broken is at a critical moment of unambiguous decisiveness. When this occurs, a powerful force within the Jewish soul is released, and nothing can stand before it. However, it concomitantly destroys the entire structure of life in a manner that does not allow for repair and the continuation of ordinary life. The author of the *Tanya* explains here that there is a way to channel this concealed force so that it can permeate everyday life, so that it does not appear in a onetime explosion that takes away life, but in a manner that sustains regular life. Some people naturally possess such a channel, which serves as a constant source of life for them. They do not require the great amount of effort described here. However, the author of the *Tanya* proposes a way for the ordinary person to attain this, a way that does not require him to develop a new ability, but only to transfer that which already exists, although it is not in use, from its place "above time" to "within time," to everyday life.

To this end, the *Tanya* prescribes contemplation, thinking deeply and for as long as possible. That is the only way to transfer the matters concealed in the "understanding of the heart" to everyday life. With this, a person does not create something new but transforms a momentary spark into a permanent relationship. This does not involve waiting for a flash of illumination; rather, a person is striving to build a connection with his soul. The only way to accomplish this is by engaging in contemplation as much and as deeply as possible. God tells us, "Open a doorway of repentance to Me like the eye of a needle, and I will open doorways for you through which carts and wagons can enter" (*Shir HaShirim Rabba* 5:2). A large aperture is not necessary, but it must be permanently open at both ends. We must make the initial perforation ourselves. It can be as small as the eye of a needle, but it must allow passage from one side to the other.

עַד שֶׁתֵּצֵא פְּעוּלָתָהּ מֵהַכֹּחַ אֶל הַפּוֹעַל מַמָּשׁ, דְּהַיְינוּ לִהְיוֹת "סוּר מֵרָע וַעֲשֵׂה טוֹב" בְּמַחֲשָׁבָה דִּבּוּר וּמַעֲשֶׂה, מִפְּנֵי ה' הַצּוֹפֶה וּמַבִּיט וּמַאֲזִין וּמַקְשִׁיב וּמֵבִין אֶל כָּל מַעֲשֵׂהוּ, וּבוֹחֵן כִּלְיוֹתָיו וְלִבּוֹ.

until it truly emerges from the potential to the actual. This entails avoiding evil and doing good in thought, speech, and action, induced by the awareness of being **before God, who watches and scrutinizes, hears and listens, understanding all** of a person's **actions and examining** the thoughts of **his inner being and** the emotions of **his heart.**

When a person's concealed fear traverses into the realm of his active thought, and when he focuses on this thought for an extended period of time, it can be fully actualized, so that he turns from evil and does good in his thought, speech, and deed. And that is because this person has a clear sense of God's presence. When a person clearly knows that God is here and is aware of his acts and thoughts, that person will inevitably fear sin. ☞

וּכְמַאֲמַר רַבּוֹתֵינוּ ז"ל: "הִסְתַּכֵּל בִּשְׁלֹשָׁה דְּבָרִים כו', עַיִן רוֹאָה וְאוֹזֶן שׁוֹמַעַת" כו' (אבות פרק ב משנה א).

As our Rabbis stated, "Apply your mind to three things and you will not come into the clutches of sin: Know what there is above you: **an eye that sees, an ear that hears...**" (Mishna *Avot* 2:1).

וְגַם כִּי אֵין לוֹ דְּמוּת הַגּוּף. הֲרֵי אַדְּרַבָּה, הַכֹּל גָּלוּי וְיָדוּעַ לְפָנָיו בְּיֶתֶר שְׂאֵת לְאֵין קֵץ מֵרְאִיַּת הָעַיִן וּשְׁמִיעַת הָאֹזֶן עַל דֶּרֶךְ מָשָׁל.

Although God **has no bodily form** with which to see and hear, but rather, **on the contrary, everything is revealed and known before Him with infinitely greater magnitude than, for example,** could be gained by the physical **sight of the eye and hearing of the ear.**

26 Nisan

22 Nisan (leap year)

People are particularly concerned about being seen and heard by others. As Rabbi Yoḥanan ben Zakkai said to his disciples: "Know that when a person commits a transgression, he says [to himself: I hope] that no one will see me" (*Berakhot* 28b). However, everything is revealed and known to God, precisely because He does not have corporeal eyes and ears.

GOD WHO WATCHES AND SCRUTINIZES

☞ A story from the early days of Hasidism tells about a hasid who returned home after a long stay with his Rebbe. When his father-in-law asked him what he had learned, he answered, "I learned that there is a God." His father-in-law burst out laughing and called his housemaid and asked her, "Is there a God?" She replied that there certainly is. His father-in-law turned to him and asked, "For this, you had to go so far away? Even the maid says there is a God." The hasid replied, "She says there is a God, but I know there is a God." The author of the *Tanya* is addressing this difference. Knowing that there is a God is like knowing that one has an arm: not saying that one has an arm nor even swearing that one has an arm, but knowing it and feeling it. Knowledge is connection, so that the object of knowledge becomes part of the knower. A person must know that there is a God who "watches and scrutinizes, hears and listens, understanding all one's actions," not merely because this phrase is found in the Rosh Ha-Shana prayers, but because he knows it to be a fact.

Physical senses are limited, because they can perceive only finite, material experience. Even within the physical realm, they are extremely limited. For example, our eyes only see a very narrow range of wavelengths on the electromagnetic spectrum. But divine knowledge is not constrained.

רַק הוּא עַל דֶּרֶךְ מָשָׁל: כְּמוֹ אָדָם הַיּוֹדֵעַ וּמַרְגִּישׁ בְּעַצְמוֹ כָּל מַה שֶׁנַּעֲשָׂה וְנִפְעָל בְּאֶחָד מִכָּל רמ"ח אֵיבָרָיו, כְּמוֹ קוֹר אוֹ חוֹם, וַאֲפִילוּ חוֹם שֶׁבְּצִפָּרְנֵי רַגְלָיו עַל דֶּרֶךְ מָשָׁל, אִם נִכְוֶה בָּאוּר

This may be conveyed **through an analogy: Just as a person knows and senses anything that occurs with or is experienced by any of his 248 limbs, such as cold or heat – including even heat in his toenails, for example, if he is singed by fire –**

When any part of a person's body is singed, even if it is just a toenail, he does not need anyone to tell him that this has occurred, nor does he need to see it; he knows it independently and immediately. He also cannot ignore it because he is preoccupied with other parts of the body. Similarly, a Jew cannot sin, even in the most private setting, without God knowing and paying attention. Every individual is a part of the Jewish people. Therefore, even if an individual Jew is not worth more than a toenail, when he is damaged the Divine Presence feels pain. ☞

וְכֵן מַהוּתָם וְעַצְמוּתָם וְכָל מַה שֶׁמִּתְפַּעֵל בָּהֶם, יוֹדֵעַ וּמַרְגִּישׁ בְּמוֹחוֹ.

so too he knows and senses in his mind his limbs' **character and essence, as well as all of their reactions.**

A person feels the very being and essence of his limbs.

THE "HEAD" OF ISRAEL FEELS THE PAIN OF EVERY JEW

☞ Just as a person feels his body's pain, so too a leader of the Jewish people, who is their "head," feels their pain. Rabbi Yisrael of Ruzhin once said that a person who does not feel the pain of every woman who is giving birth within a three-hundred-mile radius cannot be a Rebbe. A Rebbe feels this pain not because he has been told that someone is suffering but because, since he is the "head," he feels the pain of each limb. The second Lubavitcher Rebbe, Rabbi Dovber Schneuri, also known as the Mitteler Rebbe,

The Lubavitcher Rebbe, Rabbi Menaḥem Mendel Schneerson, states that there may be a typographical error here, and that perhaps instead of "all of their reactions" the text should read, "all of *his* reactions," in other words, all the ways the individual is affected by his limbs.[10] This is consistent with what is written below, that the relationship between the soul and body does not correspond perfectly to the relationship between God and the world because, whereas the soul is affected by the body, God is not affected by the world.

once stopped at an inn not far from the city of Smarhon. A crowd gathered, and he began to receive people for private audiences. The next day, while hundreds of people were still waiting to see him, the Rebbe suddenly ordered that his door be closed. A few of his leading hasidim entered the inn and from behind the door heard him crying and reciting psalms with all his heart. The hasidim were terrified and gathered in groups to recite psalms as well, and they too cried with all their hearts. Eventually, the Rebbe grew weak and had to lie down. When he arose, he recited the prayers customarily said on the Days of Awe. When the hasidim learned of this, they recited the afternoon prayer of a public fast day; it was customary in any case for a person who had a private audience with the Rebbe to fast that day. After the prayer service, the Rebbe came out and gave a long hasidic discourse on the verse "Wall of the daughter of Zion, let tears fall like a stream" (Lam. 2:18), about how tears wash away the letters of evil speech and wrongful thoughts. The next day, he was again compelled to remain in bed, and only on the fourth day did he receive people again. A few days later, one of his followers, Rabbi Pinḥas of Shklow, dared to ask the Rebbe what had happened. The Rebbe replied, "When people come to meet me for a private audience, each individual reveals to me the innermost flaws of his heart, and I must scrutinize myself and identify that point within myself in some way. I cannot provide a true answer to the individual until I have first corrected the matter within myself. On my second day here, a man came in. I was shocked to hear his words, and I could not find within myself even a trace of that matter. It occurred to me that this might be a concealed evil that lies deep within me, and this thought shook me to the core of my soul and led me to repent with all my heart" (*Sefer HaMa'amarim Kuntresim*, part 2, p. 712).

And if the righteous of Israel are the head of the Jewish people, certainly God is the "life of all life": all life lives within Him. With a person's every breath, he is breathing within God, and even when he sins, he does so within God. A person cannot separate himself from God. If he were not bound to God, he would be total nothingness. The fact that a person is alive and can act and think is because he is bound to God. And thus, if he sins, God knows and God is pained.

---

10. This version appears in first manuscript version of *Tanya*, manuscript 7.

וּכְעֵין יְדִיעָה זוֹ עַל דֶּרֶךְ מָשָׁל, יוֹדֵעַ הַקָּדוֹשׁ בָּרוּךְ הוּא כָּל הַנִּפְעָל בְּכָל הַנִּבְרָאִים, עֶלְיוֹנִים וְתַחְתּוֹנִים, לִהְיוֹת כּוּלָּם מוּשְׁפָּעִים מִמֶּנּוּ יִתְבָּרֵךְ.

By way of analogy, with a knowledge similar to this the Holy One, blessed be He, knows all that transpires with all of the creations of both the higher and lower worlds, since they are all sustained by Him.

Just as a person knows his own body, God knows everything that happens to all creatures.

כְּמוֹ שֶׁכָּתוּב: "כִּי מִמְּךָ הַכֹּל" (דברי הימים א כט, יד). וְזֶה שֶׁנֶּאֱמַר: "וְגַם כָּל הַיְצוּר לֹא נִכְחַד מִמֶּךָּ". וּכְמוֹ שֶׁכָּתַב הָרַמְבַּ"ם (הלכות יסודי התורה פרק ב הלכה י) [וְהִסְכִּימוּ לָזֶה חַכְמֵי הַקַּבָּלָה, כְּמוֹ שֶׁכָּתַב הָרַמַ"ק בַּ'פַּרְדֵּס'], שֶׁבִּידִיעַת עַצְמוֹ כִּבְיָכוֹל יוֹדֵעַ כָּל הַנִּבְרָאִים הַנִּמְצָאִים מֵאֲמִיתַּת הִמָּצְאוֹ וְכוּ'.

As it is written, "Everything comes from You" (I Chron. 29:14). This is the meaning of the statement "Even all that was formed is not concealed from You" (Rosh HaShana *Musaf* prayer). And this accords with the statement of Rambam (with which the sages of the Kabbala concurred, as Rabbi Moshe Kordevero wrote in *Pardes* Rimmonim, Sha'ar Mahut VeHanhaga 13), that by knowing Himself, as it were, He knows all the creations that exist by virtue of His existence, and so forth (*Sefer HaMadda, Hilkhot Yesodei HaTorah* 2:10).

All of creation comes only from God, since there is no reality separate from Him. Similarly, *Shir HaYiḥud* states, "Nothing in the world is separated from You; not even the slightest place exists in which You are absent." Therefore, by knowing Himself, God knows everything.[11]

רַק שֶׁמָּשָׁל זֶה אֵינוֹ אֶלָּא לְשַׁבֵּר אֶת הָאֹזֶן.

Yet this analogy is only meant to attune the ear to what it is able to hear.

---

11. See chap. 2, in the gloss.

This analogy comes from the Talmud: "Just as the Holy One, blessed be He, fills the entire world, so too the soul fills the entire body" (*Berakhot* 10a). Just as a person's soul perceives his body, so too God perceives and knows all the world's creatures. We require this analogy that stems from our world since we lack the ability to directly perceive the Divine.

אֲבָל בֶּאֱמֶת אֵין הַמָּשָׁל דּוֹמֶה לַנִּמְשָׁל כְּלָל. כִּי נֶפֶשׁ הָאָדָם, אֲפִילוּ הַשִּׂכְלִית וְהָאֱלֹהִית, הִיא מִתְפַּעֶלֶת מִמְּאוֹרְעֵי הַגּוּף וְצַעֲרוֹ מֵחֲמַת הִתְלַבְּשׁוּתָהּ מַמָּשׁ בַּנֶּפֶשׁ הַחִיּוּנִית הַמְלוּבֶּשֶׁת בַּגּוּף מַמָּשׁ.

But in truth, **the analogy** of the soul and body **does not correspond to the subject at hand whatsoever.** That is **because the human soul, including even the intellectual and divine soul, reacts to occurrences** that transpire with **the body and its distress, since** the divine soul **is actually clothed within the vital soul, which is actually clothed in the body.**

The analogy of the soul in the body sheds light on the concept that God knows about us because our very existence derives from Him and endures within Him. However, in an important respect, the analogy does not apply. The difference is that the human soul – and not only the animalistic, vital soul but even the intellectual soul and the divine soul – is affected by the circumstances of the body.[12] Not only does the soul know what is going on in the body, it is also moved, activated, and changed by the circumstances of the body. That is because the divine soul and the intellectual soul are clothed in the vital soul, which is in turn clothed in the body. Thus, to a certain extent the divine soul unites with the body. As a result, not only does the soul animate the body, but the body animates the soul.

אֲבָל הַקָּדוֹשׁ בָּרוּךְ הוּא אֵינוֹ מִתְפַּעֵל חַס וְשָׁלוֹם מִמְּאוֹרְעֵי הָעוֹלָם וְשִׁינּוּיָיו, וְלֹא מֵהָעוֹלָם עַצְמוֹ, שֶׁכּוּלָם אֵינָן פּוֹעֲלִים בּוֹ שׁוּם שִׁינּוּי חַס וְשָׁלוֹם.

But **the Holy One, blessed be He, is not affected, God forbid, by occurrences and changes in the world, nor by the** existence of **the world itself. None of these effect any change in Him, God forbid.**

---

12. See *Likkutei Torah*, Lev. 47c.

God brings about everything that happens in the world, and these events have no effect on Him. Nor is He affected by the very existence of the world. Unlike the mutual connection between the body and soul, the connection between God and the world is unidirectional. Rambam explains: "'The Lord God is true' (Jer. 10:10) [means that] He alone is the truth, and no other being possesses a truth like His truth. As the Torah states, 'There is no other than He' (Deut. 4:35). That is to say, there is no true being like Him other than He" (*Sefer HaMadda, Hilkhot Yesodei HaTorah* 1:4). In the presence of God, the world has no objective existence. Our existence and that of the entire world are real only by virtue of the truth of God's existence. But the truth of His existence does not have any need of us. As our Sages state, "He is the place of the world, and His world is not His place" (*Bereshit Rabba* 68:9).

| וְהִנֵּה כְּדֵי לְהַשְׂכִּיל זֶה הֵיטֵב בְּשִׂכְלֵנוּ, כְּבָר הֶאֱרִיכוּ חַכְמֵי הָאֱמֶת בְּסִפְרֵיהֶם. | In order to help us conceptualize this well intellectually, the sages of the Kabbala have treated this subject in their works at length. |

The kabbalists have addressed at length these relationships between God – the Encompasser who is not encompassed, the Creator who is not affected by His creations – and the world. This fundamental topic[13] constitutes the basis for all of the frameworks of relationship between the Divine and the human. This dynamic incorporates a paradox intrinsic to all of these connections: because the gulf between God and the world is not bidirectional and cannot be bridged, we can speak of closeness to God, of attachment to Him, and of serving Him.

| אַךְ כָּל יִשְׂרָאֵל מַאֲמִינִים בְּנֵי מַאֲמִינִים, בְּלִי שׁוּם חֲקִירַת שֵׂכֶל אֱנוֹשִׁי, וְאוֹמְרִים: "אַתָּה הוּא עַד שֶׁלֹּא נִבְרָא הָעוֹלָם" וְכוּ', | Yet all Jews are believers, descendants of believers, who do not resort to any human intellectual inquiry, and they recite in the morning prayers, "**You are He from before the universe was created; You are He after the universe was created**," |

---

13. See *Derekh Mitzvotekha, Mitzvat Ha'amanat Elokut.*

This is one of the most difficult and complex ideas addressed in the kabbalistic literature. Since there is nothing similar to God in our realm of existence, He is incomprehensible to ordinary human cognition. Nevertheless, all Jews are "believers, descendants of believers" (*Shabbat* 97a), who know and accept this kabbalistic secret, and each day Jews recite the passage from the prayer book that expresses this idea. As emphasized in the hasidic works, God's relationship with the world causes no change in God at all. Just as He was before the world was created, so is He now after the world exists. And all Israel, who are "believers, the children of believers," know this secret. They know of God's existence within the world and His separateness from the world, and the fact that His existence within the world does not in any way impinge upon His separate existence, and they express this every day when they recite the words "You are He from before the universe was created; You are He after the universe was created."

כַּנִּזְכָּר לְעֵיל פֶּרֶק כ'. **as mentioned above in chapter 20.**

Chapter 20 explained the relationship between God and the world as being analogous to the relationship between a statement a person makes and his essential character. First, God "speaks" the world, which is absolutely dependent on Him, into existence, and second, the existence of the world is nothing in relation to Him. Thus, God's absolute oneness is established; the existence of the world is of no consequence with respect to it, as expressed by the phrase "You are He from before the universe was created; You are He after the universe was created." ☞

"A PERSON'S SOUL WILL TEACH HIM"

☞ The point of departure of the current discussion is that the knowledge that "You are He from before the universe was created; You are He after the universe was created" is implanted in every Jewish soul. More broadly, this idea is the basis for the entire concept of the *beinoni* described in the *Tanya*. A Jew does not need to receive this knowledge from others, because "a person's soul will teach him" (see *Zohar Ḥadash*, *Lekh Lekha* 40b). As the Midrash says regarding Abraham, "God summoned his two kidneys like two teachers, and they poured forth and taught him Torah and wisdom" (*Bereshit Rabba* 61:1). This constitutes the highest level of learning, when a person learns and absorbs directly from the original source, without any buffer. This is similar to the revelation at Sinai, when "all the people saw the thunder" (Ex. 20:15). The

27 Nisan / 23 Nisan (leap year)	וְהִנֵּה כָּל אָדָם מִיִּשְׂרָאֵל, יִהְיֶה מִי שֶׁיִּהְיֶה, כְּשֶׁיִּתְבּוֹנֵן בָּזֶה שָׁעָה גְדוֹלָה בְּכָל יוֹם:

When any Jew, no matter who he is, contemplates this for a lengthy period of time **every day,**

A Jew should engage in contemplation in accordance with the level of his soul and its sensitivity, and with whatever knowledge he possesses. The amount of contemplation, time, and effort required is inversely related to the strength and sensitivity of his soul. The less capable the soul, the more the person must engage in contemplation. But at any rate, every soul needs a "lengthy period every day" to engage in such contemplation. That is because the goal is not to gain an abstract grasp of the idea of God but to strive to blend one's abstract knowledge with simple, "real" awareness. The process is not just one of learning but one of internalization and actualization, because not everything a person knows in theory is received with simple understanding in his heart. In order to reach this level of understanding regarding God, a person must exert himself and meditate a great deal, thinking and contemplating deeply for repeated lengthy periods until the matter is truly settled in his heart.

Mekhilta comments that they could see sounds and hear sights. Such a breach of the sensory boundaries occurs when an experience is so strong that it does not pass through the physical and spiritual senses but goes directly to the center of consciousness. When a person learns from books or teachers, the information passes through the soul's learning mechanisms, which have their own apparatus. However, when a person's soul teaches him, the information does not need to pass through any of these. As the author of the *Tanya* remarked toward the beginning of this chapter, the prophet Jeremiah describes the knowledge of the future as, "No longer will they teach, each man his neighbor...for all of them will know Me" (Jer. 31:33).

This capacity is found in every Jewish soul, and it teaches every individual. However, some students are better and others are weaker. As a whole, the Jews are "a wise and understanding people" (Deut. 4:6), receiving directly from the original source. Therefore, they are "believers, descendants of believers." Nevertheless, every individual must exert himself by engaging in inquiry and study so that his soul will reveal these secrets to him and teach him about God's existence. Rabbi Naḥman of Breslov said regarding the verse "I know that the Lord is great" (Ps. 135:5) that the emphasis must be on "I." A person is not told this by someone else, nor is it a matter of common knowledge. Rather, "I know" (see *Likkutei Moharan Kamma* 72, s.v. "ki yesh kama behinot"). This intrinsic, individual knowledge is described in the verse "If you seek it like silver and search for it like for hidden treasures, then you will understand the fear of the Lord" (Prov. 2:4–5). The knowledge that a person has toiled on his own to discover, unlike that which he hears from others, is considered that which "I know."

אֵיךְ שֶׁהַקָּדוֹשׁ בָּרוּךְ הוּא מָלֵא מַמָּשׁ אֶת הָעֶלְיוֹנִים וְאֶת הַתַּחְתּוֹנִים, וְאֶת הַשָּׁמַיִם וְאֶת הָאָרֶץ מַמָּשׁ, מְלֹא כָל הָאָרֶץ כְּבוֹדוֹ מַמָּשׁ,

how the Holy One, blessed be He, literally fills the upper and lower worlds, as well as the heavens and earth, earth literally, how "**the entire world is filled with His glory**" in actuality,

The word *mamash*, "literally," is repeated here three times to emphasize that this must be as palpable to a person as the most significant realities in his life. This sense of tangibility is the starting point; the process cannot go on if the beginning is not real. As long as a person does not have this tangible sense, then everything that follows is only an approximation.

וְצוֹפֶה וּמַבִּיט וּבוֹחֵן כִּלְיוֹתָיו וְלִבּוֹ, וְכָל מַעֲשָׂיו וְדִבּוּרָיו וְכָל צְעָדָיו יִסְפּוֹר –

and how God **watches and scrutinizes, examining** the thoughts of a person's **inner being** and the emotions of **his heart, and all his actions and speech, and** how God **counts** a person's **every step,**

God scrutinizes a person's inner being and his heart, his emotions, and the concealed expressions of his soul, as well as his deeds and words, which are the soul's external garments. God knows everything, and watches and examines everything. When a person contemplates God's greatness on the one hand and His closeness on the other hand, then the idea of divine providence – that God sees all of a person's actions and knows all his thoughts – ceases to be a distant, abstract concept, and becomes "real."

אֲזַי תִּקָּבַע בְּלִבּוֹ הַיִּרְאָה לְכָל הַיּוֹם כֻּלּוֹ, כְּשֶׁיַּחֲזוֹר וְיִתְבּוֹנֵן בָּזֶה אֲפִילוּ בְּהִתְבּוֹנְנוּת קַלָּה.

then the fear of God **will be affixed in his heart throughout the entire day, whenever he will resume contemplating this, even casually.**

Even when a person goes on to engage in other matters, the fear of God will remain fixed in his heart.

Once a person has contemplated properly so that the object of his contemplation has become established within him as an experience of reality, he need not repeat the process again, at least that day. Rather, it is enough for him to recall his earlier experience and consciousness, and he will return to that same awareness.

בְּכָל עֵת וּבְכָל שָׁעָה, יִהְיֶה "סוּר מֵרָע וַעֲשֵׂה טוֹב" בְּמַחֲשָׁבָה דִּבּוּר וּמַעֲשֶׂה, — As a result of engaging in such contemplation, **at all times and in all hours, he will avoid evil and do good in thought, speech, and action**

If it were always necessary to repeat the process of extended contemplation before taking any action, it would be almost impossible to accomplish anything. Rather, once such an awareness has been reached, a slight trigger will restore it. This may be compared to the formation of a conditioned reflex. Initially, there must be a clear and complete awareness, which results in a reaction. After that, it is not necessary to reach the same depth; rather, it is sufficient to have one thought about the matter for the same reaction to occur. After a person has experienced something once, something of it remains within him. Subsequently, if he does not consciously try to ignore it, and even more so if he actively tries to remember it, the power of the initial experience remains alive and real within him.

שֶׁלֹּא לִמְרוֹת חַס וְשָׁלוֹם עֵינֵי כְבוֹדוֹ, אֲשֶׁר "מְלֹא כָל הָאָרֶץ", וּכְמַאֲמַר רַבָּן יוֹחָנָן בֶּן זַכַּאי לְתַלְמִידָיו, כַּנִּזְכָּר לְעֵיל. — **so that he will not rebel, God forbid, against the "eyes" of His glory, which "fills the entire world," in accordance with Rabbi Yoḥanan ben Zakkai's statement to his disciples, as cited above** (chap. 41).

When a person recognizes experientially that "His glory fills the entire world" (Isa. 6:3), he cannot commit a transgression, because of the shame that doing so would cause him. Rabbi Yoḥanan ben Zakkai told his students, "May it be His will that the fear of Heaven be upon you like the fear of a mortal" (*Berakhot* 28b). Once a person reaches a state in which his fear of Heaven is as real and clear to him as his fear of human beings, then, at least for a short while, he no longer needs to go through the whole process again from the beginning. He requires only a moment to recall that "God is present," and then the awakening of experiential enlightenment will return.

וְזֶה שֶׁאוֹמֵר הַכָּתוּב: "כִּי אִם לְיִרְאָה אֶת ה' אֱלֹהֶיךָ לָלֶכֶת בְּכָל דְּרָכָיו" (דברים י, יב), שֶׁהִיא יִרְאָה הַמְּבִיאָה לְקִיּוּם מִצְוֹתָיו יִתְבָּרֵךְ בְּסוּר מֵרָע וַעֲשֵׂה טוֹב.

This is the fear **referred to in the verse "Only to fear the Lord your God, to walk in all His ways"** (Deut. 10:12). **That is a fear that leads** a person to **keep** God's **commandments through avoiding evil and doing good.**

The author of the *Tanya* now returns to the question raised at the beginning of the chapter. The verse states, "What does the Lord your God ask of you but to fear the Lord your God," implying that this is a minor matter. Yet how can the fear of God be considered something minor? The answer, states the author of the *Tanya*, is implicit in the following words of the verse: "to walk in all of His ways." It is true that the type of fear of God that is a deep, inner experience is not a minor matter. But the fear of God discussed here, a simple sense of the Divine Presence that leads a person to go in His ways, is a minor matter.

וְהִיא יִרְאָה תַּתָּאָה הַנִּזְכֶּרֶת לְעֵיל **This is the lower** level of **fear discussed above** (chap. 41),

This is the type of "fear" – which means simply having a sense of God's presence – that the verse is referring to. That is in contrast to a higher fear, which is a sense of divine exaltedness. ☞

AVOIDING EVIL BECAUSE OF LOWER FEAR AND BECAUSE OF HIGHER FEAR

☞ The practical expression of each type of fear of God is the avoidance of evil. In the case of lower fear, a person avoids evil because he senses God's presence. In the case of higher fear, which is an understanding of and sense of God's exaltedness, the issue before a person is not that God sees him, but that when a person has the proper awareness it is not possible for him to transgress. God and sin cannot exist in a single reality. Higher fear is neither alarm nor dread, but a sense of shame. To illustrate these two types of fear by analogy, if a person is standing in a lavish stateroom and wants to spit on the floor but doesn't do so because he sees a guard watching him, that is a lower fear. However, if a person appreciates the glory and splendor around him, it is inconceivable to him to spit. That is the level of higher fear.

וּלְגַבֵּי מֹשֶׁה, דְּהַיְינוּ לְגַבֵּי בְּחִינַת הַדַּעַת שֶׁבְּכָל נֶפֶשׁ מִיִּשְׂרָאֵל הָאֱלֹהִית, מִילְתָא זוּטַרְתִּי הִיא, כַּנִּזְכָּר לְעֵיל

and relative to Moses – that is to say, relative to **the level of knowledge** that embodies the aspect of Moses **in every Jew's divine soul** – the lower fear of God is in fact **a minor matter, as stated above.**

This sentence is not referring to Moses the individual but to the aspect of Moses in every Jew. And the fear discussed here is not higher but lower fear. In the context of the living connection to God and recognition of His presence that every Jew possesses, lower fear is not a great and lofty matter, but something minor and easily attainable.

[שֶׁהַדַּעַת הוּא הַמְקַשֵּׁר מַצְפּוּנֵי בִּינַת הַלֵּב אֶל בְּחִינַת גִּילּוּי בְּמַחֲשָׁבָה מַמָּשׁ, כַּיָּדוּעַ לְיוֹדְעֵי חֵן.]

(That is **because the** faculty of **knowledge binds the hidden recesses of the understanding of the heart to** its actualized **revelation in thought, as is known to those who are initiated in the esoteric wisdom** of Kabbala.)

The role of *Da'at*, knowledge, both in the *sefirot* and in the human soul, is to connect the internal aspect of *Bina*, understanding, which is hidden in the fiftieth gate of *Bina*, with the external aspect of *Bina*, called *tevuna*, which is revealed in thought. Every Jew possesses knowledge of God by virtue of the aspect of Moses within him. In the context of this knowledge, lower fear is a minor matter, because the faculty of knowledge can go far beyond it.

God demands the level of lower fear from everyone because, by virtue of the knowledge that each person possesses, he can easily attain that lower fear by transferring to God the fear of authority in general that he already possesses. And this can be required of even the lowliest individual. Of course, a degree of toil and exertion is required in order to achieve "knowledge," in order to reach a clear sense, even momentarily, of God's presence. The remainder of the chapter will address how a person attains this sense of God's presence through the process of contemplation.

וְעוֹד זֹאת יִזְכּוֹר, כִּי כְּמוֹ שֶׁבְּמֶלֶךְ בָּשָׂר וָדָם עִיקַּר הַיִּרְאָה הִיא מִפְּנִימִיּוּתוֹ וְחַיּוּתוֹ וְלֹא מִגּוּפוֹ, שֶׁהֲרֵי כְּשֶׁיָּשֵׁן אֵין שׁוּם יִרְאָה מִמֶּנּוּ.	**One should also bear in mind that** this **is comparable to** a person's **essential fear of a mortal king.** That is a fear of the king's **inner self and life force and not of his body,** as may be seen from the fact that **when** the king **sleeps** a person **is not afraid of him.**	28 Nisan 24 Nisan (leap year)

An individual's fear of a human king is due to the king's personality and awareness, not his body or clothing. Thus, when the king is asleep and unaware, one does not fear him.

וְהִנֵּה פְּנִימִיּוּתוֹ וְחַיּוּתוֹ אֵין נִרְאָה לְעֵינֵי בָשָׂר, רַק בְּעֵינֵי הַשֵּׂכֶל עַל יְדֵי רְאִיַּת עֵינֵי בָשָׂר בְּגוּפוֹ וּלְבוּשָׁיו, שֶׁיּוֹדֵעַ שֶׁחַיּוּתוֹ מְלוּבָּשׁ בְּתוֹכָם.	The king's **inner self and life force cannot be seen by corporeal eyes, but only by the mind's eye,** which comes as a result of his **corporeal eyes seeing** the king's **body and garments,** following which a person **then realizes that** the king's **life force is clothed in them.**

When a person sees a king, he experiences fear. However, when we analyze this, we see that the person is afraid of what he does not see, and he is not afraid of what he does see. He is not afraid of the king's body, just as he is not afraid of the king's clothes hanging in his closet. Rather, he is afraid of the king's inner essence, which remains invisible. The same is true concerning God. The process of contemplation begins with the external. But the fear of God concerns the internal realm that this externality expresses.

וְאִם כֵּן, כָּכָה מַמָּשׁ יֵשׁ לוֹ לִירָא אֶת ה'	**If that is the case** with a mortal king, then **literally in the same way one should fear God**

The author of the *Tanya* speaks mainly about fear in the context of the initial relationship between a person and God. This is because fear is the simplest and most basic way of relating. It involves just feeling another's presence; nothing else is required. On the other hand, in order to love, there must be something more. There must be a reason to love. Thus, the relationship proceeds in steps rising from level to level. When we go in order and step by step, we must start with the essential tangibility of the Divine Presence. This is lower fear. It is not a terror that paralyzes a person's ability to respond (a fear that only a person of great stature can live with). Rather, it is a simple level of fear, whose one clear sign is that it leads to the avoidance of sin. In this-worldly terms, it is a person's feeling that he is not alone: it appears to him that someone is present or that someone is about to enter the room, and that is enough to prevent him from acting in certain ways or to motivate him to perform certain actions.

At this first stage, there is the sense of being watched by God. On the next level, which a person can attain by searching diligently and studying well, he gains an appreciation of God who is watching him, and his awareness is more clear and developed.

עַל יְדֵי רְאִיַּת עֵינֵי בָשָׂר בַּשָּׁמַיִם וָאָרֶץ וְכָל צְבָאָם, אֲשֶׁר אוֹר אֵין סוֹף בָּרוּךְ הוּא מְלוּבָּשׁ בָּהֶם לְהַחֲיוֹתָם. **as a result of seeing with eyes of flesh** the heavens and earth and all their host, in which the light of *Ein Sof*, blessed be He, is enclothed in order to grant them life.

Just as it is possible to relate to a person although one sees only his body and not his soul, so too we do not need to see God in order to relate to Him; it is enough for us to see His "garment." And what is His garment? It is here, all around us. The entire world is His garment. Therefore, we cannot say that we do not see God. Certainly, we never see His inner being. But we see the garment. And just as we experience fear when we see the garment of a king or a policeman, so too must we fear God when we see the world and recognize that it clothes the divine light.

הַגָּהָה: (וְגַם נִרְאֶה בִּרְאִיַּת הָעַיִן שֶׁהֵם בְּטֵלִים לְאוֹרוֹ יִתְבָּרֵךְ בְּהִשְׁתַּחֲוָואָתָם כָּל יוֹם כְּלַפֵּי מַעֲרָב בִּשְׁקִיעָתָם. כְּמַאֲמַר רַבּוֹתֵינוּ ז"ל (בבא בתרא כה, א) **Gloss: Also, the eye can see with its vision that** the heavens and their host are subsumed in God's **light when they prostrate themselves every day toward the west** – i.e., when they set, **as our Rabbis (Bava Batra 25a) stated**

עַל פָּסוּק "וּצְבָא הַשָּׁמַיִם לְךָ מִשְׁתַּחֲוִים" (נחמיה ט, ו). regarding the verse "And the host of the heavens prostrates itself to You" (Neh. 9:6).

The world, the garment of God, is not an inanimate object that God's power sustains. Rather, when we look at the host of Heaven, we see that they all move toward the west until they are swallowed up and disappear into it; it is as though they are bowing toward the west.

שֶׁהַשְּׁכִינָה בַּמַּעֲרָב. That is **because the Divine Presence** resides **in the west.**

The source of the divine power in the world (the Divine Presence), which constitutes all reality, giving it life, is in the west (*Bava Batra* 25a). The entire host of the heavens, which, in a sense, guides the rest of the world, bows down to it and is subsumed into it.

וְנִמְצָא הִילּוּכָם כָּל הַיּוֹם כְּלַפֵּי מַעֲרָב הוּא דֶּרֶךְ הִשְׁתַּחֲוָאָה וּבִיטּוּל. Hence, their passage the entire day toward the west is a form of prostration and self-nullification.

This prostration and self-nullification occur not only as they set, but during their entire daily trajectory toward the west, which is the opposite of their nature.[14]

וְהִנֵּה גַּם מִי שֶׁלֹּא רָאָה אֶת הַמֶּלֶךְ מֵעוֹלָם וְאֵינוֹ מַכִּירוֹ כְּלָל, אַף עַל פִּי כֵן כְּשֶׁנִּכְנָס לַחֲצַר הַמֶּלֶךְ, וְרוֹאֶה שָׂרִים רַבִּים וְנִכְבָּדִים מִשְׁתַּחֲוִים לְאִישׁ אֶחָד, תִּפּוֹל עָלָיו אֵימָה וָפַחַד. Even someone who has never seen the king and does not recognize him at all will nevertheless be overcome with trepidation and fright when he enters the king's court and sees many noble ministers prostrating themselves to one man.

Although this person does not sense the presence of the king, when he sees all those around him, including wise and prominent individuals, feeling awe and trepidation, he feels it as well.[15]

---

14. *Likkutei Biurim*.
15. Although (the court of the king) is not the place in which the king is revealed (that place is his throne), and it is "this world," in which divinity is not

In this gloss, the author of the *Tanya* adds that is possible not only to see heaven and earth with "corporeal eyes" and learn from them about the existence of God who sustains them, but it is possible to perceive divine guidance with his eyes of flesh as he sees externality nullify itself before the inner, divine existence, and he thus perceives God's action, sovereignty, and providence.[16]

וְאַף שֶׁהוּא עַל יְדֵי הִתְלַבְּשׁוּת בִּלְבוּשִׁים רַבִּים, הֲרֵי אֵין הֶבְדֵּל וְהֶפְרֵשׁ כְּלָל בִּירְאַת מֶלֶךְ בָּשָׂר וָדָם בֵּין שֶׁהוּא עָרוֹם וּבֵין שֶׁהוּא לָבוּשׁ אֶחָד וּבֵין שֶׁהוּא לָבוּשׁ בִּלְבוּשִׁים רַבִּים.

Even though the light of *Ein Sof* is enclothed in many garments so that one does not perceive the divine vitality within every creation, there is, in fact, no difference or distinction whatsoever – when it comes to fearing a mortal king – whether he is naked, clothed in a single garment, or clothed in a multitude of garments.

Although a person does not see the essence of a king or policeman but only his body and garments, he fears them. The same should be true about God, and yet, as we see, it is not so. One reason is that a human being is not covered with as many garments as God. Our world consists of multiple layers covering the divine light (in accordance with the order of progression that the Kabbala describes). The author of the *Tanya* comments, however, that there should be no difference between many garments and few. He brings the example of a mortal king. To a person who is aware of the presence of the king, whether the king is wearing five garments or fifty is unimportant. Likewise, when a person knows that this world constitutes the outer garments of the divine king, it should not matter how many garments there are. Since God is enclothed within them, He is present in the reality of this world.

---

revealed, and one must bring proofs to force the prostration and nullification to the king (The Lubavitcher Rebbe, Rabbi Menaḥem Mendel Schneerson).

16. *Likkutei Biurim*.

> אֶלָּא הָעִיקָּר הוּא הַהֶרְגֵּל, לְהַרְגִּיל דַּעְתּוֹ וּמַחֲשַׁבְתּוֹ תָּמִיד לִהְיוֹת קָבוּעַ בְּלִבּוֹ וּמוֹחוֹ תָּמִיד. אֲשֶׁר כָּל מַה שֶּׁרוֹאֶה בְּעֵינָיו – הַשָּׁמַיִם וְהָאָרֶץ וּמְלוֹאָהּ – הַכֹּל הֵם לְבוּשִׁים הַחִיצוֹנִים שֶׁל הַמֶּלֶךְ הַקָּדוֹשׁ בָּרוּךְ הוּא.

Rather, the main thing is habituation; a person must **habituate his mind and thought constantly so that** he has an awareness that is permanently affixed in his heart and mind that everything he sees with his eyes – the heavens, the earth, and all its fullness – all constitute the outer garments of the King, the Holy One, blessed be He.

The way to see beyond these many garments is to engage in contemplation for sustained periods of time. A person must engage in ongoing effort so that the view that everything he sees constitutes the outer garments of the King is not just something that he affirms or thinks on an external level but is part of his inner consciousness. Just as God asked Adam, "Where are you?" (Gen. 3:9), humanity asks God the same question, and He replies, "I am here, with you and all around you. In all that you see, you are seeing Me." The question of why we do not perceive is a separate issue that is discussed elsewhere, but it is certainly not because God does not want us to. God shows Himself everywhere, on every level, and to whatever extent a person can appreciate. However, for a person to see God, he must maintain this thought and engage in the process of connecting the inner to the outer, of connecting what he sees with his corporeal eyes to what he sees with his mind's eye.

> וְעַל יְדֵי זֶה יִזְכֹּר תָּמִיד עַל פְּנִימִיּוּתָם וְחַיּוּתָם.

In this way, he will constantly be **aware of their inner essence and life force.**

Through contemplation, a person will become conscious of the inner essence and life force of the heavens, the earth, and everything in them: that they are merely the outer garments of God, the King. Consequently, his faith will no longer be a totally abstract concept but an abstraction of his corporeal sight, which is the essential experience of a person's awareness of his surroundings.

וְזֶה נִכְלָל גַּם כֵּן בִּלְשׁוֹן אֱמוּנָה, **This** contemplation **is also implicit in the word** *emuna,* **faith,**

Likewise, at the end of chapter 33, the author concludes that the contemplation described there relates to faith. Yet the connection between faith and contemplation is unclear. Contemplation is a matter of understanding, and faith and understanding apparently negate each other: when a person understands, there is no need for faith. Nevertheless, the author of the *Tanya* asserts that contemplation is part of faith.[17]

שֶׁהוּא לְשׁוֹן רְגִילוּת, שֶׁמַּרְגִּיל הָאָדָם אֶת עַצְמוֹ, כְּמוֹ אוּמָן הַמְאַמֵּן יָדָיו וכו׳. **which connotes that a person habituates himself, as in the word** *uman,* **"craftsman," which refers to someone who trains [***me'amen***] his hands, and so forth.**

Therefore, the habituation and practice involved in contemplation are alluded to in the term "faith" [*emuna*]. Even though a craftsman possesses a natural talent for his craft, he must nevertheless train [*me'amen*] his hands so that he will be able to put his knowledge into practice.[18] ☞

IMUN (PRACTICE) AND EMUNA

☞ These far-reaching words are intrinsic to the structure and methodology of the entire *Tanya*. The linguistic root of the word *emuna*, "faith," is also the root of *emet*, "truth," and *imun*, "practice." In order to achieve a full faith, a person must practice his faith. For that faith to grow and develop, he must habituate and train himself. It appears to people that something simple, basic, and natural such as faith can be attained easily and naturally, whereas the need to practice to achieve something indicates that it is not natural or obvious. However, in reality, even the simplest things, the most basic processes of our existence, require constant, repetitive practice in order to become incorporated within the soul until they no longer require thought. This can be seen in a child learning to walk. Learning to walk, which seems to us so natural and simple, requires strenuous practice for hours and days. An even more pertinent example is that of how a baby learns to see. Sight is perhaps

---

17. The Lubavitcher Rebbe, Rabbi Menaḥem Mendel Schneerson.
18. The Lubavitcher Rebbe, Rabbi Menaḥem Mendel Schneerson.

In the conclusion of this chapter, which has dealt with lower fear, the author of the *Tanya* speaks of an especially external stage of this fear, the most basic stage, which can be expressed through action alone. The Lubavitcher Rebbe, Rabbi Menaḥem Mendel Schneerson, explains, "That which was said [in this chapter] about the fear and faith that result from this contemplation applies only to a person whose intellect rules and guides him. Also, not everyone can always engage in intellectual contemplation, and for some people such contemplation is ineffective. [Nevertheless,] a person must always have the fear [of God]."

וְגַם לִהְיוֹת לְזִכָּרוֹן תָּמִיד לְשׁוֹן חֲכָמֵינוּ ז"ל: קַבָּלַת עוֹל מַלְכוּת שָׁמַיִם, שֶׁהוּא כְּעִנְיַן: "שׂוֹם תָּשִׂים עָלֶיךָ מֶלֶךְ" (דברים יז, טו), כְּמוֹ שֶׁנִּתְבָּאֵר בְּמָקוֹם אַחֵר וכו'.

Also, a person should **constantly bear in mind the wording of our Sages** in the phrase **"accepting the yoke of the kingdom of Heaven,"** which **corresponds to** the commandment **"You shall surely set a king over you"** (Deut. 17:15), **as explained elsewhere, and so on** (chap. 41).

25 Nisan
(leap year)

Just like the lower fear – the tangible awareness of the Divine Presence, of the fact that He sees, watches, and scrutinizes – so too the higher fear of accepting God's sovereignty[19] is not a onetime affirmation but requires continuous reinforcement. Analogously, the verse "You shall

---

the most natural and basic sense, yet it involves a very complex process. The visual signals that enter a person's eyes do not yet constitute sight. A person needs to learn how to see; he must learn and practice to use both eyes correctly and in coordination with one another so that the signals will merge into a complete, recognizable image. Young children require much practice to perceive dimensions such as area, distance, height, and width. There are animals that cannot see certain dimensions, such as depth, because their brains have no system for perceiving them. Thus, just as a lengthy process of training and practice is required in order to acquire the simplest, most natural sensory processes, contemplation, which is a highly complex, abstract spiritual endeavor, requires extensive practice with faith and persistence, in order for a person to reach the point of knowing the Divine.

---

19. The concept of accepting the yoke of God's kingship can be found, e.g., in *Berakhot* 13a.

surely set [*som tasim*] a king over you"[20] doubles the verb to indicate that this is a repeated, ongoing, and continuously renewed process.

There are moments of crisis or change in a person's life when he decides to accept God's kingship, a decision that interrupts and changes the course of his life. Here the author is discussing a person's life after he has made that decision. This is an ongoing resolution that a person constantly renews as he accepts God's authority constantly. This is not the psychology of a person who secludes himself and engages in lofty ideas. Rather, it is a person's feeling that he must apply these ideas in reality. The verse states, "What does the Lord your God ask of you? Only to fear the Lord your God, to walk in all His ways." What kind of fear does God require of a person? The answer is: a fear that leads him to walk in all of God's ways. Once an individual makes this decision, he must constantly return to this contemplation and each time accept God's sovereignty on a different level, in a different situation and frame of mind. This may be compared to a person who has decided to go on a diet. Once he makes that decision, he must accept a regimen and maintain it by means of a continuous resolution that hinges on restraint, habit, training, and persistence. ☞

"TRAIN THE LAD IN ACCORDANCE WITH HIS WAY"

☞ The author of the *Tanya* explains this verse in the introduction to *Sha'ar HaYihud VeHa'emuna*. Every path of spiritual progress requires leaps. There is no true ascent from one level to another without an intermediate empty space. If a person is holding an object and wants to exchange it for another, he puts down the first and for a moment he does not yet have the other. Or when a person wants to enter a body of water, there is a moment when he can no longer feel the solid ground beneath him. Such a liminal moment, which is necessary for progress, is a point of crisis, as referred to in the verse "The righteous person falls seven times and rises" (Prov. 24:16). This crisis is part of the process of progressing – not only for an evil person or someone who has failed, but for everyone. Even a person who has ascended to the highest levels experiences moments when he forgets everything he knows. At such a moment of chaos, all he can do is return to his earliest path. This is why it is so important to initially "train the lad," to educate a young child, in a fashion that will be "in accordance with his way," his own, individual way. That will leave such an impression

---

20. It is stated in *Ketubot* 17a, "[The meaning of the verse] 'Set a king over you,' is that his awe shall be upon you."

כִּי הַקָּדוֹשׁ בָּרוּךְ הוּא מַנִּיחַ אֶת הָעֶלְיוֹנִים וְהַתַּחְתּוֹנִים וּמְיַיחֵד מַלְכוּתוֹ עָלֵינוּ וכו' וַאֲנַחְנוּ מְקַבְּלִים וכו'. **This is because the Holy One, blessed be He, sets aside the upper and lower worlds** in order to confer His kingship upon us, and so forth. **And we** in turn **accept** His yoke, **and so on.**

God created all worlds, and He maintains and gives them life. Yet He expressly establishes His kingship over us: He is called "the God of Israel...the Rock of Israel" (II Sam. 23:3) and "King of Israel and its Redeemer" (Isa. 44:6). And we in turn accept the yoke of His kingdom.

וְזֶהוּ עִנְיַן הַהִשְׁתַּחֲוָואוֹת שֶׁבִּתְפִלַּת שְׁמוֹנֶה עֶשְׂרֵה **This is the significance of the prostrations** that we perform **in the Shemoneh Esrei prayer**

The prostrations in the *Shemoneh Esrei* are an expression of the self-nullification that a person is meant to reach while reciting this prayer (see also chap. 39). The Talmud says that ordinarily a person bows four times during the *Shemoneh Esrei*, the High Priest bowed with each of its blessings, and a king would bow only once, but he would remain bowed over until the end of the prayer (*Berakhot* 34b). This indicates that the more authority a person has, the more he must nullify himself before God.

---

that "even when he grows old, he will not turn from it." A seed of truth must remain within the individual, which will be able to blossom within him.

When the Ba'al Shem Tov was traveling on a ship during his attempt to reach the Land of Israel, a storm broke out. The Ba'al Shem Tov wanted to pray, but he, the great man before whom the heavens were generally open, was deprived of all of his spiritual attainments. He could not remember anything of Torah, prayer, or meditative unifications. He asked his daughter and his scribe, who were traveling with him, what they knew, but they too had forgotten everything. Then with great effort, the scribe recalled the Hebrew alphabet. The Ba'al Shem Tov told him to recite it, and the Ba'al Shem Tov repeated each letter after him: "*Alef... bet... gimmel... dalet...,*" with great fervor. Then the heavens once again opened before him. That illustrates the essence of this chapter. There must be one point, one letter, that remains, which cannot disappear. When a person has such a point to return to, he can always begin again and learn everything. That is the idea of lower fear; it may be the lowest and most humble level but it is certain, completely clear, and fixed firmly within the individual.

אַחַר קַבָּלַת עוֹל מַלְכוּת שָׁמַיִם בְּדִבּוּר, בִּקְרִיאַת שְׁמַע, לַחֲזוֹר וּלְקַבֵּל בְּפוֹעַל מַמָּשׁ, בְּמַעֲשֶׂה וכו', כְּמוֹ שֶׁיִּתְבָּאֵר בְּמָקוֹם אַחֵר. **after** orally accepting the yoke of Heaven's kingship through the recitation of the *Shema*. In the *Shemoneh Esrei* prayer, a person **accepts** the yoke **again, actually and literally, by** performing **the action** of prostration, **and so on, as explained elsewhere.**

The purpose of reciting the *Shema* is to accept God's kingship through speech, specifically when reciting the first verse "Hear, Israel: The Lord is our God, the Lord is one" (Deut. 6:4). And the purpose of the prostration in the *Shemoneh Esrei* is to accept God's kingship through action.

In continuation of the previous chapter's discussion of the fear of God, this chapter has dealt principally with the lower fear of God. It began with the Talmud's discussion of the verse "What does the Lord your God ask of you? Only to fear the Lord your God." The Talmud asks: Is the fear of God such a minor matter that the verse states, "only to fear"? The author of the *Tanya* builds this entire chapter around the Talmud's answer: "Indeed, for Moses, the fear of God was a minor matter." "Moses" refers to the aspect of knowledge that Moses, the faithful shepherd, channels to every Jewish soul. This knowledge is not any kind of schooling that one receives, but the individual's spiritual capacity to know God, to consciously connect to God, his tangible sense of God's presence. However, since a person's soul is clothed and concealed in his physical body, this knowledge is not assured. To achieve it, an individual requires great exertion, of both the soul and the flesh. This is particularly true for a low and sinful soul. But a person is assured that with exertion, courage, and strength he will find success. A person must exert himself by focusing his thoughts for extended periods on topics of faith and the acceptance of the kingdom of Heaven. His goal is to gain a tangible, ultimately truthful awareness of reality, a penetrating recognition of God's presence. From the perspective of such an awareness, the lower fear of God, which helps a person fulfill all the commandments by avoiding evil and performing good deeds, is indeed a minor matter.

The extensive discussion of the lower fear of God in chapters 41–42, which serves as the introduction to the part of the *Tanya* that addresses all aspecs of divine service, is based on the idea that the foundation of all aspects of divine service is this type of fear. If a person does not establish this as a tangible point of reference, everything he subsequently builds will be in disarray. It is easier to talk about abstract spiritual concepts and about cleaving to God than to experience a feeling that permeates our reality. Therefore, before the author of the *Tanya* will go on to address subsequent levels of spiritual work in the following chapters, he has first discussed this initial, most elementary requirement of lower fear, a relationship with God that results from a point of clear awareness. This point may be infinitesimally small, but as long as it is genuine, it is unmovable and constitutes the anchor for everything that follows. Even if for some period – whether brief or extended – and even if in the makeup of his soul a person must begin from the end (as will be discussed in the next chapter), ultimately the structure must stand on an unmoving foundation.

Chapter 43

THE PREVIOUS CHAPTER DISCUSSED THE IMPORTANCE of the "lower fear" of God and how to attain it. The lower fear of God is the bedrock that a person must establish within himself, from which he may rise in his service of God. This chapter will conclude the description of this lower fear, and it will go on to discuss the "higher fear" of God. After that, paralleling the description of two levels of fear of God, the chapter will describe two levels of love of God: "world-centered love" and "great love."

וְהִנֵּה עַל יִרְאָה תַּתָּאָה זוֹ, שֶׁהִיא לְקִיּוּם מִצְוֹתָיו יִתְבָּרֵךְ בִּבְחִינַת "סוּר מֵרָע וַעֲשֵׂה טוֹב",

Regarding this lower fear of God, **which** induces a person to **keep** God's **mitzvot in terms of** having the desire to **"turn aside from evil and do good"** (Ps. 34:15), — 29 Nisan / 26 Nisan (leap year)

The lower fear of God is the fundamental force that protects a person by impelling him to "turn aside from evil and do good."

אָמְרוּ: "אִם אֵין יִרְאָה אֵין חָכְמָה" (אבות פרק ג משנה יז).

the Sages **said, "If there is no fear, there is no wisdom"** (*Avot* 3:17).

However, this mishna then states: "If there is no wisdom, there is no fear." That being the case, where does one begin: from fear or from wisdom? Later on in this chapter, the author of the *Tanya* will explain that this mishna is referring to two different types of fear: lower fear and higher fear. If there is no lower fear of God, then there is no wisdom; and if there is no wisdom, then there is no higher fear of God. Lower fear consists of a fear of sinning and a powerful awareness of God's presence. A person may elicit that lower fear by accepting the yoke of

God's sovereignty in a spirit of self-abnegation. That constitutes the starting point of serving God. Only after he does so is his wisdom, his intellectual awareness, meaningful.

וְיֵשׁ בָּהּ בְּחִינַת קַטְנוּת וּבְחִינַת גַּדְלוּת: **This** lower level of fear **has two expressions: smallness and largeness:**

The realm of the lower fear of God has various levels, as does any other emotion. These are principally divided into two: the smaller level of lower fear and the larger level of lower fear.

The previous chapter discussed the smaller level of the lower fear of God. That is a sense of God's presence similar to a person's sense that someone is gazing at him and that he cannot hide. This fear of God is not an exalted feeling. It is a sense of apprehension, a person's awareness that "that which fills the entire world is His glory" (Isa. 6:3), in the sense that he cannot hide and the only way to assuage the terror he feels as a result of realizing that he is in God's presence is to accept the yoke of the kingdom of Heaven. The chapter will discuss the larger level of the lower fear of God.

דְּהַיְינוּ, כְּשֶׁנִּמְשֶׁכֶת בְּחִינַת יִרְאָה זוֹ מֵהַהִתְבּוֹנְנוּת בִּגְדוּלַּת ה', **That is to say, when the aspect of this fear** of God **is drawn** into a person as a result of his **contemplating God's greatness,**

This trait of fear is in keeping with a person's contemplation and awareness of God's greatness.

דְּאִיהוּ מְמַלֵּא כָּל עָלְמִין, וּמֵהָאָרֶץ לָרָקִיעַ מַהֲלַךְ ת"ק שָׁנָה וכו', וּבֵין רָקִיעַ לְרָקִיעַ כו', רַגְלֵי הַחַיּוֹת כְּנֶגֶד כֻּלָּן וכו', **of his contemplating that "He fills all worlds,"** and that **from the earth to the firmament is a journey of five hundred years, and so forth,** and a similar distance exists **between each of the firmaments, and so forth,** and **the feet of the ḥayot** angels **correspond** in distance **to all** the **firmaments, and so forth,**

Now the author of the *Tanya* will provide a model of how a person may contemplate God's greatness in order to draw this larger level of the fear of God onto himself. God "fills all worlds." A person may appreciate God's greatness by considering the magnitude of these worlds, as described by the Talmud: "From the earth to the firmament is a journey of five hundred years, and the thickness of the firmament is a journey of five hundred years, and so too the journey between each firmament, and above them are the holy *ḥayot*. The feet of the *ḥayot* correspond in distance to all these [below], the ankles of the *ḥayot* correspond to all of these," and so forth (*Ḥagiga* 13a). This description is of course not a physical one, as evident from the fact that angels are spiritual beings. Rather, it is a way of describing God's greatness. Although the earth and the firmament are immense, they are dwarfed by the levels above them, each of which is as large as all the levels and worlds below it.

וְכֵן הִשְׁתַּלְשְׁלוּת כָּל הָעוֹלָמוֹת לְמַעְלָה מַעְלָה עַד רוּם הַמַּעֲלוֹת. **and likewise the succession of all the worlds rising upward to the highest heights.**

The Talmud continues its description of the worlds up to the throne of glory, which corresponds in size to all of them, above which dwells "God the King, alive and eternal, lofty and exalted" (*Ḥagiga* 13a). A person contemplates the greatness of the physical world and its component parts, and then he contemplates the concealed, spiritual worlds, one higher than the next, relative to which the entire physical cosmos is less than a drop in the ocean. When a person contemplates this intensely and experiences its beauty, when he considers that all of this is God's handiwork and how infinitesimally small he is in relation to it, he experiences the fear of God, which in its refined state is a type of exalted awe. As Rambam writes, "When a person contemplates [God's] works and His great and wonderful creatures … and when he thinks of all these matters, he will immediately be overwhelmed and stricken with awe, and he will realize that he is an infinitesimal creature, humble and dark" (Rambam, *Sefer HaMadda, Hilkhot Yesodei HaTorah* 2:2).

אַף עַל פִּי כֵן נִקְרָא יִרְאָה זוֹ יִרְאָה חִיצוֹנִית וְתַתָּאָה, מֵאַחַר שֶׁנִּמְשֶׁכֶת מֵהָעוֹלָמוֹת, שֶׁהֵם לְבוּשִׁים שֶׁל הַמֶּלֶךְ הַקָּדוֹשׁ בָּרוּךְ הוּא אֲשֶׁר מִסְתַּתֵּר וּמִתְעַלֵּם וּמִתְלַבֵּשׁ בָּהֶם לְהַחֲיוֹתָם וּלְקַיְּמָם, לִהְיוֹת יֵשׁ מֵאַיִן וכו'.

Still and all, this fear is called only **an external and lower fear, since it is drawn** into a person as a result of his contemplating **the worlds, which are** merely **garments of the King, the Holy One, blessed be He, who conceals, hides, and clothes Himself within them in order to grant them life and sustain them so that they may** come into **existence from nothingness, and so forth.**

This fear is external and on a lower level because it results not from contemplating God Himself but from contemplating His world, which comprises His garments. Great and lofty though they be, they are only an external appearance; they are God's world and not God Himself. Thus, the fear of God that results from this contemplation is superficial, albeit on a relatively high level, and so it is the lower fear of God.

By way of analogy, when a person enters the king's palace, if he behaves properly because he is afraid of the guards, that is the smaller form of lower fear. However, if he behaves properly because he senses the grandeur and splendor of the palace and apprehends his own smallness, that is a larger form of fear. Still, it remains a lower type of fear, because it does not relate to the king himself but only to his chambers, to the external rather than to the internal.[1]

רַק שֶׁהִיא הַשַּׁעַר וְהַפֶּתַח לְקִיּוּם הַתּוֹרָה וְהַמִּצְוֹת.

However, this lower fear **is the gate and entranceway to keeping the Torah and mitzvot.**

Lower fear precedes all other stages of serving God. It is the starting point, the gateway to the central work of keeping the Torah and commandments.

This relates to the talmudic statement "Rabba bar Rav Huna said:

---

1. The reason that it is called the "lower fear" of God is that it is a fear that God, who is the One who gives life to the worlds and sustains them, may decide to cease to do so (*HaLekah VeHalibbuv*).

A person who has Torah but does not have the fear of Heaven is like a treasurer who was given the keys to the inner [doors but] was not given the keys to the outer [doors]. With what [key] will he enter?" (*Shabbat* 31a–31b). The Torah is the inner key, but without the fear of God, a person cannot reach it. The Talmud then states, "Rabbi Yannai [would] proclaim: Woe to [a person] who does not have a courtyard, yet who makes a courtyard fence." This refers to a person who has no fear of Heaven but who engages in studying Torah. When a person studies Torah without the fear of God, he and the Torah remain separate. He remains "a basket filled with books" (*Megilla* 28b), and he cannot understand what he has learned. Although he knows Torah, he is not connected to it; it is not his. When he will depart this world, he will leave his Torah knowledge buried together with his body. Conversely, when a person who has acquired Torah dies, Heaven proclaims, "Praiseworthy is the person who arrives here with his studies in his hand" (*Pesaḥim* 50a, and elsewhere). The lower, external fear of God serves as the doorway that leads from this world, the external reality in which we live, to the world of the Torah.

אַךְ הַיִּרְאָה עִילָּאָה 'יְרֵא בֹשֶׁת' וְ'יִרְאָה פְּנִימִית', שֶׁהִיא נִמְשֶׁכֶת מִפְּנִימִית הָאֱלֹהוּת שֶׁבְּתוֹךְ הָעוֹלָמוֹת,

But the higher fear of God, which is called **fear out of shame and inner fear, which is drawn down** to a person as a result of his contemplating **the internal** aspect of **the Divine within the worlds,**

In contrast to lower, external fear, which is drawn down to a person when he contemplates the worlds, which are God's garments and handiwork, the higher fear of God is drawn down to a person from his contemplation of the inner being, i.e., God Himself. ☞

OUTER FEAR AND INNER FEAR

☞ In *Siddur im Divrei Elokim Ḥayyim* (151:3), the author of the *Tanya* employs another analogy to distinguish between external (or lower) fear and inner (or higher) fear. The external fear of God is like the awe a person feels before a powerful king. That fear is due to the king's external attributes of immense sovereignty. (That corresponds to the latter letter *heh* in the name of *Havaya*.) Conversely,

עָלֶיהָ אָמְרוּ: "אִם אֵין חָכְמָה אֵין יִרְאָה" (אבות שם). the Sages **said regarding this** higher fear of God, **"If there is no wisdom, there is no fear"** (Avot 3:17).

A person requires the lower fear of God in order to acquire wisdom. He must then contemplate that wisdom deeply in order to attain the higher fear of God.

דְּחָכְמָה הִיא כֹּ"חַ מַ"ה. That is **because** the letters of the word for "wisdom," *ḥokhma*, may be rearranged to spell *koaḥ ma*, "the power of what."

The author of the *Tanya* explains elsewhere that "what," *ma*, is an expression of humility, which Moses and Aaron expressed when they said, "And what are we?" (Ex. 16:7),[2] meaning, "We are nothing." In this sense, wisdom is a person's capacity to make himself a nothing. Wisdom is the initial ability to absorb from another. It links a person to a state higher than himself that he cannot conceive. Therefore, in his mind that higher state is a nothingness and that nothingness becomes within him a wisdom. Therefore, that wisdom must in itself be a "nothingness." In later stages of perception – i.e., in the stages associated with understanding, which involve analysis and interconnections, the stages of unpacking information from existent information – there is an advantage to having much information and the ability to relate to it. But at the stage of wisdom, the more a person knows, the less he can absorb. This does not mean that a wise person is necessarily one who

---

the inner, higher fear of God is fear out of shame, similar to the shame that a person feels in the presence of a great tzaddik. He feels ashamed because of the tzaddik's inner being, not because of his outer appearance. In regard to God, a person is ashamed before the light of the Infinite One, which is clothed in wisdom, *ḥokhma*, whose letters may be rearranged to spell *koaḥ ma*, "the power of what," the word "what" indicating self-abnegation. When a person nullifies himself, he is enlivened by the level of wisdom: "Wisdom gives life" (Eccles. 7:12). And wisdom gives a person this shame as well. (That level corresponds to the letter *yod* in the name of *Havaya*.)

---

2. See chap. 3.

does not know. However, at this stage, as he absorbs he is able to nullify his knowledge and his existence. That is why it is said that an arrogant person is a fool. His "I" fills him entirely and he cannot nullify it, as a result of which he cannot receive any wisdom. Such a person may travel all over the world but never see anything new. That is because in order to see something new a person must be able to receive, and he can receive only when he can nullify his own being. Thus, young children, who are more open to novel experiences, are able to learn new things easily.

"וְהַחָכְמָה מֵאַיִן תִּמָּצֵא" (איוב כח, ב). This concept is expressed in the verse **"But wisdom, where [*me'ayin*] will it be found?"** (Job 28:12), which may be translated, "And wisdom is found from *ayin*, nothingness."

A person's capacity to attain wisdom depends on his ability to nullify himself. Therefore, it may be said that the two are one and the same: *ḥokhma* is *koaḥ ma*. Wisdom comes from "nothingness." It draws down from the unknown realm higher than intellect into the realm of the known, from the realm that we relate to as nothingness to the realm that we relate to as existence. Therefore, the more a person is able to nullify himself, the more he is able to apprehend wisdom.

וְ"אֵיזֶהוּ חָכָם הָרוֹאֶה אֶת הַנּוֹלָד" (תמיד לב, א), פֵּירוּשׁ, שֶׁרוֹאֶה כָּל דָּבָר אֵיךְ נוֹלַד וְנִתְהַוָּה מֵאַיִן לְיֵשׁ, בִּדְבַר ה' וְרוּחַ פִּיו יִתְבָּרֵךְ, כְּמוֹ שֶׁכָּתוּב: "וּבְרוּחַ פִּיו כָּל צְבָאָם" (תהלים לג, ו). Similarly, the Sages taught, **"Who is wise? A person who sees that which is born"** (*Tamid* 32a). This means that he sees how every entity is born and brought into existence from nothingness via the word of God and the breath of His mouth. As the verse states, "By the breath of His mouth, [He created] **all their hosts**" (Ps. 33:6).

One explanation of this talmudic statement is that a wise person anticipates the future, understanding what will happen before it actually occurs. However, the author of the *Tanya* explains this differently: The wise person can see the process by which everything is formed and created. He sees how the entirety of reality, from the highest worlds down to this world, emerges from nothingness into existence. Just as speech and the breath of the mouth are merely an external expression of the speaker, so too, all that exists is merely an expression of the divine speech that speaks it into being.

> וְאִי לָזֹאת, הֲרֵי הַשָּׁמַיִם וְהָאָרֶץ וְכָל צְבָאָם בְּטֵלִים בִּמְצִיאוּת מַמָּשׁ בִּדְבַר ה' וְרוּחַ פִּיו, וּכְלָא מַמָּשׁ חֲשִׁיבֵי, וְאַיִן וְאֶפֶס מַמָּשׁ, כְּבִיטוּל אוֹר וְזִיו הַשֶּׁמֶשׁ בְּגוּף הַשֶּׁמֶשׁ עַצְמָהּ.

It follows that the heavens, earth, and all their host are actually nullified in God's word and the breath of His mouth. They are considered literally nothing, literally absolute nothingness, in the same way that the light and rays of the sun are nullified within the body of the sun itself.

Since all the worlds are products and outcomes of "the breath of God's mouth," in relation to that breath they are void, no more than shadows. Just as there is no independent sunlight in the sun because everything there is one, so too there are no separate entities within the divine essence. ☞

SEEING WHAT IS BORN

☞ When a person reflects deeply on the idea that "that which is born" does not refer to something that is born once, but to something that is being born now and at every moment, that the whole world is constantly being created by the word of God and the breath of His mouth, he achieves an inner, higher fear. By way of analogy, when some people see the king's palace with its elegant halls, towering pillars, and marvelous embellishments, they are overcome with awe. But there is a higher, more profound level, when a person realizes that all of this is only the garment and adornment, and that the king himself is inside. The heavens and the earth are not only objects that the King has created. They are the outward manifestations of the King. In this sense, the magnitude and magnificence of heaven and earth and all their host are merely God's garment and adornment, inconsequential and nullified in relation to the divine essence that brings them into being. A person who experiences this no longer relates to God's deeds in terms of "How great are Your works" (Ps. 92:6) and "How manifold are Your deeds" (Ps. 104:24). Rather, he "sees that which is born"; he sees the Creator within creation. Existence grows increasingly transparent

וְאַל יוֹצִיא אָדָם עַצְמוֹ מֵהַכְּלָל, שֶׁגַּם גּוּפוֹ וְנַפְשׁוֹ וְרוּחוֹ וְנִשְׁמָתוֹ בְּטֵלִים בִּמְצִיאוּת בִּדְבַר ה' וְדִבּוּרוֹ יִתְבָּרֵךְ מְיֻחָד בְּמַחֲשַׁבְתּוֹ כוּ', וְכַנִּזְכָּר לְעֵיל [פְּרָקִים כ' וְכ"א] בַּאֲרִיכוּת, בְּדֶרֶךְ מָשָׁל מִנֶּפֶשׁ הָאָדָם, שֶׁדִּבּוּר אֶחָד מִדִּבּוּרוֹ וּמַחֲשַׁבְתּוֹ כְּלֹא מַמָּשׁ כוּ'.

A person should not exclude himself from this principle, for his body and the elements of his soul – his *nefesh*, *ruaḥ*, and *neshama* – too are nullified in the word of God, and God's word is united with His thought, and so on, and as mentioned above at length (in chaps. 20–21) **by way of analogy to the human soul: that a single utterance of** a person's **speech and his thought are truly like nothing** compared to his soul, **and so forth.**

By way of analogy: A person imagines a world, he populates it with creatures of his own invention, and he gives these creatures permission to think, speak, build, destroy, fight, and so on. How would one of these creatures view itself and its existence? Its entire world is the result of one thought, and it exists only within that thought, which exists within the person who thought it. ☞

to him. The fact that existence is an expression of "God's word and the breath of His mouth" grows increasingly clear until he no longer sees existence but nothingness. On one level, a person perceives the world, believes that there is a Creator, and he is moved by this fact. However, on this level, a person ceases to see the world and increasingly understands that there is only God.

THE ANALOGY OF THE STORYTELLER

☞ A story creates a new world with its own places, creatures, and language. The existence of that world is not separate from its narrator. It exists within him, and it continues to exist as long as he creates the characters and their actions. In the larger picture, in the reality beyond the story, there is only the creator who tells the story. Similarly, the entire world is only the thought and word of God, the story that God tells. This is clearly stated in the book of Genesis: "God said: Let there be light, and there was light" (Gen. 1:3); "Let the earth produce living creatures…and it was so" (Gen. 1:24). The world and its creatures are created by God's word, and they continue to exist as long as God continues to tell the story, as long as these matters remain in His mind, as it were. This implies that God can end the story or start a new one. And indeed, there is a kabbalistic concept (see *Torah Or* 51d; Ramban and Ibn Ezra, Lev. 25:2) that our world is the second in a series of cosmic cycles. In other words, there was a world before this one, and there may be more worlds after

This view of reality leads to the higher fear of God, because it is not a fear of ceasing to exist, which is the basis of all forms of lower fear, but the opposite. A being created by the word of God and who exists by virtue of His breath is not God's creation but God's word. A being created by God is liable to cease to exist. That fact is the basis for the lower fear of God. But God's word is inseparable from God. Therefore, the existence and reality of a person who is the word of God is part of God's reality. If a person tries to establish his existence on a basis separate from God, he is absolute nothingness, but as "the word of God," he is part of God's truth. A person who has the profound insight that all existence including himself is an existence that God brings into being with His word has a corresponding type of fear of God, with a corresponding understanding of himself and God and the relationships between himself and God. This is not yet an aspect of love of God. It is still an aspect of the fear of God, but it is a higher fear, in which a person's existence, seen in the light of the supreme, divine being, in which a person realizes, in the light of his awareness of the supreme, divine being, that his existence has more dimensions than he had previously conceived.

וְזֶהוּ שֶׁאָמַר הַכָּתוּב: "הֵן יִרְאַת ה' הִיא חָכְמָה" (איוב כח, כח).

That is the meaning of **the verse "Behold, the fear of the Lord, it is wisdom"** (Job 28:28).

---

it, variations of the story as it is told anew in different ways, with different characters and different outcomes.

This concept does not posit that our world is unreal. By way of analogy, Pieter Bruegel's paintings contain an exceptionally detailed world. Its elements truly exist – but only within the painting. Their existence is not on the same order as that of the person who painted them. Rambam says this in another way at the beginning of his *Mishneh Torah*: "All beings from heaven and earth, and that which is in between, exist only due to the true [existence] of [God's] own being. Were we to suppose that He is not, nothing else could have been called into being" (*Sefer HaMadda, Hilkhot Yesodei HaTorah* 1:1–2).

Elsewhere, Rambam says that because all of our terms refer only to our reality created by God, it is impossible to refer to God in terms of positive attributes, even to say that He exists, because these terms relate only to the framework of our world, and we cannot say that God exists in the same manner that an entity in our world exists. We can describe God only by means of negation: stating, for instance, that He is not nonexistent.

Higher fear is wisdom. That is because, like wisdom, it is a sense of the nullification of the self and of all reality within the divine essence. It is not a person's instinctive fear as his ego faces the universe. Rather, it is an awareness that comes to a person only after he exerts himself in studying Torah and serving God. Before reaching this awareness, a person must climb to the highest level of wisdom, in which he no longer sees the physical world as existence and the divine as nothingness, but the opposite: he sees that the divine alone is existence and this world is nothingness.[3] This is the highest degree of enlightenment, which only the greatest people achieve. ☞

אַךְ אִי אֶפְשָׁר לְהַשִּׂיג לְיִרְאָה וְחָכְמָה זוֹ, אֶלָּא בְּקִיּוּם הַתּוֹרָה וְהַמִּצְוֹת עַל יְדֵי 'יִרְאָה תַּתָּאָה' הַחִיצוֹנִית. וְזֶה שֶׁאָמְרוּ: "אִם אֵין יִרְאָה - אֵין חָכְמָה" (אבות פרק ג משנה יז).

However, a person **cannot achieve this fear and wisdom without keeping the Torah and mitzvot as a result of** his having attained **the lower, external level of fear. This is** what is meant **by the Sages' statement "If there is no fear, there is no wisdom"** (*Avot* 3:17).

As stated at the beginning of this chapter, the present section of the Mishna is speaking of the lower fear of God. If a person does not possess the simple, external fear of punishment, he cannot possess wisdom. Without this fear, he cannot attain the wisdom of the Torah

---

I SEE ONLY THE DIVINE VOID

☞ In the final hours of his life, in a dilapidated shack in the village of Pena, the author of the *Tanya* pointed upward and asked his grandson (who would later become the third Lubavitcher Rebbe, the Tzemaḥ Tzedek), "Do you see the ceiling rafter?" Taken aback, his grandson answered that certainly he saw it. The Rebbe told him, "All I see is the divine void that gives vitality to the rafter" (see *Sefer Shivḥei HaRav*). There is a transcendental level on which all outer garments are removed and the world becomes completely transparent to divinity. The verse states regarding that level, "A person shall not see Me and live" (Ex. 33:20), because when a person sees beyond all the partitions, he can no longer exist within them.

---

3. With regard to higher knowledge and lower knowledge, see *Likkutei Torah*, Deut. 83a.

and its commandments, and so he certainly cannot achieve the higher fear of God, which is wisdom.

Until now, this chapter has dealt with the lower and higher fear of God. The author of the *Tanya* has written significantly less about the higher fear of God than about the lower fear of God. This is understandable in light of the purpose of this work and the nature of the people to whom it is addressed. The *Tanya* is not concerned with abstract theories, but with the issues that people face, and it is addressed to *beinonim*, as indicated by the book's alternative title, *Sefer shel Beinonim*. For a *beinoni*, the higher fear of God is something that can be considered and perhaps understood, but it is not part of his being and not among his experiences. The *beinoni* lives and struggles on planes where the lower fear of God exists, in its smaller or larger form, but in general the higher fear of God is not there. Hasidim related that alongside the *Sefer shel Beinonim*, the author of the *Tanya* wanted to write, and perhaps even did write, a book called *Sefer shel Tzaddikim*.[4] In that book, the relationship between higher and lower fear would certainly have been presented differently.

The complete structure of serving God is not comprised of fear alone, but of love as well. From this point on, until the end of the chapter, the author of the *Tanya* will discuss the love of God. Similar to his analysis of the fear of God, he will begin by differentiating between two fundamental levels of the love of God.

30 Nisan | וְהִנֵּה בָּאַהֲבָה יֵשׁ גַּם כֵּן שְׁתֵּי מַדְרֵגוֹת: 'אַהֲבָה רַבָּה' וְ'אַהֲבַת עוֹלָם'. | **With regard to the love** of God, **there are also two levels:** *ahava rabba,* "great love," **and** *ahavat olam,* "world-centered love."

---

4. The Lubavitcher Rebbe, Rabbi Menaḥem Mendel Schneerson, writes in his *Reshimot*, his notebooks, "I heard from my teacher and father-in-law, the Frierdiker Rebbe, Rabbi Yosef Yitzḥak Schneerson, that the author of the *Tanya* began writing a *Sefer shel Tzaddikim* as well, but it was burned in a fire." The story is told that Rabbi Aryeh Leib of Shpola came to the author of the *Tanya* and asked him, "Has the Rebbe begun writing a *Sefer shel Tzaddikim*? The world is not worthy of such a book. This matter has provoked the heavenly prosecution, and it has been decreed that it shall be burned, and I will ascend to heaven upon that flame." And indeed, Rabbi Aryeh Leib of Shpola passed away at the time of the fire (see *Iggerot Kodesh*, vol. 9, letter 2853).

The Talmud (*Berakhot* 11b) presents two versions of the opening words of the blessing before the recitation of the *Shema*: "You have loved us with *ahavat olam*" and "You have loved us with *ahava rabba*." A number of *Ge'onim* and *Rishonim* (*Tosafot, Rosh*) reconciled these two texts in various ways. Some ruled that we should say *ahava rabba* in the morning prayer and *ahavat olam* in the evening prayer. Others ruled that we should say *ahavat olam* on weekdays and *ahava rabba* on the Sabbath. Here the author of the *Tanya* will explain that these two readings refer to the two levels of the love of God. *Ahava rabba* expresses the "great" love of God, and *ahavat olam* expresses the "worldly" love of God.[5]

אַהֲבָה רַבָּה הִיא "אַהֲבָה בַּתַּעֲנוּגִים" (שיר השירים ז, ז). *Ahava rabba* is the higher level of love. It **is a "love of delights"** (Song 7:7).

The "love of delights"[6] is a love that does not involve any anguished longing to attain what one loves. That anguished longing involves a person's need for something that he lacks, as described in the verse "My soul thirsts for You; my flesh yearns for You" (Ps. 63:2). Moreover, as he draws closer to what he loves, his thirst and longing only increase. But the "love of delights" is solely pleasure. There is no sense of lack. A person does not need or expect anything. He does not need the object of his love to make any kind of gesture, nor to remain with him always. It is enough for him that his loved one exists. That itself provides him with all the happiness he needs. His love satisfies him in itself. The more he knows and understands the object of his love, the more content he is.

Usually, when a person sees a beautiful flower in the field, he wants to pick it. But for a person who possesses the "love of delights," it is

---

5. See *Kitzurim U'Biurim LeSefer HaTanya*.
6. See *Torah Or* 47c, which says that "love of delights" is a third level of love, above *ahavat olam* and *ahava rabba*. A note states there in parentheses, "Chapter 43 of the *Tanya* requires consideration, for it appears to say that *ahava rabba* is [the same as] 'love of delights.' It must be that there are two aspects of *ahava rabba*. The first is mentioned in the *Tanya*, chap. 19, and does not contain an expression of 'delight.' The higher level is *ahava rabba*, [which does contain] delight. See also the discourse on the verse 'My sister, my love, my faultless dove' (Song 5:2), which explained that 'my sister' refers to innate love, and 'my dove' refers to 'love of delights.'"

enough for him that the flower exists. This kind of love contains a trace of the World to Come, because in heaven the tzaddik loves God and does not need anything else. Likewise, even in this world a person who possesses the "love of delights" has everything he needs. As the verse states, "Whom else do I have in heaven? With You, I desire nothing on earth…God is the strength of my heart and my portion forever" (Ps. 73:25–26). God is present, and that is enough.

וְהִיא שַׁלְהֶבֶת הָעוֹלָה מֵאֵלֶיהָ It is a fiery flame that rises on its own

This love is not something that a person creates or cultivates. It is like a flame that a person does not need to light or fan. This image, which is used to describe the lighting of the candelabrum, is also connected to the Sages' words about the fire on the altar: that even in a case when fire descends from heaven, it is still a mitzva for a person to bring fire (see *Yoma* 21b; *Torah Or* 32b). In the case of *ahava rabba*, however, the fire comes from above regardless of the human effort from below.

וּבָאָה מִלְמַעְלָה בִּבְחִינַת מַתָּנָה לְמִי שֶׁהוּא שָׁלֵם בְּיִרְאָה. and comes from above as a gift to a person who is perfect in his fear of God.

This love that comes on its own does not result from the work that a person has performed in this world, but it is a gift from above that comes when a person is perfect in his fear of God. When a person has perfected his fear of God – which means that he has perfected himself, because, as the verse states, "What does the Lord your God ask of you? Only to fear the Lord your God" (Deut. 10:12) – he receives the gift of the "love of delights."

כַּנּוֹדָע עַל מַאֲמַר רַבּוֹתֵינוּ ז״ל: דַּרְכּוֹ שֶׁל אִישׁ לְחַזֵּר אַחַר אִשָּׁה (קידושין ב, ב), **שֶׁאַהֲבָה נִקְרֵאת 'אִישׁ' וְ'זָכָר', כְּמוֹ שֶׁכָּתוּב: "זָכַר חַסְדּוֹ"** (תהלים צח, ג). **וְ"אִשָּׁה יִרְאַת ה׳"** (משלי לא, ל) **כַּנּוֹדָע.** This is known to be alluded to in our Rabbis' statement "It is the way of a man to pursue a woman" (*Kiddushin* 2b). Love is referred to as "man" or *zakhar*, male, as the verse states, "He recalled [*zakhar*] His kindness" (Ps. 98:3), whereas "a woman fears the Lord" (Prov. 31:30), as is known.

This statement of the Rabbis alludes to serving God. Kindness and love are "male" attributes, whereas fear is a "female" attribute. The phrase "a woman fears the Lord" may be translated as "'woman' is [the level of] the fear of the Lord." The *sefira* of Ḥesed, Kindness and Love, is identified with the right side, which in kabbalistic thought is male, the side of the giver. Conversely, the *sefira* of Gevura, Restraint and Fear, is identified with the left side, which in kabbalistic thought is the female side, the side of the receiver. When a person perfects his ability to be a receiver, which is the level of fear, then supernal love pursues him in order to give to him. When a person has attained all the necessary stages to experience prophecy, "the Holy Spirit immediately rests upon him."[7] Likewise, when a person perfects his fear of God, he is ready to receive *ahava rabba*.

וּבְלִי קְדִימַת הַיִּרְאָה אִי אֶפְשָׁר לְהַגִּיעַ לְ'אַהֲבָה רַבָּה' זוֹ, כִּי אַהֲבָה זוֹ הִיא מִבְּחִינַת אֲצִילוּת, דְּלֵית תַּמָּן קִצּוּץ וּפֵירוּד חַס וְשָׁלוֹם. **Without first** experiencing **the existence of the fear** of God, a person **cannot attain this *ahava rabba*, since this love is on the level of** the **world of Atzilut, where there is no severing or separation, God forbid.**

The world of *Atzilut* is a realm of unity and wholeness, and this is where *ahava rabba* belongs. *Ahava rabba* is a gift from a higher world, given in rare cases to people who have reached a level tantamount to the level of a higher world. This love is inherently connected to the person's soul. Therefore, it is unrelated to, and independent of, his desires, which take on various forms. *Ahava rabba* does not relate in any way to our split-off, finite world. Rather, it relates to the world of *Atzilut*, where there are no limits or barriers. There, the various forces (and their interactions) of the *sefirot* are not distinct from one another as they are in our world, but they function as a single unit. ☞

Just as the author of the *Tanya* did not say a great deal about the higher fear of God, neither does he say a great deal about *ahava rabba*

THE WORLD OF ATZILUT AND UNITY

☞ The world of *Atzilut* is a realm of perfection and unity, where there is no division between "I" and "He," between the self and God. The beings of the world of *Atzilut* have no sense of self because the *sefirot* in that world are the garments in

---

7. See Rambam, *Sefer HaMadda, Hilkhot Yesodei HaTorah* 7:1.

for several reasons: first, because it is a very rare state; second, because it is a gift, and this book is not concerned with what a person receives but with what he must do; and third, because a person who is on this level certainly does not need to read about it in a book. The description here comes only to complete the picture outlined in these chapters of serving God via all the aspects of fear and love, from the lowest to the highest.

אַךְ 'אַהֲבַת עוֹלָם' הִיא הַבָּאָה מֵהִתְבּוֹנְנָה וְדַעַת בִּגְדוּלַּת ה' אֵין סוֹף בָּרוּךְ הוּא, הַמְמַלֵּא כָּל עָלְמִין וְסוֹבֵב כָּל עָלְמִין, וְכוּלָּא קַמֵּיהּ כְּלָא מַמָּשׁ חֲשִׁיב, וּכְבִיטּוּל דִּבּוּר אֶחָד בְּנֶפֶשׁ הַמַּשְׂכֶּלֶת, בְּעוֹדוֹ בְּמַחֲשַׁבְתָּהּ אוֹ בְּחֶמְדַּת הַלֵּב, כַּנִּזְכָּר לְעֵיל.

However, *ahavat olam*, the lower level of love, **is the love of God that comes from** a person's **understanding and knowledge of the greatness of the infinite God, blessed be He,** who "**fills all worlds and encompasses all worlds**," before whom **everything is literally considered nothingness, just as a single utterance within the rational soul is nullified while it is still in its thought or in the desire of the heart, as explained above** (chaps. 20–21).

Ahavat olam, world-centered love, is the love of God that comes from the world, i.e., from understanding God's greatness as it relates to the world. That is because it is specifically in the world that His greatness appears. Divine greatness has meaning only as it is revealed in the worlds and in relation to them,[8] that is to say, in the divine light that which God clothes Himself. Since they have no characteristics of their own, they are called by the names of God. Thus, *Ḥesed* in *Atzilut* is called *E-l*, *Gevura* is called *Elokim*, *Tiferet* is called *Havaya*, and so on (see *Derekh Mitzvotekha*, *Shoresh Mitzvat HaTefilla*, chaps. 3–6). The world of *Atzilut* is the world of complete perfection, of a total absence of the self. In order to touch such a world, a person must be on a level similar to that of that world. On that level, there is no self and all partitions are removed. It is the state of the perfect fear of God. That is because, through that fear of God, a person completely rectifies his character and his life until he reaches perfection. At that moment, he makes contact with the perfect world of *Atzilut*, and then he is able to receive a gift at the level of *ahava rabba*.

---

8. Regarding the verse "The Lord is great and exceedingly praised in the city of

fills and surrounds all worlds, before which everything is as nothing. This is comparable to how a person's utterance is subsumed within the totality of all the possible words that he could potentially speak before he does so, while that word is still in his thought or the desire of his heart.

אֲשֶׁר עַל יְדֵי הִתְבּוֹנְנוּת זוֹ מִמֵּילָא תִּתְפַּשֵּׁט מִדַּת הָאַהֲבָה שֶׁבַּנֶּפֶשׁ מִלְּבוּשֶׁיהָ. דְּהַיְינוּ שֶׁלֹּא תִתְלַבֵּשׁ בְּשׁוּם דָּבָר הֲנָאָה וְתַעֲנוּג גַּשְׁמִי אוֹ רוּחָנִי לְאַהֲבָה אוֹתוֹ, וְלֹא לַחְפּוֹץ כְּלָל שׁוּם דָּבָר בָּעוֹלָם בִּלְתִּי ה' לְבַדּוֹ מְקוֹר הַחַיִּים שֶׁל כָּל הַתַּעֲנוּגִים,

When a person engages in **this contemplation, the attribute of love within** his **soul will shed its garments. That is to say, it will no longer clothe itself in anything** that provides **pleasure or delight, whether physical or spiritual, in order to love** that thing, **and it will not at all desire anything in the world but God alone,** who is **the source of vitality of all delights,**

Contemplation does not mean mere thought about something, but deep reflection and an effort to have the object of one's contemplation permeate one's very being. Then the trait of love in the soul will remove its garments. The attribute of love within the soul, like any other attribute, is not defined by the objects of the person's love, but it only clothes itself in them. The objects in which love clothes itself are only an expression of the love, which depends on many factors, both internal and external, in a person's life. When a person engages in contemplation, he can remove these outer garments, as will be explained. When this is accomplished, the attribute of love within the soul no longer craves anything in this world. The word "crave" refers to the innermost aspect of desire, which relates to the innermost aspect of entities and not to their outer garments.[9] Then the soul will only want God, the source of all delights. A person desires something that he believes to be worthy of desire. When he finds something that he believes to be even more worthy, he revokes his previous love and desire. And this goes on until a person has

---

our God" (Ps. 48:2), the *Zohar* states (3:5a): "When is the Lord great? When He is 'in the city of our God.'" See *Likkutei Torah*, Deut. 29b.

9. See *Likkutei Torah*, Num. 38c.

revoked all other loves before the great Beloved, God Himself, who is the source of all life and existence. ☞

שֶׁכּוּלָּם בְּטֵילִים בִּמְצִיאוּת וּכְלָא מַמָּשׁ קַמֵּיהּ חֲשִׁיבֵי וְאֵין עֲרוֹךְ וְדִמְיוֹן כְּלָל בֵּינֵיהֶם חַס וְשָׁלוֹם,

because all delights are subsumed and are considered as literally nothingness before Him. There is no basis for comparison or similarity between them whatsoever, God forbid,

CONTEMPLATION THAT LEADS TO LOVE

☞ The connection between this contemplation of the nullification of all reality before God and the love of God is apparently unclear. It is more understandable that such contemplation creates fear (as described above), because it causes a person to feel the divine power and exaltedness in contrast to his own smallness. Yet here the author of the *Tanya* describes the contemplation of divine greatness as leading in another direction: not to a sense of distance, but to a sense of being close to God, whose "glory fills the entire world" (Isa. 6:3), and regarding whom the verse states, "There is no other besides Him" (Deut. 4:35). Just as the perception of being distant from God is the root of the fear of God, the perception of being close to God is the root of the love of God (see *Torah Or* 45c). The revelation that everything that we see is nothing but a tiny fragment of God's greatness leads to the emotionally tinged realization that the soul's entire capacity to love and desire all objects of this world will melt away before the desire for God Himself, who is the source of them all. When a person realizes that all of the objects he desires and thinks about are only small fragments that conceal the divine essence, and that the most beautiful, pleasant, and desirable object is the divine light, and everything else is only an envelope and cover, he concludes: Why should I want something that is only a garment and covering when I can relate to the inner essence of these objects, which is God Himself?

There is a hasidic teaching (see *Keter Shem Tov* 194; *Likkutei Torah*, Deut. 14b; the Arizal's *Likkutei Torah, Parashat Ekev*) on the verse "Man does not live by bread alone; rather, it is by everything that emanates from the mouth of the Lord that man lives" (Deut. 8:3). A person does not live by means of bread as bread, but by that which emanates from God's mouth (the divine speech in the ten divine utterances) that exists within the bread. That is to say, that which gives a person life and which he wants is in essence not the bread but only that which God's mouth brings forth. A person does not want the outer garment but he longs for that which is within. However, because of the material garment, because of his education, because of his habituation, because of his conception of the world, he errs and prefers the covering over the substance. The fact that a person cannot relate to the content but only to the external garment and envelope is a spiritual aberration. It is as if a person were to desire the chocolate wrapper and not the chocolate itself. In this sense, contemplation acts to strip away from our reality the things whose temporary, superficial cover

Since God is the source of life, and life means pleasure, He is the source of all delights.[10] There is no comparison between the desired objects of this world and the divine essence, which is the inner essence of everything.

כְּמוֹ שֶׁאֵין עֲרוֹךְ לְאַיִן וָאֶפֶס הַמּוּחְלָט לְגַבֵּי חַיִּים נִצְחִיִּים. just as there is no value to absolute nothingness compared to eternal life.

All worldly realities and delights, which are transient, seem trivial and unworthy of attention compared to the one eternal object of love, God Himself. ☞

we love, so that we can relate to the substance, which is what we really desire: to reveal that everything that we want, the particular objects of our love, our temporary longings – in all of these, we find God alone. This contemplation is not intended to reveal that "exalted above all nations is the Lord" (Ps. 113:4), but to reveal that "there is no other besides Him," to reveal the insignificance of the envelope compared to the actuality of the content. When a person contemplates all this and truly reflects on it deeply, his attribute of love will no longer clothe itself in objects that provide pleasure or delight, whether physical or spiritual. Rather, he will desire God alone, who is the source of the life of all delights.

THE DESIRE THAT QUELLS ALL DESIRES

☞ There is a hasidic concept that love of God is also a kind of lust, but one that extinguishes all other lusts. The point of this teaching is that in order to attain the love of God, a person is not necessarily required to go through the stage of giving up his love of the things of this world. He does not have to afflict himself in order to reach the pleasure of loving God. On the contrary, in a sense, all that is necessary is that each instance of his desire and delight will be deeper than the previous instance. The hasidim in Lithuania told of a hasid who prayed to have his evil inclination removed. His prayer was answered, but he then discovered that he had become impassive even with regard to serving God. That is because a person who is unable to experience desire cannot yearn for anything, so that he cannot even love God. The mishna in Avot, "Beloved are Israel in that a desirable vessel was given to them" (3:14), may be read as: "Beloved are Israel in that a vessel was given to them, and that vessel was desire." Desire is a vessel in which a person can place the objects of his desire in accordance with his spiritual level and contemplation. Everyone possesses desire, but the objects of desire vary depending on a person's level, personality, and age. A

---

10. See *Likkutei Torah*, Ex. 1a.

וּכְמוֹ שֶׁכָּתוּב: "מִי לִי בַשָּׁמַיִם וְעִמְּךָ לֹא חָפַצְתִּי בָאָרֶץ כָּלָה שְׁאֵרִי וּלְבָבִי צוּר לְבָבִי" וְגוֹ' (תהלים עג, כה-כו), וּכְמוֹ שֶׁיִּתְבָּאֵר לְקַמָּן.

As the verse states, "Whom else do I have in heaven? With You, I desire nothing on earth. My flesh and my heart may fail, but God is the strength of my heart and my portion forever" (Ps. 73:25–26), **as will be explained below** (chap. 48).

Ahavat olam, "world-centered love," is so called because it is essentially a love of the world. When a person's love of this world grows more intense, that experience is transformed into a love of God. A person's contemplation teaches him that he should desire God and nothing else. That is not because desiring other things is forbidden, but because there is not enough in heaven and earth to satisfy a person's love, since heaven and earth are insignificant compared to the supreme essence. It is said of Jehoshaphat, king of Judah: "His heart was elevated in the ways of the Lord" (II Chron. 17:6). There is an approach to serving God in which a person should never be satisfied with what he has. Should he be satisfied with his lot in this world and in the World to Come, he will be unable to truly serve God. Unlike divine service that stems from contraction, from a sense of one's smallness, this divine service

small child's yearning for a toy is no weaker than his father's desire for money or respect. Each individual has his own ideas of what is worth desiring. As a person's understanding grows purer and his senses grow more refined, even in the realm of worldly pleasures, his desire abandons one object and goes to another. And when a person no longer desires any worldly pleasures, it is not because his desire has weakened; on the contrary, it is because he has a stronger desire. Some people are content with little; they desire a modest amount of money. Others desire a thousand times more. Still others will never be satisfied with less than all the gold and silver in the world, and for some people, even that will never be enough. A person who pursues wealth, immorality, or idol worship does so not because he has strong desires; on the contrary, his desires are so limited that he is content with shards of sparkling vessels, with insignificant fragments of the supernal essence. He is "content with little." When a person contemplates and understands that the source of life and pleasure is to be found in God, he abhors all worldly pleasures, not because they are bad or wrong, but because they are small and fleeting. They are shadows of vessels compared to what is contained within the vessels. They are absolutely nothing with respect to the love of God.

stems from expansion, from the fact that a human being is great and wants more. He is unsatisfied with anything limited. Some people have a burning desire for a life in which they must reach God, who is the essence of life. They are not willing to settle for anything less. Only when a person's heart is elevated above the heavens, when he wants more, when he thinks, "Whom else do I have in heaven? With You, I desire nothing on earth," and he desires only God, then "God is … [his] portion forever." ☞

וְגַם מִי שֶׁאֵין מִדַּת אַהֲבָה שֶׁבְּנַפְשׁוֹ מְלוּבֶּשֶׁת כְּלָל בְּשׁוּם תַּעֲנוּג גַּשְׁמִי אוֹ רוּחָנִי, יָכוֹל לְהַלְהִיב נַפְשׁוֹ כְּרִשְׁפֵּי אֵשׁ וְשַׁלְהֶבֶת עַזָּה וְלַהַב הָעוֹלֶה הַשָּׁמַיְמָה עַל יְדֵי הַהִתְבּוֹנְנוּת הַנִּזְכֶּרֶת לְעֵיל, כְּמוֹ שֶׁיִּתְבָּאֵר לְקַמָּן.

Even a person in whose soul the attribute of love is not clothed at all in any physical or spiritual delight can kindle his soul like sparks of fire, a fierce conflagration and a flame that rises heavenward through the contemplation mentioned above, as will be explained below (chap. 44).

Some people possess a cold nature, and they never uncover love in themselves for any other being, material or spiritual, for any matter, holy or mundane. In these people, the attribute of love appears to be dormant. They know that love exists. But their relationships lack passion and pleasure. It would appear that *ahavat olam*, which cultivates a person's existing faculties of love, cannot develop in such people. Nevertheless, when even such a person engages in contemplation, he can set his soul

---

"WITH YOU, I DESIRE NOTHING ON EARTH"

☞ Alongside the rejection and contempt for this-worldly matters expressed in the book of Ecclesiastes, there is another perspective, which is less talked about. That is the exalted aspect of the book of Ecclesiastes. It is the description of a person who is never satisfied, "even if he had lived a thousand years two times over" (Eccl. 6:6). Such a person has no choice but to turn to matters of eternity, of eternal life, because only there can he really find the world in a way that fulfills him, because only there can he find the source of reality: not matters of history or geography, but where things exist as they really are. In that eternal reality, he has not only bits and pieces of reality, comparable to toys that a child plays with, but the reality itself.

ablaze. When a person engages in contemplation of the love of God, he not only shifts love for some smaller object of love with the love of God. Rather, this contemplation transforms the essence of a person's soul, because he is focusing on God, who is the life force within the soul, the "I" within a person's "I." Therefore, when even a person whose soul does not clothe itself in the love of small things engages in this contemplation, he realizes that the divine essence is the only reality from which he cannot hide, which he cannot avoid relating to. At that moment, for perhaps the first time in his life, the entire attribute of love in his soul is ignited, and its object is the divine essence. "With my soul, I desired You" (Isa. 26:9); this may be interpreted to mean, "You are my soul, and therefore I desired You" (as will be stated in chap. 44).

This concludes the *Tanya*'s description of the four aspects of the love and fear of God. The chapter goes on to end with a comment on the order in which a person implements these in his service of God. The normative order is in concert with the text of the kabbalistic statement recited before performing a mitzva, "For the sake of uniting the Holy One, blessed be He, with His Divine Presence, with *fear* and *love* and *love* and *fear*." The order is: (a) the lower fear of God, which is the fear of God's presence; (b) *ahavat olam*, "world-centered love"; (c) an additional level of love, *ahava rabba*, "great love"; and finally, (d) the higher fear of God. That is the appropriate order for a person who is mapping out his path in advance. He begins with the lower fear of God because, as mentioned in chapter 41, that is "the beginning of divine service and its core and root." The correct and surest way to rise to God is to begin with the fear of God at the foundation. However, the author of the *Tanya* adds that in reality the order may be different.

---

1 Iyar
27 Nisan
(leap year)

וְהִנֵּה בְּחִינַת אַהֲבָה זוֹ **This aspect of love**

"This aspect of love" refers to *ahavat olam*, "world-centered love." "Love of delights" – that being *ahava rabba*, "great love" – is, on the other hand, essentially unrelated to anything of this world. It is a connection between an individual and God, an individual who is alone with God, so to speak. Therefore, it barely has any connection to the other aspects of serving God.

פְּעָמִים שֶׁקּוֹדֶמֶת לְיִרְאָה, כְּפִי בְּחִינַת הַדַּעַת הַמּוֹלִידָהּ, כַּנּוֹדָע	will occasionally **precede the fear of God, in accordance with the quality of the** *Da'at* – **the "knowledge" – that engenders** that love, **as is known.**

This change in order, of love preceding the lower fear of God, is in accordance with the nature of the *sefira* of *Da'at*, Knowledge, which engenders both love and fear. As is explained in several places,[11] among all the *sefirot* involving the cognitive faculties, it is the *sefira* of Knowledge that engenders the *sefirot* of emotion. Contemplation in itself, as it takes place in the *sefira* of *Bina* (Understanding), is abstract and objective; it has no valence or any preferences. Therefore, contemplation can create various responses to the object of contemplation: distance, closeness, excitement, and so forth. Only in the next *sefira* down, *Da'at*, Knowledge, are the matters being contemplated connected to the soul's attributes, which dictate the form of the person's response to the topic being contemplated. Accordingly, everything that is formed inside a person, everything that is connected and set down within him, everything he knows and feels – attraction or repulsion, love or fear – depends mainly on his faculty of knowledge.

[שֶׁהַדַּעַת כּוֹלֵל חֲסָדִים וּגְבוּרוֹת, שֶׁהֵם אַהֲבָה וְיִרְאָה,	(**That is because the** attribute of *Da'at* **encompasses the aspects of** *ḥasadim* **and** *gevurot*, **which constitute love and fear,**

Love and fear are the essence of, respectively, Ḥesed and Gevura.[12] As is explained elsewhere, the *sefira* of Knowledge, which has the character of attachment and relationship, contains the two modes of response: for and against. Since knowledge includes these two opposites, different reactions can result from the same instance of contemplation: either a feeling of love and desire to approach that which it is "for," or a feeling of fear and moving away from that which it is "against."

---

11. Chap. 3; *Iggeret HaKodesh*, epistle 15.
12. See *Iggeret HaKodesh*, epistle 15.

וּפְעָמִים שֶׁהַחֲסָדִים קוֹדְמִים לֵירֵד וּלְהִתְגַּלּוֹת.] — and occasionally the aspects of *ḥasadim* are first to descend and become manifest.)

Generally, fear precedes love. That is because in many ways it is a simpler and more preliminary feeling. In order to feel fear, a person need only be uncertain about something, whereas in order to feel love, a person requires a clear and tangible picture about something. A person who enters a dark place fears what might be there. No one enters a dark and unfamiliar place with a sense of love for something good that might be there. The feeling of fear requires less connection to the object and less contemplation, and the object need not be especially tangible. Thus, it is natural for fear to precede love. All that is required is an indefinable sense of unease, the sense of some other presence, of no longer being free to do whatever one wishes. The person need not have a clear awareness of what that entity is. Conversely, in order to love, a person must have a clear, tangible picture. Nevertheless, since a person's faculty of knowledge is linked to the structure of his soul (since it is one of the *sefirot* that comprise his soul), and it is linked to the particular circumstances of time, place, societal influence, and environment, it is possible that his contemplation will first yield love, and only afterward fear.

וְלָכֵן אֶפְשָׁר לְרָשָׁע וּבַעַל עֲבֵירוֹת שֶׁיַּעֲשֶׂה תְּשׁוּבָה מֵאַהֲבָה — For this reason, it is possible for a person who is wicked and a transgressor to repent out of love

In general, repentance is a movement that does not proceed in a step-by-step order. Therefore, it is possible for repentance to begin with love.

הַנּוֹלְדָה בְּלִבּוֹ בְּזָכְרוֹ אֶת ה׳ אֱלֹהָיו. — engendered in his heart when he remembers the Lord his God.

Ideally, in repentance, fear should come first. An evildoer should first arrive at the feeling that he is on the wrong path. He should fear what may happen to him if he will continue in this way, and as a result he should experience regret and repentance. And only afterward should he experience the love of God. However, in reality, a person who is far from God will, in addition to realizing what he has done and where he is, become aware of God, and his heart will yearn for Him. It is even possible that a wicked person, someone who has committed transgressions, will reach the state of *ahava rabba*, and his soul will depart his body, as occurred to Rabbi Elazar ben Durdaya (as will be mentioned below). ☞

וּמִכָּל מָקוֹם, הַיִּרְאָה גַּם כֵּן כְּלוּלָה בָּהּ מִמֵּילָא, — **At any rate, the fear** of God **is automatically encompassed in** this love **as well,**

Regarding the love of God that precedes the fear of God, the author of the *Tanya* states that fear is embedded within that love. Any love that has no fear within it whatsoever – whether love between man and God or between man and man – is not love but self-gratification. It is comparable to a person who "loves" a steak and tears into it without restraint.

רַק שֶׁהִיא בִּבְחִינַת קַטְנוּת וְהֶעְלֵם, דְּהַיְינוּ יִרְאַת חֵטְא שֶׁלֹּא לִמְרוֹד בּוֹ חַס וְשָׁלוֹם, — **except that** this fear **is present in a minor, hidden form: namely, as fear of sin so as not to rebel against Him, God forbid,**

HE MIGHT REPENT OUT OF LOVE

☞ I (the author of this commentary) had a close friend who lived on a secular kibbutz and who, after twenty years of distress and doubt regarding his view of religion, broke away from his natural environment and entered the world of Hasidism. Once, as we were learning, I asked him what had impelled him to take this step. He said, "For all those years, I was haunted by a verse in the book of Job: 'You yearn for Your handiwork' (Job 14:15). If God is yearning for me, His handiwork, how can I not come to Him?" I felt humbled by this man. I saw that he was a great person who could not rest, who was aroused by the thought that God is yearning for him, and he cannot say no to God! Here was a Jew who was haunted by a subtle feeling, a feeling that even a person who has served God his entire life with fear and love may not feel, a feeling that, although subtle, is powerful. This thought did not leave him alone until he turned his entire life around. It was a feeling that he, his life, and his world were not enough, because God was yearning for him!

This love of God is not removed from the reality of life in this world. This love too influences a person so that he does not sin. Like any genuine love, it keeps a person from harming and saddening his beloved. This is not the fear of God, but it is at any rate the fear of sin. The person does not reach the full understanding that a particular act comprises a sin and is forbidden, but he will not do something that transgresses God's will.

וְהָאַהֲבָה הִיא בְּהִתְגַּלּוּת לִבּוֹ וּמוֹחוֹ. **whereas the love is manifest consciously in** a person's **heart and mind.**

The person's dominant, tangible emotion is love, whereas his emotion of fear is ancillary and parallel to it. Because he loves God so much, he will not do anything against His will. However, his active and vibrant feeling is not fear but love.

אַךְ זֶהוּ דֶּרֶךְ מִקְרֶה וְהוֹרָאַת שָׁעָה, בְּהַשְׁגָּחָה פְּרָטִית מֵאֵת ה׳ לְצוֹרֶךְ שָׁעָה, **However, this** instance of love preceding fear is something **irregular and** in the nature of **a temporary measure,** brought about **through God's divine providence** to meet **the need of the hour,**

In particular situations, for particular people and at particular times, love precedes fear. Normatively, a person learns and progresses step by step on the established, step-by-step path. However, sometimes a person must skip the initial stage of the fear of God because it is not compatible with his level of understanding or with his spiritual character. He does not skip that level forever but only temporarily, and begins instead with love.

A man once brought his young son to his Rebbe. The child was intelligent, but his parents had not yet succeeded in teaching him to read the letters of the *alef-bet*. After the Rebbe spoke to the boy for a few minutes, he advised his parents to teach him Talmud. They did so, and after some time the child also learned the letters. The reason the child had not learned the alphabet was that he had a tremendous capacity for learning, and so learning the letters of the alphabet bored him and he found it meaningless. Therefore, the Rebbe suggested that he skip that stage and immediately begin to learn Talmud, which would fascinate him. Later on, he could go back and learn the letters.

The same applies to the love and fear of God. Some people at a particular time in their lives may need to achieve a great love of God before they can achieve a small amount of the fear of God.

כְּמַעֲשֶׂה דְּרַבִּי אֶלְעָזָר בֶּן דּוּרְדַּיָּא. such as the case of Rabbi Elazar ben Durdaya.

Rabbi Elazar ben Durdaya became the exemplar of repentance. For many years, he would engage the services of every prostitute he could find. One day, a prostitute told him that he was so degraded that he would never be able to repent. This touched him, and he sought a way to repent. He begged God for mercy and searched for help everywhere, but did not find a pathway. Finally, he realized that this was up to him alone. He placed his head between his knees and wept bitterly until his soul left his body. A divine voice proclaimed, "Rabbi Elazar ben Durdaya is destined for life in the World to Come." In a very short time, in a single leap, Rabbi Elazar ben Durdaya rose to the level of loving God, of pouring out his soul before God, a level that other people achieve only after many years of hard work, if they achieve it at all. This is why, when Rabbi Yehuda HaNasi heard this story, he wept and said, "There is one who acquires his [share in the World to Come only] after many years [of toil], and there is [one who] acquires his [share in the World to Come] in one moment" (*Avoda Zara* 17a).

Some have asked why the author of the *Tanya* quotes a story of repentance – which presumably is impelled by the fear of God – when he is discussing the love of God. The answer is that this is a story about repentance that was inspired by the love of God.[13] The impetus that led Rabbi Elazar ben Durdaya to repent in this way was his love for God, and therefore this is also a tremendous story of the love of God.[14]

---

13. When a person's repentance is motivated by love, his intentional sins are counted as merits; see *Yoma* 86b; chap. 7.
14. The Lubavitcher Rebbe, Rabbi Menaḥem Mendel Schneerson, remarks, "See the letter from the Rebbe Rayatz [Rabbi Yosef Yitzḥak Schneerson] at the end of *Kuntres HaAvoda* that states that the author of the *Tanya* is referring here to Rabbi

אֲבָל סֵדֶר הָעֲבוֹדָה הַקְּבוּעָה וּתְלוּיָה בִּבְחִירַת הָאָדָם, צָרִיךְ לְהַקְדִּים תְּחִלָּה קִיּוּם הַתּוֹרָה וְהַמִּצְוֹת עַל יְדֵי יִרְאָה תַּתָּאָה, בִּבְחִינַת קַטְנוּת עַל כָּל פָּנִים, בִּ"סוּר מֵרָע וַעֲשֵׂה טוֹב",

But the normative **sequence of serving God, which is determined by and contingent on a person's choice, is of necessity** that a person **begin by keeping the Torah and mitzvot through the lower fear** of God **at least in its minor form, by avoiding evil and doing good.**

Rabbi Elazar ben Durdaya did not plan his repentance in advance. Rather, it came to him. He was driven to such a tremendous awakening and depth of emotion that his love of God preceded everything else. However, when a person plans his campaign of action, the first stage is to keep the Torah and mitzvot as a result of being impelled by the lower fear of God, even if only on its basic level of avoiding evil and performing good deeds. He may even do so not because he fears punishment, but because he fears stepping out of an established framework.

לְהָאִיר נַפְשׁוֹ הָאֱלֹהִית בְּאוֹר הַתּוֹרָה וּמִצְוֹתֶיהָ,

This enables a person **to illuminate his divine soul with the light of the Torah and its mitzvot**

A person must begin with fear in order for his soul to be illuminated by the light of the Torah and its mitzvot, as he avoids evil and performs good deeds. This is the framework necessary to maintain the likelihood that his soul will proceed on the proper path.

וְאַחַר כָּךְ יָאִיר עָלֶיהָ אוֹר הָאַהֲבָה

and then the light of love will shine on his soul.

After a person has conducted himself in the framework of avoiding evil and doing good, the light of the love of God will then shine upon his soul. This is the royal road to educating oneself: A person initially enters the realm of avoiding evil and performing good deeds, of accepting God's kingship on the level of the lower fear of God, illuminating

---

Elazar ben Durdaya's love [for God]. Therefore, one should not be troubled by the fact that on the surface this story is about repentance, for it concerns both matters."

himself in the light of the Torah and mitzvot. And after that, he comes to the love of God.

[כִּי 'וְאָהַבְתָּ' בְּגִימַטְרִיָּא בּ' פְּעָמִים 'אוֹר', כַּיָּדוּעַ לְיוֹדְעֵי חֵן]. (That is **because the numerical value of the** word *ve'ahavta*, "you shall love," **is twice the** numerical value of the word *or*, light, **as is known to those who are initiated in the esoteric wisdom** of Kabbala [see *Pri Etz Ḥayyim, Sha'ar Keriat Shema*, e.g., chaps. 23, 35].)

This may be explained in several ways.[15] One approach is that the two iterations of "light" refer to the light of the Torah and the light of the mitzvot. When a person combines these two, he can reach the level of loving God: "You shall love the Lord" (Deut. 6:5). Alternatively, the Torah and its mitzvot constitute one light, and "You shall love the Lord" constitutes the other light. The love is itself light, but it can be actualized and receive meaning only when it is preceded by the light of Torah and its mitzvot. The love of God is therefore a double light, because in a person's love of God (even more than in the love of another human being), it is possible that he only thinks that he loves, that he is having a genuine experience, when in fact he is merely experiencing a passing mood, a feeling of inspiration that stems from his love of himself. In order for his love to be true and lasting, a person requires a suitable framework of life to contain it. He requires a suitable light below so that the light of love can truly be absorbed into his inner being. ☞

TWICE "LIGHT"

☞ In his commentary on the *Tanya*, Rabbi Shmuel Gronem Esterman states that this is referring to direct light and reflected light. The direct light refers to a person's keeping the Torah and mitzvot (which corresponds to the lower fear of God). That leads to a reflected light, which is the person's love of God. And see *Torah Or* (32c, 36a, s.v. "*roni vesimḥi*"), which states that in order for a person to be able to be a "lamp of the Lord" (Prov. 20:27) – meaning, to cause God's name to shine as a result of his devotion when he recites the *Shema* and the *Amida* – he must first draw upon

---

15. See *HaLekaḥ VeHalibbuv*; *Pri Etz Ḥayyim, Sha'ar Keriat Shema*, chaps. 23, 25.

This chapter presented a broad overview of how to serve God. The first part of the chapter discussed the fear of God, and the second part discussed the love of God. This overview categorizes two types of fear of God – lower and higher – and two types of love of God, *ahavat olam* ("world-centered love") and *ahava rabba* ("great love"). These pairs, which describe the ways that a human being relates to God, correspond to the two descriptions of God as filling the universe and surrounding the universe, i.e., the Divine within reality and the Divine beyond reality. Lower fear comes from an initial, empiric conception of this world, which begins with knowledge of the world and which precedes a comprehension of divinity: "If there is no [lower] fear, there is no wisdom [of knowing God]." Higher fear, fear out of shame before the Divine, comes from awareness of the divine reality beyond this world and beyond what a person in this world can perceive. It is the ultimate state of awareness: "If there is no wisdom [of knowing God], there is no fear [of His awesomeness]." *Ahava rabba*, "great love," is a flame that rises of itself. It does not depend on a person's actions but solely on the divine will. *Ahavat olam*, "world-centered love," on the other hand, results from a person's contemplation of the world, of stripping the world and its desires of all of their outer garments, so that he no longer wants garments and envelopes, because he thinks, "Whom else do I have in heaven? With You, I desire nothing on earth." At the end of the chapter, the author discusses the order in which a person normatively proceeds in his service of God. First he achieves lower fear, in which he turns aside from evil and performs good deeds; and then he achieves love. But in exceptional cases, love may be revealed in the soul prior to the stages of fear. The next chapter will discuss more specifically and more deeply the stages of the love of God.

---

himself the aspect of "You light my lamp, Lord my God" (Ps. 18:29), which he does by keeping the Torah and mitzvot and by purifying his body and animal soul as a result of avoiding evil and performing good deeds (*Torah Or* 32c, 36a).

Chapter 44

AS PART OF A DISCUSSION OF SERVICE OF THE HEART, in particular fear and love of God, that spans several chapters, the previous chapter began to explain love of God. It stated that the love of God exists on two levels that parallel the two levels of the attribute of fear: *ahavat olam* (world-centered love) parallels lower fear, and *ahava rabba* (great love) parallels higher fear. This broad two-tiered division also corresponds to the relationship between God and the world: He permeates all worlds and encompasses all worlds. This chapter will continue to address the attribute of love, enumerating its unique qualities, as revealed in specific details, as well as in the broadest generalities, which cross all interpersonal barriers, and those between human beings and God.

וְהִנֵּה כָּל מַדְרֵגַת אַהֲבָה מִבּ' מַדְרֵגוֹת אֵלּוּ: 'אַהֲבָה רַבָּה' וְ'אַהֲבַת עוֹלָם', נֶחֱלֶקֶת לְכַמָּה בְּחִינוֹת וּמַדְרֵגוֹת לְאֵין קֵץ,	**The entire** spiritual **level of love, composed of the levels of** *ahava rabba* **(great love) and** *ahavat olam* **(world-centered love), is subdivided into multiple aspects and levels without end,**	2 Iyar ___ 28 Nisan (leap year)

Any division that results in the existence of two opposite poles – such as up and down, right and left, and so on – is necessarily a generalization. Each pole groups together many different components. In reality, however, there are numerous degrees and different aspects among these components. Regarding the topic of love, different people love in different ways. There are almost as many types of love as there are people who experience love.

כָּל חַד לְפוּם שִׁיעוּרָא דִּילֵיהּ — as each individual may understand in keeping with his particular capacity.

Each person will understand this in keeping with the composition of his individual character and his present life experiences.

כְּמוֹ שֶׁכָּתוּב בַּזֹּהַר הַקָּדוֹשׁ (חלק א קג, א) עַל פָּסוּק: "נוֹדָע בַּשְּׁעָרִים בַּעְלָהּ" (משלי לא, כג) - "דָּא קֻדְשָׁא בְּרִיךְ הוּא דְּאִיהוּ אִתְיְדַע וְאִתְדַּבַּק לְכָל חַד לְפוּם מַה דִּמְשַׁעֵר בְּלִבֵּיהּ" וכו'. As the holy *Zohar* (1:103a) states regarding the verse "Her husband is renowned at the gates [*she'arim*]" (Prov. 31:23), "'Her husband' refers to the Holy One, blessed be He, who makes Himself known to and attaches Himself to each individual according to what that individual perceives [*mesha'er*] in his heart...."

God is called the "Husband" of the Divine Presence (which gives life to every soul from within herself). Being "renowned at the gates" means that God is known to every creature in the world in the measure and manner that each conceives of Him in its intellect and emotion. Sometimes this awareness is clear, and at other times it is blurred. Sometimes it perceives one particular aspect, and sometimes it covers several. A person's awareness receives its particular character in keeping with the scope and nature of his spiritual personality. A person who can conceive only of a small God attaches to Him in a small way, with a diminished level of love and fear. Conversely, a person who has a strong awareness experiences the love of God powerfully, and in a deep way. ☞

HE MAKES HIMSELF KNOWN TO EACH INDIVIDUAL

☞ Rabbi Nahman of Breslov says regarding the verse "For I know the Lord is great" (Ps. 135:5) that the emphasis is on the word "I," because no one else can know that which "I know." This is not because it is a secret that is forbidden to reveal, but because it is impossible to fully express what a person knows and perceives in his heart. Other people may understand this perception in general terms, but they cannot "know" it. People can help each other in a general sense, and at times, when individuals become very close, they can help each other in more personal ways, and a person can give another individual a key to his heart. But only the individual himself

וְלָכֵן נִקְרָאִים דְּחִילוּ וּרְחִימוּ "הַנִּסְתָּרוֹת לַה' אֱלֹהֵינוּ" (דברים כט, כח),

Therefore, the fear and love of God are referred to as "the concealed aspects, which **are for the Lord our God**" (Deut. 29:28),

What a person perceives in his heart is inherently private, and cannot be conveyed to anyone else. Only God, who examines each person's thoughts and emotions, knows the fear and love in his heart. ☞

וְתוֹרָה וּמִצְוֹת הֵן "הַנִּגְלוֹת לָנוּ וּלְבָנֵינוּ לַעֲשׂוֹת" כו'.

whereas the performance of **Torah and mitzvot is** described at the end of the verse as "**the revealed** aspects, which **are for us and for our children** forever **to perform** all the matters of this Torah."

Although the fear and love of God are mitzvot, they are described apart from the other mitzvot, because they are "concealed." As for the "revealed" mitzvot, they are Torah learning and the mitzvot that involve an element of action, the parameters of which can be measured objectively.

These revealed aspects of the Torah have an advantage over the concealed aspects in that they are equally incumbent upon all Jews. This makes it possible for all Jews to assist each other and help keep each other within the objectively measurable boundaries. This is not

can actually know what is in his own heart. What is the subjective, individual meaning of a person's feelings? What does he refer to when he says the word "green" or "sweet"? No one else can ever know. This inability to share one's perceptions is all the more true regarding the subtleties of love and fear of God, which certainly do not depend on his intellectual, abstract understanding but on what he perceives in his heart: his unique, personal experience that is shared by no one else.

ONLY GOD KNOWS WHAT IS INSIDE THE HEART

☞ A simple person in whom others do not perceive anything great, a person who does not know how to express himself, even to himself, may have so much in his heart that he perceives even more than someone else who is recognized for his holiness. Some tzaddikim who were endowed with this kind of perception would cultivate close relationships with such people. This is because the tzaddikim saw their concealed greatness, which even they themselves were unable to discover for themselves.

the case with regard to the "concealed aspects." One person cannot perceive what is in another person's heart, so generally people are unable to help others with these matters.

> כִּי תּוֹרָה אַחַת וּמִשְׁפָּט אֶחָד לְכֻלָּנוּ, בְּקִיּוּם כָּל הַתּוֹרָה וּמִצְוֹת בִּבְחִינַת מַעֲשֶׂה.

This is **because there is one Torah and one law common to us all** in terms of the fulfillment of the entire Torah and mitzvot in the aspect of action.

The "revealed aspects" of the Torah are related to action. With regard to action, the Torah applies equally to everyone. The mitzva of donning *tefillin* is the same for every man. Everyone can fulfill his obligation with the exact same pair of *tefillin*. The same is true with regard to all practical mitzvot; a person may add to a mitzva in some fashion, or adorn it, but the mitzva itself is the same for everyone. This uniformity creates a common denominator among people. Everything related to this common denominator is a "revealed aspect." It is not something personal, private, or concealed, but something common and revealed to all.

> מַה שֶּׁאֵין כֵּן בִּדְחִילוּ וּרְחִימוּ, שֶׁהֵם לְפִי הַדַּעַת אֶת ה' שֶׁבְּמוֹחַ וְלֵב כַּנִּזְכָּר לְעֵיל.

That is **unlike fear and love, which** vary **in accordance with the knowledge of God within** each person's **mind and heart, as stated above** (chap. 42).

Fear and love are "concealed aspects" not only because they are internal, spiritual experiences that cannot be seen, in contrast to physical actions, but also because they have no definite criteria. It is impossible to assess how much someone should love, in what way he should love, or why he should love. These matters are connected to the unique structure of each soul and its condition at each particular point in time. These factors determine the soul's chance of achieving faith, and love and fear of God. Whereas an arm is always ready to have *tefillin* placed upon it and a doorpost is always ready for a *mezuza*, not every soul is prepared at all times in the same manner to love and fear God. Love and fear grow out of an extremely complex structure, the most intricate and sensitive layer of human existence, which is indefinable and constantly changing. Every change in a person's viewpoint or knowledge alters this experience.

אַךְ אַחַת הִיא אַהֲבָה הַכְּלוּלָה מִכָּל בְּחִינוֹת וּמַדְרֵגוֹת 'אַהֲבָה רַבָּה' וְ'אַהֲבַת עוֹלָם'. **Yet there is one** type of **love that is comprised of all the aspects and grades of** both *ahava rabba* and *ahavat olam*.

Beyond all of the differences and levels, of whatever nature or intensity, in what one person experiences and another experiences, in what is experienced at one time and what is experienced at another – there is one encompassing level of love that includes the entire range of love from one extreme to the other, from *ahavat olam* to *ahava rabba*.[1]

וְהִיא שָׁוָה לְכָל נֶפֶשׁ מִיִּשְׂרָאֵל, **It is equally** intrinsic **to the soul of every Jew,**

This level of love is not something based on the form of an individual's particular soul. It is due to the character of the soul by virtue of a person being a human being. Therefore, this level of love is alike in every soul. It is not equal in level or intensity in every Jew, but it is equal in its essence. Not everyone experiences the same feeling, but there is a root that everyone feels in a similar way. There is a level of love of God that is common to every Jewish soul. Also in other fields there are some matters to which each individual reacts differently, and others to which everyone has the same response. In some cases, the human response and the animal response are different, and in others, every living creature has the same response.

וִירוּשָׁה לָנוּ מֵאֲבוֹתֵינוּ. **and it is our inheritance from our forefathers.**

This love is an inheritance. It is an experience which is embedded in our souls. We do not need to create it. This does not mean, however, that this trait of love is necessarily actualized, since the actualization of a feeling, like an action, is largely the outcome of our free will. Nevertheless, the possession of this inheritance means that we always

---

1. The idea of *ahavat olam* is to ascend to the source of all worlds, and the idea of *ahava rabba*, or "love of delights," is the flow from above to below. As will be explained below, this love contains both aspects (*Kitzurim U'Biurim*).

have the potential to reach this level of love without being dependent on our own effort and will.

וְהַיְינוּ מַה שֶּׁאוֹמֵר הַזּוֹהַר (חלק ג סח, א) עַל פָּסוּק "נַפְשִׁי אִוִּיתִיךָ בַּלַּיְלָה" וְגוֹ' (ישעיה כו, ט): "דִּירָחִים לְקֻדְשָׁא בְּרִיךְ הוּא רְחִימוּתָא דְּנַפְשָׁא וְרוּחָא כְּמָה דְּאִתְדַּבְּקוּ אִילֵּין בְּגוּפָא וְגוּפָא רָחִים לוֹן" וְכוּ'.

Regarding this love, the *Zohar* (3:68a) states regarding the verse "With my soul, I desired You at night..." (Is. 26:9): "One should love the Holy One, blessed be He, with a love of the soul and spirit, in the same way that they are attached to the body and the body loves them...."

The body loves the soul because the soul is its life force and sustains its existence.

וְזֶה שֶׁכָּתוּב: "נַפְשִׁי אִוִּיתִיךָ" 'כְּלוֹמַר, מִפְּנֵי שֶׁאַתָּה ה' נַפְשִׁי וְחַיַּי הָאֲמִתִּים - לְכָךְ אִוִּיתִיךָ.

This is the meaning of the verse "With my soul, I have desired You," which is read to mean, "Because You, God, are my true soul and life, therefore I have desired You."

The first phrase in the verse is read as "With my soul, I have desired You." However, literally it says, "My soul, I have desired You," which seems to be grammatically incorrect. The author of the *Tanya* explains that "my soul" refers to God. Thus, there are two separate statements in this phrase. The first is "my soul." A person addresses the root and inner essence of his desires, life, and being: God. The second statement is "I have desired You." In other words, "Because You, God, are my soul, I desire You." That is because a person loves and desires his life and the soul of his soul.

This love does not depend on a person's individual spiritual capacity, but on the fact that he has a soul, because whoever has a soul loves it. This love of the divine soul within oneself constitutes an elevation of a person's love for himself. That love no longer relates to external aspects, such as the form of his body and even the form of his soul; rather, it relates to his "self," which at its root and heart is beyond all appearances. God is the heart of the Jewish people: "God is the strength of my heart and my portion forever" (Ps. 73:26).[2] Accordingly, a person's love of

---

2. See *Pesikta DeRav Kahana* 5:6 and *Shir HaShirim Rabba* 5:2: "Rabbi Ḥiyya bar

God does not mean that he loves something external; rather, he loves his own inner essence, the life within his life. ☞

The love expressed in the words "My soul, I have desired You" is on a level that transcends the individual. Consequently, it is not a feeling that belongs only to one person and not another. Some people like a particular type of flower, while others do not. However, every individual admires his own soul. Therefore, this is a universal type of love, shared by a person on the lowest level and a person on the highest level.

THE CONCEPT OF THE SELF

☞ The outcry, "My soul, I have desired You," expresses the deepest concept of the self. However, on many other levels as well, a person must search in order to discover his self, and as he grows he must keep searching. There is a story that demonstrates to some degree how difficult this is. The author of the *Tanya* raised his grandson, who would later become the Tzemaḥ Tzedek, after his mother died. (The bond between them was particularly special, both because of their spiritual connection, which was revealed when the Tzemaḥ Tzedek was extremely young, and because of other factors related to the self-sacrifice on the part of the child's mother for the sake of her father; see *Sefer HaToledot Admor HaZaken*.) One day, when the boy was about three years old, his grandfather asked him, "Where is Zeide (Grandpa)?" The boy reached out and touched him, saying, "Here is Zeide." His grandfather said to him, "No, this is Zeide's body. Where is Zeide?" The boy thought for a while and then touched his grandfather's head: "Here is Zeide." Again, his grandfather demurred: "No, that is Zeide's head. Where is Zeide?" The boy thought some more, and suddenly, he called out, "Zeide!" When the author of the *Tanya* turned to him in response, he said, "There! There is Zeide!" This story, which contains tremendous wisdom, not just the cleverness of a small child, expresses the difficulty involved in defining the self: It is not just a part of the body or the soul, nor is it just a particular feeling or thought. In order to find and recognize who he is and come into contact with himself, a person must exert himself, searching extensively. There is a well-known children's story about a forgetful boy who is afraid that he will not remember where he has put his belongings, so before he goes to sleep, he writes a note to himself, listing where he put his hat, clothes, and so on. When he wakes up in the morning, he finds all the items, but then he realizes that he does not know where he himself is, because he did not write his own whereabouts on the note. The Rebbe of Aleksander told the above story and commented that this is the true story of Hasidism. Even if a person knows the location of everything in the world, the question remains: "Where am I?" A person who is on the hasidic path lives with this question, whether he has an answer to it or not.

Abba says: Where do we find that the Holy One, blessed be He, is called the heart of Israel? From the verse 'God is the strength of my heart and my portion forever.'"

פֵּירוּשׁ, שֶׁאֲנִי מִתְאַוֶּה וְתָאֵב לְךָ כְּאָדָם הַמִּתְאַוֶּה לְחַיֵּי נַפְשׁוֹ וּכְשֶׁהוּא חַלָּשׁ וּמְעֻנֶּה מִתְאַוֶּה וְתָאֵב שֶׁתָּשׁוּב נַפְשׁוֹ אֵלָיו.

This means that I crave and desire You in the same way a person craves his own life. When he is weak and infirm, he yearns and desires that his soul be restored to him.

The verse that describes a person's desire for his "soul" is referring to a desire for life. Usually, a person does not feel a desire for life, just as he is not generally conscious of the pleasure of being alive.[3] When a person is busy and healthy, he does not think about the fact that he is alive; he is too preoccupied with the particulars of life to treat it as an object of desire. But he begins to relate to it in this way, yearning for it, when he is weak and infirm. In such a situation, he desires life in the simplest sense; he wants to live. When a person is in pain or suffering, when the fear of death hangs over him or when he is exhausted and feels his life beginning to fade away, he longs for his soul to return to him.

When a person has a comfortable life, his inner desire is unfocused. When asked what he wants, his response involves various particulars. However, when he is in distress and is unable to deal with particulars, he immediately focuses on the most fundamental matter. When asked what he wants, he answers, "I want to live." For a person to know that he wants to live and for him to genuinely feel "My soul, I have desired You," he must understand what is important and what is not.

וְכֵן כְּשֶׁהוּא הוֹלֵךְ לִישֹׁן, מִתְאַוֶּה וְחָפֵץ שֶׁתָּשׁוּב נַפְשׁוֹ אֵלָיו כְּשֶׁיֵּעוֹר מִשְּׁנָתוֹ.

Likewise, when he goes to sleep, he yearns and longs for his soul to be restored to him when he awakes from his slumber.

When a person goes to sleep, he relinquishes his life to a certain degree, because "sleep is one-sixtieth of death" (*Berakhot* 57b). Because he is aware of this lack, he prays, "My soul, I have desired You at night." Before he goes to sleep – as in times of illness or danger or whenever some lack makes itself felt – he asks for life itself. This is a simple request, without qualifications or intricate details. A person asks for his soul in the most basic sense of the word: He asks for life itself.

---

3. See *Or HaTorah, Vayikra* 3, p. 741.

כָּךְ אֲנִי מִתְאַוֶּה וְתָאֵב לְאוֹר אֵין סוֹף בָּרוּךְ הוּא, חַיֵּי הַחַיִּים הָאֲמִתִּיִּים, לְהַמְשִׁיכוֹ בְּקִרְבִּי, **So too, I yearn and desire to draw into myself the light of *Ein Sof*, blessed be He, the ultimate source of life,**

When a person delves into the meaning of the "life" that he is seeking, he understands that there is a true life within his life, and that this is the light of *Ein Sof*. Then he feels a lack of life and a desire for life, as does someone who is awakened at night. But he does not feel this only with regard to the superficial experience of life. Rather, he craves the life of all lives, the inner essence of life: God Himself.

A verse in the book of Psalms states, "Even on my bed I remember You; I meditate on You during the night watches" (Ps. 63:7). When a person goes to sleep thirsty, he wakes up with a powerful thirst. When he recalls God before he goes to sleep, he will be thinking of God when he wakes up. This is the meaning of "My soul, I have desired You at night": When a person wakes up, he awakens from a state of lack and he awakens into a clear sense that he must connect to God.

It is also clear from the foregoing why "My soul, I have desired You" occurs "at night." Nighttime has the quality of absence and lack, and "My soul, I have desired You," can occur only when a person feels that something is missing. Desire has no meaning unless there is a lack, just as light has no meaning except against the background of darkness.[4]

עַל יְדֵי עֵסֶק הַתּוֹרָה, בְּהָקִיצִי מִשְּׁנָתִי בַּלַּיְלָה. דְּאוֹרַיְיתָא וְקֻדְשָׁא בְּרִיךְ הוּא - כּוּלָּא חַד, **by engaging in Torah study when I awake from my night's sleep, since the Torah and the Holy One, blessed be He, are all one,**

Here the author of the *Tanya* adds a remark that concerns not the awakening of love but its actualization. After a person has awakened love, how can he realize and fulfill this connection to the ultimate

---

4. See *Torah Or* 37b; *Likkutei Torah*, Lev. 20b. This is why the love of "My soul, I have desired you," is called "night," in contrast to *ahava rabba*. It is a love that belongs to darkness, a minor love. One engages in it only in order to receive a reward. See also *Siddur im Divrei Elokim Ḥayyim* 279c.

source of life? The *Zohar* states[5] that the Torah and God are one. Clinging to the Torah (through learning it) is tantamount to clinging to the infinite light. It is the act of drawing down life, one's soul, from the source of life.

כְּמוֹ שֶׁכּוֹתֵב הַזֹּהַר שָׁם (חלק ג סח, א): "דִּבְעֵי בַּר נַשׁ מֵרְחִימוּתָא דְּקֻדְשָׁא בְּרִיךְ הוּא לְמֵיקַם בְּכָל לֵילְיָא לְאִשְׁתַּדְּלָא בְּפוּלְחָנֵיהּ עַד צַפְרָא" כו'.

as the *Zohar* states there (3:68a), "**Out of love for the Holy One, blessed be He, a person must rise each night to toil in His service until morning….**"

A person wakes up at night because his love for God is impelling him. He can no longer sleep, because he feels that something is missing in his life. This is the awakening of the love described in the verse "My soul, I have desired You." He rises and asks the ultimate source of life, God, for additional life. And then he sits down and learns Torah. ☞

GOD IS MY SOUL

☞ As mentioned earlier, the love described in "My soul, I have desired You," is a love that exists within every Jew by virtue of the fact that he is a Jew, by virtue of the fact that his soul is fundamentally part of the Divine. The awakening of this love depends only on a person's awareness of who he is and what life is. There are many degrees of awareness, ranging from the faint knowledge that there is something beyond the self, to the level at which a person can say, "God is the strength of my heart and my portion forever," all the way up to the level of a tzaddik, who is a "chariot" of the Divine Presence. A tzaddik does not have to subdue any particular aspects of himself in order to reach the Godly self, because for him the self is God. God is the One thinking, acting, and desiring within him. There are a number of different souls on different planes within every human being. There are *nefesh, ruaḥ, neshama*, and beyond that the *neshama* of the *neshama* and each individual lives in a particular level of his soul. The *Zohar* states (2:94b): "When a person is born, he is given a *nefesh*. When he becomes worthy, he is given a *ruaḥ*. When he becomes more worthy still, he is given a *neshama*. A person who lives at the level of *neshama* is a truly great person; the revelation of the *neshama* is said to be an even higher level than the revelation of Elijah. Above this level is that of *ḥaya* within the *nefesh*, which is the level of the world of *Atzilut*, and above everything else is *yeḥida* within the *nefesh*, where all souls are one. This is the level of *Kenesset Yisrael* (the congregation of Israel), the word of God, and the source of all life and of the soul. At this level, a

---

5. *Zohar* 1:24a. See also chap. 23.

CHAPTER 44

3 Iyar
29 Nisan
(leap year)

וְאַהֲבָה רַבָּה וּגְדוֹלָה מִזּוֹ, וְהִיא מְסוּתֶרֶת גַּם כֵּן בְּכָל נֶפֶשׁ מִיִּשְׂרָאֵל בִּירוּשָׁה מֵאֲבוֹתֵינוּ,

There is an even **greater and more profound love than this, and it also is concealed within the soul of every Jew, as an inheritance from our forefathers.**

The *Tanya* earlier said that the level of love expressed in the phrase "My soul, I have desired You" "is equally [intrinsic] to the soul of every Jew." Now, regarding another level of love that the *Tanya* is about to discuss, the *Tanya* says that "it also is concealed within the soul of every Jew." The level of love discussed previously, which is a kind of development of the love of oneself, belongs to the character of a Jew, and it is therefore intrinsic to all Jewish souls. It is not a secret and it is not concealed. Even if this love is not apparent, every individual possesses the means with which to awaken and reveal it. However, the love that will be discussed here, which is on a higher level, is not manifest in every person; rather, it is concealed. Nevertheless, it is also "an inheritance from our forefathers," in the sense that we are not able to create it ourselves. This potential is something that we inherited as a gift from our ancestors. ☞

person is aware that God is "my soul." As the verse describing the messianic future states, "No longer will they teach, each man his neighbor and each man his brother, saying: 'Know the Lord,' because all of them will know Me" (Jer. 31:33). At this level, a person feels God as the active force, the self, within him. This perception exists at every level in every Jew when he gives up his private pursuits and external means of expression, and relates to his soul like a thirsty person, like a person who wakes up at night feeling that something is missing and yearning for life's very essence. This is what is described in the verse, "My soul, I have desired You at night."

AN INHERITANCE FROM OUR FOREFATHERS

☞ The statement that every Jew is required to discover these two aspects of love within himself comes after the repeated emphasis that this love is inherited from our ancestors and is concealed in every Jewish soul. It is only possible to instruct people to bring a matter to fruition when that matter is clearly known to exist. Every person has his own particular challenges for which some general advice may not be correct. But regarding spiritual matters that pertain to everyone, even if they are obscure, one can meaningfully talk about them and toil in a deliberate and organized manner in order to discover them. Some spiritual matters may cause one person immense excitement, but leave another cold. On the other hand, there are elements that are stamped in human nature, sensitivities that exist in every

הִיא מַה שֶׁכָּתוּב בְּרַעְיָא מְהֵימְנָא (זהר ח"ג רפא, א): "כִּבְרָא דְּאִשְׁתַּדַּל בָּתַר אֲבוֹי וְאִמֵּיהּ דְּרָחֵים לוֹן יַתִּיר מִגּוּפֵיהּ וְנַפְשֵׁיהּ וְרוּחֵיהּ" כו'.

This is described by *Raya Meheimna* (*Zohar* 3:281a), in its description of the love for God that Moses attained, "as a son who tends to his father and mother, loving them more than his own body, soul, and spirit...."

The love mentioned earlier, which in a sense stems from love of oneself, reaches as far as love of the self can go. The love being discussed here, however, is like a son's love for his father and mother, and thus it reaches beyond the individual's existence. A child's fierce concern for his parents is more important to him than his concern for himself. This is the love of a person who is willing to give his life, spirit, and soul for the object of his love.

כִּי "הֲלֹא אָב אֶחָד לְכֻלָּנוּ" (מלאכי ב, י).

For "isn't there one Father for all of us? Didn't one God create us?" (Mal. 2:10).

This love is described in the *Zohar* as the love experienced by Moses, the faithful shepherd. However, since God is the Father of every Jew and we are all His children (see Deut. 14:1), it may be said that this love is relevant to all Jews. ☞

וְאַף כִּי מִי הוּא זֶה וְאֵיזֶהוּ אֲשֶׁר עָרַב לִבּוֹ לָגֶשֶׁת לְהַשִּׂיג אֲפִלּוּ חֵלֶק אֶחָד מִנִּי אֶלֶף מִמַּדְרֵגַת אַהֲבַת 'רַעְיָא מְהֵימְנָא',

Although who is the person whose heart dares attempt to comprehend even one thousandth of the level of love attained by the faithful shepherd, Moses?

person by virtue of his being a human being. If these latter matters are not manifest, it is necessary to discover them and then to cultivate them. There is a fundamental difference between a child learning to speak and a parrot learning to speak. The ability to speak is inherent within the child's nature, and when that ability is awakened and practiced, he learns; but no matter how much the parrot is trained, he will never learn more than how to imitate some of the sounds of speech. Therefore, before the author of the *Tanya* instructs the reader to discover in himself the aspects of love that have been mentioned, he states that these aspects of love are an intrinsic part of every Jew, and therefore whatever a person develops out of these tendencies will not be castles in the air but the development of a real capacity.

מִכָּל מָקוֹם, הֲרֵי אֶפֶס קָצֵהוּ וְשֶׁמֶץ מֶנְהוּ מֵרַב טוּבוֹ וְאוֹרוֹ מֵאִיר לִכְלָלוּת יִשְׂרָאֵל בְּכָל דּוֹר וָדוֹר, כְּמוֹ שֶׁכָּתוּב בַּתִּקּוּנִים: "דְּאִתְפַּשְׁטוּתֵיהּ בְּכָל דָּרָא וְדָרָא לְאַנְהֲרָא לוֹן" וְכוּ'.

Nevertheless, Moses **radiates a minute margin and speck of his immense goodness and light to the collective of Israel in each and every generation. As the** *Tikkunei* **Zohar states, an emanation of Moses is found in each and every generation to illuminate us**....

THE TWO LEVELS OF LOVE AND SELF-SACRIFICE

☞ Love is measured in accordance with what a person is willing to sacrifice for it. Consequently, the love that is under discussion here is much greater than the love discussed previously, because that which a person is willing to give for it is much greater. There are two aspects of self-sacrifice corresponding to these two aspects of love. First, there is physical self-sacrifice. A person is aware of his soul's existence and submits his body to hard work, suffering, and sometimes even death, for the sake of his soul. This is not easy, but the decision is relatively clear-cut. Analogously, if a person must either give up a limb or give up his life, the decision to give up his limb is difficult, but it is also the obvious choice, because he knows that the limb is not who he is. This is like the self-sacrifice involved in the love of "My soul, I have desired You." When a person knows that God is the ultimate source of true life, he is prepared to maintain his connection with God and even to give up his life in this world for it. The decision is simple, because the choice to renounce the God of Israel and continue living does not exist; it constitutes a contradiction, like the choice to continue living without a soul.

But there is a higher level of self-sacrifice, whereby a person is willing to give up not only his body and not only his life, but also his soul – his *nefesh, ruaḥ,* and *neshama,* his life and the source of his life – for God. He is willing to give up not only his physical life in this world, but also his World to Come, his "self," in its deepest sense, for the sake of Heaven. An example of such self-sacrifice is that of Abraham at the binding of Isaac. Abraham was required to sacrifice not only his life in this world, but his very connection with God. He was obliged to forgo all the promises that God had made to him, everything that he believed in and had preached, his innermost world, for the sake of fulfilling God's will. Even for Moses, such a level of self-sacrifice was not easy. When God commanded him, "Go, and I will send you" (Ex. 3:10), he struggled: "I am not a man of words" (Ex. 4:10); "Please send by means of whom You will send" (Ex. 4:13). He tried to evade this command because what God was asking of him would entail a terrible sacrifice. He was being required to give up his true inner life, which was his connection to God, and to act instead "as a nurse carries the suckling babe" (Num. 11:12), interacting with people living this-worldly lives: a man fighting with his wife, quarreling neighbors, and people craving meat. Moses was required to care for the people by immersing himself in the physical world every day for forty years, until his death. For

Although we cannot possibly compare ourselves to Moses, nevertheless, as the faithful, eternal shepherd of Israel in all generations, he illuminates and transmits knowledge and faith into every one of us.[6] However, this influence is not as it was during Moses's lifetime. Currently, it is manifested in two ways. The first is through the leaders and sages of each generation, who comprise the aspect of Moses in that era. Everything that they teach the people contains an element of Moses's influence that has passed through them. The second way is through Moses's direct, spiritual influence on every individual. There is a spark of Moses in every Jewish soul. That spark is a part of a person's soul that guides and teaches him.

רַק שֶׁהֶאָרָה זוֹ הִיא בִּבְחִינַת הֶסְתֵּר וְהֶעְלֵם גָּדוֹל בְּנַפְשׁוֹת כָּל בֵּית יִשְׂרָאֵל. **However, this illumination is extremely concealed and hidden within the souls of the entire house of Israel.**

We inherit from our ancestors not just the love on the level of "My soul, I have desired you," which is the inner essence of the love of oneself, but even the love on the level possessed by Moses. While this tremendous level of love is found in every Jew, it is nevertheless concealed.

Moses, this was the ultimate self-sacrifice, but because God desired it, he yielded. Later, Moses was once again required to sacrifice, and this time in an even more extreme way. The children of Israel committed a terrible sin, and it seemed as though they could not continue to exist. At that time, God told Moses: "Allow Me, and My wrath will be enflamed against them, and I will destroy them; and I will make you into a great nation" (Ex. 32:10). Moses's unhesitating refusal constituted the highest, most tremendous level of self-sacrifice. He said to God, "If You will bear their sin... and if not, erase me now from Your book that You have written" (Ex. 32:32). In other words, if You can no longer sustain Israel, then erase me, too; erase me absolutely from all existence. Moses was prepared for this, because he knew that this was what God really wanted from him.

---

6. It is not clear which statement of the *Tikkunei Zohar* the author of *Tanya* is referring to. See also *Zohar* 3:216b, 3:273a (the Lubavitcher Rebbe, Rabbi Menaḥem Mendel Schneerson).

CHAPTER 44

וּלְהוֹצִיא אַהֲבָה זוֹ הַמְסוּתֶּרֶת מֵהֶעְלֵם וְהֶסְתֵּר אֶל הַגִּילּוּי, לִהְיוֹת בְּהִתְגַּלּוּת לִבּוֹ וּמוֹחוֹ,	**To bring this concealed love out of hiding and concealment into revelation so that it may be revealed in one's heart and mind,**

We must actualize this potential, which is concealed within us, and transform it into a real, perceptible experience.

לֹא נִפְלֵאת וְלֹא רְחוֹקָה הִיא (דברים ל, יא), אֶלָּא קָרוֹב "הַדָּבָר מְאֹד בְּפִיךָ וּבִלְבָבְךָ" (שם יד).	**"It is not obscured from you and it is not distant."** Rather, **"the matter is very near to you, in your mouth and in your heart,** to perform it" (Deut. 30:11).

The revelation of this love is not obscured and distant, but nearby. The motto of the *Tanya* – "in your mouth and in your heart, to perform it" (Deut. 30:14) – is now given an additional meaning. In previous chapters it was said that anyone can do this with his mouth and heart. Here, the verse provides instruction on how this may be done. There are three stages: The first stage is "in your mouth": A person discusses and interprets the idea through speech. The second stage is "in your heart": The idea must be internalized in one's thoughts and feelings. The third stage is "to perform it": It is not enough for a person to speak and meditate on a matter on an abstract level. Rather, from the very beginning, his thinking and orientation must lead to action.

דְּהַיְינוּ, לִהְיוֹת רָגִיל עַל לְשׁוֹנוּ וְקוֹלוֹ, לְעוֹרֵר כַּוָּונַת לִבּוֹ וּמוֹחוֹ,	**This entails becoming accustomed to talking out loud about these matters to arouse the intent of one's heart and mind,**

The importance of speaking verbally about something is that doing so brings it into the realm of consciousness. When people never speak about a particular matter and do not discuss it and do not think about it, even if it is true and important, it effectively does not exist. This is true in every field, not only regarding distant, exalted matters, but also those that are close to us. It pertains to both the holy and the mundane, to mitzvot and to sins. ☞

Speech is especially significant in affecting a person's feelings. It is said that the mind is what leads to the formation of a person's attributes. However, this does not mean that knowing about the existence of something creates the emotion. Rather, the emotion is formed when the person has something more than a thought, when he has a tangible awareness. People are made in such a way that they do not develop feelings toward theoretical, mental concepts, but only toward that which they perceive as real. What constitutes a person's sense of reality is culturally bound and connected to a person's upbringing in a complex manner. However, when a person's subjective experience, his thought, or his imagination, has a foothold in the objective, external world (so that it acts as an "echo" of that outside reality), this creates a person's sense of reality. Talking about a subject moves it from the confines of subjectivity, of existing only in thought, into an objective reality. This is especially true when one talks about it with someone else. When a person talks about God's existence and greatness, that creates a tangible, objective reality that he can relate to strongly and with emotion. When a person discusses the concealed love of God,

BECOMING ACCUSTOMED TO TALKING

☞ It is well known that in some totalitarian regimes, all references to topics that are undesirable to the rulers are deleted from all the books. A dystopian novel (*1984* by George Orwell) presents an extreme description of how, by deleting certain words from the dictionary, it is possible to direct the thoughts and desires of all humanity. The underlying idea is that when people stop using a certain word or when they no longer speak about a particular subject, it loses its vitality and meaning, and disappears from consciousness. A number of tzaddikim have explained the verse "Faithfulness is lost, and it is removed from their mouths" (Jer. 7:28), as follows: "Why was the people's faithfulness lost? Because it was removed from their mouths." When people no longer talk to each other about faith, when the subject ceases to be a topic of conversation, it withdraws from the heart as well and is forgotten. The more subtle the topic, the more one must speak about it and constantly reinterpret it, "becoming accustomed to talking out loud" about it until it reaches the realm of reality and possibility. This approach can explain the reason for some of the mitzvot that involve speech and repetition, such as reciting the *Shema*. When particular words are

this causes it to enter the world, changing it from being concealed in a person's thoughts to being manifest in his heart.

לְהַעֲמִיק מַחֲשַׁבְתּוֹ בְּחַיֵּי הַחַיִּים אֵין סוֹף בָּרוּךְ הוּא, כִּי הוּא אָבִינוּ מַמָּשׁ הָאֲמִתִּי וּמְקוֹר חַיֵּינוּ, וּלְעוֹרֵר אֵלָיו הָאַהֲבָה כְּאַהֲבַת הַבֵּן אֶל הָאָב. **in order to immerse one's thoughts in the source of life, *Ein Sof*, blessed be He,** He should contemplate **that He,** God, **literally is our true Father and the source of our life, awakening** his **love for** God **like the love of a son for his father.**

Once, when the hasidim of Kotzk were praying, one of them began to cry out fervently, as some hasidim used to do, "*Tatte! Tatte!* (Father! Father!)." One of the other hasidim jokingly remarked, in the words of the Talmud concerning a person who strikes his father, "But perhaps He is not his father?" (*Ḥullin* 11b). When the Rebbe of Kotzk was told of this, he said, "When a person cries out '*Tatte*' so many times, God becomes his *Tatte*." When a person speaks continuously about his Father, he awakens both himself and God, his Father.

---

repeated at set times, even if this is only an externally experienced statement, it prepares the person for the internal content, and without these experiences the internal content cannot develop.

For example, in a sense, people may be considered "poor" depending on how they express their poverty. A person who constantly talks about how poor he is and how he comes from a vulnerable sector of society, and so forth, becomes so conscious and sensitive to these matters that he suffers from the disadvantages that he speaks of. Another individual, who objectively is in the same economic situation but does not live in an environment where these issues are raised, is unaware of this approach, of these definitions and feelings, and therefore does not feel or frame his situation in the same way. Ideas enter a person's private consciousness by virtue of the fact that they are in the public consciousness; people talk about matters and cause each other to consider them. Likewise, when an individual does not talk to himself about something or refine it in his mind, over time it may disappear from the reality of his life. This phenomenon explains why, in many areas of life, people require an explicit declaration from another person when entering into an agreement, and are not satisfied with a vague declaration of intent, even if the other party is someone they trust.

וּכְשֶׁיַּרְגִּיל עַצְמוֹ כֵּן תָּמִיד, הֲרֵי הַהֶרְגֵּל נַעֲשֶׂה טֶבַע. **When he makes this a constant habit** for himself, the habit will become his **nature.**

When a person becomes accustomed to speaking about a particular subject and living it, then his external habits of speech and thought will be transformed to become his inner nature, and the matters he speaks of will influence him, all the more so if he wants them to.

4 Iyar
30 Nisan (leap year)

וְאַף אִם נִדְמֶה לוֹ לִכְאוֹרָה שֶׁהוּא כֹּחַ דִּמְיוֹנִי, לֹא יָחוּשׁ, **Even if it appears to him that apparently this is an imaginary feeling, he need not be concerned,**

Here, the author of the *Tanya* touches on a profound and fundamental point. If a person has spoken and thought about a matter only on a superficial level, then one might think that the emotion that develops is likewise only the semblance of a real emotion, not flowing from within. Perhaps, after talking and thinking so much about the subject, it only appears to him that there is an emotion acting within him. The reason one need not be concerned about expressing himself in an "artificial" way is a fundamental part of the approach of the *Tanya* in general. A person should certainly be concerned about that which is false, but not about that which is artificial. The premise of the *Tanya* is that the vast majority of human beings cannot reach certain concepts naturally and spontaneously, and therefore they must contrive these, to one degree or another. The fact that something is artificial does not detract from its authenticity. Unlike some approaches that demand spontaneity and see it as the test of truth, this approach maintains that spontaneity only reveals that a matter is close to a person's heart; however, it does not indicate anything about its truth or importance.

מֵאַחַר שֶׁהוּא אֱמֶת לַאֲמִיתּוֹ מִצַּד עַצְמוֹ, **since it is intrinsically absolutely genuine,**

How can a person know that his love of God is real? The answer is that since this love is intrinsically real, even if the person's awakening to it comes through pretense, through acting "as if," then the person's inner experience is real.

בִּבְחִינַת 'אַהֲבָה מְסוּתֶּרֶת'. **on the level of concealed love.**

As explained previously, this is the love of God that exists within every Jew simply because he is a Jew. Even if he wanted to, he could not remove it.

רַק שֶׁתּוֹעֶלֶת יְצִיאָתָהּ אֶל הַגִּילוּי כְּדֵי לַהֲבִיאָהּ לִידֵי מַעֲשֶׂה, שֶׁהוּא עֵסֶק הַתּוֹרָה וְהַמִּצְוֹת, שֶׁלּוֹמֵד וּמְקַיֵּים עַל יְדֵי זֶה, כְּדֵי לַעֲשׂוֹת נַחַת רוּחַ לְפָנָיו יִתְבָּרֵךְ, **However, the benefit of** the concealed love **emerging into consciousness is to induce action, namely, engaging in Torah and mitzvot that** a person studies and fulfills as a result of this love, **for the sake of giving gratification to** God,

As long as this love remains concealed, it has no practical ramifications. But when a person achieves an awakening of love as a conscious, active experience, and with that he engages in Torah study and mitzva observance, these are entirely different. While a person is only fulfilling a duty, even if he theoretically recognizes its value, he will carry it out, as people tend to do, in accordance with the minimal requirements. However, when a person does something that he himself desires, the quality and quantity of his actions will be completely different. The awakening of this love does not create something in a person that was not there previously, but develops and reveals the possibilities that already exist in his being, so that they will influence not only his inner consciousness, but all of his actions.

כְּבֵן הָעוֹבֵד אֶת אָבִיו. **as a son tends to his father.**

This love is compared to a son's relationship with his father. What is special about this relationship is that it has nothing to do with manifested feelings. A son remains a son forever, whether he is a good son or a bad one, whether he is loving or not. The question of whether and how strongly he identifies as a son does not change the nature of the father-son relationship in any way. Although this relationship is a fact, it has no inherent way of being expressed. In order to manifest it, a person must awaken and develop it with deliberate toil through habits of speech and thought.

וְעַל זֶה אָמְרוּ: "מַחֲשָׁבָה טוֹבָה הַקָּדוֹשׁ בָּרוּךְ הוּא מְצָרְפָהּ לְמַעֲשֶׂה" (קידושין מ, א). — Regarding this, the Sages stated that the Holy One, blessed be He, links a good thought to an action (see Kiddushin 40a),

This concealed love is like that of a son for his father. A person does not feel it as a living feeling but he accustoms himself to talking and thinking about it. God connects that good thought to deed. Although intent is not as powerful as love or fear revealed in the heart but is merely a good thought of performing a mitzva, it connects with the mitzva just as the attributes of revealed love and fear connect with a mitzva.

When the relationship between thought and deed is spontaneous, so that it progresses on its own from one level to the next level, when a person's thought truly brings him to perform the action, there is no place to speak of God connecting it to a deed, because in truth that thought constitutes the "wings" of his deed. However, when, as described here, a person needs to think about the idea of "You are children to the Lord" and habituate himself to talk about this and perform the deeds as a person who feels this way would, at that time it is necessary for God to connect the thought to the deed. At that time, there is a gap between the person's thought (his understanding) and his deed. It would be fitting for this gap to be filled by actual feeling. But if that does not happen, God links his thought to his deed with a "leap" that closes the gap between them. Here the Tanya states that this connection has the character of the relationship between son and father, between the Jewish people and God. Since this connection is not an artificial addition that a person manufactures but is part of his nature, God knows how one's intentions elevate his actions, even if the person himself is unaware of this, even if he does not feel how his intent elevates his deed, and God links his thought to deed. In the very formation of the relationship of "you are children to the Lord," God has already connected the thought to deed.

לִהְיוֹת גַּדְפִּין לְפָרְחָא, כַּנִּזְכָּר לְעֵיל. — to constitute wings for the action to soar upward, as stated above (chaps. 16, 39).

This image of wings pertains to the analogy mentioned in chapters 16 and 39, as well as below. A "good thought," even if it is not a tangible feeling of love or fear in one's heart, nevertheless performs the function of love and fear, elevating an act from the physical world to the realm of the Divine.

וְהֲנָחַת רוּחַ הוּא כְּמָשָׁל שִׂמְחַת הַמֶּלֶךְ מִבְּנוֹ שֶׁבָּא אֵלָיו בְּצֵאתוֹ מִבֵּית הָאֲסוּרִים, כַּנִּזְכָּר לְעֵיל. **The gratification** that a person gives God **is analogous to the joy the king receives from his son returning to him upon leaving prison, as stated above** (chaps. 31, 41).

A person expresses the love of God that is like that of a son for his father when he learns Torah and fulfills mitzvot in order to give pleasure to God. The analogy refers to a king whose son was in prison, and it conveys the immense joy the king felt when his son was released and came back to him. ☞

God derives pleasure not from the performance of a particular act by a specific individual, but rather from the liberation of the soul that results from this act. When a person performs a mitzva, he releases the "son" from the "prison" of this world, from the limitations of the

LEAVING PRISON

☞ An additional analogy is given: There was once a king who exiled his son, sending him to live in a remote part of the country. After a while, the son forgot that he was a prince, and began to behave, speak, and think like the country folk. Eventually, the king commanded that his son be returned to him. He sent distinguished ministers to him to say, "The king has decided to fulfill all your desires. What do you wish for?" Instead of asking to be returned to his position beside the king, he thought for a while and said, "I would like a good bottle of wine to have with my supper."

The king's son was in a double exile: In addition to being in exile, he did not know that he was in exile. In order to be redeemed, he would have to return to the royal mores: to behave, speak, and think like a prince. The "prison" mentioned here is a reference to the fact that people become caught up in this-worldly matters and forget who they are. A person forgets that he has a soul that is loftier than an angel, and he equates himself instead with animals. He eats and sleeps like the animals, mates like them, builds houses like them, and even flies like them. There is nothing wrong with any of these actions per se; the problem is that he is a human being, and when he behaves this way and does nothing more, he degrades the image of man and the image of that which is above.

body and from all the illusions and concealment of this world. Then, the "King" rejoices that His son has left prison and returned to Him.

The mitzvot are like flashes of light in the darkness of the world. When a person performs a mitzva, he releases from within himself a "part" of the Divine from the prison of this world, illuminating it in its pristine state, through the light of the mitzva. This is the release from "prison."

אוֹ לִהְיוֹת לוֹ 'דִּירָה בַּתַּחְתּוֹנִים', כַּנִּזְכָּר לְעֵיל. **Alternatively,** God's gratification stems from **having a dwelling in the lower worlds (as stated above** [chap. 36]**).**

There are two aspects to the gratification that God derives when human beings serve Him. The first is that which was described in the previous paragraph: the liberation involved in the act of performing a mitzva, of liberating the holiness found within the individual and within objects, which then rises upward. Here, the author of the *Tanya* discusses the second element, that of building a sanctuary and drawing down holiness. Commentaries on the verse "They shall make for Me a sanctuary, and I will dwell among them" (Ex. 25:8), note that it does not say that God will dwell "*betokho* (in it)," but "*betokham* (among them)." Whenever and wherever a person learns, prays, or performs a mitzva, he creates a sanctuary for God.[7] God is pleased when people create a tabernacle for Him, when out of destruction and turmoil a space is cleared so that He may come to dwell in it.

God's gratification does not stem from the act itself but from the fact that it fulfills His will and is an expression of love for Him. A person should cultivate this element of "for You are our Father" (Isa. 63:16) within himself, delving into it until his heart awakens and he acts in order to please God like a son serving his father.

וְהִנֵּה גַּם לִבְחִינַת 'נַפְשִׁי אִוִּיתִיךָ' הַנִּזְכֶּרֶת לְעֵיל, קָרוֹב הַדָּבָר מְאֹד לְהוֹצִיאָהּ מֵהַהֶעְלֵם אֶל הַגִּילּוּי **Also with regard to the type** of love expressed as **"With my soul, I have desired You" (discussed above), it is very possible to bring it out of concealment into consciousness**

---

7. See *Tanḥuma, Naso* 16; *Bereshit Rabba* 3:9; *Bemidbar Rabba* 13:6.

The idea that love for God can be awakened by means of habit, by means of talking about the subject and deepening one's thinking about it, was stated with regard to love for God that is like the love of a son for his father. Here, the author of the *Tanya* says that this applies to every type of "concealed love." Like the "son-father love," the love described earlier of "with my soul, I have desired You" is also a general type of love that is concealed in the heart of every Jew. God is "my soul," a person's true life, and hence a person desires Him. Since this type of love is intrinsic to a person, it may be brought from concealment into consciousness. A person evokes the concealed love of God within him in the same way that he evokes most of his inner experiences. Few people achieve spontaneous, independent inner experiences without any connection to or awareness of external reality and events. Usually, in order to have an inner experience, a person needs to prepare a conscious foundation to which his love can attach itself. If someone does not possess an emotion at all, he cannot create it within himself. But regarding an emotion that does exist within him, even if it is at present concealed, he can enhance and strengthen it until it becomes manifested. ☞

עַל יְדֵי הַהֶרְגֵּל תָּמִיד בְּפִיו וְלִבּוֹ שָׁוִין. **through constant practice, with his mouth** and his heart mirroring one another.

"His mouth and his heart mirroring one another" is a matter of habit.[8] The quality and depth of feeling are of secondary significance. The important thing is that a person's speech is not detached from what he

---

BRINGING LOVE OUT OF CONCEALMENT INTO CONSCIOUSNESS

☞ In a sense, this is what happens with regard to every kind of love. So-called "love at first sight" happens rarely, if ever; rather, relationships usually evolve. People are together, and with time their relationship becomes deeper, more significant, and closer to their hearts. Likewise, with regard to love of God, a person maintains a friendship with like-minded people, and he thinks and talks about the subject until his heart awakens and he truly feels this love.

---

8. This was explained above with regard to the love that is like that of a son, and it must be repeated with regard to the love of "My soul, I have desired You." See

feels in his heart. A person can accustom himself to maintaining this connection between his speech and his heart.

"His mouth and his heart mirroring one another" is a necessary condition. When a person speaks about loving God and at the same time tries as hard as he can to feel what he is describing, the love concealed within him receives a real, enduring enhancement, and it eventually emerges from the hidden realm into full manifestation.

אַךְ אִם אֵינוֹ יָכוֹל לְהוֹצִיאָהּ אֶל הַגִּילּוּי בְּלִבּוֹ, **But if one cannot bring it out into** conscious **manifestation in his heart,**

Up to this point, the *Tanya* has been discussing how to bring the love for God to a revealed state, and the toil involved in achieving this. However, it is possible that a person will not be able to achieve this manifestation. There are those who, although they do everything they are able, may talk and think about the love for God, but do not make significant progress in this direction. ☞

A PERSON WHO CANNOT AROUSE HIS LOVE FOR GOD

☞ As has already been explained, a person has control over his thoughts but not over his emotions. He can choose a thought that he wants to think about, and despite distractions and difficulties, he can hold on to this thought for some time. Not all human beings are equal in this regard; there are those who naturally have a great ability to concentrate, and others who have to work hard, practicing a great deal, to gain this skill. However, anyone who tries consistently will be able to overcome distractions, which will fade away until he is able to focus his thoughts on the subject of love for God. Nevertheless, when it comes to emotions (rather than merely thinking about emotions), such as love, hate, and fear, a person has almost no control over what happens inside himself. Furthermore, with regard to such matters, other people cannot help him very much. Since everyone is different, there are no set rules that apply to everyone. There is no "button" that can be pressed to automatically trigger specific emotions. A given external stimulus does not necessarily cause all human beings to have the same feelings. The author of the *Tanya* states that a person should feel love toward God in the way that a son feels love for his father. Yet, in our culture, there are many people who are unable to achieve this feeling even toward their actual father. In every culture there are certain words, concepts, and emotions to which people do not relate, and as a result, they cannot develop these further.

---

the comment of the Lubavitcher Rebbe, Rabbi Menaḥem Mendel Schneerson, in *Lessons in Tanya*, p. 655.

אַף עַל פִּי כֵן, יָכוֹל לַעֲסוֹק בַּתּוֹרָה וּמִצְוֹת לִשְׁמָן, עַל יְדֵי צִיּוּר עִנְיַן אַהֲבָה זוֹ בְּמַחֲשֶׁבֶת שֶׁבְּמוֹחוֹ,	nevertheless, he can engage in Torah and mitzvot for their own sake by conceptualizing this love in the thought of his mind,

How can a person who is unable to achieve the revelation of love in his heart serve God with love, as the *Tanya* requires? He can at least understand it intellectually, thinking about it and trying as hard as possible to gain insight into the concept that he wishes to experience emotionally.

וּמַחֲשָׁבָה טוֹבָה הַקָּדוֹשׁ בָּרוּךְ הוּא מְצָרְפָהּ כוּ' (קידושין מ, א).	and the Holy One, blessed be He, **links a good thought** to action (*Kiddushin* 40a).

A "good thought" is a thought that, even if it does not develop into an emotion, constitutes the foundation of a person's actions. It concerns the emotions that he should feel, and therefore ultimately it connects to his actions just as emotions do, because it leads to action. As a result, the action is no longer purely external and physical; rather, it is accompanied by an inner experience. Like emotion, thought possesses a certain radiance and warms a person's inner being in a way that can connect it to his deeds. And indeed, in such a case God does link the thought to an action (*Kiddushin* 40a).

וְהִנֵּה ב' בְּחִינוֹת אַהֲבוֹת אֵלּוּ, אַף שֶׁהֵן יְרוּשָׁה לָנוּ מֵאֲבוֹתֵינוּ וּכְמוֹ טֶבַע בְּנַפְשׁוֹתֵינוּ,	Although these two types of love are our inheritance from our forefathers and are like inborn traits within our souls,	5 Iyar 1 Iyar (leap year)

The first type of love mentioned in this chapter is that of "My soul, I have desired You." This requires a person to deepen his feelings toward himself, since God is "my soul." The second type is "as a son who tends to his father," which means that a person loves God as his Father, Creator, Maker, and the source of his being. Every Jew inherits the potential to experience these two types of love, regardless of his aptitude and regardless of his level of divine service. It is found within each individual and becomes part of his being.

וְכֵן הַיִּרְאָה הַכְּלוּלָה בָּהֶן שֶׁהִיא לְיָרֵא מִלִּיפָּרֵד חַס וְשָׁלוֹם מִמְּקוֹר חַיֵּינוּ וְאָבִינוּ הָאֲמִתִּי בָּרוּךְ הוּא, **and so is the fear contained within them**, namely, **the fear of becoming detached, God forbid, from our source of life and our true Father, blessed be He.**

This love for God that we inherit contains an aspect of fear. As mentioned above, every case of true love includes an element of fear, at least in the sense that the lovers do not want to spoil their relationship. When the object of a person's love is important to him, he fears that it will be taken from him. Particularly with regard to the love a person feels for his own life and for his true Father, he is afraid of becoming disconnected. This fear is the source of the experience associated with the fear of transgressing the negative commandments. It is the fear of separation, which grows in accordance with the magnitude of one's love for God.

אַף עַל פִּי כֵן, אֵינָן נִקְרָאוֹת בְּשֵׁם דְּחִילוּ וּרְחִימוּ טִבְעִיִּים, אֶלָּא כְּשֶׁהֵן בְּמוֹחוֹ וּמַחֲשַׁבְתּוֹ לְבַד וְתַעֲלוּמוֹת לִבּוֹ. **Yet they are referred to as** a person's **natural,** innate **fear and love only when they remain exclusively in his mind and thought,** dormant and **in the hidden recesses of his heart,**

These two types of love are innate – which, as explained above, is a lower level than cognitively aware fear and love. They are referred to as "innate" only when they are not revealed in one's heart. Love and fear are only fundamentally "innate" as long as they remain within us just as we inherited them, as emotions that are concealed in the heart and are present in thought alone.

וְאָז מְקוֹמָן בְּעֶשֶׂר סְפִירוֹת דִּיצִירָה, וּלְשָׁם הֵן מַעֲלוֹת עִמָּהֶן הַתּוֹרָה וְהַמִּצְוֹת הַבָּאוֹת מֵחֲמָתָן וּבְסִיבָּתָן. **and then their place is in the ten *sefirot* of the world of *Yetzira* (Formation), to where they raise up with them the Torah and mitzvot of which they have been the inspiration and cause.**

As was explained in previous chapters, a person's intention coupled with love and fear, with which he learns Torah and fulfills mitzvot, elevates the Torah and mitzvot from this world to higher worlds. Innate love and fear belong to the level of the world of *Yetzira*, and therefore, when they elevate Torah and mitzvot, they raise them to the world of *Yetzira*. ☞

אֲבָל כְּשֶׁהֵן בְּהִתְגַּלּוּת לִבּוֹ נִקְרָאוֹת 'רְעוּתָא דְלִבָּא' בַּזּוֹהַר (חלק ב רי, ב), וּמְקוֹמָן בְּעֶשֶׂר סְפִירוֹת דִּבְרִיאָה,

But when they are manifest in a person's **heart**, they are referred to by the *Zohar* (2:210b) as **"the heart's desire,"** and their place is in the ten *sefirot* of the world of *Beria* (Creation),

This is referring to when the love and fear described above are revealed in a person's heart. They are no longer just like a thought, like a latent emotion in the heart. Rather, they are emotions that a person has worked on and directed with his contemplation. They become

---

INNATE LOVE AND FEAR

☞ Natural, innate emotions, as explained above, do not go beyond the realm of thought and the concealed areas of the heart. They exist within a person's fundamental emotional structure, but are not manifested as a tangible feeling. Fear and love of this type are considered innate, because they are part of the soul's natural being, and not a part of the soul's ascent to higher levels of consciousness. Nevertheless, as discussed above, although these types of love and fear are "innate," they do not remain in the reality of the physical world. Rather, they elevate the Torah and mitzvot that a person engaged in through them from this world, the world of *Asiya*, at least to the world of *Yetzira*. The two types of love – that of "My soul, I have desired You," and that which is like a son's love for his father – are at their core a natural love for oneself. Nevertheless, they can evolve to a certain degree. They have a connection to and can strive to reach the source of a person's core self. A person's connection to his true, original self involves a process of seeking and making choices. This includes giving up certain things and holding onto others, searching for the source, and abandoning that which is incidental. This emotion is always present in the human soul, for it is part of one's "innate" being, yet it is not a natural, innate feeling akin to a person's feelings about eating and drinking, and so forth. It belongs to the person's higher, spiritual nature, which is also "innate." Therefore, although it is only an "innate" emotion, it elevates a person's deed, removing it from the ordinary world of *Asiya* and bringing it into the world of *Yetzira*.

fundamental, directed feelings that are manifest in the heart. They are not merely thoughts about what the heart is supposed to feel, but rather they are the actual will and passion of the heart. Their place is in the world of *Beria*. This is a higher world; it is the realm of the intellect, above the attributes. There, the traits of love and fear are cognitive and not innate. There, inner experiences become conscious and revealed in the heart. ☞

An innate feeling is almost automatic. In a sense, it constitutes the beginning of human existence rather than its outcome. It is therefore on a lower level than a feeling that is part of the intellectual realm, a person's mature consciousness. For example, there is a mitzva to recite the afternoon prayer on the Sabbath, and there is a mitzva to eat a third meal on the Sabbath. The enthusiasm that a person feels during the third meal relates to his natural, innate feelings. The innate soul does not need to be taught to eat or to enjoy food. On the other hand, when a person prays or recites psalms with a similar level of enthusiasm, this is certainly a higher level. Ostensibly, these two mitzvot each awaken an emotion of the same intensity; however, in one case this emotion is reinforced by the person's raw, base, and basic nature, while in the other, the emotion is formed and reinforced by his consciousness. Clearly, the second emotion is on a higher level. It is a level of love and fear that results from a person's inner being: not only from his physical

THE HEART'S DESIRE

☞ In a sense, the heart's desire reflects the highest level a human being can reach. The heart's desire is a revelation of desire that is above the intellect; it cannot be revealed in the mind, but is revealed in the heart. A person's mind can be revealed in the feeling of his heart. Beyond that, the heart is so deep that it can reveal even that which is above the mind. Humans have the ability to perceive something with our feelings that we cannot define with our intellect, something that comes from above, from a level that encompasses all levels, whose reality can be felt even if one does not understand it. Even God Himself, who cannot be perceived with thought, neither as One who fills all worlds nor as One who encompasses all worlds, is perceivable on the level of "the heart's desire." Thought cannot grasp Him, but the heart's desire can. That which cannot be perceived with intellectual understanding is perceived with the understanding of the heart. That which is not understood by the mind is affixed to "the heart's desire," the soul's yearning to be attached to God (see *Torah Or* 27a; *Likkutei Torah*, Num. 81d).

nature but from his consciousness and thoughts, which develop and enhance the nature of his higher, divine qualities.

וּלְשָׁם הֵן מַעֲלוֹת עִמָּהֶן הַתּוֹרָה וְהַמִּצְוֹת הַבָּאוֹת מֵחֲמָתָן מִפְּנֵי שֶׁיְּצִיאָתָן מֵהַהֶעְלֵם וְהֶסְתֵּר הַלֵּב אֶל בְּחִינַת גִּילּוּי הִיא עַל יְדֵי הַדַּעַת,

and that is the place **to which they elevate with them the Torah** study and **mitzvot** performance **of which they were the cause. This is because their emergence from the concealment and hiddenness of the heart to the level of being revealed is** achieved **through the attribute of Da'at,**

A person's love and fear of God elevate his Torah learning and mitzva performance to the world of *Beria*. The love and fear described here are "our inheritance from our forefathers and are like inborn traits within our souls," and therefore belong to the world of *Yetzira*. However, while this natural, hereditary link to the source of our being, to the power of the Divine Presence within our soul, exists within us, it is not active. In its natural, primal form, it contains only the beginning. These beginnings have no biological or psychological mechanism that rouses them to evolve, grow, and become active. In order to develop them further, a person needs to put in extraordinary, conscious effort through acquiring knowledge and deep thought.

THEIR EMERGENCE FROM CONCEALMENT TO REVELATION IS ACHIEVED THROUGH DA'AT

☞ Unlike animals, every human being simply by being a human being has certain potentialities within him, concealed in the physiological mechanisms of his brain. A person has the innate potential to engage in mathematics, to read and write, and so on. However, these natural faculties are only foundations. They constitute the space on which specific "buildings" may be built, but they themselves are not enough to ensure that these buildings will be built. For a "building" to be built, a person must perform an action: an action that is not innate or automatic but deliberate and conscious, with knowledge and hard work in the realm of thought. Human beings have the capacity to translate concepts from one language to another. We can read black marks on paper and understand words and sentences, and we can read a written description and visualize the image it portrays. This human ability is inherited from our ancestors. It is natural and innate within all of us. Yet when a child is being taught to read and to understand what he is reading, it is no longer

Likewise, within every Jew, there is the "inherited" love for God of "My soul, I have desired You." Fundamentally, the individual has a connection to God, just as he has a connection to himself. Nevertheless, "translating" this love into the language of experience constitutes a different stage, one that requires effort in the realm of acquiring knowledge. Regarding this, too, human beings are not all equal. There are those who cannot think of anything else once the matter enters their mind; nothing else is able to fill their soul. On the other hand, there are those who have to work at it constantly, and even then, they do not necessarily achieve a perceptible experience.

וּתְקִיעַת הַמַּחֲשָׁבָה בְּחוֹזֶק, וְהִתְבּוֹנְנוּת עֲצוּמָה, מֵעוּמְקָא דְלִבָּא יָתִיר וְתָדִיר, — **and** through **forceful fixation of one's thought and intense contemplation from the depths of the heart, immensely and diligently,**

This work is carried out through knowledge and fixating one's thoughts, which means concentrating on the subject. Such concentration does not come naturally to most people, so it must be carried out vigorously and forcefully. Intense contemplation is required in order to see the subject of one's contemplation, over and over, from all aspects, from the depth of the heart. If a person wants to experience the feeling in the depths of his heart, then his contemplation and the fixation of his thoughts must come forcefully from deep within his heart. This work should be carried out to a greater degree and more frequently than his usual endeavors, with consistency and focus. This is not a process of relaxation, but an intensive effort involving extensive, hard work, in which a person concentrates and stabilizes his thoughts so that love can burst forth from deep within himself.

בְּאֵין סוֹף בָּרוּךְ הוּא, אֵיךְ הוּא חַיֵּינוּ מַמָּשׁ וְאָבִינוּ הָאֲמִתִּי בָּרוּךְ הוּא. — of *Ein Sof*, **blessed be He, how He literally is our life and our true Father, blessed be He.**

---

a matter of nature. Learning and development require intent and conscious effort. Some people need years of exertion, while for others the process is almost effortless. Either way, it is an additional stage, which no longer involves inborn traits but acquiring knowledge and focusing one's thoughts.

A person should contemplate how the Infinite One is literally our life, as expressed in the verse "My soul, I have desired You," and He is our Father, and we relate to him as a son tending his father.

A person who is learning to read requires concentration, care, and constancy until he acquires the skill. After a while, it no longer requires effort, but comes naturally to him. The same is true with regard to a person who achieves a growing revelation of love of God in his heart by means of hard work, by means of knowledge, forceful fixation of his thoughts, and intense contemplation. After that, the love is no longer an expression of human nature, but rather of human greatness. The love and fear are no longer innate, but cognitive.

וּמוּדַעַת זֹאת מַה שֶּׁכָּתוּב בַּתִּיקוּנִים (תיקוני זהר תיקון כג, א), כִּי בְּעוֹלָם הַבְּרִיאָה מְקַנְּנָא תַּמָּן אִימָּא עִילָּאָה, שֶׁהִיא הַהִתְבּוֹנְנוּת בְּאוֹר אֵין סוֹף חַיֵּי הַחַיִּים בָּרוּךְ הוּא.

It is known what the *Tikkunei Zohar* (23a) states that **in the world of *Beria* resides the *sefira* of *Bina*, known as the supernal mother, which** corresponds to the contemplation of the light of *Ein Sof*, the source of life, blessed be He.

The *sefira* of *Bina* in the world of *Atzilut* is called the "supernal mother." In human terms, with regard to the individual's divine service, this corresponds to contemplation of the light of *Ein Sof*, which is the source of life.

וּכְמַאֲמַר אֵלִיָּהוּ (תיקוני זהר יז, א): "בִּינָה לִבָּא וּבָהּ הַלֵּב מֵבִין".

This accords with Elijah's statement "***Bina* corresponds to the heart, and with it the heart understands**" (*Tikkunei Zohar* 17a).

"Understanding of the heart" is an experiential level of understanding. At this high level, a person feels understanding and understands feeling. This is the level of cognitive love and fear explained above, which relate to "the heart's desire." ☞

INNATE FEAR AND LOVE VS. COGNITIVE FEAR AND LOVE

☞ The relationship between these two stages may be explained as follows: Within a person, there is a natural, innate emotion that emerges spontaneously, and there is

וְלֹא עוֹד, אֶלָּא שֶׁב' בְּחִינוֹת אַהֲבוֹת אֵלּוּ הַנִּזְכָּרוֹת לְעֵיל, הֵן כְּלוּלוֹת מִן בְּחִינַת 'אַהֲבָה רַבָּה' וּגְדוֹלָה וּמְעוּלָה מִדְּחִילוּ וּרְחִימוּ שִׂכְלִיִּים,

Moreover, these two types of love discussed above are comprised of the level of *ahava rabba*, and that is greater and more sublime than cognitive fear and love,

The two types of love that have been discussed in this chapter are that of "My soul, I have desired You," and that of a son serving his father. They are inherited and are innate within the root and essence of the soul, and they belong to the level of *ahava rabba*.[9] This level is certainly greater and more sublime[10] than that of cognitive love and fear, which derive from intellectual contemplation.[11] "Greater" refers to the fact that its impact on the soul is stronger, and "more sublime" refers to the fact that it is more profound and lofty. While conditional love is usually "greater," or more intense than unconditional love, unconditional love is always "more sublime" than conditional love.

another emotion, which is also innate and genuine but is not spontaneous. It does not reveal itself and flow of its own accord. In order to reveal the second emotion, the conscious effort of the rational soul is needed. This effort, which requires both understanding and contemplation, belongs to the level of the world of *Beria*, from where the forces of understanding and contemplation stem, and to where the resulting actions, the mitzvot, reach. A person who contemplates and attains this level of love has progressed from the level of dealing with things that he has received as gifts at birth to the level of acquiring through his own efforts. Moreover, with his hard work, a person gives God the greatest gift of love: he gives himself. There is a hasidic explanation (*Agra deKhala*, *Bereshit* 4d) for why God desired Abel's offering and not Cain's: It was because "Abel, he also brought [*veHevel hevi gam hu*]" (Gen. 4:4), which can be homiletically translated, "Abel also brought himself." This was an offering that God truly desired. What can a human being possibly offer God, who possesses the entire world and all its contents? Only himself. In this sense, the love for God that a person needs to create in himself and in his world through thought and contemplation is on the highest possible level; it is the level where he offers himself.

---

9. As explained in chap. 43.
10. For it appertains to the world of *Atzilut* (the Lubavitcher Rebbe, Rabbi Menaḥem Mendel Schneerson).
11. See *Torah Or* 73a.

CHAPTER 44

אֲשֶׁר הָאַהֲבָה נִקְרֵאת לְעֵיל בְּשֵׁם 'אַהֲבַת עוֹלָם'. — which is the type of **love referred to above** (chap. 43) as *ahavat olam* (world-centered love).

This cognitive love, which results from contemplation, is called world-centered love because it relates to the divine essence that is revealed within the world, rather than to the divine essence itself. It is unlike the two types of love discussed here, which stem from the essential connection between a person and the Almighty, as a result of the person's deepening, making a foundation, and verifying the essential inner identification between the root and essence of his soul and God Himself. *Ahavat olam* arises from contemplating the greatness of God in this world. This contemplation excites the soul, affecting each person in a distinct way, and to a different extent, in accordance with his personal situation, the way he contemplates, and his unique worldview through which he perceives God's greatness.[12]

Ahava rabba, and the two types of love that it encompasses, is greater and more sublime, because it does not relate to God's greatness as it is revealed in the world, but rather to the divine essence itself. The psalmist says, "Whom else do I have in heaven? With You, I desire nothing on earth" (Ps. 73:25). This does not mean only that the individual does not desire that which is found in heaven or on earth; rather, heaven and earth themselves hold no interest for him when he is in the state of *ahava rabba*, the essential connection to God himself.

רַק שֶׁאַף עַל פִּי כֵן, צָרִיךְ לִטְרוֹחַ בְּשִׂכְלוֹ לְהַשִּׂיג וּלְהַגִּיעַ גַּם לִבְחִינַת 'אַהֲבַת עוֹלָם' הַנִּזְכֶּרֶת לְעֵיל, הַבָּאָה מֵהִתְבּוֹנְנָה וְדַעַת בִּגְדוּלַּת ה', — **Still, nevertheless, one must also exert his intellect to apprehend and attain the level of *ahavat olam* discussed above, which is engendered by the understanding and knowledge of God's greatness,**   6 Iyar
2 Iyar
(leap year)

If *ahava rabba*, which is inherited from our ancestors and is innate within our souls, is more intense and sublime, why should a person

---

12. This love is not inferior to purely cognitive *ahavat olam*. It contains elements of both concealed love, which is true, innate, and unchanging, and *ahavat olam*, as will be explained below (*Pelaḥ HaRimon, Parashat Vayera*).

invest so much effort to contemplate God's greatness? Why should he work so hard learning and contemplating in order to reach *ahavat olam*, if it is on a lower level? Why should one attempt to reach other worlds, or the realm of the infinite, when the greatest and most sublime love is found within his own soul, where God is his "life" as well as his Father?

כְּדֵי לְהַגְדִּיל מְדוּרַת אֵשׁ הָאַהֲבָה **in order to intensify the blaze of love**

As mentioned above, the Talmud states that "Even though fire descends from the heavens [onto the altar], [still there is a special] mitzva for a person to bring fire" (*Yoma* 21b). *Ahava rabba* is a fire that descends from heaven. It is greater and more sublime than that which a person can achieve alone, yet in order to intensify the blaze of love, a person must add to it the love that he himself creates, *ahavat olam*, by means of his own learning and contemplation.

Regarding the natural, innate aspect of love: Even when it is great and sublime, even when it is fully manifest, it fills only a part of a person's being. There are other parts of him that cannot be stimulated by it. In order for a person to further strengthen his love for God in all ways and in all directions, he must associate more and more parts of himself with this love. For instance, a son's love for his father is essentially the love of a created being for its creator, for the one who brought it into the world. This love is fundamental, elementary, and unconditional. It is a connection between essences, unrelated to the sons' capabilities and the development of those capabilities. It is independent of the particular qualities of the father or the son, just as a person's love of himself does not depend on his individual qualities. With regard to self-love, there is no difference between a great person and a simple person, a wise person and a foolish person, a righteous person and a wicked person, since neither one's shortcomings nor his virtues affect it. Nevertheless, this kind of love can be enhanced. That occurs when, in addition to recognizing that his father is the one who gave him life, the son also recognizes his father's virtues. That recognition adds an additional aspect to his love, related to the father's qualities. It is not as fundamental as the son's fundamental love, but it includes a new dimension, which could not have developed previously.

בְּרִשְׁפֵּי אֵשׁ וְשַׁלְהֶבֶת עַזָּה וְלַהַב הָעוֹלֶה הַשָּׁמַיְמָה **into sparks of fire and a fierce conflagration and flame that rises heavenward**

This increase of self-love in *ahavat olam* is like the intensification of a fire. The previous chapter discussed the relationship between *ahavat olam* and *ahava rabba*. *Ahava rabba* requires nothing additional, because it comprises a relationship that already exists. One's father is one's father; this is a factual, essential connection, and there is nothing that can be, or that needs to be added to it. By contrast, *ahavat olam* is based on a sense of lack and yearning that is built into the world's essence. The Divine is lacking and concealed in the world, and the soul suffers as a result, and longs to fill the lack. This is a fiery love; the whole world burns with the fire of this love, it is all composed of a flammable material that is ignited in the process of its refinement. *Ahavat olam* adds this fire and tension onto *ahava rabba*, which is on a higher level. ☞

עַד שֶׁ"מַיִם רַבִּים לֹא יוּכְלוּ לְכַבּוֹת אֶת הָאַהֲבָה וּנְהָרוֹת לֹא יִשְׁטְפוּהָ" וכו' (שיר השירים ח, ז). **until "much water cannot extinguish the love and rivers cannot wash it away..." (Song 8:7). That is because there is a superiority and advantage**

"MY SISTER, MY LOVE"

☞ This phrase refers to two types of love of God (see *Likkutei Torah*, Lev. 39c). "My sister" refers to a fundamental connection that is unconditional with regard to both the "brother" and the "sister"; it is a relationship that cannot be severed. "My love," on the other hand, is a conditional relationship that is first formed and then built. Nevertheless, or perhaps because of this fact, the relationship of "my love" is the more intense one. Thus, the recurring phrases in the Song of Songs, "my sister, my love," and "my sister, my bride," express the combination of these two different types of relationships. *Ahava rabba* is the relationship of "my sister." It is stable, deep, and strong, but it is also quiet, with no outbursts. It is not like an all-consuming fire, but is fully satiated within itself. By contrast, *ahavat olam*, which is the relationship of "my love," has an entirely different structure. It is a relationship of mutual choice between us and God, as in the verse "I will betroth you to Me forever" (Hos. 2:21). It is a personal connection that pertains to the particular individual and a choice that he makes. In contrast to the natural, innate relationship, which produces the level of depth and eternity within love, choice creates intensity in love, the fierce flame.

כִּי יֵשׁ יִתְרוֹן וּמַעֲלָה לִבְחִינַת אַהֲבָה כְּרִשְׁפֵּי אֵשׁ וְשַׁלְהֶבֶת עַזָּה וְכוּ', הַבָּאָה מֵהִתְבּוֹנְנָה וְדַעַת בִּגְדוּלַּת אֵין סוֹף בָּרוּךְ הוּא עַל שְׁתֵּי בְחִינוֹת אַהֲבָה הַנִּזְכָּרוֹת לְעֵיל כַּאֲשֶׁר אֵינָן כְּרִשְׁפֵּי אֵשׁ וְשַׁלְהֶבֶת כוּ',

to love like sparks of fire and a fierce conflagration and so on, which is engendered by the understanding and knowledge of the greatness of *Ein Sof*, blessed be He, to the other two types of love discussed above, which are not like sparks of fire and a fierce conflagration and so on,

The two types of love discussed above are that of "My soul, I desired you," and that of a son tending to his father. Usually, these are not comparable to sparks of fire. However, when one brings them to the point of revelation by contemplating the greatness of "our Father," then they too become like sparks of fire and a fierce conflagration.[13]

כְּיִתְרוֹן וּמַעֲלַת הַזָּהָב עַל הַכֶּסֶף וְכוּ', כְּמוֹ שֶׁיִּתְבָּאֵר לְקַמָּן.

analogous to the advantage and superiority of gold over silver, and so forth, as will be explained below (chap. 50).

The love that is like sparks of fire which is kindled by understanding and knowledge is compared to "gold." In the language of the Kabbala, gold is *Gevura*, Restraint, and silver is *Ḥesed*, Kindness. This corresponds to the colors that symbolize the *sefirot*: *Ḥesed* is white, like silver, and *Gevura* is red, like gold. The love that is like sparks of fire relates to *Gevura* and the ascent from below to above – like fire, which rises from the physical world and dissipates as it gets higher. *Ahava rabba*, on the other hand, is compared to silver and the aspect of *Ḥesed*. It is like water, which descends from above, from the diffusion of God's essence to successively lower levels, to the level of "my soul," resulting in "I have desired you," as explained above. The advantage of the love that is like sparks of fire is "analogous to the advantage and superiority of gold over silver." It is like the advantage of choosing a relationship

---

13. The Lubavitcher Rebbe, Rabbi Menaḥem Mendel Schneerson. See also *Torah Or* 8c.

rather than being born into it. It does not relate to the essence of the relationship, but to the level of attachment. ☞

וְגַם כִּי זֶה כָּל הָאָדָם וְתַכְלִיתוֹ, לְמַעַן דַּעַת אֶת כְּבוֹד ה' וִיקַר תִּפְאֶרֶת גְּדוּלָּתוֹ

Furthermore, that is the entirety of man and his purpose: to know the glory of God and the glory of His splendid majesty,

There is another aspect to the superiority of this type of love. Man was born to know and recognize God's greatness. This type of love is based on a person's individual awareness that "I know that the Lord is great" (Ps. 135:5). The love of "My soul, I have desired You," and that of a son who tends to his father involve knowledge of God in terms of God's personal connection with the individual, of God as that person's root and source. On the other hand, a person's knowledge of God's glory is connected to *ahavat olam*, which comes (as explained above) when a person contemplates the fundamental greatness and might of God Himself, without connection to oneself, without relating to God as "my soul," or "my Father."

אִישׁ אִישׁ כְּפִי אֲשֶׁר יוּכַל שְׂאֵת, כְּמוֹ שֶׁכָּתוּב בְּרַעְיָא מְהֵימְנָא פָּרָשַׁת בֹּא (זוהר ח"ב, מב, א): "בְּגִין דְּיִשְׁתְּמוֹדְעוּן לֵיהּ" וְכוּ', וְכַנּוֹדָע.

each person in accordance with his capacity. As the *Zohar* (2:42a) states in *Raya Meheimna, Parashat Bo*, God created the world "so that they would recognize Him...," as is known.

Regardless of the commandment to love God, knowing God too is an obligation. God desires that we know and recognize Him. This is a

---

MORE PRECIOUS

☞ The sixth Lubavitcher Rebbe, Rabbi Yosef Yitzḥak Schneerson, once said: What is the difference between the level of a person's divine service during the exile and during the redemption? During the redemption, one's divine service is certainly on a higher level; however, during the exile, it is more precious. The same is true here; the intrinsic relationship that we inherit is on a higher level, but that which we choose, to God, and in a sense, also to us, is more precious.

positive commandment that is one of the 613 mitzvot, implicit in the verse "Know the God of your father and serve Him" (I Chron. 28:9).[14]

Continuing the discussion in the preceding chapters, this chapter dealt with the love of God and its two general categories: *ahava rabba* and *ahavat olam*. It began by discussing *ahava rabba*, which is innate and expresses the intrinsic connection between God and a Jewish soul. It is inherited from our ancestors and is like an inborn trait in our souls. This chapter then discussed the two levels of this love: "My soul, I have desired You," and the love of a son who tends to his parents. These two types of love express the profound identity between the divine self and the individual self. However, as stated at the end of the chapter, although *ahava rabba* is greater and more sublime than all aspects of *ahavat olam* that a person can reach by contemplating God's greatness, one must nevertheless exert himself mentally in order to reach the *ahavat olam* type of love as well. Each of these two types of love contains elements that the other does not. Together, they form a complex system of love of God that has both stability and passion.

---

14. See *Makkot* 24a.

Chapter 45

THE PREVIOUS CHAPTERS DEALT WITH THE SPIRITUAL intention a person should have when he engages in Torah and mitzvot, and with the service of the heart in general, which is the fear and love of God, including the innate aspects of the fear and love of God, existing within every Jew as an inheritance from our ancestors. We inherited the love of God from Abraham, and the fear of God from Isaac. This chapter will deal with the third aspect of service of the heart, which we also inherited from our ancestors: the attribute of compassion, which comes from Jacob.

עוֹד יֵשׁ דֶּרֶךְ יָשָׁר לִפְנֵי אִישׁ, לַעֲסוֹק בַּתּוֹרָה וּמִצְוֹת לִשְׁמָן, עַל יְדֵי מִדָּתוֹ שֶׁל יַעֲקֹב אָבִינוּ עָלָיו הַשָּׁלוֹם, שֶׁהִיא מִדַּת הָרַחֲמִים,

In addition, there is a straight path that is available to a person to engage in Torah and mitzvot for their own sake, via the attribute of our forefather Jacob, may he rest in peace. That is the attribute of compassion.

7 Iyar
3 Iyar
(leap year)

The straight path, *derekh yashar*, alludes to the names Yeshurun and Israel, which are additional names of Jacob. This path is the middle "column" in terms of the *sefirot*. The structure of the *sefirot* is comprised of three columns: right, left, and middle. Abraham, Isaac, and Jacob, each of whom are present within the soul of every Jew, are connected to and give expression to these three columns. Abraham is the attribute of Kindness, *Ḥesed* (love), in the right column; Isaac is Restraint, *Gevura* (fear), in the left column; and Jacob is the attribute of compassion, and Beauty (*Tiferet*), in the middle column, which is also called the "straight path."

This phrase describes the nature of the path; it is not crooked. Although the way of divine service is generally straight (as may be seen from the verse "The ways of the Lord are straight" (Hos. 14:10), people can nevertheless walk on it in twisted ways: "God made man straight, but they have sought out many schemes" (Eccl. 7:29). Often, people come to God only after many questions and much wandering on twisted paths. Yitro, for example, began to serve God only after worshipping every idol in the world (*Sota* 11a). This path goes "straight" from the lowest point to the highest, and furthermore it does so without requiring a person to pass through any way stations. ☞

What does it mean to worship God by means of the attribute of

THE WAY OF COMPASSION

☞ What does the path of compassion add in addition to the types of love and fear described in the previous chapters? This path is unique in that, as the *Tanya* explains here, it is a "straight path," comprising direct, unmediated attachment to God. Unlike love and fear of God, compassion does not require any prior connection. Love and fear require some measure of recognition of God's greatness and strength. Fear calls for a tangible awareness of the divine reality, so that the person knows that there is One who should be feared, and love necessitates the recognition of His greatness (as stated in the previous chapter: "You are our life," "You are our Father"). However, in order to arouse one's own compassion, a person has no need for any prior comprehension or knowledge of God, but must simply be pitiful and wanting. And this is not difficult, since with regard to God, everyone, from mortals to lofty angels, is pitiful and wanting. In fact, the farther away someone is, the more compassion he needs, and the lower someone is, the more the Divine Presence weeps over him, arousing more compassion.

Compassion is the simplest and easiest way to attain spiritual awakening. The sight of a bird with a broken wing is enough to arouse a person's compassion. There is no need for him to engage in extensive contemplation about life, the world, and God. A person experiences some level of emotional awakening almost automatically, without any deliberate effort. Even people who do not have a sensitive nature can experience a sense of compassion, even a strong one, when observing this injured bird. If this is the case with regard to compassion for other creatures, how much more is it in regard to a person's compassion for himself.

A person once came to Rabbi Naḥman of Breslov for a private audience. The Rebbe was not able to find any way to reach his heart. Finally, he said to the visitor, "You are on such a pitifully low level that I see nothing good in you." For that individual, this statement was the key. The thought that he was entirely distant and detached from God brought about an emotion within him from which he was able to embark on his spiritual path. It awakened the last

compassion? It is clear what worshipping Him through fear and love means; one should fear God and love Him. However, serving Him with the attribute of compassion does not seem to make sense, for compassion is something we feel for one who is lacking, and God is not lacking.

לְעוֹרֵר בְּמַחֲשַׁבְתּוֹ תְּחִלָּה This entails **first awakening in one's mind**

The author of the *Tanya* explains that, as in the case of love and fear, a person can think about particular topics in order to arouse this feeling. This will be explained below.

רַחֲמִים רַבִּים לִפְנֵי ה׳ עַל נִיצוֹץ אֱלֹהוּת הַמְחַיֶּה נַפְשׁוֹ, **great compassion before God for the divine spark that grants life to one's soul,**

While there is no place for compassion for God Himself, there is certainly place for compassion for the divine spark that is found within us. It has already been explained that there is a divine spark in every individual. However, as in the analogy given in previous chapters about the king's son who is imprisoned and exiled, the divine spark is usually concealed and exiled in the body and the physical world. It is clothed in "garments" that are not its own and it lives a life that is not its own, a life that is not connected to holiness, love for God and fear of God. This spark is pulled down further and further by the individual, to the distant and forsaken realm where

remaining spark of life within him, and he could no longer bear to continue in the same way. The psalmist says, "Even when I walk through the valley of the shadow of death...You are with me" (Ps. 23:4). Sometimes, it is actually because a person knows that he is in the valley of death that he is able to feel that God is with him. His sense of lack, distance, and humiliation may wake him up and lead him to ask himself, "Where am I?" However, as long as he does not know that he is in the valley of death, and believes himself to be sitting comfortably in the Garden of Eden, he does not ask for compassion, nor does he arouse it, and therefore God does not reveal His closeness to him.

this individual lives, which is entirely inappropriate for it. For all of this, it must certainly be pitied.[1] ☞

אֲשֶׁר יָרַד מִמְּקוֹרוֹ, חַיֵּי הַחַיִּים אֵין סוֹף בָּרוּךְ הוּא, הַמְמַלֵּא כָּל עָלְמִין וְסוֹבֵב כָּל עָלְמִין וְכוּלָּא קַמֵּיהּ כְּלָא חֲשִׁיב,

contemplating **how it descended from its origin, the source of life,** *Ein Sof,* **blessed be He, who fills all worlds and encompasses all worlds, and before whom everything is considered as nothingness,**

As stated above, the way for a person to evoke feeling within his soul is through thought and contemplation. A person arouses the feeling of compassion for the divine spark within him by imagining in his mind how much it lacks and how distant it is from God. The author of the *Tanya* will describe something of this distance in order to provide the foundation and substance of this thought. God gives life to every entity in existence, from the greatest to the smallest. He is above and beyond

AWAKENING IN ONE'S THOUGHTS

☞ Sometimes a person cannot arouse fear or love of God in his thoughts, because this does not appear to be connected to the reality of his life at that moment. He may feel that he is so deeply immersed in *kelippot*, outer husks, that any sense of fear or love of God does not figure in his experience. He is even ashamed to think such thoughts of the love and fear of God, because he has no connection to them, nor any grasp of them. However, there is a point that a person can always access, which is always ready and accessible no matter what his personal situation: a sense of compassion, not for himself but for the divine spark within him. The present state of the person does not matter: it makes no difference who he is, what his circumstances are. Perhaps he is distant and unworthy, but what a pity that God must continue walking with him! A part of the Divine above is present within us everywhere. Even if a person is on the lowest level possible, it is part of him, it is in his innermost being. Relating to this part of himself by means of the attribute of compassion is the door to all other connections, which can ascend to the highest heights.

---

1. Through this pity, one comes to *ahava rabba* (world-centered love), as will be explained at the end of the chapter. The author of the *Tanya* states, "This entails first awakening in one's thought," because this is the prelude to love, and it has been established that without fear and love, one's divine service does not ascend, as implied in *Kuntres Aḥaron*, s.v. "*utzedaka*" (*Likkutei Biurim*).

all existence and distinct from it. He is the foundation and "place" of the entire universe, whose very existence depends on Him. In relation to Him, everything else is as nothing.

| וְנִתְלַבֵּשׁ בְּמִשְׁכָא דְחִוְיָא, | to become enclothed in the serpent's skin, that is, the human body, |

The divine spark descended from this lofty level and is enclothed in a "serpent's skin," which is the body of a Jew,[2] which derives from *kelippat noga*, the glowing husk. It is called "the serpent's skin" because the serpent itself signifies the three impure *kelippot*, and its skin signifies the *kelippat noga*.[3]

| הָרָחוֹק מֵאוֹר פְּנֵי הַמֶּלֶךְ בְּתַכְלִית הָהֶרְחֵק. | which is at the farthest, utmost distance from the radiance of the King's countenance. |

The source of this divine spark, which gives a person life, is extremely lofty; it is above the confines of the world, nay above any world whatsoever. It is tantamount to being a part of the Divine above. Yet at this point this spark does not consciously stand before God. Furthermore, it has descended and been exiled into the lowest world in order to give life to the human body. The body is not merely a physical form akin to other creatures. The unique human combination of body and soul, ignoring its various merits, allows the body to fall to lower levels of evil that animals can never reach; in particular the level of the primordial serpent, which is the root of evil.

| כִּי הָעוֹלָם הַזֶּה הוּא תַּכְלִית הַקְּלִיפּוֹת הַגַּסּוֹת כו'. | That is because this world comprises the ultimate of the coarse *kelippot* (husks of impurity), and so forth. |

---

2. See the introduction to *Tikkunei Zohar*; see also chap. 31.
3. The body is called "skin" and a garment of the *neshama* (as in the verse "You clothed me with skin and flesh" (Job 10:11). It is called "the serpent's," because it is detestable (the Lubavitcher Rebbe, Rabbi Menaḥem Mendel Schneerson). And that is the plain meaning here as well.

This physical world is the lowest possible world. It is bound up with evil and is subject to the rule of evil and the *kelippot*.[4] However, it is not intrinsically evil. Put another way, this world is the lowliest reality from which a person can still rise.

וּבִפְרָט כְּשֶׁיִּזְכּוֹר עַל כָּל מַעֲשָׂיו וְדִבּוּרָיו וּמַחְשְׁבוֹתָיו מִיּוֹם הֱיוֹתוֹ אֲשֶׁר לֹא טוֹבִים הֵמָּה And a person's compassion will be aroused **especially when he recalls all of the wrongful actions, speech, and thoughts** that he has committed **since the day he came into being**

The exile of the soul in this world, which comprises the utmost limit of the *kelippot*, and its exile in the human body, or "serpent's skin," is not the divine spark's final descent. It is followed by another descent that is the result of the person's actions, when he actually does evil by means of one of the soul's three "garments": act, speech, or thought. The body and the world are "coarse" substances, and to be within coarse physicality in itself constitutes a colossal descent for the spark of the infinite. But when, in addition, a person commits a transgression, beyond simply being made of a coarse substance, he creates real damage. As a sinner, he is not only limited and base, but also lowly and despicable, and this decline into sin is immeasurably larger for the soul than its having merely descended into a physical body.

וּ"מֶלֶךְ אָסוּר בָּרְהָטִים" (שיר השירים ז, ו), בִּרְהִיטֵי מוֹחָא. **and** how **"the King is bound in the tresses [*rehatim*]"** (Song 7:6), meaning that He is bound **by the streams [*rehitei*] of the mind's** thoughts.

"Streams of the mind"[5] refers to a person's thoughts as they run through the various pathways in his mind. Here, the word *rehitei* means water channels, as in the verse "in the receptacles [*barehatim*], in the water troughs" (Gen. 30:38). Wherever a person's thoughts run (and they can run lower, further, and faster than anything the body is capable

---

4. This may be a reference to chap. 36 (the Lubavitcher Rebbe, Rabbi Menaḥem Mendel Schneerson).

5. See *Tikkunei Zohar* 144b.

of), God is attached to them. A person cannot split his essence, setting aside the divine spark while he runs off to sin by himself. Therefore, as low as a person goes, he brings God down with him. God takes part in everything he does, says, and even thinks about. This is because everything that takes place is possible only by virtue of God's power. Therefore, in a sense, He is a party to a person's sin, because if He were not, the person would not be able to perform that sin. Thus, wherever a person goes and wherever his mind runs, he binds the King to that place.

כִּי "יַעֲקֹב חֶבֶל נַחֲלָתוֹ" (דברים לב, ט). וְכִמְשַׁל הַמּוֹשֵׁךְ בְּחֶבֶל וכו'. That is **because "Jacob is the allotment [ḥevel] of His inheritance"** (Deut. 32:9), **as in the analogy of a person who pulls a cord [ḥevel], and so on.**

This "cord"[6] ties the individual, wherever he is, to God. Through it, as through an umbilical cord, he continuously receives life from God. As a person moves, acts, and thinks, he cannot detach himself from this vital connection, for it is his life, and the source of his existence. Wherever he goes, the cord moves with him, bringing along that which is connected at the other end. Thus, when a person lowers himself, in speech or thought, to the realm of evil and the *kelippot*, he is not just lowering his own personal essence. Since "Jacob is the ḥevel of His inheritance," a person is always tied to the Divine Presence, to the all-encompassing divine essence. Therefore, he draws it after him wherever he goes.

וְהוּא סוֹד גָּלוּת הַשְּׁכִינָה, This descent **constitutes the mystic exile of the Divine Presence.**

The descent described here is what is meant by the term "exile of the Divine Presence." Why should the Divine Presence be exiled? What is the connection between the Divine Presence and Israel's sins and exile? As will be explained below, the answer is contained

---

6. This may be a reference to the idea that is explained at length in *Iggeret HaTeshuva*, chaps. 5–7 (the Lubavitcher Rebbe, Rabbi Menaḥem Mendel Schneerson).

in the words of the verse stating that God "dwells with [the children of Israel] in the midst of their impurity" (Lev. 16:16). God is bound to us and dwells with us always, even when we defile ourselves. When a Jew defiles himself, that constitutes the "exile of the Divine Presence," since the Divine Presence descends with him even to the lowest point in all the worlds.

When a person contemplates this thought, he feels a sense of compassion. This is especially true when he considers the basic human condition, which constitutes a tremendous descent for the divine spark, the proud, supernal soul whose true world is the infinite world but which must now dwell in the prison of the body and the material world, amid all the thoughts, troubles, and desires of the human being, especially if the human being causes the place to become lowly and abhorrent. This is not sorrow or remorse, since he does not look at himself and wonder, "What have I done to myself?" Rather, the focus of his contemplation shifts away from his sins and his responsibility for his situation to a different point: the divine spark, the divine soul, which is more sublime than anything else. He looks upon it from the outside, as it were, and thinks, "This poor spark, this poor prince, who must sit in exile in this world, subject to the degradation of human sins."

וְעַל זֶה נֶאֱמַר: "וְיָשֹׁב אֶל ה' וִירַחֲמֵהוּ" (ישעיה נה, ז). About this it states, "Let him return to the Lord and have mercy on Him" (Isa. 55:7).

The simple reading of the verse is "Let him return to the Lord, and He will have mercy on him," but according to the above interpretation, the individual returns to God and in so doing has mercy on Him. This correlates with the message of the present chapter: The divine spark, which is part of God, has descended very low, and needs to return home "to the Lord," to its source. To assist that return, a person must "have mercy" on that divine spark. Moreover, as will be explained at the end of the chapter, the verse also teaches that when a person has this compassion, he will come to love Him and cleave to Him.

לְעוֹרֵר רַחֲמִים רַבִּים עַל שֵׁם ה' הַשּׁוֹכֵן אִתָּנוּ, כְּדִכְתִיב: "הַשּׁוֹכֵן אִתָּם בְּתוֹךְ טוּמְאֹתָם" (ויקרא טז, טז).

This verse can be interpreted to mean that a person should **arouse immense compassion for God's name, which dwells in our midst, as it is written, "Who dwells with them in the midst of their impurity"** (Lev. 16:16).

What does having compassion for God mean in practice, and how does one have that compassion? That compassion is on behalf of "the name of God" – i.e., the Divine Presence in our midst. God takes responsibility for us, His children and servants, and He goes into exile together with us – for our sake – into our sins and our defilement. ☞

וְזֶה שֶׁאָמַר הַכָּתוּב: "וַיִּשַּׁק יַעֲקֹב לְרָחֵל וַיִּשָּׂא אֶת קֹלוֹ וַיֵּבְךְּ" (בראשית כט, יא).

This is also the meaning of **the verse "Jacob kissed Rachel, and raised his voice, and wept"** (Gen. 29:11).

8 Iyar

BY WAY OF COMPASSION FOR ONESELF

☞ In this type of divine service, a person relates to the divine essence via the compassion he has for himself, his situation, and his place. As explained above with regard to love (see chap. 43), this involves a person's arousing an emotion toward the Divine via his compassion for himself. When he identifies with the part of his soul where the divine spark dwells, his awareness of his distance from God, and of his own wretchedness and inadequacy grows into compassion for the "name of the God" within him, which has become exceedingly distant from its source, because it dwells in the midst of impurity. The person feels compassion for the "insulted King" (see *Otzar HaMidrashim*, p. 107). The magnitude of an offense is measured in accordance with the value of the one who was hurt and the value of the one who caused the offense, as can be seen in the halakhic principle "[It is] all based on the one who humiliated and the one who was humiliated" (*Ketubot* 40a). No one has been more insulted than the name of God, which is compelled to dwell in the midst of the person's impurity. That is why God is called the "insulted King." When a person recognizes the greatness of the King and the baseness of the place and the matters into which he brings the King, then even if this person is unable to feel remorse or repentance, he can feel a tremendous amount of compassion for this great, exiled King who has been so degraded. The more a person thinks about this, the more compassion he feels, until he can no longer bear it and he must do something to transform the misery and insult: by keeping the Torah and mitzvot, and through *ahava rabba*, "great love."

Jacob and Rachel are not just individual people, but are also universal states of being that always exist in essence of Jewish existence. Thus, the meeting between Jacob and Rachel is an encounter between different elements of the Jewish existence, and it has personal significance for every Jew at all times.

כִּי רָחֵל הִיא כְּנֶסֶת יִשְׂרָאֵל מְקוֹר כָּל הַנְּשָׁמוֹת. This is **because Rachel represents the congregation of Israel, the source of all souls,**

Rachel, in her supernal character, is the congregation of Israel, the Divine Presence grieving over the sorrow of her children. These "children" are the individual souls residing in different bodies at different times. "A voice is heard in Rama, wailing, bitter weeping, Rachel weeping for her children" (Jer. 31:14). She goes into exile with her children.

וְיַעֲקֹב, בְּמִדָּתוֹ הָעֶלְיוֹנָה, שֶׁהִיא מִדַּת הָרַחֲמִים שֶׁבָּאֲצִילוּת, הוּא הַמְעוֹרֵר רַחֲמִים רַבִּים עָלֶיהָ. and **Jacob, in his supernal attribute, the attribute of compassion** in the world **of** *Atzilut*, **is the one who arouses immense compassion for her.**

The relationship of Jacob and Rachel is, in its inner being, the relationship between the *sefirot* of the world of *Atzilut*: specifically, the relationship between the attribute of compassion within the world of *Atzilut* and Kingship (*Malkhut*), which is *Kenesset Yisrael*, which is the Divine Presence. In particular, it concerns the relationship between the attribute of compassion in *Atzilut* with that of "Rachel," which is the name given to the aspect of the Divine Presence that descends all the way to the lower worlds and even into exile.

"וַיִּשָּׂא אֶת קֹלוֹ" - לְמַעֲלָה לִמְקוֹר הָרַחֲמִים הָעֶלְיוֹנִים, הַנִּקְרָא 'אַב הָרַחֲמִים' וּמְקוֹרָם. The verse can then be read: He **"raised his voice" upward to the source of supernal compassion known as the Father of compassion, and** compassion's **source.**

Jacob, who is the attribute of *Tiferet*, of compassion, in the world of *Atzilut*, raises his voice higher than the world of *Atzilut* and draws down compassion from the level of "Father of compassion," the highest level of the thirteen attributes of compassion. These thirteen attributes exist above the world of *Atzilut*. The attribute of compassion in the world of *Atzilut*, like the other *sefirot* and attributes of that world, is manifested to the extent determined by Ḥokhma, Wisdom. However, this is not the case with regard to "Father of compassion," which is on the level of *Keter*, Crown, higher than Ḥokhma in *Atzilut*. That is the level of the Father, which is the source of compassion in *Atzilut* where compassion is infinite. Compassion at this level is of the kind described by the verse "His mercy extends to all His creations" (Ps. 145:9). It is not mercy for one particular creation or another, but for all God's creations. All His creatures need compassion, for anything that is not divine has this need, and this is the function of "Father of compassion."[7]

> "**וַיֵּבְךְּ**", לְעוֹרֵר וּלְהַמְשִׁיךְ מִשָּׁם רַחֲמִים רַבִּים עַל כָּל הַנְּשָׁמוֹת, וְעַל מְקוֹר כְּנֶסֶת יִשְׂרָאֵל, לְהַעֲלוֹתָן מִגָּלוּתָן וּלְיַחֲדָן בְּיִחוּד הָעֶלְיוֹן אוֹר אֵין סוֹף בָּרוּךְ הוּא, בִּבְחִינַת נְשִׁיקִין.

"**And he wept**" in order to awaken **and draw down from there great compassion upon all souls and upon the source of the congregation of Israel, to lift them out of their exile and unify them in the supernal union of the light of** *Ein Sof*, **blessed be He**, and this union is **referred to as "kisses."**

The continuation of the verse teaches that Jacob draws compassion down from its source. The verse states, "Jacob kissed Rachel, and raised his voice, and wept." In other words, by kissing Rachel, Jacob, who is compassion, can reach the supernal union mentioned earlier. He can raise his voice until it reaches its primary source, the "Father of compassion," and convey compassion from there down to the level of Rachel.

---

7. This is why during the ten days of repentance we say "*Av HaRaḥaman*," "the compassionate Father," and on Yom Kippur, during *Musaf* and *Ne'ila*, when we say the *Kedusha* of "*Keter*," we say "*Av HaRaḥamim*," "Father of compassion"; see *Likkutei Torah*, Num. 23a, *Derushim LeRosh HaShana* 62d.

שֶׁהִיא אִתְדַּבְּקוּת רוּחָא בְּרוּחָא, כְּמוֹ שֶׁכָּתוּב: "יִשָּׁקֵנִי מִנְּשִׁיקוֹת פִּיהוּ" (שיר השירים א, ב). דְּהַיְינוּ הִתְקַשְּׁרוּת דִּבּוּר הָאָדָם בִּדְבַר ה' זוֹ הֲלָכָה,	This "kiss" constitutes the fusion of spirit with spirit, as it states, "May he kiss me with the kisses of his mouth" (Song 1:2). This is the binding of human speech with the word of God, which is *halakha*,

In the realm of divine service, a "kiss with God" refers to studying Torah.[8] When a person learns Torah, when he speaks the Torah that God speaks, when he repeats and speaks together with God His inner speech, "a great voice that has not ceased" (Deut. 5:19), this constitutes the cleaving of mouth to mouth. That is the kiss with God described in the verse "May he kiss me with the kisses of his mouth."[9]

וְכֵן מַחֲשָׁבָה בְּמַחֲשָׁבָה,	as well as the binding of human thought with divine thought through Torah study,

When a person studies and thinks about Torah, he is thinking God's thoughts together with Him. This too constitutes connection and union with God, in this case by means of thought.

וּמַעֲשֶׂה בְּמַעֲשֶׂה, שֶׁהוּא מַעֲשֵׂה הַמִּצְוֹת, וּבִפְרָט מַעֲשֵׂה הַצְּדָקָה וָחֶסֶד.	and human action with divine action through the act of performing mitzvot, and in particular the act of charity and kindness.

This refers to a union with God's deeds through an individual's physical act when he fulfills a practical commandment. Every act of God in the process of creating and sustaining the world is one of kindness, through which He gives to those who do not have. Therefore, the act

---

8. Commenting on the verse "'May he kiss me with the kisses of his mouth, as your love [*dodekha*] is better than wine' (Song 1:2) the Midrash states that the words of the beloved ones [*dodim*], the Sages, are better than the wine of the Torah" (*Bemidbar Rabba* 14:4).

9. The author of the *Tanya* additionally equates *halakha* with the binding of human speech and the word of God (see *Shabbat* 138b).

of a person who gives charity[10] to a recipient who does not have is like a divine act. Binding "action with action" thus creates an unparalleled cleaving to God.

דְּחֶסֶד דִּדְרוֹעָא יְמִינָא וְהוּא בְּחִינַת חִיבּוּק מַמָּשׁ, כְּמוֹ שֶׁכָּתוּב: "וִימִינוֹ תְּחַבְּקֵנִי" (שיר השירים ב, ו). **This is because kindness** corresponds **to the right arm of God, so to speak, and it has the quality of an actual embrace, as it states, "And His right embraces me"** (Song 2:6).

The attribute of supernal Ḥesed is called the supernal right arm.[11] When a person acts with kindness in the lower realm, he connects with Ḥesed and with God's right arm. When a person gives charity to a person who does not have, his right arm unites with God's right arm, and he is in an embrace with God, so to speak. God's great and broad arm is revealed in the world in various forms. When an individual in this world gives charity with his own arm, he merits that his arm becomes a revelation of the divine arm. At that moment, his arm is the physical expression of God's great, broad arm, and he connects and unites with the divine arm, which truly embraces him. ☞

COMPASSION FOR THE SPARKS OF HOLINESS IN THE WORLD

☞ This idea does not apply only to the mitzva of giving charity. Every mitzva involves an element of kindness (see chap. 37), an act of generosity toward an object. There is a divine spark trapped inside every object, whether it is a stone, vessel, plant, or beast. The spark moves from item to item, from inanimate object to plant to animal and back again, until a human being has compassion for it and performs a mitzva with it, thereby releasing it from its prison. Thus, the act of a mitzva is an expression of compassion toward the sparks lost in the chaos, since it attends to them and raises them, returning them to holiness. Some tzaddikim felt this compassion; they heard these trapped sparks crying out for someone to perform a mitzva with them in order to lift them up and return them to their source.

On the second day of Creation, "God made the firmament, and divided between the water that was under the firmament and the water that was above the firma-

---

10. See chap. 37.
11. The entire body is subsumed within the right side, as stated in *Iggeret HaKodesh*, epistle 32 (*Likkutei Biurim*).

וְעֵסֶק הַתּוֹרָה, בְּדִבּוּר וּמַחֲשֶׁבֶת הָעִיּוּן, הֵן בְּחִינַת נְשִׁיקִין מַמָּשׁ. **Engaging in Torah** study **through speech and penetrating thought: these constitute actual kisses.**

Just as connecting to God by performing practical mitzvot constitutes a real "embrace," connecting and uniting with Him by engaging in Torah is a real "kiss." When a human mouth speaks the Divine word, there is a "kiss," a mouth-to-mouth connection between the human mouth and the "mouth" of God, as it were. An even more profound kiss takes place when a person's thought touches upon divine thought, however imperfectly. A person achieves this level of attachment, of real kisses and real embrace, by way of the "straight path," the attribute of Jacob. This is the attribute of compassion for the Divine Presence, which is Rachel. As it says in the verse, "Jacob kissed Rachel, and raised his voice, and wept."

The motivation to attain an actual kiss and embrace does not come from deep contemplation of God's greatness, nor from love or fear of God, but rather from a person's simple compassion on the humiliated divine glory. This is the fundamental compassion that a person feels for his own soul, for the world and for God, who is compelled to descend and humiliate Himself along with the individual. When a person can no longer bear this, a strong need to act forms in his soul to truly "embrace" and "kiss." ☞

---

ment" (Gen. 1:7); God separated between the upper waters and the lower waters. Ever since that time, the lower waters have been weeping that they too "want to be before the King" (see *Bereshit Rabba* 5:4; *Tikkunei Zohar* 19b; *Likkutei Torah*, Num. 3b). This is why Sukkot, which is the time of "His right embraces me," is also the time of the water libation, when the lower waters ascend to be "before the King." This whole world is made up of "lower waters," which weep. The entire world and all its creatures are crying and begging for compassion. We too desire to be above, before the King.

COMPASSION THAT REACHES HIGHER AND DEEPER

☞ An additional aspect of compassion is revealed here. It is not only a spiritual capacity that can begin where love and fear cannot begin, but a spiritual capacity that can reach where love and fear cannot: i.e., with regard to Torah and mitzvot in realized actuality. A person can immerse himself in love of God and completely forget

וְהִנֵּה עַל יְדֵי זֶה יָכוֹל לָבוֹא לִבְחִינַת 'אַהֲבָה רַבָּה' בְּהִתְגַּלּוּת לִבּוֹ, כְּדִכְתִיב: "לְיַעֲקֹב אֲשֶׁר פָּדָה אֶת אַבְרָהָם" (ישעיה כט, כב), כְּמוֹ שֶׁנִּתְבָּאֵר בְּמָקוֹם אַחֵר.

Through this awakening of compassion, **one can achieve the level of** *ahava rabba* as a conscious manifestation in one's heart, as it states, "Jacob who redeemed Abraham" (Isa. 29:22), **as explained elsewhere** (chap. 32; *Kuntres Aharon*, s.v. "*U'Tzedaka KeNahal Eitan*").

Abraham signifies love and Jacob signifies compassion. Thus, Jacob redeeming Abraham[12] represents compassion redeeming, or liberating, love. A person's love for God can be "trapped," so that he is unable to actualize it and it does not speak to him. In a situation like this, there is still room for the revelation of compassion, which can subsequently about existence: "Whom else do I have in heaven? With You, I desire nothing on earth" (Ps. 73:25). He does not feel the need or desire to engage in any action that involves other people or the world. In this case, the only attribute that can move him to relate to the world and involve himself with it is compassion. For example, initially Moses did not want to lead the nation. He wanted to be himself and to remain alone. He did not understand the people, nor did he want anything to do with them. However, God compelled him, and he went. At every opportunity, Moses repeated this point: "Why did You send me?" (Ex. 5:22); "What shall I do for this people?" (Ex. 17:4). However, after a time, a change took place. When God threatened Israel and the situation seemed dire, Moses was filled with great compassion and offered himself so that they could continue to exist. When God said, "Allow Me, and My wrath will be enflamed against them, and I will destroy them; and I will make you into a great nation" (Ex. 32:10), Moses was no longer willing to yield. When the children of Israel were in danger, a new force arose within him, that of compassion. Moses sacrificed his soul and his very essence in order to descend to a lower level and engage with Israel, the earth, and the world. God responded, "Go, lead the people" (Ex. 32:34). With the power of compassion for Israel, the Divine Presence, Rachel, Moses drew down from the highest realm of all, reaching God's thirteen attributes of compassion – "May the power of the Lord now grow as you have spoken, saying: The Lord is patient and vast in kindness..." (Num. 14:17-18). This reaction evokes the thirteen attributes of compassion, which are higher than everything else.

---

12. This is explained in several places in hasidic teachings (*Likkutei Hagahot LaTanya*).

redeem and reveal his love for God. The problem with love is that it is difficult for a person to cultivate it for things that are not close to him, matters that do not touch him in a direct, sensory way. All love requires effort in order to bring the love itself toward the object of one's love. This is especially true regarding love for God; due to its abstract nature, it requires much refining and cultivation of the soul. By contrast, the path of compassion is always accessible and immediate, since it does not require refinement of engagement with abstract, spiritual matters. Once compassion is awakened, and it creates closeness and partnership, opening the heart, its compassion can gradually and subtly transform itself into love. This is the redemption of love by means of compassion.

This chapter dealt with the attribute of compassion. At the beginning of the chapter, this attribute was defined as "a straight path that is available to a person." Every human being, no matter who he is, can go on this path toward cleaving to the Divine. Compassion is like the central beam of the Tabernacle, which ran from end to end. On the one hand, it is found among the greatest tzaddikim, as the only way to lead them to be involved in what happens in the world. On the other hand, it can be found among the lowest of the low. Compassion is the last spark of humanity left within a person. Whereas love and fear require preexisting frameworks of understanding and sensitivity, compassion is a direct, unmediated connection between a human being, whatever level he may be on, and that which is above him, all the way up to the thirteen attributes of compassion. Compassion is based on lack. And when compared to God, everyone is lacking, and everyone needs and deserves compassion. Therefore, as was explained in this chapter, the way to evoke compassion is to think about lack, imagining how far the divine spark in one's soul has descended. It came down from the infinite, ultimate source of life until it was enclothed in the "serpent's skin," which represents the exile of the Divine Presence. The compassion that a person feels for himself, for the divine spark within him, for the exiled Divine Presence, leads to the revelation of the direct connection, to true clinging to God with embraces and kisses, Torah and mitzvot, culminating in *ahava rabba* (great love).

Chapter 46

THE PREVIOUS CHAPTER DISCUSSED A KIND OF SERVICE of God that is "a straight path available to a person," involving the attribute of compassion. As was explained, this path provides a direct route rising from below to above that is accessible at any time and any place to every human being. Every individual, no matter what level he is on, is capable of experiencing compassion. This refers to experiencing compassion for the sparks of holiness that have descended and moved extremely far away from the holiness of his actions and thoughts. In this chapter, the author of the *Tanya* will discuss another path of divine service, which is also "a straight path available to a person" and which, furthermore, is "suitable for everyone and very, very near."

| וְיֵשׁ דֶּרֶךְ יָשָׁר לִפְנֵי אִישׁ | There is another **straight path before a person** | 9 Iyar
4 Iyar
(leap year) |

"A straight path" also means the path of a person who is straight. Only such a person can walk upon this path that reaches directly from below to above. As the author of the *Tanya* will explain, this path requires that the person walking on it be straight, since this path does not require any prior intellectual or emotional preparation as it originates in the most natural, elemental force in the soul. Walking on this path requires that a person not be encumbered by any crookedness in his heart which would prevent him from feeling and responding in a natural and straightforward manner.

שָׁוֶה לְכָל נֶפֶשׁ. **which is suitable for everyone.**

As has been explained, each human being is different, especially with regard to the subtleties of the soul in divine service. There are almost no rules that are equally true for all people. Each unique stimulus causes different reactions in different individuals. These chapters attempt to provide a description of universal keys that will open doors not just for one person but for many people. These matters are explained in a way that is accessible to all.

וְקָרוֹב הַדָּבָר מְאֹד מְאֹד **The matter is very, very near**

The author of the *Tanya* reiterates the motto of the book: "The matter is very near to you …" (Deut. 30:14), with the insertion of an additional "very."

לְעוֹרֵר וּלְהָאִיר אוֹר הָאַהֲבָה הַתְּקוּעָה וּמְסוּתֶרֶת בְּלִבּוֹ, **to awaken and shine the light of the love for God that is embedded and concealed in a person's heart,**

One of the foundations of this divine service that is "suitable for everyone" is that a person does not need to create something new in his soul that did not exist beforehand. Rather, he must awaken, reveal, and activate forces that were already in existence, but concealed within him. A principle that applies to every soul must necessarily be based on the natural state of every soul and the forces within it. But even though a force exists in the soul, uncovering it is not necessarily easy. Particularly with regard to divine service, it is difficult for a person to achieve an awakening without a suitable conceptual framework and without hard work. Every individual must seek the key to these forces.

לִהְיוֹת מְאִירָה בְּתוֹקֶף אוֹרָהּ כְּאֵשׁ בּוֹעֲרָה בְּהִתְגַּלּוּת לִבּוֹ וּמוֹחוֹ, לִמְסוֹר נַפְשׁוֹ לַה', וְגוּפוֹ וּמְאוֹדוֹ **to shine its light powerfully, as a blazing fire, revealed in a person's heart and mind, so that he is prepared to sacrifice his soul to God, as well as his body and might,**

This passage refers to the three levels of love of God mentioned in the recitation of *Shema*: "with all your heart, with all your soul, and with all your might [*bekhol me'odekha*]" (see Deut. 6:5). The term "might" has two meanings, both of which apply here.[1] The first is "money"; a person should express his love of God through his willingness to give up his physical possessions. The second is an absence of limits. Once a person has sacrificed everything he can for the sake of his love for God, including his heart and soul, he then he gives a little bit more. It is not what a person is able to do within the bounds of his normal thoughts and experiences, but what he can do after he has exhausted them. The additional effort, even if it is miniscule, is the *"me'od,"* the real litmus test, the true test of divine service.

בְּכָל לֵב וּבְכָל נֶפֶשׁ וּמְאֹד, מֵעוּמְקָא דְּלִבָּא בֶּאֱמֶת לַאֲמִיתוֹ. **with all his heart and all his soul and might, from the depths of the heart with absolute sincerity.**

The requirement described here is very demanding. It comes in addition to the three levels mentioned in the *Shema*. His service must be from the depths of the heart and with sincerity regarding every level of worship, each level deeper and more sincere. This demand seems extreme. Even after a person prays, reaches a spiritual awakening, and is moved, yet more is required of him. He must supply the entirety of his heart, soul, and might. And furthermore, his love for God must come from the depths of his heart and with absolute sincerity.

Absolute sincerity is a key point in divine service, particularly with regard to the requirement to constantly ascend and add to one's service. A person can be moved in different ways and for different reasons, whether profound or superficial. For instance, if he is in a positive frame of mind and sitting with an agreeable group of people when he hears a touching melody, he may believe that the love of God is illuminating his entire heart and soul. However, sometimes this is not actually the case. His soul may not have been awakened; in fact, perhaps nothing inside him was awakened at all. He experienced something, but it was a response to a transient, external stimulus rather than to his soul. The requirement of absolute truth is therefore one that goes beyond an experience. A person must always strive for more depth and permanence,

---

1. See *Berakhot* 54a; *Likkutei Torah*, Num. 91b.

so that his love for God may truly come from the depths of his heart, and not just as something performed by rote. ☞ ☞

וּבִפְרָט בִּשְׁעַת קְרִיאַת שְׁמַע וּבְרְכוֹתֶיהָ, כְּמוֹ שֶׁיִּתְבָּאֵר. **This love should be awakened especially at the time of reciting the *Shema* and its blessings, as shall be explained** below (chap. 49).

The commandment to love God applies at all times and in all places, but particularly at the time of reciting the *Shema* and its blessings. The straightforward reason is that when a person recites, "You shall love the Lord your God" (Deut. 6:5), he should actually feel love for God, at that time at least, for if he does not, he is essentially lying, and as he continues to recite *Shema* each day, in the evening and the morning, he will become more and more accustomed to lying before God. Someone like this will end up spending his whole life lying, both to God and to himself. There is also a more spiritual reason, which relates to the order of the prayers and the place of the *Shema* within them. A person progresses through the prayers step by step, and his soul shifts from state to state, on a set path. This framework is relevant to everyone, in spite

LOVE BY ROTE

☞ Performing mitzvot by rote does not necessarily refer only to the realm of action, but can also relate to love and fear of God. A person can easily fall into a routine of "rote love" and "rote fear." In Tractate *Sota* (22b), there is a list of pseudo-righteous people. Among them is the one who says, "[Tell me] what my obligation [is] and I will perform it." This person believes himself to be perfect, and says, "Just tell me that there is another mitzva for me to do and I will perform it immediately." At the end of the list are those who abstain due to love and those who abstain due to fear. Love can certainly become part of a person's routine. Some kiss their *tzitzit* three times, whereas he kisses it four times. The hasidim used to joke about a passage in one of the festival prayer books that read, "Here, they cry in Prague." It was the custom of Prague Jewry to cry when they reached that passage. Thus, both love and fear can become routine. Just as one has a routine regarding prayer, praying at specific times and for certain amounts of time, and reciting from the same pages each time, there can be routine in love and fear as well. A person can love and fear God with all his heart, soul, and might, from the depths of his heart, and it may appear to him as though nothing is missing. Therefore, the requirement of sincerity is crucial, because in order to be sincere, a person must constantly be searching within himself and striving to awaken his enthusiasm.

of the great differences between individuals, particularly with regard to the subtleties of emotion in prayer. A certain person may become particularly inspired by a particular passage, whether in its concealed or revealed sense, while another passage will not move him or affect him at all. And an entirely different part of the prayers will speak to a different individual. Nevertheless, there is an overall pattern of ascent in prayer, of moving toward ever higher intensity. The culmination of emotion occurs around the *Shema* and its blessings, because the next and highest stage, the *Amida*, is the point of nullification, of "a still, small voice." The recitation of *Shema* and its blessings is therefore a time meant for the revelation of love and fear, when a person should take heed, contemplate deeply, and awaken feelings of love for God.

וְהוּא כַּאֲשֶׁר יָשִׂים אֶל לִבּוֹ מַה שֶׁאוֹמֵר הַכָּתוּב: "כַּמַּיִם הַפָּנִים לְפָנִים כֵּן לֵב הָאָדָם אֶל הָאָדָם" (משלי כז, יט). פֵּירוּשׁ: כְּמוֹ שֶׁבִּדְמוּת וְצוּרַת הַפָּנִים שֶׁהָאָדָם מַרְאֶה בַּמַּיִם - כֵּן נִרְאֶה לוֹ שָׁם בַּמַּיִם אוֹתָהּ צוּרָה עַצְמָהּ,

This can be achieved **when** a person takes to heart what the verse states, "As water reflects a face to the face, so does the heart of a person to a person" (Prov. 27:19). This means that just as the water reflects the very same form as the image and form of the face that a person shows the waters,

TO WHOM IS THE AUTHOR OF THE *TANYA* SPEAKING?

☞ Whom is the author of the *Tanya* addressing here, and in general throughout the book? Evidently, this passage is not aimed at people who are deliberating whether or not to keep the commandments, whether or not they want to serve God. The book does not mention, for example, the fact that it is important to avoid desecrating the Sabbath, not because it is not important, but because this work takes that as a given. The *Tanya* addresses the Jew who is observant of the mitzvot, who is as particular about performing minor mitzvot as major ones. He fears Heaven and is a hasid. This is the starting point of this work. Consequently, the requirements found in it go beyond basic conduct and dwell on higher matters, such as love of God with all one's heart, soul, and might, from the depths of one's heart, and with absolute sincerity.

This does not mean that the *Sefer shel Beinonim* is not directed toward every individual, for, as it said in chapter 14, every person can be a *beinoni*. However, it does not address each individual as he is, but as the person he could be. This is the approach of the book, and the general educational approach of the author of the *Tanya*: to look at the higher, spiritual, divine side of the person, for that is his true place.

Water is like a mirror; the face that a person shows the water is the one that he can see reflected in it.

כָּכָה מַמָּשׁ לֵב הָאָדָם הַנֶּאֱמָן בְּאַהֲבָתוֹ לְאִישׁ אַחֵר, הֲרֵי הָאַהֲבָה זוֹ מְעוֹרֶרֶת אַהֲבָה בְּלֵב חֲבֵירוֹ אֵלָיו גַּם כֵּן, לִהְיוֹת אוֹהֲבִים נֶאֱמָנִים זֶה לָזֶה.

in literally the same way, the love in the heart of a person who devotedly loves someone else will also arouse love in his friend's heart toward him, to devotedly love each other.

According to the most straightforward understanding of the verse "As water reflects a face to the face, so does the heart of a person to a person," what a person feels toward another, the other person feels toward him. Even if he does not reveal his love to the other person and that person does not know of it, the feeling passes back and forth like an echo, and like a reflection on the water.[2]

"SO DOES THE HEART OF A PERSON TO A PERSON"

☞ This emotional response is not conscious and does not result from any preparation. Similarly, there are numerous other emotional responses that do not depend on any rational system. They are ingrained in us as human beings, just as certain responses are ingrained in animals. These responses do not appear to have any kind of causal connection to what we consciously think, rather they are a kind of reflex that we are unable to account for. It is well known that laughter and yawning can be contagious. Someone starts laughing and others are drawn in and begin to chuckle too, not because something made them laugh, but because a force they cannot explain compelled them to react that way. These phenomena seem to be part of the basic social structure of any society. This is why large groups of humans, and animals as well, are able to operate together. The actions of the individual are joined to society and to the whole, and everyone's actions are coordinated, forming one, unified being that can act in a particular, coordinated way.

---

2. The resemblance to water extends to all the specifics of this matter. Water reflects the image of the face that looks into it, and it would be impossible for water not to do this, because it is part of its nature. Likewise, this reflection is ingrained in the nature of every person, and it does not require even a small amount of effort, but only that one be aware of it. This is not true when one thinks about other matters, for it is impossible to think two different thoughts at the same time (the Lubavitcher Rebbe, Rabbi Menaḥem Mendel Schneerson).

The response that is similar to the reflection of a face in water is essentially that of gratitude. This does not mean learned, conventional gratitude, but gratitude that is part of the human character; it is a fundamental part of what makes a person human. It relates to the principle of reciprocity by which God rules the world. It is written in the Torah, and taught in many places by the Sages, how crucial it is not only to act this way, but to experience reciprocity as an essential feeling. If one lacks this feeling, it is as though he has a disease, like an illness where a person is unable to feel certain parts of his body, his natural impulses, or elements of his environment. This gratitude does not derive from the higher, divine soul; rather, it is a basic, natural attribute, which is found even in animals. It is just as natural as the physical phenomenon of the reflection of a face in water. ☞

בִּפְרָט כְּשֶׁרוֹאֶה אַהֲבַת חֲבֵירוֹ אֵלָיו. **This is especially true when** a person **perceives his friend's love toward him.**

When a visible, conscious element is added to the natural, concealed, unconscious reaction, the overall response is stronger and more significant.

"YOU SHALL NOT TAKE A BRIBE"

☞ The prohibition against taking a bribe (Deut. 16:19) also stems from the principle of "As water reflects a face to the face." When a person senses, whether in a revealed or a concealed way, that another person loves him, he cannot remain indifferent to him, and inevitably, he too begins to feel something, a bias in favor of that person. Because this phenomenon is so natural and unconscious, the Sages' extreme stringency with regard to anything even remotely similar to a bribe is understandable. Bribery does not only refer to a case where a person who is supposed to be objective consciously and intentionally sells himself for monetary gain; rather, it is any kind of gift received by such a person from one party. For the essence of human nature is that a person who receives a gift cannot remain objective. This refers not only to the giving of physical objects, but also to words. The Talmud gives a number of examples of "verbal bribery," and tells of Sages who disqualified themselves from judging those who spoke to them, or behaved toward them in a manner that conveyed honor or closeness (Ketubot 105b). For one cannot remain indifferent toward the person who treated him this way; the incident affects how he relates to and understands the issue being decided. The Sages are concerned not only about a person who intentionally sells out, but about people's natural, irrational reactions; these are as natural as the reflection of a face in water.

5 Iyar
(leap year)

וְהִנֵּה זֶהוּ טֶבַע הַנָּהוּג בְּמִדַּת כָּל אָדָם, אַף אִם שְׁנֵיהֶם שָׁוִים בְּמַעֲלָה, וְעַל אַחַת כַּמָּה וְכַמָּה אִם מֶלֶךְ גָּדוֹל וְרַב מַרְאֵה אַהֲבָתוֹ הַגְּדוֹלָה וְהָעֲצוּמָה

Now, this is the ingrained behavior of every person's personality, even in a case where **both** people are of equal stature. How much more so it would apply **if a great and powerful king would show his great and immense love**

All human beings react this way toward all others, even when the recipient of the love is not of lower status and is not obligated to be grateful for that which the other person bestows upon him. The greater the person who shows his love, the more wonderful his love is considered with regard to the one receiving it. If the giver is a great and powerful king, then his love, and his expression of it, is much more significant than love that comes from someone else.

לְאִישׁ הֶדְיוֹט **to a common man**

All the more so, this love is significant when the great and powerful king shows it to one who has no special rank or status. For it is also significant whom the king shows his love to; there is a difference between showing it to his ministers and his children, and showing it to an ordinary commoner.

וְנִבְזֶה וּשְׁפַל אֲנָשִׁים, וּמְנֻוָּל הַמּוּטָל בָּאַשְׁפָּה. **who is ignoble and the lowliest of men, a degenerate cast onto the dunghill.**

Not only does this common person possess no special virtue or honor, but moreover, through his actions and behavior, he has brought himself to a contemptible, low, and filthy place.[3]

וְיוֹרֵד אֵלָיו מִמְּקוֹם כְּבוֹדוֹ, עִם כָּל שָׂרָיו יַחְדָּיו, וּמְקִימוֹ וּמְרִימוֹ מֵאַשְׁפָּתוֹ וּמַכְנִיסוֹ לְהֵיכָלוֹ, **If the king would stoop down to him from his place of glory, together with all his ministers, and raise him up, lifting him from his dunghill and**

---

3. "Common man" refers to small-mindedness; "lowliest of men" refers to his attributes; and "a degenerate cast onto the dunghill" refers to the garments of his soul: thought, speech, and action (*HaLekaḥ VeHalibbuv*).

CHAPTER 46

הֵיכַל הַמֶּלֶךְ, חֶדֶר לִפְנִים מֵחֶדֶר, מָקוֹם שֶׁאֵין כָּל עֶבֶד וְשַׂר נִכְנָס לְשָׁם. וּמִתְיַיחֵד עִמּוֹ שָׁם בְּיִחוּד וְקֵירוּב אֲמִיתִּי, וְחִיבּוּק וְנִישׁוּק, וְאִתְדַּבְּקוּת רוּחָא בְּרוּחָא, בְּכָל לֵב וְנֶפֶשׁ,

bringing him in to his palace, the king's palace, to the innermost chamber, where no servant nor minister may enter, to be secluded with him privately in true intimacy, embracing, kissing, and fusing spirit with spirit, with all his heart and soul,

The great and powerful king comes to this individual, who is in such a low place, and brings him into the king's most personal, private space.[4]

עַל אַחַת כַּמָּה וְכַמָּה שֶׁתִּתְעוֹרֵר מִמֵּילָא הָאַהֲבָה, כְּפוּלָה וּמְכוּפֶּלֶת, בְּלֵב הַהֶדְיוֹט וּשְׁפַל אֲנָשִׁים הַזֶּה אֶל נֶפֶשׁ הַמֶּלֶךְ, בְּהִתְקַשְּׁרוּת הַנֶּפֶשׁ מַמָּשׁ, מִלֵּב וְנֶפֶשׁ, מֵעוּמְקָא דְלִבָּא לְאֵין קֵץ. וְאַף אִם לִבּוֹ כְּלֵב הָאֶבֶן - הַמֵּס יִמַּס וְהָיָה לְמַיִם. וְתִשְׁתַּפֵּךְ נַפְשׁוֹ כַּמַּיִם בִּכְלוֹת הַנֶּפֶשׁ מַמָּשׁ לְאַהֲבַת הַמֶּלֶךְ.

how much more so would the love be aroused on its own many times over in the heart of this common and lowly man for the soul of the king, with an actual binding of souls, from the heart and soul, from the endless depths of the heart. Even if his heart were made of stone, it would certainly melt into water, and his soul would pour out like water, literally pining away with love for the king.

The idea that this arouses a much greater love is found at the end of the song *Dayeinu* in the Passover Haggada.

וְהִנֵּה בְּכָל הַדְּבָרִים הָאֵלֶּה, וּבְכָל הַחִזָּיוֹן הַזֶּה, וְגָדוֹל יוֹתֵר מְאֹד בְּכִפְלֵי כִפְלַיִם לְאֵין קֵץ - עָשָׂה לָנוּ אֱלֹהֵינוּ.

Now our God did for us all these things and this entire spectacle, and so much more, many times over to no end.

10 Iyar

6 Iyar (leap year)

This analogy, of the great king descending in order to lift up the lowliest people toward him from their place of filth, reflects only a miniscule portion of the relationship between us and God. For the distance

---

4. See I Sam. 2:8; Ps. 113:7–8.

between a human being and God is infinitely greater than the distance between two human beings, no matter who they may be. ☞

From here, the author of the *Tanya* progresses from the analogy of the mortal king to what it signifies: God's greatness on the one hand, and Israel's lowliness in Egypt on the other.

כִּי לִגְדוּלָּתוֹ אֵין חֵקֶר, וְאִיהוּ מְמַלֵּא כָּל עָלְמִין וְסוֹבֵב כָּל עָלְמִין. This is **because His greatness is unfathomable. He fills all worlds and encompasses all worlds.**

WHY IS IT NOT THAT SIMPLE BETWEEN US AND GOD?

☞ Why, despite the tremendous distance and the great closeness between the Creator and humankind, does this matter of "As water reflects a face to the face" not work with the same degree of simplicity, with a steady flow of love and gratitude, which occurs so naturally between human beings? If a person feeds an abandoned dog and gives it water, it will be grateful to that person for the rest of its life. Yet, a Jew, who is certainly on a higher level than a dog, does not necessarily react in this way.

The explanation may be found in a verse: "God made man straight, but they have sought out many schemes" (Eccl. 7:29). God made us straight, and we should indeed respond simply and naturally to His love for us. However, the crookedness in a person's heart distorts his picture of reality, preventing him from responding in the natural, healthy way.

There is an additional explanation of this matter, which applies to love for God in particular. In order for a person to recognize that he has received some kind of good, he needs to attain a certain level of knowledge. If he is merely a common, lowly individual, he cannot understand what has been done for him, and if he does not know this, he cannot be grateful. An injured dog that receives care and food understands, in a very tangible way, the benefit that it has received, and therefore it is grateful. However, the lowly, contemptible person who is lifted up by the great King and brought into His innermost chamber may not be able to grasp what has happened to him, due to his extremely low level as well as the immeasurable distance between them.

Many hasidic books present the following parable: Once, a king went out into a field, and while he was there, he met a peasant, who insulted him. The king's men were outraged and demanded that the peasant be punished immediately. However, the king declared that there was no punishment with which this man could suitably atone for his terrible transgression. The peasant had no understanding of the concept of kingship, so he did not understand what he had done, and therefore, it was impossible to punish him properly. Instead, they took the peasant, bathed him, dressed him, and brought him to the royal city, where they taught him all about the monarchy, until he began to gain an understanding of the king's greatness and glory. When he had a sense of what he had done, this in itself was his punishment.

When the disparity between the giver and the receiver is so great, there is no way to express the good that is bestowed, for it has no meaning in the receiver's world. Even

God is greater than any creature can ever understand.[5] His greatness is within all worlds, yet He Himself is also above and beyond the reality of the worlds.

וְנוֹדַע מִזֹּהַר הַקָּדוֹשׁ וְהָאֲרִ"י ז"ל רִיבּוּי הַהֵיכָלוֹת וְהָעוֹלָמוֹת עַד אֵין מִסְפָּר. **It is known from the holy *Zohar* and the Arizal the countless multitudes of sanctums and worlds.**

The multitude and magnitude of the worlds and sanctums beyond our world are far beyond what we are capable of grasping and appreciating. What we do know, we learn from the kabbalistic works, the *Zohar* and the Lurianic Kabbala.

וּבְכָל עוֹלָם וְהֵיכָל רִיבּוֹא רְבָבוֹת מַלְאָכִים לְאֵין קֵץ וְתַכְלִית. **In each world and sanctum, there are myriads upon myriads of angels with no end or limit.**

Each world, and each sanctum, is itself an entire universe, and, like our physical world, each one contains an endless number of beings. ☞

---

in a case where a person has received a tremendous amount of goodness, if he is unable to understand it, he is likewise unable to recognize whoever bestowed it upon him. This can be seen in the behavior of the Israelites in the desert. God strikes the Egyptians with ten plagues, delivers Israel from slavery, splits the sea before them, and sends them manna to eat (along with all the other wonders detailed in the song *Dayeinu*), yet after all this, they grumble and complain as though they were the victims of some great injustice, and they rise up against God and Moses. According to the explanation given here, the gap between God and the Israelites was extremely large, and in order for the people to grasp what had been done for them, a certain amount of time and distance needed to pass. If one were to take a lowly peasant and place him in the middle of the king's court, he would be so dazed that he would have no idea what had happened. A certain period of learning needs to take place in order for one to begin to truly understand it. In certain cases, this could take a millennium or two.

MYRIADS UPON MYRIADS OF ANGELS WITH NO END

☞ It must be explained why the author of the *Tanya* goes into detail describing the worlds, sanctums, and angels, for these chapters are concerned not with depicting God's greatness and glory, but with how to worship Him. Furthermore, it has been

---

5. See Ps. 145:3.

וּכְמוֹ שֶׁנֶּאֱמַר בַּגְּמָרָא (חגיגה יג, ב): כְּתִיב: "הֲיֵשׁ מִסְפָּר לִגְדוּדָיו?" (איוב כה, ג), וּכְתִיב (דניאל ז, י): "אֶלֶף אַלְפִין יְשַׁמְּשׁוּנֵיהּ וְרִבּוֹ רִבְבָן קָדָמוֹהִי" כו', וּמְשַׁנֵּי: אֶלֶף אַלְפִין וכו', מִסְפַּר גְּדוּד אֶחָד. אֲבָל לִגְדוּדָיו, אֵין מִסְפָּר.

As the Talmud states, posing a contradiction (Ḥagiga 13b), "One verse states: 'Is there a number to His troops?' (Job 25:3), yet another verse states: 'A thousand thousands ministered to Him, and ten thousand times ten thousand stood before him' (Dan. 7:10), implying that they have a number..." and the Talmud resolves the contradiction, "'A thousand thousands ministered to Him' is referring to the number of angels in a single troop, but there is no number to His troops.'"

explained in previous chapters that serving God through being stirred up by the idea of His glorious kingdom is a superficial kind of worship, for the worlds and everything in them, although they may contain "a thousand thousands," "ten thousand times ten thousand," or even an uncountable number of beings, are insignificant in comparison to God. They are insignificant when it comes to the individual engaging in divine service. However, since love of God and divine service are not intellectual matters, one must read these words primarily in an emotional context rather than an intellectual one.

The description of the worlds, sanctums, and angels that appears here does not imply that one should love God because He has so many angels at his command, but to enable human beings like us, who live in this lowly realm, to relate to Him in some way. In order to feel a connection, one needs a tangible image that contains some emotional significance and which, even if it is not a deep vision, nevertheless speaks to the individual. It is impossible to truly relate to God, just like it is extremely difficult to relate to a great and powerful king. It is easier to connect to the king's servants, or even to his garments. A simple person cannot fully grasp the essence of the king and of what kingship means, or the abstract concepts of the power and glory of royalty. However, he can attain some sense of this when he sees a parade of the royal guard. Similarly, for most people, extremely large numbers are meaningless. A million is a quantity that bears no relation to reality, because a person cannot conceptualize a million objects. In order to gain a real sense of a multitude, one needs to relate to a smaller number.

While followers of Chabad have always treated simple people, and simple fear of God, with a degree of respect, other hasidim used to joke about a certain Maggid who would exhort the people, "Imagine God as though He were a great and terrible duck!" Yet in truth, this is not as ridiculous as it sounds. When people try to think

The Talmud discusses an apparent contradiction between two verses concerning the number of angels. The first verse implies that there are so many of them that they have no number, while the other indicates that although it is a very large number, there is a limited, countable number of angels. The Talmud explains this contradiction in several ways. One explanation is that while the number of angels in one troop is countable, the number of troops is so great that it is impossible to count them.[6]

Troop: This term refers to the source of nourishment and life for one group, or camp, of angels. The children of Israel camped under four different banners in the wilderness, with several tribes under each banner, and the angels are similarly divided into groups. The division of the tribes into four groups was not random, but in accordance of God in the abstract, they usually cannot develop any kind of true connection within themselves. They do not feel strongly about the matter, and experience neither love nor fear. However, it is quite possible that if the same people were to imagine a great and terrible duck, they would be overcome with dread.

In this section of the *Tanya*, the author does not discuss those sublime feelings of exaltation that require subtle, deep understanding, but rather most innate human emotions, which arise from the simplest and most primitive relationships. He speaks of self-love and of the love of a son for his father (chaps. 43–44), and of simple compassion for the fallen, poor, and wretched (chap. 45), and here, he describes the natural, fundamental feeling of gratitude. These emotions do not appear only in a uniquely virtuous person, but in every soul. Some people may attain them on a higher or deeper level, but essentially, they are equally present in every human being, like it says at the beginning of the chapter: "There is a straight path before a person, which is suitable for everyone." The detailed imagery appears here so that divine greatness may be grasped in a tangible way, making it possible for the individual to work at developing that which he understands into real feeling.

One only needs to go outside and look up at the sky, as far as he can see, in order to achieve a certain appreciation of God's greatness. In the words of the psalmist, "When I see Your heavens, the work of Your fingers…What is a mortal that You remember him?" (Ps. 8:4–5). This is all the more true when a person considers the fact that the entire physical cosmos, which is so large that he cannot see it or grasp its size, is only a tiny island relative to the space of the spiritual worlds. Each world has a world above it, and each sanctum has a sanctum above it.

---

6. This is not saying that there is an infinite amount; rather, there are a certain number of angels, but this number is uncountable (*Hemshekh Ayin Bet* 2:333).

with their spiritual essences, and the same is true with regard to the arrangement of the angels in the higher worlds.[7]

וְכוּלָּם קַמֵּיהּ כְּלָא מַמָּשׁ חֲשִׁיבֵי, וּבְטֵלִים בִּמְצִיאוּת מַמָּשׁ,

Yet, before Him, they are all literally considered nothingness, and their very existence is literally nullified.

After contemplating the vast number of worlds and their magnitude, the next stage is to contemplate the fact that whatever the individual has managed to grasp is all total nothingness in relation to God. ☞

כְּבִיטּוּל דִּבּוּר אֶחָד מַמָּשׁ לְגַבֵּי מַהוּת הַנֶּפֶשׁ הַמְדַבֶּרֶת וְעַצְמוּתָהּ,

in the same way a single utterance is literally negligible in relation to the character of the soul that speaks, and its essence,

The author of the *Tanya* gives an example to illustrate this idea of all the worlds being subsumed under God. All the worlds exist by virtue of divine speech, which is what gives them life. As is explained elsewhere, this divine speech relates to the divine essence just like one utterance of a person relates to the entire array of utterances he is able to pronounce, and to the essence of his soul, which contains innumerable words and can speak endlessly. This is how one should understand the relationship between all the worlds, which are the result of only one divine utterance, and the divine powers of speech and creation. All the more so, this clarifies the relationship between the worlds and the essence of God Himself.

בְּעוֹד שֶׁהָיָה דִּיבּוּרָהּ עֲדַיִין בְּמַחֲשַׁבְתָּהּ אוֹ בִּרְצוֹן וְחֶמְדַּת הַלֵּב, כַּנִּזְכָּר לְעֵיל בַּאֲרִיכוּת.

when its utterance was still becoming crystallized in its faculty of thought or in the desire and impulse of the heart, as discussed above (chaps. 20, 21) at length.

Human speech is not entirely similar to divine speech, so to make the analogy more exact, the author of the *Tanya* adds that this does not refer to human speech that has already been vocalized, for this

---

7. See *Derekh Mitzvotekha, Ma'amar Shoresh Mitzvat HaTefilla* 20.

exists separately from the person who spoke it. Rather, it refers to potential human speech within the soul, in the form of the thought that precedes speech or, more fundamentally, the spiritual force that precedes thought, "the desire and impulse of the heart." This constitutes the impelling source of thought and speech. This analogy is more exact. Just as thought, and certainly the power of will in the soul, do not exist separately from the person who thinks and desires, divine speech and all the worlds have no existence apart from the divine essence that "speaks" them, and therefore, they are all considered to be nothingness.

וְכוּלָם שׁוֹאֲלִים: "אַיֵּה מְקוֹם כְּבוֹדוֹ?" **All** the angels ask, **"Where is the place of His glory?"** 7 Iyar (leap year)

They seek the essential point, the node of divine glory.

וְעוֹנִים: "מְלֹא כָל הָאָרֶץ כְּבוֹדוֹ" (ישעיה ו, ג), הֵם יִשְׂרָאֵל עַמּוֹ. and they answer, **"that which fills the entire earth is His glory"** (Isa. 6:3), **referring to Israel, His nation.**

The earth mentioned in this verse refers to the Jewish people.[8] Thus, the answer to the question "Where is the place of His glory," meaning, where is the point of God's inner desire to be found in reality, is here, with Israel, in the lowly, physical realm where they reside.

כִּי הִנִּיחַ הַקָּדוֹשׁ בָּרוּךְ הוּא אֶת הָעֶלְיוֹנִים וְאֶת הַתַּחְתּוֹנִים, וְלֹא בָּחַר בְּכוּלָּם, That is **because the Holy One, blessed be He, disregarded the higher worlds and the lower worlds, and did not choose any of them**

NOTHINGNESS

☞ This has been compared to the specks of dust that can be seen when a ray of sunlight enters a dark place. One ostensibly observes something real floating around in the light, yet that is the only place where these tiny specks exist; they are considered real only within that ray of light.

---

8. The Jewish people are called "a desired land" (Mal. 3:12); see also *Torah Or* 53d.

God did not choose to have this deep relationship with the higher worlds because of their supremacy, nor did He choose the lower worlds because they constitute the lowest and final point in the succession of the worlds.

The concept of "choice" does not refer to a decision that comes as a result of weighing up advantages and disadvantages. Rather, it is free of any external preferences and stems from the will in the soul, which is deeper than any other force, including emotion and consciousness. This kind of choice is made because it fits with one's own self. This is also the case with regard to God's choosing of Israel, His nation. ☞

כִּי אִם בְּיִשְׂרָאֵל עַמּוֹ. **except for Israel, His nation.**

The following parable has been cited in this regard:[9] There was once a king whose palace contained everything precious in the world. In its inner halls were the king's trusted servants and honored ministers, and in the innermost room, there was a cage that held a talking parrot. The king was asked why he had chosen to place the parrot there. After all, he had many servants, including writers, linguists, and poets, who could certainly speak and sing more beautifully than the parrot. The king answered, "It is true that it does not speak as beautifully as they do, but the parrot is a wonder; it is a parrot, yet it speaks." Similarly, God's special affection toward us is not because we sing more beautifully than the angels, nor because we can study Torah like them, but because God looks at us and

WHAT DOES GOD WANT; WHAT DOES GOD CHOOSE?

☞ A hasid once came to his Rebbe and began to recount his troubles, "Rebbe, I have a terrible headache. I cannot study and I cannot pray. What will be?" The Rebbe answered him, "What makes you think that God desires your learning and your prayers? Perhaps He desires your headache." If God wanted prayers, He could create another billion angels to pray before Him, and if He wanted Torah study, He could create two billion angels, each one more intelligent than any human being, to study without interruptions, worries, or headaches. However, if God, for whatever reason, wants the headache that comes from the effort of trying to pray or learn, this is something that He cannot assign to an angel.

---

9. *Or Torah* of the Maggid of Mezeritch, *Aggadot Ḥazal* 388; *Torah Or* 25d; *Likkutei Torah*, Num. 19:4.

says, "See this creature that I have created, with his problems, urges, and troubles; despite them all, he stands and prays." This is why Israel is in the innermost sanctum, while the angels are outside.

וְהוֹצִיאָם מִמִּצְרַיִם "עֶרְוַת הָאָרֶץ", מְקוֹם הַזּוּהֲמָא וְהַטּוּמְאָה,	He took them out of Egypt, "the nakedness of the land," the place of filth and impurity,

In a spiritual sense, Egypt is the lowest place. In the example given above, it is the dunghill onto which the common, ignoble, lowly person was cast. As explained above, the spiritual place where a person is found indicates his current state. One who is in a place of filth and impurity is himself filthy and impure.

לֹא עַל יְדֵי מַלְאָךְ וְלֹא עַל יְדֵי כו' אֶלָּא הַקָּדוֹשׁ בָּרוּךְ הוּא בִּכְבוֹדוֹ וּבְעַצְמוֹ יָרַד לְשָׁם,	not by means of an angel nor by means of a seraph or an agent. Rather, the Holy One, blessed be He, Himself, in all His glory, descended there,

God Himself[10] brought Israel out of that low place and their lowly state.

כְּמוֹ שֶׁכָּתוּב: "וָאֵרֵד לְהַצִּילוֹ" וְגוֹ' (שמות ג, ח),	as it is written, "I have descended to rescue it…" (Ex. 3:8),

This is like in the analogy above, where the king stoops down to the lowly individual from his place of glory.

כְּדֵי לְקָרְבָם אֵלָיו בְּקֵירוּב וְיִחוּד אֲמִיתִּי, בְּהִתְקַשְּׁרוּת הַנֶּפֶשׁ מַמָּשׁ,	in order to bring them intimately close to Him in true union of actual soul bonding,

This language was also used in the analogy of a king embracing a commoner. It describes an essential, profound connection between beings.

---

10. The source of the phrase used in the *Tanya* is in the Passover Haggada; see also *Mekhilta, Bo* 13.

בִּבְחִינַת נְשִׁיקִין פֶּה לְפֶה, לְדַבֵּר דְּבַר ה׳ - זוֹ הֲלָכָה, **through the** intimacy corresponding to the concept **of kissing of mouths,** achieved **by speaking the word of God, which is the** *halakha,*

In the previous analogy, this intimacy is described in terms of embracing and kissing, which, as stated in the previous chapter, is the speaking of the word of the Lord, which is the *halakha*. The Torah is God's speech that He inserts into the world. When a person speaks words of Torah, his speech joins God's speech. It is as though God's mouth touches his mouth and unites with it. This resembles a kiss between a human being and God. The statement that this refers particularly to *halakha*[11] teaches that this mouth-to-mouth connection comes about specifically when a person states orally the words of Torah on the level of a halakhic ruling, even if he does not relate to its reason or wisdom.

וְאִתְדַּבְּקוּת רוּחָא בְּרוּחָא הִיא הַשָּׂגַת הַתּוֹרָה וִידִיעַת רְצוֹנוֹ וְחָכְמָתוֹ, **and** also **fusing spirit with spirit,** which is achieved through **comprehending the Torah and knowing His will and wisdom,**

There is an even deeper connection, which fuses a person's spirit, his inner spiritual faculties, with the inner essence of the divine being, which brings the world into existence and sustains it. This clinging to God comes about when a person comprehends the Torah and knows God's will and wisdom. The Torah is the world's inner essence. It is God's essential will, expressed through divine wisdom and in the structure of inner existence as it must be in keeping with God's will. One who learns and thinks about Torah is therefore together with God in His innermost sanctum. God so to speak reveals to him His personal plans, His will, His secret, until the point that it is as though they are thinking the same thing: i.e., the Torah. When a person thinks of Torah, no matter what level he is on, he unites in some way with the will and wisdom of God.

דְּכוֹלָּא חַד מַמָּשׁ. **for they are all literally one.**

---

11. The Talmud states that "the word of God" refers to the *halakha* (*Shabbat* 138b).

God's Torah, His will, His wisdom, and He Himself are truly all one being. Therefore, one who engages in Torah becomes united with God Himself at that moment.

וְגַם בִּבְחִינַת חִיבּוּק הוּא: קִיּוּם הַמִּצְוֹת מַעֲשִׂיּוֹת בִּרְמַ״ח אֵבָרִים דִּרְמַ״ח פִּיקוּדִין הֵן רְמַ״ח אֲבָרִין דְּמַלְכָּא, כַּנִּזְכָּר לְעֵיל.

Likewise, the intimacy corresponding to the concept of embracing is achieved through the mitzvot performed by an action with the 248 limbs of the human body, since the 248 positive commandments comprise the 248 "limbs" of the King, as stated above (chap. 23).

As in the analogy of the mortal king, intimacy is achieved through kissing and embracing. When a person performs the 248 mitzvot that involve action with his 248 limbs, he is "embracing" God.[12] The 248 limbs in the human body correspond to 248 limbs of the divine structure, which is revealed within existence through the Torah's commandments. When a person performs a mitzva, he encounters and connects and binds an earthly limb to a heavenly limb, arm to arm, body to body, and this is a true embrace.

וְדֶרֶךְ כְּלָל נֶחְלָקִין לְשָׁלֹשׁ בְּחִינוֹת: יָמִין וּשְׂמֹאל וְאֶמְצַע, שֶׁהֵן חֶסֶד, דִּין רַחֲמִים,

The mitzvot are broadly classified into three categories: right, left, and center, corresponding to the attributes of kindness, judgment, and compassion,

This division is similar to the division of the ten *sefirot*, which make up the overall structure of the divine being in the world, into three columns: right, left, and middle. The right column is made up of Ḥokhma (Wisdom), Ḥesed (Kindness), and Netzaḥ (Dominance); the left is made up of Bina (Understanding), Gevura (Restraint), and Hod (Splendor); and the middle is made up of Da'at (Knowledge), Tiferet (Beauty), Yesod (Foundation), and Malkhut (Kingship). Each column is characterized by its central *sefira*. On the right is the column

---

12. Mishna *Ohalot* 1:8.

of *Ḥesed*, Kindness; on the left is the column of judgment, which is also called *Gevura*; and in the middle is the column of compassion, which is also called *Tiferet*. Like the divine being, the mitzvot, or "limbs of the King," are also divided into three general categories, as in Mishna *Avot* (1:2): "Torah, the Temple service, and the practice of acts of kindness." The right consists mainly of mitzvot of charity and kindness. These acts involve giving, and are characterized by movement from above to below. The mitzvot of the left are primarily those that relate to the Temple service and offerings, including the service of the heart, which is prayer. These are mitzvot that elevate the lower reality, such as a Temple offering or one's soul. Finally, the mitzvot of the middle category are chiefly those related to Torah study. These mitzvot are concerned with reconciliation.

תְּרֵין דְּרוֹעִין וְגוּפָא וכו'. that are represented in the human body as **the two arms and the body, and so forth.**

As expressed in the introduction to *Tikkunei Zohar* (17a), "*Ḥesed* is the right arm; *Gevura* is the left arm; *Tiferet* is the body." All the mitzvot together form two arms and a body, and our inner connection is structured the same way. Thus, a full embrace is created when we fulfill the mitzvot.

11 Iyar

וְזֶה שֶׁאוֹמְרִים: "אֲשֶׁר קִדְּשָׁנוּ בְּמִצְוֹתָיו". כְּאָדָם הַמְקַדֵּשׁ אִשָּׁה לִהְיוֹת מְיֻחֶדֶת עִמּוֹ בְּיִחוּד גָּמוּר. כְּמוֹ שֶׁכָּתוּב: "וְדָבַק בְּאִשְׁתּוֹ וְהָיוּ לְבָשָׂר אֶחָד" (בראשית ב, כד).

The formula for the blessing **recited before a mitzva, "Who has sanctified us [*kideshanu*] with His mitzvot,"** can also be read to mean "who has betrothed us [*kideshanu*]," **as a man betroths a woman to become united with him in total union, as the verse states, "He shall cleave to his wife, and they shall become one flesh"** (Gen. 2:24).

The term "sanctified" is likened to betrothal. We are betrothed through the mitzvot, becoming exclusive to the Creator. This is akin to a woman who is the partner only of her husband, and who is united with him, becoming "one flesh." ☞

כָּכָה מַמָּשׁ, וְיָתֵר עַל כֵּן לְאֵין קֵץ, הוּא יִחוּד נֶפֶשׁ הָאֱלוֹקִית הָעוֹסֶקֶת בַּתּוֹרָה וּמִצְוֹת, וְנֶפֶשׁ הַחִיּוּנִית וּלְבוּשֵׁיהֶן, הַנִּזְכָּרִים לְעֵיל, בְּאוֹר אֵין סוֹף בָּרוּךְ הוּא.

It is literally the same, and infinitely more so, regarding the union of the divine soul, when engaged in Torah and mitzvot, as well as the vital soul, and their garments mentioned above, with the light of *Ein Sof*, blessed be He.

This is parallel to the betrothal of a woman. "Garments" of the soul refers to thoughts, speech, and bodily actions. The divine soul can act upon the reality of this world only by means of the vital soul and the body, and when this action involves the fulfillment of mitzvot, which constitutes the divine will itself, then the divine soul, the vital soul, and their garments are completely united with the light of the Infinite One.

The important point is that this connection is not actualized by means of some kind of mystical, spiritual union, but by performing a mitzva that comprises an action. Only through the actual act of a mitzva does a human being's body and soul unite with God's essential, basic will, which is the foundation and purpose of all existence.

AS A MAN BETROTHS A WOMAN

☞ This idea is expressed symbolically in the observance of several mitzvot. For example, regarding the mitzva of *tefillin*, which concerns specifically one's personal connection to God, when wrapping the straps around one's finger like rings, some say the following verses: "I will betroth you to Me forever; I will betroth you to Me with righteousness, with justice, with grace, and with mercy. I will betroth you to Me with faithfulness" (Hos. 2:21–22). This action is thus equated to putting on a wedding ring, and the observance of this mitzva is likened to the act of betrothal. Similarly, the rings of the *lulav*, which bind the four species together, symbolize our union with God. Just as there are symbols of marriage within the mitzvot, there are likewise allusions to the acceptance of Torah and mitzvot in the wedding ceremony. Many Jewish wedding customs, such as the bride circling the groom, and the finger on which the ring is placed, allude to the fact that the phrase "On the day of his wedding" (Song 3:11), refers to the giving of the Torah (Mishna *Ta'anit* 4:8).

**8 Iyar
(leap year)**

וְלָכֵן הִמְשִׁיל שְׁלֹמֹה עָלָיו הַשָּׁלוֹם בְּשִׁיר הַשִּׁירִים יִחוּד זֶה לְיִחוּד חָתָן וְכַלָּה: בִּדְבִיקָה חֲשִׁיקָה וַחֲפִיצָה, בְּחִבּוּק וְנִישׁוּק.

That is why King **Solomon, may he rest in peace, portrayed** in Song of Songs **this union using the metaphor of the union of groom and bride, with attachment, desire, and longing, through embracing and kissing.**

The Song of Songs is an analogy for the relationship between God and the Jewish people. This does not refer only to the emotion of love, such as "attachment, desire, and longing," but also to outward expressions of love, "embracing and kissing," which signify the performance of Torah and mitzvot. ☞

This is one interpretation of the phrase "who has sanctified us with His mitzvot," which is mentioned in the blessing recited before a mitzva. It concerns the most intimate kind of attachment and closeness. Now, the author of the *Tanya* will explain a different perspective.

וְזֶה שֶׁאוֹמְרִים: "אֲשֶׁר קִדְּשָׁנוּ בְּמִצְוֹתָיו", שֶׁהֶעֱלָנוּ לְמַעֲלַת קוֹדֶשׁ הָעֶלְיוֹן בָּרוּךְ הוּא, שֶׁהִיא קְדוּשָׁתוֹ שֶׁל הַקָּדוֹשׁ בָּרוּךְ הוּא בִּכְבוֹדוֹ וּבְעַצְמוֹ.

This implies an additional meaning of the blessing **recited, "who sanctified us with His mitzvot": He elevated us to the height of supernal holiness, blessed be He, which is the holiness of the Holy One, blessed be He, Himself, in all His glory.**

The phrase "who has sanctified us with His mitzvot" can therefore be interpreted in two ways. The first concerns God's descent toward

---

HE PORTRAYED THIS UNION IN SONG OF SONGS

☞ There are two levels to the analogy in the Song of Songs: general and particular. On a general level, as can be seen in the Aramaic translation, the book depicts the love between God and the Jewish people. On a particular level, the book conveys the love between God and each individual Jewish soul, and this is more emotionally charged. The author of the *Tanya* was also a profound composer; according to tradition, he composed ten hasidic melodies. One of these is to the verse "The sound of my beloved is knocking: Open for me, my sister, my love" (Song 5:2). If one listens closely to this melody, he will perhaps gain a sense of what the author of the *Tanya* means when he speaks of love of God "with attachment, desire, and longing."

us like a groom coming toward a bride, as the Mishna states, "'On the day of his wedding'; this is the giving of the Torah." The second interpretation, which complements the first, relates to an ascent. God raises us up toward Him to become holy through His mitzvot, for the mitzvot constitute the supernal will, and they are like a crown, which is above and distinct from the body.

וּקְדוּשָׁה הִיא לְשׁוֹן הַבְדָּלָה, מַה שֶּׁהַקָּדוֹשׁ בָּרוּךְ הוּא הוּא מוּבְדָּל מֵהָעוֹלָמוֹת. **Holiness implies separation in the sense that the Holy One, blessed be He, is separated from the worlds.**

The term "holy" means distinct, and refers to that which is above and separate from all else. Therefore, as explained elsewhere, this term relates only to God, because only He is truly holy. Only God is separate, independent, and unattached to anything else. Anything that is referred to as "holy" is called this only in connection with God, as it is written, "You shall be holy, for I, the Lord your God, am holy" (Lev. 19:2). This is the meaning of "who sanctified us with His mitzvot": the union – *tzavta* – involved in the act of a mitzva is holy, for it constitutes attachment to God and separation from the world.

וְהִיא בְּחִינַת סוֹבֵב כָּל עָלְמִין, מַה שֶּׁאֵינוֹ יָכוֹל לְהִתְלַבֵּשׁ בָּהֶן. **It is** referred to **as the quality of** divinity which **"encompasses all worlds," as it is unable to become enclothed in them.**

"Holy" means distinct; it relates to that which is beyond all realms and definitions. Therefore, according to the mystical teachings, it is not possible to say that the divine holiness is within the world, but only beyond it. It transcends any attachment to the world.

כִּי עַל יְדֵי יִחוּד הַנֶּפֶשׁ וְהִתְכַּלְלוּתָהּ בְּאוֹר אֵין סוֹף בָּרוּךְ הוּא, הֲרֵי הִיא בְּמַעֲלַת וּמַדְרֵגַת קְדוּשַׁת אֵין סוֹף בָּרוּךְ הוּא מַמָּשׁ, מֵאַחַר שֶׁמִּתְיַיחֶדֶת וּמִתְכַּלֶּלֶת בּוֹ יִתְבָּרֵךְ, וְהָיוּ לַאֲחָדִים מַמָּשׁ. That is **because by the union and incorporation of the soul in the light of *Ein Sof*, blessed be He, it too** actually **attains the height and level of the holiness of *Ein Sof*, blessed be He, since it is unified and included within Him, and they literally become one.**

The language of the blessing "who has sanctified us with His mitzvot" does not refer only to the union that takes place below, whereby God descends toward us and sanctifies us like a groom going toward his bride. Rather, it also pertains to the union above, where we ignore existence through fulfilling the mitzvot, becoming sanctified and separate from all existence, and connecting to God. We say, "who has sanctified us with His mitzvot," because through the mitzva, we connect to divine holiness, which means divine separation, the fact that God is entirely distinct from any existence in the world.

וְזֶה שֶׁכָּתוּב: "וִהְיִיתֶם לִי קְדֹשִׁים כִּי קָדוֹשׁ אֲנִי ה', וָאַבְדִּל אֶתְכֶם מִן הָעַמִּים לִהְיוֹת לִי" (ויקרא כ, כו).

This is the meaning of the verse "You shall be holy to Me; for I, the Lord, am holy and have separated you from among the peoples to be Mine" (Lev. 20:26).

"You shall be holy to Me" is interpreted not only as a command, but as a declarative sentence meaning: You shall be different and distinct. The reason given for this is: "For I, the Lord, am holy and have distinguished you from the peoples," through the commandments. This kind of distinction is not made by constructing a barrier; rather, it is an essential distinction relating to holiness, and it is formed by the very presence of a connection with God. When a person performs a mitzva, he moves beyond all other domains toward that which is holy.

וְאוֹמֵר: "וַעֲשִׂיתֶם אֶת כָּל מִצְוֹתָי וִהְיִיתֶם קְדֹשִׁים לֵאלֹהֵיכֶם, אֲנִי ה' אֱלֹהֵיכֶם" וְגוֹ' (במדבר טו, מ-מא). פֵּירוּשׁ: כִּי עַל יְדֵי קִיּוּם הַמִּצְוֹת הֲרֵינִי אֱלוֹהַּ שֶׁלָּכֶם,

It further states, "You shall perform all My commandments, and be holy to your God. I am the Lord your God..." (Num. 15, 40–41). This means to say, "Through your performing the mitzvot, I am your God,"

The clarification "this means to say" comes to explain the difficulty regarding the possessive pronoun *Elokeikhem*, "your God." One may ask how it is possible to refer to God as though He belongs to someone. Therefore, the author of the *Tanya* adds an explanation: "As a result of your performing the mitzvot, I am your God." Moreover, from a linguistic perspective, the possessive form indicates only that the object relates to the person and the person relates to the object. For example, this is how we understand the appellations "my lord," and "my king"; the individual in question is the lord or the king over me. So too, this is how the phrase "your God" should be understood: the God who is connected to you, and to whom you are connected, through your performance of the mitzvot. ☞

The author of the *Tanya* claims that there are two ways in which this is possible. The first appeared in the clarification: "Through your performing the mitzvot, I am your God." When we keep the mitzvot, a connection is formed that does not come from us, but from God. Since He creates the connection, and he is the One establishing the commandments, the distance between us no longer matters. The constraint comes from our side, but from God's perspective there is none; when we simply accept and follow His command, the outcome is a relationship with "your God."

כְּמוֹ אֱלֹהֵי אַבְרָהָם אֱלֹהֵי יִצְחָק וְכוּ׳, שֶׁנִּקְרָא כֵּן מִפְּנֵי שֶׁהָאָבוֹת הָיוּ בִּחִינַת מֶרְכָּבָה לוֹ יִתְבָּרֵךְ, וּבְטֵלִים וְנִכְלָלִים בְּאוֹרוֹ. — in the same way He is called "God of Abraham, God of Isaac…" He is called this, because the forefathers were on the level of being a chariot to Him and were subsumed and incorporated in His light.

The second way in which God can be "your God," which in a sense is the first way, concerns the connection created by human beings.

YOUR GOD

☞ The fundamental problem with this explanation is defining the relationship between us and God. Since God is holy and separate, how is such a relationship possible? The connection that we feel occasionally, as though we comprehend and connect with Him, is our own personal experience, and the human experience is subjective and does not necessarily correspond to objective reality. Therefore, even when a person experiences attachment and transcendent enlightenment, it is entirely unclear what he has actually connected to, whether to God or something else. In fact, it is more likely that he has not connected to God, for by nature, that which can be attained and united with is not that which is beyond and separate. However, in a sense, this fundamental problem is answered by the Torah in its entirety; we learn from the giving of the Torah that this relationship is entirely possible.

This kind of connection is possible, as will be explained below, only when the person truly leaves behind all the ordinary constraints of humanity and existence. God is called "God of Abraham, God of Isaac, and God of Jacob," which indicates that He is connected in some sense to the forefathers. This kind of connection is total; the human being is a chariot to God. Being a chariot means not being oneself, and instead being a perfect vessel for God. This is why it is possible to say "God of Abraham": Abraham who is a chariot is not the man Abraham, who is like all the other people in the world, but rather Abraham who is a vessel for God. Abraham is a vessel of expression and reflection of divine kindness on earth, and therefore, Abraham is himself divine kindness. The appellation "God of Abraham" is not a reference to Abraham the man, but to this divine attribute and to the Divine itself.

וְכָכָה הוּא בְּכָל נֶפֶשׁ מִיִּשְׂרָאֵל בִּשְׁעַת עֵסֶק הַתּוֹרָה וְהַמִּצְוֹת. **So it is with the soul of every Jew while he engages in Torah and mitzvot.**

Like our forefathers, so too their descendants: all Jews say, "the Lord our God." Although not all Jews are chariots of the Divine Presence like the patriarchs were, each Jew becomes one when he fulfills a mitzva. The difference is that the forefathers were chariots of the Divine Presence[13] due to their own power, due to their own particular consciousness and will, and therefore, they were chariots at all times, at every stage of their lives. By contrast, ordinary Jews become chariots only by virtue of the mitzvot that God commanded; therefore, they are chariots only while performing a mitzva.

Since this point of connection, which is present within every Jewish soul, does not come from the individual, it is entirely conditional on the performance of a mitzva. When one engages in Torah and mitzvot, he becomes a chariot of the Divine Presence; he is transformed into part of the divine being, and he is holy. A moment later, when he is no longer engaged in Torah and mitzvot, he may even be found in the depths of the netherworld. ☞

---

13. *Bereshit Rabba* 47:6, 82:6; see also chap. 23.

וְלָכֵן חִייְבוּ רַבּוֹתֵינוּ ז"ל לָקוּם
וְלַעֲמוֹד מִפְּנֵי כָּל עוֹסֵק בְּמִצְוָה
אַף אִם הוּא בּוּר וְעַם הָאָרֶץ
(ביכורים ג, ג; קידושין לג, א),

That is why the Rabbis (*Bikkurim* 3:3; *Kiddushin* 33a) **required standing up for anyone engaged in a mitzva, even if he is a boor and an ignoramus,**

When a Jew performs a mitzva with intention, he nullifies himself to the divine will and at that moment he becomes a chariot of the Divine Presence. In addition to the honor one shows elders and Torah scholars, particular honor is afforded to a person who is in the middle of doing a mitzva, even if he is unlearned, since this standing up and giving honor pertains to the mitzva that the person is engaged in.

וְהַיְינוּ מִפְּנֵי ה' הַשּׁוֹכֵן וּמִתְלַבֵּשׁ
בְּנַפְשׁוֹ בְּשָׁעָה זוֹ.

since it is actually **for God who dwells and enclothes Himself in his soul at that time.**

A person who performs a mitzva may be a boor and an ignoramus, and he may even be wicked and sinful. However, while he engages in the mitzva, he is not merely connected to the Divine; he becomes a revelation of the divine essence. We express honor to the divine light that shines within his soul, the Divine that is now acting through him.

WHILE ENGAGING IN TORAH AND MITZVOT

☞ Once, a group of hasidim came to the Ḥozeh of Lublin, and one of them gave the Ḥozeh a *kvittel* (a note containing a petitionary prayer) on behalf a friend of his. The Ḥozeh glanced at the note and immediately spat in disgust. That evening, the hasid once more handed the note to the Seer, and this time, when the Seer looked at the note, he declared, "This man shines and illuminates all the worlds!" The Rebbe then explained that the first time the hasid had given him the note, the man mentioned in it had been playing cards, but the second time, he had been lighting the Hanukkah candles. This is the difference between the patriarchs and ordinary Jews. "The God of Abraham" is Abraham's God at all times, but "the Lord our God," which is said by all Jewish people, is true only at that moment, when the person is standing in prayer or performing a mitzva; however, when he goes out to the street, it may no longer be true.

רַק שֶׁאֵין נַפְשׁוֹ מַרְגֶּשֶׁת מִפְּנֵי מָסַךְ הַחוֹמֶר הַגּוּפָנִי שֶׁלֹּא נִזְדַּכֵּךְ וּמַחְשִׁיךְ עֵינֵי הַנֶּפֶשׁ מֵרְאוֹת אֱלֹהִים, **Yet his soul does not feel** this union **because of the screen of unrefined corporeal physicality that dims the eyes of the soul from seeing visions of God,**

All human beings, small or great, are equal in that when they perform a mitzva they are revealing the divine essence and glory through their act. The difference between people lies in their subjective feelings. The ability to see and feel depends on two things: The first is the special capacity of the soul to see visions of God, which certain exceptional people are born with. The second is a person's hard work,[14] for the body in its initial state does not allow the soul to see visions of God, even if it has the potential to do so. Because it is imprisoned within the physical body, the soul cannot see the significance of mitzva observance, or how the divine light illuminates a person when he fulfills a mitzva. Therefore, one needs to expend a great deal of effort to cultivate the soul, molding, adjusting, and refining it so that it can see beyond the pervasive physical reality.

כְּמוֹ הָאָבוֹת וְכַיּוֹצֵא בָּהֶן שֶׁרָאוּ עוֹלָמָם בְּחַיֵּיהֶם. **in the same way as the forefathers and those like them, who saw their** spiritual **world during their lifetime.**

As mentioned in the wording of the Grace after Meals, God blessed Abraham, Isaac, and Jacob "in everything, from everything, with everything." This blessing was a special gift to the forefathers whereby they were able to see and feel, each in his own way, "their spiritual world during their lifetime."[15] They saw and felt God dwelling and being revealed within them when they carried out His will. They did not see this in another realm, in the Garden of Eden or the World to Come, but in their lives in this world, at the time that they were doing God's will.

---

14. The term for work, *avoda*, including when it relates to the soul, should be understood in the same sense as the term for processing hides to produce leather; see *Torah Or* 5b.
15. *Berakhot* 17a.

| וְזֶה שֶׁאָמַר אָסָף בְּרוּחַ הַקֹּדֶשׁ, | That is the meaning of what *Asaf*, the psalmist, **wrote with divine inspiration regarding the entire congregation of Israel in the exile,** | 12 Iyar
9 Iyar
(leap year) |

Asaf is not expressing himself through these words, nor do they relate only to his place and time, which was in the Land of Israel during Temple times. Rather, he is the voice of the entire Jewish people, *Kenesset Yisrael*, including when they are in exile. This is why the author of the *Tanya* remarks here, unusually, that Asaf's words were divinely inspired, to teach that they are not a personal expression of the psalmist, but rather divine inspiration, which sees beyond the particular individual and time.[16]

The author of the *Tanya* emphasizes this point because his object

---

SEEING OR NOT SEEING ONE'S SPIRITUAL WORLD DURING ONE'S LIFETIME

☞ The main difference between the level of the patriarchs and our level is not in the observance of the mitzvot, but in our comprehension and feeling when fulfilling them. The real question is not what is achieved, but the state of the person achieving it. In order to achieve something, one must be on a level where he is able to form a connection with it. This difference can be seen between adults and children, and all the more so between humans and animals. To understand a drawing, even a very simple one, and to be able to identify what is portrayed in it, the observer must be at a certain level. Any creature with eyes, whether human or animal, can physically see the drawing, but the degree to which one understands it depends on his soul and its level of knowledge and understanding. Experiments have shown that some animals are unable to perceive anything unless it is moving. This does not mean that the object is invisible to that animal; however, since its concept of reality is that anything that is not moving is unimportant, it does not see it. The object may have been sensed externally, but not internally. Likewise, there are many things that we know to exist, in both the spiritual and physical realms, yet we know that we are unable to comprehend them; they definitely exist, but we lack the ability to connect with them. When the level of an object is higher, the level of the observer is more significant with regard to the question of whether or not he will be able to grasp what he sees. God dwells within every person who is fulfilling a mitzva, but the degree to which one feels this depends on his own personal level.

---

16. See the comment of the Lubavitcher Rebbe, Rabbi Menaḥem Mendel Schneerson, cited in *Likkutei Biurim*.

is not to deal with lofty levels of spiritual refinement such as those of the Land of Israel and the Temple era. Rather, he is speaking equally to all Jewish souls, even the ones in exile, and even those who are like "boors" or "beasts." ☞

"וַאֲנִי בַעַר וְלֹא אֵדָע, בְּהֵמוֹת הָיִיתִי עִמָּךְ, וַאֲנִי תָמִיד עִמָּךְ" (תהלים עג, כב-כג). כְּלוֹמַר, שֶׁאַף עַל פִּי שֶׁאֲנִי כִּבְהֵמָה בִּהְיוֹתִי עִמָּךְ, וְלֹא אֵדַע וְלֹא אַרְגִּישׁ בְּנַפְשִׁי יִחוּד זֶה, שֶׁתִּפּוֹל עָלֶיהָ אֵימָתָה וָפַחַד תְּחִלָּה, וְאַחַר כָּךְ אַהֲבָה רַבָּה בְּתַעֲנוּגִים, אוֹ כְּרִשְׁפֵּי אֵשׁ, כְּמִדַּת הַצַּדִּיקִים שֶׁנִּזְדַּכֵּךְ חוֹמְרָם,

"I am a boor, unknowing; I am like the beasts before You. Yet I am always with You" (Ps. 72:22–23). That is, even though I am like a beast when I am with You, not knowing and not feeling this union in my soul, so that it should first be overcome with trepidation and fright and then with the great love of delight or the love of sparks of fire, as characterized the tzaddikim whose physicality has been refined,

Asaf wrote this verse about the time of exile and concealment. Even when one is "with" God, when he is engaged in performing a mitzva, he is a "beast." When a Jew performs a mitzva, his soul should experience fear due to God's closeness, and this fear should be followed by love. It may be a love of gratification and pleasure due to the closeness, or alternatively, one of longing, but even allowing for each individual's particular circumstances, some type of love should arise from the closeness and the union with the divine being that occurs during

THE ILLUMINATING HOLINESS OF THE LAND OF ISRAEL

☞ It is a given that there is a greater illumination of holiness in the Land of Israel (see *Torah Or* 13a), especially when the Jewish people are there, and even more so when there is a Temple, whose entire essence is "I will dwell among them" (Ex. 25:8). One who does not sense this should not see this as a problem with the Land of Israel, but with himself. There is an analogy for this idea in the book of Isaiah (29:11–12): That which is concealed is like a sealed scroll, which even a literate person is unable to read. An unsealed scroll, on the other hand, is available to be read by everyone except those who cannot read. If one is unable to read such a scroll, then the problem is not with scroll, but with the person.

the observance of a mitzva. In the case of tzaddikim, the "screen of unrefined corporeal physicality" mentioned above has been refined, and therefore, they see and feel this closeness.

The feeling and experience of one mitzva could fill a person entirely, to the point where he is unable to bear any more. When a person performs a mitzva, he himself becomes a chariot of the Divine Presence, as explained above. We learn about this chariot from the visions of the prophets, yet the prophets only see the chariot, while the individual performing a mitzva actually is the chariot. He is the seraphim and the holy creatures. Ostensibly, therefore, he should also feel like the seraphim and the holy creatures. However, as the verse states, "I am a boor, unknowing; I am like the beasts before You"; the person may be like an animal that is brought into the king's palace and is moved neither by the king's greatness nor the fearfulness and the glory of the kingdom. Animals behave in exactly the same way in the king's palace as they do in a barn. Likewise, a person who engages in a mitzva and feels nothing is "like the beasts before You." A donkey that sees a Torah scroll is not inspired, nor should it be, because it is, after all, a donkey. So too, there are people who see a Torah scroll and are unmoved.

וְכַנּוֹדָע, שֶׁדַּעַת הוּא לְשׁוֹן הַרְגָּשָׁה בַּנֶּפֶשׁ, **as it is known that "knowledge," referred to in the verse, connotes the feeling of the soul,**

"Knowledge" does not allude to information that is recorded in a person's brain like in a computer's memory, like when one "knows" historical or geographical facts, which do not affect him personally. Rather, in the above verse, knowledge is referred to in the experiential, emotional sense of the word.

וְהוּא כּוֹלֵל חֶסֶד וּגְבוּרָה, **and it includes Ḥesed and Gevura.**

Knowledge includes the two extremes of emotion, Ḥesed and Gevura. There is "knowledge out of love," when a person knows something in terms of his love and desire for it, and the pleasure derived from being close to it. Additionally, there is "knowledge out of fear," where one knows a certain matter through the dread and pain that it brings. The phrase, "I am a boor, unknowing," refers to one who acts but does not know; he feels neither the dread of the act, nor the pleasure of the soul's longing that the act involves.

אַף עַל פִּי כֵן - "אֲנִי תָמִיד עִמָּךְ". The verse continues, **nevertheless, "I am always with You,"**

The fact that a person is "like the beasts" does not negate the fact that he is "with" God. One can be a boor and a beast, and still be "always with You."

כִּי אֵין הַחוֹמֶר מוֹנֵעַ יִחוּד הַנֶּפֶשׁ בְּאוֹר אֵין סוֹף בָּרוּךְ הוּא, **for the physicality does not obstruct the union of the soul with the light of *Ein Sof*, blessed be He,**

Physicality prevents one from seeing and understanding. It affects a person's subjective feelings, yet it does not change the essence of the matter. A person who is holding highly sensitive explosive materials may be overcome with terror, yet a donkey that is carrying the same item on its back feels no different than it does when it carries any other burden. The explosives are no less dangerous when they are on top of the donkey, but the donkey is unaware of the danger, because it is an animal. The same is true with regard to holiness. It is written regarding Abraham, "Behold, a dread, a great darkness, fell upon him" (Gen. 15:12). Yet there are many people who feel nothing when they perform mitzvot. Nevertheless, they too are like chariots of the Divine Presence when they engage in these acts. The fact that one does not feel does not prevent the connection, which is the wondrous union of the soul with God's infinite light, from being formed through the act of the mitzva.

הַמְמַלֵּא כָּל עָלְמִין, וּכְמוֹ שֶׁכָּתוּב: "גַּם חוֹשֶׁךְ לֹא יַחְשִׁיךְ מִמֶּךָּ" (תהלים קלט, יב). **which fills all worlds, as the verse states, "Even darkness does not darken for You"** (Ps. 139:12).

This union occurs with the infinite light, which has no limits. It is both beyond and inside every place, filling all of reality. Thus, nothing in reality can conceal or prevent it. Darkness and light are equal before the Creator. A person who "knows" and a person who does not "know" are both exactly the same distance away from holiness. However, while the one who knows feels the immense burden, the holiness and terror involved in his act, the one who does not know performs the mitzva as if he were carrying out any ordinary action. ☞

Thus, "Even darkness does not darken"; the union and connection formed by the mitzvot cannot be hampered by the "screen of physicality," or by the fact that the person is a boor or a beast. Furthermore, just as this is the case with regard to the union and pleasure of a mitzva, it is also true with regard to sin; the distance and disconnection that arise as the result of a transgression are present even if we do not feel the terror or pain of these matters. Every transgression harms the soul and cuts it off from its source, even if the person does not feel this. Just as dead flesh does not feel anything, and just as a fool has no sense of

---

WHEN IGNORANCE IS AN ASSET

☞ It is said that this lack of discernment is actually an asset, because it enables human beings to act. When a person performs a mitzva, he is intimately connected to the most elevated and supernal entity. If that individual were not in the "dark," if he were able to "see," he would not be able to act. Only very few people are able to know what they are doing, yet act as if they do not know. God commands Moses to tell Aaron, "When you kindle the lamps, the seven lamps shall illuminate toward the front of the candelabrum" (Deut. 8:2), and the next verse states, "Aaron did so" (Deut. 8:3). Rashi explains, "This comes to praise Aaron, who did as he was commanded and did not change anything." The hasidim ask what is so impressive about this; after all, no one would have thought that Aaron would have done something different from that which Moses had instructed him. They answer that Rashi's point is that if Moses had given these instructions to Rabbi Levi Yitzḥak of Berditchev, he would have spilled the oil, knocked over the candelabrum, and extinguished the lamps out of sheer excitement. While Aaron's level of elation must surely have been just as high as that of Rabbi Levi Yitzḥak of Berditchev, he nevertheless did not change a thing. Aaron's greatness is that although he could "see" (the letters of Aaron's name can be switched to make the word *nireh*, seen), he contained his excitement and did exactly as he was told. The highest level a person can reach is when he knows and feels everything, the Divine within all worlds and beyond all worlds, yet he can continue to live in the world. This challenge of continuing to live with the world is not a challenge that many people face; rather, it is an issue for a few select individuals in every generation. There were people in almost every generation who reached the point where they could no longer be involved with other people or with the physical world. The *Tanya*, however, like Asaf, addresses the entire Jewish people and relates to being a "boor" or a "beast," yet always being with God.

the consequences of his actions, a person can act in ways that hurt and sometimes even kill his soul, and not feel it.

וּבָזֶה יוּבָן חוֹמֶר עוֹנֶשׁ אִיסּוּר מְלָאכָה בְּשַׁבָּתוֹת וְחָמֵץ בְּפֶסַח, הַשָּׁוֶה לְכָל נֶפֶשׁ. **This enables understanding** why the **punishment** for violating **the prohibition of labor on the Sabbath and consuming leaven on Passover is equally severe for everyone.**

One who violates one of the Torah prohibitions that requires the severe punishments of stoning or *karet*, spiritual excision, will be liable for the relevant punishment, whether he is a great rabbi or an ignoramus. The punishment is the same for everyone, whether or not the person senses the severity of the prohibition and fears this terrible punishment.

לְפִי שֶׁאַף בְּנֶפֶשׁ בּוּר וְעַם הָאָרֶץ גָּמוּר מֵאִיר אוֹר קְדוּשַׁת שַׁבָּת וְיוֹם טוֹב, וְנִידּוֹן בְּנַפְשׁוֹ בְּכָרֵת וּסְקִילָה עַל חִילוּל קְדוּשָׁה זוֹ. That is **because the light of the holiness of the Sabbath and the festival illuminates even the soul of a boor and total ignoramus, and** therefore even **his soul is condemned to** *karet*, **excision, and stoning, for desecrating this holiness.**

One receives *karet* if he violates the prohibition against eating leaven on Passover, and stoning if he desecrates the Sabbath by performing labor on that day. The holiness that is felt by a tzaddik on the Sabbath is vastly different from that which is felt by an ordinary person, and certainly that which is felt by an ignoramus. Rabbi Ḥayyim of Chernovitz, author of *Siddduro shel Shabbat*, was said to have grown an entire head taller every Sabbath; his weekday clothes and his Sabbath clothes were entirely different sizes. On the other hand, there are those for whom the Sabbath is like any other day. Essentially, however, the holiness of the Sabbath is divine, whether one is an ignoramus or a tzaddik; anyone who performs labor on the Sabbath desecrates it, regardless of what he feels.

וְגַם מַשֶּׁהוּ חָמֵץ, אוֹ טִלְטוּל מוּקְצֶה, פּוֹגֵם בַּקְּדוּשָׁה שֶׁעַל **Even** consuming **a miniscule amount of leaven** on Passover **or moving** some

נַפְשׁוֹ, כְּמוֹ בִּקְדוּשַׁת נֶפֶשׁ הַצַּדִּיק, כִּי תּוֹרָה אַחַת לְכוּלָּנוּ. thing *muktze* (set aside) on the Sabbath **blemishes the holiness of his soul in the same way** it blemishes the holiness of the tzaddik's soul, for there is one Torah for us all.

These are rabbinic prohibitions and do not result in stoning or *karet*,[17] yet an ignoramus who violates them still blemishes the holiness of his soul.[18] "There is one Torah for us all," because in a way we are all equal in Torah. The objective connection established by the Torah, whereby the divine soul becomes attached to divine holiness when a mitzva is performed, and detached from it when the person sins, is not conditional on the individual's feelings. The difference between a tzaddik and someone else, between a person on a higher level and one on a lower level, does not lie in this connection, but in one's sensitivity to its existence or absence. A tzaddik, who lives life on a high plane, and whose entire existence is love and fear of God,[19] feels the pain of separation from the Divine in its full, real, tangible sense, while someone else might feel it only slightly or not at all. Nevertheless, no matter what a person feels, it is just a feeling, his reaction to the matter. The connection itself, however, is what the Torah takes from God, before whom all are equal. In this respect, "There is one Torah for us all," not one for the tzaddikim and a different one for the simple people.

וּמַה שֶּׁכָּתוּב "בְּהֵמוֹת" (תהלים עג, כב), לְשׁוֹן רַבִּים, **(That which the verse** cited above **uses the plural, "beasts"** [Ps. 73:22],

The verse begins in the singular form: "I am a boor, unknowing," so why does it go on to use the plural form of the word "beast," *behemot*?

---

17. The Lubavitcher Rebbe, Rabbi Menaḥem Mendel Schneerson, notes that this accords with the ruling in *Shulḥan Arukh HaRav* (308, 447), also written by the author of the *Tanya*.
18. Rabbinic prohibitions, too, apply equally to tzaddikim and ignoramuses (the Lubavitcher Rebbe, Rabbi Menaḥem Mendel Schneerson).
19. See *Iggeret HaKodesh*, epistle 27.

לְרַמֵּז כִּי לְפָנָיו יִתְבָּרֵךְ, גַּם בְּחִינַת דַּעַת הָעֶלְיוֹן, הַכּוֹלֵל חֶסֶד וּגְבוּרָה, נִדְמָה כִּבְהֵמוֹת וַעֲשִׂיָּיה גּוּפָנִית לְגַבֵּי אוֹר אֵין סוֹף, alludes to the fact that before the blessed One, even the level of higher knowledge, which includes Ḥesed and Gevura, is also deemed to be on the level of "beasts" and corporeal action relative to the light of Ein Sof,

We, in our suffering and exile, are considered mindless beasts who do the mitzvot without the knowledge required to feel their essence and importance. Moreover, the higher knowledge of the world of *Atzilut*, which is the inner essence of the higher attributes, including higher love and fear, is deemed to be on the same level as our knowledge. This higher knowledge is likened to our knowledge, for despite the tremendous difference between them, both are like "beasts" with regard to God. This is why *behemot* is written in the plural form, for there is an additional type of beast above, which is just like the one below.

כְּמוֹ שֶׁכָּתוּב: "כֻּלָּם בְּחָכְמָה עָשִׂיתָ" (תהלים קד, כד). as it is written, "With wisdom have You made them all" [Ps. 104:24].

The expression "With wisdom have You made" (rather than "With wisdom have You thought") is understood as being like "With a hoe have You made": not as God's instrument of thought but as His instrument of deed. Relative to God, the divine wisdom in *Atzilut* and in the world of physical action are on the same level. The distinctions we make within our own microcosm between our intellect and our senses of sight and touch are from His standpoint insignificant. It is like when a person looks down at all the small objects below him; he does not distinguish or consider the differences between them. There are vast differences between the influenza virus and the common cold virus, but from the perspective of a human looking at them, these hierarchical distinctions have no meaning. The same is true of all the worlds with respect to God. Since He made them all with wisdom, all successive levels, including higher wisdom, belong to the realm that is by analogy like deeds for us.

וְנִקְרָא "בְּהֵמָה רַבָּה", This level is referred to as the "Great Beast,"

This higher "beast" is on the level of the attributes in the *sefira* of *Keter*, Crown, which are drawn into supernal *Da'at*. In its root, it is even higher than the world of *Atzilut*.

כְּמוֹ שֶׁנִּתְבָּאֵר בְּמָקוֹם אַחֵר (לִיקוּטֵי תּוֹרָה, וַיִּקְרָא לג, ד), וְהוּא שֵׁם ב״ן, בְּגִימַטְרִיָּא בְּהֵמָ״ה, — as explained elsewhere [*Likkutei Torah*, Lev. 35d]. It corresponds to the divine name *Ban*, which has the numerical value of the word *behema*,

The *gematria* of *Ban* is 52. *Ban* is a "full *gematria*" of the name of *Havaya*. A full *gematria*, or *milui*, is calculated when each letter in a word is itself written out as a full word. For example, the letter *alef* is spelled out as *alef, lamed, peh*. The letter *heh* can be spelled out in several ways, one of which is *heh-heh*. When it is spelled that way, the "full *gematria*" of the name of *Havaya* is 52. (The Kabbala enumerates four ways to spell the name *Havaya*, having the numerical values of 72, 63, 52, and 45.)

שֶׁלִּפְנֵי הָאֲצִילוּת.] — which precedes the world of *Atzilut*.)

The level of the "great beast" is exceedingly high, even higher than the world of *Atzilut*. (*Atzilut* corresponds to humanity, *adam*, whose *gematria* is 45, *mem-heh*, which is a *milui* of the name of *Havaya*.) This higher level, which is above wisdom and which precedes the world of *Atzilut*, is called "beast" just like the lowly human, who resides in the physical world and who is called a boor and "like the beasts." Just as we are living in exile, forced into this lowly realm, the rest of existence is also intrinsically closed off and incapable of understanding the Divine.

However, another aspect of this reality is that precisely for this reason, it is possible for a lowly human, even one who knows nothing, to achieve connection to God. Since from God's perspective there is no difference between the great worlds and the small worlds, between the most lofty and the most lowly, He can dwell among us. The impediment to understanding how the Infinite One can dwell in a human being who is a boor and like the beasts does not stem from an understanding of divine greatness, but rather from an inability to understand it. With regard to finite greatness, there is a difference between great and small.

Thus, while one may be able to understand that God is occupied with the Milky Way, he may not be able to comprehend that it is also important to God whether an individual made a blessing after he drank a glass of milk. However, when we are able to grasp that God's greatness is beyond all measure, there is no longer a difference between great and small, between a heavenly beast and an earthly beast, or between the bacteria found in one drop of water and the stars in all the cosmos. Thus, one can understand that it is possible for God to descend and dwell among us, and it is possible for us to be intimately embraced while also being unable to grasp what that means. This is similar to a baby, who is embraced and loved by its mother, despite, or even because of the fact that it has no understanding of the essence of their connection, nor of the meaning of the embraces and kisses: "Like a weaned child with its mother, like a weaned child is my soul" (Ps. 131:2).

The phrase "I am like the beasts, yet I am always with God" contains the two extremes upon which this chapter is based. At the beginning, the chapter was concerned with the "straight path," awakening love for God by means of a basic principle of the soul and of all reality: "As water reflects a face to the face, so does the heart of a person to a person." This is the principle of "measure for measure," basic gratitude toward whoever has done good for him. This principle is so natural that it does not require deep reflection or elevation; one needs only to pay attention to it. A person must only look at the face in the water, so to speak, in order to awaken within himself the most basic, profound love for God. The central part of the chapter dealt with the description and explanation of the objects of this process. This is referring not only to "contemplation" of the holiness of the mitzvot, the supernal union, and the extraordinary connection that is formed through the fulfillment of a mitzva. Rather, it also includes a comparison: "Who am I? From what place did God take me out, bringing me toward closeness, embracing, and kissing?" Tremendous love for God arises on the "straight path" from between these two extremes, the fact that He both brought us out of Egypt and gave us the Torah.

Chapter 47

THE PREVIOUS CHAPTER DESCRIBED A TYPE OF DIVINE service that is based on innate human nature: the way of "As water reflects a face to the face, so does the heart of a person to a person" (Prov. 27:19). This is the way of "measure for measure," of gratitude that increases in accordance with the level of the giver and the act of giving itself. The way to awaken this type of love for God is to contemplate the fact that He, the King of kings, came down and took us out of Egypt, the land of shame, and brought us especially close to Him, forming a deep connection with us by giving us the Torah and the mitzvot. The greatest obstacle to serving God in this way is that His love for us that was revealed through the exodus from Egypt is too distant from people's daily lives to arouse emotion since it is an image from ancient history, of a reality that existed thousands of years ago. As such, it is difficult to internalize this on a personal level such that it elicits emotion. This chapter will explain how the description of the exodus and the giving of the Torah is actually a description of the daily personal reality of every single individual.

וְהִנֵּה בְּכָל דּוֹר וָדוֹר וְכָל יוֹם וָיוֹם חַיָּיב אָדָם לִרְאוֹת עַצְמוֹ כְּאִילּוּ הוּא יָצָא הַיּוֹם מִמִּצְרָיִם. **In each and every generation, every single day, a person must view himself as though he** personally **left Egypt today.**

13 Iyar
10 Iyar (leap year)

The exodus from Egypt was not just a one-time historical event; rather, it is a perpetual experience that occurs, in a spiritual sense, in every generation, every day, within every human being. Therefore, each day, one must once again see himself as though he left Egypt that day,[1] and not only that, but he should experience an actual "exodus from Egypt"; one must "depart from Egypt" in some way every day. It is not always the same "Egypt" (*Mitzrayim*), but every day, a person faces certain constraints [*metzarim*] and limitations from which he needs to emerge. ☞

וְהִיא יְצִיאַת נֶפֶשׁ הָאֱלוֹהִית מִמַּאֲסַר הַגּוּף, מִשְׁכָא דְחִוְיָא, This refers to the exodus of the divine soul from imprisonment in the body, the serpent's skin,

The human body is the skin of the primordial serpent. It is the *kelippa* (literally, "husk," a term to connote a force for evil) of the serpent that exists within a person, imprisoning the soul, enveloping it, and concealing the Divine from it. Humans are on different levels in terms of the dominance of the body over the soul. Nevertheless, simply by virtue of a person's being inside a body, he is subordinate to, and enslaved by, corporeal conceptions. These are associated with the body's sensory systems, through which a person perceives everything, including spiritual forces. In this matter, there is no variation between people. Even a great, righteous person is always confined within his sensory organs. Nevertheless, the idea that the body's perception is limited does not refer only to its external, sensory organs; rather, the soul itself, and its

RECEIVING THE TORAH EVERY DAY

☞ A similar statement is made with regard to the giving of the Torah: One should receive it anew every day (see Rashi, Deut. 26:16). The question arises: If we already received the Torah once, why do we need to receive it again? Likewise, if we already left Egypt once, why do we need to leave it again every day? The answer is that today, we need to receive the Torah on a different level, and we should not be satisfied with the Torah we received in the past. The same is true with regard to the exodus. Before, we emerged from *metzarim* (constraints) of particular types and magnitudes, but now, there are different *metzarim* that we need to leave behind. Even if a person already left Egypt, if he does not leave again today, but remains as he is, continuing with the same habits and ways of thinking, then he is still in Egypt. Everyone is constantly growing and being renewed, so what was once the "exodus" for a particular individual is no longer enough.

---

1. The source of this is Mishna *Pesaḥim* 10:5.

desires, thoughts, and experiences, are limited, enslaved to the body's physical perception of the world. The soul desires, thinks, and experiences through the body. The body does not necessarily tend toward doing evil, but it dims the light of the soul. The soul can comprehend the spiritual realm only through the body, and this involves a certain degree of darkness. As Rambam says in his *Introduction to Avot*: Just as a blind man cannot comprehend the concept of color, a person who has been placed inside a body cannot comprehend spiritual reality.

This imprisonment is the personal "Egyptian exile" of the soul that has been placed inside the body. The physical reality limits, envelops, and conceals the soul and its domain. It conceals the infinite Divine from the soul and purports to be a real, tangible entity in itself. The divine soul's exodus is thus an exodus from all "*metzarim*." Furthermore, it applies at all times, for every day constitutes a new constraint from which one must emerge. ☞

לִיכָּלֵל בְּיִחוּד אוֹר אֵין סוֹף בָּרוּךְ הוּא עַל יְדֵי עֵסֶק הַתּוֹרָה וְהַמִּצְוֹת **in order to become incorporated within the unity of the light of *Ein Sof*, blessed be He.** This is achieved **through engaging in Torah** study **and** performing **mitzvot,**

When a person performs a mitzva, this constitutes his "exodus" from the constraints that appear to differentiate between the external world and the Divine. When one engages in God's Torah and mitzvot, he identifies and unites with God, for the words of the Torah are God's, and

---

SERPENT'S SKIN

☞ This refers to the garment of *kelippa* that Adam received after the sin of the tree of knowledge, which happened because of the primordial serpent. Since then, every human being, as a result of being in this world, is placed in this garment, which includes the body, the animal soul, and the entire material world. It is also called *kelippat noga*, a glowing husk, which contains both good and evil from the tree of knowledge of good and evil. Evidently, before the sin, the soul was not inside a garment of *kelippa*, but instead wore a holy, heavenly garment, and only after the serpent caused Adam to sin was he placed in this garment. Therefore, it is called the serpent's skin (see also chap. 45).

the mitzvot are commanded by Him. At that moment, the divine soul fulfills itself, for it is a part of God above, and now, it unites with Him.

בִּכְלָל, in general,

Every engagement with Torah and mitzvot contains an element of "leaving" the physical experience and this world, and connecting with God.

וּבִפְרָט בְּקַבָּלַת מַלְכוּת שָׁמַיִם בִּקְרִיאַת שְׁמַע, שֶׁבָּהּ מְקַבֵּל וּמַמְשִׁיךְ עָלָיו יִחוּדוֹ יִתְבָּרֵךְ בְּפֵירוּשׁ, בְּאָמְרוֹ: "ה' אֱלֹהֵינוּ ה' אֶחָד" (דברים ו, ד). and particularly through accepting the kingship of Heaven while reciting the *Shema*, in which he accepts and draws upon himself God's unity explicitly, when he says, "The Lord is our God, the Lord is One" (Deut. 6:4).

One's daily recitation of the *Shema* is his daily exodus from Egypt. This involves more than just remembering the exodus; it constitutes a true return to the exodus. When a person accepts God's kingship upon himself in the *Shema*, he also openly and consciously accepts upon himself, to the extent that he is able, freedom from worldly limitations and *metzarim*. The spiritual orientation of the *Shema* is the same as that of the exodus from Egypt. It involves emerging from oneself, rising up from the world of matter, multiplicity, and separation, and entering the realm of oneness, where boundaries are transcended.

וּכְמוֹ שֶׁנִּתְבָּאֵר לְעֵיל כִּי 'אֱלֹהֵינוּ' הוּא כְּמוֹ "אֱלֹהֵי אַבְרָהָם" וְכוּ' This has the same implication as explained above (chap. 46), whereby the words "our God" in the *Shema* have the same connotation as the phrase "God of Abraham...."

The possessive pronoun "our God" should be understood in the same way as the phrase "God of Abraham," which connects God to Abraham in the most complete way. This constitutes the most perfect level of connection and union. It is called the level of the "chariot," for it is as though the chariot is nullified to the rider, and they become one and the same, such that Abraham is the divine attribute of Ḥesed, Kindness, and the divine attribute of Ḥesed is Abraham.

לְפִי שֶׁהָיָה בָּטֵל וְנִכְלָל בְּיִחוּד אוֹר אֵין סוֹף בָּרוּךְ הוּא. **He is called "God of Abraham" because** Abraham **was subsumed and incorporated within the unity of the light of** *Ein Sof,* **blessed be He.**

The term "God of Abraham" can be used only when the man Abraham no longer exists as a separate entity. His entire being is continuously and utterly nullified to the divine unity, and is nothing but a means of expression for the divine essence and its greatness.

רַק שֶׁאַבְרָהָם זָכָה לָזֶה בְּמַעֲשָׂיו, The **only** difference is **that Abraham merited this through his deeds,**

Abraham merited this through his own deeds, and not by virtue of divine enlightenment from above. This means that his entire personality and being were subsumed. His nullification was not related to a particular act (a mitzva) and to the specific time when it was carried out, which is the case when an ordinary person is subsumed, as will be explained below.

וְהִילּוּכוֹ בַּקּוֹדֶשׁ מִמַּדְרֵגָה לְמַדְרֵגָה, כְּמוֹ שֶׁכָּתוּב: "וַיִּסַּע אַבְרָם הָלוֹךְ וְנָסוֹעַ" וְגוֹ' (בראשית יב, ט). **and his progressing in holiness from level to level, as the verse states, "Abram journeyed, steadily journeying to the Negev"** (Gen. 12:9),

Abraham's external journeys, which are described in the Torah, are also his internal journeys, his soul's progress from one level to the next as he moves deeper toward the love[2] in his divine soul. Abraham journeys

---

2. This is symbolized by Abraham's journey "to the Negev." North and south correspond to right and left, and in the *sefirot*, to Ḥesed and Gevura (Restraint). When one stands facing east, the south (Negev) is to his right and the north is to his left.

closer and closer to the essence of divine Ḥesed until he unites with it and becomes its "chariot," and his entire essence and personality are only a vessel for the revelation of the Divine Presence through Ḥesed. Abraham was not born a "chariot," nor did he receive this attribute as a gift; he achieved it through hard work and "journeying to the Negev."

אֲבָל אֲנַחְנוּ, יְרוּשָׁה וּמַתָּנָה הִיא לָנוּ, שֶׁנָּתַן לָנוּ אֶת תּוֹרָתוֹ, וְהִלְבִּישׁ בָּהּ רְצוֹנוֹ וְחָכְמָתוֹ יִתְבָּרַךְ, whereas for us it is an inheritance and gift. For God gave us His Torah and enclothed within it His will and wisdom,

When we reach the level of God being "our God," it is not by virtue of our own work. God gave us His Torah, the expression of His essence, in a vessel that we are able to receive, understand, and even touch. This is what is meant by "enclothing"; the divine will and wisdom are enclothed in the Torah like a person who leaves his house and shows himself to others with clothes on his body. The nature of clothing is that it both conceals and reveals; it conceals the inner essence and reveals that which the other can comprehend. Another example is that of a parable. Like a garment, a parable allows the message to be revealed, yet at the same time, it does fully reveal that which it explains. Thus, the Torah is the "ancient proverb" (I Sam. 24:13),[3] a parable of the most ancient One, God. Like clothing, the Torah reveals to us only certain, superficial images; however, the actual will and wisdom of God are enclothed within these images.

God's supernal will and wisdom are beyond the bounds of comprehension, yet we are able to relate to the will and wisdom in the Torah. One cannot ignite his soul with the supernal divine light which "rested from all His works" (Gen. 2:3). Certain virtuous individuals merit to receive a light that is somewhat similar to this. However, even a young girl can light Sabbath candles. This marvel is expressed in the form of the letter *alef*: There is a *yod* at the top and a *yod* at the bottom, and a slanting line that joins them. The top and bottom signify the wisdom of above and the wisdom of below, the upper waters and the lower waters, and the beginning and end of an act. The line that connects

---

3. See *Torah Or* 98b.

them is the observance of a mitzva, when a person willingly accepts God's kingship.

הַמְיֻחָדִים בְּמַהוּתוֹ וְעַצְמוּתוֹ	which are unified with His essence
יִתְבָּרֵךְ בְּתַכְלִית הַיִּחוּד. וַהֲרֵי זֶה	and being in absolute union. Thus,
כְּאִלּוּ נָתַן לָנוּ אֶת עַצְמוֹ כִּבְיָכוֹל,	it is as though He gave us His self, so to speak.

The divine will and wisdom that are enclothed in the Torah are not merely will and wisdom in their highest form; they are actually unified with God's essence. "The giving of the Torah" refers to the gift that God included within the Torah: His own will and wisdom, and His desire and longing for the world. In fact, His very self may be found there.[4]

| כְּמוֹ שֶׁכָּתוּב בַּזֹּהַר הַקָּדוֹשׁ (חלק ב קמ, ב) עַל פָּסוּק "וְיִקְחוּ לִי תְּרוּמָה" (שמות כה, ב) [דְּ"לִי", כְּלוֹמַר אוֹתִי, וַהֲוָה לֵיהּ לוֹמַר: 'וּתְרוּמָה', אֶלָּא מִשּׁוּם דְּכוֹלָא חַד, עַיֵּין שָׁם הֵיטֵב]. | As it states in the holy *Zohar* (2:140b) regarding the verse, "They shall take for Me [*li*] a gift," (Ex. 25:2) (that the word "*li*" here means "Me," and not "for Me." Accordingly, the verse should have stated "Take Me and a gift," inserting the word "and." However, it did not, because God and the Torah are all one. Study it there well.) |

According to this interpretation, the verse actually states, "They shall take Me [and] a gift" since the verse does not include the word "and." Consequently, there is only one matter here: the mitzva. Taking a gift to God is the act of the mitzva, and since His will and wisdom that are enclothed in the Torah are unified with His essence, the act involved in this mitzva essentially equates taking God Himself.[5]

---

4. See *Likkutei Torah*, Num. 48d, which explains the Sages' words in *Shabbat* 105a: "[The word] *anokhi* [that begins the Ten Commandments is an] abbreviation [for]: I myself wrote [and] gave [*ana nafshi ketivat yehavit*]" (the Lubavitcher Rebbe, Rabbi Menaḥem Mendel Schneerson). See also *Degel Maḥaneh Efrayim* 431, s.v. "*vekatavta*." This idea is brought in several places in the name of the *Ba'al Shem Tov*. See Also *Meor Einayim, Yitro*.

5. The *Zohar* (3:179a) explains that "gift" is a reference to the Torah. Accordingly,

וְזֶה שֶׁכָּתוּב: "וַתִּתֶּן לָנוּ ה' אֱלֹהֵינוּ בְּאַהֲבָה" כו', "כִּי בְאוֹר פָּנֶיךָ נָתַתָּ לָנוּ ה' אֱלֹהֵינוּ" כו'.

This is the meaning of **what is recited** in the liturgy of the festivals, "**You gave us Lord our God with love...**" and in the prayer of the eighteen blessings, "**For in the light of Your countenance You gave us Lord our God....**"

Consequently, one should understand these phrases as follows: "You granted us that the Lord will be our God, with love," and, "For in the light of Your countenance You granted us that the Lord would be our God." The greatest possible gift from God is His being "our God." This gift is "living Torah." Since the Torah, which is His will and wisdom, is truly unified with His essence and being, the giving of the Torah essentially means that God gives Himself to us.

וְלָזֶה אֵין מוֹנֵעַ לָנוּ מִדְּבֵיקוּת הַנֶּפֶשׁ בְּיִחוּדוֹ וְאוֹרוֹ יִתְבָּרֵךְ, אֶלָּא הָרָצוֹן. שֶׁאִם אֵין הָאָדָם רוֹצֶה כְּלָל חַס וְשָׁלוֹם לִדְבֵקָה בּוֹ כו',

Therefore, nothing can prevent our soul from bonding with God's unity and light except our will, such as if a person has no desire at all, God forbid, to bond with Him, etc.

When God gave us the Torah, the barrier that separated the upper worlds from the lower worlds, and God from the world, was eradicated.[6] Since that time, the wall between us and God is no longer an objective, real barrier, but one that is made of our lack of will. God does not compel us to unite with Him; rather, He sanctifies us, making us truly one with Him, only when we willingly choose to observe His mitzvot.

אֲבָל מִיָּד שֶׁרוֹצֶה וּמְקַבֵּל וּמַמְשִׁיךְ עָלָיו אֱלֹהוּתוֹ יִתְבָּרֵךְ, וְאוֹמֵר: "ה' אֱלֹהֵינוּ ה' אֶחָד" (דברים ו, ד), הֲרֵי מִמֵּילָא נִכְלֶלֶת נַפְשׁוֹ בְּיִחוּדוֹ יִתְבָּרֵךְ,

Nevertheless, the moment he desires it and accepts and draws upon himself God's divinity, reciting, "**The Lord is our God, the Lord is One**" (Deut. 6:4), his soul is automatically incorporated into God's unity,

---

the verse means: Take Me by means of a gift, the Torah, for the Torah and God's essence are one (*Likkutei Biurim*).

6. See *Kohelet Rabba* 3:17.

This occurs as soon as a person associates himself with God, who is one. Since the individual wants it, the door is opened, and since he is doing nothing to block it, there is no longer any barrier between him and God.

דְּרוּחַ אַיְיתֵי רוּחַ וְאַמְשִׁיךְ רוּחַ (זוהר ח"ב, קסב, ב). **as spirit** from below **evokes spirit** from above **and draws forth spirit** (*Zohar* 2:162b).

The way a person relates to others influences how those others relate to him. Likewise, through discovering and through doing God's will, he draws down the revelation of God's will. When a person willingly accepts what God wants from him and affirms his acceptance of God's kingship, God's will and his own will become one.

וְהִיא בְּחִינַת יְצִיאַת מִצְרַיִם. **This constitutes a form of leaving Egypt.**

Desiring and accepting the divine will, and connecting with the Divine, is a spiritual form of leaving Egypt. Connecting to God, who is one, means being freed from all other ties. This connection releases the divine soul from its imprisonment in the body and in the world.

וְלָכֵן תִּקְנוּ פָּרָשַׁת יְצִיאַת מִצְרַיִם בִּשְׁעַת קְרִיאַת שְׁמַע דַּוְוקָא, אַף שֶׁהִיא מִצְוָה בִּפְנֵי עַצְמָהּ וְלֹא מִמִּצְוֹת קְרִיאַת שְׁמַע, **That is why** the Sages **specifically instituted** reciting **the passage** of remembering **the exodus from Egypt while reciting the *Shema*, even though** remembering the exodus **is a mitzva in its own right and not** a component **of the mitzva of reciting the *Shema*,**

The main part of the mitzva of reciting the *Shema* is the first two passages, where it is explicitly stated that one must say these verses every day, morning and evening. Remembering the exodus from Egypt, which is mentioned in the passage that deals with the *tzitzit*, is a separate positive commandment that is seemingly unrelated to the recitation of the *Shema*.

כְּדְאִיתָא בַּגְּמָרָא (ברכות יב, ב; כא, א) וּפוֹסְקִים (על שולחן ערוך אורח חיים סימן סז), אֶלָּא מִפְּנֵי שֶׁהֵן דָּבָר אֶחָד מַמָּשׁ.

as stated in the Talmud (*Berakhot* 12b, 21a) and by the halakhic **authorities** (*Shulḥan Arukh, Oraḥ Ḥayyim* 67), **nevertheless**, the Sages linked them, **because they actually comprise a single concept.**

The exodus and the recitation of the *Shema* comprise a single concept. The only boundaries between a Jew and God are those that are formed by the person's will, or, in the words of the prophet, "Your iniquities have been separating between you and your God" (Isa. 59:2). If a person desires it and is willing to accept it upon himself, he can leave Egypt. Consequently, the recitation of the *Shema*, which constitutes the acceptance of the yoke of God's kingship and the expression of one's desire to cling to Him, is itself the equivalent of the exodus, the soul's breaking free of its constraints.

וְכֵן בְּסוֹף פָּרָשַׁת יְצִיאַת מִצְרַיִם, מְסַיֵּים גַּם כֵּן: "אֲנִי ה' אֱלֹהֵיכֶם" (במדבר טו, מא). וְהַיְינוּ, גַּם כֵּן כְּמוֹ שֶׁנִּתְבָּאֵר לְעֵיל.

Accordingly, the end of the passage of the exodus from Egypt also concludes with the same theme as the *Shema*: **"I am the Lord your God"** (Num. 15:21). **This should also** be understood **as was explained above.**

As mentioned above, the exodus is mentioned in the passage of the *Shema* that deals with the *tzitzit* (ritual fringes). The exodus from Egypt, and the connection to the Divine wherein God is "your God," are literally one concept.

This chapter dealt entirely with one point, which extends and completes what was explained in the previous chapter. The previous chapter dealt with love "as water reflects a face to the face"; when a person contemplates God's love for him, this awakens his love for God within him. This chapter emphasized the individual's contemplation of God's love for him. In every generation, within every person, and every single day, there is a renewed expression of the greatest revelation of God's love, which occurred at the exodus from Egypt. God brought us out of Egypt and gave us His Torah, and since that time, the revelation of this matter to the individual, in a way that is capable of moving the soul, depends only on the individual himself. When one accepts the yoke of God's kingship upon himself through the recitation of "Hear, Israel: The Lord is our God, the Lord is one," a door is opened, giving the person a chance to see God's love. He can see that God delivered him from all the difficulties and limitations he has faced, brought him close with the greatest closeness and connection. After this discovery of God's love for him, an exceedingly strong love of God will be awakened within him, too, like the reflection of a face in the water. He will feel it with all his heart, soul, and might.

Chapter 48

THE PREVIOUS CHAPTERS FOCUSED ON LOVE OF GOD as a person's response to God's love for him: "as water reflects a face to the face" (Prov. 27:19). This love is evoked in the same way that the reflection in a mirror shows the image of the face before it. In the face of God's love, the kindness and good that He bestows on a person, love for God is awakened in the individual, as well as gratitude and a desire to be close to Him in turn. In light of this, to achieve love of God, a person must contemplate God's love for him. The intensity of this love as a result of such contemplation can be understood when compared to the love of a human king: The greater the king, and the lower and more limited the level of the individual, and the greater the kindness the king does for him, the more intense and powerful the love that the individual will feel toward the king.

In chapter 47, the nature of this contemplation revolved around the kindness of God involved in the exodus from Egypt and the giving of the Torah and the close relationship with the Divine that resulted from these momentous events. In this chapter, the author of the *Tanya* will focus on the contemplation of God's greatness and the nature of His eternity and the infinite light that emanates from Him, a light that fills and encompasses all worlds.

As stated in the previous chapters, such contemplation is not meant to be merely theoretical or even deeply emotional. It should result in a practical outcome: Just as God constricts His infinite powers in order to connect with us, we too are expected to constrain our impulses and desires out of our love for Him. We should be ready and willing to limit our desires to the point of total self-sacrifice for the sake of our all-encompassing love of God.

14 Iyar
11 Iyar (leap year)

וְהִנֵּה כַּאֲשֶׁר יִתְבּוֹנֵן הַמַּשְׂכִּיל בִּגְדוּלַּת אֵין סוֹף בָּרוּךְ הוּא, כִּי כִּשְׁמוֹ כֵּן הוּא, אֵין סוֹף וְאֵין קֵץ וְתַכְלִית כְּלָל לָאוֹר וְחַיּוּת הַמִּתְפַּשֵּׁט מִמֶּנּוּ יִתְבָּרֵךְ בִּרְצוֹנוֹ הַפָּשׁוּט,

When the intelligent person reflects on the greatness of *Ein Sof*, blessed be He, he will realize that as His name implies, so is He. Namely, God is **infinite, and there is no end or limit whatsoever to the light and light force that emanate from God's simple will,**

In Hebrew, the name of an object expresses its essence, and this is the case with regard to God's name as well. The name *Ein Sof*, which connotes the Infinite One, is an expression of God's essence in relation to the world. The name constitutes the light and life force that He issues forth to the countless worlds and this light is like God Himself: infinite and without any limit whatsoever. ☞

וּמְיוּחָד בְּמַהוּתוֹ וְעַצְמוּתוֹ יִתְבָּרֵךְ בְּתַכְלִית הַיִּחוּד.

which is united with His essence and being in perfect unity.

The light and life force emanate from God's will, which has no limitations or any particular form. Unlike the will of a human being, the will of God, who is omnipotent and infinite, is not limited in any way and it is inseparable from Him. Like God Himself, His name and His will are infinite.

NO END OR LIMIT

☞ This description, that there is "no end or limit whatsoever to the light and life force," negates any possibility of limitation in quantity, size, intensity, or any other aspect. The concept of infinity is found in other contexts, but there it is always limited in some way. In mathematics, for example, the concept of infinity has specific properties that define it. Although in one sense infinity is a number or a set of numbers that can continue indefinitely, in other ways it is limited by its very definition. Yet the infinite light of *Ein Sof* truly has no end or limit of any kind.

CHAPTER 48

וְאִילּוּ הָיְתָה הִשְׁתַּלְשְׁלוּת הָעוֹלָמוֹת מֵאוֹר אֵין סוֹף בָּרוּךְ הוּא, בְּלִי צִמְצוּמִים, **Had the worlds devolved from the light of *Ein Sof*, blessed be He, without constrictions,**

There is an inherent difference, a gap that cannot be bridged, between the light of *Ein Sof* and the created beings, between the infinite and the finite. For the finite worlds to have been brought into existence, for them to be able to receive the life from *Ein Sof*, who is infinite, there had to have been constrictions of that light as it descended through the worlds. The light of *Ein Sof*, by definition, shines unrestrained, without boundaries, while created beings, by nature, have limits. Without constrictions, the creation could not possibly have contained the light.

רַק כְּסֵדֶר הַמַּדְרֵגוֹת מִמַּדְרֵגָה לְמַדְרֵגָה, בְּדֶרֶךְ עִלָּה וְעָלוּל, לֹא הָיָה הָעוֹלָם הַזֶּה נִבְרָא כְּלָל כְּמוֹ שֶׁהוּא עַתָּה בִּבְחִינַת גְּבוּל וְתַכְלִית, **but according to a sequence of levels, descending from level to level by means of cause and effect, this world would not have been created in its current limited and finite state at all,**

In a causal system, there is always a direct relationship between the cause and the effect. This is the implication of the term *hishtalshelut* that the author of the *Tanya* uses here in reference to the devolvement of the worlds, which shares a root with the Hebrew word for chain, *shalshelet*. Such a system is like a chain in which each link is joined to the next, and there are no breaks between the highest link and the lowest.[1] If the worlds had devolved from *Ein Sof* without qualitative leaps from one state of reality to a completely different state of reality, without undergoing any concealments, but only by means of a direct causal progression maintaining one state of reality, the process of devolvement would not have resulted in the formation of this finite world.

---

1. See *Likkutei Torah*, Song 42b.

מֵהָאָרֶץ לָרָקִיעַ - מַהֲלַךְ ת"ק שָׁנָה. וְכֵן בֵּין כָּל רָקִיעַ לְרָקִיעַ וְכֵן עוֹבִי כָּל רָקִיעַ וְרָקִיעַ. | where the walking distance from the earth to the firmament is five hundred years, and the same distance exists between each and every one of the firmaments, and so too is the thickness of each and every one of the firmaments.

Our world has boundaries on all sides. It is a realm of physical space and dimensions. As the Sages describe it, the distance from the earth to the firmament is distance one would walk for five hundred years; so is the distance from one firmament to the next, as well as the thickness of each firmament.[2] This distance is extremely far, yet it is still measurable, specific, and limited. The realities of all the worlds are likewise measurable and limited. The expanses that the Talmud describes are certainly beyond the grasp of the physical, human senses, and one will struggle to comprehend such dimensions in physical terms. When the Talmud goes on to measure the feet and ankles of holy entities such as *ḥayot*, which are also a walking distance of five hundred years each, even that is not possible. It must be acknowledged, then, that even regarding the first measurements, the Sages refer not only to physical distances but also to dimensions beyond that which is physical, to spiritual realms, to the very highest planes of existence, which transcend the physical plane. Yet the fact that the Sages describe these realms with physical measurements shows that even these realms are finite.

וַאֲפִילוּ עוֹלָם הַבָּא וְגַן עֵדֶן הָעֶלְיוֹן, מְדוֹר נִשְׁמוֹת הַצַּדִּיקִים הַגְּדוֹלִים וְהַנְּשָׁמוֹת עַצְמָן, וְאֵין צָרִיךְ לוֹמַר הַמַּלְאָכִים, הֵן בִּבְחִינַת גְּבוּל וְתַכְלִית, | Even the World to Come and the higher level of the Garden of Eden, the dwelling place of the souls of the great tzaddikim, and even the souls themselves, and, needless to say, the angels are limited and finite,

The higher level of the Garden of Eden is the realm where the souls of the righteous bask in the radiance of the Divine Presence. Not only

---

2. See *Ḥagiga* 13a.

is this abode of these souls finite, but even the souls themselves are finite, and not only when enclothed in a body. The angels, which are on a lower level than these souls, are certainly finite.

כִּי יֵשׁ גְּבוּל לְהַשָּׂגָתָן בְּאוֹר אֵין סוֹף בָּרוּךְ הוּא, הַמֵּאִיר עֲלֵיהֶן בְּהִתְלַבְּשׁוּת חָכְמָה בִּינָה דַּעַת כו'.

for there is a limit to their apprehension of the light of *Ein Sof*, blessed be He, which shines on them through being enclothed in the *sefirot* of Ḥokhma, Bina, Da'at, and so forth.

The limitations of an angel do not fall into the same parameters with which we measure an area of land. Some variables are measured in kilometers; others are measured according to their weight, luminosity, or some other factor. Higher, spiritual beings, while abstract and limitless in terms of material definitions, are limited in other dimensions. Although they are not definable on a scale of centimeters, pounds, or seconds, they are limited with regard to the extent of their comprehension. Because there is a limit to their existence, there is a limit to their apprehension, and the limit of their comprehension is what determines the limit of their existence.

וְלָכֵן יֵשׁ גְּבוּל לַהֲנָאָתָן שֶׁנֶּהֱנִין מִזִּיו הַשְּׁכִינָה וּמִתְעַנְּגִין בְּאוֹר ה', כִּי אֵין יְכוֹלִין לְקַבֵּל הֲנָאָה וְתַעֲנוּג בִּבְחִינַת אֵין סוֹף מַמָּשׁ, שֶׁלֹּא יִתְבַּטְלוּ מִמְּצִיאוּתָן וְיַחְזְרוּ לִמְקוֹרָן.

Therefore, there is a limit to their pleasure as they enjoy the splendor of the Divine Presence and delight in the divine light, for they are not able to receive pleasure and delight at an actual infinite level without being nullified from their existence by returning to their source.

Since the angels and souls are essentially limited, they can comprehend and take pleasure only in a limited portion of the infinite divine light. Unable to grasp the infinite, they are unable to receive anything that is beyond their capacity to contain. Even the highest, most ethereal creatures have an upper limit in terms of how much they are able to comprehend. If they receive anything beyond that, they will be consumed.

The Talmud recounts that before God created human beings, He created a group of ministering angels and asked them, "Shall We make man in Our image?" (Gen. 1:26), and they answered, "What is a mortal that You remember him, a man that You take him into account?" (Ps. 8:5). At this, God stretched out His small finger among them and burned them with fire.[3]

Even the supernal angels, the creatures most remote from the physical realm, and with whom God even consulted, as it were, regarding the creation of humankind, cannot bear a level of enlightenment that is beyond their comprehension, even if it is no greater than the measure of one small finger. Certainly, then, all the other creatures, worlds, and souls endure only an extremely limited degree of illumination. Even if it seems immense from their perspective, it is greatly restricted with respect to God.

15 Iyar
12 Iyar
(leap year)

וְהִנֵּה פְּרָטִיּוּת הַצִּמְצוּמִים, אֵיךְ וּמָה, אֵין כָּאן מְקוֹם בֵּיאוּרָם,

While this is not the place to explain the intricate details of how the constrictions occurred and what their nature is,

The kabbalistic works explain some of the details of the constrictions and their progression from the infinite to the finite, including what occurred at each stage in the creation of the worlds. The *Tanya*, which is primarily meant to guide the individual in his divine service, does not attempt to explain these matters unless they are necessary for understanding the topic under discussion. Thus, the author of the *Tanya* mentions the constrictions here, not in order to explain this subject as a particular topic of theoretical study, but only in order to shed light on the subject at hand and to relate it to the topic of divine service.

אַךְ דֶּרֶךְ כְּלָל הֵן הֵם בְּחִינַת הֶסְתֵּר וְהֶעְלֵם הַמַּשְׁכַת הָאוֹר וְהַחַיּוּת שֶׁלֹּא יָאִיר וְיִמָּשֵׁךְ לַתַּחְתּוֹנִים בִּבְחִינַת גִּלּוּי לְהִתְלַבֵּשׁ וּלְהַשְׁפִּיעַ בָּהֶן וּלְהַחֲיוֹתָם, לִהְיוֹת יֵשׁ מֵאַיִן, כִּי אִם מְעַט מִזְעֵר אוֹר וְחַיּוּת,

nevertheless, in general they constitute that which conceals and hides the flow of light and life force so that the light and life force will not overtly radiate and flow to the lower creations. Rather, they are enclothed and channeled into them to grant them life so that they may be brought into

---

3. *Sanhedrin* 38b.

בִּכְדֵי שֶׁיִּהְיוּ בִּבְחִינַת גְּבוּל וְתַכְלִית. existence out of nothingness with only a minuscule amount of light and life force so that they will be limited and finite.

Through constriction, the transition from giver to receiver is by nature indirect and involves a leap from one state of reality to another. By contrast, the relationship between a cause and an effect is direct and constant.[4] Then there is always a relationship between the giver and the receiver, since they share the same state of being and the receiver is able to perceive the giver. Constriction, on the other hand, creates an immeasurable, essential gap between them because they are two entirely different realities.

Through the constriction, only a miniscule amount of light and life force pass from the Creator to His creations so that they are limited with respect to God, who is infinite and without limit.

שֶׁהִיא הָאָרָה מוּעֶטֶת מְאֹד וּמַמָּשׁ כְּלֹא חֲשִׁיבֵי לְגַבֵּי בְּחִינַת הָאָרָה בְּלִי גְבוּל וְתַכְלִית, וְאֵין בֵּינֵיהֶם עֵרֶךְ וְיַחַס כְּלָל. This is a minute illumination, which is considered literally as nothingness relative to the unlimited, infinite illumination, and there is no proportional relationship or point of reference between them whatsoever.

No relationship exists between the limited and the limitless. There is only empty space. On one side of the space, there is the creation, and on the other, the Creator. In the middle lies the mysteries of creation, of crossing from the infinite to the finite. This transition entails constriction and the leap from one state of being to another entirely different state of being so that there is no connection whatsoever between the two sides.

כַּנּוֹדָע פֵּירוּשׁ מִלַּת 'עֵרֶךְ' בְּמִסְפָּרִים, שֶׁאֶחָד בְּמִסְפָּר יֵשׁ לוֹ עֵרֶךְ לְגַבֵּי מִסְפָּר אֶלֶף אֲלָפִים, שֶׁהוּא חֵלֶק אֶחָד מִנֵּי אֶלֶף אֲלָפִים. As is known, the term "proportional value" with regard to numbers means, for example, that the number one relative to the number one million has a value of one millionth.

---

4. See *Iggeret HaKodesh*, epistle 20.

It is easy to determine the relative value of any two numbers. Although the difference between the number one and the number one million is extremely large, their values are still comparable. Each number is numerically related to every other number.

אֲבָל לְגַבֵּי דָּבָר שֶׁהוּא בִּבְחִינַת בְּלִי גְבוּל וּמִסְפָּר כְּלָל – אֵין כְּנֶגְדּוֹ שׁוּם עֵרֶךְ בְּמִסְפָּרִים. שֶׁאֲפִילוּ אֶלֶף אַלְפֵי אֲלָפִים וְרִבּוֹא רְבָבוֹת אֵינָן אֲפִילוּ כְּעֵרֶךְ מִסְפָּר אֶחָד לְגַבֵּי אֶלֶף אַלְפֵי אֲלָפִים וְרִבּוֹא רְבָבוֹת, אֶלָּא כְּלָא מַמָּשׁ חֲשִׁיבֵי.

However, with regard to an entity that is infinite and has no numeration whatsoever, no number has a proportional value relative to it. Even a billion or a trillion do not have the value of even one billionth or trillionth in comparison to infinity. **Rather, they are considered literally as nothing.**

It is impossible to determine any numerical ratio relative to infinity. All numbers are numerically related to all other numbers, but there is no relationship between any number and infinity. Relative to infinity, every number is equal to zero.

13 Iyar (leap year)

וְכָכָה מַמָּשׁ הִיא בְּחִינַת הֶאָרָה מוּעֶטֶת זוֹ הַמִּתְלַבֶּשֶׁת בָּעוֹלָמוֹת עֶלְיוֹנִים וְתַחְתּוֹנִים, לְהַשְׁפִּיעַ בָּהֶם לְהַחֲיוֹתָם, לְגַבֵּי עֵרֶךְ אוֹר הַגָּנוּז וְנֶעְלָם, שֶׁהוּא בִּבְחִינַת אֵין סוֹף, וְאֵינוֹ מִתְלַבֵּשׁ וּמַשְׁפִּיעַ בָּעוֹלָמוֹת בִּבְחִינַת גִּלּוּי לְהַחֲיוֹתָם,

In literally the same way, this infinitesimal illumination, which is enclothed in the higher and lower worlds to be channeled into them and sustain them, is as nothing in relation to the quality of the hidden and concealed light, which is infinite and does not become enclothed or channeled into the worlds in a revealed manner to sustain them

This finite reality must be sustained by means of a light and life force that are also limited and constricted. The infinite divine light is far beyond all of reality and is not measured in the same terms. It is impossible for there to be a measurable relationship between the infinite light and the worlds, which, despite their immense size, are limited.

CHAPTER 48

אֶלָּא מַקִּיף עֲלֵיהֶם מִלְמַעְלָה, וְנִקְרָא 'סוֹבֵב כָּל עָלְמִין'.

but rather surrounds them from above and is referred to as "encompasses all worlds."

The concept of the divine light encompassing all worlds is mentioned frequently in the writings of the author of the *Tanya* and is crucial to understanding them. It is usually mentioned in contrast to "filling all worlds," which refers to the immanent aspect of the Divine, where it permeates every single minutia of reality, giving it existence and sustaining it. By contrast, there is a higher, transcendent divine essence that surrounds and encompasses all of reality.

That the light fills all worlds relates to the inner vitality of everything, which is revealed more as one delves deeper into a creation's essence. That it encompasses all worlds, on the other hand, pertains to that which is concealed, never to be revealed within reality but always beyond it. ☞

וְאֵין הַפֵּירוּשׁ 'סוֹבֵב וּמַקִּיף מִלְמַעְלָה' בִּבְחִינַת מָקוֹם חַס וְשָׁלוֹם,

This does not mean that it encompasses and "surrounds from above" in the sense of physical space, God forbid,

It is easy to visualize concepts in terms of images and diagrams drawn from the material reality, where there are objects that are inside and others that are outside. In view of this, one might envision the concept of encompassing the worlds by imagining a large circle drawn around

---

THE LIGHT THAT ENCOMPASSES ALL WORLDS

☞ The concept of encompassing all worlds does not refer to that which is elsewhere, on some other plane. The light that encompasses is equally present in heaven and on earth, in the living and in the inanimate, in the physical and in the spiritual.

This is similar to the concept of ether. Physicists once believed that ether was the medium through which all matter moves. It was said to be found in the space within and between entities, even though ether itself was not considered matter and was imperceptible. Another example from the same field is the force of gravity. Unlike electricity, which requires an object through which it must be conducted and does not act equally on everything, gravity is not affected by different objects and their particular measurements. It acts equally on all objects, whether they are heavy or light, big or small.

an inner light. But it is important to keep in mind that such physical images do not reflect the true reality. One should not think that the encompassing light is found only above and around and not below and within.

כִּי לֹא שַׁיָּיךְ כְּלָל בְּחִינַת מָקוֹם בְּרוּחָנִיּוּת. **because the dimension of** physical **space does not apply whatsoever to the spiritual realm.**

One cannot say that God is found in heaven and not on earth. The definition of space, where a certain object is found in a particular geographical place and not in any other place, belongs only to the realm of physical matter. Consequently, the spiritual concepts of "fills all worlds" and "encompasses all worlds" have no relation to geographical space and certainly this is the case with regard to the Divine. These terms are employed only to convey how the relationship between the Divine and the world exists on two planes: within everything and beyond everything. The first is metaphorically called "fills all worlds" and the second, "encompasses all worlds." Yet these terms are certainly not meant to be understood in the physical sense. ☞

אֶלָּא רוֹצֶה לוֹמַר 'סוֹבֵב וּמַקִּיף מִלְמַעְלָה' לְעִנְיַן בְּחִינַת גִּילּוּי הַשְׁפָּעָה, **Rather, it means that it "encompasses and surrounds from above" in reference to the manifestation of the flow** of sustenance,

---

FILLING AND ENCOMPASSING

☞ *Nefesh HaḤayyim* is a work that was written by Rabbi Ḥayyim of Volozhin in a certain sense as a counterpoint to the *Tanya* and is therefore structured in a similar way. When it comes to these kabbalistic concepts, that of "encompasses all worlds" and that of "fills all worlds," *Nefesh HaḤayyim* presents these terms in the opposite sense to the *Tanya*. There, encompasses all worlds refers to the immanent nature of holiness, while fills all worlds refers to its transcendent nature (see *Nefesh HaḤayyim* 3:4, 6–7). This inversion does not indicate a difference, but rather an inherent similarity. The fact that the two works switch the terms used for these concepts indicates that the terminology is merely external. "Fills" and "encompasses" are only metaphors, and their physical-spatial connotations do not necessarily connect to their internal, spiritual meanings.

The flow of sustenance and life force that brings the world into existence cannot be divided or defined according to worldly limits. It is found in every place toward which it is channeled, both inside and outside, within and around, whether the recipient is aware of it or not. Yet the manifestation of this flow of sustenance within the worlds may be described in terms of inside and outside, "encompassing" and "filling." The manifestation of this sustenance, unlike the sustenance itself, is defined by the knowledge of its recipient. If the recipient does not know of it and cannot define it in his own terms, it may be said that it only "encompasses and surrounds from above."

In the same vein, a person can transmit content, knowledge, and emotion through words. These words will have an impact on the listener to the extent that the listener can understand these words. In this sense, the individual is a vessel that can receive this influence, this flow of words. But content can also be transmitted in the sense of encompassing. A particular melody or mood can affect a person even if he does not understand its "language." Some kind of indefinable, incomprehensible force takes effect beyond the barriers of knowledge and intellectual awareness.

כִּי הַהַשְׁפָּעָה שֶׁהוּא בִּבְחִינַת גִּילּוּי בָּעוֹלָמוֹת נִקְרֵאת בְּשֵׁם 'הַלְבָּשָׁה', שֶׁמִּתְלַבֶּשֶׁת בָּעוֹלָמוֹת, כִּי הֵם מַלְבִּישִׁים וּמַשִּׂיגִים הַהַשְׁפָּעָה שֶׁמְּקַבְּלִים. **because the flow of sustenance that is manifest in the worlds is referred to by the term "enclothed," since it is clothed within the worlds, for** the worlds **clothe and perceive the** flow they receive.

Every revelation is an enclothing because the recipient incorporates the essence of the flow within himself. By contrast, that which is unattainable and beyond all perception is referred to as "encompassing." In view of this, encompassing and filling can occur in the same place, but one is absorbed internally, while the other only surrounds. The difference between them is not spatial, but depends on the receiver's capacity to receive or enclothe the flow of sustenance. When the recipient can take in and relate to the flow he receives, he can absorb it internally. When he cannot relate to it with his limited intellect or emotion, the flow is said to encompass him.

Another example of enclothing in this sense is speech, which enclothes thought. This does not refer to the physical location of either thought or speech, but rather thought constitutes the internal content of speech, and speech reveals the thought to the outside world.

In the same vein, the divine sustenance gives life to the world, and it is apparent that this flow constitutes the world's content and meaning in its every aspect, both overall and in its minutiae. This is the internal flow that fills the worlds and is enclothed within the worlds.

מַה שֶּׁאֵין כֵּן הַהַשְׁפָּעָה שֶׁאֵינָהּ בִּבְחִינַת גִּילּוּי, אֶלָּא בְּהֶסְתֵּר וְהֶעְלֵם, וְאֵין הָעוֹלָמוֹת מַשִּׂיגִים אוֹתָהּ, אֵינָהּ נִקְרֵאת 'מִתְלַבֶּשֶׁת' אֶלָּא 'מַקֶּפֶת' וְ'סוֹבֶבֶת'. By contrast, the flow that is not manifest but is concealed and hidden, not perceived by the worlds, is not referred to as "enclothed" in the worlds but rather as "surrounds" and "encompasses."

Something that cannot be incorporated into that which it influences because it is above and beyond all its dimensions, yet nevertheless has an impact on it, is considered to be encompassing and surrounding.

A surrounding flow is no less impactful than an internal flow. Sometimes it is even stronger and influential. Yet the recipient is unable to perceive it. Something envelops and surrounds him, leading him to certain feelings and actions, but he has no awareness of it. When a flow surrounds not just one person or group, but all the worlds, this is

---

SURROUNDING FLOW AND INTERNAL FLOW

☞ What defines these terms is not fixed and absolute. Something that is surrounding for one person may be internal for another, who is able to perceive it. Likewise, this reality can vary within the individual himself. As he grows, that which was surrounding for him can become internal. This phenomenon is so characteristic to progress that it actually constitutes a test of progress. It is said that when a person is advancing properly, he must sense how yesterday's heaven becomes today's earth.

This is comparable to the interactions between a teacher and a student. When the teacher explains something to the student, the part of the teacher's words that is absorbed by the student, which he understands and can consciously develop, has been internalized – "enclothed" – by the student. The part that the student is

referred to as "encompassing all worlds." It surrounds and affects the worlds, yet none of them can perceive it.

הִלְכָּךְ, מֵאַחַר שֶׁהָעוֹלָמוֹת הֵם בִּבְחִינַת גְּבוּל וְתַכְלִית, נִמְצָא שֶׁאֵין הַשְׁפָּעַת אוֹר אֵין סוֹף מִתְלַבֵּשׁ וּמִתְגַּלֶּה בָּהֶם בִּבְחִינַת גִּילּוּי רַק מְעַט מִזְעֵר, הָאָרָה מוּעֶטֶת, מְצוּמְצֶמֶת מְאֹד, וְהִיא רַק כְּדֵי לְהַחֲיוֹתָם בִּבְחִינַת גְּבוּל וְתַכְלִית.

Therefore, since the worlds are limited and finite, it follows that only an exceedingly minute and constricted illumination of the flow of the light of *Ein Sof*, whose essence is infinite, becomes enclothed and manifest within them in a revealed way, and this is only in order to sustain them as limited and finite creations.

Essentially, there can be no defined relationship between the infinite and the finite. The connection that can exist between them is not a connection to God Himself, but merely to a diminished, constricted illumination of the divine light. This minute illumination is sufficient to light up all the finite, limited worlds, bringing them into existence and sustaining them, each with its own limitations and purpose.

---

unable to absorb, the teacher's intentions and direction, some of which are included in his words and some of which are not, as well as the expanse of his knowledge, is said to surround him. It is all there, but it is imperceptible to the student.

Often, the most real and important thing that passes between a teacher and a student, and between people in general, is not what the recipient hears and understands, but rather that which he does not understand and of which he is not even cognizant. When teaching a child to read, one first teaches him the shapes of the letters. The student absorbs this information, yet only at a much later stage does he fully grasp the internal significance of reading and writing, the transmission of words and meanings. Though that is essential to the learning process even now, at this early stage, the child receives it only in a surrounding manner.

This is the meaning of the talmudic statement, "A person does not understand the view of his teacher until [after] forty years" (*Avoda Zara* 5b). This does not mean that a person comprehends nothing for forty years, but in the initial stages of his learning, he understands only certain units of knowledge, some of the details of what he is taught. He grasps the full extent of his teacher's teachings only at a later stage.

Of course, one can never comprehend the entirety of God's knowledge, yet even in this regard there are occasional shifts, or leaps, in which that which surrounds suddenly becomes internal, while new, unfamiliar elements begin to encompass and surround, waiting to be absorbed within.

אֲבָל עִיקַּר הָאוֹר בְּלִי צִמְצוּם כָּל כָּךְ נִקְרָא 'מַקִּיף' וְ'סוֹבֵב', מֵאַחַר שֶׁאֵין הַשְׁפָּעָתוֹ מִתְגַּלֵּית בְּתוֹכָם, מֵאַחַר שֶׁהֵם בִּבְחִינַת גְּבוּל וְתַכְלִית.

But the principal light, which has not been constricted to such an extent, is referred to as encompassing and surrounding, since its flow is not manifest within the worlds because they are limited and finite.

There is an infinite gap between the infinite and the finite, and this creates the essential distinction between the internal flow and the surrounding flow, between that which fills all worlds and that which encompasses all worlds. The internal flow must necessarily be finite and limited, just as its recipients, their lives and reality, are finite and limited, relative to the encompassing, infinite light, which is completely distinct and unknowable. Yet even the surrounding light, that which encompasses all worlds, is a form of revelation, and therefore it too is characterized by some degree of limitation. This is the implication of the author of the *Tanya*'s description of the surrounding light, "the principal light, which has not been restricted to such an extent." ☞

Though unknowable, the surrounding light is manifest in the world and acts upon everything. Moreover, it is actually the essence of reality. Just as the primary essence of the light is encompassing, so too the essence of reality, the great secret of our existence, encompasses. What we can actually perceive and understand in our reality is in this sense less important and less real. What is truly important, what truly determines our reality, is the encompassing essence that we are entirely unable to perceive, understand, or resonate with.

All finite reality is thus a paradox whose solution is found not within the world but beyond it. The reality of matter, of the self, and ultimately

PERCEPTION THROUGH NEGATION

☞ Even if we are unable to understand or internalize the idea of light that surrounds, we can sense it in some way, because we feel our own limitations in relation to it. One might say that we understand it by knowing what it is not. We can comprehend the fact that it is not perceptible, not limited, and so on. This is not true understanding, but it is a feeling that can be quite tangible, the sense that there is something else beyond all that we comprehend, beyond the limits of our consciousness. When we are able to feel this, we are really perceiving, to the extent that this is possible, that which surrounds our reality, that which is infinite.

of a world that can deny the existence of the Creator who brings it into being is itself an expression of the infinite, of *Ein Sof*. The fact that God has constricted His divine light to allow for the existence of the worlds is itself a manifestation of His divine light. This finite, limited, most distant point is where the most complete, and only, expression of the Divine is found.[5]

A being that recognizes the force that gives it life and nullifies itself in the face of it is giving expression to the light that fills it and and is constricted within it. On the other hand, a being that cannot recognize the force that brought it into existence and sustains it, living instead with the awareness that it is a separate, independent entity, is itself giving expression to the existence of the Divine, which encompasses all worlds and cannot be perceived or understood yet sustains everything in existence.

| וְהַמָּשָׁל בָּזֶה, הִנֵּה הָאָרֶץ הַלֵּזוּ הַגַּשְׁמִיּוּת. אַף שֶׁמָּלֵא כָל הָאָרֶץ כְּבוֹדוֹ, | **To illustrate this, consider this physical earth: Although the earth is filled with His glory,** | 16 Iyar
14 Iyar
(leap year) |

The author of the *Tanya* offers a simple example of encompassing light from the reality that all can see, that of our physical world. The physical earth, which expresses and reveals only the most minimal life force, is filled at all times with the infinite divine light, the glory of God Himself.

| וְהַיְינוּ אוֹר אֵין סוֹף בָּרוּךְ הוּא, כְּמוֹ שֶׁכָּתוּב: "הֲלֹא אֶת הַשָּׁמַיִם וְאֶת הָאָרֶץ אֲנִי מָלֵא, נְאֻם ה'" (ירמיה כג, כד), | **which is the light of *Ein Sof*, blessed be He, as the verse states, "Do I not fill the heavens and the earth? – the utterance of the Lord"** (Jer. 23:24), |

The author of the *Tanya* adds that the glory of God is the light of God Himself and not merely the illumination of His glory. The words of the verse "Do I not fill…?" are unequivocal: God Himself, in His infiniteness, exists and is found within this physical earth just as He exists in every other reality and on every other plane.[6]

---

5. See also *Sha'ar HaYiḥud VeHa'emuna*, chap. 4.
6. It is noteworthy that in several places the author of the *Tanya* points out that

אַף עַל פִּי כֵן, אֵין מִתְלַבֵּשׁ בְּתוֹכָהּ בִּבְחִינַת גִּילּוּי הַהַשְׁפָּעָה, רַק חַיּוּת מְעַט מִזְעֵר, בִּבְחִינַת דּוֹמֵם וְצוֹמֵחַ לְבַד.

only a minuscule amount of life force, on the level of that which can sustain **inanimate and vegetative matter alone, is nevertheless enclothed within** the world as a revealed flow.

The divine life force that is manifest in the physical world is infinitesimal. Only that which is necessary for the sake of a creation's existence and growth is apparent. The world cannot perceive the divine light itself except in a constricted, limited sense within the world's bounds. At the very most, God is revealed in the world as its Creator and Ruler, but beyond that, it is as though He is not there.

וְכָל אוֹר אֵין סוֹף בָּרוּךְ הוּא נִקְרָא סוֹבֵב עָלֶיהָ, אַף שֶׁהוּא בְּתוֹכָהּ מַמָּשׁ, מֵאַחַר שֶׁאֵין הַשְׁפָּעָתוֹ מִתְגַּלֵּית בָּהּ יוֹתֵר, רַק מַשְׁפִּיעַ בָּהּ בִּבְחִינַת הֶסְתֵּר וְהֶעְלֵם,

All the light of *Ein Sof*, blessed be He, that is not manifest in the world is referred to as encompassing the world, **even though it is actually within it, since its flow is not manifest beyond this but only flows within it in a concealed and hidden way,**

The difference between filling and encompassing is therefore not a matter of location but of enclothing, of the ability to absorb and reveal the flow. When the recipient can relate to it, when he is aware of it and expresses this awareness in his life and actions, the flow is considered to be filling him. By contrast, any flow whose essence the recipient does not internalize and reveal by means of his spiritual faculties, intellect, and emotions, is an encompassing flow. Although the verse states, "Do I not fill the heavens and the earth?" the flow of the divine light, and its existence relative to the world, is encompassing since the essence of

---

the verse "That which fills the entire world is His glory" (Isa. 6:3) does not signify God's essence and being, but only the light that emanates from Him, the light that fills all worlds. In those sources, the author also states that the verse "Do I not fill the heavens and the earth?" refers to the light that encompasses all worlds. See, e.g., *Torah Or* 30b.

the Divine, in its infiniteness, is not revealed in heaven or on earth. On the other hand, that which is enclothed, which is apparent in heaven and on earth and possesses a certain life force, such as a physical form with a defined size and shape or the capacity to grow, constitutes the constricted flow that the world receives, which is internal and filling.

"Do I not fill" refers to the aspect of the light that encompasses all worlds, because the infinite, divine essence fills and permeates all of reality equally. Reality does not divide it or absorb it at any point. The divine essence is, as it were, invisible to reality. "Do I not fill the heavens and the earth?" does not say anything in particular with regard to heaven and earth, since their reality cannot relate to what that means. Therefore, even though their entire reality comes from the Divine, it is as though He does not exist for heaven and earth. ☞

| וְכָל הַשְׁפָּעָה שֶׁבִּבְחִינַת הֶסְתֵּר נִקְרָא 'מַקִּיף מִלְמַעְלָה', | and any flow in a state of concealment, imperceptible by the receiver, is referred to as encompassing from above |

"Above" in this context does not relate to physical space because above and below are the same with regard to that which is encompassing so that the author of the *Tanya* could have said "encompassing from below"

EVERYWHERE AND NOWHERE

☞ There are real-world examples of things that exist but cannot be seen, which pass by but do not touch anything. In mathematics, the concept of transcendental numbers is based on the idea that there are systems and units that ostensibly do not relate to one another at all. Therefore, the question of whether a particular unit in one system is small or large is not a valid question in relation to another system because the scale used in the former system may not apply to the other. Two distinct entities may be the same size and may be found in the same place, and moreover, something can exist in reality and not be found there. It may exist and be very close by yet will be found on a totally separate plane of reality.

These examples show that this concept does not apply only to the distant, abstract realm of the mystical, but it is also found in our world and relates to matters with which we live and come into contact. This is how one should view the "I" in "Do I not fill the heavens and the earth"; God literally fills all worlds, and yet, because He does not come into contact with any part of them, it is as though He does not exist. This is the implication of the divine light encompassing all worlds.

just as well. Whether it says above, below, or adjacent, the meaning is the same: God is not found on the same plane as the worlds. The worlds may be able to perceive themselves and the others, but this does not include that which encompasses, although the Divine is found within them.

כִּי עָלְמָא דְּאִתְכַּסְיָא הוּא לְמַעְלָה בְּמַדְרֵגָה מֵעָלְמָא דְּאִתְגַּלְיָא. **because the concealed world is on a higher level than the revealed world.**

The term "above" is used here in the sense of spiritual level, not in terms of physical location, to describe that which is on another plane. It is concealed and separate from all revealed levels. Similarly, the nothingness that is beyond existence is described as being dark, without light. As the *Zohar* expresses it, "[This] supernal crown, although it is an ancient light, a pure, polished light, it is black."[7] In the physical realm too, we label all electromagnetic waves with wavelengths longer than infrared or shorter than ultraviolet as darkness. Since we cannot see the light of those waves, they appear dark. The term "above," like the term "darkness," is just a way of using language to express that which is invisible and beyond the realm of concepts that human beings can perceive.

וּלְקָרֵב אֶל הַשֵּׂכֶל יוֹתֵר הוּא בְּדֶרֶךְ מָשָׁל: This concept can **be made more intelligible by way of an analogy:**

The author of the *Tanya* brings an analogy to help us grasp the concepts of encompassing and filling in a deeper and more tangible way and achieve a clearer intellectual understanding. Furthermore, it prevents the individual from applying these ideas to the physical realm, which would be a crude and incorrect interpretation. The analogy does not come from the physical realm, but it is familiar, since it is drawn from the human experience.

כְּמוֹ הָאָדָם שֶׁמְּצַיֵּיר בְּדַעְתּוֹ אֵיזֶה דָּבָר שֶׁרָאָה אוֹ שֶׁרוֹאֶה, **It is comparable to a person who depicts in his mind an object he has seen or** currently **sees.**

---

7. *Tikkunei Zohar* 135b.

When a person sees an image or tries to remember a picture he saw in the past, an image forms in his mind that comprises his personal perception of what he saw.

הִנֵּה אַף שֶׁכָּל גּוּף עֶצֶם הַדָּבָר הַהוּא וְגַבּוֹ וְתוֹכוֹ וְתוֹךְ תּוֹכוֹ, כּוּלּוֹ מְצוּיָּיר בְּדַעְתּוֹ וּמַחֲשַׁבְתּוֹ, מִפְּנֵי שֶׁרָאָהוּ כּוּלּוֹ אוֹ שֶׁרוֹאֵהוּ, הִנֵּה נִקְרֵאת דַּעְתּוֹ מַקֶּפֶת הַדָּבָר הַהוּא כּוּלּוֹ, וְהַדָּבָר הַהוּא מוּקָף בְּדַעְתּוֹ וּמַחְשַׁבְתּוֹ, **Although the entire body of that object, including its exterior, interior, and innermost core, are wholly depicted in his mind and thoughts because he has seen it entirely or** currently **sees it, it is considered that his mind encompasses that object in its entirety, and that object is encompassed in his mind and thoughts.**

When a person thinks about a safety pin, for example, he calls up an image of a safety pin in his mind, which he can scrutinize from all angles and in any way he wishes. That image is said to be encompassed in his thoughts. This is true of any subject of a person's thoughts, whether it is a physical object or a spiritual topic. It is encompassed within his mind commensurate with the extent of his understanding and perception.

In this analogy, the concepts of surrounding and internal lose their physicality. When one contemplates a complex machine, for example, it is possible that his mind encompasses only its exterior and not its interior. He perceives its external form, and perhaps also its function, yet he is unable to grasp its internal workings. In this case, while he is encompassing the device's exterior, its interior in a sense encompasses him. It is there, hovering over him, encompassing him, but he is unable to let it in since he cannot apprehend it. Such a circumstance, where it is not obvious what is encompassing and what is being encompassed, has no meaning in the physical realm.

רַק שֶׁאֵינוֹ מוּקָף בְּפוֹעַל מַמָּשׁ, רַק בְּדִמְיוֹן מַחֲשֶׁבֶת הָאָדָם וְדַעְתּוֹ. **Yet it is not actually and literally encompassed, only in the imagination of the person's thoughts and mind.**

In the analogy, the subject of the person's thoughts is not actually and literally found inside his head. Rather, he can call up an image of it in his mind and contemplate it in his thoughts. When one thinks about a particular object, and all the more so about an abstract concept, he does not actually contain it inside him. It is merely an image, a reflection of that thing within his consciousness. The object itself has its own essential, meaningful existence outside and independent of the person's reality.

15 Iyar
(leap year)

אֲבָל הַקָּדוֹשׁ בָּרוּךְ הוּא, דִּכְתִיב בֵּיהּ: "כִּי לֹא מַחְשְׁבוֹתַי מַחְשְׁבוֹתֵיכֶם" כו' (ישעיה נה, ח), הֲרֵי מַחֲשַׁבְתּוֹ וְדַעְתּוֹ, שֶׁיּוֹדֵעַ כָּל הַנִּבְרָאִים, מַקֶּפֶת כָּל נִבְרָא וְנִבְרָא מֵרֹאשׁוֹ וְעַד תַּחְתִּיתוֹ וְתוֹכוֹ וְתוֹךְ תּוֹכוֹ, הַכֹּל בְּפֹעַל מַמָּשׁ.

By contrast, the Holy One, blessed be He, about whom it states, "For My thoughts are not your thoughts..." (Isa. 55:8), His thoughts and knowledge, which knows all created beings, actually and literally encompasses each and every creation from top to bottom, including its interior and innermost core.

We cannot compare our thoughts to God's, because they are so essentially different, in a completely different category. The analogy of human thought certainly cannot correspond precisely to the reality of divine thought.

Our thoughts are in another realm and on a different plane than the reality. In a certain sense, they are less real than the reality because they contain only an external, marginal component of the subject being pondered. God's thoughts, on the other hand, are more real than the reality. They do not merely take in a likeness of the world but encompass all of reality so that the entire world, including its exterior and its interior, its major components and its intricate details, is a reflection and a likeness within divine thought.

Rambam conveys this idea in the introduction to his work *Mishneh Torah*: "All entities are dependent on Him, while He is not dependent on them nor a single one of them. Therefore, the truth of His being is incomparable to the truth of any other individual being. This is implied in the prophet's statement 'But the Lord God is truth' (Jer. 10:10). That is, He alone is true, and no other entity possesses truth that compares to His truth."[8]

God is the one true reality, and all created beings are secondary, for they have no independent existence apart from God's reality and truth. ☞

לְמָשָׁל, כַּדּוּר הָאָרֶץ הַלֵּזוּ, הֲרֵי יְדִיעָתוֹ יִתְבָּרֵךְ מַקֶּפֶת כָּל עוֹבִי כַּדּוּר הָאָרֶץ וְכָל אֲשֶׁר בְּתוֹכוֹ וְתוֹךְ תּוֹכוֹ עַד תַּחְתִּיתוֹ, הַכֹּל בְּפוֹעַל מַמָּשׁ, שֶׁהֲרֵי יְדִיעָה זוֹ הִיא חַיּוּת כָּל עוֹבִי כַּדּוּר הָאָרֶץ כּוּלּוֹ וְהִתְהַוּוּתוֹ מֵאַיִן לְיֵשׁ.

For instance, consider **this planet Earth**. God's knowledge actually and literally encompasses the entire breadth of the Earth and all that is in it and its innermost core to its lowest depths in its entirety. This is because this knowledge constitutes the life force of the entire breadth of the entire planet Earth and its creation, when it was **brought forth into existence from nothingness**.

17 Iyar

Here the author of the *Tanya* adds an idea that is not emphasized by Rambam. The world exists because God thinks of it, because it is present within His mind. God thinks about something, and His knowledge constitutes its formation from nothingness. God's knowledge thus constitutes the existence of every minutia and aspect of reality, because

---

INVENTIONS OF THE MIND

☞ To better understand God's thoughts and knowledge in relation to created beings, consider the human imagination. This does not refer to thoughts about an object that exists in the external reality but rather to a thing that is created and contained entirely within one's thoughts. What is the connection between our thoughts and that which is created within them?

When a person thinks or dreams about something, it exists within the thought or dream but has no reality outside it. The dream is the reality, and all that is inside the dream has been formed within it and relies on it for its existence. The creations of our thoughts exist only within our thoughts. Moreover, any element that the thought does not encompass does not exist. Every facet must be included in the thought in order for that detail to exist.

---

8. *Sefer HaMadda, Hilkhot Yesodei HaTorah* 1:3–4.

each and every one exists only by virtue of their being encompassed in His knowledge. If it is not known to Him, it does not exist. ☞

רַק שֶׁלֹּא הָיָה מִתְהַוֶּה כְּמוֹת שֶׁהוּא עַתָּה, בַּעַל גְּבוּל וְתַכְלִית וְחַיּוּת מוּעֶטֶת מְאֹד, כְּדֵי בְּחִינַת דּוֹמֵם וְצוֹמֵחַ, אִם לֹא עַל יְדֵי צִמְצוּמִים רַבִּים וַעֲצוּמִים שֶׁצִּמְצְמוּ הָאוֹר וְהַחַיּוּת שֶׁנִּתְלַבֵּשׁ בְּכַדּוּר הָאָרֶץ, לְהַחֲיוֹתוֹ וּלְקַיְּמוֹ בִּבְחִינַת גְּבוּל וְתַכְלִית, וּבִבְחִינַת דּוֹמֵם וְצוֹמֵחַ בִּלְבָד.

Yet it would not have come into being in its current state as a finite and limited entity with an exceedingly minute degree of life force sufficient only for inanimate and vegetative matter of which the world is comprised without numerous and immense constrictions that constricted the light and life force that is enclothed in the planet Earth to grant it life and sustain it in its finite and limited state with the qualities of inanimate and vegetative matter alone.

As stated above, all of reality exists only within the confines of divine knowledge, which encompasses all worlds. But the formation and differentiation of particular entities, as they perceive themselves within their reality as distinct from all other entities, is brought about through the inner divine light, which is exceedingly constricted commensurate with the specific boundaries of each creation. In the supernal, divine

---

DIVINE PROVIDENCE

☞ In light of the concept that an entity exists in reality only if it exists in God's thoughts, the answer to the question of whether God is aware of the movements of every single ant in the Amazon contains an additional twist: If God does not know about it, then the ant does not exist. The ant crawls across the edges of a leaf because God knows about it. Everything that exists, and everything that happens, is found within the divine knowledge. In contrast to the famous statement of Descartes, "I think, therefore I am," one might declare, "God thinks, therefore I am." In view of this, there is no difference between small objects and large objects. If something exists, from the microscopic virus to the Milky Way galaxy, this means that God is thinking about it. On the other hand, if something is not in God's mind, it does not exist.

knowledge that encompasses all worlds,⁹ everything, small and large, light and dark, is the same, as the verse states, "If you have sinned, how have you acted against Him?... If you are righteous, what have you given Him?" (Job 35:6–7). But each inanimate object, plant, and so forth is formed through constrictions because God is concerned that it be exactly as it is supposed to be. This constitutes His involvement in the many immense constrictions that occur within the boundaries of the worlds, what is referred to as the Divine filling all worlds.

The concept of constriction in relation to God does not mean that He does not know about something, for this is impossible. Rather, it is expressed in the fact that He does know – that He knows things that are limited and that He knows them in their limited form. It is expressed in the fact that He is concerned with what a particular worm eats on any given day and what a particular individual does and does not do. In the words of the *Zohar*, God is involved in the "everyday affairs" of ordinary individuals,¹⁰ unlike a king who involves himself only with major affairs of state.

In a very limited sense, even a human being can think about an entire system of worlds and at the same time think about his shoelace. He is able to think of the totality of everything and, simultaneously, of one particular detail. From the perspective of the knower, these two things are the same. The difference between them lies within the object itself, in which the constriction is revealed. This is the secret of creation, that God Himself, who is infinite, knows all and can do all, yet He is involved in mundane, everyday matters.

אַךְ יְדִיעָתוֹ יִתְבָּרֵךְ הַמְיוּחֶדֶת בְּמַהוּתוֹ וְעַצְמוּתוֹ,	**However, God's knowledge, which is unified with His essence and being,**	16 Iyar (leap year)

This self-knowledge, that which God Himself thinks to Himself, as it were, which is not constricted within the worlds, encompasses. It is separate and distinct from the worlds and not enclothed within them.¹¹

---

9. This is referred to as higher knowledge. See *Torah Or* 14d.
10. *Zohar* 3:149b; see also *Likkutei Torah*, Lev. 25d.
11. Consequently, what happens in the world is not predetermined, even though God knows everything before it occurs. Likewise, God's knowledge does not

כִּי הוּא הַמַּדָּע וְהוּא הַיּוֹדֵעַ וְהוּא הַיָּדוּעַ. וּבִידִיעַת עַצְמוֹ כִּבְיָכוֹל יוֹדֵעַ כָּל הַנִּבְרָאִים, וְלֹא בִּידִיעָה שֶׁחוּץ מִמֶּנּוּ כִּידִיעַת הָאָדָם. כִּי כּוּלָם נִמְצָאִים מֵאֲמִיתָּתוֹ יִתְבָּרֵךְ. **because He is the knowledge, He is the knower, and He is the known object itself, and through knowledge of His self, as it were, He knows all created beings, and not with a knowledge that is external to Himself – as in the case of human knowledge, because all creations are derived from God's reality,**

The knowledge possessed by God's essence and being is one with His actual essence and being. In the human mind, there is a difference between the subject, or the self, and the object of one's thoughts, which is outside the self. Certainly there is a difference between knower, knowledge, and knowing. God's knowledge of reality, however, is not a knowledge of something extrinsic. The whole of reality is real only within the truth of the divine reality. God knows all His creations and all of reality just as a human being knows his own imaginative creations, which exist only in the way he imagines them. The world, and everything that happens in it, exists only within God's mind, where He conceives of all creations and events within His thoughts. In this sense, God, His knowledge, and the object of His knowledge are all one.

וְדָבָר זֶה אֵין בִּיכוֹלֶת הָאָדָם לְהַשִּׂיגוֹ עַל בּוּרְיוֹ וכו'. **and this concept is beyond human ability to clearly comprehend and so on** – is viewed as encompassing and surrounding.

Despite all the comparisons, God's knowledge is completely alien in comparison to human knowledge, and therefore we are unable to attain a true picture of it. This is even more striking because it is not a distant and concealed matter, but rather it is closer to us than anything. God's knowledge is found in all of reality, down to the most minute details of our existence. Nevertheless, our knowledge cannot grasp it. This is the idea of "encompasses all worlds."

---

compel the formation of anything, even though He knows each creation before it is formed. see *Hemshekh Ayin Bet* 1:60.

| הַגָּהָה: [כְּמוֹ שֶׁכָּתַב הָרַמְבַּ"ם ז"ל וְהִסְכִּימוּ עִמּוֹ חַכְמֵי הַקַּבָּלָה, | **Gloss: As Rambam, of blessed memory, stated, and the sages of the Kabbala concurred with him,** |

The idea that God is the knower, the knowledge, and the known, is stated by Rambam,[12] and although their general approach to Jewish thought is entirely different from his, the kabbalists agree with Rambam with regard to this matter.

| כְּמוֹ שֶׁכָּתוּב בַּפַּרְדֵּס מֵהָרַמַּ"ק ז"ל, וְכֵן הוּא לְפִי קַבָּלַת הָאֲרִ"י ז"ל, | **as stated in *Pardes Rimmonim* by Rabbi Moshe Kordevero, of blessed memory. It is also in accord with the esoteric teachings of the Arizal,** |

Rabbi Moshe Kordevero describes a similar idea to Rambam's statement that God is the knower, knowledge, and known, but in connection with all the *sefirot*, all of God's divine attributes.[13] Likewise, within the broader conception of Lurianic Kabbala, Rambam's words are shown to be correct and relevant. The Lurianic Kabbala builds a more comprehensive worldview than previous approaches. Thus, it does not negate the truths put forward by earlier kabbalists, nor even those of Rambam and other, entirely different approaches. Rather, all of them have a place.

This is similar to the relationship between the theory of relativity and Newtonian physics. Relativity does not negate the old laws of physics but only establishes the fact that they refer to certain cases within an immeasurably more complex system.

| בְּסוֹד הַצִּמְצוּם וְהִתְלַבְּשׁוּת אוֹרוֹת בְּכֵלִים, | **which convey the secret of the *tzimtzum*, constriction, and the enclothing of the lights within vessels,** |

---

12. *Sefer HaMadda, Hilkhot Yesodei HaTorah* 2:10.
13. For example, it may also apply to the attribute of Ḥesed: He is the benefactor of Ḥesed, the object of Ḥesed, and the Ḥesed itself. See *Pardes Rimmonim, Sha'ar Mahut VeHanhaga* 13 and *Sha'ar Atzmut VeKelim* 3; *Sha'ar HaYiḥud VeHa'emuna*, chap. 7.

According to several commentaries,[14] the author of the *Tanya* is relating here to the words of the Maharal, mainly in the introduction to *Gevurot Hashem*. The Maharal states there that one cannot impose any kind of boundary on God, including an intellectual one. In light of this, the statement that He is knowledge, knower, and so forth constitutes a limitation and should not be said in reference to God. In general, the author of the *Tanya* agrees with the Maharal. But he explains here that according to Lurianic Kabbala there is also a place for Rambam's words. This refers to the world of *Atzilut*, where the divine light is constricted into the ten *sefirot*, the "lights within vessels," in such a way that He, the light, and the vessels are all one.[15] This is where Rambam's statement that God is knowledge, knower, and knowing applies.

as explained above in chapter 2.	כְּמוֹ שֶׁנִּתְבָּאֵר לְעֵיל פֶּרֶק ב'.]
Since this aspect of God's **knowledge is infinite, it is not referred to in terms of being enclothed within the Earth, which is limited and finite,**	הֲרֵי יְדִיעָה זוֹ, מֵאַחַר שֶׁהִיא בִּבְחִינַת אֵין סוֹף, אֵינָהּ נִקְרֵאת בְּשֵׁם 'מִתְלַבֶּשֶׁת' בְּכַדּוּר הָאָרֶץ, שֶׁהוּא בַּעַל גְּבוּל וְתַכְלִית,

Since this knowledge is God's knowledge of Himself, and He is infinite, it too is bound to the infinite, and this infinite knowledge cannot fit into the earth's boundaries and limitations.

| but rather is referred to as **"encompasses and surrounds,"** even though this knowledge actually and literally envelops the entire breadth and interior of the Earth, **and thus brings it into existence from nothingness, as explained elsewhere** (*Sha'ar HaYihud VeHa'emuna*, chap. 7). | אֶלָּא מַקֶּפֶת וְסוֹבֶבֶת, אַף שֶׁיְּדִיעָה זוֹ כּוֹלֶלֶת כָּל עוֹבְיוֹ וְתוֹכוֹ בְּפוֹעַל מַמָּשׁ, וּמְהַוָּוה אוֹתוֹ עַל יְדֵי זֶה מֵאַיִן לְיֵשׁ, וּכְמוֹ שֶׁנִּתְבָּאֵר בְּמָקוֹם אַחֵר. |

We are encompassed by God's knowledge, and He is not encompassed

---

14. See, e.g., *Derekh Mitzvotekha, Mitzvat Ha'amanat Elokut* 3.
15. *Tikkunei Zohar* 3b.

by our knowledge. His knowledge of us, and of all creatures, is knowledge of both the exterior and the interior. Our entire existence is found within His knowledge, and our whole being is His knowledge.

This is the solution to the apparent contradiction, where the verse "Do I not fill the heavens and the earth?" refers to One who encompasses all worlds. As it states in *Shir HaYiḥud,* a poem dedicated to the theme of Jewish faith, "His glory encompasses all and fills all.... No one in the midst [of existence] is separated from You. Even the narrowest place does not exist without Your presence," yet at the same time, as the *Sha'ar HaYiḥud* goes on to state, "no wisdom can grasp You; no mind can attain You."

God fills all of existence. There cannot be a place where He is not found. He is both above and below, both here and there, yet He is not in any place, for all places exist only within His knowledge. God fills the heavens and the earth, yet no being is able to apprehend this aspect of Him; no point in reality can grasp it. This is what it means that God's light encompasses all worlds.

In explaining God's immense love for us, in order to evoke love for God within us in turn, the author of the Tanya has described God's greatness, how He constricted His infinite light so that He could relate to individual beings and give them life. This constriction has two distinguishing factors: As a result of the constriction, the divine light fills all worlds and encompasses all worlds. These concepts do not relate to physical space but to revelation and concealment, to the divine flow that can be detected within the world and the divine flow that cannot be perceived in the worlds but rather encompasses and surrounds them.

This chapter mostly focused on the light that encompasses all worlds, explaining that it is not merely a flow that surrounds from the outside, but rather sustains all creations both from within and in relation to everything else. The concept of encompassing all worlds can be understood by the idea of divine knowledge: Divine knowledge of a world constitutes the world itself. It is the knowing that is also the known. Although it is the essence of all reality, it is at the same time beyond reality.

Since the author of the Tanya does not generally delve into theoretical analysis for its own sake, he will go on to explain, in the next chapter, the meaning of these ideas in relation to divine service. Like a reflection in the water, this must also involve constriction, and the relinquishment of all a person has in order to cling to God alone.

Chapter 49

THE PREVIOUS CHAPTER EXPLAINED THE CONCEPT OF constriction as a transition from the infinite to the limited, as a passage that leads from God, who is beyond the worlds, to a reality where He is the Creator and Ruler of the universe, giving life to every single creature and minutiae of reality, a transition from the light that encompasses all worlds to that which fills all worlds.

In this chapter, the author of the *Tanya* brings the theoretical concepts underlying the connection between God and the world to their practical implications in a person's divine service. First, picking up the thread of the previous chapters, he discusses the various stages and levels of constriction in detail, beginning with the infinite and ending with the material reality in which we live. Then, in the spirit of the key phrase that characterizes these chapters, "as water reflects a face to the face…" (Prov. 27:19), he goes on to describe the response to God that should be held in a person's heart.

וְהִנֵּה אַף כִּי פְּרָטֵי בְּחִינַת הַהֶסְתֵּר וְהַהֶעְלֵם אוֹר אֵין סוֹף בָּרוּךְ הוּא, בְּהִשְׁתַּלְשְׁלוּת הָעוֹלָמוֹת עַד שֶׁנִּבְרָא עוֹלָם הַזֶּה הַגַּשְׁמִי - עָצְמוּ מִסַּפֵּר,

Although the intricate details entailed in the concealment and obscuring of the light of *Ein Sof*, blessed be He, by means of the devolvement of the worlds, culminating in the creation of this physical world, are too numerous to describe,

18 Iyar

17 Iyar (leap year)

Each world constitutes a concealment of the Divine, of the light of *Ein Sof*, and the succession of the worlds, one beneath the other, is the process of this concealment, whereby the light is constricted one step at a time. This process takes place through myriad layers of concealment, and the number of worlds, concealments, and transitions that exist between the light of *Ein Sof* and this material world is incalculable.

וּמִינִים מִמִּינִים שׁוֹנִים, **and are comprised of a multitude of diverse types,**

Constriction does not refer only to a reduction in size, but to the concealment and obscuring of the inner light. Each world has its own, unique way of constricting, in accordance with its nature and level.

כַּיָּדוּעַ לַטּוֹעֲמִים מֵעֵץ הַחַיִּים, **as is known to those who have tasted from the tree of life,**

There is a double meaning here. Tasting from the tree of life generally refers to individuals who study Kabbala.[1] It can also be referring to *Etz Ḥayyim*, the title of Rabbi Ḥayyim Vital's well-known work that means "Tree of Life," which summarizes the teachings of the Arizal and focuses specifically on the order of the worlds' devolvement.

The kabbalistic works do indeed detail the succession of the worlds extensively, but the concepts involved are highly abstract, and the average person finds them difficult to grasp. Only the few individuals who devote most of their time and energy to studying them are able to truly apprehend them.

אַךְ דֶּרֶךְ כְּלָל הֵם שְׁלֹשָׁה מִינֵי צִמְצוּמִים עֲצוּמִים כְּלָלִיִּים, לִשְׁלֹשָׁה מִינֵי עוֹלָמוֹת כְּלָלִיִּים, וּבְכָל כְּלָל יֵשׁ רִבּוֹא רְבָבוֹת פְּרָטִיִּים. **they are generally categorized as three types of immense, overarching constrictions of the divine light to constitute three types of comprehensive worlds, and each category consists of myriads upon myriads of specific constrictions.**

The author of the *Tanya* does not go into detail here about this subject, because it is essentially theoretical. He focuses mainly on the general concepts that have practical implications and meaning in relation

---

1. See *Iggeret HaKodesh*, epistle 26, citing the *Zohar*.

to the individual's divine service. He goes on to explain how every world is one form of constriction that is a composite of many specific constrictions and layers of concealment. In this sense, the Hebrew word for world, *olam*, is related to the word *he'elem*, concealment. Since there are three worlds that occupy three planes of reality, there are three general levels of constriction.

וְהֵם שְׁלֹשָׁה עוֹלָמוֹת: בְּרִיאָה, יְצִירָה, עֲשִׂיָּה. כִּי עוֹלָם הָאֲצִילוּת הוּא אֱלֹהוּת מַמָּשׁ. **These constitute the three worlds** of *Beria, Yetzira,* and *Asiya,* **for the world of** *Atzilut* **is one of actual divinity.**

Although four worlds are usually mentioned in the description of the succession of worlds, only three are mentioned here. This is because the world of *Atzilut*, the highest of the four worlds, is not a world that emerged through constriction and creation of existence from nothingness. Rather, it is a world that constitutes an extension of God, so to speak, that emanates directly from God's essence, the word *atzilut* denoting emanation. Relative to the worlds of created beings, it constitutes a pure revelation of actual divinity. ☞

וּכְדֵי לִבְרוֹא עוֹלָם הַבְּרִיאָה, שֶׁהֵן נְשָׁמוֹת וּמַלְאָכִים עֶלְיוֹנִים, אֲשֶׁר עֲבוֹדָתָם לַה' בִּבְחִינַת חָכְמָה בִּינָה דַעַת, הַמִּתְלַבְּשִׁים בָּהֶם, וְהֵם מַשִּׂיגִים וּמְקַבְּלִים מֵהֶם, **In order to create the world of** *Beria,* **which is** the world of **the souls and the supernal angels whose service of God is in the** intellectual **sphere of** the *sefirot* of **Ḥokhma, Bina, and Da'at, which are clothed in them, and they apprehend and receive** their sustenance **from those** *sefirot,*

ACTUAL DIVINITY

☞ This is a precise description of the world of *Atzilut*: "divinity" and not "the Divine." Not even the world of *Atzilut* is truly infinite. It is still a world that receives its life force from *Ein Sof*, and it too constitutes a constriction of the infinite. Nevertheless, it is not as much of a constriction as the worlds of *Beria, Yetzira*, and *Asiya* (as explained in chap. 39), but rather its existence constitutes a transparent revelation of the Divine.

In the world of *Beria*, the Divine is revealed on the level of the divine intellect. The created beings that exist in this world perceive the Divine in an intellectual manner, through the cognitive *sefirot* of Ḥokhma, Bina, and Da'at and thus receive their vitality and sustenance through these *sefirot*. This is the realm of the supernal angels, for regular angels exist in the world of *Yetzira*.[2]

The world of *Atzilut* constitutes a transparent revelation of the Divine, and is divinity itself, in the sense that the divine essence is found there without any concealment, partition, or distance, and everything that is created there has no existence that is separate from Him.[3] Therefore, there are no limits to their perception of divinity. By contrast, in the world of *Beria*, there are limits to the understanding and awareness of the Divine of the created beings that exist in that realm. While this apprehension is far beyond human understanding, it is still a limited understanding that is attained in the intellectual sphere of the *sefirot* of Ḥokhma, Bina, and Da'at.

הָיָה תְּחִלָּה צִמְצוּם עָצוּם כַּנִּזְכָּר לְעֵיל. **there** had to **first be an immense constriction, as stated above** (chap. 48).

The immense constriction necessary to form the essence of the world of *Beria* constricted God's presence to nothingness. From that point, the process of bringing forth existence from nothingness could then begin. This constriction took place in the transition from the world of *Atzilut* to the world of *Beria*.

וְכֵן מִבְּרִיאָה לִיצִירָה. כִּי אוֹר מְעַט מִזְעֵר הַמִּתְלַבֵּשׁ בְּעוֹלַם הַבְּרִיאָה, עֲדַיִין הוּא בִּבְחִינַת אֵין סוֹף לְגַבֵּי עוֹלַם הַיְצִירָה, וְאִי אֶפְשָׁר לְהִתְלַבֵּשׁ בּוֹ אֶלָּא עַל **Similarly, from** the world of *Beria* **to** the world of *Yetzira* there was an immense constriction, **because** even **the minuscule amount of light enclothed within the world of** *Beria* **is still considered infinite relative to the world of** *Yetzira*, **and it is impossible**

---

2. See gloss to chap. 39.
3. In other words, God, the light (the life force that emanates from Him), and the vessel (the created being that receives the light) are one. See *Tikkunei Zohar* 3b.

יְדֵי צִמְצוּם וְהֶעְלֵם. וְכֵן מִיְּצִירָה לַעֲשִׂיָּה **for it to become enclothed within the world of** *Yetzira* **except through constriction and concealment. Likewise, the progression from the world of** *Yetzira* **to the world of** *Asiya* **entailed an additional stage of constriction.**

There is also an immense constriction in the transition between the world of *Beria* and the world of *Yetzira*, even though the world of *Beria* itself has undergone constriction. The world of *Yetzira* cannot contain any of the light of the world of *Beria*. It cannot be perceived in the world of *Yetzira*, nor enclothed within it, until it undergoes further constriction. The same is true of the transition between the world of *Yetzira* and the world of *Asiya*, which entailed another immense constriction.

[וּכְמוֹ שֶׁנִּתְבָּאֵר בְּמָקוֹם אַחֵר בֵּיאוּר שְׁלֹשָׁה צִמְצוּמִים אֵלּוּ בַּאֲרִיכוּת, לְקָרֵב אֶל שִׂכְלֵנוּ הַדַּל.] (**These three constrictions are explained elsewhere at length in order to acclimate our meager intellect** to these lofty concepts.)

Our intellect is weak and limited when it comes to grasping these concepts since they refer to beings and worlds that are beyond our reality and understanding. We cannot grasp their essence directly, but only through metaphor.

וְתַכְלִית כָּל הַצִּמְצוּמִים הוּא כְּדֵי לִבְרֹא גּוּף הָאָדָם הַחוּמְרִי **The ultimate purpose of all these constrictions was to create the material human body**

The human body is where the soul is enclothed. Even if we cannot comprehend the nature of all these constrictions, we can grasp their purpose, for the reality of a soul within a body is a part of the human experience.

וּלְאַכְפְּיָיא לְסִטְרָא אָחֳרָא so that he might **subdue the** *sitra aḥara*,

The purpose of combining the physical body and the divine soul within man is so that the soul would be able to subdue and subjugate the *sitra aḥara* to the side of holiness. On a higher level, one can even transform the *sitra aḥara*, turning it into a force for good.

וְלִהְיוֹת "יִתְרוֹן הָאוֹר מִן הַחוֹשֶׁךְ" thus **achieving the advantage of**
(קהלת ב, יד) **light** that emerges **from darkness.**

The author of the *Tanya* compares the subjugation of the *sitra aḥara*, which is the purpose of all the constrictions, to the advantage of light that emerges from darkness.[4] This does not refer only to the objective advantage of light over darkness, but to the relative advantage of light that emerges from within darkness. This is the same advantage of the soul within the body and within the material world. In a certain sense, it is also the advantage described with the words of the Mishna: "One hour of tranquility in the World to Come is better than an entire lifetime in this world" (Mishna *Avot* 4:17).

בְּהַעֲלוֹת הָאָדָם אֶת נַפְשׁוֹ הָאֱלֹהִית This is accomplished **when a human elevates his divine soul,**

When one subdues the *sitra aḥara*, it does not cease to exist in the person or in the world. It is not even hidden. It is still present and active, yet it acts, though unwillingly, on behalf of holiness. At that point, not only is there a light that repels the darkness, but there is

---

LIGHT THAT EMERGES FROM DARKNESS

☞ There are several aspects to the advantage of light that emerges from darkness. The light contained in the darkness emanates from the divine essence and is on a higher level than revealed light. All light is revelation, yet every revelation is merely external and partial in relation to the essence that is not revealed. This essence is concealed in the darkness and is usually not attainable. But when one overcomes the *sitra aḥara*, and the darkness itself gives off light, the essence, which is beyond both the light and the darkness, is revealed.

---

4. Based on Eccles. 2:14.

also the advantage of a light that comes from within the darkness and together with it. ☞

וְהַחִיּוּנִית וּלְבוּשֶׁיהָ וְכָל כֹּחוֹת הַגּוּף כּוּלָן - לַה׳ לְבַדּוֹ, כַּנִּזְכָּר לְעֵיל בַּאֲרִיכוּת, along with his vital soul and its garments, as well as all the body's faculties, to God alone, as explained above at length (chap. 37),

The darkness that comes with the light, with the person's ascending divine soul, is the vital, animal soul and its garments: thought, speech, and action. Through actions that he performs for the sake of Heaven, the individual, who contains both a divine soul and an animal soul within a physical body, elevates the entire range of the material world from his divine soul, which is a portion of God on high, to his physical body. He, together with every part of the world with which he comes into contact while performing a mitzva, ascends to God alone.

כִּי זֶה תַּכְלִית הִשְׁתַּלְשְׁלוּת הָעוֹלָמוֹת. because this was the purpose of the succession of the worlds.

The succession of the worlds, beginning from the highest realm, ultimately leads to the creation of the complex human reality. On one hand, there is the holy soul, which originates from the loftiest plane, and on the other, man has a physical body that exists in the lowest, material realm. In other words, there is a reality of evil and darkness, and within it there is a seed, or code, of potential elevation. The purpose of the succession of the worlds is the realization of this potential. This unique, complex reality is ostensibly a balance between good and evil. By choosing good over evil, by performing good deeds in this dark, evil world, one overcomes the *sitra aḥara* and elevates himself, as well as the entire world, to the side of holiness. A person who does this successfully provides justification for the existence of the worlds. He gives meaning to each world and to every element that led at the end of the entire order of succession, to that bottommost reality in which he exists and impacts.

The higher worlds are constructed on established laws, and as a result, they serve only as vessels and transitions for the succession and not as ends in themselves. Only in our world, though it is the lowest, most physical, and most concealed realm, can there be a created being who is capable of free choice. By means of this free choice, through overcoming the *sitra aḥara*, through the advantage of light that emerges from darkness, one can give meaning to the whole of reality and change the direction of the flow and illumination so that they go from below to above. This is the purpose of the succession of the worlds.

This concludes the author of the *Tanya*'s description of God's immense love for us that began in the previous chapter. This love was expressed when He brought us out of Egypt and gave us the Torah[5] and is magnified by descriptions of His greatness on the one hand and His descent to us, who exist in the lowest possible realm, by way of innumerable constrictions and worlds on the other. The author of the *Tanya* now goes on to discuss the individual's response to this love and how to reciprocate it.

וְהִנֵּה, "כַּמַּיִם הַפָּנִים לַפָּנִים" (משלי כז, יט): "As water reflects a face to the face" (Prov. 27:19), so should a person reflect God's conduct toward him:

As explained in the previous chapters, when a person contemplates God's disposition toward him, he should relate to God in the same way. This is akin to water reflecting the image of the face peering into it.

כְּמוֹ שֶׁהַקָּדוֹשׁ בָּרוּךְ הוּא כִּבְיָכוֹל הִנִּיחַ וְסִילֵּק לְצַד אֶחָד, דֶּרֶךְ מָשָׁל, אֶת אוֹרוֹ הַגָּדוֹל הַבִּלְתִּי תַּכְלִית, וּגְנָזוֹ וְהִסְתִּירוֹ, בְּג' מִינֵי צִמְצוּמִים שׁוֹנִים, Just as the Holy One, blessed be He, as it were, figuratively speaking, laid down and set to one side His great, endless light and hid and concealed it through the three aforementioned different forms of constrictions

This dual phrasing, "as it were" and "figuratively speaking," emphasizes that the descriptions used to explain the concept of constriction, particularly when one uses imagery, are only metaphors.[6] Constriction

---

5. See chap. 47.

6. Here, where the author of the *Tanya* describes constrictions as God's light being retracted to one side, the act of setting aside was actually done equally in all directions. See *He'arot VeTikkunim LaTanya*.

itself is not the simple idea that the analogies seem to convey. The constriction is not meant to be understood literally but rather the light was concealed from the created beings in the lower realms.⁷

וְהַכֹּל בִּשְׁבִיל אַהֲבַת הָאָדָם הַתַּחְתּוֹן לְהַעֲלוֹתוֹ לַה׳, **all for the sake of His love for mortal man, in order to elevate him to God,**

All these constrictions and concealments were effected only in order to make space for human beings in this world. A human being cannot exist as a soul inside a body unless the divine light is concealed and not in evidence. In view of this, it is as though God squeezes Himself into a corner in order to make room for us to exist.⁸

כִּי 'אַהֲבָה דּוֹחֶקֶת הַבָּשָׂר' (בבא מציעא פד, א), **for "love compresses the flesh"** (*Bava Metzia* 84a),

It is human nature to diminish oneself out of love, to make room for that which a person desires, for the love to "compress the flesh." Similarly, it is as though God's love for us squeezes His essence into Himself so that He can connect to humankind.⁹

עַל אַחַת כַּמָּה וְכַמָּה, בְּכִפְלֵי כִפְלַיִים לְאֵין קֵץ, כִּי רָאוּי לָאָדָם גַּם כֵּן לְהַנִּיחַ וְלַעֲזוֹב כָּל אֲשֶׁר לוֹ, מִנֶּפֶשׁ וְעַד בָּשָׂר, **how much more so, to an exponentially infinite degree, is it proper for a person to also set aside and relinquish all that he has, whether of the soul or of the flesh,**

When a person contemplates this concept in depth, how God constricted Himself to such an extent that he, a mortal man, could exist, he

---

7. See *Sha'ar HaYiḥud VeHa'emuna*, chap. 7.
8. The constriction was not done for its own sake but rather so that as a result light could be contained and within the created being and sustained therein (Rabbi Menaḥem Mendel Schneerson, the Lubavitcher Rebbe).
9. The Midrash conveys this idea with the statement "See how beloved is Israel: The glory about which it is said, 'Do I not fill the heavens and the earth?' (Jer. 23:24), from where was it taken? This glory was compressed so that it could speak from above the ark cover, between the two cherubs" (*Sifra*, Lev. 2:12). See *Likkutei Hagahot LaTanya*.

should respond in kind. The words "as water reflects a face to the face" indicate a relationship between equals.¹⁰ But in a relationship where one side is far greater than the other, as is the case with our connection to God, this expectation is infinitely more applicable. If God, who is infinitely greater, could do this for us, then surely we should renounce all our concerns, whether they are spiritual, physical, familial, social, financial, or material.

| וּלְהַפְקִיר הַכֹּל בִּשְׁבִיל לְדָבְקָה בּוֹ יִתְבָּרֵךְ, בִּדְבִיקָה חֲשִׁיקָה וַחֲפִיצָה, | and forego everything in order to cleave to God with attachment, longing, and desire, |

If God has constricted Himself to the point that He has altered His essential, infinite nature in order to descend to the individual down below, then he too should take action for God. Since God has done so much in order to move toward him, he must likewise leave everything behind and cling to God.¹¹

| וְלֹא יִהְיֶה שׁוּם מוֹנֵעַ מִבַּיִת וּמִבַּחוּץ, לֹא גוּף וְלֹא נֶפֶשׁ וְלֹא מָמוֹן וְלֹא אִשָּׁה וּבָנִים. | so that there will be no hindrance from within or without, neither from body nor soul, neither from money, wife, nor children. |

These are the main factors tying a person to this world, and he should be willing to disengage from all of them for the sake of his love of God. Everything else is inconsequential in the face of that love, just as all else is inconsequential to God in comparison to His immense love for us.¹²

---

10. See chap. 46.
11. The author of the *Tanya* uses three terms to describe what a person should renounce for the sake of God: "soul," "flesh," and "everything." We could say that these expressions correspond to the three general categories of constriction: *Beria*, *Yetzira*, and *Asiya*, as well as the three ways to bind with God: "attachment, longing, and desire." Attachment corresponds to *Asiya*, longing to *Yetzira*, and desire to *Beria* (*Likkutei Levi Yitzhak*).
12. This certainly does not mean that one should separate from the world. On the contrary, this "disengagement" should be effected while being engaged with one's community and society at large. The Torah certainly demands that one's

וּבָזֶה יוּבַן טוּב טַעַם וָדַעַת לְתַקָּנַת חֲכָמִים, שֶׁתִּקְּנוּ בִּרְכוֹת קְרִיאַת שְׁמַע, שְׁתַּיִם לְפָנֶיהָ כו',	This provides an understanding and reasoning regarding an enactment of the Sages, where they instituted the recitation of **two blessings before the** *Shema* **and so forth.**

19 Iyar

The first blessing that precedes the *Shema* is *Yotzer Or* in the morning prayer, and its counterpart in the evening prayer, *Ma'ariv Aravim*,[13] which speaks of the creation of the worlds and God's authority over them. The second blessing is *Ahavat Olam*, which tells of God's love for us.

דִּלְכְאוֹרָה אֵין לָהֶם שַׁיָּיכוּת כְּלָל עִם קְרִיאַת שְׁמַע, כְּמוֹ שֶׁכּוֹתֵב הָרַשְׁבָּ"א וּשְׁאָר פּוֹסְקִים.	**On the surface, it seems that they have no relevance whatsoever to the recitation of the** *Shema*, **as Rashba** (*She'eilot U'Teshuvot HaRashba* 1:47, cited by *Beit Yosef, Oraḥ Ḥayyim* 46) **and other halakhic authorities have noted.**

In terms of content, there is no connection between the blessings of the *Shema* and the *Shema* itself. Other blessings that are recited before the performance of a mitzva mention and explain the essence of the mitzva, but the blessings said before the recitation of the *Shema* do not appear to be related to the mitzva at all; they do not even mention it.

וְלָמָּה קָרְאוּ אוֹתָן 'בִּרְכוֹת קְרִיאַת שְׁמַע'? וְלָמָּה תִּקְּנוּ אוֹתָן לְפָנֶיהָ דַּוְוקָא?	**Why did** the Sages **call them "blessings of the** *Shema*," **and why did they institute** their recitation **specifically before the** *Shema*?

One cannot claim that these blessings constitute a separate matter

---

wife and children should take precedence over everything else. However, one should relate to his personal affairs as labor of the hands, leaving his mind and heart free to cling to holy matters (*HaLekaḥ VeHalibbuv*).

13. The term "and so forth" in the text of the *Tanya* here may come to include the blessings recited in the evening prayer (Rabbi Menaḥem Mendel Schneerson, the Lubavitcher Rebbe).

altogether, because both according to their title and their place in the prayers, they are connected to the *Shema*. Moreover, according to the *halakha*, they are not merely adjoined to the *Shema*, but rather they are an essential part of this mitzva.

The blessings recited on mitzvot are meant to prepare a person to be a worthy vessel for the observance of the particular mitzva. The blessings of the *Shema* too constitute a preparation for the observance of the mitzva of reciting the *Shema*. The author of the *Tanya* goes on to explain what this preparation is and how these blessings provide it.

אֶלָּא מִשּׁוּם שֶׁעִיקַּר קְרִיאַת שְׁמַע לְקַיֵּים "בְּכָל לְבָבְךָ" כו' (דברים ו, ה) בִּשְׁנֵי יְצָרֶיךָ כו' (ברכות פרק ט משנה ה), דְּהַיְינוּ לַעֲמוֹד נֶגֶד כָּל מוֹנֵעַ מֵאַהֲבַת ה'.

It is because the primary objective **of reciting the *Shema* is to fulfill** the commandment to love God **"with all your heart** and with all your soul, and with all your might" (Deut. 6:5). **"With all your heart"** means **"with your two inclinations…"** (Mishna Berakhot 9:5), **which entails withstanding any hindrance to loving God.**

The "two inclinations" are our good inclination and our evil inclination. Loving God "with your two inclinations" means that there is no other love in one's heart. The evil inclination tempts a person to pursue other desires, to love other things. This is the "hindrance" that the author of the *Tanya* mentions. It is a reference to the other kind of love, a love of other things, which stems from the evil inclination. Loving God with all your heart, then, means that even the place in the heart that wants to love other things is filled entirely with love of God.

וּ'לְבָבְךָ' - הֵן "הָאִשָּׁה וִילָדֶיהָ", שֶׁלִּבּוֹ שֶׁל אָדָם קְשׁוּרָה בָּהֶן בְּטִבְעוֹ,

Specifically, **"your heart"** alludes to one's **wife and her children, since a person's heart is naturally bound to them,**

Loving with all one's heart means even with the part of the heart that loves and is intrinsically attached to other things. In a certain sense, it is the ability to give up those other things for the sake of love of God. These things are not insignificant. It is easy to forgo something that does not truly matter to a person, but giving up something important, to which one's heart is attached, such as one's wife and children, to whom he is naturally and essentially connected, is the true ramification of the commandment to love God with all one's heart.

This does not mean that a person should not love anything that is found in this world, such as his wife and children, but that these other loves should not be independent or separate from his love of God. Certainly they should not be in conflict with it. All the love that a person feels should be encompassed within his love of God and unified with it.

כְּמוֹ שֶׁאָמְרוּ רַבּוֹתֵינוּ ז״ל (שבת קנב, א) עַל פָּסוּק (תהלים לג, ט): "הוּא אָמַר וַיֶּהִי" – זוֹ אִשָּׁה, "הוּא צִוָּה וַיַּעֲמוֹד" – אֵלּוּ בָּנִים.   **As the Rabbis stated** (*Shabbat* 152a) **regarding the verse** (Ps. 33:9): **"For He spoke and it was done"**: This is a **woman** that a man marries. **"He commanded and it took form"**: These are **the children** whom one works hard to raise."

The Sages explain that one's connection to his wife and children is not rational or acquired but is basic and inherent to human existence. It is part of the essence of humankind that God created when He "spoke and it was done." It is thus a strong and solid bond that is extremely difficult to break.

וְ"נַפְשְׁךָ" וּ"מְאֹדֶךָ" – כְּמַשְׁמָעוֹ, חַיֵּי וּמְזוֹנֵי,   **"Your soul" and "your might" are to be understood literally as your life and livelihood,**

The Mishna goes on to explain the next words of the *Shema*: "'With all your soul' [means] even if God takes your soul. 'With all your might' [means] with all your money." In other words, "with all your soul" refers to life itself, and "with all your might" relates to one's possessions and means of sustenance in this world.

לְהַפְקִיר הַכֹּל בִּשְׁבִיל אַהֲבַת ה׳.   **so that one foregoes everything for the love of God.**

Essentially, the verse "with all your heart, and with all your soul, and with all your might" refers to all those things that are truly important to a person, and to which he is attached in varying degrees, depending on the nature of the thing. It includes a person's wife and children, his health and livelihood, even his life itself. All of it should be considered completely forfeit relative to his love of God.

18 Iyar
(leap year)

וְאֵיךְ יָבוֹא הָאָדָם הַחוֹמְרִי לְמִדָּה זוֹ? **Yet how can a corporeal person attain this lofty standard of love?**

The requirement to disassociate from all things material, from connections and feelings that bolster a person's existence in this world, all the markers of his reality, is an ambitious one. Moreover, it does not pertain only to externalities but even to the bonds of his soul. How can a human being, who is part of the physical world, sever these ties?

לְכָךְ סִידְּרוּ תְּחִלָּה בִּרְכַּת ׳יוֹצֵר אוֹר׳, **That is why the Sages introduced the blessing of *Yotzer Or* before the recitation of the *Shema*.**

This blessing is not part of the recitation of the *Shema* itself but rather constitutes a level of preparation for the soul in order to free a person from his connections to the material world and enables him to perceive the divine realm. Rather than seeing only his own daily existence, he embraces existence of the wondrous, divine life force that burgeons within him at that very moment. He recognizes God's kindness and love for him, and, in turn, he is able to reflect back that love and fulfill the words he recites in the *Shema*: "You shall love the Lord your God with all your heart, and with all your soul, and with all your might."

"WITH ALL YOUR HEART, AND WITH ALL YOUR SOUL, AND WITH ALL YOUR MIGHT"

☞ The Torah consistently speaks in concise terms. It says, for example, "In pain you shall give birth to children" (Gen. 3:16). The verse describes a woman's experience during childbirth with one simple word: *be'etzev*, "in pain." The Sages, on the other hand, express it thus: "Of the one hundred cries a woman lets out while sitting on the birthing stool, ninety-nine are for death and one is for life" (*Vayikra Rabba* 27:7). In view of this, one may begin to understand the scope of the Torah's commandment to love God "with all your heart, and with all your soul, and with all your might."

וְשָׁם נֶאֱמַר וְנִשְׁנָה בַּאֲרִיכוּת עִנְיַן וְסֵדֶר הַמַּלְאָכִים הָעוֹמְדִים בְּרוּם עוֹלָם, לְהוֹדִיעַ גְּדוּלָּתוֹ שֶׁל הַקָּדוֹשׁ בָּרוּךְ הוּא אֵיךְ שֶׁכּוּלָּם בְּטֵלִים לְאוֹרוֹ יִתְבָּרֵךְ, וּמַשְׁמִיעִים בְּיִרְאָה כוּ', וּמַקְדִּישִׁים כוּ' וְאוֹמְרִים בְּיִרְאָה: "קָדוֹשׁ" כוּ'.

There this blessing **describes and expounds at length the account of the order of angels who stand on the pinnacle of the world to proclaim the greatness of the Holy One, blessed be He, how all** the supernal angels, the seraphim, **are subsumed in God's light, "and fearfully declare…and sanctify… and assert with fear, 'Holy, holy, holy, is the Lord of hosts.'"**

PREPARATION FOR THE SOUL

☞ This preparation to ready the soul to love God is not carried out only once or twice in a lifetime, but every day, morning and evening, when reciting the blessings of the *Shema*. This frequent repetition, day after day, is not easy. It is human nature to become accustomed to habitual behavior, and when one becomes used to such behavior, he is no longer moved by it in the same way as he was before. The most surprising and impactful experience is less surprising on the second day and even less so on the third, and by the fourth day, the person already believes that this is the way it should always be. When the children of Israel journeyed through the wilderness, manna descended from the heavens every morning, and a pillar of cloud went before them during the day and a pillar of fire by night. Yet the people complained, experienced lust, and had little faith, as if all this were normal.

Over time, every miracle ceases to appear miraculous. People become accustomed to it and believe that this is the way it should be. Habit erodes everything, slowly eating away at a person's ability to feel excited and motivated. In order to achieve that feeling, particularly in matters that have become habitual, a person has to prepare himself, and he must do this every time, with a conscious, repeated effort.

Those things that evoke love of God are always present and plentiful, but like all things that are truly important, they are so self-evident that one does not pay attention to them. He needs to say the blessings of the *Shema* every day, twice a day, in order to contemplate them with focused concentration. Perhaps at some point, the wall created by habit will crack and the individual will be able to feel something.

The need for this daily preparation is repeated in numerous places in the *Tanya*, the "Book of *Beinonim*," because it pertains specifically and fundamentally to *beinonim*. It does not concern a person who has sinned and whose eyes have subsequently been opened for the first time to the light of truth. The *beinoni*, on the other hand, who does not sin in deed, speech, or thought, is liable to become stuck in a routine of Torah study and mitzva performance, of service of God and even love of God, without attaining the authentic experience and power of loving Him "with all your heart and with all your soul." It is of this that the *Tanya* speaks: how to bring a decent, honest, kind, pleasant individual like this to lofty heights.

The blessing of *Yotzer Or* "describes and expounds at length," because contemplation requires a person to say the words repeatedly and to spend a lengthy amount of time on such repetition. This blessing describes how the supernal angels stand on the lofty heights of the universe in order to make us aware of God's greatness. Contemplating the supernal angels, who are in awe of God's greatness and completely subsumed in the divine light, allows us to join them, so to speak. We too feel His greatness and holiness, and we too sing God's praises.

כְּלוֹמַר, שֶׁהוּא מוּבְדָּל מֵהֶן וְאֵינוּ מִתְלַבֵּשׁ בָּהֶן בִּבְחִינַת גִּילּוּי, **"Holy" means that He is separate from them and is not overtly enclothed in them,**

The concept of holiness indicates that which is separate or distinct, and that which is beyond all limits and definitions. When the angels declare, "Holy, holy, holy," they are saying that God's reality is distinct and sublime, that He is on a much higher level than the angels and all the worlds, distant and separate from them at all times and on all planes.[14]

אֶלָּא "מְלֹא כָל הָאָרֶץ כְּבוֹדוֹ" הִיא 'כְּנֶסֶת יִשְׂרָאֵל' לְמַעְלָה, וְיִשְׂרָאֵל' לְמַטָּה, כַּנִּזְכָּר. **but rather,** as they continue and proclaim, **"His glory fills the entire world,"** **which refers** both **to the congregation of Israel on high and the Jewish people below, as explained above** (chap. 46).

After the angels proclaim, "Holy, holy, holy," they say, "His glory fills the entire world [*ha'aretz*]." According to the teachings of Kabbala, *ha'aretz*, which the Sages refer to as the Divine Presence and the kabbalists refer to as *Malkhut*, is the congregation of Israel, the source of all Jewish souls in the upper world. God's glory is likewise found in the lower

---

14. This does not mean to say that the angels apprehend God's holiness but rather that they do not understand it – and that is precisely due to His holiness. This explains how they are able to "declare" and "assert" even though they are nullified before Him. They are declaring the very fact that they are nullified before Him (the Lubavitcher Rebbe, Rabbi Menaḥem Mendel Schneerson).

realm, within the body of a Jew in this world, and it is revealed when they engage in Torah study and mitzvot.

The angels say, "Holy," because relative to them God is holy and distinct. If that is the case, where is God to be found? The angels answer, "His glory fills the entire world." His glory is revealed on earth, in the lowest and most material realm, because that is where He chose to dwell, within the Torah and mitzvot that the Jewish people fulfill in this physical world.

וְכֵן הָאוֹפַנִּים וְחַיּוֹת הַקּוֹדֶשׁ "בְּרַעַשׁ גָּדוֹל וכו' בָּרוּךְ כְּבוֹד ה' מִמְּקוֹמוֹ". לְפִי שֶׁאֵין יוֹדְעִים וּמַשִּׂיגִים מְקוֹמוֹ,

Likewise, "the angels known as ophanim and holy ḥayot raise themselves with a great clamor opposite the seraphim, and facing them, they offer praise and declare, 'Blessed is the glory of the Lord from His place,'" since they do not know or apprehend where His place is,

The ophanim and holy ḥayot are angels that are on a lower level than the seraphim. They do not grasp how God is holy and distinct from them, how "His glory fills the entire world," with the same level of clarity.

The seraphim have an intelligent, orderly worldview; they understand that God is holy and distinct, and that they cannot truly apprehend or perceive Him. They comprehend that there is a "place" in the lower realm where God has chosen to dwell. This is why they say: "Holy, holy, holy," and "God's glory fills the entire world." The ophanim and holy ḥayot, on the other hand, do not possess an intelligent picture of God's holiness but rather a strong feeling that He is present. Consequently, they rise up "with a great clamor opposite the seraphim," which are on a higher level than they are. Since they do not understand where the place of God's holiness is, they say: "Blessed is the glory of the Lord from His place," wherever that place may be.

וּכְמוֹ שֶׁאוֹמְרִים "כִּי הוּא לְבַדּוֹ מָרוֹם וְקָדוֹשׁ".

as we say in the continuation of the blessing: "For He is alone, exalted, and holy."

There are three elements to this phrase: "He is alone" means He exists and is an entity in and of Himself, "exalted" means that He is above reality, and "holy" means that He is distinct from all else.

The general theme of the *Yotzer Or* blessing is God's greatness, if not in terms of His infiniteness, then at least in relation to the enormous scope of the universe.[15] The blessing describes the sun and the moon, and above them, the angels and seraphim, and how they all proclaim the same thing: God is above and beyond all planes of reality. After saying these words and contemplating how the entire universe and all its contents, all the way to the highest possible realm, exist and live by means of His power alone and are insignificant in relation to Him, one can gain some grasp of God's greatness.

וְאַחַר כָּךְ בְּרָכָה שְׁנִיָּה: "אַהֲבַת עוֹלָם אֲהַבְתָּנוּ ה' אֱלֹהֵינוּ". **Then one recites the second blessing:** "You have loved us with an everlasting love, Lord, our God."

The first blessing of the *Shema* speaks of God's greatness and exaltedness above everything else. The second blessing focuses on His closeness. Only by grasping both His greatness and loftiness on the one hand, and His closeness on the other, can our connection to God be formed, overcoming all other desires and bonds for the sake of love of God alone.

כְּלוֹמַר, שֶׁהִנִּיחַ כָּל צְבָא מַעְלָה הַקְּדוֹשִׁים וְהִשְׁרָה שְׁכִינָתוֹ עָלֵינוּ, לִהְיוֹת נִקְרָא אֱלֹהֵינוּ, **This means that He set aside all the holy supernal hosts and bestowed His Divine Presence on us so that He is referred to as "our God"**

Although God is the Creator of all the luminaries and worlds, as we expressed in the *Yotzer Or* blessing, He chooses to be called *Elokeinu*, "our God." He is not called "God of the higher worlds and angels" but rather "our God." He left the higher worlds, so to speak, and brought

---

15. As the *Zohar* states (3:5a) regarding the verse "The Lord is great and exceedingly praised in the city of our God": "When is the Lord great? When He is 'in the city of our God.'" See also chap. 43; *Likkutei Torah*, Deut. 29b; *Torah Or* 56b.

Himself closer to the Jewish people, who are in this world, and attached Himself to us.

כְּמוֹ "אֱלֹהֵי אַבְרָהָם" כו' כַּנִּזְכָּר לְעֵיל in the same sense as the phrase "**God of Abraham...**," as stated above (chap. 46).

The term *Elokeinu*, "our God," may be understood in the same sense as the phrase "God of Abraham, God of Isaac, and God of Jacob." Our forefathers were chariots of God, vehicles for the Divine in this world so that they were subsumed and encompassed in His light. Since they were completely subsumed within Him, and possessed no element that was separate from Him, He is called "God of Abraham, God of Isaac, and God of Jacob." ☞

וְהַיְינוּ כִּי 'אַהֲבָה דּוֹחֶקֶת הַבָּשָׂר' (בבא מציעא פד, א). This is because "**love compresses the flesh**" (*Bava Metzia* 84a),

---

OUR GOD AND NOT THE GOD OF THE ANGELS

☞ The exact wording in the prayer book is "our God and the God of our forefathers." First we say "our God" and then "the God of our forefathers." The emphasis is on God's relationship with us, and only then comes the explanation of how this relationship became possible: because He is the "God of our forefathers." God did not choose us because we are superior to all other creations, but because this is what He chose: to humble Himself and to be called our God.

The Sages say, "Wherever you find [a reference to] the greatness of the Holy One, blessed be He, you [also] find [a reference to] His humility" (*Megilla* 31a; see also *Torah Or* 16a). His greatness and His humility are not mutually exclusive. On the contrary, precisely in the place where one is found, the other is also found. Wherever one finds God exalted over all the world, that is precisely where one finds His humility. When God is called the King of the universe, this is not a sign of His greatness but His humility, that He is willing to humble Himself and be called by this title.

To illustrate, a group of children are playing, and they are looking for someone to be the king in their game. A man walks past, and they ask him to play with them and be their king. If he agrees, this is not a sign of his greatness, but rather of his humility, because he is willing to play with small children and become the "king" in their world. This is all the more true with regard to God: He is willing to be called King of the universe, and this is an expression of His unparalleled humility.

All love contracts and minimizes the individual before his beloved. Even God, as it were, compresses His infinite self, as a result of His love for us, of being "our God."

וְלָכֵן נִקְרָא 'אַהֲבַת עוֹלָם', שֶׁהִיא בְּחִינַת צִמְצוּם אוֹרוֹ הַגָּדוֹל הַבִּלְתִּי תַכְלִית לְהִתְלַבֵּשׁ בִּבְחִינַת גְּבוּל הַנִּקְרָא עוֹלָם, בַּעֲבוּר אַהֲבַת עַמּוֹ יִשְׂרָאֵל, כְּדֵי לְקָרְבָם אֵלָיו, לִיבָּלֵל בְּיִחוּדוֹ וְאַחְדוּתוֹ יִתְבָּרֵךְ.

and thus this love **is called** *ahavat olam,* **world-centered love, which constitutes a constriction of His great, endless light so that it may become enclothed in the limitation that is called "world" for the sake of** His **love for His nation, Israel, in order to bring them close to Him so that they may become incorporated in His unity and oneness.**

This love that God has for us is called *ahavat olam,* love for the world in which He constricts Himself in order to come close to us. The Hebrew term for world, *olam,* has the same root as the term for concealment, *helem,* conveying the concealment of the infinite Creator within a finite, limited time and space. *Ahavat olam* means "world-centered love," a love that creates a world, that causes God to constrict Himself within its confines. This love is God's love for the Jewish people. Through this world, through Torah study and the fulfillment of mitzvot, the Jewish people are able to come extremely close to God and become incorporated within His unity.

וְזֶה שֶׁאוֹמְרִים: "חֶמְלָה גְדוֹלָה וִיתֵרָה", פֵּירוּשׁ: יְתֵרָה עַל קִרְבַת אֱלֹהִים שֶׁבְּכָל צְבָא מַעְלָה.

This is the meaning of what we say in the continuation of the blessing: "You have bestowed on us a great and exceeding compassion," meaning God's **compassion for us exceeds God's closeness to all the heavenly hosts,**

The *Ahavat Olam* blessing goes on to state that God has a great and exceeding compassion for us. "Great" compassion refers to His compassion for all of reality, encompassing both the higher and lower worlds.

For God, there is no difference between the smallest earthworm and the archangel Michael. Both are on the level of the "world," which exists on account of His compassion for its creations. Yet His compassion for His nation, the Jewish people, exceeds His compassion for the rest of the world. Not only does He sustain us, but He also brings us closer to Him than any of the supernal angels, though they exist on a higher plane and possess a greater apprehension of the Divine.

"וּבָנוּ בָחַרְתָּ מִכָּל עַם וְלָשׁוֹן", הוּא הַגּוּף הַחוֹמְרִי, הַנִּדְמֶה בְּחוֹמְרִיּוּתוֹ לְגוּפֵי אוּמּוֹת הָעוֹלָם. "**and You have chosen us from among all the nations and languages**," which refers to **the corporeal body** of a Jew, which resembles the bodies of the nations of the world in its physicality.

Choosing one object among equivalent objects is an arbitrary action that simply favors one particular object over everything else. True free choice is possible only between comparable objects, where there is no apparent advantage of one over another. If one thing is significantly more beneficial or detrimental, there really is no choice at all.

Likewise, God does not "choose" the souls of Israel, which are a portion of the Divine on high and are therefore inherently holy. Therefore, the phrase "and You have chosen us" refers to the bodies of Israel, which are essentially no different from the bodies of all the other nations. One cannot say that a particular body, brain, or arm is better than that of another person. God's choice, then, concerns only a Jew's physical body, which is not unique and is no better than that of a gentile.

"וְקֵרַבְתָּנוּ וכו', לְהוֹדוֹת" וכו'. וּפֵירוּשׁ הוֹדָאָה יִתְבָּאֵר בְּמָקוֹם אַחֵר. The blessing continues, "**And You brought us close** to Your great name **to give thanks** to You…," and the **explanation of** this **thanks will be explained elsewhere**,

The Talmud uses a similar term, *modeh*, to say that one Rabbi concedes to another. This does not involve understanding and accepting the other person's approach but only acknowledgment with regard to his conclusion. When one person concedes to another, this means that he accepts the other person's opinion even though according to his own understanding, the outcome should be different. In the same way, we must concede that God chose us from among all the nations.

Hoda'a is like a choice. It is not that one of the options possesses an obvious advantage, but on the contrary, we thank because we were chosen despite the fact that there is no obvious benefit of one over the other. The essence of giving thanks to God with glory and praise occurs when everything is not as clearly understood and felt as it should be. One may see things differently, or even understand and feel the exact opposite, yet he concedes that God is right.[16] ☞

NETZAḤ AND HOD

☞ Although in the order of *sefirot*, *Netzaḥ* (Dominance) and *Hod* (Splendor) are relatively lower than the others, they contain an advantage in that that they act in opposition, so to speak, to all the rules.

Netzaḥ is triumph, whether in war or in the struggle within reality. Yet the struggle is meaningful only as long as there is a chance of winning. The Ba'al Shem Tov said that the term *nitzaḥon*, victory, has the same numerical value as *tzeḥok*, laughter. The connection between these terms has far-reaching implications in several areas, but the simplest one is that the essence and power of victory exists as long as one is on the winning side, as long as he is still able to laugh in the face of a challenge, because he is the one who is triumphant.

This is *Netzaḥ*, the power to vanquish. Above it is *Hod*. *Hod* signifies existence against all odds. It is present when there are hardships and nothing is going well, when one knows that he is lost and has no chance, yet nevertheless he goes on. In view of this, *hoda'a* does not pertain to the moment of victory but to that of defeat. When there is no chance for success and everything is going wrong, we persist even when there seems to be no rational reason to go on. At that moment, we concede to God: Though the challenges seem insurmountable, still we persist in trying to attach to Him and be unified with Him.

In this sense, *hoda'a* contains a power greater than all other forces. This power is implied in the verse "Judah: You, your brothers shall acknowledge you [*yodukha*]" (Gen. 49:8). Judah, whose name connotes *hoda'a* and who was the chosen leader among his brothers, was also the one who conceded (specifically, he conceded that he was the father of Tamar's child, as recounted in Gen. 38). This quality of concession that Judah perfected is the characteristic of *Hod*.

---

16. See also *Torah Or* 45c; *Siddur im Divrei Elokim Ḥayyim, Sha'ar Lag BaOmer*.

"וּלְיַחֶדְךָ" כו', לִיכָּלֵל בְּיִחוּדוֹ יִתְבָּרֵךְ כַּנִּזְכָּר לְעֵיל. "and proclaim Your unity…," meaning, to be incorporated in God's unity, as stated above.

Proclaiming God's unity, making Him "one" in the full depth and extent of the term means recognizing that everything, which seems separate from Him, is all encompassed within the One. Most importantly, the person himself who is proclaiming God's unity is included in that oneness. He, his possessions, his thoughts, and his feelings are all subsumed within the divine unity.

Thus the theme of the second blessing of the *Shema*, *Ahavat Olam*, is that God brought us closer to Him than He brought any of His other creations. His relationship to us is one of choice and concession, of *hoda'a*, which is beyond all emotion and reason, so that we may be incorporated within His unity.

וְהִנֵּה, כַּאֲשֶׁר יָשִׂים הַמַּשְׂכִּיל אֵלֶּה הַדְּבָרִים אֶל עוּמְקָא דְלִבָּא וּמוֹחָא, **When the intelligent person reflects on these matters in the depths of his heart and mind,** 20 Iyar / 20 Iyar (leap year)

The blessings that precede the *Shema*, *Yotzer Or* and *Ahavat Olam*, were instituted in order to inspire the individual to love God with all his heart, soul, and might. For this to occur, it is not enough to merely recite the words without thought. One must contemplate them in the depths of his heart and mind. ☞

☞ How does one engage in such contemplation? How can a person internalize certain matters, such as those mentioned here, within the depths of his heart and mind? More generally, what is contemplation and how does it connect to prayer?

Despite everything that has been written on this topic, both in the *Tanya* and in other works, nowhere are there systematic instructions regarding how to achieve contemplation. Yet it is clear from what has been written in various works on the subject that there is a method to it. The author of the *Tanya* himself alludes to this.

Contemplation does not involve just thinking about an idea or even understanding it, nor does it mean emptying the mind of all other thoughts, a method employed in some types of meditation. Contemplation is active and structured thinking about a defined subject, but it is not only intellectual. The purpose of contemplation is not only to understand on a cerebral level but to internalize the subject of the thought and impact the soul. It should build something deep in the heart and mind that leads to an emotional response. This requires work, which constitutes maintaining the framework and sticking to the subject. When a person takes a subject and thinks about it, it should not be too general, such as "God's greatness," but should involve a certain degree of specificity. It should be determined by the individual ahead of time: "This is what I am going to think about now." Then he should sit and think about it, going over it again and again from one angle and then another. If he continues doing this repeatedly over time, the idea, which previously had been only a thought, will become a tangible reality for him in his mind and soul, and he will experience an emotional shift.

To aid in this effort, below are several insights on the subject of contemplation and how to employ it to achieve authentic results.

CONTEMPLATION EVEN OF THIS-WORLDLY AFFAIRS

This paradigm does not pertain only to the higher worlds but is part of the daily life of every individual. The author of the *Tanya* explains in all his works that we do not need to create new mechanisms for divine service but rather we can, and should, use our existing mechanisms. The process we employ can be the same with regard to the spiritual and the physical, to that which is holy and that which is not. Here too is an established mechanism: A person can evoke an emotional response through contemplation.

In light of this, everyone has engaged in contemplation in his life. If a person has ever loved, hated, felt angry or grateful, he reached that point through contemplation. Love, like all other emotional responses, is not evoked in an instant. That first flash creates, at most, attraction, interest, impetus, but more is required for it to become a deep, authentic experience. A second thought is also insufficient. Rather, it requires the repeated reconstruction of that first flash, that first thought. This is how the emotion and experience of love are created.

A more common example is that of a person who becomes angry or hateful. He is wronged, and whether the wrongdoing is real or imagined, the anger will pass if he does not think about it. But if he continues to think over and over about what the other person said or did to him, he will eventually become agitated. The event itself that caused the emotional reaction does not create deep-seated anger. At most, it may lead to an emotional outburst. True anger or hatred develops only when a person ruminates on the matter continually.

One could say the same of anxiety. When something happens to disturb a person's peace of mind, such as when a spouse does not arrive home on time, it is worrying, but it does not derail the person. But if he begins to consider all the possibilities of what might have happened and to analyze why and how the spouse might be late, if he has a good imagination as well as persistence, he may begin to panic and become severely anxious as a result of his fears.

People who have a well-developed imagination are subject to emotional extremes, for better or worse. But they will not come to such a state without contemplation. It is not always beneficial or indeed recommended, but it does constitute contemplation, thought that leads to a deep and authentic emotional experience.

All such emotions result from inner work, whether it is done intentionally or not, whether for holy purposes or not. It makes sense that the Hebrew verbs that describe emotional responses are reflexive: *hitragez* is to become angry; to fall in love is *hitahev*. This form indicates an action that the person does to himself: He made himself angry; he caused himself to love. This is the only way to create emotional experiences, both regarding mundane affairs and matters of holiness.

CONTEMPLATING GOD'S GREATNESS

Contemplating God's greatness presents a unique challenge. When a person thinks about an object that is found in the realm of his daily experience, it is easy for him to recreate an image of it in his mind time after time. But when the matter is more abstract and is not within the realm of his sensory perception or his regular thoughts, the time and effort required are much greater. Some people's intellect and imagination allow them to visualize abstract concepts, and it is easier for them to internalize these ideas and achieve an emotional experience as a result. But it is harder for others, who may worry less but find it more difficult to feel authentic emotional responses.

Yet internal divine service such as this, that which pertains to the self alone, does not hinge on the possession of particular talents, but stems from the person's very soul, from his being. The belief, at least in Chabad Hasidism, is that with hard work, every single person is able to achieve meaningful results from such an effort in accordance with his own level and character.

Over the course of the generations, there have been numerous celebrated hasidim who were considered simple individuals, not particularly intellectual or learned, yet in the context of Hasidism, they were outstanding. One such personality, for instance, was Reb Yekutiel Liepler, a disciple of Rabbi Shneur Zalman of Liadi (see *Likkutei Dibburim*, 19-20 Kislev 5693 2:18; see also chap. 42 and the commentary there). Such individuals are proof of the power of contemplation. They did not reach their lofty level because of the inherent capabilities of their souls, or other gifts from above, but because they took this matter literally, and seriously, and worked ceaselessly. They would sit for three or four hours before the prayer services began and force themselves to engage in contemplation. For someone who does not have the right nature for such lengthy and deep focus, it is extremely difficult to do. Usually, when a person like this sits down to contemplate these matters, within moments his thoughts wander to a topic that is easier to consider. But if he possesses the willpower and persists in clinging to the particular matter that he wanted to contemplate, over time a picture forms within his mind and heart, and if he persists, that picture continues to grow. Even if he still appears simple with regard to other matters, he too grows and achieves heights he might never have attained otherwise.

CONTEMPLATING LOVE OF GOD

As with all other types of contemplation, contemplation of love must relate to a specific topic. Accordingly, the blessings of *Yotzer Or* and *Ahavat Olam* are a topic that one should develop and expand. The first step in developing it has been outlined in this chapter. But as the author of the *Tanya* stated in the introduction to this work, people are very different from one another, particularly regarding this matter, which involves emotional subtleties. Different people become excited by different things. It is therefore difficult, indeed almost impossible, to expand on any topic in a way that will be equally meaningful to everyone. When more details are given, people become lost, and less of the content is meaningful for them. The author of the *Tanya* therefore presents only a general model that each individual must continue to develop in his effort to instill the words "in the depths of his mind and heart."

In Chabad Hasidism there were, and still are, hasidim who would sit for extended periods before and during the prayer service. When they would reach *Yotzer Or*, they would contemplate this matter, God's love for us, His greatness and desire to be close to us. When they recited *Ahavat Olam*, they would contemplate the matter again. They would contemplate it over and over until they were stirred by feelings of love and fear, and only then would they begin their prayers. Beyond the effort it requires, praying this way also takes a long time. It can last for four or five hours, and one certainly cannot do it in the short time that communal prayer services usually take. There is no fixed solution for this; it varies from time to time, from person to person, and even from generation to generation.

The accepted practice in our day actually seems to be almost the opposite of what was customary in other times. During the talmudic era, for example, when a person did not feel ready to pray, he was not required to pray. If a person was tired, busy, or stressed, it was preferable that they did not pray at that moment in time. The Talmud states that Rabbi Yehuda would pray only once every thirty days, when he finished reviewing what he had learned and his mind was free (*Rosh HaShana* 35a; *Iggeret HaKodesh*, epistle 26). These examples constitute the theoretical and halakhic basis for customs like those found among hasidim in some places.

Another approach, which is more accepted in our day, is that one recite the prayers anyway, at the established times, three times every day, whether he feels ready for prayer or not. The basis for this approach is the assumption that usually we do not really focus when we engage in prayer. If a person prays with the proper intentions, it is impossible to dictate when he will be ready for prayer. But if he does not pray with the proper intentions in any case, we can oblige him to recite the words at fixed times.

This idea is akin to preparing a student to take a test after he has failed it several times. The tutor spends a long time with the student, systematically going over all the questions that might be on the test. The assumption is since they have gone over so many questions, they must surely have covered the actual test questions among them. It is not a targeted approach. It assumes that if a person prays three times a day, a thousand times a year, then on at least one of those occasions, his emotions and his words will converge.

Consequently, a set formula was instituted for the prayers. The assumption is that if a person repeats the same words several times every day, then the right words will be said at the right time at least once. When this happens, it justifies all the repetition and exertion. An awakening from above is only the beginning of the process. It needs to be channeled and given shape in the moment and beyond.

It is not enough just to say the words. To develop authentic emotion, one must also repeat the basic concepts and the principles on which they are constructed. There are those who experience an awakening

CHAPTER 49

אֲזַי מִמֵּילָא, "כַּמַּיִם הַפָּנִים לַפָּנִים", תִּתְלַהֵט נַפְשׁוֹ וְתִתְלַבֵּשׁ בְּרוּחַ נְדִיבָה, לְהִתְנַדֵּב לְהַנִּיחַ וְלַעֲזוֹב כָּל אֲשֶׁר לוֹ מִנֶּגֶד,

then inevitably, "as water reflects a face to the face" (Prov. 27:19), **his soul will be ignited and enveloped in a generous spirit to willingly disregard and forego all that he possesses,**

After contemplating God's love of for us, which is described in the blessings of the *Shema*, the individual's soul will be ignited with love of God in turn, and he will offer up something that belongs to him, an object that has value and importance to him. The author of the *Tanya* is not talking about a person who already recognizes that there is nothing else but God, because to someone like that, nothing is important except God, and he does not need to give up anything of his own. This discussion concerns a person who wants to achieve love of God and has even begun to feel something, yet he is still attached to the world, to people, actions, and objects. This person is told to contemplate how

from above, and only years later, they realize how close they came to truly unifying with the Divine, yet they did not achieve it because they were not ready. They were not holding onto the other end of the thread in order to form a real connection. This is the intrinsic value of the repetition of words, and even more, of concepts and thought processes. Even if in a particular moment, they do not find expression within so that the person experiences a tangible emotional response, repetition provides the opportunity for this to occur.

The author of the *Tanya*'s approach, which is expressed in several places in the *Tanya*, and on an even more practical level, in his letters to his hasidim, is that one should in any case spend a long time in prayer. In one letter (*Iggeret HaKodesh*, epistle 1), he wrote that one who does not pray for at least an hour and a half every day would not be permitted to come to him to hear his teachings. He allowed only those people who had to earn their livelihood, whose time was not their own, to pray briefly, but this pertained only to weekdays, not to the Sabbath and festivals, when they too had to pray at length.

The time frame of an hour and a half or more is clearly not referring only to the recitation of the words, which itself does not take long, but rather to contemplation of prayer and internalizing the concepts within the depths of one's heart and mind. The Chabad custom today is to begin the Sabbath morning prayers at ten o'clock. This allows the individual to spend two or more hours studying hasidic works, preparing his soul for prayer. After this preparation, when the heart is ignited, he can begin to pray properly for two, three, or even five hours in accordance with his capacity. Even if one cannot engage in this preparation, even if one is not inspired on every occasion, the framework has been put into place; the path and the impetus toward an awakening from within have been established.

God constricts Himself out of His love for him, which is greater than His love of all the higher worlds, and how He breaks down all barriers in order to come close to him. Subsequently, the person's love is also ignited, and he willingly abandons all he has and clings beyond all measure and limitation to God alone.

וְרַק לְדָבְקָה בּוֹ יִתְבָּרֵךְ, וְלִיכָּלֵל בְּאוֹרוֹ בִּדְבִיקָה חֲשִׁיקָה וכו׳ so that he may cleave only to God and be incorporated in His light with an attachment, longing, and desire

Thus, the individual contemplates what he has said in the blessings of *Shema*, about God's greatness and holiness on the one hand, and about the fact that He leaves all the higher worlds for us on the other hand. When he instills these matters deep within his heart and mind, he attains such a tremendous feeling of gratitude and love that he is prepared to give up everything he has for the sake of this love, for the sake of his attachment to God.

בִּבְחִינַת נְשִׁיקִין, וְאִתְדַּבְּקוּת רוּחָא בְּרוּחָא כַּנִּזְכָּר לְעֵיל. in a manner of kissing and the fusion of spirit with spirit, as explained above (chaps. 45, 46).

A kiss is a metaphor for the union between the soul and the Divine, the merging and unification of spirit with spirit, which results when a person utters the word of God with God, so to speak – a unification of breath with breath. As will be explained below, when a person studies Torah and utters the words, a union takes place, a fusing of spirit with spirit. The person's spirit merges with God's spirit, his essence with the essence of the Divine.

אַךְ אֵיךְ הִיא בְּחִינַת ׳אִתְדַּבְּקוּת רוּחָא בְּרוּחָא׳? Yet how is this fusion of spirit with spirit achieved?

What is the author of the *Tanya* asking here? It would seem that once a person contemplates God's love for him and attains love of God in turn, the outcome will occur automatically. Yet even though the work of contemplation was undertaken in order to achieve love of God, the love itself is not the answer. Love of God is an awakening within the person, and accordingly, the blessings of the *Shema* and the contemplation of these blessings are an awakening to an awakening. Yet just as the awakening that constituted the contemplation is not the goal, neither is the love of God.

Thus far, the individual has achieved love of God; he desires to cling to Him and is willing to give up everything for Him, with all his heart, soul, and might. Yet this is not the end. It is merely the longing that is supposed to draw the person forward, toward the "fusion of spirit with spirit." This raises one of the toughest questions with regard to the essence of Judaism: How can we actualize an attachment to God, the fusing of spirit with spirit, in a way that expresses and sustains a love that is felt "with all your heart, and with all your soul, and with all your might"?

לָזֶה אָמַר: "וְהָיוּ הַדְּבָרִים הָאֵלֶּה כו' עַל לְבָבֶךָ, וְדִבַּרְתָּ בָּם" כו'. **For this reason,** the next passage of the *Shema* states, **"These matters** that I command you today **shall be upon your heart....** You shall inculcate them in your children, **and you shall speak of them..."** (Deut. 6:6–7).

The Hebrew word *bam*, in the phrase "and you shall speak of them [*bam*]," literally means "in them," implying that one speaks within the words, because they are God's words. In other words, even as one says the words, one senses that they exist in a reality that is beyond him yet in which he now finds himself. The Maggid of Mezeritch comments on the verse "It was as the musician played, and the hand of the Lord was upon him" (II Kings 3:15) that although a musical instrument emits the sounds, it is not the creator of the tune but merely a vessel for its production.[17] Similarly, one who speaks words of Torah should see himself only as a medium for God's words, an instrument for the words that God places in his mouth.[18] The person's task is merely to try not to ruin them by negating himself and being as much as possible. A perfect vessel is one that is itself completely nullified to that which

---

17. See *Or Torah* 387a.
18. See Isa. 59:21; see also *Iggeret HaTeshuva*, chap. 9; *Likkutei Torah*, Lev. 27a.

it contains, so that it can hold a thing as it is, intact, without adding, removing, or changing it. If one achieves this level of perfection, then when he speaks words of Torah, it is as though they emanate directly from God. ☞

וּכְמוֹ שֶׁכָּתוּב בְּ'עֵץ חַיִּים' (שַׁעַר ל דְּרוּשׁ ב) שֶׁ'יִּחוּד הַנְּשִׁיקִין', עִיקָרוֹ הוּא יִחוּד חָכְמָה בִּינָה דַּעַת בְּחָכְמָה בִּינָה דַּעַת וְהוּא עִיּוּן הַתּוֹרָה,

This may be understood **in accordance with what is stated in** *Etz Ḥayyim* **(30:2), that the union of kissing is primarily a unification of** a person's faculties of **wisdom, understanding, and knowledge** with God's attributes of *Ḥokhma*, *Bina*, and *Da'at*, which is achieved **through study of Torah,**

The author of the *Tanya* explains how the "union of kissing," the fusion of spirit with spirit, between man and God, is achieved. When a person employs his faculty of wisdom to study Torah, "these matters that shall be upon your heart," which is God's wisdom, this constitutes joint thinking. The individual is thinking what God is thinking, so to speak, and is united with Him in thought and wisdom. This is the union of spirit with spirit.

THE NULLIFIED VESSEL

☞ One of the biggest questions in modern technology is how to transmit electricity without resistance. When a current flows through an object, the material resists the flow to a certain degree, and some of the energy is lost as a result. To combat this, scientists are working on developing superconductors that would be able to transmit electric currents without any energy loss. When we speak "within" words of Torah, we need to know how to make ourselves into superconductors that can convey the Torah's contents without diminishing it in any way.

Taking the analogy even further, when a material is cooled until it is close to absolute zero, a state that is akin to complete stillness, it has no resistance. As soon as its temperature rises and it begins to come alive, it develops resistance just by virtue of its existence. In this sense, when the soul speaks within the words of Torah, it is revivified in the body and the world at large. Yet as a result, it develops resistance – concealment and obstructions – so that ultimately the words of the Torah that emerge from the person's mouth may seem no different from anything else he utters.

CHAPTER 49

וְהַפֶּה הוּא מוֹצָא הָרוּחַ וְגִילּוּיוֹ, בִּבְחִינַת גִּילּוּי, וְהַיְינוּ בְּחִינַת הַדִּבּוּר בְּדִבְרֵי תוֹרָה,

and the mouth, is the outlet of the breath and its emergence into a revealed state, which corresponds to the category of speech employed in speaking **words of Torah,**

Just as in the physical realm the mouth releases the breath and the sounds that make up speech, so too in the spiritual realm the mouth is the revelation of the union of spirit with spirit. Speech is the revelation of thought, and the mouth is the vessel for that speech, revealing the union of spirit with spirit, which is achieved through Torah study and thoughts of Torah. Thus, the "union of kissing" is attained through Torah study through the cognitive faculties of wisdom, understanding, and knowledge, and this union is revealed through speaking words of Torah. When a person speaks words of Torah, which are the words of God, with his own mouth, he is saying them together with God. At that moment, he is joined with God mouth to mouth, so to speak.

"כִּי עַל מוֹצָא פִּי ה' יִחְיֶה הָאָדָם"
(דברים ח, ג).

"for it is by everything that emanates from the mouth of the Lord that man lives" (Deut. 8:3).

21 Iyar
(leap year)

The words of Torah that a person speaks "emanate from the mouth of the Lord," and the person receives his life force from them. The union that results from speaking words of Torah, the "union of kissing," is the most spiritual of all connections. The person is completely unified with the holiness contained within him and the holiness that encompasses him.

וּמִכָּל מָקוֹם, לֹא יָצָא יְדֵי חוֹבָתוֹ בְּהִרְהוּר וְעִיּוּן לְבַדּוֹ, עַד שֶׁיּוֹצִיא בִּשְׂפָתָיו

At any rate, one does not fulfill his obligation of Torah study **with thought and deliberation alone unless he pronounces** the words **with his lips**

The union that results from the study and understanding of Torah is deeper and more complete than the bond that forms through the performance of mitzvot.[19] Thoughts of Torah are entirely bound up within the Torah, and at the same time, the Torah is bound up within one's thoughts. A thought about an object acts upon that object and is acted upon by the object; it both surrounds it and is surrounded by it. This kind of union is incomparable to any other known relationship model. As the author of the *Tanya* states above:[20] "This constitutes a wondrous union, of which no likeness or [equal] estimation can be found at all in the physical realm, [a union where the human intellect and divine wisdom of the Torah] are literally one and the same from every side and angle." In light of this, the author of the *Tanya* emphasizes that studying Torah aloud, actually uttering the words of Torah that one is studying, has its own inherent value in addition to revealing the union formed within the thoughts of Torah.

One hasidic master provides an analogy to illustrate this concept. When two drops of mercury coalesce to form one larger drop, we cannot say that one drop has absorbed or incorporated the other. Rather, a new entity has been created, and the distinction between the two drops no longer exists. This is the fusion of spirit with spirit of which the author of the *Tanya* speaks.

כְּדֵי לְהַמְשִׁיךְ אוֹר אֵין סוֹף בָּרוּךְ הוּא לְמַטָּה, עַד נֶפֶשׁ הַחִיּוּנִית, הַשּׁוֹכֶנֶת בְּדַם הָאָדָם, **in order to draw down the light of *Ein Sof*, blessed be He, until it reaches the vital soul that resides in a person's blood,**

The vital soul gives life to the human body,[21] as explained in chapter 1. Speech and action are bodily processes that are activated by the vital soul. Thus, when a person speaks words of Torah, he includes his body in his attachment to God.

מִתְהַוֶּה מִדּוֹמֵם צוֹמֵחַ חַי, כְּדֵי לְהַעֲלוֹת כּוּלָן לַה', עִם כָּל הָעוֹלָם כּוּלּוֹ, **which is produced from inanimate, vegetative, and living matter in order to elevate them all to God, along with the entire world,**

---

19. See chap. 5.
20. Chap. 5.
21. See chap. 1.

Whatever a person eats is absorbed and incorporated into his blood, his body, with which he is able to speak. In that case, along with the body, which speaks words of Torah, all the inanimate, vegetative, and living matter that gives life to the body ascends too. Furthermore, they do not ascend alone. They signify the entire world and raise it up together with them.[22]

וּלְכָלְלָן בְּיִחוּדוֹ וְאוֹרוֹ יִתְבָּרֵךְ אֲשֶׁר יָאִיר לָאָרֶץ וְלַדָּרִים בִּבְחִינַת גִּילוּי, "וְנִגְלָה כְּבוֹד ה' וְרָאוּ כָל בָּשָׂר" וכו' (ישעיה מ, ה), שֶׁזֶּהוּ תַּכְלִית הִשְׁתַּלְשְׁלוּת כָּל הָעוֹלָמוֹת - לִהְיוֹת כְּבוֹד ה' מָלֵא כָּל הָאָרֶץ הַלֵּזוּ דַּוְקָא, בִּבְחִינַת גִּילוּי

and incorporate them in God's unity and light, which will shine on the earth and on those that dwell on it in a revealed manner, as the verse states, "The glory of the Lord will be revealed, and all flesh will see together that the mouth of the Lord has spoken" (Isaiah 40:5). **This is the ultimate purpose of the devolvement of all the worlds: so that the glory of God may specifically fill this** physical **earth in a manifest state**

The purpose of the existence of all the worlds, which is for God's glory to shine, is not rooted in the higher, spiritual worlds but in this physical world. In light of this, though the connection to God that is found within Torah thoughts is sublime and spiritual, it is for this very reason that it is not a fulfillment of God's intent when He created the world, for it does not touch upon the world; the world remains outside of it. By contrast, the unity formed through speech, through speaking words of Torah, is generated within the physical reality.

Sound is formed by means of a person's muscles, and the activation of each muscle employs the body's energy and resources, which are themselves generated through all that the person has eaten, gathered, and interacted with in the material world. When speech constitutes Torah, not only does it give meaning to the spirit but also to physical matter, and not only to physicality of the individual, but to all matter

---

22. See *Iggeret HaTeshuva*, chap. 12.

in existence. Human beings are not self-contained. One lives within the world and is connected to it, just as all objects within the world are interconnected and interdependent. When a person speaks words of Torah and connects with God, he draws the whole world along with him. When his body is elevated, it is not elevated alone because his life in this world is dependent on an immense system involving the sun's light, the earth, and innumerable other components that enable each muscle in his body to move and his mouth to speak words of Torah. When he ascends to the Divine by means of a particular word, he does not rise alone. He lifts up the entirety of the physical world together with him through countless concealed threads.

This does not apply only to material objects. A person's soul, with its faculties and experiences, is not detached or isolated from everything. Rather, it is interwoven with other souls and all the spiritual worlds as a whole. When one performs a holy act, that holiness is connected to and stems from the worlds and spiritual processes that led him to that place. Holiness that a person creates is connected, materially and spiritually, not only to him but also to his parents and grandparents, and through it he justifies not only his own existence but also the existence of all generations that came before him.

This idea is related to the significance of saying Kaddish for a person who has died, and it is related to the concept that "the son confers merit upon the father" (*Sanhedrin* 104a). The source for the recitation of Kaddish is a story in one of the minor tractates:[23] A man who had died appeared to Rabbi Akiva and said that his soul could not be rectified until his son would recite words of holiness amid a quorum of Jews. The deceased had not performed even one act of holiness in his life, so it would seem that his soul could not be rectified or elevated at all. This story teaches that if a person performs an act of holiness, he can confer merit on his father. Just as the child's body is bound to his parents, who gave him life, his soul is likewise bound to them. Even if the father's soul is no longer in his body, he is able to receive merit from the child.

The Talmud states regarding the verse "For that is all of man" (Eccles. 12:13): "The entire world was created [to serve] as companions for him" (*Berakhot* 6b). The entire world was created just for

---

23. *Kalla Rabbati* 2:9.

the individual, just so that he would have company. Similarly, the Mishna describes the virtues of a person who studies Torah, among them that "he is worth the whole world" (*Avot* 6:1). All of creation was worthwhile because of that individual. It may be said that the moment any person performs a mitzva, he justifies the existence of the entire world, the physical and the spiritual, in the present and in the past.

We have no way of measuring the value of a mitzva, just as we have no way of measuring the value of a human being. Nonetheless, it is important to recognize that each mitzva, or word of Torah, is connected to a complex array of other elements, and that it penetrates and illuminates the entire world. A dark, meaningless, unfathomable world can suddenly begin to shine brightly when a holy act or thought lights it up and fills it with meaning.

| לְאַהֲפְכָא חֲשׁוֹכָא לִנְהוֹרָא וּמְרִירָא לְמִיתְקָא, כַּנִּזְכָּר לְעֵיל בַּאֲרִיכוּת. | and transform darkness into light and bitterness into sweetness, as explained above at length (chaps. 36–37). |

This is the advantage of light that comes from darkness.[24] When bitterness is transformed into sweetness, darkness into light, this has a much greater impact than something that was sweet or light to begin with.

| וְזֶהוּ תַּכְלִית כַּוָּנַת הָאָדָם בַּעֲבוֹדָתוֹ, לְהַמְשִׁיךְ אוֹר אֵין סוֹף בָּרוּךְ הוּא לְמַטָּה. | This is the ultimate intention of a person in his service of God, namely to draw the light of *Ein Sof* below. |

The purpose of the creation of the world is not the fusing of spirit with spirit, of the divine soul with God, but rather it is the drawing down of the divine unity into the world. It is not the elevation of the individual to a higher world but the bringing down of God's glory into this lower world.

---

24. Introduction to the *Zohar* 4b; see also *Kitzurim VeHe'arot LeSefer Likkutei Amarim*.

רַק שֶׁצָּרִיךְ תְּחִלָּה 'הַעֲלָאַת מַיִּין נוּקְבִין' לִמְסוֹר לוֹ נַפְשׁוֹ וּמְאוֹדוֹ, כַּנִּזְכָּר לְעֵיל. **But** in order to achieve this purpose, **it is necessary first to cause feminine waters to ascend by sacrificing his soul and everything** material that he possesses **to Him, as explained above.**

"Feminine waters" is a kabbalistic concept that refers to the lower reality, that of the creative worlds, which have the quality of receiving, a feminine quality. Elevating the feminine waters, then, refers to the elevation of the receiver toward the giver, which corresponds to the upper realms. More specifically, the author of the *Tanya* is referring to the spiritual work of contemplating the blessings of the *Shema* and the *Shema* itself in order to attain love of God "with all your heart, and with all your soul, and with all your might."

A person's ultimate purpose, what constitutes his divine service, is the drawing down of God's glory into the world, and it is the purpose of the existence of all the worlds. Yet this cannot happen without raising the feminine waters, without the individual down below making an effort to reach out to the Divine. Without self-sacrifice on his part, he cannot become a vessel and conduit worthy of having the divine light flow through him, illuminating both the physical and the spiritual realms as a result.

Ultimately, revelation and lifegiving sustenance comes from above. But it cannot issue forth unless the individual breaks through the wall below. In this vein, the Sages said, "Open for Me an opening of repentance like the eye of a needle, and I will open for you openings through which carts and wagons can enter" (*Shir HaShirim Rabba* 5:2). Only when one performs a mitzva below will God perform similar acts in turn, so to speak. Only when a person gives up his soul and his material possessions for the sake of God does God move into his world.

In order for this world to exist, there is necessarily a screen between this reality and God. If that screen were removed, there would be no world. Yet the purpose of the world is to reveal God's glory in the world, specifically there, where it is profoundly concealed. It is a paradox, and it seems impossible to achieve. Nevertheless, there is one way to accomplish it, and that is when the world approximates infinity.

There are many examples where there is no connection between two domains, and the only way to link them is to create something in one of the domains that contains a trace of the essence of the other. When there is some common denominator between them, the two can be joined together.

There is no tangible contact between the Divine, that which is infinite, and the world, which is limited. In order to forge a connection between them, the world must construct something that marginally resembles that which is infinite. There is only one way to achieve this: when a person in the lower, limited world breaks through the boundaries of his own essence and creates within himself an opening to infinity. When one gives up his soul and his material possessions, when he sacrifices what he has beyond natural limits, God in turn goes beyond His limits, so to speak, and reveals the Divine within the world. This is indeed an impossible phenomenon as long as the individual has not created this possibility, but once he has done so, it becomes all too possible.

This concept is manifest in the process of repentance. Regarding the repentance of Manasseh, king of Judah, the verse states, "He prayed to Him, and He acceded [*vaye'ater*] to his entreaty" (II Chron. 33:13). The Talmud reads the word *vaye'ater* as if it says *vayeḥater*, with the letter *ḥet* replacing the *ayin*. It states: "'And He made an opening [*vayeḥater*] for him': This teaches that the Holy One, blessed be He, crafted for him a type of opening in Heaven in order to accept him in repentance" (*Sanhedrin* 103a).

From God's perspective, repentance means accepting the penitent. He breaches the entire system of time and causality and creates a new being for whom all that occurred in the past does not exist. This cannot happen unless the penitent himself does a comparable act, breaking down the structures of his very being. When one is able to "make an opening," performing an act that is beyond his own limitations, God too can "make an opening" in Heaven, breaking the structure of reality and accepting the person's repentance, ostensibly without the knowledge of the attribute of justice.

The author of the *Tanya* concludes this chapter by saying that in order to raise "feminine waters," in order to reach out to the Divine from this lower reality, one must sacrifice his soul and everything he possesses, literally his "might." There is no fixed measure to such a sacrifice. It depends on the individual's heart and soul, and it changes like the horizon. Every time a person achieves love for God with all his heart and soul, no matter how high he has reached, there is always a little more to go. That is what is referred to as "with all your might." Even if all your energy has been exhausted, and it seems you have nothing left to give, yet still you make a supreme effort, "with all your might," you will find you can go further and achieve more.

The author of the *Tanya* is striving to unlock the secret of how to go one step further. These are the feminine waters that rise up and open the gate from above.

With this chapter, the discussion of God's love for us and our love for Him in turn concludes. The beginning of the chapter described how God constricted His light in order to reach humankind. When contemplating this phenomenon, a person is spurred to constrict himself, renouncing all worldly matters and clinging to God alone. Achieving this love and forging this connection is the central theme of the blessings of the *Shema* and the focus of the recitation of the *Shema* itself.

Chapter 50

THE PREVIOUS CHAPTERS DISCUSSED THE VARIOUS degrees and ways of loving God (see chaps. 43–49). Now the author of the *Tanya* concludes this subject, as well as the topic of divine service through love and fear (which began in chapter 41), by describing an all-encompassing love that transcends all the other types of love mentioned so far. This all-encompassing love employs all the spiritual faculties so that there is no other emotion or level one can attain other than a yearning to be unified with God, a yearning that is so intense that it can only lead to the expiration of the soul.

וְהִנֵּה כָּל בְּחִינוֹת וּמַדְרֵגוֹת אַהֲבָה הַנִּזְכָּרוֹת לְעֵיל הֵן מִסִּטְרָא דִּימִינָא, **All the aforementioned aspects and levels of love** emanate **from the right side** of the array of the *sefirot*,   21 Iyar   22 Iyar (leap year)

The various types of love of God that were discussed in the previous chapters belong overall to two categories: *ahavat olam*, world-centered love, and *ahava rabba*, great love. Each these levels of love is of a particular scope, intensity, and class, but all of them are from the right side of the array of the *sefirot*, which is the side of Ḥesed (Kindness). ☞

THE ARRAYS OF THE *SEFIROT*

☞ Like the ten cosmic *sefirot*, the soul's faculties can be arranged into three arrays, three groups of *sefirot*. The right array is that of Ḥesed, composed of the *sefirot* of Ḥokhma, Ḥesed, and Netzaḥ. The left array is that of Gevura, composed of the *sefirot* of Bina, Gevura, and Hod. The array in the middle is composed of the *sefirot* of Da'at,

וּבְחִינַת כֹּהֵן, אִישׁ חֶסֶד. — represented by **the priest,** who is referred to as **a man of kindness.**

The right array, that of *Ḥesed*, is also that of the priest, who is known as a "man of kindness."[1] The core theme of the priestly service is *Ḥesed* and the *sefirot* associated with it, whereas the Levite service is characterized by *Gevura*, as the author of the *Tanya* will go on to explain. *Ḥesed* is the attribute of flow and propagation from above to below. This is the service of the priest: to draw down blessing from above. The Sages even refer to the priest as an "agent of the Merciful One" (*Kiddushin* 23b). The priest is not the agent of any person, to make contact with the Divine on an individual's behalf or even for the sake of Israel as collective. He is an agent of God, tasked with conveying the flow of divine sustenance and vitality from above to below.

וְנִקְרָא 'כֶּסֶף הַקֳּדָשִׁים', מִלְּשׁוֹן "נִכְסוֹף נִכְסַפְתָּ לְבֵית אָבִיךָ" (בראשית לא, ל). — It is also **called the consecrated silver,** because the word for silver, *kesef,* **is related to the word** *kasof,* **"longing," as in the verse "You longed [*nikhsof nikhsafta*] for your father's house"** (Gen. 31:30).

Tiferet, Yesod, and *Malkhut.* In these groupings, all the types of love that the author of the *Tanya* has discussed thus far are associated with the right array, and all the levels of fear relate to the left. Yet this division is not so rudimentary. Human beings are not one-dimensional, but possess varying and sometimes even opposing traits. Furthermore, the traits do not function independently but always in conjunction with the other traits to some degree.

This concept is reflected in the text for the counting of the Omer that appears in most prayer books. One counts for seven weeks, and each week is characterized by one of the seven lower *sefirot*. Each day of the week is subdivided into the seven lower *sefirot* as well. The first week, for instance, corresponds to *Ḥesed*. Sunday is *Ḥesed* within *Ḥesed*, Monday is *Gevura* within *Ḥesed*, and so on. The next week corresponds to *Gevura*. Sunday is *Ḥesed* within *Gevura*, Monday is *Gevura* within *Gevura*, and so on. In view of this, although the levels of love usually relate to the array of *Ḥesed* on the right, there is a type of love that stems from the left, as the author of the *Tanya* will go on to explain. In any event, all of the types of love discussed in the previous chapters emerge from the right side, the side of *Ḥesed*.

---

1. See Deut. 33:8.

This level of love that stems from the right side is also called "consecrated silver,"[2] which the author of the *Tanya* interprets as a sense of longing for that which is sacred, the soul's desire to cling to its Father in Heaven. "Your father" in the verse represents the *sefira* of Ḥokhma, which is the first *sefira* in the right array. This type of love is also referred to as "love that is like water."

By contrast, love that belongs to the left side is called "love that is like sparks of fire."[3] Love that is like water flows continuously from above to below. The most salient element of this love is that of drawing close, of identifying and uniting with the object of the love, the overall drive to come closer, to touch and to connect. This is the nature of all the types of love that have been discussed so far, whether *ahavat olam* or *ahava rabba*. In all its forms, it is a serene love that brings peace. When people speak of happiness, they are usually talking about the experience of such love.

Because of the strong element of connection involved in this love, reciprocity is essential. There must be a response from the other side, so that the emotions find a tangible expression.

אַךְ יֵשׁ עוֹד בְּחִינַת אַהֲבָה הָעוֹלָה עַל כּוּלָנָה, כְּמַעֲלַת הַזָּהָב עַל הַכֶּסֶף, **Yet there is another level of love that is superior to all the rest, like the superiority of gold over silver,**

If all the types of love mentioned in the previous chapters are like silver, then this love is like gold. Granted, silver is a precious metal, and love that is like silver comprises exceedingly high levels. Nevertheless, there is another type of love that is superior to them all in terms of the intensity of the emotion and its power to cause an individual to change.[4]

---

2. The Lubavitcher Rebbe, Rabbi Menaḥem Mendel Schneerson, points out that it is possible that the author of the *Tanya* is alluding to the verse "All the consecrated silver that is brought to the House of the Lord..." (II Kings 12:5), referring to the silver that the Israelites donated to the Temple and so belonged to the priests. See also *Torah Or* 86d.
3. See *Sefer HaArakhim, Ahavat Hashem* 6; *Ahava KaMayim*.
4. Whether this love is also superior to the love of delights discussed in chapter 9, see *Pelaḥ HaRimmon, Parashat Vayera* 30b, and *Torah Or* 47c, which explain that there are two types of love of delights. One can delight in the name of *Havaya*,

וְהִיא אַהֲבָה כְּרִשְׁפֵּי אֵשׁ **and that is love like sparks of fire,**

This love surpasses love that is like water because the constant happiness that characterized the love that is like water, the love that stems from Ḥesed, is accompanied by an element of peace and tranquility, which brings with it the danger of becoming complacent. This is the feeling that "I am here and You, God, are there. We are connected to one another, and with that I am content." By contrast, love that is like sparks of fire does not allow a person peace of mind. He cannot be satisfied with the level he has attained, and he consumes anything that does not align with his yearning for the Divine. Everything else ceases to have importance or value, not only because he does not think about them, but because he actively engages in eradicating them. This kind of love is not peaceful, it is not enjoyable, nor does it provide a feeling of contentment. On the contrary, one may suffer as a result of it. He may be burned by it. Yet it is more essential to the human experience than love like water, in the same way that gold is superior to silver. ☞

LOVE LIKE FIRE VERSUS LOVE LIKE WATER

☞ Like fire and water, these two types of love are natural opposites. The author of the *Tanya* explains elsewhere (*Likkutei Torah*, Lev. 40c) that the nature of water is to combine different elements, whereas the nature of fire is to separate them. Love that is like water is therefore the desire to come closer and connect. When the individual is near the object of his love, he feels content and desires nothing more. This kind of attraction is understated. It draws the one who loves and the object of the love together until the love reaches the climactic point of complete attachment.

The book of Psalms describes love that is like water: "Instead I have composed and quieted my soul like a weaned child on its mother; like a weaned child is my soul" (Ps. 131:2). The verse depicts a baby longing for his mother, who gathers him into her arms. When the child is united with her, he is content and wants nothing more. He feels as though he has everything he could possibly desire. His heart is full.

By contrast, love that is like fire constitutes the drive to separate the soul's faculties from the physical vessels that contain them, to expire and literally be consumed in the Divine.

These two types of love are apparent in the source of creation, and this constitutes a love of delights that is inferior to the love that the author of the *Tanya* goes on to describe: "love that is like sparks of fire." But when one delights "upon," or higher than, *Havaya*, when one reaches that which transcends the source of the worlds, this is a love of delights that is superior to the love that is like fire.

מִבְּחִינַת גְּבוּרוֹת עֶלְיוֹנוֹת דְּבִינָה עִילָּאָה. which emanates **from the level of the supernal *Gevurot* of supernal *Bina*.**

Love that is like fire stems from the side of *Gevura*, though not from the attribute of *Gevura* itself, which is characterized by emotional constriction, but rather from the higher aspects of *Gevura*, the source of the *Gevurot* in *Bina*. The *sefira* of *Bina* is in the left array of the *sefirot*, which is the side of *Gevura*. *Bina* is called the "mother" of all seven attributes below it, including both *Gevura* and *Ḥesed*. This means that love, which is an aspect of *Ḥesed*, can stem from *Bina*, but it also contains an element of *Gevura*. This is love from the left side, a love that is like fire, which differs from the aforementioned types of love that stemmed from *Ḥesed*, from the right side of the array.

דְּהַיְינוּ שֶׁעַל יְדֵי הִתְבּוֹנְנוּת בִּגְדוּלַת אֵין סוֹף בָּרוּךְ הוּא, דְּכוּלָּא קַמֵּיהּ כְּלָא מַמָּשׁ חָשִׁיב, **That is, through contemplation of the greatness of *Ein Sof*, blessed be He, before whom everything is literally considered nothingness,**

Contemplation, which employs the faculty of understanding, an attribute of *Bina*, is the first step. A person cannot achieve an emotional connection unless he first contemplates the object of that emotion, not as an external concept but as an internal experience. Contemplating the physical world. Love that is like water is the magnetic attraction between two bodies. The two objects start by moving toward each other, getting closer and closer, until they are joined. Once that occurs, the process is done. Fire and the fuel that feeds it are also attracted to each other, but the encounter between them is vastly different. It is not silent but forceful and explosive. Certain chemicals are attracted to each other, but when they bond, the result is by no means peaceful. The elements cannot remain as they were before because the bond consumes their original essence. This is love that is like fire. It does not conclude in simple connection. The love consumes the person and sets him ablaze to the point that he throws off all his garments and ignites his very soul. This is not because the individual is small and lowly, but because the process is one of destruction, consuming the person's being. This is a love for that which is beyond everything in existence, and it requires a person to relinquish everything for the sake of it.

God's greatness will evoke different responses in a person. It may lead to fear or to love. In every instance of contemplation, there is a moment of choice, where the person directs his thoughts toward a particular emotional connection. The direction of the person's thoughts depends on his nature, his spiritual state at the time, and the focus of his contemplation.

תִּתְלַהֵט וְתִתְלַהֵב הַנֶּפֶשׁ לִיקַר תִּפְאֶרֶת גְּדוּלָּתוֹ, וּלְאִסְתַּכְּלָא בִּיקָרָא דְּמַלְכָּא כְּרִשְׁפֵּי אֵשׁ שַׁלְהֶבֶת עַזָּה הָעוֹלָה לְמַעְלָה, וְלִיפָּרֵד מֵהַפְּתִילָה וְהָעֵצִים שֶׁנֶּאֱחֶזֶת בָּהֶן. וְהַיְנוּ, עַל יְדֵי תִּגְבּוֹרֶת יְסוֹד הָאֵשׁ אֱלֹהִי שֶׁבַּנֶּפֶשׁ הָאֱלוֹהִית.

the soul will ignite and become inflamed to ascend toward the glory of the splendor of His greatness and to gaze at the king's glory. It is like sparks of fire and a fierce conflagration that rises upward and strives to detach itself from the wick or tinder that it grasps. That is to say, this love is generated by strengthening the element of divine fire within the divine soul.

When a person chooses to contemplate God's greatness, how everything is literally nothingness before Him, his soul is ignited. The divine soul is like fire bound to the wick, which is the body and this world. When the element of fire in the soul is intensified through such contemplation, this element awakens a yearning in the soul to separate itself from the body and ascend to its source to become subsumed in the Divine.

All the levels of love that the author of the *Tanya* discussed until now have involved some kind of implementation, such as studying Torah or performing mitzvot, through which one achieves attachment to God, which is all that the person desires. Love that is like fire constitutes a different process. Contemplating the greatness of God, before whom everything else is literally considered nothingness, evokes the feeling that there is nothing for the person in this reality and so he no longer wants to be there. It generates a fierce and passionate desire to escape the bounds of one's existence, to escape the boundaries of this world and be consumed in the divine essence, where there is no other besides Him.

CHAPTER 50

וּמִזֶּה בָּאָה לִידֵי צִמָּאוֹן, וּכְמוֹ שֶׁכָּתוּב: "צָמְאָה לְךָ נַפְשִׁי" (תהלים סג, ב), וְאַחַר כָּךְ לִבְחִינַת "חוֹלַת אַהֲבָה" (שיר השירים ב, ה).

From this the soul **comes to a thirst** for God, **as it is written, "My soul thirsts for you"** (Ps. 63:2), **and subsequently to a state of "lovesickness"** (Song 2:5).

When a person is in a place that is hot and arid, he becomes thirsty. Likewise, when the element of fire is strengthened within the soul, a feeling of thirst is created, the sense that something is lacking, together with a strong desire to fill that lack. Unlike other types of love, this love does not bring contentment. On the contrary, as it grows stronger, it becomes more demanding. The thirst becomes more severe, and the love does not quench it but rather intensifies it.

This thirst cannot be quenched. When the thirst, the burning need that gets progressively stronger, cannot be gratified or reconciled in any way, it develops into a spiritual illness that is incapable of being cured, an ailment called "lovesickness." This is not random or accidental. It is the very essence of this type of love, which becomes incurable. ☞

FEAR THAT IS LIKE FIRE VERSUS LOVE THAT IS LIKE FIRE

☞ The contrast between fire and water is generally that of *Gevura* and *Ḥesed*, the attributes of restraint and kindness, fear and love, respectively. Here, however, the author of the *Tanya* is not discussing fear that is like fire, but love that is like fire. There is a vast difference between the two. While fear always moves inward, in the direction of contraction, nullification, and withdrawal, love moves outward, toward expansion and closeness. Yet unlike love that is like water, which is the desire to come closer to God and unite with Him here in this world, love that is like fire burns the connection to the world in its race toward the Divine. This is love from the realm of *Gevura*. The element of fire is intensified, causing the love to detach from the world and become consumed within the Divine.

LOVESICKNESS

☞ The Ba'al Shem Tov once met a well-known doctor and discussed medicine with him. During their conversation, the Ba'al Shem Tov told the doctor, "I am deficient in something. Please check my pulse and tell me what disease I have."

The doctor examined the Ba'al Shem Tov and declared that he was indeed sick,

וְאַחַר כָּךְ בָּאָה לִידֵי כְּלוֹת הַנֶּפֶשׁ מַמָּשׁ, כְּמוֹ שֶׁכָּתוּב: "גַּם כָּלְתָה נַפְשִׁי" (תהלים פד, ג). Then the soul **comes to literally expire, as it is written, "Indeed my soul languishes"** (Ps. 84:3).

When thirst becomes severe and hopeless, the result is illness, and when the illness advances, the patient faces death. When lovesickness for God increases, and the thirst for Him cannot be quenched, when a person no longer desires or feels anything else, it is as though he has expired. The soul leaves this world, consumed by love of God.

When one places a small candle flame next to a large flame, it appears as though the large flame swallows up the small flame. The small flame disappears, leaving an unlit wick. In a sense, this is also what happens in the case of love that is like fire. There is no solution to the process of this love, and it seems to have only one possible conclusion: the extinguishing of the small flame. Since the thirst will only increase and the love can never be fulfilled, the only resolution lies in self-annihilation so that there is no longer a person experiencing this love. The soul that loves like fire cannot reconcile its yearning within existence. It can only move toward its own annihilation, its existence as an independent entity in danger of perishing.

וְהִנֵּה מִכָּאן יָצָא שׁוֹרֶשׁ הַלְוִיִּם לְמַטָּה **From this,** the source of this love, **emerged the root of the Levites** here **below.**

Unlike the love that stems from the right array of the *sefirot*, the side of Ḥesed, which pertains to the priestly service, love that is like fire relates to the service of the Levites. A person's divine service contains aspects of both, the priest's service and that of the Levite. Both served God in the Temple, yet the worship of one was not like the worship of the other. The service of the priest expressed the characteristic of Ḥesed,

---

but the doctor did not know what malady he was suffering from. The Ba'al Shem Tov later said that it made perfect sense that the doctor did could not diagnose his ailment because the Ba'al Shem Tov was sick with love of God, an illness beyond the doctor's understanding and one not mentioned in any medical textbook (*Shivḥei HaBesht*, Rubinstein edition, p. 385).

of bringing the world closer to God and bringing down the divine sustenance and vitality from above. The service of the Levite, on the other hand, relates to the attribute of *Gevura* and involved singing, yearning, and thirsting.

[וּלְעָתִיד, שֶׁהָעוֹלָם יִתְעַלֶּה, יִהְיוּ הֵם הַכֹּהֲנִים, (In the future, when the world will be elevated, the Levites will be the priests,

In our present-day world, the priests' service is considered the central element of Temple service, whereas the service of the Levites is auxiliary. In the messianic future, the roles will be reversed, so that the Levites' service will be the primary component. When this fallen world is repaired and elevated, there will be a different reality, where the Levites will be on a higher level than the priests.

וּכְמוֹ שֶׁכָּתַב הָאֲרִ"י ז"ל עַל פָּסוּק: "וְהַכֹּהֲנִים הַלְוִיִּם" (יחזקאל מד, טו) – שֶׁהַלְוִיִּם שֶׁל עַכְשָׁיו יִהְיוּ כֹּהֲנִים לֶעָתִיד]. as the Arizal stated regarding the verse "But the priests, the Levites" [Ezek. 44:15], that the Levites of the present will become priests of the future.)

CONSUMED BY LOVE

☞ The description of this self-destruction is both terrible and wonderful. One of the most remarkable and beautiful descriptions of the pining of the soul due to love of God appears in the commentary of the *Or HaHayyim* on the verse "The Lord spoke to Moses after the death of the two sons of Aaron, when they approached before the Lord and they died" (Lev. 16:1). Among other things, the *Or HaHayyim* states, "Although they felt their death approaching, they did not flinch at the connection, pleasantness, delight, companionship, affection, longing, and sweetness, until their souls expired from them."

The *Or HaHayyim* explains that the death of Aaron's sons occurred in a fire of love of God that burns and consumes the soul. As the author of the *Tanya* says below, it is impossible to put this experience into words. Nonetheless, one who reads the words of the *Or HaHayyim* can sense that he is speaking from personal experience rather than describing something that happens to others. Yet the Torah states that Aaron's sons performed an act "that He had not commanded them" (Lev. 10:1). They allowed themselves to be consumed by passion, and this is considered a sin. Yet it is certainly the most beautiful and exalted sin compared to the countless other acts that God did not command.

That the Levites will one day become the priests is part of an overall picture of the world that will exist in the future.[5] Our world is primarily tasked with bringing Heaven down to earth. It is active, dynamic, and ever changing, and it relies on a constant equilibrium between various forces. In the supernal world, and in our world in the future, where Heaven and earth are one and those who seek perfection will find it, there will be no such balance. Our world cannot endure those who are identified with the *Gevura* and judgment, with the heavenly ideal of strict adherence to the letter of the law, but rather needs to straddle the line between kindness and judgment. In the future, however, the world will be constructed on this side of the *sefirot*, the side of *Gevura*. ☞ ☞

In the future, all structures will be reversed. Currently, in our flawed and deficient world, we are wary of the attribute of judgment, because we cannot bear it. To be judged is to be found wanting because we are so flawed. In the perfect world of the future, we will seek out the attribute of judgment. In this world, our main task is to interact with reality and channel it toward service of God, but in the World to Come, the task will be to accept what is found within reality. The Levites of the present day will be the priests in the future because even if it is not apparent within the present reality, the Levites of today are superior to the priests in the same way that gold is superior to silver.

---

5. See *Likkutei Torah* by the Arizal, Ezek. 2; *Sha'ar HaPesukim* 47a. The Lubavitcher Rebbe, Rabbi Menaḥem Mendel Schneerson, explains that one can interpret this statement, "The Levites of today will become priests of the future," as referring to those who are Levites now and will be reincarnated as priests in the future so that they will be reborn as priests. We know that the Torah was given "for us and for our children forever" (Deut. 29:28), which indicates that there will be no changes to the Torah in the future (Rambam, *Sefer HaMadda, Hilkhot Yesodei HaTorah* 9). Thus, it is not that Levites will perform the priestly service but that those who are Levites now will be reincarnated as priests in the future. Levites perform the Temple service, recite prayers, and observe the other mitzvot in accordance with the root of their souls, which stem from *Gevura*. A priest, on the other hand, is a "man of kindness," as stated above. In the future, the Levite souls will be higher than the priestly souls, and thus those who had been Levites will be born into priestly families.

CHAPTER 50

וַעֲבוֹדַת הַלְוִיִּם הָיְתָה לְהָרִים קוֹל רִנָּה וְתוֹדָה, בְּשִׁירָה וְזִמְרָה, בְּנִגּוּן וּנְעִימָה, **The service of the Levites was to raise the sound of joy and thanksgiving, with song and music, melodiously and pleasantly,**

From the service of the Levites in the Temple, we learn about the Levite service of our souls, the love that is like fire. "Song" refers to music created with the voice, while "music" is created with instruments. The terms "joy and thanksgiving" and "melodiously and pleasantly" refer to the movements of the music. A melody does not move in one direction, and because it contains opposing dynamics, it is both powerful and riveting. It rises and falls, goes forth and comes back. The purpose of the Levites' musical service is to awaken these dynamics within the soul.

בִּבְחִינַת 'רָצוֹא וָשׁוֹב', **in the manner of "running and returning"** (Ezek. 1:14),

A DAY THAT IS ENTIRELY SABBATH

☞ It is said that in the future the *halakha* will be in accordance with Beit Shammai, while our world needs the *halakha* of Beit Hillel, which is characterized by the attribute of *Ḥesed* and does not have the tension of the attribute of *Gevura* that characterizes the approach of Beit Shammai (see *Zohar* 3:245a; *Iggeret HaKodesh*, epistle 13). The rulings of Beit Hillel take into account the reality in which we exist today, but in the future the world will be able to accept the rulings of Beit Shammai.

This is one explanation for the Sages' statement "These and those are the words of the living God" (*Eiruvin* 13b). Both the rulings of Beit Hillel and those of Beit Shammai represent God's word, only the ruling that the *halakha* is in accordance with Beit Hillel relates to a specific time period. In our reality, the *halakha* is in accordance with Beit Hillel, but at a different time, in a different reality, in a more perfect world, the *halakha* is in accordance with Beit Shammai.

THE FUTURE: A DAY THAT IS ENTIRELY SABBATH

☞ This dichotomy also exists in our world, in the distinction between this world that was created in six days and the world of the Sabbath. One is a world of action, creation, and change, and the other is one of being, of rest. A different system of rules and priorities prevails within each. Our world corresponds to the world of six days, the world of action, while the World to Come will be a "day that is entirely Sabbath" (Mishna *Tamid* 7:4).

The phrase "running and returning" is used in kabbalistic works to refer to this dynamic. "Running" indicates the pining of the soul to the point of expiration, in the manner described in the verse "Their hearts cried to the Lord" (Lam. 2:18). "Returning" is depicted in a different verse: "The people saw, and trembled, and stood at a distance" (Ex. 20:15).

שֶׁהִיא בְּחִינַת אַהֲבָה עַזָּה זוֹ כְּשַׁלְהֶבֶת הַיּוֹצֵא מִן הַבָּזָק, כִּדְאִיתָא בַּגְּמָרָא [פֶּרֶק ב' דַּחֲגִיגָה (יג, ב)]. which is the level of this fierce love like the flame emitted from between pieces of earthenware, as the Talmud states (in the second chapter of Ḥagiga 13b).

The phrase "running and returning" appears in Ezekiel's vision of the divine chariot: "The divine creatures were running and returning like the appearance of a flash of lightning [*bazak*]" (Ezek. 1:14). The Talmud asks: What is the meaning of the phrase "running and returning"? Rav Yehuda states that it is like fire that is emitted from a furnace, whose flame is continuously bursting forth and withdrawing.

The Talmud goes on to ask the meaning of the next part of the verse, "like the appearance of a flash of lightning." Rabbi Yosei bar Ḥanina explains that it is like the fire that is emitted from between shards of earthenware used for refining gold. (*Bazak*, translated in the verse as a lightning flash, and can also mean a shard of earthenware.) Rashi explains, "Gold refiners would pierce holes in earthenware vessels and place them on burning coals with gold inside them…. A flash of light would rise through the holes that was multicolored and constantly emerging and withdrawing."

This is the manner in which the service of the Levites awakened the divine soul to pine for God to the point of expiration. While the role of the priest is to bring blessings down from above into this reality, the role of the Levite is to take the supplicant out of the midst of the current reality and raise him toward Heaven.

וְאִי אֶפְשָׁר לְבָאֵר עִנְיָן זֶה הֵיטֵב בְּמִכְתָּב, It is impossible to explain this subject clearly in writing,

This kind of love is superior to the types of love discussed above, just as gold is superior to silver. The essence of love that is like fire, the soul's desire for annihilation, cannot be explained by means of the written word. As the author of the *Tanya* explained in the introduction to *Likkutei Amarim*, the written word, unlike speech, does not entail personal contact or connection. It merely offers a formulation of the overall message.

רַק כָּל אִישׁ נִלְבָּב וְנָבוֹן הַמַּשְׂכִּיל עַל דָּבָר, וּמַעֲמִיק לְקַשֵּׁר דַּעְתּוֹ וּתְבוּנָתוֹ בַּה׳, יִמְצָא טוֹב וָאוֹר הַגָּנוּז בְּנַפְשׁוֹ הַמַּשְׂכֶּלֶת, כָּל חַד לְפוּם שִׁיעוּרָא דִּילֵיהּ.	but any ardent and astute individual, who is intelligent in grasping a subject and delves deeply to attach his knowledge and understanding to God, will discover the goodness and light hidden in his rational soul, each according to his capacity.

This passage mentions each of the cognitive faculties: wisdom, understanding, and knowledge. When a person is endowed with these faculties and employs them, contemplating God's greatness and binding his mind to the Divine, he will "discover the goodness and light hidden in his rational soul." When it comes to such contemplation and perception, there is no single parameter that pertains to everyone, so the insight one gleans cannot be conveyed adequately through words or superficial descriptions. Words that hit the mark for one person may be meaningless to another. Only one who has experienced it can understand it. Only then can he relate to it and perceive what is beyond the words that attempt to define it.

This passage describes an inner journey, a road whose subtle markers are impossible to describe in writing. A person cannot understand these markers unless he himself has traversed that road.

[וְיֵשׁ מִתְפַּעֵל כו׳ וְיֵשׁ מִתְפַּעֵל כו׳].	(**One** person **is moved** in one way, **and another is moved** in a different way.)

There are no uniform rules that dictate what moves the soul or the ways in which it is moved. Each person's unique character determines what moves him and how. Likewise, what a person does as a result and how he does it is entirely individual. As stated above, it is impossible to fully explain this matter in writing, because that which evokes the feeling of thirst for the Divine to the point of lovesickness and the expiration of the soul is so personal that no objective parameter can be given for it. Yet there are certain conditions that must be met in order to achieve it, and while they are not the source of this love, they are prerequisite conditions, and they can be defined objectively to some extent. ☞

IMPOSSIBLE TO EXPLAIN

☞ It is impossible to explain in writing what happens within the human soul when it desires to break through the bounds of this world and run toward God. In fact, it is impossible to explain it at all. It is a spiritual movement that makes no sense, that does not lead to any particular point, nor even to attachment to God. Attachment is achieved by the priest, not the Levite, and it is achieved through action, not desire. The passion and intensity of this experience have no parallel in anything in reality. They are like fire, an aspect of *Gevura*, which leads a person, both body and soul, to a state in which he is incapable of anything. It leads to "My soul thirsts for you" (Ps. 63:2), to "I am lovesick" (Song 2:5), and to the final edge of experience: "Indeed my soul languishes" (Ps. 84:3), to the expiration of the soul.

When Rabbi Elimelekh of Lizhensk prayed, particularly the more moving passages, he would take out a watch from his pocket and peer at it. He did this to remain grounded, to maintain contact with the physical reality as he recited the words, interrupting the one-way charge toward the expiration of the soul. There were individuals who did not stop, who could not or did not want to suspend this running, and ultimately departed from this world, unable to return. Some tzaddikim would bid farewell to their families every time they prayed because they did not know whether they would return, whether they would be able to continue living after that prayer. Of course, this happens only to individuals on the loftiest levels. It occurs when they remain thus in prayer, in endless connection with God.

Although his fundamental approach to divine service is rational and orderly, the author of the *Tanya* was himself extraordinarily passionate. More than once he would faint or disconnect from reality during prayer. His family and those who were close to him took special measures to protect him, lining his room with cushions, for instance, so that he would not injure himself in his fervor. Once, he remained immersed in a state of connection to God for an exceptionally long period of time while praying. The other worshippers had left the synagogue while he remained there alone for a long time, holding onto the pulpit. When his followers returned, they did not find him there. They searched the surrounding area and eventually found him in a field far from the synagogue. In his rapture, he had unconsciously broken off the part of the pulpit that he had been clutching and walked out of the synagogue with it.

אַחֲרֵי קְדִימַת יְרִאַת חֵטְא, לִהְיוֹת 'סוּר מֵרָע' בְּתַכְלִית, שֶׁלֹּא לִהְיוֹת 'עֲוֹנוֹתֵיכֶם מַבְדִּילִים' כו' חַס וְשָׁלוֹם.

However, **the prerequisite for attaining this love is fear of sin, utterly avoiding evil, so that your iniquities will not separate you from your God, God forbid.**

The prerequisite that one must utterly avoid evil pertains to all categories of love of God.[6] If fear of sin, which causes a person to avoid evil completely, does not precede the love of God, that is not true love but love that is false. To acquire love of God and closeness to Him, a person must first make room within by clearing out all the garbage. Only then is he able to build a genuine edifice of love.

This is particularly pertinent to love that is like fire, which involves a desire to depart from reality, a yearning for the expiration of the soul. For this to be a genuine feeling and a true ascent rather than madness or illusion, there cannot be even a slight blemish within the soul. If such a blemish exists, the person will not be able to cut off all ties to this reality and truly rise. In order to attain the love of the pining of the soul and the ascent toward a state where nothing concerns him but being subsumed in the Divine, a person must reach a state where not a single thread binds him to the side of evil and the lower world. ☞

וְהִנֵּה סֵדֶר הָעֲבוֹדָה בְּעֵסֶק הַתּוֹרָה וְהַמִּצְוֹת הַנִּמְשֶׁכֶת מִבְּחִינַת אַהֲבָה עַזָּה זוֹ,

The order of the service of God through Torah study and the mitzvot, which is drawn forth from this fierce love,

22 Iyar
23 Iyar
(leap year)

CLEANSING THE BODY AND SOUL

☞ For there to truly be no iniquities separating a person from God, he must cleanse the interior of his soul. The body itself does not sin. It is only an instrument that participates in sin when the soul causes it to commit a transgression. If a person cleanses only his body, his soul remains unclean. When a person fasts, his body is afflicted, but his soul and his entire being are not rectified as a result of this alone. To attain love that is like fire, the desire to ascend and be consumed in nothingness, the soul itself must be absolutely cleansed.

---

6. See chap. 14; *Iggeret HaTeshuva*, chap. 5.

The solution for love of God on all its levels, its sole origin and expression, lies in the Torah and the mitzvot.[7] Love is the desire to draw closer and become truly attached, and the only way to become attached to God is through Torah and mitzvot.

הִיא בִּבְחִינַת 'שׁוֹב' לְבַד. **is exclusively in the manner of "returning."**

Divine service generally consists of the dynamic between "running" and "returning." This constitutes the rhythm of life, like the heartbeat and breath in the body. In divine service, these movements involve rising from below and returning from above. In very general terms, the divine service of love, which is prayer, constitutes "running" from below to above, from created being to God. The actualization of that love, through the observance of Torah and mitzvot, constitutes "returning." The totality of life in divine service is the combined rhythm of these two movements. They must therefore correspond to each other in terms of their scope, intensity, and nature. When love consists exclusively of "running," there must be a corresponding motion of "returning," through the fulfillment of Torah and mitzvot. When the love is like fire, which cannot exist in the reality of this world at all, the divine service that follows it must necessarily comprise a complete return to reality.

כְּמוֹ שֶׁכָּתוּב בְּסֵפֶר יְצִירָה: "וְאִם רָץ לִבְּךָ - שׁוּב לְאֶחָד". **As it is written in *Sefer Yetzira* (1:8), "If your heart runs, return to the One."**

Love that is like fire and attachment to God do not go in the same direction. The yearning of love that is like fire cannot be satisfied. It has no inherent resolution. It burns like fire, and thus by nature it is constantly rising out of the vessels that contain it while at the same time consuming them, because it is an entirely destructive force. The resolution of this love cannot come about by exhausting it, because that would constitute the soul's expiration. It can only be gratified

---

7. See chap. 40.

through "returning to the One,"[8] breaking the process and returning to the all-encompassing unity, to the perspective that God is one on earth just as He is in Heaven and therefore running in any direction is purposeless. The ultimate human objective is the divine objective, and this is achieved with the "returning" that follows the "running," wherein the supernal unity is revealed in the lower world.

פֵּירוּשׁ, וְאִם רָץ לִבְּךָ - הִיא תְּשׁוּקַת הַנֶּפֶשׁ שֶׁבַּלֵּב בֶּחָלָל הַיְמָנִי, כְּשֶׁמִּתְגַּבֶּרֶת וּמִתְלַהֶבֶת וּמִתְלַהֶטֶת בִּמְאֹד מְאֹד, עַד כְּלוֹת הַנֶּפֶשׁ מַמָּשׁ, לְהִשְׁתַּפֵּךְ אֶל חֵיק אָבִיהָ, חַיֵּי הַחַיִּים בָּרוּךְ הוּא, וְלָצֵאת מִמַּאֲסָרָהּ בַּגּוּף הַגּוּפָנִי וְגַשְׁמִי לְדָבְקָה בּוֹ יִתְבָּרֵךְ; "And if your heart runs" refers to the yearning of the soul that resides in the right chamber of the heart. When this yearning intensifies and is set ablaze and ignites until the soul pines to literally pour itself into the bosom of its father, the infinite source of life, blessed be He, and emerge from its confinement in the corporeal, physical body in order to cling to God,

The phrase quoted from *Sefer Yetzira*, "and if your heart runs," means that the heart's desire races and increases in order to emerge from the vessel of the heart. The soul desires to be freed from the limitations of the body, from the obligation to live in this world, and yearns to cling to God, the source of all life.

אֲזַי זֹאת יָשִׁיב אֶל לִבּוֹ   then he must take to heart

This phrases is often interpreted as referring to the contemplation that leads to internalizing matters in the heart. Here the author of the *Tanya* is indicating that after a person's heart runs in order to part from the vessel of the heart, one needs to return it to the heart, to the vessel, to the body, to this world.

---

8. In our version of *Sefer Yetzira*, the text actually reads, "Return to the place," but the version quoted by the author of the *Tanya* is the same one that appears in, e.g., *Likkutei Torah*, Lev. 6a, Num. 56a. There is also a version that states, "Go back"; see *Tikkunei Zohar* 6a; *Sefer HaMa'amarim* 5659 by the fifth Lubavitcher Rebbe, Rabbi Sholom Dovber Schneerson, p. 211 in the gloss.

מַאֲמַר רַבּוֹתֵינוּ ז״ל, כִּי עַל כָּרְחֲךָ אַתָּה חַי (אבות פרק ד משנה כב), בַּגוּף הַזֶּה, לְהַחֲיוֹתוֹ כְּדֵי לְהַמְשִׁיךְ חַיִּים עֶלְיוֹנִים מֵחַיֵּי הַחַיִּים בָּרוּךְ הוּא לְמַטָּה עַל יְדֵי תּוֹרַת חַיִּים,

our Rabbis' statement "For against your will you live" (Mishna *Avot* 4:22), that despite the yearning to be subsumed, the soul must remain **in this body to keep it alive in order to draw down supernal life from the infinite source of life, blessed be He, through the life-giving Torah,**

The Mishna teaches that a person is obligated to sustain his physical body, the abode of his soul, by drawing down the life force into the body and the material realm. This is accomplished when a person fulfills the Torah with his body and with every part of the world with which he interacts.

These words, "against your will you live," expresses the great paradox of the life of the soul and its constant yearning. The gratification of this fierce love of God, the union of the soul with the Divine, is not found in continuing along the path of "running" but in the opposite direction by fulfilling the Torah through the soul's connection to this world, this body. In the larger picture, this is the paradox of existence. It is through returning to life in this reality "against your will," through the "returning" that follows the "running," that one lives. ☞

RUNNING AND RETURNING

☞ Running and returning is more than a specific phenomenon. It is the secret of life, the wonder of existence. Every entity in existence functions in accordance with the pulse of running and returning. If a person cannot breathe, he tries to inhale as much air as possible. This act, which gives life, could also lead to death if it continues beyond a certain point. There must be an equilibrium: an inhale followed by an exhale followed by an inhale. The dynamic of "running" cannot be resolved by moving in one direction to its utmost end, because that can only lead to expiration, but rather by moving in the opposite direction, which in a certain sense is the opposite of what this entity desires.

The course of life does not incline to any one particular side, although the vicissitudes of life may be, and indeed are supposed to be, larger each time. The range between up and down must become greater, and in a sense more intense with each pulse. Yet the gap between the two points, between the zenith and the nadir, and the movement from one to the other, is what constitutes life itself. Running and returning, inhaling and exhaling, contraction and relaxation, are all part of the heartbeat of life. A melody is not a mel-

לִהְיוֹת דִּירָה בַּתַּחְתּוֹנִים לְאַחְדוּתוֹ יִתְבָּרַךְ, בִּבְחִינַת גִּלּוּי, כְּמוֹ שֶׁנִּתְבָּאֵר לְעֵיל.

so that there is a dwelling place in the lower worlds for God's unity in a revealed state, as explained above.

This is the purpose of returning in the overall scope of the existence of all the worlds: When the world moves toward concealment of God's oneness, the next movement will be the creation of a dwelling place on earth for the revelation of His oneness. This is the world's ultimate purpose: to make room for the Divine to have a dwelling place on earth.[9]

וּכְמוֹ שֶׁכָּתוּב בַּזֹּהַר הַקָּדוֹשׁ (חלק ב קלה, א): "לְמֶהֱוֵי אֶחָד בְּאֶחָד". פֵּירוּשׁ, שֶׁהַיִּחוּד הַנֶּעְלָם יִהְיֶה בִּבְחִינַת עָלְמָא דְּאִתְגַּלְיָא.

As it is written in the holy *Zohar* (2:135a), the purpose of creation was "that there be one in one," meaning that the unity that is concealed will be manifest on the level of the revealed world.

The objective is for the divine unity to no longer be concealed but rather to be revealed within the world and within our reality. This passage from the *Zohar* is recited before the Sabbath evening prayer

---

ody if the notes move only in one direction, whether ascending or descending. At some point, the sound ceases to be music. So too with life itself: It must keep moving, in one direction or another.

In this sense, reality is paradoxical. This perspective relates to the kabbalistic concept of "circles and a line." A straight line represents one fragment within reality, whereas a circle constitutes its entirety of reality. The preservation of the circle, and its very formation, lies in the constant transition of movement from one direction to the opposing direction, the constant struggle between the force moving inward and the force moving outward. Life cannot move in one direction on a straight line. One moves forward, then back, up, then down. As long as this dynamic exists, as long as there is balance, the circle endures.

The larger scope of reality is a realm of circles; in the smaller scale, it constitutes a series of straight lines. The essence of life, like that of the movement of a circle, lies in running and returning. Every move in one direction is necessarily completed by a move in the opposite direction.

---

9. See chap. 36.

in most communities that pray according to the Sephardic custom. The Sabbath, particularly at night, represents this state of perfection described as "one in one." In *Siddur Admor HaZaken*, the author of the *Tanya* explains that this means that just as there is One above so is there the "secret of the One," as stated in this passage of the *Zohar*, below. Our goal is to connect the two so that rather than standing in contrast to each other, they resemble each other.

וְזֶה שֶׁאוֹמְרִים: "לְכָה דוֹדִי" וְכוּ'. **This is** also **the meaning** of the liturgy **that we recite** on the Sabbath: "**Come, my beloved,** toward the bride...."

This liturgy is recited when one ushers in the Sabbath. In its simplest sense, it is our call to God to come toward us. But it also contains our move toward Him, or in any case our preparation for coming toward Him.[10]

It is explained elsewhere that the word for bridegroom, *ḥatan*, also connotes a descent, from the Aramaic term *ḥut*, whereas the word for bride, *kalla*, comes from the term for destruction, *kilayon*, a hint at *kelut hanefesh*, the expiration of the soul. The bride must be a *kalla*, to reach a point where the soul will expire from this love, but the goal is for the groom to come toward the bride. This is why the text says here that the resolution of this love, which reaches the point of the soul's expiration, is "against your will you live," bringing the Divine down to the world to be "one in one," in order that God's oneness will be revealed on earth.

וּבָזֶה יוּבָן מַאֲמַר רַבּוֹתֵינוּ ז"ל: "עַל כָּרְחָךְ אַתָּה חַי וְעַל כָּרְחָךְ" וְכוּ', וְאֶלָּא אֵיךְ יִהְיֶה רְצוֹנוֹ? **Now one can understand our Rabbis' statement** "**For against your will you live, and against your will** you **die**" (*Avot* 4:22). **What then should** a person's **will be**?

This statement is puzzling: "Against your will you live" indicates that a person wants to die, to leave this world, yet he is compelled to live. On the other hand, "against your will you die" has the opposite meaning,

---

10. See *Shir HaShirim Rabba* 7:12; *Shabbat* 119a.

implying that the person wants to live, but he is compelled to die. What should a person want? To live or not to live?

The answer is just as the Mishna describes it: One should desire both. This is the nature of life. When the soul pines, the divine service should be in the manner of "against your will you live," and in the next moment, when the soul returns and lives in this world, the person's desire and divine service must be in terms of "against your will you die."

This is the "running and returning" of divine service. "Running" refers to the service of prayer and self-sacrifice when reciting the *Shema*, when the love that is like fire is evoked. The focus is parting from this life like sparks of fire, which cannot be contained in any vessel, whether the mind or the heart, but must burst forth. "Returning" is divine service through Torah study and performance of mitzvot. This service grounds a person in this world and draws down the divine light to be contained within the vessels of the mind and heart.[11] It is the divine service of "against your will you live": Although the individual would prefer to part from the world, he must live and revitalize reality because God commanded it. We draw down life and existence from the Source of life, through the life-giving Torah. Through its fulfillment, the divine light is enclothed within the vessels of this world, and the purpose of the creation of the world, providing a dwelling place for the Divine in this lower world.

וּכְמוֹ שֶׁנִּתְבָּאֵר בְּמָקוֹם אַחֵר בַּאֲרִיכוּת עַל מִשְׁנָה זוֹ, "עַל כָּרְחָךְ אַתָּה חַי" בְּעֶזְרַת חַיֵּי הַחַיִּים בָּרוּךְ הוּא. This is **explained elsewhere at length** (*Torah Or* 25b, 36c; *Likkutei Torah*, Lev. 48d) **regarding this** statement of the **Mishna, "For against your will you live," with the help of the infinite source of life, blessed be He.**

"Against your will you live, and against your will you die" summarizes the vicissitudes of a life of divine service. "Running" is about the desire to reach God and not to live in this reality. It is yearning for God

---

11. See also *Derekh Mitzvotekha, Mitzvat Tumat Metzora*, p. 100; *Torat Ḥayyim, Parashat Vayishlaḥ, Ma'amar Vayikaḥ*, chap. 7; *Sefer HaMa'amarim 5649* by the fifth Lubavitcher Rebbe, Rabbi Sholom Dovber Schneerson, *Aḥarei Mot*, pp. 233ff.

until the point of expiration. But then, when there is no more place to run, the soul discovers that God is here, not there. Thus ensues the movement that constitutes "returning."

This dynamic is expressed in the prayers, specifically in *Kedusha*, where the myriad angels, the seraphim, ophanim, and holy ḥayot, together with the Jewish people below, declare, "Holy, holy, holy." All attempt to raise themselves, to reach God. Then comes the response: "The entire world is filled with His glory." They raise themselves higher and ask, "Where is the place of His glory?" The answer is "Blessed is the Lord's glory from His place." God is here, right now.

This is the essence of *Kedusha*: the question and the answer, the "Holy" and the "Blessed."

In the second section of the *Tanya*, *Sha'ar HaYiḥud VeHa'emuna*, the author of the *Tanya* explains the first verse of the *Shema*, "Hear, Israel: The Lord is our God, the Lord is one," and the phrase that is said immediately afterward, "Blessed be the name of His glorious kingdom forever and ever." "The Lord is one," which expresses God's unity, signifies the annihilation of existence in the face of the Divine. "Blessed be the name of His glorious kingdom forever and ever" heralds the return, reconsecration, and reevaluation of this world.

It is for this reason that we say this phrase softly during the year. In our ordinary reality we are urged, and even required, to ascend. Moving downward is the natural state of our being, the direction in which our bodies pull us in this world, so we are encouraged always to ascend. On one day a year this is not the case, and then we say, "Blessed be the name of His glorious kingdom forever and ever," out loud and unabashedly. A person who can say after the race that he wants to return to the reality of this world, after he has refrained from eating and drinking, after he has conducted himself like the angels, does not need to be ashamed. The "returning" that follows the "running" justifies the existence of all the worlds, higher and lower.

This chapter describes a love for God that transcends all other types of love. This love rises like sparks of a fire that is trying to escape the wick that fuels it, the physical body and life in this world, because of the soul's thirst, lovesickness, and yearning to be subsumed in the

Divine. This type of love cannot be actualized within this reality, within a person's life in this world. Consequently, it cannot be adequately described with words but can only be experienced within the heart. Every individual feels it in his own way, on his own level, when he seeks to connect with God. Nonetheless, the "running" must be followed by a "returning," not as a continuation of the race to depart this world, not as the next stage, nor even as the answer to a question, but rather as an answer that is given to a question that has no answer. It is only when the running is depleted, when the path has come to an end, that there must be a return, which constitutes divine service through Torah study and mitzvot.

Finally, this chapter, which sums up the previous ten chapters that discussed serving God with fear and love, concluded that even when one feels this love, the love that is like sparks of fire, perfection and attachment to God can be achieved only in the reality of this world, in drawing down life from the source of life so that He will have a dwelling place below.

Chapter 51

THE PREVIOUS CHAPTER DISCUSSED THE HIGHEST level of love for God and serving Him. In a sense, that concluded the topic of a person's love and fear in his service of God. However, the *Tanya* did not end there. At the end of that chapter, the author of the *Tanya* wrote that love for God, and especially a love in which a person's soul pines for God, ultimately leads to a solution and resolution that points in the opposite direction: Its culmination is in the person's return to the world of action (which is solely on the level of "returning"). The three final chapters (of which this is the first) will continue this discussion. At the beginning of the book, the *Tanya* quoted a verse as its motto: "The matter is very near to you, in your mouth and in your heart, to perform it" (Deut. 30:14). Throughout, the *Tanya* has referenced this verse in whole or in part, directly or indirectly. Toward the end of the *Tanya*, its author refers to the final term of this verse, which is its very essence: "to perform it." When this term was discussed earlier in chapter 35, the author of the *Tanya* quoted from the *Zohar* to explain why the purpose of the universe and humankind is reached specifically in action in this physical world. That quote describes how the Divine Presence rests upon a person when he performs a mitzva. In these final chapters, the author of the *Tanya* will encapsulate the topic of the Divine Presence dwelling in the world as a result of a person's "performing it."

| 23 Iyar |
| 24 Iyar (leap year) |

וְהִנֵּה לְתוֹסֶפֶת בֵּיאוּר לְשׁוֹן הַיָנוּקָא דִּלְעֵיל, **To gain further insight into the words of the child** in the *Zohar* (2:187a) cited **above** (chap. 35),

"The words of the child" refers to a passage in the *Zohar*. Chapter 35 above explained that this teaching of the child compares the light of the Divine Presence to the light of an oil lamp. The flame adheres to the wick and remains lit only when there is oil in the lamp. Similarly, the Divine Presence rests upon a human body, which is compared to a wick, only when a person performs good deeds, which are compared to oil. The present chapter will return to this idea from additional angles. And to that end, the author will first clarify a broader topic.

צָרִיךְ לְבָאֵר תְּחִלָּה, לְהָבִין קְצָת עִנְיַן 'הַשְׁרָאַת הַשְּׁכִינָה' שֶׁהָיְתָה שׁוֹרָה בְּבֵית קָדְשֵׁי קָדָשִׁים, וְכֵן כָּל מְקוֹם הַשְׁרָאַת הַשְּׁכִינָה מַה עִנְיָנוֹ. **it is first necessary to explain** something **in order to understand** somewhat **the topic of the "resting of the Divine Presence," which rested in the** housing **of the Holy of Holies, and likewise** to understand **the meaning of every place that "the resting of the Divine Presence"** is mentioned.

The concept of the Divine Presence resting somewhere is mentioned many times in the sources, whether concerning a physical location or a soul. What this means needs to be clarified precisely.

הֲלֹא "מְלֹא כָל הָאָרֶץ כְּבוֹדוֹ" (ישעיה ו, ג), וְ"לֵית אֲתָר פָּנוּי מִינֵיהּ"? **For is it not the case that "the entire world is filled with His glory"** (Isa. 6:3) **and "there is no space void of Him"** (*Zohar*)?

Since the Divine Presence is everywhere, we cannot say that it is found in a particular place, e.g., in the Holy of Holies. If we say that something is found in a specific place, that means that it is not in another place. However, no place is empty of the Divine Presence.[1]

---

1. *Tikkunei Zohar* 57.

אַךְ הָעִנְיָן, כְּדִכְתִיב: "וּמִבְּשָׂרִי אֶחֱזֶה אֱלוֹהַּ" (איוב יט, כו). **But this** concept can be understood based on an analogy implied by **the verse, "and from my flesh I will view God"** (Job 19:26).

From of a person's "flesh," his personal essence, he can see and grasp the higher essence. This terminology is frequently used in hasidic literature[2] to introduce a particular type of explanation that uses the paradigm of the human body and soul as a model and example to explain higher reality. ☞

שֶׁכְּמוֹ שֶׁנִּשְׁמַת הָאָדָם הִיא מְמַלְּאָה כָּל רְמַ"ח אֶבְרֵי הַגּוּף, מֵרֹאשׁוֹ וְעַד רַגְלוֹ, This means **that just as the human soul permeates all 248 limbs of the body, from head to foot,**

The soul exists in the entire human body. If any limb did not contain the soul of life, it would wither and die.

FROM MY FLESH I WILL VIEW GOD

☞ Clearly, higher reality is separate from us, and we can only grasp it through lower reality. All of our tools of comprehension, our senses and our cognitive understanding, come from the lower, material realms. But the phrase, "From my flesh I will view God," emphatically states more than that: that a person's ability to see the spiritual and supernal can come only from within him. The kabbalistic works speak of the physical body in this sense, while Hasidism, especially the writings of Chabad, also speak of the soul in this sense. This idea is predicated on the fact that our reference point is mainly the reference point of our mind and senses. Thus, anything that we can understand necessarily fits into this framework of "From my flesh I will view." On a deeper level, this approach is based on the fundamental concept that "He made man in the image of God" (Gen. 9:6). Therefore, the human framework familiar to us is truly – to the extent that it is possible to relate to this and speak of it – the divine framework. An additional aspect of seeing "from my flesh" (from one's essence) is that every deep understanding of existence, of understanding matters and their significance – in lower reality and, even more, in higher reality – accords essentially with our own inner frameworks. That understanding is achieved via that unmediated sense of self-knowledge that does not pass through the senses and the external garments.

---

2. See the beginning of *Iggeret HaKodesh*, epistle 15, and the commentary there.

וְאַף עַל פִּי כֵן, עִיקַּר מִשְׁכָּנָהּ וְהַשְׁרָאָתָהּ הִיא בְּמוֹחוֹ, and nevertheless, its primary abode and resting place is in a person's **brain,**

This is because the brain is the center of a person's consciousness and vitality.[3]

וּמֵהַמּוֹחַ מִתְפַּשֶּׁטֶת לְכָל הָאֵבָרִים, and from the brain it extends to all the limbs.

The presence of the soul emanates from the brain, and gives life to all the limbs. An approximate analogy would be electrical energy which in itself does not create heat or cold. However, when the electric current comes to the home, it is transmitted into different appliances, where it functions in different ways. It cools and heats, washes, cooks, and so forth.

The soul is the essence of life. And with regard to this level of being alive, all parts of the body are equal. In this respect, there is no difference between the toenail and the brain.[4]

וְכָל אֵבָר מְקַבֵּל מִמֶּנָּה חַיּוּת וְכֹחַ הָרָאוּי לוֹ לְפִי מִזְגוֹ וּתְכוּנָתוֹ - **Each limb receives from** the soul **the life force and capacity befitting its composition and character.**

Every limb receives its vitality and power appropriate for it from the overall living soul. And the extent to which the soul spreads into a particular limb, as is fitting and appropriate for the limb in accordance with its nature and composition, constitutes that limb's vitality.[5] That is to say, the nature and composition of each limb is not brought about by the limb itself but already exists in the flow of vitality from the soul. In other words, the flow of soul into the limbs is not comparable to

---

3. "Its abode" means: within. "Its resting place" means: encompassing (the Lubavitcher Rebbe, Rabbi Menahem Mendel Schneerson).
4. The Lubavitcher Rebbe, Rabbi Menahem Mendel Schneerson.
5. The Lubavitcher Rebbe, Rabbi Menahem Mendel Schneerson.

water that appears to have different colors only after it has been poured into jars of different colors.[6]

הָעַיִן לִרְאוֹת, וְהָאֹזֶן לִשְׁמוֹעַ, וְהַפֶּה לְדַבֵּר, וְהָרַגְלַיִם לַהֲלוֹךְ - For example, **the eye** receives the life force and capacity enabling it **to see, and the ear to hear, the mouth to speak, and the feet to walk.**

These body parts receive their energy and capabilities from the soul. This can be compared to an electric current. The current itself does not heat or cool down a room. But when it enters a house and branches out to different appliances, it is expressed through the various functions of those appliances. It thereby heats or cools a room, washes laundry, and so on.[7]

כַּנִּרְאֶה בְּחוּשׁ, שֶׁבַּמּוֹחַ מַרְגִּישׁ כָּל הַנִּפְעָל בִּרְמַ"ח אֵבָרִים וְכָל הַקּוֹרוֹת אוֹתָם. **As our experience indicates, it is with the brain that one is conscious of** **everything that affects the 248 limbs, and anything that occurs to them.**

The brain is the center of all the particular powers in the various parts of the body. Instructions and desires travel from the brain to the body parts, and responses and sensory information then travel back to the brain. The brain is the center of a person's consciousness overall, and the center of the nervous system. It is clear from the foregoing that the spiritual life force that is enclothed in the body is not one capacity that is split among the various organs. Rather, it is inherently complex. Even while it is still at its point of origin, the brain, before it is enclothed within the various body parts, it is complex and divided into the various intrinsic faculties, such as the ability to see, the ability to walk, and so forth.

---

6. The Lubavitcher Rebbe, Rabbi Menaḥem Mendel Schneerson.
7. The author of the Tanya mentions these four body parts (the eye, the ear, the mouth, and the feet) because they correspond to thought, speech, and action. Sight and hearing evoke thought, the mouth is used for speech, the feet represent action (the Lubavitcher Rebbe, Rabbi Menaḥem Mendel Schneerson).

וְהִנֵּה אֵין שִׁינּוּי קַבָּלַת הַכֹּחוֹת וְהַחַיּוּת שֶׁבְּאֵבְרֵי הַגּוּף מִן הַנְּשָׁמָה מִצַּד עַצְמָהּ וּמַהוּתָהּ, **The differentiation among the bodily limbs in receiving the capacity and life force does not derive from the soul's intrinsic essence,**

On the one hand, even before the soul is drawn into the body parts, their faculties are separated from one another. On the other hand, it cannot be said that this division and split exists in the soul itself, in its intrinsic essence.

שֶׁיִּהְיֶה מַהוּתָהּ וְעַצְמוּתָהּ מִתְחַלֵּק לִרְמַ"ח חֲלָקִים שׁוֹנִים, מִתְלַבְּשִׁים בִּרְמַ"ח מְקוֹמוֹת כְּפִי צִיּוּר חֶלְקֵי מְקוֹמוֹת אֶבְרֵי הַגּוּף. **such that its intrinsic essence would be divided into 248 different parts, clothed in 248 different locations, according to the layout of the various locations of the bodily limbs.**

If we were to say that the soul's intrinsic essence is composed of different faculties, sight, hearing, walking, and so forth, this would mean that the soul's essence is divided into many parts, corresponding to the number and form of the body parts. Each part of the soul would have its own unique nature, qualities, and way of functioning.

שֶׁלְּפִי זֶה נִמְצָא עַצְמוּתָהּ וּמַהוּתָהּ מְצֻיָּיר בְּצִיּוּר גַּשְׁמִי וּדְמוּת וְתַבְנִית כְּתַבְנִית הַגּוּף חַס וְשָׁלוֹם, **According to this, it would be the case that the** soul's **intrinsic essence would be portrayed with a physical portrayal, and a likeness and structure like the structure of the body, God forbid.**

This is impossible, because the soul is a spiritual entity, and no physical form can be associated with it.

אֶלָּא כּוּלָהּ עֶצֶם אֶחָד רוּחָנִי פָּשׁוּט, וּמוּפְשָׁט מִכָּל צִיּוּר גַּשְׁמִי, וּמִבְּחִינַת וְגֶדֶר מָקוֹם וּמִדָּה וּגְבוּל גַּשְׁמִי, **Rather, the soul is entirely a single, simple spiritual entity, devoid of any physical depiction or defined location, dimension, and physical limitation,**

The soul is not complex or divisible. The limitations that apply to physical objects do not apply to it.

מִצַּד מַהוּתָהּ וְעַצְמוּתָהּ. וְלֹא שַׁיָּיךְ בְּמַהוּתָהּ וְעַצְמוּתָהּ לוֹמַר שֶׁהִיא בַּמּוֹחִין שֶׁבָּרֹאשׁ יוֹתֵר מִבָּרַגְלַיִם, מֵאַחַר שֶׁמַּהוּתָהּ וְעַצְמוּתָהּ אֵינָהּ בְּגֶדֶר וּבְחִינַת מָקוֹם וּגְבוּל גַּשְׁמִי.

from the aspect of its intrinsic essence. Therefore, **it cannot be stated that** the soul's **intrinsic essence is** located **in the brain in the head more so than** it is **in the feet, since its intrinsic essence is not defined and on the level of physical space and limitation.**

One cannot say that the soul is more present in one body part than in another, or that it is present in different ways in different body parts, because the parameters of spatiality do not apply to it.

Thus, the question is: If the soul does not relate to the body parts, if it does not, as it were, recognize them by name, shape, and qualities, how do the body parts receive their vitality from it, the vitality that is directed to them each in accordance with its particular nature and composition, and without which vitality they cannot exist as they are?

רַק שֶׁתַּרְיַ"ג מִינֵי כֹּחוֹת וְחַיּוּת כְּלוּלִים בָּהּ בְּמַהוּתָהּ וְעַצְמוּתָהּ לָצֵאת אֶל הַפּוֹעַל וְהַגִּילּוּי מֵהַהֶעְלֵם

Rather, 613 types of faculties and life forces are incorporated within the soul's **intrinsic essence, to be actualized and revealed**

The answer is that all of the parts of the body, all 248 organs and 365 sinews, are formed and encompassed in potential within the soul's character. There, they are prepared to go from potential to actual.

לְהַחֲיוֹת רַמַ"ח אֵבָרִין וְשַׁסַ"ה גִּידִין שֶׁבַּגּוּף עַל יְדֵי הִתְלַבְּשׁוּתָם בַּנֶּפֶשׁ הַחִיּוּנִית, שֶׁיֵּשׁ לָהּ גַּם כֵּן רַמַ"ח וְשַׁסַ"ה כֹּחוֹת וְחַיּוּת הַלָּלוּ.

to animate the 248 limbs and 365 sinews of the body by being enclothed in the vital soul, which also has these 248 and 365 types **of faculties and life forces.**

The vital, or animal, soul directly vitalizes and activates the body. The higher soul is a unified spiritual entity that does not relate to and does not connect with the differentiation and distinctions among the body parts. But the vital soul is the midpoint between the higher, divine soul and the body. The vital soul is also a spiritual entity, but it is on a lower level and is less primary. It splits and flows to the different faculties in accordance with the needs of each of the body parts, giving them life and activating them.

24 Iyar

וְהִנֵּה עַל הַמְשָׁכַת כָּל הַתרי"ג מִינֵי כֹּחוֹת וְחַיּוּת מֵהֶעְלֵם הַנְּשָׁמָה אֶל הַגּוּף לְהַחֲיוֹתוֹ, עָלֶיהָ אָמְרוּ שֶׁעִיקַּר מִשְׁכָּנָהּ וְהַשְׁרָאָתָהּ שֶׁל הַמְשָׁכָה זוֹ וְגִלּוּי זֶה הוּא כּוּלּוֹ בַּמּוֹחִין שֶׁבָּרֹאשׁ.

Regarding the drawing down of all 613 types of faculties and life forces from the concealment in the soul to the body, in order to animate it, they said that the principal abode and resting of this drawing down and this revelation is entirely in the brain within the head.

The force in the soul that acts and activates the body does not flow directly from the soul's intrinsic essence to the various body parts. Rather, it first passes through a central point in the human body: the brain, housed in the head.

וְלָכֵן הֵם מְקַבְּלִים תְּחִלָּה הַכֹּחַ וְהַחַיּוּת הָרָאוּי לָהֶם, לְפִי מֶזֶג וּתְכוּנָתָם. שֶׁהֵן: חָכְמָה בִּינָה דַּעַת, וְכֹחַ הַמַּחֲשָׁבָה, וְכָל הַשַּׁיָּיךְ לַמּוֹחִין.

That is why the brain is first to receive the capacity and life force befitting its composition and character, that being wisdom, understanding, and knowledge, as well as the faculty of thought and everything that pertains to the brain.

First of all, the brain receives the capacity for thought and cognition that are germane to the brain.

וְלֹא זוֹ בִּלְבַד, אֶלָּא גַּם כְּלָלוּת כָּל הַמְשָׁכוֹת הַחַיּוּת לִשְׁאָר הָאֵבָרִים, גַּם כֵּן כְּלוּלָה וּמְלוּבֶּשֶׁת בַּמּוֹחִין שֶׁבָּרֹאשׁ.

Not only that, but the totality of all of the flows of life force to the other limbs is also incorporated and enclothed in the brain within the head.

Not only does the brain receive its own life force, but all of the forces that act within the body are first revealed in the brain. The powers relevant to the brain itself, wisdom, understanding, knowledge, and the faculty of thought, which are the faculties of the brain itself, are fully revealed there, while the other faculties, which belong to the 248 body parts, are not in the brain in a manifest way ready to perform their action. Rather, they only radiate and extend from the brain like a ray of the sun from the sun.

וְשָׁם הוּא עִיקָרָהּ וְשָׁרְשָׁהּ שֶׁל הַמְשָׁכָה זוֹ, בִּבְחִינַת גִּילּוּי הָאוֹר וְהַחַיּוּת שֶׁל כָּל הַנְּשָׁמָה כּוּלָּהּ. — **There**, in the brain, **is the core and root of this drawing down, on the level of a manifestation of the light and life force of the very entirety of the soul.**

The essence and entirety of the life force that is drawn from the soul to the body is revealed in the manifestation of the life force in the brain.

וּמִשָּׁם מִתְפַּשֶּׁטֶת הֶאָרָה לִשְׁאָר כָּל הָאֵבָרִים וּמְקַבֵּל כָּל אֶחָד כֹּחַ וְחַיּוּת הָרָאוּי לוֹ כְּפִי מִזְגּוֹ וְתִכוּנָתוֹ. — **From there, the illumination** of the soul **extends to all the other limbs, and each one receives the capacity and life force befitting its composition and character.**

Thus, in the life force within the brain, along with the revelation of the light of the entire soul, there is also a particular drawing down and particular illumination toward each body part.

כֹּחַ הָרְאִיָּה מִתְגַּלֶּה בָּעַיִן, וְכֹחַ הַשְּׁמִיעָה בָּאוֹזֶן וְכוּ׳. — For example, **the capacity for sight is manifest in the eye, and the capacity for hearing is manifest in the ear, and so forth.**

The eye and the ear are the proper vessels for sight and hearing, respectively. Thus, the spiritual capacity for sight is revealed within the eye and the spiritual capacity for hearing is revealed within the ear. The proper spiritual power is revealed within each one of the body parts.

וְכָל הַכֹּחוֹת מִתְפַּשְׁטִים מֵהַמֹּחַ כַּנּוֹדָע כִּי שָׁם הוּא עִיקַר מִשְׁכַּן הַנְּשָׁמָה כֻּלָּהּ, בִּבְחִינַת גִּלּוּי, שֶׁנִּגְלֵית שָׁם כְּלָלוּת הַחַיּוּת הַמִּתְפַּשֵּׁט מִמֶּנָּה.

Yet **all the faculties extend from the brain, as is known, because** the brain **is the principal abode of the entirety of the soul on a manifest level, where the totality of the life force that extends from the soul is manifest.**

The essence and beginning of the drawing forth is in the brain. As mentioned, the essential soul itself is not revealed at all, whether in a toenail or in the brain. However, illumination from the soul is drawn forth in a manifest state. And the totality of this illumination of the life force and its being revealed in the body is in the brain.

רַק כֹּחוֹתֶיהָ שֶׁל כְּלָלוּת הַחַיּוּת מְאִירִים וּמִתְפַּשְׁטִים מִשָּׁם לְכָל אֶבְרֵי הַגּוּף, כְּדִמְיוֹן הָאוֹר הַמִּתְפַּשֵּׁט וּמֵאִיר מֵהַשֶּׁמֶשׁ לְחַדְרֵי חֲדָרִים

It is merely the faculties of the totality of the life force that radiate and extend from there to all the limbs of the body, just as the light of the sun spreads and shines into innermost rooms.

The forces of vitality in the limbs are only an illumination and extension of the total illumination of the soul shining in the brain. The analogy of the sunlight emphasizes that although the forces of vitality in the limbs appear independent, they are not separate from the soul, just as light cannot be separated from its source, even if it appears to be so, as when an innermost room is lit by sunlight while the sun itself cannot be seen.

[וַאֲפִילוּ הַלֵּב מְקַבֵּל מֵהַמֹּחַ, וְלָכֵן הַמֹּחַ שַׁלִּיט עָלָיו בְּתוֹלַדְתּוֹ, כַּנִּזְכָּר לְעֵיל].

(**Even the heart receives** its life force **from the brain. And therefore** the brain **innately controls it, as stated above** [chap. 12].)

The heart too is the center of life. It is the center of blood circulation, which brings life to the body. Yet it too receives nerve signals from the brain, which regulate and activate it. The brain is the central organ of the nervous system. It is the center for every sensation and for consciousness, for the transfer of life force to all the limbs, and for the coordination among them. In this sense, just as the brain controls all the limbs, it controls the heart as well.

Thus it is only the illumination of the soul that is revealed within the body and which affects the various limbs. However, this illumination of the soul, including even the aspect of the soul that acts within the body, does not function in a decentralized way, such that each part of the body receives its particular spiritual power directly from that illumination. Rather, all the powers come to one central point, the brain, from which the soul is drawn toward all the body parts, to each in accordance with its nature and purpose.

This concludes the first part of the chapter which employed an analogy, taken from the human context, to outline in the broadest way the relationship among three concepts: intrinsic essence, permeation (*hashra'a*), and manifestation. The chapter taught that these concepts differ from each other in various ways. "Intrinsic essence" refers to an entity that can be in different places and in different states without being revealed. It exists within everything, but it is not manifest in any specific object. This is life itself, which is found in the whole body equally, as much in the sole of the foot as in the brain, yet which is not revealed in any specific place. Another concept and level is that of "permeation," the Divine Presence resting in the world, and the soul resting in the body. This pertains to a location. The analogy speaks of the soul dwelling in the brain, from which it is revealed and from where it affects all the limbs. The third level is "manifestation." According to this analogy, the soul is revealed in the life force of the body parts and in their various actions. Permeation and manifestation are distinct from one another. Sometimes manifestation exists without permeation, and sometimes permeation exists without manifestation.

The soul might be manifest in a different place from where it resides. For example, a painter's hand can serve as a tool for the revelation of the inner being of the soul more than any other part of his body, including his brain. The manifestation of his soul, of the existence of the life within him, certainly needs to pass through his brain, but it is not necessarily revealed there but rather in another limb in the body, namely his hand. There were great artists who possessed a brutish nature that astonished people. They wondered how one person could be both refined and coarse at the same time. The explanation is that it is possible for the interior of the soul to be manifest in this way as well. The soul always resides in the brain, but it is possible for the interior of the soul to be revealed only through a different part of the body. The Talmud (*Sota* 10a) lists five people, Samson, Saul, Absalom, Zedekiah, and Asa, who "were created [with a characteristic that is] akin to the representation of the [One on] High." That is to say, in a certain area of their being, they were perfect. As we see from those people, it is possible that a higher virtue will be revealed only in one part of a person and not in his entire being. "Samson [was glorified] in his strength": With his hands, Samson manifested supernal powers that were not manifest in his brain. There can be manifestation without permeation, when the permeation within a person is not apparent.

Another example concerns two mountains referred to in the Torah: Mount Sinai and Mount Moriah. Mount Sinai was a place of manifestation. The revelation there at the giving of the Torah was beyond any revelation that took place on Mount Moriah, where the Temple stood. However, after that revelation, Mount Sinai reverted to being an undistinguished place for sheep and cattle to graze. Mount Moriah, on the other hand, is the place where the Divine Presence always rests, even when there is no revelation there.

25 Iyar
25 Iyar (leap year)

וְכָכָה מַמָּשׁ עַל דֶּרֶךְ מָשָׁל, **In the very same way, figuratively speaking,**

It has already been mentioned that this phrase contains a paradox. Here, it reflects the complex nature of the matter at hand, the permeation and manifestation of the Divine Presence. On the one hand, the entire explanation is only "figurative," but on the other hand it is "the very same." Even if it is impossible to fully understand the analogy, it must be accepted as "the very same" until further explanations are provided.

אֵין סוֹף בָּרוּךְ הוּא מְמַלֵּא כָּל עָלְמִין לְהַחֲיוֹתָם וּבְכָל עוֹלָם יֵשׁ בְּרוּאִים לְאֵין קֵץ וְתַכְלִית, רִבּוֹא רְבָבוֹת מִינֵי מַדְרֵגוֹת, מַלְאָכִים וּנְשָׁמוֹת כו'. *Ein Sof*, **blessed be He, fills all worlds to grant them life. Each world contains an endless number of creations, and myriads upon myriads of varied levels of angels and souls, and so forth.**

The Talmud states, "Just as the Holy One, blessed be He, fills the entire world, so too the soul fills the entire body" (*Berakhot* 10a).[8]

A "world" is defined as a realm of beings, conscious and partially conscious, that are arranged within a particular system. It is not necessarily a physical realm, but it comprises the dimensions that allow certain things to exist in reality. In this sense, as we see in our world, each world contains innumerable levels and different entities: angels, souls, and so forth.

| וְכֵן רִיבּוּי הָעוֹלָמוֹת, אֵין לוֹ קֵץ וּגְבוּל, גָּבוֹהַּ עַל גָּבוֹהַּ כו׳. | Likewise, the multitude of worlds has no end or limit, one above the other and so forth. |

In addition to the multitude of creations in each world, there is an infinite number of worlds. Although we speak of numbers of worlds, two or four worlds, there are in fact an untold number, each with a different composition and on a different level. The difference in worlds is in their nature and their level. There are worlds that are higher than high, and worlds that are even higher than that,[9] without end. Each world is inhabited by many different creatures and entities: physical entities and an even greater number of spiritual entities. The "universe" that physicists refer to, which itself is beyond measure, is just a thin layer within one system of worlds, and above that system of worlds there are countless others.

| וְהִנֵּה מַהוּתוֹ וְעַצְמוּתוֹ שֶׁל אֵין סוֹף בָּרוּךְ הוּא שָׁוֶה בָּעֶלְיוֹנִים וְתַחְתּוֹנִים, כִּמְשַׁל הַנְּשָׁמָה הַנִּזְכָּר לְעֵיל. | Now the essence and being of *Ein Sof*, blessed be He, is uniform in both the higher and lower worlds, as in the analogy of the soul presented above. |

It cannot be said that God's essence is found in a higher world to a greater degree than in a lower world. Likewise, the life force that the soul conveys to the body illuminates the toes just as much as it illuminates the brain.

---

8. See *Likkutei Torah*, Lev. 31a.
9. As the verse states, "For higher than high is watching, and high ones are over them" (Eccles. 5:7).

As above, from the perspective of God's being and essence, "there is nowhere that is devoid of Him." This means that from the aspect of His being and existence, there is no place, entity, or level of existence that is empty of Him; from infinitely high to infinitely low, from the great archangel Michael to the smallest worm. As Rambam says, "All beings exist due only to the truth of His Own Being. If a person might conjecture that He were not, then nothing could exist."[10] Worlds, entities, can exist only given divine existence, since only divine being and essence grant life and existence to all existence, from beginning to end and in every direction.

וּכְמוֹ שֶׁכָּתוּב בַּתִּיקוּנִים (הקדמת תיקוני זהר יז, א): דְּאִיהוּ סְתִימוּ דְּכָל סְתִימִין. **As written in the *Tikkunei Zohar* (17a), "He is the most hidden of all hidden."**

If God is equally present in all worlds, then He is concealed in all of them.

פֵּירוּשׁ: דַּאֲפִילוּ בְּעָלְמִין סְתִימִין דִּלְעֵילָא הוּא סָתוּם וְנֶעְלָם בְּתוֹכָם כְּמוֹ שֶׁהוּא סָתוּם וְנֶעְלָם בַּתַּחְתּוֹנִים. **This means that even in the hidden higher worlds He is hidden and concealed within them, in the same way that He is hidden and concealed in the lower worlds.**

The expression, "He is the most hidden of all hidden," could be understood to mean that God is more concealed than all that is concealed, but concealed in the same way. Thus, the author of the *Tanya* adds this sentence. That is to say, not only is God more hidden than they are, but He is hidden from them to such a degree that there is no difference between His being concealed in the lower worlds and His being concealed in the higher, hidden worlds.

The distinction between hidden worlds and revealed worlds is significant only with respect to us. A "revealed world" is one which an entity of our magnitude can understand, whereas a "hidden world" is beyond the limits of our comprehension. In this sense, the division between the revealed worlds and the hidden worlds is not fixed. It varies from person to person, and even from moment to moment within the life of

---

10. Rambam, *Sefer HaMadda, Hilkhot Yesodei HaTorah* 1:1–2.

a particular individual, in accordance with his level. This division is also a division of level; the hidden worlds are also higher worlds. The author of the *Tanya* is saying that even if a person were able to comprehend all the revealed worlds and the hidden worlds beyond them, endlessly higher and higher, God Himself is still "the most hidden of all hidden." There too He is concealed just as He is concealed in our world.

כִּי לֵית מַחֲשָׁבָה תְּפִיסָא בֵּיהּ כְּלָל, אֲפִילוּ בְּעוֹלָמוֹת עֶלְיוֹנִים, **For no thought can grasp Him at all, even in the higher worlds.**

This is not referring only to human thought, but to any thought, on any level, and in any world. As stated in the liturgical hymn recited during the Days of Awe, God is "the constant One who considers small and great equally." He is separate and concealed from the higher worlds just as He is from our world. The angel Michael does not know God's essence any more than does the lowliest creature on earth. The ministering angels ask one another, "Where is the place of His glory?" in the same way that a small child asks this, at his level of comprehension. As stated above, the impossibility of understanding God is not a question of the level of one's thought. In essence, no thought whatsoever can perceive Him.[11]

וְנִמְצָא כְּמוֹ שֶׁמָּצוּי שָׁם, כָּךְ נִמְצָא בַּתַּחְתּוֹנִים מַמָּשׁ. **Thus, in literally the same way that He is present there in the higher worlds, He is present in the lower worlds.**

There is no difference between God's presence in the highest heights and in the lowest abyss. In terms of comprehension, no one comprehends, and in terms of existence, He is present everywhere. With regard to God's essence and being, the divine life force is just as present within a grain of sand as it is within the heavenly angels. ☞

IN THE SAME WAY THAT HE IS PRESENT IN THE HIGHER WORLDS, HE IS PRESENT IN THE LOWER WORLDS

☞ This too can be seen "from my flesh." The soul itself is equally present throughout the whole body. But its essence is not revealed at all, and this applies equally to all parts of the body. The intrinsic essence of the soul is always present in every part of

---

11. *Sha'ar HaYiḥud VeHa'emuna*, chap. 9, discusses the analogy of wisdom, which is intangible.

26 Iyar
(leap year)

וְהַהֶבְדֵּל שֶׁבֵּין עוֹלָמוֹת עֶלְיוֹנִים וְתַחְתּוֹנִים הוּא מִצַּד הַמְשָׁכַת הַחַיּוּת, אֲשֶׁר אֵין סוֹף בָּרוּךְ הוּא מַמְשִׁיךְ וּמֵאִיר בִּבְחִינַת גִּילּוּי מֵהַהֶעְלֵם

The difference between the higher and lower worlds exists from the aspect of the channeling of the life force which *Ein Sof*, blessed be He, channels and radiates so that it is **revealed**, having come **out of concealment**

Nevertheless, we see a difference between the various levels and worlds. This difference is not due to the divine essence itself but to its illumination and the extent to which this illumination is manifest within the worlds. The greater the revelation of the divine light, the higher the level the world is considered to be on. In this sense, there are differences between higher level and lower level, between one world and another. Nevertheless, the revelation is not a revelation of the divine essence and being, but only of the light of the essence. This light does not touch the divine essence. It does not add or detract anything from fundamental being or essence.

---

us, and we cannot fathom existing without it. However, while on the one hand it is extremely close to us, on the other hand we know nothing about it. Apparently, nothing is closer to us than our soul. Nevertheless, we know nothing about it. We can faintly and partially perceive certain ways in which the soul is manifest. Although we have been contemplating this problem for generations, we are still unable to arrive at any characterization of the soul itself.

In the context of serving God, the Rabbis have offered an explanation of the verse, "If I ascend to Heaven, You are there; if I lie down in the netherworld, You are here" (Ps. 139:8). If a person were to ascend to Heaven, to the highest heights, he would discover God there, and if he were to go down into the abyss, to the very lowest point, he would find Him there, too.

Any attempt to define where God is, to distinguish between the "here" and the "there," is impossible. A person rises to the highest heights and sees that God is no more there than He is anywhere else. And a person descends to the depths and sees that He is there as well, as He is in any other place. It is said that one of the reasons that the wicked do not leave Gehenna is because they do not believe. If they believed, Gehenna would cease to be Gehenna for them. At the moment that people believe that even "if I lie down in the netherworld, You are here," that God is there as well, there would no longer be a "netherworld," because "even when I walk through the valley of the shadow of death...You are with me" (Ps. 23:4). It is no longer the valley of the shadow of death.

| שֶׁזֶּה אֶחָד מֵהַטְּעָמִים שֶׁהַהַשְׁפָּעָה וְהַמְשָׁכַת הַחַיּוּת מְכוּנָּה בְּשֵׁם 'אוֹר', עַל דֶּרֶךְ מָשָׁל,] | (this is one of the reasons that the flow and channel of life force is referred to metaphorically as light), |

The author of the *Tanya* notes that the divine flow is often referred to in terms of light: "the light of *Ein Sof*," "supernal lights," "direct light," "reflected light," and so forth.[12] The "light" expresses the idea that there is a source of light, an independent "luminary," and the light that emanates from it does not change or affect it in any way. This relationship between the source of the light, which is concealed and distinct, and the light itself, which illuminates and is revealed within other objects, expresses the relationship between the divine essence and its influence upon the worlds.[13]

| לְהַחֲיוֹת הָעוֹלָמוֹת וְהַבְּרוּאִים שֶׁבָּהֶם, שֶׁהָעוֹלָמוֹת הָעֶלְיוֹנִים מְקַבְּלִים בִּבְחִינַת גִּילּוּי קְצָת יוֹתֵר מֵהַתַּחְתּוֹנִים, | to grant life to the worlds and creations within them. The higher worlds receive their life force somewhat more openly than do the lower worlds, |

Regarding this illumination that gives life to the worlds and creatures, there is a disparity between one world and another, and between one creation and another. As stated, no world can contain and grasp the divine essence itself. The worlds all receive just a little light, and the only difference between them is that the "higher" worlds receive a little more.

| וְכָל הַבְּרוּאִים שֶׁבָּהֶם מְקַבְּלִים כָּל אֶחָד כְּפִי כֹּחוֹ וּתְכוּנָתוֹ, | and all of the creations within them receive the flow, each according to its capacity and character, |

---

12. As the author of the *Tanya* mentions here, this is only "one of the reasons." There are others; see *Sha'ar HaYihud VeHa'emuna*, chap. 10, which describes the unity as the unification of the light in the luminary; *Torah Or* 97a, that it is the encompassing light; *Ma'amrei Admor HaZaken* 5562, p. 40; see also *Sefer HaArakhim*, vol. 2, s.v. "or."

13. See *Likkutei Torah*, Lev. 52c.

Light is received by each world in general, and as a result, these worlds are able to exist. Moreover, each individual creation within the worlds also receives light. The degree of this light is in accordance with each creation's particular characteristics and its capacity to bear the light.[14]

שֶׁהִיא תְּכוּנַת וּבְחִינַת הַמְשָׁכָה הַפְּרָטִית אֲשֶׁר אֵין סוֹף בָּרוּךְ הוּא מַמְשִׁיךְ וּמֵאִיר לוֹ. — which is the character and category of a particular flow which *Ein Sof*, blessed be He, channels and radiates to it.

The illumination received by each creation, in accordance with its makeup and character, is in keeping with the structure and quality of its vessel, which also receives its own specific drawing down and illumination.

Accordingly, the revelation of the divine light is twofold. First, it forms a vessel of a certain size and capability, and second, it maintains and serves and acts within that vessel, in accordance with the capacity and manner that each particular vessel can receive. This revelation creates the worlds, which are different and distinct from one another, each with its own particular dimensions and quality of being. Subsequently, in accordance with the relevant capacity, a certain degree of consciousness can come within that existence. To use the human analogy, the body itself is formed as it is from the same source as its life force. This force acts within the body, forming it and causing it to grow, one way in the toenail and another in the brain. Next, the soul illuminates within the body, operating in one way in the brain and in another way in the toenail, in each part according to its nature and function. Here as well, there is a doubleness: the formation of the vessel and its function, which are two stages that by definition come one after the other.

Thus, the illumination of life acts twice: in the vessels and in the lights. The relationship between the light and vessel may be seen also more abstractly as the relationship between a concept and a word. The concept enters the word, but the word, which stores the concept, also

---

14. In the analogy of the human being above, the phrase used was "its composition and character." Here the phrase used is "particular characteristics and its capacity" (the Lubavitcher Rebbe, Rabbi Menaḥem Mendel Schneerson).

requires a certain characterization in order to become a vessel in a specific and appropriate manner. The composition and wondrousness of the word itself, as in any "vessel," is no less than the wondrousness in the light.¹⁵

וְהַתַּחְתּוֹנִים, אֲפִילוּ הָרוּחָנִיִּים אֵינָם מְקַבְּלִים בִּבְחִינַת גִּילּוּי כָּל כָּךְ רַק בִּלְבוּשִׁים רַבִּים, אֲשֶׁר אֵין סוֹף בָּרוּךְ הוּא מַלְבִּישׁ בָּהֶם הַחַיּוּת וְהָאוֹר אֲשֶׁר מַמְשִׁיךְ וּמֵאִיר לָהֶם לְהַחֲיוֹתָם.

By contrast, **the lower worlds, even the spiritual ones, do not receive** their life force **so openly, but rather through many garments in which** *Ein Sof,* blessed be He, enclothes the life force and light which He channels and radiates in order **to grant them life.**

The lower worlds, even the spiritual ones such as the spiritual world of *Asiya,* do not receive their life force in the same manner as the higher worlds. The life force of the lower worlds is shrouded by many concealments. ☞

HIDDEN HIGHER WORLDS AND REVEALED LOWER WORLDS

☞ There is a complex relationship here. The lower worlds, which are visible to us, are actually concealed, and the higher worlds, which are hidden, are in fact revealed. The following ancient analogy elucidates this (see *Torah Or* 62b, and elsewhere): A "revealed world" is comparable to the land, and a "hidden world" is comparable to the sea. The sea is considered "concealed" because the creatures that live in it are inside it, whereas on land, creatures generally live on the surface. Sea creatures are engulfed in the sea, and this makes the sea a realm of concealment. On land, the creatures are visible, and thus it is a visible world. Nevertheless, to take this analogy one step further, sea creatures know the sea better than land creatures know the land. Land creatures reside only on the outer layer of their world, whereas the realm of the sea is more visible and accessible to sea creatures. The relationship between that which is revealed and that which is hidden is therefore complex. The enshrouded, impenetrable, incomprehensible realm essentially contains more revelation, and because it contains revelation, it is a "hidden world." In our world, objects are visible on the surface, but because the creatures in it are all on the surface and cannot disappear within it, and since in a certain sense it is impossible to reveal anything further, it is a "revealed world."

---

15. See *Iggeret HaKodesh,* epistle 5.

27 Iyar
(leap year)

וְכָל כָּךְ עָצְמוּ וְגָבְרוּ הַלְּבוּשִׁים אֲשֶׁר אֵין סוֹף בָּרוּךְ הוּא מַלְבִּישׁ וּמַסְתִּיר בָּהֶם הָאוֹר וְהַחַיּוּת, עַד אֲשֶׁר בָּרָא בּוֹ עוֹלָם הַזֶּה, הַחוֹמְרִי וְהַגַּשְׁמִי מַמָּשׁ,

The garments in which *Ein Sof*, blessed be He, enclothes and conceals the light and life force intensified and grew so strong until He created this world, which is actually physical and material.

The many garments obscure and dim the divine essence, which is the source of the light. God created our world (*ha'olam hazeh*), the revealed world with this limited, dim light. The author of the *Tanya* explains that the description "actually physical and material" refers to the lowest possible point from which it is impossible to descend further, and where there is apparently no longer contact with any other reality. This is the fundamental difference between the material world and the spiritual world (which includes the spiritual world of *Asiya*). All the spiritual worlds are connected to each other in a sense, at least by means of negative definitions, since material definitions do not apply to them. On some level they can perceive the realities of other spiritual worlds. In contrast, it is nearly impossible to see any connection between the physical and the spiritual. The two have almost no common ground. From the perspective of the physical realm, the spiritual realm does not exist, and from the perspective of the spiritual realm, the physical realm looks lifeless, completely disconnected, like a dead body showing no signs of life.[16]

---

16. Presumably, the *Tanya*'s intent and specific phrasing here – "actually physical and material" – refers to the process of coming into being from nothingness to tangibility only the inanimate part of the material globe of the earth. This explains several specific phrases in the language (of the author of the *Tanya* further on in the chapter) such as "existence from nothingness," "which is visible to corporeal eyes" (which is "*Malkhut* of *Malkhut* of *Asiya*"). By contrast, when referring to the world of *Asiya* in general, which includes the spiritual (world) of *Asiya*, the author of the *Tanya* writes further on (chaps. 52–53), "*Malkhut* of *Asiya*" and not "*Malkhut* of *Malkhut* of *Asiya*" (the Lubavitcher Rebbe, Rabbi Menaḥem Mendel Schneerson).

וּמְהַוֵּוהוּ וּמְחַיֵּיהוּ בַּחַיּוּת וְאוֹר אֲשֶׁר מַמְשִׁיךְ וּמֵאִיר לוֹ, אוֹר הַמְלוּבָּשׁ וּמְכוּסֶּה וּמוּסְתָּר בְּתוֹךְ הַלְּבוּשִׁים הָרַבִּים וְהָעֲצוּמִים הַמַּעֲלִימִים וּמַסְתִּירִים הָאוֹר וְהַחַיּוּת, **He sustains it and grants it life through the life force and light which He channels and radiates to it, which is enclothed, cloaked, and concealed within the many immense garments which hide and conceal the light and life force,**

Without being noticed by the physical realm, the light is enclothed within it. God makes the existence of such a world possible. The divine light is veiled and concealed, such that neither the divine nor the light can be seen. Similarly, the light that reaches us from the moon is a reflection of the sunlight and so diminished that it is difficult for us to associate it with the sunlight or the sun itself.

עַד שֶׁאֵין נִרְאֶה וְנִגְלֶה שׁוּם אוֹר וְחַיּוּת, רַק דְּבָרִים חוֹמְרִיִּים וְגַשְׁמִיִּים **to the extent that no light or life force is detectable – only physical and material entities**

When we see physical entities, we do not see their spiritual life force, the divine light that is the essential source of their life and their existence.

וְנִרְאִים מֵתִים. **that appear to be lifeless.**

Something lifeless is seen only in terms of its inanimate matter. We do not see a spiritual life force within it as we do in plants and animals.[17]

NO LIGHT OR LIFE FORCE IS DETECTABLE

The material world, which is the lowest and most impermeable realm that could possibly exist, is therefore also the pinnacle of divine creation. God created a world that is completely impermeable to the Divine. He gives it life and sustains

---

17. Although inanimate matter also receives light from *Malkhut* within *Malkhut* of *Asiya*, plant and animal life and human beings receive a greater and more revealed life force (the Lubavitcher Rebbe, Rabbi Menaḥem Mendel Schneerson).

אַךְ בְּתוֹכָם יֵשׁ אוֹר וְחַיּוּת הַמְהַוֶּה אוֹתָם מֵאַיִן לְיֵשׁ תָּמִיד, שֶׁלֹּא יַחְזְרוּ לִהְיוֹת אַיִן וָאֶפֶס כִּשְׁהָיוּ.

However, within them lies the light and life force which perpetually brings them into existence from nothingness, so that they will not revert to their original state of absolute nothingness.

We can see that living beings such as animals have life force. But even inanimate matter exists, and nothing exists on its own. All of existence is supported by the divine life force within. Thus, not only is the world not "lifeless," but it breathes in life at all times. For the sake of its very existence, it must receive in each instant a new life force in order to vitalize it and sustain it in existence, in order to maintain it every aspect of it so perfectly that it has no awareness that He is doing so. Ostensibly, this is a world that cannot be. It is absurd that its entire existence contradicts its awareness, and that all its awareness and perceptions contradict its existence. The existence of physicality is thus the greatest wonder in creation. It is an entity that on the one hand is entirely dependent on the Creator, and on the other hand does not at all recognize that it is not the origin of everything. The existence of such an entity is the glory of God. Only He could do such a thing. Only from the aspect of the Infinite One can there be something that is from Him and within Him, a part and direct continuation of His being, yet able to deny all this.

The author of the *Tanya* says here that God does not merely resurrect the dead. That is a simple matter for Him. God can even create the dead! To do that – to bring about absence, darkness – is the real marvel of creation. To make things that appear lifeless, to make a world in which the Creator, God Himself, the Source of all life, is not seen at all. That is a wonder in which the power of the Infinite One can be clearly seen.

It is possible to interpret the verse, "He put 'the world' [*ha'olam*] as well in their heart, notwithstanding that man will not discover from beginning to end the accomplishment that God has accomplished" (Eccles. 3:11) in this vein. *Ha'olam* can be read as *he'elem*, "concealed," because God also put concealment into the hearts of human beings, and as a result, they do not know "the accomplishment that God has accomplished." The crux of creation is the fact that "man will not discover." This is the secret of the world: It is a reality in which we do not see God, in which His existence is impossible. This is a paradox, because when a person claims that there is nothing else besides physicality, he is having recourse to something non-physical in making that claim. The fact that a philosophy of materialism can exist hinges on the fact that "He put the world as well in their heart... that man will not discover," that a person can use his soul to prove that he has no soul. As above, this is the purpose of the process of creation, for matter to appear to have an independent reality, and seemingly lifeless, and without God.

so that it does not return to nothingness. That is because in relation to God Himself, now too after the world has been created, there is nothing besides God, just as there was nothing besides Him prior to Creation.

| וְאוֹר זֶה הוּא מֵאֵין סוֹף בָּרוּךְ הוּא, רַק שֶׁנִּתְלַבֵּשׁ בִּלְבוּשִׁים רַבִּים. | **This light** emanates **from Ein Sof, blessed be He, but it is enclothed in many garments.** |

This light animates the worlds so that they will not return to chaos and nothingness. It gives them existence, form, and continuity: all that we call reality. As the author of the *Tanya* explains elsewhere,[18] every act of creation, from nothingness into existence, is effected only by the power of the Divine, by *Ein Sof* Himself. If the light of *Ein Sof* that shines upon the worlds were revealed without garments, there would be no concealment and therefore no world.

| וּכְמוֹ שֶׁכָּתוּב בְּעֵץ חַיִּים, שֶׁאוֹר וְחַיּוּת כַּדּוּר הָאָרֶץ הַחוֹמְרִי הַנִּרְאֶה לְעֵינֵי בָשָׂר, הוּא מִמַּלְכוּת דְּמַלְכוּת דַּעֲשִׂיָּה, | **As stated in *Etz Ḥayyim* (50:1), the light and life force** present within **the physical planet Earth, which is visible to corporeal eyes, emanates from** the *sefira* of *Malkhut* within *Malkhut* of the world of *Asiya*, |

This is the final level of illumination in the unfolding succession by whose power the physical world lives. The world of *Asiya* is the last of the four worlds, and *Malkhut* is the last of the *sefirot*, and *Malkhut* within *Malkhut* is the last level within that.[19] There are thus three immense constrictions, becoming progressively more hidden, each one leaving behind only the physical, inanimate matter on that level, leading to the ultimate descent: the material from which the three inner, spiritual layers – human beings, animals, and plants – are removed, so that all that remains is the inanimate.

---

18. *Iggeret HaKodesh*, epistle 20.
19. *Etz Ḥayyim* 59:1. There are other versions of this text in *Etz Ḥayyim* 43:1. This is mentioned in *Mishnat Ḥasidim, Masekhet Asiya Gufanit* 1:2 (the Lubavitcher Rebbe, Rabbi Menaḥem Mendel Schneerson).

וּבְתוֹכָהּ מַלְכוּת דִּיצִירָה וכו', within which lies the *sefira* of *Malkhut* of the world of *Yetzira*, and so forth, such that within all of them are ten *sefirot* of the world of *Atzilut*, which are one with their Emanator, *Ein Sof*, blessed be He.

עַד שֶׁבְּתוֹךְ כּוּלָּן עֶשֶׂר סְפִירוֹת דַּאֲצִילוּת הַמְיֻחָדוֹת בְּמַאֲצִילָן אֵין סוֹף בָּרוּךְ הוּא.

Within this light is hidden a deeper level of light, that of *Malkhut* of *Yetzira*. Within *Malkhut* of *Yetzira* is *Malkhut* of *Beria*, and within that is *Malkhut* of *Atzilut*. Thus, the light of the ten *sefirot* of *Atzilut* is found at the core of every reality, even one that is ultimately inanimate and superficial. What sets the world of *Atzilut* apart from all of the created worlds is that it does not, as it were, have an independent and separate existence, not only in that which is concealed but also in that which is revealed. The ten *sefirot* of *Atzilut* are completely and utterly united with the Emanator. He and His "vessels," the *sefirot*, are one. The life force of the truly material world cannot be seen, yet in its very core it is truly the very same life force that animates the world of *Atzilut*. The world of *Atzilut* is all unity and holiness. It is completely transparent to the divine life force that acts within it.

All the worlds essentially have the same composition, yet this composition is expressed in the language of analogy. On certain levels, the analogy becomes so complex and obscure that the inner reality of what it points to can no longer be seen. Moreover, sometimes what is read out of it is the total opposite of the original meaning. This can be seen in the Sages' description of the Torah standing before God and weeping, "Your children have rendered me like a harp on which clowns play" (*Sanhedrin* 101a). They enjoy the poetry, the analogy, but they do not consider the intended meaning, or they think about something else entirely, sometimes its opposite, and what is antithetical to it. Nevertheless, as long as there is an analogy and its meaning, there is a relationship between them. There are simple, obvious relationships, and there are more complex relationships, like the relationship between God and this world. Nevertheless, in them the intended meaning is always one.

In explanation of the topic of the indwelling of the Divine Presence, which is not equally present everywhere, but is found in a specific place within reality, this chapter brought the analogy of "from my flesh I will see," of the relationship between a person's soul and body. It explained that there is a difference between the divine essence and divine revelation. God's essence and being are everywhere, at all times, and in every entity, in good and evil, above and below. It could not possibly be otherwise, because every entity exists only from God and within Him. Yet precisely for that reason, the Divine Presence is not revealed anywhere. That essential being that is equally present in all elements, in all revelations, and in all aspects, is likewise hidden from them all in precisely the same measure. And there is another level of divine revelation. Each world and each individual creation is like a limb of the body, as described in the analogy; each is a vessel that receives a certain illumination appropriate for it. The higher worlds receive more of the light and the lower worlds receive less, until in the lowest worlds, the worlds of physical matter, hardly any light is visible, because of the multiplicity of garments. This level of divine revelation is the revelation of particular faculties and, as in the analogy, the capacity of sight in the eye and the capacity to walk in the legs, and so forth. But where is the essence of the revelation and its origin? Where is the revelation of the totality of the soul? This is an analogy for the question; where is the place of the indwelling of the Divine Presence? That is what the next chapter will discuss.

Chapter 52

THE PREVIOUS CHAPTER INTRODUCED THE IDEA OF the indwelling of the Divine Presence. It compared God's light in this world to the soul's light within the human body. The soul fills the whole body, yet its beginning, its abode, and chief dwelling place are in the brain. Likewise, the light of the Infinite One fills and animates all the worlds. In this chapter, the author of the *Tanya* will continue to draw insights from this analogy. While the infinite light fills all the worlds, there is one place, both spiritual and physical, where this all-encompassing life force is revealed. This is the "resting place of the Divine Presence."

וּכְמוֹ שֶׁבְּנִשְׁמַת הָאָדָם עִיקַּר גִּילּוּי כְּלָלוּת הַחַיּוּת הוּא בַּמּוֹחִין, וְכָל הָאֵבָרִים מְקַבְּלִים אוֹר וְכֹחַ לְבַד, הַמֵּאִיר לָהֶם מִמְּקוֹר גִּילּוּי הַחַיּוּת שֶׁבַּמּוֹחִין,

Just as, in a person's soul, the principal manifestation of the life force as a whole is in the brain, and all the organs only receive the light and power that shine onto them from the source of the manifestation of the life force in the brain,

26 Iyar

28 Iyar (leap year)

The all-encompassing life force that flows into the body in order to give it life is manifest in the brain. The overall power of life is revealed in the brain. Awareness of existence, the sensory centers, and the response to everything that happens in the entire body exist in the brain.

כָּכָה מַמָּשׁ עַל דֶּרֶךְ מָשָׁל so too, figuratively speaking,

As elsewhere in the *Tanya*, this paradoxical expression describes the paradoxical relationship between the analogy and what the analogy points to. The resemblance between the two continues up to a certain point. It is not boundless. It is therefore important to mention that the comparison is only metaphorical, that the analogy and what it points to are not in fact completely alike. Nevertheless, there is a degree of correspondence between them, and within that particular zone they are "the very same."

עִיקַּר גִּילּוּי כְּלָלוּת הַמְשָׁכַת הַחַיּוּת, לְהַחֲיוֹת הָעוֹלָמוֹת וְהַבְּרוּאִים שֶׁבָּהֶם, הוּא מְלוּבָּשׁ וְנִכְלָל בִּרְצוֹנוֹ וְחָכְמָתוֹ וּבִינָתוֹ וְדַעְתּוֹ יִתְבָּרֵךְ הַנִּקְרָא בְּשֵׁם 'מוֹחִין'.

the principal manifestation of the overall drawing forth of life force in order to grant life to the worlds and the creatures within them is enclothed and incorporated in God's will, His wisdom, His understanding, and His knowledge, which as a whole are referred to by the term *mohin* ["brain"].

God's "will" is the *sefira* of *Keter*, Crown, and His "wisdom, understanding, and knowledge" are the *sefirot* of *Ḥokhma*, *Bina*, and *Da'at*. This system of *sefirot* is called *mohin* (literally "brains"). It is analogous to the human brain, as explained in the previous chapter, from which the totality of the revelation of the soul's life force flows into the body. The life forces split up from the brain and spread out to the various parts of the body. ☞

HIS WILL, WISDOM, UNDERSTANDING, AND KNOWLEDGE

☞ Generally, the author of the *Tanya* enumerates the first three *sefirot*. But here he enumerates four. When three are enumerated, they are not always the same three. Sometimes the first three are presented as *Keter* (will), *Ḥokhma*, and *Bina*, and sometimes they are presented as *Ḥokhma*, *Bina*, and *Da'at*. These two enumerations do not negate each other, but should be seen as two aspects of one entity: the assemblage called *mohin*, or brains. One is the objective view, from the outside.

Therefore, it includes the sefira of *Keter*, the supernal will, which is above and beyond the intellect. It does not include *Da'at*. The other aspect is a subjective view from within. Consequently, it does not include the transcendent sefira of *Keter*, but it does include the sefira of *Da'at*. Thus, whenever the "first" *sefirot* are mentioned, three are enumerated. Here, however, because the author of the *Tanya* is discussing the assemblage of *mohin*, he lists four *sefirot* and integrates both viewpoints.

וְהֵן הֵן הַמְלוּבָּשִׁים בַּתּוֹרָה וּמִצְוֹתֶיהָ. **These four *sefirot* are enclothed in the Torah and its mitzvot.**

On each level and in every world, God's will, wisdom, understanding, and knowledge are enclothed and revealed in the "garments" of Torah and its mitzvot. The Torah is the garment, the vessel that reveals via the intellect, and in a way that allows God's will, wisdom, understanding, and knowledge to be put into practice in our lowly world.

By itself, our physical world is passive and indifferent. It does not exhibit any preference or will. A woolen thread does not care whether it is made into a sweater or a pair of *tzitzit*. It is passive. It takes whatever shape it is woven into. Likewise, the world at large is not disposed toward good or evil. It cannot be said to favor one way over another. The Torah, however, is just the opposite. It is the world's intellect and direction. Its whole essence is to determine what the Creator wants from His creations and how to achieve this. The Torah paints a picture of the world as it should be, and then guides it to this point. This will and wisdom are at the core of the Torah. Accordingly, the Torah is the *moḥin* of each world, for it sees how things are supposed to be. It is the center of life, and all other creations draw their individual forms from it.

וְגִילּוּי כְּלָלוּת הַמְשָׁכָה זוֹ הוּא מְקוֹר הַחַיּוּת, אֲשֶׁר הָעוֹלָמוֹת מְקַבְּלִים כָּל אֶחָד בִּפְרָטוּת. **The manifestation of the totality of this drawing-forth is the source of the life force that the worlds receive, each one individually.**

The manifestation of the totality of this life force, which is enclothed and revealed in the Torah and its mitzvot, is the universal source from which every world and every creation receives its particular life force.

רַק הֶאָרָה מִתְפַּשֶּׁטֶת וּמְאִירָה מִמְּקוֹר זֶה. **Only a glimmer spreads and shines from this source.**

The life force that each individual creation receives is not an extension of the source itself, but a diminished, partial glimmer of it.

כְּדִמְיוֹן אוֹר הַמִּתְפַּשֵּׁט מֵהַשֶּׁמֶשׁ, עַל דֶּרֶךְ מָשָׁל, This is **similar to the light that spreads out from the sun, by way of analogy.**

The connection between the source of the life and the life drawn into the worlds is comparable to the connection between the sun and its light that spreads out and reaches our globe. In both of these, there is a one-way relationship. Sunlight cannot exist without a constant connection to the sun, whereas regardless of what happens to the sunlight, the sun itself is not altered. Sunlight might illuminate a polished mirror or a black surface. Likewise, it might shine upon a baby or a pile of garbage. However, this does not at all affect the sun in any way.

וְכֹחוֹת אֶבְרֵי הַגּוּף מֵהַמּוֹחַ הַנִּזְכָּר לְעֵיל. It is similar to **the faculties of the limbs of the body** receiving life force **from the brain, as stated above** (chap. 51).

All the life force that the body receives from the soul is concentrated in the brain. This analogy, which was expounded upon in the previous chapter, demonstrates the relationship between three matters: 1) the essence of the soul, which is indivisible and does not relate to any particular place, time, or particular parameter; 2) the place where the soul rests within the body; and 3) the activity of the powers of the soul within the body, which give life and existence to each organ of the body in accordance with its nature. Similarly, the divine essence itself does not spread out to the world or shine in a revealed manner in it. The world's components and parts are completely unable to relate to it. Consequently, as in the body, there is one fundamental point in the world, on the border between entities, from which the light is particularized and distributed to all the worlds. ☞

וּמָקוֹר זֶה הוּא הַנִּקְרָא 'עָלְמָא דְאִתְגַּלְיָא', This source is referred to as the "**manifest world.**"

This does not mean that everything is revealed within the "manifest world," for in this world there are various different levels that are not manifest to the same extent. Even in the physical world, there are millions of different creatures and beings that have not been discovered and are unknown, and this is even more true with regard to the "manifest" spiritual worlds. Nonetheless, the source of all the worlds, which are inherently able to be manifest, is referred to in the kabbalistic works as "the manifest world."

וּ׳מַטְרוֹנִיתָא׳ וְ׳אִימָּא תַּתָּאָה׳, And it is also referred to as *matronita* [queen] and "lower mother."

In the *Zohar*, this source is referred to as the *matronita*, variously noblewoman, or queen, who receives from the king, God.[1] It is likewise identified with the lower aspect of the "mother," or *Bina*, Understanding. This lower aspect is the *sefira* of *Malkhut*, Kingship.

וּ׳שְׁכִינָה׳, מִלְּשׁוֹן ״וְשָׁכַנְתִּי בְּתוֹכָם״ (שמות כה, ח), It is also referred to as **the Divine Presence** [*Shekhina*], **as in the phrase, "and I will dwell** [*v'shakhanti*] **in their midst"** (Ex. 25:8).

The Sages called this source the Divine Presence.[2]

SIMILAR TO THE LIGHT EMITTED BY THE SUN

☞ Another analogy can be drawn from the material realm. It concerns electrical energy whose voltage is so high that it would destroy any device it was to enter. This is why there are series of transformers that step down and transfer electrical energy so that it is able to power different kinds of devices. Similarly, the "transformer" of a particular world is that world's source of life force and manifestation.

---

1. See *Zohar* 3:146a; *Iggeret HaKodesh*, epistle 25.
2. *Iggeret HaKodesh*, epistle 25. There is no mention here of the fact that this is referring to *Malkhut* of the world of *Atzilut* and the word of God, although that is stated in *Iggeret HaKodesh*. Only at the end of this chapter is *Malkhut* of the world of *Atzilut* mentioned. This is because, since there the author of the *Tanya* cites the *Etz Ḥayyim*, he employs the kabbalistic term *Malkhut*, which is used in that work. The *Tanya* itself, however, is not written with kabbalistic terminology (the Lubavitcher Rebbe, Rabbi Menaḥem Mendel Schneerson).

עַל שֵׁם שֶׁמָּקוֹר זֶה הוּא רֵאשִׁית הִתְגַּלּוּת אוֹר אֵין סוֹף, אֲשֶׁר מַמְשִׁיךְ וּמֵאִיר לָעוֹלָמוֹת בִּבְחִינַת גִּילּוּי. וּמִמָּקוֹר זֶה נִמְשָׁךְ לְכָל אֶחָד הָאוֹר וְחַיּוּת פְּרָטִי הָרָאוּי לוֹ, וְשׁוֹכֵן וּמִתְלַבֵּשׁ בְּתוֹכָם לְהַחֲיוֹתָם.

It is **called this because this source is the inception of the revelation of the light of** *Ein Sof,* **which extends and shines on the worlds on a revealed level. And from this source is drawn to every individual** entity **the specific light and life force befitting it. And** the light **dwells and is enclothed within** the worlds and their entities **to vivify them.**

All of these names demonstrate the many aspects of this one source. "Manifest world": the inception of the revealing of the light of *Ein Sof.* "*Matronita*": that continues and shines on the worlds on a revealed level. "Lower mother": from this source is drawn to every individual [being] the specific light and life force befitting it. "Divine Presence": that is dwelling and enclothed within them to vivify them.[3]

THE MANY NAMES OF *MALKHUT*, THE DIVINE PRESENCE

☞ There is a locus that is each world's source of life, on the level of the "brain" of that world, from which life extends and particularizes into each creature and reality that exists within that world. Earlier, this was compared to the light that spreads out from one source and is drawn into every object on its level. It has already been said that this is not the original source, because there is no differentiation within the original source, and therefore there is no way to understand or relate to it. The original source is the highest and most concealed of all. By contrast, the secondary source, which is called the Divine Presence, is the center that creates differentiation. It is the center from which begins the differentiation between large and small, between understanding and not understanding, between a human being and an angel. It is the source from which all life-forms and beings emerge. This is why the Divine Presence has so many names: e.g., the manifest world, *matronita*, lower mother, and so forth, because it is not the source of one object or one aspect of reality, but rather of all life-forms.

Furthermore, the multiplicity of aspects and names also stems from the fact that this locus of particularization and spreading forth of the life-forms is also the point where all higher forces are gathered. *Malkhut* is not a primary source, which only gives and does not receive, rather it is

---

3. The Lubavitcher Rebbe, Rabbi Menaḥem Mendel Schneerson.

וְלָכֵן נִקְרָא 'אֵם הַבָּנִים' עַל דֶּרֶךְ מָשָׁל וּ'כְנֶסֶת יִשְׂרָאֵל', **Therefore, it is also metaphorically referred to as "mother of children" and the "congregation of Israel."**

The Divine Presence is the source of all revelation. It is the source of the divine light that flows to and dwells within the worlds, and also the source of Jewish souls.[4] Thus, it is called "mother of children," a phrase from Psalms 117:9. It is like a mother from whom all of her children suckle and receive sustenance. These "children" are a metaphor for the souls of Israel. The Divine Presence is likewise called "the congregation of Israel," because it gathers and unites within itself all the levels of the

the point from which all of life spreads out. It is also the point to which all of the forces of life from above gather. In this same point where they are assembled, they are particularized. Thus, this point is also called Kenesset Yisrael, the congregation of Israel, and it is called "the sea," for all "streams" converge into it. It gathers everything like a reservoir, and from it the parts spread out in all directions. This is comparable to a person. The brain is not the primary source of all of the life in the human being, but rather it is only the focal point where the entity of the soul shines when it is manifest. And from there, it can be apportioned to the limbs. In some ways, it serves as a storehouse, as the center of distribution rather than the center of creation.

In every world, this point is like a "Temple" in which the supernal life dwells. In relation to that world, this point has something of the presence of the Infinite One. That is not to say that a dimension of Ein Sof is itself manifest in that world (as Ein Sof). But in the appropriate garment and in the appropriate realm regarding that world, it serves as being the dimension of Ein Sof. That is to say, regarding each world, on the level and scope that is appropriate for it, it is the source of the infinite from which everything emerges, from which all life and existence are drawn. For instance, God gives life to the human brain and to the brain of the frog. The brain is the locus of all life and comprehension, in a frog as much as in a human being. The frog's brain and perception are nothing like those of the human, for the frog receives a different light than does a human. However, the brain itself has the same essence in the frog as in the human. The same is true with regard to different people; the brain of a holy person, who receives a greater degree of light by virtue of his holiness, fulfills the same role as the brain of a person who uses his mind only for trivial pleasures. The brain is the center of life in both cases. For both individuals, it is the medium for receiving and giving life. With regard to the specific content that it conveys, however, that is another matter.

---

4. This is because the Jewish nation, at its root, represents the entire world; see chap. 37.

Jewish people, all of the lights and forms and hues found among all the souls of Israel.

שֶׁמִּמָּקוֹר זֶה נֶאֶצְלוּ נְשָׁמוֹת דַּאֲצִילוּת, וְנִבְרְאוּ נְשָׁמוֹת דִּבְרִיאָה וכו'.

This is due to the fact that **from this source the souls of *Atzilut* were emanated and the souls of *Beria* were created, and so forth.**

All the souls of Israel, whether they are from the world of *Atzilut*, *Beria*, *Yetzira*, or *Asiya*, shine forth from this one source. They all emerge in their root from "the mother of children," the mother of all the levels found within the Jewish people. As explained, this point is also called "the congregation of Israel," because it gathers all the souls together into one entity.[5] This level, the quality of all the souls of Israel as a single entity, is identical at its root to the source of the divine light, that being the Divine Presence, which gives life to the entire world.

וְכוּלָּן אֵינָן רַק מֵהִתְפַּשְׁטוּת הַחַיּוּת וְהָאוֹר מֵהַמָּקוֹר הַזֶּה הַנִּקְרָא 'שְׁכִינָה', כְּהִתְפַּשְׁטוּת הָאוֹר מֵהַשֶּׁמֶשׁ.

They all exist **only as a result of the spreading of the life force and the light from this source called "Divine Presence," similar to light spreading out from the sun.**

All that the Divine Presence bestows upon the created being is only illumination. This is like the sun's illumination of our planet and those who dwell upon it. Just as the sun itself is not in all the places where its light shines, so too the Divine Presence is not manifest in its entirety everywhere that life extends from it into souls and all creations. In the analogy of the human being, the brain does not send parts of itself to all the body parts. There is no piece of the brain in the hand or the foot. Rather, the brain is in its own space, and it sends messages to the body parts, and from there onward to whatever a person creates or does with the different aspects of his character.

---

5. Or because it gathers the aspect of "Israel" above with the souls below; see *Torah Or* 84b.

CHAPTER 52

אֲבָל הַשְּׁכִינָה עַצְמָהּ, שֶׁהִיא רֵאשִׁית הַגִּילּוּי וְעִיקָּרוֹ, מַה שֶּׁאֵין סוֹף בָּרוּךְ הוּא מֵאִיר לָעוֹלָמוֹת בִּבְחִינַת גִּילּוּי, וְהִיא מְקוֹר כָּל הַמְשָׁכוֹת הַחַיּוּת שֶׁבְּכָל הָעוֹלָמוֹת

However, regarding the Divine Presence itself, which is the inception and essence of the revelation that *Ein Sof*, blessed be He, shines onto the worlds on a revealed level, and which is the source of all life force being drawn down into all the worlds

27 Iyar
29 Iyar
(leap year)

Thus, all the worlds receive and live from the light of the Divine Presence. Just as the source of the light is the constant source of all of the existence and tangibility of the light, which cannot exist without it, so too the Divine Presence itself is the source of life in all the worlds.

[שֶׁכָּל הַחַיּוּת שֶׁבָּהֶם אֵינוֹ רַק אוֹר הַמִּתְפַּשֵּׁט מִמֶּנָּה, כָּאוֹר הַמִּתְפַּשֵּׁט מֵהַשֶּׁמֶשׁ],

(because all the life force within them is only the light that spreads from it, like light spreading out from the sun),

The light that "fills all worlds" spreads forth from the Divine Presence. It does not draw directly from the divine essence itself. The specific life force in all levels of reality is only an illumination of the source, which is the Divine Presence.

אִי אֶפְשָׁר לָעוֹלָמוֹת לִסְבּוֹל וּלְקַבֵּל אוֹר שְׁכִינָתָהּ, שֶׁתִּשְׁכּוֹן וְתִתְלַבֵּשׁ בְּתוֹכָם מַמָּשׁ, בְּלֹא לְבוּשׁ הַמַּעֲלִים וּמַסְתִּיר אוֹרָהּ מֵהֶם, שֶׁלֹּא יִתְבַּטְּלוּ בִּמְצִיאוּת לְגַמְרֵי בִּמְקוֹרָם, כְּבִיטּוּל אוֹר הַשֶּׁמֶשׁ בִּמְקוֹרוֹ בְּגוּף הַשֶּׁמֶשׁ,

the worlds could not bear and receive the light of its presence so that it might **actually dwell and be enclothed within them, without a garment to hide and conceal its light from them,** in order **to prevent them from being totally nullified out of existence in their source, as sunlight is nullified in its source, i.e., in the body of the sun,**

The light of the Divine Presence, which is the level of the "brain" of the world, the light of the beginning, the light of the seven days of

Creation, the all-encompassing light that illuminates the entirety of reality, cannot be revealed to its full extent and power within the world. Were it to be revealed, the world would not be able to exist. The entire existence of the world, its structure, and its most minute details, hinge on the fact that there is distance, that there is a barrier that constricts and hides the manifestation of light from the worlds. If the Divine Presence were revealed within the world, all the components of reality would be nullified, just as all shadows and different shades of light are nullified within the revelation of the unobstructed light itself.

שֶׁאֵין נִרְאֶה שָׁם אוֹר זֶה, רַק עֶצֶם גּוּף הַשֶּׁמֶשׁ בִּלְבַד. **where this** sun **light is not apparent, but only the actual body of the sun.**

The light of the sun is not visible on its surface. All that is visible on the surface of the sun is the sun itself. Moreover, were we to return some sunlight to the sun – e.g., by means of a mirror – we would not expect this light to be discernible on the sun. It can be seen in other places, but not on the sun. In other words, sunlight gains an independent existence only when it leaves the sun, when the sun itself is at a distance from it. Only as long as the sun itself is not manifest, do sunlight and the various shades and forms of light exist: bright light, dim light, reflected light, and so forth. However, when the sun itself is manifest, sunlight no longer has substance. Furthermore, all energy and all life on earth derive from sunlight, yet we cannot endure the sun itself. If the sun were located on earth or close to it, it would consume everything. In order for there to be life, which exists only by means of the sun, there must be a certain distance, as well as numerous veils and defenses, between us and the sun.

1 Sivan (leap year)

וּמַהוּ הַלְּבוּשׁ שֶׁיּוּכַל לְהַסְתִּירָהּ וּלְהַלְבִּישָׁהּ וְלֹא יִתְבַּטֵּל בִּמְצִיאוּת בְּאוֹרָהּ? **What garment is capable of concealing and enclothing** the Divine Presence **without becoming nullified out of existence** as a result of being **in its light?**

Thus, the world cannot enclothe the Divine Presence. The question, therefore, is: What garment can conceal the essence of the Divine Presence and enclothe it and reveal it, without being nullified in its light? If the entire world does not suffice to enclothe the Divine Presence, because it would be burned up and nullified, what can do so? As above, the resting place of the Divine Presence in each world is the "Holy of Holies" of that world, but a world cannot entirely and constantly be in the "Holy of Holies," for in the Holy of Holies there is no world. Similarly, the human soul cannot cleave to the Divine Presence with its entire being, because then it would no longer be able to retain its own existence. The soul must be distant and detached in order to exist in its own being. Thus the broad question is: How can the Divine Presence be manifest in reality without reality being nullified? If everything is nullified before the Divine Presence, how can anything enclothe it? How can the Divine Presence be concealed, and how can it be revealed?

הוּא רְצוֹנוֹ יִתְבָּרֵךְ וְחָכְמָתוֹ וכו' הַמְלוּבָּשִׁים בַּתּוֹרָה וּמִצְוֹתֶיהָ, הַנִּגְלֵית לָנוּ וּלְבָנֵינוּ.	It is God's will, wisdom, and so forth, which are enclothed in the Torah and its mitzvot, which is revealed to us and our children.

The answer is: God's will, wisdom, understanding, and knowledge are enclothed in the Torah and its mitzvot. God's will, wisdom, understanding, and knowledge constitute the level of the supernal *moḥin* in which, as explained above, the essence and totality of the flow of life are enclothed. This is the level of the resting place of the Divine Presence, giving life to the worlds. The author of the *Tanya* is not referring to the heavenly Torah, but to the Torah and mitzvot in our possession.[6] The commandments that we are able to understand and perform are the ones that enclothe the Divine Presence.

דְּאוֹרַיְיתָא מֵחָכְמָה נָפְקַת, הִיא חָכְמָה עִילָּאָה דִּלְעֵילָּא לְעֵילָּא מֵעָלְמָא דְּאִתְגַּלְיָא.	That is "because the Torah emerged from Ḥokhma" (Zohar 2:121a), referring to the supernal wisdom that totally transcends the manifest world.

---

6. The phrase "The revealed are for us and for our children" comes from Deut. 29:28.

How is the Torah able to serve as the garment for the Divine Presence? As stated above, the "manifest world" refers to the Divine Presence. The Torah emerges in its source from divine wisdom, which is above and beyond the illumination of the Divine Presence. Consequently, the Torah can be the vessel that contains the Divine Presence, which is the essential and overall divine revelation that gives life to all the worlds. This is because the Torah itself is not a product of the worlds; its existence is not a part of the worlds, since it expresses the divine essence itself. As a result, it retains its own existence even when it enclothes the Divine Presence. And when it clothes and conceals the Divine Presence, as it were, it is able to reveal the light of the Divine Presence in this world and in all the worlds. ☞ ☞

IT EMERGED FROM ḤOKHMA THAT TRANSCENDS THE WORLD

☞ If the Torah is on such a high level, beyond even the light of the Divine Presence, then just as we, and the whole world, are nullified before the Divine Presence, we should likewise be nullified before the light of Torah. However, as has been said, the light in the Torah is so lofty that we have virtually no connection to it. Just as the essential divine existence on the level of "Do I not fill the heavens and the earth" (Jer. 23:24), which refers to God encompassing all worlds, does not affect and burn us, nor are we consumed in its light, likewise the light of divine wisdom does not, from our viewpoint, change anything, because it is above and beyond all the systems in which our lives are organized. As explained in several places (see *Torah Or* 16a), the phrase, "Do I not fill the heavens and the earth," indicates that divinity fills the heavens and the earth equally, because neither are on the same plane of existence as the divine "I." Consequently, heaven and earth are not burned in its presence, and it is not affected by their existence and activity. When a person speaks words of profound wisdom to an audience, there are some among the listeners whose wisdom and character are nullified before the depth of this wisdom. Some are elevated by the words, some are harmed by them, and still others experience their minds growing foggy as a result of hearing them. However, all of these responses pertain only to people who understand. A person who does not understand at all is not harmed at all. Only when there is a connection can there be an outcome, whether it be nullification, or even damage. Hearing the greatest and most awesome secret does not have any effect on a person who does not know the language in which it is spoken. The best joke will only make a person laugh if he understands it. On a more abstract level, entities act upon each other when they are on the same plane, when they have a shared dimension. However, when they are in two different dimensions, they do not directly affect each other at all.

There is a custom to recite passages from the *Zohar* at particular times, to say these words even if one does not understand the content, or even the language. In some synagogues, it is customary for the

"דְּאִיהוּ חַכִּים וְלָא בְּחָכְמָה יְדִיעָה **"Because He is wise, but not with a known wisdom,** He is understanding, but not with a known understanding" (*Tikkunei Zohar* 17b).
וכו' (תיקוני זהר יז, ב).

whole congregation to recite the *Idra Rabba* and *Idra Zuta*. The passages are divided among those present so that together they will complete the entire *Idra*. The *Idra* deals with very cryptic matters. It has images and descriptions that can easily be misconstrued to resemble true idol worship. Because of this, Rabbi Shimon bar Yoḥai is depicted in the introduction to *Idra Rabba* as admonishing his students not to understand it literally. The text (*Zohar* 3:128a) describes how his students placed their hands upon his heart and he made them swear in the words of the verse, "Cursed is the man who will craft an idol or a cast figure...the handiwork of a craftsman, and places it in secret" (Deut. 27:15). How then can simple Jews, who certainly are not on that level of abstract understanding, recite the entire *Idra*? Perhaps the students of Rabbi Shimon bar Yoḥai needed to swear because of the very fact that they were capable of understanding. Consequently, they needed to be warned against reading the words in their literal sense. However, Jews who do not even understand Aramaic, the language in which this is written, need not be warned, because they cannot be harmed at all.

Likewise, divine wisdom in itself, in whatever form, is far beyond human existence, and therefore human existence is not harmed by it. However, this is not the case with regard to matters that descend to our realm, to the existence, life, or world that we experience. When we encounter a higher level of life, we cannot endure it; we are burned by it. Similarly, a human being consumes oxygen. A higher amount of oxygen accelerates his inner workings, and an excessive amount can be extremely harmful, but this is only because he also consumes oxygen in his regular life.

WHERE IS THE DIVINE PRESENCE HIDDEN?

☞ The answer to this question is: in the Torah. The Torah, which is divine wisdom, is essentially from another realm, it is not from the human realm. Therefore, it does not harm or destroy us.

But the Torah descends step by step, with one garment added to another, and this allows a human being to relate to it. If so, why does it not burn a person who understands it or who does what is written in it? It is because its garments, on all levels, are utterly incomprehensible in their supernal context (or conversely they are understood in a way that leaves no room for doubt). Consequently, a person can study Tractate *Bava Metzia* and know all the *halakhot* in *Ḥoshen Mishpat*, and the divine wisdom will not burn him. In Tractate *Ḥagiga* (13a) it is related that the Sages considered suppressing the book of Ezekiel. One reason was an incident that took place when a child read about the divine chariot and comprehended the *ḥashmal* (Ezek. 1:27), and fire came out of the *ḥashmal* and burned him. Nonetheless, the words of Ḥananya ben Ḥizkiya led to the decision

"Known wisdom"[7] refers to all that can be understood. Higher wisdom, God's wisdom, is certainly not such. It is unknown in the sense that it cannot be known; our "knowing" does not apply to it. It belongs to a different class, totally different from our wisdom. This is the wisdom from which the Torah emerges. Thus, the source and inner content of the Torah before us is the supernal wisdom, which is essentially unknown to us. The Midrash says, "The withered vestige of supernal wisdom is Torah" (*Bereshit Rabba* 17:5, 44:17). The Torah that we possess is like a shriveled fruit that is not connected to the tree, like a dream as compared to prophecy. The Torah that we have, which we understand, bears some similarity to higher wisdom, something reminiscent of it. However, it is fundamentally different from supernal wisdom.

not to hide the book: "If this [child happened to be] wise, [are] all [people] wise [enough to understand this book]?" In other words, the chance of a situation like this happening again is so minimal that it is not appropriate to take it into consideration when making the decision of whether to hide the book. Indeed, the book of Ezekiel is taught today in numerous schools to children, and no fire emerges to burn them. In order for something to truly change a person and pose any kind of risk to him, it must be something he can connect to. A person cannot be harmed by something if it is beyond him. It can affect him only if he is on a level where he can understand and relate to it.

The Divine Presence, as the source of our present existence and life, must be deeply concealed, because life is not something that one needs to understand in order to live it. A person who suddenly receives a higher level of life is immediately consumed and destroyed within it, whether he understands it or not, just as sunlight is nullified within the sun. On the other hand, with regard to supernal wisdom, if a person does not understand it, he does not connect to it. Therefore, precisely because this wisdom is so elevated, the chance that a person will be consumed by it is almost non-existent. This is true even when higher wisdom takes on lower forms, such as in the revealed Torah. Although we personally connect to and understand the divine wisdom itself, we nevertheless do not comprehend its inner content, but only its ramifications in the realm of our physical lives. We understand the "ancient parable," the analogy of the Torah, but never what it signifies.

THE TORAH IS ENCLOTHED IN PHYSICAL CONSTRUCTS

☞ The Talmud (*Shabbat* 88b) tells that when Moses ascended to Heaven to receive the Torah, the angels protested: "[The Torah is a] hidden treasure that was concealed by You 974 generations before the creation of the world. Do You seek to

---

7. This phrase also appears in *Zohar Ḥadash* 58a.

CHAPTER 52

וּכְמוֹ שֶׁנִּתְבָּאֵר לְעֵיל, שֶׁאוֹר אֵין סוֹף בָּרוּךְ הוּא מְלוּבָּשׁ וּמְיוּחָד בְּחָכְמָה עִילָּאָה, וְהוּא יִתְבָּרֵךְ וְחָכְמָתוֹ – אֶחָד,

As was explained above (chap. 18), **the light of** *Ein Sof,* **blessed be He, is enclothed in and united with the supernal wisdom, and God and His wisdom are one.**

On this high level, God and wisdom are one.[8]

רַק שֶׁיָּרְדָה בְּסֵתֶר הַמַּדְרֵגוֹת מִמַּדְרֵגָה לְמַדְרֵגָה בְּהִשְׁתַּלְשְׁלוּת הָעוֹלָמוֹת

However, His wisdom **descended in concealed stages, from stage to stage, through the unfolding succession of the worlds.**

As stated above, the Torah "emerged from *Ḥokhma.*" Its source is higher wisdom, from which it descended in "concealed stages." This term, which is taken from Song of Songs (2:14), expresses the nature of the descent: Each higher step is so far above the subsequent step that it is concealed from it. Moreover, each concealment constitutes a concealment added to the previous concealment. The higher, divine wisdom is not manifest in the worlds on the supernal level at which God and His wisdom are one. Rather, the essence of this wisdom is enclothed and concealed by way of multiple stages and concealments, in accordance with each world's character.

עַד שֶׁנִּתְלַבְּשָׁה בִּדְבָרִים גַּשְׁמִיִּים, שֶׁהֵן תרי״ג מִצְוֹת הַתּוֹרָה.

It descended until it became enclothed in physical matters, which are the 613 mitzvot of the Torah.

The essence, the divine wisdom, is revealed in our world through physical permutations that result in the 613 commandments, such as the *halakha* concerning an ox that gored a cow, *tefillin, tzitzit.* ☞

---

8. As Rambam says, "He is the knowledge and He is the knower…." According to the works of Kabbala, this is the level of the world of *Atzilut*, where "He and His 'life force' [the lights of the *sefirot*] are one; He and the vessels of the *sefirot* are one." And *Atzilut* is the aspect of *Ḥokhma* within the worlds. See the gloss to chap. 2.

| 28 Iyar |
| 2 Sivan (leap year) |

וּבִירִידָתָהּ בְּהִשְׁתַּלְשְׁלוּת מֵעוֹלָם לְעוֹלָם, גַּם הַשְּׁכִינָה יָרְדָה וְנִתְלַבְּשָׁה בָּהּ בְּכָל עוֹלָם וְעוֹלָם.

As the Torah **successively descended from world to world, the Divine Presence also descended and became enclothed in** the Torah, **in each world respectively.**

The Torah descends, as explained above, in concealed stages, and is enclothed within every world. The Divine Presence descends together with it and is likewise enclothed within each world.

וְזֶהוּ הֵיכַל קָדְשֵׁי קָדָשִׁים שֶׁבְּכָל עוֹלָם וְעוֹלָם.

This is the shrine of the Holy of Holies in each world

The Torah is called God's Temple because it is where the Divine Presence rests. On each level of reality, there is a shrine of the Holy of Holies in which the Divine Presence rests. This shrine is the Torah in each world, in which the *moḥin* are enclothed. It is the center of that realm's life and existence. The beginning and totality of the life force that belongs in that world flows into it and throughout it.

give it to flesh and blood?" God told Moses to provide them with an answer, and this is the gist of what he said:

"The Torah states, 'I am the Lord your God, who took you out of the land of Egypt' (Ex. 20:2). Did you descend to Egypt? The Torah states, 'Remember the Sabbath day, to keep it holy' (Ex. 20:8). Do you perform labor from which you require rest? The Torah states, 'You shall not murder. You shall not commit adultery. You shall not steal' (Ex. 20:13). Is there jealousy among you, or an evil inclination among you?"

Indeed, if this is the Torah, what will the angels do with it? They cannot wear *tzitzit*, don *tefillin*, or return a lost donkey to its owner. Nonetheless, it is important to understand the angels' line of thought. They were aware that they are unable to return lost donkeys, yet they knew that Torah has an expression in the higher realms. It is not expressed there by means of "an ox that gored a cow," nor through *tefillin* or *tzitzit*. However, that which is revealed in material configurations in our world is manifest in other configurations in the higher worlds. The Torah has expression and significance in every realm, and it proceeds from one level to the next, from one form of expression to the next. In the material world, it is revealed in physical manifestations, through positive and negative commandments that pertain to physical matters. However, the Torah has a form of expression on the level of the angels as well. There are no *tzitzit* or *tefillin* there, nor are there lost donkeys to be returned, but Torah exists there in a different sense. Thus the angels were able to complain when God gave the Torah to human beings, maintaining that He could have given it to them instead. The form of the Torah that we possess is not its only form. Rather, the form that we have is a kind of pro-

וּכְמוֹ שֶׁכָּתוּב בַּזֹּהַר (חלק ג קסא, ב) וְעֵץ חַיִּים (שער מו פרק ו), שֶׁהַשְּׁכִינָה שֶׁהִיא 'מַלְכוּת דַּאֲצִילוּת' as written in the *Zohar* (3:161b) and *Etz Ḥayyim* (46:6), **the Divine Presence, which is the *sefira* of *Malkhut* of the world of *Atzilut***

At its root, the Divine Presence is in the *sefira* of *Malkhut* of *Atzilut*. This refers to the capacity of sovereignty within the world of *Atzilut*.

[שֶׁהִיא בְּחִינַת גִּילּוּי אוֹר אֵין סוֹף בָּרוּךְ הוּא וְחַיּוּת שֶׁמֵּאִיר לְעוֹלָמוֹת, (which is the level of the revelation of the light of *Ein Sof*, blessed be He, and the life force that shines onto the worlds,

"*Malkhut* of *Atzilut*" is a symbolic term. In a more abstract sense, *Malkhut* of *Atzilut* is the divine power with which God relates to the reality of the worlds and through which He reveals the divine light and the life force that He bestows upon the worlds.[9]

jection of the Torah onto the dimensions of our material world. However, in another realm with different parameters, the same matters possess a totally different meaning. The shadow of a geometric shape can appear as a circle, an ellipse, or a straight line, depending on the angle of the light shining on it. Likewise, the inner essence of the Torah is one. Within the dimensions of our world it takes on a certain form that we recognize, but in the higher worlds it takes on completely different forms.

The angels could have replied to Moses, "While it is true that we have no father or mother, in our Torah there is no commandment to honor one's father and mother," and other, similar arguments. Nonetheless, the Sages say, "The Holy One, blessed be He, desired a dwelling place in the lower worlds" (*Tanḥuma, Beḥukotai* 3; see chap. 36). This refers to our physical world, the lowest level where the Torah can possibly exist. The Torah, as has been explained, is a garment for the Divine Presence, and it was in this world that God desired that the Torah be given. The shortcoming of the angels, the reason why they did not receive the Torah, is that they reside in a world that is an intermediary, and therefore their Torah too is an intermediary. It merely transmits entities but does not absorb them. Only in our world, where the Torah descends to the lowest, most concentrated point, into a physical world, is the purpose – "a dwelling place in the lower worlds" – achieved. The Torah was written for and given to the lowest of beings: those who departed from Egypt, who work for six days before resting on the Sabbath, and who possess an evil inclination.

---

9. See *Sha'ar HaYiḥud VeHa'emuna*, beginning of chap. 7, on the phrase, "There is no king without a nation."

וְלָכֵן הִיא נִקְרֵאת 'דְּבַר ה'' וְ'רוּחַ פִּיו', כִּבְיָכוֹל עַל דֶּרֶךְ מָשָׁל, **and which is therefore figuratively referred to as "the word of God" and the "breath of His utterance," so to speak,**

Although the Divine Presence, *Malkhut* of *Atzilut*, is referred to as "the word of God" and "the breath of His utterance," it is important to remember that these terms are only figurative. We cannot attribute physical speech, which is comprised of sound waves, to God. Human speech is merely a metaphor for divine speech.

כְּמוֹ שֶׁבָּאָדָם הַדִּבּוּר הוּא מְגַלֶּה מַחֲשַׁבְתּוֹ הַסְּתוּמָה וְנֶעֱלָמָה לְהַשּׁוֹמְעִים,] **in the same way that a person's speech reveals his impenetrable, hidden thoughts to his listeners).**

Speech is communication, the transmission of content from the inside to the outside. It is the way in which a person reveals to others that which is concealed within him. The Divine Presence is called "the word of God" because it is the revelation of God's infiniteness to the worlds, to the reality outside the divine "I." It is the manifestation of the Divine outside the divine unity that is on the level of the world of *Atzilut*, which is why the Divine Presence is called *Malkhut* of *Atzilut*. Communication, even in our world, is not limited to one mode of transmission of content. There is communication in action, allusions, the written word, and oral speech. The term, "the word (*devar*) of God," is merely a metaphor that expresses the idea that God conveys content from one place to another. In that sense, the connotation of oral communication is only secondary. The primary meaning of the root *dalet-bet-resh* – "*dabar*" – relates to governance and the transmission of entities, whether of people or of content. These meanings can be seen in the term *dovra*, "barge," and in the talmudic phrase "[There must be] one [clear and authoritative] leader (*dabar*) for the generation" (*Sanhedrin* 8a).

הִיא מִתְלַבֶּשֶׁת בְּהֵיכַל קָדְשֵׁי קָדָשִׁים דִּבְרִיאָה, שֶׁהִיא חָכְמָה בִּינָה דַּעַת דִּבְרִיאָה **The Divine Presence is enclothed in the shrine of the Holy of Holies of the world of *Beria*, which is the *Ḥokhma*, *Bina*, and *Da'at* of *Beria*.**

The Divine Presence, which is *Malkhut* of *Atzilut*, "the word of God," is enclothed within a shrine, the level of the *moḥin* of the world of *Beria*. The brain is the "highest" part of a human being because it is the locus of consciousness and operations. The manifestation of the Divine Presence in each world is on the level of *Ḥokhma* in that world. The Divine Presence is enclothed in that level and makes it the level of the Holy of Holies of that world.

וּבְהִתְלַבְּשׁוּתָן בְּמַלְכוּת דִּבְרִיאָה – נִבְרְאוּ הַנְּשָׁמוֹת וְהַמַּלְאָכִים שֶׁבַּבְּרִיאָה. **When** these three *sefirot* are **enclothed in** *Malkhut* of *Beria*, then **the souls and angels** of the world **of** *Beria* **are created.**

Ḥokhma, *Bina*, and *Da'at* of *Beria* are the level of the "Holy of Holies" of the world of *Beria*. When this "Holy of Holies" descends to the level of "*Malkhut* of *Beria*," which is the final level of the world of *Beria*, the level of its "speech," it reveals from the world of *Beria* whatever it can outward. This is comparable to human speech, which transmits content from the inside to the outside, from one individual to another. Souls and angels are also formed in the course of this descent and enclothement. These souls and angels are the level of creations of each world,[10] which have a separate existence, as it were, from the totality of the world to which they belong.

וְגַם מִשָּׁם נִמְשַׁךְ הַתַּלְמוּד שֶׁלְּפָנֵינוּ, **The Talmud that we possess is also derived from there.**

As stated above, the Torah that we possess emanates from an exceedingly high place. It passes through each world – *Atzilut*, *Beria*, *Yetzira*, and *Asiya* – and each one reveals its portion in the Torah. Thus, in our world and in our Torah the elements of all the worlds assemble. The Talmud that we possess belongs, in its source and in its fundamental character, to the world of *Beria*. The Mishna belongs to the world of *Yetzira*, and *Tanakh* to the world of *Asiya*.

---

10. See *Iggeret HaKodesh*, epistle 25 (cited by the Lubavitcher Rebbe, Rabbi Menaḥem Mendel Schneerson).

וּכְמוֹ שֶׁנִּתְבָּאֵר לְעֵיל בְּשֵׁם הַתִּיקּוּנִים (תיקוני זהר תיקון ו), שֶׁבְּעוֹלַם הַבְּרִיאָה מְאִירוֹת וּמַשְׁפִּיעוֹת שָׁם חָכְמָתוֹ וּבִינָתוֹ וְדַעְתּוֹ שֶׁל אֵין סוֹף בָּרוּךְ הוּא, בִּבְחִינַת צִמְצוּם עָצוּם, בִּכְדֵי שֶׁיּוּכְלוּ הַנְּשָׁמוֹת וְהַמַּלְאָכִים, שֶׁהֵם בַּעֲלֵי גְּבוּל וְתַכְלִית, לְקַבֵּל הַשְׁפָּעָה מִבְּחִינַת חָכְמָה בִּינָה דַּעַת אֵלּוּ.

As explained above (chap. 39) in the name of the *Tikkunei Zohar* (23a), in the world of *Beria*, the Ḥokhma, Bina, and Da'at of *Ein Sof*, blessed be He, shine and flow in an immensely constricted form so that the souls and angels, which have finite limitations, can receive the flow from the level of these constricted Ḥokhma, Bina, and Da'at.

Ḥokhma, Bina, and Da'at of *Ein Sof* are themselves on the level of *Ein Sof*. Thus, no finite creature is able to grasp them at all. As a result, they require immense constriction. It is stated in *Tikkunei Zohar* that Bina (*moḥin*) is associated with and revealed in the world of *Beria*: "The higher mother, Bina, resides on the throne, *Beria*." The attributes, love, fear, and so forth, belong in, and are revealed in, the world of *Yetzira*: "Six *sefirot* reside in Metatron [the world of *Yetzira*]." *Malkhut* relates to the world of *Asiya* (and the world of *Atzilut* is associated with that which is beyond revelation and comprehension). Thus the character of the world of *Beria* is intellectual understanding. And the essence of the creations within it, the souls and angels, is in the realm of intellectual understanding.

וְלָכֵן נִמְשַׁךְ מִשָּׁם הַתַּלְמוּד, שֶׁהוּא גַּם כֵּן בְּחִינַת חָכְמָה בִּינָה דַּעַת, שֶׁהַתַּלְמוּד הוּא טַעֲמֵי הַהֲלָכוֹת עַל בּוּרְיָין,

Therefore the Talmud is drawn down from there, since it is also a category of Ḥokhma, Bina, and Da'at, because the Talmud consists of the clearly defined reasons for the *halakhot*.

Thus the Talmud is derived from the world of *Beria*. The concept of "Talmud" refers to intellectual inquiry through Ḥokhma, Bina, and Da'at. This does not necessarily relate to a specific text called "Talmud." The terms "Gemara" and "Talmud" appeared in ancient sources before the Talmud was completed,[11] because the character of Talmud has always

---

11. See, for example, *Berakhot* 22a.

existed. It is part of the Oral Torah and the way we connect with it. It signifies intellectual engagement with the Torah in order to understand and clarify what is written in it: the *halakhot*, their sources, and the reasoning behind them.

וְהַטְּעָמִים הֵם בְּחִינַת חָכְמָה בִּינָה דַּעַת, **The reasons are on the level of Hokhma, Bina, and Da'at.**

The rationales for the *halakhot* are "Torah" on the intellectual plane. On this level are revealed the reasons for the *halakhot*, as well as the insights that make it possible to infer one matter from another, to grasp the Torah's wisdom, and to reveal it in each world on its appropriate level. This level is called "Talmud," and it corresponds mainly to the world of *Beria*.

וְהַהֲלָכוֹת עַצְמָן הֵן מִמִּדּוֹתָיו שֶׁל אֵין סוֹף בָּרוּךְ הוּא, שֶׁהֵן: חֶסֶד, דִּין, רַחֲמִים כו', **The *halakhot* themselves come from** below that, from **the attributes of *Ein Sof*, blessed be He, which are** the *sefirot* of ***Hesed*** **(kindness), *Din* (judgment), *Rahamim* (compassion), and so on.**

The rationales of the *halakhot*, the Talmud, are associated with the realm of the intellect. The halakhic rulings of what to do and what not to do relate to the world of the attributes.

שֶׁמֵּהֶן נִמְשָׁךְ: הַהֶיתֵּר וְהָאִיסּוּר, וְהַכָּשֵׁר וְהַפָּסוּל, וְהַחִיּוּב וְהַפְּטוּר, כְּמוֹ שֶׁכָּתוּב בַּתִּיקּוּנִים (תיקון ו). **From these are derived the** halakhic rulings of **permitted and prohibited, valid and invalid, and liable and exempt, as written in** *Tikkunei Zohar* **(23b).**

The connection of the *halakhot* to the attributes is that from the attributes are drawn forth what is permitted and what is forbidden, what is valid what is invalid, what is obligatory and what is permissible. A halakhic ruling is essentially an expression of love and fear. Simply put, the *halakha* indicates what God loves and what He does not love. When it states, "God wants something this way," the individual who loves God acts accordingly. When it states, "God does not want something that way," the person who is connected to God and fears being parted from Him refrains from that. The *halakhot* themselves are independent of logic and explanation. Rather, they are in the context of parameters such as love and fear. In this vein, the medieval scholars refer to deeds that are beloved by God and deeds that are abhorred by God. ☞

29 Iyar　וּבְהִתְלַבְּשׁוּת מַלְכוּת דַּאֲצִילוּת בְּמַלְכוּת דִּבְרִיאָה, מִתְלַבֶּשֶׁת בְּהֵיכַל קָדְשֵׁי קָדָשִׁים דִּיצִירָה, שֶׁהוּא חָכְמָה בִּינָה דַּעַת דִּיצִירָה. וּבְהִתְלַבְּשׁוּתָן בְּמַלְכוּת דִּיצִירָה - נוֹצְרוּ הָרוּחוֹת וְהַמַּלְאָכִים שֶׁבִּיצִירָה.

When *Malkhut* of *Atzilut* is enclothed in *Malkhut* of *Beria*, it then goes on to become enclothed in the shrine of the Holy of Holies of the world of *Yetzira* – that being Ḥokhma, Bina, and Da'at of Yetzira. And when all of these *sefirot* are enclothed in *Malkhut* of *Yetzira*, the spirits and angels of the world of *Yetzira* are formed.

The author of the *Tanya* now resumes his description of the descent of the Divine Presence through the worlds, from *Malkhut* of *Atzilut* to the world of *Asiya*. After the Divine Presence has descended and become enclothed in *Malkhut* of *Beria*,[12] it proceeds to the world of

---

HALAKHIC RULINGS ARE A COMBINATION OF THE ATTRIBUTES

☞ The relationship of the attributes as expressed in the *halakhot* is complex. They involve not only love and hate, but love, fear, compassion, and others. Kindness involves doing a deed that is beloved by God. Fear involves avoidance of a deed that is hated by God, while compassion involves a blend of these two attributes. Every halakhic ruling, whether it declares a matter permitted or prohibited, valid or invalid, a mitzva or a transgression, is an expression of a particular combination of attributes. For example, one thing may be valid but not a requirement, another may be obligatory and a mitzva. There are mitzvot that are performed out of love, because one wants to do them, and there are mitzvot that we perform because they are necessary in certain circumstances. It is a mitzva to give a woman a document of divorce, yet this is not an obligation that every man should strive to fulfill. There are acts that constitute a mitzva under certain conditions and a serious transgression under other conditions. The *halakhot* are expressions of complex interrelationships, of kindness and judgment blended together, of compassion, dominance, splendor, and foundation, of kindness within judgment, restraint within compassion, and so on.

---

12. See the comment of the Lubavitcher Rebbe, Rabbi Menaḥem Mendel

Yetzira. The kabbalistic texts explain that the three worlds of *Beria*, *Yetzira*, and *Asiya* correspond to the three levels of the soul: *nefesh*, *ruaḥ*, and *neshama*. This is why the author of the *Tanya* earlier referred to the *neshamot*, "souls," of the world of *Beria*, while here he mentions the *ruḥot*, "spirits," of the world of *Yetzira*.

וְגַם מִשָּׁם הִיא הַמִּשְׁנָה שֶׁלְּפָנֵינוּ, שֶׁהִיא הֲלָכוֹת פְּסוּקוֹת, הַנִּמְשָׁכוֹת גַּם כֵּן מֵחָכְמָה בִּינָה דַּעַת שֶׁל אֵין סוֹף בָּרוּךְ הוּא, — Also from *Malkhut* of *Yetzira* is the Mishna that we possess, which consists of halakhic rulings. These too are ultimately drawn from the *Ḥokhma*, *Bina*, and *Da'at* of *Ein Sof*, blessed be He.

The Mishna as we know it derives from *Malkhut* of *Yetzira*, although its ultimate source is from *Ḥokhma*, as the entire Torah, including the Mishna, is the *Ḥokhma* of *Ein Sof*.

רַק שֶׁבְּחִינַת חָכְמָה בִּינָה דַּעַת, שֶׁהֵם טַעֲמֵי הַהֲלָכוֹת, הֵם מְלוּבָּשִׁים וּגְנוּזִים בְּגוּפֵי הַהֲלָכוֹת וְלֹא בִּבְחִינַת גִּילּוּי. — However, the levels of *Ḥokhma*, *Bina*, and *Da'at*, which are the rationales for the *halakhot*, are enclothed and hidden within the *halakhot* themselves, and are not revealed.

In the halakhic rulings in the Mishna there are reasons for why one matter is prohibited and another permitted. However, these are not revealed on the same level as the halakhic ruling itself. A halakhic ruling only states, "Do this, and do not do that." That is the main focus of the Mishna. Certainly, the ruling itself requires study, but this study does not seek to understand the reasons for the *halakha*. This study relates to the halakhic ruling, to know what one must do in different situations. Clarifying the reasons and rationales pertains to the level of the Talmud.

Schneerson, published in *Lessons in Tanya* (and in *Likkutei Biurim LaSefer Ha-Tanya*).

וְגוּפֵי הַהֲלָכוֹת, שֶׁהֵן בִּבְחִינַת גִּילּוּי, הֵן הֶאָרַת מִדּוֹתָיו שֶׁל אֵין סוֹף בָּרוּךְ הוּא בִּבְחִינַת גִּילּוּי, כְּמוֹ שֶׁנִּתְבָּאֵר לְעֵיל בְּשֵׁם הַתִּיקוּנִים (תיקוני זהר שם).

By contrast, **the *halakhot* themselves, which are in a revealed form** in the Mishna, **are the very illumination of the attributes of *Ein Sof*, blessed be He, on the revealed level, as explained above** (chap. 39), **citing *Tikkunei Zohar*** (23a),

The *halakhot*, "Do this, and do not do that," are an expression of God's attributes, for God loves "this" and dislikes "that."

דְּשִׁית סְפִירָן מְקַנְּנִין בִּיצִירָה, **six *sefirot* nest in** the world of ***Yetzira*.**

The three worlds of *Beria*, *Yetzira*, and *Asiya* receive their life force and existence from the world of *Atzilut*. Each of the three worlds receives the essence of its life and its unique nature from a different aspect of the world of *Atzilut*. The world of *Beria* receives this from the *sefira* of *Bina*; the world of *Yetzira* from the six *sefirot* of Ḥesed, Gevura, Tiferet, Netzaḥ, Hod, and Yesod (Kindness, Restraint, Beauty, Dominance, Splendor, and Foundation); and the world of *Asiya* from the *sefira* of *Malkhut*. This is why it is stated here in the name of *Tikkunei Zohar* that the six *sefirot*, which are the attributes of the world of *Atzilut*, are found in the world of *Yetzira* and illuminate it.

שֶׁהֵן דֶּרֶךְ כְּלָל שְׁנֵי קַוִּין, יָמִין וּשְׂמֹאל:

These **six *sefirot* are, broadly** speaking, in **two** vertical **lines: right and left.**

When the six *sefirot*, the attributes, are arranged in the form of two inverted triangles, one below the other, they are divided overall in two vertical lines. The right line is that of the attribute of Ḥesed, and the left is that of Gevura. Although there is a third line in the middle, that of Tiferet, since it is the midpoint, a composite of the right and the left lines, it is possible to speak in general of two lines.

לְהָקֵל - מִסִּטְרָא דְּחֶסֶד, דְּהַיְינוּ לְהַתִּיר שֶׁיּוּכַל לַעֲלוֹת אֶל ה', אוֹ לְהַחְמִיר כוּ'.

This allows **being lenient, from the side of *ḥesed*,** i.e., permitting something **so that it can ascend to God, or being strict, etc.**

In general, a halakhic decisor has two paths before him: leniency and stringency. For example, if he is asked whether or not a certain food is kosher, he could be lenient and permit the food, or he could be stringent and prohibit it. The two paths are the two lines, the line of *Ḥesed*, kindness, and the line of *Gevura*, judgment. The line of kindness involves being lenient and permitting, such that the object is free of the bonds of the *kelippa* ("husk") and it is able to ascend and draw nearer to God. The line of judgment and *Gevura* is to prohibit, to tie down the object below, so that it cannot detach itself from the *kelippa* and come closer to God.

The attribute of kindness in a lenient halakhic ruling is not found in a particular individual's dispensation to eat, but primarily in the kindness and freedom bestowed upon the permitted food itself. As was explained above (chap. 7), *asur*, "prohibited," also means "bound," for the object is bound to the *kelippot*, tied to impurity. In contrast, the word *mutar*, permitted, also means unbound, for when something is permitted according to the *halakha*, it is released from its bondage to evil and allowed to ascend. ☞

As stated earlier, the permitted and the forbidden express God's attributes. The permitted is on the side of kindness, for the matter in

THE LAW OF THE GOOSE

☞ There is an amusing story, perhaps it is also a joke, about a great rabbi who permitted the consumption of an injured goose. People argued against him, citing the Shakh, a noted seventeenth-century talmudist and halakhist, who is of the opinion that a goose with that particular injury is not kosher. The rabbi responded, "When I come before the heavenly court, the Shakh will bring a claim against me for not ruling in accordance with his approach, and we will argue the case before the court. However, if I prohibit the goose, the goose will make a claim against me in the heavenly court for declaring it non-kosher. Personally, I would prefer to debate the Shakh than a goose." The goose, like all physical reality, is attached to the *kelippot*. A ruling that prohibits it binds it permanently to the *kelippot*, far away from the light of God's countenance. A ruling that permits it, however, frees it to rise up from the *kelippa* and draw near to God. The problem of "forbidden" and "permitted," "impure" and "pure," is therefore not merely a question of whether or not a person can derive benefit from a particular object. Rather, it is an essential question with far-reaching ramifications. In the words of the Jerusalem Talmud, "Just as it is forbidden to declare the impure pure, it is forbidden to declare the pure impure" (*Terumot* 5:3). The halakhic ruling is a critical declaration that must be handled with great caution, not only when declaring a matter permitted, but also when prohibiting something.

question is desired and beloved by God, while the prohibited belongs on the side of judgment, meaning that the object is undesired and unworthy of being before Him. However, even a person who studies Mishna and *halakha* expresses his attributes through that and, as explained in the introduction to the *Tanya*, the root of his soul: whether it is on the right or the left. Although the study of *halakha* is logical, every logical inquiry contains tangential aspects that depend on the root of the soul. A person whose soul is on the side of *Gevura* tends to be stringent and create distance, while a person whose soul is on the side of *Ḥesed* tends to be lenient and bring closer.

וְהַכֹּל עַל פִּי חָכְמָה עִילָּאָה, דַּאֲצִילוּת וּבִינָה וְדַעַת כְּלוּלוֹת בָּהּ, וּמְיוּחָדוֹת בְּאֵין סוֹף בָּרוּךְ הוּא. **All this,** Mishna and Talmud, **is in accordance with the supernal Ḥokhma of Atzilut, in which Bina and Daʿat are incorporated. And all of these are unified in Ein Sof, blessed be He.**

The entire structure of the Torah – the study of Talmud, which is on the level of the world of *Beria*; the halakhic rulings of the Mishna, which are on the level of the world of *Yetzira*; and the halakhic act itself, which is on the level of the world of *Asiya* – are in keeping with the supernal *Ḥokhma* of *Atzilut*. The Torah with all of its components and levels is God's wisdom, for "the Torah emerged from *Ḥokhma*." Moreover, *Bina* and *Daʿat* are included in *Ḥokhma*. The Torah and God are one, and therefore the Torah is united with *Ein Sof* on every level where it is found and not only on the level of *Ḥokhma* of *Atzilut*.

כִּי בְּתוֹךְ כּוּלָן מְלוּבָּשׁוֹת חָכְמָה בִּינָה דַעַת דַּאֲצִילוּת, שֶׁאוֹר אֵין סוֹף בָּרוּךְ הוּא מְיוּחָד בָּהֶן בְּתַכְלִית הַיִּחוּד. **That is because within them all are enclothed the Ḥokhma, Bina, and Daʿat of Atzilut, with which the light of Ein Sof, blessed be He, is unified in absolute union.**

The Torah is always in the Holy of Holies of each world, and the Divine Presence rests in each world. The light of *Ein Sof* is united with an absolute oneness to the Holy of Holies of each world, and in the Torah that enclothes *Ein Sof* in each world. *Ein Sof* also enclothes everyone who learns and observes the Torah in each world.

וְכֵן בְּדֶרֶךְ זֶה יָרְדָה הַשְּׁכִינָה וְנִתְלַבְּשָׁה בְּהֵיכַל קֹדֶשׁ קָדָשִׁים דַּעֲשִׂיָּה.

Similarly, the Divine Presence descended in this manner and it was enclothed in the shrine of the Holy of Holies of the world of *Asiya*.

According to what has been described, the Divine Presence descended from the shrine of the Holy of Holies of the world of *Atzilut* to *Malkhut* of *Atzilut*. From there, it descended to the Holy of Holies of the world of *Beria*, and from there to *Malkhut* of *Beria*. From there, it descended to the Holy of Holies of the world of *Yetzira*, and from there to *Malkhut* of the world of *Yetzira*. And it became enclothed in the *sefirot* of *Ḥokhma*, *Bina*, and *Da'at* of the world of *Asiya*.

וְכָל עוֹלָם מִג׳ עוֹלָמוֹת אֵלּוּ מִתְחַלֵּק לְרִבְבוֹת מַדְרֵיגוֹת, הַנִּקְרָאוֹת גַּם כֵּן עוֹלָמוֹת פְּרָטִים.

Each of these three worlds is divided into myriads of levels, which are also called specific worlds

The worlds of *Beria*, *Yetzira*, and *Asiya* are inclusive, and within each of them is are a multitude of particular aspects and levels, each of which is also defined as a "world." And the progression and order of the indwelling of the Divine Presence in the worlds is the same for all of the particular worlds within the four overall worlds, and in each particular level within each particular world. ☞

MYRIADS OF LEVELS THAT ARE CONSIDERED SPECIFIC WORLDS

☞ In our world, the profusion of worlds and levels within it, and the myriad ways that the Torah is manifest, and that the Divine Presence indwells, is especially significant. As the lowest of all worlds, it is the repository of all of the forms, all of the details and particulars of all the multitude of worlds and levels, in general and in particular. Here are found the fragments, sparks, and ramifications of all of the worlds. The "loose ends" of all the worlds are tied together here. Thus, everything we encounter in our world is significant in so many ways both for our world and the entirety of worlds.

This complex reality is a unique quality of our lowly, physical world. Because it is so low and physical, it is able to contain a complexity so vast that no spiritual world can contain. (The differences between our world and the World to Come are discussed in *Likkutei Torah*, Num. 75c.) A spiritual world is a static realm whose specifications are fixed and unchanging,

וּמַלְכוּת דַּאֲצִילוּת הַמְלוּבֶּשֶׁת בְּמַלְכוּת שֶׁל כָּל עוֹלָם פְּרָטִי and *Malkhut* of *Atzilut*, which is enclothed in the *sefira* of *Malkhut* of every particular world.

Every world, whether abstract or particular, is an entire universe unto itself. Each one contains the level of a "head" and the level of a "foot." The head is its Holy of Holies, its Ḥokhma, Bina, and Da'at, and the "foot" is its *Malkhut*. Furthermore, the repeating uniform structure of all the worlds is indicative of the revealed and concealed ties between all the worlds; the "head" of one world connects to the "head" of another world, the "foot" of one world connects to the "foot" of another world, and *Malkhut* of *Atzilut* connects to each *Malkhut* of every other world. The Divine Presence itself pervades everything from the very highest to the very lowest. It is enclothed in *Malkhut* and in the very reality, even in the minute details, of all the worlds, including ours.

and because its specifications are always in one circumscribed area, they are referred to as "pure." For instance, abstract geometric shapes such as the triangle and the square can be precisely defined. Despite the multitude of possible forms each shape can take, the nature and rules defining it are relatively simple. But in our world, the difference between two creatures of the same species is so manifold that it cannot be characterized precisely. The reason for this is that creatures in our world are not pure. They are comprised of many aspects of various levels and a spectrum of realms. A unique amalgam of attributes, levels, and channels forms the unique nature and parameters of each creation. Thus no being in our world can be compared in a meaningful way to any other being. This is especially true of complex beings such as humans.

Understanding this difficulty is one of the fundamental goals of the *Tanya*. In the introduction, the author of the *Tanya* debates the merits of writing such a book in view of the nature of humankind. Moreover, while he did write it, he presents within the book numerous approaches to divine service as well as many attributes that are involved in it, such as love, fear, and compassion, but he does not state which of these approaches a person should adhere to. He does not express an unequivocal preference for one way over the others. After all, if human beings are so different from each other, the rules that apply to them are true only in a general sense, and no guarantees can be given concerning what is right and what is wrong for each individual. Furthermore, not only are there differences between individuals, but there are also variations within individuals at different times. Every day, and sometimes every hour, is like a new world. Thus, even if a person remains in the same place, he may over the course of time discover that he has become a new person in a completely different world. This makes it almost im-

הַגָּה"ה: (וּבָזֶה יוּבַן לְשׁוֹן הַכָּתוּב [תהלים קמה, יג]: "מַלְכוּתְךָ מַלְכוּת כָּל עוֹלָמִים"),

Gloss: Now we may understand the verse "Your kingship is a kingship of all worlds" (Ps. 145:13).

God's kingship, which is *Malkhut* of *Atzilut*, is in fact the *Malkhut* of all the worlds. Within all worlds and on the level of *Malkhut* in all the worlds, notwithstanding all the subtleties and differences, only one *Malkhut* is revealed: God's kingship.

יוֹרֶדֶת וּמִתְלַבֶּשֶׁת בְּהֵיכַל קָדְשֵׁי קָדָשִׁים, שֶׁהוּא חָכְמָה בִּינָה דַּעַת שֶׁבָּעוֹלָם שֶׁלְּמַטָּה מִמֶּנּוּ בְּמַדְרֵגָה.

It descends and is enclothed in the shrine of the Holy of Holies, namely *Ḥokhma*, *Bina*, and *Da'at*, of the world on the level below it.

The Divine Presence, which is enclothed in *Malkhut* of each particular world, descends to the world below it. Thus, all of the worlds affect one another, level after level, in such a way that the "final stage of action" of

---

possible to generalize with regard to particular individuals or with regard to the same individual at different times.

Some of this variety can be seen in those prayer books that include the intentions of the Arizal for the counting of the Omer. Each day of the Omer is a new day, a day that corresponds to a totally different system of elements and worlds. Consequently, the blessing recited on the first day and the blessing recited on the second day are similar only in their general, superficial format. However, the prayer book that details their differences reveals how the letters and vowels are to be read differently each time. The names are to be recited differently and the letters are to be combined differently. The world in which we are counting today is different from the one in which we counted yesterday. In view of this, it is surprising that there is any connection between one moment and another, one place and another, and one person and another. Many have discussed the mystery of continuity despite the countless disparities due to creation constantly being renewed at every moment, yet moments are not entirely severed from the moments that came before them, because despite our differences they are common paths that are more or less right for everyone. The author of the *Tanya* is aware of the depth of the problem, of the possibility and even the necessity for many paths to exist. And he indeed seeks these ways and connections everywhere. Throughout the entire book, he tries on the one hand to present approaches that are as general as possible. Yet at the same time, he reiterates that one must take note of the tremendous diversity that exists in all the worlds, and also in our world, and which therefore exists in each person's path to divine service.

one world constitutes "the origin of thought" of the next. The lowest point of one realm is the starting point of the world below it. Each world's "feet" are the "crown" of the world beneath it.

וְהִנֵּה מֵהַשְּׁכִינָה, הַמְלוּבֶּשֶׁת בְּהֵיכַל קָדְשֵׁי קָדָשִׁים שֶׁל כָּל עוֹלָם וְעוֹלָם כְּלָלִי אוֹ פְּרָטִי, נִמְשָׁךְ וּמִתְפַּשֵּׁט מִמֶּנָּה אוֹר וְחַיּוּת לְכָל הָעוֹלָם וְהַבְּרוּאִים שֶׁבּוֹ, נְשָׁמוֹת וּמַלְאָכִים וְכוּ'.

From the Divine Presence, which is enclothed in the shrine of the Holy of Holies of each world, whether that world is **general or specific**, light and life force are drawn down and spread out to that entire world and the creatures within it, such as **souls and angels and so forth.**

Each world's Holy of Holies is the focus of its life, its brain, from which life, which is the Divine Presence enclothed within that world, spreads out to all its sections and levels, as well as to its creatures. Nevertheless, this is like the "speech" of that world, since it creates beings that are seemingly separate from it: souls, angels, and so forth.

כִּי כֻּלָּם נִבְרְאוּ בַּעֲשָׂרָה מַאֲמָרוֹת שֶׁבְּמַעֲשֵׂה בְרֵאשִׁית, שֶׁהֵם דְּבַר ה' הַנִּקְרָא בְּשֵׁם שְׁכִינָה.

That is **because they were all created with the ten utterances of the act of creation, which are the word of God, which is called the Divine Presence.**

All creations were formed by means of the ten utterances. As mentioned above, the Divine Presence, *Malkhut* of *Atzilut*, is the word of God. Just as a person's speech reveals his thoughts to others, the Divine Presence is the overall divine revelation, as it were, outward, in creation and in all creatures, which perceive themselves to have been created from nothingness.

This chapter continued discussing the indwelling of the Divine Presence: what it is and how it resides in all the worlds. The previous chapter cited the analogy of "From my flesh I will view" (Job 19:26), the parallel between the Divine Presence and the human soul, and this chapter focused on its meaning. The Divine Presence, which constitutes the essence and beginning of the divine manifestation that flows into all the worlds, is enclothed in God's will, wisdom, understanding, and knowledge. These are called the *moḥin*, and they are enclothed in the Torah and its commandments. The author of the *Tanya* explains how and why specifically the Torah, which derives from God's supernal wisdom, can serve as a vessel and a garment for the Divine Presence in each world on its own level. He then described the indwelling of the Divine Presence in the worlds, enclothed in the Torah: in the world of *Beria* (on the level of the Talmud), in the world of *Yetzira* (on the level of the Mishna), and in the world of *Asiya*. The descent in all the worlds, not only in the three general worlds of *Beria*, *Yetzira*, and *Asiya* but in each individual level within them, each of which is also called a "world," occurs in such a way that the *Malkhut* of a higher world is enclothed in the Holy of Holies of the world below it, from which it spreads out and gives life to all the details and components of that world, until it reaches *Malkhut*, or "speech," in that world, giving life to that world's creations, the souls and angels, and then the Divine Presence continues to descend, to the worlds below it. This chapter described in a general way the spiritual worlds above our world. In the next chapter, the author of the *Tanya* will discuss our world and reality, the indwelling of the Divine Presence in the here and now.

Chapter 53

THE PRECEDING CHAPTERS DISCUSSED THE DYNAMICS of the manifestation of the Divine Presence: what it is and how it appears in each of the worlds. While these chapters do not summarize all of the issues discussed in the book, they bring the ideas that they do discuss to their practical expression. This follows the language of the verse upon which the *Tanya* is founded: "The matter is very near to you, in your mouth and in your heart, to perform it." "To perform it" relates to the material world of *Asiya*. The present chapter, which concludes the *Tanya*, will discuss the manifestation of the Divine Presence in our world, the material world of *Asiya*.

This concluding chapter serves as a kind of landing, but not one following which the reader sets down the book and transitions to other things. Rather, it translates the concepts of all the chapters into the lower, tangible reality of our lives. This allows the book to continue with us, and it allows us to continue with it, on all our paths through the vicissitudes of life in this world.

וְהִנֵּה כְּשֶׁהָיָה בַּיִת רִאשׁוֹן קַיָּים, **When the First Temple stood,** — 1 Sivan / 3 Sivan (leap year)

There was a difference between the manifestation of the Divine Presence in the First Temple and in the Second Temple, because the latter was less complete than the former.

שֶׁבּוֹ הָיָה הָאָרוֹן וְהַלּוּחוֹת בְּבֵית קָדְשֵׁי קָדָשִׁים, **which contained the Ark of the Covenant and the tablets in the abode of the Holy of Holies,**

The First Temple was unique in that it contained the Ark of the Covenant containing the tablets in the Holy of Holies. The physical structure of the Second Temple was more grand and elaborate than that of the First Temple. Yet, it lacked this inner aspect. Thus, the First Temple was perfect both internally and externally. Not only was the building perfect, but all of the details of the Sanctuary were as well. ☞

הָיְתָה הַשְּׁכִינָה, שֶׁהִיא מַלְכוּת דַּאֲצִילוּת, שֶׁהִיא בְּחִינַת גִּילּוּי אוֹר אֵין סוֹף בָּרוּךְ הוּא, שׁוֹרָה שָׁם וּמְלוּבֶּשֶׁת בַּעֲשֶׂרֶת הַדִּבְּרוֹת בְּיֶתֶר שְׂאֵת וְיֶתֶר עָז בְּגִילּוּי רַב וְעָצוּם יוֹתֵר מִגִּילּוּיָהּ בְּהֵיכָלוֹת קָדְשֵׁי הַקֳּדָשִׁים שֶׁלְּמַעְלָה בָּעוֹלָמוֹת עֶלְיוֹנִים.

the Divine Presence, which is *Malkhut* of *Atzilut,* which is the level of the manifestation of the light of *Ein Sof,* blessed be He, would dwell there and be enclothed in the Ten Commandments with especial magnitude and power, in an immensely greater intense revelation than its manifestation in the palaces of the Holy of Holies above in the supernal worlds.

When the Temple stood and the Ark of the Covenant and the tablets were in the physical Holy of Holies in this world, the revelation of the Divine Presence in this world was even more perfect than it is in all the higher worlds. The Holy of Holies in the physical Temple contained the highest revelation of the Divine Presence from the highest point

THE PERFECTION OF THE TEMPLE AND THE PERFECTION OF THE WORLD

☞ When the ark and the tablets, through which came a revelation of the Divine Presence, are part of the physical existence of the world, every structure in the world is perfect and complete. And so, as will be explained, when the First Temple was destroyed and the Holy of Holies, the ark, and the Tablets of the Covenant no longer had their presence in the physical world, the structure of the world overall was no longer perfect. This is similar to the analogy of a person's brain afflicted with a defect. A person receives a blow to the head or becomes ill, and some of his brain cells are destroyed. Even if the brain continues to function, it is not the same as it was in its uninjured state. This is true with regard to the worlds as well. Although there are different forms of the manifestation of the Divine Presence, they are only a lesser level of the perfection of the manifestation of the Divine Presence that was manifest in the First Temple.

of all the worlds, the revelation of the Divine Presence in the Holy of Holies of the world of *Atzilut*.

כִּי עֲשֶׂרֶת הַדִּבְּרוֹת הֵן כְּלָלוּת הַתּוֹרָה כּוּלָּהּ, **That is because the Ten Commandments comprise the essence of the entire Torah,**

The Ten Commandments, written on the Tablets of the Covenant, are the essence and soul of the entire Torah.[1] All the commandments, with their respective explanations in the Oral Torah, are alluded to in the words and letters of the Ten Commandments.[2]

דְּנָפְקָא מִגּוֹ חָכְמָה עִילָּאָה, דִּלְעֵילָּא לְעֵילָּא מֵעָלְמָא דְּאִתְגַּלְיָא. **which emerged out of supernal Ḥokhma, which totally transcends the manifest world.**

The source of the Torah is the supernal Ḥokhma that transcends all the revealed worlds, all existence that can be revealed at all. It not only transcends the lower worlds, but even the highest. Given this, since the Ten Commandments contain the entire Torah, they must contain a revelation that is higher than all revelation that is possible within the higher worlds.

וּכְדֵי לְחָקְקָן בְּלוּחוֹת אֲבָנִים גַּשְׁמִיִּים לֹא יָרְדָה מִמַּדְרֵגָה לְמַדְרֵגָה כְּדֶרֶךְ הִשְׁתַּלְשְׁלוּת הָעוֹלָמוֹת עַד עוֹלָם הַזֶּה הַגַּשְׁמִי. **In order to engrave them on physical tablets of stone,** the Divine Presence **did not descend from level to level according to the** sequential **succession of worlds to reach this physical world.**

---

1. See *Likkutei Torah*, Num. 59c, which states that the letters were engraved into the stone of the tablets. This is a singularly higher level than the rest of the Written Torah, which is not engraved but is written in ink on parchment.
2. Accordingly, the 613 commandments are listed and organized in the letters of the Ten Commandments in the liturgical poems of Rav Se'adya Gaon. *Otzar HaḤayyim* of Rabbi Yitzḥak Isaac Yehuda Yeḥiel Saffrin from Kamarna explains the various commandments and their connection to the letters in the Ten Commandments according to Kabbala. Also see above, chapter 20.

The "sequential succession of worlds" is the way that the divine light descends within the worlds, descending and contracting from a higher world to a lower one, until the physical world, the lowest world of all. This sequential descent is the natural process, the way in which life comes into being and all worlds function. The revelation of divine light that descends in this way is in accord with the level of each world and each created being according to each level and its "vessels." This is distinct from the manifestation of the Divine Presence that existed in the Ten Commandments. This revelation was not manifest according to levels and vessels at all, neither in this world nor in the higher worlds.

כִּי עוֹלָם הַזֶּה הַגַּשְׁמִי מִתְנַהֵג בְּהִתְלַבְּשׁוּת הַטֶּבַע הַגַּשְׁמִי, That is **because this physical world operates clothed within** the laws of **physical nature,**

Our world is unique not only because it is a physical, material world that can be touched, weighed, and measured. It is also unique in that it operates according to very specific rules that govern everything within it. Accordingly, the more precise definition of our world is: material that operates according to fixed rules. The laws of nature are an intrinsic aspect of the physical nature of our world.

"וְהַלּוּחוֹת - מַעֲשֵׂה אֱלֹהִים הֵמָּה" (שמות לב, טז), "וְהַמִּכְתָּב מִכְתַּב אֱלֹהִים הוּא" (שם) לְמַעְלָה מֵהַטֶּבַע שֶׁל עוֹלָם הַזֶּה הַגַּשְׁמִי, whereas **"the tablets were the work of God, and the writing was the writing of God"** (Ex. 32:16), **beyond the nature of this physical world,**

In contrast, "The tablets were the work of God" (Ex. 32:16). Even though the tablets were made from physical material, they were not part of the nature of the physical world. The physical world is part of the process of the sequentially descending worlds, the world of cause and effect. The tablets, on the other hand, since they are "the work of God," were not created through the process of sequential succession. They were not formed through geological forces, but directly through "the work of God." Therefore, they did not follow the rules of the physical world. We defined the physical world as having two parameters: material and the laws governing the material. The tablets possessed only one element: material. They were not governed by the rules of the material, however, and thus they were not part of the material world. ☞

הַנִּשְׁפָּע מֵהֶאָרַת הַשְּׁכִינָה שֶׁבְּהֵיכַל קָדְשֵׁי קָדָשִׁים דַּעֲשִׂיָּה, שֶׁמִּמֶּנָּה נִמְשָׁךְ אוֹר וְחַיּוּת לְעוֹלָם הָעֲשִׂיָּה, שֶׁגַּם עוֹלָם הַזֶּה בִּכְלָלוֹ.

which receives its flow from the illumination of the Divine Presence that dwells **in the palace of the Holy of Holies of** *Asiya*. From that illumination of the Divine Presence, **light and life force are drawn** down **to the world of** *Asiya,* **which includes this world** of ours **as well.**

THE DIVINE WRITING

☞ The verse states that the tablets were "inscribed on both their sides; from this side and from that side they were inscribed" (Ex. 32:15). Ostensibly, the letters were carved through the full thickness of the tablets, from one side through to the other. This is why the Talmud says that "the *mem (sofit)* [a square] and *samekh* [a circle] that were in the tablets were miraculously suspended" (*Shabbat* 104a). However, the miracle is greater than this. If the miracle were just in those two letters of *mem* and *samekh*, the writing would be read in its mirrored reverse on the other side. However, as described in other places (see *Likkutei Torah*, Num. 18c), the tablets were readable from all sides, meaning that they only had a front side. When perceived from behind or from the sides they could still be read as from the front. This illustrates that the basic natural laws of our reality, the distinctions between front and back, left and right, did not apply to the tablets. This is also said regarding the ark: "the space taken by the ark and cherubim is not included in the measurements" (*Bava Batra* 99a).

Along these lines, there are a number of things that are found within our world yet are not a part of its reality. As a result, the laws of our world do not apply to them. Included in this is the manna (see *Likkutei Torah*, Deut. 17a), as well as the Torah more generally, for its source is the supernal wisdom that transcends the descending unfolding of our reality. To use an analogy from the field of numbers, there are rational and irrational numbers. An irrational number, although its value is found approximately between two other numbers, it can never coincide with a "real," rational number. For example, the value pi (π), which is the quantitative relationship between the circumference of a circle and its radius, has a particular numerical value found between two other values, yet it never actually coincides with a rational number. It is as if it passes between these other values and never touches them at any point. There are similar things in reality, like the inscriptions on the tablets and the tablets themselves, that come from beyond the world and then pass through the world, never once touching the world at any point.

The light from the illumination of the Divine Presence descends from the palace of the Holy of Holies of *Asiya* level by level. It does so in the spiritual worlds of *Asiya* until it includes this physical world as well. The animating life force of this world is life force that comes through the descending levels of being, a "natural" path in which there is a fixed, defined connection between each level, between each cause and effect.

אֶלָּא בְּחִינַת חָכְמָה עִילָּאָה דַּאֲצִילוּת, שֶׁהִיא כְּלָלוּת הַתּוֹרָה שֶׁבַּעֲשֶׂרֶת הַדִּבְּרוֹת, נִתְלַבְּשָׁה בְּמַלְכוּת דַּאֲצִילוּת וּדְבְרִיאָה לְבַדָּן.

But the level of supernal *Ḥokhma* of *Atzilut*, which comprises the totality of the Torah within the Ten Commandments, became enclothed in *Malkhut* of *Atzilut* and *Beria* alone.

The Tablets of the Covenant did not become enclothed in *Malkhut* of *Yetzira* and *Asiya* (as will be explained later) even when they entered the physical world. That is because the tablets did not continuously enclothe themselves through descending levels, level by level, until reaching the physical world within *Asiya*, the place where the tablets rest in the ark in the Holy Temple.

וְהֵן לְבַדָּן, הַמְיוּחָדוֹת בָּאוֹר אֵין סוֹף שֶׁבְּתוֹכָן, הֵן הַנִּקְרָאוֹת בְּשֵׁם 'שְׁכִינָה' הַשּׁוֹרָה בְּקָדְשֵׁי קָדָשִׁים דְּבֵית רִאשׁוֹן.

It is they alone, unified with the light of *Ein Sof* within them, that are referred to as the "Divine Presence" that rested in the Holy of Holies of the First Temple.

In the Holy of Holies in the First Temple, there was a revelation that is different from all other realities. The world reveals the divine power that descends from one level to the next until it reaches the level of the world of *Asiya*, including the physical world within *Asiya*. This central point of divine revelation in the physical world is the source of all life force and revelation for all creatures in the world, each on its level. In contrast to this, in the Holy of Holies, in the ark and the tablets it contains, there was a skipping (as it were), like a line that breaks through and traverses directly from the most supernal realms to the physical world, skipping the many levels in between. It is a revelation that takes place in the physical world (the tablets and the ark), but without undergoing the processes of constriction and transformation that exist for all other entities in this world. It is a point in this world that has nothing to do with this world at all but is penetrated by the supernal divine world, like a higher type of existence embedded in a material form. This revelation, although it is present in our world, truly belongs to other levels of existence in terms of its relationships to existence and in terms of its meaning.

עַל יְדֵי הִתְלַבְּשׁוּתָהּ בַּעֲשֶׂרֶת הַדִּבְּרוֹת הַחֲקוּקוֹת בַּלּוּחוֹת שֶׁבָּאָרוֹן, בְּנֵס וּמַעֲשֵׂה אֱלֹהִים חַיִּים [הוּא עָלְמָא דְּאִתְכַּסְיָא הַמְקַנֵּן בְּעוֹלָם הַבְּרִיאָה, כַּנּוֹדָע לְיוֹדְעֵי חֵן].

This was **through** the Divine Presence **becoming enclothed in the Ten Commandments, which were engraved on the tablets miraculously and as a work of the Living God.** (This refers to the concealed world that nests in the world of *Beria*, as is known to those initiated in the esoteric wisdom.)

"Living God" indicates the level and *sefira* of *Bina*, Understanding,[3] of the world of *Atzilut*. This concealed world is revealed in the world of *Beria*. The tablets, the ark, and the cherubs in the Holy of Holies, correspond to the heavenly "chariot," which is also called the "throne of glory." The throne of glory is an aspect of the world of *Beria*, which is called the "throne" or "chariot" of the world above it, the world of *Atzilut*. A chariot is nullified to the person riding in it, and it carries him to faraway places. The world of *Beria* is like a chariot, or a throne, on which the world of *Atzilut* "sits" in order to illuminate the worlds. This is why the Divine Presence speaks from between the two cherubs atop the ark: The tablets and the ark, which reside in the Holy of Holies, are the site and the means of the revelation of the Divine Presence or, in other words, the revelation of the "concealed world." ☞ ☞

WHAT MAKES THE TABLETS, AND THE TORAH ITSELF, GREATER THAN THE WORLD?

☞ The verse states, "The tablets were the work of God, and the writing was the writing of God" (Ex. 32:16). Yet the entire world is the work of God, so what is special about the tablets? Why is the Divine Presence revealed in the tablets in the Holy of Holies,

---

3. See *Meorei Or*, s.v. "Elokim."

whereas in all other areas of the world the Divine Presence is concealed? This question is essentially that which was propounded at the beginning of these three chapters on the Divine Presence, and it concerns the entire relationship between the Torah and the world. The Torah is the word of God, but the world is also the word of God. So what is the difference between them?

As is explained here and elsewhere, the world is the work of God, but because of concealment, constriction, and sin, it does not fully reflect the essence of its Creator. God's power within His creations is not revealed. Our world is a creation that has been distorted. This stems in part from the transition from a higher, spiritual existence to material reality, by way of many levels that involve constrictions and transformations. This distortion is essential to meeting the purpose of our world, which must be ambiguous in order to be a place of free will. Accordingly, the world must be a physical domain in which the Divine Presence is concealed and impenetrable. Even without the distortion of sin, it is always a complex and multifaceted realm that may be understood in multiple ways. Although it bespeaks God and reveals His power, which is constantly acting upon His creations, it signifies something else as well, a different explanation for its structure and affairs, an explanation that conceals and obscures the presence of the One who gives life to, sustains, and governs His world.

Torah, as manifested within the reality of our world, reveals forty-nine aspects of purity and forty-nine aspects of impurity. However, whereas in the Torah itself it is clear which aspects are pure and which are impure, in our world these always appear ambiguous. In our world, two doors are always equally open to a person. The possibility of free will relies on the fact that everything that happens in the world can be explained in more than one way. The rebuke in the book of Leviticus is based entirely on this concept: "If you walk contrarily with Me..., so I also will walk with you contrarily" (see Lev. 26:21). When a person sins, God sends him a warning, but the person does not necessarily interpret it as such. He may tell himself that it occurred by chance. Then, when God sends him further punishments, precisely as He warned He would, the person can always interpret them once again as happenstance and refrain from taking any action. This is the foundation of our world: The door is open to anyone who chooses to sin. There is no instantaneous outcry against his actions. If the world were not ambiguous in this way, if it were as clear as day what is good and what is evil, what constitutes life and what constitutes death, a person would never debase or corrupt himself. A stone would not allow itself to be used for idol worship, and a stick would not allow itself to be used for violence. Regarding the future, the verse states, "The stone will cry from the wall" (Hab. 2:11). In the future, the world will lose its ambiguity and all objects will cry out and, through their very essence, point in the right direction. In our world, however, there is nothing to indicate what is holy and what is unholy.

The existence of free will depends on the perpetual struggle between a person's good inclination and his evil inclination. For this reason, "A person who is greater than another has a greater [evil] inclination" (*Sukka* 52a). No human being is born with inherent holiness unless he possesses a corresponding potential for impurity. Even the greatest individual was created with an inner balance such that he will be able to choose between good and evil. This even includes Adam, who was formed by God. This is how our reality is structured: There is equilibrium between that which is revealed and that which is concealed so that one can freely choose between good and evil without any degree of coercion.

SIN'S DISTORTION OF THE WORLD

☞ In addition to the essential concealment that is a result of the world's structure as a place of free will, there is an additional distortion that is caused by sin. Although the world is a place of ambiguity, the verse states that "God made man straight" (Eccles. 7:29). God made human beings essentially righteous so that they would be able to choose a path of goodness and righteousness. If a person were to remain "straight," he would continue on his straight path even in a world of concealment where he cannot clearly see where he is going. However, because a person does not remain straight, because he tarnishes himself, he damages his ability to see and walk in the way of the righteous. In order to walk straight when he cannot see everything, a person must be very pure. Even a minor infraction can potentially spoil many years of spiritual progress. A tzaddik once stated that a single instance of eating in a coarse manner can spoil all that a person has achieved in forty years of divine service. After the death of Rabbi Elimelekh of Lizhensk, one of his disciples traveled to Rabbi Elimelekh's brother, Rabbi Zusha of Anipoli. He got lost along the way and was forced to sleep in a forest. When he awoke, he could not find any water, and thus he was compelled to continue on his way without washing his hands. When he eventually arrived, Rabbi Zusha looked at him and said, "My brother worked on your soul for twenty years, and now it must start again from the beginning." Thus, the world is a realm of concealment. Yet if a person is unblemished and upright, he will proceed on the right path, even if he cannot see. However, when a person sins and creates blemishes, he adds distortion to distortion and concealment to concealment.

The distortion that a person creates through his sins acts inwardly on his soul as well as outwardly on the world. Our deeds, as well as our speech and thoughts, create real changes in the world. These changes accrue until eventually even an upright person no longer has a clear view. If the world were clear, a person would arrive, look at himself, and see the image of God. However, as the world becomes more distorted, our experience becomes increasingly like walking through a house of mirrors at a funfair amid distorted images, lights, and sounds. Our world has been repeatedly distorted throughout the generations, and one can no longer see things as they truly are, but only in an altered and corrupted form. In such a world, a person must try to recreate the true image, the source, the Garden of Eden from which the journey began, when the distortion was more limited and the image was clearer.

In this material world, which is full of ambiguities and distortions, the Tablets of the Covenant in the Holy of Holies are the only thing that comprise an unequivocal "act of the living God." They are a pure creation that contains no distortions. "Written with the finger of God" (Ex. 31:18) means that the ambiguities and distortions of the world, of sin and of imperfection, are not present here. The site of the Holy of Holies, with the ark and the tablets, is the one place in the physical cosmos that is connected to the highest level of existence. Everywhere else, there is some obstruction, a fog beyond which one cannot see. The "Holy of Holies" is the one opening that is not distorted or blurred. Through it, God's glory is revealed on earth.

The Ten Commandments were written in a physical form on a physical material. Matter itself is not inherently deficient. It is merely a form of reality. Therefore, if an object is created by "the finger of God," even if it is physical matter, it nonetheless reflects the divine essence that is beyond all worlds.

This is the concept of a miracle. Nature is based on constant balance. Nothing in nature is clear-cut, and anything that is perceived as supernatural, as a miracle, is such because God has intervened and modified the system so that it no longer works according to its internal rules. Instead, it acts in accordance with a different paradigm.

Reality is comprised of concepts, rules, and laws. But there is something that cuts through all of reality, since it is not subject to these rules. Almost every game is based around specific rules. The players play as long as balance is maintained and all moves are made in accordance with the rules. In chess, for example, if someone moves the king not in keeping with the rules, the game is over. The same is true with regard to the intervention of "the finger of God." God extends His finger, so to speak, into the reality of this world, and it erases something or writes something new in the most fundamental rules of our reality. It creates a new object that never existed previously.

The magicians of Egypt understood this. After observing unusual phenomena and identifying explanations for some of them, they encountered a phenomenon for which they had no explanation. They made their calculations, taking into account all the laws of nature and elements of reality, and it became clear to them that this was something new that was not acting in accordance with the rules. At that point, they said, "It is the finger of God" (Ex. 8:15). God had come into the mechanism, adding additional letters.

In a different way, this is also true regarding "the finger of God" that wrote on the tablets. Within the unfolding succession of reality, the progression of cause and effect, an object suddenly appeared from a different level. It did not go through the usual order of succession. No change or distortion had occurred in it, and it conveyed exactly what it was: an "act of the living God." As in a game, from the moment that this entity entered reality, it broke the rules and created new rules, and it was now at the center. Although it is physical and part of reality, it expresses, through its very existence, the transcendent reality, the divine being that is present in the worlds.

The place where the tablets are found, which on the one hand is part of the world, and on the other hand expresses the Divine, is the place that enclothes and reveals *Malkhut* of *Atzilut*. That is because *Malkhut* of *Atzilut* is the gateway from the world of *Atzilut* into the created worlds. Likewise, although the tablets are made of stone, they are "written with the finger of God."

וּבְבַיִת שֵׁנִי, שֶׁלֹּא הָיָה בּוֹ הָאָרוֹן וְהַלּוּחוֹת, אָמְרוּ רַבּוֹתֵינוּ ז"ל שֶׁלֹּא הָיְתָה שְׁכִינָה שׁוֹרָה בּוֹ.	In the Second Temple, which did not have the ark and the tablets, the Sages stated that the Divine Presence did not rest there	2 Sivan 4 Sivan (leap year)

The difference between the First and Second Temples did not relate to the Sanctuary itself, nor to the service that took place there. Rather, the difference lay in the unequivocal manifestation of the Divine Presence within the ark and the tablets that occurred solely in the First Temple (see *Yoma* 52b).

פֵּירוּשׁ, מַדְרֵגַת שְׁכִינָה שֶׁהָיְתָה שׁוֹרָה בְּבַיִת רִאשׁוֹן, שֶׁלֹּא כְּדֶרֶךְ הִשְׁתַּלְשְׁלוּת הָעוֹלָמוֹת.	**meaning,** it did not have **the same level of Divine Presence that had resided in the First Temple, which did not conform to the** sequential **succession of worlds.**

This does not mean that there was no revelation of the Divine Presence whatsoever in the Second Temple. However, the Divine Presence rested in the First Temple in a different way. The "unfolding succession of the worlds" refers to the causal way in which the worlds are structured and operate. In contrast to this, when the Torah was given, a light pierced the realities and rules of all the worlds. This illumination came from a higher level and broke through the "clouds" of worldly reality. It passed through each world, one after another, without stopping, changing, or becoming distorted, until it ultimately reached our world. The tablets in the First Temple were the reality and "testimony" that remained in our world of this illumination. However, the Second Temple did not have the ark or the tablets, and as a result the Divine Presence did not rest there in the same way.

אֶלָּא בְּבַיִת שֵׁנִי הָיְתָה שׁוֹרָה בְּדֶרֶךְ הִשְׁתַּלְשְׁלוּת וְהִתְלַבְּשׁוּת מַלְכוּת דַּאֲצִילוּת בְּמַלְכוּת דִּבְרִיאָה, וְדִבְרִיאָה בְּמַלְכוּת דִּיצִירָה, וְדִיצִירָה בְּהֵיכַל קָדְשֵׁי קָדָשִׁים דַּעֲשִׂיָּה, וְקָדְשֵׁי קָדָשִׁים דַּעֲשִׂיָּה הָיָה מִתְלַבֵּשׁ בְּקָדְשֵׁי קָדָשִׁים שֶׁבְּבֵית הַמִּקְדָּשׁ שֶׁלְּמַטָּה.

Rather, in the Second Temple, the Divine Presence **rested according to the sequential succession and enclothement of** *Malkhut* of *Atzilut* within *Malkhut* of *Beria*, and *Malkhut* of *Beria* within *Malkhut* of *Yetzira*, and *Malkhut* of *Yetzira* was invested **in the palace of the Holy of Holies of** *Asiya*, **and the Holy of Holies of** *Asiya* **was enclothed within the Holy of Holies of the Temple below.**

In the Second Temple, the Divine Presence rested in accordance with the unfolding succession of the worlds. *Malkhut* of *Atzilut* is the manifestation of the Divine Presence. It is enclothed in *Malkhut* of *Beria*. *Malkhut* of *Beria* is enclothed in *Malkhut* of *Yetzira*, and *Malkhut* of *Yetzira* is enclothed in the Palace of the Holy of Holies of *Asiya*, which refers to Ḥokhma, Bina, and Da'at (Wisdom, Understanding, and Knowledge) of the spiritual world of *Asiya*. The Holy of Holies of *Asiya* was enclothed[4] in the Holy of Holies in the Temple in our material world.

וְשָׁרְתָה בּוֹ הַשְּׁכִינָה, מַלְכוּת דִּיצִירָה הַמְלוּבֶּשֶׁת בְּקָדְשֵׁי קָדָשִׁים דַּעֲשִׂיָּה.

Thus, **the Divine Presence rested there** as *Malkhut* of *Yetzira* **enclothed within the Holy of Holies of** *Asiya*.

Consequently, the Divine Presence rested in the Second Temple in a manifest state, without the covering and garment of *Malkhut* of *Asiya*. As stated, the resting of the Divine Presence refers to the manifestation of the divine power that gives existence and life to a certain place, time, or soul. Thus, in the Second Temple too, as in the first, the Divine Presence rested within the Holy of Holies.

---

4. It was not enclothed by way of *Malkhut* of *Asiya*.

| וְלָכֵן לֹא הָיָה רַשַּׁאי שׁוּם אָדָם לִיכָּנֵס שָׁם, לְבַד כֹּהֵן גָּדוֹל בְּיוֹם הַכִּפּוּרִים. | **That is why no one was permitted to enter** the Holy of Holies **except for the High Priest on Yom Kippur.** |

In the Second Temple, the holiness and light of the Holy of Holies were not the same as in the First Temple. Nevertheless, the Holy of Holies was still a Holy of Holies, and it was treated with the same restrictions regarding holiness and separation. The difference is that in the First Temple, the illumination within the Holy of Holies was on a higher level. It was higher even than the illumination of holiness in the spiritual worlds of *Asiya* and *Yetzira*. Therefore, not only with regard to our world but also with regard to the higher worlds, the First Temple was deemed to be of especial holiness, and likewise it was seen as the resting place of the Divine Presence. In contrast, in the Second Temple, the holy illumination pertained to our world only. It was a "Holy of Holies" with regard to our world, although not with regard to the higher worlds. This is similar to the human brain. As stated above, the brain is the locus of a person's life, where all of his faculties are to be found. The illumination of life in a person's brain relates to his individual essence, and constitutes the core of his essence, before that essence is broken down and sent to the various body parts and faculties. This is the individual's "Holy of Holies." Sometimes, however, a person receives illumination of a higher realm. At that moment, his brain is not only the locus of his own existence, his own "Holy of Holies." Rather, it is a "Holy of Holies" that is at the center of higher and vaster realms that transcend the boundaries of his private world.

| וּמִשֶּׁחָרַב בֵּית הַמִּקְדָּשׁ אֵין לוֹ לְהַקָּדוֹשׁ בָּרוּךְ הוּא בְּעוֹלָמוֹ אֶלָּא ד' אַמּוֹת שֶׁל הֲלָכָה בִּלְבָד (ברכות ח, א). | **Since** the day **the** Second **Temple was destroyed, the only** place **the Holy One, Blessed be He, has in His world is the four cubits** within which the study **of** *halakha* is undertaken (*Berakhot* 8a). |

The Temple was the heart of the material world. There, the soul of the world shone in a revealed state, just as a person's soul shines in a revealed state within his brain. Once the Temple was destroyed, there was no longer a specific physical place for the revelation of the Divine

Presence. Four cubits is the measure of personal space as defined in *halakha* for various purposes, and it is therefore the measure that defines something as a space. "Four cubits of *halakha*" is thus metaphorically any place in the physical world where *halakha* applies. There, the word of God, which is the Divine Presence, is manifest. This is because *halakha* is the manifestation and essence of the word of God, which is the divine will and wisdom. It is the Divine Presence as it is revealed in the Torah. At present, the world's "Holy of Holies," the place where consciousness on our plane reaches its peak, is the "four cubits of *halakha*."

וַאֲפִילוּ אֶחָד שֶׁיּוֹשֵׁב וְעוֹסֵק בַּתּוֹרָה – שְׁכִינָה עִמּוֹ, כִּדְאִיתָא בְּבְרָכוֹת פֶּרֶק קַמָּא (פרק ראשון [ו, א]). Therefore, "even when just one person sits and engages in Torah study, the Divine Presence is with him," as taught in the first chapter of *Berakhot* (6a).

The resting of the Divine Presence in the four cubits of *halakha* does not depend on the presence of the Temple structure. It does not even require a quorum of ten Jews. All it requires is the study of, and engagement with, the *halakha* written in the Torah.

פֵּירוּשׁ 'שְׁכִינָה עִמּוֹ' This means that "the Divine Presence is with him"

We have already discussed the resting of the Divine Presence in the First Temple, in the ark and the tablets, and in the Second Temple. Now, we must clarify what is meant by the resting of the Divine Presence within the four cubits of *halakha*. On what level and in what way does that take place?

כְּדֶרֶךְ הִשְׁתַּלְשְׁלוּת וְהִתְלַבְּשׁוּת: מַלְכוּת דַּאֲצִילוּת בְּמַלְכוּת דִּבְרִיאָה וִיצִירָה וַעֲשִׂיָּה. according to the sequential succession and enclothement of *Malkhut* of *Atzilut* within *Malkhut* of *Beria* and subsequently within *Malkhut* of *Beria*, *Malkhut* of *Yetzira*, and *Malkhut* of *Asiya*.

The resting of the Divine Presence in the four cubits of *halakha* takes place through enclothement in *Malkhut* of *Asiya* (an enclothing that did not occur even in the Second Temple). The Divine Presence that rests with a person who engages in Torah study is therefore not the revelation of a higher world that occurs by means of a leap into our realm by a totally distinct essence, which is how the Divine Presence was revealed in the Temple. Rather, the Divine Presence is with the person, and its revelation and illumination pertain to this world with its particular scope and nature. In other words, the Divine Presence is enclothed within the rules, laws, and boundaries of our innately physical realm.

כִּי תַרְיַ"ג מִצְוֹת הַתּוֹרָה, רוּבָּן כְּכוּלָּן הֵן מִצְוֹת מַעֲשִׂיּוֹת. That is **because virtually all of the 613 mitzvot of the Torah are mitzvot** performed with physical **action.**

The 613 mitzvot are all the commandments contained in the Torah, both positive and negative. All are concerned with physical action and the realm of physical action.

וְגַם הַתְּלוּיוֹת בְּדִבּוּר וּמַחֲשָׁבָה, כְּמוֹ: תַּלְמוּד תּוֹרָה, וּבִרְכַּת הַמָּזוֹן, וּקְרִיאַת שְׁמַע, וּתְפִלָּה, הָא קַיְימָא לָן דְּהִרְהוּר לָאו כְּדִבּוּר דָּמֵי, וְאֵינוֹ יוֹצֵא יְדֵי חוֹבָתוֹ בְּהִרְהוּר וְכַוָּונָה לְבַד עַד שֶׁיּוֹצִיא בִּשְׂפָתָיו, **Even** regarding **the** mitzvot **contingent on speech and thought – such as** Torah study, Grace after Meals, reciting the *Shema*, and prayer – **we have an established** principle, **that contemplation** of the mitzva **is not tantamount to speech, and one does not fulfill his obligation** in these mitzvot **with contemplation and intent alone, but only when he pronounces** the words **with his lips.**

Some mitzvot are not performed with actions, but with speech and thought; one must say something, and understand, and feel what one says. Torah study is ostensibly a mitzva of comprehension, and the essence of prayer is a person's internal connection to God. Nevertheless, the obligation to carry out these mitzvot is not fulfilled through thought or intent alone.

וְקַיְימָא לָן דַּעֲקִימַת שְׂפָתָיו הֲוֵי מַעֲשֶׂה. **And we have an established** principle **that the moving of one's lips is** considered **an action.**

Speech, in which the words are expressed with the lips, is considered an action.[5] It is not as discernible as other actions, but it is still an action and it belongs in the physical realm of *Asiya*.

Essentially, the mitzvot in the Torah all involve action, and consequently they belong especially to the world of *Asiya*, and specifically to the realm of physical action.

וְתרי"ג מִצְוֹת הַתּוֹרָה עִם שֶׁבַע **The 613 mitzvot of the Torah** together
מִצְוֹת דְּרַבָּנָן בְּגִימַטְרִיָּא כֶּתֶר, **with the seven mitzvot** instituted **by the Rabbis have the numeric value of 620, which is equal to the numeric value of *Keter* (crown),**

It is generally agreed upon that there are 613 mitzvot in the Torah.[6] In addition, there are seven mitzvot that were established by the Sages. Added together, these make 620, which is the *gematriya* of the word *Keter*.[7] In addition to the elucidations, ordinances, and safeguards that the Sages appended to the mitzvot written in the Torah, they established these seven mitzvot, which are separate from the 613 Torah commandments.[8]

---

5. In keeping with the view of Rabbi Yoḥanan in *Bava Metzia* 90b (*Likkutei Hagahot LaTanya*).
6. See *Makkot* 23b.
7. See *Shenei Luḥot HaBerit, Torah Or* 34a.
8. These seven mitzvot are: 1) washing one's hands before eating bread; 2) *eiruv*; 3) reciting blessings; 4) lighting Sabbath candles, 5) reading the *megilla* (the book of Esther) on Purim; 6) the festival of Hanukkah; and 7) reciting *Hallel*. The book *Mitzvot Hashem* (by Rabbi Yonatan Steif) explains that these rabbinic commandments are listed in the group of seven and not others because, although they do not derive from the Torah, the Sages ruled that one must recite a blessing on them. *Torah Or* and *Likkutei Torah* (Ex. 6d) state that these are specifically active mitzvot. The *Sefer Mitzvot Gadol* lists only five rabbinic mitzvot, and *Sha'arei Kedusha* lists several others. It may be said, however, that these two books also hold that there are seven rabbinic mitzvot, but that the object of these two books is not to count the rabbinic mitzvot, but to teach and explain the Sages' ordinances. When these seven mitzvot are added to the 613 Torah commandments, the result is 620, corresponding to 620 "pillars of light" (from the comment of the Lubavitcher Rebbe, Rabbi Menaḥem Mendel Schneerson, on *Sefer HaMa'amarim* 5708).

שֶׁהוּא רָצוֹן הָעֶלְיוֹן בָּרוּךְ הוּא which is God's supernal will

The number 620 alludes to the *sefira* of *Keter*, which corresponds to God's supernal will, just as the *sefira* of Ḥokhma is His wisdom, and so forth. A physical crown that is placed on a person's head is external to the person and encircles his physical being. Likewise, God's supernal will appearing in each person is separate from the person and encompasses his spiritual being: his mind and attributes. It does not come from his inner faculties. The supernal will is not the will that comes from the intellect, when a person wants what he intellectually understands he should want. Rather, he directly comprehends what it is that he really should want. The mitzvot express God's primary, supernal will: what He wants of His world and what He wants to happen in the world. Therefore, the term that encompasses all the mitzvot, both those that are written in the Torah and those that are rabbinic, is *Keter*.

הַמְלוּבָּשׁ בְּחָכְמָתוֹ יִתְבָּרֵךְ, enclothed in His wisdom,

God's primary, supernal will is revealed within our world when that will is enclothed in His wisdom. We know His will, what He desires and how He desires it, because it is enclothed in a comprehensible way in the Written and Oral Torah, which stem from His supernal wisdom.

הַמְיוּחָדוֹת בָּאוֹר אֵין סוֹף בָּרוּךְ הוּא בְּתַכְלִית הַיִּחוּד. both unified in the light of *Ein Sof*, blessed be He, in an absolute union.

God's will and wisdom are totally unified in the light of *Ein Sof*. As stated earlier, wisdom is totally subsumed in the divine light. Thus the light of the wisdom within the Torah is essentially the light of *Ein Sof* Himself. It is the light of the indefinable, limitless, supernal essence that penetrates our world.

וְ"ה' בְּחָכְמָה יָסַד אָרֶץ" (משלי ג, יט), הִיא תּוֹרָה שֶׁבְּעַל פֶּה דְּנָפְקָא מֵחָכְמָה עִילָּאָה, The verse states, "**The Lord founded the earth with wisdom**" (Proverbs 3:19), in which "earth" **refers to the Oral Torah, which emerged from supernal Ḥokhma,**

The above does not refer only to the Written Torah, but also to the Oral Torah. The verse mentioned here reflects the special connection, which is expressed in several ways, between wisdom and the earth, between the *sefira* of Ḥokhma and the *sefira* of Malkhut. The earth symbolizes the Divine Presence, the aspect of divine speech, which is the Oral Torah. The Oral Torah signifies the spoken word: the expression of the Torah and of divine wisdom in the world of action. The Oral Torah applies the Written Torah, which is abstract and general, to the details of worldly reality. This physical realization of the Torah in the world is directly and uniquely linked to supernal Ḥokhma.

כְּמוֹ שֶׁכָּתוּב בַּזֹּהַר (חלק ג רנו, ב): דְּאַבָּא יָסַד בְּרַתָּא. as the *Zohar* (3:256b) states: "The father founded the daughter."

This is another expression of the connection between Ḥokhma and Malkhut. The *Zohar* compares this connection to the special bond that exists between a father and a daughter. Ḥokhma is like the "father," and the earth, which is the aspect of Malkhut, is like the "daughter." As applied here, there is a special connection between the Oral Torah, which is expressed through physical speech with one's mouth, which is like the "daughter," and the supernal source of the Torah in supernal Ḥokhma, which is like the "father." Accordingly, the initial source of divine Ḥokhma reveals itself on earth within the Oral Torah.

Thus, the four cubits of *halakha* are where God reveals His supernal will within the reality of this lower realm. This revelation occurred in the Holy of Holies in the First Temple, on a level far beyond that of the worlds. Subsequently, it also appeared, to a lesser degree, in the Second Temple. And since the destruction of the Second Temple, it is manifest in the only "place" in this world where divine holiness is found with no distortions or constrictions, the place where the Torah (Ḥokhma) reveals itself on earth: within the four cubits of *halakha*.

3 Sivan
5 Sivan (leap year)

וְזֶה שֶׁאָמַר הַיָּנוּקָא: דִּנְהוֹרָא עִילָּאָה דְּאַדְלִיק עַל רֵישֵׁיהּ, הִיא שְׁכִינְתָּא, אִצְטְרִיךְ לְמִשְׁחָא (זוהר ח"ג, קפז, א).

This explains **what the child said:** that "**the supernal light kindled upon** the Jew's **head,** namely, **the Divine Presence, requires oil**" (*Zohar* 3:187a)

Here, the author of the *Tanya* returns to the explanation that he began in chapter 51 regarding that which is written in chapter 35. The quote from the *Zohar* cited here continues, "That is because a person's body is the wick, and the light shines upward. [Concerning this], King Solomon cried out, saying, 'May the oil on your head not be lacking' (Eccles. 9:8), because the light upon [a person's] head requires oil – namely, good deeds." The human being is the lamp of God, which shines God's light onto the world. As it is written, "The spirit of man is the lamp of the Lord" (Prov. 20:27). The body and the vital soul are the wick, and the flame is the light of the Divine Presence, which is the light of the person's divine soul. Thus there is a wick and a flame. However, oil is also necessary so that the wick is not burned up and the light can continue to shine.

פֵּירוּשׁ, לְהִתְלַבֵּשׁ בְּחָכְמָה הַנִּקְרֵאת "שֶׁמֶן מִשְׁחַת קֹדֶשׁ" (שמות ל, כה), כְּמוֹ שֶׁכָּתוּב בַּזֹּהַר.

meaning, oil alludes to **being enclothed in wisdom, which is** referred to by the *Zohar* (3:34) **as "oil of sacred anointment"** (Ex. 30:25).

Oil is the symbol of wisdom.

וְאִינּוּן עוֹבְדִין טָבִין הֵן תַּרְיַ"ג מִצְוֹת, הַנִּמְשָׁכוֹת מֵחָכְמָתוֹ יִתְבָּרֵךְ

This oil is identified by the child as "good deeds," the 613 mitzvot, which are derived from God's wisdom

Good deeds are the expression of supernal Ḥokhma, the "oil," in a person's life and actions. True good deeds are the mitzvot. The mitzvot are derived from the supernal Ḥokhma of the world of *Atzilut*, which is entirely subsumed in the Divine.

כְּדֵי לֶאֱחוֹז אוֹר הַשְּׁכִינָה בַּפְּתִילָה, הִיא נֶפֶשׁ הַחִיּוּנִית שֶׁבַּגּוּף, הַנִּקְרֵאת פְּתִילָה עַל דֶּרֶךְ מָשָׁל.

in order to enable the light of the Divine Presence to cling to the wick, which symbolizes **the vital soul within the body.** The vital soul **is figuratively referred to as a wick.**

The oil of "the spirit of man, [which] is the lamp of the Lord," enables the light of the Divine Presence to cling to the wick. The wick is the vital soul within the body.

כִּי כְּמוֹ שֶׁבְּנֵר הַגַּשְׁמִי הָאוֹר מֵאִיר עַל יְדֵי כִּלְיוֹן וּשְׂרֵיפַת הַפְּתִילָה, הַנֶּהְפֶּכֶת לָאֵשׁ, כָּךְ אוֹר הַשְּׁכִינָה שׁוֹרָה עַל נֶפֶשׁ הָאֱלֹהִית עַל יְדֵי כִּלְיוֹן נֶפֶשׁ הַבַּהֲמִית,

That is because, **just as the light of a physical candle shines via the consumption and combustion of the wick, which is transformed into fire, so too the light of the Divine Presence rests on the divine soul through the consumption of the animal soul,**

For a physical lamp to emit light, something must burn: the wick. Likewise, for the divine soul to shine, the animal soul, which is the person's essence as a physical entity, must burn. This refers to the destruction of a person's connection to, and desire for, physical matters.

וְהִתְהַפְּכוּתָהּ מֵחֲשׁוֹכָא לִנְהוֹרָא וּמִמְּרִירוּ לְמִתְקָא,

and through **its transformation from darkness to light and from bitterness to sweetness.**

Of course, we cannot, nor do we want to, completely annihilate the animal soul, for it is what sustains our existence as human beings, as a soul within a body. Rather, this is referring to the destruction of the aspect of the animal soul that conceals the Divine. The vital soul, which sustains a person's physical side, conceals and darkens the divine light. By concealing the meaning and inner essence of life, it expresses life's bitter and difficult aspects. Thus the desired destruction of the vital soul, or animal soul, occurs not through annihilation, but via the transformation of the veil of darkness into light, and the transformation of bitterness into the sweetness that is present in the essence of all things.

בַּצַּדִּיקִים, This is what occurs in the **righteous**

As was stated at the beginning of the *Tanya* (see chaps. 10–12), the essential transformation of the nature of the animal soul from darkness to light and from bitterness to sweetness is the work of the tzaddik.

Only the tzaddik, as he is defined by the author of the *Tanya*, can accomplish this fundamental transformation of matter and of the vital soul. Even though the vital soul remains an animal soul, its desires and urges are completely changed. It no longer desires physical objects per se. Rather, all it yearns for is holiness.

| אוֹ לְפָחוֹת עַל יְדֵי כִּלָּיוֹן לְבוּשֶׁיהָ, שֶׁהֵן: מַחֲשָׁבָה דִּבּוּר וּמַעֲשֶׂה, וְהִתְהַפְּכוּתָן מֵחֹשֶׁךְ הַקְּלִיפּוֹת לְאוֹר ה' אֵין סוֹף בָּרוּךְ הוּא, | **or at least through the consumption of the garments** of the animal soul, **which are thought, speech, and action, and their transformation from the darkness of the** *kelippot* **into the light of God,** *Ein Sof,* **blessed be He,** |

Someone who is not a tzaddik but is on the level of a *beinoni*, a person who cannot change the essence of his animal soul, can with hard work reach a point where his actual life is a life of holiness. A person's actual way of living affects his soul's garments, and the work of the *beinoni* is, at the very least, to destroy these garments. When the *beinoni* destroys the animal soul's garments in all their forms of expression, and he instead reveals only his divine soul and enclothes it in his thought, speech, and action, he takes his life as he is living it out of the realm of the *kelippa* and transforms it into holiness. The animal soul of the *beinoni* does not change its essence. However, when it is engaged only in matters of divine service, whether directly or indirectly, its garments of thought, speech, and action are eliminated and consumed. While it is true that the *beinoni* acts only on the manifestations of his animal soul, in this case his animal soul is fundamentally no longer the same as it had been previously. Its external part has been consumed, and it transforms the darkness of the *kelippot* into the light of God. The difference between the tzaddik and the *beinoni* is that in the case of the tzaddik, there is a complete reversal of the soul's inner essence, while for the *beinoni* only the soul's external manifestations experience reversal.

| הַמְלוּבָּשׁ וּמְיוּחָד בְּמַחֲשָׁבָה דִּבּוּר וּמַעֲשֶׂה שֶׁל תרי"ג מִצְוֹת הַתּוֹרָה בַּבֵּינוֹנִים. | **which is enclothed in and united with the thought, speech, and actions of the 613 mitzvot of the Torah. This is what occurs in the** *beinoni.* |

When the *beinoni* fulfills the Torah and the mitzvot, he can "burn" the animal soul's garments even when the animal soul itself is not burned. He can bring about their transformation from darkness to the light of the Infinite One, even when the essence of the animal soul itself is unchanged. That is because the light of the Infinite One is enclothed in and united with the thought, speech, and action of the 613 mitzvot of the Torah. That is what occurs in the *beinoni*. The *beinoni* can change his behavior and "burn" all the thoughts, speech, and actions that are not performed for God. Instead, he can turn them into thoughts, speech, and actions in which God Himself is enclothed and with which He is united. Through the *beinoni's* destruction of the animal soul's garments and his fulfillment of the 613 mitzvot in thought, speech, and action, the light of the Divine Presence rests upon him and holds fast in him. As the verse states, "The spirit of man is the lamp of the Lord."

כִּי עַל יְדֵי הִתְהַפְּכוּת נֶפֶשׁ הַבַּהֲמִית, הַבָּאָה מִקְּלִיפַּת נוֹגַהּ מֵחֲשׁוֹכָא לִנְהוֹרָא וכו׳, That is **because through the transformation of the animal soul, which stems from the *kelippat noga* (glowing husk), from darkness to light and so forth,**

As explained previously, the animal soul within a Jew is affiliated with *kelippat noga*, which is defined as the dimension of the mundane, the realm between holiness and *kelippa*. As long as nothing is done to elevate the animal soul, it belongs to the *kelippa*, which dims and conceals light. However, when a person performs one of the 613 Torah commandments with his animal soul through his thought, speech, or action, the animal soul is transformed from darkness to light. This does not require the transformation of the animal soul's inner essence, because even on its deepest, most essential level, it is not utterly evil. When the animal soul expresses itself with holiness, when it acts with holiness, it reveals its inner essence as purely holiness. Thereafter, it no longer dims the divine being within itself but rather shines the divine being upon the world.

נַעֲשֶׂה בְּחִינַת הַעֲלָאַת ׳מַיִין נוּקְבִין׳, **the elevation of the *mayim nukvin* is brought about,**

The elevation of the *kelippa*, at least of a person's own *kelippa*, from below toward the source of all holiness, constitutes the elevation of *mayim nukvin*. *Mayim nukvin* is water that does not flow downward like physical water, which descends from above and bestows life below. *Mayim nukvin* already exists below. It is hidden deep within the earth, within materiality and physical reality. *Mayim nukvin* can, however, ascend – not alone, but by means of a human being and his thoughts, speech, and actions. When this water emerges from the earth and rises, it causes a corresponding awakening above and an even stronger drawing down of holy light (referred to as *mayim dukhrin*).

לְהַמְשִׁיךְ אוֹר הַשְּׁכִינָה, הִיא בְּחִינַת גִּילוּי אוֹר אֵין סוֹף בָּרוּךְ הוּא, עַל נַפְשׁוֹ הָאֱלֹהִית שֶׁבַּמּוֹחִין שֶׁבְּרֹאשׁוֹ. — engendering the flow of the Divine Presence's light, which represents the manifestation of the light of *Ein Sof*, blessed be He, on the person's **divine soul in the brain in his head.**

The supernal light of holiness, the light of the Divine Presence, is impelled to rest upon a person from above as a result of the elevation of the *mayim nukvin*, the burning of the concealing *kelippa*, the awakening of holiness from below. The soul that receives this illumination of supernal holiness is the divine soul, which dwells (as was explained in chapter 9) in the individual's brain. From there, it extends to his whole being, which is completely transformed into "the spirit of man, [which] is the lamp of the Lord."

The author of the *Tanya* has thus explained the statement of the child in the *Zohar* regarding "the supernal light kindled upon his head." In order to shine, this light, the light of the Divine Presence upon one's head, requires oil. That oil refers to good deeds, the mitzvot that a person performs in the lower world with his body and his animal soul. With that, the individual transforms the darkness of *kelippat noga* into light. This means that he burns and destroys the aspect of *kelippa* and darkness that was previously manifest in his body and his animal soul, and he illuminates the aspect of holiness that was concealed in them.

וּבָזֶה יוּבָן הֵיטֵב מַה שֶּׁכָּתוּב: "כִּי ה' אֱלֹהֶיךָ אֵשׁ אוֹכְלָה הוּא" (דברים ד, כד), וּכְמוֹ שֶׁנִּתְבָּאֵר בְּמָקוֹם אַחֵר.

This explanation **enables a clear understanding of the verse, "For the Lord your God is a consuming fire"** (Deut. 4:24), **and as explained elsewhere.**

"The Lord your God" is like "a consuming fire,"[9] which must perpetually consume something in order to exist. Thus, for God to be "your God," something within you needs to be burnt. In other words, the process of connecting to God within our reality is like the process of burning, of fire consuming and destroying the substance and exterior of a being in the midst of a process of a deep connection with it.

This chapter, the last in *Likkutei Amarim*, concludes with a discussion of the manifestation of the Divine Presence in the physical world. There are various levels to this. The highest level was the resting of the Divine Presence within the Holy of Holies in the First Temple. Next, in a more limited way, it rested in the Holy of Holies in the Second Temple. The third level is that of the present day, when all God has on earth is the four cubits of *halakha*. As was explained, "The Lord founded the earth with wisdom." Supernal wisdom is the source of the Torah, which is unified with God. The "earth" is the Oral Torah, the *halakha*. This is the Torah that is revealed and that receives a physical form within the space of four cubits on this earth. Accordingly, whenever a person learns Torah, the Divine Presence is with him. That person brings the Divine Presence to his place. The meaning of the statement in the *Zohar* is now clear. There, the child states that the light that shines on a person's head, that being the manifestation of the Divine Presence, requires oil. The human being is like God's lamp. When the lamp is burning, it radiates God's light and reveals the Divine Presence. However, in order to burn, it needs oil and a wick. The wick is the person's vital, animal soul, while the oil refers to his good deeds, his performance of the mitzvot, which are drawn from supernal wisdom (which too is called "oil").

---

9. The author of the *Tanya* states that the explanation of this verse is discussed elsewhere. He may be referring to *Likkutei Torah*, Lev. 25c (the Lubavitcher Rebbe, Rabbi Menaḥem Mendel Schneerson).

In order for the fire to take hold and for the oil to be burned as in a lamp, the wick must be consumed. The verse states, "The Lord your God is a consuming fire." So that the Divine Presence may rest within us and so that we may maintain a connection with "the Lord your God," we must continually supply a flammable substance that is consumed in God's light. Here the author of the Tanya returns to the *beinoni*. The substance that is ablaze, the "wick" that grips the fire, is the *beinoni*'s vital animal soul, which desires other things. When the *beinoni* burns and consumes his animal soul, he ignites the light of the Divine Presence within it and within the entire world.

נִשְׁלַם חֵלֶק רִאשׁוֹן בְּעֶזְרַת ה' יִתְבָּרֵךְ וְיִתְעַלֶּה. **This concludes the first section of** *Tanya,* **with God's help, may He be blessed and exalted.**

Afterword

The first section of the *Tanya*, which the author calls *Sefer shel Beinonim*, dealt mainly with the person who is a *beinoni*, an earthly human being. The second section, *Sha'ar HaYiḥud VeHa'emuna*, deals with reality from the perspective of the Divine. It discusses the divine oneness expressed in the phrase "There is no other besides Him," and the essential nature of the worlds, which are purely the word of God. The word of God speaks the world into existence. In addition, it speaks to the world so that the world will respond. The first section of the *Tanya* dealt with this response. Who is the one that responds? The world cannot respond, because it itself is part of the divine speech. Likewise, the creatures within the world cannot respond, because they too are an inherent part of the world and are part of the divine speech. The only one who can respond is the human being, the creature known as "the speaker." The human being's divine soul is so lofty that it is near to God, yet the human being is so far away, so concealed within the darkness of the body and the animal soul, that he cannot see the divine light and he cannot hear the speech that creates the world around him. He is the one who can respond to the divine speech. The individual who answers, who speaks from within the reality of his life in this world, is the *beinoni* described in the *Tanya*.

Summary of Chapters

Two Souls

> **Chapter 1**   There are two souls. The first is the animal soul, which originates from *kelippa*.

The Divine Soul

> **Chapter 2**   The other is the divine soul, which is actually a portion of God on high.
>
> **Chapter 3**   The divine soul possesses ten faculties, which are divided into two general categories: cognitive and emotive.
>
> **Chapter 4**   The garments of the divine soul are thought, speech, and action.
>
> **Chapter 5**   Torah is the sustenance of the divine soul.

The Animal Soul

> **Chapter 6**   The animal soul, its faculties, and its garments stem from *kelippa*.
>
> **Chapter 7**   There are two levels of kelippa: the three utterly impure *kelippot* and *kelippat noga*, the "luminescent husk," in which some good is mixed.
>
> **Chapter 8**   Some things are prohibited, some are permitted, and some fall into the category of permissible, depending on the intent, for example, idle chatter or studying non-Torah subjects.

The Battle

> **Chapter 9**   The two souls wage war against each other for control over the body.

The Righteous

Chapter 10 Good prevails in the righteous; some possess a vestige of evil, while others possess no trace of evil at all.

The Wicked

Chapter 11 Evil prevails in the wicked; some possess a vestige of good, while others possess no trace of good at all.

The *Beinoni*

Chapter 12 Good always prevails in the *beinoni*, but only within the soul's garments, not its faculties.

Chapter 13 The good inclination and the evil inclination are like judges within the *beinoni*, and the verdict always rendered in support of the good inclination.

Chapter 14 Every individual has the ability to attain the rank of *beinoni*.

The Divine Service of the *Beinoni*

Chapter 15 There are two levels in the category of *beinoni*: one who serves God and one who does not.

Chapter 16 The *beinoni* serves God by contemplating God's greatness and engendering love of God within himself. Alternatively, he serves God through the innate, concealed love within him.

Chapter 17 This type of divine service is accessible to all: Every individual is able to contemplate God's greatness and evoke a love that at the very least moves him to perform His will.

The Concealed Love

Chapter 18 One may serve God through the love that is concealed within the heart of the collective of Israel.

Chapter 19 This love constitutes the innate desire to cling to God and to avoid being parted from Him at all costs, even if it requires the ultimate self-sacrifice.

God's Unity and Oneness

Chapter 20 Divine service engendered by the concealed love is based on a grasp of God's unity: There is no other besides Him.

Chapter 21 God's speech and thoughts are united with Him, much like a person's speech and thoughts before they are articulated, while they are still unformed in his faculty of wisdom.

Chapter 22 The *kelippot* and the *sitra aḥara* were created through concealment. They receive their life force from the "back side," and they are not nullified in the face of the Divine.

Chapter 23 God's unity is revealed through Torah and mitzvot, which are truly unified with the Divine, even in this world.

Chapter 24 Conversely, when a person violates a prohibition, he is separated from God's unity.

Chapter 25 A person's concealed love prevents him from committing transgressions, even at the cost of sacrificing his life.

Eradicating Sadness

Chapter 26 Divine battles cannot be won through sadness. Consequently, one must eradicate it from his house.

Chapter 27 If sadness is the result of evil thoughts and lusts, one must force himself not to dwell on them.

Chapter 28 Sadness may also result from experiencing foreign thoughts during prayer.

Eradicating Dullness of the Heart

Chapter 29 One should humble himself to counteract dullness of the heart.

Chapter 30 One should be of humble spirit in the presence of all people.

Joy

Chapter 31 True joy will follow bitterness and regret over one's sins and authentic humility.

Love of One's Fellow Jew

Chapter 32 One should evoke love of his fellow Jew as one loves himself

Returning to Joy

Chapter 33 Faith in God's unity brings joy.

Chapter 34 One who transforms himself into a sanctuary for the Divine Presence experiences joy.

Action

Chapter 35 The Divine Presence rests where mitzvot are performed.

Chapter 36 God desires a dwelling place in the lower realms.

Chapter 37 The future redemption and the subsequent divine revelation depend on our actions during the exile.

Intent

Chapter 38 A prayer or blessing uttered without intent is like a body without a soul.

Chapter 39 Serving God with intent has an impact on the realms of *Yetzira, Beria,* and *Atzilut.*

Chapter 40 Torah and mitzvot ascend beyond this world on the wings of intent, which stems from love and fear.

The Ways of Divine Service

Chapter 41 The first stage of divine service is fear of God, which is referred to as the work of a servant. Everyone must be both a servant and a child of God.

Chapter 42 Lower fear is the bedrock of divine service that every Jew must evoke within himself in order to advance to higher levels.

Chapter 43 There are two levels of fear of God: lower fear and higher fear. Likewise, there are two levels of love of God: world-centered love and great love.

Chapter 44 There are two types of love that pertain to the level of great love: the love of a soul for the Divine, for its own essence, and the love of a child for his father.

Chapter 45 The third aspect of divine service is the attribute of compassion.

Chapter 46 One can awaken love of God within himself through the principle of "as water reflects a face to the face": By contemplating God's love for him, he will naturally feel a love for God.

Chapter 47 One should also contemplate the exodus from Egypt, which revealed God's love for us.

Chapter 48 One should likewise contemplate God's infinite greatness, which is embodied in the fact that He constricted His light, which permeates all the worlds.

Chapter 49 When contemplating this phenomenon, a person constricts himself, in turn, renouncing all worldly matters for the sake of God.

Chapter 50 There is another level of love that is superior to all the other levels, just as gold is superior to silver: love that is like sparks of fire.

The Indwelling of the Divine Presence

Chapter 51 The indwelling of the Divine Presence can be compared to the relationship between the soul and the body: The soul is enclothed in the brain, and from there it extends to the whole body.

Chapter 52 The Divine Presence is enclothed in God's will and wisdom, and the Torah and its commandments serve as the vessels for that will and wisdom in this world.

Chapter 53 The Divine Presence rested in the Holy Temple constituting the highest revelation of the Divine in this world.

Glossary

Adnut Literally, "mastery," referring to the divine name *Adonai*, which connotes God's mastery over the universe

aggadot The nonlegalistic teachings of the Midrash and Talmud, often containing maxims, anecdotes, and parables

alef First letter of the Hebrew alphabet

Amida Silent prayer recited three times daily

Arizal Rabbi Yitzhak Luria of Tzefat (1534–1572), the most influential kabbalist of modern times

Asiya The world of Action, the fourth and lowest of the spiritual worlds

Atzilut The world of Emanation, the highest of the four spiritual worlds and closest to the source of creation

ayin Nothingness; the sixteenth letter of the Hebrew alphabet

Ba'al Shem Tov Rabbi Yisrael ben Eliezer (1698–1760), founder of the hasidic movement

beinoni (pl. beinonim) Literally, "intermediate"; a person who is on a level where he is neither wicked nor righteous

Beria The world of Creation, the second of the four spiritual worlds

bet The second letter of the Hebrew alphabet

Bina Understanding, one of the ten divine attributes known as *sefirot*

Chabad An acronym of the three cognitive attributes, *Hokhma, Bina,* and *Da'at*; the name attributed to Lubavitch Hasidism, founded by Rabbi Shneur Zalman of Liadi

Da'at Knowledge, one of the ten divine attributes known as *sefirot*

dalet The fourth letter of the Hebrew alphabet

Ein Sof God's infinite being

Elokim The name of God that embodies the attribute of judgment

emuna Faith

etrog Citron, one of the four species waved on the festival of Sukkot

gematriya (pl. gematriyot) A method of interpretation employed by assigning numerical values to the letters of the Hebrew alphabet

Gevura Restraint, one of the ten divine attributes known as *sefirot*

gimmel The third letter of the Hebrew alphabet

halakha (pl. halakhot) Jewish law

hasid Literally, "pious individual"; a follower of Hasidism, the movement initiated by the Ba'al Shem Tov

Havaya A reference to the four-letter name of God known as the Tetragrammaton

haya The second highest of the five soul levels

hayot Angelic creatures that appear in Ezekiel's mystical vision

heh The fifth letter of the Hebrew alphabet

Hesed Kindness, one of the ten divine attributes known as *sefirot*

het The eighth letter of the Hebrew alphabet

Hod Splendor, one of the ten divine attributes known as *sefirot*

Hokhma Wisdom, one of the ten divine attributes known as *sefirot*

Kabbala The mystical teachings of the Torah

karet The punishment of premature death and excision from the World to Come

kelippa (pl. kelippot) Literally, "husk"; the aspect of the universe that is unholy and conceals the Divine

kelippat noga Literally, "glowing husk"; a form of *kelippa* that contains an element of goodness that can be elevated

Keter Crown, one of the ten divine attributes known as *sefirot*

lamed The twelfth letter of the Hebrew alphabet

Malkhut Kingship, one of the ten divine attributes known as *sefirot*

mem The thirteenth letter of the Hebrew alphabet

Mishna A concise summary of the teachings of the Sages on all topics of the Torah, which was redacted in the beginning of the third century CE by Rabbi Yehuda HaNasi

mitzva (pl. mitzvot) A Torah commandment

mohin Literally "brains"; the *sefirot* corresponding to the cognitive faculties

Ne'ila The concluding prayer service of Yom Kippur

nefesh The soul; specifically, the lowest of the five levels of the soul

neshama The soul; specifically, the third of the five soul levels

Netzaḥ Dominance, one of the ten divine attributes known as *sefirot*
parasha (pl. parashot) Torah portion
peh The seventeenth letter of the Hebrew alphabet
resh The twentieth letter of the Hebrew alphabet
ruaḥ Second of the five soul levels
samekh The fifteenth letter of the Hebrew alphabet
Seder Ceremonial meal held on the first or the first and second nights of Passover commemorating the exodus from Egypt
sefira (pl. sefirot) One of the ten divine attributes with which God creates, sustains, and directs the worlds
Shema Prayer recited three times daily in which one declares one's faith in the oneness of God
Shemoneh Esrei prayer The main part of the daily prayer service, recited three times every weekday
shofar Ram's horn sounded on the festival of Rosh HaShana
sitra aḥara Literally, "the other side"; a general term for evil, including all aspects of the universe that counter the Divine
sukka Hut or shelter with a roof of branches and leaves used as a temporary residence during the festival of Sukkot
tallit Prayer shawl
Tanakh An acronym for *Torah, Nevi'im, Ketuvim* (Torah, Prophets, Writings), comprising the twenty-four books of the Scriptures
tefillin Leather boxes worn on the arm and forehead containing certain biblical passages that declare the unity of God and the miracles of the exodus from Egypt
teshuva Repentance
tzaddik (pl. tzaddikim) Righteous individual; a person born with the extraordinary ability and brilliance to perceive God
tzimtzum Literally, "constriction"; the concealment of the Divine to allow for the existence of the worlds
tzitzit Strings that are affixed to four-cornered garments
vav The sixth letter of the Hebrew alphabet
yeḥida The highest of the five soul levels
yesh Existence, substance, entity
Yesod Foundation, one of the ten divine attributes known as *sefirot*
Yetzira The world of Formation, the second of the four spiritual worlds
yod The tenth letter of the Hebrew alphabet

Works Cited in This Volume

Agra DeKhala Teachings on the weekly Torah portion by Rabbi Tzvi Elimelekh of Dinov (1783–1841), author of the famous work *Benei Yissaskhar*

Amud Ha'Avoda Hasidic work by Rabbi Barukh of Kosov (d. 1782)

Asara Ma'amarot Kabbalistic work by Rabbi Menaḥem Azaria of Fano

Avaneha Barzel Stories and insights from Rabbi Naḥman of Breslov and his disciple, Rabbi Natan of Nemirov. written by Rabbi Avraham Ḥazan

Ba'al Halakhot Gedolot A halakhic work dating back to the geonic period, ascribed to Rav Shimon Kayyara

Ba'al Shem Tov al HaTorah A compendium of teachings on the Torah and the festivals by the founder of the hasidic movement, anthologized by Shimon Menaḥem Mendel Vodnik

Beit Rebbe Biography of the author of the *Tanya*, Rabbi Shneur Zalman of Liadi (1745–1812), and his successors by Chaim Meir Heilman

Biur al HaTanya Commentary on the *Tanya* by Rabbi Shmuel Gronem Esterman

Biurim al HaTanya Commentary on the *Tanya* by Rabbi Yaakov Bachrach of Kidan

Degel Maḥaneh Efrayim A work of hasidic teachings on the Torah by Rabbi Moshe Ḥayyim Efrayim of Sudilkov (c. 1737–1800)

Derekh Mitzvotekha Hasidic discourses on the esoteric meaning of the mitzvot by the third Lubavitcher Rebbe, Rabbi Menaḥem Mendel Schneerson (1789–1866), also known as the Tzemaḥ Tzedek

Divrei Sofrim A work of hasidic teachings and insights by Rabbi Tzadok HaKohen Rabinowitz of Lublin (1823–1900)

Ein Yaakov A sixteenth-century compilation of all aggadic material in the Talmud together with commentaries

Eser Tzaḥtzaḥot A collection of teachings, practices, and tales of the early hasidim

Etz Ḥayyim The fundamental work of the Arizal's Kabbala, compiled by his disciple, Rabbi Ḥayyim Vital

Gevurot Hashem Commentary on the exodus from Egypt and the Passover Haggada by Rabbi Judah Loew, the Maharal of Prague (c. 1520–1609)

Guide of the Perplexed Classic work of Jewish philosophy by Rambam (1138–1204)

Hagahot LeDibbur HaMathil Pataḥ Eliyahu Comments of the fifth Lubavitcher Rebbe, Rabbi Shalom Dovber Schneerson (1860–1920), on *Pataḥ Eliyahu*, a section of *Torah Or*, by the author of the *Tanya*

HaKuzari Classic work of Jewish thought by Rabbi Yehuda HaLevi

HaLekaḥ VeHalibbuv A commentary on the *Tanya* by Rabbi Alexander Sender Yudeson (d. 1982)

HaMa'asar HaRishon An account of the incarceration of the author of the *Tanya* by Rabbi Yehoshua Mondshein

HaMasa HaAḥaron An account of the author of the *Tanya*'s last journey and death during the Napoleonic war

HaTomim A periodical published in Warsaw between 1935 and 1937 by the association of students of the Chabad yeshiva network

HaYom Yom An anthology of hasidic aphorisms and customs arranged according to the days of the year, compiled by Rabbi Menaḥem Mendel Schneerson, the Lubavitcher Rebbe (1902–1994)

Hemshekh Mayim Rabbim A compilation of hasidic discourses by the fourth Lubavitcher Rebbe, Rabbi Shmuel Schneerson, all of which were taught as a continuation of a specific discussion in 1875

Hemshekh Samekh Vav A compilation of hasidic discourses by the fifth Lubavitcher Rebbe, Rabbi Shalom Dovber Schneerson, all of which were taught between 1905 and 1908

Ḥiddushei Aggadot Commentary on the aggadic portions of the Talmud by the Maharsha, Rabbi Shmuel Eliezer Eidels

Idra Rabba A section of the *Zohar* on *Parashat Naso*, in which kabbalistic mysteries that Rabbi Shimon bar Yoḥai revealed to nine of his students are transcribed

WORKS CITED IN THIS VOLUME 745

Iggeret HaKodesh The fourth section of the *Tanya* containing the compiled epistles of Rabbi Shneur Zalman of Liadi to his disciples
Iggeret HaTeshuva The third section of the *Tanya*
Iggerot Kodesh A comprehensive collection of correspondence written by the rebbes of Chabad
Kedushat Levi A classic hasidic work on the Torah by Rabbi Levi Yitzḥak of Berditchev (1740–1810)
Keter Shem Tov Collection of teachings of the Ba'al Shem Tov (c. 1698–1760), compiled from the works of his disciples, by Rabbi Aharon HaKohen
Kisse Melekh Commentary on the *Zohar* and *Tikkunei Zohar* by Rabbi Shalom Buzaglo
Kitvei HaMaggid MiDubno The collected writings of the Maggid of Dubno, Rabbi Yaakov Krantz, compiled by Eliezer Steinman
Kitzurim U'Biurim LeSefer HaTanya A condensed version of the *Tanya* with commentaries
Kitzurim VeHe'arot LeSefer Likkutei Amarim Pamphlet containing the letters of the Tzemaḥ Tzedek, the third Lubavitcher Rebbe, pertaining to the *Tanya*
Kol Sippurei Rabbi Naḥman MiBreslov The complete collection of the tales of Rabbi Naḥman of Breslov in chronological order, edited by Tzvi Mark and Dov Elboim
Kuntres Aharon The fifth and final section of the *Tanya*
Kuntres U'Mayan MiBet Hashem Hasidic treatise of Rabbi Shalom Dovber Schneerson, the fifth Lubavitcher Rebbe
Lessons in Tanya A popular commentary on the *Tanya* by Rabbi Yosef Weinberg
Likkutei Amarim Also known as *Maggid Devarav LeYaakov*, a collection of teachings of Rabbi Dov Ber, the Maggid of Mezeritch (c. 1700–1770), compiled by his disciple, Rabbi Shlomo of Lutzk
Likkutei Biurim LaSefer HaTanya Explanations on the *Tanya* culled from other works of Chabad Hasidism, including the discourses of the seventh Lubavitcher Rebbe, Rabbi Menaḥem Mendel Schneerson (1902–1994), compiled by Rabbi Yehoshua Korf
Likkutei Dibburim A series of books containing the teachings of the sixth Lubavitcher Rebbe, Rabbi Yosef Yitzḥak Schneerson (1880–1950)

Likkutei Hagahot LeTanya A collection of marginalia from various copies of the *Tanya* transcribed by illustrious figures

Likkutei Levi Yitzḥak He'arot LeSefer HaTanya A collection of marginalia from the *Tanya* of Rabbi Levi Yitzḥak Schneerson

Likkutei Moharan The magnum opus of Rebbe Naḥman of Breslov (1772–1810) containing all his major lessons

Likkutei Siḥot The collected discourses of the seventh Lubavitcher Rebbe, Rabbi Menaḥem Mendel Schneerson (1902–1994) on the Torah and festivals

Likkutei Torah Hasidic discourses by the author of the *Tanya*, Rabbi Shneur Zalman of Liadi (1745–1812) on the last three books of the Torah and the festivals

Likkutei Torah A collection of mystical teachings of the Arizal (1534–1572) on the Torah (not to be confused with the work written by the author of the *Tanya* of the same name)

Likkutim Yekarim Collected teachings of the Maggid of Mezeritch and the Ba'al Shem Tov

Ma'amar Bati LeGani The title of the last hasidic discourse of the sixth Lubavitcher Rebbe, Rabbi Yosef Yitzḥak Schneerson (1880–1950), and the first, as well as subsequent, discourses of his successor Rabbi Menaḥem Mendel Schneerson

Ma'amarei Admor HaEmtza'i Hasidic discourses of Rabbi Dovber Schneuri, the second Lubavitcher Rebbe

Ma'amarei Admor HaZaken Discourses of the author of the *Tanya*, Rabbi Shneur Zalman of Liadi (1745–1812)

Ma'or Einayim Hasidic teachings on the Torah by Rabbi Menaḥem Naḥum Twersky of Chernobyl (1730–1798)

Me'orei Or Kabbalistic reference book by Rabbi Meir Paprish (1624–1662)

Mesillat Yesharim A classic ethical *mussar* text by Rabbi Moshe Ḥayyim Luzzatto (1707–1746)

Mikhlol HaMa'amarim VeHaPitgamim An index of rabbinic phrases and idioms by Moshe Savar

Mishlei Yaakov Parables of Rabbi Yaakov Krantz, the Maggid of Dubno

Mishnat Ḥasidim Exposition of the Arizal's kabbalistic teachings by Rabbi Raphael Immanuel Ḥai Ricchi (1687–1743)

Mishneh Torah Code of Jewish law composed by Rambam (1138–1204), containing fourteen books, including *Sefer HaMadda* (the Book of Knowledge), which addresses fundamentals of Judaism

Nefesh HaḤayyim A pietistic work by Rabbi Ḥayyim of Volozhin based on the musical teachings of the Vilna Gaon

Niflaot HaRebbe An anthology of stories about Rabbi Yaakov Yitzḥak HaLevi Horowitz, the Ḥozeh of Lublin, compiled by Moshe Menaḥem Walden

Notzar Ḥesed A commentary on *Pirkei Avot, the Ethics of the Fathers*, by Rabbi Yitzḥak Yehuda Yeḥiel Safrin of Kamarna

Ohev Yisrael Hasidic teachings on the Torah by Rabbi Avraham Yehoshua Heshel of Apta (1748–1825)

Or HaḤayyim A commentary on the Bible by Rabbi Ḥayyim ibn Atar

Or HaTorah Compilation of hasidic discourses on the *Tanakh* and festivals by the third Lubavitcher Rebbe, Rabbi Menaḥem Mendel Schneerson (1789–1866), also known as the Tzemaḥ Tzedek

Or Torah A collection of the thoughts of Rabbi Dov Ber, the Maggid of Mezeritch, compiled by his students

Otzar HaḤayyim A mystical work on the 613 mitzvot by Rabbi Yitzḥak Yehuda Yeḥiel Safrin of Kamarna

Otzar HaMidrashim A collection of two hundred minor midrashim, compiled by Yehuda David Eisenstein

Otzar Iggerot Kodesh A collection of letters by the Lubavitcher Rebbe, Rabbi Menaḥem Mendel Schneerson

Pardes Rimmonim The primary exposition of the kabbalistic system of Rabbi Moshe Kordevero, famously known as the Ramak (1522–1570)

Pelaḥ HaRimmon Hasidic discourses on Genesis, Exodus, and Song of Songs by Rabbi Hillel of Paritch

Pri Etz Ḥayyim Mystical teachings of the Arizal on rituals and holidays as recorded by his disciple Rabbi Hayyim Vital

Raya Meheimna Subsection of the *Zohar* presenting a kabbalistic exposition of the commandments and prohibitions of the Torah

Reshimot Devarim Stories and memories of the Habad hasidim in Yeshivat Tomkhei Temimim, recorded by Rabbi Yehuda Chitrik

Reshit Ḥokhma Work of Kabbala, ethics, and morality written by Rabbi Eliyahu de Vidas (1518–1587)

Sefer HaArakhim An encyclopedic work of hasidic concepts compiled by Rabbi Yoel Kahn and Rabbi Shalom Dovber Lipsker

Sefer HaHakira Treatise on Creation from a philosophical perspective by the Rabbi Menahem Mendel Schneerson, the third Lubavitcher Rebbe, also known as *Derekh Emunah*

Sefer HaMa'amarim A series of works containing the collected hasidic discourses of the Lubavitcher Rebbes, arranged by year

Sefer HaMitzvot Work by Rambam (1138–1204), listing and briefly describing all the commandments of the Torah

Sefer Haredim Treatise on the 613 commandments by Rabbi Elazar Ezkari (1533–1600) of Tzefat

Sefer Hasidim Considered a foundation work of the teachings of the Hasidei Ashkenaz (Pious Ones of Germany), containing ethical, ascetic, and mystical teachings by Rabbi Yehuda of Regensburg (1150–1217), also known as Rabbi Yehuda HeHasid

Sefer HaToledot A series of biographical works on the founders of Hasidism and the Rebbes of Chabad, edited by Rabbi Avraham Hanokh Glitzenstein (1929–2015)

Sefer Mitzvot Gadol Halakhic work by thirteenth-century scholar Rabbi Moshe of Coucy, containing an enumeration of the 613 commandments

Sefer Yetzira Ancient mystical work attributed to the biblical Abraham

Sha'ar HaGemul Treatise on divine justice by Nachmanides

Sha'ar HaMitzvot The fifth section of the work *Shemoneh She'arim*, containing the kabbalistic teachings of the Arizal on the commandments

Shenei Luhot HaBerit Work of Kabbala, ethics, and *halakha* by Rabbi Yeshaya HaLevi Horowitz, famously known as the Shelah (c. 1655–1730)

Shevet Mussar Prominent ethical work by Eliyahu HaKohen HaItamri (1659–1729)

Shivhei HaBesht Biographical stories of the Ba'al Shem Tov and his disciples

Shulhan Arukh HaRav The code of Jewish law compiled by the author of the *Tanya*, Rabbi Shneur Zalman of Liadi

Siddur Admor HaZaken Prayer book edited in accordance with the teachings of the author of the *Tanya*, Rabbi Shneur Zalman of Liadi (1745–1812)

Siddur im Divrei Elokim Ḥayyim   Prayer book based upon the Arizal version of the text with an esoteric commentary by the author of the *Tanya*, Rabbi Shneur Zalman of Liadi

Sippurei Ḥasidim   Collection of hasidic stories compiled by Rabbi Shlomo Yosef Zevin

Sippurei Ma'asiyot   The mystical tales of Rabbi Naḥman of Breslov

Tanya BeTzeruf Likkutei Peirushim   An edition of *Tanya* which includes a collection of commentaries from the Rebbes of Chabad, culled from their various teachings

Tanya Mahadura Kamma   A collection of manuscript versions of the *Tanya* before its initial publication

Teshuvot UVeiurim   Halakhic rulings and explanations on the *Shulḥan Arukh* culled from the letters of the Lubavitcher Rebbe, Rabbi Menaḥem Mendel Schneerson, 1987 edition

Tiferet Shlomo   Hasidic teachings on the Torah by Rabbi Shlomo Rabinowitz of Radomsk (1803–1866)

Toledot Yaakov Yosef   The first hasidic work ever published containing the teachings of the Ba'al Shem Tov as recorded by his disciple, Yaakov Yosef of Polonne (1710–1784)

Torah Or   Hasidic discourses by the author of the *Tanya*, Rabbi Shneur Zalman of Liadi (1745–1812), on the books of Genesis and Exodus, as well as on Hanukkah and the book of Esther

Torat Ḥayyim   The collected discourses of the second Lubavitcher Rebbe, Rabbi Dovber Schneuri (1773–1827), on the books of Genesis and Exodus

Torat Menaḥem   The comprehensive collection of discourses and speeches of the seventh Lubavitcher Rebbe, Rabbi Menaḥem Mendel Schneerson (1902–1994)

Torat Shalom   The collected speeches of the fifth Lubavitcher Rebbe, Rabbi Sholom Dovber Schneerson (1860–1920)

Yeshuot Meshiḥo   An explanation of rabbinic statements concerning redemption by Don Yitzḥak Abarbanel

Yosef Ometz   Treatise on Ashkenazic customs and practices by Rabbi Yosef Han Neerlingen of Frankfurt (1570–1637)

Zohar   One of the fundamental texts of Kabbala (Jewish mysticism), consisting of the teachings of Rabbi Shimon bar Yoḥai (second century CE), as recorded by his close disciples

Zohar Ḥadash A section of the *Zohar* containing material that was not included in the first edition

About the Author

Rabbi Adin Even-Israel Steinsaltz was a teacher, philosopher, social critic, and prolific author who has been hailed by *Time Magazine* as a "once-in-a-millennium scholar." His lifelong work in Jewish education earned him the Israel Prize, his country's highest honor.

Born in Jerusalem in 1937 to secular parents, Rabbi Steinsaltz studied physics and chemistry at Hebrew University. At the age of twenty-four, he became Israel's youngest school principal and went on to establish several experimental schools. In 1965, he began his monumental Hebrew translation and commentary on the Talmud. By 2010, all forty-four volumes were completed, and they have since been translated into English and French. His classic work of Kabbala, *The Thirteen Petalled Rose*, was first published in 1980 and has been translated into eight languages. In all, Rabbi Steinsaltz authored some sixty books and hundreds of articles on subjects ranging from zoology to theology, and he often engaged in social commentary as well.

Continuing his work as a teacher and spiritual mentor, Rabbi Steinsaltz established a network of schools and educational institutions in Israel and the former Soviet Union. He served as scholar-in-residence at the Woodrow Wilson Center for International Studies in Washington, D.C., and the Institute for Advanced Studies at Princeton University. His honorary degrees include doctorates from Yeshiva University, Ben-Gurion University of the Negev, Bar-Ilan University, Brandeis University, and Florida International University.

Rabbi Steinsaltz lived in Jerusalem until his passing in August of 2020. He and his wife had three children and many grandchildren.

ליקוטי אמרים

וממרירו למתקא בצדיקים או לפחות ע"י כליון לבושיה שהן מחשבה דבור ומעשה והתהפכותן מחשך הקליפות לאור ה' א"ס ב"ה המלובש ומיוחד במחשבה דבור ומעשה של תרי"ג מצות התורה בבינונים כי ע"י התהפכות נפש הבהמית הבאה מקליפ' נוגה מחשוכא לנהורא וכו' נעשה בחי' העלאת מ"ן להמשיך אור השכינה היא בחי' גילוי אור א"ס ב"ה על נפשו האלהית שבמוחין שבראשו ובזה יובן היטב מ"ש כי ה' אלהיך אש אוכלה הוא וכמ"ש במ"א:

נשלם חלק ראשון בעז"ה ית' וית'

בחי' גילוי אור א"ס ב"ה שורה שם ומלובשת בעשרת הדברות ביתר שאת
ויתר עז בגילוי רב ועצום יותר מגילויה בהיכלות ק"ק שלמעלה בעולמות
עליונים כי עשרת הדברות הן כללות התורה כולה דנפקא מגו חכמה עילאה
דלעילא לעילא מעלמא דאתגליא וכדי לחקקן בלוחות אבנים גשמיים לא
ירדה ממדרגה למדרגה כדרך השתלשלות העולמות עד עוה"ז הגשמי כי
עוה"ז הגשמי מתנהג בהתלבשות הטבע הגשמי והלוחות מעשה אלהים
המה והמכתב מכתב אלהים הוא למעלה מהטבע של עוה"ז הגשמי הנשפע
מהארת השכינה שבהיכל ק"ק דעשיה שממנה נמשך אור וחיות לעולם
העשיה שגם עוה"ז בכללו אלא בחי' חכמה דאצילות עילאה שהיא כללות
התורה שבי' הדברות נתלבשה במלכות דאצי' ודבריא' לבדן והן לבדן
המיוחדות באור א"ס שבתוכן הן הנקראות בשם שכינה השורה בק"ק דבית
ראשון ע"י התלבשותה בי' הדברות החקוקות בלוחות שבארון בנס ומעשה
אלהים חיים [הוא עלמא דאתכסיא המקנן בעולם הבריאה כנודע לי"ח]
ובבית שני שלא היה בו הארון והלוחות אמרז"ל שלא היתה שכינה שורה
בו. פי' מדרגת שכינה שהיתה שורה בבית ראשון שלא כדרך השתלשלות
העולמות אלא בבית שני היתה שורה כדרך השתלשלות והתלבשות
מלכות דאצי' במלכות דבריאה ודבריא' במלכו' דיצירה וידיצי' בהיכל
ק"ק דיצי' וק"ק דעשי' היה מתלבש בק"ק שבבהמ"ק שלמטה ושרתה
בו השכינה מלכות דיצירה המלובשת בק"ק דעשיה. ולכן לא היה רשאי
שום אדם ליכנס שם לבד כהן גדול ביה"כ ומשחרב בית המקדש אין לו
להקב"ה בעולמו אלא ד"א של הלכה בלבד ואפילו אחד שיושב ועוסק
בתורה שכינה עמו כדאית' בברכו' פ"ק פי' שכינה עמו כדרך השתלשלות
והתלבשות מלכות דאצילות במלכות דבריאה ויצירה ועשיה כי תרי"ג
מצות התורה רובן ככולן הן מצות מעשיות וגם התלויות בדבור ומחשבה
כמו ת"ת ובהמ"ז וק"ש ותפלה הא קיימא לן דהרהור לאו כדבור דמי ואינו
יוצא ידי חובתו בהרהור וכוונה לבד עד שיוציא בשפתיו וקי"ל דעקימת
שפתיו הוי מעשה ותרי"ג מצות התורה עם שבע מצות דרבנן בגימטריא
כת"ר שהוא רצון העליון ב"ה המלובש בחכמתו יתברך המיוחדות באור
א"ס ב"ה בתכלית היחוד וה' בחכמה יסד ארץ היא תורה שבעל פה דנפקא
מחכמה עילאה כמ"ש בזהר דאבא יסד ברתא. וז"ש הינוקא דנהורא
עילאה דאדליק על רישיה היא שכינתא אצטריך למשחא פי' להתלבש
בחכמה הנק' שמן משחת קדש כמ"ש בזהר ואינון עובדין טבין הן תרי"ג
מצות הנמשכות מחכמתו ית' כדי לאחוז אור השכינה בפתילה היא נפש
החיונית שבגוף הנקראת פתילה עד"מ כי כמו שבנר הגשמי האור מאיר
ע"י כליון ושריפת הפתילה הנהפכת לאש כך אור השכינה שורה על
נפש האלהית על ידי כליון נפש הבהמית והתהפכותה מחשוכא לנהורא

ליקוטי אמרים

כח אייר פשוטה

ב סיון מעוברת

שנתלבשה בדברים גשמיים שהן תרי"ג מצות התורה. ובירידתה בהשתלשלו' מעולם לעולם גם השכינה ירדה ונתלבשה בה בכל עולם ועולם וזהו היכל ק"ק שבכל עולם ועולם וכמ"ש בזהר וע"ח שהשכינה שהיא מלכות דאצילות [שהיא בחי' גילוי אור א"ס ב"ה וחיות שמאיר לעולמות ולכן היא נקראת דבר ה'. ורוח פיו כביכול עד"מ כמו שבאדם הדבור הוא מגלה מחשבתו הסתומה ונעלמה להשומעים] היא מתלבשת בהיכל ק"ק דבריאה שהיא בחי' חב"ד דבריאה ובהתלבשותן במלכות דבריאה נבראו הנשמות והמלאכי' שבבריאה וגם משם נמשך התלמוד שלפנינו וכמש"ל בשם התיקונים שבעולם הבריאה מאירות ומשפיעות שם חכמתו ובינתו ודעתו של א"ס ב"ה בבחי' צמצום עצום בכדי שיוכלו הנשמות והמלאכים שהם בעלי גבול ותכלית לקבל השפעה מבחי' חב"ד אלו ולכן נמשך משם התלמוד שהוא ג"כ בחי' חב"ד שהתלמוד הוא טעמי ההלכות על בוריין והטעמים הם בחי' חב"ד וההלכות עצמן הן ממדותיו של א"ס ב"ה שהן חסד דין רחמים כו' שמהן נמשך ההיתר והאיסור והכשר והפסול והחיוב והפטור כמ"ש בתיקוני'. ובהתלבשות מלכות דאצי' במלכות דבריאה

כט אייר פשוטה

מתלבשת בהיכל ק"ק דיצי' שהוא חב"ד דיצירה ובהתלבשותן במלכות דיצירה נוצרו הרוחות והמלאכים שביצירה וגם משם היא המשנה שלפנינו שהיא הלכות פסוקות הנמשכות ג"כ מחב"ד של א"ס ב"ה רק שבחי' חב"ד שהם טעמי ההלכות הם מלובשים וגנוזי' בגופי ההלכות ולא בבחי' גילוי וגופי ההלכו' שהן בבחי' גילוי הן הן הארת מדותיו של א"ס ב"ה בבחי' גילוי כמש"ל בשם התיקוני' דשית ספירן מקננין ביצירה שהן דרך כלל שני קוין ימין ושמאל לחסד מסטרא דחסד דהיינו להתיר שיוכל לעלות אל ה' או להחמיר כו'. והכל ע"פ חכמה דאצי' ובינה ודעת כלולות בה ומיוחדות בא"ס ב"ה כי בתוך כולן מלובשות חב"ד דאצילות שאור א"ס ב"ה מיוחד בהן בתכלית היחוד וכן בדרך זה ירדה השכינה ונתלבשה בהיכל ק"ק דעשיה וכל עולם מג' עולמות אלו מתחלק לרבבות מדריגות הנקראות גם כן עולמות פרטים ומלכות דאצילו' מלובשת במלכות* של כל עולם פרטי יורדת ומתלבשת בהיכל ק"ק שהוא חב"ד שבעולם שלמטה ממנו במדרגה. והנה מהשכינה המלובשת בהיכל ק"ק של כל עולם ועולם וחיות לכל העולם והברואים שבו נשמות ומלאכים וכו' כי כולם נבראו בעשרה מאמרות שבמעשה בראשית שהם דבר ה' הנקרא בשם שכינה:

הגהה

* (ובזה יובן לשון הכתוב מלכותך מלכות כל עולמים):

פרק נג

א סיון פשוטה

ג סיון מעוברת

והנה כשהיה בית ראשון קיים שבו היה הארון והלוחות בבית ק"ק היתה השכינה שהיא מלכות דאצילות שהיא

ליקוטי אמרים

וגשמיים ונראים מתים אך בתוכם יש אור וחיות המהוה אותם מאין ליש תמיד שלא יחזרו להיות אין ואפס כשהיו ואור זה הוא מא"ס ב"ה רק שנתלבש בלבושים רבים וכמ"ש בע"ח שאור וחיות כדור הארץ החומריי הנראה לעיני בשר הוא ממלכות דעשיה ובתוכה מלכות דיצירה* וכו' עד שבתוך כולן י"ס דאצילות המיוחדות במאציל א"ס ב"ה:

* [בדפוסים הקודמים הי' כתוב "מלכות דמלכות דעשיה" ונ"ל דצ"ל "מלכות דיצירה" וכ"ה באגה"ק סי' כ"ה המתחיל להבין אמרי בינה כו' אשר נמצא לפנינו גוף כתי"ק]:

פרק נב וכמו שבנשמת האדם עיקר גילוי כללות החיות הוא במוחין וכל האברים מקבלים אור וכח לבד המאיר להם ממקור גילוי החיות שבמוחין ככה ממש עד"מ עיקר גילוי כללות המשכת החיות להחיות העולמות והברואים שבהם הוא מלובש ונכלל ברצונו וחכמתו ובינתו ודעתו ית' הנק' בשם מוחין והן הן המלובשים בתורה ומצותיה וגילוי כללות המשכה זו הוא מקור החיות אשר העולמות מקבלי' כל א' בפרטות רק הארה מתפשטת ומאירה ממקור זה כדמיון אור המתפשט מהשמש עד"מ וכחות אברי הגוף מהמוח הנ"ל ומקור זה הוא הנקרא עלמא דאתגליא ומטרונית' ואימא תתאה ושכינה מלשון ושכנתי בתוכם על שם שמקור זה הוא ראשית התגלות אור א"ס אשר ממשיך ומאיר לעולמות בבחי' גילוי וממקור זה נמשך לכל א' האור וחיות פרטי הראוי לו ושוכן ומתלבש בתוכם להחיותם ולכן נקרא אם הבנים עד"מ וכנסת ישראל שממקור זה נאצלו נשמות דאצי' ונבראו נשמות דבריאה וכו' וכולן אינן רק מהתפשטות החיות והאור מהמקור הזה הנק' שכינה כהתפשטות האור מהשמש אבל השכינה עצמה שהיא ראשית הגילוי ועיקרו מה שא"ס ב"ה מאיר לעולמות בבחי' גילוי והיא מקור כל המשכות החיות שבכל העולמות [שכל החיו' שבהם אינו רק אור המתפשט ממנה כאור המתפשט מהשמש] א"א לעולמות לסבול ולקבל אור שכינתה שתשכון ותתלבש בתוכם ממש בלא לבוש המעלים ומסתיר אורה מהם שלא יתבטלו במציאות לגמרי במקורם כביטול אור השמש במקורו בגוף השמש שאין נראה שם אור זה רק עצם גוף השמש בלבד. ומהו הלבוש שיוכל להסתירה ולהלבישה ולא יתבטל במציאות באורה הוא רצונו ית' וחכמתו וכו' המלובשים בתורה ומצותיה הנגלית לנו ולבנינו דאורייתא מחכמה נפקת היא חכמה עילאה דלעילא מעלמא דאתגליא דאיהו חכים ולא בחכמה ידיעא וכו' וכמש"ל שאור א"ס ב"ה מלובש ומיוחד בחכמה עילאה והוא ית' וחכמתו אחד רק שירדה בסתר המדרגות ממדריגה למדריגה בהשתלשלות העולמות עד

כו אייר פשוטה
כח אייר מעוברת

כז אייר פשוטה
כט אייר מעוברת

א סיון מעוברת

ליקוטי אמרים

הפועל והגילוי מהההעלם להחיות רמ"ח אברין ושס"ה גידין שבגוף ע"י התלבשותם בנפש החיונית שיש לה ג"כ רמ"ח ושס"ה כחות וחיות הללו.

כד אייר פשוטה

והנה על המשכת כל התרי"ג מיני כחות וחיות מהעלם הנשמה אל הגוף להחיותו עליה אמרו עיקר שכינתה והשראתה של המשכה זו וגילוי זה הוא כולו במוחין שבראש ולכן הם מקבלים תחלה הכח והחיות הראוי להם לפי מזגם ותכונתם שהן חב"ד וכח המחשבה וכל השייך למוחין ולא זו בלבד אלא גם כללות כל המשכות החיות לשאר האברים ג"כ כלולה ומלובשת במוחין שבראש ושם הוא עיקרה ושרשה של המשך זו בבחי' גילוי האור והחיו' של כל הנשמ' כולה ומשם מתפשטת הארה לשאר כל האברים ומקבל כל א' כח וחיו' הראוי לו כפי מזגו ותכונתו כח הראיה מתגלה בעין וכח השמיעה באוזן וכו'. וכל הכחות מתפשטים מהמוח כנודע כי שם הוא עיקר משכן הנשמה כולה בבחי' גילוי שנגלית שם כללו' החיות המתפשט ממנה. רק כחותיה של כללות החיות מאירים ומתפשטים משם לכל אברי הגוף כדמיון האור המתפשט ומאיר מהמשך לחדרי חדרים [ואפילו הלב מקבל מהמוח ולכן המוח שליט עליו בתולדתו כנ"ל]:

כה אייר פשוטה

וככה ממש עד"מ א"ס ב"ה ממלא כל עלמין להחיותם ובכל עולם יש ברואים לאין קץ ותכלית ריבוא רבבות מיני מדרגות מלאכים ונשמות כו' וכן ריבוי העולמות אין לו קץ וגבול גבוה על גבוה כו'. והנה מהותו ועצמותו של א"ס ב"ה שוה בעליונים ותחתונים כמשל הנשמה הנ"ל וכמ"ש בתיקונים דאיהו סתימו דכל סתימין פי' דאפי' בעלמין סתימין דלעילא הוא סתום ונעלם בתוכם כמו שהוא סתום ונעלם בתחתוני' כי לית מחשבה תפיסא ביה כלל אפי' בעולמות עליונים. ונמצא כמו שמצוי שם כך נמצא בתחתונים ממש. וההבדל שבין עולמו' עליונים ותחתונים הוא מצד המשכת החיות אשר א"ס ב"ה ממשיך ומאיר בבחי' גילוי מהההעלם [שזה אחד מהטעמי' שההשפעה והמשכת החיות מכונה בשם אור עד"מ] להחיות העולמות והברואים שבהם שהעולמו' העליוני' מקבלים בבחי' גילוי קצת יותר מהתחתוני' וכל הברואי' שבהם מקבלים כל א' כפי כחו ותכונתו שהיא תכונת ובחי' המשכה הפרטית אשר א"ס ב"ה ממשיך ומאיר לו. והתחתונים אפי' הרוחניים אינם מקבלים בבחי' גילוי כ"כ רק בלבושים רבים אשר א"ס ב"ה מלביש בהם החיות והאור אשר ממשיך

כה אייר מעוברת

כו אייר מעוברת

כז אייר מעוברת

ומאיר להם להחיותם וכ"כ עצמו וגברו הלבושים אשר א"ס ב"ה מלביש ומסתיר בהם האור והחיות עד אשר ברא בו עוה"ז החומרי והגשמי ממש מהוהו ומחייהו בחיות וממשיך ואור מאיר לו המלובש מכוסה ומוסתר בתוך הלבושים הרבים והעצומים המעלימים ומסתירי' האור והחיות עד שאין נראה ונגלה שום אור וחיות רק דברים חומריים

ליקוטי אמרים

הלוים שהלוים של עכשיו יהיו כהנים לעתיד] ועבודת הלוים היתה להרים קול רינה ותודה בשירה וזמרה בניגון ונעימה בבחי' רצוא ושוב שהיא בחי' אהבה עזה זו כשלהבת היוצא מן הבזק כדאיתא בגמ' [פ"ב דחגיגה] וא"א לבאר ענין זה היטב במכתב רק כל איש נלבב ונבון המשכיל על דבר ומעמיק לקשר דעתו ותבונתו בה' ימצא טוב ואור הגנוז בנפשו המשכלת כל חד לפום שיעורא דיליה [יש מתפעל כו' ויש מתפעל כו'] אחרי קדימת יראת חטא להיות סור מרע בתכלית שלא להיות עונותיכם מבדילים כו' ח"ו. והנה סדר העבודה בעסק התורה והמצוות הנמשכת מבחי' אהבה עזה זו היא בבחי' שוב לבד כמ"ש בספר יצירה ואם רץ לבך שוב לאחד פי' ואם רץ לבך היא תשוקת הנפש שבלב בחלל הימני כשמתגברת ומתלהבת ומתלהטת במאד מאד עד כלות הנפש ממש להשתפך אל חיק אביה חיי החיים ב"ה ולצאת ממאסרה בגוף הגופני וגשמי לדבקה בו ית' אזי זאת ישיב אל לבו מאמרז"ל כי ע"כ אתה חי בגוף הזה להחיותו כדי להמשיך חיים עליוני' מחיי החיים ב"ה למטה ע"י תורת חיים להיות דירה בתחתוני' לאחדותו ית' בבחי' גילוי' כמש"ל וכמ"ש בז"הק למהוי אחד באחד פי' שהיחוד הנעלם יהיה בבחי' עלמא דאתגליא וז"ש לכה דודי וכו' ובזה יובן מארז"ל ע"כ אתה חי וע"כ וכו' ואלא איך יהיה רצונו וכמ"ש במ"א באריכות על משנה זו ע"כ אתה חי בעזרת חיי החיים ב"ה:

פרק נא והנה לתוספת ביאור לשון הינוקא דלעיל צריך לבאר תחלה להבין קצת ענין השראת השכינה שהיתה שורה בבית ק"ק וכן כל מקום השראת השכינה מה ענייננו הלא מלא כל הארץ כבודו ולית אתר פנוי מיניה. אך הענין כדכתיב ומבשרי אחזה אלוה שכמו שנשמת האדם היא ממלאה כל רמ"ח אברי הגוף מראשו ועד רגלו ואעפ"כ עיקר משכנה והשראתה היא במוחו וממוחו מתפשטת לכל האברים וכל אבר מקבל ממנה חיות וכח הראוי לו לפי מזגו ותכונתו העין לראות והאזן לשמוע והפה לדבר והרגלים להלוך כנראה בחוש שבמוח מרגיש כל הנפעל ברמ"ח אברים וכל הקורות אותם. והנה אין שינוי קבלת הכחות והחיות שבאברי הגוף מן הנשמה מצד עצמה ומהותה שיהיה מהותה ועצמותה מתחלק לרמ"ח חלקי' שונים מתלבשי' ברמ"ח מקומו' כפי ציור חלקי מקומו' אברי הגוף שלפי זה נמצא עצמותה ומהותה מצוייר בציור גשמי ודמות ותבנית כתבנית הגוף ח"ו אלא כולה עצם אחד רוחני פשוט ומופשט מכל ציור גשמי ומבחי' וגדר מקום ומדה וגבול גשמי מצד מהותה ועצמות' ולא שייך במהות' ועצמותה לומר שהיא במוחין שבראש יותר מברגלים מאחר שמהותה ועצמותה אינו בגדר ובחי' מקום וגבול גשמי רק שתרי"ג מיני כחות וחיות כלולים בה במהותה ועצמותה לצאת אל

ליקוטי אמרים

אהבת עולם אהבתנו ה' אלהינו. כלומר שהניח כל צבא מעלה הקדושים והשרה שכינתו עלינו להיות נקרא אלהינו. כמו אלהי אברהם כו' כנ"ל. והיינו כי אהבה דוחקת הבשר ולכן נקרא אהבת עולם שהיא בחי' צמצום אורו הגדול הבלתי תכלית להתלבש בבחי' גבול הנקרא עולם בעבור אהבת עמו ישראל כדי לקרבם אליו ביחודו ואחדותו ית'. וז"ש חמלה גדולה ויתירה פי' יתירה על קרבת אלהים שבכל צבא מעלה. ובנו בחרת מכל עם ולשון הוא הגוף החומרי הנדמה בחומריותו לגופי אומות העולם. וקרבתנו וכו' להודות וכו' ופי' הודאה יתבאר במ"א. וליחדך כו' ליכלל ביחודו ית' כנ"ל. והנה כאשר ישים המשכיל אלה הדברים אל עומקא דלבא ומוחא אזי ממילא כמים הפנים לפנים תתלהט נפשו ותתלבש ברוח נדיבה להתנדב להניח ולעזוב כל אשר לו מנגד ורק לדבקה בו ית' וליכלל באורו בדביקה חשיקה וכו' בבחי' נשיקין ואתדבקות רוחא ברוחא כנ"ל.

אך איך היא בחי' אתדבקות רוחא ברוחא לזה אמר והיו הדברים האלה כו' על לבבך ודברת בם כו' וכמ"ש בעה"ח שיחוד הנשיקין עיקרו הוא יחוד חב"ד בחב"ד והוא עיון התורה והפה הוא מוצא הרוח וגילויו בבחי' גילוי והיינו בחי' הדבור בד"ת. כי על מוצא פי ה' יחיה האדם ומ"מ לא יצא ידי חובתו בהרהור ועיון לבדו עד שיוציא בשפתיו כדי להמשיך אור א"ס ב"ה למטה עד נפש החיונית השוכנת בדם האדם המתהוה מדומם צומח חי כדי להעלות כולן לה' עם כל העולם כולו ולכללן ביחודו ית' ואורו ית' אשר יאיר לארץ ולדרים בבחי' גילוי ונגלה כבוד ה' וראו כל בשר וכו' שזהו תכלית השתלשלות כל העולמות להיות כבוד ה' מלא כל הארץ הלזו דוקא בבחי' גילוי לאהפכא חשוכא לנהורא ומרירו למיתקא כנ"ל בארוכות. וזהו תכלית כוונת האדם בעבודתו להמשיך אור אין סוף ברוך הוא למטה הוא רק שצריך תחלה העלאת מ"ן למסור לו נפשו ומאדו כנ"ל:

פרק נ

והנה כל בחי' ומדרגות אהבה הנ"ל הן מסטרא דימינא ובחי' כהן איש חסד ונק' כסף הקדשים מלשון נכסוף נכספת לבית אביך. אך יש עוד בחי' אהבה העולה על כולנה כמעלת הזהב על הכסף והיא אהבה כרשפי אש מבחי' גבורות עליונות דבינה עילאה דהיינו שע"י התבוננות בגדולות א"ס ב"ה דכולא קמיה כלא ממש חשיב תתלהט ותתלהב הנפש ליקר תפאר גדולתו ולאסתכלא ביקרא דמלכא כרשפי אש שלהבת עזה זה העולה למעל' ולפרד מהפתילה והעצים שנאחזת בהן והיינו על ידי תגבורת יסוד האש אלהי שבנפש האלהית ומזה באה לידי צמאון וכמ"ש צמאה לך נפשי ואח"כ לבחי' חולת אהבה ואח"כ באה לידי כלות הנפש ממש כמ"ש גם כלתה נפשי והנה מכאן יצא שורש הלוים למטה [ולעתיד שהעולם יתעלה יהיו הם הכהנים וכמ"ש האר"י ז"ל ע"פ והכהנים

פרק מט והנה אף כי פרטי בחי' ההסתר וההעלם אור א"ס ב"ה בהשתלשלות העולמות עד שנברא עו"הז הגשמי עצמו מספר ומינים ממינים שונים כידוע לטועמים מעץ החיים: אך דרך כלל הם שלשה מיני צמצומים עצומים כלליים. לשלשה מיני עולמות כלליים. ובכל כלל יש רבוא רבבות פרטיים. והם שלשה עולמות בי"ע. כי עולם האצילו' הוא אלהות ממש. וכדי לברוא עולם הבריא' שהן נשמות ומלאכים עליונים אשר עבודתם לה' בבחי' חב"ד המתלבשים בהם והם משיגים ומקבלים מהם היה תחלה צמצום עצום כנ"ל. וכן מבריאה ליצירה. כי אור מעט מזער המתלבש בעולם הבריא' עדיין הוא בבחי' א"ס לגבי עולם היצירה. ואי אפשר להתלבש בו אלא ע"י צמצום והעלם וכן מיצירה לעשיה [וכמ"ש במ"א בביאור שלשה צמצומים אלו בארוכות לקרב אל שכלנו הדל] ותכלית כל הצמצומים הוא כדי לברוא גוף האדם החומרי ולאכפייא לס"א ולהיות יתרון האור מן החושך בהעלות האדם את נפשו האלהית והחיונית ולבושיה וכל כחות הגוף כולן לה' לבדו כנ"ל באריכות. כי זה תכלית השתלשלות העולמות. והנה כמים הפנים לפנים כמו שהקב"ה כביכול הניח וסילק לצד אחד דרך משל את אורו הגדול הבלתי תכלית וגנזו והסתירו בג' מיני צמצומים שונים. והכל בשביל אהבת האדם התחתון להעלותו לה'. כי אהבה דוחקת הבשר. עאכ"ו בכפלי כפליים לאין קץ כי ראוי לאדם ג"כ להניח ולעזוב כל אשר לו מנפש ועד בשר ולהפקיר הכל בשביל לדבקה בו ית' בדביקה חשיקה וחפיצה ולא יהיה שום מונע מבית ומבחוץ לא גוף ולא נפש ולא ממון ולא אשה ובנים. ובזה יובן טוב טעם ודעת לתקנת חכמים שתקנו ברכות ק"ש שתים לפניה כו' דלכאורה אין להם שייכות כלל עם קריאת שמע כמ"ש הרשב"א ושאר פוסקי'. ולמה קראו אותן ברכות ק"ש ולמה תקנו אותן לפניה דווקא. אלא משום שעיקר ק"ש לקיים בכל לבבך כו' בשני יצריך כו' דהיינו לעמוד נגד כל מונע מאהבת ה'. ולבבך הן האשה וילדיה. שלבבו של אדם קשורה בהן בטבע. כמשארז"ל ע"פ הוא אמר ויהי זו אשה הוא צוה ויעמוד אלו בנים. ונפשך ומאדך כמשמעו חיי ומזוני להפקיר הכל בשביל אהבת ה'. ואיך יבא האדם החומרי למדה זו לכך סידרו תחלה ברכת יוצר אור. ושם נאמר ונשנה באריכות ענין וסדר המלאכים העומדים ברום עולם להודיע גדולתו של הקב"ה איך שכולם בטלים לאורו ית' ומשמיעים ביראה כו' ומקדישים כו' ואומרים ביראה קדוש כו' כלומר שהוא מובדל מהן ואינו מתלבש בהן בבחי' גילוי אלא מלא כל הארץ כבודו היא כנסת ישראל למעלה וישראל למטה כנ"ל. וכן האופנים וחיות הקודש ברעש גדול וכו' ברוך כבוד ה' ממקומו לפי שאין יודעים ומשיגים מקומו וכמ"ש כי הוא לבדו מרום וקדוש. ואח"כ ברכה שניה

ליקוטי אמרים

מתלבשת אלא מקפת וסובבת הלכך מאחר שהעולמות הם בבחי' גבול ותכלית נמצא שאין השפעת אור א"ס מתלבש ומתגלה בהם בבחי' גילוי רק מעט מזער הארה מועטת מצומצמת מאד מאד והיא רק כדי להחיותם בבחי' גבול ותכלית. אבל עיקר האור בלי צמצום כ"כ נק' מקיף וסובב מאחר שאין השפעתו מתגלית בתוכם מאחר שהם בבחי' גבול ותכלית.

<small>טז אייר פשוטה</small>

והמשל בזה הנה הארץ הלזו הגשמיות אף שמלא כל הארץ כבודו. והיינו אור א"ס ב"ה כמ"ש הלא את השמים ואת הארץ אני מלא נאם ה'. אעפ"כ אין מתלבש בתוכה בבחי' גילוי ההשפעה רק חיות מעט מזער בחי' דומם וצומח לבד וכל אור א"ס ב"ה נק' סובב עליה אף שהוא בתוכה ממש. מאחר שאין השפעתו מתגלית בה יותר רק משפיע בה בבחי' הסתר והעלם וכל השפעה שבבחי' הסתר נקרא מקיף מלמעלה כי עלמא דאתכסי' הוא למעלה במדרגה מעלמ' דאתגליא ולקרב אל השכל יותר הוא בדרך משל. כמו האדם שמצייר בדעתו איזה דבר שראוה או שרואה הנה אף שכל גוף עצם הדבר ההוא וגבו ותוכו כולו מצוייר בדעתו ומחשבתו מפני שראהו כולו או שרואהו הנה נקראת מקפת דעתו הדבר ההוא כולו. והדבר ההוא מוקף בדעתו ומחשבתו רק שאינו מוקף בפועל ממש רק בדמיון מחשבת האדם ודעתו. אבל הקב"ה דכתיב ביה כי לא מחשבותי מחשבותיכם כו' הרי מחשבתו ודעתו שיודע כל הנבראים מקפת כל נברא ונברא מראשו

<small>יד אייר מעוברת</small>

<small>טו אייר מעוברת</small>

ועד תחתיתו ותוכו ותוך תוכו הכל בפועל ממש. למשל כדור הארץ הלזו הרי ידיעתו ית' מקפת כל עובי כדור הארץ וכל אשר בתוכו ותוך תחתיתו הכל בפועל ממש שהרי ידיעה זו היא חיות כל עובי כדור הארץ כולו והתהוותו מאין ליש שלא רק היה מתהוה כמות שהוא עתה שהוא בעל גבול ותכלית וחיות מועטת מאד כדי בחי' דומם וצומח. אם לא ע"י צמצומים רבים ועצומים שצמצמו האור והחיות שנתלבש בכדור הארץ להחיותו ולקיימו בבחי' גבול ותכלית ובבחי' דומם וצומח בלבד אך ידיעתו ית'

<small>יז אייר פשוטה</small>

<small>טז אייר מעוברת</small>

המיוחדת במהותו ועצמותו. כי הוא המדע והוא היודע והוא הידוע ובידיעת עצמו כביכול יודע כל הנבראים ולא בידיעה שחוץ ממנו כידיעת האדם. כי כולם נמצאים מאמיתתו ית'. ודבר זה אין ביכולת האדם להשיגו על בוריו וכו'* הרי ידיעה זו מאחר שהיא בבחי' א"ס אינה נקרא' בשם מתלבשת בכדור הארץ שהוא בעל גבול ותכלית אלא מקפת וסובבת. אף שידיעה זו כוללת כל עביו ותוכו בפועל ממש ומהוה אותו עי"ז מאין ליש וכמ"ש במ"א:

הגהה

(כמ"ש הרמב"ם ז"ל והסכימו עמו חכמי הקבלה כמ"ש בפרד"ס מהרמ"ק ז"ל וכ"ה לפי קבלת האר"י ז"ל בסוד הצמצו' והתלבשות אורות בכלים כמש"ל פ"ב):

ומקבל וממשיך עליו אלהותו ית' ואומר ה' אלהינו ה' אחד הרי ממילא נכללת נפשו ביחודו ית' דרוח אייתי רוח וממשיך רוח והיא בחי' יציאת מצרים ולכן תקנו פ' יציאת מצרים בשעת ק"ש דווקא. אף שהיא מצוה בפני עצמה ולא ממצות ק"ש כדאיתא בגמרא ופוסקים אלא מפני שהן דבר אחד ממש. וכן בסוף פ' יציאת מצרים מסיים ג"כ אני ה' אלהיכם והיינו גם כן כמש"ל:

פרק מח והנה כאשר יתבונן המשכיל בגדולת א"ס ב"ה כי כשמו כן הוא א"ס ואין קץ ותכלית כלל לאור וחיות המתפשט ממנו ית' ברצונו הפשוט ומיוחד במהותו ועצמותו ית' בתכלית היחוד ואילו היתה השתלשלות העולמות מאור א"ס ב"ה בלי צמצומי' רק כסדר המדרגות ממדרגה למדרגה בדרך עלה ועלול לא היה העוה"ז נברא כלל כמו שהוא עתה בבחי' גבול ותכלית מהארץ לרקיע מהלך ת"ק שנה וכן בין כל רקיע לרקיע וכן עובי כל רקיע ורקיע ואפי' עו"הב וג"ע העליון מדור נשמות הצדיקי' הגדולים והנשמו' עצמן ואצ"ל המלאכי' הן בבחי' גבול ותכלית כי יש גבול להשגתן באור א"ס ב"ה המאיר עליהן בהתלבשות חב"ד כו'. ולכן יש גבול לההנאתן שנהנין מזיו השכינה ומתענגין באור ה' כי אין יכולין לקבל הנאה ותענוג בבחי' א"ס ממש שלא יתבטלו ממציאותן ויחזרו למקורן. והנה פרטיות הצמצומים איך ומה אין כאן מקום ביאורם. אך דרך כלל הן הם בחי' הסתר והעלם המשכת האור והחיות שלא יאיר ויומשך לתחתונים בבחי' גילוי להתלבש ולהשפיע בהן ולהחיותם להיות יש מאין. כי אם מעט מזער אור וחיות בכדי שיהיו בבחי' גבול ותכלית שהיא הארה מועטת מאד ממש כלא חשיבי לגבי בחי' הארה בלי גבול ותכלית ואין ביניהם ערך ויחס כלל כנודע פי' מלת ערך במספרים שאחד במספר יש לו ערך לגבי מספר אלף אלפים שהוא חלק אחד מני אלף אלפים אבל לגבי דבר שהוא בבחי' בלי גבול ומספר כלל אין כנגדו שום ערך במספרים שאפי' אלף אלפי אלפים וריבוא רבבות אינו אפי' כערך מספר אחד לגבי אלף אלפים וריבוא רבבות אלא כלא כלא ממש חשיבי. וככה ממש היא בחי' ההארה מועטת זו המתלבשת בעולמות עליונים ותחתונים להשפיע בהם להחיותם לגבי ערך אור הגנוז ונעלם שהוא בבחי' א"ס ואינו מתלבש ומשפיע בעולמות בבחי' גילוי להחיותם אלא מקיף עליהם מלמעלה ונקרא סובב כל עלמין. ואין הפי' סובב ומקיף מלמעלה בבחי' מקום ח"ו כי לא שייך כלל בחי' מקום ברוחניות. אלא ר"ל סובב ומקיף מלמעלה לענין בחי' גילוי השפעה כי ההשפעה שהוא בבחי' גילוי בעולמו' נקראת בשם הלבשה שמתלבשת בעולמות כי הם מלבישים ומשיגים ההשפעה שמקבלים משא"כ ההשפעה שאינה בבחי' גילוי אלא בהסתר והעלם ואין העולמות משיגים אותה אינה נקראת

יד אייר פשוטה
יא אייר מעוברת

טו אייר פשוטה
יב אייר מעוברת

יג אייר מעוברת

אלהיכם וגו' פי' כי ע"י קיום המצות אלוה שלכם הריני כמו אלהי אברהם אלהי יצחק וכו' שנקרא כן מפני שהאבות היו בחי' מרכבה לו ית' ובטלים ונכללים באורו. וככה הוא בכל נפש מישראל בשעת עסק התורה והמצות ולכן חייבו רז"ל לקום ולעמוד מפני כל עוסק במצוה אף אם הוא בור ועם הארץ והיינו מפני ה' השוכן ומתלבש בנפשו בשעה זו רק שאין נפשו מרגשת מפני מסך החומר הגופני שלא נזדכך ומחשיך עיני הנפש מראות מראות אלהים כמו האבות וכיוצא בהן שראו עולמם בחייהם. וז"ש אסף ברוח הקדש בעד כל כנסת ישראל שבגולה ואני בער ולא אדע בהמות הייתי עמך ואני תמיד עמך. כלומר שאע"פ שאני כבהמה בהיותי עמך ולא אדע ולא ארגיש בנפשי יחוד זה שתפול עליה אימתה ופחד תחלה ואח"כ אהבה רבה בתענוגים או כרשפי אש כמדת הצדיקי' שנזדכך חומרם וכנודע שדעת הוא לשון הרגשה בנפש והוא כולל חסד וגבורה. אעפ"כ אני תמיד עמך כי אין החומר מונע יחוד הנפש באור א"ס ב"ה הממלא כל עלמין וכמ"ש גם חושך לא יחשיך ממך. ובזה יובן חומר עונש איסור מלאכה בשבתות וחמץ בפסח השוה לכל נפש לפי שאף בנפש בור ועם הארץ גמור מאיר אור קדושת שבת וי"ט ונידון בנפשו בכרת וסקילה על חילול קדושה זו. וגם משהו חמץ או טלטול מוקצה בקדושה שעל נפשו פוגם בקדושת נפש הצדיק כי תורה אחת לכולנו. [ומ"ש בהמות לשון רבים לרמז כי לפניו ית' גם בחי' דעת העליון הכולל חו"ג נדמה כבהמות ועשייה גופנית לגבי אור א"ס כמ"ש כולם בחכמה עשית ונק' בהמה רבה כמ"ש במ"א. והוא שם ב"ן בגימ' בהמ"ה שלפני האצילות]:

פרק מז והנה בכל דור ודור וכל יום ויום חייב אדם לראות עצמו כאילו הוא יצא היום ממצרים. והיא יציאת נפש האלהית ממאסר הגוף משכא דחויא ליכלל ביחוד אור א"ס ב"ה ע"י עסק התורה והמצות בכלל ובפרט בקבלת מלכות שמים בק"ש שבה מקבל וממשיך עליו יחודו ית' בפירוש באמרו ה' אלהינו ה' אחד. וכמש"ל כי אלהינו הוא כמו אלהי אברהם וכו' לפי שהיה בטל ונכלל ביחוד אור א"ס ב"ה רק שאברהם זכה לזה במעשיו והילוכו בקודש ממדרגה למדרגה. כמ"ש ויסע אברם הלוך ונסוע וגו': אבל אנחנו ירושה ומתנה היא לנו שנתן לנו את תורתו והלביש בה רצונו וחכמתו ית' המיוחדים במהותו ועצמותו ית' בתכלית היחוד והרי זה כאלו נתן לנו את עצמו כביכול. כמ"ש בזה"ק ע"פ ויקחו לי תרומה [דלי כלומר אותי וה"ל ותרומה אלא משום דכולא חד ע"ש היטב]: וז"ש ותתן לנו ה' אלהינו באהבה כו' כי באור פניך נתת לנו ה' אלהינו כו' ולזה אין מונע לנו מדביקות הנפש ביחודו ואורו ית' אלא הרצון שאם אין האדם רוצה כלל ח"ו לדבקה בו כו'. אבל מיד שרוצה

ליקוטי אמרים

מאשפתו ומכניסו להיכלו היכל המלך חדר לפנים מחדר מקום שאין כל עבד ושר נכנס לשם ומתייחד עמו שם ביחוד וקירוב אמיתי וחיבוק ונישוק ואתדבקות רוחא ברוחא בכל לב ונפש עאכ"ו שתתעורר ממילא האהבה כפולה ומכופלת בלב ההדיוט ושפל אנשים הזה אל נפש המלך בהתקשרות הנפש ממש מלב ונפש מעומקא דלבא לאין קץ. ואף אם לבו כלב האבן המס ימס והיה למים ותשתפך נפשו כמים בכלות הנפש ממש לאהבת המלך: והנה בכל הדברים האלה ובכל החזיון הזה וגדול יתר מאד בכפלי כפליים לאין קץ עשה לנו אלהינו כי לגדולתו אין חקר ואיהו ממלא כל עלמין וסובב כל עלמין ונודע מז"הק והאר"י ז"ל ריבוי ההיכלות והעולמות עד אין מספר ובכל עולם והיכל ריבוא רבבות מלאכים לאין קץ ותכלית. וכמ"ש בגמ' כתיב הישׁ מספר לגדודיו וכתיב אלף אלפין ישמשוניה וריבו רבבן קדמוהי כו' ומשני אלף אלפין וכו' מספר גדוד אחד אבל לגדודיו אין מספר וכולם קמיה כלא ממש חשיבי ובטלים במציאות ממש כביטול דבור א' ממש לגבי מהות הנפש המדברת ועצמותה בעוד שהיה דיבורה עדיין במחשבתה או ברצון וחמדת הלב כנ"ל בארוכות: וכולם שואלים איה מקום כבודו ועונים מלא כל הארץ כבודו הם ישראל עמו. כי הניח הקב"ה את העליונים ואת התחתונים ולא בחר בכולם כי אם בישראל עמו והוציאם ממצרים ערות הארץ מקום הזוהמא והטומאה לא ע"י מלאך ולא ע"י כו' אלא הקב"ה בכבודו ובעצמו ירד לשם כמ"ש וארד להצילו וגו' כדי לקרבם אליו בקירוב ויחוד אמיתי בהתקשרות הנפש ממש בבחי' נשיקין פה לפה לדבר דבר ה' זו הלכה ואתדבקות רוחא ברוחא היא השגת התורה וידיעת רצונו וחכמתו דכולא חד ממש. וגם בבחי' חיבוק הוא קיום המצות מעשיות ברמ"ח אברים דרמ"ח פיקודין הן רמ"ח אברין דמלכא כנז"ל. ודרך כלל נחלקין לשלש בחי' ימין ושמאל ואמצע שהן חסד דין רחמים תרין דרועין וגופא וכו'. וז"ש אשר קדשנו במצותיו כאדם המקדש אשתו להיות מיוחדת עמו ביחוד גמור כמ"ש ודבק באשתו והיו לבשר אחד. ככה ממש ויתר על כן לאין קץ הוא יחוד נפש האלהית העוסקת בתורה ומצות ונפש החיונית ולבושיהן הנ"ל באור א"ס ב"ה. ולכן המשיל שלמה ע"ה בשיר השירים יחוד זה ליחוד חתן וכלה בדביקה חשיקה וחפיצה בחיבוק ונישוק. וז"ש אשר קדשנו במצותיו שהעלנו למעלת קודש העליון ב"ה שהיא קדושתו של הקב"ה בכבודו ובעצמו וקדושה היא לשון הבדלה מה שהקב"ה הוא מובדל מהעולמות והיא בחי' סובב כל עלמין מה שאינו יכול להתלבש בהן. כי ע"י יחוד הנפש והתכללותה באור א"ס ב"ה הרי היא במעלת ומדרגת קדושת א"ס ב"ה ממש מאחר שמתייחדת ומתכללת בו ית' והיו לאחדים ממש. וז"ש והייתם לי קדושים כי קדוש אני ה' ואבדיל אתכם מן העמים להיות לי ואומר ועשיתם את כל מצותי והייתם קדושים לאלהיכם אני ה'

ליקוטי אמרים

פרק מה עוד יש דרך ישר לפני איש לעסוק בתורה ומצות לשמן ע"י מדתו של יעקב אע"ה שהיא מדת הרחמי' לעורר במחשבתו תחלה רחמים רבים לפני ה' על ניצוץ אלהות המחיה נפשו אשר ירד ממקורו חיי החיים א"ס ב"ה הממלא כל עלמין וסובב כל עלמין וכולא קמיה כלא חשיב ונתלבש במשכא דחויא מאור פני המלך בתכלית ההרחק כי העו"הז הוא תכלית הקליפו' הגסות כו' ובפרט כשיזכור על כל מעשיו ודבוריו ומחשבותיו מיום היותו אשר לא טובים המה ומלך אסור ברהטים ברהיטי מוחא כי יעקב חבל נחלתו. וכמשל המושך בחבל וכו' והוא סוד גלות השכינה. וע"ז נאמר וישוב אל ה' וירחמהו לעורר רחמים רבים על שם ה' השוכן אתנו כדכתיב השוכן אתם בתוך טומאתם. וזש"ה וישק יעקב לרחל וישא את קולו ויבך. כי רחל היא כנסת ישראל מקור כל הנשמות. ויעקב במדתו העליונה שהיא מדת הרחמים שבאצילות הוא המעורר רחמים רבים עליה. וישא את קולו למעלה למקור הרחמים העליונים הנק' אב הרחמים ומקורם. ויבך לעורר ולהמשיך משם רחמים רבים על כל הנשמות ועל מקור כנסת ישראל להעלותן מגלותן ולייחדן ביחוד העליון אור א"ס ב"ה בבחי' נשיקין שהיא אתדבקות רוחא ברוחא כמ"ש ישקני מנשיקות פיהו דהיינו התקשרות דבור האדם בדבר ה' זו הלכה וכן מחשבה במחשבה ומעשה במעשה שהוא מעשה המצות. ובפרט מעשה הצדקה וחסד. דחסד דרועא ימינא והוא בחי' חיבוק ממש כמ"ש וימינו תחבקני. ועסק התורה בדבור ומחשבת העיון הן בחי' נשיקין ממש. והנה ע"י זה יכול לבוא לבחי' אהבה רבה בהתגלות לבו כדכתיב ליעקב אשר פדה את אברהם כמ"ש במ"א:

פרק מו ויש דרך ישר לפני איש שוה לכל נפש וקרוב הדבר מאד מאד לעורר ולהאיר אור האהבה התקועה ומסותרת בלבו להיות מאירה בתוקף אורה כאש בוערה בהתגלות לבו ומוחו למסור נפשו לה' וגופו ומאודו בכל לב ובכל נפש ומאד מעומקא דלבא באמת לאמיתו ובפרט בשעת ק"ש וברכותיה כמו שיתבאר. והוא כאשר ישים אל לבו מ"ש הכתו' כמים הפנים לפנים כן לב האדם אל האדם פי' כמו שכדמות וצורת הפנים שהאדם מראה במים כן נראה לו שם במים אותה צורה עצמה ככה ממש לב האדם הנאמן באהבתו לאיש אחר הרי האהבה זו מעוררת אהבה בלב חבירו אליו ג"כ להיות אוהבים נאמנים זה לזה בפרט כשרואה אהבת חבירו אליו. והנה זהו טבע הנהוג במדת כל אדם אף אם שניהם שוים במעלה ועל אחת כמה וכמה אם מלך גדול ורב מראה אהבתו הגדולה והעצומה לאיש הדיוט ונבזה ושפל אנשים ומנוול המוטל באשפה ויורד אליו ממקו' כבודו עם כל שריו יחדיו ומקימו ומרימו

מאד בפיך ובלבבך דהיינו להיות רגיל על לשונו וקולו לעורר כוונת לבו ומוחו להעמיק מחשבתו בחי החיים א"ס ב"ה כי הוא אבינו ממש האמיתי ומקור חיינו ולעורר אליו האהבה כאהבת הבן אל האב. וכשירגיל עצמו כן תמיד הרי ההרגל נעשה טבע. ואף אם נדמה לו לכאורה שהוא כח דמיוני לא יחוש מאחר שהוא אמת לאמיתו מצד עצמו בבחי' אהבה מסותרת רק שתועלת יציאתה אל הגילוי כדי להביא לידי מעשה שהוא עסק התורה והמצות שלומד ומקיים ע"י זה כדי לעשות נחת רוח לפניו ית' כבן העובד את אביו. ועל זה אמרו מחשבה טובה הקב"ה מצרפה למעשה להיות גדפין לפרחא כנ"ל. והנחת רוח הוא כמשל שמחת המלך מבנו שבא אליו בצאתו מבית האסורים כנ"ל או להיות לו דירה בתחתונים כנ"ל והנה גם לבחי' נפשי אויתיך הנ"ל קרוב הדבר מאד להוציאה מההעלם אל הגילוי ע"י ההרגל תמיד בפיו ולבו שוין. אך אם אינו יכול להוציאה אל הגילוי בלבו אעפ"כ יכול לעסוק בתורה ומצות לשמן ע"י ציור ענין אהבה במחשבה שבמוחו ומחשבה טובה הקב"ה מצרפה כו': והנה ב' בחי' אהבות אלו אף שהן ירושה לנו מאבותינו וכמו טבע בנפשותינו וכן היראה הכלולה בהן שהיא לירא מליפרד ח"ו ממקור חיינו ואבינו האמיתי ב"ה אעפ"כ אינן נקראות בשם דחילו ורחימו טבעיים אלא כשהן במוחו ומחשבתו לבד ותעלומות לב ואז מקומן בי"ס דיצירה ולשם הן מעלות התורה והמצות הבאות מחמתן ובסביבתן. אבל כשהן בהתגלות לבו נק' רעותא דלבא בזוהר ומקומן בי"ס דבריאה ולשם הן מעלות עמהן התורה והמצות הבאות מחמתן. מפני שיציאתן מההעלם והסתר הלב אל בחי' גילוי היא ע"י הדעת ותקיעת המחשבה בחוזק והתבוננות עצומה מעומקא דלבא יתיר ותדיר בא"ס ב"ה איך הוא חיינו ממש ואבינו האמיתי ב"ה ומודעת זאת מ"ש בתיקונים כי בעולם הבריאה מקננא תמן אימא עילאה שהיא ההתבוננות באור א"ס חי החיים ב"ה וכמאמר אליהו בינה לבא ובה הלב מבין. ולא עוד אלא שב' בחי' אהבות אלו הנ"ל הן כלולות מן בחי' אהבה רבה וגדולה ומעולה מדחילו ורחימו שכליים אשר האהבה נק' לעיל בשם אהבת עולם רק שאעפ"כ צריך לטרוח בשכלו להשיג ולהגיע גם לבחי' אהבת עולם הנ"ל הבאה מהתבוננה ודעת בגדולת ה' כדי להגדיל מדורת אש האהבה ברשפי אש ושלהבת עזה ולהב העולה השמימה עד שמים רבים לא יוכלו לכבות וכו' ונהרות לא ישטפוה וכו' כי יש יתרון ומעלה לבחי' אהבה כרשפי אש ושלהבת עזה וכו' הבאה מהתבוננה ודעת בגדולת א"ס ב"ה על שתי בחי' אהבה הנ"ל כאשר אינן כרשפי אש ושלהבת כו' כיתרון ומעלת הזהב על הכסף וכו' כמ"ש לקמן וגם כי זה כל האדם ותכליתו למען דעת את כבוד ה' ויקר תפארת גדולתו איש איש כפי אשר יוכל שאת כמ"ש בר"מ פ' בא בגין דישתמודעון ליה וכו' וכנודע:

ד אייר פשוטה
ל ניסן מעוברת

ה אייר פשוטה
א אייר מעוברת

ו אייר פשוטה
ב אייר מעוברת

קודמים לירד ולהתגלות] ולכן אפשר לרשע ובעל עבירות שיעשה תשובה מאהבה הנולדה בלבו בזכרו את ה' אלהיו ומ"מ היראה ג"כ כלולה בה ממילא רק שהיא בבחי' קטנות והעולם דהיינו יראת חטא למרוד בו ח"ו והאהבה היא בהתגלות לבו ומוחו אך זהו דרך מקרה והוראת שעה בהשגחה פרטית מאת ה' לצורך שעה כמעשה דר"א בן דורדייא. אבל סדר העבודה הקבועה ותלויה בבחירת האדם צריך להקדים תחלה קיום התורה והמצות ע"י יראה תתאה בבחי' קטנות עכ"פ בסור מרע ועשה טוב להאיר נפשו האלהית באור התורה ומצותיה ואח"כ יאיר עליה אור האהבה [כי ואהבת בגימטריא ב"פ אור כידוע לי"ח]:

פרק מד והנה כל מדרגת אהבה מב' מדרגות אלו אהבה רבה ואהבת עולם נחלקת לכמה בחי' ומדרגות לאין קץ כל חד לפום שיעורא דיליה כמ"ש בזה"ק ע"פ נודע בשערים בעלה דא קב"ה דאיהו אתידע ואתדבק לכל חד לפום מה דמשער בלביה וכו'. ולכן נקראי' דחילו ורחימו הנסתרות לה' אלהינו ותורה ומצות הן הנגלות לנו ולבנינו לעשות כו'. כי תורה אחת ומשפט אחד לכולנו בקיום כל התורה ומצות בבחי' מעשה משא"כ בדחילו ורחימו שהם לפי הדעת את ה' שבמוח ולב כנ"ל. אך אחת היא אהבה הכלולה מכל בחי' ומדרגות אהבה רבה ואהבת עולם והיא שוה לכל נפש מישראל וירושה לנו מאבותינו. והיינו מ"ש הזהר ע"פ נפשי אויתיך בלילה וגו' דירחים לקב"ה רחימותא דנפשא ורוחא כמה דאתדבקו אילין בגופא וגופא רחים לון וכו'. וז"ש נפשי אויתיך כלומר מפני שאתה ה' נפשי וחיי האמיתים לכך אויתיך פי' שאני מתאוה ותאב לך כאדם המתאוה לחיי נפשו וכשהוא חלש ומעונה מתאוה ותאב שתשוב נפשו אליו וכן כשהוא הולך לישן מתאוה וחפץ שתשוב נפשו אליו כשיעור משנתו כך אני מתאוה ותאב לאור א"ס ב"ה חיי החיים האמיתיים להמשיכו בקרבי ע"י עסק התורה הקיציץ משנתי בלילה דאורייתא וקב"ה כולא חד. כמ"ש הזהר שם דבעי בר נש מרחימותא דקב"ה למיקם בכל לילא לאשתדלא בפולחניה עד צפרא כו'. ואהבה רבה וגדולה מזו והיא מסותרת ג"כ בכל נפש מישראל בירושה מאבותינו היא מ"ש בר"מ כברא דאשתדל בתר אבוי ואימיה דרחים לון יתיר מגרמיה ונפשיה ורוחיה כו' כי הלא אב אחד לכולנו. ואף כי מי הוא זה ואיזהו אשר ערב לבו לגשת להשיג אפי' חלק אחד מני אלף ממדרגת אהבת רעיא מהימנא. מ"מ הרי אפס קצהו ושמץ מנהו מרב טובו ואורו מאיר לכללות ישראל בכל דור ודור כמ"ש בתיקונים דאתפשטותיה בכל דרא ודרא לאנהרא לון וכו'. רק שהארה זו היא בבחי' הסתר והעלם גדול בנפשות כל בית ישראל ולהוציא אהבה זו המסותרת מההעלם וההסתר אל הגילוי להיות בהתגלות לבו ומוחו לא נפלאת היא ולא רחוקה היא אלא קרוב הדבר

בגדולת ה' דאיהו ממלא כל עלמין ומהארץ לרקיע מהלך ת"ק שנה וכו' ובין רקיע לרקיע כו' רגלי החיות כנגד כולן וכו' וכן השתלשלות כל העולמות למעלה מעלה עד רום המעלות אעפ"כ נקרא יראה זו יראה חיצונית ותתאה מאחר שנמשכת מהעולמות שהם לבושים של המלך הקב"ה אשר מסתתר ומתעלם ומתלבש בהם להחיותם ולקיימם להיות יש מאין וכו' רק שהיא השער והפתח לקיום התורה והמצות. אך היראה עילאה ירא בשת ויראה פנימית שהיא נמשכת מפנימית האלהות שבתוך העולמות עליה אמרו אם אין חכמה אין יראה דחכמה היא כ"ח מ"ה והחכמה מאין תמצא ואיזהו חכם הרואה את הנולד פי' שרואה כל דבר איך נולד ונתהוה מאין ליש בדבר ה' ורוח פיו ית' כמ"ש וברוח פיו כל צבאם ואי לזאת הרי השמים והארץ וכל צבאם בטלים במציאות ממש בדבר ה' ורוח פיו וכלא ממש חשיבי ואין ואפס ממש כביטול אור וזיו השמש בגוף השמש עצמה ואל יוציא אדם עצמו מהכלל שגם גופו ונפשו ורוחו ונשמתו בטלים במציאות בדבר ה' ודבורו ית' מיוחד במחשבתו כו' וכנ"ל [פ' כ' וכ"א] באריכות בד"מ מנפש האדם שדבורו אחד מדבורו ומחשבתו כלא ממש כו' וזש"ה הן יראת ה' היא חכמה. אך אי אפשר להשיג ליראה וחכמה זו אלא בקיום התורה והמצות ע"י יראה תתאה החיצונית וז"ש אם אין יראה אין חכמה. והנה באהבה יש ג"כ שתי מדרגות אהבה רבה ואהבת עולם. אהבה רבה היא אהבה בתענוגי' והיא שלהבת העולה מאליה ובאה מלמעלה בבחי' מתנה למי שהוא שלם ביראה כנודע על מאמר רז"ל של איש דרכו לחזר אחר אשה שאהבה נקראת איש וזכר כמ"ש זכר חסדו ואשה יראת ה' כנודע ובלי קדימת היראה אי אפשר להגיע לאהבה רבה זו כי אהבה זו היא מבחי' אצילות דלית תמן קיצוץ ופירוד ח"ו אך אהבת עולם היא הבאה מהתבונה ודעת בגדולת ה' א"ס ב"ה הממלא כל עלמין וסובב כל עלמין וכולא קמיה כלא ממש חשיב וכביטול דבור אחד בנפש המשכיל בעודו במחשבתה או בחמדת הלב כנ"ל אשר ע"י התבוננו' זו ממילא תתפשט מדת האהבה שבנפש מלבושיה דהיינו שלא תתלבש בשום דבר הנאה ותענוג גשמי או רוחני לאהבה אותו ולא לחפוץ כלל שום דבר בעולם בלתי ה' לבדו מקור החיים של כל התענוגים שכולם בטילים במציאות וכלא ממש קמיה חשיבי ואין ערוך ודמיון כלל ביניהם ח"ו כמו שאין ערוך לאין ואפס המוחלט לגבי חיים נצחיים וכמ"ש מי לי בשמים ועמך לא חפצתי בארץ כלה שארי ולבבי צור לבבי וגו' וכמ"ש לקמן וגם מי שאין מדת אהבה שבנפשו מלובשת כלל בשום תענוג גשמי או רוחני יכול להלהיב נפשו כרשפי אש ושלהבת עזה ולהב העולה השמימה ע"י התבוננו' הנ"ל כמ"ש לקמן והנה בחי' אהבה זו פעמים שקודמת ליראה כפי בחי' הדעת המולידה כנודע [שהדעת כולל חסדים וגבורות שהם אהבה ויראה ופעמים שהחסדים

ל ניסן פשוטה

א אייר פשוטה
כז ניסן מעוברת

ליקוטי אמרים

ממש מלא כל הארץ כבודו ממש וצופה ומביט ובוחן כליותיו ולבו וכל מעשיו ודבוריו וכל צעדיו יספור אזי תקבע בלבו היראה לכל היום כולו כשיחזור ויתבונן בזה אפילו בהתבוננות קלה בכל עת ובכל שעה יהיה סור מרע ועשה טוב במחשבה דבור ומעשה שלא למרות ח"ו עיני כבודו אשר מלא כל הארץ וכמאמר רבן יוחנן בן זכאי לתלמידיו כנ"ל וז"ש הכתוב כי אם ליראה את ה' אלהיך ללכת בכל דרכיו שהיא יראה המביאה לקיום מצותיו ית' בסור מרע ועשה טוב. והיא יראה תתאה הנ"ל ולגבי משה דהיינו לגבי בחי' הדעת שבכל נפש מישראל האלהית מילתא זוטרתי היא כנ"ל [שהדעת הוא המקשר מצפוני בינת הלב אל בחי' גילוי במחשבה ממש כידוע לי"ח] ועוד זאת יזכור כי כמו שבמלך בשר ודם עיקר היראה היא מפנימיותו וחיותו ולא מגופו שהרי כשישן אין שום יראה ממנו. והנה פנימיותו וחיותו אין נראה לעיני בשר רק בעיני השכל על ידי ראיית עיני בשר בגופו ולבושיו שיודע שחיותו מלובש בתוכם וא"כ ככה ממש יש לו לירא את ה' ע"י ראיית עיני בשר בשמים וארץ וכל צבאם אשר אור א"ס ב"ה מלובש בהם להחיותם:* ואף שהוא ע"י התלבשות בלבושים רבים הרי אין הבדל והפרש כלל ביראת מלך בשר ודם בין שהוא ערום ובין שהוא לבוש לבוש אחד ובין שהוא לבוש בלבושים רבים אלא העיקר הוא ההרגל להרגיל דעתו ומחשבתו תמיד להיות קבוע בלבו ומוחו תמיד אשר כל מה שרואה בעיניו השמים והארץ ומלואה הכל הם לבושים החיצונים של המלך הקב"ה וע"י זה יזכור תמיד על פנימיותם וחיותם וזה נכלל ג"כ בלשון אמונה שהוא לשון רגילות שמרגיל האדם את עצמו כמו אומן המאמן ידיו וכו'. וגם להיות לזכרון תמיד לשון חז"ל קבלת עול מלכות שמים שהוא כענין שום תשים עליך מלך כמ"ש במ"א וכו' כי הקב"ה מניח את העליונים והתחתונים ומייחד מלכותו עלינו וכו' ואנחנו מקבלים וכו' וזהו ענין ההשתחואות שבתפלת י"ח אחר קבלת עול מלכות שמים בדבור בק"ש לחזור ולקבל בפועל ממש במעשה וכו' כמ"ש במ"א:

פרק מג והנה על יראה תתאה זו שהיא לקיום מצותיו ית' בבחי' סור מרע ועשה טוב אמרו אם אין יראה אין חכמה ויש בה בבחי' קטנות ובחי' גדלות דהיינו כשנמשכת בבחי' יראה זו מהתבוננות

כח ניסן פשוטה

כד ניסן מעוברת

כה ניסן מעוברת

הגהה

(וגם נראה בראיית העין שהם בטלים לאורו ית' בהשתחוואתם כל יום כלפי מערב בשקיעתם כמארז"ל ע"פ וצבא השמים לך משתחוים שהשכינה במערב ונמצא הילוכם כל יום כלפי מערב הוא דרך השתחואה וביטול והנה גם מי שלא ראה את המלך מעולם ואינו מכירו כלל אעפ"כ כשנכנס לחצר המלך וראה שרים רבים ונכבדים משתחוים לא' תפול עליו אימה ופחד):

כט ניסן פשוטה

כו ניסן מעוברת

ממ"ה הקב"ה אשר מלא כל הארץ כבודו עומד עליו ורואה במעשיו מיד יגיע אליו היראה וכו' ויש נפש שפלה בטבעה ותולדתה ממקור חוצבה ממדרגות תחתונות די"ס דעשיה ולא תוכל למצוא במחשבתה האלהות כ"א בקושי ובחזקה ובפרט אם הוטמאה בחטאת נעורי' שהעוונות מבדילים כו' [כמ"ש בס"ח סי' ל"ה] ומ"מ בקושי ובחזק' שתתחזק מאד מחשבתו באומץ ויגיעה רבה ועומק גדול להעמיק בגדולת ה' שעה גדולה בודאי תגיע אליו עכ"פ היראה תתאה הנ"ל וכמשארז"ל יגעתי ומצאתי תאמין וכדכתי' אם תבקשנה ככסף וכמטמונים תחפשנה אז תבין יראת ה' פי' כדרך שמחפש אדם מטמון ואוצר הטמון בתחתיות הארץ שחופר אחריו ביגיעה עצומה כך צריך לחפור ביגיעה עצומה לגלות אוצר של יראת שמים הצפון ומוסתר בבינת הלב של כל אדם מישראל שהיא בחי' ומדרגה שלמעלה מהזמן והיא היראה הטבעית המסוטרת הנ"ל רק שכדי שתבא לידי מעשה בבחי' יראת חטא להיות סור מרע במעשה דבור ומחשבה צריך לגלותה ממצפוני בינת הלב שלמעלה מהזמן להביאה לבחי' מחשבה ממש שבמוח להעמיק בה מחשבתו משך זמן מה ממש עד שתצא פעולתה מהכח אל הפועל ממש דהיינו להיות סור מרע ועשה טוב במחשבה דבור ומעשה מפני ה' הצופה ומביט ומאזין ומקשיב ומבין אל כל מעשהו ובוחן כליותיו ולבו וכמאמר רז"ל הסתכל בשלשה דברים כו' עין רואה ואוזן שומעת כו' וגם כי אין לו דמות הגוף הרי אדרבה הכל גלוי וידוע לפניו ביתר שאת לאין קץ מראיית העין ושמיעת האזן עד"מ רק הוא עד"מ כמו אדם היודע ומרגיש בעצמו כל מה שנעשה ונפעל באחד מכל רמ"ח איבריו כמו קור או חום ואפי' חום שבצפרני רגליו עד"מ אם נכוה באור וכן מהותם ועצמותם וכל מה שמתפעל בהם יודע ומרגיש במוחו וכעין ידיעה זו עד"מ יודע הקב"ה כל הנפעל בכל הנבראים עליונים ותחתונים להיות כולם מושפעי' ממנו ית' כמ"ש כי ממך הכל וז"ש וגם כל היצור לא נכחד ממך וכמ"ש הרמב"ם [והסכימו לזה חכמי הקבלה כמ"ש הרמ"ק בפרד"ס] שבידיעת עצמו כביכול יודע כל הנבראים הנמצאים מאמיתת המצאו וכו' רק שמשל זה אינו אלא לשכך את האזן אבל באמת אין המשל דומה לנמשל כלל כי נפש האדם אפי' השכלית והאלהית היא מתפעלת ממאורעי הגוף וצערו מחמת התלבשותה ממש בנפש החיונית המלובשת בגוף ממש אבל הקב"ה אינו מתפעל ח"ו ממאורעי העולם ושינוייו ולא מהעול' עצמו שכולם אינו פועלים בו שום שינוי ח"ו וכדי להשכיל זה היטב בשכלנו כבר האריכו חכמי האמת בספריהם אך כל ישראל מאמינים בני מאמיני' בלי שום חקירת שכל אנושי ואומרי' אתה הוא עד שלא נברא העולם וכו' כנ"ל פ"כ: והנה כל אדם מישראל יהיה מי שיהיה כשיתבונן בזה שעה גדולה בכל יום איך שהקב"ה מלא ממש את העליונים ואת התחתונים ואת השמים ואת הארץ

כו ניסן פשוטה
כב ניסן מעוברת

כז ניסן פשוטה
כג ניסן מעוברת

ליקוטי אמרים

התורה והתפלה להעלות ניצוץ אלהות שבתוכה למקורו תהא רק כדי לעשות נחת רוח לפניו ית' כמשל שמחת המלך בבוא אליו בנו יחידו בצאתו מן השביה ובית האסורים כנ"ל. והנה כוונה זו היא אמיתית באמת לאמיתו לגמרי בכל נפש מישראל בכל עת ובכל שעה מאהבה הטבעית שהיא ירושה לנו מאבותינו. רק שצריך לקבוע עתים להתבונן בגדולת ה' להשיג דחילו ורחימו שכליים וכולי האי ואולי וכו' כנ"ל:

פרק מב והנה במ"ש לעיל בענין יראה תתאה יובן היטב מ"ש בגמ' על פסוק ועתה ישראל מה ה' אלהיך שואל מעמך כי אם ליראה את ה' אלהיך אטו יראה מילתא זוטרתי היא אין לגבי משה מילתא זוטרתי היא וכו' דלכאורה אינו מובן התירוץ דהא שואל מעמך כתיב. אלא הענין הוא כי כל נפש ונפש מבית ישראל יש בה מבחי' משרע"ה כי הוא משבעה רועים הממשיכים חיות ואלהות לכללו' נשמות ישראל שלכן נקראים בשם רועים ומשרע"ה הוא כללו' כולם ונקרא רעיא מהימנא דהיינו שממשיך בחי' הדעת לכללות ישראל לידע את ה' כל אחד כפי השגת נשמתו ושרשה למעלה וינקתה משרש נשמת משרע"ה המושרשת בדעת העליון שבי"ס דאצילות המיוחדות במאצילן ב"ה שהוא ודעתו אחד והוא המדע כו'. ועוד זאת יתר על כן בכל דור ודור יורדין ניצוצין מנשמת משרע"ה ומתלבשין בגוף ונפש של חכמי הדור עיני העדה ללמד דעת את העם ולידע גדולת ה' ולעבדו בלב ונפש כי העבודה שבלב היא לפי הדעת כמ"ש דע את אלהי אביך ועבדהו בלב שלם ונפש חפיצה ולעתיד הוא אומר ולא ילמדו איש את רעהו לאמר דעו את ה' כי כולם ידעו אותי וגו' אך עיקר הדעת אינה הידיעה לבדה שידעו גדולת ה' מפי סופרים ומפי ספרים אלא העיקר הוא להעמיק דעתו בגדולת ה' ולתקוע מחשבתו בה' בחוזק ואומץ הלב והמוח עד שתהא מחשבתו מקושרת בה' בקשר אמיץ וחזק כמו שהיא מקושרת בדבר גשמי שרואה בעיני בשר ומעמיק מחשבתו בו כנודע שדעת הוא לשון התקשרות כמו והאדם ידע וגו' וכח זה ומדה זו לקשר דעתו בה' יש בכל נפש מבית ישראל בינקתה מנשמת משרע"ה רק מאחר שנתלבשה הנפש בגוף צריכה ליגיעה רבה ועצומה כפולה ומכופלת. האחת היא יגיעת בשר לבטש את הגוף ולהכניעו שלא יחשיך על אור הנפש כמש"ל בשם הזהר דגופא דלא סליק ביה נהורא דנשמתא מבטשין ליה והיינו על ידי הרהורי תשובה מעומק הלב כמ"ש שם. והשנית היא יגיעת הנפש שלא תכבד עליה העבודה ליגע מחשבתה להעמיק ולהתבונן בגדולת ה' שעה גדולה רצופה כי שיעור שעה זו אינו שוה בכל נפש יש נפש זכה בטבעה שמתבוננת תמיד יגיע אליה היראה ופחד ה' כמ"ש בש"ע א"ח סימן א' כשיתבונן האדם שהמלך הגדול

לרוות נפשו הצמאה לה' אלא כברא דאשתדל בתר אבוי ואמי' דרחים לון יתיר מגרמיה ונפשיה כו' [כמ"ש לעיל בשם רעיא מהימנא]. מ"מ יש לכל אדם להרגיל עצמו בכוונה זו כי אף שאינה באמת לאמיתו לגמרי בלבו שיחפוץ בזה בכל לבו מ"מ מעט מזער חפץ לבו בזה באמת מפני אהבה הטבעית שבלב כל ישראל לעשות כל מה שהוא רצון העליון ב"ה. ויחוד זה הוא רצונו האמיתי והיינו יחוד העליון שבאצילות הנעשה באתערותא דלתתא ע"י יחוד נפש האלהית והתכללותה באור ה' המלובש בתורה ומצות שעוסקת בהן והיו לאחדי' ממש כמש"ל כי ע"ז מתיחדים ג"כ מקור התורה והמצות שהוא הקב"ה עם מקור נפשו האלהית הנקרא בשם שכינה שהן בחי' ממלא כל עלמין ובחי' סובב כל עלמין כמ"ש במ"א בארוכות.

אבל יחוד נפשו והתכללותה באור ה' להיות לאחדים בזה חפץ כל אדם מישראל באמת לאמיתו לגמרי בכל לב ובכל נפש מאהבה הטבעית המסותרת בלב כל ישראל לדבקה בה' ולא ליפרד ולהיות נכרת ונבדל ח"ו מיחודו ואחדותו ית' בשום אופן אפי' במסירת נפש ממש ועסק התורה ומצות והתפלה הוא ג"כ ענין מסירת נפש ממש כמו בצאתה מן הגוף במלאת שבעים שנה שאינה מהרהרת בצרכי הגוף אלא מחשבתה מיוחדת ומלובשת באותיות התורה והתפלה שהן דבר ה'. ומחשבתו ית' והיו לאחדים ממש שזהו כל עסק הנשמות בג"ע כדאיתא בגמרא ובזהר אלא ששם מתענגים בהשגתם והתכללותם באור ה' וזהו שתקנו בתחלת ברכות השחר קודם התפלה אלהי נשמה וכו' ואתה נפחתה כו' ואתה עתיד ליטלה ממני כו' כלום' מאחר שאתה נפחתה בי ואתה עתיד ליטלה ממני לכן מעתה אני מוסרה ומחזירה לך לייחדה באחדותך וכמ"ש נפשי אשא אליך ה' והיינו על ידי התקשרות מחשבתי ודיבורי בדיבוריך באותיות התורה והתפלה ובפרט באמירה לה' לנכח כמו ברוך אתה וכה"ג והנה בהכנה זו של מסירת נפשו לה' יתחיל ברכות השחר ברוך אתה כו' וכן בהכנה זו יתחיל ללמוד שיעור קבוע מיד אחר התפלה וכן באמצע היום קודם שיתחיל ללמוד צריכה הכנה זו לפחות כנודע שעיקר ההכנה לשמה לעכב הוא בתחל' הלימוד בבינונים וכמו בגט וס"ת שצריכים לשמה לעכב ודיו שיאמר בתחלת הכתיבה הריני כותב לשם קדושת ס"ת או לשמו ולשמה כו' וכשלומד שעות הרבה רצופות יש לו להתבונן בהכנה זו והנ"ל בכל שעה ושעה עכ"פ כי בכל שעה ושעה היא המשכה אחרת מעולמות עליונים להחיות התחתונים והמשכת החיות שבשעה שלפניה חוזרת למקורה [בסוד רצוא ושוב שבס' יצירה] עם כל התורה ומעשים טובים של התחתונים כי בכל שעה שולט צירוף אחד מי"ב צירופי שם הוי"ה ב"ה בי"ב שעות היום וצירופי שם אדנ"י בלילה כנודע. והנה כל כוונתו במסירת נפשו לה' ע"י

קדוש' כו' [ובר"מ שם ד' קי"א ע"ב] שכל אדם צ"ל בשתי בחי' ומדרגות והן בחי' עבד ובחי' בן ואף דיש בן שהוא ג"כ עבד הרי א"א אפשר לבא למדרגה זו בלי קדימת היראה עילאה כידוע ליודעים והנה אף מי שגם במוחו ובמחשבתו אינו מרגיש שום יראה ובושה מפני פחיתות ערך נפשו ממקור חוצבה ממדרגות תחתונו' די"ס דעשיה אעפ"כ מאחר שמתכוין בעבודתו כדי לעבוד את המלך הרי זו עבודה גמורה כי היראה והעבודה נחשבות לשתי מצות במנין תרי"ג ואינן מעכבות זו את זו. ועוד שבאמת מקיים גם מצות יראה במה שממשיך היראה במחשבתו כי בשעה ורגע זו עכ"פ מורא שמים עליו עכ"פ כמורא בשר ודם הדיוט לפחות שאינו נק' מלך המביט עליו שנגמנע בעבורו מלעשות דבר שאינו הגון בעיניו שזו נק' יראה כמו שאמר רבן יוחנן בן זכאי לתלמידיו יהי רצון שיהא מורא שמים עליכם כמורא בשר ודם כו' תדעו כשאדם עובר עבירה אומר שלא יראני אדם כו' רק שיראה זו נקראת יראת תתאה ויראת חטא שקודמת לחכמתו ויראה עילאה הוא ירא בושת כו' דאית יראה ואית יראה כו' אבל בלי יראה כלל לא פרחא לעילא באהבה לבדה כמו שהעוף אינו יכול לפרוח בכנף אחד דדחילו ורחימו הן תרין גדפין [כמ"ש בתיקונים] וכן היראה לבדה היא כנף אחד ולא פרחא בה לעילא אף שנק' עבודת עבד וצריך להיות ג"כ בחי' בן לעורר האהבה הטבעית עכ"פ המסותרת בלבו שתהא בהתגלות מוחו עכ"פ לזכור אהבתה לה' אחד במחשבתו וברצונו לדבקה בו ית' וזאת תהיה כוונתו בעסק התורה או המצוה הזו לדבקה בו נפשו האלהית והחיונית ולבושיהן כנ"ל. אך אמנם אמרו רז"ל לעולם אל יוציא אדם עצמו מן הכלל לכן יתכוין ליחד ולדבקה בו ית' מקור נפשו האלהית ומקור נפשות כל ישראל שהוא רוח פיו ית' הנק' בשם שכינה על שם ששוכנת ומתלבשת תוך כל עלמין להחיותן ולקיימן והיא המשפעת בו כח הדבור הזה שמדבר בדברי תורה או כח המעשה הזה לעשות מצוה זו ויחוד זה הוא ע"י המשכת אור א"ס ב"ה למטה ע"י עסק התורה והמצות שהוא מלובש בהן ויתכוין להמשיך אורו ית' על מקור נפשו ונפשות כל ישראל ליחדן וכמ"ש לקמן פי' יחוד זה באריכות ע"ש. וזהו פי' לשם יחוד קב"ה ושכינתיה בשם כל ישראל* ואף שלהיות כוונה זו אמיתית בלבו שיהיה בלבו באמת חפץ היחוד העליון הזה צריך להיות בלבו אהבה רבה לה' לבדו לעשות נחת רוח לפניו לבד ולא

יט ניסן פשוטה
טו ניסן מעוברת

כ ניסן פשוטה
טז ניסן מעוברת

כא ניסן פשוטה

הגהה

◄ (וגם על ידי זה יתמתקו גם כן הגבורות בחסדים ממילא בהתכללות המדות ויחודם על ידי גילוי רצון העליון ב"ה המתגלה למעלה באתערותא דלתתא הוא גילויו למטה בעסק התורה והמצוה שהן רצונו ית' וכמ"ש באדרא רבא ובמשנת חסידים מסכת א"א פ"ד שתרי"ג מצות התורה נמשכות מחיוורתא דא"א שהוא מקור רצון העליון מקור החסדים):

ליקוטי אמרים

והאהבה לועשה טוב. אעפ"כ לא די לעורר האהבה לבדה לועשה טוב ולפחות צריך לעורר תחלה היראה הטבעית המסותרת בלב כל ישראל שלא למרוד בממ"ה הקב"ה כנ"ל שתהא בהתגלות לבו או מוחו עכ"פ דהיינו להתבונן במחשבתו עכ"פ גדולת א"ס ב"ה ומלכותו אשר היא מלכות כל עולמים עליונים ותחתונים ואיהו ממלא כל עלמין וסובב כל עלמין וכמ"ש הלא את השמים ואת הארץ אני מלא ומניח העליונים ותחתונים ומייחד מלכותו על עמו ישראל בכלל ועליו בפרט כי חייב אדם לומר בשבילי נברא העולם והוא גם הוא מקבל עליו מלכותו להיות מלך עליו ולעבדו ולעשות רצונו בכל מיני עבודת עבד. והנה ה' נצב עליו ומלא כל הארץ כבודו ומביט עליו ובוחן כליות ולב אם עובדו כראוי. ועל כן צריך לעבוד לפניו באימה וביראה כעומד לפני המלך ויעמיק במחשבה זו ויאריך בה כפי יכולת השגת מוחו ומחשבתו וכפי הפנאי שלו לפני עסק התורה או המצוה כמו לפני לבישת טלית ותפילין וגם יתבונן איך שאור אין סוף ב"ה הסובב כל עלמין וממלא כל עלמין הוא רצון העליון הוא מלובש באותיו' וחכמת התורה או בציצית ותפילין אלו ובקריאתו או בלבישתו הוא ממשיך אורו ית' עליו דהיינו על חלק אלוה ממעל שבתוך גופו ליכלל וליבטל באורו יתברך ודרך פרט בתפילין ליבטל וליכלל בבחי' חכמתו ובינתו שבנפשו האלהית בבחי' חכמתו ובינתו של א"ס ב"ה המלובשות דרך פרט בפ' קדש והיה כי יביאך דהיינו שלא להשתמש בחכמתו ובינתו שבנפשו בלתי לה' לבדו וכן ליבטל ליכלל בבחי' הדעת שבנפשו הכולל חו"ג שהן יראה ואהבה שבלבו בבחי' דעת העליון הכולל חו"ג המלובש בפ' שמע והיה אם שמוע והיינו כמ"ש בש"ע לשעבד הלב והמוח כו'. ובעטיפת ציצית יכוין כמ"ש בזהר להמשיך עליו מלכותו ית' אשר היא מלכות כל עולמים וכו' לייחדה עלינו ע"י מצוה זו והוא כענין שום תשים עליך מלך ואזי אף אם בכל זאת לא תפול עליו אימה ופחד בהתגלות לבו מ"מ מאחר שמקבל עליו מלכות שמים וממשיך עליו יראתו ית' בהתגלות מחשבתו ורצונו שבמוחו וקבלה זו היא אמיתית בלי שום ספק שהרי היא טבע נפשות כל ישראל שלא למרוד במלך הקדוש ית' הרי התורה שלומד או המצוה שעושה מחמת קבלה זו ומחמת המשכת היראה שבמוחו נקראות בשם עבודה שלימה ככל עבודת העבד לאדונו ומלכו משא"כ אם לומד ומקיים המצוה באהבה לבדה כדי לדבקה בו ע"י תורתו ומצותיו אינה נקראת בשם עבודת העבד והתורה אמרה ועבדתם את ה' אלהיכם וגו' ואותו תעבודו וגו' וכמ"ש בזהר [פ' בהר] כהאי תורא דיהבין עליה עול בקדמיתא בגין לאפקא מיניה טב לעלמא כו' הכי נמי אצטריך לב"נ לקבלא עליה עול מלכות שמים בקדמיתא כו' ואי האי לא אשתכח גביה לא שריא ביה

יא ניסן מעוברת

יח ניסן פשוטה
יב ניסן מעוברת

יג ניסן מעוברת

יד ניסן מעוברת

ליקוטי אמרים

ח ניסן מעוברת

יעופף [וכמ"ש הרח"ו ז"ל בשער היחודים פי"א] שהכנפים בעוף הן זרועות האדם כו' ובתיקונים פי' שהעוסקים בתורה ומצות בדחילו ורחימו נקראים בנים ואם לאו נק' אפרוחים דלא יכלין לפרחא* כי כמו שכנפי העוף אינם עיקר העוף ואין חיותו תלוי בהם כלל כדתנן ניטלו אגפיה כשרה והעיקר הוא ראשו וכל גופו והכנפיי' אינם רק משמשים לראשו וגופו לפרחא בהון וכך ד"מ התורה ומצות הן עיקר היחוד העליון ע"י גילוי רצון העליון המתגלה על ידיהן והדחילו ורחימו הם מעלים אותן למקום שיתגלה בו הרצון אור אין סוף ברוך הוא והיחוד שהן יצירה

טז ניסן פשוטה
ט ניסן מעוברת

ובריאה* והנה אף דדחילו ורחימו הם ג"כ מתרי"ג מצות אעפ"כ נקראין גדפין להיות כי תכלית האהבה היא העבודה מאהבה ואהבה בלי עבודה היא אהבה בתענוגים להתענג על ה' מעין עוה"ב וקבלת שכר והיום לעשות' כתי' ולמחר לקבל שכרם ומי שלא הגיע למדה זו לטעום מעין עוה"ב אלא עדיין נפשו שוקקה וצמאה לה' וכלתה אליו כל היום ואינו מרווה צמאונו במי התורה שלפניו הרי זה כמי שעומד בנהר וצועק מים מים לשתות כמו שקובל עליו הנביא הוי כל צמא לכו למים. כי לפי פשוטו אינו מובן דמי שהוא צמא ומתאווה ללמוד פשיטא שילמוד מעצמו ולמה לו לנביא לצעוק עליו הוי וכמ"ש במ"א באריכות:

יז ניסן פשוטה
י ניסן מעוברת

פרק מא ברם צריך להיות לזכרון תמיד ראשית העבודה ועיקרה ושרשה. והוא כי אף שהיראה היא שרש לסור מרע

בכל עולם מהן לפי מעלתו ואף שנפש האדם העוסק בתורה ומצוה זו אינה מאצילות מ"מ הרי רצון העליון המלובש במצוה זו והוא עצמו הדבר הלכה והתורה שעוסק בה הוא אלהות ואור א"ס המאציל ב"ה שהוא ורצונו אחד וברצונו ית' האציל מדותיו המיוחדות בו ית' וע"י גילוי רצונו המתגלה ע"י עסק תורה ומצוה זו הן נכללות ונמתקות הגבורות בחסדים בעת רצון זו):

הגהה

(ובתיקון מ"ה דעופא הוא מט"ט רישא דיליה י' וגופא וא"ו ותרין גדפין ה' ה' כו' והיינו עולם היצירה שנקרא מט"ט ובו הן גופי הלכות שבמשנה ורישא דיליה הן המוחין ובחי' חב"ד שהן פנימיות ההלכות וסודן וטעמיהן ותרין גדפין דחילו ורחימו הן ה' עילאה שהיא רחימו וה' תתאה היא יראה תתאה עול מלכות שמים ופחד ה' כפחד המלך ד"מ שהיא יראה חיצונית ונגלית משא"כ יראה עילאה ירא בושת היא מהנסתרות לה' אלהינו והיא בחכמה עילאה יו"ד של שם הוי' ב"ה כמ"ש בר"מ):

הגהה

(או אפילו בעשיה בי"ס דקדושה מקום מצות מעשיות וכן מקרא אבל במשנה מתגלה היחוד ואור אין סוף ברוך הוא ביצירה ובתלמוד בבריא' דהיינו שבלימודו מקרא מתפשט היחוד ואור א"ס ב"ה מאצילו' עד העשיה ובמשנה עד היצירה לבדה ובתלמוד עד הבריאה לבדה כי כולן באצילות אבל קבלה אינה מתפשטת כלל מאצילות לבי"ע כמ"ש בפרע"ח):

ליקוטי אמרים

וכמ"ש בזוהר על פסוק מה יתרון לאדם בכל עמלו שיעמול תחת השמש דאפילו עמלא דאורייתא אי עביד בגין יקריה כו' וז"ש אשרי מי שבא לכאן ותלמודו בידו פי' שלא נשאר למטה בעו"הז. ואף דאורייתא וקב"ה כולא חד שהוא ורצונו אחד הרי קב"ה איהו ממלא כל עלמין בשוה ואעפ"כ אין העולמות שוים במעלתם והשינוי הוא מהמקבלים בב' בחי' הא' שהעליונים מקבלים הארה יותר גדולה לאין קץ מהתחתונים והשנית שמקבלים בלי לבושים ומסכים רבים כ"כ כבתחתונים ועו"הז הוא עולם השפל בב' בחי' כי ההארה שבו מצומצמת מאד עד קצה האחרון ולכן הוא חומרי וגשמי וגם זאת היא בלבושים ומסכים רבים עד שנתלבשה בקליפת נוגה להחיות כל דברים הטהורים שבעו"הז ובכללה הוא נפש החיונית המדברת שבאדם ולכן כשמדברת דברי תורה ותפלה בלא כוונה אף שהן אותיות קדושות ואין קליפת נוגה שבנפש החיונית מסך מבדיל כלל להסתיר ולכסות על קדושתו ית' המלובשת בהן כמו שהיא מסתרת ומכסה על קדושתו ית' שבנפש החיונית כשמדברת דברים בטלי' ושבנפש החיונית שבשאר בעלי חיים הטהורים דאף דלית אתר פנוי מיני' מ"מ איהו סתימו דכל סתימין ונק' אל מסתתר וגם ההארה והתפשטות החיות ממנו ית' מסתתרת בלבושים ומסכים רבים ועצומים עד שנתלבשה ונסתתרה בלבוש נוגה משא"כ באותיות הקדושות של דברי תורה ותפלה דאדרבה קליפת נוגה מתהפכת לטוב ונכללת בקדושה זו כנ"ל מ"מ ההארה שבהן מקדושתו ית' היא בבחי' צמצום עד קצה האחרון מאחר שהקול והדבור הוא גשמי אבל בתפלה בכוונה ותורה בכוונה לשמה הרי הכוונה מתלבשת באותיות הדבור הואיל והיא מקור ושרש להן שממחמתה ובסיבתה הוא מדבר אותיות אלו לכן היא מעלה אותן עד מקומה בי"ס דיצירה או דבריאה לפי מה שהיא הכוונה בדחילו ורחימו שכליים או טבעיים כו' כנ"ל ושם מאיר ומתגלה אור א"ס ב"ה שהוא רצון העליון ב"ה המלובש באותיות התורה שלומד ובכוונתן או בתפלה ובכוונתה או במצוה ובכוונתה בהארה גדולה לאין קץ מה שלא יכול להאיר ולהתגלות כלל בעוד האותיות והמצוה בעו"הז הגשמי לא מינה ולא מקצתה עד עת קץ הימין שיתעלה העולם מגשמיותו ונגלה כבוד ה' וגו' כנ"ל באריכות:* ובזה יובן היטב הא דדחילו ורחימו נקראי' גדפין ד"מ כדכתי' ובשתים

הגהה

(ושם מאיר ומתגלה ג"כ היחוד העליון הנעשה בכל מצוה ות"ת שהוא יחוד מדותיו ית' שנכללות זו בזו ונמתקות הגבורות בחסדים ע"י עת רצון העליון א"ס ב"ה המאיר ומתגלה בבחי' גילוי רב ועצום באתערותא דלתתא היא עשיית המצוה או עסק התורה שבהן מלובש רצון העליון א"ס ב"ה אך עיקר היחוד הוא למעלה מעלה בעולם האצילות ששם הוא מהות ועצמות מדותיו ית' מיוחדו' במאצילן א"ס ב"ה ושם הוא מהות ועצמות רצון העליון א"ס ב"ה והארתן לבד היא מאירה בבי"ע

יד ניסן פשוטה

טו ניסן פשוטה

ז ניסן מעוברת

ליקוטי אמרים

יא ניסן פשוטה
ג ניסן מעוברת

לעלות וליכלל ביחודו ית' שהן עשר ספי' הקדושות וכמ"ש בתיקונים דבלא דחילו ורחימו לא פרחא לעילא ולא יכלא לסלקא ולמיקם קדם ה'. והיינו אפי' אם אינו עוסק שלא לשמה ממש לשום איזו פניה ח"ו אלא כמ"ש ותהי יראתם אותי מצות אנשי' מלומדה פי' מחמת הרגל שהורגל מקטנותו שהרגילו ולימדו אביו ורבו לירא את ה' ולעבדו ואינו עוסק לשמה ממש כי לשמה ממש אי אפשר בלא התעוררות דחילו ורחימו הטבעיים עכ"פ להוציאן מהסתר הלב אל הגילוי במוח ותעלומות לבו עכ"פ כי כמו שאין אדם עושה דבר בשביל חבירו למלאות רצונו אא"כ אוהבו או ירא ממנו כך אי אפשר לעשות לשמו ית' באמת למלאות רצונו לבד בלי זכרון והתעוררות אהבתו ויראתו כלל במוחו ומחשבתו ותעלומות לבו עכ"פ וגם אהבה לבדה אינה נק' בשם עבודה בלי יראה תתאה לפחות שהיא מסותרת בלב כל ישראל כמ"ש לקמן וכשעוסק שלא לשמה ממש לשום איזו פניה לכבוד עצמו כגון

יב ניסן פשוטה
ד ניסן מעוברת

להיות ת"ח וכהאי גוונא אזי אותה פניה שמצד הקליפה דנוגה מתלבשת בתורתו והתורה היא בבחי' גלות בתוך הקליפה לפי שעה עד אשר יעשה תשובה שמביאה רפואה לעולם שבשובו אל ה'. גם תורתו שבה עמו ולכן אמרו רז"ל לעולם יעסוק אדם וכו' שמתוך שלא לשמה בא לשמה בודאי שבודאי סופו לעשות תשובה בגלגול זה או בגלגול אחר כי לא ידח ממנו נדח אך כשעושה סתם לא לשמה ולא שלא לשמה אין הדבר תלוי בתשובה אלא מיד שחוזר ולומד דבר זה לשמה הרי גם מה שלמד בסתם מתחבר ומצטרף ללימוד זה ופרחא לעילא מאחר שלא נתלבש בו עדיין שום קליפה דנוגה ולכן לעולם יעסוק אדם כו' וכן הענין בתפלה שלא בכוונה כמ"ש בזהר:

יג ניסן פשוטה
ה ניסן מעוברת

פרק מ אך כל זמן שלא חזר ולמד דבר זה לשמה אין לימודו עולה אפי' בי"ס המאירות בעולם היצירה והעשיה כי הספירות הן בחי' אלהות ובהן מתלבש ומתיחד אור א"ס ב"ה ממש ובלא דחילו ורחימו לא יכלא לסלקא ולמיקם קדם ה' כמ"ש בתיקונים רק לימודו עולה להיכלות ומדורין שהן חיצוניות העולמות שבהן עומדים המלאכים וכמ"ש הרח"ו ז"ל בשער הנבוא פ"ב שמהתורה שלא בכוונה נבראים מלאכים בעולם היצירה ומהמצות בלי כוונה נבראים מלאכים בעולם העשייה וכל המלאכים הם בעלי חומר וצורה אבל תורה שלא לשמה ממש כגון להיות ת"ח וכה"ג אינה עולה כלל למעלה אפי' להיכלו' ומדור המלאכים דקדושה אלא נשארת למטה בעו"הז הגשמי שהוא מדור הקליפות*

הגהה

◂ (כמ"ש בזהר ח"ג דף ל"א ע"ב ודף קכ"א עמוד ב' עי' שם ההיא מלה סלקא ובקעא רקיעין כו' ואתער מה דאתער אי טב טב כו' ע"ש ודף ק"ה ע"א מלה דאורייתא אתעביד מיניה קלא וסליק כו' וד' קס"ח ע"ב קלין דאורייתא וצלותא בקעין רקיעין כו'):

ליקוטי אמרים

מלובשות י״ס דאצי׳ ומיוחדות בהן בתכלית וי״ס דאצי׳ מיוחדות בתכלית במאצילן א״ס ב״ה משא״כ הנשמ״כ אינן נכללות באלהות די״ס אלא עומדות בהיכלות ומדורין דבריאה או יצירה ונהנין מזיו השכינה הוא אור א״ס ב״ה המיוחד בי״ס דבריאה או דיצי׳ והוא זיו תורתן ועבודתן ממש [ע׳ זהר ויקהל דר״י] כי שכר מצוה היא מצוה עצמה: ועולם האצילות שהוא למעלה מהשכל וההשגה וההבנה לשכל נברא כי חכמתו ובינתו ודעתו של א״ס ב״ה מיוחדות שם בו בתכלית היחוד ביחוד עצום ונפלא ביתר שאת ויתר עז לאין קץ מעולם הבריאה כי שם ירדו להאיר בבחי׳ צמצום כדי שיוכלו שכלים נבראי׳ לקבל מהן חב״ד לידע את ה׳ ולהבין ולהשיג איזו השגה באור א״ס ב״ה כפי כח שכלים הנבראים שהם בעלי גבול ותכלית שלא יתבטלו במציאותם ולא יהיו בגדר נבראים כלל רק יחזרו למקורם ושרשם שהוא בחי׳ אלהות ממש. והנה צמצום זה היא סבת ההארה שמאירות שם חב״ד של א״ס ב״ה לנשמות אלו בעולם הבריאה. משא״כ באצילות שאינם בבחי׳ צמצום כ״כ א״א לשכלים נבראים לקבל מהן ולכן לית מחשבתא דילהון תפיסא שם כלל לכן הוא מדור לצדיקי׳ הגדולים שעבודתם היא למעלה מעלה אפי׳ מבחי׳ דחילו ורחימו הנמשכות מן הבינה ודעת בגדולתו ית׳ כמו שעולם האצילות הוא למעלה מעלה מבחי׳ בינה ודעת לשכל נברא אלא עבודתם היתה בבחי׳ מרכבה ממש לא״ס ב״ה וליבטל אליו במציאות ולהכלל באורו ית׳ הם וכל אשר להם ע״י קיום התורה והמצות ע״ד שאמרו האבות הן המרכבה והיינו לפי שכל ימיהם היתה זאת עבודתם. אך מי ששרש נשמתו קטן מהכיל עבודה תמה זו ליבטל וליכלל באורו ית׳ בעבודתו בקביעות רק לפרקים ועתים שהם עת רצון למעלה וכמו בתפלת שמונה עשרה שהיא באצילות ובפרט בהשתחוואו׳ שבה שכל השתחוואה היא בבחי׳ אצילות [כמ״ש בפרע״ח בקבל׳ שבת] כי היא ענין ביטול באורו ית׳ להיות חשיב קמיה כלא ממש אזי ג״כ עיקר קביעות נשמתו הוא בעולם הבריאה [רק לפרקים בעת רצון תעלה נשמתו לאצילות בבחי׳ מ״נ כידוע לי״ח]: והנה שכר מצוה מצוה פי׳ שמשכרה נדע מהותה ומדרגתה ואין לנו עסק בנסתרות שהם צדיקי׳ הגדולים שהם בבחי׳ מרכבה רק הנגלו׳ לנו שאחריהם כל אדם ימשוך לידע נאמנה מהות ומדרגת עבודת ה׳ בדחילו ורחימו בהתגלות לבו הנמשכות מן הבינה ודעת בגדולת א״ס ב״ה דבריאה ועבודה בדחילו ורחימו הטבעיים שבמוחו בי״ס דיצירה אבל עבודה בלי התעוררות דחילו ורחימו אפי׳ במוחו בבחי׳ גילוי דהיינו לעורר האהבה הטבעית המסותרת בלב להוציאה מהעלם והסתר הלב אל הגילוי אפי׳ במוחו ותעלומות לבו עכ״פ רק היא נשארת מסותרת בלב כתולדתה כמו שהיתה קודם העבודה הרי עבודה זו נשארת למטה בעולם הפירוד הנק׳ חיצוניות העולמות ואין בה כח

ט ניסן פשוטה
כח אדר ב מעוברת

כט אדר ב מעוברת

א ניסן מעוברת

י ניסן פשוטה
ב ניסן מעוברת

ליקוטי אמרים

ודעתו וכך הן על ד"מ היראה והאהבה הטבעיות המסותרות בלב כל ישראל כי הן ירושה לנו מאבותינו וכמו טבע בנפשותינו כנז"ל:

פרק לט ומפני זה ג"כ נקראים המלאכים בשם חיות ובהמות כדכתי' ופני אריה אל הימין וגו' ופני שור מהשמאל וגו' לפי שאינם בעלי בחירה ויראתם ואהבתם היא טבעית להם כמ"ש בר"מ פ' פנחס ולכן מעלת הצדיקים גדולה מהם כי מדור נשמות הצדיקים הוא בעולם הבריאה ומדור המלאכי' בעולם היצירה:* וההבדל שביניהם הוא כי בעולם היצירה מאירות שם מדותיו של א"ס ב"ה לבדן שהן אהבתו ופחדו ויראתו כו'. וכמ"ש [בתיקונים וע"ח] דשית ספירין מקננין ביצירה ולכן זאת היא עבודת המלאכים תמיד יומם ולילה לא ישקוטו לעמוד ביראה ופחד וכו' והיינו כל מחנה גבריאל שמהשמאל ועבודת מחנה מיכאל היא האהבה כו'. אבל בעולם הבריאה מאירות שם חכמתו ובינתו ודעתו של א"ס ב"ה שהן מקור המדות ואם ושרש להן וכדאיתא בתיקונים דאימא עילאה מקננא בתלת ספירן בכרסיא שהוא עולם הבריאה ולכן הוא מדור נשמות הצדיקים עובדי ה' בדחילו ורחימו הנמשכות מן הבינה ודעת גדולות א"ס ב"ה שאהבה זו נקרא רעותא דלבא כנ"ל ומרעותא דלבא נעשה לבוש לנשמה בעולם הבריאה שהוא גן עדן העליון כדלקמן וכמ"ש בזהר ויקהל אך היינו דווקא נשמות ממש שהן בבחי' מוחין דגדלות א"ס ב"ה אבל בבחי' הרוח של הצדיקים וכן שאר כל נשמות ישראל שעבדו את ה' בדחילו ורחימו המסותרות בלב כללו' ישראל אין לשם רק בשבת ור"ח לבד דרך העמוד שמג"ע התחתון לג"ע העליון שהוא עולם הבריאה הנקרא ג"ע העליון להתענג על ה' וליהנות מזיו השכינה כי אין הנאה ותענוג לשכל נברא אלא במה שמשכיל ומבין ויודע ומשיג בשכלו ובינתו מה שאפשר לו להבין ולהשיג מאור א"ס ב"ה ע"י חכמתו ובינתו ית' המאירות שם בעולם הבריאה ומה שזוכות נשמות אלו לעלות למעלה מהמלאכים אף שעבדו בדחילו ורחימו טבעיים לבד היינו מפני שע"י דחילו ורחימו שלהם אתכפיא ס"א המלובשת בגופם בין בבחי' סור מרע לכבוש התאוות ולשברן ובין בבחי' ועשה טוב כנ"ל והם היו בעלי בחירה לבחור ברע ח"ו ובחרו בטוב לאכפיא לס"א לאסתלקא יקרא דקב"ה כו' כיתרון האור כו' וכנ"ל והנה כל זה הוא במדור הנשמות ומקום עמידתן אך תורתן ועבודתן נכללות ממש בי"ס שהן בחי' אלהות ואור א"ס מתייחד בהן בתכלית היחוד והיינו בי"ס דבריאה ע"י דחילו ורחימו שכליים ובי"ס דיצירה ע"י דחילו ורחימו טבעיי' ובתוכן

ז ניסן פשוטה
כז אדר ב מעוברת

הגהה
(והיינו בסתם מלאכים אבל יש מלאכים עליונים בעולם הבריאה שעבודתם בדחילו ורחימו שכליים כמ"ש בר"מ שם שיש שני מיני חיות הקדש טבעיים ושכליים וכמ"ש בע"ח):

ח ניסן פשוטה

14

ליקוטי אמרים

בו ית' ולא שדביקות המחשבה ושכל האדם בו ית' היא מצד עצמה למעלה מדביקו' קיום המצות מעשיו' בפועל ממש כמ"ש לקמן אלא מפני שזהו ג"כ רצונו ית' לדבקה בשכל ומחשבה וכוונת המצות מעשיו' ובכווג' ק"ש ותפלה ושאר ברכות והארת רצון העליון הזה המאירה ומלובשת בכוונה זו היא גדולה לאין קץ למעלה מעלה מהארת רצון העליון המאירה ומלובשת בקיום המצות עצמן במעשה ובדבור בלי כוונה כגודל מעלת אור הנשמה על הגוף שהוא כלי ומלבוש הנשמה כמו גוף המצוה שהוא כלי ומלבוש לכוונתה ואף שבשתיהן במצוה ובכוונתה מלובש רצון אחד פשוט בתכלית הפשיטות בלי שום שינוי וריבוי ח"ו ומיוחד במהותו ועצמותו ית' בתכלית היחוד אף על פי כן ההארה אינה שוה בבחינת צמצום והתפשטות* ונחלקת גם כן לארבע מדרגות כי גוף המצות עצמן ממש הן ב' מדרגות שהן מצות מעשיות ממש ומצות התלויות בדבור ומחשבה כמו תלמוד תורה וק"ש ותפלה וברכת המזון ושאר ברכות. וכוונת המצות לדבקה בו ית' שהיא כנשמה לגוף נחלקת ג"כ לשתי מדרגות כמו שתי מדרגות הנשמה שהן

הגהה

(וכמ"ש בע"ח שכוונת המצות ותלמוד תורה היא במדרגת אור וגוף המצות הן מדרגות וכחי' כלים שהם בחי' צמצום שע"י צמצום האור נתהוו הכלים כידוע לי"ח):

בגוף החומרי שהן חי ומדבר. כי מי שדעתו יפה לדעת את ה' ולהתבונן בגדולתו ית' ולהוליד מבינתו יראה עילאה במוחו ואהבת ה' בחלל הימני שבלבו להיות נפשו צמאה לה' לדבקה בו ע"י קיום התורה והמצות שהן המשכת והארת אור א"ס ב"ה על נפשו לדבקה בו ובכוונה זו הוא לומד ומקיים המצות וכן בכוונה זו מתפלל ומברך הרי כוונה זו על ד"מ כמו נשמת המדבר שהוא בעל שכל ובחירה ובדעת ידבר. ומי שדעתו קצרה לידע ולהתבונן בגדולת א"ס ב"ה להוליד האהבה מבינתו בהתגלות לבו וכן היראה במוחו ופחד ה' בלבו רק שזוכר ומעורר את האהבה הטבעית המסותרת בלבו ומוציאה מהעלם והסתר הלב אל הגילוי במוח עכ"פ שיהיה רצונו שבמוחו ותעלומות לבו מסכים ומתרצה ברצוי גמור באמת לאמיתו למסור נפשו בפועל ממש על יחוד ה' כדי לדבק בו נפשו האלהית ולבושיה ולכללן ביחודו ואחדותו שהוא רצון העליון המלובש בת"ת ובקיום המצות כנ"ל וגם היראה כלולה בה לקבל מלכותו שלא למרוד בו ח"ו ובכוונה זו הוא סור מרע ועושה טוב ולומד ומתפלל ומברך בפירוש המלות לבדו בלא דחילו ורחימו בהתגלות לבו ומוחו הרי כוונה זו עד"מ כמו נשמת החי שאינו בעל שכל ובחירה וכל מדותיו שהן יראתו מדברים המזיקים אותו ואהבתו לדברים הנאהבים אצלו הן רק טבעיים אצלו ולא מבינתו

ולקרות וכן בברכת המזון דאורייתא ובשאר ברכות דרבנן ובתפל' ואם הוציא בשפתיו ולא כיון לבו יצא ידי חובתו בדיעבד ואין צריך לחזור לבד מפסוק ראשון של ק"ש וברכה ראשונה של תפלת שמונה עשרה וכדאי' [ברפ"ב דברכות] ע"כ מצות כוונה מכאן ואילך מצות קריאה וכו'. והיינו משום שהנשמה אינה צריכה תיקון לעצמה במצות רק להמשיך אור לתקן נפש החיונית והגוף ע"י אותיות הדבור שהנפש מדברת בה' מוצאות הפה וכן במצות מעשיות שהנפש עושה בשאר אברי הגוף: אך אעפ"כ אמרו

כב אדר ב מעוברת

תפלה או שאר ברכה בלא כוונה הן בגוף בלא נשמה פי' כי כמו שכל הברואים שבעוה"ז שיש להם גוף ונשמה שהם נפש כל חי ורוח כל בשר איש ונשמת כל אשר רוח חיים באפיו מכל בעלי חיים וה' מחיה את כולם ומהוה אותם מאין ליש תמיד באור וחיות שמשפיע בהם שגם הגוף החומרי ואפי' אבנים ועפר הדומם ממש יש בו אור וחיות ממנו ית' שלא יחזור להיות אין ואפס כשהיה ואעפ"כ אין ערך ודמיון כלל בין בחי' אור וחיות המאיר בגוף לגבי בחי' אור וחיות המאיר בנשמה שהיא נפש כל חי ואף שבשניהם

ג ניסן פשוטה

אור אחד שוה בבחי' הסתר פנים ולבושי' שום שהאור מסתתר ומתעלם ומתלבש בו כי שניהם הם מעוה"ז שבכללותו מסתתר בשוה האור והחיות שמרוח פיו ית' בבחי' הסתר פנים וירידת המדרגות בהשתלשלות העולמות ממדרגה למדרגה בצמצומים רבים ועצומים עד שנתלבש בקליפת נוגה להחיות כללית עוה"ז החומרי דהיינו כל דברים המותרים והטהורים שבעולם הזה וממנה ועל ידה מושפעים דברים הטמאים כי היא בחי' ממוצעת כנ"ל אעפ"כ ההארה שהיא המשכת החיות אשר ה' מאיר ומחיה דרך לבוש זה

כג אדר ב מעוברת

אינה שוה בכולן בבחי' צמצום והתפשטות כי בגוף הגשמי והדומם ממש כאבנים ועפר ההארה היא בבחי' צמצום גדול אשר אין כמוהו והחיות שבו מועטת כל כך עד שאין בו אפי' כח הצומח ובצומח ההארה אינה בצמצום גדול כל כך. ודרך כלל נחלקות לארבע מדרגות דומם צומח חי מדבר כנגד ד' אותיות שם הוי"ה ב"ה שממנו מושפעים וכמו שאין ערך ודמיון ההארה והמשכת החיו' שבדומם וצומח לההארה והמשכת החיות המלובש' בחי' ומדבר אף שבכולן אור אחד שוה בבחי' הסתר פנים ומלובש בלבוש אחד בכולן שהוא לבוש נוגה כך אין ערך ודמיון כלל בין הארת והמשכת אור א"ס ב"ה שהוא פנימיות רצונו ית' בלי הסתר פנים ולבוש כלל המאירה ומלובשת במצות מעשיות ממש. וכן במצות התלויות בדבור ובביטוי שפתים בלי כוונה שהוא נחשב כמעשה ממש כנ"ל לגבי ההארה והמשכת אור א"ס ב"ה המאירה ומלובשת בכוונת המצות מעשיות שהאדם מתכוין בעשייתן כדי לדבקה בו ית' ע"י קיום רצונו שהוא ורצונו אחד וכן בכוונת התפלה וק"ש וברכותיה ושאר ברכות שבכוונתו בהן מדבק מחשבתו ושכלו

ד ניסן פשוטה

כד אדר ב מעוברת

ליקוטי אמרים

הפנימי' של נפש החיונית וגם מהותן ועצמותן של בחי' חב"ד מקליפת נוגה שבנפש החיונית נכללות בקדושה ממש כשעוסק בתורה בעיון ושכל ואף שמהותן ועצמותן של המדות חג"ת כו' לא יכלו להם הבינונים להפכם לקדושה היינו משום שהרע חזק יותר במדות מבחב"ד מפני יניקתן שם מהקדושה יותר כידוע לי"ח: זאת ועוד אחרת והיא העולה על כולנה במעלת עסק ת"ת על כל המצו' ע"פ מ"ש לעיל בשם התיקוני' דרמ"ח פיקודין הן רמ"ח אברי' דמלכא וכמו באדם התחתון ד"מ אין ערוך ודמיון כלל בין החיות שברמ"ח איבריו לגבי החיות שבמוחין שהוא השכל המתחלק לג' בחי' חב"ד ככה ממש ד"מ להבדיל ברבבות הבדלות לאין קץ בהארת אור א"ס ב"ה המתלבשות במצות מעשיות לגבי הארת אור א"ס שבבחי' חב"ד שבחכמת התורה איש איש כפי שכלו והשגתו. ואף שאינו משיג אלא בגשמיות הרי התורה נמשלה למים שיורדים ממקום גבוה כו' כמ"ש לעיל ואעפ"כ ארז"ל לא המדרש עיקר אלא המעשה והיום לעשותם כתיב ומבטלין ת"ת לקיום מצוה מעשיית כשא"א לעשותה ע"י אחרים משום כי זה כל האדם ותכלית בריאתו וירידתו לעו"הז להיות לו ית' דירה בתחתונים דוקא לאהפכא חשוכא לנהורא וימלא כבוד ה' את כל הארץ הגשמית דייקא וראו כל בשר יחדיו כנ"ל משא"כ כשאפשר לעשותה ע"י אחרים אין מבטלין ת"ת אף שכל התורה אינה אלא פירוש המצות מעשיות והיינו משום שהיא בחי' חב"ד של א"ס ב"ה ובעסקו בה ממשיך עליו אור א"ס ב"ה ביתר שאת והארה גדולה והארה לאין קץ מהארה והמשכה ע"י פקודין שהן אברי' דמלכא וז"ש רב ששת חדאי נפשאי לך קראי לך תנאי כמ"ש במ"א בארוכות: והנה המשכה והארה זו שהאדם ממשיך ומאיר מהארת אור א"ס ב"ה על נפשו ועל נפשות כל ישראל היא השכינ' כנסת ישראל מקור כל נשמות ישראל כמ"ש לקמן ע"י עסק התורה נקראת בלשון קריאה קורא בתורה פי' שע"י עסק התורה קורא להקב"ה לבוא אליו כביכול כאדם הקורא לחבירו שיבא אליו וכבן קטן הקורא לאביו לבא אליו להיות עמו בצוותא חדא ולא ליפרד ממנו ולישאר יחידי ח"ו וז"ש קרוב ה' לכל קוראיו לכל אשר יקראוהו באמת ואין אמת אלא תורה דהיינו שקורא להקב"ה ע"י התורה דוקא לאפוקי מי שקורא אותו שלא על ידי עסק התורה אלא צועק כך אבא אבא וכמו שקובל עליו הנביא ואין קורא בשמך כו' וכמ"ש במ"א. ומזה יתבונן המשכיל להמשיך עליו יראה גדולה בשעת עסק התורה כמש"ל [פ' כ"ג]:

פרק לח והנה עם כל הנ"ל יובן היטב פסק ההלכה הערוכה בתלמוד ופוסקי' דהרהור לאו כדבור דמי ואם קרא ק"ש במחשבתו ובלבו לבד בכל כח כוונתו לא יצא ידי חובתו וצריך לחזור

כט אדר פשוטה

א ניסן פשוטה

ב ניסן פשוטה
כא אדר ב מעוברת

ליקוטי אמרים

ולהעביר רוח הטומאה ממנה בשמירת' כל שס"ה מצות ל"ת שלא יינקו ממנה שס"ה גידיה כי כללות ישראל שהם ששים רבוא נשמות פרטיות הם כללות החיות של כללות העולם כי בשבילם נברא וכל פרט מהם הוא כולל ושייך לו חלק אחד מששים רבוא מכללות העולם התלוי בנפשו החיונית להעלותו לה' בעלייתה דהיינו במה שמשתמש מעוה"ז לצורך גופו ונפשו החיונית לעבודת ה' כגון אכילה ושתיה ודומיהם ודירה וכל כלי תשמישיו אלא ששים רבוא נשמות פרטיות אלו הן שרשי' וכל שרש מתחלק לששים רבוא ניצוצות שכל ניצוץ הוא נשמה אחת וכן בנפש ורוח בכל עולם מארבע עולמות אצילו' בריאה יצירה עשיה וכל ניצוץ לא ירד לעוה"ז אף שהיא ירידה גדולה ובחי' גלות ממש כי גם שיהיה צדיק גמור עובד ה' ביראה ואהבה רבה בתענוגים לא יגיע למעלות דביקותו בה' בדחילו ורחימו בטרם ירידתו לעוה"ז החומרי לא מינה ולא מקצתה ואין ערך ודמיון ביניהם כלל כנודע לכל משכיל שהגוף אינו יכול לסבול כו' אלא ירידתו לעולם הזה להתלבש בגוף ונפש החיונית הוא כדי לתקנם בלבד ולהפרידם מהרע של שלש קליפות הטמאות על ידי שמירת שס"ה ל"ת תעשה וענפיהן ולהעלות נפשו החיונית עם חלקה השייך לה מכללות עוה"ז ולקשרם וליחדם באור א"ס ב"ה אשר ימשיך בהם ע"י קיומו כל רמ"ח מצות עשה בנפשו החיוני' שהיא היא המקיימ' כל מצות מעשיות כנ"ל וכמ"ש [בע"ח שער כ"ו] כי הנשמה עצמה אינה צריכה תיקון כלל כו' ולא הוצרכה להתלבש בעוה"ז וכו' רק להמשיך אור לתקנם כו' והוא ממש דוגמת סוד גלות השכינה לברר ניצוצין וכו'. ובזה יובן מה שהפליגו רז"ל במעלת הצדקה מאד מאד ואמרו ששקולה כנגד כל המצות ובכל תלמוד ירושלמי היא נק' בשם מצוה סתם כי כך היה הרגל הלשון לקרוא צדקה בשם מצוה סתם מפני שהיא עיקר המצות מעשיות ועולה על כולנה שכולן הן רק להעלות נפש החיונית לה' שהיא היא המקיימת אותן ומתלבשת בהן ליכלל באור א"ס ב"ה המלובש בהן ואין לך מצוה שנפש החיונית מתלבשת בה כל כך כבמצות הצדקה שבכל המצות אין מתלבש בהן רק כח א' מנפש החיונית בשעת מעשה המצוה לבד אבל בצדקה שאדם נותן מיגיע כפיו הרי כל כח נפשו החיונית מלובש בעשיית מלאכתו או עסק אחר שנשתכר בו מעות אלו וכשנותנן לצדקה הרי כל נפשו החיונית עולה לה'. וגם מי שאינו נהנה מיגיעו מ"מ הואיל ובמעות אלו היה יכול לקנות חיי נפשו החיונית הרי נותן חיי נפשו לה'. ולכן אמרו רז"ל שמקרבת את הגאולה לפי שבצדק' אחת מעלה הרבה מנפש החיונית מה שלא היה יכול להעלות ממנה כל כך כחות ובחי' בכמה מצות מעשיות אחרות. ומ"ש רז"ל שת"ת כנגד כולם היינו מפני שת"ת היא בדבור ומחשבה שהם לבושים

ע"י נפש החיונית הבהמית המלובשת באברי הגוף ממש וכל מה שמדבר בכח גדול יותר הוא מכניס ומלביש יותר כחות מנפש החיונית בדיבורים אלו וז"ש הכתוב כל עצמותי תאמרנה וגו' וז"ש רז"ל אם ערוכה בכל רמ"ח איברים משתמרת ואם לאו אינה משתמרת כי השכחה היא מקליפת הגוף ונפש החיונית הבהמית שהן מקליפת נוגה הנכללת לפעמים בקדושה והיינו כשמתיש כחן ומכניס כל כחן בקדושת התורה או התפלה:

זאת ועוד אחרת שכח נפש החיונית המתלבשת באותיות הדבור בת"ת | כד אדר פשוטה
או תפלה וכיוצא בהן או מצות מעשיות הרי כל גידולו וחיותו מהדם | יד אדר ב מעוברת
שהוא מקליפת נוגה ממש שהן כל אוכלין ומשקין שאכל ושתה ונעשו דם
שהיו תחת ממשלתה וינקו חיותם ממנה ועתה היא מתהפכת מרע לטוב
ונכללת בקדושה ע"י כח נפש החיונית הגדל ממנה שנתלבש באותיות אלו
או בעשיה זו אשר הן הן פנימיות רצונו ית' בלי שום הסתר פנים וחיותן
נכלל ג"כ באור א"ס ב"ה שהוא רצונו ית' ובהיותן נכלל ועולה ג"כ כח
נפש החיונית וע"י זה תעלה ג"כ כללות קליפת נוגה שהיא כללות החיות | טו אדר ב מעוברת
של עוה"ז הגשמי והחומרי וכאשר כל הנשמה ונפש האלהית שבכל ישראל
המתחלקת בפרטות לששים רבוא תקיים כל נפש פרטית כל תרי"ג מצות
התורה שס"ה ל"ת להפריד שס"ה גידים של דם נפש החיונית שבגוף שלא
יינקו ויקבלו חיות בעבירה זו מאחת משלש קליפות הטמאות לגמרי שמהן
נשפעים שס"ה ל"ת דאורייתא ושס"ה דרבנן שהן ונפיהן ושוב לא תוכל
נפש החיונית לעלות אל ה' כי אם נטמאה בטומאת השלש קליפות הטמאות
שאין להן עליה לעולם כ"א ביטול והעברה לגמרי כמ"ש ואת רוח הטומאה
אעביר מן הארץ ורמ"ח מצות עשה להמשיך אור א"ס ב"ה למטה להעלות
לו ולקשר וליחד בו כללות הנפש החיונית שברמ"ח אברי הגוף ביחוד גמור
להיות לאחדים ממש כמו שעלה ברצונו ית' להיות לו דירה בתחתונים והם
לו למרכבה כמו האבות. ומאחר שכללות נפש החיונית שבכללות ישראל | כה אדר פשוטה
תהיה מרכבה קדושה לה' אזי גם כללות החיות של עוה"ז שהיא קליפת | טז אדר ב מעוברת
נוגה עכשיו תצא אז מטומאתה וחלאתה ותעלה לקדושה להיות מרכבה
לה' בהתגלות כבודו וראו כל בשר יחדיו ויופיע עליהם בהדר גאון עוזו
וימלא כבוד ה' את כל הארץ וישראל יראו עין בעין כבמתן תורה דכתיב
אתה הראת לדעת כי ה' הוא האלהים אין עוד מלבדו ועל ידי זה יתבלעו
ויתבטלו לגמרי כל השלש קליפות הטמאות כי יניקתן וחיותן מהקדושה
עכשיו היא ע"י קליפת נוגה הממוצעת ביניהן ונמצא כי כל תכלית של | יז אדר ב מעוברת
ימות המשיח ותחיית המתים שהוא גילוי כבודו ואלהותו ית' ולהעביר רוח
הטומאה מן הארץ תלוי בהמשכת אלהותו ואור א"ס ב"ה לנפש החיונית
שבכללות ישראל בכל רמ"ח אבריה ע"י קיומה כל רמ"ח מצות עשה

ליקוטי אמרים

כדכתיב וכל העם רואים את הקולות את הנשמע ופי' רז"ל מסתכלים למזרח ושומעין את הדבור יוצא אנכי כו'. וכן לארבע רוחות ולמעלה ולמטה ודפי' בתיקונים דלית אתר דלא מליל מיניה עמהון כו' והיינו מפני גילוי רצונו ית' בעשרת הדברות שהן כללות התורה שהיא פנימית רצונו ית' וחכמתו ואין שם הסתר פנים כלל כמ"ש כי באור פניך נתת לנו תורת חיים ולכן היו בטלים במציאות ממש כמארז"ל שעל כל דיבור פרחה נשמתן כו' אלא שהחזירה הקב"ה להן בטל שעתיד להחיות בו את המתים והוא טל תורה שנקרא עוז כמארז"ל כל העוסק בתורה טל תורה מחייהו כו'. רק שאח"כ גרם החטא ונתגשמו הם והעולם עד עת קץ הימין שאז יזדכך גשמיות הגוף והעולם ויוכלו לקבל גילוי אור ה' שיאיר לישראל ע"י התורה שנק' עוז ומיתרון ההארה לישראל יהיה חשך האומות גם כן כדכתיב והלכו גוים לאורך וגו' וכתיב בית יעקב לכו ונלכה באור ה' וכתיב ונגלה כבוד ה' וראו כל בשר יחדיו וגו' וכתיב לבוא בנקרת הצורים ובסעיפי הסלעי' מפני פחד ה' והדר גאונו וגו' וכמ"ש והופע בהדר גאון עוזך על כל יושבי תבל ארצך וגו':

יא אדר ב מעוברת

פרק לז והנה תכלית השלימות הזה של ימות המשיח ותחיית המתים שהוא גילוי אור א"ס ב"ה בעוה"ז הגשמי תלוי במעשינו ועבודתנו כל זמן משך הגלות כי הגורם שכר המצוה היא המצוה בעצמה כי בעשייתה ממשיך האדם גילוי אור א"ס ב"ה מלמעלה למטה להתלבש בגשמיות עוה"ז בדבר שהיה תחלה תחת ממשלת קליפת נוגה ומקבל חיותה ממנה שהם כל דברים הטהורים ומותרי' שנעשית בהם המצוה מעשיית כגון קלף התפילין ומזוזה וספר תורה וכמאמר רז"ל לא הוכשר למלאכת שמים אלא טהורים ומותרים בפיך. וכן אתרוג שאינו ערלה* ומעות הצדקה שאינן גזל וכיוצא בהם ועכשיו שמקיים בהם מצות ה' ורצונו הרי החיות שבהם עולה ומתבטל ונכלל באור א"ס ב"ה שהוא רצונו ית' המלובש בהם מאחר שאין שם בחי' הסתר פנים כלל להסתיר אורו ית' וכן כח נפש החיונית הבהמית שבאברי גוף האדם המקיים המצוה הוא מתלבש ג"כ בעשיה זו ועולה מהקליפה ונכלל בקדושת המצוה שהיא רצונו ית' ובטל באור א"ס ב"ה וגם במצות תלמוד תורה וק"ש ותפלה וכיוצא בהן אף שאינן בעשיה גשמית ממש שתחת ממשלת קליפת נוגה מ"מ הא קיימא לן בדהרהור לאו כדבור דמי ואינו יוצא ידי חובתו עד שיוציא בשפתיו וקיימא לן דעקימת שפתיו הוי מעשה כי אי אפשר לנפש האלהית לבטא בשפתיים ופה ולשון ושיניים הגשמיים כי אם

כג אדר פשוטה
יב אדר ב מעוברת

יג אדר ב מעוברת

הגהה

* (שהערלה היא משלש קליפות הטמאות לגמרי שאין להם עליה לעולם כמ"ש בע"ח וכן כל מצוה הבאה בעבירה ח"ו)

ועד רגליו וז"ש דשכינתא שריא על רישיה על דייקא וכן אכל בי עשרה שכינתא שריא. והנה כל בחי' המשכת אור השכינה שהוא בחי' גילוי אור א"ס ב"ה אינו נקרא שינוי ח"ו בו ית' ולא ריבוי כדאיתא בסנהדרין דאמר ליה ההוא מינא לרבן גמליאל אמריתו כל בי עשרה שכינתא שריא כמה שכינתא אית לכו והשיב לו משל מאור השמש הנכנס בחלונות רבים כו' והמשכיל יבין:

פרק לו והנה מודעת זאת מארז"ל שתכלית בריאת עולם הזה הוא שנתאוה הקב"ה להיות לו דירה בתחתונים. והנה לא שייך לפניו ית' בחי' מעלה ומטה כי הוא ית' ממלא כל עלמין בשוה. אלא ביאור הענין כי קודם שנברא העולם היה הוא ית' לבדו יחיד ומיוחד וממלא כל המקום הזה שברא בו העולם וגם עתה כן הוא לפניו ית' רק שהשינוי הוא אל המקבלים חיותו ואורו ית' שמקבלים ע"י לבושים רבים המכסים ומסתירים אורו ית' כדכתיב כי לא יראני האדם וחי וכדפי' רז"ל שאפי' מלאכים הנק' חיות אין רואין כו' וזהו ענין השתלשלות העולמות וירידתם ממדרגה למדרג' ע"י ריבוי הלבושים המסתירים האור והחיות שממנו ית' עד שנברא עוה"ז הגשמי והחומרי ממש והוא התחתון במדרגה שאין תחתון למטה ממנו בענין הסתר אורו ית' וחשך כפול ומכופל עד שהוא מלא קליפות וס"א שהן נגד ה' ממש לומ' אני ואפסי עוד. והנה תכלית השתלשלו' העולמו' וירידתם ממדרגה למדרגה אינו בשביל עולמות העליוני' הואיל ולהם ירידה מאור פניו ית' אלא התכלית הוא עוה"ז התחתון שכך עלה ברצונו ית' להיות נחת רוח לפניו ית' כד אתכפיא ס"א ואתהפך חשוכא לנהורא שיאיר אור ה' אין סוף ב"ה במקום החשך והס"א של כל עוה"ז כולו ביתר שאת ויתר עז ויתרון אור מן החשך מהארתו בעולמות עליונים שמאיר שם ע"י לבושים והסתר פנים המסתירים ומעלימים אור א"ס ב"ה שלא יבטלו במציאות. וזה נתן הקב"ה לישראל את התורה שנקר' עוז וכח וכמארז"ל שהקב"ה נותן כח בצדיקים לקבל שכרם לעתיד לבא שלא יתבטלו במציאות ממש באור ה' הנגלה לעתיד בלי שום לבוש כדכתיב ולא יכנף עוד מוריך [פי' שלא יתכסה ממך בכנף ולבוש] והיו עיניך רואות את מוריך וכתיב כי עין בעין יראו וגו' וכתיב לא יהיה לך עוד השמש לאור יומם וגו' כי ה' יהיה לך לאור עולם וגו'. ונודע שימות המשיח ובפרט כשיחיו המתים הם תכלית ושלימות בריאות עולם הזה שלכך נברא מתחילתו* וגם כבר היה לעולמים מעין זה בשעת מתן תורה כדכתי' אתה הראת לדעת כי ה' הוא האלהים אין עוד מלבדו הראת ממש בראיה חושית

כא אדר פשוטה
ז אדר ב מעוברת

ח אדר ב מעוברת

ט אדר ב מעוברת

הגהה

כב אדר פשוטה
יא אדר ב מעוברת

∗ (וקבלת שכר עיקרו באלף השביעי כמ"ש בלקוטי תורה מהאר"י ז"ל):

ליקוטי אמרים

רצון העליון ב"ה וירידת המדרגות עד שיוכלו להתהוות ולהבראות יש מאין ודבר נפרד בפני עצמו ולא יבטלו במציאות כנ"ל משא"כ המצות שהן פנימיות רצונו ית' ואין שם הסתר פנים כלל אין החיות שבהם דבר נפרד בפני עצמו כלל אלא הוא מיוחד ונכלל ברצונו ית' והיו לאחדים ממש ביחוד גמור. והנה ענין השראת השכינה הוא גילוי אלהותו ית' ואור א"ס ב"ה באיזה דבר והיינו לומר שאותו דבר נכלל באור ה' ובטל לו במציאות לגמרי שאז הוא שורה ומתגלה בו ה' אחד אבל כל מה שלא בטל אליו במציאות לגמרי אין אור ה' שורה ומתגלה בו ואף צדיק גמור שמתדבק בו באהבה רבה הרי לית מחשבה תפיסא ביה כלל כי באמת כי אמיתת ה' אלהים אמת הוא יחודו ואחדותו שהוא לבדו הוא ואפס בלעדו ממש. וא"כ זה האוהב שהוא יש ולא אפס לית מחשבה דיליה תפיסא ביה כלל ואין אור ה' שורה ומתגלה בו אלא ע"י קיום המצות שהן רצונו וחכמתו ית' ממש בלי שום הסתר פנים* והנה כשהאדם עוסק בתורה אזי נשמתו שהיא נפשו האלהית עם שני לבושיה הפנימים לבדם שהם כח הדבור והמחשבה נכללות באור א"ס ב"ה ומיוחדות בו ביחוד גמור והיא השראת השכינה על נפשו האלהית כמארז"ל שאפי' אחד שיושב ועוסק בתורה שכינה עמו. אך כדי להמשיך אור והארת השכינה גם על

יח אדר פשוטה

יט אדר פשוטה

הגהה

(וכאשר שמעתי ממורי ע"ה פי' וטעם למ"ש בע"ח שאור א"ס ב"ה אינו מתייחד אפי' בעולם האצילות אלא ע"י התלבשותו תחלה בספי' חכמה והיינו משום שא"ס ב"ה הוא אחד האמת שהוא לבדו הוא ואין זולתו וזו היא מדרגת החכמה וכו'):

גופו ונפשו הבהמית שהיא החיונית המלובשת בגופו ממש צריך לקיים מצות מעשיות הנעשות ע"י הגוף ממש שאז כח הגוף ממש שבעשיה זו נכלל באור ה' ורצונו ומיוחד בו ביחוד גמור והוא לבוש השלישי של נפש האלהית ואזי גם כח נפש החיונית שבגופו ממש שמקליפת נוגה נתהפך מרע לטוב ונכלל ממש בקדושה כנפש האלהית ממש מאחר שהוא הפועל ועושה מעשה המצוה שבלעדו לא היתה נפש האלהית פועלת בגוף כלל כי היא רוחנית והגוף גשמי וחומרי והממוצע ביניהם היא נפש החיונית הבהמית המלובשת בדם האדם שבלבו וכל הגוף ואף שמהותה ועצמותה של נפש הבהמית שבלבו שהן מדותיה הרעות עדיין לא נכללו בקדושה מ"מ מאחר דאתכפיין לקדושה ובע"כ עונין אמן ומסכימין ומתרצין לעשיית המצוה ע"י התגברות נפשו האלהית שבמוח ששליט על הלב והן בשעה זו בבחי' גלות ושינה כנ"ל ולכך אין זו מניעה מהשראת השכינה על גוף האדם בשעה זו דהיינו שכח נפש החיונית המלובש בעשיית המצוה הוא נכלל ממש באור ה' ומיוחד בו ביחוד גמור וע"ז ממשיך הארה לכללות נפש החיונית שבכל הגוף וגם על הגוף הגשמי בבחי' מקיף מלמעלה מראשו

כ אדר פשוטה

ליקוטי אמרים

ידות לה' להיות מכון לשבתו ית' כנודע מאמר רז"ל שמצות צדקה שקולה כנגד כל הקרבנו' ובקרבנות היה כל החי עולה לה' ע"י בהמה אחת וכל הצומח ע"י עשרונות סלת אחד בלול בשמן כו' ומלבד זה הרי בשעת התורה והתפלה עולה לה' כל מה שאכל ושתה והנה מארבע הידות לבריאות גופו כמ"ש לקמן. והנה בכל פרטי מיני שמחות הנפש הנ"ל אין מהן מניעה להיות נבזה בעיניו נמאס ולב נשבר ורוח נמוכה בשעת השמחה ממש מאחר כי היותו נבזה בעיניו כו' הוא מצד הגוף ונפש הבהמית והיותו בשמחה הוא מצד נפש האלהית וניצוץ אלהות המלובש בה להחיותה כנ"ל [בפ"ל"א] וכה"ג איתא בזהר בכיה תקיעא בלבאי מסטרא דא וחדוה תקיעא בלבאי מסטרא דא:

ג אדר ב מעוברת

פרק לה והנה לתוספת ביאור תיבת לעשותו וגם להבין מעט מזעיר תכלית בריאת הבינונים וירידת נשמותיהם לעו"הז להתלבש בנפש הבהמית שמהקליפה וס"א מאחר שלא יוכלו לשלחה כל ימיהם ולדחותה ממקומה מחלל השמאלי שבלב שלא יעלו ממנה הרהורים אל המוח כי מהותה ועצמותה של נפש הבהמית שמהקליפה היא בתקפה ובגבורתה אצלם כתולדתה רק שלבושיה אינם מתלבשים בגופם כנ"ל וא"כ למה זה ירדו נשמותיהם לעו"הז ליגע לריק ח"ו להלחם כל ימיהם עם היצר ולא יכלו לו ותהי זאת נחמתם לנחמם בכפליים לתושיה ולשמח לבם בה' השוכן אתם בתוך תורתם ועבודתם והוא בהקדים לשון הינוקא [בזהר פ' בלק] על פסוק החכם עיניו בראשו וכי באן אתר עינוי דבר נש כו' אלא קרא הכי הוא ודאי דתנן בר נש לא יהך בגילוי' דרישא ארבע אמות מאי טעמא דשכינתא שריא על רישיה וכל חכם עינוהי ומילוי ברישיה אינון בההוא דשריא וקיימא על רישיה וכד עינוי תמן לנדע דההוא נהורא דאדליק על רישיה אצטריך למשחא בגין דגופא דב"נ איהו פתילה ונהורא אדליק לעילא ושלמה מלכא צוח ואמר ושמן על ראשך אל יחסר דהא נהורא דבראשו אצטריך למשחא ואינון עובדין טבאן וע"ד החכם עיניו בראשו עכ"ל. והנה ביאור משל זה שהמשיל אור השכינה לאור הנר שאינו מאיר ונאחז בפתילה בלי שמן וכך אין השכינה שורה על גוף האדם שנמשל לפתילה אלא ע"י מעשים טובים דוקא ולא די לו בנשמתו שהיא חלק אלוה ממעל להיות היא כשמן לפתיל' מבואר ומובן לכל משכיל כי הנה נשמת האדם אפי' הוא צדיק גמור עובד ה' ביראה ואהבה בתענוגי' אעפ"כ אינה בטילה במציאות לגמרי ליבטל ויכלל באור ה' ממש להיות לאחדים ומיוחדים ביחוד גמור רק הוא דבר בפני עצמו ירא ה' ואוהבו. משא"כ המצות ומעשים טובים שהן רצונו ית' ורצונו ית' הוא מקור החיים לכל העולמות והברואים שיורד אליהם על ידי צמצומים רבים והסתר פנים של

טז אדר פשוטה
ד אדר ב מעוברת

ה אדר ב מעוברת

יז אדר פשוטה
ו אדר ב מעוברת

ליקוטי אמרים

יג אדר פשוטה

כפולה ומכופלת כי מלבד שמחת הנפש המשכלת בקרבת ה' ודירתו אתו עמו. עוד זאת ישמח בכפליים בשמחת ה' וגודל נחת רוח לפניו ית' באמונה זו דאתכפיא ס"א ממש ואתהפך חשוכא לנהורא שהוא חשך הקליפות שבע"ז החומרי המחשיכים ומכסים על אורו ית' עד עת קץ כמ"ש קץ שם לחשך [דהיינו קץ הימין שיעביר רוח הטומאה מן הארץ ונגלה כבוד ה' וראו כל בשר יחדיו וכמ"ש לקמן] ובפרט בחו"ל שאויר ארץ העמים טמא ומלא קליפות וס"א ואין שמחה לפניו ית' כאורה ושמחה ביתרון אור הבא מן החשך דייקא. וז"ש ישמח ישראל בעושיו פי' שכל מי שהוא מזרע ישראל יש לו לשמוח בשמחת ה' אשר שש ושמח בדירתו בתחתוני' שהם בחי' עשיה גשמיית ממש. וז"ש בעושיו לשון רבים שהוא עו"ז הגשמי המלא קליפות וס"א שנק' רשות הרבים וטורי דפרודא ואתהפכן לנהורא ונעשים רשות היחיד ליחודו ית' באמונה זו:

יד אדר פשוטה
ל אדר א מעוברת

פרק לד והנה מודעת זאת שהאבות הן הן המרכבה שכל ימיהם לעולם לא הפסיקו אפי' שעה אחת מלקשר דעתם ונשמתם לרבון העולמים בביטול הנ"ל ליחודו ית'. ואחריהם כל הנביאים כל אחד לפי מדרגת נשמתו והשגתו ומדרגת משרע"ה היא העולה על כולנה שאמרו עליו שכינה מדברת מתוך גרונו של משה ומעין זה זכו ישראל במעמד הר סיני רק שלא יכלו לסבול כמאמר רז"ל שעל כל דיבור פרחה נשמתן כו' שהוא ענין ביטול במציאות הנ"ל לכן מיד אמר להם לעשות לו משכן ובו קדשי הקדשים להשראת שכינתו שהוא גילוי יחודו ית' כמ"ש לקמן ומשארב בהמ"ק אין להקב"ה בעולמו משכן ומכון לשבתו הוא יחודו ית' אלא ארבע אמות של הלכה שהוא רצונו ית' וחכמתו המלובשים בהלכות הערוכות לפנינו ולכן אחר שיעמיק האדם מחשבתו בענין ביטול הנ"ל כפי יכלתו זאת ישיב אל לבו כי מהיות קטן שכלי ושרש נשמתי מהכיל להיות מרכבה ומשכן ליחודו ית' באמת לאמיתו מאחר דלית מחשבה דילי תפיסא ומשגת בו ית' כלל וכלל שום השגה בעולם ולא שמץ מנהו מהמשגת האבו' והנביאים אי לזאת אעשה לו משכן ומכון לשבתו הוא העסק בת"ת כפי הפנאי שלי בקביעות עתים ביום ובלילה כדת הניתנה לכל אחד ואחד בהלכות תלמוד תורה וכמאמר רז"ל אפי' פרק אחד שחרית כו' ובזה ישמח לבו ויגיל ויתן הודאה על חלקו בשמחה ובטוב לבב על שזכה להיות אושפיזכן לגבורה פעמים בכל יום כפי העת והפנאי שלו כמסת ידו אשר הרחיב ה' לו:

א אדר ב מעוברת

טו אדר פשוטה
ב אדר ב מעוברת

ואם ירחיב ה' לו עוד אזי טהור ידים יוסיף אומץ ומחשבה טובה כו' וגם שאר היום כולו שעוסק במשא ומתן יהיה מכון לשבתו ית' בנתינת הצדקה שיתן מיגיעו שהיא ממדותיו של הקב"ה מה הוא רחום וכו' וכמ"ש בתיקונים חסד דרועא ימינא ואף שאינו נותן אלא חומש הרי החומש מעלה עמו כל הארבע

פרק לג עוֹד זאת תהיה שמחת הנפש האמיתי' ובפרט כשרואה בנפשו בעתים מזומנים שצריך לזככה ולהאירה בשמחת לבב אזי יעמיק מחשבתו ויצייר בשכלו ובינתו ענין יחודו ית' האמיתי איך הוא ממלא כל עלמין עליונים ותחתונים ואפי' מלא כל הארץ הלזו הוא כבודו ית' וכולא קמיה כלא חשיב ממש והוא לבדו הוא בעליונים ותחתונים ממש כמו שהיה לבדו קודם ששת ימי בראשית וגם במקום הזה שנברא בו עולם הזה השמים והארץ וכל צבאם היה הוא לבדו ממלא המקום הזה וגם עתה כן הוא לבדו בלי שום שינוי כלל מפני שכל הנבראים בטלים אצלו במציאות ממש כביטול אותיות הדבור והמחשבה במקורן ושרשן הוא מהות הנפש ועצמותה שהן עשר בחינותיה חכמה בינה ודעת כו' שאין בהם בחי' אותיות עדיין קודם שמתלבשות בלבוש המחשבה [כמ"ש בפ' כ' וכ"א באריכות ע"ש] וכמ"ש ג"כ במ"א משל גשמי לזה מענין ביטול זיו ואור השמש במקורו הוא גוף כדור השמש שברקיע שגם שם מאיר ומתפשט ודאי זיוו ואורו וביתר שאת מהתפשטותו והארתו בחלל העולם אלא ששם הוא בטל במציאות במקורו וכאילו אינו במציאות כלל: וככה ממש דרך משל הוא ביטול העולם ומלואו לגבי מקורו שהוא אור א"ס ב"ה וכמ"ש באריכו'. והנה כשיעמיק בזה הרבה ישמח לבו ותגל נפשו אף גילת ורנן בכל לב ונפש ומאד באמונה זו כי רבה היא כי היא קרבת אלהים ממש וזה כל האדם ותכלית בריאתו ובריאת כל העולמות עליונים ותחתוני' להיות לו דירה זו בתחתוני' כמ"ש לקמן באריכות. והנה כמה גדולה שמחת הדיוט ושפל אנשים בהתקרבותו למלך בשר ודם המתאכסן ודר אתו עמו בביתו וק"ו לאין קץ לקרבת ודירת ממ"ה הקב"ה וכדכתיב כי הוא זה אשר ערב לבו לגשת אלי נאם ה': ועל זה תיקנו ליתן שבח והודיה לשמו ית' בכל בקר ולומר אשרינו מה טוב חלקנו וכו' ומה יפה ירושתנו כלומר כמו שהאדם שש ושמח בירושה שנפלה לו הון עתק שלא עמל בו כן ויותר מכן לאין קץ יש לנו לשמוח על ירושתנו שהנחילונו אבותינו הוא יחוד ה' האמיתי אשר אפי' בארץ מתחת אין עוד מלבדו וזו היא דירתו בתחתונים וז"ש רז"ל תרי"ג מצות ניתנו לישראל בא חבקוק והעמידן על אחת שנאמר וצדיק באמונתו יחיה כלומר כאלו אינה רק מצוה אחת היא האמונה לבדה כי ע"י האמונה לבדה יבא לקיום כל התרי"ג מצות דהיינו כשיהיה לבו שש ושמח באמונתו ביחוד ה' בתכלית השמחה כאלו לא היתה עליו רק מצוה זו לבדה והיא לבדה תכלית בריאתו ובריאת כל העולמות הרי בכח וחיות נפשו בשמחה רבה זו תתעלה נפשו למעלה מעלה על כל המונעים קיום כל התרי"ג מצות מבית ומחוץ. וזהו שאמר באמונתו יחיה דייקא כתחיית המתים דרך משל כך תהיה נפשו בשמחה רבה זו והיא שמחת

יא אדר פשוטה
כט אדר א
מעוברת

יב אדר פשוטה

ליקוטי אמרים

חלק ראשון

לכ"ק אדמו"ר הזקן

הרב רבי שניאור זלמן מליאדי

בעל התניא והשו"ע

כרך ב
פרקים לג-נג